Better Homes and G[a...]

BIG
BOOK OF
HOME
HOW-TO

Meredith® Books
Des Moines, Iowa

Better Homes and Gardens® Books
An imprint of Meredith® Books

Big Book of Home How-To
Senior Associate Design Director: Tom Wegner
Graphic Designer: Tim Abramowitz
Copy Chief: Terri Fredrickson
Copy and Production Editor: Victoria Forlini
Editorial Operations Manager: Karen Schirm
Managers, Book Production: Pam Kvitne,
   Marjorie J. Schenkelberg, Rick von Holdt
Contributing Copy Editor: Ro Sila
Contributing Proofreaders: Julie Cahalan,
   David Craft, Stacey Schildroth
Indexer: Donald Glassman
Editorial and Design Assistants: Renee E. McAtee,
   Karen McFadden

Additional Editorial Contributions
Greenleaf Publishing, Inc.
Publishing Director: Dave Toht
Associate Editor: Steve Cory
Associate Designer: Jean DeVaty
Illustrator: Tony Davis

Meredith® Books
Editor in Chief: Linda Raglan Cunningham
Design Director: Matt Strelecki
Executive Editor, Gardening and Home Improvement:
   Benjamin W. Allen
Executive Editor, Home Improvement: Larry Erickson

Publisher: James D. Blume
Executive Director, Marketing: Jeffrey Myers
Executive Director, New Business Development: Todd M. Davis
Executive Director, Sales: Ken Zagor
Director, Operations: George A. Susral
Director, Production: Douglas M. Johnston
Business Director: Jim Leonard

Vice President and General Manager: Douglas J. Guendel

Meredith Publishing Group
President, Publishing Group: Stephen M. Lacy
Vice President-Publishing Director: Bob Mate

Meredith Corporation
Chairman and Chief Executive Officer: William T. Kerr

In Memoriam: E.T. Meredith III (1933-2003)

All of us at Better Homes and Gardens® Books are
dedicated to providing you with the information and
ideas you need to enhance your home and garden.
We welcome your comments and suggestions. Write
to us at:
   Better Homes and Gardens Books
   Home Improvement Books Department
   1716 Locust St.
   Des Moines, IA 50309–3023

If you would like to purchase any of our home
improvement, gardening, cooking, crafts, or home
decorating and design books, check wherever quality
books are sold. Or visit us at: bhgbooks.com

Note to the Readers: Due to differing conditions,
tools, and individual skills, Meredith Corporation
assumes no responsibility for any damages, injuries
suffered, or losses incurred as a result of following the
information published in this book. Before beginning
any project, review the instructions carefully, and if
any doubts or questions remain, consult local experts
or authorities. Because codes and regulations vary
greatly, you always should check with authorities to
ensure that your project complies with all applicable
local codes and regulations. Always read and observe
all of the safety precautions provided by
manufacturers of any tools, equipment, or supplies,
and follow all accepted safety procedures.

TABLE OF CONTENTS

YOU AND YOUR HOME

BUYING A HOME

Whether you're a first-time home buyer or a repeat customer, the labyrinth of steps and documents leading up to the holy grail of the closing can be intimidating. But buying a home is actually a logical, straightforward process—nerve-wracking because so much is riding on it, but not difficult to understand. These are the basic steps:

■ Choose a community (or two or three), considering such factors as commuting distance, congestion, proximity to shopping, quality of schools, parks, etc.

■ Prequalify for financing to find out how much house you can afford. This can give you an advantage over competing bidders once you find a home you love.

■ Find a broker. Look for one with substantial experience and a good reputation. A broker's first duty is to the seller; but because brokers do not get paid unless the deal goes through, there is often room to negotiate. Or hire a "buyer's broker" to guard your interests (the commission will be split with the seller's broker).

■ Make an offer. This is more an expression of good faith than a binding contract. Realize that other buyers may be bidding and that offers and counteroffers may continue for a while before an agreement is reached.

■ Hire a lawyer for "due diligence," a process that includes the title search (verifying that the seller actually owns the property, and checking for liens or claims); and an inspection (assessing the physical condition of the house). If you prefer, you can sign the contract first and work out the due diligence details later; just include a contingency clause in the contract that ensures that you will get your deposit back if the title and inspection do not check out okay.

■ Negotiate the contract through your lawyer. Usually the seller's lawyer will draw up a contract and you and your lawyer will suggest modifications—for instance, listing things that need to be fixed, clarifying ownership of appliances, suggesting a closing date that works best for your family.

■ Sign the contract and make a deposit, often 10 percent of the purchase price. Most contracts have contingency clauses that say you can terminate the contract and get your deposit back if you cannot obtain a loan by a certain date.

■ If you have not prequalified, it's now time to apply for a mortgage. Once your loan is approved, you will get a mortgage commitment from the lender detailing the terms of the loan, the interest rate, and the up-front costs.

■ Have the property appraised. As part of the approval process, the lender will usually hire an appraiser—whose fee you will pay—to make sure the value of the property is high enough to protect the lender's risk.

■ Attend the closing. This is when title is transferred to you and money changes hands among the parties involved. You will sign many documents. Among them is a promissory note that says how much you owe and when you need to make payments. The mortgage describes what the lender would do if you were to default—how and when it would handle a foreclosure.

■ Typically, the mortgage covers 80 percent of the purchase price. At closing you must pay the balance of your down payment. You may have already made a 10-percent deposit; at closing you would pay the remaining 10 percent.

■ At closing you may also pay a loan origination fee and points to the lender. A point is 1 percent of the total loan amount, charged as prepaid interest to reduce the rate at which your loan is amortized.

■ Other fees will include the appraisal, a document preparation fee for the bank's attorney, and title insurance. If your down payment is low, you also may be required to pay mortgage insurance (often included in the monthly payment), which protects the lender against loss in the event of default.

■ You must buy homeowner's insurance, not only for your own protection in the event of fire, accident, or weather damage, but because the lender will require it.

■ You will have to prepay a few months' worth of real estate taxes and a few months of interest on the loan, to be held ("in escrow") by the lender or its escrow agent.

■ At the end of the closing process, the seller's lender will give you a document called a mortgage satisfaction, which is proof that the seller's mortgage has been paid.

■ All together, these closing costs have typically added up to 6 to 8 percent of the cost of the house, though competition has reduced that amount in recent years. The seller will be responsible for the broker's commission.

WORKING WITH A REAL ESTATE BROKER

Look at a dozen or more houses. If the broker says there are a lot of people interested in a particular house, don't feel pressured to rush your decision. While some anxiety is normal, you should feel comfortable about your final choice. Once you find a house you like, go back and look at it two or three more times. (If possible, check out the house soon after a rainstorm because leaks will be more apparent.) If the broker balks at extra visits, walk away.

SHOPPING FOR A MORTGAGE

Your mortgage payment is a big part of your monthly budget, so it's worthwhile to invest some time researching the market and comparison-shopping.

■ Contact several lenders. Take the time to get a basic idea what's available in the mortgage market.

■ If you're new to this, check with a nonprofit organization that offers courses for home buyers.

■ Find out how your credit report looks. There are several major credit reporting companies; each charges a modest fee for a copy of your report. Check with each company to make sure there is nothing inaccurate in its report. At the same time, find out what your credit score is. This is a number from 300 to 800 calculated by a computer based on a number of details in your credit history. Sometimes this will be included free with the credit report. Often people think they have bad credit and end up with a more expensive loan when they actually could have qualified for a conventional loan. Because credit scores are so widely used today, it's important to be aware of where you stand and to clean up any inaccuracies. For a conventional loan, you'll usually need a score of 620 or higher. If your score is lower, the loan terms will be more expensive—called "subprime."

■ Add everything up, including the interest rate, the points, and fees, to find out the total cost of financing. There is a lot of variability out there, so do some comparison-shopping.

■ Ask whether there are early termination fees, prepayment penalties, or other charges associated with the loan.

■ Most people prefer a fixed-rate loan. The right loan for you will depend on your budget, your aversion to risk, and the length of time you're likely to own your home. Your lender can explain the benefits of various loan types.

REFINANCING

In years when interest rates are low, refinancing applications can outpace new-purchase mortgages. A common motivation for refinancing is to get cash for remodeling; the downside to this, of course, is increased personal debt and the chance that your home might depreciate in value, leaving you with a loan worth more than your house.

The old rule was to refinance only if the interest rate dropped by at least 2 percentage points. However, recent trends show homeowners refinancing at rates only 1.25 percent lower than the original loan. What's important is whether refinancing improves your overall financial picture.

Most consumers seeking to refinance focus on rates, but it's important to look at closing costs as well. These can vary widely, so it's best to shop around.

Because there are a lot of bad deals out there, do some research to make sure you're dealing with a reputable broker and lender. If you were happy with your original lender, consider checking there after you've done some research on rates and closing costs available elsewhere (for example, on the Internet). Sometimes the original lender will bend a little to keep your business, and the process will be easier for you. However, quite often the original lender has sold the loan to another lender.

Be careful about shortening the term of your loan, which raises monthly payments. Many people have trouble meeting these higher payments, especially in times of unexpected expense or interrupted income. It often makes better sense to make additional principal payments when you have extra money, without saddling yourself with a heavier monthly obligation.

Paying an extra amount toward your principal each month reduces your overall loan cost without incurring the expenses associated with refinancing.

EXPERTS' INSIGHT

AVOIDING PREDATORY LENDERS

You should be the one to initiate the refinancing process, not someone soliciting via phone or internet—who may be offering a higher rate of interest than the market average. Once you decide to refinance, choose a reputable broker or an established lending institution.

■ Don't assume you won't qualify for a conventional loan until you have checked it out; even if your credit is blemished, they may be able to work something out with you.

■ As with all legal documents, don't sign anything with blank spaces that can later be filled in.

■ If you're having second thoughts, get a second opinion. Check the Internet to find non-profit groups that offer information on loans and mortgage counseling. If you're feeling pressured, walk away. Keep in mind that you have a legal right to cancel a refinancing loan for three days after closing.

WORKING UP TO CODE

Most likely, a local building department in your city or county has the authority to determine how all new building must be done in your locale. (Some rural areas have no building department.) A building department has exhaustive and detailed lists of regulations (codes) covering new home construction and remodeling projects, including wiring, plumbing, roofing, structural framing, and the installation of permanent appliances (like air-conditioners).

Though it may seem a hassle, your building department is there for your protection. The regulations are not arbitrary, but are based on decades of building experience. A project that is built up to code will likely be safe and durable; a project built without benefit of codes may be both dangerous and flimsy. When it comes time to sell your home, you could be in legal trouble if it is found that significant work was done without being inspected.

The consequences of ignoring these regulations can be harsh. You may be required to have the work professionally checked, or you may be ordered to tear out the work and start again. Also, insurance companies may balk at paying a claim for damage done to your house if you have not followed regulations.

As a general rule, the building department and its codes come into play whenever a new permanent structure is built, or when new electrical, plumbing, or gas service is installed.

So for instance, you probably do not need a permit in order to replace an existing toilet, sink, tub, or light fixture. However, if you run new electrical cable or new pipes in order to install fixtures where there were none before, then you need a permit. A sand-laid patio (rather than one that involves a concrete slab), a simple storage shed with no wiring or plumbing, or a small deck that is not attached to the house may be exempt from inspections. However, always check with the building department to be sure.

Most codes are based on national standards but may be modified to suit local conditions. For example, construction techniques required for earthquake-prone areas are different than those for other areas, and construction in areas that are consistently wet may require weather-resistant materials in outdoor applications. Whenever you're undertaking home improvements, make sure you know what local building codes apply to your project. In addition, be aware that codes may vary significantly from town to town—even within the same county.

Working with a building department involves several steps. First, go to your local building department and ask for general guidelines for the project you are proposing. They may have copies of regulations for common projects, or they may direct you to reference works.

Second, make a detailed, neat drawing of the project, including a materials list, and show it to an inspector in the office. The inspector may ask for changes and clarifications.

Finally, once your plans are approved, one or more inspections will be scheduled—typically, one inspection for the rough installation, and one for the finished project.

EXPERTS' INSIGHT

WORKING WITH AN INSPECTOR

Some inspectors are more friendly than others, but they are all there for your protection. Treat the inspector with respect, and you will likely have a mutually beneficial relationship.

■ Go to your inspector with a plan to be approved or amended; don't expect the building department to plan the job for you.

■ To avoid wasting the inspector's time, find out as much information as possible about your project before you talk to the inspector. Consult the building department's literature, national codes, or how-to books.

■ Draw plans that are close to professional quality. Everything should be to scale and should be drawn clearly. You may need to make both a top view drawing and one or more other drawings.

■ Never argue with an inspector. Always be courteous. Follow instructions. Assume the inspector knows more than you do. Inspectors are wary of homeowners, because many take on projects beyond their abilities. Show the inspector you are serious about doing things the right way.

■ Be sure you clearly understand when you need to have inspections. Do not cover up any work that needs to be inspected.

■ If you are hiring a contractor, it is usually best to have the contractor, not you, deal directly with the inspector.

DO IT YOURSELF OR HIRE A PRO?

This book is designed for avid do-it-yourselfers. If you are the kind of homeowner who wants to help only with planning a project and doing the finishing touches after the majority of the work is done, see the tips below. Read the step-by-step instructions for projects in this book and then decide whether you want to tackle the job.

In an all-too-common scenario, a homeowner gets excited about an ambitious project and tears into walls or floors. Once the demolition is finished and some initial work is done, however, it becomes difficult to keep up the energy level. After a long day of work, the TV and the armchair are much more appealing than the tool belt. So the house remains an unfinished mess for weeks or

months longer than was originally planned. Home life can become very difficult; many marriages founder under the stress of remodeling projects.

Remodeling always takes longer and is more difficult than new construction, because you run into so many obstacles. This is especially true if your home is an older one with plaster walls.

To gauge whether you are really ready to take on a large project, first try some modest repairs or installations. Once you (and your spouse) are convinced that you have the needed skills and can complete projects in a timely manner, it may be time to attempt a more serious job.

Professionals often charge what look to be fearsome rates. However, before you decide to

save money by doing it yourself, consider all the factors: A pro can probably do things much more quickly than you. If you can make extra money by working overtime or taking on extra work in your field, chances are it will be easier to do so and hand over the remodeling project to a pro.

Some contractors are willing to lower their prices if the homeowner agrees to perform certain tasks. This sort of "sweat equity" arrangement can be beneficial, but only if the terms are clearly spelled out. The contract should state precisely what you will do, and when you will do it. Ideally, there should be a clear division between the contractor's work and yours. For instance, you might agree to install moldings and paint the walls, or to install the flooring.

FINDING AND HIRING A CONTRACTOR

To achieve a happy relationship and professional results, follow these steps to find and hire a pro:
■ Get the names of several contractors by asking friends for recommendations. Take a look at examples of their work to see if it meets your expectations.
■ Get rough estimates from all contractors who interest you. It will help you narrow the field of candidates and judge how candid they are about money matters.
■ For a major job, get at least three bids. Give a contractor about three weeks to produce the bid. Read the bids closely; they should detail the materials that will be used. If one contractor is much lower than the others, check to make sure he or she is truly capable and experienced.
■ When accepting bids, find out how long the contractor has been in business—the longer the better.

Ask who finances the contractor's company (usually it's a bank). Ask the bank about the contractor's general solvency. You don't want a contractor to go bankrupt in the middle of your project.
■ Determine whether the contractor carries insurance. Every contractor's insurance should cover property damage, liability, and workers' compensation. If the contractor is not covered, you could be liable for hefty fees in case of an accident.

Writing the Contract

Once you've chosen a bid, negotiate a contract. It should have these important elements:
■ Itemize in detail all work to be done. Specify the type and brand of materials and finishes to be used. Include a specific timetable.

You may want to work in a penalty for late completion, or a reward for early completion.
■ A fixed-price contract should specify the total cost of the job. A cost-plus contract should specify the cost of materials and labor. Payments should be dependent on work completed.
■ Include a right of rescission, permitting you to rescind, or back out of, a contract within 72 hours of signing it.
■ A certificate of insurance guarantees that the contractor is covered. Include in the contract a warranty ensuring that the labor and materials are free from defects for at least a year.
■ An arbitration clause delineates the method for resolving disputes.
■ A release of liens clause ensures that you won't be responsible for liens filed against the contractor by suppliers or subcontractors.

STAYING SANE WHILE REMODELING

Whether you are doing it yourself or hiring a pro, a remodeling project can be stressful. Your normal routines are interrupted, you're engulfed by noise and dust, and your home is in turmoil. Kitchen remodels are the most stressful. Suddenly, the source of meals, snacks, and beverages is out of commission or barely accessible.

Careful planning and a few simple steps can minimize your family's emotional and physical discomfort. Here are some tips:

■ Do what you can to move the job along quickly. Even if it means paying a little more, you may save money in the long run because, in the case of a kitchen remodel, you will eat out less often. For a do-it-yourself project, consider hiring a pro to complete a specific aspect, such as running plumbing lines or roughing in the wiring. Often, hiring a laborer can also speed things up. If you are hiring a contractor, build incentives for timely completion into the contract.

■ Cultivate realistic expectations about how long the project will take—usually, longer than you think. If the estimate is two weeks, prepare yourself emotionally for three or four weeks.

■ For a kitchen remodel, take the time to set up a fairly pleasant temporary kitchen in another room that will be fairly quiet and free of dust. A pleasant "camping out" ambience can actually make for relatively fun and memorable family times.

■ Some or all family members may be able to actually leave the house for a couple of weeks, either for a vacation or to visit relatives.

Be aware, however, that most remodels involve many small decisions that are best considered when you are on the site.

■ Take extraordinary steps to minimize dust; see page 11.

■ Require that floors be swept and vacuumed and tools put neatly away at the end of every work day.

■ Go ahead and entertain informally. Under the circumstances, guests will not expect neatness, so having dinner guests can actually be easier than when the house is in good shape and you have to clean up. Guests often find a remodel project interesting. Outdoor entertaining is often the easiest.

■ If you have small children, demand that the area be kept clear of all sharp or otherwise dangerous objects.

WORKING WITH A CONTRACTOR

Once you've hired a contractor and written a clear contract, prepare for an unusual relationship. You'll be living in close quarters with one or more strangers. Together, you'll be completing complex projects involving your living space. To keep things on an even keel and achieve the best results, follow these tips:

■ Communication is the key. Start with a contract that spells out precisely the work to be done (see page 9). Don't be surprised, however, if some aspects of the job turn out differently than you expected—that's normal for a remodeling project. If you are displeased with the way things are turning out, tell the contractor as soon as possible. The longer you wait, the more difficult—and expensive—corrections will be.

■ Whenever there is a change in plans, put the new expectations in writing. A "change work" agreement should be just as precise and detailed as the original contract.

■ Keep close tabs on escalating costs created by mid-project changes. If, for example, unexpected structural or plumbing problems are discovered when walls are opened, it will cost extra to fix them. In order to keep within budget, you may need to settle for some less expensive installations.

■ Coordinate your schedules so you and your contractor are together long enough to communicate daily, but avoid getting in each others' hair. Perhaps the contractor could arrive about a half hour before you leave for work in the morning, or maybe you could make a point of returning from

work before the contractor leaves. That way, you can quickly assess the work done and discuss any decisions that must be made.

If you do not go to work, arrange to be out of the house or in another part of the house for most of the day.

■ Be empathetic. Statistically, most contractors fail simply because it is a very difficult business. For instance, a mistake may be the contractor's fault, or it may instead be the fault of a supplier or subcontractor.

■ On the other hand, be firm and stand up for your rights. Don't let the contractor bully you into changes you do not want. If you feel you are being taken advantage of, don't hesitate to say so. If the problem persists, call in another contractor for arbitration.

MINIMIZING THE MESS OF HOME IMPROVEMENT

Though the final results of an upgrade will be beautiful, no doubt you will make a mess along the way. Out-of-control debris, clutter, and dust can make home life miserable. Follow these tips to minimize the anguish.

■ Contain the job. Having part of your home look like a construction site is usually bearable. If the mess migrates to the rest of the home, things get pretty depressing. Clearly mark off where the work zone ends and living quarters begin. That way, the mess becomes a place you visit, rather than the place where you live.

■ Take extraordinary measures to protect valuable wood or carpeted floors. Usually, one layer of protection is not enough. For a painting project, tape down plastic or protective paper, then lay a thick canvas drop cloth over that. If the top layer is plastic, you are liable to step in wet paint and then track it around. For a major renovation, carefully fit pieces of plywood or thick cardboard to the floor, followed by a drop cloth. Or purchase interlocking foam floor protectors made for the purpose.

■ Keep the dust from traveling. Construction typically produces a fine dust that will seep into every corner of your house if it gets a chance. (This is particularly true when cutting into a plaster wall or sanding drywall joint compound.) It's not enough to close a door. Seal off the construction site with plastic taped to the doorway. Place a fan or two in a window to blow dust out of the house.

■ Do as much work as possible outdoors or in the garage. Even if it means taking extra steps before cutting boards, you will save hassle in the long run if you keep the dust out of your house.

■ Sweep and vacuum every day. At the end of a workday, cleaning up may be the last thing you want to do, but it's worth the effort to make the site well swept and organized for the next day. Make it a regular routine to spend the last 15 minutes of each day cleaning up. You'll find the site easier to live with and much more pleasant to return to in the morning.

■ Use the right cleaning tools. A wet/dry vacuum cleaner with a fine filter is ideal for eliminating dust. Or scatter sweeping compound to minimize flying dust while sweeping. Have several scrubbing devices on hand for cleaning buckets and tools.

WORKING SAFE AND SMART

Home improvement projects can be dangerous. Many tasks call for sharp tools or power tools that can cause injuries. Follow these safety rules:

■ Before using a power tool, read its instruction manual and follow the manufacturer's safety cautions. Tighten any adjustments and check that the guard is working before you operate a tool.

■ Keep power tools dry, and plug them into grounded electrical outlets. Take care not to cut the power cord.

■ Keep fingers well away from a power blade. Clamp small pieces of wood before cutting them, rather than holding them.

■ Wear work gloves when handling rough materials, but take them off and firmly roll up your sleeves if operating a power tool.

■ Wear eye and ear protection when cutting with a power tool.

■ Unplug a power saw before changing the blade.

■ Properly support a board to be cut so you will avoid kickback (see page 268).

■ When working on wiring, shut off the power to the circuit first. When working with plumbing, shut off the water first.

■ When working on a ladder, don't lean out to either side. Keep your body weight between the sides of the ladder. It may take longer to get off the ladder and move it to reach farther, but it is well worth your time. Falls are one of the most common causes of injuries in the home.

Avoid Physical Strain

You are probably not accustomed to physical construction work, so it is quite possible for you to strain muscles or joints while engaging in remodeling work. Often, you feel fine while doing the work but wake up the next day in pain. Don't take chances. Follow these guidelines to avoid injury:

■ Don't overexert yourself when lifting heavy objects, or when repeatedly lifting lighter loads. Get a helper to do some of the work, and take plenty of breaks.

■ Working in an awkward position can put a strain on your back and other areas of your body. Take the time to move or to arrange things so that you are as comfortable as possible.

■ Lift with your legs, not your back. When picking up a heavy object, keep your back as upright and straight as possible. Bend your knees to reach the object.

GETTING TO KNOW YOUR HOME

An educated homeowner is prepared for emergencies and is able to handle repairs and upgrades with confidence. This book will help you understand your home's structural, electrical, plumbing, and heating/cooling systems. If you feel ignorant about important aspects of your home, hire a contractor or a professional house inspector to explain things.

Here's a basic list of things a homeowner should understand and be able to do:

■ Find and understand your electrical service panel. If your service is less than 100 amps, consult with an electrician to see if you need larger service. The panel should be easy for an adult to access, yet out of reach for small children. Know which breaker or fuse controls which parts of your electrical system, and understand how to flip a breaker or change a fuse when a circuit blows.

■ Know what sort of electrical cable runs through your walls, and be sure that the cables are kept safe from harm, especially when driving fasteners into walls.

■ In case of a plumbing crisis, know how to shut off water to individual fixtures and (more importantly) how to shut off water to the entire house (see page 138). Often there are two shutoffs—one in the crawlspace or basement or just outside the house, and one underground near the street.

■ Learn the basics of your plumbing system: what material the pipes are made of, where the vent pipes go, and where the main drain goes. If you have a septic system, locate it and contact a service company to make sure it is in good working order.

■ Understand your home's framing. If any floors sag, check to see whether they can be buttressed. If termites are a problem in your area, have your home inspected for them regularly.

■ Inspect your siding, roofing, and gutter system yearly for signs of damage. Often a timely repair will save money in the long run.

■ To be comfortable, a home must be well sealed with caulk and weatherstripping, and it must be properly ventilated. See pages 502–520 for tips and information.

■ Understand your HVAC system—what type it is, as well as how the pipes or vents are routed. Some systems require annual maintenance, which you neglect at your peril. It may be possible to improve your system's efficiency with a few simple steps. Solutions are found on pages 521–562.

IDENTIFYING A BEARING WALL

Every wall fits one of two structural categories—bearing walls, which support a load above, and nonbearing walls, which support only themselves. If you remove or make a big opening in a bearing wall, you could literally bring down the house.

To determine whether a wall is bearing or not, do some sleuthing in the basement or attic—wherever there are exposed joists or rafters. If the joists run parallel to the wall in question, you can be sure it's not a bearing wall.

However, if they are perpendicular to the wall—as shown below right—you can reasonably expect that the wall is bearing a load.

If you cannot see the joists, use a stud finder to locate them and determine the direction they run. Or use the techniques shown on page 14.

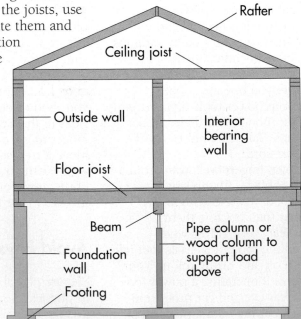

Rafter

Ceiling joist

Outside wall

Interior bearing wall

Floor joist

Beam

Foundation wall

Pipe column or wood column to support load above

Footing

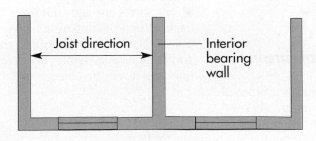

Joist direction

Interior bearing wall

ASSESSING BASEMENTS AND FOUNDATIONS

*T*he foundation of your house has several tough assignments. First, it supports the weight of the entire house. It also acts as a retaining wall and must be firm enough to hold back the earth—and moisture—around its perimeter. Finally, it may shelter a basement.

Basement/foundation walls begin with a concrete footing designed to stably distribute a load of thousands of pounds per square foot. The footing also supports the thinner slab used for most basement floors. Footings may or may not be protected from moisture by drain tiles laid in sand or gravel to remove water.

The walls may be made of concrete block, poured concrete, brick, stone, or even treated wood. Regardless of the material, the walls' exterior should be covered with a layer of waterproofing before the soil is replaced.

Basements suffer from a special ill that doesn't afflict other spaces in your home—moisture. Differences between the temperature below ground and that of the air upstairs or outside often create a slight mustiness, especially in muggy summer weather. This is normal.

However, if floors or walls in your basement chronically sweat—or worse, if puddles collect on the floor—the problem should be dealt with. To solve basement moisture problems or leaks, see pages 640–641.

On top, the walls support a wood sill plate upon which joists are laid for the subfloor and finish floor. (See pages 370 and 480–481 for more about sill plates and floors.)

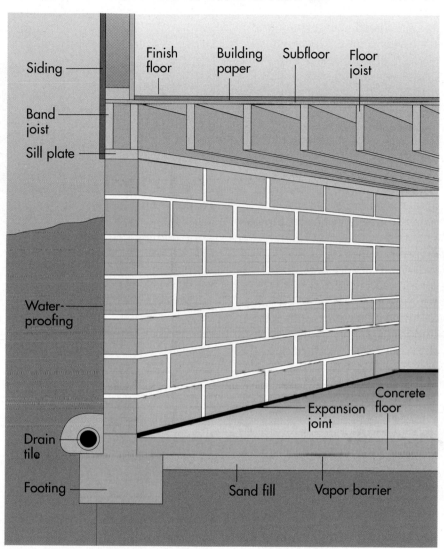

Siding · Band joist · Sill plate · Finish floor · Building paper · Subfloor · Floor joist · Water-proofing · Drain tile · Footing · Expansion joint · Concrete floor · Sand fill · Vapor barrier

EXPERTS' INSIGHT

CRAWLSPACES

If your house has a crawlspace underneath, the house either rests atop short supporting walls or is held up by a series of concrete or masonry piers.

Local climate and soil conditions determine how a crawlspace should be constructed. In some areas, it should be sealed off tightly, with only a few vents. In other areas, larger openings are needed. See pages 514–515 for ways to insulate a crawlspace.

Before crawling under your home, make sure it's safe. In some areas, poisonous insects and other critters pose a danger.

If your floor sags, resupporting it may involve jacking the floor up and installing a new post. Or, you may need to pour a new pier or part of a foundation wall.

Crawlspaces provide ample opportunities for wood-eating bugs. Have yours inspected regularly by an exterminator.

UNDERSTANDING INTERIOR WALL SURFACES

Most homes built after World War II have walls made of drywall, also known as Sheetrock® or wallboard. Most residential drywall is ½ inch thick. Installed on studs that are spaced 16 inches apart, this provides a fairly durable wall—one that will last for many decades, as long as it is not abused. However, slamming doorknobs or roughhousing adolescents can easily punch a hole through drywall. Fortunately, repairs are fairly easy, though time-consuming (see pages 862–865).

Drywall is only gypsum covered on each side with paper, so it's not very strong. If you need to hang anything heavy on a wall, it is important to find a stud and fasten the nail or screw to the stud.

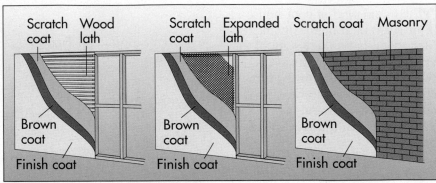

Plaster walls.
Most plaster walls begin with the same framing that's used for drywall construction. To hold and strengthen the plaster, the studs must be covered with lath, usually made of narrow strips of wood, but more recent applications may use a heavy metal mesh instead. The lath then is covered by three successive layers of plaster. The scratch coat of plaster, the first to go down, grips the lath. The brown coat smooths out the surface. Finally, the finish coat is applied to produce a texture ranging from rough to glassy smooth. If your home has solid masonry walls, the plaster might be applied directly to the masonry.

FINDING STUDS

Studs are usually—but not always—spaced at regular intervals. After you've found one, you can often plot others by measuring.

Begin your search near the wall's center, not at the ends, where spacing might be irregular. Also, ignore the studs on either side of a door or window opening.

Electronic stud finders offer the easiest way to find studs and joists. However, they usually do not work in a plaster wall, because of the wood lath.

Once you've found one stud, measure 16 inches—the most common spacing—in one direction or the other. If you cannot find a second stud, try 24 inches, a spacing used in some newer houses.

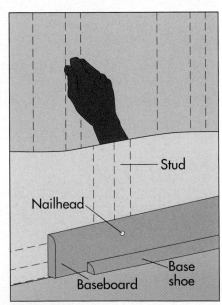

Sound it out.
Often you can "sound out" a wall by rapping along it with your knuckles. A solid thunk indicates a stud. If rapping doesn't tell you anything, look for nails in the baseboard. They're usually driven into the studs.

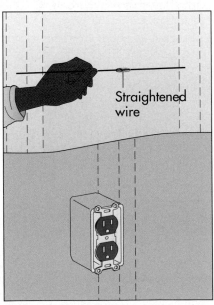

Probe with a wire.
You can also drill a small, angled hole and probe with a straightened wire coat hanger to find the stud. Or, take the face plate off an electrical receptacle to check: Wall boxes usually are nailed to the side of a stud.

HANGING LIGHT OBJECTS

Choose hanging hardware that is appropriate for the object to be hung. It should be strong enough, but there's no need to go overboard, for instance using beefy screws to hang a small picture. Often, an appliance or fixture will come with its own hanging hardware. If you have lath-and-plaster walls, a screw driven into the lath will hold much better than a screw driven into drywall, though not as well as a screw driven into a stud. Make sure you hit a lath, not a space between.

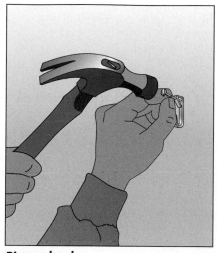

Picture hooks.
Ordinary nailed picture hooks hold items up to about 10 pounds. These have the advantage of poking only tiny holes in the wall. Hooks that are attached to adhesive cloth can be used only on very lightweight objects.

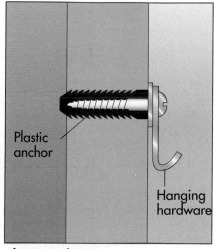

Plastic anchors.
Plastic anchors grip by expanding as you drive screws into them. Drill the right-sized hole, and tap the anchor into the hole until it is flush with the wall surface. Then drive the screw.

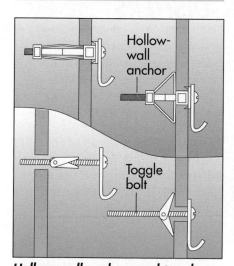

Hollow-wall anchors and toggle bolts.
Hollow-wall anchors open behind the wall surface for an installation that cannot pull loose. Toggle bolts screw into wings that pop open inside the wall. Assemble with the hanging hardware before inserting.

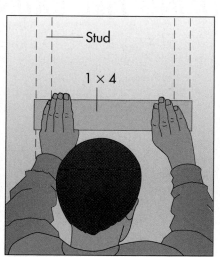

Attaching to two or more studs.
Bridging studs with a 1×4 or a strip of plywood adds strength and freedom from stud spacings. Nail or screw the hanger to the bridging.

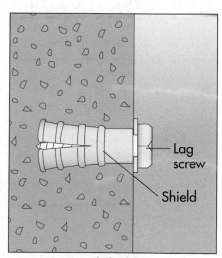

Lag screws and shields.
For hanging heavy items, buy lag screws with masonry shields. Drill the right-sized hole, then tap in the shield. When you drive the lag screw, the shield expands to grip the wall. For medium-weight items, use masonry screws, which are typically blue or green; these need no anchor. Drill the right-sized hole, then drive the screw.

SAFETY IN THE HOME

Keeping a home safe is often a simple matter of common sense and attentiveness—having fire extinguishers readily available and keeping harmful chemicals out of reach of children, for instance. However, many dangers are less obvious—like carbon monoxide gas (see page 18) and radon (page 19). The next six pages will acquaint you with some types of household hazards and their safeguards. In addition, here are some commonsense safety tips:

■ With your family, develop, discuss, and practice an emergency evacuation plan in case of fire. Make sure everyone has at least two routes for exiting the house, in case one route is blocked.

■ Install smoke alarms throughout the home, and install at least one fire extinguisher, preferably in the kitchen.

■ If you use a wood-burning stove or any other type of supplemental heat (especially kerosene or electric), take special precautions, because these units are notorious for starting fires.

■ Do not overload an electrical outlet. A cheap multiplug adapter, with four or five cords plugged into it, is a hazard. Instead, install a new outlet or purchase a power strip with its own breaker designed to handle a number of plugs.

■ Replace or repair any frayed or damaged wires. Don't use a thin household-type extension cord for a heavy appliance. If the cord gets warm when in use, it is unsafe.

■ If a circuit often overloads so you need to flip the breaker or change the fuse, call an electrician to fix the problem.

■ Don't use a lightbulb of a higher wattage than is recommended for the light fixture or lamp. If you do, it will overheat. In a closet or utility space, make sure you don't have a bare lightbulb within a foot of clothing or other flammable objects.

■ Have your furnace or boiler checked yearly, both to ensure that it is burning safely and to make sure it does not produce carbon monoxide. Place carbon monoxide detectors in at least two places in your home.

■ Be aware of dangers specific to your locale and your type of home construction. For example, an older home may have asbestos pipe insulation, or paint that contains lead. Radon is a problem in some areas, and some fairly new homes may be in danger of developing mold or mildew.

CHOOSING AND USING FIRE EXTINGUISHERS

Not all fire extinguishers are the same. Choose one designed to extinguish the type of fire you are most likely to have. Check the extinguisher's label for information.

For example, class A fire extinguishers contain pressurized water to put out simple fires involving wood and cloth. Class B extinguishers contain sodium bicarbonate or foam to suffocate flames. They can handle fires that involve flammable substances such as grease, oil, gasoline, and solvents. Class C extinguishers contain dry chemicals so that they can put out electrical fires. (Class A units would only spread such a fire.)

For general protection, purchase an "ABC" unit, which can handle most any type of fire. For a kitchen, you may choose a "BC" extinguisher, since most fires there are electrical or involve burning grease. Sometimes the label rates how well an extinguisher can put out fires of each type.

Spend a little more for an extinguisher that has a high "UL" number, which indicates how much extinguishing agent it contains. The higher the number, the longer the unit will last and the larger the unit will be. Make sure the extinguisher is small enough so that all family members can use it.

Check your fire extinguishers regularly to make sure they are still at full pressure. A quick glance at the gauge will suffice; if you mount the extinguisher so that the gauge is visible, checking it will be simple.

Most household extinguishers are disposable; throw yours out if you use it even for a very short burst, because it likely will not work the next time. A more expensive rechargeable model must be serviced by an authorized dealer between uses.

Read the label ahead of time to learn how to use the extinguisher; when a fire occurs, you will not have time. In most cases, there is a safety pin that must be pulled before you can squeeze the trigger.

Hold the extinguisher 5 or 6 feet away from the fire. Any closer could cause the fire to disperse, and any farther away might not be effective. Aim the spray at the base—the source— of the fire; hitting the flames in the middle will do little good. Use a sweeping motion when spraying to cover the area thoroughly. You can either use short bursts or a long spray.

INSTALLING SMOKE DETECTORS

*T*here are two basic types of smoke detectors—photoelectric and ionization units. Photoelectric units include a beam of light and a photoelectric cell. When smoke enters the unit, it scatters the light, causing part of it to contact the photoelectric cell and trigger the alarm. Photoelectric smoke detectors react more readily to slow, smoldering fires than to fast, flaming blazes.

An ionization unit ionizes the air inside the detector and gives it an electrical charge. Smoke particles cut down current flow, which sounds a warning. Ionization detectors respond more quickly than photoelectric units to fast, flaming fires.

Combination units are also available that provide the benefits of both types. These are more expensive, however.

Each type has its advantages and drawbacks. While battery-operated photoelectric models are available, many models depend on house current, which means you lose protection during a power outage or electrical fire, and you must locate them near an electric outlet. Ionization units run on house current, batteries, or both. Besides reacting more slowly to smoldering fires, they're also more susceptible to false alarms, especially from a steamy shower or from someone smoking nearby.

Consider installing at least one of each—an ionization detector in your bedroom hallway plus a photoelectric unit in the living area. A deluxe system might also include a series of heat sensors wired in tandem with smoke detectors so that all the alarms will sound if any one senses heat or smoke. These require extensive wiring.

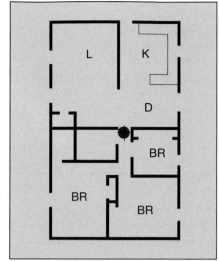

Where to place them.
Smoke detectors take only a few minutes to mount. Knowing where to place them, however, helps you decide how many you need.

Attach each unit to a ceiling, or high on a wall about 8 to 10 inches below ceiling level. Ideally, you should have at least one detector on each floor in hallways leading to bedrooms and at the top of stairwells. Analyze your home's air currents and avoid dead

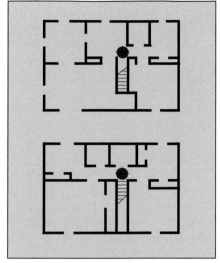

corners where there is poor air circulation. Also, keep detectors away from smoky kitchen, furnace, garage, or fireplace areas.

In a single-floor home with bedrooms clustered together, you can install one unit in a hallway between the bedroom and living areas. If your sleeping areas are spread out or are on different levels, you should use at least two detectors. Mount one at the top of the stairway.

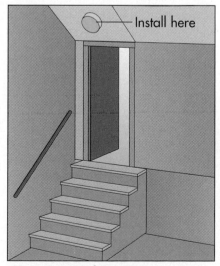

Basements and garages.
Protect your basement and utility areas as well. Because smoke and heat always rise, install at the top of the basement stairway, if possible.

How smoke travels.
Once smoke reaches the ceiling, it spreads out horizontally. This makes the center of a room the optimum location for a smoke detector.

Making a Home Safe for Children

Small children love to experiment and explore, climbing into new places and tasting anything in reach. A child who is only crawling today may be standing up and reaching tomorrow, so parents need to plan ahead. Fortunately, a host of new products on the market make it easier than ever to shield children from danger. Here are some steps you can take:

■ A bathtub has hard and slippery surfaces. Cover the spout with an inflatable or foam spout cover. If the handles can be reached by a child, turn them off firmly; a child who turns on the hot water could be scalded. Apply slip-resistant strips to the bottom of the tub or buy a nonslip tub mat. Consider installing a grab bar or two. Keep all electrical appliances well away from the tub.

And, of course, never leave a young child unattended in the tub.
■ Turn the home's hot-water temperature down so it is just warm enough for a shower, and not so hot as to scald a child.
■ Many products commonly found in a bathroom, such as aftershave and perfume, can be harmful if swallowed or if they get in a child's eyes. Keep them out of reach.
■ At a certain stage, a child finds stairways irresistible. Use gates to keep the stairs out of bounds. Purchase only new gates, which meet modern safety standards.
■ Electrical cords are a potential hazard, especially if a child handles the plug with wet fingers. A child also might pull down a toaster or other appliance by the cord. Position furniture such that the child cannot reach plugs.

■ Cover unused electrical outlets with special plastic safety plugs or covers.
■ If you have heating units that get very hot—a wood-burning stove, a kerosene unit, electrical baseboard heaters, or even steam radiators—take special precautions to keep the child away.
■ If you are cooking while the child is in the kitchen, use the back burners whenever possible. Turn pan handles toward the back, and move hot pots out of a child's reach.
■ If a stove knob is left uncovered, a child can easily turn on a stove burner. Special covers are available to protect the knobs.
■ While the child is in the putting-everything-in-the-mouth stage, move all knickknacks up and out of reach.

Carbon Monoxide Protection

Because it is invisible and odorless, carbon monoxide (CO) can be detected only with a carbon monoxide detector.

Symptoms of overexposure to carbon monoxide include headaches, nausea, dizziness, fatigue, and blurred vision. In a home where CO levels are slightly high, family members may experience some of these symptoms at a low level for years and not know the cause.

Carbon monoxide commonly enters a home because a furnace or water heater is improperly vented. Have your gas company come to your home to give a free inspection. Vent pipes might be clogged, inadequately joined, or installed in the wrong configuration. In any of these cases, repairs are simple. An inspection by a heating

professional can also reveal any CO problems.

Venting configurations can be complicated, especially if two appliances—most commonly a furnace and a water heater— are in the same room. Have a pro check the venting carefully.

Be sure to follow correct maintenance procedures for your furnace. A forced-air system is the most likely to cause problems. Make sure filters are changed regularly and that air can flow freely through the vents.

Any appliance that uses flammable fuels can be the source of CO poisoning.

A fireplace may also be the culprit. If the chimney does not draw well, or if the chimney bricks are not well mortared, CO from burning wood can leak into living areas—even if you do not smell

smoke. This often occurs on upper floors, so install a CO detector there as well.

Many homeowners neglect to install carbon monoxide detectors, but these are an essential line of defense. Place one detector near but not in the room that contains the water heater and heating unit. Place another in the main floor's living room. If you use your garage as a work space, place one there as well. You may want to place CO detectors next to your smoke detectors.

If your home tests for high levels of CO, open windows to provide some ventilation. If that does not solve the problem, evacuate the house. In either case, call in a heating contractor to make repairs.

TESTING FOR RADON

Like carbon monoxide, radon is a colorless and odorless gas, so it can affect your family's health in subtle or dramatic ways with no warning.

Usually, there are no immediate, apparent symptoms of radon poisoning. However, breathing radon for extended periods increases the risk of cancer.

Radon is a naturally occurring result of the decay of radium, an element that can be found in most any locale. According to some estimates, 1 in 15 houses in the United States is affected by radon poisoning.

Though it is present most everywhere, radon is more of a problem in some locales than in others. Before buying a home, check with an inspector to see whether radon is a danger in that neighborhood. Some communities require a radon test before selling a home.

To test for radon, you may choose to hire a company that specializes in testing for radon and other airborne dangers. Before hiring the company, check with your building department and the Better Business Bureau to make sure it is on the level: Radon detection and protection is fertile ground for unscrupulous contractors.

Alternatively, purchase a radon testing kit. Typically, a kit consists of a canister filled with charcoal. Leave the canister open for a few days in the house, then send it to a testing agency.

Radon typically seeps up through the ground and into a home via small openings in a basement or crawlspace. If a home is otherwise well sealed, radon will remain in the air. A well-ventilated home is somewhat less likely to be affected, but the real solution is to stop the radon from entering the home.

Sealing out radon is largely a low-tech affair. Check your basement or crawlspace, as well as lower parts of your first-floor siding or masonry, for any points of access. Use latex/silicone caulk to seal small gaps, such as around pipes and cables that enter from the outside. Stuff larger gaps with insulation or foam sealant.

If your basement walls are often moist, they could also be allowing radon into the home. Paint them with waterproofing basement paint. If you have a sump pump, install a tight-fitting lid. Then take steps to increase your home's ventilation.

TESTING FOR LEAD

Children are particularly susceptible to lead poisoning. Once it enters the human body, lead is very slow to leave, so prolonged exposure to even very low levels has an accumulative effect. Lead poisoning typically affects the brain. Symptoms may include nausea, headache, fatigue, short attention span, and clumsiness.

Prior to the 1970s, many homes were finished with paint that contained high levels of lead. As long as it remains on the wall, lead paint is not a problem. However, paint chips or dust, caused by flaking walls or two surfaces rubbing together (as with a sash window), are exceedingly poisonous if swallowed by a child.

A hardware store may carry a lead testing kit, which unfortunately is not guaranteed to be accurate. To be sure, hire a company to collect chips and send them to a lab for testing.

If you have lead paint in sound condition, the solution may be simply to paint over it. Scraping or sanding will create dangerous dust and chips. If the paint is peeling or otherwise unsound, contact a company that specializes in lead abatement.

A few older homes have lead pipes. A lead pipe is gray, and you can easily gouge it with a sharp object. In some older cities, the main supply pipe, which runs from the street to the house, is lead. Copper pipe installed before the 1970s may have joints held together with soldering that contains lead.

Some cities treat these problems by adding a trace element of phosphate to the water. This coats the lead pipes or joints so that virtually no lead leaches into drinking water. To be safe, however, contact your building department to see about having your water tested.

To further ensure that there's no lead in your drinking and cooking water, allow water to run for a minute or so before using it; water that has sat in pipes all night is more likely to pick up lead. Cook with cold water rather than hot water, which is also more likely to be contaminated.

Until the 1970s, automobiles ran on gasoline that contained lead. Consequently, soil near a busy street may be contaminated. Simply keeping a house and clothing clean can go a long way toward eliminating the possibility of lead poisoning.

ASSESSING POTENTIAL ASBESTOS HAZARDS

Until the 1970s, it was common to wrap pipes with insulation made of asbestos. Asbestos was also used as wall insulation, as a siding material, and as an ingredient of many floor tiles and sheet goods. Even the "cottage cheese" texture on some ceilings may contain asbestos.

Asbestos is an ideal material for many purposes because it is virtually impossible to burn. However, we now know that tiny particles of asbestos, when inhaled, can cause cancer of the lung or stomach. In many cases, symptoms are not apparent until 10 years or more after exposure. It's well worth your efforts to have your home inspected for asbestos and to require an inspection if buying a home.

When the dangers of asbestos first became apparent, companies and individuals spent thousands of dollars removing it. This proved a difficult process because even microscopic particles must be captured during removal.

Today, many experts say that covering, rather than removing, is the best solution. They've concluded that the very act of removing asbestos poses far more dangers than does undisturbed existing asbestos. Asbestos in good condition poses little danger, and asbestos that is adequately covered poses virtually no danger.

If your heat or water pipes are wrapped in old, cloth-covered insulation, it may be asbestos. If the material is brown, it's probably a type of cardboard. However, if it is light gray or white, chances are it is asbestos. Soak a small section thoroughly with water and, wearing long sleeves and gloves and a dust mask, cut out a small section. Place it in a plastic bag and take it to your building department to see if it is asbestos.

Loose-fill insulation in an older attic also may contain asbestos. Wet and collect a sample and have it tested. Older asphalt or vinyl tiles and sheet goods may contain asbestos. Wear a respirator when removing these products.

Local codes may require that asbestos be removed rather than encapsulated. You will have to hire an abatement company certified to do such work.

Otherwise, you may be able to deal with the problem yourself; consult with your building department first. Perhaps you will be allowed to wrap asbestos pipe insulation with plastic and tape approved for such use. You also may be permitted to seal over asbestos insulation with plastic, and then cover the plastic with plywood.

GUARDING AGAINST FORMALDEHYDE AND MOLD

Many modern composite building materials, including plywood, particleboard, oriented-strand board (OSB), and medium-density fiberboard (MDF), are made using resins that contain formaldehyde. These products are used to make cabinets, to cover subfloors and exterior walls and roofs, and to serve many other common purposes in home construction. Urea-formaldehyde foam insulation (UFFI) is no longer made, but was used to build many homes. Cloth that is used for draperies, carpet, and furniture also may contain formaldehyde.

So for most of us, formaldehyde is a fact of life; there's no way to completely eliminate it from the air. However, newer or recently remodeled homes generally have more formaldehyde; levels tend to degrade significantly as the years go by.

About 10 percent of the population is sensitive to formaldehyde exposure. For this group, formaldehyde can produce symptoms such as runny nose, difficulty breathing, coughing, headache, skin rash, and dizziness.

An environmental testing company can test your home for formaldehyde. Ask your building department for recommendations.

If you do have high levels of formaldehyde, it may not be a problem unless a family member is sensitive to it. To relieve symptoms of such sensitivity, improve ventilation in the home, and use a dehumidifier or air conditioner to keep the home drier.

Lately, there have been reports of homes with severe cases of mold. This typically propagates inside walls, ceilings, and floors, and becomes visible only when the problem is out of control.

These problems typically occur in newer homes that are tightly caulked and weatherstripped, but that lack adequate ventilation due to poor construction methods. Homes built correctly according to code will not have these problems.

Be aware that this super-mold problem, though very real, is quite rare. If you find mold or mildew on a wall or ceiling, simply wash it with a bleach solution. Then correct whatever is causing the area to remain moist for long periods.

DEALING WITH HAZARDOUS MATERIALS

We deal with some type of hazardous wastes almost daily. The chart below lists common waste products and how to dispose of them safely and responsibly.

Some items need special attention. For example, rags soaked in a flammable substance such as mineral spirits can burst into flames spontaneously if they're left in a bundle. That's why it's important to spread them out outdoors until all the solvent has evaporated.

Some of the substances cited below are best treated by rinsing with water until they are heavily diluted. Once diluted, flush them through a lower-floor toilet, which empties out quickly into the main drain. Pour, flush, wait for the tank to fill, and flush again.

For more difficult disposal problems, consult with your building department. In some locales, a special disposal truck visits your home for hazardous material pickup several times a year. Or there may be an annual hazardous waste dropoff day, or a designated site where you can deliver the materials anytime.

DISPOSING OF HAZARDOUS WASTES

Waste	OK in Trash	Dilute and Flush	Evaporate and Place in Trash	Recycle or Return	Special Disposal Problem
Aerosol cans, empty	●				
Automobile items					
Antifreeze			●		
Battery				●	
Diesel Fuel					●
Gasoline					●
Motor oil				●	
Tires					●
Cleaners and solvents					
Brush cleaner					●
Degreaser solvent					●
Drain cleaner		●			
Dry-cleaning fluid			●		
Mildew remover	●				
Oven cleaner		●			
Paints and finishes					
Latex paint			●		
Oil-based paint					●
Mineral spirits			●		
Paint stripper		●			
Paint thinner			●		
Rust remover		●			
Wood preservative					●
Pesticides					
Insecticide					●
Pet pest collar					●
Rat poison					●
Weed killer					●

KEEPING YOUR HOME SECURE

How do you guard your home from intruders? The best solution is a combination of safeguards like the following:

■ Start with solid entry doors equipped with high-quality locks. The doors should be solid-core or made with heavy panels. A deadbolt lock with a bolt that slides deep into the door's frame is far superior to a handle lock or a rim lock (see page 429). Equip the garage door with a solid lock as well. If an entry door has its hinges facing out rather than in, a burglar can easily pop the hinge pins and open the door. Install special hinges that make this impossible.

■ Windows are the next most common point of illegal entry. Choose from a wide assortment of locking and securing options; see pages 450–452. Pay special attention to basement windows and consider installing glass block.

■ When you are gone, create the illusion that your home is occupied. Program timers to turn lights on and off (see page 23). You may want to put a radio or even a TV on the timer as well. Have a neighbor collect newspapers and mail; piled-up papers are a dead giveaway that you're out of town.

■ Hide your valuables in unusual locations. Better yet, buy a safe. A fire-resistant safe can also keep your precious photographs safe from harm. If you buy a money chest, install it in a masonry wall, where it will be difficult to remove. The most secure method is to have a safe set into the concrete of a foundation wall.

■ Consider having an alarm system installed. A typical system has sensors at every door and window, as well as a control panel that is turned off and on by use of a secret code. When a window or door is opened and the control panel is not turned off, a loud alarm sounds, and the security company is alerted. The company may send its own personnel, or it may contact the police.

■ In addition, consider installing an intercom system as well as security lighting, as described on these pages.

CHOOSING AN INTERCOM SYSTEM

An entryway intercom lets you check the identity, from a safe distance, of anyone who visits your home. It also can be used to control a buzzer-latch on an entry garden gate. A complete intercom system can also monitor a sleeping baby, pipe music through the house, and generally ease communication.

Intercoms vary in complexity, but the hard-wired types operate on low voltages, stepped down via a transformer, from your home's electrical system. This makes them relatively easy and safe to install (see pages 116–117). Follow the manufacturer's instructions. Your biggest challenge will be unobtrusively routing or fishing wires from one room to another. Newer wireless intercoms skip this step by using your household wiring to carry voice communication, but they don't give you the option of buzzing open locked doors.

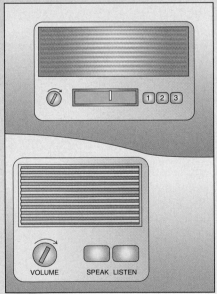

The basic components.
The master station contains circuitry that lets you call any or all of the substations. It also may include a radio. Substations have a combined speaker and microphone with switches that transfer from listen to talk modes. Outdoor substations often include a button to sound the doorbell or chimes. Others just beep or buzz.

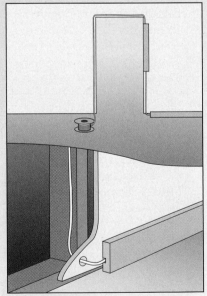

Running the wires.
Low-voltage wiring is similar to that used for telephones. Often, you can run it along moldings.

USING LIGHTS FOR SAFETY AND SECURITY

Thoughtfully planned outdoor lighting not only lights your path, but also repels potential intruders. Photoelectric cell lights in the yard and at the eaves detect movement and turn on when they sense movement. If the lights flood the yard, a burglar will likely be deterred. (For more about exterior lighting, see pages 128–129.)

When you are away from the house, hook interior lights to timers to orchestrate the illusion that the home is occupied. For example, you might program lights to let a living room lamp burn until bedtime, then turn on your usual night-light. More expensive versions control several lights on different programs. You can override most timers when you wish. Check with your local home center or hardware store for other up-to-the-minute devices and techniques.

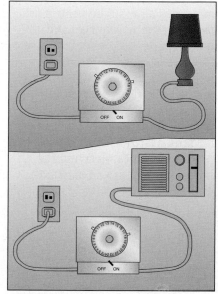

Using timers.
Plug a clock timer into an electric outlet, set the times, then plug in a floor or table lamp. To make it sound as if you are home during the day, program a timer to turn on a radio in the morning and then to turn it off at night.

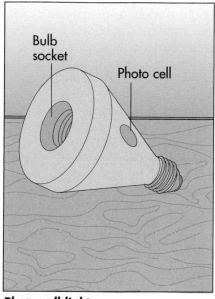

Photo-cell lights.
Inexpensive photoelectric cells sense darkness and turn lights on and off so you don't need to switch them.

Placing outdoor lights.
Position lights not only to illuminate your way at night but also to make any possible intruder feel exposed. Photoelectric cells ensure that strategic outdoor fixtures will turn on, whether you're home or not.

Programmable timer.
You can replace a regular wall switch with a programmable timer that turns lights off and on at preset hours.

Porch or eaves lights.
A pair of eaves fixtures at one corner or above a porch or deck can illuminate two sides of your home with 40- or 60-watt floodlight bulbs. Inexpensive units can be controlled by a motion sensor or by an interior light switch.

DESIGNING FOR UNIVERSAL ACCESS

Until recently, people with physical disabilities have been treated as a special class requiring unusual housing to accommodate their needs. With research sponsored by the Veterans' Administration, and especially with the passage of the Americans with Disabilities Act (ADA), emphasis has shifted from specialized facilities and housing to a design approach that

integrates accessibility into public facilities, the workplace, and housing.

There is growing interest in homes "for the rest of your life." A small initial investment in accessibility and adaptability can make a home more manageable for senior citizens with diminished physical abilities, delaying the need to move into an assisted-living facility.

Before building or purchasing your next home, consider the handicap accessibility features shown on these pages. While designed to accommodate persons in wheelchairs, these plans serve those walking with canes and walkers. The ADA website (www.usdoj.gov/crt/ada) has downloadable drawings that show correct dimensions for all sorts of situations.

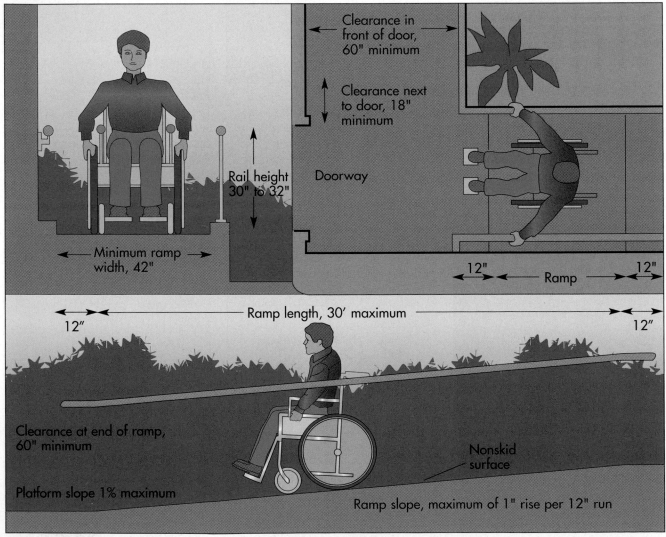

Accessible walks and ramps.
ADA requirements for outdoor walkways are meant to help an able-armed person in a wheelchair to negotiate turns and inclines. Railings must be placed at the

correct height so a person can grab them easily. A ramp should be smooth and free of obstructions. Concrete is preferable, but wooden ramps are also allowed. Turns must be large enough that the

wheelchair can negotiate them with ease. Be sure to position a walkway so that a disabled person can open the door.

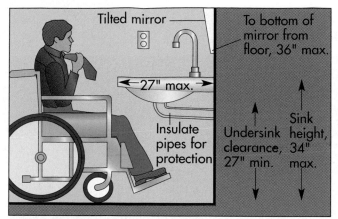

Accessible sink.

A wide assortment of ADA-approved fixtures and special covers ensure that a disabled person can wheel up to a sink and reach the controls without bumping his or her knees on the plumbing.

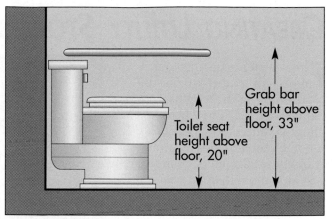

Accessible toilet.

A high-rise toilet brings the seat more closely in line with wheelchair height for an easy transfer. A grab bar, firmly fastened to wall studs, aids the process.

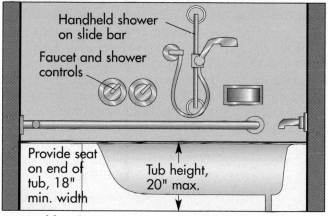

Accessible tub.

Equip a tub with an ADA-approved handheld sprayer, a pivot seat that lets the user swing into the tub, and a grab bar. Place controls within easy reach.

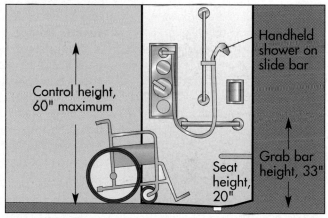

Accessible shower.

Equip the shower with a no-lip floor, a handheld sprayer, accessible controls, and a nonslip seat (18-inch minimum width).

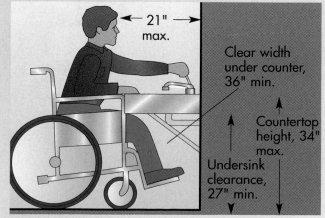

Accessible kitchen.

In a well-designed kitchen, a disabled person can prepare food, cook, and clean up afterwards. Special ADA-approved appliances make installation

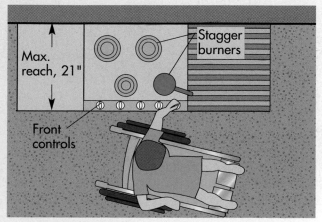

not much more difficult than for a standard kitchen. An accessible counter is narrower than a standard counter. The stove is also narrow, with staggered burners for easy access.

CREATING UTILITY STORAGE

Time spent organizing your tools and lumber will pay off handsomely in the long run. Work can be positively fun when the things you need are in easy reach. A home center will carry a variety of utility storage units, which may cost little more than buying materials to make them yourself.

If you have the space, create a dedicated workroom, complete with workbench (see page 27), shop tools, and organized storage. Plan the layout carefully. If, for instance, you want to run full sheets of plywood through a table saw, you will need more than 8 feet of space in front of and behind the saw. If space is limited, it may help to have movable rather than stationary shop tools.

An unfinished garage ceiling is ideal for storing things that you do not need to reach often, such as seasonal gear. Adding cross ties and nailing up plywood opens an entire level of new space.

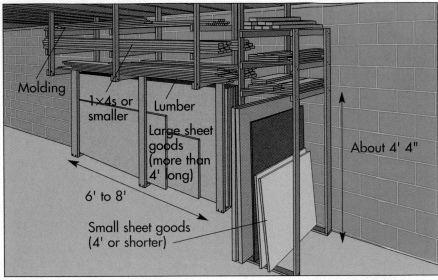

Lumber storage.
A storage setup with shelves up high keeps scrap lumber and sheet goods handy without taking up too much space or looking cluttered. Make plenty of shelves; if you end up stacking the lumber in more than a few layers, it will be difficult to get the bottom pieces out.

Plan the arrangement so it is easy to move pieces in and out. That means you will need ample room to the right or left of the sheet goods. Elevate the sheet goods on boards laid on the floor; if plywood or particleboard gets wet even once, it can be ruined. Place the larger sheets to the rear so you can see the smaller sheets.

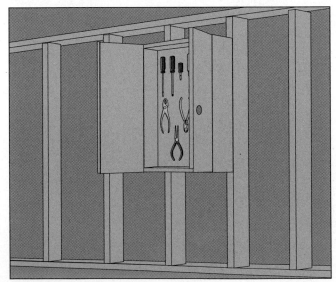

Small-tool storage.
Locking cabinets are best for storing expensive tools, chemicals, paint, and other items that might attract children. For easy access, attach a sheet of pegboard to the studs, and use special hangers for the tools. For portable storage, use a large toolbox or a bucket with a pocketed fabric apron.

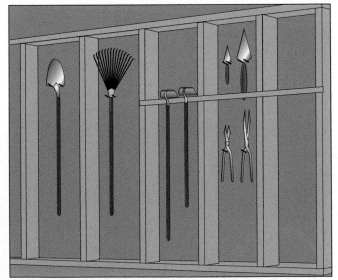

Large-tool storage.
Shovels, rakes, and other large tools are best protected from damage if they are hung, rather than simply propped in a corner. Inexpensive storage is easy to create with nails and scrap lumber. Or purchase special hangers designed for large tools.

BUILDING A SAWHORSE

Sawhorses are portable workbenches that will hold lumber at a comfortable height, making it easier to produce accurate cuts. The sooner you buy or build a pair, the better.

If the top piece is a flat-laid 2×4 or 2×6 (as in the first example at right), a single horse can act as a small workbench. You may want to add a second (replaceable) top layer so you can cut into it. Also consider attaching a shelf to the legs for storing tools.

YOU'LL NEED...
TIME: 1 to 2 hours to build sawhorses from scratch.
SKILLS: Basic carpentry skills.
TOOLS: Tape measure, hammer, drill and drill bits, saw.

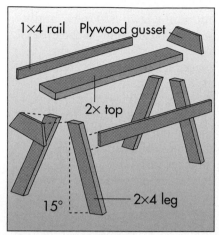

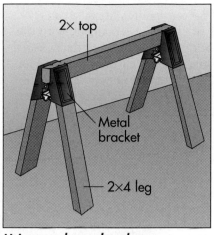

All-wood sawhorse.
Make the length of your sawhorse legs 30 inches, cutting the ends at a 15-degree angle. Make the length and width of the top rail any size you want, but a 2×8 board 4 feet long makes a stable platform on which to set and work on paneling and sheet goods.

Using sawhorse brackets.
A collapsible sawhorse is not as stable as an all-wood model, but it can be stored in a small space. Your options are a sawhorse kit that includes brackets and lumber; brackets only (you cut the lumber to suit); or all-metal collapsible sawhorses.

BUILDING A WORKBENCH

A clean and spacious work surface makes any repair job or construction job more pleasant.

Commercial units range from simple steel-and-particleboard arrangements to elaborate versions that would satisfy a cabinetmaker.

The workbench shown at right is a simple cut-and-assemble job, yet it's plenty serviceable. Specify your own dimensions to fit the available shop space.

The height is important so you won't be bending over more than you need to, and depends on your height. A range of 34 to 40 inches should be in your comfort zone. Width should be 24 to 36 inches. Length will depend on space, although 6 to 8 feet gives you plenty of working area to handle standard-length materials that don't need much cutting.

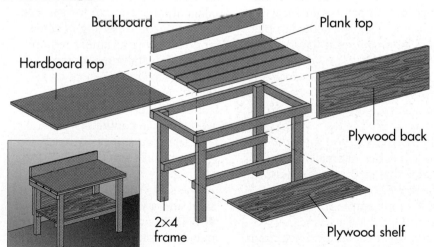

A simple workbench.
Cut the legs from 2×4s or 4×4s, and use 2×4s to support the top and the shelf. Use 2×6s for the top planks and ¾-inch plywood for the backboard, back, and shelf. Top it off with ¼-inch tempered hardboard, which can be replaced when it is worn out.

Assemble the framing with

carriage bolts, and nail or screw on the shelf and planking. If you have a clamp-on vise, extend the front of the planking and top so it overhangs the frame by 3 inches to accept the clamp.

Give all the lumber two coats of penetrating sealer, then assemble the parts. Sand smooth any rough or sharp edges.

PLANNING OUTDOOR LIVING AREAS

Your family's lifestyle can change dramatically with the addition of a patio or deck. You'll find that a well-planned outdoor living area takes pressure off the interior spaces by providing alternative spots for cooking, eating, and relaxing. If you have small children, your life will be easier if they have a play area that is easily viewed by adults who are relaxing or preparing food.

Take your time thinking about and talking over a master plan for your outdoor space. On page 29 you'll see some potential solutions for typical lots. Each has the three ingredients you should include in your plan: an outdoor living area, storage facilities, and a service area. Add a play area if you have children. If you like to grow your own food or love flowers, don't forget to include plans for vegetable and flower gardens.

■ Start with the outdoor living area. The slope of your lot will help you decide whether to plan a deck or a patio. On flat lots, you have a complete range of choices, from brick-in-sand patios to an on-grade deck. If you must work on a slope, you may find that an elevated deck is the only practical alternative. Or, you may choose to build a series of small decks or patios that step gracefully down the slope.

■ Plan for ample room for your typical outdoor activities. A barbecue area should have room for the barbecue unit, plus one or two people to stand and cook; you may want to provide a small counter as well. A dining area should accommodate the table, the chairs, room for scooting the chairs out, and a path for bringing food to the table when people are seated.

■ To make sure the space will be comfortable, set patio furniture out on the lawn and have family members test it out. If the area is too heavily sloped to do this, experiment in another area with the same dimensions.

■ Study the area's relationship to the interior floor plan. You'll want convenient access, so take advantage of existing doors or consider installing a sliding glass door (see pages 448–449). Most people prefer a plan that allows easy access from the kitchen to the outdoor dining area.

■ Consider the view from the inside, which may be obstructed by the railing of a deck. The solution may be to lower the deck by two or three steps.

■ Plan the location and size of storage units to hold your yard and garden or recreational equipment. If a deck is raised 3 feet or more above the ground, the area beneath may fit the bill.

■ Don't neglect the service area. Make it large enough for garbage cans, firewood, potting benches, or whatever your family requires. Consider installing a screen—either a small solid fence or a lattice structure—to hide or partially hide your equipment and your garbage containers. Make sure that you can easily reach garbage bins from the house and can easily wheel them to the street. At the same time, keep bins out of sight and away from living areas.

■ Before you dig holes or trenches, learn the locations of any underground lines. Your utility companies will tell you (at no charge) where the electrical cables and gas pipes run, as well as how deeply they are sunk. Your building department should know the locations of the main water supply. If you have a septic system, be sure you maintain access to the tank, and avoid building on top of the field.

■ Use graph paper to sketch out ideas to scale. Or you may want to stake out the areas on a trial-and-error basis.

■ Finally, plan for privacy and screening. Consider the plantings you have and those you want to add, as well as fences you might want to build.

With goals established, you're ready to work out the details, such as the exact size of your deck or patio, what materials to use, and the cost. With the know-how that follows, doing it yourself will yield worthwhile results—convenience, comfort for years to come, and more money in your pocket.

EXPERTS' INSIGHT

SETBACK REQUIREMENTS

Many a homeowner has made the mistake of building a structure that extends a foot or so beyond the legal boundary.

Check your plat of survey to find your exact property line. If you are unsure, consult with your building department.

In many locales, it's not enough to simply stay on your property. Setback regulations may require that a building or patio be a certain distance short of the property line. Again, check with your building department before construction.

You may also have an easement to think about. If, for instance, a neighbor needs to cross your property to take out the garbage, you may be restricted as to what sorts of things you can build in this path.

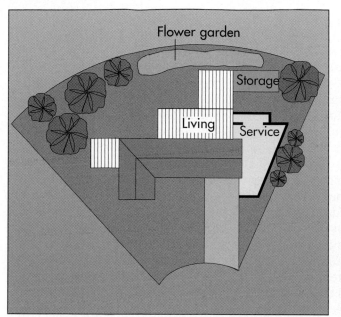

A long house with ample yard space on either side.
Sometimes you can have more than one living area. In this plan, a small deck or patio provides privacy for lounging or intimate dining, while a larger area provides spillover for parties. The large deck leads to a flower garden, which is on display for visitors as well as for those inside the house. The service area is largely out of sight, yet accessible to the driveway.

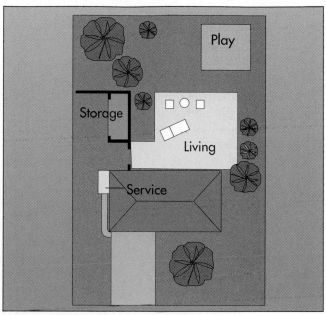

A traditional rectangular yard.
Many homes have yards shaped like this, with a front yard, narrow spaces on both sides, and a fairly large backyard. If all you need is space for the garbage, the service area can be small and tucked away. A large, nearly square deck or patio can accommodate dining, lounging, and barbecuing. The play area is in plain sight from the deck or from a back window.

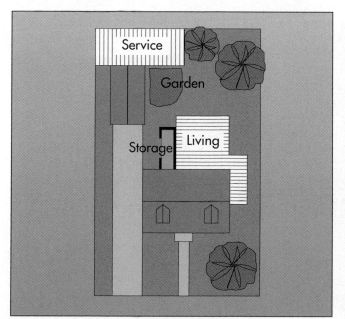

A compact arrangement with detached garage.
Where overall area is limited, plan the spaces and paths carefully. This living area, though small, provides both a dining/barbecuing area and a smaller section on the side for a lounge chair. The service area, behind the garage, is largely hidden yet next to the garden.

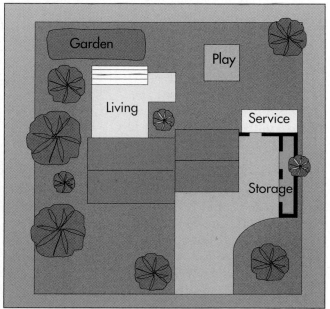

A square space.
If a home is located in the center of a squarish space, there may be no one large yard area. The best solution may be to scatter the living, service, and storage areas. Here, storage and service areas are clearly separate from the living area—and also easily reached from the driveway.

Planning a Kitchen

Before you get specific about style, materials, and the exact features and appliances you might want to add to your kitchen, assess your needs. Here are some things to consider:

■ Make a list of the items you use often and of those items you seldom use. Plan a cabinetry layout that puts often-used items within easy reach.

■ Consider how much counter space you need and where to best locate it. A cutting area near the sink or the garbage container, for instance, is helpful.

■ Keep the traffic between the back door and the rest of the house away from the food preparation area. Design in a permanent detour. Also, if there's a bottleneck between the dining area and the sink, doing the dishes for a large dinner will be difficult and could take some of the fun out of entertaining.

■ Kitchen lighting should be bright, but not glaring. In most cases, a combination of overhead, hanging, and undercabinet lighting is the best arrangement.

■ Even if you usually do not eat meals in the kitchen, having a spot for a couple of kids to snack or for guests to talk with the cook makes the kitchen a friendlier place. Islands or peninsulas work well as informal eating areas.

When it comes time to draw up your plans, a great many resources are at your disposal. Home centers, cabinetmakers, and kitchen specialty stores often have computer programs that simulate various configurations tailored for your space. Many also give you an instant quote on what the proposed kitchen would cost.

A lower-tech option may be more useful and enjoyable: Purchase a set of kitchen design templates. With these scale-drawn cutouts of cabinets and appliances, you can move the pieces around until you achieve the most useful and pleasing configuration.

Plan countertops so you can reach items easily. For average-size adults, tables should be 29 to 31 inches high. Counters are typically 36 inches high; a surface that's 34 inches high can be used as both a counter and a table.

Wall cabinets range from 30 to 42 inches in height. Unless you are tall, the top shelf of a 42-inch-high wall cabinet will be difficult to reach without a boost up.

Keep the swing of appliance doors in mind. Make sure you can walk through the space while a dishwasher or oven door is open.

Measuring for New Cabinets

Standardized dimensions and modular designs greatly simplify the job of tailoring cabinets to your kitchen. Order a series of units that comes close to fitting the space, then make up the difference with fillers between the cabinets.

Plot your kitchen area on graph paper, making both a floor plan and an elevation drawing. Be sure to include door swings, heating vents, window casings, pipes, electrical outlets and switches, and appliance sizes.

Visit a cabinet dealer for more ideas, then plan your layout using the information at right. The height measurements shown accommodate the reach of an average-height person and are accepted as standards throughout the kitchen and appliance industries.

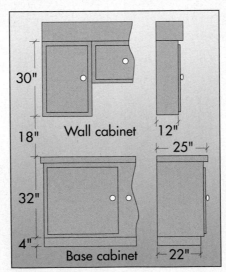

Base cabinets.
Base cabinets usually are 34½ inches high by 23 inches deep. (The countertop will be 36 inches high and 25 inches deep.) Some units have several drawers; others have one drawer and a set of doors. A sink base typically has only doors.

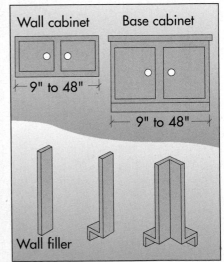

Wall cabinets and fillers.
Manufacturers offer plenty of choices when it comes to cabinet widths—from 9 to 48 inches wide. Filler strips fit between cabinets or cabinets and walls, letting you adjust a bank of cabinets to the space available. Ripsaw each strip to the width required.

DESIGNING A KITCHEN LAYOUT

Measure your kitchen, including exact lengths of walls, widths and locations of doors and windows, location of existing plumbing, and heights of windowsills and the ceiling. Be precise and thorough—even include the molding around doors and windows. Carefully note the dimensions of existing appliances that you will have to accommodate in the plan. Use manufacturer's literature to find the correct opening sizes for each new appliance.

A typical kitchen design seeks to create a "work triangle" so that the refrigerator, sink, dishwasher, and range (or cooktop and oven) are conveniently nearby without being crowded. It should be easy to open the refrigerator door and move items to a countertop. The dishwasher should be next to the sink. Provide at least 18 inches of counter space on either side of the sink and the range.

Plot these dimensions on graph paper and take the sketch to a home center. You'll see samples of many cabinet styles, ranging from unfinished pine to hardwoods and ultramodern European designs. After selecting a product line that suits your taste and budget, sit down with the designer.

The designer will key your sketch dimensions into a computer-aided design (CAD) program. Working from the list of cabinet sizes available in your chosen line, you can plug cabinets into the layout. When you're done, the design for your kitchen will appear. Changing cabinet widths, heights, or even styles is as simple as a few key strokes. You can even view the design in three dimensions. "Move" around the room and see how it looks.

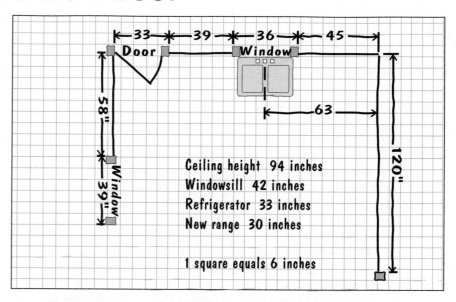

Ceiling height 94 inches
Windowsill 42 inches
Refrigerator 33 inches
New range 30 inches

1 square equals 6 inches

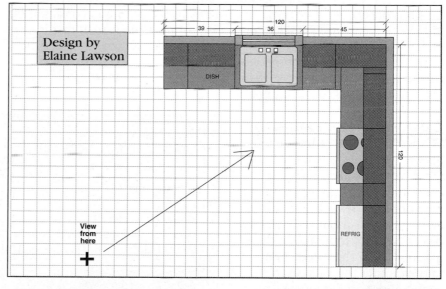

Design by Elaine Lawson

PLANNING A BATHROOM

Bathrooms are small, but they're densely packed with potential projects. In fact, most of the installations needed for a kitchen are also needed in a bathroom.

Begin the planning process by assessing your needs:

■ Should the bathroom be configured so that two people can use it at the same time?

■ Do you just want the basic ensemble of toilet, tub/shower, and sink, or would you like something extra, such as a spa, a double sink, or a luxury shower?

■ Does your bathroom need more light? If you have a window, is it in a place where water collects and causes problems?

■ Is better ventilation needed, or perhaps another electrical outlet, or more counter space around the sink?

■ Do you have enough towel racks and other storage room?

■ Is the shower or tub large enough?

■ What style is your bath calling out for?

If you examine your present bathroom, you may be surprised at how much of it can be salvaged. If the basic layout works—the fixtures are placed comfortably apart and there is enough room left for storage and towel racks—then you can keep your basic plumbing and only replace fixtures. Even if your bathroom as a whole needs remodeling, one or more of the fixtures may be worth keeping. Perhaps the color and condition of wall or floor tile is such that it can be preserved. Often you can find new fixtures, tiles, and wall treatments to go with them.

If you do decide to move fixtures around, be prepared for major plumbing chores. The first question to ask is whether you can run a drain to the new fixture location. You may need to hire a professional plumber to tell you whether you need to install a new plumbing vent—a major project involving running a sizeable pipe through walls and possibly the roof (see pages 212–213). If the space seems unworkable, consider moving walls to make more room.

Lighting is important in a bathroom. Usually, you want a good general overhead light, another overhead light in the tub area, and lights above or alongside the medicine cabinet and mirror. Choose these carefully; you should aim for adequate illumination without glare.

Comfortable clearances.

When it comes to bathroom fixtures, an inch or two can make the difference between feeling comfortable or cramped. Map out the floor of your bathroom on graph paper. Cut out scale-size pieces of paper to represent the fixtures. Move the pieces around until you find the most usable configuration. If a door swings inward, make sure it won't bump into a fixture or built-in unit. The dimensions given in these drawings show the minimum requirements for ease of use. Fixtures placed closer to each other than these minimums will make you feel squeezed. Usually, it's best to give yourself more room than the minimum, but don't go overboard and space things too far apart. Watch the details: Plan your towel racks and hooks at the same time as you plan your fixtures.

WIRING BASICS

How Circuits Work

Electricity is the flow of electrons through a conductor. In home electrical systems, wires, consisting of highly conductive copper wrapped in insulation for safety, are the conductors—the assigned pathway through which the electricity travels. A host of other items—a fork, a screwdriver, you—also can serve as conductors, sometimes with disastrous results. It's the goal of a safe electrical system to prevent this from happening.

Electricity always flows in a loop, known as a circuit. When a circuit is interrupted at any point, the electricity shuts off. As soon as the circuit is reconnected, the flow begins again.

Electricity is generated by your local electric company. Overhead and underground wires bring power from the utility company lines to a home's service head, also called a weatherhead because it can withstand wind, heat, and ice. Although the utility company sends high-voltage electricity along some of its power lines, by the time it reaches your house, it is 120 volts per wire.

The electricity passes through an electric meter, which measures how much enters the house. It proceeds to a service panel (also called the breaker box or fuse box), which distributes electricity throughout the house along individual circuits. Each circuit flows out of the service panel, through a number of fixtures and receptacles, and back to the service panel. (For more on service panels, see pages 36-37.)

To make a circuit, electricity is carried out of the service panel on "hot" wires that usually have black insulation, although they sometimes may be red, and is returned to the panel on neutral wires that have white insulation.

The service panel contains

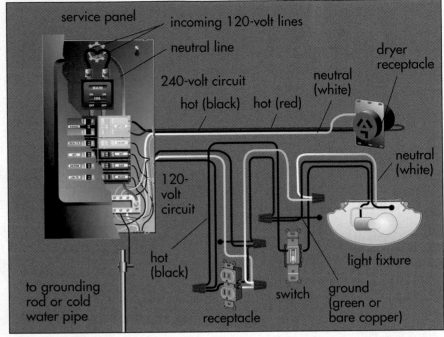

Following the flow

The flow of electricity in typical household circuits starts with the two 120-volt lines and single neutral line that enter the top of the service panel. Both 120-volt lines are used to make the 240-volt circuit, though only one neutral

circuit breakers or fuses—both are safety devices that shut off the power in case of a short circuit or other fault in the circuit (see pages 36-37, 75–76).

Each circuit has a number of outlets that lead to smaller circuits through which the electricity flows. These outlets might include receptacles, fixtures, and switches. For example, a wall switch interrupts (off) or completes (on) the circuit to one or more light fixtures. A heavy-use appliance—such as a dishwasher, garbage disposal, or microwave oven—may need a circuit to itself.

Most circuits carry current of 120 volts which will give most people quite a jolt but will not seriously harm them if they should accidentally come into contact

line is needed for the electricity to complete its loop. The 120-volt circuit has one hot wire (black) and one neutral wire (white), plus a copper ground wire (green). In case of a short, the ground wire carries the current safely into the ground.

with it. Most homes also have one or two 240-volt lines, which double the power by using two hot wires with one neutral wire. Because of the higher power, take special care when dealing with these.

Every electrical system must be grounded for safety. Grounding allows excess current to travel harmlessly into the earth in case of overload or a short circuit. Usually this is done by connecting a wire to a cold water pipe, to a grounding rod sunk deep into the ground, or sometimes to both.

Circuits in your home may be grounded with a grounding wire that is bare copper or green, or they may be grounded by means of the metal receptacle boxes and the metal sheathing that contains the wires (see pages 48–51).

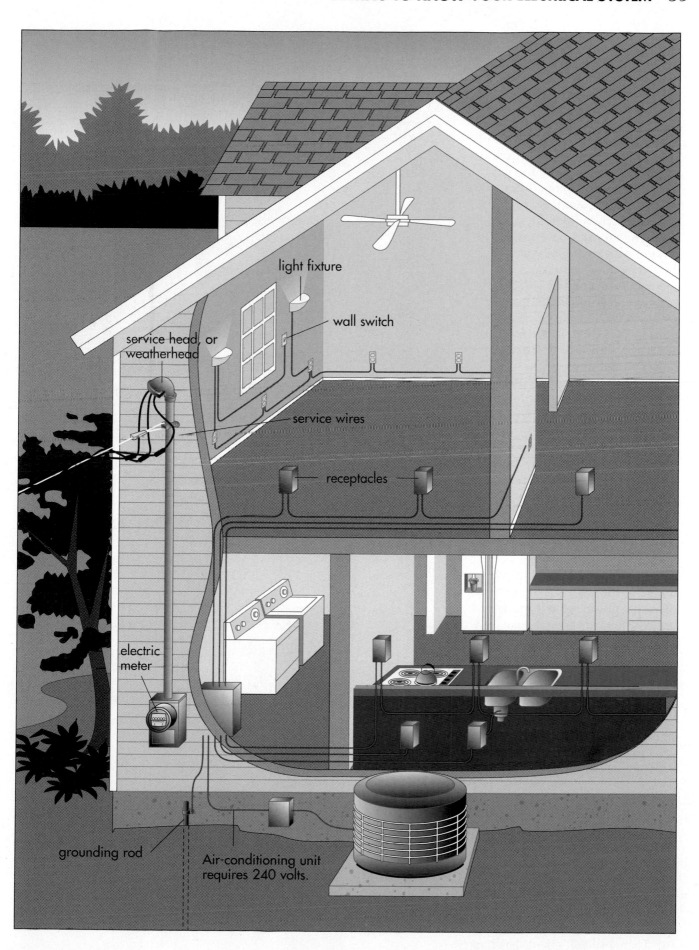

light fixture

wall switch

service head, or weatherhead

service wires

receptacles

electric meter

grounding rod

Air-conditioning unit requires 240 volts.

SERVICE PANELS

Electrical projects always begin at the service panel, which is either a breaker box or a fuse box. When a short or an overload shuts down power to a circuit, this is where you go to restore the flow. It's also where you cut off power to a circuit before starting a project.

Power arrives from the meter through two main power wires, each of which carry 120 volts of electricity into the house. Usually these are black and/or red. In addition there is a white main neutral wire that carries electricity back to the utility. The main hot wires are connected to a main power shutoff. When you turn this off, you don't de-energize the hot wires, but you cut power to everything else in the box.

Breaker boxes

Emerging from a breaker box's main shutoff are two hot bus bars. The 120-volt breakers are each attached to one of these bars. (This means that if one of the main hot wires gets damaged outside your house, you will lose power to about half of the circuits in your house.) Each 240-volt breaker gets twice the power by being attached to both bus bars. When a circuit is overloaded or a short occurs, its breaker trips and shuts off power before the wires heat up and become a danger.

The main neutral wire is connected to the neutral bus bar. This bar is connected to a system ground wire, which leads to a grounding rod (see art on page 34). White wires for every circuit, and possibly bare or green ground wires, also connect to the neutral bus bar. As a result, each 120-volt circuit has a black or colored wire leading from a circuit breaker, a white wire leading to the neutral bus bar, and possibly a bare copper or green-covered ground wire also connected to the neutral bar. Each 240-volt circuit has two

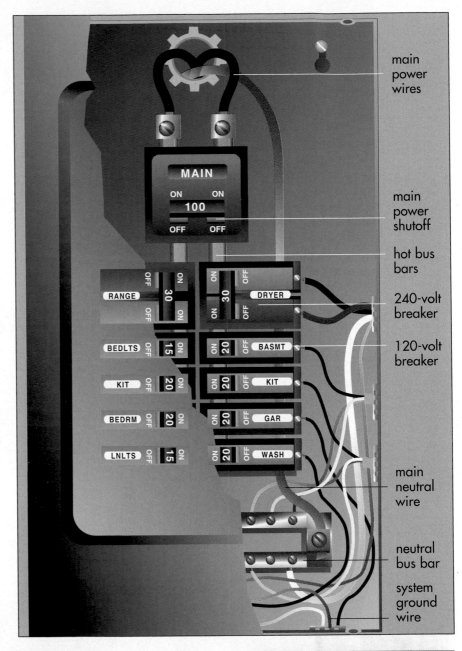

main power wires

main power shutoff

hot bus bars

240-volt breaker

120-volt breaker

main neutral wire

neutral bus bar

system ground wire

wires leading to a circuit breaker. In addition, the 240-volt circuit has a neutral and, possibly, a ground wire connected to the neutral bus bar. Systems with conduit or armored cable do not need separate ground wires—the conduit or metal sheathing act as ground conductors (see page 92).

For how to troubleshoot the several types of circuit breakers and how to check for the cause of shorts, see pages 75.

CAUTION!
LEAVE INCOMING WIRES FOR THE UTILITY COMPANY
If you suspect that the wires entering your house may be damaged in any way, do not attempt to work on them yourself. Have the utility company inspect them. Usually it will inspect and repair them for free.

Fuse boxes

If you have an older home that has not been rewired in the last 25 or 30 years, chances are that its electrical heart is a fuse box rather than a breaker box.

Fuse boxes are wired and work the same way as breaker boxes (see page 36), but instead of tripping as a breaker does, a fuse "blows" when there's too much current in its circuit. When this happens, you must eliminate the short or the overload, remove the blown fuse, and screw in or plug in a new one.

Power comes into a fuse box through two main power wires. (In a house with no 240-volt equipment, there may be only one of these.) Current flows through a main disconnect, in this case a pullout block that holds a pair of cartridge fuses.

Next in line are a series of plug fuses that protect the black hot wires of the individual circuits, often called branch circuits. Unscrewing a fuse disconnects its circuit. A neutral bus bar receives the main neutral wire and a neutral wire for each of the branch circuits. A system ground wire leads from the neutral bus bar to a grounding rod outside the house.

For tips on troubleshooting a fuse box, see page 76.

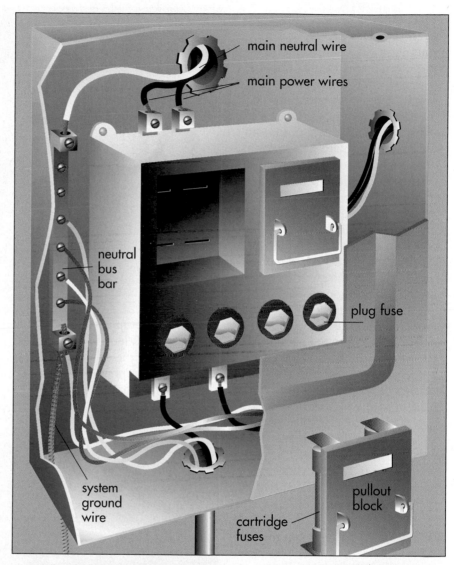

main neutral wire

main power wires

neutral bus bar

plug fuse

system ground wire

cartridge fuses

pullout block

> ## CAUTION!
> **NEVER "UPGRADE" A FUSE**
> If you have a chronically overloaded circuit, you might be tempted to install a bigger fuse—replace a 15-amp fuse with a 20-amp fuse, for example. Don't do it. Wiring that gets more current than it was designed to handle heats up and can catch fire. Always replace a blown fuse with one of the same amperage rating.

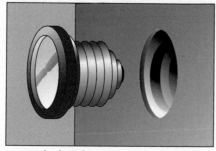

Typical plug fuse

A plug fuse is threaded and screws into the fuse box. Handle only the rim. Do not touch the threads while removing or replacing the fuse. For information on identifying and replacing a blown fuse, see page 76.

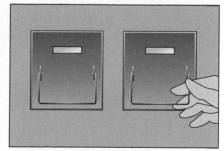

Handling pullout blocks

Larger 240-volt circuits, as well as main shutoff fuses, often are protected by pullout blocks that contain cartridge fuses. If you need to pull out a cartridge fuse that is not in a pullout block, do not use your fingers. Get a fuse puller (see pages 43 and 76).

GROUNDING AND POLARIZATION

Older homes often have receptacles and fixtures that are ungrounded, and many local codes do not require that they be rewired so they're grounded. Still, grounding is worth adding to your system because it adds protection against electrical shock. Grounding provides a third path for electricity to travel along, so if there is a leak of any sort, it will flow into the earth rather than into the body of a person who touches a defective fixture, appliance, or tool.

An electrical system is grounded with a grounding rod driven at least 8 feet into the ground outside the house or by connecting to a cold water pipe. Each individual branch circuit must be grounded as well, either with a separate wire that leads to the neutral bar of the service panel or with metal sheathing that runs without a break from each outlet to the panel. (In theory, electrical outlets can be grounded individually, but this is impractical.)

Some locations in your house—especially where the outlet and/or appliances may become wet—require ground-fault circuit-interrupter (GFCI) receptacles (see pages 112–113). Older, ungrounded circuits usually are protected by polarization, which is less effective than grounding but better than nothing. Grounded and polarized receptacles work only if they are wired correctly. See pages 70–71 to test for this.

> **CAUTION!**
> *DON'T ALTER PRONGS ON PLUGS*
> *Never clip or file down the prongs on a grounded or polarized plug. Go to the heart of the problem: Test and upgrade your circuit and receptacle.*

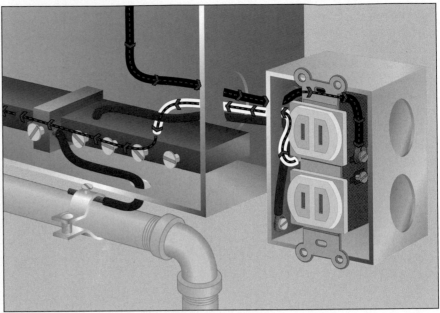

A polarized receptacle
A polarized outlet has one slot that is longer than the other. This is to ensure that the plug is inserted so that its hot current flows through black or red wires, and neutral current flows through white wires. Although not as safe as a grounded system, polarization is the next best thing.

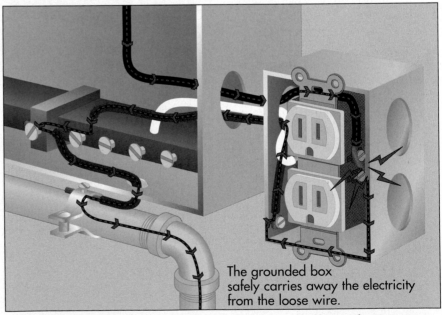

The grounded box safely carries away the electricity from the loose wire.

A grounded receptacle
The grounding circuit must follow an unbroken path to the earth. A third, rounded prong on a modern plug fits into the round slot in the receptacle. This slot connects to a wire—or to metal conduit or sheathing—that leads without interruption to the neutral bus bar of the breaker box. The system ground wire then leads from the bus bar to the earth. Instead of a grounding rod, a cold water pipe often is used for grounding because it is connected to water supply pipes that go deep under the ground.

LIMITATIONS OF OLDER SYSTEMS

An older home may have electrical service that is inadequate or even unsafe. It can be confusing, as well. If you are unsure about your home's wiring, have a professional check it out.

Some older systems have only two wires—one hot (rather than two) and a neutral—entering the house. This means you will not be able to have any 240-volt circuits for large appliances.

Modern electrical service provides at least 100 amps of power, which is enough to power a medium-size house with an average number of appliances. A house built in the 1950s or before may only have 30-amp service (the circuit box will have only two fuses) or 60-amp service (four fuses). With so few circuits, the number of fixtures and appliances you can run will be limited.

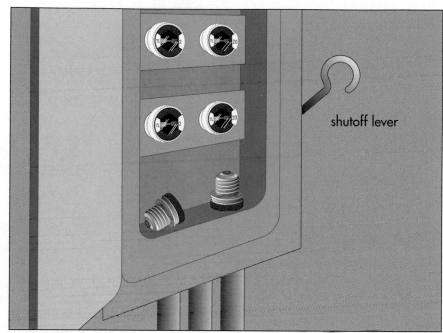

Limited service
This 60-amp service panel has four 15-amp fuses and a switch lever for shutting off all power. If

you have this or a 30-amp (two-fuse) box, it's a good idea to have a professional upgrade you to a 100-amp service panel with breakers.

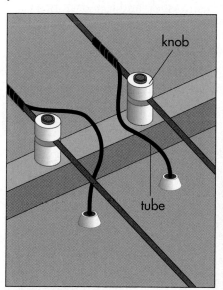

Knob-and-tube wiring
This type of wiring was common in houses built before World War II. The individual wires are wrapped in a rubberized cloth and have no additional protection. There is no ground wire. These wires should be replaced with modern cable, particularly in areas where they are exposed, such as attics and basements.

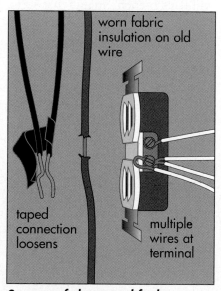

Sources of shorts and faults
Loose taped wires, old wire damaged because it's exposed, and multiple wires slipping off a single terminal screw may seem like minor problems, but are not. Drastic consequences, such as fire and electrocution, are the reasons codes are strict about good wiring practices. See pages 57–59 for the correct way to connect wires.

Ungrounded, unpolarized circuits
If your outlets have two slots that are the same size, then they are neither polarized nor grounded (see page 38). This leaves you with no protection against shocks from defective fixtures or appliances using that outlet. At the very least you need to install polarized outlets.

HOUSEHOLD CIRCUITS

The electrical service in your house is divided into branch circuits, each of which supplies power to a defined area of your home. It is important to make sure that no branch circuit is carrying too great a load, or you will be constantly resetting breakers or replacing fuses. Some appliances need to have a circuit for themselves. An electric stove or dryer will have its own 240-volt circuit; other heavy-use appliances may require their own 120-volt circuits. More often a circuit supplies a number of outlets using a range of power.

To find out if a circuit is overloaded, add up the total power drawn by the circuit as outlined below. Check the breaker or fuse to see how many amps the circuit can deliver. If your total use exceeds the amperage the circuit can supply, change your usage. The solution may be as simple as plugging an appliance into a different receptacle—or you may have to add another circuit to your electrical system (see pages 80–83).

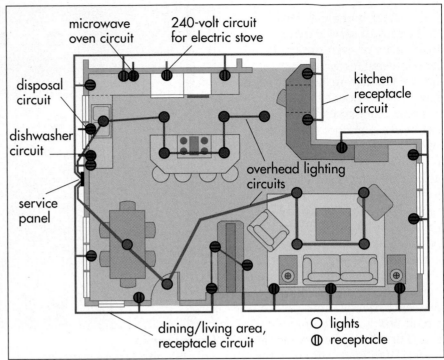

Typical circuit plan

A well-planned electrical system will have branch circuits that serve easily defined areas or purposes. Unfortunately, many homes— especially if they have been remodeled by do-it-yourselfers— have circuits that roam all over the house. Note that some appliances, such as the microwave oven, dishwasher, and disposal, need their own circuits. The electric stove needs its own 240-volt circuit. Otherwise, circuits are roughly organized by the rooms they serve and by their anticipated demand.

MEASUREMENTS

To figure your circuit loads, total the watts being used. Check the specification label on each appliance. Also note the wattage of the lightbulbs in fixtures on the circuit. Divide the total by 120 (the number of volts). The resulting number will tell you how many amperes ("amps") the circuit draws when all appliances and lights are on and whether or not you are placing too great a demand on it. Here are some typical watt and amperage figures for common household appliances.

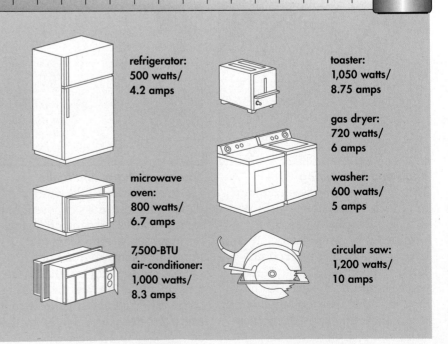

refrigerator: 500 watts/ 4.2 amps

microwave oven: 800 watts/ 6.7 amps

7,500-BTU air-conditioner: 1,000 watts/ 8.3 amps

toaster: 1,050 watts/ 8.75 amps

gas dryer: 720 watts/ 6 amps

washer: 600 watts/ 5 amps

circular saw: 1,200 watts/ 10 amps

MAPPING YOUR CIRCUITS

When you look inside the door of your service panel, do you see a detailed description of what each branch circuit controls? If not, make a chart yourself. You'll be glad you mapped the circuits the next time you have to turn off a circuit for repairs or improvements.

Begin by making a map of each floor in the house. Take care to include all receptacles, switches, appliances, and fixtures. Be aware that 240-volt receptacles will have their own circuits. With a large house, you may have to make more than one drawing per floor.

Mapping is best done with a helper to flip switches and test outlets while you stay at the box and write down findings. If you must work alone, plug in a radio turned to peak volume to find the general area covered by the circuit. The radio will go silent when you switch off the current. Test outlets to find the extent of the circuit.

1. Test each outlet.
Mark each circuit breaker or fuse with a number. Turn on all the appliances and lights on one floor. Plug a lamp into every receptacle and turn on. Turn off one circuit and have your helper write the circuit number next to each outlet that went dead.

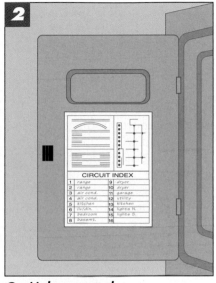

2. Make a record.
Continue the test with every circuit for every floor. Transfer the findings onto a sheet of paper you will affix to the inside of the circuit box door.

THE NEC

Electrical codes are based on the National Electrical Code (NEC), which is published by a non-profit organization and is upgraded periodically. The NEC takes up a huge book that covers every conceivable electrical situation. It provides the model on which virtually all local codes are based.

Some communities simply adopt the code as their own; others modify it. Any time you want to make a change in your electrical service, check the NEC and local codes before you begin.

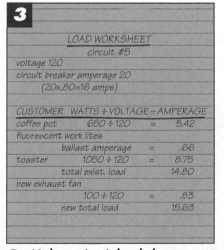

3. Make a circuit load sheet.
To really get a fix on how your house uses electricity, combine the information you have just gathered with the power-use information printed on appliances. Write up a load sheet, as shown. It will help you assess capacity for future additions to your electrical system.

CAUTION!
HANDLE YOUR SERVICE PANEL WITH RESPECT
Take special care when working around a service panel. Remove cover plates only when you absolutely have to and replace them as soon as you can. Keep the door shut whenever you are not inspecting the panel. Lock it, if you think your kids may get at it. Remember that even if you have shut off the main power breaker or switch, there is still power entering the box.

Essential Tools

You don't need to purchase an arsenal of specialized tools to do the electrical projects in this book. For most repairs, a minor outlay will be enough to equip you adequately.

Needle-nose and **lineman's pliers** are musts. You need the first to bend wires into the loops required for many electrical connections. Lineman's pliers make it possible to neatly twist wires together. Both also are used to cut wires. **Side-cutting pliers** make it easy to snip wires in tight places and are ideal for cutting sheathing off cable.

To strip wires use an **adjustable wire stripper** or a **combination tool** (which also crimps and cuts wire). If you're working with nonmetallic cable, use a **cable ripper** to remove the sheathing easily without nicking the wires. A simple **neon tester** will tell you if an outlet or fixture is live. A

beaded chain simplifies fishing thin, low-voltage wires or phone wires through walls.

General carpentry tools that come in handy when doing electrical work include an **electric drill** with a **spade bit** to make holes for cable to pass through; a **utility knife, screwdrivers**, a **keyhole saw** for cutting drywall, a **level**, a **hacksaw** for cutting conduit and metal-sheathed cable, and a **tape measure**.

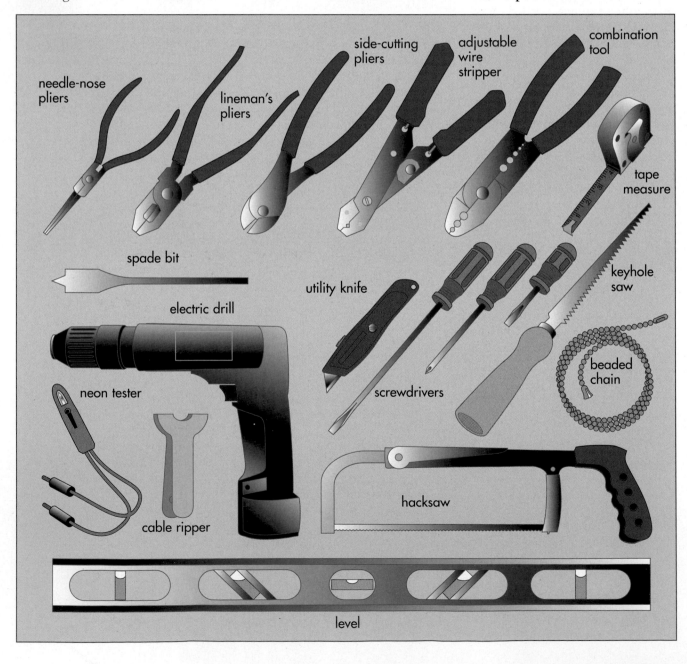

SPECIALIZED TOOLS

As you take on more complicated electrical projects, you will find that other tools are invaluable. Some of these tools are essential to such projects; others simply help you do a better, faster job.

If you need to drill holes deeper than the length of your spade bit, get a **bit extension.** A **soldering gun** with a spool of **lead-free, rosin-core solder** will be necessary if local codes require soldering.

Always use a **fuse puller** to remove a cartridge-type fuse; don't pull it by hand. A **BX cutter** (this tool can be rented) makes easy and safe work of cutting metal-sheathed cable. A **tubing cutter** quickly makes clean cuts in conduit. When working with conduit, use a **conduit bender** to shape the material without crimping it and **tongue-and-groove pliers** for tightening connectors. For running cable through finished walls and

ceilings or wire through conduit, a **fish tape** makes the job easier.

A **continuity tester** has a small bulb and battery for testing fuses, switches, and sockets with the power off. A **voltmeter** works with the power on or off and indicates the amount of voltage at an outlet. A **receptacle analyzer** runs a number of tests, telling you if your receptacle has a good connection and if it is properly grounded and polarized.

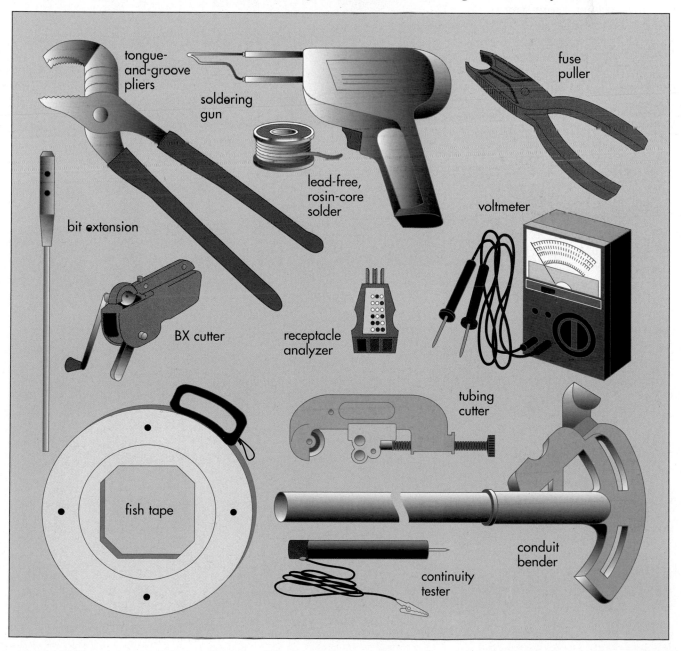

tongue-and-groove pliers

soldering gun

fuse puller

bit extension

lead-free, rosin-core solder

voltmeter

BX cutter

receptacle analyzer

tubing cutter

fish tape

continuity tester

conduit bender

Choosing Switches

Manufacturers offer a sometimes bewildering array of switches. To begin with you have a choice of colors—brown, ivory, and white are the most readily available. But the differences extend far beyond appearance.

For most of your needs you'll probably choose a **single-pole toggle,** which is available for a low price. "Toggle" simply refers to a switch that flips up and down.

Three-way and **four-way** switches are needed if you want to control a light from two or more separate switches. To learn about wiring them, see pages 120–124.

If you want to add a switch without putting in a larger box, a **double** switch may be the solution. It takes up the same amount of space as a single switch.

A **rocker** switch functions the same way as a standard toggle switch but is slightly easier to use.

A **dimmer** switch allows you to adjust lighting levels to suit your needs. A sliding dimmer brightens the light as you slide it upward. The rotary type comes in two versions. One version turns lights on or off with a push; the light level is altered by turning the knob. The other type dims the light as the knob is rotated counterclockwise until it turns off.

Experts' Insight

LOOK FOR THE UL SYMBOL
The UL symbol means that electrical materials have been checked for any defects by Underwriters Laboratories, an independent testing organization. Local codes may prohibit using items not UL-listed.

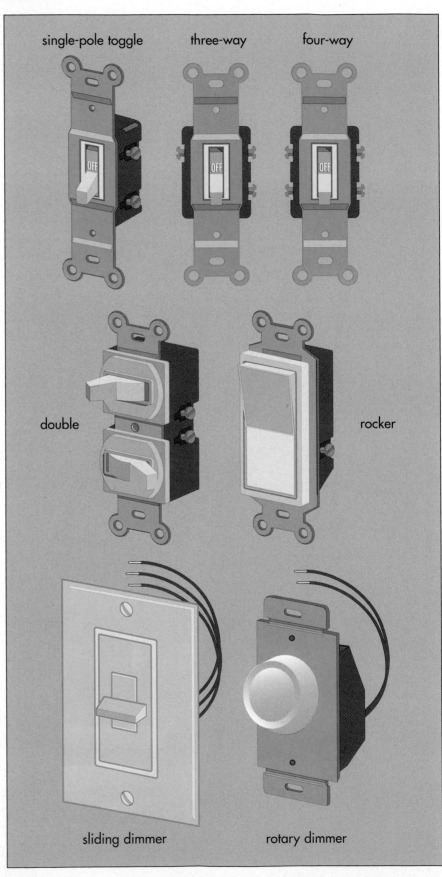

single-pole toggle   three-way   four-way

double   rocker

sliding dimmer   rotary dimmer

SELECTING SPECIALTY SWITCHES

Of the many available switches built to suit special needs, the ones on this page are some of the most common. Take a trip to a home center or a lighting store and you may find the switch that does exactly what you want. To find out how to install these switches, see page 108.

If you have power tools or other devices that you don't want children to play with, consider installing a **tamperproof** switch. It can be operated only with a key and wired to control the receptacle to which such items are connected.

For security in your backyard, or to have a light automatically greet you as you approach your house, choose a **motion-sensor security** switch. Its wide-angle infrared beam detects motion and turns a light on automatically. With most units, you can choose how long the light will stay on.

A **pilot-light** switch has a little bulb that glows when power is flowing through the switch. Use it when a fixture or appliance is out of sight. Closet lights, attic exhaust fans, basement lights, and garage lights often are controlled by pilot-light switches.

If you need to squeeze both a switch and an outlet into a single box, use a **switch/receptacle.** Also use this switch to easily add a receptacle to a room. This switch can be wired so the receptacle is live all the time or wired so the switch controls the receptacle.

A **programmable** switch comes with digital controls and can be programmed to turn lights on and off up to four times a day. This type of switch is useful for security and deterring burglars when you are away from home.

A **time-delay** switch has a dial that can be set to leave a fixture running for up to 60 minutes. Use one for a vent fan, space heater, heat lamp, or garage light.

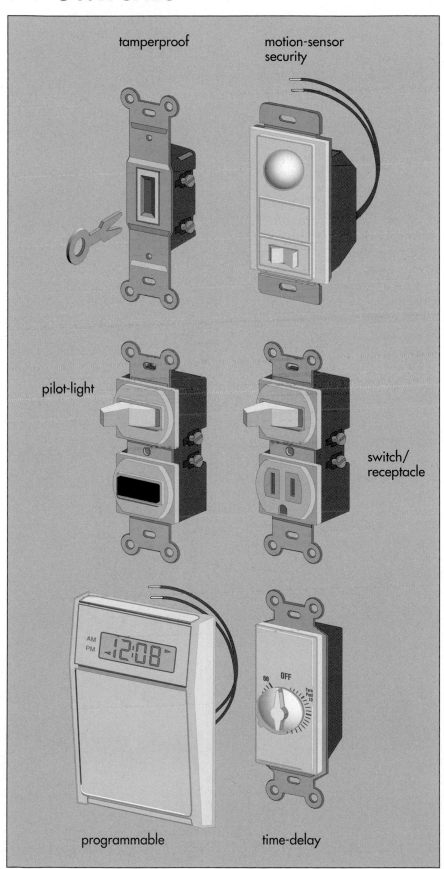

tamperproof

motion-sensor security

pilot-light

switch/ receptacle

programmable

time-delay

CHOOSING RECEPTACLES

A standard duplex receptacle has two outlets for receiving plugs. Each outlet has a long (neutral) slot, a shorter (hot) slot, and a half-round grounding hole. This ensures that the plug will be polarized and grounded (see page 38). Receptacles are rated for maximum amps. A **20-amp grounded receptacle** has a T-shaped neutral slot; use it only on 20-amp circuits. For most purposes, a **15-amp grounded receptacle** is sufficient. When replacing a receptacle in an ungrounded outlet box, use a **15-amp ungrounded receptacle,** intended only for use in older homes without ground wires in the circuits. Use a three-pronged plug adapter on an ungrounded receptacle only if the wall-plate screw is grounded (see page 71 to test this). The switch in a combination **switch/receptacle** can be hooked up to control the receptacle it's paired with.

A **20-amp single grounded receptacle** makes it nearly impossible to overload a critical circuit. For outdoors, in basements, or within 6 feet of a water fixture, install **ground-fault circuit-interrupter (GFCI)** receptacles (see pages 112–113). Select a **240-volt receptacle** based on the appliance amperage rating. Plugs required for appliances of 15, 20, 30, and 50 amps will have different prong configurations.

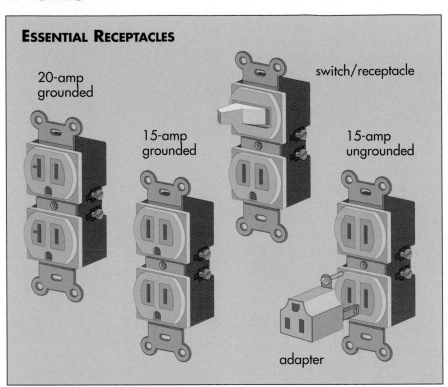

ESSENTIAL RECEPTACLES

20-amp grounded

15-amp grounded

switch/receptacle

15-amp ungrounded

adapter

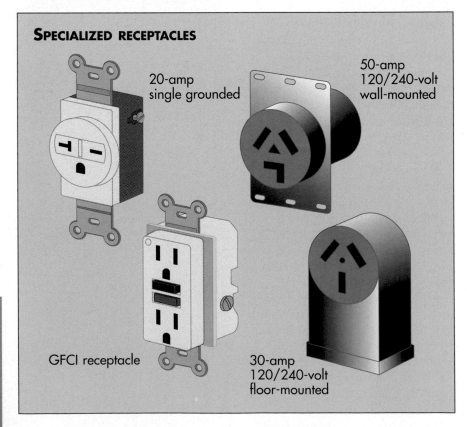

SPECIALIZED RECEPTACLES

20-amp single grounded

50-amp 120/240-volt wall-mounted

GFCI receptacle

30-amp 120/240-volt floor-mounted

> ### CAUTION!
> *REPLACE, DON'T CHANGE*
> *Replace a receptacle with one that is just like the old one. Change types only if you are certain that the wiring is suitable. Do not replace an ungrounded outlet with a grounded one unless you know the box is grounded.*

CHOOSING WIRE AND CABLE

Wire, cord, and cable (generically referred to as "conductors") are the pathways along which electricity travels. Wire is a solid strand of metal encased in insulation. Cord is a group of small strands encased in insulation. Cable is made of two or more wires wrapped in protective sheathing of metal or plastic.

Most local codes allow you to use nonmetallic sheathed cable (NM cable) inside walls, floors, and other places where it can't be damaged and won't get wet. Information printed on the sheathing tells you what is inside. The top example at right has two 14-gauge wires plus a bare ground wire, and is thus referred to as "14-2 G" cable ("G" for ground). Cable marked "14-3 G" has three wires plus a ground wire. Flexible armored cable (BX) contains wires wrapped in a flexible metal sheathing. It can be used for short runs in exposed areas such as attics or basements. BX needs no separate ground wire because the metal sheathing itself conducts the ground. Underground feed (UF) cable is watertight with the sheathing molded around the wire. Many municipalities permit this for underground lines.

Different gauge wires carry different amounts of electricity—14-gauge carries a maximum of 15 amps, 12-gauge carries up to 20 amps, and 10-gauge wire up to 30 amps. Doorbells and other low-voltage circuits typically use 18-gauge wire. Unsheathed wires are pulled through flexible or rigid conduit. Flexible metal conduit, or Greenfield, looks like armored cable but doesn't contain wires. It is cut to length, wires are pulled through it, and the completed pieces installed (see pages 92–93). With conduit, you pull wires through it after it's installed (see pages 94–97).

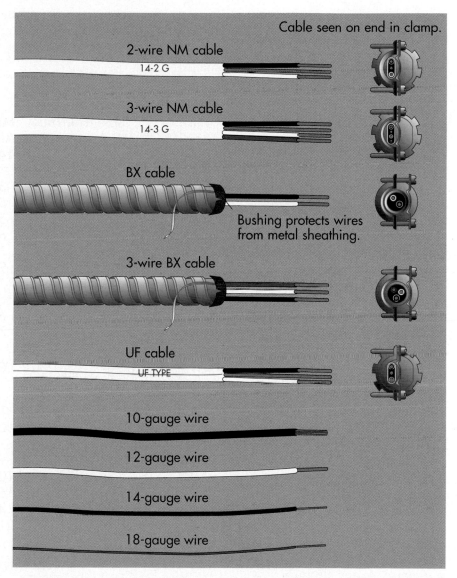

Cable seen on end in clamp.

2-wire NM cable — 14-2 G
3-wire NM cable — 14-3 G
BX cable
Bushing protects wires from metal sheathing.
3-wire BX cable
UF cable — UF TYPE
10-gauge wire
12-gauge wire
14-gauge wire
18-gauge wire

WHAT THE COLORS MEAN

Color	Function
white	neutral, carrying power back to the service panel
black	hot, carrying power from the service panel
red and other colors	also hot, color-coded to help identify which circuit they are on
white with black tape	a white wire that is being used as a hot wire
bare or green	a ground wire

CHOOSING BOXES

An electrical box has one primary function—to house electrical connections. Those connections might be to a switch, a receptacle, the leads of a light fixture, or other sets of wires.

Electrical codes require that all wire connections or cable splices be inside an approved metal or plastic box. You cannot bury a box inside a wall; they all must be accessible. This protects your home from the danger of fire and makes it easier to inspect and upgrade your wiring in the future.

Codes govern how many connections you're allowed to make within a box, depending on its size. If you must make more connections, you have to use a larger box (see chart at right).

There are boxes to suit most any depth of wall or ceiling, boxes to support heavy fixtures such as ceiling fans, and boxes for remodeling work and new construction. If, for instance, you'll be pulling cables through a finished wall, you can choose from a number of retrofit boxes that can be mounted with a minimum of damage to the wall.

Boxes for switches and receptacles serve as the workhorses in any electrical installation. Some of the metal ones can be "ganged" into double, triple, or larger multiples by removing one side and linking them together. Switch/receptacle boxes made of plastic are accepted by most codes, but they can't be ganged. If you are using conduit, Greenfield, or BX, you must use metal boxes to ground the system.

Utility boxes are surface-mounted in basements and garages to hold switches or receptacles. Boxes for fixtures or junctions may support lighting fixtures or split circuits into separate branches.

MEASUREMENTS
CHOOSING THE CORRECT BOX SIZE

Type of Box	Size in Inches (Height × Width × Depth)	Maximum Number of Wires Allowed in a Box		
		14-gauge	12-gauge	10-gauge
switch/ receptacle	3×2×1½	3	3	3
	3×2×2	5	4	4
	3×2×2¼	5	4	4
	3×2×2½	6	5	5
	3×2×2¾	7	6	5
	3×2×3½	9	8	7
utility	4×2⅛×1½	5	4	4
	4×2⅛×1⅞	6	5	5
	4×2⅛×2⅛	7	6	5
fixture/ junction	4×1¼ round or octagonal	6	5	5
	4×1½ round or octagonal	7	6	6
	4×2⅛ round or octagonal	10	9	8
	4×1¼ square	9	8	7
	4×1½ square	10	9	8
	4×2⅛ square	15	13	12
	4¹¹⁄₁₆×1½ square	14	13	11
	4¹¹⁄₁₆×2⅛ square	21	18	16

EXPERTS' INSIGHT

BOX CAPACITY

Overcrowd a box and you risk damaging wire connectors, piercing insulation, and cracking a switch or receptacle, any of which could cause a short. That is why codes spell out how many wires you can install in a box.

The chart above gives standard requirements. Other items may add to the total number of wires a box can hold. As you count wires, keep in mind these rules:

■ Don't count fixture leads (the wires that are connected to the fixture).

■ Count a wire that enters and leaves without a splice as one.

■ Count each cable clamp, stud, or hickey inside the box as one wire.

■ Count each receptacle or switch as one.

■ Count grounding wires entering a box as one, but do not count grounding wires that begin and end in the box.

NEW INSTALLATION SWITCH/RECEPTACLE BOXES

These boxes are designed for quick installation when the framing is exposed. They all have built-in gauges to make it easy for you to install them flush with the surface of the finished wall.

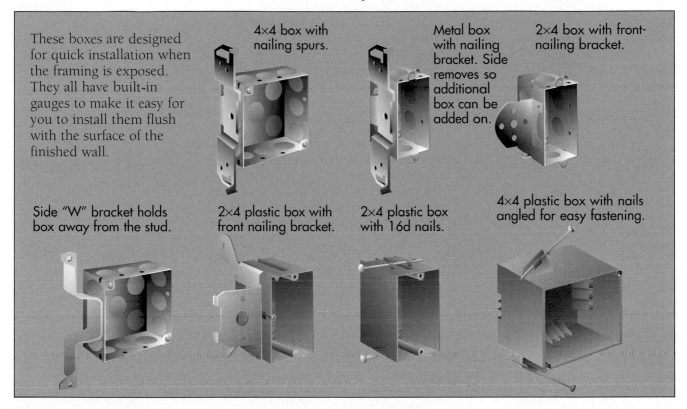

4×4 box with nailing spurs.

Metal box with nailing bracket. Side removes so additional box can be added on.

2×4 box with front-nailing bracket.

Side "W" bracket holds box away from the stud.

2×4 plastic box with front nailing bracket.

2×4 plastic box with 16d nails.

4×4 plastic box with nails angled for easy fastening.

RETROFIT SWITCH/RECEPTACLE BOXES

When installing new electrical service where the walls are finished, use boxes designed to minimize damage to the wall. If the special clips do not work, you may be able to attach the boxes to framing pieces with screws driven through holes inside the boxes.

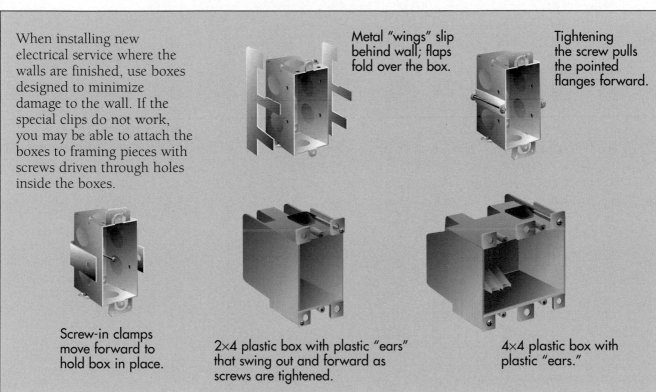

Metal "wings" slip behind wall; flaps fold over the box.

Tightening the screw pulls the pointed flanges forward.

Screw-in clamps move forward to hold box in place.

2×4 plastic box with plastic "ears" that swing out and forward as screws are tightened.

4×4 plastic box with plastic "ears."

New Installation Fixture/Junction Boxes

"New installation" wiring refers to work done on a freshly framed wall. With no drywall or plaster in the way, it is easy to install ceiling fixture boxes that are solid enough to hold a heavy chandelier or a fan. Remember that all junction boxes must remain accessible—never cover them with drywall.

Telescoping brackets allow you to position these boxes anywhere between joists.

Metal octagonal box requires framing behind it if it is to support a heavy fixture.

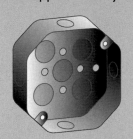

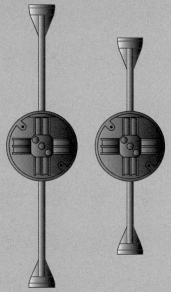

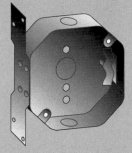

Round plastic fixture box has a bracket with sharp points so you can quickly tap it in place, then secure it with screws.

Octagonal junction box with side bracket is nailed to framing.

Retrofit Fixture/Junction Boxes

The retrofitting of adding new wiring to old walls is challenging. Often it's not easy to secure a fixture box when there's drywall or plaster in the way. For heavy ceiling fixtures, use a brace bar that can be slipped into the hole and expanded from joist to joist (see page 103).

A shallow box like this is sometimes needed in older homes with plaster walls.

"Wings" come forward as you tighten their screws, clasping the box to the plaster or drywall.

Most retrofitting starts with standard junction boxes located in accessible areas.

SPECIALIZED BOXES

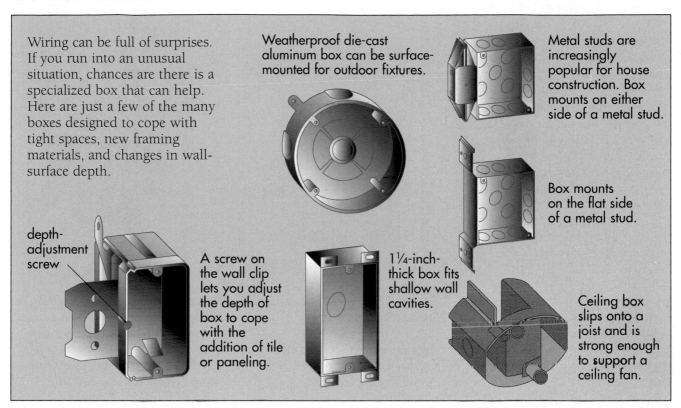

Wiring can be full of surprises. If you run into an unusual situation, chances are there is a specialized box that can help. Here are just a few of the many boxes designed to cope with tight spaces, new framing materials, and changes in wall-surface depth.

Weatherproof die-cast aluminum box can be surface-mounted for outdoor fixtures.

Metal studs are increasingly popular for house construction. Box mounts on either side of a metal stud.

Box mounts on the flat side of a metal stud.

depth-adjustment screw

A screw on the wall clip lets you adjust the depth of box to cope with the addition of tile or paneling.

1¼-inch-thick box fits shallow wall cavities.

Ceiling box slips onto a joist and is strong enough to support a ceiling fan.

BOX ACCESSORIES

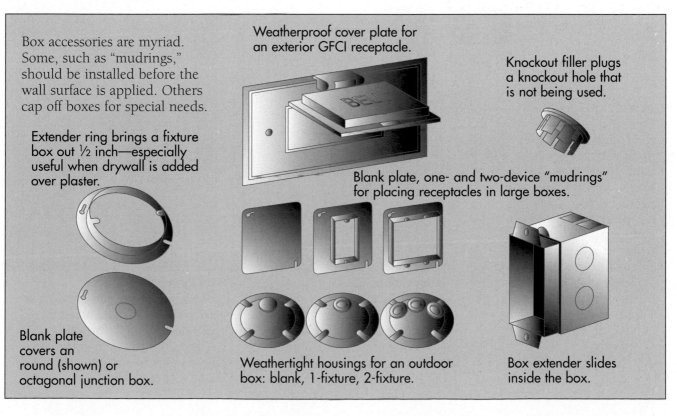

Box accessories are myriad. Some, such as "mudrings," should be installed before the wall surface is applied. Others cap off boxes for special needs.

Weatherproof cover plate for an exterior GFCI receptacle.

Knockout filler plugs a knockout hole that is not being used.

Extender ring brings a fixture box out ½ inch—especially useful when drywall is added over plaster.

Blank plate, one- and two-device "mudrings" for placing receptacles in large boxes.

Blank plate covers an round (shown) or octagonal junction box.

Weathertight housings for an outdoor box: blank, 1-fixture, 2-fixture.

Box extender slides inside the box.

INSTALLING BOXES IN UNFINISHED SPACE

To wire a room with unfinished walls, such as a basement remodeling or a room addition, you'll need boxes fastened to the framing. When attaching the boxes, be sure they protrude from the framing the same thickness as your drywall or paneling—usually ½ inch. Run cable from box to box and to the service panel.

After you've roughed in the wiring, but before you install the switches and receptacles, put up the drywall on the walls and ceiling. Finish and prime the surfaces, and install the devices in the boxes.

YOU'LL NEED...

TIME: About 3 hours for installing 10 boxes.
SKILLS: Basic carpentry skills.
TOOLS: Tape measure, hammer or drill with screwdriver bit.

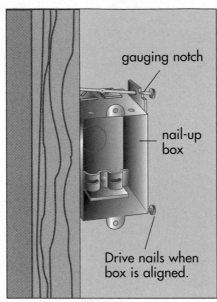

Nonmetallic handy box
Many boxes have a series of gauging notches on their sides. Determine the thickness of the drywall and/or paneling you will be installing, and align the box to the appropriate notch as you attach it. A nail-up box like this one is the easiest to install.

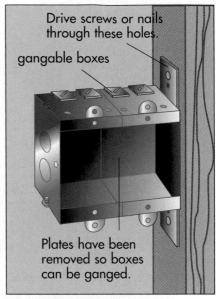

Gangable boxes
These have detachable sides, so you can attach them together to form double- or triple-size boxes. To attach such boxes without special mounting hardware, simply drive screws or nails through the holes and into the framing.

MEASUREMENTS

PLACING BOXES

In a typical room, place switch boxes 48–50 inches above the floor and receptacles 12–16 inches above floor level. Check with local codes to see how many receptacles you will need. In most cases they must be placed so that no point along any wall is more than 6 feet from a receptacle. This means that you'll have to install at least one receptacle every 12 feet along the wall. For kitchens and bathrooms, special requirements apply.

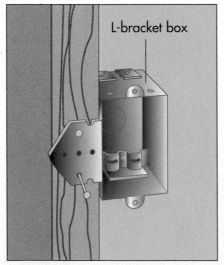

L-bracket box
Some L-bracket boxes adjust to suit the thickness of your wall material. Others accommodate only one thickness. Hold the box in position against the framing, and drive two nails or screws through the holes in the bracket.

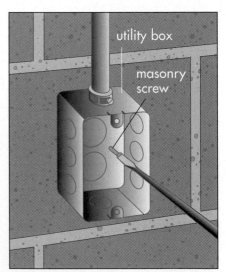

Utility box
Use a utility box and conduit or armored cable in an area where you don't need a finished appearance. If you're attaching boxes to masonry, use anchors or masonry screws.

Fixture and junction boxes are easy to install in unfinished space. Install boxes so they will be flush with the finished surface of the ceiling or wall. Do not place any electrical box where it will be covered by drywall or paneling.

If there is a joist at the spot where you want the box, use a box with a **hanger bracket** or an **L-bracket.** This page shows various types available—some designed for installing from below, some for installing from above. These fasten to the joist with screws or nails. When attaching, allow for the thickness of the ceiling material.

If you need to install a fixture box between joists, use a box with a **bar hanger.** Attach the ends of the brackets to the joists, and slide the box into the desired position.

Junction boxes protect wire connections or cable splices. Some junction boxes come with brackets. Others just nail or screw to a joist, stud, or rafter.

Regardless of the type of box you're installing, always secure it with two fasteners. If the box will be supporting a ceiling fan or other heavy fixture, make sure it's anchored securely enough to carry the weight. If a box has been correctly mounted but still doesn't feel firm enough, add a framing piece and secure it to that as well.

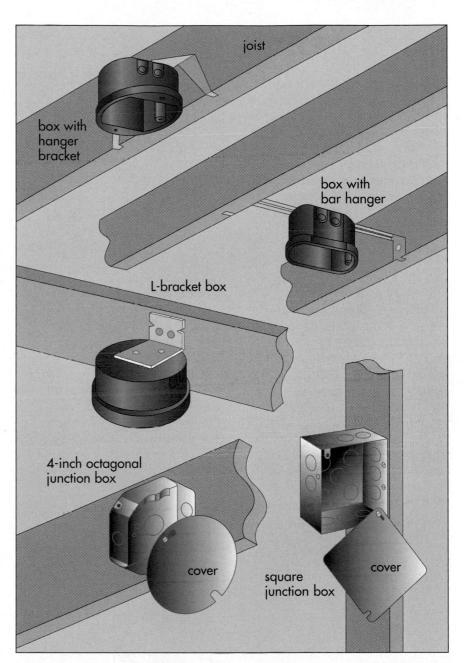

joist

box with hanger bracket

box with bar hanger

L-bracket box

4-inch octagonal junction box

cover

square junction box

cover

OVERHEAD LIGHT PLACEMENT

■ One pleasing way to light a room is with recessed can lights (see pages 104–105) or small fixtures. To plan for a group of symmetrically placed lights, make a map of your ceiling and experiment by drawing circles, each of which represents the area lit up by a recessed fixture.

■ When you experiment with your design, try to arrange the lights so they are half as far from the walls as they are from each other. A pleasingly symmetrical pattern usually results. Start by arranging lights 6 feet apart and 3 feet from walls. Position them at least 4 feet apart. Add to your plan any suspended or track lighting you need for task illumination or to accent an attractive area of the room.

■ Don't expect to achieve an arrangement that's perfectly symmetrical; few ceilings will allow for that. Also keep in mind that with recessed lighting, you may not be able to put all the lights exactly where you want them because there will be joists in the way (see page 104). In most cases, a less-than-perfect arrangement will not be noticeable.

INSTALLING BOXES IN FINISHED SPACE

*I*nstalling electrical work is a greater challenge when the walls and ceilings are finished. Often patching and painting can take far more time than the electrical work itself! Plan the placement so you avoid making unnecessary holes.

Wherever possible, avoid making contact with the framing. Using special boxes designed for installation in finished space, you often can simply make a hole the size of the box and secure the box to the wall or ceiling surface.

Before you begin, plan how you're going to get cable to the new location (see pages 84–85).

YOU'LL NEED...

TIME: About 30 minutes a box, not including running new wire.
SKILLS: Simple skills are required.
TOOLS: Keyhole saw, screwdriver, needle-nose pliers, utility knife, and neon tester.

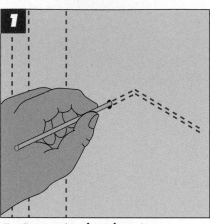

1. Determine box location.
Drill a small hole in the wall. Insert a bent wire and rotate it. If you hit something, you've probably found a stud. Try 6 inches to one side. If you strike wood again, you may have hit a fire block. Drill another hole 3 inches higher or lower. Keep trying until you can rotate the bent wire freely.

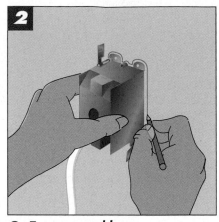

2. Trace around box.
Some boxes come with a template that can be held against the surface and traced around. Otherwise, use the box itself and center it on the hole you could rotate the wire in. Make sure the template or box is plumb before you mark the outline.

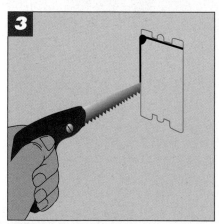

3. Cut the opening.
Carefully cut around the traced outline. If the surface is drywall, use a utility knife. If you are cutting into plaster walls, use a keyhole saw. If the plaster is crumbly, mask the outline with tape. For a wood-surfaced wall, drill a ¼-inch access hole in each corner and use a saber saw. Run cable (see pages 84–87).

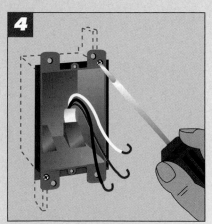

4. Fasten with side clamps...
Side-clamp boxes grip the wall from behind when you tighten the screws. Pull 8 inches of cable through the box and insert the box. Hold the box plumb as you tighten the clamps. Alternate from side to side as you work so the box seats evenly. Avoid overtightening the clamps.

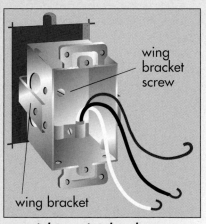

wing bracket screw

wing bracket

...or tighten wing bracket screws.
Loosen the screw centered in the receptacle box until the wing bracket is at maximum extension from the back. Hold the wings against the body of the box and push the box into the hole. Tighten the screw until the box is held firmly in place.

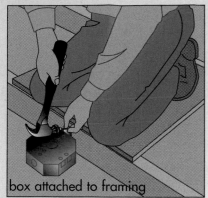

box attached to framing

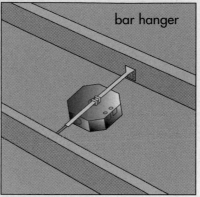

bar hanger

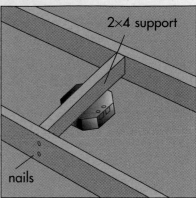

2×4 support

nails

With access from above
A ceiling box must support a fixture, so it must be securely attached to the framing. If you are fortunate enough to have

attic space above, the job can be done without damaging your ceiling. Mark the location of each box on the ceiling, and drive nails as reference points.

Cut the hole for the box. If there is a nearby joist, attach an L-bracket box directly to it. If not, either use a bar hanger or frame in a 2×4 support.

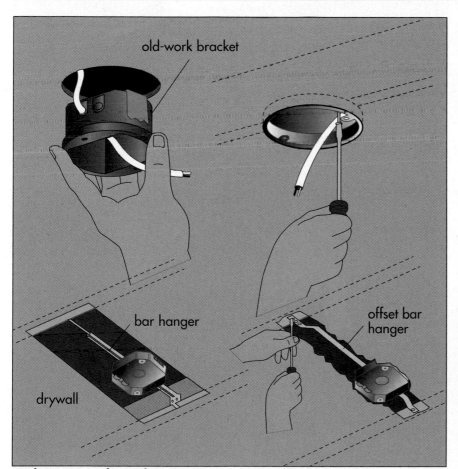

old-work bracket

bar hanger

drywall

offset bar hanger

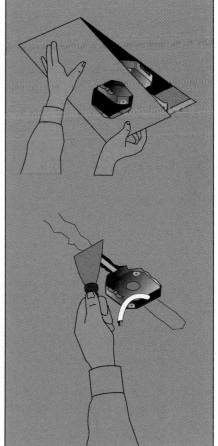

With no access from above
If you cannot work from above, use one of these methods. For light fixtures that weigh less than 5 pounds, use an old-work bracket. Cut the hole the size of the box, slip the bracket in, telescope it to fit between two joists, and attach the box to it.

For heavier fixtures, such as chandeliers and ceiling fans, make an opening in the ceiling and install hanging hardware. With a drywall ceiling, cut out a large rectangle and install a bar hanger. With plaster, chip out a path and use an offset bar hanger.

Repair the ceiling.
After checking the electrical installation, patch the ceiling. With drywall, you may be able to use the same piece you cut out. Nail the panel to the joists, and tape the seam with joint compound. For a plaster ceiling, fill with patching compound.

STRIPPING WIRE

Before making electrical connections, you'll need to remove some of the sheathing that encases the three or four wires of the cable and strip some of the insulation that coats the individual wires. Stripping techniques are simple, but exercise care when removing sheathing in order to avoid damaging any of the underlying insulation. Also be careful to strip the insulation without nicking the copper wire—this would weaken it.

Strip wires before inserting them into the box. That way, if you make a mistake, you can cut off the damaged portion and try again.

YOU'LL NEED...

TIME: About 5 minutes or less.
SKILLS: Simple stripping.
TOOLS: Cable ripper, utility knife, side cutters and combination tool or adjustable wire stripper.

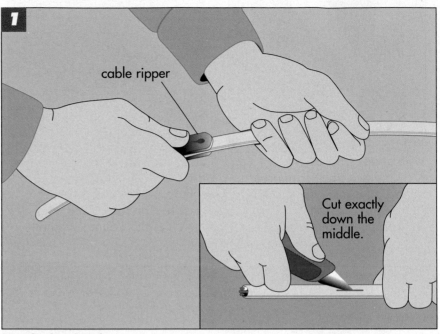

cable ripper

Cut exactly down the middle.

1. Slit the sheathing.
The easiest way to remove plastic sheathing from nonmetallic sheathed cable is to use an inexpensive cable ripper. Slip 6 to 8 inches of cable into the ripper's jaws, squeeze, and pull. This slits open the sheathing without damaging the insulation of internal wires. The same job can be done with a knife, but you must be careful: Run the blade right down the middle so it doesn't strip insulation from the wires.

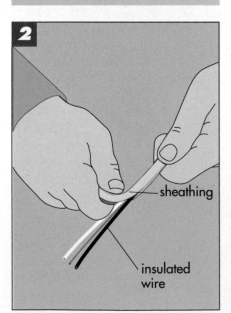

sheathing

insulated wire

2. Peel back the sheathing.
Pull back the sheathing you have just slit, as well as the paper wrapping or strips of thin plastic, if any. You'll find two or three separately insulated wires, as well as a bare ground wire.

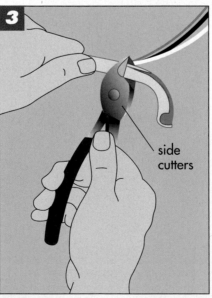

side cutters

3. Cut away the sheathing.
Cut off the sheathing and paper. Remove the slit sheathing with a pair of side cutters. Or use a utility knife, taking care to point the blade away from the wires.

CAUTION!
This job is simple but it must be done with great care or you could end up with dangerous electrical shorts. If you think you may have accidentally damaged some insulation, cut the cable back to a place behind the potentially dangerous spot and start again.
Another possible problem: If you cut into the copper wire while stripping the insulation, you can weaken the wire so that it is liable to break while you are making a connection later.

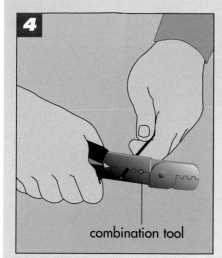

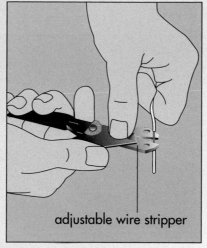

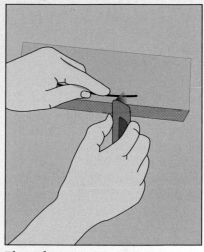

4. Strip the wire.
To strip insulation from wires, use a combination tool, which has separate holes for the different sizes of wires. Locate the wire in the correct hole, clamp down, give it a twist, and

pull the tool away from you. With an adjustable stripper, set it for the wire size, twist, then pull the tool away from you. Stripping also can be done with a utility knife, but be careful not to dig into the copper wire.

Place the wire on a scrap piece of wood, hold the blade at a slight angle, and strip the insulation by slicing off thin strips until you reach wire.

JOINING WIRES

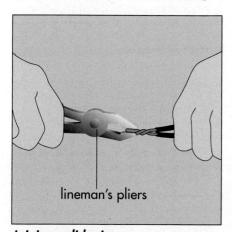

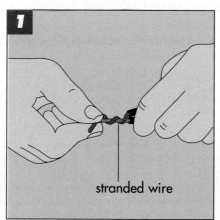

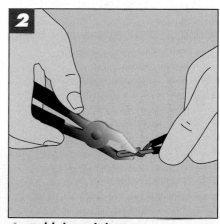

Joining solid wires
Join solid wires by using a pair of lineman's pliers. Cross the two wires, grab both wires with the pliers, and twist clockwise. Both wires should twist—do not just twist one wire around the other. Twist for several revolutions, but don't twist so tightly that the wires are in danger of breaking. Screw a wire connector onto the two wires (see page 58).

1. Joining stranded to solid wires
Often a stranded wire (made of many thin wires) has to be spliced to a solid wire, as when hooking up a light fixture or dimmer switch. Because the stranded wire is more flexible, the two won't twist together. Wrap the stranded wire around the solid wire.

2. Fold the solid wire over.
Bend the solid wire so it clamps down on the stranded wire. Screw a wire connector onto the two wires (see page 58), and wrap the connection with electrician's tape.

WORKING WITH WIRE

The final—and most gratifying—phase of an electrical installation comes when you tie all those wires together and attach them to the switches, light fixtures, and receptacles. Don't take shortcuts with wire connections and splices. Cap splices with wire connectors rather than only tape, and wrap tape around each connector. Make pigtails (see page 59) wherever they are needed instead of trying to connect two or more wires to a terminal. Finally, don't overcrowd a box with too many wires (for limits, see chart on page 48).

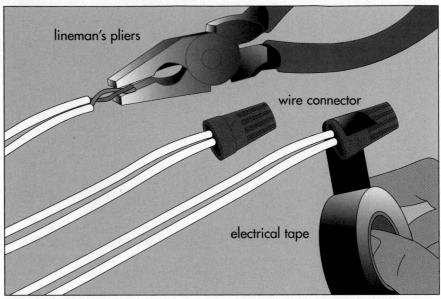

lineman's pliers

wire connector

electrical tape

HOW MANY WIRES IN A CONNECTOR?

Wire connector	12-gauge wires	14-gauge wires
red	2–4	2–5
yellow	2–3	2–4
orange	2	2–4

Using wire connectors
To complete a splice of two or more wires, use wire connectors. These come in a variety of sizes. Select the size you need depending on how many wires you will connect as well as the thickness of the wires (see chart, left). Wire connectors firm up the splice and

protect bare wires better than tape. First twist the wires firmly together. Do not depend on the connector to do the joining. Twist the wire connector on, turning it by hand until it tightens firmly. As a final precaution, wrap the connector clockwise with electrical tape, overlapping the wires.

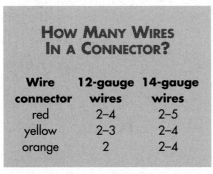

1 needle-nose pliers

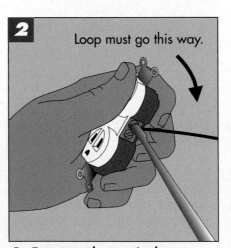

2 Loop must go this way.

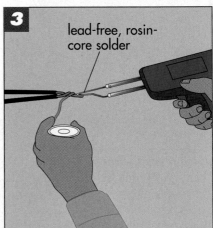

3 lead-free, rosin-core solder

1. To connect a wire to a terminal, form a loop.
Strip just enough wire to wrap around the terminal—about ¾ inch. Then form it into a loop using needle-nose or lineman's pliers. It takes practice to make loops that lie flat and are neither too big nor too small.

2. Fasten to the terminal.
Hook the wire clockwise around the terminal so that tightening the screw will close the loop. With receptacles, the black wires go to the brass side, white to silver. Tighten firmly, but avoid overtightening, which can damage the device. If you do crack a device in any way, throw it out.

3. Solder a splice.
A few codes require that splices be soldered. More often, soldering house wiring is prohibited. If you need to solder a splice, start by twisting the wires together. Heat the wires with a soldering iron, then touch lead-free, rosin-core solder to the splice. The solder should melt into the splice.

CONNECTING WIRES

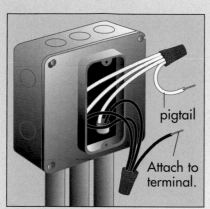

pigtail

Attach to terminal.

Solder and tape.

Attach to terminal.

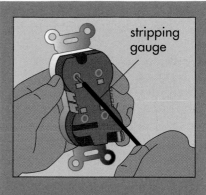

stripping gauge

Add a pigtail where two or more wires attach to a terminal...

Never attach more than one wire to a terminal. Codes prohibit it, and it's unsafe because terminal screws are made to hold only one wire. An easier way to join many wires to a terminal is to cut a short piece of wire (about 4 inches), strip both ends, and splice it to the other wires as shown to form a pigtail.

...or make a soldered splice.

Twist wires together so that one extends 1 inch beyond the splice. Solder the twist and loop the extended wire. Tape the soldered splice before screwing the wire to the terminal.

CAUTION!
Make sure local codes permit soldering.

CAUTION!
Most receptacles and switches have connection holes in the back. To make a connection, strip the wire (a stripping gauge often is provided, showing you how much insulation to remove) and poke it into the correct hole. On a receptacle the holes are marked for white and black wires. However most professionals do not use these holes. Wires inserted this way are simply not as secure as those screwed to a terminal.

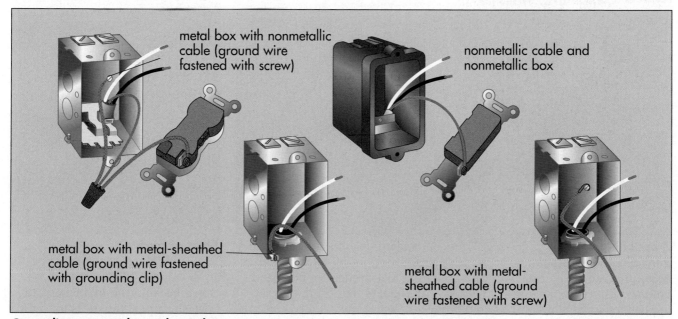

metal box with nonmetallic cable (ground wire fastened with screw)

nonmetallic cable and nonmetallic box

metal box with metal-sheathed cable (ground wire fastened with grounding clip)

metal box with metal-sheathed cable (ground wire fastened with screw)

Grounding receptacles and switches

How you ground devices like receptacles and switches depends on the type of wiring you're using as well as the type of box. With flexible armored cable (BX), Greenfield, or rigid conduit, the metal of the wiring casing and the metal of the box substitutes for the grounding wire. Simply by attaching the device firmly to the box, you have grounded it. Some local codes require that you also attach a short grounding wire, as shown. If you're working with nonmetallic sheathed cable (Romex) and metal boxes, connect short grounding wires to the box and to the device. With nonmetallic boxes, the cable's grounding wire connects directly to the device.

REPLACING PLUGS AND CORDS

Faulty plugs pose the most common shock and fire hazards in the house. Plugs get stepped on, bumped against, and yanked out by their cords. It's a good idea to regularly inspect your plugs, especially if you have some old ones, for loose connections, damaged wire insulation, and prongs that have been bent so often they are in danger of breaking.

Fortunately, it is easy to replace faulty plugs to make your home significantly safer.

YOU'LL NEED...

TIME: About half an hour to replace a plug.
SKILLS: Stripping, tying, and wrapping wire.
TOOLS: Wire stripper, screwdriver, and needle-nose pliers.

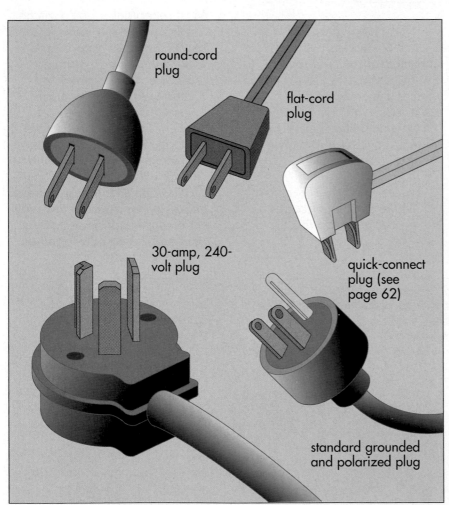

Types of plugs
Round-cord plugs often accommodate fairly thick wire and are used for moderately heavy appliances such as irons. Flat-cord plugs are suitable for lamps, radios, and other low-amperage devices. Newer lamp and extension cord plugs are polarized, with one blade wider than the other (see page 38).

Standard grounded plugs have a third, round prong for grounding; the two flat prongs are polarized.

Appliances that use 240 volts require heavy-duty three-pronged plugs of various configurations. The one shown here is for a 30-amp, 240-volt dryer.

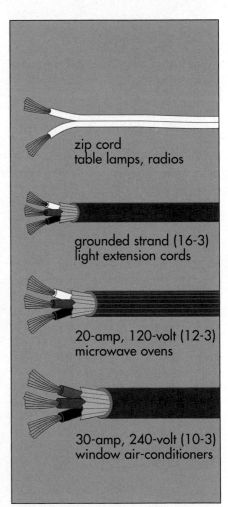

Types of cords
For flexibility, cord wires are stranded, not solid. Zip cord, so called because the two wires can be easily zipped apart, is for light duty. Use cords with 16-gauge wire for appliances pulling 15 amps or less and 12-gauge wire for 20 amps or less. For 240-volt appliances, use wire that is 10-gauge or thicker.

1. To replace a round-cord plug, strip and insert the cord.

Snip off the old plug. Remove the cardboard cover from the new plug, and slide the snipped-off end of the cord through. Strip off 3 inches of outer insulation and about ½ inch of wire insulation.

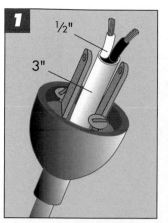

Pull both ends tight.

2. Tie Underwriters knot.

This special knot will ensure that tugging the cord won't loosen any electrical connections. Make the knot close to the end of the stripped outer insulation.

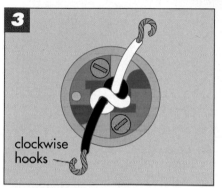
clockwise hooks

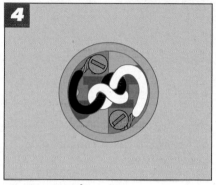

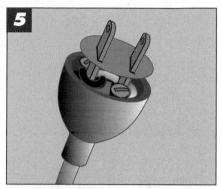

3. Bend hooks.

Twist the wire strands tight. With a pair of needle-nose pliers, shape clockwise hooks to wrap around the screw shafts.

4. Connect the wires.

Hook the wires on the screw shafts (attach the black wire to the brass-colored screw), and tighten. Tuck in stray strands.

5. Replace the cover.

Check to be sure all wires and strands are neatly inside the plug. Slip on the cardboard cover.

SAFETY

DON'T CHANGE THE PLUG TO FIT THE RECEPTACLE

■ If your appliance or tool has a plug with a third, round prong, then it should only be plugged into 3-hole outlets that are properly grounded. If you remove the grounding prong, or if you use a plug adapter that is not connected to a ground, you will disable a feature designed to protect against electrical shock.

■ Some appliances and tools are "double insulated" and do not need the extra protection of a grounding prong. You can plug them into an ungrounded outlet and still be protected from shock.

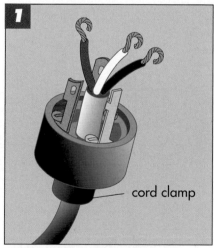
cord clamp

1. To repair a 240-volt plug, slide the plug onto the cord.

A 240-volt plug has a steel clamp that grips the cord, so you don't have to tie an Underwriters knot. Slide the plug onto the cord and strip about ½ inch of insulation from the ends of the three wires. Twist the strands tight, and use needle-nose pliers to form hooks.

2. Attach the wires.

Attach the black and red wires to brass-colored terminals, and the green one to the silver-colored terminal. Tuck in any loose strands as you tighten the terminal screws. Tuck all the wires in place, tighten the cord clamp, and slip on the cardboard cover.

WIRING QUICK-CONNECT, FLAT-CORD PLUGS

Keep a few quick-connect plugs on hand and you'll never again be tempted to put off replacing a faulty or questionable plug. Installing one is only slightly more difficult and time-consuming than changing a lightbulb.

Replacing a standard flat-cord plug is more like doing actual electrical work, but it takes only a little more time.

YOU'LL NEED...

TIME: About 5 minutes to install a quick-connect; 15 minutes for a flat-cord plug.
SKILLS: No skill at all for the quick-connect plug; stripping wire and connecting to a screw for the flat-cord plug.
TOOLS: Knife or scissors for the quick-connect; wire strippers and screwdriver for the flat-cord.

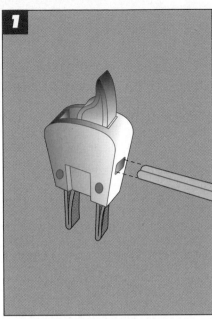

1. To wire a quick-connect plug, open the lever.
Snip off the old plug. Lift the lever on top of the new plug and insert the zip cord into the hole.

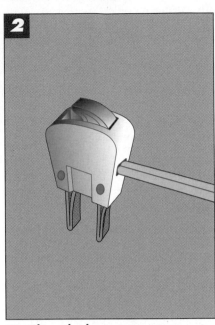

2. Close the lever.
Closing the lever pierces and holds the wire. Push the lever firmly down and you're done.

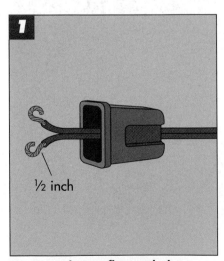

½ inch

1. To replace a flat-cord plug, slip on a shell and twist the wires.
Snip the old plug off. Slip the new shell onto the cord. Peel apart the wires, and strip away about ½ inch of insulation. Twist the strands tight with your fingers and use needle-nose pliers to form hooks that will wrap most of the way around each screw.

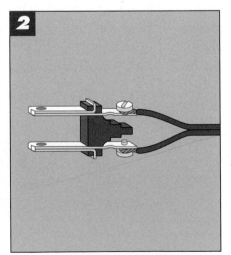

2. Connect the wires.
Wrap the wires clockwise around the screw threads, and tighten the screws to secure the connection. Tuck in any loose strands.

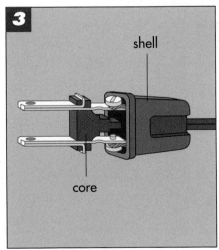

shell

core

3. Snap the shell on.
Grasp the shell of the plug and push the core toward it until it snaps into place. Put your appliance back into service.

REPLACING LAMP SOCKETS

Most standing lamps consist of a body, a base where the cord enters, a harp to support the shade, and a socket that receives the cord at one end and the lightbulb at the other. The cord usually runs through a hollow threaded rod from the base to the socket.

When a lamp won't work and you know the bulb and plug are OK, check the cord for damage. If the insulation is worn and cracked, replace the entire cord (see page 64). If the cord is OK, the problem is most likely in the socket.

Most lamps have felt bases that must be removed before repairing the lamps. Remove the felt by paring it off with a utility knife. After the repair, reapply the felt with white glue.

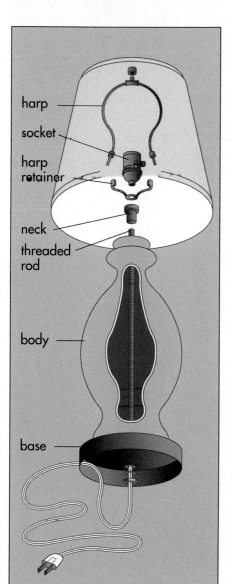

harp
socket
harp retainer
neck
threaded rod
body
base

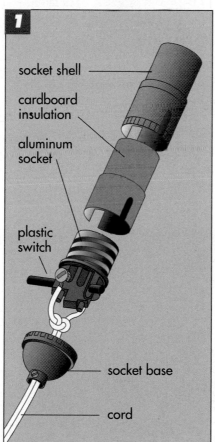

1

socket shell
cardboard insulation
aluminum socket
plastic switch
socket base
cord

1. Disassemble the socket.
Unplug the cord and remove the harp, if it is in the way. Examine the socket shell and find the word "press." Push hard here and the unit will pull apart into the components shown. Remove the cord from the socket.

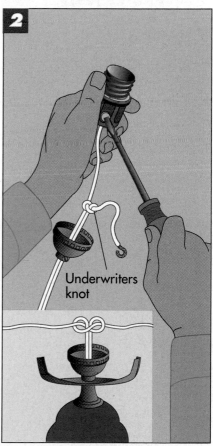

2

Underwriters knot

2. Connect the new socket.
Slip the new socket base onto the cord and tie an Underwriters knot (see page 61). Strip about ½ inch of insulation from the wires, twist the strands tight, and form them into hooks with a pair of needle-nose pliers. Wrap the wires clockwise around the shafts of the screws and tighten the screws. Reassemble the cardboard insulation and the outer shell. Attach the new socket to the lamp.

REWIRING LAMPS

Like plugs, lamp cords get stepped on and yanked. And if a lamp has a tendency to heat up, the cord's insulation can become cracked near the socket. Replace any cord with damaged insulation; it is dangerous.

Replacing a cord is not difficult. In fact, you may want to do it simply in order to have a cord that makes a lamp more attractive.

YOU'LL NEED...

TIME: About 45 minutes.
SKILLS: Stripping wire and connecting wire to screws.
TOOLS: Wire strippers, needle-nose pliers, and screwdriver.

CAUTION!

UNPLUG IT FIRST!
Never work on a lamp or appliance while it is plugged in. Always unplug it first.

Pull cord through top.

Splice new cord to old to feed here.

1. Feed the new cord through.
Disconnect the old cord from the lamp socket, and snip off the plug. Tie the new cord to the old one with a piece of string or some tape. The trick is to make the connection thin enough so it slides through the center rod. Pull the new cord through as you withdraw the old one.

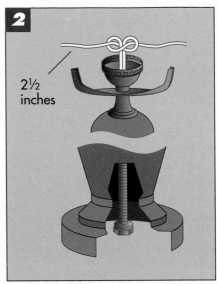

2½ inches

2. Secure the cord.
Snip off the old cord and discard it. Tie an Underwriters knot, as shown, leaving about 2½ inches of each wire to work with. Strip ½ inch of insulation from the end of each wire.

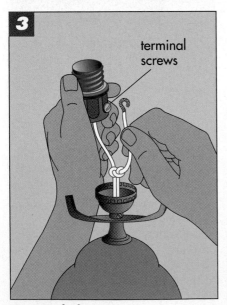

terminal screws

3. Attach the wires.
Twist the strands tight with your fingers. Use needle-nose pliers to form hooks and wrap them around the terminal screws. Tuck any loose strands in as you tighten the terminal screws.

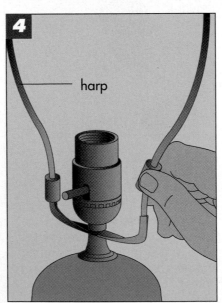

harp

4. Reassemble the lamp.
Reassemble the socket and install the harp as shown. Attach a new plug (see pages 60–62). You're ready to put in a bulb, attach the shade, and plug in your lamp.

CAUTION!

REPLACE DAMAGED LAMP CORD—DON'T TAPE IT

■ *It may not look dangerous, but nicked and cracked lamp wire insulation is the cause of many fires. Also you or your children could receive painful shocks if you touch a bare spot.*

■ *If you see a damaged spot and need to keep using the lamp, wrap electrician's tape around the damaged area. But be aware that this is a temporary solution. The tape can easily come unwrapped. And if one part of the cord is damaged, chances are other parts are as well. Replace the cord as soon as possible.*

CHECKING INCANDESCENT FIXTURES

Though they vary widely in style, most incandescent fixtures have the same arrangement of components (see illustration, below right).

Mounting screws hold a canopy plate against the ceiling. The canopy has one or more sockets for bulbs. A translucent diffuser or globe cuts down on the glare of bare lightbulbs. In newer fixtures, a ring of fiber insulation provides added protection from heat damage to the wires and ceiling.

If a fixture shorts out, causing a circuit to blow and/or creating sparks, the problem is probably in the fixture. If it simply refuses to light, the wall switch may be faulty (see pages 68–69).

(see pages 68–69).

YOU'LL NEED...
TIME: To inspect a typical fixture, about ½ hour.
SKILLS: No special skills needed.
TOOLS: Screwdriver and steel wool.

CAUTION!
USE THE RIGHT BULBS
A label on the fixture will tell you the maximum bulb wattage allowed. Don't install higher-wattage bulbs or your fixture will overheat, burn up bulbs quickly, and become dangerous.

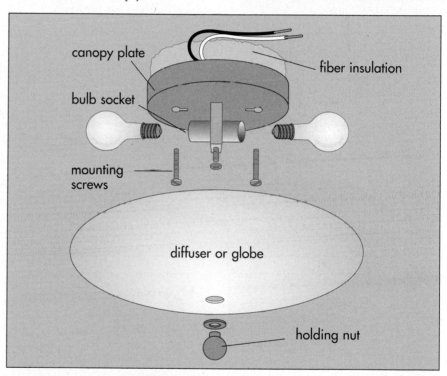

canopy plate
fiber insulation
bulb socket
mounting screws
diffuser or globe
holding nut

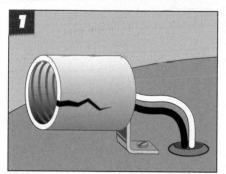

1. Inspect the socket.
Shut off the circuit that supplies power to the fixture. Inspect the socket. If it is cracked, or if its wires are scorched or melted, replace it or the entire fixture. If it's OK, remove the bulb and check the contact at the socket's base. If there's corrosion, scrape the contact with a flat screwdriver or steel wool, and pry up on it. Turn on circuit and retry.

2. Check the wiring.
If the problem remains, shut off the circuit again, loosen or remove the mounting screws, and drop the fixture from its outlet box. Check for loose connections and for nicked insulation. If you see drywall paper that is slightly

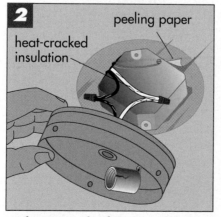

peeling paper
heat-cracked insulation

peeling near the fixture or heat-cracked wire insulation, your fixture is overheating. This means either that it is faulty or you need to reduce the wattage of the bulbs. Wrap any bare wires with electrical tape.

SAFETY

KEEP THE FIBER INSULATION
Although it makes installation a bit more difficult, don't remove the fiber insulation in the canopy plate. It provides extra protection against shorts.

TROUBLESHOOTING FLUORESCENT FIXTURES

The heart of a fluorescent fixture is its ballast, an electrical transformer that steps up voltage and sends it to a pair of lamp holders. The current passes through the lamp holders and excites a gas inside the fluorescent tube, causing its phosphorus-coated inner surface to glow with cool, diffused light.

Because they produce far less heat, fluorescent tubes last much longer than incandescent bulbs and consume considerably less electrical energy. However, problems with the fixtures sometimes arise. The ballasts burn out after years of steady use, and the lamp holders are easily cracked if they get bumped.

Older units have starters that must be replaced periodically.

YOU'LL NEED...
TIME: To inspect a fixture and replace a ballast (for example), about an hour.
SKILLS: No special skills needed.
TOOLS: Screwdriver.

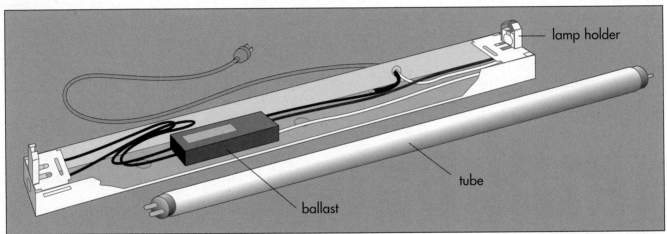

lamp holder

tube

ballast

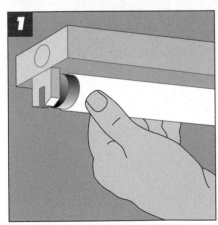

1. Wiggle the tube.
Fluorescent tubes rarely burn out abruptly; they flicker or dim. If a tube suddenly stops lighting, try wiggling and rotating its ends to make sure it's properly seated.

CAUTION!
Never get rid of burned out tubes by breaking them. They contain mercury. Dispose of them whole or request disposal guidelines.

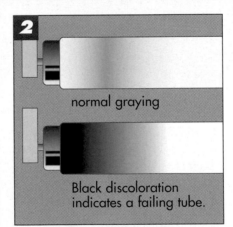

normal graying

Black discoloration indicates a failing tube.

2. Replace a worn-out tube.
A working tube usually has a grayish tinge near its ends. If the tube is uniformly dim, it may simply need washing. To wash a tube, remove it from the fixture, wipe it with a damp cloth, and then replace the tube. If the tube ends turn dark gray or black, the tube is failing and needs to be replaced. Purchase a tube that is the same length and wattage as the old one.

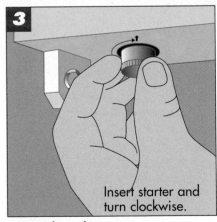

Insert starter and turn clockwise.

3. Replace the starter.
Older, delayed-start fluorescent lights flicker momentarily as they light up. If the flickering continues for more than a few seconds, make sure the starter is seated properly. Push it in and turn clockwise. When the ends of a tube light up but its center does not, the starter is defective. Press in and turn counterclockwise to remove it. Insert a new starter and turn clockwise.

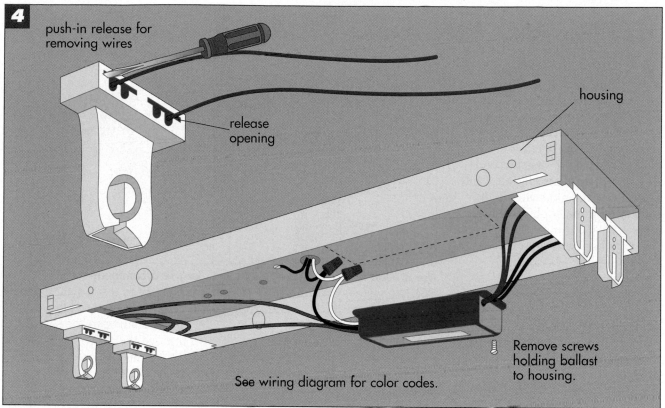

4

push-in release for removing wires

housing

release opening

See wiring diagram for color codes.

Remove screws holding ballast to housing.

4. Replace the ballast.

If the fixture hums or oozes a tarlike goop, the ballast needs replacing. (You may be better off replacing the entire unit. Compare prices.) **NOTE:** *Shut off the power.* To remove the ballast, release the wires at the sockets by pushing a screwdriver into the release openings. Unscrew the ballast and disconnect wires to power source. Reassemble with the new ballast.

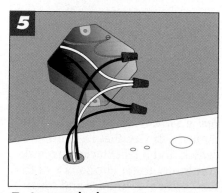

5

5. Inspect the box.

If none of these steps locates the problem, you may not have power going into the fixture. Remove the fixture, and look for loose connections and broken or bare wires in the outlet box.

EXPERTS' INSIGHT

TROUBLESHOOTING CHART FOR FLUORESCENT FIXTURES

Symptom	Solution
Tube does not light	1. Rotate the tube to make sure it is properly seated. 2. Replace any damaged lamp holders. 3. Replace starter, if there is one. 4. Check wall switch and outlet box to see that there is power to the fixture.
Tube flickers only lights partially	1. Rotate the tube to make sure it is properly seated. 2. Replace any tubes that are discolored or have damaged pins. 3. Replace the starter, if there is one.
Black substance or humming sound	1. Replace the ballast or the entire fixture.

TESTING AND REPLACING SWITCHES

After getting flipped thousands of times, a switch can wear out. Unless the problem is a loose wire connection, there is usually no way to repair a faulty switch; you'll need to replace it.

It is easy to test switches and easy to replace them. If you want to replace your old switch with something more sophisticated—for example, a dimmer—check out the switch options presented on pages 44–45.

YOU'LL NEED...

TIME: About 30 minutes to test and replace a switch.
SKILLS: Using testers (we'll show you how) and connecting wires to screw terminals.
TOOLS: Neon tester, continuity tester, and screwdriver.

CAUTION!

Hold only the metal flanges of the switch when pulling it out of a box. Be very careful not to touch the terminal screws or to allow the screws to touch the edge of the box.

TOOL TIP

SAFE USE OF A CONTINUITY TESTER

Never use a continuity tester on wires that might be live. Always shut off power and disconnect wires before testing. The continuity tester uses a battery that generates a small current to test for the flow of electricity from one point to another. It is not made to carry household current.

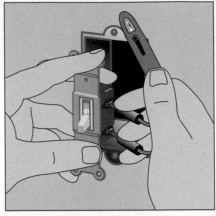

Use a neon tester...
NOTE: *Shut off power.* Remove the cover plate and the screws holding the switch. Pull the switch out from the box. Turn the switch to OFF and restore power to the circuit. Touch the probes of a neon tester to the switch's screw terminals. If the tester glows, the box has power. Turn the switch on. Touch the probes to the terminals again. If the tester glows this time, the switch is blown and must be replaced.

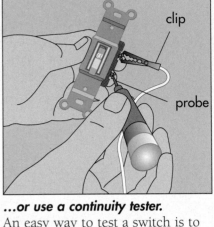

...or use a continuity tester.
An easy way to test a switch is to use a continuity tester. Shut down the circuit leading to the switch and remove the switch from the box. Disconnect all wires. Attach the tester clip to one of the terminals and touch the probe to the other. If the switch is working, the tester will glow when the switch is on and not glow when the switch is off.

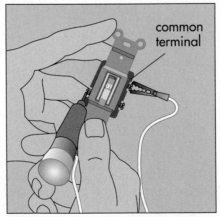

Test a three-way switch.
To check out a three-way switch, shut off the circuit and attach the clip to the common terminal (it's usually labeled on the switch body). Touch the probe to one of the other screw terminals and flip the switch. If it's OK, the tester will light when touching one of the two terminals. Flip the switch. The tester should light when the other terminal is touched.

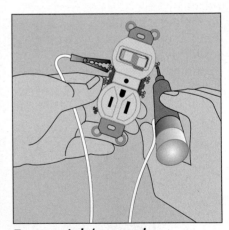

Test a switch/receptacle.
To test a device that has both a switch and a receptacle, attach the continuity tester clip to one of the top (switch) terminals and touch the probe to the top terminal on the other side. If the switch is working, the tester will glow when the switch is on, and not glow when it is off.

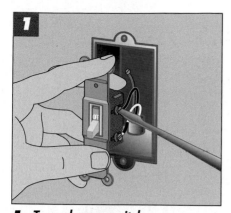

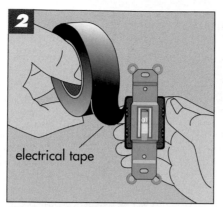

electrical tape

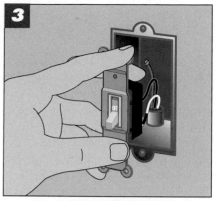

1. To replace a switch, remove the old switch.

NOTE: *Shut off power.* If a switch is damaged, remove the screws holding the switch to the box and gently pull out the device. Loosen the screw terminals and disconnect the wires.

2. Attach wires to the new switch.

Inspect the wires in the box and wrap any damaged insulation with electrical tape. Attach the wires to the terminals of the new switch and wrap electrical tape around the body of the switch so the terminals are covered.

3. Reinstall the switch.

Carefully tuck the wires and switch back into the box and connect the switch to the box by tightening the mounting screws. Don't force anything; switches crack easily.

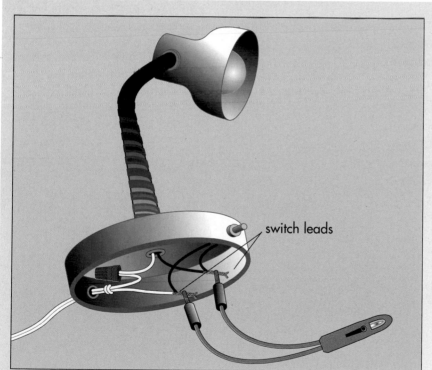

switch leads

Test a fixture-mounted switch.

Small switches that mount on fixtures work by pull chain, flipping up and down, or twisting. These switches are not long-lived, so if the light does not work and the bulb is not blown, there is a good chance that the problem is with the switch. To test, shut off power to the fixture (or unplug it).

Remove the connectors holding the switch's leads. Leave the bare wires twisted together, and arrange them so the connections are not in danger of touching each other or anything else. Restore power to the fixture and carefully touch a neon tester to the connections. If the switch is turned on and the tester lights, the switch is bad.

Replace a fixture-mounted switch.

NOTE: *Shut off power.* Remove the fixture and disconnect the wires. Release the pull-chain switch by loosening the terminal screws and two screws in the base of the socket. Install a replacement switch and remount the fixture.

Other porcelain fixtures have an integrated switch. In such cases, replace the entire fixture. Lamp pull chains cannot be repaired. Buy a new pull-chain socket and replace the old one (see page 63).

TESTING AND REPLACING RECEPTACLES

Receptacles can be damaged in ways that are not readily apparent. Small cracks can lead to a short. As receptacles grow old, they may hold plugs in place less firmly. The good news is that receptacles are inexpensive and easy to replace. Don't hesitate to replace one for any reason, such as because it is paint-glopped or the wrong color. However, if you want to replace your receptacle with one of a different type—for example, replace an ungrounded receptacle with a grounded one—read pages 38 and 46 first.

YOU'LL NEED...

TIME: About 5 minutes to test and 15 minutes to replace a receptacle.
SKILLS: Using a tester (we'll show you how) and connecting wires to terminals.
TOOLS: Neon tester, receptacle analyzer, and screwdriver.

1. To test for a faulty receptacle, see if receptacle is live.
With the power to the circuit on, insert one probe of a neon tester into each slot of the receptacle. Do not touch the metal probes; only touch the insulated wires of the tester. If the tester glows, the receptacle is working. Test both plugs of a duplex receptacle.

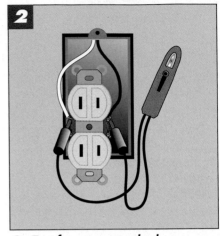

2. Test for power to the box.
If the receptacle is not live, check its power source. Shut off power to the outlet at the service panel, remove the cover plate, disconnect the screws holding the receptacle to the box, and pull the receptacle out. Restore power, and touch one probe of the neon tester to a brass screw terminal and the other to a silver-colored terminal. The tester light will glow if power is coming to the receptacle.

1. To replace a receptacle, remove the old receptacle.
NOTE: *Shut off power.* Note which wires are attached to which terminals. If necessary, make notations on pieces of tape and wrap them on the wires. Loosen the terminal screws and disconnect the wires.

2. Wire the new receptacle.
Inspect the wires in the box, and wrap electrical tape around any damaged insulation. Attach the wires to the receptacle, positioning each wire so it hooks clockwise on the terminal screw. Firmly tighten the terminal screws.

3. Wrap with tape and install.
Wrap the body of the receptacle with electrical tape, so that all the terminals are covered. Carefully tuck the wires and the receptacle into the box and connect the receptacle to the box by tightening the mounting screws. Don't force the receptacle into place—it may crack.

Test for grounding and polarization.

Do not turn off the power. Insert one prong of a neon tester into the short (hot) slot and the other into the grounding hole. If the tester glows, the receptacle is grounded and the slots are polarized. If the tester doesn't glow, put one probe in the grounding hole, the other in the long slot. If the tester glows, hot and neutral wires are reversed. If the tester doesn't glow in either place, the device isn't grounded.

Test a two-slot receptacle.

With the power on, insert one probe of a neon tester into the short (hot) slot, and touch the other probe to the cover plate screw (above). The screw head must be clean and paint-free. Or, remove the cover plate and insert one probe in the short slot and touch the other to the metal box (above right). If the neon tester glows, the box is grounded, and you can install a grounded three-hole receptacle.

If the tester doesn't glow, insert one prong into the long (neutral) slot and touch the other to the cover-plate screw or the box. If the tester glows, the box is grounded, but the receptacle is not correctly polarized; the hot and neutral wires are reversed. If the tester doesn't glow in either position, the box is not grounded. Do not install a three-hole receptacle.

TOOL TIP

USING A RECEPTACLE ANALYZER

With this handy device, you can perform a series of tests almost instantly without having to dismantle anything.

Leave the power on, but unplug all equipment and flip all switches to off on the circuit of the receptacle you will be testing. Plug the analyzer in. A combination of glowing lights will tell you what is happening with your receptacle (far right).

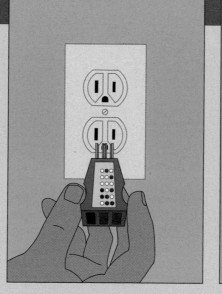

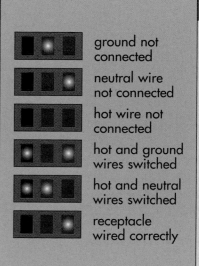

ground not connected

neutral wire not connected

hot wire not connected

hot and ground wires switched

hot and neutral wires switched

receptacle wired correctly

TROUBLESHOOTING THERMOSTATS

A thermostat is a switch that senses temperature and turns your heater or air-conditioner on and off according to the control settings. Most homes have low-voltage units like the one described here. A transformer reduces power from 120 volts to around 24 volts and sends it to the thermostat. Some systems have two transformers: one for heating and one for air-conditioning.

Possible causes of thermostat problems include faulty wiring, a corroded thermostat, and a worn-out transformer.

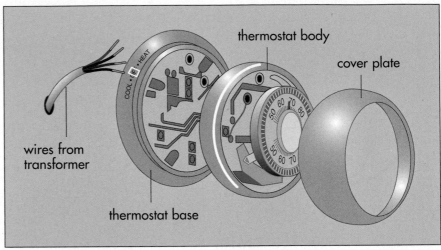

wires from transformer

thermostat body

cover plate

thermostat base

You'll Need...

TIME: Most inspections and repairs can be done in an hour.
SKILLS: No special skills needed.
TOOLS: Voltmeter or multitester, continuity tester, screwdriver, artist's brush, and a short piece of wire.

Anatomy of a thermostat
A low-voltage system begins with a transformer that is either mounted to a panel on the furnace or connected to an electrical box. Anywhere from two to six thin wires (depending on how many items are being controlled) lead to the thermostat base where they are connected to terminals. The thermostat body contains the heat-sensing device and the control dial. Because the voltage is so low, it is not necessary to shut off power to the thermostat while working on it—unless you are working on the transformer.

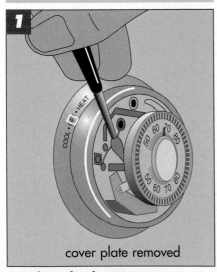

cover plate removed

1. Clean the thermostat.
Dust can cause a thermostat to malfunction. Remove the cover plate and brush the inner workings with an artist's brush. Pay special attention to dust and dirt on contacts.

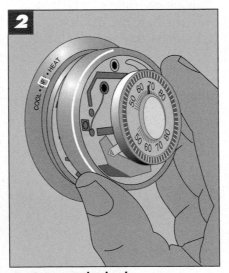

2. Remove the body.
Unscrew the screws that hold the thermostat body to the base, and pull the body away. Check to see that the base is securely fastened to the wall. If it is loose, the thermostat could tilt, which would throw off the settings. Blow on the body to remove more dust, but do not handle the parts inside—they are sensitive.

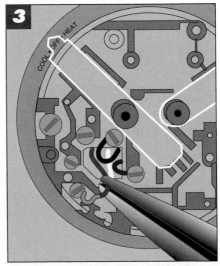

3. Inspect connections to the base.
Look for loose, corroded, or broken wires coming into the base. If any are damaged, clip them, strip insulation from the ends, and reattach. Tighten all the terminal screws to make sure the connections are secure.

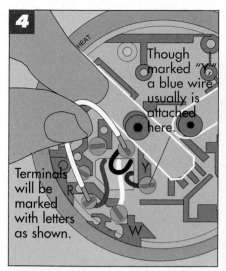

Though marked "Y" a blue wire usually is attached here.

Terminals will be marked with letters as shown.

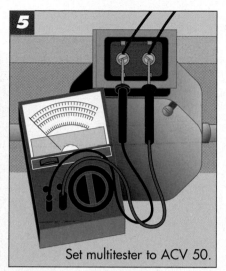

Set multitester to ACV 50.

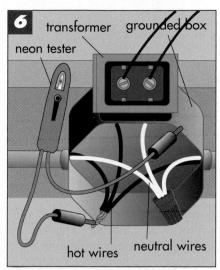

transformer   grounded box
neon tester
hot wires   neutral wires

4. Hot-wire the terminals.

Cut a short piece of wire and strip insulation from both ends. Use it to "jump" between terminals. Touch one end to the "R" terminal and one to "W," and the heater's burner should come on. Touch "Y" and "G," and the fan should come on. If they do not, the thermostat is faulty and should be replaced.

5. Test the transformer.

If the thermostat checks out, test the transformer. Touch one probe of a voltmeter or multitester to each of the low-voltage terminals on the transformer. Set dial to ACV 50. If the meter does not detect current, the transformer is defective and needs to be replaced.

6. Check power to transformer.

Before you go out and buy a new transformer, open up the transformer box and make sure that there is power leading to the transformer. Touch one probe of a neon tester to the hot wires and the other to the box (if grounded) or the neutral wires.

Installing a Programmable Thermostat

A programmable thermostat automatically changes the temperature in your home for sleeping and waking hours. It also can deliver different temperatures when you're away.

There are many options to choose from. Some control heat only and some also control air-conditioning. Some can be completely programmed in one sitting; others require a week-long run-through.

Write down the brand names and model numbers of your old thermostat and heating and air-conditioning units. Take this list when you shop for a thermostat to assure it will be compatible with your system. Here is a guide for installation, but follow the manufacturer's instructions that come with the unit.

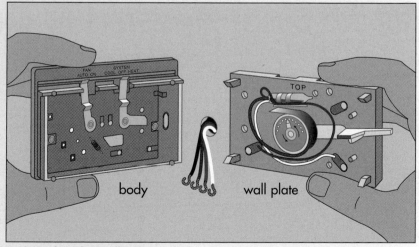

body   wall plate

Removal and installation

As you remove wires from the old thermostat, label them. Remove the old thermostat. Pull the wires through the new wall plate and mount the plate securely to the wall. Check that it is level. Push any excess wire back into the wall and hook up the wires according to the manufacturer's instructions.

Attach the body to the cover plate. Set the clock and program the unit according to the manufacturer's instructions. Attach the cover.

ADDING SURGE PROTECTION

Occasionally your electrical service can experience sudden increases in power, known as surges. A surge almost certainly will not harm lights and appliances, but it could damage sensitive electronic equipment, such as a computer.

To protect a few pieces of equipment, purchase a surge protector that simply plugs into an outlet. Or you can replace an existing receptacle with a surge-protecting receptacle.

Install it as you would a normal receptacle, except that you will be connecting wires to wires rather than to screw terminals.

YOU'LL NEED...

TIME: About 15 minutes.
SKILLS: Joining wires.
TOOLS: Screwdriver, wire stripper, and lineman's pliers.

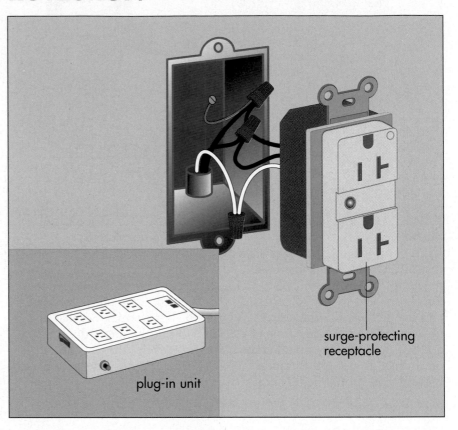

surge-protecting receptacle

plug-in unit

ADDING SURGE ARRESTERS TO CIRCUITS

To protect a circuit against surges, install this device in your service panel. At the service panel, shut off the main circuit breaker, and take off the panel cover. Remove the ½-inch knockout that is nearest to the circuit you want to protect. Insert the surge arrester through the knockout hole, and fix it in place by tightening the nut. Wire as shown, connecting the white wire to the neutral bus bar and the black wire(s) to breakers. Before connecting, cut wires as short as possible for maximum protection.

YOU'LL NEED...

TIME: About an hour.
SKILLS: Understanding of your service panel.
TOOLS: Screwdriver, tongue-and-groove pliers, and wire stripper.

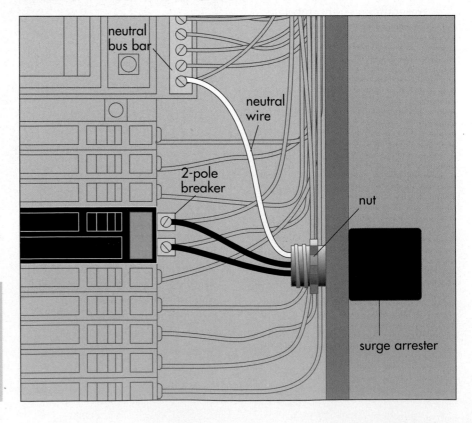

neutral bus bar

neutral wire

2-pole breaker

nut

surge arrester

TROUBLESHOOTING CIRCUIT BREAKERS

Think of a circuit breaker as a heat-sensing switch. As the illustrations at right show, when the toggle is on, current flows through a set of contacts attached to a spring and lever. The contacts are held together by tension in the bimetal strip through which the current flows.

If there is a short or an overload in the circuit, the bimetal strip heats up and bends. As it bends it releases a lever that opens the spring-loaded contact. The contact remains open until the toggle is manually reset by the homeowner.

YOU'LL NEED...

TIME: A few seconds to reset a breaker and about 10 minutes per device to inspect for shorts.
SKILLS: No special skills needed.
TOOLS: Screwdriver.

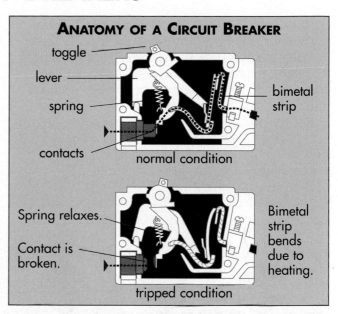

ANATOMY OF A CIRCUIT BREAKER

toggle

lever

spring

bimetal strip

contacts

normal condition

Spring relaxes.

Contact is broken.

Bimetal strip bends due to heating.

tripped condition

Identify a tripped breaker.

A tripped breaker will identify itself in any of the four ways shown at left. To find out whether the problem has corrected itself, reset the breaker. If the problem persists, the breaker will shut itself off again. Usually the problem is an overload, and you only need to unplug or turn off one of the circuit's big energy users. If the circuit breaker keeps tripping even though it isn't overloaded, suspect a short. A defective plug, cord, or socket may be the problem.

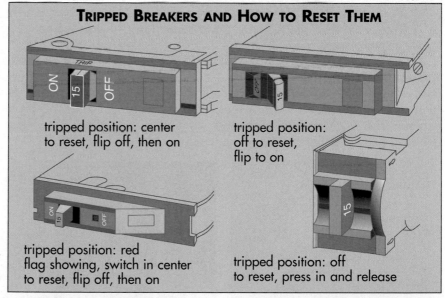

TRIPPED BREAKERS AND HOW TO RESET THEM

tripped position: center to reset, flip off, then on

tripped position: off to reset, flip to on

tripped position: red flag showing, switch in center to reset, flip off, then on

tripped position: off to reset, press in and release

Check connections in boxes.
Short circuits can occur in electrical boxes. Here, a wire has pulled loose from the switch and has shorted out against the box.

wire pulled loose

frayed insulation

Inspect wiring.
Frayed or nicked insulation will expose wire and could cause a short. Wrap damaged insulation with layers of electrical tape.

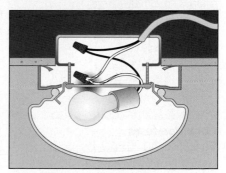

Watch for overheated fixtures.
High-wattage bulbs can melt insulation. Never use bulbs with higher wattage ratings than those for which the fixture is rated.

TROUBLESHOOTING FUSES

Fuses serve the same purpose as circuit breakers, but instead of tripping as a breaker does, a fuse contains a strip of metal that melts when too much current in the circuit produces heat. When this happens, you must eliminate the short or overload and replace the blown fuse.

YOU'LL NEED...
TIME: 10 minutes to inspect your fuses.
SKILLS: Using continuity tester.
TOOLS: Fuse puller and continuity tester.

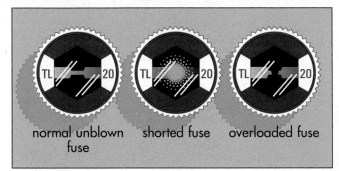

normal unblown fuse   shorted fuse   overloaded fuse

Understanding blown fuses
By examining a fuse you usually can tell what made it blow—an overload or a short. A short circuit usually explodes the strip, blackening the fuse window. An overload usually melts it, leaving the window clear.

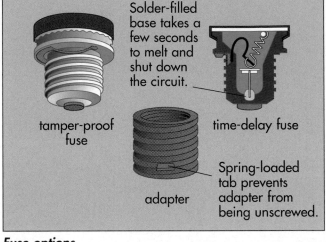

Solder-filled base takes a few seconds to melt and shut down the circuit.

tamper-proof fuse   time-delay fuse

adapter   Spring-loaded tab prevents adapter from being unscrewed.

Fuse options
A tamper-proof fuse is an important safety device that makes it impossible to install a fuse with a higher amperage rating than the circuit is designed for. It comes with a threaded adapter that fits permanently into the box. The adapter accepts only a fuse of the proper rating.

When an electric motor on a washing machine or refrigerator starts up, it causes a momentary overload that can blow fuses unnecessarily. A time-delay fuse avoids this problem by not blowing during the surge. Only a sustained overload will blow the fuse.

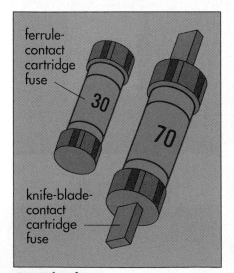

ferrule-contact cartridge fuse

knife-blade-contact cartridge fuse

Cartridge fuses
Fuses for 30- to 60-amp circuits typically are the ferrule-contact cartridge type. Knife-blade-contact fuses carry 70 amps or more. Handle both with extreme caution. Touching either with your bare hand could fatally shock you.

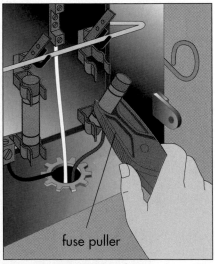

fuse puller

Removing cartridge fuses
For safety keep a plastic fuse puller with your spare fuses and use it as shown. Note, too, that the ends of a cartridge fuse get hot, so don't touch them immediately after you've pulled the fuse.

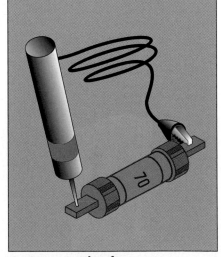

Testing cartridge fuses
To see if a cartridge fuse has blown, check it with a continuity tester. Clamp or hold the clip on one end and touch the probe to the other. The bulb will light if it is not blown.

ADVANCED WIRING

PLANNING PATHS FOR NEW CIRCUITS

Electric cable often does not run in a straight line. Instead, it zigzags from one outlet to another in a circuit. Sharp turns and long trips do not bother electricity. You can snake cable up and down walls, along or across joists, and around obstructions without impeding the flow of electrons.

In the home shown here, two general-purpose 120-volt circuits go from the service panel through the bottom plate of the stud wall and travel around perimeter walls to receptacle outlets. Two others go up into the ceiling for lighting and a 240-volt circuit follows along a floor joist to serve an electric stove receptacle.

Saving money by planning

Even though electricity isn't affected by bends and detours, cable is priced by the foot, and costs for extra feet can add up fast—in labor as well as materials. So to be economical, keep your runs as short and direct as possible.

In new work, that's not too difficult. In this illustration of a well-planned new home, most of the cables travel directly to their destinations. The plan saved money by installing the dryer outlet near the service panel, minimizing the amount of heavier, more costly cable needed for its 240-volt circuit.

The plan also saved the electrician time because there was no need for many bends in the conduit to carry the wire through exposed locations. For example, the cable for the 240-volt receptacle for the electric stove takes as direct a path as possible along the basement sill plate.

Drawing up your plan

In planning an electrical layout, especially if you'll be running more than one circuit, draw a floor plan of your home to scale, then mark the routes cable will travel. See page 40 for an example of circuits planned for one of the more complex areas of a home— the kitchen and family room.

To estimate how much cable you'll need, measure the distances involved, and add 10 percent for bends, unexpected detours, and waste. Be sure to add in another 6 to 8 inches to make connections each time cable enters or leaves a junction or outlet box.

Working in finished spaces

If you plan to fish through finished walls or ceilings, be prepared to use more cable than you would have to if the framing were exposed.

You'll also have some detective work ahead of you. Because cutting holes in walls and patching afterward takes so much time and effort, saving cable is a low priority when wiring in finished space. Search out the path that involves the least damage to your walls and the greatest ease in running the cable.

Your first task is to determine exactly what's in the space through which you want to run cable. If it's an exterior wall, for instance, there will probably be insulation, which makes fishing more difficult.

In addition, many older homes have fire blocking spanning the studs about halfway up the wall. If faced with these barriers, you will have to notch the wall surface at those points. See pages 54–55 and 84–87 for tips on running cable in finished spaces.

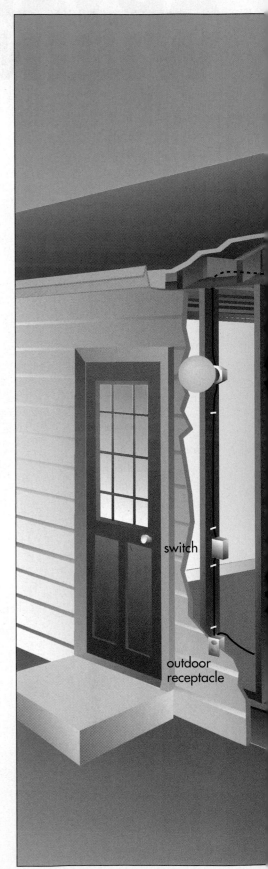

switch

outdoor receptacle

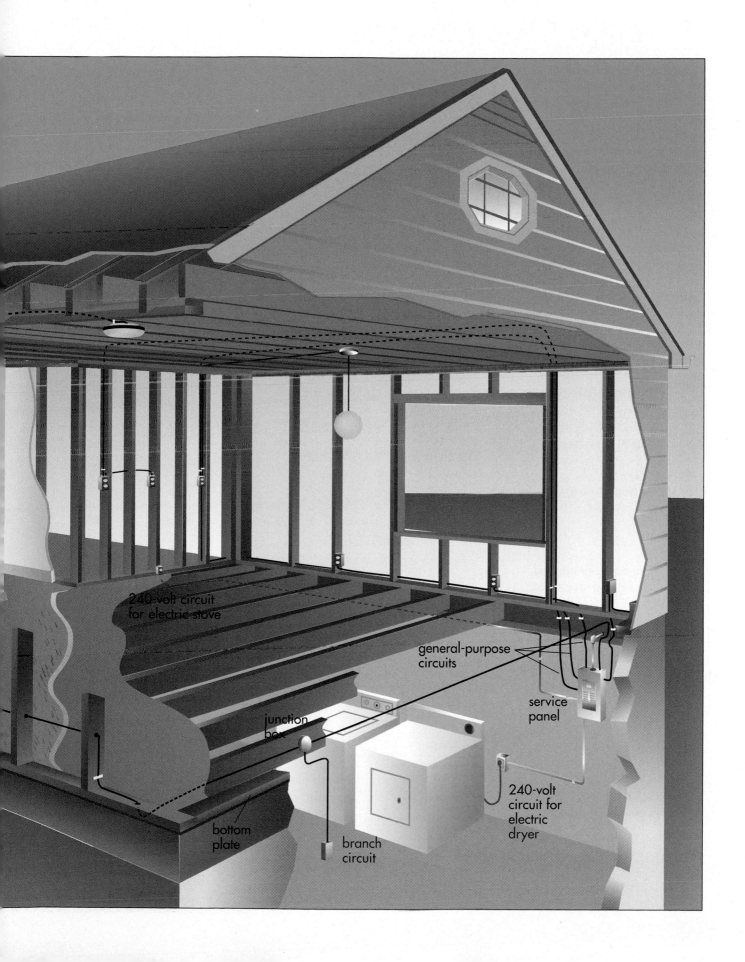

240-volt circuit
for electric stove

general-purpose
circuits

service
panel

junction
box

240-volt
circuit for
electric
dryer

bottom
plate

branch
circuit

PLANNING MAJOR CIRCUITS

Adding a new circuit to your home's service panel is an advanced project for which you may want to call in a professional —especially if your service panel is already crowded. Begin by seeing if you can add to an existing circuit. Failing that, make sure the service can be expanded. Look for an amperage rating on the main fuse, main circuit breaker, or disconnect switch. Older 60-amp service can't be easily upgraded; call in an electrician. Newer 100-amp service may have enough reserve to handle a new circuit or two, and 150- or 200-amp service usually has plenty of capacity.

YOU'LL NEED...

TIME: After running the cable to the service panel, 3 hours.
SKILLS: Understanding of electrical principles and general electrical skills.
TOOLS: Voltmeter and basic electrician's tools.

2. *Estimate capacity needed.*
If you can't add to an existing circuit, check the chart at right for the capacity your new circuit is likely to require. Rooms like living rooms and bedrooms that have about 10 light or receptacle outlets require only 15-amp capacity. Ideally, you should have one general-purpose circuit for every 500 square feet of living space. Some local codes require that lighting and receptacles be on separate general-purpose circuits.

The kitchen is appliance-intensive and needs at least two 20-amp circuits. A bathroom gets by on one 15-amp circuit protected by a ground-fault circuit interrupter. Circuits for the garage, laundry room, and workshop need 15- to 20-amp capacity.

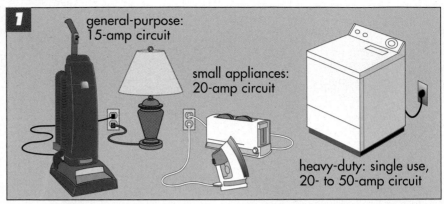

general-purpose: 15-amp circuit

small appliances: 20-amp circuit

heavy-duty: single use, 20- to 50-amp circuit

1. *Try adding to a circuit.*
Different circuits have different capacities. If your need for extra capacity is modest, a few extra receptacles for a bedroom, for example, see if you can add to a general-purpose or small appliance circuit. (Never add on to a heavy-duty, single-use circuit.) Figure the total circuit load by totaling the demand of the appliances and fixtures (see page 40). Then check the chart at right to see if the demand is within safe capacity. The safe capacity of a circuit, as prescribed by the National Electric Code, is 20 percent less than maximum capacity.

CIRCUIT CAPACITY

Circuit rating	Maximum capacity	Safe capacity
15 amps	1,800 watts	1,440 watts
20 amps	2,400 watts	1,920 watts
25 amps	3,000 watts	2,400 watts
30 amps	3,600 watts	2,880 watts

CIRCUIT NEED SELECTOR

Location	Circuits
living and dining rooms, bedrooms, hallways, finished basements	A 15-amp general-purpose circuit for each 500 square feet. Separate circuits for lights and receptacles may be required by code. For a room air-conditioner, install a small appliance circuit.
kitchen	At least two 20-amp small-appliance circuits and a 15-amp lighting circuit. An electric range needs a 240-volt circuit. A microwave oven may need its own circuit.
bathroom	A 15-amp general-purpose circuit with GFCI protection.
garage	A 15- or 20-amp general-purpose circuit (depending on tools and machinery, if any), with GFCI protection.
laundry	A 20-amp small appliance circuit for the washer and a gas dryer. An electric dryer needs a 240-volt circuit.
workshop	A 20-amp GFCI circuit. For larger shops run two 20-amp circuits or a separate circuit for lighting.
outdoors	One 20-amp GFCI circuit.

3. *Check the total service capacity.*
Now that you know what additional circuit capacity you'll need, can your service capacity handle it? If you add up the amperage ratings for all the circuit breakers or fuses, plus the circuits you want to add, you may discover that the total equals or even exceeds the amperage rating of your service panel. Does that mean you can't add new circuits?

Not likely. Few if any of the circuits ever work at full amperage capacity. And some of your electrical fixtures and appliances never run at the same time—a furnace blower and an air-conditioner, for example. That's why codes allow you to de-rate your service capacity. De-rating is a standardized reduction used when computing service capacity. The chart shows a de-rating calculation for a 2,000-square-foot

3

DE-RATING SERVICE CAPACITY

Formula		Compute	
Add			
general-purpose circuits (square footage x 3 watts)	6,000 W	The first 10,000 watts at 100 percent	10,000 W
small-appliance circuits (number x 1,500 watts)	7,500 W	the remaining 13,500 watts at 40 percent	+ 5,400 W
heavy-duty circuits (total of appliance name-plate ratings in watts)	10,000 W	De-rated total:	15,400 W
		Divide	
		The total de-rated wattage by voltage (240)	÷ 240 V
Total:	23,500 W	De-rated amperage	64.2 A

house with 100-amp service, five small-appliance circuits, and two heavy-duty circuits.

In assigning wattage values, don't count each general-purpose circuit. Instead, use 3 watts per square foot of house area. Small-appliance circuits rate at 1,500 watts each. Use the full wattage rating for heavy-duty circuits.

If two items never run simultaneously, ignore the one that draws less. Rate only the first 10,000 watts of the total at full value, then calculate 40 percent of the remainder. Divide the total by 240 volts. The answer, 64.2 amps, shows that the system could accommodate more circuits.

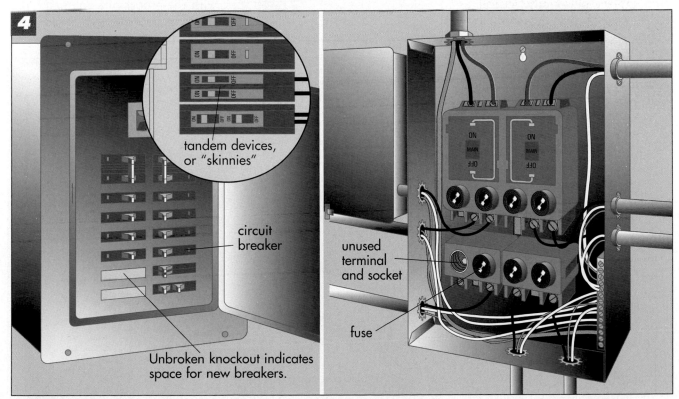

4

tandem devices, or "skinnies"

circuit breaker

Unbroken knockout indicates space for new breakers.

unused terminal and socket

fuse

4. *Check for room in the box.*
Once you've decided the type and capacity of your new circuit, see if you have room for it in your service panel. If your panel has circuit breakers, you might find a

blank space or two. (Unbroken knockouts on the panel indicate space for a breaker underneath.) If not, you may be able to double up two circuits by replacing an existing breaker with a tandem

device, also called a skinny. In a fuse box you might find an unused terminal and socket that could be used. More likely, you'll have to add a secondary fuse box called a subpanel (see page 83).

ADDING MAJOR CIRCUITS

1. To install new circuits, shut off power to the box.
Before working on the box itself, work backward from the new electrical installation. Mount boxes, connect them with cable, and run wiring back to the service panel (see pages 50–59 and 84–99) in what the pros call a "home run." Next comes the serious business of adding and tying into a new circuit. First, look for your home's main disconnect switch. You may have a switch outside the house near the meter (as shown) or inside near the service panel. If you have such a remote disconnect, flip the switch or pull the fuse. Then open the service panel and test it.

If your main disconnect is part of the service panel, seek advice from an electrician, an electrical inspector, or your utility company. To make sure there is no power coming into the service panel, you may have to ask the utility company to have the meter pulled and reconnected later.

EXPERTS' INSIGHT

Outdoor Shutoff Switches
■ If your indoor service panel is located more than 5 feet from the meter, an outdoor shutoff switch is required.
■ If you have an outdoor shutoff switch, it's a good idea to keep it secured with a padlock. Otherwise, anyone passing through your backyard can easily turn off the power to your entire house.

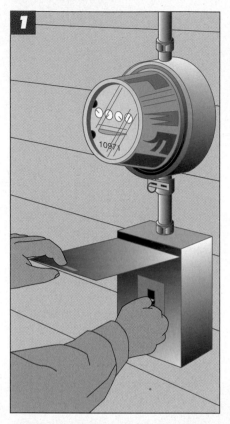

CAUTION!
Remember that the main breaker or main fuse in a service panel does not de-energize the main power cables coming into the box. If you cannot shut off power to the service panel, work carefully or call the power company to disconnect your service temporarily.

2. Test to make sure power is off.
Check that power is off, that main breakers are off or the main fuses are removed. Stand on a board, rubber mat, or other insulator. Being careful not to touch electrical or plumbing fittings, remove the cover plate. Test the terminals of the main power lines with the probes of a voltmeter. If you've got a reading, there is power to that point.

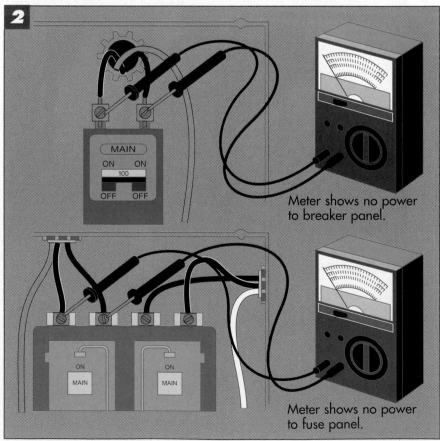

Meter shows no power to breaker panel.

Meter shows no power to fuse panel.

3. Hook up the new breakers.

Punch out the center from a convenient knockout on the circuit panel box. If needed, pry out one or more of the knockout's concentric rings to make a hole the size of the cable connector you'll be using.

Strip the cable sheathing, allowing for enough wire to reach the neutral bus bar as well as the blank space where you'll install the new breaker. Connect the cable to the box. Inside the service panel, run the white and ground wires (bare copper or green) to the neutral bus bar. (No ground wire is used if you are using conduit or BX.) For a 120-volt circuit, attach the black or red wire to the terminal of a single-pole breaker. To finish the job, simply clip the breaker onto one of the hot bus bars.

Some 240-volt appliances, such as water heaters, do not require a third neutral wire. For this type, connect two hot wires to a two-pole breaker (twice as wide as a single-pole breaker), and attach the ground wire to the neutral bar.

Most 240-volt circuits run a white neutral wire and are sometimes called 120/240-volt circuits. Connect the two hot wires to the two-pole breaker and the white wire to the neutral bar. GFCI breakers install somewhat differently (see pages 112–113).

4. Add a subpanel.

If you have a crowded fuse box or are adding several circuits far from the main service panel, connect them to a remote subpanel. Then make just one home run back to the main panel.

You will need a new panel with breakers or fuses, as well as three-wire cable with wire sized to handle the total amperage that the entire subpanel will draw. Connect the cable at the main service panel with terminal lugs.

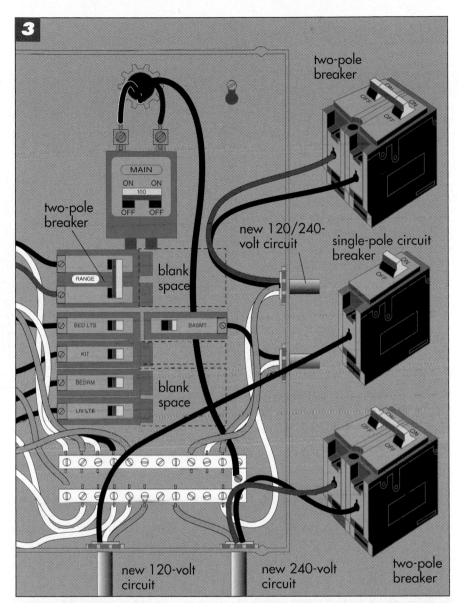

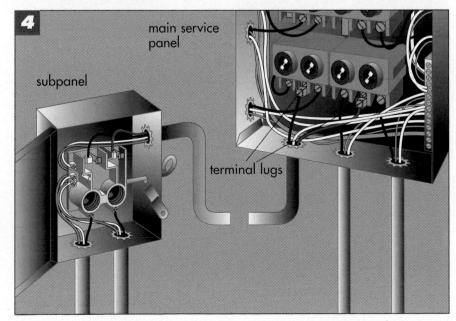

RUNNING CABLE IN FINISHED SPACE

Do some detective work before running cable through finished walls and ceilings. As far as possible, determine what's in the wall or ceiling cavity. Look for access from an unfinished attic floor or basement ceiling. Check to see if there is insulation or blocking in the way. Determine whether or not there is a way to run cable parallel to the joists and studs. **TIP:** *Make as few holes as possible; often the most time-consuming part of running cable is patching walls and ceilings.* Use patching plaster, drywall tape, and compound to patch any holes.

You'll Need...
TIME: About 3 hours.
SKILLS: Drilling and patching.
TOOLS: Power drill, ¾- and 1-inch bits, fish tape, keyhole saw, utility knife, chisel, hammer, and standard carpentry tools.

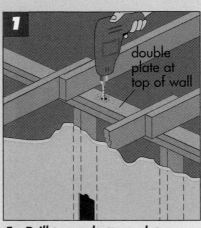

1. Drill top or bottom plates...
If there is access from above or below, drill into the top or bottom plates of the wall frame. For a double plate or awkward angle, use a bit extension. After drilling the hole, feed the cable to the box opening. If you hit blocking (horizontal pieces between the studs), see Step 4.

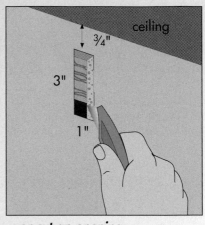

...or cut an opening.
When there is no room for drilling through the plates from above or below, bore from the side instead. At the top of the wall, cut an opening to expose the single or double plate. At the bottom, there will only be a single plate; remove the baseboard, and make the cutout ¾ inch above the floor.

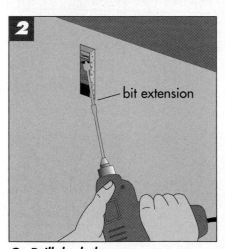

2. Drill the hole.
Using a bit extension, bore into the bottom of the plate, angling toward the center.

Caution!
Bore slowly to avoid burning out the drill. Watch out for nails. Wear goggles when working with power tools.

3. Push the cable through.
Push the cable up or down to the box opening. Then loop it through the plate. Pulling cable through walls is a two-person job. One person tugs—not too hard or the sheathing might tear—from the attic or basement. The other coils cable and feeds it through the opening, taking care to avoid kinks and knots.

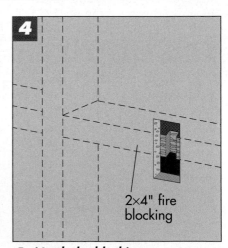

4. Notch the blocking.
To locate fire blocking, slip a tape measure through the hole and push it until it strikes the blocking. Measure to that point and make an opening that straddles the blocking. Chisel a notch that is large enough to accommodate the cable easily. After you've run the cable, but before you patch the hole, install a nail plate (see page 88).

Short runs of cable

Often it is easiest to fish cable from a nearby outlet. Before tapping into an outlet, make sure you won't be overloading the circuit (see pages 78–81).

NOTE: *Shut off the power, remove the cover plate, and see if the receptacle has a set of unused terminals. If it doesn't, add pigtails (see page 59) before reconnecting.*

YOU'LL NEED...

TIME: About 2 hours, not including wall patching.
SKILLS: Pulling wire and patching drywall or plaster.
TOOLS: Fish tape, keyhole saw, standard carpentry tools.

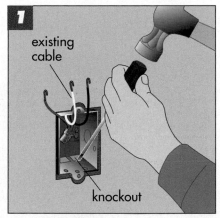

1. Open the box.
Disconnect the receptacle. Check for a cable clamp or other device that will attach the new cable to the box. If necessary, remove a knockout with a hammer and screwdriver and install a clamp.

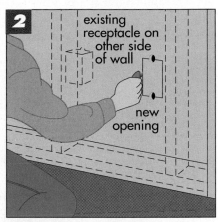

2. Cut the new opening.
Use a box as a template to mark the new outlet opening, and cut it open with a utility knife or keyhole saw. If possible, locate the new box in the same wall cavity as the source box.

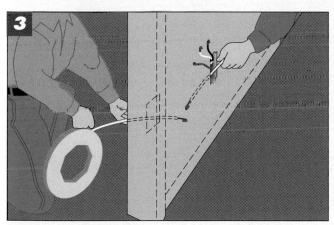

3. Connect fish tapes.
Thread one fish tape (or bent coat hanger) through the knockout hole, and another through the new opening. Wiggle one or both until they hook.

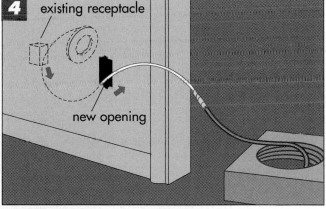

4. Pull tape and connect to cable.
Pull the tape from the existing box through the new opening. Strip some sheathing from the cable, hook the wires on the fish tape end, and wrap with tape.

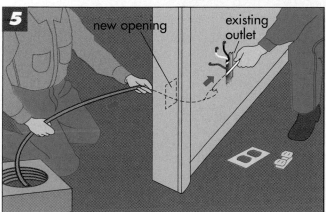

5. Pull the cable through.
Finally, pull the cable through the new opening and into the old box. Connect the cable to the old box (see page 91) and install the new box (see page 54).

CUT NOTCHES

To run cable past studs, cut openings that span each of the studs. Save the cutouts. Chisel a notch in the stud. Install a nail plate to protect the cable (see page 88) and patch the wall.

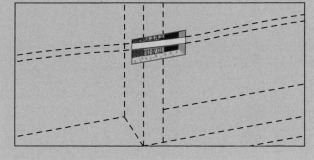

RUNNING CABLE ALONG BASEBOARDS

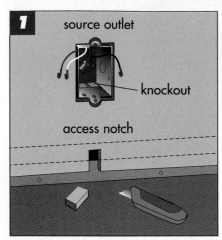

source outlet

knockout

access notch

1. Remove trim, notch for access.
After cutting the hole for your new outlet, remove trim. Avoid damaging the wall or cracking the trim. Pop nails loose one at a time, levering the wood away from the wall with a pry bar. Once the board is free, make a notch in the wall below the outlet that will be the power source. If possible, cut the notch so the baseboard covers it when you replace the baseboard.

YOU'LL NEED...

TIME: 2 hours.
SKILLS: Cutting holes, fishing cable, and simple carpentry.
TOOLS: Utility knife, keyhole saw, chisel, and common carpentry tools.

EXPERTS' INSIGHT

Use armored flexible cable
Use only armored flexible cable (BX) for this operation—never nonmetallic sheathed cable, which can be easily pierced with a nail. Plan the location of the cable and the location of the nails so there is no danger of hitting the cable with a nail. Be especially careful when renailing baseboard, casing, and trim.

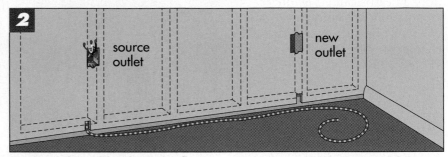

source outlet

new outlet

2. Feed the cable along the floor.
If your home has drywall, you may find a gap at the wall's base that's large enough to accommodate the cable. If there's no gap, cut a channel in the drywall for it. Feed the cable through a knockout hole in the source box, and pull it out of the wall below. As you run the cable along the floor, be sure that it is set back from the wall surface.

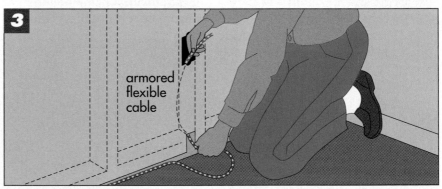

armored flexible cable

3. Bring cable to the new outlet.
If the new opening is low enough, simply push the cable up through the wall to the opening. To pull the cable up to a higher opening, use a fish tape (see page 85).

door jamb

4. Go around a door.
Carefully remove the casing from one side of the door jamb. Push the cable into the space between the jamb and the wall material, notching where necessary. When replacing the casing, be careful not to pierce the cable with the casing's nails.

RUNNING CABLE FOR CEILING FIXTURES

To run cable for a switch-controlled ceiling fixture, first determine the location and direction of the wall studs and ceiling joists. If possible, run wires parallel with framing members to save time-consuming work patching and painting. When cutting notches in drywall, make clean cuts and save the cutout pieces, if possible. Later, glue them back in place with construction adhesive, and finish with drywall tape and compound. Notches in plaster will require more work to repair. Fill the void with nonshrinking patching plaster.

YOU'LL NEED...
TIME: With a helper, 3 hours.
SKILLS: Cutting clean holes in walls, and fishing cable.
TOOLS: Utility knife, keyhole saw, chisel, and fish tape.

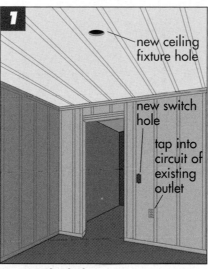

1. Cut the holes.
Decide where to locate the fixture. If a framing member is in the way, move the location of the switch or fixture a few inches. If you have to run cable across framing members, make notches at each joist or stud (see page 85). Next, cut the holes for the switch and the fixture (see pages 54–55).

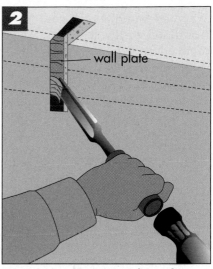

2. Cut an opening at the ceiling.
Where the wall and the ceiling meet, make a 1-inch-wide opening. Extend the opening at least 1 inch below the wall plate, and 2 inches at the ceiling. Chisel a channel into the framing deep enough to accommodate the cable.

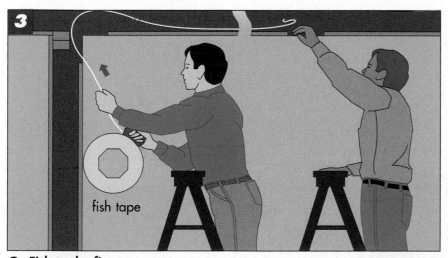

3. Fish to the fixture.
Slowly feed fish tape into the ceiling opening. If the tape meets resistance and coils up, pull back a few feet, shake the tape, and try again. Shaking also makes the tape rattle in the wall—a sure way to locate the tape. For longer runs, use two tapes, feeding in one from either end and snagging them together (see page 85).

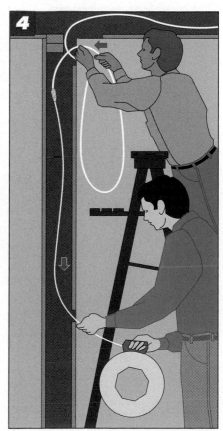

4. Run cable to the switch.
Typically the wall cavity will be clear enough to push the cable down through the wall to the switch opening. Or work a fish tape up, and pull the cable to the switch box opening. Staple the cable into the notches before patching the wall and ceiling.

RUNNING CABLE IN UNFINISHED SPACE

If you're working on a new addition, or if you've gutted a room and removed the old walls, running cable will be much easier. Begin by installing the electrical boxes. Place all the receptacles and switches at uniform height (12 to 18 inches from the floor for receptacles, 48 inches for switches). Make sure the boxes protrude forward from the face of the studs so your drywall will be flush with the front of them. Once the boxes are in place, bore holes in the middle of framing members.

You'll Need...
Time: 1 hour to install two boxes and run 10 feet of cable.
Skills: Drilling holes and fastening boxes in place.
Tools: Drill with spade bit, hammer, and chisel.

center of the stud

1. Bore the holes to run cable.
With an electric drill and a sharp ³/₄-inch spade bit, you can bore holes for a run of cable quickly. Have extra bits on hand for large jobs. Align the holes with each other by eye or use a chalk line to mark a guide. Bore as near the center of each stud as possible to maintain the strength of the framing and lessen the chance of drywall or trim nails piercing the cable. See Step 4 if the corners are solid wood.

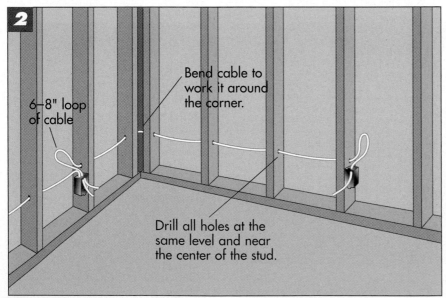

6–8" loop of cable

Bend cable to work it around the corner.

Drill all holes at the same level and near the center of the stud.

2. Run the cable.
Run the cable fairly tightly so that it does not hang between studs. At the corners you may need to bend the cable sharply to keep it at least 1¼ inches from the outer face of the framing. At each box leave a loop of 6 to 8 inches of cable, but do not kink it. This loop gives a margin of error if the wire is damaged when stripped, and makes future repairs and improvements easier.

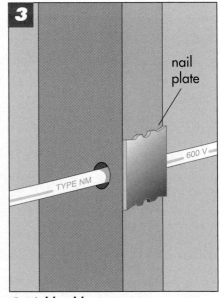

nail plate

600 V

TYPE NM

3. Add cable protectors.
If some of the holes end up less than 1¼ inches from the face of a framing member, install a nail plate. Inexpensive and easy to install, it shields live electrical wires from being pierced by nails or screws. Simply tap the nail plate into place with a hammer.

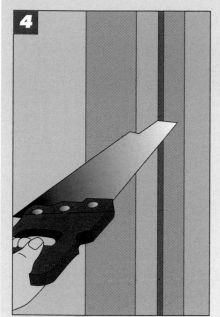

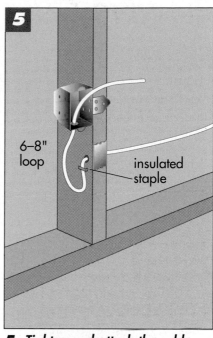

4. Cut notches at corners.
If the corner is solid wood, cut a notch to run cable around corners. Use a hand saw or a reciprocating saw to make two cuts in each stud, wide enough and deep enough for the cable

to fit easily. Chisel out the wood between the two cuts. At inside corners, leave plenty of room—the cable cannot make sharp 90-degree turns. After running the cable, protect it by covering each notch with a nail plate.

5. Tighten and attach the cable.
Pull the cable fairly taut as you install it. At each box, leave a 6- to 8-inch loop and attach the cable with an insulated staple.

6–8" loop

insulated staple

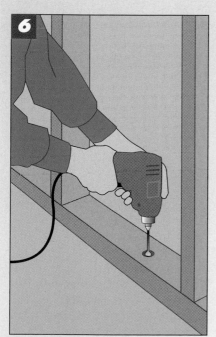
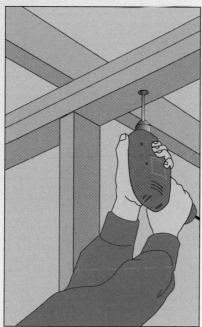
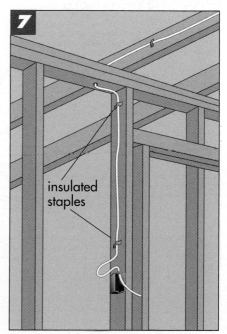

6. Drill plates for vertical runs.
Drill holes in top and bottom wall plates with a ¾-inch spade bit. Drill the holes near the center of the plates. If necessary,

use a drill extension to bore through 2×4 plates. To avoid burning up the bit, stop periodically to let it cool. Drill at high speed and push gently.

7. Run and secure the cable.
On vertical runs, secure the cable with insulated staples every 4 feet or so, wherever you change direction, and 8 to 12 inches from each box. Avoid sharp bends in the cable.

insulated staples

RUNNING CABLE IN ATTICS AND FLOORS

How cable is run in an attic depends on how accessible and usable the attic is. Some local codes allow cable to be surface-mounted in seldom-used spaces. Cable can be attached to the top of the joists with insulated staples. Then 1×2 guard strips are nailed on either side. These strips will protect the cable from damage if anyone steps or sets a heavy object there.

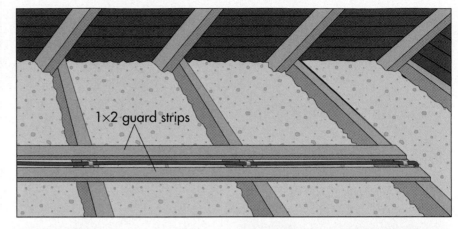

1×2 guard strips

Running cable through holes

If your attic is readily accessible, bore holes through the joists, at least 1½ inches below the top of the joists (see near right). For best protection, and to add a utilitarian floor, install plywood over joists. If the attic has flooring, remove some of it to install the cable or take an alternate route along framing members. In a basement, run cable through holes in the joists (see far right).

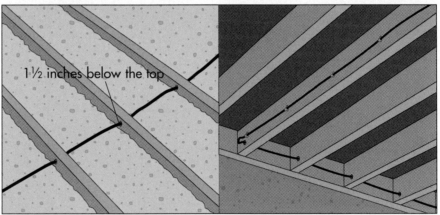

1½ inches below the top

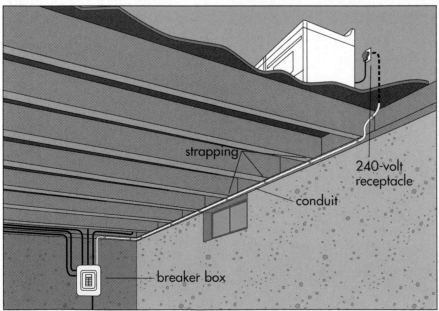

strapping

240-volt receptacle

conduit

breaker box

Strapping thicker cable

Because the heavy cable (8-gauge or larger) used for 240-volt appliance circuits is too stiff to thread easily through holes in joists, some towns allow wiring to be strapped to the underside of joists and along joist plates. Check your local code; conduit may be required for all exposed runs.

EXPERTS' INSIGHT

Special protection

Many special rules may apply when running cable in a permanently unfinished space. Check the local codes before you do any work. Some codes require that cable must be protected in an attic when it is within 6 feet of the entrance; in a garage or basement when it is within 8 feet of the floor. The most commonly accepted form of protection is conduit.

CONNECTING CABLE TO BOXES

This page shows the most common systems for connecting nonmetallic cable to boxes. Other connectors are needed for metallic sheathed cable, Greenfield, and conduit (see pages 93 and 96). Leave ½ inch or more of sheathing inside the outlet box.

▶ Nonmetallic box with clamp

Some nonmetallic boxes come with internal clamps. However, clamping may not be necessary. Some local codes require only that the cable be secured within 8 inches of the box.

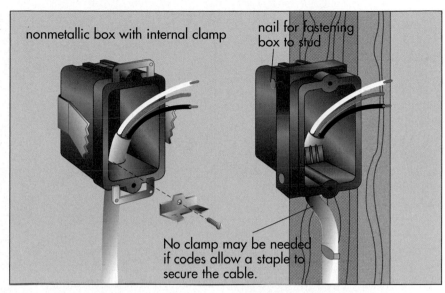

nonmetallic box with internal clamp

nail for fastening box to stud

No clamp may be needed if codes allow a staple to secure the cable.

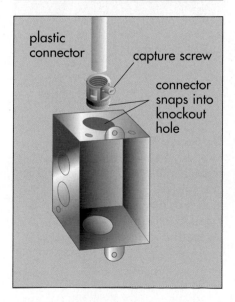

internal saddle clamp

holds 1 or 2 cables

◀ Metal box with saddle clamp

Some metal boxes come with internal saddle clamps. By tightening the saddle-clamp screw, one or two cables can be secured quickly.

▶ Metal box with clamp connectors

Remove a knockout hole in the box, insert a clamp connector into the hole, and secure it with a locknut. Slide the cable through the clamp connector and into the box. Tighten the saddle onto the cable. In some situations it is easier to clamp the connector to the cable first, then slide it into the box and screw on the locknut.

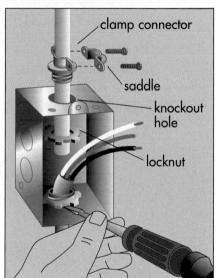

clamp connector

saddle

knockout hole

locknut

◀ Plastic connector

A plastic connector works like a clamp connector, but it is quicker and easier to use. Snap it into the knockout hole, insert 6 to 8 inches of cable, and tighten the capture screw. Other types grab the cable when you pry up on a wedge or squeeze the unit with pliers.

▶ Quick clamp

Some boxes come with internal quick clamps. Pry up a spring-metal tab and slip the cable through. The clamp springs back by itself to hold the cable securely.

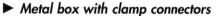

plastic connector

capture screw

connector snaps into knockout hole

quick clamp

WORKING WITH BX, GREENFIELD

*F*lexible armored cable, or BX, is composed of a bendable metal sheathing containing insulated and ground wires. Greenfield, or flexible conduit, is a hollow, flexible metal sheath. Like conduit, it is a tube through which wires are pulled. Check local codes regarding use of these materials—restrictions vary. (See page 47 for the different types of wire and cable available.)

> ### CAUTION!
> *Whenever you work with these materials, you end up with cut ends that are sharp. If wires are allowed to rub against them, insulation could be stripped, resulting in an electrical short. Follow the procedures here carefully to protect wires at all times.*

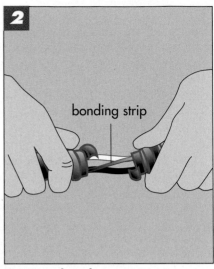

1. Cut notch in the sheathing.
To get through the metal covering, hold a hacksaw at a right angle to the spirals and cut partway through the armor. With BX, be especially careful not to nick the insulation on the wires inside. For a safe and easy way to cut cable, use a BX cutter (see inset above).

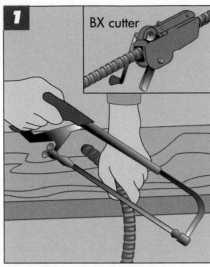

2. Complete the cut.
Twist the armor and it will snap free. The paper-wrapped wires (and aluminum bonding strip, if there is one) can be snipped with ordinary wire cutters. To expose the wires for connecting to boxes and fixtures, cut off the armor at a second point about a foot away.

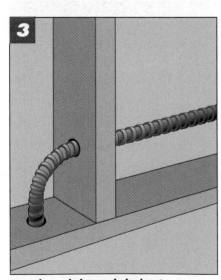

3. Thread through holes in framing members.
Run armored cable and flexible conduit through holes bored in the middle of framing members. Where necessary, use notches. BX and Greenfield are heavier and stiffer than nonmetallic cable, so it will take more room every time you want to change direction.

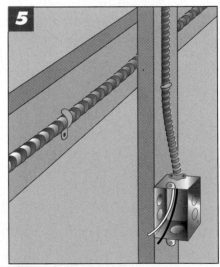

4. Protect the cable.
Even armored sheathing can be pierced with a nail, so anywhere that the cable is within 1¼ inches of the framing surface, protect it with a nail plate designed for the purpose. For short runs (see inset), flexible armored cable may be left exposed—check your local codes.

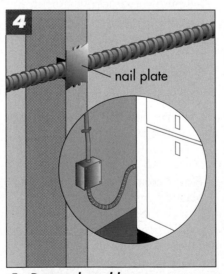

5. Secure the cable.
Support metal-clad cable with specially designed straps or staples every 4 feet or so and within 12 inches of boxes. If you're fishing through existing walls or ceilings, secure the run as best you can.

CONNECTING BX, GREENFIELD

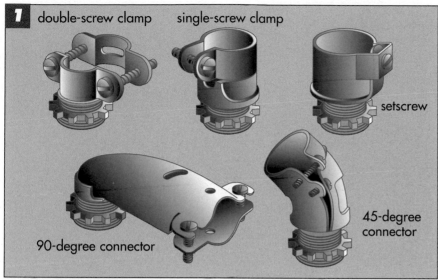

1 double-screw clamp   single-screw clamp

setscrew

90-degree connector

45-degree connector

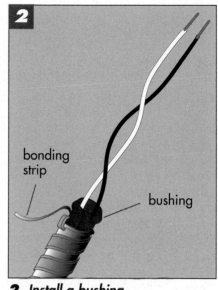

2

bonding strip

bushing

1. To connect cable to boxes, choose the connectors.

In most cases, use a simple straight connector that holds the cable in place either by clamping it or with a setscrew. In some tight situations, you may need to use a

45-degree or 90-degree connector. To install a connector, choose the side of the box you wish to access, and remove the knockout. Cut the cable to length and trim off the armored sheathing (see page 92).

2. Install a bushing.

Pull the brown paper surrounding the wires in BX back about an inch inside the armor. This leaves room to slip in a bushing. If your cable has a bonding strip, fold it back as shown.

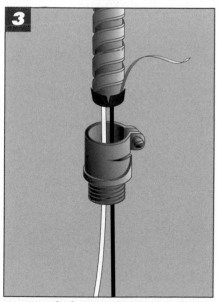

3

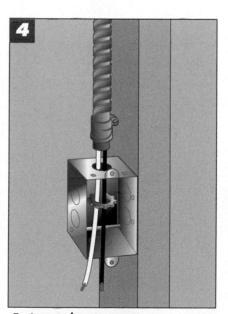

4

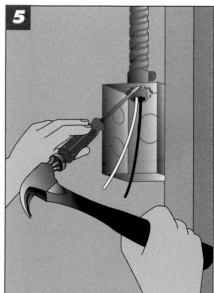

5

3. Attach the connector.

Slip on a connector, making sure the bushing is in place. Tighten the clamp or setscrew. Armored cable and conduit are self-grounding so you don't need a grounding wire. Some codes require that the bonding strip be attached to the tightening screw.

4. Insert the connector.

Slip the wires and connector into a knockout hole, slip on a locknut, and tighten with your fingers. As with all wiring, connections should be made only in boxes.

5. Tighten the locknut.

Tighten the locknut with a hammer and screwdriver. Finally, tug on the cable to make sure everything is securely fastened.

CUTTING AND ASSEMBLING CONDUIT

Codes sometimes require conduit, especially for exposed areas. Conduit has definite advantages: It protects the wires well, and the electrical system can be upgraded later simply by pulling new wires through the conduit. Conduit is the most difficult way to install wiring because it's hard to bend. But it is still within the reach for do-it-yourselfers. For small jobs, use elbows and connectors at each turn to avoid bending conduit.

Codes allow many wires to be pulled through conduit. But the more wires you pull, the more crowded the conduit, so buy larger conduit than is required by code— say, ¾-inch instead of ½-inch.

You'll Need...

Time: About 2 hours for a run with three bends and two boxes.
Skills: Careful measuring, clean cutting, and screwing pieces together.
Tools: Tubing cutter or hacksaw, pliers, and screwdriver.

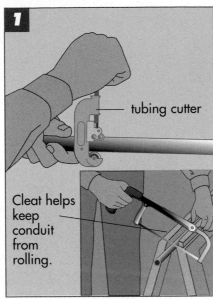

1. Measure and cut.
Measure the distance for the run— don't forget to subtract for the connector or elbow you will be using. Cut with a tubing cutter by clamping it to the conduit and rotating it a few times. Tighten and rotate until the cut is made. Or cut with a hacksaw. Hold conduit against a cleat or use a miter box to keep it from rolling as you saw.

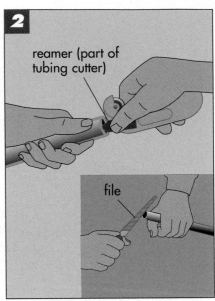

2. Ream the ends.
Sharp edges can chew up wiring insulation in a hurry. Remove all burrs and rough spots from the inside of the conduit, using the reamer that's attached to the tubing cutter or a file. File rough spots on the outside as well, so the conduit can slip easily into a connector.

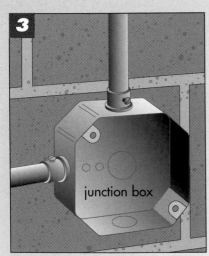

3. Install a junction box.
Where you have more than four turns to negotiate, install a junction box. When it's time to pull the wires, it will let you start another run. More boxes and few bends ease wire-pulling.

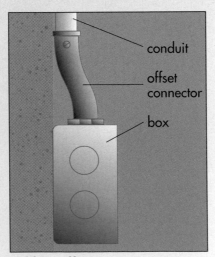

Add an offset.
Use an offset connector to keep the conduit flush against the wall when it's attached to a box. The conduit can be bent to form an offset (see page 95), but adding an offset connector is easier.

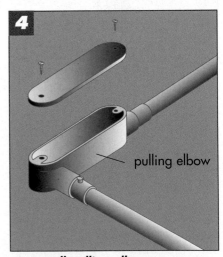

4. Install pulling elbows.
A pulling elbow makes negotiating corners easier. Remove the cover to pull the wires through. Don't make any connections inside a pulling elbow; wires must pass through without a break.

BENDING CONDUIT

For larger jobs, it is expensive and time-consuming to use connectors at each corner. Instead, bend the conduit. Bending isn't difficult, but getting the bend in just the right location is tricky and requires some practice.

Runs begin and end at places where you can get at wires to pull them. Codes generally forbid a total of more than 360 degrees of bends in a run. Add up the degrees of the bends you'll be making in a single run before you start bending to ensure the total is less than 360 degrees.

YOU'LL NEED...

TIME: About 30 minutes to measure, bend a piece, and connect it on either end.
SKILLS: This is a specialized skill that requires practice.
TOOLS: Conduit bender, tape measure, and black marking pen.

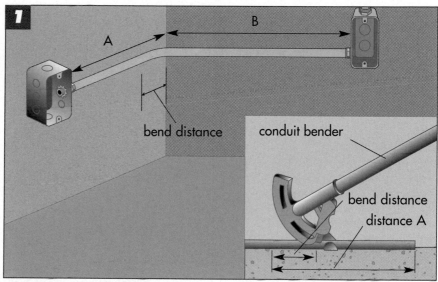

1. Measure for a corner.
To get conduit around a corner, first measure from the box to the top of the bend (distance A). Then subtract the bend distance and mark the conduit. (The bend distance for ½-inch conduit is 5 inches. For ¾- and 1-inch conduit, allow 6 and 8 inches, respectively.) Slip the conduit bender onto the tubing and align it as shown. After making the bend, trim section B by holding the bent conduit in place for measuring, and cutting the end so it just reaches the box.

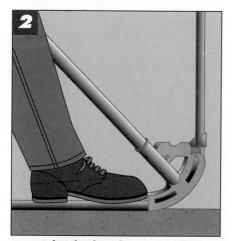

2. Make the bend.
With one foot on the rear of the bender, pull slowly and steadily on the handle. Be careful. Tugging too sharply will crimp the tubing and you'll have to start over again with another piece. (Codes forbid installing crimped conduit.) Making crimp-free bends takes practice, so don't be surprised if your first efforts fail.

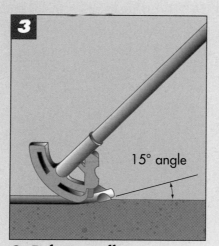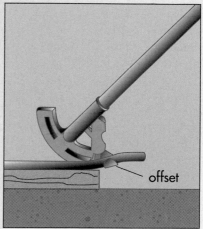

3. To form an offset, start with a 15-degree bend...
When mounting conduit on a flat surface, you'll need to form an offset at each box. Offsets must be aligned with other bends in the tubing. A stripe painted along the length of the conduit helps you do this. First make a 15-degree bend.

...then bend in the other direction.
Roll the conduit over, move the bender a few inches farther from the end, and pull until the section beyond the first bend is parallel to the floor.

CONNECTING CONDUIT

1. Use couplings to join sections.
To join sections end to end, use either setscrew or compression couplings, securely fitted.

> ### CAUTION!
> *Make all connections mechanically strong. Pulling wires through conduit can put a strain on connections. Grounding depends on secure metal-to-metal connections.*

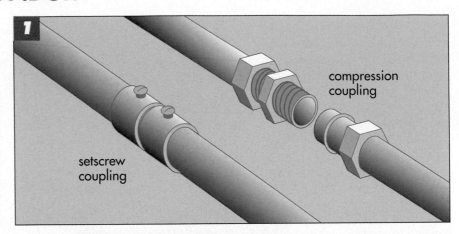

2. Anchor the conduit.
Anchor conduit runs with at least one strap every 8 feet and a strap within 3 feet of every box. For masonry walls, use screws and plastic anchors. When attaching to framing, simply drive barbed straps into the wood.

To mount conduit inside walls, bore holes in the studs (see pages 84–90), or notch the framing and secure it with straps or metal plates every 8 feet.

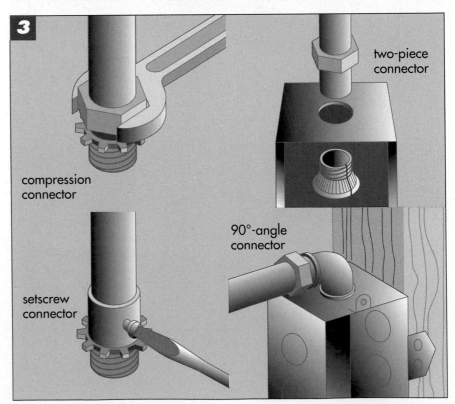

3. Connect to boxes.
The various types of box connectors differ mainly in the way they attach to conduit. Compression connectors grab the conduit as you tighten the nut with a wrench. To install a setscrew connector, slip it on and tighten the screw. Both types are available in 90-degree versions.

All these connectors attach to the box with the same threaded stud and locknut arrangement used with cable connectors (see page 91). Insert the stud into a knockout hole, turn the locknut finger tight, then tap the nut with a hammer and screwdriver to tighten it. A two-piece connector comes in handy when space is tight inside a box. Instead of a locknut, it has a compression fitting. As you tighten the nut, the fitting squeezes the conduit.

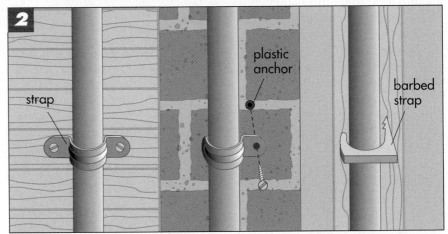

PULLING WIRE THROUGH CONDUIT

Now comes the moment when you realize why codes are so specific about bends, crimps, and burrs in conduit. Pulling wire can be surprisingly hard work. If you suspect that the wire is scraping against something that might damage the insulation, stop work, locate the trouble spot (you can find it easily by using the wire as a measuring device), and remove it. Purchase pulling grease, and lubricate the wires with it if you need to make a long pull.

YOU'LL NEED...

TIME: About an hour to pull cable through 60 feet of conduit.
SKILLS: Patience and some pulling muscle.
TOOLS: Fish tape, pulling grease, and electrical tape.

1. Push through short runs.
For short runs with only a couple of bends, you can probably just push the wires from one box to the other. Feed the wires carefully to protect the insulation.

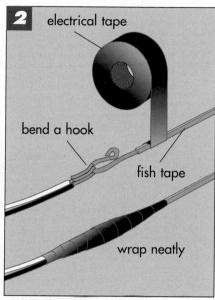

electrical tape
bend a hook
fish tape
wrap neatly

2. Attach a fish tape.
If you can't push the wires, you'll need a fish tape and an assistant. Snake the fish tape through the conduit, hook the wires to the fish tape and secure with electrician's tape. Wrap the connection neatly so it can slide through the conduit.

3. Pull the wires through.
As one worker feeds the wire in and makes sure there are no kinks, the other pulls. Pull the wires with steady pressure—avoid tugging. As the wires work past bends, expect to employ more muscle. If you have lots of wires or a long pull, lubricate the wires with pulling grease. Where possible, use gravity to aid the process. Feed the wires from above and pull from below.

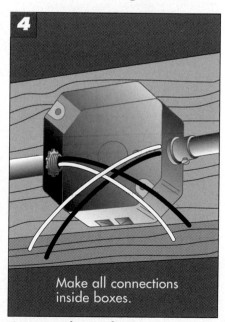

Make all connections inside boxes.

4. Leave plenty of wire.
Leave 6 to 8 inches of wire at each box. Never splice wire inside conduit—all wires must run continuously from box to box.

RUNNING WIRES UNDERGROUND

If you want to install a lamppost in the front yard or install new power to the garage, run the wiring underground.

Check local codes to see if you can simply run waterproof cable (labeled "UF") underground or if you need to protect cable with conduit. Also find out how deep the wiring needs to be.

The potential for shock is greater outdoors, so buy watertight fittings designed for outdoor use. Protect all exterior receptacles with ground-fault circuit interrupters (see pages 112–113).

If you are installing only a light or two, you probably can extend power from an existing circuit. If the outdoor outlets will receive heavy use, you'll need to establish a new circuit. See page 81 to assess the amount of demand you're likely to place on it.

YOU'LL NEED...

TIME: Two days to tap into an outlet, dig 30 feet of trench, and install a lamppost.
SKILLS: Making electrical connections, working with conduit, trenching, and mixing and pouring concrete.
TOOLS: Wire stripper, lineman's pliers, conduit bender, and carpentry tools.

CAUTION!

Before you start digging trenches, contact your utility companies to find out where all the underground pipes and cables are in your yard.

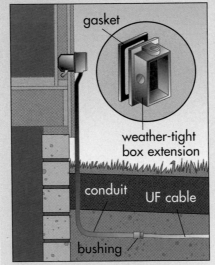

Tap an exterior receptacle...
Add a weather-tight extension to an existing exterior receptacle, and run conduit from it. Attach it so the gasket will keep out moisture. Unprotected UF cable should exit from the conduit about 18 inches below grade through a special insulating bushing. Check to see if your local codes allow cable.

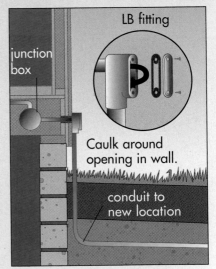

...or connect inside the house.
If no exterior receptacle is handy, find a nearby junction box or run a new circuit from the service panel. At the point where the wiring leaves the house, install an LB fitting. Do not make connections inside the connector—wires must run from box to box.

Add a light to an existing switch.
If you want a lawn light that will come on when you turn on an exterior light, tap into an existing fixture. Remove the fixture from its electrical box and install a weather-tight box extension into which you can run the wiring. Run conduit down the side of your house or hide cable inside the wall cavity.

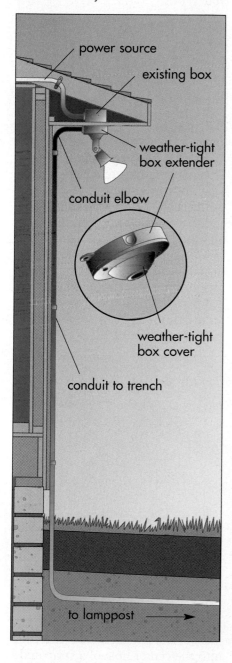

power source

existing box

weather-tight box extender

conduit elbow

weather-tight box cover

conduit to trench

to lamppost →

1. To install a lamppost, first dig a post hole and trench.
Various types of lampposts come with their own installation instructions. However, they all need to be firmly anchored to the ground. The simplest way to do this is to dig a deep post hole with a clamshell-type digger, set the post in it, and fill with concrete or tamped soil. If your trench must pass under a sidewalk or driveway, dig the trench on either side of the obstruction. Cut a piece of conduit about a foot longer than the span. Flatten one end to form a point. Drive the piece under and past the obstruction, cut off the flattened end, and connect it to conduit with couplings (see page 96).

2. Plumb the post.
After you run the wire (see page 97) and before you fill the hole, plumb and brace the post using scrap lumber. Attach the braces to the post with clamps and screw or nail them to the stakes. Add water to premixed concrete, shovel it into the hole, and trowel smooth.

3. Make the electrical connection.
Wire the light (see page 100) using wire connectors (see page 58). A light-sensing photocell accessory switches on the light at nightfall. If you also wire it to a conventional indoor switch, the switch can override the photocell when the light isn't needed.

TIME-SAVER

DIGGING TRENCHES
For short runs where the digging is easy, a shovel will suffice, although you'll end up with a trench wider than needed. For large jobs, rent a walk-behind trencher, which makes a trench up to 2 feet deep. Give trees a wide berth to avoid damage to roots and time-consuming chipping.

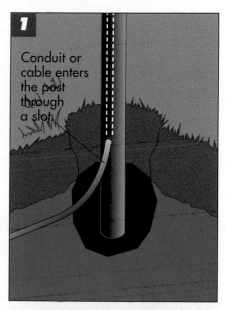

1

Conduit or cable enters the post through a slot

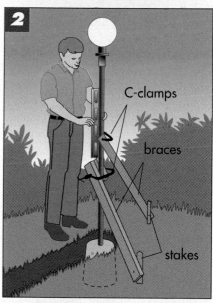

2

C-clamps

braces

stakes

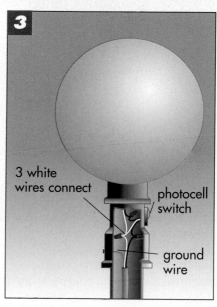

3

3 white wires connect

photocell switch

ground wire

HANGING CEILING FIXTURES

*D*ramatically change the appearance of a room by adding or replacing a ceiling light. Although the choices are many, from simple ceiling fixtures to elaborate chandeliers, all are installed in essentially the same way: Power is drawn from a ceiling-mounted box designed to support a particular fixture. If you are replacing a ceiling fixture, take the time to inspect the wires and the area around the outlet box for heat damage (see page 65).

YOU'LL NEED...

TIME: An hour to mount a simple fixture; more time is needed for elaborate units.
SKILLS: Basic carpentry and wiring skills
TOOLS: Screwdriver and pliers.

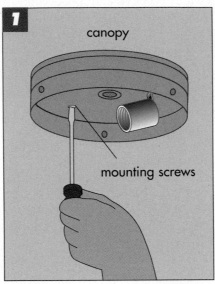

1. Remove a flush-mounted fixture. NOTE: *Shut off the power.* Remove the globe or diffuser and the bulb(s). Remove the screws or the cap nut holding the canopy in place and drop the fixture down. Disconnect the black and white wires. Check wires for cracks in the insulation (see page 65). To replace wire, see pages 84–90.

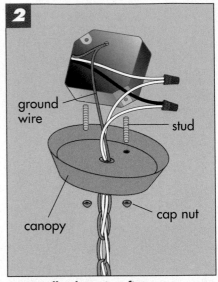

2. Install a hanging fixture.
This hanging fixture attaches with a pair of studs screwed to the box. Connect the black and white wires and the ground wire, coil them up into the box, and push the canopy into place so the studs poke through. If the unit does not easily push up flush to the ceiling, drop it down and rearrange the wires. Secure the canopy by twisting cap nuts onto the studs.

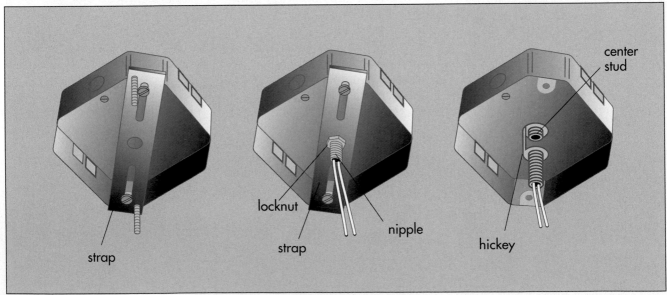

Mounting systems
If the holes in the canopy don't match those in the box, choose from the three mounting systems shown above. Adapt the box for fixtures with side mounting bolts by fastening a **strap** to the box. Some straps have several screw-in holes to choose from. For center-mounted fixtures, screw a **nipple** into the center hole of a strap and secure it in place with a locknut. If the box has a center stud, attaching a **hickey** is another way to adapt the box.

INSTALLING TRACK LIGHTING

Track lighting gives you a great deal of flexibility. After it is installed, you easily can change the number of lights, their positions, or the direction they point—even the type of light.

The initial hookup is much like other ceiling fixtures (see page 100). But installing the tracks involves measuring your ceiling and establishing lines for correct placement so the track is pleasingly aligned with your room. Have two ladders and one helper on hand for marking placement. (If you do not have an existing box to tie into, see pages 84–90.)

YOU'LL NEED...

TIME: If you are working from an existing ceiling box, 4–6 hours for a 12-foot system.
SKILLS: Connecting wires in a box, and careful measuring of and attaching to a ceiling.
TOOLS: Tape measure, Phillips screwdriver, and drill with screwdriver bit.

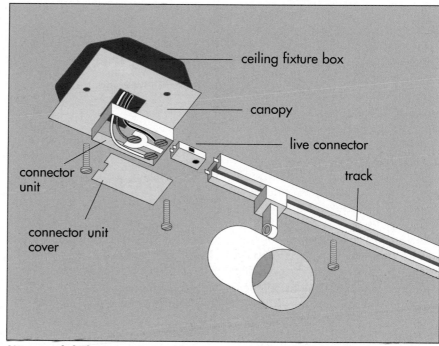

How track lighting goes together.
Instructions for your unit will tell you specifically how to make connections, but most track lights go together in the following way. A connector unit connects to the ceiling electrical box and transfers power to the tracks. Inside the tracks are two metal strips that run along its length. They are electrified by wires from the box. The lights themselves have two contacts at their base. When the contacts meet the electrified strips, the light comes on. A cover caps off the connector unit.

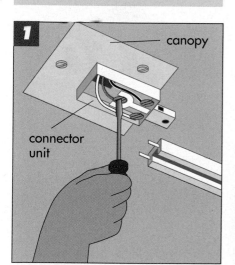

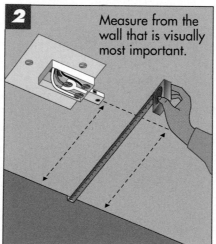

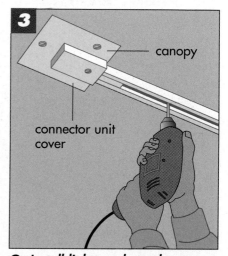

1. Install the connector unit.
NOTE: *Shut off the power.* Attach the black, white, and ground wires from ceiling fixture box to the connector unit terminals. Hook wires clockwise on the screw shafts before tightening. Fasten the connector unit to the canopy.

2. Lay out and install tracks.
To establish a line that the track will follow, measure off a wall at several points, and strike a line between them. Connect the track to the connector plate. Screw the track into ceiling joists or use toggle bolts.

3. Install lights and attach cover.
Restore power to the circuit. Install lights according to instructions—in most cases, you twist them in place. Attach the canopy and any connector covers by snapping into place.

INSTALLING CEILING FANS

Whether it's keeping warm air down for heat in the winter, or circulating cool air in the summer, a ceiling fan can cut energy costs and help keep your home more comfortable all year long. Installing a ceiling fan is an ideal one-day project for homeowners with little or no wiring experience. Most fans have pull switches that turn the unit off and on and that control fan speed. You can also install wall switches to control the fan (see pages 118–124).

Turn off the electricity. When unpacking your fan, lay fan blades on a flat surface to check that they are not warped. If one is warped, ask your retailer to replace the entire set. Then check the blade irons. They are typically set at a 12-degree angle, though on small fans they can be pitched as high as 25 degrees. Set them on top of each other. If one doesn't match the others, have your retailer replace it.

YOU'LL NEED...

TIME: About 4 to 6 hours if you need to run new wiring.
SKILLS: Simple carpentry and wiring skills.
TOOLS: Screwdriver, utility knife, keyhole saw, wrench, socket driver, and needle-nose pliers.

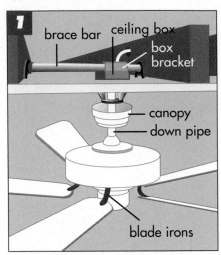

1. Select a brace bar.
If you don't have access from above, you'll need a ceiling fan support, known as a brace bar, which can be inserted from the room below. Typically, it consists of an adjustable bar installed between two joists.

HOW TO CHOOSE A BRACE BAR AND CEILING BOX

You'll find many types of brace bars and ceiling boxes to choose from at your local hardware store or home center. Be sure both can support the size of fan you are installing.

You may not need a brace bar if you have access from above. You can add in framing and attach the ceiling box directly to it using general-purpose screws. Never install a fan support bracket or fixture box that is held up only by the ceiling material.

Ceiling boxes may be reinforced plastic or sturdy metal designed to support fans. If you are putting in a fan where there was once just a light fixture, you may need to replace the ceiling box, install a brace bar to support the added weight, or do both.

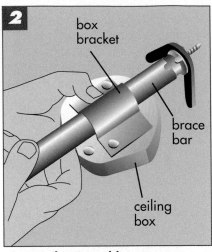

2. Test the assembly.
Do a dry run of assembling the brace bar, ceiling box, and box bracket. Be sure you fully understand how the brace bar is fastened in place and how the box is attached. Follow the instructions that come with it. Once installed, these items are hard to remove.

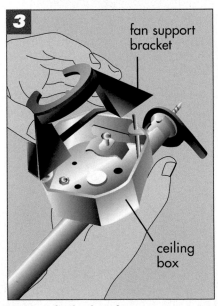

3. Test-fit the bracket.
Check that the fan support bracket fits and can be attached easily once the box is in place. Push out a ceiling box knockout (a tab covering a hole in the back or one of the sides), and install a cable clamp. Disassemble the brace bar, ceiling box, and box bracket.

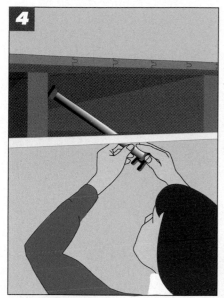

4. Position brace bar.

Between joists, cut a hole in the ceiling about 5 inches in diameter (see page 55 for tips on locating it). Most brace bars have a screwlike fastener at each end that fixes the bar in place. Slip the bar through the hole and position it perpendicular to the joists.

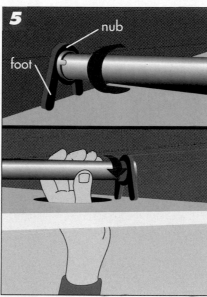

5. Fasten the bar.

Turn the outermost piece of the brace bar until it locks into the nub. Continue turning until the first foot is fastened. Next turn the innermost bar to fasten the other foot.

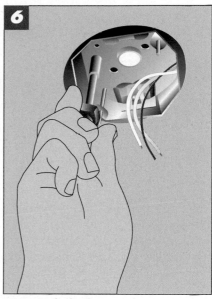

6. Attach the box.

Pull wires into the receptacle box. Loosely fasten one side of box bracket and position the bracket on the brace bar. Feed the second bracket bolt through the box and fasten nuts on both of the bolts using a socket driver or pliers.

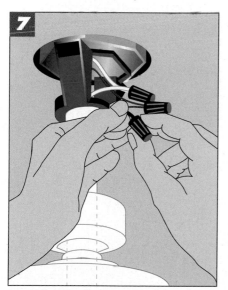

7. Wire the fan.

Attach the fan support bracket and the down pipe. Using wire connectors, connect the fan leads to the circuit wires. Be sure to attach white to white, black to black, and the ground wire to the green lead. Manufacturers usually provide instructions. Wire the fan following the instructions.

CHOOSE A CEILING FAN: CLEARANCES AND CAPACITIES

For safety, and to give the fan adequate space to effectively move air, use the clearances shown below. Select fan blades to suit the square footage of the room.

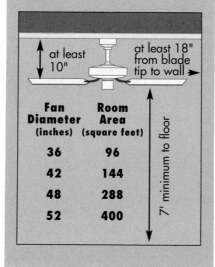

at least 10"

at least 18" from blade tip to wall

7' minimum to floor

Fan Diameter (inches)	Room Area (square feet)
36	96
42	144
48	288
52	400

EXPERTS' INSIGHT

Balancing a wobbly fan
All may not be gentle breezes when you turn on your fan. Particularly at high speed, it may rock and roll. Don't panic. It might not be a manufacturer's defect or the result of shoddy installation. One of these two steps should fix the problem:
■ Check for any loose screws where the blades attach to the blade irons and the blade irons attach to motor.
■ Buy an inexpensive ceiling fan balancing kit and follow its simple procedures for checking the blades.

INSTALLING RECESSED CEILING LIGHTS

Recessed fixtures have much to recommend them: They are inexpensive, unobtrusive, and if you have no fixture box already in place, a recessed light is the easiest fixture to install because it comes with a box attached. Purchase a unit with a silver reflector for greater brightness or choose a black reflector for more subdued lighting. Make sure the fixture you buy will fit in your ceiling space. If your ceiling joists are smaller than 2×10, for instance, you will need a fixture with a side-mounted box.

YOU'LL NEED...

TIME: After running cable from the switch, about 1½ hours.
SKILLS: Cutting a clean hole in the ceiling and attaching wires.
TOOLS: Keyhole saw, screwdriver, and drill with screwdriver bit.

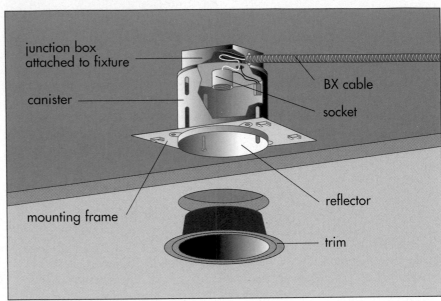

Anatomy of a recessed fixture
Designed for installation where there is no access from above (a common problem when adding recessed lighting in the first-floor ceiling of a two-story house), this unit sits atop drywall or plaster. The fixture can be installed from below. The mounting frame spreads out the weight of the unit.

CAUTION!
KEEP IT COOL

If you don't take precautions, a recessed light can build up a lot of heat, which can lead to prematurely burned-out bulbs, damage to your ceiling, melted wire insulation, or even fire. Allow the fixture room to breathe. Keep any ceiling insulation at least 3 inches away from it and don't place it in a cramped space. Use bulbs of the recommended type and wattage. You can increase the wattage if you use a floodlight bulb because it directs more heat away from the fixture than a regular bulb. Don't leave any flammable materials, such as scraps of insulation paper, anywhere near the fixture.

1. Cut a hole.
Determine the general location of the fixture and drill an exploratory hole. To make sure a joist is not in the way, use a bent wire, so when spun it will follow the circumference of the fixture. If the site is clear, mark and cut an opening with a keyhole saw.

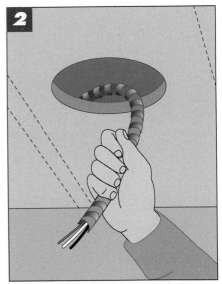

2. Rough in the wiring.
NOTE: *Shut off the power.* For the rough wiring, simply run cable to the hole where the fixture will go. Leave a foot or so of extra cable sticking through the hole. See pages 118–124 for ways to wire a switched ceiling fixture.

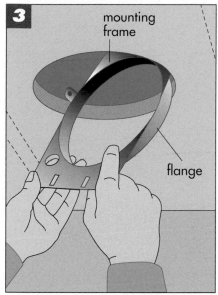

3
mounting frame

flange

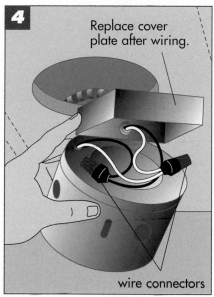

4
Replace cover plate after wiring.

wire connectors

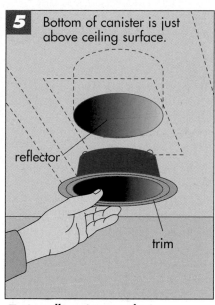

5
Bottom of canister is just above ceiling surface.

reflector

trim

3. Secure the mounting frame.

Slip the mounting frame up through the hole (it will just fit). Pull the cable down through the mounting frame. Place frame so the flange sits in the hole. Strip about 6 inches of sheathing from the cable and about ¾ inch of insulation from each wire (see pages 56–57).

4. Wire the fixture.

Remove the cover plate from the fixture's electrical box. Secure the cable to the box and connect the wires in the box. Follow the same procedures as if wiring a regular box—see pages 59 and 91. Push the wires into the box and replace the cover plate.

5. Install canister and trim.

Slide the canister up through the mounting plate until it is slightly recessed above the surface of the ceiling. Secure it to the mounting plate by tightening the screws provided. Attach the reflector. Screw in a lightbulb, and attach the trim.

Another configuration

There are several types of recessed lights, all with their own ways of connecting to the ceiling. Here is one that works well if you have access to the space above your ceiling. Once the fixture is positioned over the hole, sliding brackets attached to the canister extend out to reach joists on either side. When these brackets are secured to the joists, the unit is more firmly attached than most recessed fixtures. As with all recessed fixtures, it comes with its own electrical box.

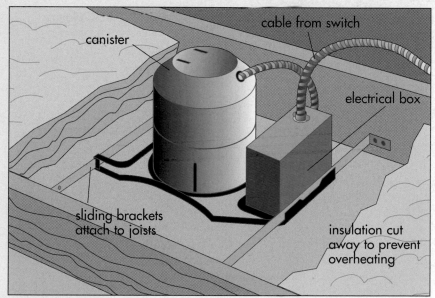

cable from switch

canister

electrical box

sliding brackets attach to joists

insulation cut away to prevent overheating

Installing this type

Pound a nail up through the ceiling at the point where you want the light. Go into the space above, find the nail, cut back the insulation, and cut a hole. Install the reflector in the canister. Set the canister in the hole, slide out the brackets, and attach to the joists with nails or general-purpose screws. Wire the box, screw in a bulb, and attach trim.

ADDING WALL SCONCES

Wall sconces are ideal for hallways, stairways, and any room that needs indirect accent lighting. Installing a wall sconce is similar to adding a new light fixture. The only difference is location and the type of fixture box used. As with ceiling lights, you can control as many lights as you want with one switch, or control one or more of them from two different locations by using three-way switches. See pages 120–124 for the various options.

It's ideal if you can secure the fixture box to a framing member as well as the drywall or plaster. Use one of the standard retrofit boxes shown on page 49.

YOU'LL NEED...

TIME: About a full day to install a new switch and two sconces, not including any wall patching.
SKILLS: Basic electrical skills, plus cutting and patching walls.
TOOLS: Keyhole saw, screwdriver, lineman's pliers, drill, and fish tape.

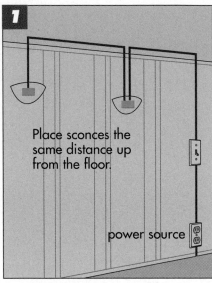

Place sconces the same distance up from the floor.

power source

1. Cut holes and run cable.
NOTE: *Shut off the power.* Find a junction box or a receptacle with power you can use. Cut a vertical hole for the switch box and horizontal holes for the sconce boxes (see page 54). Run cable from the power source to the switch and from the switch to the openings cut in the wall for the sconces (see pages 82–83).

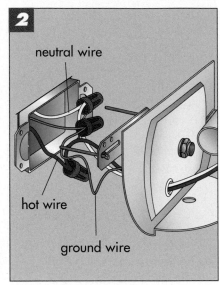

neutral wire

hot wire

ground wire

2. Wire the sconces.
Fasten cable to the boxes, allowing an extra 8 inches of cable to protrude at each box. Attach the boxes to the walls. Strip the sheathing and the wire insulation, and make the connections (see pages 56–57). Note that wires travel both into and out of the first sconce fixture box. Wire the switch (see page 118).

EXPERTS' INSIGHT

THE USES OF SCONCE LIGHTING

■ Wall sconces provide a splash of indirect light that creates the illusion that a room is larger than it is. For this reason, and because they are commonly placed slightly higher than eye level, keep the bulb wattage low.
■ In most cases wall sconces work best in conjunction with other lights rather than as the primary light source for a room. They work well for ambient light but are insufficient for specific tasks, such as reading.
■ Install sconces 72 to 78 inches high. Any lower and you will bump into them; any higher and they will seem designed to light the ceiling rather than the room.
■ Typically it makes the most sense to add wall sconces to one wall where accent or indirect lighting is called for. A few sconces go a long way, so keep them spaced more than 6 feet from each other.

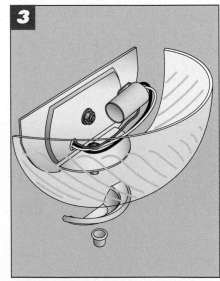

3. Install the sconces.
Tuck the wires into the box, screw a mounting strap to the box, and attach the sconce to the mounting strap. Secure the switch and its cover plate, and test.

INSTALLING UNDER-CABINET LIGHTING

A kitchen is a brighter, more pleasant place to work when its countertops are illuminated by under-cabinet fixtures. Under-cabinet lighting provides a sparkling decorative effect and gives you excellent task lighting.

A 120-volt system requires hours of fishing and installing fixture boxes in one of the most crowded and complicated areas of the house. An attractive alternative is the low-voltage system shown here. Low-voltage halogen lights operated with a remote-controlled, surface-mounted switch can be installed in a day and look as good as a more permanent system.

YOU'LL NEED...

TIME: About a day to install a switch and 10 lights.
SKILLS: Stripping and connecting wires and simple carpentry skills.
TOOLS: Screwdriver, drill, lineman's pliers, and keyhole saw.

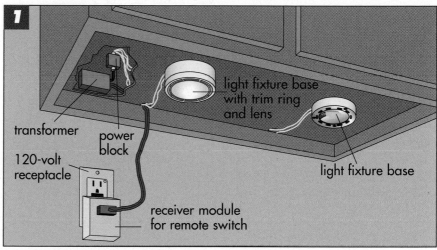

transformer
power block
120-volt receptacle
light fixture base with trim ring and lens
light fixture base
receiver module for remote switch

1. Install lights and transformer.
Determine a location for each light fixture where it won't shine in your eyes as you work. Halogen lights get hot; they can be safely attached to wooden cabinets but should be kept away from plastic and paper goods. Remove the trim ring and lens from each fixture base and attach them with screws to the underside of the cabinets. (Be sure the screws are the right length so they do not poke up into your cabinet.) Align fixtures so the bulbs aim in the same direction. Drill small holes to allow the wires to pass into your cabinet, and plug their ends into the power block located inside the cabinet. Coil excess wire inside the cabinet. Connect the power block to the transformer. Drill a hole and run a wire from the transformer to a 120-volt receptacle.

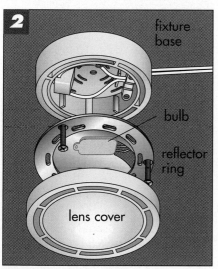

fixture base
bulb
reflector ring
lens cover

2. Assemble the lights.
Once the fixture bases are installed, snap the lens cover onto the reflector ring. Some under-cabinet lighting kits come with a warning label to attach inside the cabinet door to caution users about the heat of the units.

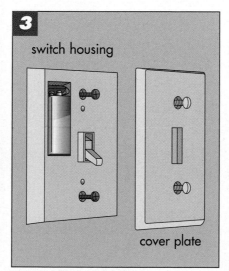

switch housing
cover plate

3. Install the switch.
The switch operates by battery power, so it can be installed anywhere in the kitchen and requires no wiring. Attach the switch housing by screwing it to the wall—use plastic anchors if you can't find a stud. Screw the cover plate to the switch housing.

EXPERTS' INSIGHT

FLUORESCENT UNDER-CABINET LIGHTING

The low-voltage halogen lighting shown here is a convenient improvement when cabinets are already installed. If you are in the process of installing cabinets, consider installing thin (1- to 1½-inch thick) fluorescent lights under the cabinets. To install fluorescent lights, run standard electrical cable behind the walls. Run wires behind the cabinets if possible so you won't have to patch the walls. Or use raceway wiring attached to the underside of the cabinets (see pages 110–111).

INSTALLING SPECIAL SWITCHES

One of the easiest ways to enhance your home's electrical system is to install special switches. Wiring them is rarely much more difficult than installing a standard switch.

Choose from a wide variety of options. The single-pole dimmer (shown at right), for instance, is touch-sensitive, like a modern elevator button. Touching its flush plate turns lights on and off. Holding a finger on it adjusts the light level. Even that minimal effort isn't necessary with the motion-sensitive switch. It turns on a light fixture whenever someone enters a room then stays on for a prescribed amount of time.

Be aware that some switches have limitations. For example, an ordinary dimmer can only handle up to 600 watts, so it may not be able to operate a chandelier. For higher-wattage fixtures, buy special dimmers able to handle 800, 1,000, or 1,500 watts. (For more information on these and other switches, see pages 44–45.)

If you have ground wires, they all should be connected together in the box, no matter what kind of switch you are installing.
NOTE: *Shut off the power before installing the switch.*

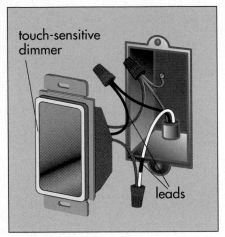

Single-pole dimmer
Most dimmers have a set of leads, or short wires, instead of screw terminals. Hook up a single-pole dimmer as shown.

Most dimmers are deeper than conventional switches, so you may have to rearrange wires in the box before you can fit one in. Don't force dimmers, because they crack easily. If there are too many wires, order a thin-profile unit.

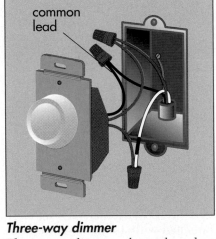

Three-way dimmer
Three-way dimmers have three hot leads. Before you remove the old switch, determine which is the common terminal—it will be printed on the switch body, and/or the screw will be darker-colored than the others. Hook the common wire to the new switch's common lead, and connect the other wires. (For more on three-way switches, see pages 121–123.)

You'll Need...
Time: To install most of the switches on these two pages, about an hour.
Skills: Connecting wires.
Tools: Screwdriver, lineman's pliers, and wire stripper.
Materials: Wire connectors, wire for pigtails, and electrical tape.

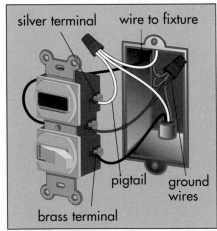

Pilot-light switch
This switch has a bulb that glows when its fixture is on. Connect the black feed wire to the brass terminal on the side that does not have a connecting tab. Pigtail two white wires, and connect them to the silver terminal. Connect the black wire that leads to the fixture to the terminal on the side with the connecting tab.

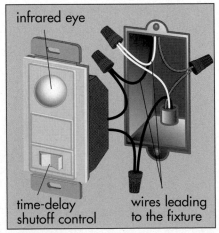

Motion-sensor switch
An infrared beam detects movement and turns on a light fixture. A time-delay feature lets you choose how long the light remains on. Connect the neutral wires to each other, not to the switch. Connect the black feed wire to one lead. To the other lead, attach the black wire that runs to the fixture.

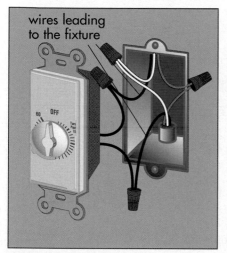

wires leading to the fixture

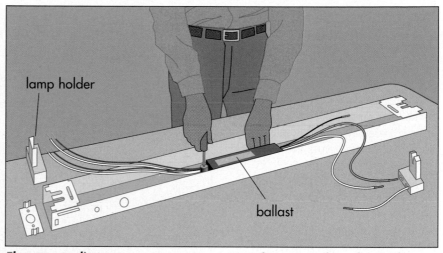

lamp holder

ballast

Time-delay switch
With this type of switch, you turn a spring-driven dial to set the switch so it will turn off a fixture after a delay ranging from 1 to 60 minutes. Connect the black leads to the black wires in the box, and connect the white wires together, not to the switch.

Fluorescent dimmer
Fluorescent dimmer switches connect in the same way as incandescent dimmers (see page 108), but you must equip each lamp with a special ballast. Remove the fixture. Mark the wires with pieces of tape so you'll know where to refasten them. Remove the lamp holders and disconnect their wires by poking

into the terminals with a nail or thin screwdriver. Remove the old ballast and install a new dimming ballast. Reconnect the lamp holders. Reinstall the fluorescent fixture. If more than one fluorescent light is connected to a dimmer switch, all the bulbs must be the same size and share the same ballast (for replacing a ballast, see page 67).

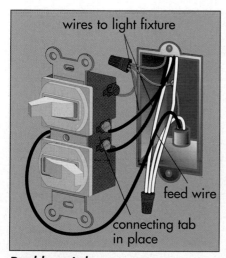

wires to light fixture

feed wire

connecting tab in place

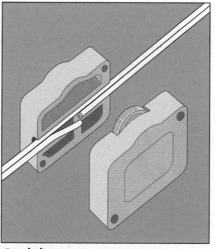

Double switch
This unit has two switches that fit into a single-switch space. Attach the feed wire to a terminal on the side with the connecting tab. (This tab enables the wire to supply power to both switches.) Connect the two wires that lead to the two fixtures to the terminals on the other side, and connect the white wires together, not to the switch.

Cord dimmer
You can purchase in-line cord dimmers for lamps that do not have switches. Some, such as this one, automatically pierce the insulation when you put the unit together. Others require stripping the wires before assembling.

Money $ Saver

These switches not only give you greater control over your lighting but can save money as well. A dimmer switch enables you to operate a bulb at less than its full intensity so you save energy and prolong the life of the bulb. Time-delay and pilot-light switches keep you from burning lights unnecessarily. Programmable switches (see page 45) save money and provide security while you are on vacation. You can program them to turn lights on and off in a pattern that makes it appear you are at home.

ADDING SURFACE-MOUNTED WIRING

If you do not want to cut into your walls, fish wires, and patch and paint afterward, consider surface-mounted wiring, often called "raceway" wiring. Surface-mounted components are available in metal or plastic and are comparatively easy to install. The system's main drawback is the way it looks. But for informal settings—a basement or a work room, for instance—it is a convenient alternative.

NOTE: *Shut off the power before tying into existing receptacles.*

YOU'LL NEED...

TIME: For a system like the one shown, about 4 hours.
SKILLS: Connecting wires and measuring and cutting the components.
TOOLS: Hacksaw, miter box, and basic electrician's tools.

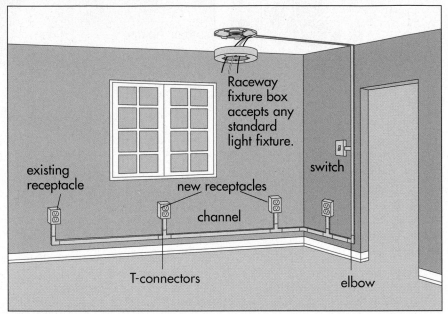

Raceway fixture box accepts any standard light fixture.

existing receptacle

new receptacles

channel

switch

T-connectors

elbow

Plan the job.
Check your local codes. They probably limit raceway wiring to dry locations where the walls are not subject to damage (as they are, for example, in a garage). Map where you want the pieces to go and measure carefully for all the runs. Take your plan to your electrical supplier and have a salesperson help you choose the parts you need.

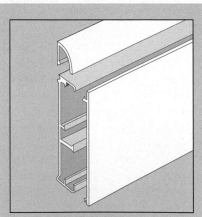

Baseboard channel
Decorative and functional plastic baseboard channel can be added onto existing baseboard or even substituted for it. This type of channel is designed to simultaneously carry household wiring, coaxial cable, and telephone and computer lines. Extension boxes with receptacles, phone jacks, and coaxial hookups can be added along its length.

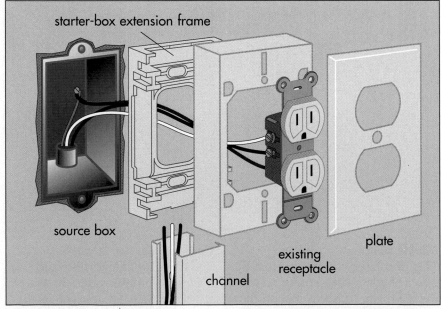

starter-box extension frame

source box

channel

existing receptacle

plate

How the pieces go together
A raceway system begins by tapping into an existing circuit at a receptacle by using a "starter box." This extends the existing outlet so it can match up with the wall-mounted channel. Twist-away holes allow you to exit the box with raceway channel from any direction. Additional receptacles—as well as switches and light fixtures—mount directly on the wall. Begin by selecting a receptacle on a circuit that has enough capacity for additional outlets (see pages 80–81).

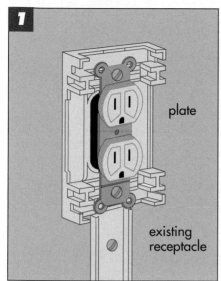

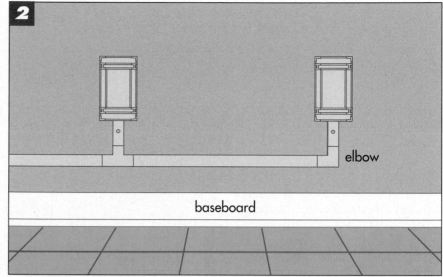

1. Start at the box.
NOTE: *Shut off the power.* Remove the receptacle and install the starter box, onto which the receptacle will be reinstalled as shown. Map out the system from this starting point.

2. Cut and assemble components. When you measure the channel sections for cutting, take into account every elbow, T, and other connector. Cut the channels with a hacksaw and a miter box. Use extension connectors to tie the ends of channels together, and T and elbow connectors at corners. Measure carefully from the floor and use a level to make sure the receptacles are at the same height.

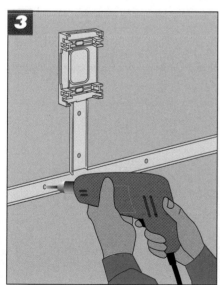

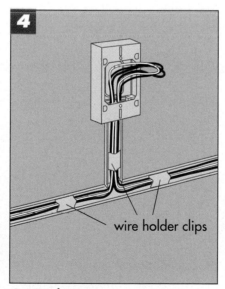

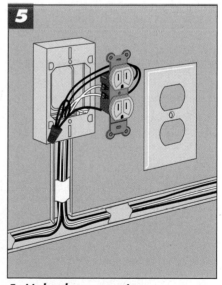

3. Attach components securely.
The channels will be bumped by furniture and normal household traffic, so take care to attach them securely. Attach channel back by locating studs and drilling screws into them where possible. Use plastic anchors for places where you can't reach studs.

4. Run the wires.
Run the wiring and hold it in place every foot or so with specially designed clips. Be sure to leave 6–8 inches of wire at each outlet so you will have room to strip and make connections.

5. Make the connections.
Connect all fixtures and receptacles (see pages 58–59). Connect to the existing receptacle, turn the power back on, and test the new fixtures and receptacles (see page 70). Install the snap-on covers for the channels, fittings, and boxes.

CHOOSING GFCI RECEPTACLES AND BREAKERS

Fuses and circuit breakers protect the wiring in your home. A ground-fault circuit interrupter (GFCI) protects people who might otherwise get a dangerous shock.

A GFCI has a microprocessor that senses tiny leakages of current and shuts off the power instantly. In most circumstances, leakage of current isn't a big problem. In properly grounded systems most of it is carried back to the service panel. What remains would scarcely give you a tickle. But if you are well grounded—standing on a wet lawn or touching a plumbing component, for example—that tiny bit of current would pass through your body on its way to the earth. As little as $\frac{1}{5}$ of an amp, just enough to light a 25-watt bulb, can be dangerous.

A GFCI is wired into both wires of a circuit so it can continuously monitor the hot and neutral current levels and compare them. These should always be equal. If the microprocessor senses a difference of just $\frac{1}{200}$ of an amp, it instantly trips the circuit. Power is

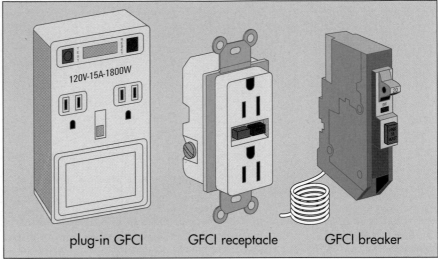

plug-in GFCI   GFCI receptacle   GFCI breaker

interrupted in $\frac{1}{40}$ of a second or less, cutting off the power before you're seriously hurt. Any ground fault is a potential hazard. If a tool or appliance is faulty, it can give you a serious shock even if its grounding wire is in good condition. So GFCI protection is a good idea anywhere you might be in contact with any dampness while using electricity.

There are three types of GFCIs: plug-ins, receptacles, and breakers. To use a portable plug-in unit, simply insert its blades into a

receptacle and plug the appliance into it. A GFCI receptacle replaces a conventional receptacle and, properly placed, can protect other receptacles on the same circuit. Install a GFCI breaker into a service panel to protect a circuit.

YOU'LL NEED...

TIME: To install either a receptacle or a breaker, 1 to 2 hours.
SKILLS: Connecting wires.
TOOLS: Screwdriver, wire stripper, and lineman's pliers.

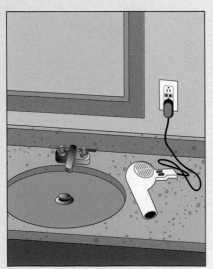

Electrical codes require GFCI receptacles in the places where you're likely to ground an electrical appliance. In a kitchen, GFCIs often are required for all receptacles within 6 feet of a sink. All bathroom receptacles, as well as all outdoor receptacles, must be GFCI-protected.

INSTALLING GFCI DEVICES

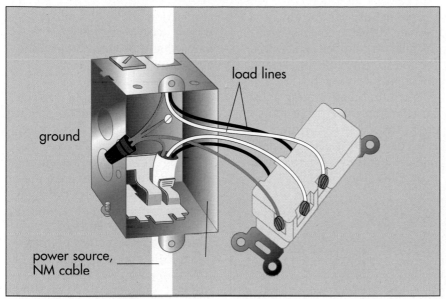

ground

load lines

power source,
NM cable

box extender

A GFCI receptacle is bulkier than a standard receptacle, so things can get tight in the box. If gently pushing wires around doesn't seat the GFCI properly, don't try forcing it in. Force can break, and wire connections can come loose. Install a box extender to store the wires safely.

Wire a GFCI receptacle.
Attach a GFCI receptacle as shown above, connecting multiple wires with pigtails. Incoming power goes to the line leads or terminals. Load lines carry it to other receptacles on the circuit. If you install a GFCI in the first receptacle of a circuit, the entire circuit will be protected. If you are installing a GFCI at the end of a line, cap off the load leads with wire connectors or buy a version that protects only one receptacle.

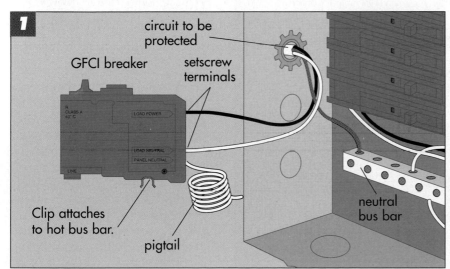

1

circuit to be protected

GFCI breaker

setscrew terminals

Clip attaches to hot bus bar.

pigtail

neutral bus bar

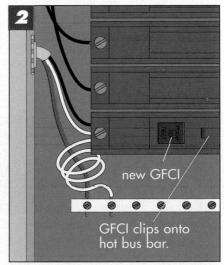

2

new GFCI

GFCI clips onto hot bus bar.

1. To install a GFCI breaker, connect hot and neutral wires.
You can clip a GFCI breaker into a service panel as you would an ordinary breaker (see page 83), but you must wire it differently.
NOTE: *Shut off the power.* Shut off the main breaker and be careful not to touch the hot wires coming into the box (see pages 82–83).

Select the circuit you wish to protect, unclip the old breaker from the hot bus bar, and slip it out of the service panel. Disconnect the hot and neutral wires from the old breaker. Attach both wires to the setscrew terminals of the new GFCI breaker as shown. Strip half an inch of insulation from the pigtail.

2. Ground and install the breaker.
Loosen a terminal on the neutral bus bar, and connect the white pigtail by inserting the wire and tightening the screw. Clipping the GFCI breaker into place attaches it to the hot bus bar. Turn the power back on, set the breaker, and push the test button. The breaker should trip.

INSTALLING TELEPHONE AND CABLE LINES

The telephone and cable companies will install cable for you, but be braced for a pretty hefty bill, even for running a simple surface-mounted extension line. The cable company may want to charge you a monthly fee for splitting the line in order to service two televisions. So, although it is not feasible for a homeowner to make major telephone installations (and perhaps illegal to make a cable installation), it does make sense for you to run cable for extra telephones or a second TV.

You'll find that running wires for telephones and cable TV is easier than electrical wiring. There is no danger of shock, and only one cable to run. Still, the same principles of installation and connection apply: You must protect wire insulation from damage and be sure connections are secure.

The simplest way to install the cable is to tack or staple it to the wall. Although a common practice, this can be unsightly and a mess when you paint walls and molding. For a neater and more permanent installation, take the time to run the cable out of sight.

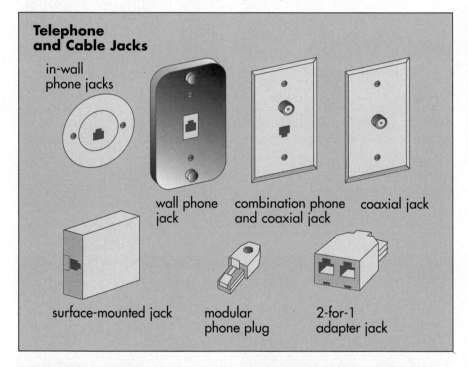

Telephone and Cable Jacks

in-wall phone jacks

wall phone jack

combination phone and coaxial jack

coaxial jack

surface-mounted jack

modular phone plug

2-for-1 adapter jack

Telephone Cable

Four-pair cable is used by the phone company.

22-AWC cable (line cord)

stranded-wire extension cable

EXPERTS' INSIGHT

THE RIGHT CABLE

■ To avoid a noisy connection and possible damage to your phone system, use cable marked 22-AWC (often sold as "line cord") to add a branch line. Stranded-wire extension cable sold in 25- and 50-foot lengths, it should only be used between the jack and the phone, not for adding new extensions. This solid-core cable is more expensive than stranded wires or (the worst of all) filament wire, but well worth the investment.

■ Purchase shielded coaxial cable for television cables. It has a metal wrapping under the insulation. Nonshielded cable will not perform as well.

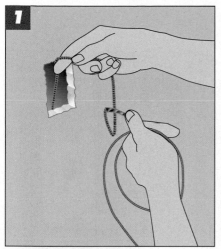

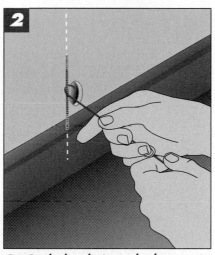

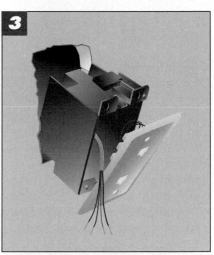

1. To run cable down a wall, attach to a chain and drop down.
Cut a hole in the wall where you want to locate an in-wall phone or cable jack. Attach a length of beaded chain to the end of the cable with electrician's tape. Drop the chain down through the hole. If you feel it hitting an obstruction, give it a wiggle.

2. Grab the chain at the bottom.
Once the chain has dropped far enough, drill a hole in the wall at the point where you want to retrieve the cable. (To hide the cable completely, remove the baseboard molding before drilling.) Insert a bent piece of coat hanger wire and root around until you hook the chain. Pull the chain through the hole until a foot or so of cable is sticking out.

3. Install box and jack.
Where you want a new phone or coaxial cable jack, cut out the wall as you would for an electrical box (see page 55). Pull about 8 inches of cable through the box. Install the box. For phone cable, strip the sheathing and insulation, and make connections as marked on the jack. At the phone junction box, connect the wires to the color-coded terminals. (For coaxial cable connections, see below.)

4. Hide cable under carpeting.
If you don't want to go to the trouble of pulling up your baseboard, it is often possible to hide most of the cable under wall-to-wall carpeting. Pry up only two feet or so of carpeting at a time or you may have trouble getting it to reattach to the tack strip. Slip the cable in place, and push the carpet firmly back in place as you go.

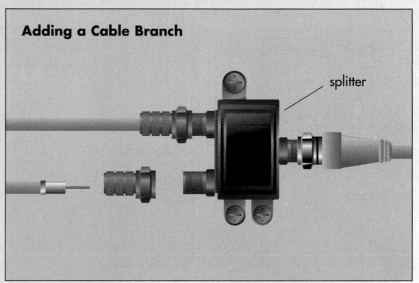

Adding a Cable Branch

splitter

Make coaxial connections.
To hook an additional television to your cable, add a two-way splitter. Mount the splitter to a wall, floor, or baseboard and run cable. Add a screw-on connector to both ends of the cable by stripping ¾ inch of insulation (cutting all the way to the wire), taking care not to bend the wire. Next strip ⅜ inch of the thin outer insulation only, leaving the metal wrapping intact. Screw the connector on—it will grab the insulation firmly. Attach the connector to the splitter.

INSTALLING DOORBELL INTERCOMS

With conventional intercom systems you have to run bell wires from intercom to intercom. You may spend hours drilling holes and fishing wire or still have foot after foot of exposed wire running along the baseboards. Newer doorbell intercoms sidestep these problems by using a combination of existing bell wire and standard 120-volt power circuits to carry your two-way conversations.

For room-to-room communication you can buy units that use only your electrical circuits and no bell wire. You mount the inexpensive units on a wall, plug them in, and start talking.

> ### YOU'LL NEED...
> **TIME:** Two hours to install a doorbell module and intercom.
> **SKILLS:** Connecting wires.
> **TOOLS:** Screwdriver and drill.

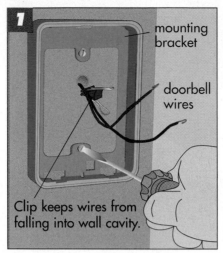

1. Install mounting bracket.
NOTE: *Shut off the power.* Test that the power to the doorbell is shut off by pressing the button—the chime or bell shouldn't sound. Remove the doorbell button and disconnect the wires from the terminals. Fasten the new doorbell mounting bracket to the wall with screws. Fasten the top screw first, check the unit for plumb, then insert the bottom screw.

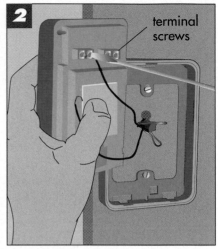

2. Install doorbell module.
Attach the bell wires to the terminal screws on the back of the doorbell module. Indoors, find your existing doorbell transformer (see page 134). Transfer the wires from its terminals to the new AC adapter that comes with the system. Plug the adapter into the nearest 120-volt receptacle. This links the doorbell module to the circuit that will carry the signal to the intercom monitor.

3. Disconnect the chime or bell.
Remove the doorbell or chime cover. Unscrew the terminal screws and remove the wires. Twist the bare ends of the wires together and cover the splice with a small wire connector (see page 59). Replace the cover; the doorbell will no longer be used.

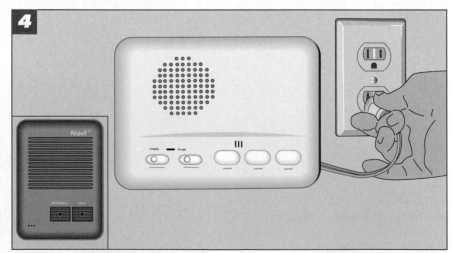

4. Plug in the intercom.
Choose a location for the intercom monitor, fasten it to the wall with the screws provided, hang the unit in place, and plug its cord into a 120-volt receptacle. Restore power to the circuit and test the unit. Pressing the button on the outdoor unit produces a gong-like sound from the monitor. The signal is carried from the outdoor unit, along the bell wire, into the household circuit, and to the intercom monitor. This allows you to talk with whoever is at the door.

INSTALLING VIDEO INTERCOM SYSTEMS

For a surprisingly small amount of work, you can install a video intercom that lets you see and hear the person at your door. For about the cost of a full-size television, this system provides a new level of convenience and security.

One of the simpler systems to install is wired by running a four-wire, 18-gauge cable from a camera outside to the monitor inside. The monitor plugs into a standard electrical receptacle. The toughest part of the job is pulling the four-wire cable from the front door to the monitor location.

YOU'LL NEED...

TIME: Several hours to install in most cases.
SKILLS: Connecting wires and running cable.
TOOLS: Screwdriver, drill, jigsaw, fish tape, and wire stripper.

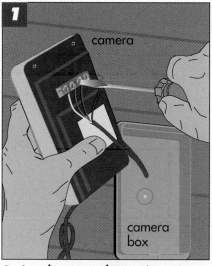

1. Attach camera box, wire camera.
Choose a location for the camera as close to eye level as possible. Cut an opening in the wall (see page 128) and run four-wire, 18-gauge cable from the box to the location of your monitor (see page 114). Attach the box to the wall; connect the wires to the terminals on the back of the camera.

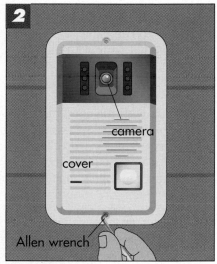

2. Install camera.
You may want to adjust the camera angle up or down if the unit cannot be placed at eye level. Place the camera unit in the camera box, install the front panel, and secure it with tamperproof screws. Tighten them with the Allen wrench that comes with the unit and insert protective caps.

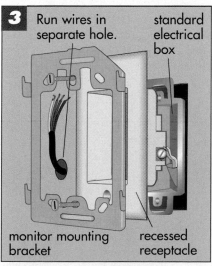

3. Wire a recessed receptacle.
A recessed receptacle (sometimes called a clock receptacle because it often is located behind electric wall clocks) allows you to install the monitor without having the electrical cord visible. Wire it as you would a standard receptacle (see page 70). Attach the mounting bracket for the monitor.

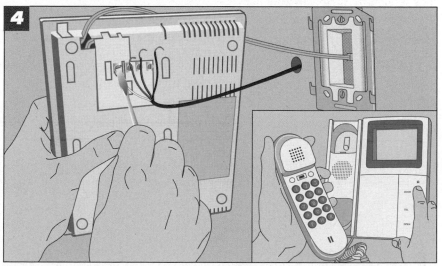

4. Wire the monitor.
Connect the four wires to the back of the monitor. Some units allow you to install electronic door unlockers. Plug the cord in. Push the monitor onto the bracket and pull downward to anchor it.

To operate the video intercom, the power switch must be on.

Adjust the volume and brightness controls. When a visitor presses the call button on the camera unit, you will hear a chime, and the visitor will appear on the monitor. Pick up the handset to speak. The visitor speaks through the microphone mounted on the camera unit.

WIRING CEILING FIXTURES WITH SWITCHES

Depending on which way is easier to run cable, you can wire a ceiling fixture with the power coming into the fixture box (as on this page), or with power coming into the switch (as on page 119).

Here, as with the configurations on the following six pages, the type of fixture doesn't matter. Whether it is a flush-mounted light, track lighting, a chandelier, or a ceiling fan, the rough wiring to the fixture is the same.

YOU'LL NEED...
TIME: Not including running the cable and installing boxes, about an hour making connections.
SKILLS: Basic electrical skills.
TOOLS: Lineman's pliers, screwdriver, wire stripper, cable ripper, and side-cutting pliers or combination tool.

power source

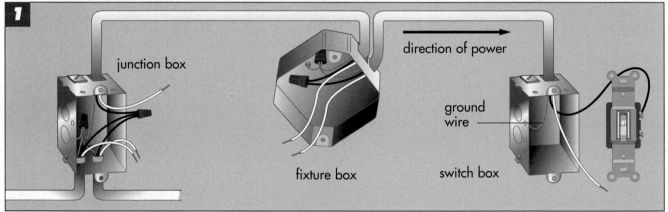

junction box

direction of power

ground wire

fixture box

switch box

1. Begin making connections.
NOTE: *Shut off power.* Install fixture and switch box, if they do not already exist (see pages 84–85 and 100). Find a junction box that has power from a circuit you can use. Run two-wire cable from the junction box to the fixture box, and from the fixture box to the switch. Connect the ground wires as shown. Connect all the black wires as shown. Note how the black wire picks up power at the junction box and carries it to the fixture box, then on to the switch.

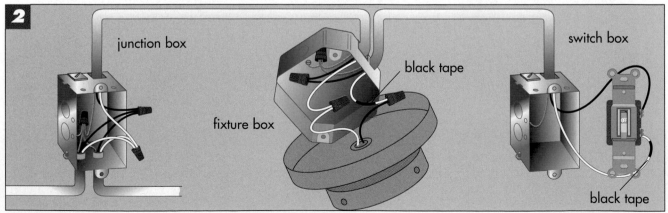

junction box

switch box

black tape

fixture box

black tape

2. Complete the connections.
Mark the white wire running from the switch box to the fixture box with black tape on both ends. Attach one end to the switch. At the fixture box, connect the black-taped white wire to the black fixture wire, and the untaped white wire to the white fixture wire. At the junction box, connect all white wires together. (For how to connect wires, see page 58.)

WIRING TWO CEILING FIXTURES

In this wiring configuration, power comes to the switch first, then goes to one or more fixtures by extending the run from one to the next. If you have multiple fixtures on a single line, make sure the wattage or amperage total of fixtures on the line doesn't exceed the maximum indicated on the body of the switch or what's available on that fuse or breaker (see page 81).

YOU'LL NEED...

TIME: Not including running the cable and installing boxes, about 1½ hours to plan and complete the connections.
SKILLS: Basic electrical skills.
TOOLS: Lineman's pliers, needlenose pliers, wire stripper, cable ripper, screwdriver, and sidecutting pliers or combination tool.

power source

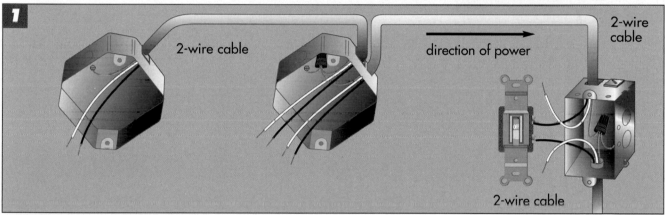

1. Begin making connections.
NOTE: *Shut off power.* Install fixture boxes and a switch box, if they do not already exist (see pages 84–85 and 100). Find a junction box that has power from

a circuit you can use. Run twowire cable from the junction box to the fixture box (see pages 54–55 for instructions on running cable), and from the fixture box to the next fixture box. Connect the

ground wires as shown (see page 58). At the switch box, hook both black wires to the terminals. The current in the black wires passes through the switch, which can allow it to flow (on) or stop (off).

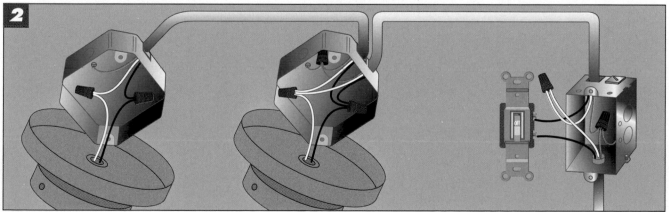

2. Complete the connections.
At the switch box, connect the two white wires together. At the first fixture box, connect all three black wires together, and connect all three white wires together. At the

second fixture box, connect the black wires together, and connect the white wires together.

Note that you also can control two or more fixtures with the power coming to the fixture, but

it's more complicated. Route the power as on page 120, and connect the second fixture's black wire to the black-taped white wire in the first fixture box. (For how to connect wires, see page 58.)

WIRING FIXTURES WITH SEPARATE SWITCHES

*I*f you are installing ceiling fixtures and a switch box, with a little more work you can provide individual switches for the fixtures. Use a two-gang box for the switches and run three-wire cable between the fixtures and to the switch. Power comes to the fixtures by means of two-wire cable. Electricians are fond of three-wire cable because in many instances it allows you to run one cable instead of two.

> ### YOU'LL NEED...
> **TIME:** Not including running the cable and installing boxes, about 1½ hours to make connections.
> **SKILLS:** Basic electrical skills.
> **TOOLS:** Lineman's pliers, cable ripper, screwdriver, wire stripper, needle-nose pliers, and side-cutting pliers or combination tool.

to junction box

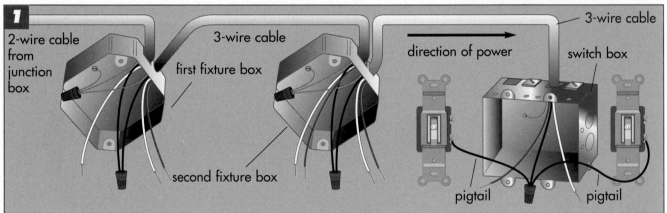

1. Begin making connections.
NOTE: *Shut off power.* Install fixture boxes and a switch box, if they do not already exist (see pages 84–85 and 100). Run two-wire cable from a junction box to the first fixture box. Run three-wire cable from the first to the second fixture box, and from there to the switch box. Connect all ground wires as shown, using green connectors. Bring power to the switches by connecting the black wires in all three boxes as shown. In the switch box, cut pigtails (the two short pieces of wire) and connect them to the switches.

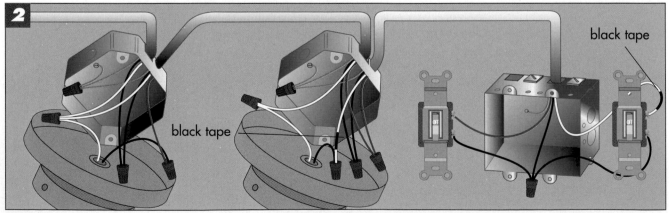

2. Complete the connections.
At the switch box, connect the red wire to a switch and the white wire to the other switch. Wrap black tape on the white wire, both at the switch box and at the second fixture box, to show that it is hot. At the second fixture box, connect the two red wires together. At both fixture boxes, connect the hot and neutral wires to the fixture wires, as shown. Or install this wiring configuration with power coming to the switch. Split the incoming black wire and run the outgoing red and black wires to the fixtures. The neutral white wire, shared by both switches, passes on through.

WIRING THREE-WAY SWITCHES

Three-way switches control power to a fixture from two points, allowing you to control a light from either side of a room. Three-way switches use a three-wire system composed of a power wire and two interconnecting wires called travelers. Unless you have metal conduit or armored cable, you also need a fourth grounding wire. Power comes in through one switch, travels to the fixture and to the second switch (see page 122 for the ABCs of three-way switching).

power source

(see page 122 for the ABCs of three-way switching).

YOU'LL NEED...

TIME: Not including running the cable and installing boxes, about 1½ hours to make connections.
SKILLS: Basic electrical skills.
TOOLS: Lineman's pliers, wire stripper, cable ripper, needle-nose pliers, side-cutting pliers, and screwdriver.

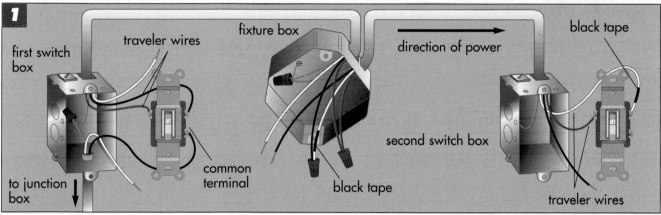

1 first switch box · traveler wires · fixture box · direction of power · black tape · second switch box · common terminal · black tape · to junction box · traveler wires

1. Begin making connections.
NOTE: *Shut off power.* Install switch boxes and a fixture box (see pages 84–85 and 100). Run two-wire cable from a junction box to the first switch box. Run three-wire cable from the first switch box to the fixture box, and from the fixture box to the second switch box. Connect all ground wires as shown (for how to connect wires, see page 58). At the first switch box, connect the hot wire to the common terminal on the switch (it is labeled and/or is darker than the other two). Attach traveler wires to the other two terminals.

At the second switch box, attach the red and white wires to the noncommon terminals of the switch. Wrap a piece of black tape on the white wire, both here and at the fixture box. At the fixture box, connect the two red wires, and connect the marked white wire to the black wire that comes from the first switch.

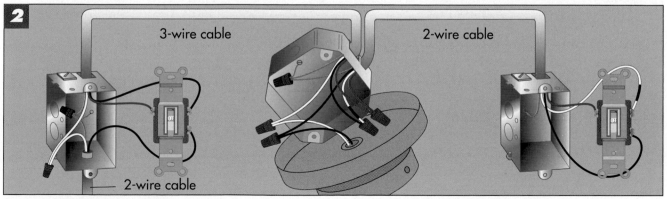

2 3-wire cable · 2-wire cable · 2-wire cable

2. Complete the connections.
At the second switch box, connect the black wire to the common terminal on the switch. This completes the hot portion of the circuit. At the first switch box, connect the two white wires. At the fixture box, connect the white and black wires to the fixture. Once completed, either switch will operate the light.

WIRING THREE-WAYS, POWER TO SWITCH

P age 121 shows how to wire three-way switches when the light is between two switches. Here you see the light beyond both switches. A dimmer is included in this example. (With most dimmers, you can use only one per circuit.)

For this configuration, you run three-wire cable only between the switches. Power comes into the first switch and out of the second on just two wires.

YOU'LL NEED...
TIME: Not including running the cable and installing boxes, about 1½ hours to make the connections.
SKILLS: Basic electrical skills.
TOOLS: Lineman's pliers, cable ripper, screwdriver, wire stripper, needle-nose pliers, and side-cutting pliers or combination tool.

power source

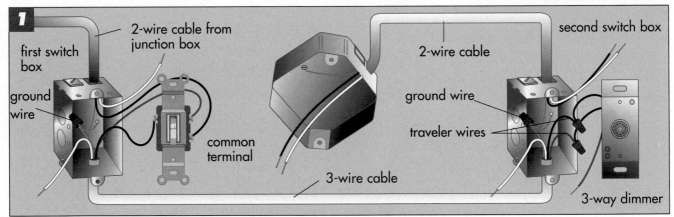

1. Begin making connections.
NOTE: *Shut off power.* Install switch boxes and a fixture box (see pages 84–85 and 100). Run two-wire cable from a junction box to the first switch box. Run three-wire cable from the first switch box to the second, and two-wire cable from the second switch box to the fixture box (see page 121). Connect ground wires as shown. At the first switch box, connect the black (hot) wire of the power source to the switch's common terminal (see page 58). Connect traveler wires to the other terminals. At the second switch box, connect the travelers. (Note: A three-way dimmer can burn out if hooked up incorrectly. Check by setting up the circuit with ordinary three-way switches and turning on the power. Then replace one switch with a dimmer.)

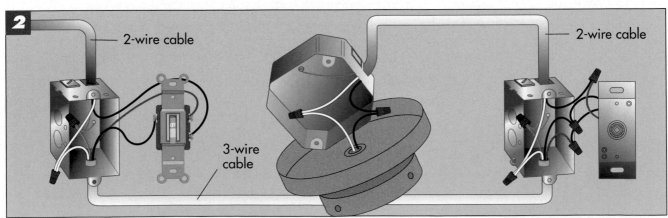

2. Complete the connections.
At the second switch box, connect the black wire that goes to the fixture box with the dimmer's common wire. Connect the two white wires.

At the first switch box, connect the white wires. At the fixture box, connect black to black wires and white to white wires. Install the switches and switch plates and the light fixture.

WIRING THREE-WAYS, POWER TO FIXTURE

In this situation, power comes to the light fixture, then proceeds to the two switches. A two-wire cable runs to the fixture and to the the first switch box. A three-wire cable runs only from switch box to switch box.

YOU'LL NEED...
TIME: After running cable and installing boxes, 1½ hours
SKILLS: Basic electrical skills.
TOOLS: See page 122.

ABCs OF THREE-WAYS
Follow these principles when installing any three-way configuration: **A.** Always attach the incoming hot (black) wire to the common terminal of one switch. **B.** Use traveler wires to connect the other terminals to each other, never to the light. **C.** Connect the common terminal of the second switch only to the black fixture wire.

power source

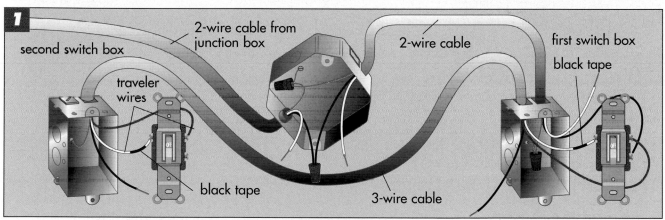

second switch box

traveler wires

2-wire cable from junction box

2-wire cable

first switch box

black tape

black tape

3-wire cable

1. Begin making connections.
At the ceiling box, connect the black, hot wires. At the first switch box, connect the hot wire to the common terminal and the traveler wires to the other terminals. Wrap a piece of black tape on either end of the white wire to show that it is hot. At the second switch box, attach the traveler wires.

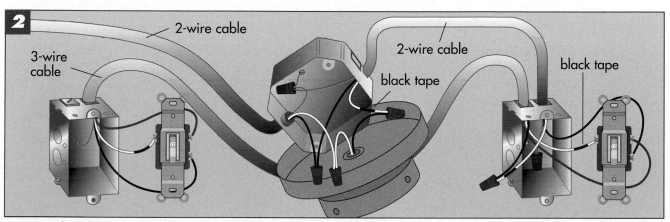

2-wire cable

3-wire cable

2-wire cable

black tape

black tape

2. Complete the connections.
At the second switch, connect the black wire to the common terminal. At the first switch box, connect the black and white wires, and wrap a piece of black tape at either end of the white wire to show that it is hot.

At the fixture box, connect white to white wire and the black-taped white wire to the black wire of the fixture.

WIRING FOUR-WAY SWITCHES

To control a fixture from three or more different switches, use one or more four-way switches. You can install any number of them between a pair of three-way switches. In four-way situations, the first and last switches must always be three-ways.

In this illustration the power flows from junction box to switch to switch to switch to the fixture. It also could be routed as shown on pages 121–123.

YOU'LL NEED...

TIME: Not including running the cable and installing boxes, about 2 hours to make the connections for a fixture and three switches.
SKILLS: Basic electrical skills.
TOOLS: Lineman's pliers, cable ripper, wire stripper, screwdriver, needle-nose pliers, and side-cutting pliers or combination tool.

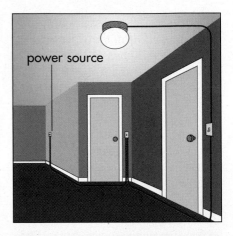

power source

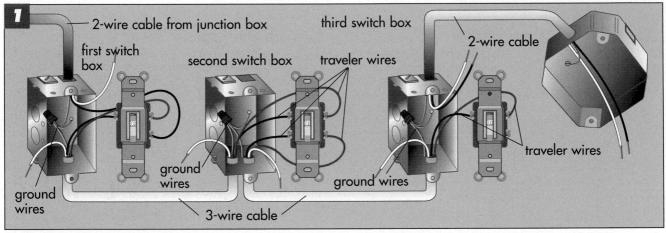

1. Begin making connections.
NOTE: *Shut off power.* Install switch boxes and a fixture box. Run two-wire cable from a junction box to the first switch box. Run three-wire cable from the first switch box to the second and third ones, and two-wire cable from the third switch box to the fixture box. Connect all ground wires.

At the first switch box, connect the black wire from the power source to the switch's common terminal. Connect the traveler wires to the other terminals.

At the second and third switches, connect the traveler wires as shown. The four-way switch carries only traveler wires. (For how to connect wires, see page 58.)

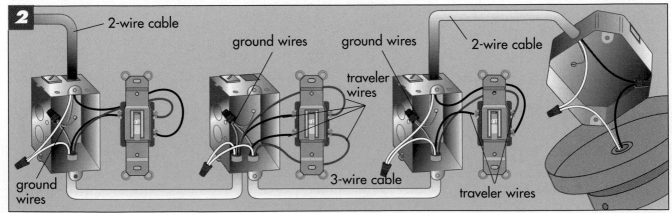

2. Complete the connections.
At the third switch, connect the fixture box's black wire to the common terminal. Connect the white wires. Connect the white wires at the first and second switch boxes. Connect the fixture to the two wires at the fixture box and install the switches and switch plates. Once completed, you can turn the fixture on and off from any of the three switches.

ADDING RECEPTACLES

Once you find a usable power source, adding a receptacle is easy to figure out. Most of the work is cutting the wall, installing a box, fishing the cable, and patching the wall.

You can tap into an existing receptacle, as shown on this page, only if it is at the end of a wiring run. If it's in the middle of a run, all of its terminals will be occupied.

YOU'LL NEED...

TIME: Not including running the cable and installing boxes, about an hour to make connections.
SKILLS: Basic electrical skills.
TOOLS: Lineman's pliers, cable ripper, screwdriver, wire stripper, needle-nose pliers, and side-cutting pliers or combination tool.

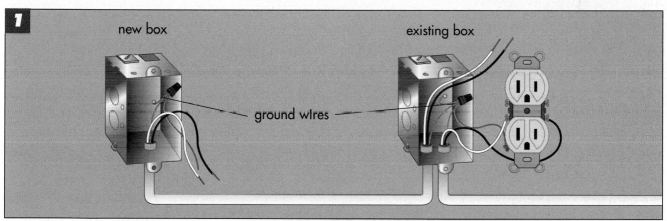

1. Begin making connections.
NOTE: *Shut off power.* Find a receptacle box where you can draw power without overcrowding the box or overloading the circuit. (You also can draw power from a junction box. Just connect to the hot and neutral wires instead of to the receptacle.) Install the new receptacle box. Run a two-wire cable from the existing box to the new box.

Remove the screws that secure the existing receptacle to the box, and pull it out so you can work on it. Connect the ground wires in both boxes as shown.

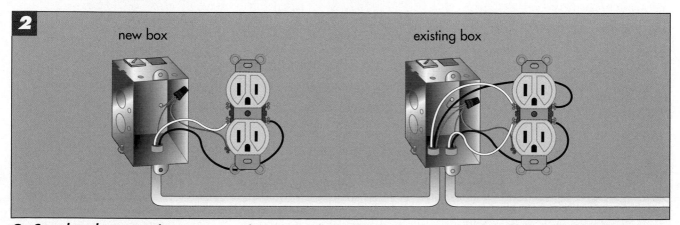

2. Complete the connections.
At the existing box, connect the black wire to the hot receptacle terminal, which is brass-colored. Connect the white wire to the other terminal. At the new box, also connect the black wire to the hot terminal and the white wire to the other terminal. Wrap both receptacles with electrician's tape so that all the terminals are covered. Fasten both receptacles in place, turn on power and test your installation. Finally, attach the receptacle plates.

ADDING 240-VOLT RECEPTACLES

Some 240-volt equipment—central air-conditioning units and electric water heaters, for example—have no plugs and are wired directly into junction boxes because they do not need to be moved. Ranges, clothes dryers, and other appliances are connected by cords and plugs and require special receptacles.

The wiring requirements for 240-volt circuits are specific. For a 30-amp dryer, use a 30-amp breaker and 10-gauge wire. For a 50-amp range, use a 50-amp breaker and 6-gauge wire. Choose a receptacle designed to provide the correct amperage for your appliance and has holes to match the prongs on the plug.

YOU'LL NEED...

TIME: To install a 240-volt receptacle after the wiring is completed, about an hour.
SKILLS: Running cable and stripping and connecting wires.
TOOLS: Screwdriver, wire stripper, and lineman's pliers.

CAUTION!

*DANGER! HIGH VOLTAGE!
Wiring for 240-volt receptacles is no different from 120-volt lines except that the danger is much, much greater. Even if you are dry and are wearing rubber-soled shoes, a jolt of this current could do you serious physical harm and perhaps even kill you. Check and double-check that the power is off before installing a 240-volt receptacle. This is one job where you may want to call in an experienced electrician, just for safety's sake.*

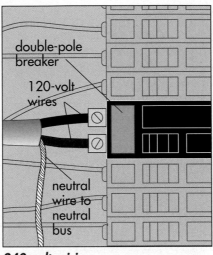

240-volt wiring
NOTE: *Shut off the power.* Wiring starts at a 240-volt breaker or fuse in the service panel and ends at a specially designed receptacle. A 240-volt circuit should supply only one appliance; no other receptacles can be attached to it. Connect 120-volt wires to a breaker and the neutral wire to the neutral bus (see pages 82–83)

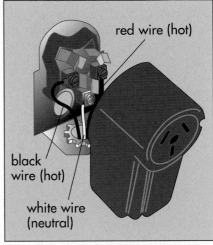

Floor-mounted 240-volt receptacle
If no outlet box is available, you can install this unit on the floor. Position it so it won't get bumped when you move the appliance. Remove the cover and connect the neutral wire to the terminal marked "white," and the red and black wires to the other terminals. All receptacles shown on this page use the neutral wire as ground.

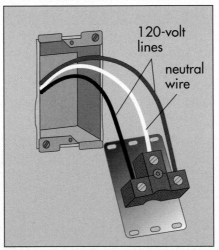

Wall-mounted 240-volt receptacle
Install a receptacle box and run 10-3 cable (for a 30-amp breaker) or 6-3 cable (for a 50-amp breaker) to it. (For information on running cable in finished spaces, see pages 84–85; for information on selecting cable, see page 47.) Strip the black, red, and white wires (see pages 56–57) to the length marked on the receptacle housing and attach.

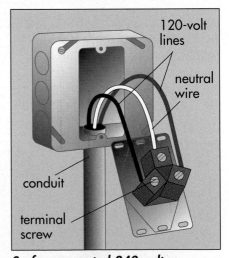

Surface-mounted 240-volt receptacle for basement or garage
Install a box (see page 50) and run conduit (see pages 94–96) to the desired location. Fish red, black, and white 10- or 6-gauge wire (see page 97). Strip wires and insert them into the slots in the terminals as shown; tighten the screws.

SPLITTING, SWITCHING RECEPTACLES

Examine a standard duplex receptacle, and you'll see that each set of terminals on either side is connected by a small metal tab—one silver-colored, one brass-colored (see Step 3 below). If you break the brass bridge, the upper and lower receptacles can be used independently, one controlled by a switch and one functioning like a

standard receptacle. A split receptacle is handy when you want to turn a lamp on and off from a wall switch, for example, but still leave half of the receptacle for general use. Sometimes you may need a split receptacle when you want to supply the two outlets of a heavily used receptacle with two different circuits.

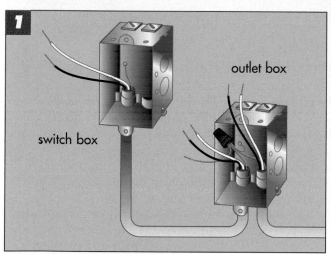

1. Install cable and boxes.
NOTE: *Shut off the power.* Disconnect the receptacle and run two-wire cable to a switch box. Connect the ground wires.

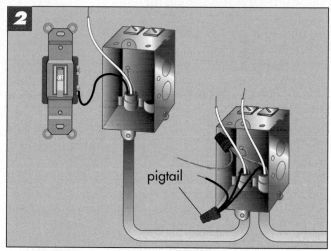

2. Attach and connect black wires.
Route power to the switch by tying the two black wires together with a pigtail at the receptacle box. At the switch box, connect the black wire.

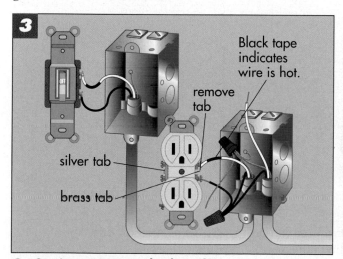

3. Continue wiring and split outlets.
Add black tape to both ends of the white wire that runs between the boxes to show that it's hot. Connect it to the switch and receptacle terminals. Connect the remaining black wire to the receptacle. Snap off the brass tab with needle-nose pliers to split the outlets. Leave the silver-colored metal tab in place.

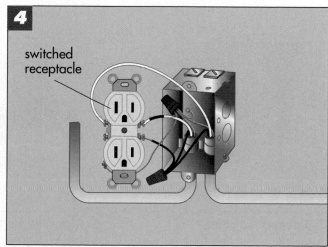

4. Complete the wiring.
Connect the white and ground wires to the receptacle, screw the receptacle and switch to their boxes, turn on the power, and test. In this example, the upper outlet will be live only when the switch is on. The lower one remains on at all times.

ADDING OUTDOOR RECEPTACLES

The easiest way to bring power to the outside of your house is to install a receptacle directly opposite an existing interior receptacle. If you need to place the outdoor receptacle elsewhere, see page 97 for ideas on fishing the cable. Be sure that the interior receptacle box you choose has room for new wires. Check that you will not be overloading the circuit (see page 81). Codes usually require a GFCI receptacle with a weatherproof cover plate with a spring-loaded door.

YOU'LL NEED...

TIME: Barring unexpected obstacles, plan on 3 hours.
SKILLS: Basic electrical skills.
TOOLS: Drill with spade bit and perhaps a bit extension; screwdriver; lineman's pliers; and a jigsaw, saber saw, or keyhole saw. If you have a masonry exterior, a masonry bit, cold chisel, and hammer.

Drill at an angle to offset the boxes from each other.

1. Drill a hole to the outside.
NOTE: *Be sure to shut off the power.* Remove the face plate and the interior outlet. To accurately locate your new receptacle, punch out a knockout hole in the back of the box, and drill a hole through the house to the outside. To make sure you have room for a box on each side (the wall may not be thick enough), drill off to the side.

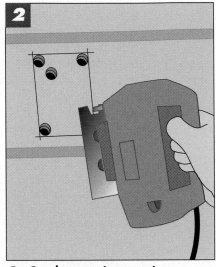

2. Cut the exterior opening.
Find the hole on the outside of your house, and draw an outline of the new box (see page 85). Drill a hole at each corner of the box, and cut out with a jigsaw. If you have a masonry exterior, drill a series of closely spaced holes with a masonry bit. Knock out the hole with a cold chisel and hammer.

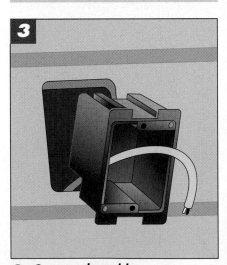

3. Connect the cable.
Cut a piece of cable long enough to allow you working room. Connect it to the interior box— you will need a helper to reach through the exterior hole and hold the locknut in position while you tighten the locknut. Connect cable to the exterior box.

GFCI receptacle

4. Make the electrical connections.
With the box pushed into place, strip the sheathing and the ends of the wires and make connections on both ends of the cable (see pages 56–59). Be sure to connect to the "line" terminals on the GFCI receptacle and the load terminals on the existing interior receptacle.

weatherproof cover plate

foam gasket

5. Install the box and cover.
Attach the box firmly in place. With a masonry wall, insert screws into the back of the box and attach them to a framing member, or mortar the box in place. Fasten the GFCI receptacle to the box. Finally, attach the gasket and weatherproof cover plate.

INSTALLING OUTDOOR LIGHTING

If you have eaves overhanging an exterior door, it makes sense to install a light there, where it will be better protected from weather than a wall-mounted unit would be. You're also likely to find it easy to run cable from an attic junction box to the eaves.

Consider installing a motion-detector floodlight. These are quite inexpensive, and if you wire it to be controlled with a regular wall switch, you can switch off the motion-sensing feature.

YOU'LL NEED...

TIME: With no unusual obstacles, plan on 4 hours.
SKILLS: Basic electrical skills, measuring and cutting eaves.
TOOLS: Screwdriver, lineman's pliers, drill, saber saw or keyhole saw, and fish tape.

Center the light above the door.

1. Cut a hole in the eaves.
NOTE: *Shut off the power.* Draw an outline of the new box—a retrofit box with wings for attaching to the eaves will probably work best. Drill starter holes, and cut the hole with a saber saw or a keyhole saw.

2. Run the cable, install the box. Fish cable and make connections to an interior switch (see pages 59 and 97). Connect the cable to the new box, and firmly attach the box to the eaves.

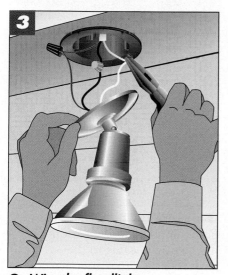

3. Wire the floodlight.
Connect the wires to the floodlight using wire connectors (see page 58), and screw the light firmly to the box. If your unit has a motion detector, wait until nighttime and adjust the direction of the sensor so it turns on as people approach the door.

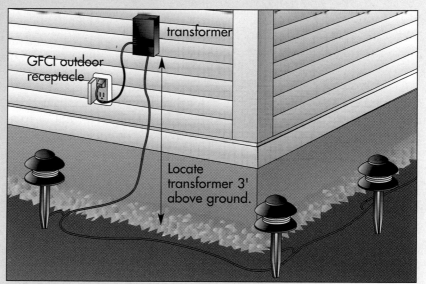
transformer

GFCI outdoor receptacle

Locate transformer 3' above ground.

INSTALL A LOW-VOLTAGE LIGHTING SYSTEM

For highlighting your landscaping, the easiest and least costly choice is low-voltage lighting. Kits containing 10 or more lights, a transformer, and lots of wire are inexpensive and readily available. Installation is simple: Assemble the lights, and attach the cable. The lights usually can be poked into the ground, and you don't need to dig a trench for the wiring—just cover it with a bit of mulch. Fasten the transformer to a wall at least 3 feet above the ground and plug it into an outdoor receptacle.

ADDING BATHROOM VENT FANS/LIGHTS

If your bathroom does not have a window that opens, most codes require that you have a vent fan to remove moisture and odor. Adding a fan can make your bathroom more pleasant, protect your walls from mildew and moisture damage, and can lower air-conditioning costs. You can wire a bathroom fan so that it operates by itself, but some codes require the fan to switch on with the light.

YOU'LL NEED...

TIME: About one day.
SKILLS: Basic electrical skills and carpentry skills.
TOOLS: Screwdriver, lineman's pliers, drill, and saber saw.

flush with surface of ceiling

1. Install the fan unit.
NOTE: *Shut off the power.* Cut a ceiling opening between joists. From the attic, nail or screw the unit's mounting brackets securely to the framing. Make sure the fan assembly is level and flush with the surface of the ceiling below before fastening.

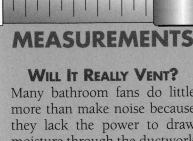

MEASUREMENTS

WILL IT REALLY VENT?

Many bathroom fans do little more than make noise because they lack the power to draw moisture through the ductwork to the outside. The larger the bathroom and the longer the duct, the more powerful the fan needs to be. When you shop for a vent fan, know the size of the bathroom and how long the ducting will be. If the salesperson cannot help you choose the right size fan, open a fan box and check the manufacturer's instructions.

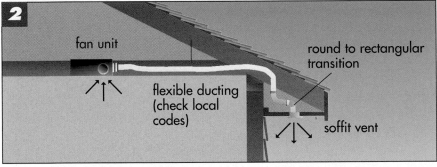

2. Run the ductwork.
In some climates, and if your attic has adequate cross-ventilation, you may be able to get by without venting to the outside—check local codes. Otherwise, run flexible ducting to a soffit or to a roof-mounted outlet. To increase the efficiency of your fan, run the ducts as straight as possible.

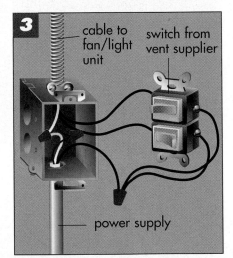

3. Wire the switches.
For a combination fan and light, fish two-wire cable to the switches, then run three wires from the switches to the unit. For a fan-only installation, run two-wire cable to the unit (for instructions on running wire in finished and unfinished spaces, see pages 84–89). If the fan has a heater, you'll probably need to run a 15- or 20-amp circuit (see pages 80–83 for information about planning and adding circuits).

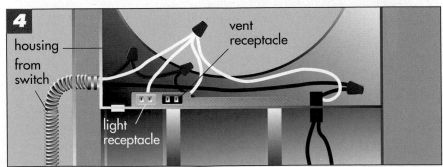

4. Wire the vent fan unit.
Inside the unit, connect the wires according to the manufacturer's directions. Typical connections are shown above. Install the working parts in the housing, and plug them into the appropriate receptacles. Turn on the power, and test the fan and light. Finally, fit the grille. Once a year, remove the grille and clean the fan blades and other parts inside the fan.

ADDING ATTIC FANS

On a hot summer day, attic temperatures can reach 150 degrees Fahrenheit. Turbine-type roof ventilators can help dissipate the heat but, because they depend on wind to supplement the upward draft of hot air, you're out of luck on a still day when the heat buildup may be most intense.

A thermostat-controlled attic fan mounted in the roof or a gable-end wall automatically turns the fan on to vent overheated attics.

YOU'LL NEED...

TIME: A full day, with a helper.
SKILLS: Basic electrical and carpentry skills.
TOOLS: Ladder to get to the roof, roof jacks to provide a safe standing place if the roof is steep, drill, saber saw or keyhole saw, utility knife, hammer, screwdriver, and lineman's pliers.

Money $ Saver

COMBINE WHOLE-HOUSE FANS AND ATTIC FANS

Depending on your climate and use pattern, it may make economic sense to combine a thermostat-controlled fan with a whole-house fan. Here's why:
■ Even after sundown, super-heated air continues to put a heavy strain on your home's air-conditioning system. Improving attic ventilation can cut cooling costs up to 30 percent.
■ A whole-house fan will pull a strong, steady draft up through the house—and push air out of the attic—on those days when you choose not to use the air-conditioning. It is not, however, efficient to use a whole-house fan while the air-conditioning is on.

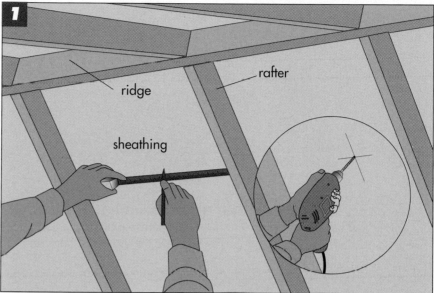

ridge

rafter

sheathing

1. Drill a locating hole.

Position your fan as close to the ridge as you can so as little hot air as possible will build up in the attic area above the fan. Choose a slope of the roof that's not visible from the street. Go into the attic and pick a pair of rafters close to the attic's center. Measure to a point midway between them. Drill up through the roof at this point. Leave the drill bit in place or push a piece of wire up through the hole as a marker.

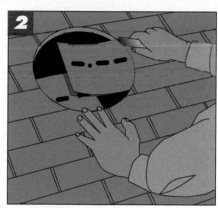

2. Cut the roofing.

Find the locating hole on the roof and set the fan in place on top of it. The flashing should tuck neatly under shingles above the fan housing. To minimize the number of shingles you will have to trim, adjust the unit up or down slightly. Trace the outline of the unit on the roofing.

Use the template that comes with the fan to mark for a circular cut on the shingles. Cut the shingles with a utility knife.

For a gable-end installation, cut through the siding only—not the sheathing—with a circular saw. If the wall has a window or louvers, adapt the opening to fit the fan.

MEASUREMENTS

HOW BIG A FAN DO YOU NEED?

To determine how powerful a unit to buy, multiply the square footage of your attic by 0.7. Add 15 percent if your roofing is dark-colored—it will absorb more heat from sunlight than a lighter, more reflective roofing color. The resulting number tells you the cubic feet per minute (CFM) that your fan should pull.

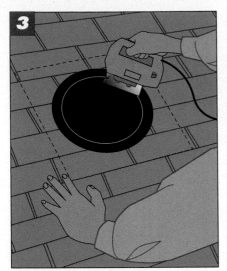

3. *Cut the sheathing.*
A second template will guide you in marking a smaller circle inside the cutaway shingles. Use a saber saw or keyhole saw to cut through the roofing paper and sheathing. Remove any nails in the shingles that lie in the top two-thirds of the unit's outline you traced onto the roof. Now you're ready to slip the unit into place.

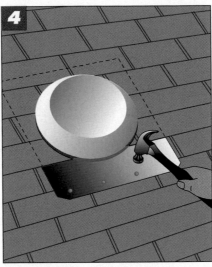

4. *Install the exhaust vent.*
Turn the fan over and coat the underside of its flashing with roofing cement. Slide it under the shingles above and on either side; the flashing should overlap the shingles below the housing. Center the fan over the hole. Pry up shingles covering the flashing and nail it in place. Drive the nails so they penetrate the sheathing, and cover them with roofing cement.

EXPERTS' INSIGHT

BUILDING A DEFENSE AGAINST HUMIDITY

If you live in an area known for high humidity, consider purchasing an attic fan that comes equipped with a humidistat in addition to a thermostat. A humidistat reads the humidity in the same way a thermostat reads the temperature, giving you another measurement for controlling the comfort level of your home.

On humid days an attic fan can make your home more comfortable by removing some of the moist air. Keeping attic moisture under control also helps keep your fiberglass insulation from compacting and losing its effectiveness.

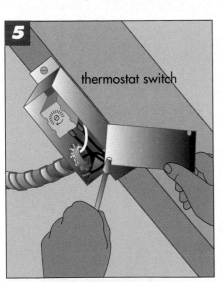

5. *Install the thermostat.*
Back in the attic, screw the thermostat switch to a stud or rafter above the fan and out of the fan's airstream. Remove the box cover plate.

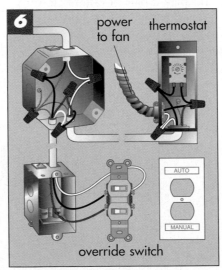

6. *Make the wiring connections.*
Run cable from a junction box to the thermostat. Install cable to an accessible switch that can be used to override the automatic control. Follow the fan manufacturer's instructions for wiring. If instructions weren't provided, make the connections as indicated above, using wire connectors.

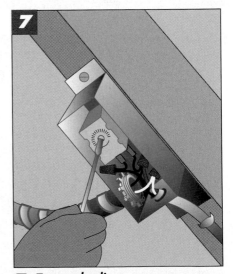

7. *Test and adjust.*
Turn on the power and test your installation. An adjusting screw in the thermostat box lets you set the temperature that will activate the fan. The temperature setting will vary depending on your roof and the fan's capacity. Consult the manufacturer's instructions for the right temperature for your attic.

ADDING WHOLE-HOUSE FANS

Before you select a whole-house fan, plan the overall venting of your house. The fan should pull air through open windows and doors on the lower floors and out through vents in the attic, eaves, and gables. Without adequate openings below and above the fan, it will not be able to do its job. Leave at least 2 feet of clearance between the fan and any obstructions. If you stack your attic with boxes, the fan may not have room to breathe, which will make it noisy as well as inefficient. Installation is not as difficult as you may think: The fan sits on top of joists in the attic, so cutting and reframing aren't necessary.

YOU'LL NEED...

TIME: About a day, if fishing the cable is straightforward.
SKILLS: Basic electrical and carpentry skills.
TOOLS: Drill, saber saw, screwdriver, and lineman's pliers.

MEASUREMENTS

CHOOSING A FAN

■ Buy a fan that's rated to pull a minimum cubic feet per minute (CFM) equal to the square footage of your house multiplied by 3.
■ Do you really plan on venting the whole house? If you plan to open the windows of just a few rooms, use only their square footage to figure the needed CFM.
■ Often a hall is the best spot for a fan. Will it fit in yours? Fans designed to vent houses larger than 1,800 square feet (5,400 CFM) generally have louver panels of 38 inches or more—too wide for some hallways.

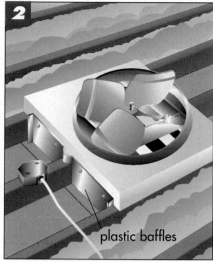

1. Establish a location.
Find a spot for the fan—the top-floor hallway ceiling is the usual place. Measure from a point common to the hall and the attic, choose a location for the fan, and clear away the insulation. Beside the joists, drill locator holes for cutting away the drywall or plaster. From below, cut a hole in the ceiling. Don't cut any joists.

2. Install the fan.
Set the fan on top of the joists, directly above the ceiling hole. Secure it by driving screws into the joists. Fasten it down tight so it cannot vibrate. Install the plastic baffles provided with the fan. They seal the cavities between the joists so the fan draws properly.

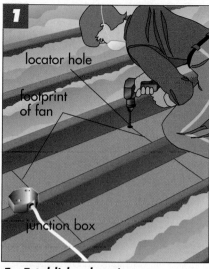

3. Install the louver panel.
From below tip the louver panel into place so it covers the entire hole. Attach it to the ceiling by driving screws up into the joists. The louver is lightly spring-loaded so it stays shut when the fan is not in use but opens when the fan is switched on.

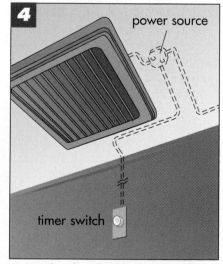

4. Make the electrical connections.
Run power up into a switch then to the fan (see page 87). Consider installing a timer switch or a programmable switch (see page 109) so you can have the fan run during those times of the day when it is most needed.

REPLACING DOORBELLS

A doorbell system starts with a transformer that reduces current from 120 volts to somewhere between 6 and 30 volts. From the transformer, light-gauge wire connects the bell, chime, or buzzer with the back in a circuit that is usually open at the button. Pressing the button, which is a spring-loaded switch, closes the circuit and sends low-voltage power to activate the bell, chime, or buzzer.

If your bell does not work, find the cause by using the process of elimination described in the steps below. A voltmeter or multitester will make the job easier, but you also can do most tests with a short piece of bell wire or a screwdriver.

Unless you are working on the transformer, there's no need to shut off power while inspecting a bell. The voltage coming from the transformer is so low you will barely feel it.

YOU'LL NEED...

TIME: You may find and solve the problem in minutes, or it could take several hours.
SKILLS: Using continuity tester and ability to work methodically.
TOOLS: Voltmeter or multitester or short length of wire, and screwdriver.

1. Check wires to the button.
To check a doorbell system, remove the button, turn it over, and examine the connections. Attach a spring clip to the wires to make sure that they cannot accidentally slip back through the hole. Scrape away any corrosion on the terminals. If the wires are corroded, cut off bad, strip (see pages 56–57), and reconnect. Tighten the connections to the terminals. Wrap any faulty insulation with electrical tape.

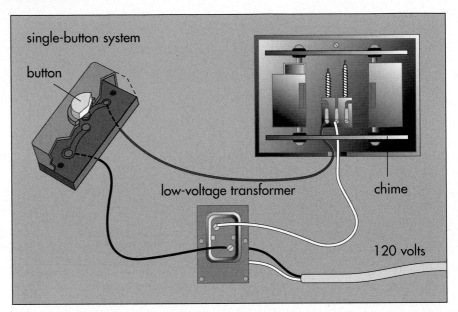

single-button system
button
low-voltage transformer
chime
120 volts

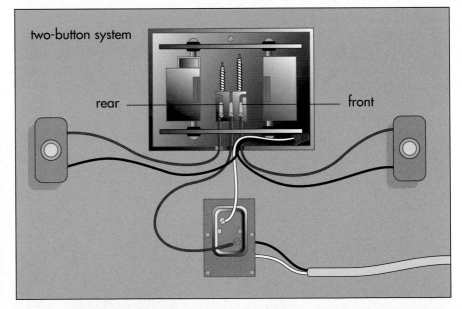

two-button system
rear
front

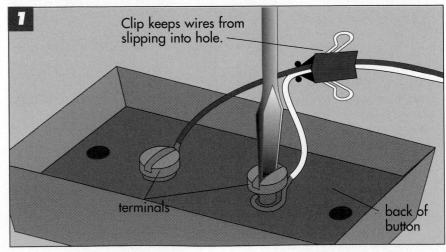

1 Clip keeps wires from slipping into hole.
terminals
back of button

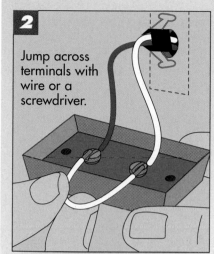

Jump across terminals with wire or a screwdriver.

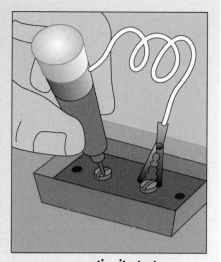

2. Test the button by jumping...

Weather and abuse make buttons the most vulnerable parts of a bell system. Test a button by jumping its terminals with a short piece of wire, as shown above. If the bell sounds, the button is faulty and should be replaced.

...or use a continuity tester.

You can also test the button by disconnecting the wires and touching both terminals with a continuity tester. If the tester glows when the button is pressed, the button is working. If the bell still doesn't sound, disconnect the button, twist its wires together, and test further.

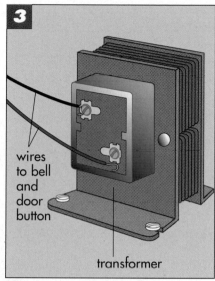

wires to bell and door button

transformer

3. Check wires to the transformer.

Find your transformer. It may be near your home's service panel or attached to a junction box in the vicinity of the door or the bell. Look for corrosion, wires that have come loose, or faulty insulation.

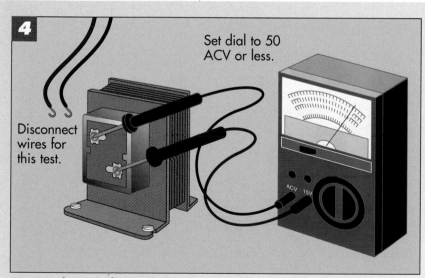

Set dial to 50 ACV or less.

Disconnect wires for this test.

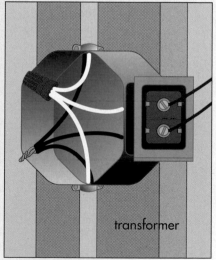

transformer

4. Test the transformer...

To check the transformer, disconnect both wires and touch each terminal with the probes of a voltmeter or multitester. Set the dial at ACV 50 or less. If the meter shows no current at all, the transformer is the culprit and should be replaced. You also can jump the low-voltage terminals with a screwdriver to test the transformer. It is OK if you see a weak spark.

...and replace if necessary.

NOTE: *Shut off the power.* Remove the cover plate of the electrical box, remove the transformer, and disconnect the wires. Wire the new transformer just like the old one, and reassemble the bell.

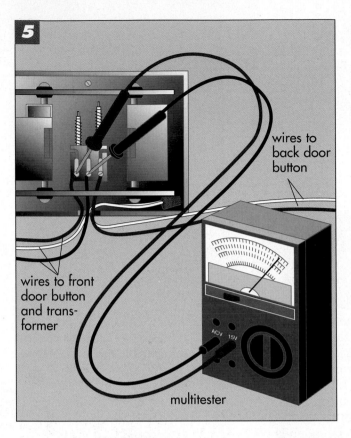

wires to back door button

wires to front door button and trans-former

multitester

5. Inspect the bell.

If the button, the wires, and the transformer are not to blame, check the bell itself. Remove the cover. Look for loose or broken connections. Even if you don't have a second button, the chime will have terminals labeled front and rear. Touch the voltmeter or multitester probes to the front and trans (meaning "transformer") terminals. If the meter registers a reading, then power is going to the bell, but the bell is defective. If you have a rear button, test again, touching rear and trans.

If you don't have a voltmeter, test the bell by removing it and temporarily wiring it directly to the transformer. If it is working, it will ring.

EXPERTS' INSIGHT

IF EVERYTHING IS OK, IT'S THE WIRES

If the button, transformer, and bell check out, a wire likely has broken. Disconnect the wires going into the bell and test current flow with a voltmeter or multitester. Or touch the front and rear wires to the transformer wire and look for a spark.

REPLACING CHIME UNITS

When shopping for a doorbell, consider your wall: Will the new unit cover up the discolored area left by the old one, or will it require you to do some touch-up painting? Make sure the doorbell you choose has the same voltage rating as its transformer.

TIME-SAVER

INSTALL A REMOTE-CONTROLLED CHIME

Running new wires is a time-consuming job. If you have damaged wires, consider installing a remote-controlled bell. This type costs more than a regular unit, but saves you the trouble of running wires.

1. Label wires and remove chime.

Shut off power to the circuit if you like, but it shouldn't be necessary because the voltage is so low. The terminals are labeled, so label the wires the same as you disconnect them. These labels also will prevent the wires from accidentally slipping through the hole and into the wall. Unscrew the chime from the wall, and remove it.

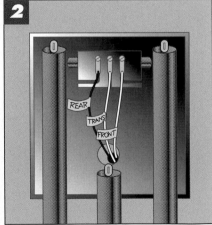

2. Install the new chime.

Attach the new chime to the wall with mounting screws. Use plastic anchors if you cannot drive a screw into a stud. Connect the low-voltage wires to the terminals, and attach the cover.

PLUMBING BASICS

GETTING TO KNOW YOUR SYSTEM

With so many pipes and fittings running unseen inside walls and floors, a plumbing system can seem complicated and mysterious. But plumbing is actually a straightforward matter of distributing incoming water to where it's wanted and facilitating the outflow of waste. Here's an overview of how household plumbing works.

Supply, drain, and vent systems

The supply system brings water into your house, divides it into hot and cold water lines, and distributes it to various fixtures (sinks, toilets, showers, tubs) and appliances (washing machines, dishwashers, water heaters, heating system boilers).

The drain system carries water away from the fixtures and appliances and out of the house. The vent system supplies air to the drain pipes so waste flows out freely. Because drains and vents use the same types of pipes and are tied together, they often are referred to as the drain-waste-vent system, or DWV.

Locating the water meter and main shutoffs

The first step toward gaining mastery over your house's plumbing system is to locate the water meter and, more important, the main shutoff.

Look for the place where water first enters your house. Usually, you'll find a pipe an inch or so thick, called a water main, coming up through the floor in your basement or first floor. If you have metered water, the pipe will enter and exit a round gauge, the water meter. This has either a digital readout that looks like a car's odometer or a series of five or six dials. The meter tells how much water passes into the house. If you have a well, or if your bill does not change no matter how much water you use, you don't have a meter.

Near the place where the water main enters your house, look for one or two valves that you can turn on and off by hand. This is the main shutoff for the house.

You may have an additional shutoff outside the house, buried in a cavity sometimes called a "buffalo box." To find it, look for a round metal cover in the ground near the street or the edge of your property. It may be overgrown with grass. Pry it up and look inside with a flashlight. There may be a valve that you can turn by hand, or you may need a special long-handled "key." Older homes in warm weather locations sometimes have an exposed valve just outside the house.

If you have an older home, don't depend entirely on the inside shutoff; it can break, leak, or stop shutting off completely. If you'll have to shut down the system often during a project, learn where your outside shutoff is and use it to shut off the water.

> ### CAUTION!
> #### ALWAYS BE PREPARED TO SHUT OFF THE WATER
> In case of a burst pipe or other emergency, be ready to shut off the main water supply quickly. Let members of your family know where the main shutoff is. Clear away boxes and furniture so it is easy to get at. If it takes a special tool to shut off your water, keep it handy.

WHERE YOUR RESPONSIBILITY ENDS

The water meter is the continental divide when it comes to assigning responsibility for plumbing repairs. Most often, the water meter and pipes leading away from the house are the responsibility of the water company. Anything on the house side of the meter is your responsibility. However, if you will be adding new fixtures (not just replacing old ones), you may be required to have a larger water main coming into the house. If so, you'll have to pay for it. Check when you get your permit.

THE NEW AND THE OLD

In the old days, plumbers installed cast-iron drain lines. They had to pack each joint with tarred oakum, then pour in molten lead—a practice dating from the time of the Romans. For supply lines and smaller drain lines, they used galvanized pipe, which is strong but can rust and corrode over time.

Plastic drain lines and copper supply lines are superior to the old materials. They last much longer and are easier to work with. However, it took many years for different localities' codes to make the switch to modern materials. In some places, for instance, cast-iron was required by code well into the 1980s. Even to this day, some municipalities require that supply lines be made with galvanized pipe.

If you have old pipe, there's no need to rip it out. Many products are available that make it easy to connect the new to the old. These products often use gaskets that can remain leakproof for many decades.

SUPPLY SYSTEM

Water enters your house through a pipe that connects either to a municipal water line or a private well. If your bill changes according to how much water you use, your water flows through a water meter. Near the meter you will find one or two main shutoffs.

From there water travels to the water heater. Water from a private well goes to a pressure tank before going to the heater.

From the water heater, a pair of water lines—one hot and one cold—branch out through the house to serve the various fixtures (toilets, tubs, sinks, showers) and water-using appliances (dishwashers, washing machines, heating system boilers).

These supply lines are always under pressure; if they are opened or a break occurs, water will shoot out and not stop until it is shut off in some way. That is why modern homes have stop (or shutoff) valves for every fixture and appliance. If your home is not equipped with them, plan to install them. They'll make maintenance and repairs more convenient and will more than pay for themselves should you face a serious break.

Older homes have plumbing systems that use galvanized pipe, which will corrode over time, leading to low pressure and leaks. Newer homes use copper and plastic supply lines, which last much longer.

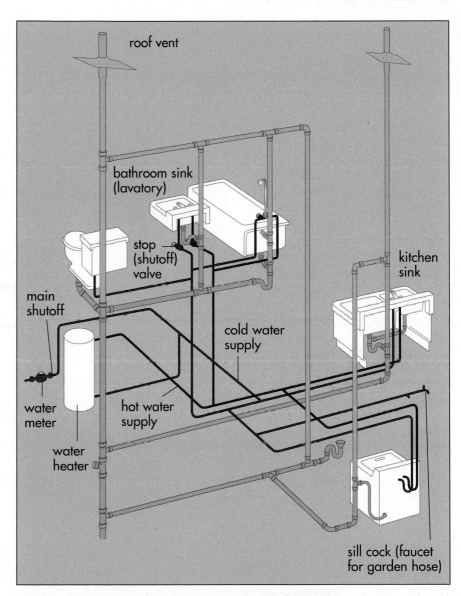

roof vent

bathroom sink (lavatory)

stop (shutoff) valve

main shutoff

cold water supply

kitchen sink

water meter

hot water supply

water heater

sill cock (faucet for garden hose)

SUPPLY SYSTEM PROBLEM SOLVER

For answers to these problems and questions   **see pages**

DRAIN SYSTEM

Drain pipes use gravity to rid the house of liquid and solid waste. This system also guards against foul-smelling and potentially harmful gases entering the house from the municipal drain system or the septic field.

All fixtures except the toilet empty into a trap (toilets have built-in traps). A trap is a curved section of drain pipe that holds enough standing water to make an airtight seal that prevents sewer gases from backing up and leaking into the home. Each time a fixture is used, the old water in the trap is forced down the line and replaced with new water.

After leaving the trap, drain water moves in pipes sloped at no less than ¼ inch per foot toward a waste stack (also called a soil pipe), a large, vertical pipe that carries water below the floor. There it takes a bend and proceeds out to a municipal sewer line or a private septic system. A clean-out is a place where you can insert an auger to clear the line. Traps serve the same function.

Drain pipes come in 1¼-inch pipe for a bathroom sink, 1½-inch for kitchen sinks and bathtubs, and 3- or 4-inch for toilets. The stack is usually a 4-inch pipe. Older homes use cast-iron pipe for the stacks and galvanized pipe for the other drain lines. New homes use plastic, and occasionally copper, for stacks and drains.

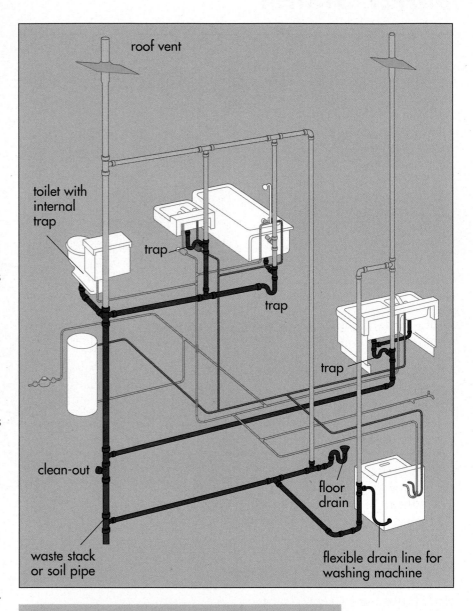

roof vent

toilet with internal trap

trap

trap

trap

clean-out

floor drain

waste stack or soil pipe

flexible drain line for washing machine

DRAIN SYSTEM PROBLEM SOLVER

For answers to these problems and questions   **see pages**

VENT SYSTEM

To flow freely, drain pipes need air. Without air, water will glug down a drain like soda pop from a bottle. A plumbing vent plays the same role as that little second opening in a gasoline can. With the stopper closed, gas pours out slowly. But once the stopper is opened, the air entering the can equalizes the pressure and allows the liquid to flow freely.

Also the air supplied by a vent prevents siphoning action, which might otherwise pull water up out of traps and toilets and allow sewage gases to escape into the house. Instead vents carry the gases through your roof. Sewer gas, composed largely of methane, is not only smelly, it is harmful and dangerous. Install a top quality venting system, even if it means a lot of work.

A main vent is an extension of the waste stack and reaches upward through the roof. Branch vents tie into the main vent. Each and every plumbing fixture and appliance must be vented properly, either by tying into a main vent or by having a vent of its own that extends through the roof.

When installing a new fixture in a new location (not just replacing an existing fixture), venting is often the most difficult problem to overcome. Local codes require that venting adhere to specific dimension requirements. Research these requirements before you begin planning. Vent pipes are made of the same materials as drain pipes, although sometimes they are of smaller dimensions.

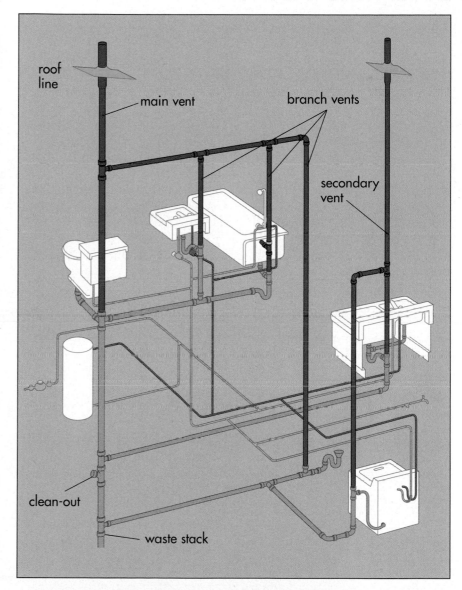

VENT SYSTEM PROBLEM SOLVER

For answers to these problems and questions   **see pages**

ESSENTIAL TOOLS

Plumbing does not require a lot of expensive tools, and even those that you may use for only one job are well worth the cost. The money you save by doing your own work will pay for them many times over. Using the tools shown on this page, you can tackle most plumbing projects.

To clear drain lines, get a **plunger.** The type shown here, with the extra flange extending downward, is ideal for toilets and also works well on bathtubs and sinks. Use a hand-cranked **drain auger** to clear away clogs that won't plunge away. For toilets, use a **closet auger**.

To disassemble and connect pipes and to make many other plumbing repairs, purchase a pair of high-quality **tongue-and-groove pliers** that adjust to grab almost any size pipe. A standard **adjustable pipe wrench** is essential for working with threaded iron pipe. An **adjustable Crescent wrench** will fit the nuts on faucets and other fixtures.

To cut pipe, use a **hacksaw.** Hacksaw blades dull quickly so have extra blades on hand.

For running new pipes through walls, you will need a **drill** with plenty of **spade bits**. To cut away drywall or plaster to make room for the plumbing, use a **keyhole saw.** A **flashlight** comes in handy when you need to peer into wall cavities and under sinks.

For delicate chores such as removing faucet O-rings and clips, have a pair of **needle-nose pliers** on hand. And have a ready supply of general-purpose tools, including **screwdrivers**, a **putty knife**, a **utility knife**, and a **tape measure**.

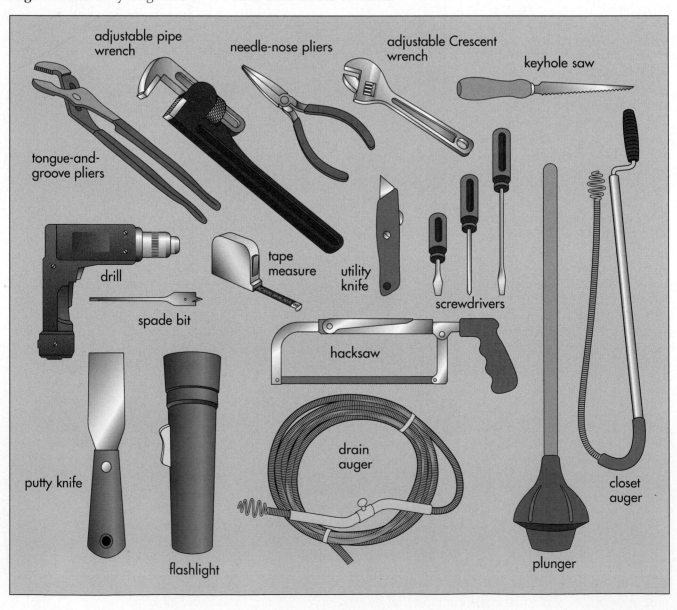

adjustable pipe wrench

needle-nose pliers

adjustable Crescent wrench

keyhole saw

tongue-and-groove pliers

drill

spade bit

tape measure

utility knife

screwdrivers

hacksaw

putty knife

drain auger

closet auger

flashlight

plunger

SPECIALIZED TOOLS

Some tools are designed for specialized plumbing tasks. Choose the ones that will help you work with your materials and fixtures.

If you will be soldering copper pipe, you must have a **propane torch.** If you have a lot to do, pay the extra money for a self-igniting model. Otherwise, get an inexpensive **spark lighter.**

To bend flexible copper tubing without kinking it, use a **tubing bender.** A two-part **flaring tool** is necessary if you want to make flare joints in copper tubing. If you plan on cutting copper pipe or tubing, buy a **tubing cutter.** It makes easier and cleaner cuts than a **hacksaw** and will not squeeze tubing out of shape. For cutting plastic supply pipes, a **plastic tubing cutter** makes the job easier. To set the proper incline for drain pipes, you'll need a **level.**

When working on faucets and sinks, you will sometimes need a **basin wrench** to get at nuts you cannot reach with pliers. If you have a damaged faucet seat that needs replacing, don't take a chance with a screwdriver—use a **seat wrench.** For those big nuts that hold on the basket strainers of kitchen sinks, you may need a **spud wrench.**

When plunging and augering don't clear out a clog, a **blow bag** will often do the trick: hook up a garden hose to it, insert it into the drain pipe, and turn on the water.

For large-scale demolition, notching studs and joists, and quickly cutting galvanized pipe, a **reciprocating saw** makes the job much easier. If you need to chip away tiles to get at plumbing, use a **cold chisel.**

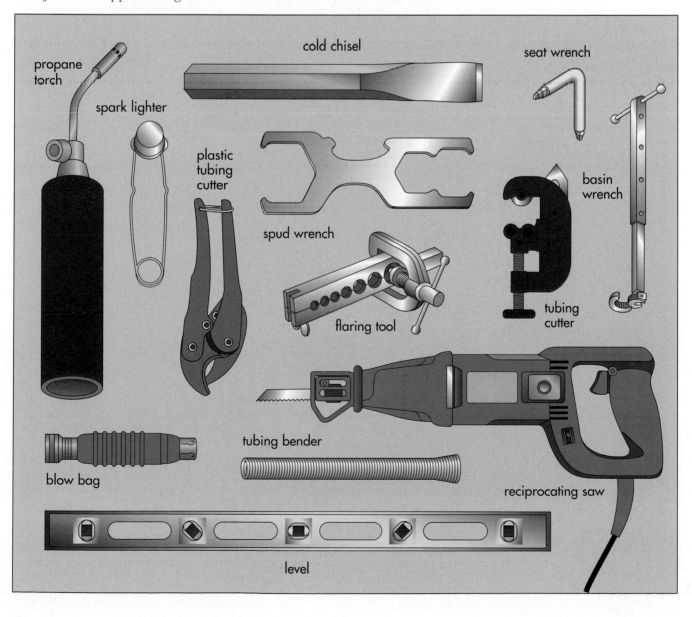

propane torch

spark lighter

cold chisel

seat wrench

plastic tubing cutter

spud wrench

flaring tool

basin wrench

tubing cutter

blow bag

tubing bender

reciprocating saw

level

PREVENTING FREEZE-UPS

Ice-cold tap water may taste refreshing, but it also can be a chilling sign that your plumbing is in trouble. Burst pipes from freezing are difficult and expensive to fix, so take precautions if there is reason to believe that your system will not survive the coldest days of the year. New homes with pipes placed near an exterior wall can be as prone to having frozen pipes as poorly insulated older homes. Often the best solution is insulating the wall or ceiling that contains the pipes. This helps keep your home warm and protects your pipes. This page shows some additional ways to prevent plumbing freeze-ups.

YOU'LL NEED...
TIME: About three hours to prepare the average home.
SKILLS: Beginner carpentry and plumbing skills.
TOOLS: Knife and flashlight.

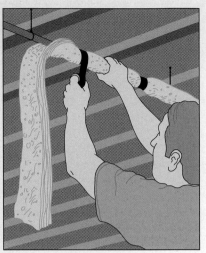

1. Insulate the pipes.
Insulation goes a long way toward preventing freeze-ups, as long as every square inch of pipe—including connections—is protected. Pipe jacketing comes in standard lengths that can be cut with a knife and secured with electrical tape. Ordinary insulation, cut in strips and bundled around pipes, works equally well for less cost but more labor. In an extremely cold wall or floor, pack the entire cavity with insulation. Also consider insulating long hot water runs, especially those that pass through unheated spaces. The added insulation will conserve water-heating energy.

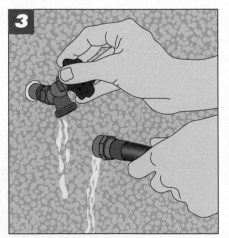

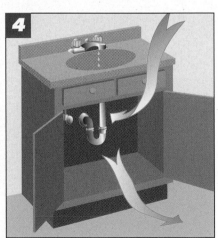

2. Wrap pipes with heat tape.
Electric heat tape draws only modest amounts of current, so it is safe and inexpensive to use. Wrap tape around the pipe, and plug the tape into a receptacle. A thermostat turns the tape on and off as needed. However tape will not work during a power outage—the very time when the protection may be most needed.

3. Protect the sill cock.
Before winter, remove and drain garden hoses to prevent them from splitting. Shut off the water leading to the sill cock, allow it to drain, and leave it open. If there is no indoor shutoff, install one (see page 196), or install a freeze-proof sill cock—an improvement that may be required by local codes.

4. Precautions for very cold days
As a preventive measure on extremely cold days, turn on the faucets that have vulnerable parts and let water trickle continuously. If there is a cabinet underneath, open its doors to let room heat warm the pipes. Use a small lamp to warm pipes that run through cold areas.

WINTERIZING A HOUSE

If you're leaving a house or cabin for an extended period of time during the winter, you don't have to leave the heat on in order to avoid plumbing disasters. You can save money by turning off your utilities and winterizing, which involves shutting off the water supply and draining the whole plumbing system. If you have a private water system, the process is slightly more involved—you'll also have to drain the holding tank and any water-treating apparatus. The result will be peace of mind that the plumbing system is safely dormant, without the expense of keeping the home fires burning.

YOU'LL NEED...

TIME: About four hours to winterize a modest house.
SKILLS: Disconnecting pipes.
TOOLS: Pipe wrench, Crescent wrench, and bucket.

1. Drain the system.
Have the water department shut off the water valve outside your home, or do it yourself. Then open every faucet in the house, starting at the top of the system. Shut down and drain the water heater (see page 202). Detach drain hoses on dish and clothes washers.

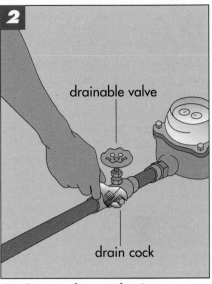

2. Open valves and unions.
Look to see if you have a drainable valve or two—often they are near the water meter. Open the drain cock on each. Drain supply lines completely. If you find a low-lying pipe that doesn't have a faucet or drain cock, open a union where two pipes join (see page 190).

3. Replace water with antifreeze.
Flush toilets, then pour a gallon of antifreeze solution (non-toxic antifreeze mixed with water, according to directions on the container) into the bowl. This will start a mild flushing action. Some of it will remain in the

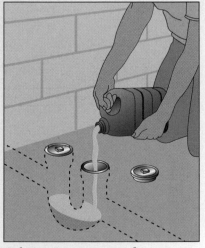

toilet's trap. Pour antifreeze solution into all fixtures with a trap—sinks, showers, bathtubs, and the washing-machine standpipe. If your house has a main house trap, fill the elbow portion with full-strength antifreeze.

HOME AGAIN

After returning to your winterized house, follow these steps, in order:

- Turn all faucets off, including the sill cock. Remove any aerators on the faucets, and clean if necessary.
- Reconnect all disconnected pipes, and close down all drainable valves.
- Turn on the main water-supply valve.
- Turn all the faucets on slowly, beginning at the sill cock. The water will "spit" out for a while, then assume a normal flow.
- Replace the aerators.

FIXING LEAKS AND FROZEN PIPES

Water escaping from a pipe can wreak havoc in your house. Even a tiny leak that is left to drip day and night will soon rot away everything in its vicinity. A pipe that freezes and bursts can produce a major flood.

As soon as you spot a leak, shut off the water to take pressure off the line. Then locate exactly where the problem is. If the pipe is not visible, this may be difficult: Water can run quite a ways along the outside of the pipe, a floor joist, or a subfloor before becoming visible. Eventually, any leaking pipe must be replaced (see pages 178–194). Here are emergency measures to temporarily stop the flow.

YOU'LL NEED...

TIME: An hour or so to clamp or apply epoxy to a leak.
SKILLS: No special skills needed.
TOOLS: Screwdriver and putty knife.

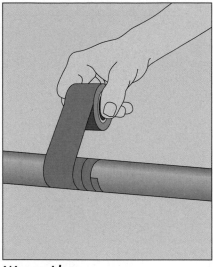

Wrap with tape.
For a pinhole leak, dry off the pipe, and wrap it tightly with several layers of duct tape. Wrap it about 6 inches on either side of the hole. This is extremely temporary, but the tape should hold while you make a trip to the hardware store for a pipe clamp and rubber gasket.

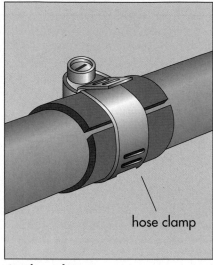

hose clamp

Apply a clamp.
An automotive hose clamp with a piece of rubber—both available at any hardware store—makes a somewhat better leak-stopper. Again, it works only for pinhole leaks. Wrap the rubber around the pipe, and tighten up the clamp. Be sure that the clamp itself is placed directly over the hole.

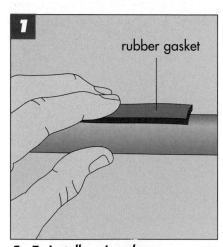

rubber gasket

1. To install a pipe clamp, position the gasket.
The best temporary solution to a leaking pipe is a pipe clamp specially made for this purpose. It will seal small gashes, cracks, and pinhole leaks. It also is semipermanent—expect it to last several years. Position the rubber gasket so the hole is centered under it.

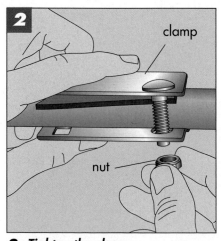

clamp

nut

2. Tighten the clamp.
Assemble the clamp pieces around the gasket and tighten. Take care that the gasket does not move as you work. Tighten all four nuts evenly, working from nut to nut until all are tight.

EXPERTS' INSIGHT

IT MAY NOT BE A LEAK...
If a pipe shows drips all along its length, it may be condensing water from humid air rather than leaking. Wrap it with insulation to stop the condensation (see page 144).

...OR IT MAY BE MORE
An isolated leak may be a sign that pipes are aging. The galvanized pipe common to older homes tends to rust from the inside out. Once a leak appears, expect others to follow. If the pipes in your house have begun to deteriorate, buy a supply of pipe clamps to fit your lines.

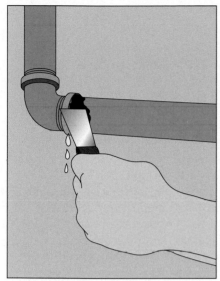

Apply plumber's epoxy at fittings.

If the leak is coming from a fitting, don't try to clamp it. Your best bet is plumber's epoxy. Unless the leak is a real gusher, don't shut off the water. The epoxy comes in two parts. Cut a piece of each and knead them together until the color is uniform. Pack the epoxy into the connection by pushing it in with your thumb or a putty knife. Pack it until the leak stops.

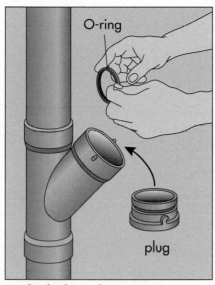

Seal a leaking clean-out.

Drain lines are less leak-prone than supply lines. Once in a while, however, a clean-out plug may seep waste water. Warn everyone in the household not to use any fixtures. Remove the plug (it may screw out or pull out). Reseal screw-in plugs by applying Teflon tape to the male threads. If it has an O-ring, replace it.

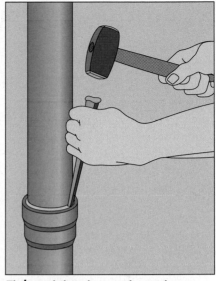

Tighten joints in cast-iron pipe.

If you have a leak at the joint of cast-iron pipes, it is usually easy to deal with. For the hub-and-spigot type shown here, use a hammer and chisel to tamp down the soft lead that fills the joint. Don't whack the pipe hard—you could crack it. If you have the no-hub system (see page 219), tightening the clamp will likely stop the leak.

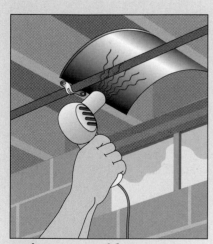

To thaw exposed frozen pipes, heat with a blow dryer...

Open the faucet the pipe supplies so any steam can escape. If it is exposed, apply heat directly with a hair dryer or a heat gun turned to its lowest setting. Move the dryer or gun back and forth—don't hold it in one spot.

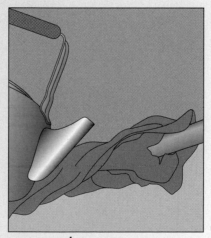

...or pour hot water.

Another solution for an exposed frozen pipe is to wrap a cloth around it, then pour boiling water over the cloth. Allow the water to cool, pour again, and repeat until the pipe is thawed. Be sure a faucet is open while you do this so steam can escape.

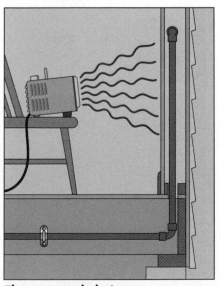

Thaw concealed pipes.

If the pipes are concealed, thawing will take more time. Open a faucet. Beam a heat lamp or electric space heater at the wall containing the pipe. Monitor closely to make sure the heat doesn't damage the wall surface.

IDENTIFYING STEM FAUCETS

When a faucet develops a leak—most often, a drip from the spout or a leak around the base—the problem is usually easy to fix. Very likely, you'll be able to purchase a repair kit for your type of faucet. Repair techniques vary from faucet to faucet, but in most cases you can easily do it yourself. When buying replacement parts, take the old unit to the store. If the faucet cannot be repaired, it is not difficult to replace it with a new one (see pages 198–199).

The first step is to identify the type of faucet you have. The anatomy drawings here and on pages 152, 154, 156, and 158 show you the various types.

The most common type is the seat-and-washer faucet, often called a compression faucet. All stem faucets have separate hot and cold controls. In its off position, the stem compresses a flexible washer on the stem into a beveled seat located in the faucet base, stopping the flow of water. As the washer wears, you have to apply more and more pressure to turn off the unit. That's when dripping usually begins.

Two newer versions are types of washerless stem faucets—cartridge and diaphragm. The cartridge type rotates rather than raising and lowering to control flow. It uses a rubber seal and O-rings. The diaphragm type uses a durable diaphragm instead of the seat washer.

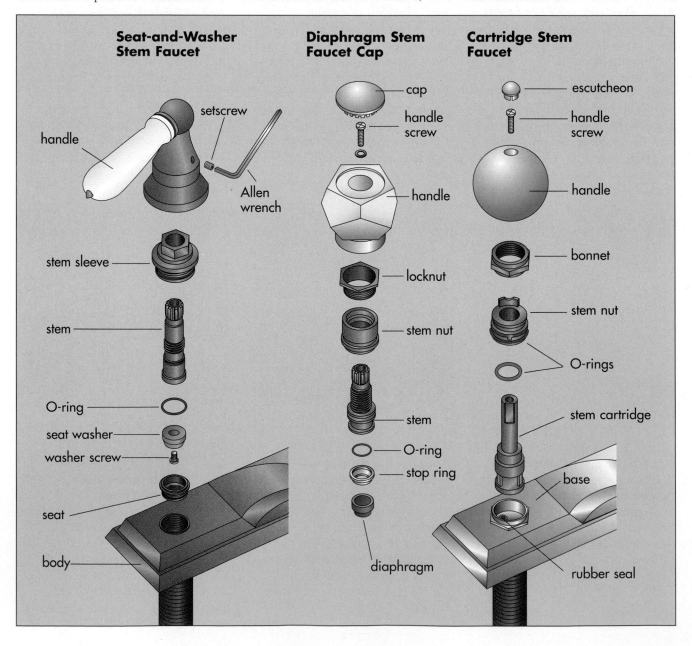

Seat-and-Washer Stem Faucet

handle
setscrew
Allen wrench
stem sleeve
stem
O-ring
seat washer
washer screw
seat
body

Diaphragm Stem Faucet Cap

cap
handle screw
handle
locknut
stem nut
stem
O-ring
stop ring
diaphragm

Cartridge Stem Faucet

escutcheon
handle screw
handle
bonnet
stem nut
O-rings
stem cartridge
base
rubber seal

PULLING OUT HANDLES AND STEMS

The first step in replacing the inner workings of a stem faucet is to pull out the handles and stems and take them to the store so you can buy proper replacement parts. If you can identify the faucet by brand name, it will be easier to find the right part. Often no brand name is visible, so you'll have to take out the stem and compare it with the drawings on pages 148, 152, 154, 156, and 158.

Note: *When working on faucets, shut off the water.*

You'll Need...

TIME: About 15 minutes, unless the parts are stuck.

SKILLS: No special skills needed.

TOOLS: Screwdriver, tongue-and-groove pliers, and possibly a handle puller.

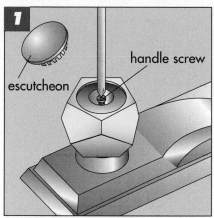

1. Remove escutcheon and screw.
If your handle is round, it is probably connected to the stem with a screw from the top. You may have to pry off an escutcheon (usually marked "H" or "C") to get to it. Some handles are attached with setscrews—see the handle on the seat-and-washer stem faucet on page 148. Remove the setscrew with an Allen wrench and pull the handle off.

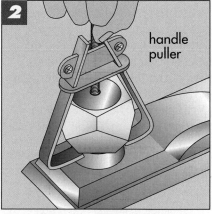

2. Pull out handle and stem.
Usually, the handle will come out if you pull it up firmly or pry it up with a screwdriver. Take care not to mar the finish on the handle. If it is really stuck, use a handle puller that grips the handle from underneath and draws the handle off the stem. Once the handle is off, unscrew the stem with pliers.

REPLACING SEAT WASHERS

Perhaps the most common plumbing repair of all is replacing a seat washer. If yours is a seat-and-washer stem faucet, the washer often becomes worn. Most commonly, there is a depression running in a ring around the washer, or the washer has begun to crumble from old age.

If a washer wears out quickly, the seat is damaged and nicks the washer every time you shut the water off, making the faucet drip (see page 159 to replace a seat).

You'll Need...

TIME: About 30 minutes, plus a trip to your supplier if you don't have the right washer.

SKILLS: No special skills needed.

TOOLS: Screwdriver.

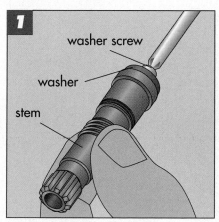

1. Remove the old washer.
Examine your washer. If it is damaged in any way, remove the washer screw and pull the old washer off. Clean away any debris or deposits from the bottom of the stem. Take your stem and old washer to your supplier if you are not sure how to select a new washer that will fit.

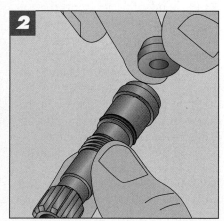

2. Insert a new washer.
Find a washer the exact same size and shape as the old one. If the old washer has been squashed out of shape, this may be difficult to determine, so double-check by slipping the new washer onto the bottom of the stem. It should fit snugly. Replace and tighten the screw, and reinstall the stem.

REPAIRING DIAPHRAGM AND CARTRIDGE STEMS

Diaphragm and cartridge stem faucets are just as easy to repair as seat-and-washer stem faucets. Often the most difficult part of the job is finding the right parts. There are hundreds of O-ring sizes. The safest way to choose is to remove the stem, take it to your supplier, and show it to a salesperson. That way, the O-rings fit the stem exactly. **NOTE:** *Be sure to shut off the water before removing stems.*

YOU'LL NEED...

TIME: Just a few minutes, once you've got the right parts, the faucet handle is removed, and the stem unscrewed.
SKILLS: No special skills needed.
TOOLS: Small screwdriver or a sharp-pointed tool.

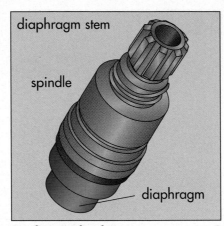

Replace a diaphragm.
Sometimes called a top hat stem, a diaphragm stem has a diaphragm that functions much like a seat washer. To replace it, simply pull off the worn diaphragm, and snap a new one on.

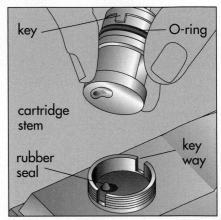

Replace O-ring, seal, and spring.
For a cartridge stem, fix leaks by replacing the seal and O-ring. Remove the rubber seal from the base of the faucet with the sharpened end of a pencil; a small spring will come out as well. Remove the O-ring by hand, or carefully pry it off with a sharp tool. Lubricate the new parts lightly with heatproof grease after you install them.

REPAIRING LEAKS FROM HANDLES

If the faucet leaks around the handle, you'll need to remove the stem to get at the source of the problem. Older faucets have packing wound around the top of the stem to keep water from seeping out the top. Don't be put off by this old-fashioned material; it is easy to replace, and new packing will last for years. Newer stems have O-rings. Once you have the stem out, inspect the rest of the faucet and replace any parts that look as if they're starting to wear out. **NOTE:** *Be sure to shut off the water.*

YOU'LL NEED...

TIME: Fifteen minutes to repack a spindle and replace an O-ring.
SKILLS: No special skills needed.
TOOLS: None.

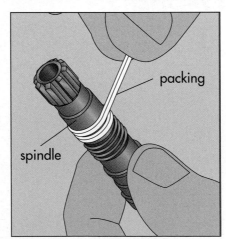

Wrap on new packing string.
If your faucet has packing wound around the spindle just under the packing nut (see page 197), remove all of it and clean the spindle. Use either Teflon tape or strand packing, and wind it fairly tight. Leave just enough room so the packing nut can be screwed on when the stem is replaced.

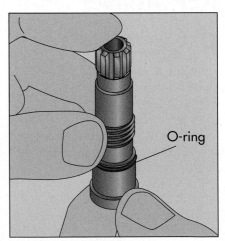

Replace the O-ring.
Newer stems have an O-ring instead of packing. Simply remove the old O-ring, and replace it with one that fits exactly. Lightly lubricate the O-ring with heatproof grease after you install it and before you reinstall the stem.

REPLACING AND GRINDING SEATS

When the spout of a stem faucet (either a seat-and-washer or a diaphragm type) leaks, be sure to inspect the seat as well as the washer or diaphragm. If the seat is pitted or scored, it is scraping the washer or diaphragm every time you turn the faucet off. It will quickly damage a seat washer, and your faucet will leak again even after you've fixed it.

If the seat is damaged, it is best to replace it. Sometimes, however, it is hard to extract the old one. In those cases, try grinding it smooth with a special tool.

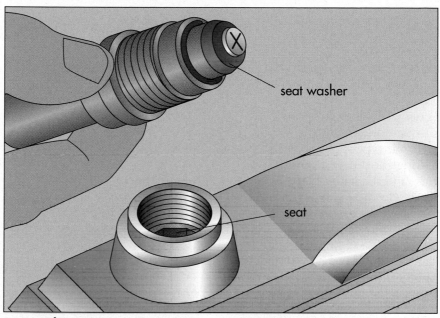

seat washer

seat

Inspect the seat.
Remove the stem (see page 148), and inspect the washer or diaphragm. If it looks cut up, the likely cause is a damaged seat. Whether the washer or diaphragm looks damaged or not, examine the seat, first by looking at it with a flashlight, then by feeling with your finger. If it appears or feels less than smooth, your washer or diaphragm will have a hard time sealing water off when you crank down on the handle. The seat needs to be replaced or ground smooth with a seat grinder.

seat wrench

Replace a damaged seat.
Though it is sometimes possible to remove a seat with a screwdriver, this is risky—you may damage the seat so that it cannot be removed. Purchase a seat wrench, which is designed to remove seats of various sizes. Insert it into the seat, push down firmly, and turn counterclockwise. Install the new seat with the same tool.

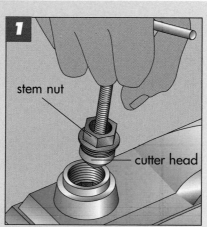

1

stem nut

cutter head

1. Use a seat grinder for a seat that cannot be removed.
Purchase a seat grinder. Slip the stem nut over the shaft of the seat grinder—it helps stabilize the grinder. Select a cutter head that fits easily inside the body and is as wide as the seat.

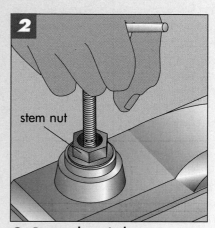

2

stem nut

2. Rotate the grinder.
Screw the stem nut into the faucet body to hold the shaft securely without wobbling. Push down gently, and turn the handle clockwise three full rotations. Remove the grinder and inspect the seat with a flashlight. If it is not smooth, try again.

REPAIRING CARTRIDGE FAUCETS

Most washerless faucets use a combination of seals and O-rings to control and direct water. A cartridge faucet (manufactured by Kohler, Moen, Price-Pfister, and others) uses a series of strategically placed O-rings and/or seals.

In the type shown, the cartridge O-rings fit snugly against the inside of the faucet body. One O-ring forms a seal between the hot and cold supply lines. The others protect against leaks from the spout and from under the handle. On swivel-spout models, another ring protects against leaks from under the spout. Raising the handle lifts the stem so it slides upward inside the cartridge. Holes in the stem align with the openings in the cartridge in various combinations.

Other types have fewer O-rings and use other types of seals. Repair kits are available for each manufacturer and model.

When this type of faucet leaks, you can replace either the O-rings or the cartridge itself if it has corroded. Because the design is simple, repairs usually don't take long. In fact, disassembly is usually the bulk of the work, and your only problem may be finding the retainer clip that holds the cartridge in the faucet.

YOU'LL NEED...

TIME: About an hour, once you have the replacement parts.
SKILLS: No special skills needed.
TOOLS: Screwdriver, needle-nose pliers, and tongue-and-groove pliers.

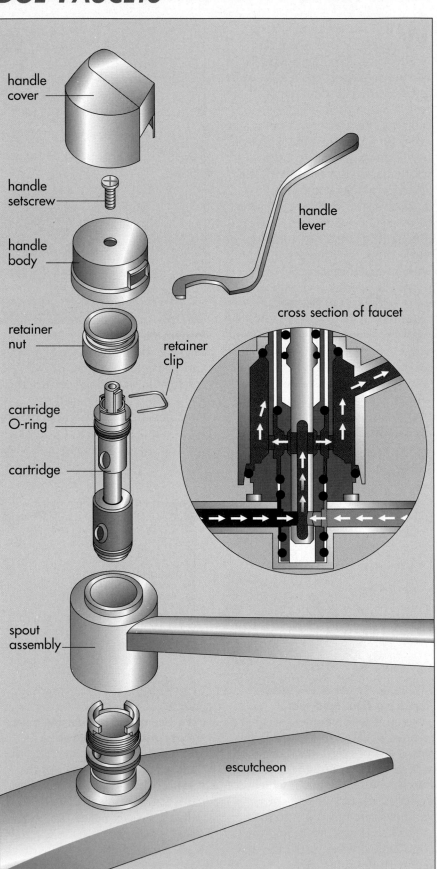

handle cover

handle setscrew

handle body

handle lever

retainer nut

retainer clip

cartridge O-ring

cartridge

cross section of faucet

spout assembly

escutcheon

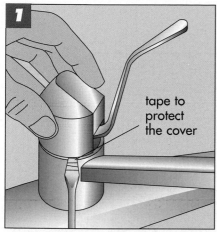

1. Remove the handle housing.
NOTE: *Shut off the water and drain the line.* Cartridge faucets vary in design from model to model, but you disassemble most of them as follows: Pry off the decorative cover that conceals the handle screw. Be careful not to crack the cover in doing so; most are made of plastic. You may need to remove an external retaining clip to get the cover off.

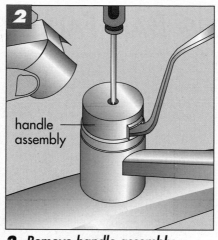

2. Remove handle assembly.
Cover the drain with a rag to avoid losing any small parts. Beneath the handle housing is a setscrew that holds the handle in place. Remove the handle screw, and lift off the handle body and lever. If there is no retainer nut (next step), lift out the spout.

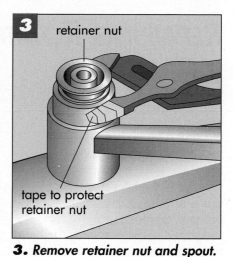

3. Remove retainer nut and spout.
Swivel-spout models will have a retainer nut. Unscrew it, then lift off the spout.

You'll need to disassemble some models differently. Pry off the cap on top of the faucet, remove the screw, and remove the handle by tilting it back and pulling up. Then remove the plastic threaded retaining ring.

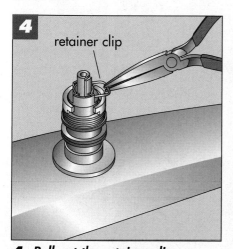

4. Pull out the retainer clip.
Depending on the model you have, you may need to lift off a cylindrical sleeve to get at the cartridge. You should now be able to see the retainer clip, a metal piece that holds the cartridge in place. Use needle-nose pliers to remove the clip from its slot. Be careful not to misplace it.

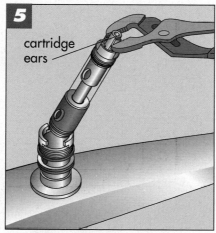

5. Remove the cartridge.
With tongue-and-groove pliers, lift the cartridge from the faucet body. Take note of the position of the cartridge ears, and be sure that when you put the cartridge back in, its ears are facing in the same direction. Otherwise, hot and cold will be reversed. If you are replacing O-rings, give them a light coating of heatproof lubricant. When reassembling the faucet, tighten firmly, but don't crank down hard—there are many plastic parts that can crack.

REPAIRING ROTATING BALL FAUCETS

Inside a rotating ball faucet a slotted ball sits atop a pair of spring-loaded seals. When the handle is lowered to the "off" position, this ball, held tight against the seals by the faucet's cap, closes off the water supply. This type of faucet is often called a Delta faucet, after its primary manufacturer.

As the handle is raised, the ball rotates in such a way that the openings align with the supply line ports. This allows water to pass through the ball and out the spout. Moving the handle to the left allows more hot water to flow out; moving it to the right adds cold water.

Most leaks can be fixed by replacing the ball and gaskets in the faucet (see page 155). In addition, seals and springs can give out and need replacement.

These faucets also can spring leaks from around the handle and, with swivel-spout models, from under the base of the spout. Handle leaks indicate that the adjusting ring has loosened or the seal above the ball is worn.

Leaks from under the spout result from O-ring failure. Inspect the rings encircling the body and—on units with diverter valves for a sprayer—the valve O-ring. Replace the O-rings if they look worn.

CAUTION!
To avoid damage to flooring and walls, turn off supply lines or the main water valve.

YOU'LL NEED...
TIME: About two hours to rebuild and reassemble a faucet.
SKILLS: Patience and an eye for detail.
TOOLS: Allen wrench, adjustable pliers, wrench that comes with the rebuild kit, and awl or other sharp-pointed tool.

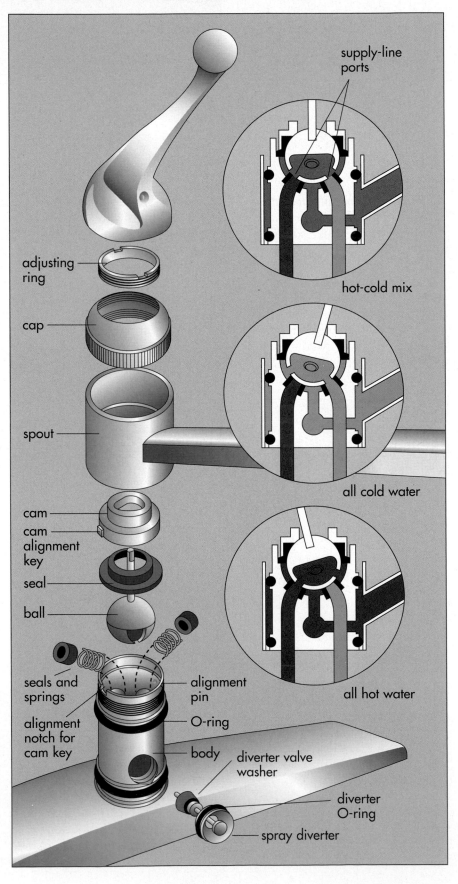

supply-line ports

hot-cold mix

all cold water

all hot water

adjusting ring

cap

spout

cam

cam alignment key

seal

ball

seals and springs

alignment notch for cam key

alignment pin

O-ring

body

diverter valve washer

diverter O-ring

spray diverter

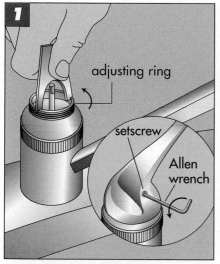

1. Remove handle and cap.
Shut off the water supply and drain the lines by lifting straight up on the handle. Using an Allen wrench, loosen the setscrew that holds the handle in place (see inset above). Loosen the adjusting ring using the wrench that comes packed with your purchased repair kit.

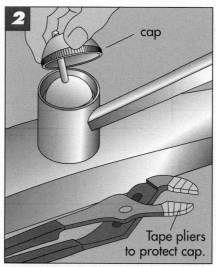

2. Disassemble cam, ball, spout.
Unscrew the cap with cloth- or tape-covered adjustable pliers. Lift out the cam assembly, the ball, and, in the case of a swivel-spout faucet, the spout. The spout fits tightly against the O-rings of the body, so it may prove stubborn. Be careful not to scratch the spout as you remove it.

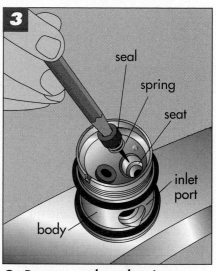

3. Remove seals and springs.
To remove worn seals and springs from the body, insert a pencil into each seal to pull it out. Check for blockage at the supply inlet ports and scrape away any buildup. Then insert new springs and seals.

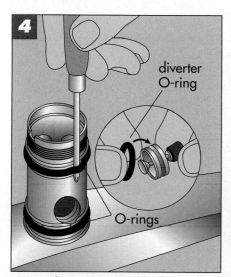

4. Replace O-rings.
If the faucet has a swivel spout, remove the O-rings by prying them away from the body using an awl or other sharp-pointed tool. Roll the new ones down over the body until they rest in the appropriate grooves. Replace the diverter O-ring in the same way. Lightly coat the O-rings and the inside of the spout with heatproof grease.

5. Reassemble.
Be sure to align the slot in the side of the ball with the pin inside the body. Also, the key on the cam assembly fits into a corresponding notch in the body. Hand-tighten the cap and tighten the adjusting ring for a good seal between the ball and the cam. If the faucet leaks, tighten further.

EXPERTS' INSIGHT

Select quality parts
Repair kits of lesser or greater quality are available for this type of faucet. Some include plastic balls; others include longer-lasting metal parts. If your hardware store only has the cheaper kit, try a plumbing supply store for a kit with longer-lasting, though more expensive, parts.

Consider a complete rebuild
When a faucet is old enough to have one part wear out, other parts will soon wear out as well. As long as you are fixing one part of the faucet, do a complete rebuild.

REPAIRING CERAMIC DISK FAUCETS

When you raise the faucet lever of a disk faucet, the upper disk in the cartridge slides across the lower disk, allowing water to enter the mixing chamber. The higher you raise the lever, the more water enters through the inlet ports of the faucet body. Moving the lever from side to side determines whether hot or cold water or a mixture of the two comes out of the spout.

The disk assembly itself, generally made of a long-lasting ceramic material, rarely needs replacing. However, the inlet ports can become clogged with mineral deposits. If this happens, simply disassemble the faucet and scrape away the crusty buildup.

If the faucet leaks at the base of the lever, one or more of the inlet seals on the cartridge may need replacing. See page 157 for how to replace the seals and the cartridge. While the faucet is dismantled, replace all of the seals. If one is worn, the others don't have long to live. Before you go to your supplier, get the brand name of your faucet from the faucet body—or take the disk assembly along. You probably can buy a repair kit with the parts you need.

YOU'LL NEED...

TIME: About an hour for repairs.
SKILLS: No special skills needed.
TOOLS: Small screwdriver and tongue-and-groove pliers.

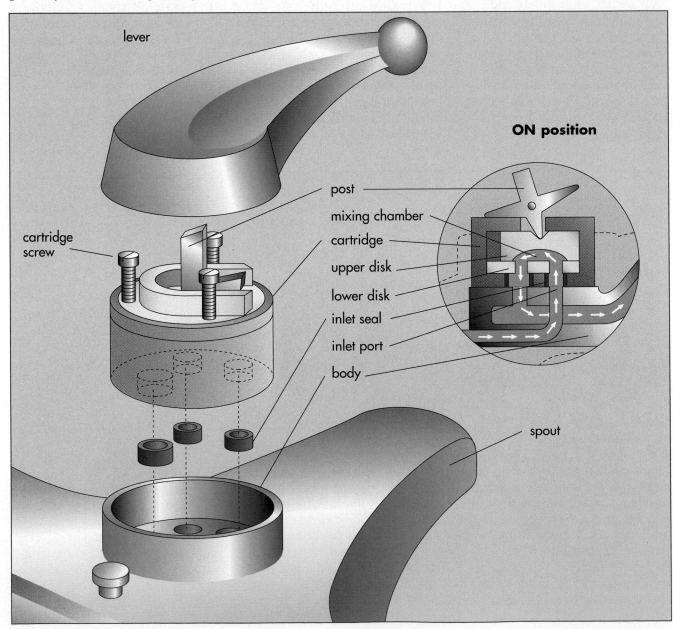

lever

ON position

cartridge screw

post
mixing chamber
cartridge
upper disk
lower disk
inlet seal
inlet port
body

spout

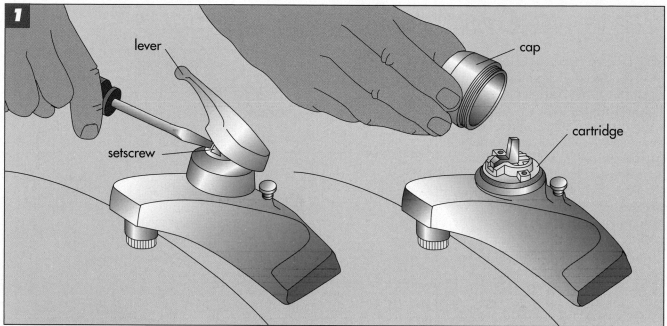

1. Remove the lever and cap.
Note: *Shut off the water.*
Under the lever you'll see a setscrew that holds the lever to the lever post. Use an appropriately sized screwdriver to unscrew the setscrew—don't try to unscrew it with a knife or you may damage it. Loosen the screw until you can raise the lever off the post. You may have to gently pry it off with a large screwdriver.

Lift off or unscrew the decorative cap that covers the cartridge. Then loosen the screws holding the cartridge to the faucet body and lift out the cartridge.

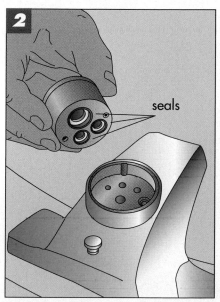

2. Remove the seals.
On the underside of the cartridge you'll find a set of seals. Pull them out with your fingers or carefully use a sharp-pointed tool, being careful not to scratch the cartridge.

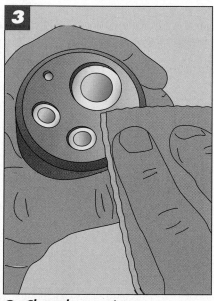

3. Clean the openings.
Check the openings for sediment buildup and clean it. Use a nonmetallic scrubber or a sponge.

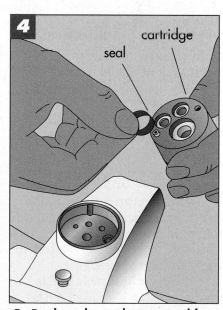

4. Replace the seals; reassemble.
Put the seals back or install replacement seals. Reassemble the faucet. Turn the water back on and test. If the faucet continues to leak after you have cleaned the cartridge and replaced the seals, install a new cartridge.

REPAIRING GASKETED CARTRIDGE FAUCETS

Gasketed cartridge faucets use a gasket with a group of openings at the bottom of the faucet cartridge to mix hot and cold water and direct water to the spout. Newer models have ceramic cartridges; older ones have plastic.

YOU'LL NEED...

TIME: About an hour, plus shopping time.
SKILLS: Basic plumbing skills.
TOOLS: Screwdriver, and tongue-and-groove pliers.

Note: *Shut off the water before disassembling.*

If you're trying to fix a leak from the body of the faucet, first try tightening the cap by hand—do not crank down on it with a wrench. If that doesn't work, disassemble the faucet and replace the two O-rings. Coat them lightly with heatproof grease.

To disassemble, pry off the escutcheon and remove the lever screw. Lift off the lever and unscrew the cap and the retainer nut. The other parts will pull out.

If you're trying to fix a drip from the spout, the cartridge probably needs to be replaced. Check the retainer nut as well. If its threads are stripped, replace it.

These parts are specific to the faucet manufacturer, so take the old parts with you when you go to the store to make sure you buy the right replacement parts.

If the faucet operates stiffly, debris may have built up in the cartridge. In most cases, it will be more trouble to clean the cartridge than it is to buy a new one and replace it.

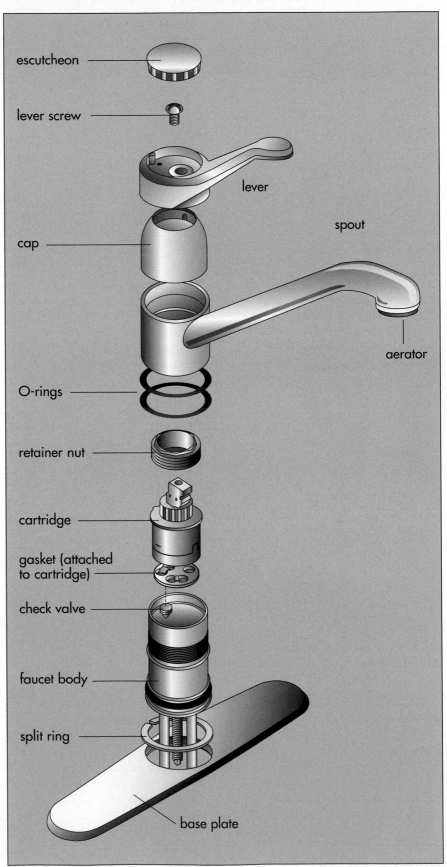

escutcheon

lever screw

lever

spout

cap

O-rings

aerator

retainer nut

cartridge

gasket (attached to cartridge)

check valve

faucet body

split ring

base plate

SEALING LEAKY BASE PLATES

If you find water in the cabinet below the sink, it could be from three places—the supply lines, the drain, or water leaking into the cabinet from under the faucet base plate. The problem may be solved by simply tightening the supply lines (see page 161). If the leak comes from the drain, see page 171. If neither of those is the cause, you may have a leaky base plate that allows splashed water to seep through mounting holes. Follow the steps on this page to solve this last problem.

YOU'LL NEED...

TIME: Two hours to remove, seal, and replace the faucet.
SKILLS: Basic plumbing skills.
TOOLS: Putty knife, and tongue-and-groove pliers or basin wrench.

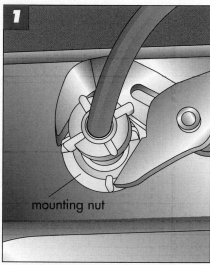

mounting nut

1. Tighten the mounting nuts.
It may be that your faucet is not held tight against the sink. Get under your sink in as comfortable a position as possible and tighten the mounting nuts. If you can't turn them with pliers, use a basin wrench (see page 143). If this does not solve the problem, try Step 2.

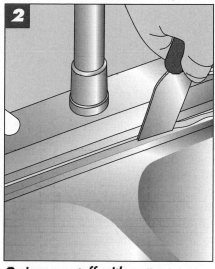

2. Loosen, stuff with putty.
First try to fix the leak without removing the faucet. Loosen the mounting nuts enough to raise the faucet base about a half inch above the sink. Scrape out any hardened gunk. Holding the base plate just above the sink, stuff plumber's putty under it evenly. Retighten the mounting nuts. If it continues to leak, proceed to Step 3.

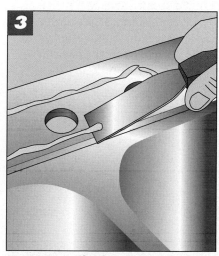

3. Remove the faucet and scrape.
NOTE: *Shut off the water and drain the line.* To entirely reseat the base plate, remove the faucet. Disconnect the supply lines, remove the mounting nuts, and pull the faucet out. Scrape any old putty away and clean the area thoroughly. Take care not to scratch the sink.

gasket

4. Replace the gasket...
If the faucet has a gasket, throw it out, and replace it with a new one. If you have trouble finding a replacement, a new gasket can be made by purchasing a piece of rubber of a similar thickness. You can use the old gasket as a pattern and cut out a new one.

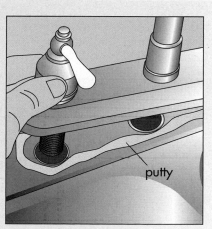

putty

...or apply new putty.
Many plumbers believe putty lasts longer than gaskets, so even if your faucet has a gasket, you may want to discard it and apply putty instead. Roll a rope of putty, about $\frac{1}{4}$ inch in diameter, and apply it to the sink or to the underside of the faucet. Reinstall the faucet, and check for leaks.

FIXING SPRAYERS, DIVERTERS, AND AERATORS

Sink sprayers can be obstructed at the connections, gaskets, and the nozzle. If your faucet has low water pressure, check the aerator. Aerators may develop leaks if their seals are worn, or they can get clogged up. See below to unclog. If water doesn't come out of the sprayer, the problem is most likely a faulty diverter valve: You can replace either the rubber seal or the diverter. Remove the diverter and take it to your supplier to be sure you get the correct replacement.

Diverters vary in shape and location, but all work in much the same way. When water isn't flowing toward the spray outlet, the valve remains open and directs the water flow toward the spout. When you press the sprayer lever, the flow of water shifts toward the sprayer head.

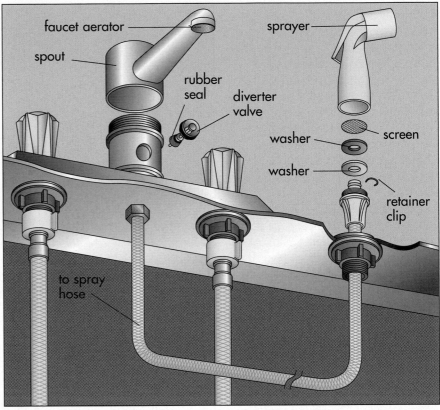

YOU'LL NEED...

TIME: One to two hours.
SKILLS: Basic plumbing skills and attention to detail.
TOOLS: Tongue-and-groove pliers, old toothbrush, and awl or nail.

From diverter to sprayer

In a typical one-handle faucet, remove the spout to find the diverter; it's usually located in front.

If you get low or no water pressure from the sprayer, first check the hose for kinks. A slow stream of water coupled with some water coming from the spout may signal a stuck valve or a worn washer or O-ring. Replace the rubber parts or the diverter valve. Or the sprayer screen may be clogged (see below).

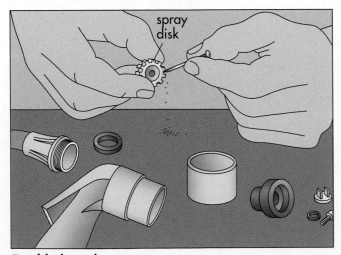

Troubleshoot the sprayer.

Minerals may be restricting the flow of water through the sprayer. Clean the spray disk with an awl or a nail as shown. Replace any worn parts and tighten all the connections.

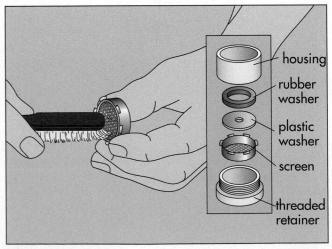

Clean the aerator.

To clean out the aerator, unscrew it from the faucet spout and disassemble it. Brush all the parts clean and soak the pieces in vinegar overnight. If it is heavily clogged, just buy a new one.

STOPPING LEAKS IN FLEXIBLE SUPPLY LINES

There are three basic types of flexible supply lines. Plain or chrome-plated copper tubing uses ferrules and nuts for connections. Flexible plastic lines use knobby ends that take the place of ferrules. Flexible supply lines—either plastic or stainless-steel-braided—use nuts preattached at each end. The last type is the easiest to use. Be sure you buy lines that are long enough.

YOU'LL NEED...

TIME: An hour for most repairs and replacements.

SKILLS: Tightening and loosening nuts in tight places.

TOOLS: Basin wrench or tongue-and-groove pliers and adjustable wrenches.

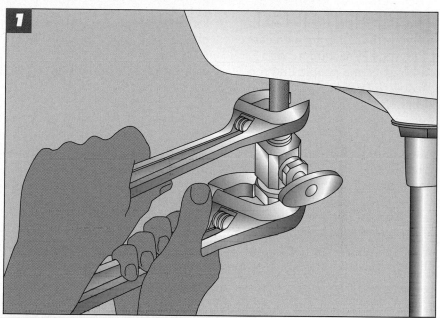

1. Tighten the nuts.
Often fixing a leak is simple—just tighten the nut at the point where you see a leak. Take care not to crank down too hard; you can crack the nut or strip the threads.

Use only adjustable wrenches, not pipe wrenches. If the leak persists, loosen the nuts and recoat the threads or ferrules with Teflon tape or pipe joint compound as shown in Step 2.

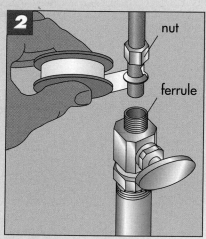

2. Coat the ferrule...
Note: *Be sure to shut off the water, and drain the line.*
If you have a tubing-and-ferrule arrangement, remove the nut and pull the line at least partway out. Take care not to kink it. Coat the ferrule with joint compound or wrap it with Teflon tape. Hook it back up, tighten, and test.

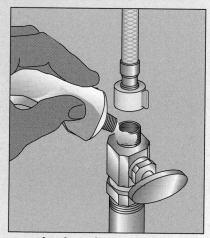

...or the threads.
If you have a plastic or braided flexible line, shut off the water, unscrew the nut, and apply joint compound or Teflon tape to the male threads of the shutoff valve or the faucet. Reconnect, tighten, and test.

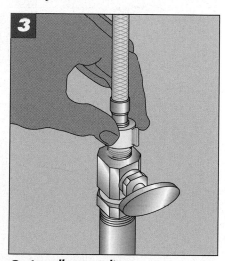

3. Install a new line.
If these measures do not solve your problem quickly, don't keep fussing with the old line. Shut off the water and remove the old supply line. Buy a new flexible line, apply Teflon tape or joint compound to the male threads, and screw the new flexible line on. Tighten both ends and test.

REPAIRING TOILETS

*B*ecause it gets used so often, your toilet has a good chance of eventually needing repair. Although some people find the prospect of working on a toilet distasteful, as long as you flush it once or twice before beginning, you will be dealing with clean water only. (If it won't flush, see page 174.) You may find some rust and sediment in the tank.

The inner parts of a toilet are fairly simple. When someone flips the flush handle, a chain reaction of events starts. The handle lifts the trip lever, which in turn pulls a chain that lifts the tank flapper off the flush valve. (In older units, a lift rod raises a tank ball.) As water rushes down through the opening into the bowl, the reservoir of water and the waste in the bowl yield to gravity and pass through the toilet's trap, down through the closet bend, and out a drain line.

Inside the tank, the float (or in older systems the float ball) descends along with the outrushing water until, at a predetermined level, the shutoff rod is attached to trips the ballcock, which is a water supply valve. At the same time, the tank flapper settles back into the flush valve, stopping water from leaving the tank. The ballcock opens to shoot a new supply of water into the tank through a refill tube and into the bowl through the overflow tube. When the float rises to its filled position, the ballcock shuts the water off.

A wax ring seals the toilet bowl to a flange on the closet bend and keeps water from leaking out onto the floor. A spud gasket seals the tank to the bowl.

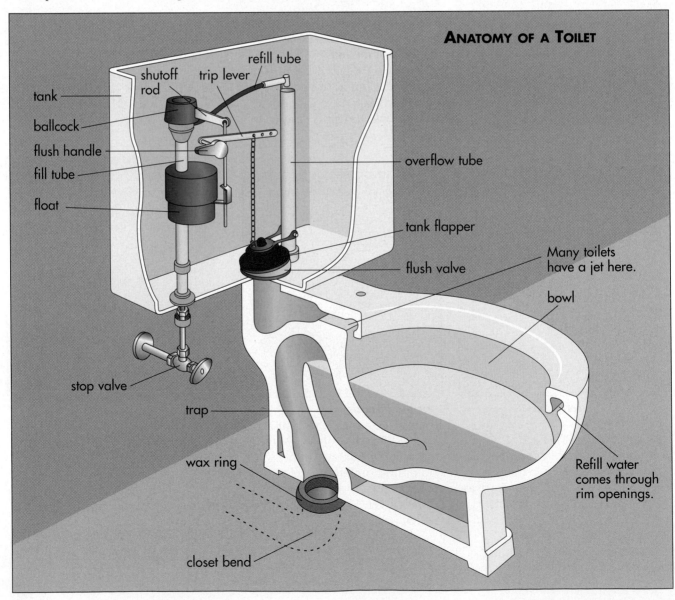

ANATOMY OF A TOILET

refill tube

shutoff rod

trip lever

tank

ballcock

flush handle

fill tube

float

overflow tube

tank flapper

flush valve

Many toilets have a jet here.

bowl

stop valve

trap

wax ring

Refill water comes through rim openings.

closet bend

TOILET REPAIR CHART

Symptom	Cause	Repair
Water continuously trickles or runs into tank and/or bowl (tank run-on).	Water level is too high.	Adjust trip lever chain, adjust water level in tank, or replace leaky float (see below).
	Flapper or tank ball isn't sealing properly.	Clean the flush valve under the flapper, or replace worn flapper.
	Ballcock is faulty.	Repair or replace ballcock.
Bowl overflows when flushed. Toilet flushes incompletely.	Trap or drain is partially clogged.	Run a toilet auger through the toilet (see page 174), or clear drain (see page 175).
	Trap or bowl is clogged.	
Tank leaks.	Water is spraying up against the lid.	Anchor the refill tube so it sprays into the overflow tube.
	Gasket between tank and bowl is faulty.	Replace the spud gasket.
	Tank is cracked.	Replace the tank.
Bowl leaks. Leak appears as a wet spot on the floor.	Wax ring is not sealing.	Pull up the toilet and replace the wax ring (see page 165).
	Bowl is cracked.	Replace the bowl.
Tank "sweats"—drops of water appear on the outside.	Condensation occurs due to difference in temperature between air and tank water.	Buy an insulation kit and install in the inside of the tank.

FIXING TANK RUN-ON

Most of a toilet's mechanical action goes on inside the flush tank, and that's where most common toilet problems develop. If water continually trickles or flows into the tank and/or bowl, start with the simplest diagnosis: The float may be rising too high, causing water to trickle down the overflow tube. If fixing that doesn't solve the problem, see if the chain is tangled or has fallen off. Check flapper and ballcock (see page 162).

YOU'LL NEED...

TIME: Five minutes to adjust the float; a half hour to adjust and clean the flush valve; one hour to replace a ballcock.
SKILLS: General mechanical aptitude.
TOOLS: Screwdriver and tongue-and-groove pliers.

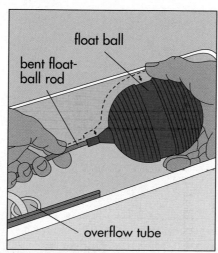

float ball
bent float-ball rod
overflow tube

Adjust the float ball.
Remove the tank lid, and look to see if the water level is too high—it should not be above the overflow tube. If it is, the water will shut off when you pull up on the float ball. Bend the rod slightly downward so the float ball sits a bit lower. With a float like the one shown on page 162, adjust the clip.

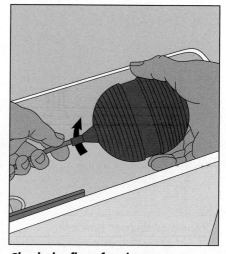

Check the float for damage.
A cracked float takes on water. When this happens, the ball won't rise enough to trip the ballcock. To check out this possibility, agitate the ball. A faulty ball will make a swishing sound. Unscrew a faulty float ball, and replace it with a new one.

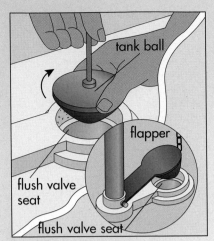

Fix a leaky flush valve seat.

If water continually trickles into the bowl, and perhaps even causes the toilet to weakly flush occasionally, the problem is probably in the flush valve. It has two parts: a flapper or a tank ball, and the flush valve seat into which the flapper or ball drops to seal the bottom of the tank while it fills. Often the seat simply needs cleaning.

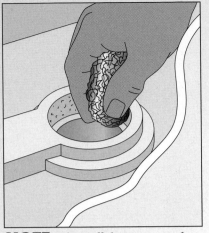

NOTE: *Shut off the water to the tank, and flush the toilet to get the water out.* Check the tank ball or flapper. If it has gunk on it, wipe it clean and smooth it using an abrasive pad. Once it's cleaned, feel the valve seat to see if it is pitted or corroded if it's metal. Flexible seats can be pried out and replaced. If you have a damaged metal seat, replace the entire flush valve.

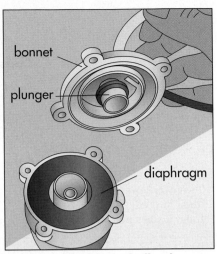

Repair a diaphragm ballcock.
NOTE: *Shut off the water and flush the toilet.* Remove the four screws on top of the ballcock, and lift off the bonnet. Clean out any deposits. Replace any worn parts, including the plunger. If a number of parts look worn, replace the entire ballcock.

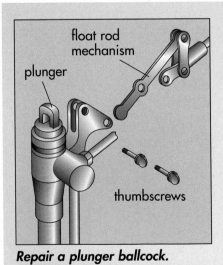

Repair a plunger ballcock.
NOTE: *Shut off the water and flush the toilet.* This is the oldest type of ballcock, and there are a number of parts that can go bad. You may need to replace it with either a diaphragm or float-cup ballcock. But first try cleaning and replacing the washers.

Remove the thumbscrews holding the float rod mechanism

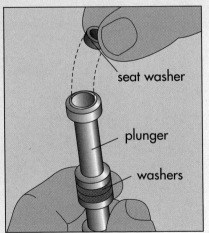

in place, then lift it out and set it aside. Remove the plunger by pulling up on it. Typically you'll find a seat washer as well as a couple of other washers. (In very old models, you may even find leather washers.) Remove and replace all of the washers, reassemble the mechanism, and turn the water back on.

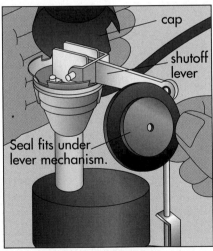

Repair a float-cup ballcock.
NOTE: *Shut off the water and flush the toilet.* This is the newest and the simplest design, and it rarely acts up. Pry off the cap, then remove the bonnet by lifting the shutoff lever on the float rod mechanism, pushing the mechanism down, and twisting counterclockwise firmly. Clean out any gunk, and replace the seal if it looks worn.

FIXING LEAKY TANKS AND BOWLS

Puddling of water on the floor near the toilet can be fixed in several ways. On a hot, humid day, condensation dripping from the cool outside of the tank or bowl could be substantial enough to make a puddle. You can simply live with it or install rigid-foam tank insulation.

A chronic leak probably means a faulty water supply connection, spud gasket, or wax ring. Often you simply need to tighten the hold-down bolts to solve the problem. A crack in a tank can sometimes be patched from the inside with silicone sealant. A cracked bowl should be replaced.

YOU'LL NEED...

TIME: About two hours to replace a spud gasket or a wax ring.
SKILLS: No special skills, but be careful not to crack the toilet.
TOOLS: Wrenches, screwdriver, and putty knife.

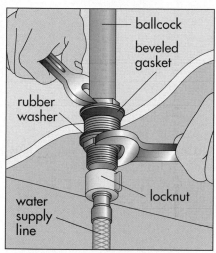

A leak at the water supply line
If the leak comes from where the water supply enters the tank, first tighten the locknut. If that doesn't work, shut off the water, flush the toilet, and sponge out the water that remains in the tank. Disconnect the water supply line, remove the locknut, and replace the old beveled gasket and rubber washer with new ones.

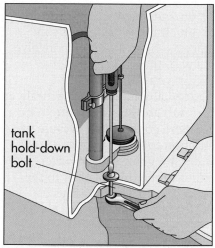

A leak between the tank and bowl
Extended use can cause the tank hold-down bolts to loosen enough to produce a leak at the spud gasket. Use a screwdriver and a wrench to tighten the bolts to squeeze the tank against the spud gasket. If the leak persists, shut off the water, flush, and sponge out any water. Detach the supply line, remove the hold-down bolts, lift out the tank, and replace the spud gasket (see page 200). Reassemble.

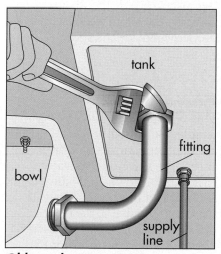

Older-style connections
With some old toilets, the tank connects to the bowl with a fitting. If leaks develop at either end of the fitting, tightening the nuts may stop the leak. If not, take the toilet apart and replace any worn parts from a plumbing supply source.

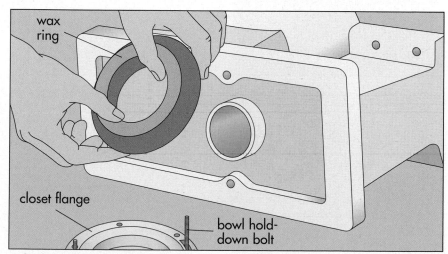

A leak at the base of the bowl
If the bowl is cracked, you'll have to replace it. If the bowl is sound, try gently tightening the hold-down nuts (see page 200). If that doesn't stop the leak, replace the wax ring. Begin by shutting off the water, flushing the toilet, and sponging out any remaining water.

Disconnect the water supply line, and remove the nuts on the hold-down bolts. Lift out the toilet. Scrape away the old wax ring and any old putty on the bottom of the bowl. Press a new wax ring in place according to the manufacturer's directions. Reinstall the toilet (see page 200).

REPAIRING TUB AND SHOWER CONTROLS

Tub and shower controls work much the same way as sink faucets, so repairing them involves many of the same operations, except you are working horizontally rather than vertically. Also tub and shower controls are a bit more complicated because in addition to mixing hot and cold water, they must divert water either to the tub spout or to the showerhead. The drawings on these pages show the inner workings of common types.

Sometimes the parts are hard to get at. You may have to chip away at tiles in order to get your tools to the shower control parts.

If a shower control body is damaged and needs to be replaced, look at the other side of the wall to see if you have an access panel. If so you may be able to work from behind and minimize damage to your shower wall. Usually replacing a shower control body means tearing up a shower wall and retiling.

YOU'LL NEED...

TIME: About two hours for most repairs, not including time spent looking for parts.
SKILLS: Basic plumbing skills and ability to work with tile.
TOOLS: Screwdriver, pliers, and wrenches.

Note: Be sure to shut off the supply stop valves, built-in shutoff valves, or the main water valve before making these repairs.

Two-handle control

The handles on these usually contain stems with washers. Each washer presses against a seat in order to shut the water off (see pages 149–158). To stop a drip, shut off the water, and remove the stem—you may have to use a special stem wrench or a deep socket, or chip away at the tiles to get at the packing nut. Replace the washer and the seat, if necessary, just as you would on a sink faucet (see page 160). If the diverter valve on the spout is not working properly, replace the spout.

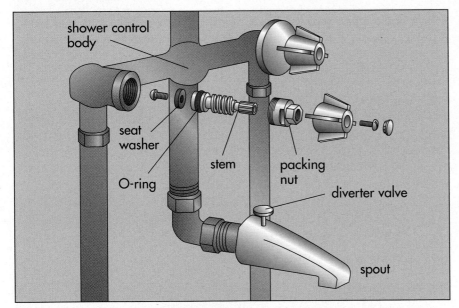

Three-handle control

This type is much like a two-handle control but it has a central handle that controls a diverter valve. The valve directs water either up or down—out the showerhead or out the spout. If the diverter valve sticks or if it does not completely divert water to either the showerhead or to the spout, shut off the water and remove the valve just as you would a regular stem (see page 160). Take it apart, clean it, and replace any washers or O-rings. Or, replace the whole stem with a new one.

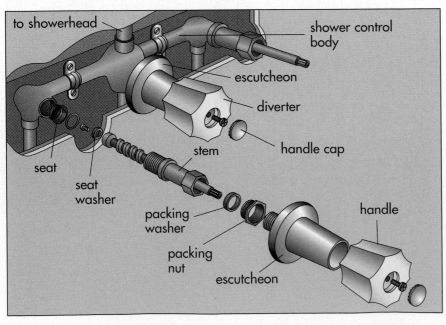

One-handle ball control

This type has seals and springs like ball-type sink faucets, so repairs are similar to those shown on pages 154–155. As the handle is raised, the ball rotates in such a way that its openings begin to align with the supply line ports, allowing water to pass through the ball and out the spout.

Impeded flow is usually the result of clogged orifices or worn seals. Shut the water off and remove the ball—a few ball controls have setscrews that you may have to remove to do this. Clean out the orifices, replace any worn rubber parts, and lubricate the new seals with heatproof grease.

While you have the faucet apart, check the ball for wear and corrosion; if you find either, replace the ball.

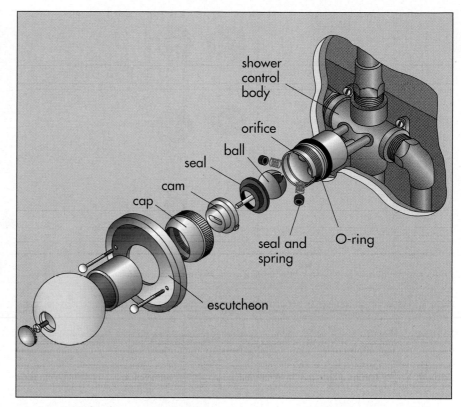

One-handle cartridge control

There are other configurations of one-handled cartridge controls besides the one shown here, so you may have to search out the location of your parts, such as the retaining clip. Parts are usually made of plastic; be careful not to crack them.

To repair a leak or limited flow, remove the handle, unscrew the retainer nut, and pull out the cartridge. Clean away any deposits and replace worn rubber or plastic parts. Lubricate all rubber parts with heatproof grease. Or simply replace the cartridge itself. When you remove the cartridge, be sure to note its original position and insert the new one the same way. If you don't, your hot and cold water will be reversed.

See pages 152–153 for more on repairing cartridge faucets.

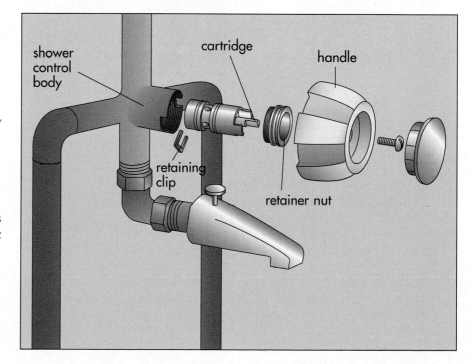

OPENING CLOGGED DRAINS

Sooner or later every homeowner encounters a clogged drain. If you hire a professional to clear it out, you will usually get a better price if you call someone who specializes in clearing drains rather than a general plumber. But it will still cost you plenty; a professional's time costs the same whether the job requires something highly specialized or something you could have done yourself.

Most clogs are not due to faulty plumbing but to the slow buildup of solids that sink drains aren't intended to cope with. Only toilets are plumbed to handle solid waste; sinks, tubs, and showers have drains designed to carry away water only. Hair, grease, soap, food scraps, and gunk will clog up a drain. With a few basic tools, you can clear most clogs and get the system flowing again.

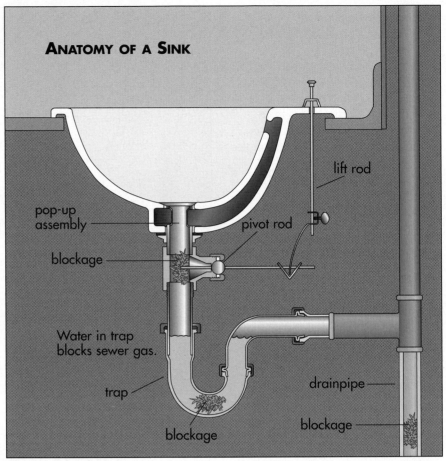

ANATOMY OF A SINK

lift rod

pop-up assembly

pivot rod

blockage

Water in trap blocks sewer gas.

trap

drainpipe

blockage

blockage

Where clogs happen
The slow buildup of soapy slime inside a drainpipe, a point of resistance such as a drain assembly, or a sharp bend in the drain can cause a clog. If a fixture is often clogged, install a strainer to keep solids from going down the drain. It will be well worth cleaning the strainer occasionally.

TOOLS TO USE

POWER AUGERS

■ For extra augering power, rent or buy a power auger or an augering attachment for a drill. The drill attachment is less expensive but not as sturdy as a power auger.

■ A high-quality tool will have a second cable that runs through the middle of the wound-wire augering cable. This keeps the auger cable from kinking, and it allows you to retrieve the auger cable if it should break. If your auger does not have this second cable and it breaks—a real possibility, especially if you are doing heavy-duty augering—you'll have a length of auger cable stuck in your pipe.

EXPERTS' INSIGHT

USING DRAIN CLEANERS

■ If your drain is completely stopped up and water is not moving through it at all, do not use a drain cleaner. It will not help the problem, and some types will actually harden if they cannot get through, making the clog worse. Drain cleaner can damage pipes, and it might splash you when you plunge or auger the drain.

■ If your drain is sluggish, use only nonacid drain cleaners (sodium hydroxide and copper sulfide are safe). Pour them in when the drain is sluggish, not when it is completely stopped. Regular use of a drain cleaner can keep the pipes clear of hair, soap, grease, and so on.

■ To maintain a smooth-flowing drain, every week or so run very hot water into the drain for a minute or two. This will clear away small amounts of grease and soap and keep them from building up.

USING SIMPLE UNCLOGGING METHODS

When a sink clogs up, first figure out where the blockage might be. It could be anywhere along the three main sections of a household drain system: in the fixture drain, in the drain stack that serves multiple fixtures, or in the main sewer line that carries waste out of the house (see page 139). Usually the problem will be close to a fixture because the drain pipe and trap near a fixture are narrower than the stack and main sewer lines they tie into. To verify that the clog is near the fixture, check other drains in your home. If more than one won't clear, something is stuck in a drain stack. If no drains work, the problem is farther down the line, probably in the main sewer line.

EXPERTS' INSIGHT

PLUNGING SINKS WITH MORE THAN ONE DRAIN

■ When plunging a double sink, it's best to have a helper block up one of the drain holes by pressing a wet rag firmly into it, while you plunge the other drain hole.

■ A dishwasher drains through a hose into the disposal or the sink plumbing (see page 236). Before plunging, use a C-clamp and two wood blocks to seal the drain hose and keep water from backing into the dishwasher.

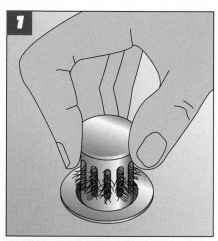

1. Clean the strainer.
Clearing a sink may involve nothing more than removing the strainer or stopper from the drain opening. Push the stopper up and pull away any soap, hair, food matter, or other debris that may clog the opening or be dangling down into the drain.

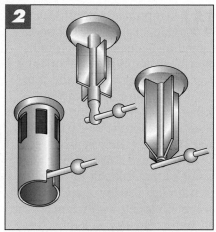

2. Detach the pop-up assembly.
The strainers in kitchen sinks and many bathroom sinks simply lift out. Others require a slight turn before they will come out. With some, you must pull out the pivot rod before the stopper will come out. If you want to auger the sink, you will have to remove the pivot rod (see below).

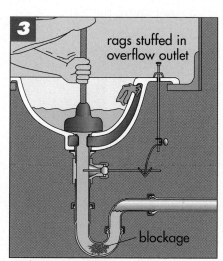

3. Plunge a sink.
A plunger uses water pressure to blast out obstructions and suction to bring stuff up. The plunger's rubber cup must seal tightly around the drain opening. Water in the sink helps create a seal; rubbing petroleum jelly on the plunger rim also helps. Stuff a rag into any openings, such as an overflow outlet. Push and pull rapidly with the plunger.

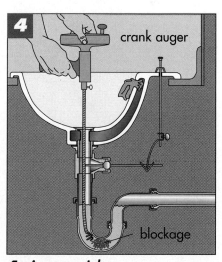

4. Auger a sink.
If plunging doesn't work, fit an auger down the drain. Cranking the auger handle rotates a stiff spring that bores through a stubborn blockage. Augering may push blockage through, or it may snag something so you can pull it up and out. If none of these techniques works, see page 172.

DISMANTLING FIXTURE TRAPS

When plunging doesn't clear a clog, or if you've dropped something valuable into a drain, your next step is to dismantle the trap. Before dismantling the trap, see if it has a nutlike clean-out fitting at its lowest point. If so, open it, and fit the auger into the hole. If there is no clean-out, don't be discouraged. Dismantling a trap is not all that difficult or time-consuming. Usually, the worst part of the job is getting a wrench into position if the trap is in an awkward place.

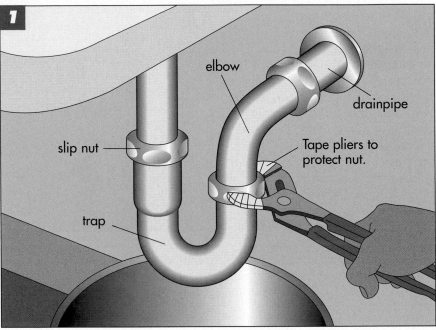

YOU'LL NEED...
TIME: About an hour to dismantle and reassemble a trap.
SKILLS: Beginner plumbing skills.
TOOLS: Tongue-and-groove pliers, Teflon tape or pipe joint compound, some extra washers, and a dishpan or bucket.

1. Open and drain the trap.
Turn off the faucet firmly. As an extra precaution, turn off the supply valves. Position a bucket to catch the water that will spill out when you remove the trap. Loosen the slip nuts that secure the trap. Protect the nuts from scratches by wrapping electrical tape around the jaws of your wrench or pliers. After a half-turn or so, the nuts can be unscrewed by hand.

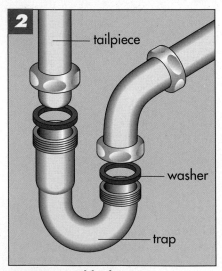

2. Disassemble the trap.
The joints of the trap have a nut and a flexible washer. Keep track of these by pushing them up the tailpiece and elbow. Dump out the water that sits in the trap.

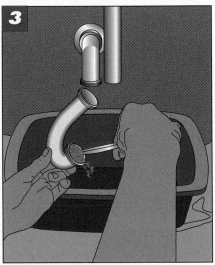

3. Clean out the trap.
Remove any gunk that has collected. Clean the inside of the trap with a small wire brush, or run a piece of cloth through it. Replace any washers that show signs of wear and slide the trap back into position.

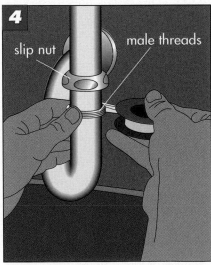

4. Reassemble.
Wrap the male threads with Teflon tape or brush on joint compound. Position trap, slide washers into place, and hand-tighten the slip nuts. Use an adjustable wrench for final tightening. Test for leaks by filling the bowl then removing the plug. Tighten slip nut if necessary.

REPLACING SINK STRAINERS

A slight leak under the sink at the tailpiece is likely the result of a poor seal between the strainer body and the sink. To check for this, plug the sink, fill the bowl, and look for drips. If water drips from where the strainer body joins the sink, disassemble the strainer and apply new putty. Leaks may also occur where the tailpiece joins the strainer body. If so, tighten the slip nut. If that does not solve the problem, replace the washer.

YOU'LL NEED...

TIME: About two hours to disassemble and reassemble a strainer.
SKILLS: Intermediate plumbing techniques.
TOOLS: Adjustable wrench (and possibly a spud wrench), putty knife, plumber's putty, and pipe joint compound or Teflon tape. You may need replacement parts.

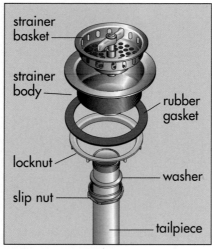

Sink strainer parts
Waste that would clog the drain is captured by the sink strainer. Its wide bowl is held snug against the sink bottom by the locknut. Putty and a rubber gasket sandwich the sink for a tight seal. The next important joint is where the strainer body meets the tailpiece. Here the seal is made watertight with a washer and a slip nut.

1. Remove the tailpiece.
Loosen the slip nut beneath the strainer body and the slip nut above the trap bend using an adjustable wrench. Finish unscrewing it by hand and remove the tailpiece.

2. Remove the locknut.
Removing the locknut can be difficult, especially if it is hard to get to. Consider purchasing a spud wrench, which is specially designed to fit on locknuts. Otherwise, place a screwdriver against a rib and tap gently with a hammer to loosen the nut.

3. Remove old putty.
Use a putty knife to scrape the old putty from the drain opening. Clean the opening thoroughly with a scouring pad soaked with paint thinner. If you will be reusing the strainer, clean off the flange of the strainer as well.

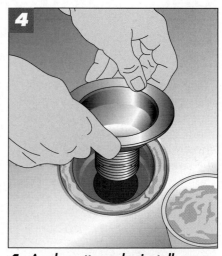

4. Apply putty and reinstall.
Make a rope of putty, and place it on the lip of the drain opening. Press the strainer into the opening. From under the sink, slip on the rubber gasket and the friction ring; screw on the locknut. Tighten the locknut until the strainer nests completely into the sink. Reinstall the tailpiece.

AUGERING TECHNIQUES

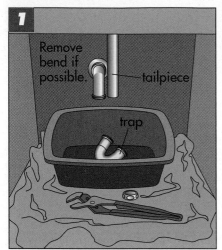

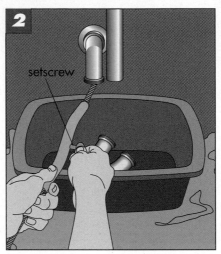

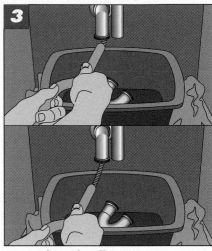

1. Set up a drop cloth and pan.
Be prepared for a mess. Place a drop cloth and a dishpan below the drain opening. Wearing gloves, remove the trap and elbow (see page 170) as well as the pipe leading to the wall. Loosen the setscrew of the auger, and push the auger cable in until you feel it meet resistance.

2. Set the screw and crank.
Give yourself 6 to 8 inches of cable to work with, and tighten the setscrew. Crank the auger handle clockwise, and push in until the auger moves forward. Once it is past an obstruction, like a bend in the pipe, you may be able to push the cable in without cranking.

3. Push and pull.
Augers can pass through soft obstructions such as soap clogs. Use a push-and-pull motion to ream out such clogs. If the auger comes to a place where it will not crank easily, pull it out; often the blockage will come out with it. Sometimes you can use the auger to clear the line by pushing the blockage through to a larger pipe.

UNCLOGGING SHOWERS

If a shower stall drains sluggishly, try filling the base with an inch of water and plunging. If the clogged shower drain does not respond to plunging, remove the strainer and attempt to clear the blockage with the two methods shown here. Begin by prying up the strainer with a screwdriver. (Some strainers may have a center screw. Remove it, then pry up.)

YOU'LL NEED...
TIME: Allow yourself two hours to try both methods.
SKILLS: Beginner plumbing skills.
TOOLS: Auger, garden hose attached to a spout, and rags.

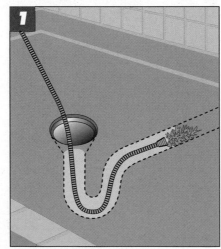

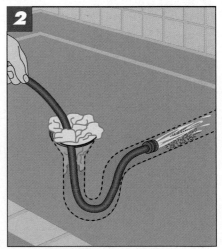

1. Run an auger.
Push an auger down the drain and through the trap. Push and pull to remove a soap clog. If the auger hits a blockage, pull out the auger. The blockage may come with it. If it doesn't, push the auger to try to force the clog into a larger pipe.

2. Push in a hose.
If all else fails, try forcing out the blockage with a hose. Stick it in as far as it will easily go and pack rags tightly around the hose at the drain opening. Hold everything in place and have a helper turn the water fully on and off a few times.

UNCLOGGING TUBS

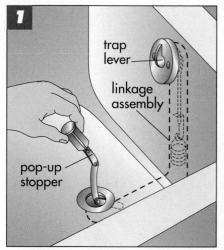

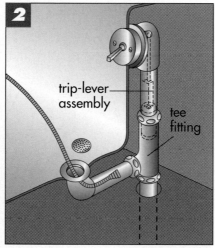

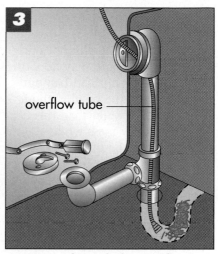

1. Plunge.
Try plunging first. If your tub has a pop-up stopper, remove it before plunging. Wiggle it to free the linkage assembly—the mechanism that connects the trap lever with the stopper mechanism. Before plunging, plug the overflow and run an inch or so of water in the tub to help the plunger seal.

2. Auger through the strainer.
If plunging doesn't work, thread in an auger. The tub will have a stopper or a trip-lever assembly like the one above. Pry up or unscrew the strainer to insert the auger. This method will reach only to the tee fitting. If the clog is farther down, you'll have to go through the overflow tube.

3. Auger through the overflow.
Remove the pop-up or trip-lever assembly by unscrewing the overflow plate and pulling out the parts (see page 238). Feed the auger down through the overflow tube and into the trap and beyond. If the auger goes in a long way and the stoppage remains, find a clean-out point on the main drain and auger there.

CLEANING DRUM TRAPS

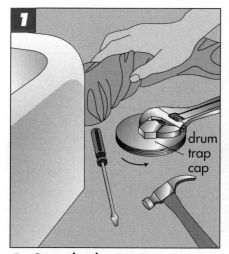

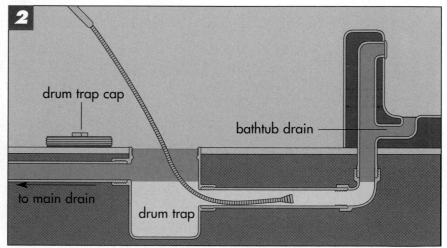

1. Open the drum trap.
Many older bathrooms have a removable metal cap on the floor, usually near the tub. This covers a drum trap. Before opening it, bail out the tub and remove standing water with rags or a large sponge.

2. Auger through the drum trap.
Removing the cap may be difficult. If a wrench does not do the trick, use a hammer and cold chisel or screwdriver. Damage the trap cap if necessary (it can be replaced easily), but don't hurt the threads on the trap. Open the trap slowly, watching for water to well up around the threads. If the trap is full, work the auger away from the tub toward the main drain. If the trap is only partially full (as shown), the obstruction is between the tub and the trap, so auger back and forth. Drum traps are no longer to code and should be replaced with a P-trap as shown on page 172.

UNCLOGGING TOILETS

When a toilet clogs, do not continue to flush it. Additional flushing will not push objects through and may flood the bathroom floor. Instead bail out the toilet until the bowl is about half full. More water than this can lead to a sloshy mess while plunging, but too little water will prevent the plunger from making a tight seal around the bowl's outlet. Add water to the toilet if necessary. Most toilet clogs occur because the toilet trap is blocked. If plunging and using a toilet auger do not clear things up, the waste-vent stack may be blocked.

CAUTION!
Never attempt to unclog a toilet with a chemical drain cleaner. Chances are, it won't do the job, and you'll be forced to plunge or auger through a strong solution that could burn your skin or eyes.

EXPERTS' INSIGHT

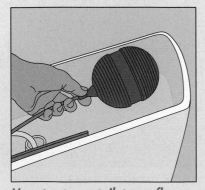

How to stop a toilet overflow
If the toilet begins to overflow, act fast. Remove everything atop the tank, and take off the lid. Pull the float up, and push down on the flapper at the tank bottom. The flush will stop.

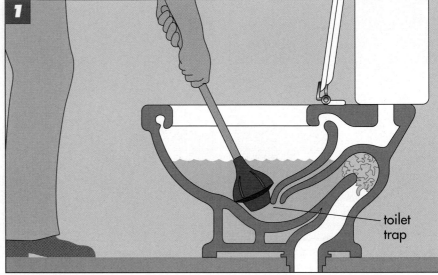

toilet trap

1. Plunge.
An ordinary plunger can clear a toilet, but the molded-cup type shown here generates stronger suction. Work up and down vigorously for about a dozen strokes, then quickly yank away the plunger.

If the water disappears with a glug, it's likely the plunging has succeeded. But don't flush yet. First pour in more water, until the bowl empties several times. If plunging doesn't work, the toilet will have to be augered.

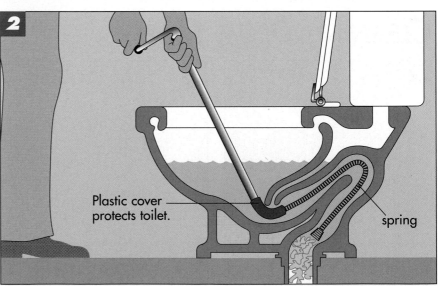

Plastic cover protects toilet.

spring

2. Use a closet auger.
A closet auger makes short work of most toilet stoppages. This specialized tool has a long handle with a plastic cover at the bend to protect your toilet from scratches. To operate the auger, pull the spring all the way up into the handle so the spring barely protrudes from the plastic protective cover. Insert the bit into the bowl outlet and crank. If you meet resistance, pull back slightly, wiggle the handle, and try again. A closet auger can grab and pull many blockages, but not solid objects such as toys. If you hear something other than the auger rattling around, remove the toilet to get at the item (see page 200).

CLEARING MAIN DRAINS AND SEWER LINES

If more than one of your fixtures is sluggish or clogged, or if plunging and augering fail to solve the problem, you may have a clogged drain or sewer line. Look for clean-outs, places where you can remove a large nut and slip in an auger.

Start with the highest clean-out you can find that is below the clogged fixture. If augering it does not work, continue working downward. Sometimes it proves best to go up on the roof and run an auger down through the vent stack. This job often warrants calling in a plumber or a drain-cleaning service, especially if the line is clogged with tree roots.

> ### CAUTION!
> Before removing any clean-out plug from a main drain line, have buckets on hand to catch the wastewater.

Auger a main drain.
Look for a clean-out near the bottom of your home's waste stack. Loosen the plug of the clean-out. If water flows out, the blockage is below. (If no water flows out, the blockage is holding the water above, so replace the

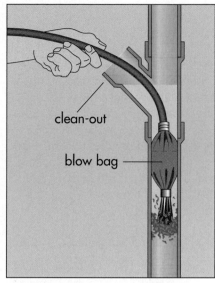

clean-out plug and auger from a higher point.) Insert the auger into the opening and run it back and forth several times (see page 172). Another solution is to use a blow bag. Once the blow bag is in place, run the water in the hose full force on and off several times.

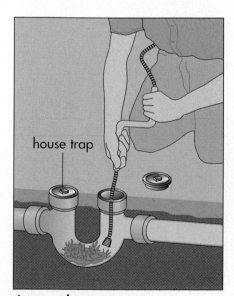

Auger a house trap.
If neither procedure works, move farther down the line. Some houses have a house trap near where the drain line leaves the house. Open one of the two plugs and thread in an auger. The blockage may be in the trap itself.

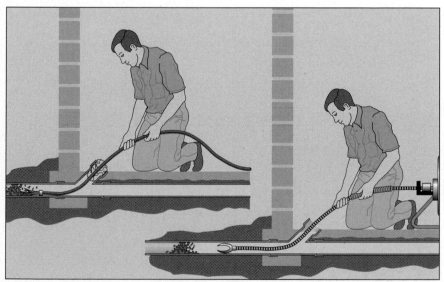

Clear a sewer line.
If the blockage still does not go away, the outdoor sewer line may be blocked. Often fine tree roots work their way into the line, creating a tough blockage that can only be removed with a heavy auger with a cutting bit.

First try feeding in a garden hose to push and flush out the obstruction. If that doesn't work, call in a professional or rent a heavy-duty power auger. Running one of these is a two-person job. Get a demonstration from the rental center on its use.

CLEANING SHOWERHEADS

*I*f your showerhead sprays unevenly, take it apart and clean it or replace it. If it leaks at the arm, or if it doesn't stay in position, tighten the retainer or collar nut. If that doesn't work, replace the O-ring—or replace the showerhead.

If you want to replace your showerhead, take the old one with you to your supplier to make sure you get one that will fit your pipe. You'll find a wide range of styles and features.

YOU'LL NEED...

TIME: About an hour for removal and scrubbing; overnight soaking for a thorough cleaning.
SKILLS: Basic plumbing skills.
TOOLS: Wrench, screwdriver, sharp-pointed tool or thin wire, and old toothbrush.

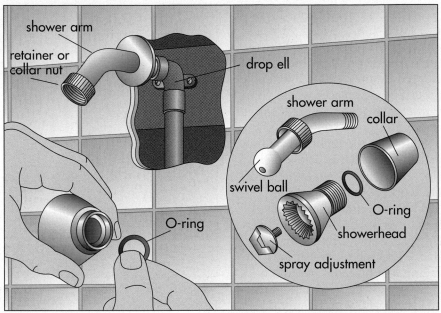

Two basic types
Newer showerheads simply screw onto the shower arm, the chromed pipe that extends from the wall. Older models require a shower arm with a ball-shaped end that acts as a swivel (see inset). In most cases you can switch to a newer style by replacing the shower arm. If you wish to replace the shower arm, remove it from the drop ell. Wrap Teflon tape around the male threads of the new shower arm before screwing it into place.

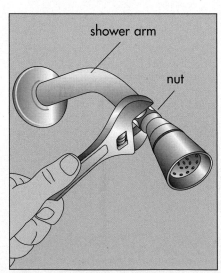

Removing a showerhead
This is a simple matter of unscrewing the nut at the shower arm. Take care not to mar the finish of the shower head or arm: Use a wrench rather than pliers. For an added precaution, cushion your wrench with a rag as you work.

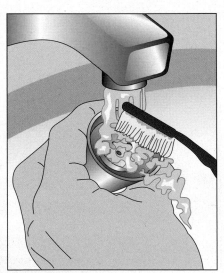

Clean the holes.
Shower heads often spray unevenly because the tiny holes have gotten clogged with mineral deposits. Use an old toothbrush to clean the head. Then run a sharp blast of water backward through the showerhead.

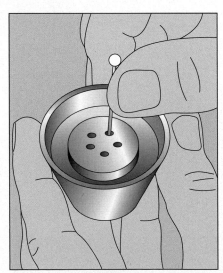

Dismantle and clean.
For a thorough cleaning, take the head apart, use a pin to poke out any mineral buildup or debris, and brush away all deposits. Then soak the parts in vinegar overnight to dissolve remaining mineral deposits. Reassemble and reinstall the showerhead.

ADVANCED PLUMBING

CHOOSING PIPE

The first step in choosing pipe is to find out which type of pipe you have in your home. It's often easiest to use the same type when adding on, but it's not mandatory. To change type, you must purchase special adapter fittings to switch from one material to another in the middle of a pipe run.

For supply lines—the pipes that carry pressurized water to your fixtures—the usual choices are copper and plastic. However if your home is old enough to have galvanized pipe and you need to install only a short run of pipe, it makes sense to continue with galvanized. In many localities, plastic supply pipe is not allowed. Keep in mind that you must learn how to solder (see pages 184–185) before you can install copper pipe.

When making final connections to a fixture or a faucet, usually it is easiest to install a flexible supply line. Use copper or plastic flexible tubing. Be careful to avoid kinks.

Plastic pipe—either PVC or ABS—is now used almost exclusively for drains. If you have old cast-iron, galvanized, or copper drain pipes, make the transition to plastic. It is much easier to install and less expensive.

Before you buy any pipe, check with the local building department to make sure you're using material approved for use in your area.

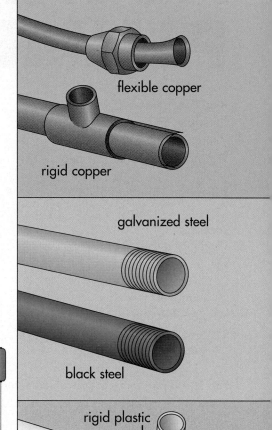

flexible copper

rigid copper

galvanized steel

black steel

rigid plastic supply

flexible plastic

plastic drain

EXPERTS' INSIGHT

GAS LINES

■ Gas lines are almost always made of black steel pipe. It has the same texture as galvanized pipe but not the shiny silver color. Black steel pipe is installed in the same way as galvanized pipe (see pages 190–191). Check for leaks by turning the gas on, pouring soapy water on all the joints, and looking for tiny bubbles.

■ Do not use copper pipe for long gas lines. A chemical reaction causes the inside of the pipe to flake, which can plug orifices and damage appliances. Contrary to some opinions, you can use galvanized pipe for gas, but it's more expensive.

MEASUREMENTS

THE MOST COMMON SIZES

Here are the pipe sizes commonly used in residential plumbing in North America. (To determine the size of your pipe, see page 182.)

■ Main water-supply line entering a house: ¾–1 inch.

■ Water-supply lines after the water heater usually are ½ inch, sometimes ¾ inch.

■ Gas lines are most often ¾ inch and sometimes are ½ inch.

■ Main drain pipes, called stacks, are 3 or 4 inches.

■ Kitchen, tub, and shower drains are almost always 1½ inches.

■ Bathroom sink drains are almost always 1¼ inches.

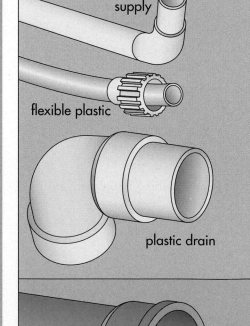

cast-iron

Material	Type	Uses	Features and Joining Techniques
Copper	Rigid	Hot and cold supply lines; rarely for DWV (drain-waste-vent) lines	Sold in 10' and 20' lengths. The most widely used pipe for supply lines. Lightweight and durable, though a bit expensive. Once the soldering technique is learned, you can cut it on the spot and put it together quickly. Type M is the thinnest, and is a good choice for home projects. Types L and K are used mainly in commercial projects.
	Flexible	Hot and cold supply lines, for short final runs to fixtures	Comes in easily bent 60' and 100' coils or by the foot. Can be soldered like rigid copper, but usually is connected with compression fittings.
Threaded Steel	Galvanized	Supply and occasionally DWV	Because it's cumbersome to work with and tends to build up lime deposits that constrict water flow, it is not used widely anymore. It takes expensive equipment to cut and thread it, so you must buy pre-cut pieces from your supplier. If you have a good selection of shorter pieces on hand, you can cut down on trips to the supplier.
	Black	Gas lines	Rusts readily, so it must not be used for water supply.
Plastic	ABS	DWV only	Black in color, in 10' or 20' lengths. Lightweight and easy to work with, you can cut it with an ordinary saw and cement it together with a special glue. Check local codes before using.
	PVC	Cold water supply and DWV	Cream-colored, blue-gray, or white, in 10' or 20' lengths. This has the same properties as ABS except that you must apply primer before cementing it. Do not mix PVC with ABS or interchange their cements.
	CPVC	Hot and cold supply lines	White, gray, or cream-colored, available in 10' lengths. Has the same properties as ABS and PVC.
	Flexible PB (polybutylene)	Hot and cold supply lines, usually for short runs	White or cream-colored, sold in 25' or 100' coils or by the foot. Flexible. Expensive and not widely used, it is joined with special fittings.
	Flexible PE (polyethylene)	Supply lines	Black-colored, sold in 25' or 100' coils or by the foot. Same properties as PB. Used for sprinkler systems.
Cast-Iron	Hub-and-Spigot	DWV	Cast-iron is extremely heavy and difficult to work with, so don't try to install any new pipes of this material. Hub-and-spigot is joined with oakum and molten lead.
	No-Hub	DWV	Joins with gaskets and clamps, but still is hard to work with. Make the transition to plastic.

CHOOSING THE RIGHT FITTING

The parts bins at a plumbing supplier contain hundreds of fittings that let you connect any pipe material in just about any way. To get the best pipe for your needs, familiarize yourself with the terms on this page. Items in bold are illustrated.

Supply fittings connect the pipes that bring water to fixtures and faucets. When changing direction in a supply run, use an **elbow (ell)**. The most common ones make 45- or 90-degree turns and have female threads on each end. A **street ell** has male and female connections to allow for insertion into another fitting. A reducing ell joins one size pipe to another. Use a **drop ell** to anchor the pipes to framing where they will protrude into a room.

Use **tees** wherever two runs intersect. A **reducing tee** lets you join pipes of different diameters; for example, adding a ½-inch branch to a ¾-inch main supply.

A **coupling** connects pipes end to end. **Reducing couplings** let you step down from one pipe diameter to a smaller one. Slip couplings (see page 216) function the same way as unions, joining sections of copper or plastic line. Use a **cap** to seal off a line.

A plastic-to-copper **transition fitting** is one of many transition fittings that connect one pipe material to another. (Do not make the transition from steel to copper without a special dielectric fitting, or the joint will corrode.)

In any run of threaded pipe, you'll need a **union** somewhere. This fitting compensates for the frustrating fact that you can't simultaneously turn a pipe into fittings at either end.

Nipples—lengths of pipe less than 12 inches long—are sold in standard sizes because short pieces are difficult to cut and thread.

Examine drainage fittings, and you'll see how they're designed to keep waste water flowing downhill. Sometimes called **sanitary fittings**, they have gentle curves rather than sharp angles, so waste will not get hung up.

Choose ¼ **bends** to make 90-degree turns, and ⅛ **bends** for 45 degrees. Also available are ⅕ bends for 72-degree turns, and ⅙ bends for 60 degrees. All types of bends also come in more gradual curves, known as **long-turn bends**, which make for a smoother flow.

Sanitary branches such as the **tee** and **cross** shown here, come in a variety of configurations that suit situations where two or more lines converge. These can be tricky to order, so make a sketch of your proposed drain lines, identifying all pipe sizes, and take it to your supplier when you order.

Toilet hookups require a **closet bend**, which connects to the main drain, and a **closet flange**, which fits onto the bend. The flange is anchored to the floor and anchors the toilet bowl. To connect a sink trap to the drainpipe, use a **trap adapter**. To make the transition from cast-iron drain to plastic drain, use a **no-hub adapter**.

EXPERTS' INSIGHT

ORDERING OR FINDING FITTINGS

When ordering materials, organize your description of a fitting in this way: first the size, then the material, and finally the type of fitting. You might, for example, ask or look for a ½-inch galvanized, 90-degree ell. With reducing fittings, the larger size comes first, then the smaller.

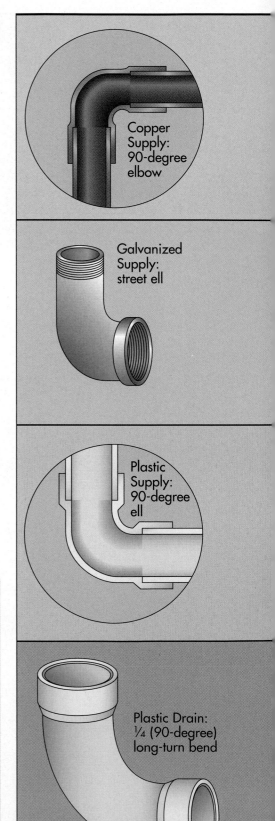

Copper Supply: 90-degree elbow

Galvanized Supply: street ell

Plastic Supply: 90-degree ell

Plastic Drain: ¼ (90-degree) long-turn bend

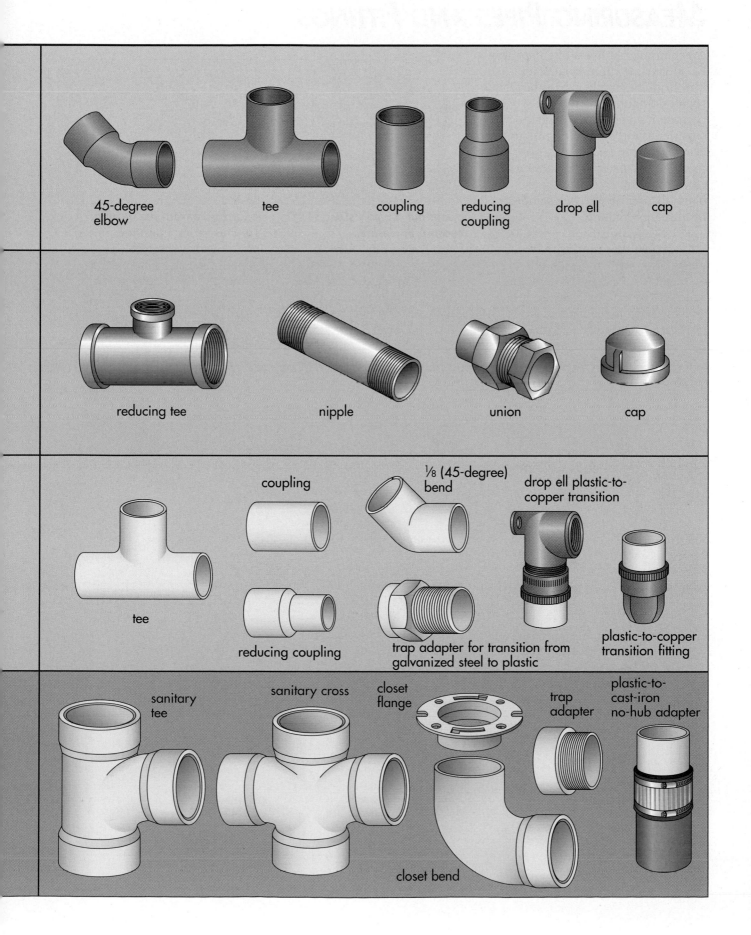

45-degree elbow

tee

coupling

reducing coupling

drop ell

cap

reducing tee

nipple

union

cap

coupling

1/8 (45-degree) bend

drop ell plastic-to-copper transition

tee

reducing coupling

trap adapter for transition from galvanized steel to plastic

plastic-to-copper transition fitting

sanitary tee

sanitary cross

closet flange

trap adapter

plastic-to-cast-iron no-hub adapter

closet bend

MEASURING PIPES AND FITTINGS

Beginning plumbers often spend more time running back and forth to their supplier than they spend doing the actual work because it takes practice and experience to be able to figure out everything you need ahead of time. The first step in becoming an efficient plumber is to learn to correctly identify the pipes and fittings a job requires.

Plumbing dimensions aren't always what they appear to be. A plastic pipe with a ⅞-inch outside diameter, for instance, is actually called a ½-inch pipe because it has a ½-inch inside diameter and pipes are usually sized according

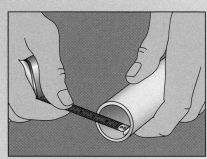

To find out a pipe's size, measure the inside...
If you have a pipe with an exposed end, simply measure the pipe's inside diameter and round off to the nearest ⅛ inch. Some manufacturers indicate the size on the fittings.

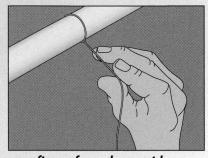

...or figure from the outside.
You also can determine pipe size by measuring its outside circumference. Wrap a string around the pipe, straighten it out, and measure it. Use the chart below to find the nominal size you'll need to order.

MEASUREMENTS: PIPE DIMENSIONS

Material	Inside Diameter (ID) Nominal Size	Approximate Outside Diameter (OD)	Approximate Circumference	Approximate Socket Depth
Copper	¼"	⅜"	1⅛"	⁵⁄₁₆"
	⅜"	½"	1½"	⅜"
	½"	⅝"	2"	½"
	¾"	⅞"	2¾"	¾"
	1"	1⅛"	3½"	¹⁵⁄₁₆"
	1¼"	1⅜"	4⁵⁄₁₆"	1"
	1½"	1⅝"	5⅛"	1⅛"
Threaded	⅜"	⅝"	2"	⅜"
	½"	¾"	2⅜"	½"
	¾"	1"	3⅛"	⁹⁄₁₆"
	1"	1¼"	4"	¹¹⁄₁₆"
	1¼"	1½"	4¾"	¹¹⁄₁₆"
	1½"	1¾"	5½"	¹¹⁄₁₆"
	2"	2¼"	7"	¾"
Plastic	½"	⅞"	2¾"	½"
	¾"	1⅛"	3½"	⅝"
	1"	1⅜"	4⁵⁄₁₆"	¾"
	1¼"	1⅝"	5⅛"	¹¹⁄₁₆"
	1½"	1⅞"	6"	¹¹⁄₁₆"
	2"	2⅜"	7½"	¾"
	3"	3⅜"	10½"	1½"
	4"	4⅜"	14"	1¾"
Cast-Iron	2"	2¼"	7"	2½"
	3"	3¼"	10⅛"	2¾"
	4"	4¼"	13⅜"	3"

to their inside diameter (ID). (See chart on page 182.) This dimension is also referred to as the nominal size, the size you ask for at a plumbing supplier.

If you are at all unsure about getting the right material, make things perfectly clear by specifying ID for most pipes. In a minority of cases—flexible copper lines, for example—pipe is ordered by using the outside diameter (OD).

If you can measure the inside dimension, you're home free. However often you won't have a way of measuring the inside of the pipe. Holding a ruler against a pipe will give you only a rough idea of the outside diameter. Instead, use a string or a set of calipers for a more exact measurement. Once you find the outside dimension, use the chart, opposite, to find the nominal size.

Fittings can be just as confusing. Their inside diameters must be large enough to fit over the pipe's outside diameter. A half-inch plastic elbow, for example, has an outside diameter of about 1¼ inches.

As a rule of thumb, the OD of copper is ⅛ inch greater than its ID, the nominal size. For plastic pipe, measure the OD and subtract ⅜ inch. For threaded and cast-iron, subtract ¼ inch.

Another mathematical pitfall for a beginning plumber is measuring the length of a pipe running from one fitting to the next. Pipes must fully extend into fixture and fitting sockets (see illustration, right), or the joint could leak. Socket depths vary from one pipe size and material to another, so you must account for the depth of each fitting's socket in the total length of pipe needed between fittings.

The only times you don't have to take socket depth into account are when you are using no-hub cast-iron pipes (see pages 178–179) or slip couplings with copper or plastic pipe (see page 216).

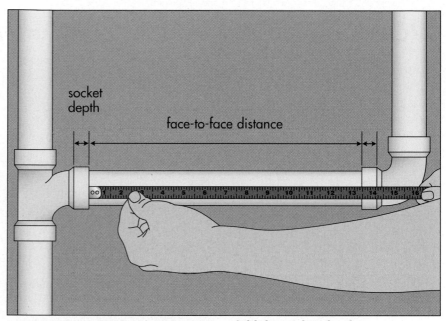

FULLY JOINED PIPE

copper

ID equals OD less ⅛"

socket depth

plastic

ID equals OD less ⅜"

threaded

ID equals OD less ¼"

Add the socket depths.

To figure the length of a pipe, first measure from face to face, as shown above. Next check the chart on page 182 for the socket depth of the material you're working with. Because pipes have fittings on both ends, multiply by 2, and add the face-to-face length.

Measure copper or plastic in place.

When working with copper or plastic—materials you can cut on the job—often the most accurate way of measuring is to insert the pipe into one fitting and mark the other end, rather than using a tape measure.

EXPERTS' INSIGHT

Don't leave the household high and dry while you drive back and forth to the plumbing supplier. When buying fittings, invest in a handful of caps (see page 181) in different sizes. That way, if you've misread a dimension—as even experienced plumbers do occasionally—you can cap off the line and turn the water on.

WORKING WITH RIGID COPPER PIPE

To solder rigid copper plumbing lines, you must learn a skill that is unlike other household repair skills. At first it may seem frustratingly slow. But once you get the knack, soldering will go faster than screwing together threaded pipe.

Sometimes soldering is called "sweating." Soldering works by using capillary action to flow molten solder into the fitting. Just as an ink blotter soaks up ink, a joint absorbs molten solder, making a watertight bond as strong as the pipe itself.

YOU'LL NEED...

TIME: With practice, an hour to connect five joints.
SKILLS: Soldering is a specialized skill that takes time to learn.
MATERIALS: Pipe and lead-free solder.
TOOLS: Tubing cutter or hacksaw, emery cloth, wire brush, flux brush, propane torch, and tongue-and-groove pliers.

EXPERTS' INSIGHT

ELIMINATING MOISTURE

If you are adding on to existing plumbing, there may be a little water inside the pipes. This must be dried up if you are to solder a tight joint.
■ Stuff in a piece of white bread (not the crust) just upstream of the connection. It will absorb the water and dissolve when the water is turned on.
■ Buy specially made waxy capsules that plug the line while you work. Later apply heat where the capsule lodged to melt the capsule away.

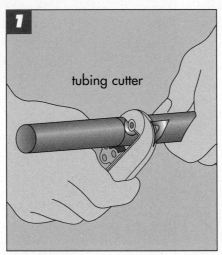

1. Cut the pipe.
Use a hacksaw or a tubing cutter (it makes cleaner cuts). Clamp the cutter onto the tubing, rotate a few revolutions, tighten, and rotate some more. Make hacksaw cuts in a miter box. Don't nick the metal—this could cause the connection to leak.

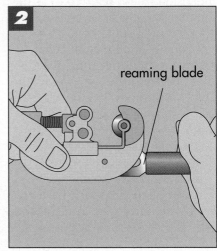

2. Remove burrs.
Remove any burrs on the inside of the pipe by inserting the reaming blade of the tubing cutter and twisting. If you don't have a tubing cutter, use a metal file.

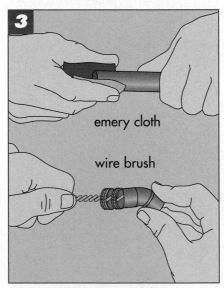

3. Polish the pipe and fitting.
Polish the outside of the pipe and the inside of the fitting with emery cloth or steel wool. This removes grease, dirt, and oxidation that could impede the flow of solder. Stop polishing when the metal is shiny. Avoid touching polished surfaces—oil from your fingers could interfere with the solder flow and cause a leak.

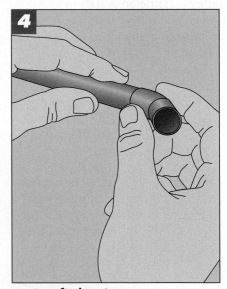

4. Dry-fit the pieces.
Dry-fit a number of pipe pieces and fittings to make sure they are the right length. If you have difficulty pushing pieces together, the pipe may have been squeezed out of shape during cutting. Cut a new piece. Once you are satisfied, take them apart and set them on a clean surface.

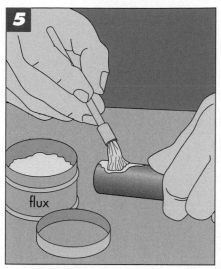

5. Apply flux.

Brush on a light, even coating of flux (also called soldering paste) to both surfaces. Flux retards oxidation when the copper is heated. As solder flows into the joint, the flux burns away. Use rosin- (not acid-) type flux for plumbing work.

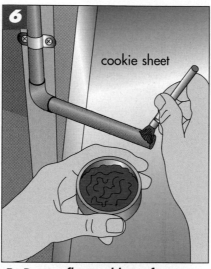

cookie sheet

6. Protect flammable surfaces.

If you're working near framing, paper-sheathed insulation, or other flammable materials, shield them from the propane torch flame with an old cookie sheet or a piece of sheet metal.

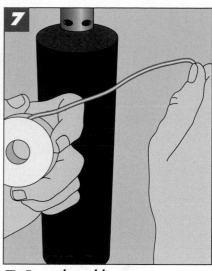

7. Form the solder.

Bend the solder so it's easy to work with but long enough to keep your fingers away from the flame. Unwind about 10 inches of solder, straighten it, and bend 2 inches at a 60-degree angle. Light the torch. Adjust the flame until the inner (blue) cone is about 2 inches long.

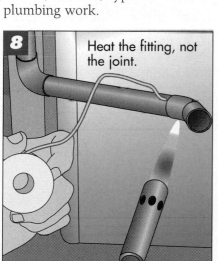

Heat the fitting, not the joint.

8. Assemble the connection.

Heat the middle of the fitting—not the joint—with the inner cone of the flame. Touch the solder to the joint. If it is hot enough, capillary action will pull solder into the joint. Remove the flame when solder drips from the pipe.

CAUTION!
Any gaps will leak. Be sure the joint has an even bead around its circumference to prevent leaks.

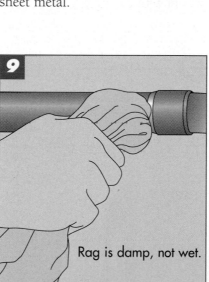

Rag is damp, not wet.

9. Wipe away excess.

For a neat, professional look, lightly brush the joint with a damp rag. Take care not to burn your fingers.

Most pros lay out an entire run of copper, first cutting and dry-fitting all of its components. After dry-fitting, they go back to clean, flux, and solder each joint.

10. Check for leaks.

Test the system by turning the water on. If you have a leak, there is no easy solution—it cannot be fixed while water is present. Shut off the water, drain the line, disassemble the joint (see page 186), and discard the old fitting. Dry the inside of the pipes. Polish the pipe end and the inside of the new fitting, apply flux, reassemble, and solder again.

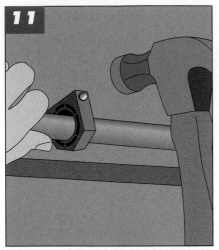

11. *Install pipe hangers.*
Copper supply lines need support at least every 6 feet. The plastic type of hanger pictured here is easy to install, helps quiet noisy pipes, and is slightly flexible so it doesn't damage the pipes.

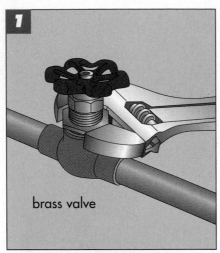

brass valve

1. *To install a brass valve, remove any heat-sensitive parts.*
A valve stem has rubber or plastic parts that will melt during soldering. Remove the stem with a wrench. Polish the pipe end and the inside of the fitting as you would with a copper joint.

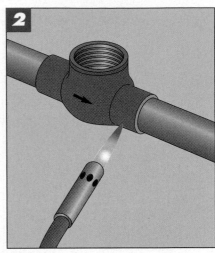

2. *Solder the joint.*
Fit the pieces together. (If the valve has an arrow, be sure it is pointing in the direction of water flow). Heat the body of the valve, moving the flame back and forth to heat both sides evenly. Brass requires more heating than copper. Apply solder as you would with a copper fitting (see page 185).

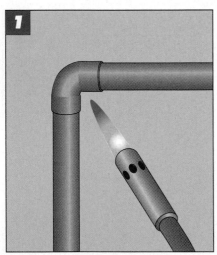

1. *To take apart soldered joints, heat the fitting.*
NOTE: *Shut off the water.* Drain the line by opening faucets above and below the run. Light a propane torch, set it so the inner (blue) cone of the flame is about 2 inches long, and heat the fitting. Point the flame at both sides of the fitting, but not directly at the soldered joint.

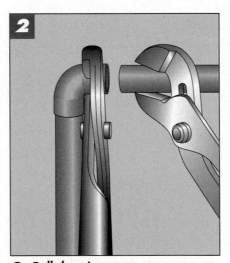

2. *Pull the pieces apart.*
While the pipe is hot, grasp the fitting and pipe with pliers, and pull the joint apart.

CAUTION!
Once the fitting is heated, you have only a few seconds to take the joint apart. Prepare a safe place to set the torch and have two pairs of pliers within easy reach. Work carefully—the pipes are very hot.

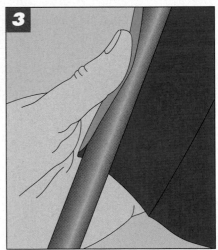

3. *Polish the pipe ends.*
To remove old solder, heat the pipe end with the torch and quickly wipe with a dry rag. Do this carefully—the pipe is very hot. Allow the pipe to cool and polish the end with emery cloth. Never reuse an old copper fitting—a watertight seal can only be made with a new fitting.

WORKING WITH FLEXIBLE COPPER TUBING

Flexible copper tubing is pliable enough to make all but the sharpest turns. This means you don't have to install a fitting every time you make a turn as you would with rigid pipe. In almost every case, you should connect flexible tubing to compression and flare fittings (see pages 188–189) rather than soldering them.

Do not use copper tubing for a gas line. Natural gas will cause the inside of the copper tube to flake, which can damage appliances.

YOU'LL NEED...

TIME: To bend and cut tubing for a short run, about 15 minutes.
SKILLS: Patience and care to keep from kinking tubing.
TOOLS: Tubing cutter and coil-spring tubing bender.

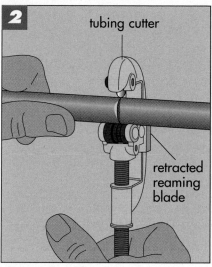

1. Uncoil the tubing.
Because flexible copper tubing is soft, always handle it gently. Uncoil tubing by straightening it out every few inches as you go. If the tubing comes in a box, grip the box and carefully pull the tubing upward.

tubing cutter

retracted reaming blade

2. Cut the tubing.
Cut flexible tubing with a tubing cutter or a hacksaw. Remove any burrs on the inside of the tubing by inserting the reaming blade of the tubing cutter and twisting (see page 184). Or use a metal file.

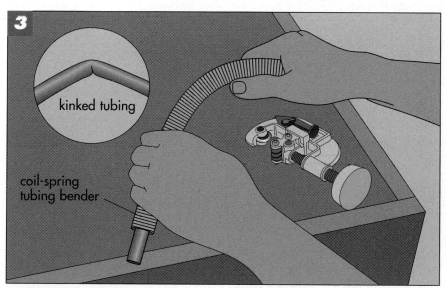

kinked tubing

coil-spring tubing bender

3. Bend the tubing.
Bend the flexible tubing in gradual, sweeping arcs or it will surprise you by suddenly kinking and you'll have to throw the piece away. Kinks seriously impede water flow and are almost impossible to reshape.

If you need to make a fairly tight turn, use a coil-spring tubing bender like the one shown here. Slide the bender to the point you need a tight bend and, with it in place, bend the tubing. With one of these tools, it is nearly impossible to kink the tubing.

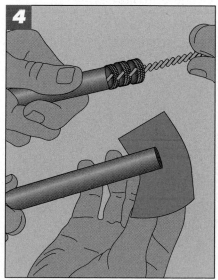

4. Polish the end.
Rub the end of the tubing lightly with emery cloth to remove dirt and grease. With compression or flare fittings, you don't need to polish as much as for a soldered joint. Join tubing by using compression fittings (see page 188) or flare fittings (see page 189), or by soldering (see pages 184–185).

USING COMPRESSION FITTINGS

*U*se compression fittings in places where you may need to take the run apart someday or where it is difficult to solder. One common location is on supply lines for a sink, which have compression fittings at both the stop valve and the faucet inlet. Flexible supply lines are an even easier way to make this connection (see page 187).

Compression fittings usually are used with flexible copper tubing, but may also be used with type-M rigid copper (see page 184). These fittings are not as strong as soldered joints so they should not be hidden inside walls.

YOU'LL NEED...

TIME: About 15 minutes to make a simple connection.
SKILLS: No special skills needed.
TOOLS: Two Crescent wrenches.

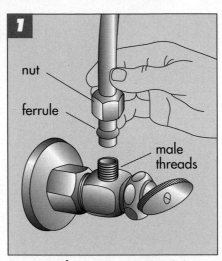

1. To make a compression joint, position the parts.
Bend the tubing into position (see page 187), and slip on the nut and the ferrule. The ferrule will not go on if the tubing end is bent or out of round. You may have to sand the tubing with emery cloth to get the ferrule to slide on. Smear pipe joint compound on the ferrule and the male threads of the fitting.

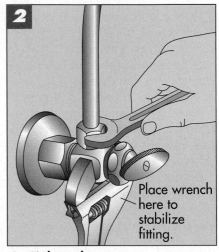

Place wrench here to stabilize fitting.

2. Tighten the nut.
Tighten the compression nut with a wrench, forcing the ferrule down into the tubing to secure and seal the connection. If the joint leaks when the water is turned on, tighten the nut a quarter turn at a time until the leak stops. Don't overtighten the joint—too much pressure can crush the tubing or crack the nut.

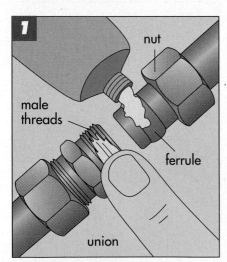

1. To join a compression union, position the parts.
Bend the tubing pieces into position (see page 187) and slip a nut and a ferrule onto each piece of tubing. Smear pipe joint compound on the ferrules and on the male threads of the union. Slide the pieces together, and hand-tighten the nuts.

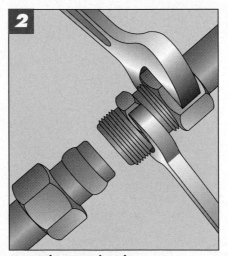

2. Tighten each side.
Place one wrench on the union. Use another wrench to tighten each side. Once snug, tighten about a half turn more. Turn on the water; if there is a leak, gently tighten more.

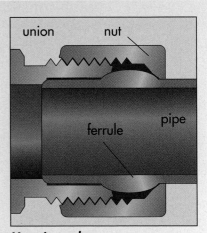

How it works
The compression nut forms a seal by squeezing the ferrule against the copper pipe. Because copper is a soft metal, the seal can be extremely tight. Still, use pipe joint compound to make sure the seal is watertight. Anchor or support the tubing within 2 feet of either side of the fitting.

USING FLARE FITTINGS

Flare fittings, like compression fittings, are useful in places where it's difficult to solder a joint. Do not hide flare fittings inside a wall. You can use flare fittings only with flexible copper tubing; they cannot be used on rigid pipe. Unlike compression fittings, this type of fitting requires a flaring tool. The two-piece tool reshapes the end of the copper tubing, "flaring" it to fit into a special flare fitting. If possible, make the flared connection first, then cut the tubing to length because sometimes tubing splits while being flared.

YOU'LL NEED...

TIME: About half an hour to join two pieces together in a union.
SKILLS: Use of the flaring tool is not difficult.
TOOLS: Flaring tool and adjustable wrenches.

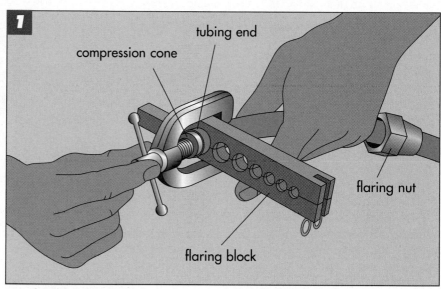

1. Flare the tubing ends.
Make sure the tubing is cut square across. Also remember to slip the flaring nut on before you flare the end of the tubing.

Choose the hole in the flaring block that matches the outside diameter of the tubing. Clamp the tool onto the tubing. Align the compression cone on the tubing's end and tighten the screw. As you turn the handle, the cone flares the tubing's end. Inspect your work carefully after removing the tubing from the flaring block. If the end has split, cut off the flared portion and repeat the process.

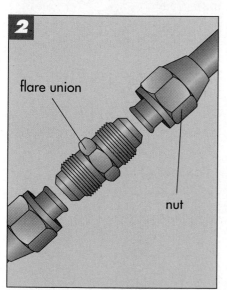

2. Assemble the pieces.
Seat the flare union against one of the flared ends of the tubing, slide the nut down, and hand-tighten. Do the same on the other side. No pipe joint compound is necessary.

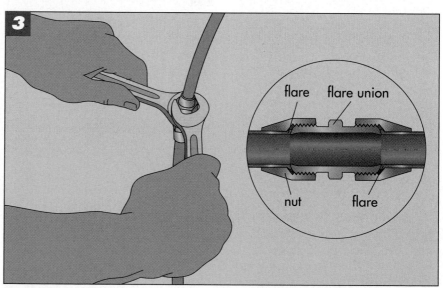

3. Tighten and test.
Place one wrench on the union and one on a nut. Don't over-tighten a flared joint. Once snug, give a half turn on each nut. Turn the water on and test. If the joint leaks, tighten it carefully until the leak stops. If tightening won't stop the leak, dismantle the joint and examine it to see if the tubing was cut squarely. Make sure that the nut was not cross-threaded on the fitting. Anchor or support the tubing within 2 feet of either side of the flare fitting.

REMOVING OLD THREADED PIPE

After your first experience with threaded pipe, you'll appreciate why this material is all but extinct in new installations. Cutting, threading, and assembling steel pipe requires muscle. Sometimes when you're trying to take old pipe apart, you'll swear it is welded together.

If your home was built before World War II, its supply pipes are likely to be threaded steel. This doesn't mean you have to use the same pipe for improvements or repairs. Special fittings let you break into a line and add copper or plastic (see pages 180–181).

Black threaded pipe, which lacks the shiny gray color of galvanized, is meant for gas only and is still commonly used. Do not use black pipe for water lines.

YOU'LL NEED...

TIME: To take apart four or five sections of pipe with fittings, about an hour.
SKILLS: Use of a pipe wrench and sometimes brute strength.
TOOLS: Two pipe wrenches, hacksaw, and maybe a propane torch.

EXPERTS' INSIGHT

SWITCHING MATERIALS

If you have good water pressure and can find no serious rust, there is no need to replace your threaded steel pipe with copper or plastic. But if water pressure is low, aerators fill up with rust, and leaks develop, it is time for a change. Replace the worst-looking pipes first. Don't cut holes into walls and get involved in a major refit unless it is absolutely necessary.

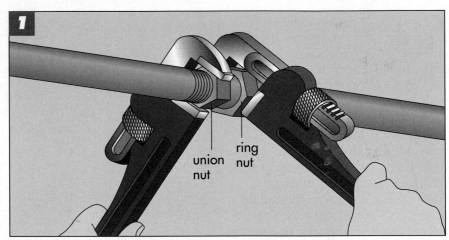

union nut · ring nut

1. Start at a union.
NOTE: *Shut off water, and drain the pipes.* Examine the way your pipes and fittings thread together and you'll see you can't simply begin unscrewing them anywhere. Somewhere in every pipe run is a union that allows you to unlock and dismantle the piping. To crack open a union, determine which of the smaller union nuts the ring nut is threaded onto. Use a wrench on the union nut to hold it stable. Put another wrench on the ring nut to turn it counterclockwise. Once it's unthreaded, you have the break you need and can start unscrewing pipes from fittings.

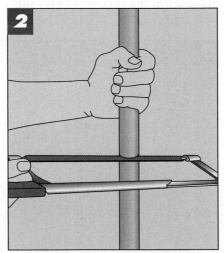

2. When necessary, cut the pipe.
If there is no union handy, cut a pipe with a hacksaw or a reciprocating saw fitted with a metal-cutting blade. When you reassemble this run you'll have to install a union using prethreaded nipples on either side of the union.

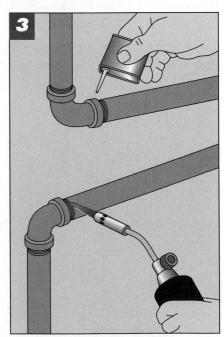

3. If the pipe won't budge
Stubborn joints may respond to penetrating oil, or try heating the fitting with a propane torch. Then use a larger pipe wrench, or slip a piece of 1¼-inch or 1½-inch pipe onto the handle of your wrench to increase its leverage.

INSTALLING THREADED PIPE

If you choose to work with threaded pipe, one difficulty is ending the run at the right place. Because the ends of the pipe are threaded, you can't just cut a piece to fit, as with copper or plastic. Purchase long pieces that take up most of the runs and have on hand plenty of couplings and a selection of nipples—or short lengths of pipe that are threaded on each end. You will then have a number of options to choose from to end the run in the right spot.

YOU'LL NEED...

TIME: In an hour you can assemble about four pipe lengths with fittings.
SKILLS: Pipe measuring and use of pipe wrench.
TOOLS: Tape measure and two pipe wrenches.

EXPERTS' INSIGHT

BOOSTING PRESSURE

■ Poor water pressure in an old house may be due to galvanized pipes that are clogged with rust. If the problem is limited to one fixture, try replacing a few of the pipes leading up to it. If the problem is throughout your house, call in a professional.

■ There are companies that specialize in unclogging galvanized pipe. They use a process that causes rust and corrosion to fall away from the inside of the pipe. The process can take months, will clog faucets, and may require repairing leaks found as gunk plugging holes is removed. In the end, however, water will flow through your pipes as if they were new.

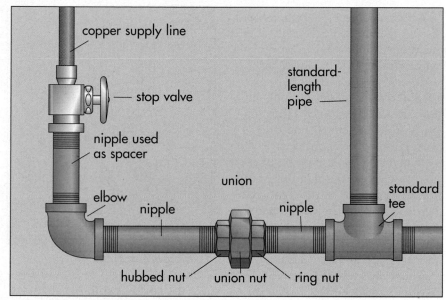

Assembling the parts

This typical installation combines standard-length pipes with joints and nipples to end up exactly at the right location. (For background on measuring pipe accurately, see pages 182–183.) Many plumbing suppliers have ready-cut galvanized pipe in standard sizes—12 inches, 48 inches, and so on—for less cost and delay than having pieces custom-cut. Try to use these pieces; if you make a mistake in measuring, you may not be allowed to return a custom-cut piece.

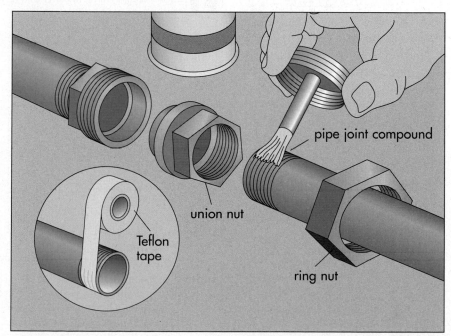

Joining the pieces

Before you thread a pipe and fitting together, seal the pipe threads using pipe joint compound or Teflon tape. Assemble the pipes and fittings one at a time, tightening each as you go. If your assembly requires a union, work from each end toward the union. The union is installed last. Support runs of threaded pipe at least every 6 feet.

WORKING WITH RIGID PLASTIC PIPE

Plastic plumbing is popular with do-it-yourselfers because it is inexpensive and easy to work with. Plastic pipe cuts with an ordinary hacksaw and goes together without special tools or techniques. You simply clean the burrs from the cut, prime, and then glue the parts together.

Installing plastic pipe requires attention to detail, planning ahead, and doing things in the right order. If you make a mistake, the parts cannot be disassembled. You'll have to cut out the faulty section, throw it out, and start again.

There are various types of plastic, so check local codes to make sure you are using the right type for your purpose. In most localities, either ABS or PVC are acceptable (sometimes even required) for drain lines. Many localities do not accept plastic pipe for supply lines; others specify CPVC. See pages 178–179 for types of plastic pipe. Do not mix ABS with PVC. Each expands at a different rate, and each uses a differently formulated cement. Plastic pipe is not as stiff as metal. Be sure to support horizontal runs every 4 to 5 feet.

> ### YOU'LL NEED...
> **TIME:** With practice you can cut and install about five fittings and five pieces of pipe in an hour.
> **SKILLS:** Measuring, cutting, and assembling components in a logical manner.
> **TOOLS:** Plastic pipe saw or hacksaw, miter box, tape measure, utility knife, pencil, emery cloth, and plastic tubing cutter for supply lines.

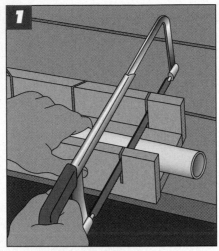

1. Measure and cut.
When measuring pipe for cutting, take the socket depth of the fitting into account (see page 183). Cut with any fine-tooth saw, using a miter box. Avoid diagonal cuts because they reduce the bonding area at the deepest part of the fitting's socket—the most critical part of the joint.

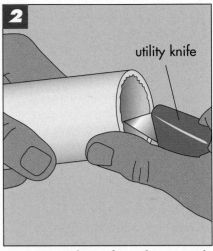

2. Remove burrs from the cut end.
After you've made the cut, use a knife or file to remove any burrs from the inside and outside of the cut end. Burrs can scrape away cement when the pipe is pushed into the fitting, seriously weakening the bond and resulting in leaks.

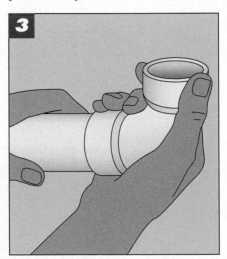

3. Test the fitting.
Dry-fit the connection. You should be able to push it in at least one-third of the way. If the pipe bottoms out and feels loose, try another fitting. Unlike copper components, plastic systems are designed with tapered walls on the inside of the socket so that the pipe makes contact well before the pipe reaches the socket shoulder.

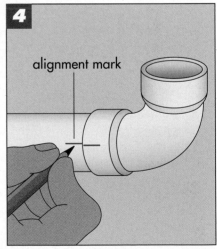

4. Mark for alignment.
When gluing the pieces together, you will have less than a minute to correctly position the pipe and fitting before the glue sets. Draw an alignment mark across the pipe and fitting of each joint. When you fit the pieces together, the mark will indicate exactly how to position the pipe and fitting.

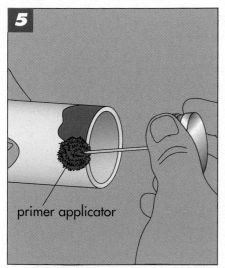

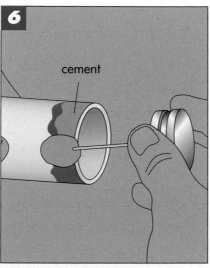

cement

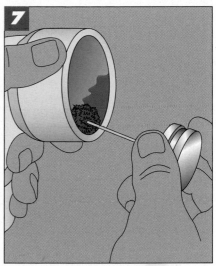

primer applicator

5. Clean and prime.
Wipe the inside of the fitting and the outside of the pipe end with a clean cloth. If you are working with PVC or CPVC (but not ABS), coat the outside of the pipe end with a special primer. Many inspectors require purple-colored primer so they can easily see that joints have been primed.

6. Apply cement to pipe.
Use the cement designed for the material you're working with. Immediately after you've primed, swab a smooth coating of cement onto the pipe end.

7. Prime and cement fitting.
Repeat the process on the inside of the fitting socket. Apply cement liberally, but don't let it puddle inside the fitting. Reapply a coating of cement to the pipe end.

EXPERTS' INSIGHT

DRY-FIT 3 OR 4 PIECES AHEAD
Whenever possible, cut and dry-fit three or four pieces before priming and gluing. That way, you can get things lined up ahead of time and avoid going back and forth between cans of primer and cement.

However, don't dry-fit more than four pieces, and don't dry-fit an entire section that must come out to an exact length. Plastic is not like copper pipe, which will solder together exactly the way it dry-fit. Once the cement is applied, plastic pipes may slide farther in than they did during the dry run, which can throw your measurements off as much as ¼ inch per fitting.

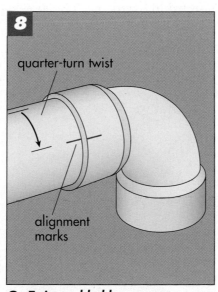

quarter-turn twist

alignment marks

8. Twist and hold.
Forcefully push the two together to ensure the pipe moves fully into the socket. Twist a quarter turn as you push to help spread the cement evenly. Complete the twist until your alignment marks come together. Hold the pipe and fitting together for about 20 seconds while they fuse into a single piece. Wipe away excess cement.

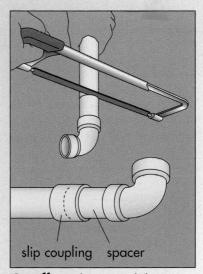

slip coupling   spacer

Cut off any incorrect joints.
If you misalign a connection, saw it off, making sure to cut squarely. Install a new fitting with a spacer and slip coupling as shown. Cemented joints are strong enough to handle after 15 minutes, but don't run water in the line for about two hours.

WORKING WITH FLEXIBLE PLASTIC TUBING

Flexible plastic tubing comes in long coils that you can snake through tight spots without using fittings. It kinks if bent too far, but doesn't kink as readily as flexible copper tubing. Codes in your area may disallow it entirely. If they do allow it, they will specify which type can be used in specific situations. PB (polybutylene) flexible plastic tubing can be used for hot and cold lines. Less expensive PE (polyethylene) tubing is affected by heat and therefore can only be used to carry cold water. Many communities allow PE use underground for wells and sprinkler systems.

Both types of plastic are easy to work with: Cut the tubing with a knife and join sections with clamps or compression fittings. Connect flexible plastic to other pipe materials with transition fittings that allow expansion and contraction. Support tubing every 32 inches and clamp it loosely. PE and PB can be punctured, so don't use either for exposed runs.

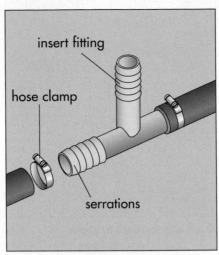

Connect PE flexible tubing with inserts and clamps.
Use insert fittings to connect PE tubing. Slip hose clamps over the ends of the tubing, push the tubing onto the insert, and tighten the clamp. Check that the serrations of the fittings are fully inserted in the tubing. The hose clamp should be positioned squarely on the serrations.

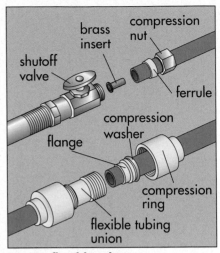

For PB flexible tubing, use compression fittings.
Attach PB to a metal shutoff valve with a compression nut and ferrule. A brass insert keeps the tubing from collapsing as the nut is tightened. Two sections of tubing can be joined by a flexible tubing union; tighten only by hand. Tees, ells, and other supply fittings fit every configuration.

YOU'LL NEED...
TIME: About two hours to connect three lengths.
SKILLS: No special skills needed.
TOOLS: Utility knife, pliers, and screwdriver.

TOOLS TO USE

PLASTIC TUBING CUTTER
If you have a lot of tubing to cut (as you will if you are installing a sprinkler system), buy a plastic tubing cutter. With this tool, you can snip the tubing easily.

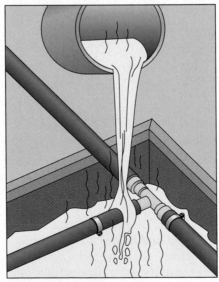

Soften PE with hot water.
Sometimes it takes a lot of muscle to push PE tubing over an insert fitting. Soak the tubing in hot water or pour hot water over the tubing to soften it so it slips on easily. Use the same technique to dismantle a stubborn connection.

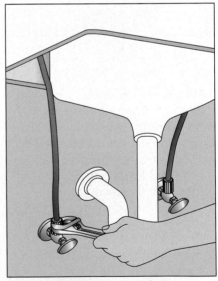

Use flexible plastic supplies.
PB makes an excellent choice for stop-to-fixture hookups, allowing you a margin of error during installation. Avoid bending it excessively or it may kink. Don't overtighten the nuts.

QUIETING NOISY PIPES

Sudden changes in water pressure can vibrate pipes, causing noise when the pipes hit the house's framing. This page tells you what causes the noise and what you can do about it.

First identify the type of noise and its cause. Water hammer is the most common pipe noise. It results from a sudden stop in the flow of water, as when you turn off a faucet. The abrupt halting of water flow creates a shock wave in the pipes, causing them to vibrate and hit against framing members.

A ticking noise can be traced to a hot water pipe that was cool, then suddenly is heated by water running through it. Pipe insulation dampens the noise. Chattering or moaning sounds may be caused by water pressure that is too high. If this is a persistent problem, call a professional to check the pressure.

YOU'LL NEED...

TIME: Several hours to install an air chamber or cushion pipes.
SKILLS: Connecting pipes.
TOOLS: Knife and hammer for pipe insulation; and basic plumbing tools for adding an air chamber.

EXPERTS' INSIGHT

DON'T BLAME PIPES

■ A machine-gun rattle, that annoying sound sometimes heard when you barely open a faucet, usually is caused by a defective seat washer.
■ Do pipes pound only when the dishwasher is running? An aging pump valve creates the same effect as a defective seat washer. Replace the pump.

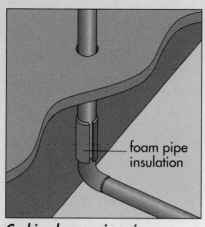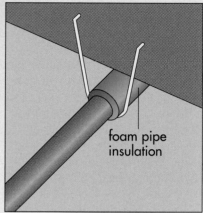

Cushion hammering pipes.
Have a helper do whatever it is that causes the noise while you search for the location of the noise. Once you find it, check to see if one of the pipes has been knocking up against or rubbing a joist. Cushion the pipe at the trouble spot with pieces of foam pipe insulation or use sound-insulating pipe hangers.

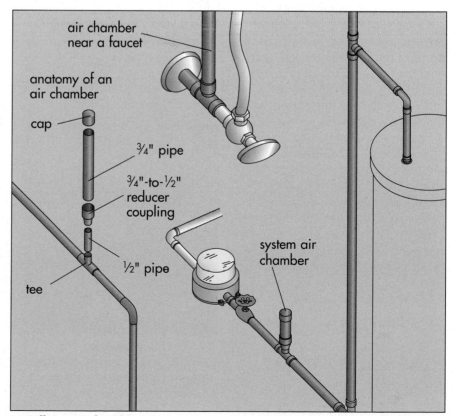

Install an air chamber.
To eliminate pipe noises, install air chambers at accessible points in your supply lines. These provide a pocket of air for water to bump against. Cut the pipe, install a tee (see pages 180–181), and solder the chamber in place. For galvanized pipe, cut the pipe and with nipples and a union, install a tee to which the chamber can be attached (see pages 180–181).

INSTALLING STOP VALVES

Any time a water line bursts, a faucet needs repair, or a toilet needs replacing, you'll be grateful to have a stop valve in the right place. Without one of these handy devices, you may have to shut off the water to the entire house simply to change a faucet washer. If you have an older home that lacks stop valves under sinks and toilets, plan to install them.

No matter what the material or size of your pipes, there's a stop valve made to order. With copper lines, use brass valves. Galvanized and plastic pipes take steel and plastic stop valves respectively. You can also use a transition fitting (see page 181) to change material just prior to the stop. If the valve will be in view, choose a chrome finish.

To make the connection from a stop valve to a sink or toilet, you can use flexible copper or plastic line. Or throw away the nut and ferrule that come with the valve and use the handy plastic or braided-metal flexible supply lines that simply screw on.

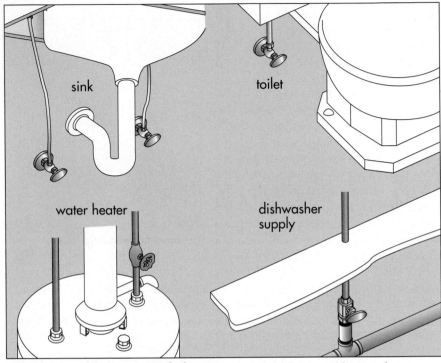

Where stop valves are needed
To determine your stop valve needs, simply take a look at your home's plumbing fixtures. Sinks, tubs, showers, and clothes washers should have one on both the hot and cold lines. Toilets and water heaters require one only on the cold water line, and dishwashers need one only on the hot line. The water meter should have a valve just inside the house from it.

YOU'LL NEED...

TIME: About two hours to cut a pipe, install a stop valve, and run flexible line to the fixture.
SKILLS: Cutting and connecting pipe.
TOOLS: Hacksaw, tongue-and-groove pliers, tubing cutter, Crescent wrench, and propane torch (for copper).

MEASUREMENTS

MATCH THE VALVE WITH THE FLEXIBLE LINE

Stop valves for sinks and toilets come with either ½- or ⅜-inch outlets. Make sure your flexible line is the same size.

1. Cut pipe or tubing.
In the example shown, the existing plumbing consists of galvanized pipe and flexible copper tubing. To make room for the stop valve, cut enough tubing off to make room for the valve. Leave enough supply to fit the compression fitting and allow for tightening the stop valve on the steel pipe.

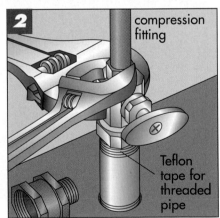

2. Install the valve.
One end of the stop valve is sized to fit regular pipe, and the other receives a compression-fitted flexible line. Wrap the galvanized pipe clockwise with Teflon tape and install the stop valve. Slip the copper line into the other end, and tighten the compression fitting, holding the stop valve in place with a second wrench.

TROUBLESHOOTING MAIN LINE VALVES

In an older home, the shutoff valves for your main line may be worn and rusted. If you have a shutoff up-line from the valve, you can easily shut off the water and replace the valve. But often there is none, so you may have to live with a less-than-perfect valve rather than paying the water company to shut off your water while you change valves.

If the shutoff valve handle breaks off in such a way that you cannot simply replace it, use pliers or a pipe wrench for those few times when you need to use the valve. However to make sure all household members can turn off the water in case of an emergency, replace the valve.

Another common problem is a slight leak from the packing nut when the valve is opened or closed. When this happens, try tightening the nut gently. Don't apply too much force when tightening or the valve may crack. If you still have a slow drip, place a bucket under it and watch for a day or two; sometimes the leak will stop on its own.

If you still have a leak, you will need to repack the valve. Shut the valve by turning it clockwise until it tightens. Unscrew the screw at the top and remove the handle. Loosen and remove the packing nut. Apply strand packing or a packing washer, and reinstall the packing nut.

You can purchase valves that screw onto galvanized pipe or brass adapters, or solder-on types for copper lines.

YOU'LL NEED...
TIME: About an hour.
SKILLS: No special skills needed.
TOOLS: Screwdriver, Crescent wrench, tongue-and-groove pliers, and pipe wrench.

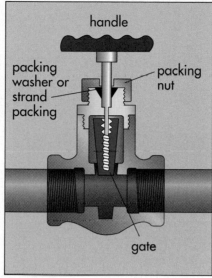

Gate valve
This style of valve, commonly found in older houses, is not as reliable as a globe or ball valve, so replace it if you have the opportunity. A wedge-shaped brass "gate" screws up and down to control water flow. If it does not fully stop water flow, it cannot be repaired. Repair a leak around the handle by replacing the packing washer or strand packing.

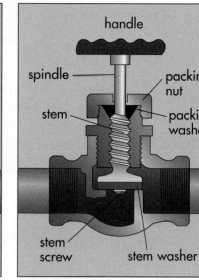

Globe valve
This works in much the same way as stem faucets (see page 148). It is more reliable and more easily repaired than a gate valve. If it does not fully stop water, and if you can shut off the flow prior to the valve, replace the stem washer. Repair a leak around the handle by replacing the packing washer.

EXPERTS' INSIGHT

AVOID CLOGGING FAUCETS
Over the years, old pipes build up rust, lime, and sediment deposits. Whenever you shut off water and turn it back on in a house with old galvanized pipe, you will cause these deposits to loosen and flow through the pipes. After turning off the main valve, take the time to remove aerators from the faucets and let the water run for a couple of minutes to flush out the gunk.

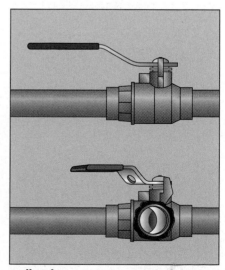

Ball valve
These cost more than the other valves but are more reliable and are easy to shut off quickly. The lever rotates a ball-like gate pierced by an opening. The gate pivots to control the flow of water.

REPLACING FAUCETS

Even though thousands of styles of faucets have been made and continue to be made, there are few variations in basic design. Bathroom faucets have pop-up drain assemblies, and kitchen faucets may have sprayers.

Also there are two possibilities for supply connections: Your faucet may have flexible copper supply inlets in the center of the unit, as shown at right, or its inlets may be located under the hot and cold handles, as seen in Step 2 on page 199.

YOU'LL NEED...

TIME: Several hours to remove an old faucet and install a new one.
SKILLS: No special skills needed, but it may be hard work getting the old faucet out.
TOOLS: Tongue-and-groove pliers, basin wrench, and screwdriver.

EXPERTS' INSIGHT

MAKING IT EASY

■ The hardest part of the job will be getting at the faucet from underneath. Remove any cabinet doors that may be in the way, hook up a work light, and make your work area as comfortable as possible.

■ If you are installing a sink at the same time as the faucet, attach the faucet to the sink before you install the sink.

■ Often even penetrating oil won't loosen old locknuts. You may have to knock the nut loose with a hammer and screwdriver.

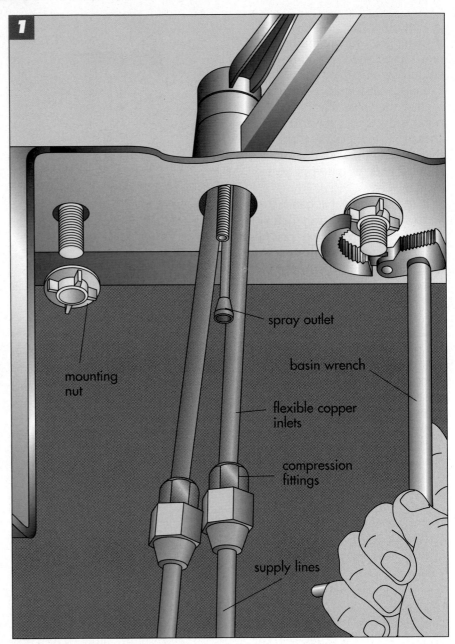

mounting nut

spray outlet

basin wrench

flexible copper inlets

compression fittings

supply lines

1. Remove the old fixture.
Note: *Shut off the water.*
(This illustration shows a faucet with flexible copper inlets.) Before you worm your way into the space below the sink, gather the tools you'll need, as well as some penetrating oil in case the mounting nuts are stuck. It helps to have someone around who can hand you tools as you work.

If your faucet has a sprayer, remove the nuts securing the hose to the faucet body and the spray head to the sink. Unhook the supply lines and move them out of the way. Use the basin wrench to loosen and remove the mounting nuts holding the faucet body to the sink.

Lift the faucet out from above. Scrape the sink top clean of old putty and mineral deposits.

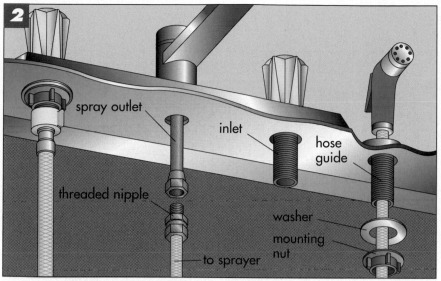

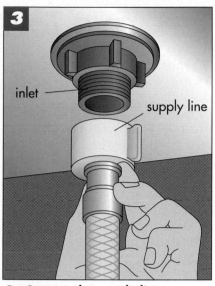

2. Attach the faucet to the sink.

(Here we show a faucet with inlets located under the handles.) Install a gasket or a rope of plumber's putty to the faucet or to the sink (see page 159). Set the faucet in place, making sure it is parallel to the backsplash. Crawl under the sink and have a helper hold the faucet in position while you work. Screw a washer and mounting nut onto each inlet and tighten with a basin wrench.

For faucets with sprayers, secure the hose guide to the sink with a washer and mounting nut. Thread the spray hose down through the hole in the guide. Apply pipe joint compound or Teflon tape to the threaded nipple at the end of the hose and secure it to the spray outlet of the faucet.

3. Connect the supply lines.

Brush the inlet threads with pipe joint compound or wrap them with Teflon tape. Twist the supply line nut onto the inlet and tighten first by hand, then with a basin wrench. Connect the other end of the supply line to the shutoff valve in the same way.

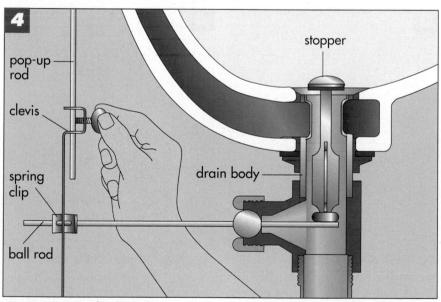

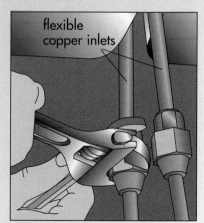

4. Connect and adjust the pop-up drain assembly.

For a bathroom faucet, insert the ball rod into the opening in the drain body and secure it with the nut provided. Slip the rod through the clevis strap and secure it with the spring clip. Lower the pop-up rod down through the hole near the rear of the faucet spout and through the holes at the upper end of the clevis strap. Lightly tighten the thumbscrew and adjust the rod so the stopper seals when the rod is pulled up. When the stopper opens and closes easily, tighten the thumbscrew further to secure the rod.

Connecting to flexible inlets

Some faucets use flexible copper inlets for the water supply. Connect supply lines to these lines in the same way as you would regular inlets, but take special care not to twist the copper tubes. If they become kinked, the faucet will be ruined. Use one wrench to hold, another to turn, as shown.

REPLACING TOILETS

Replacing a toilet is surprisingly easy. Problems arise only if the closet flange isn't at the floor surface (see below) or if the floor isn't level (shim the toilet after you set it on the hold-down bolts).

Toilets are ceramic, so work carefully. It is possible to crack a toilet if you bang it or screw down a nut too hard. Most toilets sold today have their drains centered 12 inches from the back wall. Measure yours from the wall to the hold-down bolt. If yours is centered 10 inches from the wall, either buy a 10-inch toilet or install a special offset closet flange. If you need to run supply and drain lines for a new installation, see pages 214–221.

YOU'LL NEED...

TIME: Three hours to remove an old toilet and install a new one.
SKILLS: No special skills needed—just work carefully.
TOOLS: Wrenches, screwdriver, hacksaw, tongue-and-groove pliers, and putty knife.

EXPERTS' INSIGHT

IF THE FLANGE IS LOW

If your bathroom has a new layer of flooring, the closet flange often will end up below the floor surface. In that case, a regular wax ring may not be thick enough to seal the toilet bowl to the flange. You can extend the ring upward with a special flange extender (see page 201) or double the wax ring. Place a wax ring without a plastic flange on the toilet, then place a flanged ring on top of it.

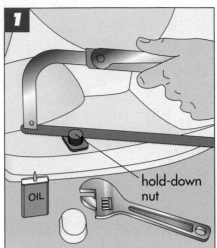

1. Remove the old toilet.
Note: *Shut off the water.*
Flush the toilet and remove remaining water with a sponge. Disconnect the water supply line and unscrew the hold-down nuts. Often these are rusted tight. If penetrating oil does not loosen them, cut the nuts with a hacksaw. Lift the toilet out.

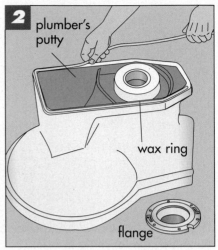

2. Prepare the new toilet bowl.
Carefully remove the new toilet bowl from its container and turn it upside down on a cushioned surface, such as a throw rug or folded drop cloth. Run a rope of plumber's putty around the perimeter of the bowl's base and fit a wax ring (sold separately) over the outlet opening.

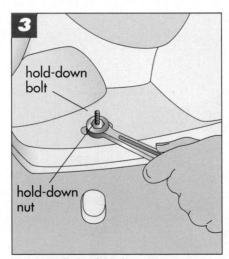

3. Install the bowl.
Return the bowl to its upright position and gently set it in place atop the closet flange. Make sure the hold-down bolts align with the holes in the base. Press down on the bowl with both hands and align it. Slip a metal washer and a nut over each bolt and tighten slowly. Don't overtighten or you could crack the bowl. Set caps on.

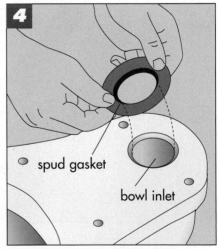

4. You're ready for the tank.
First lay the spud gasket, beveled side down, over the bowl inlet opening. This forms the seal between the tank and the bowl. Or slip the spud gasket onto the threaded tailpiece located at the bottom of the tank if you have older-style connectors.

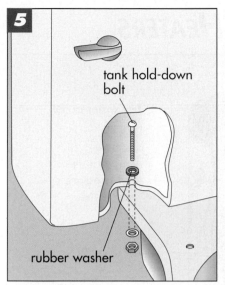

5. Install the tank.

Gently lower the tank onto the bowl, aligning the tank holes with those toward the rear of the bowl. Secure the tank to the bowl with the hold-down bolts, washers, and nuts provided with the toilet. Be sure that the rubber washer goes inside the tank under the bolt.

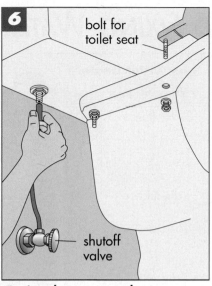

6. Attach water supply.

Complete the installation by hooking up the water supply line. The easiest way is to use a flexible plastic or chrome-braided supply line. Or use chrome-finished flexible copper tubing and compression fittings (see page 188).

WATER-SAVING TOILETS

In most localities, toilets that use only 1.6 gallons of water are required for new installations. These save money by reducing water consumption, but they do not flush strongly. They differ from older models by having a smaller tank or a mechanism that restricts the amount of water in the tank.

Don't buy a new toilet simply to save money in water use. Reduce an old toilet's consumption by setting a brick into the tank or by bending the float ball's rod so the ball sits lower in the tank. Most people don't mind the reduced flushing power of new models. If it is a problem for you, get a pressure-assisted toilet.

1. Install a closet flange extender.

If your floor surface is more than half an inch above the closet flange (as will happen when you install new tile), you must extend the flange so it's flush with the floor. A closet flange extender with flexible gaskets and a plastic extender ring make up the difference. First clean off old wax, insert new bolts, and slip on a flexible gasket and the extender ring.

2. Make a waxless seal.

The closet flange extender should now fit flush with the surface of your new flooring. (If it does not, add an additional extender ring.) Add the second flexible gasket. This gasket takes the place of the wax ring. Most kits also include handy plastic shims for leveling the toilet once it is placed on the hold-down bolts. See page 200 for completing the bowl installation.

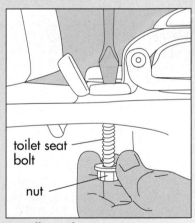

Install a toilet seat.

To remove an old toilet seat, lower the seat and cover and pry up the little lids that cover the toilet seat bolts. Hold each nut from below, unscrew each bolt, and lift out the seat.

Clean out the area around the bolt holes and install the new seat by aligning the seat with the holes and installing the bolts. Screw nuts onto the bolts and tighten the bolts just enough to firmly hold the seat.

MAINTAINING AND FIXING WATER HEATERS

Water heaters are little more than giant insulated water bottles with heaters. As hot water is used, cold water enters through a dip tube. This lowers the water temperature inside the tank, causing a thermostat to call for heat. In gas units, burners beneath the water tank kick in and continue heating the water until the desired temperature is reached. Heating elements perform the same function in electric water heaters. Most water heater problems are the result of sediment buildup or rust. You can help prevent this by opening the drain valve every few months and flushing out a few gallons of water. This purges rust and mineral buildup from the heater.

You'll Need...

Time: Allow two hours for inspection and minor repairs.
Skills: No special skills needed.
Tools: Crescent wrench and tongue-and-groove pliers.

MEASUREMENTS

Vital Numbers

The nameplate on the outside of your water heater gives the unit's vital statistics. Look for:

■ **Tank Capacity:** The more gallons it holds, the less chance you'll run out of hot water during a shower. A 40-gallon tank suits most households.

■ **R-Value:** The better insulated the unit is, the more efficient it will be. If yours has an R-value of less than 7, wrap the tank with insulation.

■ **Installation Clearances:** This tells you how much room you must leave between the unit and any combustible materials.

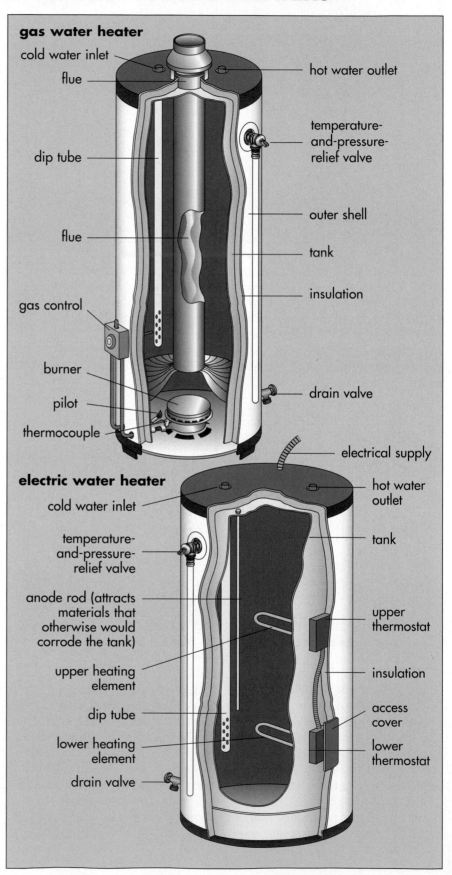

gas water heater

cold water inlet
flue
dip tube
flue
gas control
burner
pilot
thermocouple

hot water outlet
temperature-and-pressure-relief valve
outer shell
tank
insulation
drain valve

electric water heater

electrical supply

cold water inlet
temperature-and-pressure-relief valve
anode rod (attracts materials that otherwise would corrode the tank)
upper heating element
dip tube
lower heating element
drain valve

hot water outlet
tank
upper thermostat
insulation
access cover
lower thermostat

WATER HEATER REPAIR CHART

Symptom	Cause	Repair
No hot water.	No power to the heater (electric). Pilot light out (gas).	Check circuit breaker or fuse (electric). Relight pilot; replace thermocouple if pilot does not stay lit.
Water not hot enough.	Upper element burned out (electric).	Replace upper element.
Not enough hot water—hot water runs out quickly.	Thermostat set too low. Hot water must travel a long way to get to faucets. Sediment buildup in tank. Lower element burned out (electric). Burner blocked by dirt (gas). Leaking faucets. Tank not large enough for demand.	Turn thermostat up. Insulate hot water pipes (see page 144). Drain and refill tank. Replace lower element. Clean burner, or call gas company. Repair faucets. Replace with a larger tank.
Tank makes noise.	Sediment in tank.	Drain and refill tank.
Leak from temperature-and-pressure-relief valve.	Thermostat set too high. Defective temperature-and-pressure-relief valve.	Lower thermostat setting. Replace valve.
Leak around tank base.	Tank corrosion has created a leak.	Replace water heater.

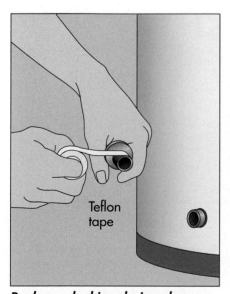

Replace a leaking drain valve.
If your water heater's drain valve leaks, shut off the cold water stop valve, shut off the gas or the electrical current, and drain the water heater. Unscrew the faulty valve. Apply Teflon tape or pipe joint compound to the male threads of a new valve, and install. Fill tank, and restore power or gas.

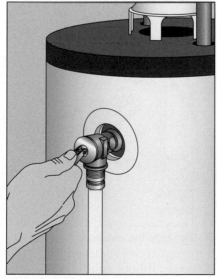

Test a relief valve.
Either on top or high on the side of the water heater, you'll find a relief valve that opens if the temperature or pressure in the tank gets too high (thus, it is called a "T-and-P-relief valve"). Test it once a year by pulling on the handle; water should rush out of the pipe it is attached to.

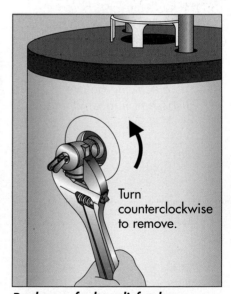

Replace a faulty relief valve.
If no water comes out, replace the valve. Shut off the cold water, turn off power or gas to the unit, and drain some of the water. Remove the attached drainpipe and the valve. Apply Teflon tape or pipe joint compound to the male threads when you install the new valve.

REPAIRING ELECTRIC WATER HEATERS

If you are not getting enough hot water, make sure the thermostat is set correctly. Also drain the heater if you suspect it is filled with sediment. If you have no hot water, check for power to the unit. If none of these measures solves the problem, you need to replace the thermostats and heating elements. To determine which thermostat and element to replace, see Experts' Insight below.

YOU'LL NEED...

TIME: About two hours.
SKILLS: Making electrical connections.
TOOLS: Screwdriver, tongue-and-groove pliers, neon circuit tester.

CAUTION!

DANGER! HIGH VOLTAGE! Electric water heaters use 240-volt current, twice the voltage in other receptacles. Be sure to remove the fuse or shut off the breaker at the service panel. Test wires for electricity before disassembling anything.

EXPERTS' INSIGHT

WHICH TO REPLACE?

Electric water heaters have two thermostats and heating elements (see page 202). To find out which pair is defective, turn on a hot water faucet. If the water gets warm but not hot, the upper thermostat and element are the culprits and should be replaced. If the water is hot for awhile then goes cold, replace the lower element and thermostat.

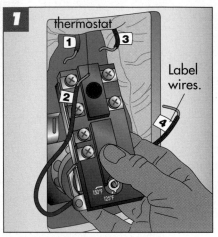

1. Remove the thermostat.
Note: *Shut off the power, shut off the water to the heater, and drain the heater.* Remove the cover plate and use a neon circuit tester to make sure the power is off. Drain the water heater (see page 206). Push aside insulation, label and disconnect the wires, and remove the thermostat.

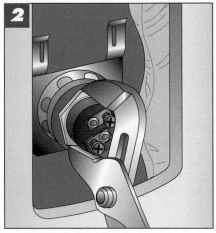

2. Remove the element.
Use tongue-and-groove pliers to unscrew the element, then pull it out. Remove the gasket if there is one. Take the old element and thermostat with you to your supplier to make sure you get the correct replacement.

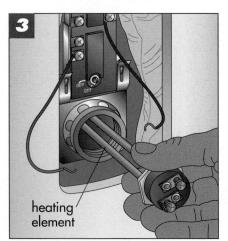

3. Replace the element.
If the replacement element has a gasket, coat both sides of the gasket with pipe joint compound and then slide the gasket onto the new element. Slide the element in and screw it in place. Tighten with tongue-and-groove pliers.

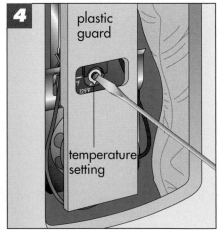

4. Install, set the thermostat.
Slide the new thermostat into place and reconnect the wires, using your labels as guides. Snap in the plastic guard. Use a screwdriver to set the thermostat. Press the red reset button on the thermostat. Make sure the drain valve is closed and turn on the shutoff valve to fill the tank. When water flows to your hot water faucets, turn off the faucets and restore electrical power.

REPAIRING GAS WATER HEATERS

If you suddenly lose hot water, or if your unit is not heating water efficiently, remove the access panel at the bottom of your water heater and check the pilot light. If it's not burning, relight it according to directions printed on the unit. If it won't relight, you need a new thermocouple. If you have yellow rather than blue flame, you need to replace the thermocouple and/or clean the burner. If you smell smoke or fumes, check your flue immediately.

YOU'LL NEED...

TIME: An hour or two for any of the operations on this page.
SKILLS: Handling compression fittings on gas tubes.
TOOLS: Wrench or pliers, thin wire, small wire brush, and vacuum cleaner.

EXPERTS' INSIGHT

REGULAR MAINTENANCE FOR YOUR GAS WATER HEATER

■ To avoid the dangerous buildup of fumes from a faulty flue, check your flue at least once a year. Be sure it is efficiently pulling fumes out of your house (see Step 4). To dismantle the flue to check for debris, see page 206.

■ Once a year, or at least whenever you replace the thermocouple, clean the burner, even if it shows no symptoms of being clogged. A clean burner will burn more efficiently and help your water heater last longer.

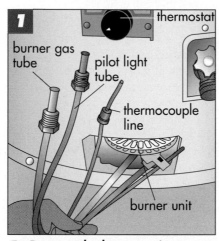

1. Remove the burner unit.
Note: *Shut off the gas.* If you need to replace a thermocouple or clean the burner, first remove the burner unit. Disconnect the pilot light tube, the burner gas tube, and the thermocouple line. Pull down on the tubes, and carefully pull the entire burner unit out.

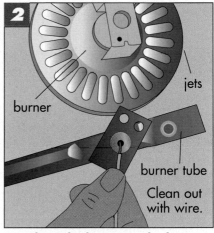

2. Clean the burner and tube.
Turn the burner counterclockwise to unscrew it from the tube. With a thin piece of wire, clean out the small orifice at the point where the tube enters the burner. Also use wire to clean the small orifice in the pilot light tube. Use a vacuum cleaner to suck out any rust and debris from the burner jets and inside the burner area of the unit.

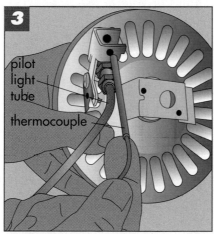

3. Replace a thermocouple.
If your pilot light won't light or is not staying lit, pull the old thermocouple from its bracket. Take it to your supplier to get one exactly like it. Push the new one into place until it clicks tight. The tip of the thermocouple should be right next to the end of the pilot gas tube so the pilot flame will touch it.

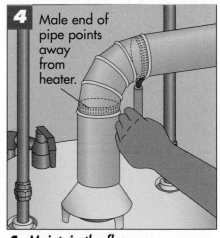

4. Maintain the flue.
A rusted, clogged, or loose-fitting flue will cause harmful fumes to enter your home. To check if the flue is drawing, light a piece of paper and blow it out. While it is smoking, hold it near the opening at the bottom of the flue. If the smoke is not sucked out, your flue needs cleaning. Also check for leaks by holding a candle near flue openings. If the flame is drawn, tighten the joint.

REPLACING GAS WATER HEATERS

Though water heaters sometimes last 25 years or more, they usually give out sooner—the victims of rust and sediment. When yours fails, there's no need to call in a plumber. Though it may seem like a complicated job, installing a gas water heater involves only two or three pipe hookups, and an electric heater requires connecting some wires. Removing the old unit is often the most difficult part of the job.

First make sure your old water heater can't be fixed. If the tank itself leaks—not the pipes—the lining has rusted and the heater must be replaced. If your heater is not producing enough hot water, it may simply be suffering from a buildup of rust and sediment, which insulates the water from the burner and forces it to work more

often to satisfy demand. Drain the heater. You may be able to flush out enough sediment to make it efficient. If it still produces too little hot water, replace it.

YOU'LL NEED...

TIME: Allow a day to remove the old heater and install the new.
SKILLS: Basic plumbing skills.
TOOLS: Wrenches for loosening unions or flexible fittings, garden hose, level, appliance dolly, and screwdriver.

CAUTION!

PRECAUTIONS WITH GAS
If you do not have a gas shutoff near the water heater, shut off the gas to your house by turning the valve on the gas meter with a large wrench. Relight all the pilot lights in your house after you turn the gas back on. Consider adding a shutoff.

EXPERTS' INSIGHT

CHOOSING THE RIGHT WATER HEATER

■ Check the nameplate on the old unit and note its capacity. You'll be safe purchasing a new one of the same size, unless you have recently installed or plan to buy an appliance that consumes a lot of hot water, such as a dishwasher. Usually, a 30- to 50-gallon unit will have enough capacity for an average home.

■ Units designed to heat water quickly, called fast recovery units, are more expensive to buy and operate, but they handle peak demand times better. Standard units don't heat as fast but are more economical to run.

■ If you have hard water, consider a unit with an extra anode rod for collecting mineral deposits (see drawing on page 202).

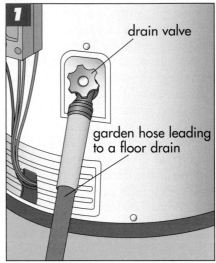

drain valve

garden hose leading to a floor drain

1. Drain the tank.
NOTE: *Shut off the main water valve to your house and shut off the gas at the heater.* Drain the water lines in your home by opening hot and cold taps in an upstairs faucet. Also open both taps positioned closest to the system's lowest point. Attach a garden hose to the water heater drain valve, open the valve, and drain the tank.

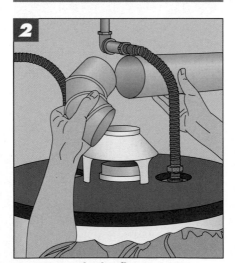

2. Dismantle the flue.
Remove the sheet-metal screws and dismantle enough ductwork to give yourself room to work. Keep track of which piece of ductwork goes where and be careful not to bend it.

3. Disconnect the gas line.
Many localities require that gas line be rigid pipe all the way to the water heater; others allow you to use a flexible gas line. Take apart a gas line union (as shown), or disconnect the flexible line.

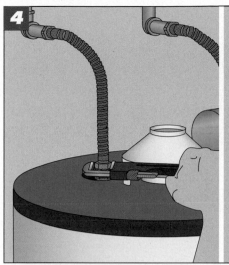

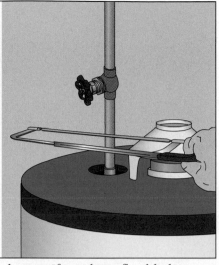

4. Disconnect the water lines.

Mark hot and cold water lines so you won't hook up the new heater backward. If you have galvanized pipe, open unions near the unit. If you have rigid copper, cut the pipe with a hacksaw or tubing cutter just below the shutoff valves. Make the cuts straight so you can tap into the lines easily with new soldered pipe or flexible water lines when you install the new heater. If you have flexible lines, disconnect them. Move the old unit out with an appliance dolly.

> **CAUTION!**
> *IT MAY BE HEAVY!*
> *If sediment buildup clogged your old heater, it will be extremely heavy. Have a helper and a good appliance dolly, and take care not to strain your back.*

5. Set the new unit in place.

Move the new water heater into place. Position it to make your gas connection as easy as possible. Check for plumb and level, shimming if necessary. If the unit is in an area prone to dampness, purchase a traylike base to protect it.

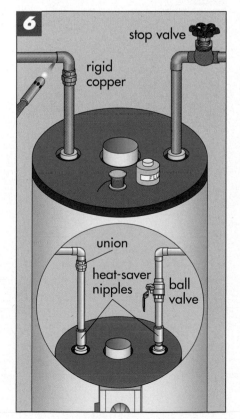

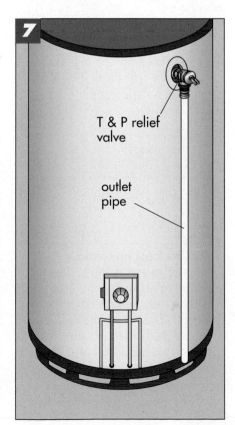

6. Connect the water lines.

Find out code requirements for the water lines. If they're permitted, flexible copper water connectors are usually the easiest way to go. Otherwise solder rigid copper or install galvanized pipe with a union. To save energy, install heat-saver nipples at each inlet. These temperature-sensitive in-line valves hold back water until it's needed. Follow directions, installing the cold water nipple with the arrow pointing down, the hot water nipple with the arrow pointing up.

7. Install T & P relief valve.

You may have to purchase a temperature-and-pressure-relief valve separately. Be sure it matches the working-pressure rating of the tank as given on the nameplate. Wrap the threads with Teflon tape and screw the valve in—either on top or near the top on the side.

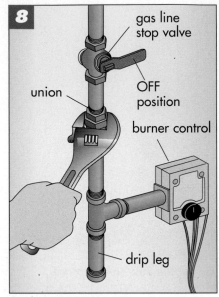

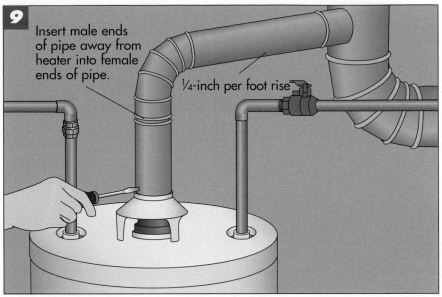

8. Hook up the gas.

Connect a gas (black pipe) nipple to the burner control of the water heater and connect the nipple to the gas line. Be sure to install a drip leg to collect sediment and moisture from the gas line.

9. Install the flue.

If your old flue worked well and your new water heater is the same height as the old one, you can reuse the old flue. Make sure it isn't blocked. Clean out any dust, rust, or sediment from the flue. If you replace or add to the vent, use galvanized pipe fittings that are designed for venting gas. When running a horizontal section, maintain at least a ¼-inch-per-foot rise. Insert male ends of the vent into female ends away from the water heater so the fumes will not have a chance to escape. Fasten each joint of the vent with two sheet-metal screws.

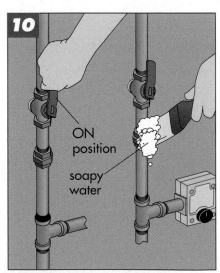

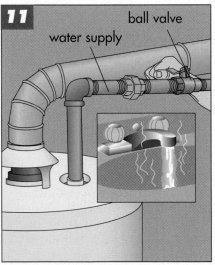

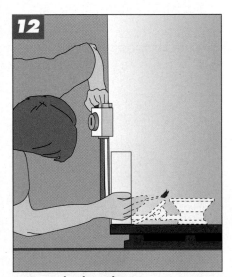

10. Check for gas leaks.

Open the gas stop valve. Test for leaks by brushing soapy water on all the connections. Watch for bubbles. If you see any, tighten the connection. If they persist, shut off the gas, disassemble, carefully clean the threads, and check again.

11. Turn on the water.

Open the water supply valve. Open the nearest hot faucet about halfway and allow the system to "bleed." First air will come out, then the spattering of water mixed with air. When the water flows freely, close the faucet.

12. Light the pilot.

Open the access panel at the bottom of the tank and light the pilot according to the directions printed on the water heater. Adjust the temperature setting.

REPLACING ELECTRIC WATER HEATERS

Installing an electric water heater is similar to installing a gas unit. The differences are that you make electrical rather than gas connections, and there is no flue on an electric water heater.

YOU'LL NEED...

TIME About a day.

SKILLS: Making electrical and plumbing connections.

TOOLS: Wrenches for unions or flexible fittings, garden hose for draining, level, appliance dolly, screwdriver, and neon tester.

CAUTION!

DANGER! HIGH VOLTAGE! Working with 240-volt circuits is a serious matter. Remove the fuse or turn off the circuit breaker, and then check to make sure the power is off.

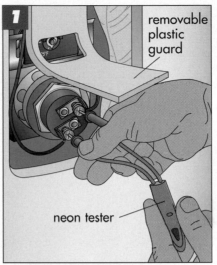

1. Remove the panel and test.
NOTE: *Shut off the power and water.* Remove the access panel for the thermostat (usually behind the lower panel), push aside any insulation, and lift or remove the plastic guard. Test for current with a neon tester to make sure you have turned off the circuit.

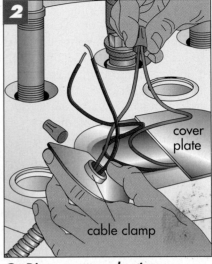

2. Disconnect, mark wires.
Remove the electrical cover plate at the side or the top of the unit. Disconnect the wires and mark them with pieces of tape so you'll know exactly where to attach them on the new unit. Loosen the screw on the cable clamp and carefully pull the cable out.

Complete steps 1, 4, and 5 on pages 206–207.

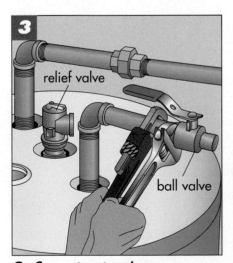

3. Connect water pipes.
Install water lines (see page 207). Supply lines can be galvanized steel pipe (see page 191), rigid copper (see pages 184–185), or flexible water connectors (see page 206–207). Install a ball valve on the supply line (see page 196). Install a relief valve, and attach an outlet pipe (see page 207).

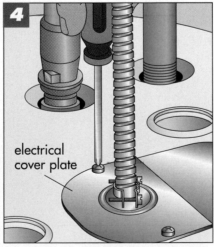

4. Make the electrical connections.
Connect the black and white wires with wire connectors, and attach the ground wire to the ground screw. Tighten the screw on the clamp to hold the cable in place, gently push the wires inside, and replace the cover plate.

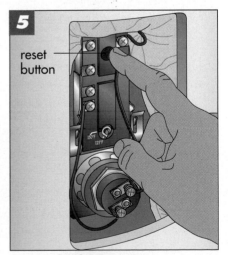

5. Set the thermostat.
Set the water heater to the temperature you want. Press the reset button, and replace the plastic guard, insulation, and access panels. Turn the water on as shown in Step 11 on page 208.

REPLACING BATHTUBS

This is a difficult, time-consuming job, but it's within the reach of a do-it-yourselfer who plans carefully and takes the time to do it right. You will need a helper. In most cases, the wall repair is just as much work as the tub installation and plumbing. Visit your local library to find books specifically about wall finishing and tiling.

YOU'LL NEED...

TIME: Several days to remove an old tub, install a new one, and fix the walls.

SKILLS: Basic plumbing skills, wall-finishing skills.

TOOLS: Screwdriver, channel-type pliers, prying bars, hammer and chisel, and carpentry and wall-preparation tools.

EXPERTS' INSIGHT

CHOOSING A TUB

■ Most tubs are 60 inches long, but 54- and 66-inch ones are available. Make sure you get a size that fits your space. Widths vary, too. This can result in a gap between the new tub and the floor tile. You may have to add some tiles or even build the wall out with a layer or two of cement board or green drywall. This could spare you retiling the entire bathroom floor.

■ Cast-iron is the most durable but also the most expensive and heaviest tub material. Fiberglass is convenient but will scratch. Baked-enamel steel tubs are fairly light and durable, but they can chip, and they are noisy when being filled.

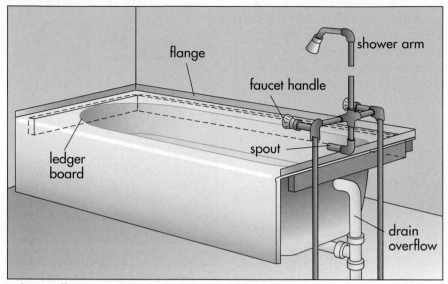

Tub installation overview

The supply system for a tub and shower includes a faucet (for possible types, see pages 166–167), a spout, and a showerhead and arm. In most cases, these do not need to be disturbed when you remove and replace a tub. (Sometimes you need to remove the spout and handles to get the old tub out.) Remove the drain assembly and detach the drain overflow to remove the tub. When you replace the tub, replace the drain assembly as well. You can choose one that has a trip lever at the top to control the drain stopper or choose a simpler model in which you control the drain at the stopper (see page 238).

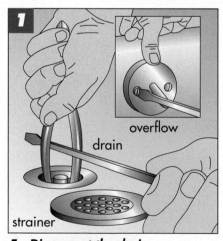

1. Disconnect the drain.
Loosen the screws and remove the overflow plate. Pull out the trip lever and linkage (see page 238). Remove the strainer and use a pair of pliers and a screwdriver to unscrew the drain piece. You may have to pull out the stopper with pieces of linkage attached to it.

2. Cut the wall away.
Chisel into the grout and pry out at least one course of tile along the edge of the tub. Cut away as much of the wall as necessary to reveal the tub flange and to get at any screws or nails that fasten the flange to the wall.

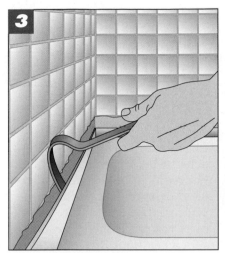

3. Remove the tub.

Depending on how it was installed, you may be able simply to pry the tub loose, or you might have to pull nails, unfasten screws, or disconnect clips that secure the tub to the wall. Pull the tub away from the wall and remove it. (See the box for removal tips.)

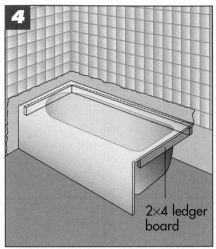

2×4 ledger board

4. Prepare for the new tub.

Consult manufacturer's directions for any special installation preparations. For a cast-iron tub, install a 2×4 ledger board, shown above. For steel or fiberglass, use the screws or clips provided with the unit. Some fiberglass bathtubs are installed in a bed of mortar to add support.

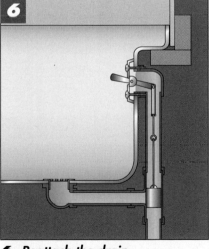

5. Set the new tub in position.

Attach a new drain assembly or check to see that the old one will fit. Slide the new tub into place, reversing whatever procedures you used to remove the old one. Check for level along its length and across its width, and shim if necessary.

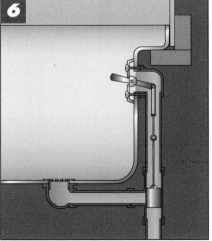

6. Reattach the drain.

Chances are you will need to have access to the drain either from below or from behind. Align the overflow and the drain with their holes. Apply plumber's putty to the threads of the drain piece. Attach the overflow plate and the drain piece and fasten them in place, taking care not to scratch the chrome or tub surfaces.

EXPERTS' INSIGHT

REMOVING OLD TUBS

■ Depending on the layout of your bathroom, you might be able to tilt the tub in one piece and carry it out the door. Have at least one helper on hand.

■ In some situations, the only solution is to cut a hole in a wall without any obstructing plumbing and slide the tub through into the next room. This is not as drastic as it sounds: You will only have to cut one or two studs, and the wall patching may actually be less than you would have with other methods of removal.

■ If the tub is cast-iron, by far the easiest way to remove it is to break it apart with a sledgehammer. Wear protective eyewear and work gloves. Remove or cover any items in the bathroom that might be scratched.

Money $ Saver

WALL-FINISHING OPTIONS

■ You may not have to tear out all of your tiles and retile the entire tub surround. If you work carefully, you can piece in cement board or green drywall (see page 227) in the places where you cut away the wall. You can then fill in the space with tiles.

■ Other good options include acrylic and fiberglass panels. These are reasonably priced, and they can be installed in a fraction of the time it takes to tile and grout.

PLANNING FOR NEW FIXTURES

Most improvements shown in this book are add-ons, where you simply hook new fittings or fixtures to existing pipes. Running new lines takes coping with the constraints of your structure and an understanding of how supply, drain, and vent pipes work.

New supply lines are the easiest to plan. They require no slope or venting, just the correct pipe size (see box). You can run them wherever you need them.

Far trickier are the drain-waste-vent (DWV) lines that carry away water, waste, and gases. The illustrations below and on page 213 show straightforward ways to tap in for a new fixture. Your situation may not be this simple and may require the skill of a professional.

For any new installation, even a minor one, you'll probably need to apply to your local building department for a permit and arrange with them to have the work inspected before you cover up any new pipes.

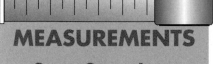

MEASUREMENTS

SIZING SUPPLY LINES

Check with your local building department for the supply line size required. As a general rule, most departments require that a line supplying one or two fixtures can be ½ inch. Any line supplying three or more fixtures must be at least ¾ inch.

Planning drain lines

The first step in planning an extension of your plumbing system is to map out exactly where existing lines run. Your home probably has a drainage arrangement similar to the one shown. Notice that some of the fixtures (toilet, double sink) cluster near a wet wall—one containing the main stack. A wet wall is usually a few inches thicker than other walls to accommodate the 3- or 4-inch-diameter stack that runs up through the roof. (To find a wet wall, note the location of the stack on the roof.)

The fixtures drain directly into the main stack or into horizontal runs that slope downward at a pitch of at least ¼ inch per running foot. Fixtures more than a few feet from the stack (like the bathtub and bathroom sink shown) must be vented with a loop that goes up and back to the stack. Called a revent or a circuit vent, this branch can be concealed inside walls and floors of normal thickness. Fixtures even farther away (like the shower and utility sink shown) may require a separate new stack. Requirements vary on revents and new vents, so check local codes.

Position the new fixtures as close as possible to an existing stack to minimize wall damage.

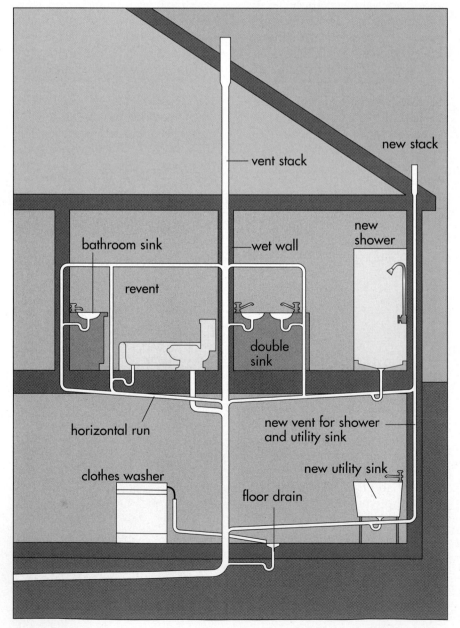

- new stack
- vent stack
- new shower
- bathroom sink
- wet wall
- revent
- double sink
- horizontal run
- new vent for shower and utility sink
- new utility sink
- clothes washer
- floor drain

VENTING POSSIBILITIES

Think of a main stack as a two-way chimney: Water and wastes go down; gases go up. Just as you wouldn't install a fireplace without a chimney, neither should you consider adding a fixture without properly venting it. Strangle the air supply of a drain, and you risk creating a siphoning effect that can suck water out of traps. This in turn breaks the seal that provides protection from gas backup—and often retards the flow of wastes as well.

Codes are specific about how you must vent fixtures. These requirements differ from one locality to another, so check your community's regulations for details about the systems shown here.

With unit venting—sometimes referred to as common venting—two similar fixtures share the same stack fitting. This method allows you to put a new fixture back to back with one that already exists. The fixtures are installed on opposite sides of the wet wall. To install a unit vent, open up the wall, replace the existing sanitary tee with a sanitary cross, and connect both traps to it. The drains of unit-vented fixtures must be at the same height.

Wet venting uses a section of one fixture's drain line to double as the vent for another. Not all codes permit wet venting. Those that do often specify that the vertical drain be at least one pipe size larger than the upper fixture drain. In no case can it be smaller than the lower drain.

Regardless of how you vent a fixture, codes limit the distance between the trap outlet and the vent. These distances depend on the size of the drain line you're running. For 1¼-, 1½-, and 2-inch drain lines—the sizes you'll most likely be working with— 2, 3, and 5 feet, respectively, are typical distances. (For help adding plastic drain line see page 218. For how to tap into a cast-iron drain, see page 219.)

Often the best way to install a new fixture is with a revent, also called a circuit vent. Clear this with your local building department first. They may not allow you to do this with heavy-use items such as toilets or showers.

Sometimes the only solution is to install a new stack running up through the roof (see page 212). In some situations—especially if the fixture is on the top floor— that may be relatively simple.

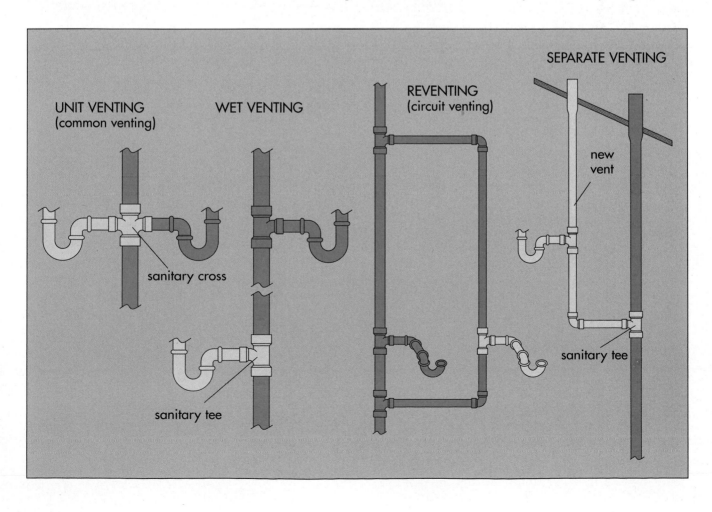

ROUGHING IN TUBS, SHOWERS, AND TOILETS

Plan the location of your bathroom fixtures carefully: A couple of inches one way or the other can make the difference between a bathroom that is comfortable and one that feels cramped and inconvenient.

Begin by mapping the floor of your bathroom on a piece of graph paper. Cut out small-scale pieces of paper that represent the fixtures. Move the pieces until you find the most usable configuration. If a door opens inward, make sure it can swing completely without hitting a fixture.

The dimensions given in the drawings at right show the minimum requirements for ease of use. Do not place fixtures closer to each other than specified. Once you decide on your floor plan, mark your floors and walls for the rough-in dimensions, using the dimensions shown below right.

EXPERTS' INSIGHT

FINDING DRAINPIPES

■ Before you figure how to rough in your new drains, you need to find the existing drain. Start at the basement or crawl space. If you see a 3- or 4-inch stack, it probably runs straight up through the roof. Or look for a plumbing access panel. You may have one on the other side of the wall behind your bathroom fixtures. (Often you'll find it in a closet.) Remove the access panel and peer inside with a flashlight.

■ If you notice a wall is thicker than the standard 4½ inches, chances are it contains drainpipes. Toilets usually are placed near stacks.

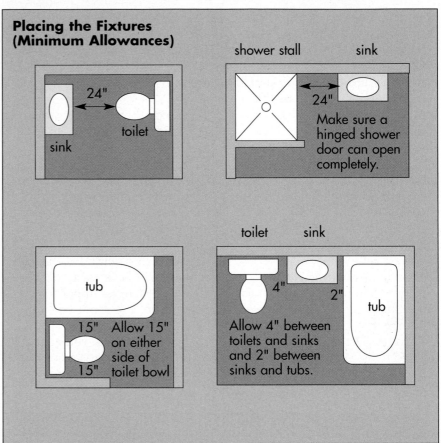

Placing the Fixtures (Minimum Allowances)

sink — 24" — toilet

shower stall — sink — 24" — Make sure a hinged shower door can open completely.

tub — 15" — Allow 15" on either side of toilet bowl — 15"

toilet — sink — 4" — 2" — tub — Allow 4" between toilets and sinks and 2" between sinks and tubs.

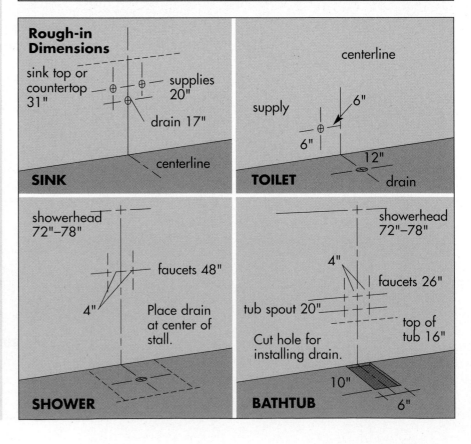

Rough-in Dimensions

SINK — sink top or countertop 31" — supplies 20" — drain 17" — centerline

TOILET — centerline — supply — 6" — 6" — 12" — drain

SHOWER — showerhead 72"–78" — faucets 48" — Place drain at center of stall. — 4" — 4"

BATHTUB — showerhead 72"–78" — 4" — faucets 26" — tub spout 20" — top of tub 16" — Cut hole for installing drain. — 10" — 6"

Once you've finished planning, cut holes in your walls and floors for installing drain lines and supply stubs, the supply lines that stick out a bit from the wall and are ready to accept stop valves.

Patching walls and floors can be more time-consuming than the plumbing itself. Where possible, limit your cuts to areas that will be covered by the fixtures. Cut drywall or plaster neatly so it can be patched easily. Don't forget to install venting (see pages 212–213).

YOU'LL NEED...

TIME: A rough estimate: two days to cut walls and rough-in a sink, toilet, and tub or shower.
SKILLS: Basic plumbing and carpentry skills.
TOOLS: Reciprocating saw, carpenter hand tools, and basic plumbing tools.

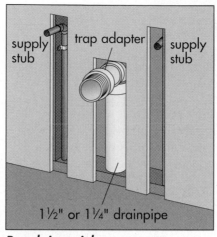

Rough-in a sink.

If you are installing a vanity cabinet, you have latitude for placing the drain and supply stubs. For a wall-hung sink or a pedestal sink, hold the fixture up against the wall and mark the best locations for drain and supply stubs (see pages 224–225). In most cases, it is best to position the supply stubs within 12 inches of the faucet.

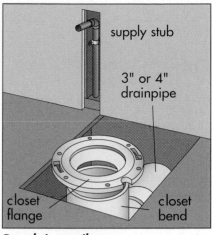

Rough-in a toilet.

Be careful to place the closet bend the correct distance from the wall—usually 12 inches to the center of the drain. (Double-check the requirements for your toilet.) A closet flange will sit on top of the floor after you have patched and surfaced it. Only a cold water supply stub is needed. Place it where it will be unnoticeable.

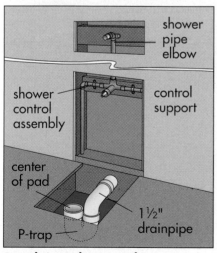

Rough-in a shower only.

To correctly position the drain, set the base in place and measure from the walls. Allow for wall surfacing (see pages 226–227). To spare patching later, cut the floor so the base will cover the hole. Install a P-trap below the level of the floor at the level required by the drain assembly kit. Install the control assembly. Its size determines how far apart the supply pipes should be. Firmly attach the shower pipe to framing.

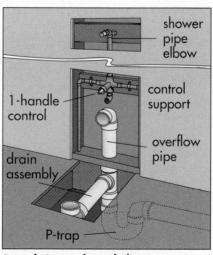

Rough-in a tub and shower.

Cut the floor so the tub will cover the hole. Install a P-trap and bathtub drain assembly. It will be somewhat unstable until you connect it to the tub. The one-handle control shown requires that supplies be plumbed horizontally into it. Attach the control and the top of the shower pipe firmly to framing; you will probably need to frame in a piece of lumber between the studs.

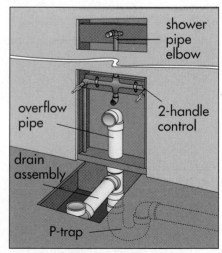

Rough-in a two-handle control.

A two-handle control is easier to install. Set the hot and cold pipes at the same height. Attach the control and the top of the shower pipe elbow to frame supports.

CAUTION!
DON'T WEAKEN JOISTS
Deep notches greatly reduce the strength of joists. Drill holes if possible, or reinforce joists after notching

TAPPING INTO EXISTING LINES

When you add a sink close to or on the other side of a wet wall—the wall containing working plumbing lines—tie into existing copper supplies and plastic drain lines. (For tapping into cast-iron, see page 219.) If you have trouble locating your drain line in the wall, see the tips on page 214.

Tapping into a wet wall is much less trouble than installing new drain, vent, and supply lines, but it is still a major project. Don't spoil the job by getting one important detail wrong: A telltale sign of an unprofessional plumbing job is when the hot and cold end up on the wrong sides of the sink. People notice if the two are switched. Plan so the hot handle is on the left.

YOU'LL NEED...

TIME: About a day.
SKILLS: Joining copper or plastic pipe, and basic carpentry skills.
TOOLS: Keyhole saw, utility knife, tubing cutter, fine-toothed saw, miter box, tongue-and-groove pliers, hacksaw or reciprocating saw, ratchet with socket, and torch.

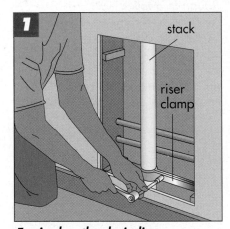

1. Anchor the drain line.
NOTE: *Shut off the water and drain the lines.* Open up the wet wall to the center of the studs on either side so you will have a nailing surface for patching later. You may have to make a separate hole for access to the supply pipes. Anchor the stack by attaching riser clamps above and below the area you will cut.

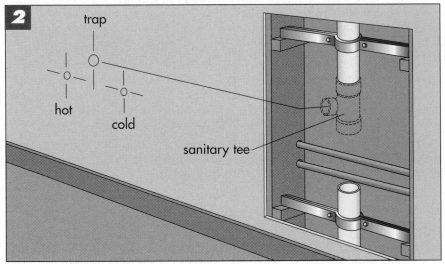

2. Lay out the installation.
Plan out the fixture's rough-in dimensions (see page 214), and mark them on the wall. Be sure the location doesn't exceed the maximum distance permitted by local codes. To determine the point at which the fixture will tie into the stack, draw a line that slopes from the center of the drain trap at $\frac{1}{4}$ inch per foot. Being careful to cut squarely, use a hacksaw or reciprocating saw to remove a section of stack 8 inches longer than the sanitary tee you'll be installing.

CAUTION!
AVOID DISASTER
Tell family members not to use any toilets positioned above the place where you have cut the stack or you will receive an extremely rude surprise. Also be aware that sewer gases can escape from an opened stack. Cap the lines with duct tape or stuff rags in them if they will be left open for more than a few minutes.

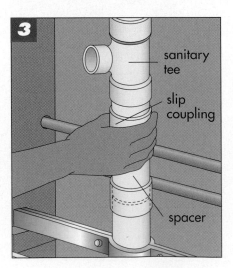

3. Install the sanitary tee.
In most cases, the sanitary tee should be sized to accept $1\frac{1}{2}$-inch pipe; for bathroom sinks, $1\frac{1}{4}$-inch is sometimes acceptable. Fit the tee, two spacers, and two slip couplings into place as shown. Slide the couplings up and down to secure the spacers. Just dry-fit the pieces at this point; don't cement them until the rest of the run is completed.

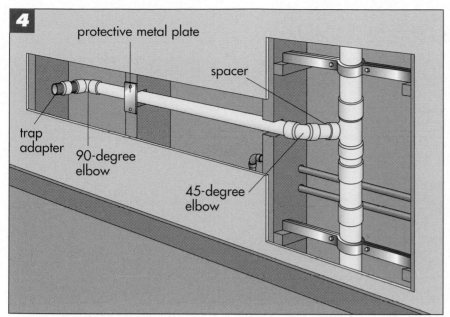

4. Install the drainpipe.
Cut out a strip of drywall and notch the studs just deep enough to support the pipes. In most cases, it works best to use a 45-degree elbow and a short spacer at the stack, and a 90-degree elbow and a trap adapter at the trap. Once you're sure the pipe slopes at ¼ inch per foot, scribe all the pieces with alignment marks, disassemble, prime, and cement the drainpipe pieces together (see page 193).

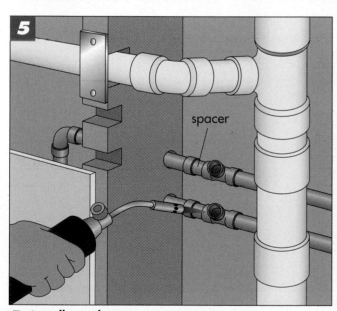

5. Install supply tees.
Tap into copper or plastic supply lines using spacers, slip couplings, and tees similar to those you used on the drainpipe. (For soldering in copper joints, see pages 184–185.) If you tap into galvanized steel supply lines, you may have to cut and remove sections of pipe and install unions. Be sure to use a transition fitting if you're mixing pipe materials (see pages 180–181).

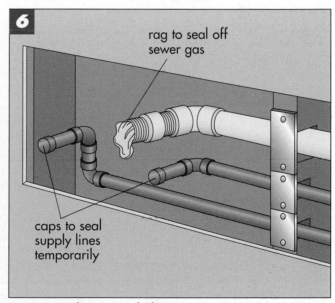

6. Run and cap supply lines.
Run pipes over to the fixture location using 90-degree elbows and pipe as needed. Use 90-degree elbows and short pieces to bring the lines past the wall surface. Stuff a rag in the drain to seal off sewer gas. Solder caps on the ends of the supply lines, turn on the water, and test for leaks. Close up the wall, add stop valves (see page 196), and you're ready to install the fixture.

ADDING PLASTIC DRAIN LINES

Cutting, moving, and refitting plastic pipe are all simple jobs—as long as you have a plastic waste stack and easy access to the drainpipe.

Don't forget that every drain line must be properly vented (see pages 212–213). Be sure you have this planned before you start cutting into the drainpipe. You may need to tap in at a second, higher point for the vent.

YOU'LL NEED...

TIME: If you have easy access to the existing drain, assume a half day for this assembly.
SKILLS: Cutting pipe straight; and measuring, aligning, and cementing plastic pipe.
TOOLS: Hacksaw or fine-toothed saw, marker, utility knife, and drill with holesaw bit or a reciprocating saw.

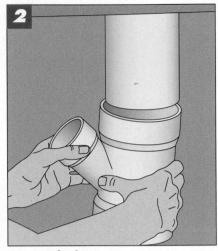

length of new fitting, minus depth of sockets

1. Cut out a section of pipe.
Measure the new sanitary tee to see how much of the old pipe you need to remove. Take into account the depth of the sockets (see page 183). Be sure that both sides of the existing pipe are supported so they'll stay in position after the cut is made. Cut with a hacksaw or fine-toothed saw and remove any burrs with a utility knife.

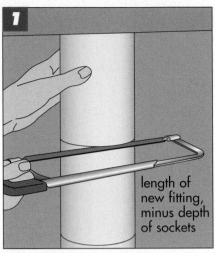

2. Dry-fit the sanitary tee.
First install the top end, then the bottom. You may have to loosen one of your support straps somewhere to give yourself enough play in the pipes to do this. Once the sanitary tee is dry-fit in the desired position, make an alignment line with a marker.

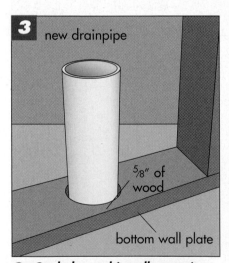

new drainpipe

5/8" of wood

bottom wall plate

3. Cut hole, and install new pipe.
Run pipes to the location of the new fixture (see pages 215–217). If you need to run the drainpipe through wall plates or framing, cut holes to accommodate the pipe. Leave at least 5/8 inch of wood on any side that will receive drywall. This way, nails or screws driven through drywall plund into the plate won't pierce the pipe.

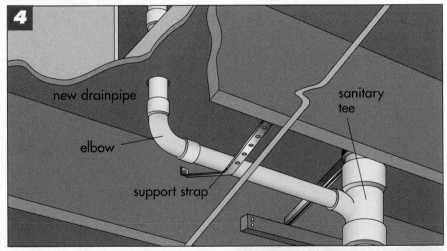

new drainpipe

elbow

support strap

sanitary tee

4. Connect the pieces between.
Connect the new drainpipe to the sanitary tee with elbows and lengths of pipe. Dry-fit the pieces, draw alignment lines, disassemble, prime, and cement the pieces together (see page 193). Support the run with at least one strap for the horizontal run.

CAUTION!
PROTECT YOUR EYES
This is a job in which plenty of dirt, burrs, and sawdust will fall from above. Wear goggles when working above your head.

TAPPING INTO CAST-IRON DRAIN LINES

Cast-iron pipe is used in many older homes for the DWV (drain-waste-vent) system. Often one or two large stacks are made of cast-iron, and the lines leading into them are galvanized steel.

Cast-iron is difficult to work with (see Caution! below). Fortunately, it is no longer required for new installations. However you may need to run a new drain into an existing cast-iron stack. Most likely you will have to tap in at two places: one for the drain and one for the vent.

This page shows how to break into a cast-iron stack to replace a cast-iron Y-fitting with a plastic sanitary tee. The same techniques can be used to install a sanitary tee, as shown on page 218.

YOU'LL NEED...

TIME: Set aside a full day so you can take your time on this difficult project.
SKILLS: Joining plastic pipe and basic carpentry skills.
TOOLS: Chain-type pipe cutter (rent or buy this tool), socket and ratchet, screwdriver, and hacksaw or fine-toothed saw.

CAUTION!

CONSIDER HIRING A PRO
Working with cast-iron is not only difficult, it is dangerous as well. Cast-iron is heavy, can shatter, and has sharp edges. This is a project that you may want to leave to a professional. Some plumbers may be willing to make the cast-iron connections only, allowing you to save money by making the plastic connections yourself.

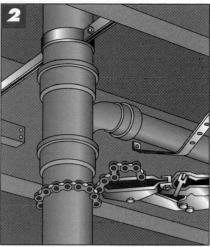

1. Support the stack.
Begin by securely supporting the stack from above and making sure that it is well-supported below. (You do not need to move either portion of the cast-iron pipe in order to make the connection.) Use riser clamps specially made for support, available at your plumbing supply store.

riser clamp

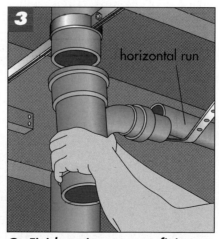

2. Cut the pipe.
Using the chain-type pipe cutter. Wrap the chain around the stack, hook it, and—with the handles open—crank the chain tight with the turn screw. Draw the handles together. This part of the job takes muscle, but if you follow the manufacturer's directions, you will get a clean cut.

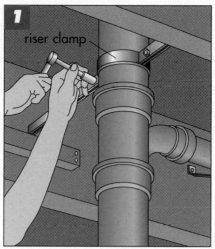

horizontal run

3. Finish cutting, remove fitting.
If you are removing a fitting, make a second cut about 4 inches below the first cut, and cut the horizontal run. If the horizontal pipe is galvanized steel, cut it with a hacksaw. Remove the 4-inch section and pull the fitting out.

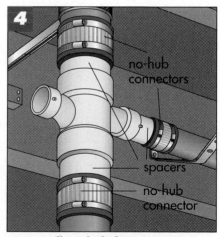

no-hub connectors
spacers
no-hub connector

4. Install no-hub fittings.
Install new plastic fittings with no-hub connectors. You may have to use short sections of pipe as spacers. To assemble a no-hub connector, slip the connector over the end of the old pipe, insert the sanitary tee with spacers in place, slide the connector so it bridges the old pipe and the spacers, and install clamps. Tighten clamps with a screwdriver.

ADDING NEW VENTS

If your new fixture is far away from an existing stack, codes may require a new vent. Though it will have to run all the way up through the roof, it may be easier to install than tying into the existing stack. If your wall has no insulation and no fire blocking, adding a new stack can be less work than cutting into a wall for a revent and patching afterward. If you have attic space with exposed pipes, consider running the new vent straight up through the attic. You can tie into the existing vent there.

YOU'LL NEED...

TIME: If there are no major obstructions, count on spending a day running the vent and a day patching the walls.
SKILLS: Basic plumbing and carpentry skills.
TOOLS: Drill with holesaw bit, knife, keyhole saw, and jigsaw.

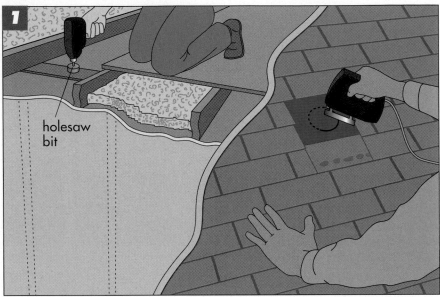

1. Cut holes in the attic, roof.
In the attic, find the top plate of the wall where the new vent is needed. Choose a spot between two studs and drill down through the plate. Size the hole just big enough to handle the outside diameter of the pipe. (Codes will probably call for a 1½- or 1¼-inch vent.) Mark the point directly above the hole and drive a nail up through the roof. Remove a shingle; cut a hole with a jigsaw or reciprocating saw. (You may need to cut a larger hole if you're increasing pipe size. See Step 3.) If a rafter is in the way, offset the vent with 45-degree elbows.

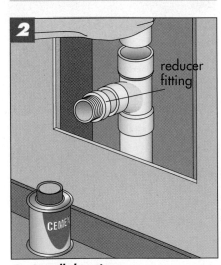

2. Install the pipe.
With a helper, slide a pipe through the holes. It usually works best to start at the attic and push down. After everything is dry-fit, mark alignment, disassemble, and prime and cement the joints. Allow extra pipe above the roof—you can trim it once the cement has set and you have checked the fit of the flashing.

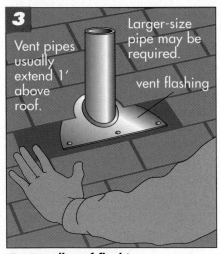

3. Install roof flashing.
Secure the vent with a riser clamp (see page 219) in the attic. In cold climates, codes call for a larger pipe size where it pierces the roof to prevent freeze-ups from clogging the vent. Slip the flashing over the vent; tuck it under the shingles uphill from the vent. Nail and seal with roofing cement.

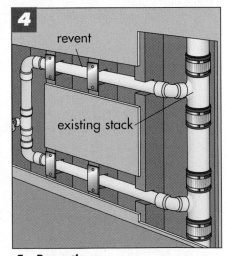

4. Reventing.
If you are close enough to an existing stack, it is often easiest to revent. However, as the illustration shows, this usually means lots of patching afterward. If you will be tying into an old cast-iron stack, you will have to go through all the hassle described on page 219.

RUNNING THE SUPPLY LINES

Once the DWV system is installed, it's time for the easier job of extending supply lines to the new location. If you are tying into old galvanized pipe, look for a convenient union, open it, and dismantle back to the nearest fittings. Otherwise, tee in the supply by cutting a supply pipe and removing both ends (see page 216). Now you are ready to connect new to old. **NOTE:** *Turn the water off and drain the lines before cutting pipe or opening unions.*

YOU'LL NEED...

TIME: About four hours to tap into two lines and run eight pieces of pipe, including fittings.
SKILLS: Measuring, cutting, and soldering copper pipe.
TOOLS: Hacksaw or tubing cutter, propane torch, tongue-and-groove pliers, and Crescent wrench.

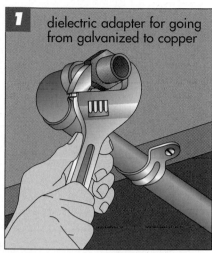

dielectric adapter for going from galvanized to copper

1. Tap in with an adapter.
To go from galvanized to copper or plastic (check to be sure your locality permits the use of plastic supplies if you choose this option), use a dielectric adapter like the one shown here. Never hook copper pipe directly to galvanized as electrolytic action will corrode the connection.

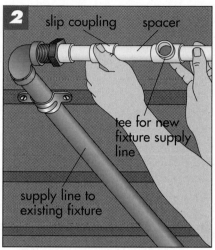

slip coupling   spacer
tee for new fixture supply line
supply line to existing fixture

2. Make new pipe connections.
Replace the run you've just removed with copper or plastic pipe and a tee fitting. Splice with a slip coupling and spacer. Solder or cement the pipes and fittings. As you install the pipes leading to the new service, slope the lines slightly so the system can be drained easily.

EXPERTS' INSIGHT

MAINTAINING PRESSURE WHEN ADDING LINES

■ For pipes supplying more than two fixtures, use ³/₄-inch rather than ½-inch pipe.
■ If you have a long run (more than 25 feet), use ³/₄-inch pipe. Usually it is best to run ³/₄-inch pipe into a bathroom, then ½-inch pipe to each fixture.
■ Don't move up from ½-inch to ³/₄-inch pipe in a line. Step down in dimension, never up.
■ If you have more than four right-angle bends, make some gradual by using 45-degree elbows. Too many sharp turns will reduce water pressure.

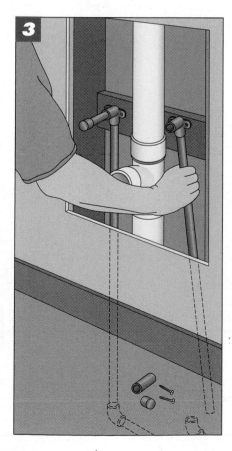

3. Add on drop ells.
At the new fixture, use drop ells instead of regular elbows. Attach them with screws to a piece of wood that is firmly anchored to the framing. Make sure they are positioned 6 to 8 inches apart.

Follow the directions given on pages 184–185 for soldering copper pipes, or see pages 192–193 for cementing plastic pipe. Before soldering copper, open every faucet on the run. Otherwise heat from the torch can burn out washers and other parts, and built-up steam can rupture a fitting or pipe wall.

Cap the lines, turn on the water, and check for leaks. Don't cover the opening yet; the inspector will probably want to look at the pipes before you patch the wall.

INSTALLING RIMMED SINKS

Setting a new sink in place is one of the truly satisfying plumbing tasks. It signals completion of a fairly easy job that gets noticed by your family.

When shopping for a new deck-mounted fixture, you'll find plenty of options—stainless steel, cast-iron, plastic composite, vitreous china, and more. Nowadays most sinks—for the kitchen and bathroom—are self-rimming,

which means you just put some putty on the rim and clamp the sink down on the countertop.

To remove an old sink, first turn off the supply stops or shut off the water to your house and drain the lines. Disconnect the supply lines and the trap joining the sink to the drainpipe. Remove any mounting clips from underneath, and pry the sink up. Add stop valve (see page 196).

1. To install a bathroom sink, first cut an opening.

If you need to cut a hole for the sink, trace the template provided with the sink. Drill an entry hole and cut with a sabersaw and fine-toothed blade.

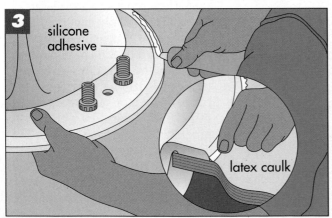

countertop

template

2. Attach faucet and drain.

Before lowering the sink into the opening, hook up the faucet (see pages 198–199) and drain assembly (see page 238). With bathroom sinks, the drain assembly consists of a basin outlet flange, a drain body, a gasket, a locknut, and a tailpiece that slides into the P-trap. (Installing these after you install the sink is not only difficult, but you also run a greater risk of damaging the parts.) Lay a bead of plumber's putty around the basin outlet, insert the flange, and screw together the other parts of the drain assembly.

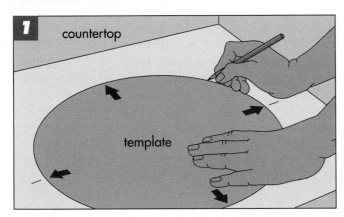

silicone adhesive

latex caulk

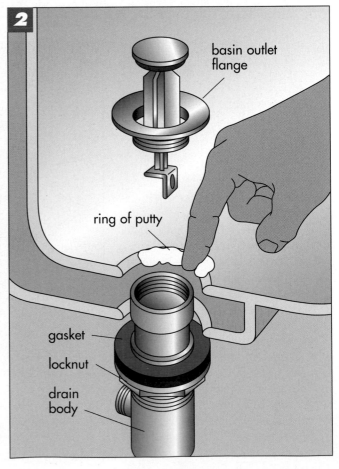

basin outlet flange

ring of putty

gasket

locknut

drain body

3. Set the sink.

Apply a thick bead of silicone adhesive around the underside of the fixture's flange, about ¼ inch from the edge. Turn the sink right side up and lower it carefully into the opening. Press down on the sink; some of the caulk will ooze out. Wipe away the excess with a damp cloth. After the silicone adhesive has set (about two hours), apply latex caulk around the sink.

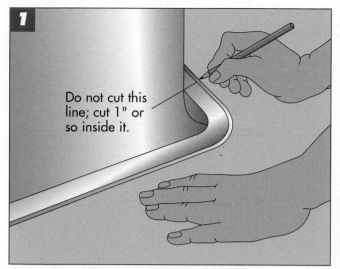

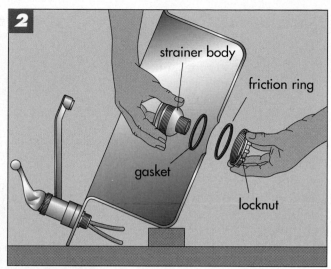

1. For a stainless-steel sink, mark and cut opening.

Turn your sink upside down on the countertop. Make sure it is in the correct position, safely set back from the cabinet beneath. Trace the outline of the sink, then draw a line that is an inch or so to the inside of that outline. Erase the first line to make sure you do not cut it. Test to make sure the sink fits. Cut the opening using a circular saw with a fine-toothed blade for the straight cuts and a sabersaw for curves. Take your time to avoid splintering the laminate.

2. Attach the faucet and strainers.

Attach a basket strainer to each bowl. Lay a bead of putty around the outlet, set the gasket in place, and lower the strainer body into the hole. With your other hand, from underneath, slip the friction ring in place, and screw on the locknut. Tighten, and clean away the putty that oozes out. You also can attach the tailpiece and trap assembly at this point. To install the faucet, see page 199.

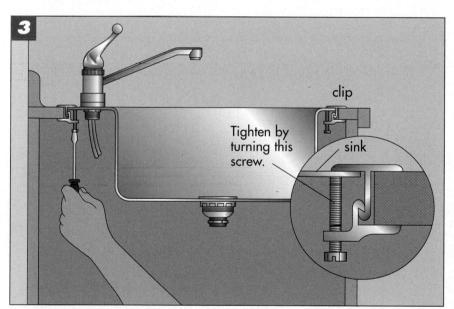

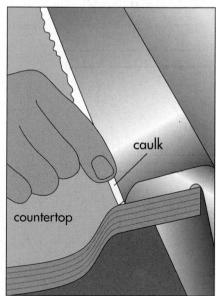

3. Set and secure the sink.

To set the sink, place a rope of plumber's putty all around the rim so it will seal everywhere. Turn the sink right side up and lower it into the opening. Secure the sink to the countertop with sink clips every 6 to 8 inches. Working from underneath the sink, tighten the clips with a screwdriver. Remove excess putty with a putty knife and a rag dipped in paint thinner.

Install a cast-iron sink.

To set a cast-iron kitchen sink, use the same technique as for the rimmed sink (see page 222). Run a bead of silicone sealant under the rim, turn the sink right side up, set it in place, and wipe away the excess sealant. Run caulk along the edge, and smooth it with a wet finger.

INSTALLING WALL-HUNG SINKS

Wall-hung bathroom sinks are not as popular as they once were but remain useful where space is limited or a retro style is called for. Installing the bracket support is the most time-consuming part of this job.

YOU'LL NEED...
TIME: A half day to add framing and install a new sink.
SKILLS: Basic plumbing and carpentry skills.
TOOLS: Keyhole saw, hammer, level, screwdriver, and tongue-and-groove pliers or pipe wrench.

CAUTION!
WATCH YOUR WEIGHT!
Bracket-supported sinks stand up well to normal everyday use, but warn members of the household not to sit on them. They could crack or pull away from the wall.

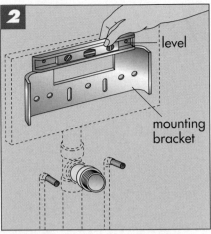

Notch studs and anchor a piece of 2×10.

1. Rough-in, provide bracing.
Note: *Be sure to shut off the water and drain the line.* To remove an old fixture, disconnect the drain and supply lines and look underneath to see if it is held in by bolts. If so, loosen or cut the bolts. Pull straight up on the sink to dislodge it.

For a new installation, run new supply lines (see pages 220–221), and provide solid framing for the hanger bracket.

level

mounting bracket

2. Finish wall, anchor bracket.
Install the drywall. You may even want to tape and paint it—it will be easier to do now than after the sink is in place. Secure the hanger bracket to the 2×10 blocking. Use plenty of screws and make sure the bracket is level. If they are not already in place, equip each supply line with a stop valve (see page 196).

3. Set sink in place.
Turn the sink on its side, and install the faucet and the drain assembly (see pages 198–199, 238). Attach flexible supply lines to the sink. Place the sink above the bracket, press it flat against the wall, and lower it onto the bracket. A flange fits into a corresponding slot in the sink.

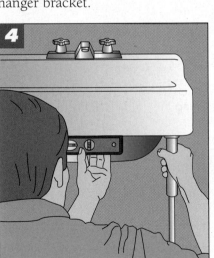

4. Attach legs.
If your sink comes with support legs, insert them into the holes in the bottom of the sink, plumb them, and adjust them so they firmly support the sink. To do this, twist the top portion of each leg. Check to see that the sink is level.

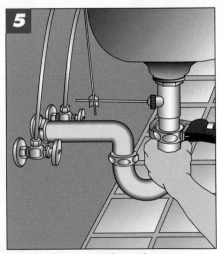

5. Hook up supplies, drain.
Connect the flexible supply lines to the stop valves. Connect the trap to the sink drain and to the drainpipe. Restore water pressure and check supply lines for leaks. To test the drain for leaks, pull the stopper lever up, fill the bowl, and open the stopper.

INSTALLING PEDESTAL SINKS

Pedestal sinks are popular because of their sleek good looks. They hide the plumbing without a cabinet. However installation is more difficult than for a regular wall-hung sink or a vanity. You have to get all the plumbing to fit inside the pedestal, and you must attach the sink at the right height so the pedestal fits just beneath it. Watch out for less expensive units that have narrower than usual pedestals.

YOU'LL NEED...

TIME: A day to move the plumbing and install the sink.
SKILLS: Basic plumbing and carpentry skills.
TOOLS: Keyhole saw, hammer or drill, screwdriver, and tongue-and-groove pliers.

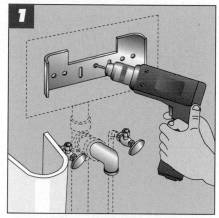

1. Install plumbing, framing.
Note: *Shut off the water.* Open the wall, and install a 2×10 (see page 224). Measure the width of the pedestal and install the drain and supply lines so they will fit inside it. Finish the walls and install stop valves (see page 196). Position the sink and pedestal against the wall to mark the bracket's location. Attach the bracket to the wall.

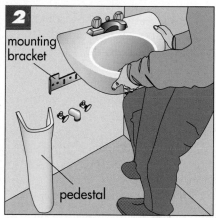

2. Assemble, install the sink.
Carefully set the sink into the bracket and fasten with the nuts and bolts or toggle bolts provided. Slide the pedestal in and caulk around the bottom with bathtub caulk. Restore water pressure and check for leaks.

ADDING VANITIES

Vanities are popular because they add much-needed storage space. They're easier to install than a wall-hung or pedestal unit because the sink sits on the vanity rather than hanging from the wall. As a result, measurements and cuts don't have to be as exact. If your vanity has a back panel, you don't have to finish the wall around the plumbing—the vanity covers it. Install a stop valve if one is not already there (see page 196). **Note:** *Be sure to shut off the water and drain the line.*

YOU'LL NEED...

TIME: A day to add the vanity and install the basic plumbing.
SKILLS: Basic plumbing and carpentry skills.
TOOLS: Sabersaw, screwdriver, channel-type pliers, caulk gun.

1. Install plumbing, cabinet.
Install the supply lines and drain line (see pages 220–221, 238). Be sure they will be covered by the cabinet and won't interfere with the sink. If the cabinet has a back, measure carefully, and cut out holes. Slide the cabinet into position and level it from side to side and front to back with shims. Anchor it to the wall by driving screws through the cabinet frame and into studs.

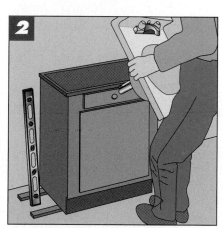

2. Hook up the sink top.
Turn the sink top on its side, and install the faucet, the flexible supply lines, and the drain assembly (see pages 198–199, 220–221, and 238). Run a bead of silicone caulk under the sink to anchor it to the cabinet. Set it on top of the cabinet, and make the final connections. Restore water pressure, and check for leaks.

INSTALLING SHOWERS

A successful shower installation requires careful planning and plenty of work. In most cases, you will need to do three kinds of tasks: frame walls, install the plumbing, and finish the walls. For information about framing, finishing, and tiling shower stall walls for the projects on this page and page 227, look for books at your local library.

First decide where you would like to put the shower. You need a space at least 32 inches square—36 inches makes for a more comfortable shower—not including the thickness of any new walls you may have to build. Be sure to leave room for the shower door to open and close. See pages 214–215 for help in planning.

Next plan the rough plumbing. The most important planning issue is how the unit will be vented (see pages 213, 220–221 for options). Make sure the drain line can be installed without seriously weakening your joists. The supply lines are usually easy to plan for—you simply tap into and extend existing lines (see pages 216–218).

Sometimes during new house construction, plumbers install plumbing lines for possible future use. You may be lucky enough to already have the drain line you need poking up through the basement floor.

The final step in planning a shower is choosing the material the shower is made from. There are several kinds, including one-, two-, and three-piece prefabricated fiberglass stalls. In addition, you can purchase knockdown units with a base and walls that you put together, freestanding metal units that require no framing, and plastic or concrete shower bases with tiled walls.

A large variety of glass doors are available, or you can simply hang a shower curtain.

EXPERTS' INSIGHT

TIPS FOR PLANNING A NEW SHOWER

■ For a coordinated look, choose the whole ensemble at once: door, enclosure, base, faucet, and showerhead.

■ Unless you have better than average ventilation or live in an extra-dry area, install a bathroom vent fan near the shower. The shower will introduce a great deal of moisture that could damage walls and lead to mildew problems if it is not properly vented.

■ Consider hiring a professional to install the shower base with drain and vent. Installing the showerhead and controls and finishing the walls are comparatively easy tasks.

■ Although 32-inch bases and prefab units are available, most adults will feel cramped in them. If at all possible, install a 36-inch base.

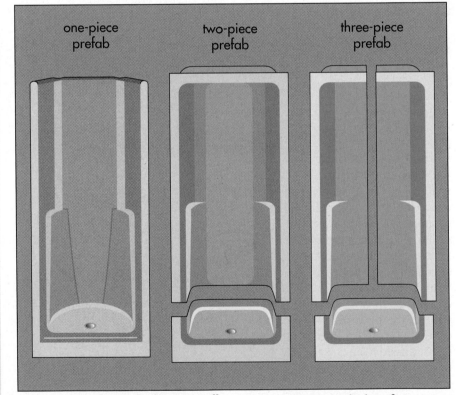

one-piece prefab two-piece prefab three-piece prefab

Three types of prefab shower stalls
Prefabricated stalls usually include the base and come with framing instructions. A freestanding one-piece unit is the easiest to install, but may be too bulky to haul into your bathroom. When logistics require, use a multipiece unit.

Other options include a freestanding metal unit, usually installed in basements as utility showers. Or you may choose to construct tiled walls around a shower base (see page 227). Tile also offers wide color options.

INSTALLING PREFAB UNITS

Purchase the unit before you build the framing. Consult the manufacturer's instructions closely regarding the exact dimensions needed. You may need to leave one wall of framing open until the unit is in place.

Install the drain in the center of the stall, following manufacturer's instructions. Frame for the unit, providing a nailing surface where needed. Check framing for plumb.

YOU'LL NEED...

TIME: Several days in most situations.
SKILLS: Good plumbing, carpentry, and wall-preparation and finishing skills.
TOOLS: A complete set of plumbing and carpentry tools (a reciprocating saw often comes in handy).

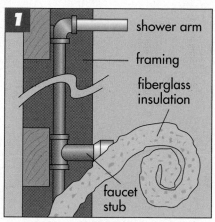

1. Anchor plumbing.
Anchor supply lines, the faucet, and the shower arm to framing—don't rely on the unit's walls for support. (See pages 214–215.)

To reduce noise, install insulation between the studs. Slice the insulation's foil or paper face so moisture will not get trapped between the insulation and the walls of the prefab shower.

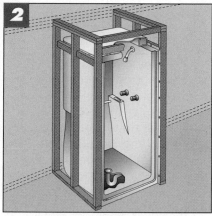

2. Attach unit, finish walls.
Drill holes in the unit's walls for the faucet and shower arm. Slide the parts into place and attach to the framing. Install the finish plumbing pieces: drain piece, shower handle, escutcheon, and showerhead. Caulk the seams and check for leaks. Finish the walls and install a shower door or curtain bar.

PREPARING FOR TILE

Install the drain and the shower base. Check for leaks by pouring water down the drain. Install any necessary new framing. Be sure to leave an opening that's the right size for your shower door. Purchase the door kit in advance so you can check the finished opening dimensions. Make sure new and old walls are plumb or you'll end up with crooked grout lines. Install the shower supply lines, faucet, and shower arm before preparing the walls for tile.

YOU'LL NEED...

TIME: Two days, once the plumbing is in place.
SKILLS: Carpentry and tiling.
TOOLS: Knife, drill, taping knife, notched trowel, and grout float.

1. Install, tape cement board.
Check for plumb and any waviness in the walls. Shim the walls as required. Use cement board for the most stable and long-lasting subsurface. Cut this material with a utility knife in the same way as drywall, and attach it with galvanized screws. Cover the screws or nails and the corner joints with wallboard compound using a taping knife.

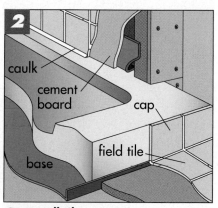

2. Install tile.
Plan your tile job carefully. Use field tiles for most of the walls, but at all exposed edges, use caps. These have one finished edge. Special corner pieces have two finished edges. Apply the adhesive with a notched trowel, set the tiles, and let them dry for 24 hours. Apply grout with a grout float, wipe away excess, and clean it several times. Apply bathroom caulk to all inside corners.

INSTALLING HAND SHOWERS

A hand shower attached to an existing shower is a luxurious addition to a shower/tub area. A hand shower attached to a tub faucet can be an economical alternative to a complete shower installation, giving you a shower without the trouble of cutting open walls and installing new plumbing. Whichever type of unit you choose, a variety of showerheads are available, ranging from the simple to the exotic. Installing them is quick and easy: a straightforward bathroom upgrade well within the skill level of any do-it-yourselfer.

YOU'LL NEED...

TIME: An hour or two for either installation.
SKILLS: No special skills needed.
TOOLS: Screwdriver, tongue-and-groove pliers, drill with masonry bit, hammer, and awl.

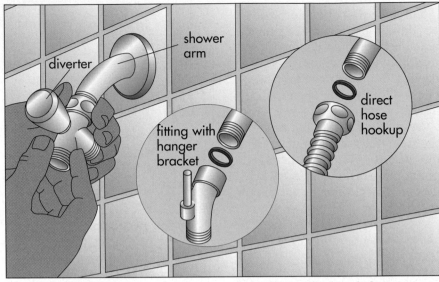

At an existing shower
Remove the showerhead. Protect chrome parts from scratches by taping the jaws of the pliers. Clean the threads. If your shower arm does not have male threads, replace it with one that does. Wrap the threads with Teflon tape, and screw on the hand shower with pliers. The hand shower connector may have a diverter (which allows you to choose either the fixed or the hand-held head), a hanger bracket (the new head fits on it), or a direct hose hookup (the hose attaches to the shower arm). For the last, install a shower hanger (see below).

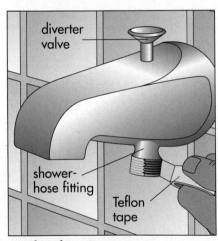

A tub-only unit
Remove the old spout by inserting the handle of a hammer into the spout opening and turning counterclockwise. Clean the pipe threads to which the spout was attached. You may need to remove the existing nipple and install one that is longer or shorter. Apply Teflon tape and screw on the new spout with diverter valve. Attach the hose to the shower-hose fitting.

Mount the shower hanger.
Be sure the wall is absolutely clean and dry before starting. Some hangers can be mounted by simply peeling the paper off the backs and sticking them in place. For a more permanent attachment, hold the hanger in position and mark for the screw holes. With a hammer and a

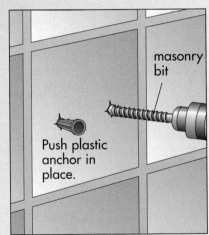

sharp-pointed awl or nail, tap a little nick in the tile—gently, so you don't crack the tile. This will keep your masonry bit from slipping on the ceramic glaze as you start the hole. Drill the holes, push plastic anchors in place, and secure the hanger with screws.

INSTALLING WATER FILTRATION SYSTEMS

*I*f you receive municipal water, information concerning water quality should be available at city hall. However if you have a well, you are on your own. Your local department of health can recommend a company to test your water to see if you need a filter. A test for bacteria is relatively inexpensive, but a full test that includes a search for pesticides, organic matter, and other potential problems can be costly. Local officials should be able to tell you if other people in your area have had similar tests done and what, if any, contaminants were found.

If the taste of your drinking water is your major concern, try a faucet filter before you get involved with a more expensive installation. If you have mineral-laden hard water that makes it difficult to wash clothes and leaves ugly deposits on fixtures, install a water softener (see page 231).

WATER FILTRATION OPTIONS

Sediment — This option uses a filter to screen out particles that can clog your aerators and may make your water look cloudy. Usually a sediment filter is used in conjunction with an activated-charcoal filter.

Activated-Charcoal — This filter will remove organic chemicals and pesticides. If your water is heavily chlorinated, it will remove much of the chlorine, improving the taste of your water. If taste is your major concern, install a small unit at the kitchen spout. A unit serving the whole house will need to have the charcoal filter replaced fairly frequently.

Reverse Osmosis — This is the most extreme measure, and it is capable of removing bacteria and harmful chemicals. It is expensive and bulky, requiring at least one holding tank. This system can be combined with an activated-charcoal system installed near the kitchen sink.

Water Softener — Also called an ion-exchange unit, this system will greatly reduce minerals such as calcium and iron. Have a water softener company install one for you—the piping is specialized and complicated.

INSTALLING WHOLE-HOUSE FILTERS

*T*his typical whole-house system combines a sediment filter with an activated-charcoal unit. The plumbing is not complicated, but you will have to shut off water to the whole house before beginning. Also, you may have to reroute or raise pipes in order to gain enough room to install the two units.

YOU'LL NEED...
TIME: Half a day.
SKILLS: Good plumbing skills.
TOOLS: Wrenches and pliers, and propane torch if you need to solder copper pipe.

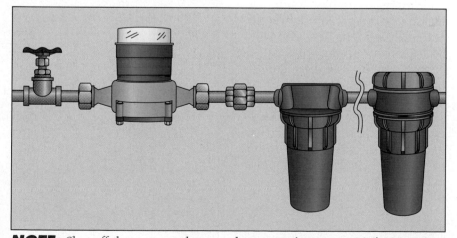

NOTE: *Shut off the water and drain the line.* At a convenient point near the outlet side of the water meter (or just inside the house, if you have no meter), break into the line by opening a union or cutting the pipe (see pages 216–219). Install a shutoff valve if you don't have one (see page 196). Remove 4 feet of pipe and work toward the meter. If you wish, add a stop valve to cut off backflow when changing filters. Then install the charcoal filter, a nipple, and finally the sediment filter. Make the last joint with a union or sleeve coupling.

INSTALLING UNDER-SINK FILTRATION UNITS

A whole-house filtration system will supply you with filtered water in every tap and likely prolong the life of your water-using appliances. Because it is difficult to install and requires regular filter changes, however, it is not installed by many homeowners. They reason that most of their water does not need to be treated because it is used for bathing, flushing away waste, and washing clothes. They choose to filter the water that counts most, their drinking and cooking water.

You can install a unit that gives you filtered water every time you turn on the cold water at your kitchen sink, or you can install a separate faucet with the filter. The first type saves you the trouble of drilling a hole and installing a separate faucet. The separate faucet will mean that you will change filter cartridges less often.

Some systems include an activated-charcoal filter. This two-canister system takes a little more time to install but adds another stage of filtration.

Before you purchase a unit, measure your space under the sink and make sure the new unit will fit. There are various types, but the connectors for all of them are fairly simple, ranging from standard compression fittings to simple connectors designed for a quick hookup to flexible supply lines. In most cases, you need only to shut off the cold water supply, cut into a flexible supply, and install the system.

YOU'LL NEED...

TIME: Usually a half hour.
SKILLS: Basic plumbing skills.
TOOLS: Tubing cutter, flashlight, and screwdriver.

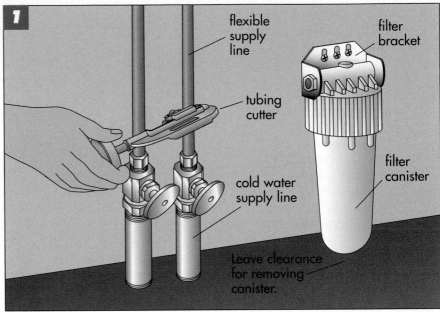

1. Filtering the cold water tap.
Anchor the filter in a location where you can get at it to replace its filter cartridges. Allow for enough clearance underneath to unscrew the canister when replacing cartridges. Use the screws provided to fasten it to the cabinet back or wall. If you do not have a flexible cold water supply line, install one (see pages 194 and 216). Cut into the cold water supply using a tubing cutter or plastic tubing cutter.

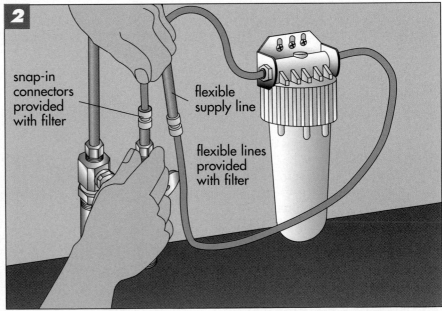

2. Hook up the filter.
Note which filter inlet is marked for the incoming supply, and connect that flexible tube to the section of supply line nearest the shutoff valve. For the connectors shown, you simply push the tubing in and they're joined. Connect the tube carrying filtered water to the section of flexible supply line for the faucet. Follow the manufacturer's directions for lubricating the canister seal and breaking in the system.

CHOOSING WATER SOFTENERS

A water softener removes minerals—especially iron, calcium, and magnesium—from water by means of ion exchange. As water passes through the unit, minerals are absorbed and replaced by sodium, which comes from salt that must be added to the storage tank from time to time.

The resulting soft water will clean clothes better than mineral-laden hard water, which does not create suds as readily. The drawback is that it adds salt to the water—probably not enough to damage your health, but enough to affect the taste of the water.

It is best to have a cold water bypass so some faucets receive unsoftened cold water. At the least, make sure your toilets and outside sill cocks do not receive softened water or you will be paying for lots of extra salt.

In most cases, it pays to have a water softener service install and maintain your system. If you were to install one yourself, you would have to make drain and electrical connections, then periodically flush and recharge your system. With a service unit, the dealer simply brings a fresh tank and takes the old one to regenerate it.

In the unit shown, a bypass valve lets you or the dealer service the unit without shutting down your home's water supply.

EXPERTS' INSIGHT

FILTERING BACTERIA

If bacteria is your problem rather than simply minerals, sediment, taste, or odor, be careful which filter you choose. Some filters may actually increase the amount of bacteria in your drinking water because they remove chlorine. Bacteria can grow in dechlorinated water if it sits for a while, even if it's in your refrigerator.

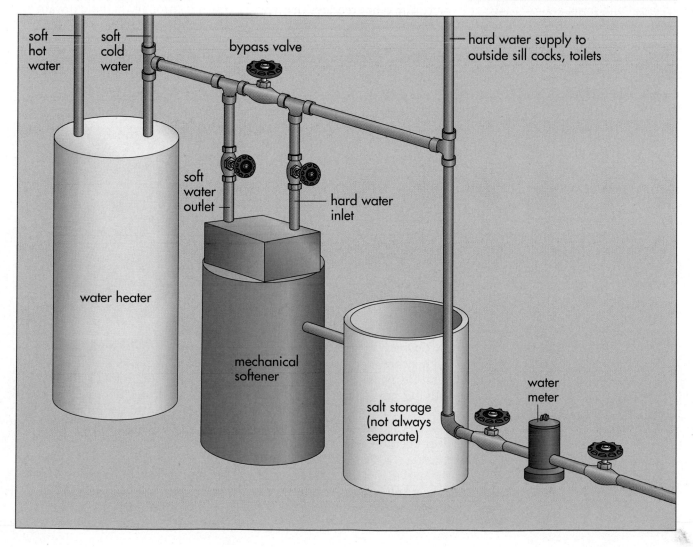

soft hot water — soft cold water — bypass valve — hard water supply to outside sill cocks, toilets — soft water outlet — hard water inlet — water heater — mechanical softener — salt storage (not always separate) — water meter

PLUMBING ICEMAKERS

If your refrigerator has an icemaker, supplying it with cold water is not difficult. The main problem will be to choose a path for the ¼-inch outside dimension flexible copper tubing. The cold water line under your kitchen sink may be the nearest source, but you may not be able to run the line so it isn't visible. If you have a basement, it's often easier to run the supply line through the floor to the pipes below.

YOU'LL NEED...

TIME: Several hours for an average installation.
SKILLS: Drilling holes and running flexible copper tubing without kinking it.
TOOLS: Drill, tongue-and-groove pliers or wrench, and screwdriver.

EXPERTS' INSIGHT

ICEMAKER TIPS

■ Some localities may not allow saddle valves. If so, or if you are concerned that your water may clog up the tiny opening in a saddle valve, break into your line and install a standard tee fitting, nipple, shutoff valve, and an adapter fitting.

■ If you don't like the taste of your water, purify the ice cubes the same way you purify your drinking water: Install a carbon filter prior to the icemaker line (see pages 229 and 230).

■ Even if you have flushed the line (Step 3), throw out the first two batches of ice to make sure the line is completely clean.

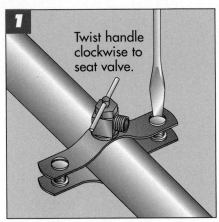
Twist handle clockwise to seat valve.

1. Install a saddle valve.
NOTE: *Shut off the water and drain the line.* There are two types of saddle valves. One uses a spike to puncture the water supply pipe. You clamp it in place and twist the valve handle until it punctures the pipe. The other requires that you drill a hole in the line, twist the valve into the hole, and clamp the unit firmly on the pipe.

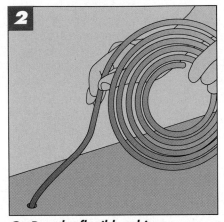

2. Run the flexible tubing.
Starting at the floor behind your refrigerator, drill a hole for the flexible copper line. Place it so the refrigerator will not bump into the line. Straighten the tubing carefully to avoid kinking it and push it through the hole toward the saddle valve. Leave an ample amount of tubing in a springlike coil so you can pull the refrigerator away from the wall without kinking the tubing.

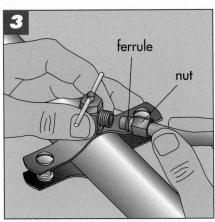
ferrule
nut

3. Connect to the saddle valve.
Taking care not to kink the tubing, bend it so you can stick it straight into the valve. Slip on a nut and ferrule, slide the tubing in, and tighten the nut. It is a good idea to flush the line before you start making ice. Place the other end of the tubing in a large bucket, and have a helper briefly turn the water back on to clear any sediment.

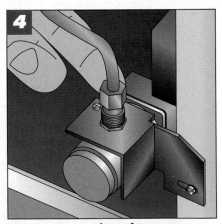

4. Connect to the refrigerator.
Position the refrigerator as if you were about to do that semiannual under-the-fridge floor cleaning. Carefully uncoil the tubing and attach it to the icemaker connection as you did at the saddle valve. Turn on the valve at the refrigerator and turn the water back on. If you used a drill-type saddle valve, open the saddle valve and turn on the icemaker.

INSTALLING GARBAGE DISPOSALS

A garbage disposal is a useful upgrade to your kitchen that is not too difficult to install. The hardest part is working under your sink, so work on plenty of towels to make it as comfortable as possible. If you're installing a new sink, attach the disposal to the sink first, then set the sink in place. Begin by removing the trap from one of the sink strainers.

YOU'LL NEED...

TIME: Several hours, not including installing an electrical receptacle and switch.
SKILLS: Basic electrical and plumbing connections.
TOOLS: Hammer, spud wrench, screwdriver, tongue-and-groove pliers, putty knife, and wire stripper.

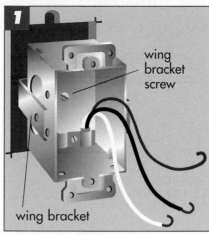

1. Supply electricity.
If there isn't one already, install an electrical box under the sink near the disposal. Install a GFCI receptacle and plug the disposal in. Or hard-wire the disposal (see Step 6 on page 234). Unless you are using a self-switching disposal, install a switch as well.

TIME SAVER

SELF-SWITCHING DISPOSAL
Most disposals will require a switched receptacle, leaving the homeowner with the difficult job of finding a good location for the switch. A wall switch usually means fishing an electrical line up the wall above the countertop. Another option is a switch on the face of the lower cabinets, but that puts it within the reach of children.

To avoid these problems, spend the extra money for a self-switching garbage disposal. Just plug it into a regular always hot receptacle. It turns on when food is pushed into it.

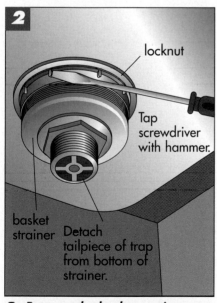

2. Remove the basket strainer.
Disconnect the trap assembly from the basket strainer and the drainpipe. Remove the locknut holding the strainer in place using a spud wrench or a hammer and screwdriver as shown. Lift out the strainer, and clean away old putty from around the sink opening using a putty knife, paint thinner, and an abrasive pad.

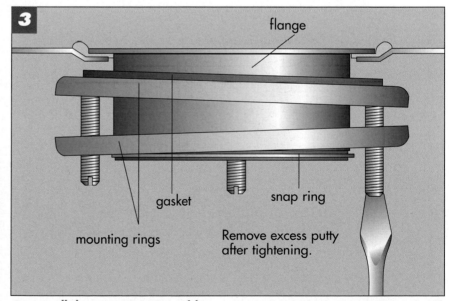

3. Install the mounting assembly.
You'll usually need to take apart the mounting assembly. To do this, remove the snap ring, mounting rings, and gasket from the flange.

Lay a rope of putty around the sink opening and seat the flange in the opening. Have a helper hold the flange in place as you work from underneath. Slip the gasket, mounting rings, and snap ring up onto the flange. The snap ring will keep the mounting assembly in place temporarily.

Tighten the mounting assembly against the sink by turning the screws counterclockwise, as shown. Tighten each screw a little at a time to assure a tight seal. With a putty knife, shave away excess putty.

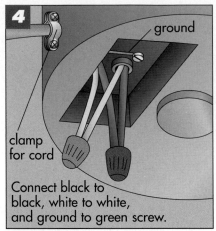

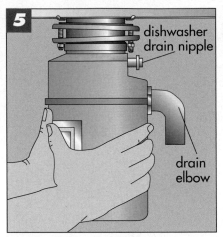

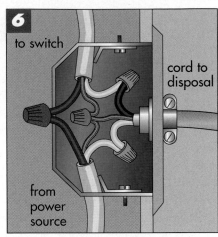

4. Connect the electrical cord.

Remove the electrical cover plate on the disposal. Strip sheathing and wire insulation from an approved appliance cord (see pages 200–201) and insert it into the opening. Tighten the clamp while holding the cord in place. Make the electrical connections in the disposal, ease the wires into place, and reinstall the cover plate.

5. Attach the disposal.

Secure the drain elbow to the disposal. If you'll drain a dishwasher through the unit, remove the knockout inside the nipple. To mount the disposal, lift it into place, and rotate it until it engages and tightens. (This may take some muscle.) Once the connection is made, rotate disposal to the best position for attaching the drain lines.

6. Make the electrical connection.

If you installed an electrical receptacle, simply insert the disposal's plug. For a hard-wired installation, *first shut off power*. Then connect the source black wire to the switch black wire, the white switch wire to the black wire leading to the disposal, the white disposal wire to the white power source wire, and all the ground wires together.

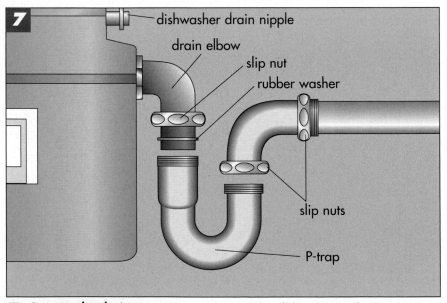

7. Connect the drain.

Fit a slip nut and a rubber washer onto the drain elbow, and fasten the trap to the elbow and the drainpipe. You may need to cut the elbow to make the connection. For double sinks connect the elbow to the second bowl drain. If you will be draining a dishwasher through the disposal, connect the dishwasher drain hose to the drain nipple of the disposal. Use an automotive clamp to attach the hose, tightening it in place with a screwdriver or ratchet and socket. Test for leaks by running water down through the disposal. Turn the electrical power back on. With standing water in the bowl, turn the disposal on, and make sure it is securely attached.

EXPERTS' INSIGHT

TIPS ON INSTALLING THE DRAINPIPES

■ On a double-bowl sink, it is possible to remove the drain elbow of the disposal and run pipe straight across to the trap of the other bowl. But the best way is to install a separate trap for the disposal so each bowl has its own trap.

■ If the original drain traps are in good condition, reuse them. In most cases if you buy one extension piece you will have enough material to complete the piping. If your old trap looks at all worn, save yourself a repair job later by replacing it while you have everything apart.

MAINTAINING GARBAGE DISPOSALS

To avoid maintenance problems, be sure you have cold water running before you turn on your disposal. Gradually feed in food waste. Do not stick a spatula or any silverware down past the splash guard. With the cold water continuing to flow, run the disposal for a few seconds after the food has been ground. If you hear a clanking sound, or if the disposal stops, remove the object that has caused the problem by following the steps shown here.

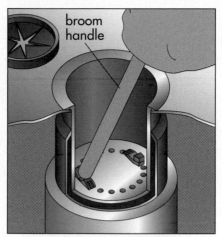

Remove stuck objects.
If a fork, bottle cap, or any other solid object drops down through the splash guard, it can cause the disposal to jam. If this happens, turn off the power (if it has not already shut itself off). Remove the splash guard and peer down the disposal with a flashlight. If you can't free the object, rotate the grinder with a broom handle.

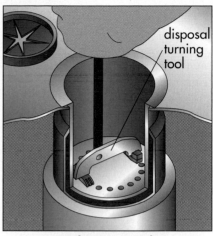

Use a special turning tool.
Your disposal may come with an Allen wrench that fits into a hole at the bottom of the disposal. If not, you can purchase a tool like the one shown. In either case, use the tool to turn the disposal back and forth. Once it's free, remove any obstructions, replace the splash guard, turn on the cold water, and test the disposal.

YOU'LL NEED...

TIME: Less than an hour to deal with most problems.
SKILLS: No special skills needed, unless you need to auger.
TOOLS: Allen wrench or disposal turning tool, flashlight, auger, and broom handle.

Reset an overloaded disposal.
If your disposal motor shuts off during operation, its overload protector has sensed overheating and has broken the electrical connection. Wait a few minutes for the unit to cool, then push the red reset button on the bottom of the disposal. If that doesn't work, check to see that you have power to the unit by inspecting the cord and the fuse or circuit breaker.

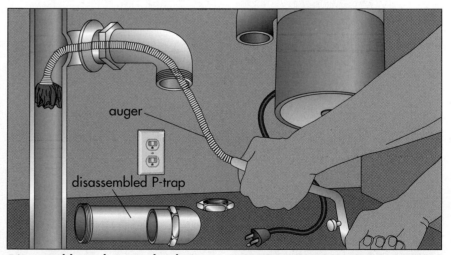

Disassemble and auger the drain.
Because a disposal gobbles up huge amounts of food waste, it's to be expected that occasionally the drain line will clog. If this happens, disassemble and remove the P-trap (make sure you have a bucket handy to catch the water that will spill), and clean out the trap (see page 170). If the trap itself is clear, thread a drain auger into the drainpipe (see page 172).

CAUTION
DON'T USE CHEMICALS
Do not attempt to clear a blocked drain line with chemicals of any type—not even "safe" chemicals. If the solution does not work, you'll be in danger of getting spattered with the stuff when you work to clear the line.

REPLACING AND INSTALLING DISHWASHERS

Replacing a dishwasher is fairly simple. Most units fit neatly into a 24-inch-wide undercounter cavity, and all are prewired and ready for simple supply, drainage, and electrical hookups. Installing a new dishwasher, however, is a much larger job: You must make room for it and bring in electrical, supply, and drain lines. To avoid straining the discharge pump, position the dishwasher as near to the sink as possible.

YOU'LL NEED...

TIME: About two hours to replace a dishwasher; a full day or more to put in a new one.
SKILLS: Simple electrical and plumbing skills for replacing; carpentry and basic plumbing and electrical skills for a new installation.
TOOLS: Drill, electrical tools, carpentry tools, screwdriver, and tongue-and-groove pliers.

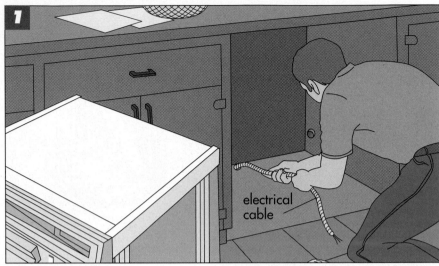

electrical cable

1. Prepare the opening.
NOTE: *Shut off the water and shut off the electrical power.*
If you are replacing an existing dishwasher, remove its lower panel and disconnect the supply line, the drain hose, and the electrical line. Remove any screws attaching it to the countertop, and carefully pull the unit out.

For a new installation, remove a 24-inch-wide base cabinet, or tailor a space to fit the dishwasher. Bore a hole large enough to allow for the supply and drain lines near the lower back of the side panel of the adjoining cabinet. The dishwasher will need its own 15- or 20-amp circuit. Run a circuit from the service panel (you may want to hire a licensed electrician to install this).

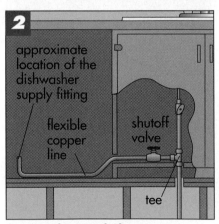

approximate location of the dishwasher supply fitting

flexible copper line

shutoff valve

tee

2. Run the supply line.
Cut into the hot water supply line, and insert a standard tee fitting, a nipple, and a shutoff valve. Run flexible copper tubing into the cavity, leaving enough line to reach the dishwasher supply fitting. (See pages 184–187 and 190–193 for information on working with various types of pipes.)

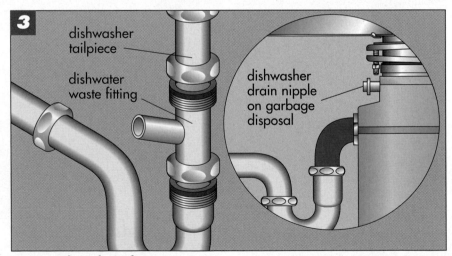

dishwasher tailpiece

dishwater waste fitting

dishwasher drain nipple on garbage disposal

3. Provide a drain fitting.
Your dishwasher can drain either into the sink drain or into a garbage disposal if you have one.

For sink drainage, install a dishwasher tailpiece. Loosen the slip nuts and remove the tailpiece, insert the dishwasher tailpiece into the trap, and cut the old tailpiece to fit above it. Connect all the pieces, and tighten the slip nuts.

To drain a dishwasher into a garbage disposal, use a screwdriver and hammer to remove the metal knockout inside the dishwasher drain nipple located near the top of the disposal. The knockout, when freed, may fall into the grinding chamber of the disposal, so be sure to take it out.

4. Attach the drain line.
Thread the drain line through the hole in the cabinet, and slip it onto the dishwasher tailpiece or drain nipple—you may have to push hard. Secure it with an automotive hose clamp.

To ensure proper operation of the appliance, the drain line must make a loop as shown at top right, so that at some point it is raised near the height of the countertop. Support the drain line securely—it will vibrate during use—by wrapping a couple of lengths of wire around it and fastening them to screws driven into the underside of the countertop. Take care that the screws do not poke through the countertop. Some local codes require an air gap (see inset) at the top of the loop. You can place this in a knockout hole in the sink or drill a hole for it in the countertop. Run one line from the drain nipple to the air gap, another from the air gap to the dishwasher drain outlet.

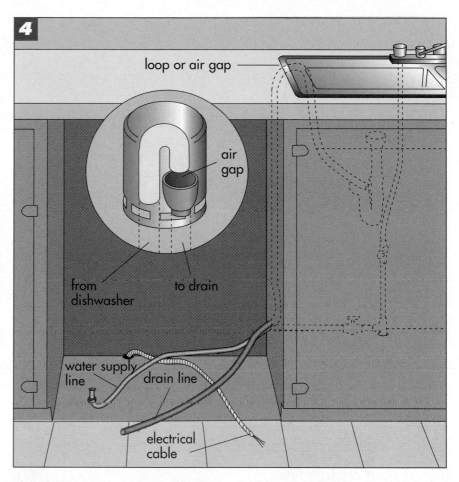

loop or air gap

air gap

from dishwasher

to drain

water supply line

drain line

electrical cable

5. Make the hookups.
Position the ends of the three lines approximately at the locations where they will be connected to the dishwasher. Remove the bottom cover plate from the dishwasher, and slide the unit carefully into place, watching to make sure no lines are damaged. Make sure the dishwasher is all the way in position.

Make the connections as shown in the detail drawings. Tighten the compression nut and drain line clamp firmly, and make secure electrical connections.

Adjust the dishwasher by turning the leveling screws on the legs; then check with a level. Anchor the dishwasher to the underside of the countertop with screws. Turn on the water and the electrical power. Before reattaching access panels, run the washer, watching carefully for leaks.

leveling screw

water supply line

drain line

electrical connection

compression nut

drain line clamp

ADJUSTING DRAIN ASSEMBLIES

If the water in your bathroom sink or tub gradually leaks out when you've stopped the drain, or if it doesn't drain out as quickly as you would like, you may need to adjust your drain assembly.

Before dismantling the assembly, pull up the strainer or stopper, and remove any hair or other debris hanging from it. Next thoroughly clean away soap or other gunk that may be keeping the strainer or stopper from seating properly.

YOU'LL NEED...

TIME: An hour for most adjustments.
SKILLS: Basic plumbing skills.
TOOLS: Screwdriver and pliers.

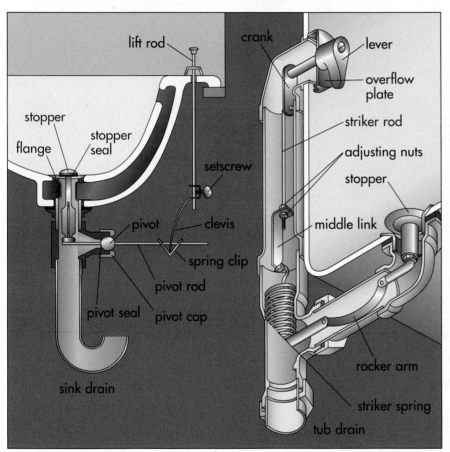

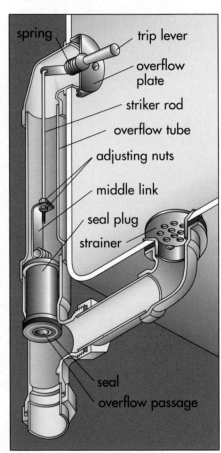

Pop-up drains

If you've cleaned out the strainer and stopper and the problem persists, check the stopper seal. If it's damaged, replace any rubber parts or replace the stopper itself. Look for signs of wear on the flange the stopper seats into.

On a bathroom sink, examine the pivot rod. When the stopper is closed, it should slant slightly up from the pivot to the clevis. If it doesn't, loosen the setscrew, raise or lower the clevis on the lift rod, and retighten the screw.

If the stopper doesn't operate as easily now as you would like, squeeze the spring clip, pull the pivot rod out of the clevis, and reinsert it into the next higher or lower hole. If water drips from the pivot, try tightening its cap. If the pivot still drips, you may need to replace the seal inside.

To adjust a tub pop-up, unscrew the overflow plate, withdraw the entire assembly, and loosen the adjusting nuts. If the stopper doesn't seat tightly, move the middle link higher on the striker rod. If the tub is slow to drain, lower the link.

Trip-lever drain

A trip lever lifts and lowers a seal plug at the base of the overflow tube. When the seal plug drops into its seat, water from the tub drain can't get past. But because the plug is hollow, water can still flow through the overflow tube through the overflow passage in the seal plug.

Dismantle and adjust a trip lever as you would a tub pop-up unit. Also check the seal on the bottom of the plug and replace it if it appears to be worn.

CARPENTRY BASICS

Chapter 6

GETTING TO KNOW YOUR HOME

When you plan a carpentry project or go to a building supply center for materials, it helps to know the common terms describing the parts of your house. Some of these terms vary from region to region, but most are understood throughout the country. Although this book deals primarily with interior carpentry projects, you need to be able to visualize how your house is put together. Even a task as simple as attaching a wall shelf or installing baseboard molding requires some knowledge of framing.

The house shown at *right* combines the elements of old and new construction—a situation you may find in your own home. The two-story section of the house shows construction methods and materials common between 1910 and 1960. The one-story addition shows materials and techniques in common use by contractors today.

Framing is the skeleton of your house, the basic structure holding it together. Vertical **wall studs** run from floor to ceiling. They're usually made of 2×4s, but often 2×6s or 2×8s are used to allow for more insulation. The horizontal pieces at the top and bottom of the walls are called **plates**. The bottom plate rests on a **concrete block** or **formed concrete** foundation. Walls may have **fire blocking** running horizontally about halfway up the wall.

Wherever there is an opening for a door or a window, a correctly sized **header**, made of a massive piece of lumber or two pieces of 2× lumber, must span the gap in the framing. For more details about framing, see pages 329–335.

Roofs are supported by either **rafters** or **trusses**, which use small-dimensioned lumber joined in such a way as to give them strength. **Collar ties** brace the rafters. The roof typically is made of plywood or shiplap covered with **roofing felt** and **shingles**. **Eaves** are trimmed with **fascia**. **Vents** draw hot air from the attic.

Joists made of 2×10s support **subfloors** and **flooring** and other interior load-bearing walls. The undersides of joists provide nailing surfaces for ceilings.

On the exterior walls, the framing is covered with at least three layers of material. First comes **sheathing**, which in older homes is made of 1× lumber run horizontally. When it's milled with an overlapping joint, it is called **shiplap**. Plywood, fiberboard, or foamboard is used in newer homes. Next comes a paperlike layer to improve insulation and reduce the effects of condensation. Older homes use **roofing felt** (also called tar paper) or a reddish-colored building paper; newer homes have **house wrap**, often made of polyethylene. Finally, the house is clad in siding. This house has horizontal **beveled siding**, but vertical siding and sheet siding are also common. Inside the walls, older homes often have gray-colored **rock wool insulation**; **fiberglass batts** are used now.

Interior wall surfaces of older homes usually are covered with **lath**, thin pieces of rough, 3⁄8-inch thick wood, run horizontally. The lath is covered with two or three layers of **plaster**. Today **drywall** is nailed or screwed to the framing and the joints and nail holes are covered with joint compound. Plastering is a specialized skill that takes years to learn, but a homeowner can apply and finish drywall (see pages 338-343).

Gaps around windows (**double-hung sash**, **casement**, **fixed-pane**, or **full-round**), doors, and along walls are covered with molding. See pages 304–307 for how to apply molding.

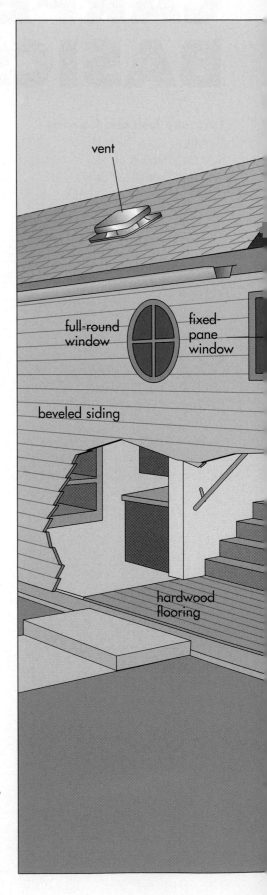

vent

full-round window

fixed-pane window

beveled siding

hardwood flooring

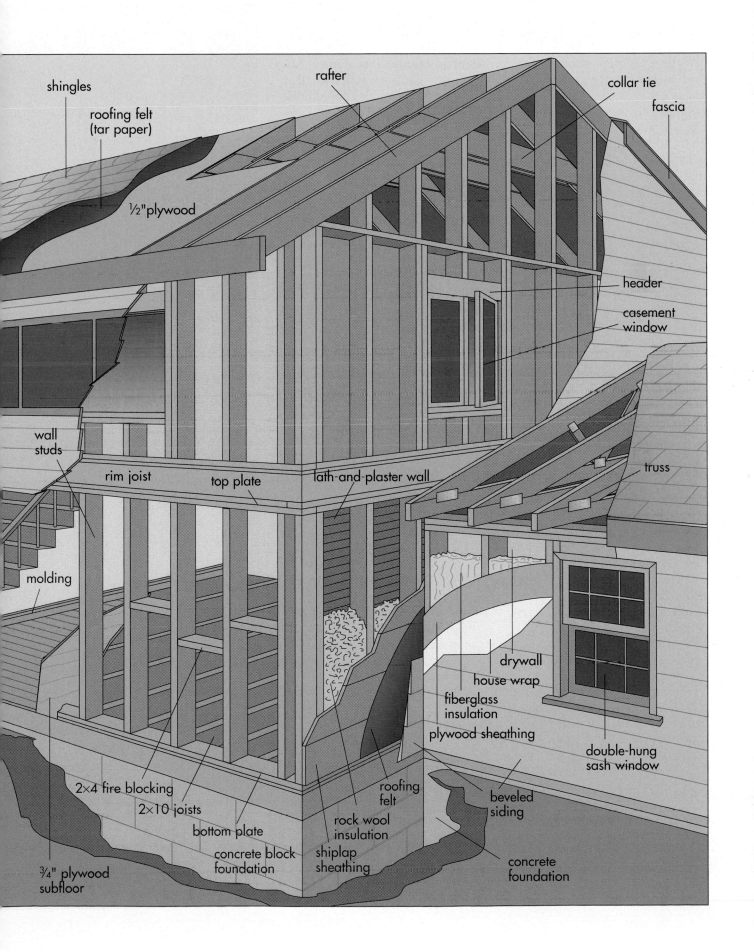

shingles

roofing felt
(tar paper)

rafter

collar tie

fascia

½" plywood

header

casement
window

wall
studs

rim joist

top plate

lath-and-plaster wall

truss

molding

drywall

house wrap

fiberglass
insulation

plywood sheathing

double-hung
sash window

2×4 fire blocking

2×10 joists

bottom plate

concrete block
foundation

roofing
felt

rock wool
insulation

shiplap
sheathing

beveled
siding

concrete
foundation

¾" plywood
subfloor

SELECTING HAND TOOLS

Often, the right hand tool makes your job easier and yields better results. Hand tools are relatively inexpensive so it's easy to gather quite a collection. To avoid becoming a tool junkie who fills the basement with tools that will never be used, assemble a basic tool kit and add to your collection only when the job at hand requires a new tool.

Typically, the top-of-the-line contractor-type tool model will be of higher quality than an average homeowner needs, but inexpensive tools will not perform well. Your best choice is a mid-priced model. If you need a tool to complete an unusual task and probably won't need it very often, go with the cheaper version.

Few tools see more action than the flexible **tape measure.** Buy a 25-foot one with a 1-inch-wide blade; this will extend farther and last longer than a ¾-inch one. Some carpenters prefer a folding ruler for smaller jobs. Purchase one with a metal pull-out extension for making precise inside-to-inside measurements (see page 260).

A **framing square** (also called a carpenter's square) is used to check corners for square and to mark for rafters and stringers. More often, you'll need a smaller square. A triangular **speed square** is easy to use, allows you to quickly figure 45-degree-angle cuts, and holds its shape after getting banged around. It slips into your back pocket and is handy for quickly marking cut lines on planks and framing material. A **combination square** is helpful for scribing lines (see page 263). A **T-bevel** can be set to duplicate an angle.

Plumb and level large and small projects with a **carpenter's level.** A 2- or 4-foot model works well for most projects. A **plumb bob** establishes true vertical lines. Snap long, straight lines with a **chalk line.** A chalk line also can double as a plumb bob.

Although you will do most of your cutting with power tools, a **handsaw** still comes in handy. You may want to choose a smaller saw that fits into a tool box. For accurate miter cuts, use a **backsaw** and **miter box.** Use a **drywall saw** to cut curves in drywall. To make rough curved cuts in wood, choose a **keyhole saw.** Cut intricate and precise curves in thin materials with a **coping saw.**

Wood chisels enable you to shape mortises and make rough notches in places where a saw will not reach. Choose chisels with metal-capped handles. Have a **utility knife** close at hand for razor-sharp cuts. Most people prefer one with a retractable blade. To shave wood along the length of a board, use a **plane** for the smoothest cut. For final shaping, use a **rasp** or a **wood file.**

Buy a **hammer** that is comfortable and solidly built. The most popular model weighs 16 ounces and has curved claws. You'll find a baffling array of specialty hammers, including framing and wallboard hammers. Stick to the basic curved-claw hammer. To sink the heads of finishing nails below the surface of the work, use a **nail set.**

Have plenty of **screwdrivers** on hand; get various sizes of both Phillips-tipped and slot-tipped types, or buy a combination screwdriver that has four tips in one tool. Make pilot holes for small screws with an **awl.**

To fasten nuts, bolts, and lag screws, use an **adjustable wrench.** For holding pieces of wood firmly, have **C-clamps** of various sizes handy. A pair of **locking pliers** helps to hold fasteners or pieces of wood tight while you work.

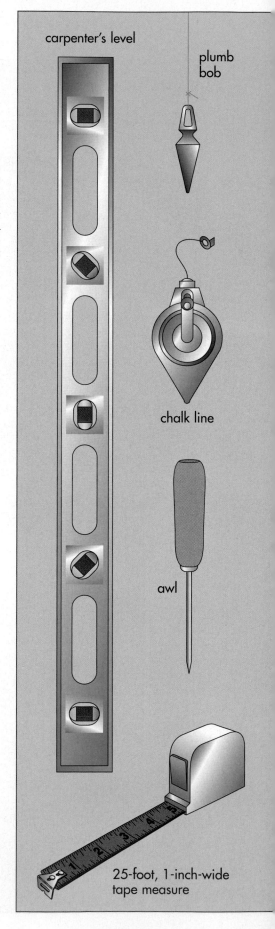

carpenter's level

plumb bob

chalk line

awl

25-foot, 1-inch-wide tape measure

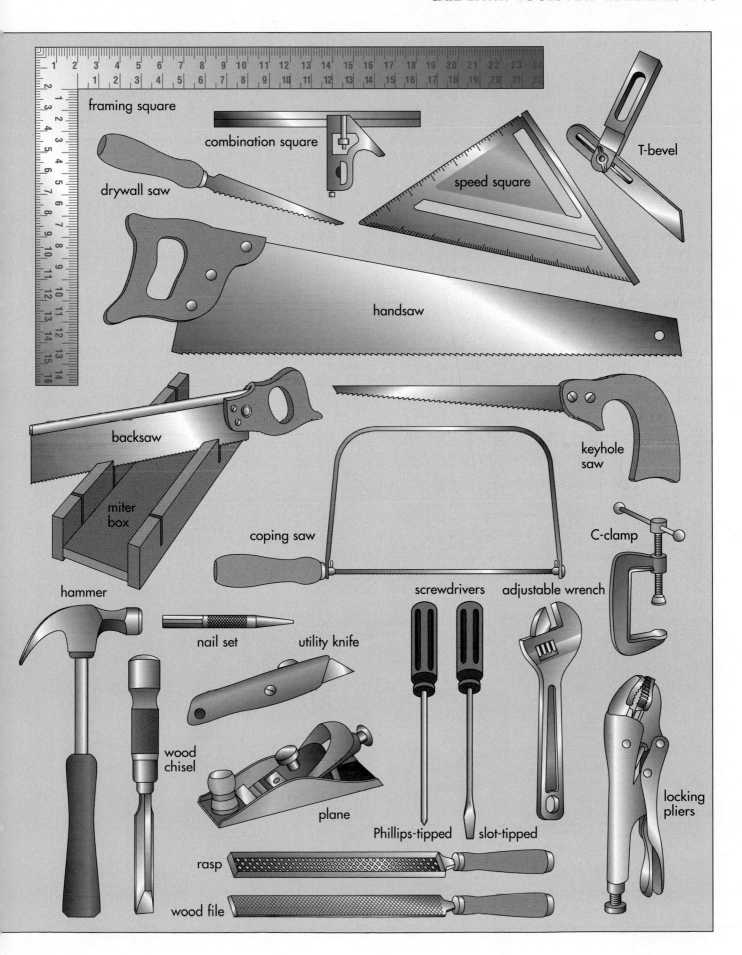

framing square

combination square

speed square

T-bevel

drywall saw

handsaw

backsaw

keyhole saw

miter box

coping saw

C-clamp

hammer

screwdrivers

adjustable wrench

nail set

utility knife

wood chisel

plane

Phillips-tipped

slot-tipped

locking pliers

rasp

wood file

Tongue-and-groove pliers are one of the most useful tools you can buy so it makes sense to pay extra for a high-quality pair. They grab most anything firmly and work well for pulling nails. **Lineman's pliers** enable you to grab things tightly from the front rather than the side of the tool and also will cut nails or screws. **Side-cutting pliers** enable you to cut nails nearly flush to the surface. They also are useful for grabbing the pointed ends of finishing nails to pull them out of the back of molding without marring the face.

A **flat pry bar** is indispensable. With it, you can pry apart fastened lumber pieces with minimal damage to the wood. It also is handy for levering heavy objects into place; for example, reattaching a door on its hinges.

A **cat's paw** (also called a nail puller) makes it easy to pull nails, although it will damage the wood (see page 289). It's indispensable if you are planning any demolition.

For patching damaged walls and for taping drywall, have a variety of sizes of **taping knives** to apply wallboard compound (see pages 342–343). If you have 6-, 8-, and 12-inch blades you will be prepared to tape or patch most any surface. If you have a lot of drywall to cut, you'll thank yourself for buying a **drywall square.** You'll find it is also very useful for marking cut lines on pieces of plywood.

Sanding large wall and ceiling areas is much easier if you have a **pole sander.** Buy a smaller sanding block for detail work (see pages 300–301).

Use a **caulking gun** to fill cracks with caulk or to apply construction adhesive. Purchase a **staple gun** to attach sheets of plastic or felt or to install fiberglass insulation batts.

A **forming tool** is easier to use than a plane for working wood, but it will not cut as straight or as smooth. It is more versatile, however, and comes in handy for fine-tuning anything from foam board to wallboard.

When you need to stabilize something that is too thick to handle with a C-clamp, use a quick-fitting **adjustable clamp.** To clamp a straightedge in place or hold thin materials that might be marred by a C-clamp (see page 243) or adjustable clamp, use a **squeeze clamp** (see page 291 for other specialized clamps).

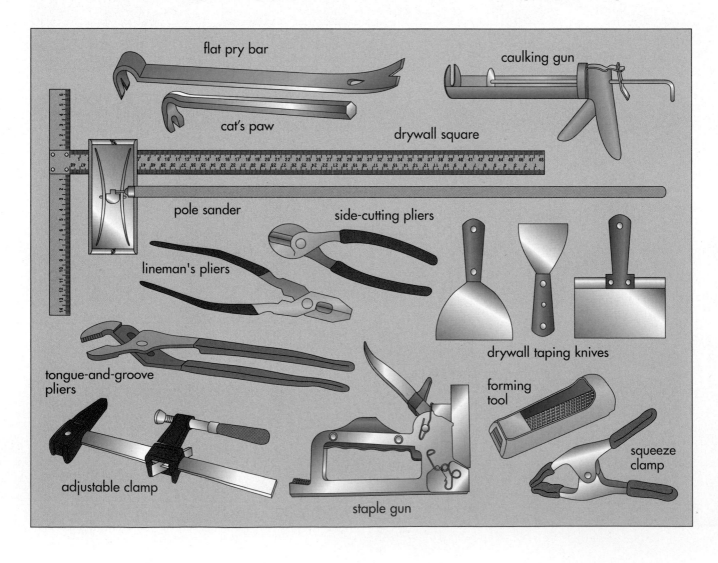

flat pry bar

caulking gun

cat's paw

drywall square

pole sander

side-cutting pliers

lineman's pliers

drywall taping knives

tongue-and-groove pliers

forming tool

adjustable clamp

squeeze clamp

staple gun

SELECTING BASIC POWER TOOLS

A circular saw, a power drill, and a sabersaw are musts for your basic tool kit. With the two saws you can make straight and curved cuts quickly in almost any material. The drill lets you make holes of almost any size and drive screws quickly and easily. With these three tools, you can handle most any household carpentry job.

A **circular saw** crosscuts, angle-cuts, rips (cuts lengthwise), and even bevels lumber easily and cleanly. Don't worry if the saw has a plastic housing; many plastics are very strong. Do take a look at the metal baseplate. A baseplate made of thin, stamped metal can warp; look for a thicker base made of extruded or cast metal. A saw that takes 7¼-inch blades is the usual choice. It lets you cut to a depth of about 2½ inches at 90 degrees and to cut through a piece of 2× lumber even when the blade is set at 45 degrees.

Horsepower is not important when choosing a circular saw. Instead, look at the amperage and the type of bearings. A low-cost saw pulls only 9 or 10 amps and runs on rollers or sleeve bearings. This means less power, a shorter life because it heats up easily, and less precise cuts because the blade wobbles somewhat. Better saws are rated at 12 or 13 amps and run on ball bearings. This combination of extra power and smoother operation makes for long life and more precise cutting. Worm-drive saws, which are the most powerful saws and have the longest-lasting bearings, are heavy and hard to use. As is often the case, a mid-priced saw is your best choice.

Be sure to get a variable-speed, reversible **power drill**. Unless you will be doing heavy-duty work, you don't need one with a ½-inch chuck; a ⅜-inch one is fine. Buy a drill that pulls at least 3.5 amps. A keyless chuck makes changing bits quick and easy, but some people prefer a keyed chuck for a tighter grip on the bit.

A **cordless drill** frees you to work without the mess of electrical cords. Buy one that uses at least 9.6 volts, preferably more. If possible, get an extra battery pack so you won't have to wait for a battery to charge.

When buying a **sabersaw**, examine the baseplate and the mechanism for adjusting it. On cheaper saws, these are flimsy and eventually wobble, making it difficult to keep the blade aligned vertically. Variable speed is a useful option. A saw pulling 3 amps or more handles most difficult jobs.

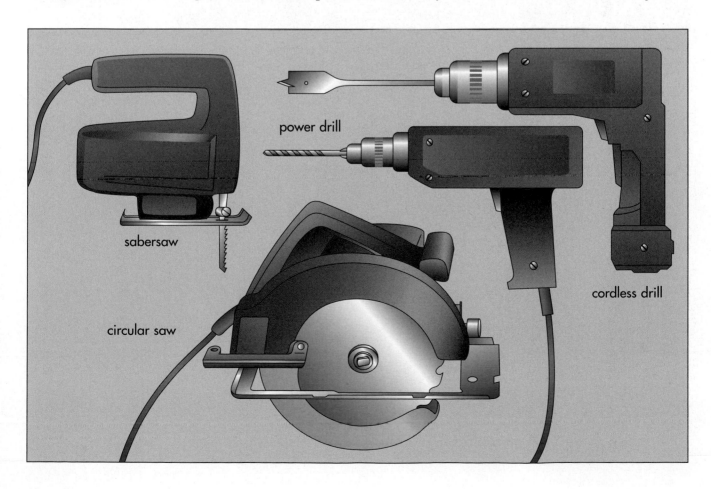

power drill

sabersaw

cordless drill

circular saw

SELECTING SPECIALIZED POWER TOOLS

The more carpentry jobs you take on, the more power tools you will need or want to own. Many of these are high-priced items, so do some careful research before making a purchase. If the tool is one you will turn to often, pay extra money to get a good-quality one that will last. If you will use it only rarely, settle for a lesser-quality tool.

To determine the quality of a tool, check the amperage rather than the horsepower. Compare models and avoid buying the one with the lowest amperage rating. A plastic housing is not necessarily a sign of poor quality. But do check any mechanisms and metal

attachments to see if they're solid. A tool with ball bearings runs smoother and lasts longer than one with other types of bearings.

For quick sanding of large areas, nothing beats a **belt sander.** Make sure it uses belts that are easily available—3×24 inches is the most common size. A good belt sander is fairly heavy and has a large dust collector. You can switch from rough to fine sanding belts; however, because a belt sander is difficult to handle for fine work, you probably will want to use another method for the final sanding—either a hand-sanding block or a smaller mechanized sander, such as a **random-orbit**

sander. It works by moving rapidly in small circles. Some people prefer the finish of an older-style vibrating sander, which simply moves back and forth. Some units switch from random-orbit to vibrating action.

With a **router,** you can mill lumber to a wide variety of shapes (see page 283). If you choose a solid model with plenty of power and a base that won't warp with age, you can produce pieces that are just as straight and smooth as millwork from a factory.

If you plan a project that calls for joining two pieces of lumber side by side, a **biscuit joiner** produces professional-looking

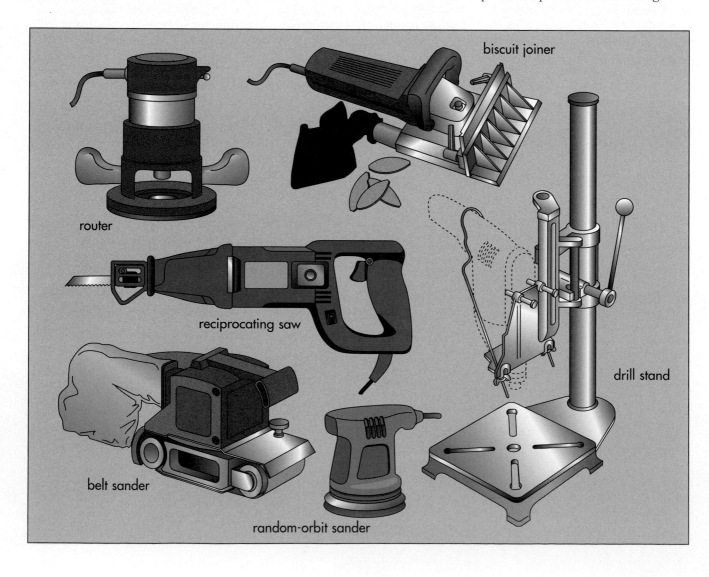

biscuit joiner

router

reciprocating saw

drill stand

belt sander

random-orbit sander

results with ease (see page 297).

Need to drill holes that are precisely vertical? You can purchase a drill press or a **drill stand** that uses a regular power drill. A stand is less expensive than a drill press, but does take more time to set up and use.

For demolition work, nothing beats a **reciprocating saw.** It can make cuts in places where no other saw will reach. If you need to remove portions of walls or floors, this tool can save you a lot of time and frustration.

If you have to cut a lot of molding or exterior siding, consider a **power miter saw.** This tool (also called a chopsaw or cutoff saw) is simply a circular saw mounted on a pivot assembly. It makes quick, precise crosscuts and miter cuts. Make sure you get a saw large enough to cut all the way through the stock you want to cut; a 10-inch blade handles most projects. Unless you will be doing complicated framing, there is no need to buy a model that makes compound miter cuts.

Use a **bench grinder** to sharpen tools and shape wood and metal

objects. Clamp it to your work bench, and it will be ready to use at a moment's notice.

With a good **tablesaw** you can make perfectly straight, long cuts. Use it for dado cuts as well. It also works for crosscuts and miter cuts (see page 281), but not as easily as a power miter saw. Choose a model that has a solid table that will not wiggle as you work on it, a fence that stays firmly in place, and a powerful motor. Keep in mind that you will need a good deal of room in your shop if you are going to use a tablesaw to cut sheets of plywood or long pieces of lumber.

A **radial-arm saw** is a general-purpose power saw. It makes long cuts like a tablesaw and crosscuts and miter cuts like a power miter saw. But like many multipurpose tools, it takes more time to do the job with it than with more specialized tools. Homeowners with limited space and funds, however, find this tool works quite well for a variety of cutting jobs; others prefer to buy the more specialized tools.

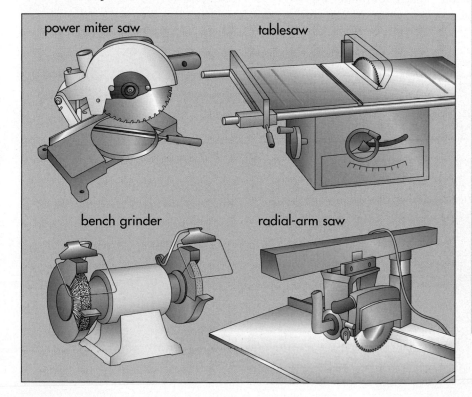

power miter saw

tablesaw

bench grinder

radial-arm saw

SELECTING AND BUYING LUMBER

As you learn carpentry techniques, it's important to become familiar with the characteristics and uses of various types of lumber and how to choose the wood that will work best for a particular project.

There are two basic types of lumber—softwoods, typically made from coniferous trees, and hardwoods, made from deciduous trees. Wood is graded according to how many knots it has and the quality of its surface (see the chart below for the most common grades). Some lumberyards have their own grading systems, but they usually simply rename these standard grades.

No matter what species of lumber you buy, be on the lookout for the types of wood problems shown at *right*. A board that is heavily **twisted, bowed, cupped,** or **crooked** usually is not usable, although some bows will lie down as you nail them in place. **Knots** are only a cosmetic problem unless they are loose and likely to pop out. **Checking,** which is a rift in the surface, also is only cosmetic. **Splits** cannot be repaired and will widen in time. Cut them off.

The nominal dimensions of wood are used when ordering lumber. Keep in mind that the actual dimensions of the lumber will be less (see the chart on page 249). Large quantities of lumber are sometimes figured by the board foot. A board foot is the wood equivalent of a piece 12 nominal inches square and 1 inch thick (see chart at *bottom*). Most lumberyards will not require you to figure board feet.

SOME COMMON GRADES OF WOOD

Grades	Characteristics
Clear	Has no knots.
Select or select structural	Very high-quality wood. Broken down into Nos. 1–3 or grades A–D; the lower grades will have more knots.
No. 2 common	Has tight knots, no major blemishes; good for shelving.
No. 3 common	Some knots may be loose, often blemished or damaged.
Construction or standard	Good strength; used for general framing.
Utility	Economy grade used for rough framing.

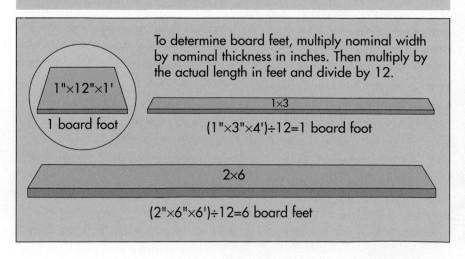

To determine board feet, multiply nominal width by nominal thickness in inches. Then multiply by the actual length in feet and divide by 12.

1"×12"×1'
1 board foot

1×3
(1"×3"×4')÷12=1 board foot

2×6
(2"×6"×6')÷12=6 board feet

twist

bow

cup

crook

check   knot

split

LUMBER SELECTOR

Type		Description and Uses	Nominal Sizes	Actual Sizes
Furring	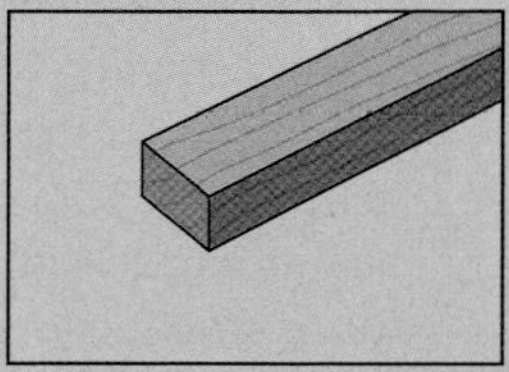	Rough wood of small dimensions. For furring drywall and paneling, interior and exterior trim, shimming, stakes, crates, light-duty frames, latticework, and edging.	1×2 1×3	¾×1½ ¾×2½
Finish lumber	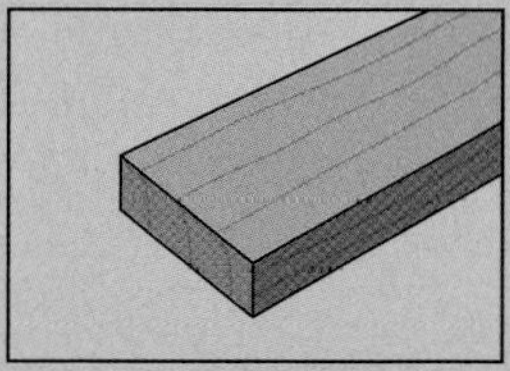	Smooth-finished lumber. For paneling, trim, shelving, light framing, structural finishing, forming, siding, decking, casing, valances, cabinets, built-ins, and furniture.	1×4 1×6 1×8 1×10 1×12	¾×3½ ¾×5½ ¾×7¼ ¾×9¼ ¾×11¼
Tongue-and-groove	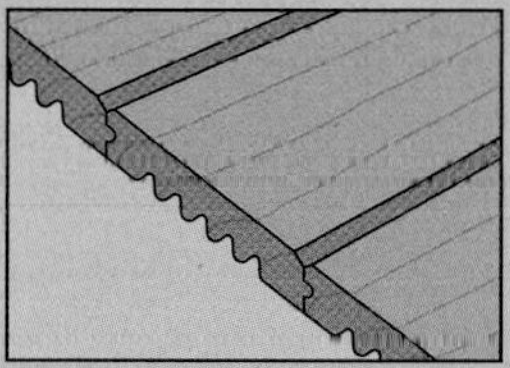	Tongues and grooves fit into each other for a tight fit. For decorative interior wall treatments, exterior siding, flooring, and subflooring.	1×4 1×6 1×8	Actual sizes vary from mill to mill
Shiplap	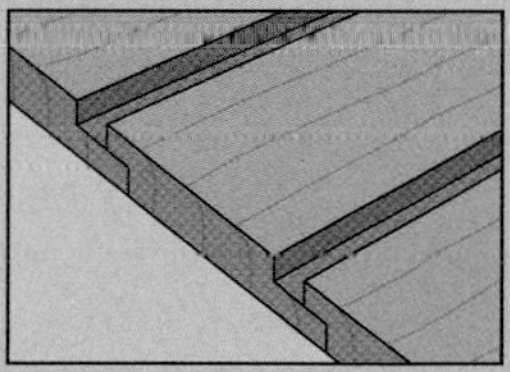	One edge fits on top of the other. For decorative wall treatments, siding, decking, exterior sheathing, subflooring, and roof sheathing.	1×4 1×6 1×8	¾×3⅛ ¾×5⅛ ¾×6⅞
Dimensional lumber	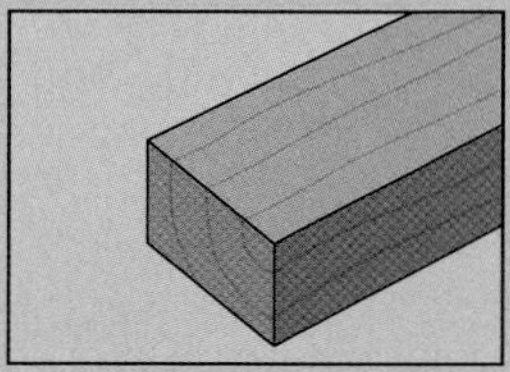	Studs are usually 2×4, sometimes 2×6. "Planks" are 6 or more inches wide. For structural framing (wall studs, ceiling and floor joists, rafters, headers, top and bottom plates), structural finishing, forming, exterior decking and fencing, and stair components (stringers, steps).	2×2 2×3 2×4 2×6 2×8 2×10 2×12 4×4 4×6 6×6	1½×1½ 1½×2½ 1½×3½ 1½×5½ 1½×7¼ 1½×9¼ 1½×11¼ 3½×3½ 3½×5½ 5½×5½
Glue-laminate	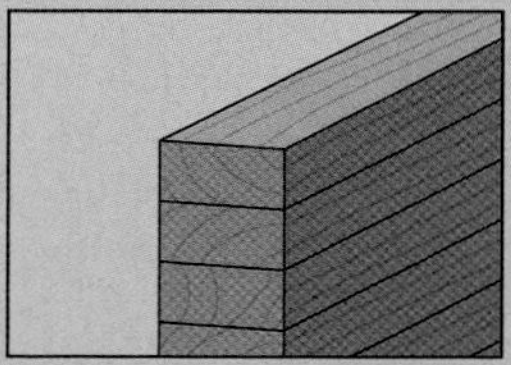	Layers of dimensional lumber laid flat on top of each other and laminated into one solid piece. Used for rafters, joists, and beams. Can be stained for exposed beams.	4×10 4×12 6×10 6×12	3½×9 3½×12 5½×9 5½×12
Micro-laminate	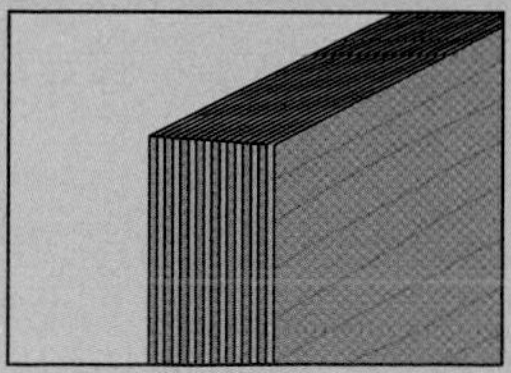	Veneers glued together with crossing grains like plywood, only thicker. For rafters, joists, and beams.	4×12	3½×11⅜

SELECTING SOFTWOODS

Unless you're installing major structural components, such as floor or ceiling joists, that will bear significant weight, you can't make a serious mistake when buying softwoods. In most cases, you simply want to buy the wood that looks best or is the least-expensive alternative.

Softwood usually is less expensive than hardwood (see page 251) because it comes from trees that grow faster. In general, the disadvantage of softwood is evident in its name; it actually is soft. If you use softwood for furniture and other objects that will get handled and bumped against, plan on applying a hard finish or paint. Even then, it will not be as durable as hardwood.

Most retail suppliers stock only a few species of softwood. The chart below summarizes the chief characteristics of each. In most cases, you won't be choosing between species, but between grades of lumber. Which grade you choose depends on the nature of your project.

Softwood grading is tricky because several grading systems exist. Most often, however, you'll find two general classifications: select and common.

Use select lumber, which comes in several subgrades, for trim or cabinetry where finished appearance counts. For all other projects, common lumber will do nicely. Common lumber is graded as No. 1, No. 2, and No. 3.

With some suppliers, you can dispense with the grades and talk about more straightforward categories, such as "clear" (without knots) and "tight-knot" (having only small knots without cracks).

Of course, the better the grade—that is, the fewer the defects—the more you pay for the product. Often, however, a better grade is only slightly more expensive. Once you gain some experience, if you sort through the lumber rack carefully, you often can find pieces that are out of their class—for instance, a piece of No. 2 common that actually could have been classified as select.

SOFTWOOD SELECTOR

Species	Characteristics	Common Uses
Cedar, cypress	Similar to redwood—only the darker wood is rot-resistant. Weak, brittle; resists warping; pleasant aroma; easy to cut.	Siding, paneling, rough trim, roof shingles and shakes, decks.
Fir, larch	Heavy, very strong, hard; holds nails well; good resistance to warping and shrinkage; somewhat difficult to cut.	Framing studs, joists, posts, and beams; flooring; subflooring.
"Hem/fir"	A general classification that takes in a variety of species. Lightweight, soft, fairly strong; warps easily; may shrink; easy to cut.	Framing, exterior fascia, flooring, subflooring, trim.
Pine	From eastern, northern, and western trees. Very light, soft, fairly weak; good resistance to warping, but with a tendency to shrink; easy to cut.	Paneling, trim (molding), flooring, cabinets.
Redwood	Durable and resistant to rot and insects if you get the darker-colored heartwood. Light, soft, not as strong as fir or Southern pine; tendency to split; easy to cut.	Exterior posts and beams, siding, paneling, decks, fences.
Southern pine	Very hard, stiff, excellent strength; holds nails well; has a tendency to crack, splinter, warp; cuts with average ease.	Framing, subflooring.
Spruce	Lightweight, soft, fairly strong; resistant to splitting and warping; easy to work.	Framing, flooring, subflooring, trim (molding).
Treated lumber	Several species can be treated—most often, fir, "hem/fir," and Southern pine are used. Green or brown color will fade in time, leaving the wood a dirty gray; extremely resistant to rot and insects.	Bottom framing plates that rest on concrete; other framing that might come into contact with water, decks, fences.

SELECTING HARDWOODS

You can buy various types of plastic-laminated products made to look like hardwood, but there is no substitute for the real thing. Hardwood flooring and trim give a home an elegance unmatched by any other product. For furniture and cabinetry, nothing quite measures up in appearance and durability.

Unfortunately, hardwood trees grow slowly, so prices tend to be higher than for softwood. But prices fluctuate widely from year to year, and often the difference is surprisingly small. Oak flooring, for example, is sometimes cheaper than softwood flooring.

The more expensive hardwoods are milled to make use of virtually every splinter of wood. Instead of the standard sizes, some hardwoods are sold in pieces of varying lengths and widths. Sometimes the boards are smooth-surfaced only on two sides (S2S), leaving the edges rough. Hardwoods may be priced by the board foot (see page 248).

Hardwood grading differs from that of softwoods. It is based primarily on the amount of clear surface area on the board. The best grade is FAS (firsts and seconds), which is the most knot-free. Select boards have defects on one side only: No. 1 Common has tiny, tight knots; No. 2 Common has larger knots.

Most lumberyards and home centers can't afford to maintain an extensive inventory of hardwood lumber and generally stock only a limited assortment of a few species. For the best selection, find a store that specializes in hardwoods. They stock or can order a wide selection of species.

EXPERTS' INSIGHT

HARDWOOD FROM MANAGED FORESTS

Concerned that your lumber may come from irreplaceable forests? The Forest Certification Resource Center lists suppliers of wood products derived from sustainable forests. You can search the FCRC's on-line data on contact it on the Internet at: http://www.certifiedwood.org/

HARDWOOD SELECTOR

Species	Characteristics	Common Uses
Birch	Hard, strong; fine-grained; resists shrinking and warping. Similar in color to maple—sometimes used as a cheaper replacement. Finishes fairly well; hard to cut.	Paintable cabinets, paneling, furniture.
Mahogany	Durable; fine-grained; resistant to shrinking, warping, and swelling. Finishes well; easy to cut. (Not to be confused with lauan mahogany, a much cheaper material that is used for veneers and plywoods.)	Fine furniture, cabinets, millwork, veneers.
Maple	Extremely hard, strong; pieces with bird's-eye or wavy grains are highly prized. Color ranges from reddish to nearly white in color. Finishes well; difficult to cut.	Flooring (basketball and bowling alley floors are made of maple), butcher blocks, veneers, millwork, and molding.
Poplar	Lightweight, soft for a hardwood; fine-grained. White to yellow-brown in color. Paints well; easy to cut.	Paintable furniture, cabinets, trim, places where a less-expensive hardwood will do.
Red oak	Hard, strong, rigid; pronounced open grain; resists warping, but may shrink if not well dried. Reddish color. Finishes well; moderately hard to cut.	Flooring, furniture, cabinets, molding, stair rails.
Walnut	Hard, heavy, extra strong; fairly pronounced, straight grain; resists warping and shrinking. Light to dark brown in color. Finishes well; cuts fairly easily.	Fine furniture and cabinets, millwork, paneling, inlays, veneers.
White oak	Hard, strong; open-grained, but not as pronounced as red oak; resists shrinking and warping. Golden color. Finishes well; moderately hard to cut.	Better than red oak for flooring—less variation in color. Millwork, molding, furniture, cabinets, stair rails, balusters.

SELECTING SHEET GOODS

Sheet goods are easy to work with and an inexpensive way to neatly cover large surface areas. For many applications, they provide the strength and appearance you need at a fraction of the cost of dimensional lumber.

Plywood is made by laminating thin layers (or plies) of wood to each other using water-resistant glue. The plies are sandwiched with the grain of each successive ply running at 90 degrees to the grain of the previous layer. This gives plywood its tremendous strength, as you will find if you try to break a piece in two. The front and back surface plies may be made of softwood, usually fir, or hardwood. A plywood face surface rated "A" is smooth and free of defects; "B," "C," and "D" faces are progressively rougher. Both faces need not be graded the same, for example, "A-C." T-111 plywood siding is made with exterior adhesive and a rough veneer.

Wood particles, sawdust, and glue are compressed and bonded together by heat to form **particleboard** and **hardboard**. This process produces a material that is hard, but easy to break. Hardboard comes in tempered (very hard) and untempered (softer) composition and is available in a variety of textures. Particleboard also comes in a variety of densities. Particleboard laminated with a plastic surface is handy for cabinet construction. **Waferboard** is made by a similar process, but with scraps of thin wood rather than sawdust, making it similar to plywood.

Drywall, sometimes called wallboard, is made of gypsum powder sandwiched between layers of heavy paper. **Cement board** is made with crushed rock and a nylon mesh.

SHEET GOODS SELECTOR

Material	Grades and Common Types	Thickness (in inches)	Common Panel Sizes (in feet)	Typical Uses
Plywood sheathing	C-D, C-D Exterior	$\frac{3}{8}$, $\frac{1}{2}$, $\frac{5}{8}$, $\frac{3}{4}$	4×8	Sheathing, subflooring, underlayment, structural supports. Tongue-and-groove and shiplap versions are available.
Finish plywood	A-B, A-C, B-C	$\frac{1}{4}$, $\frac{3}{8}$, $\frac{1}{2}$, $\frac{5}{8}$, $\frac{3}{4}$	4×8, 2×4	Cabinets, cabinet doors, shelves, soffits.
Hardwood plywood	A-A (or A-2), G1S (good one side); hardwood side sometimes labeled N	$\frac{1}{4}$, $\frac{3}{4}$	4×8, 2×4	Cabinets, cabinet doors, shelves, wall panels.
Lauan subflooring	Only one type	$\frac{1}{4}$	4×8, 2×4	Underlayment for vinyl tiles or sheet goods, backing for cabinets.
T-111 siding	Rough, with grooves variously spaced	$\frac{3}{8}$, $\frac{1}{2}$, $\frac{5}{8}$	4×8, 4×9	Exterior siding.
Waferboard	Only one type	$\frac{1}{4}$, $\frac{7}{16}$, $\frac{1}{2}$, $\frac{3}{4}$	4×8	Roof sheathing, underlayment.
Particleboard	Density of material varies	$\frac{1}{4}$, $\frac{3}{8}$, $\frac{1}{2}$, $\frac{5}{8}$, $\frac{3}{4}$	4×8, 2×4	Underlayment, core material for laminated furniture and countertops.
Hardboard	Standard, tempered, perforated	$\frac{1}{8}$, $\frac{1}{4}$	4×8, 2×4	Underlayment, drawer bottoms and partitions, cabinet backs, perforated tool organizers.
Drywall	Standard, greenboard (water-resistant)	$\frac{3}{8}$, $\frac{1}{2}$, $\frac{5}{8}$	4×8, 4×10, 4×12	Interior walls.
Cement board	Only one type	$\frac{5}{16}$, $\frac{1}{2}$	32"×60"	Backing for wall tiles, underlayment for ceramic floors.

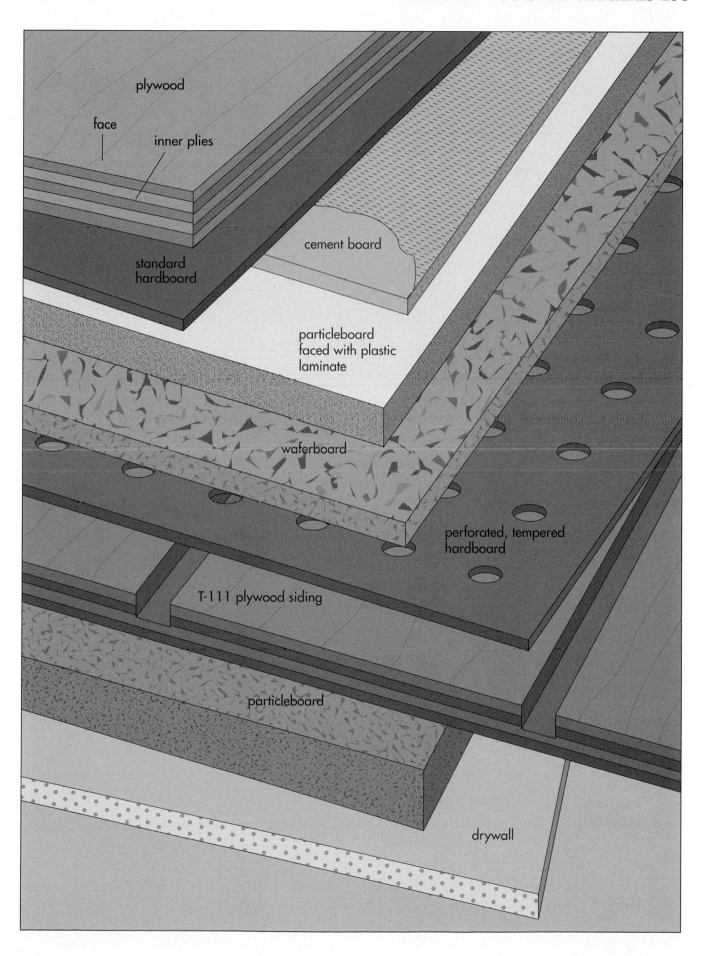

plywood

face

inner plies

standard
hardboard

cement board

particleboard
faced with plastic
laminate

waferboard

perforated, tempered
hardboard

T-111 plywood siding

particleboard

drywall

SELECTING AND ORDERING MOLDING

All rooms use at least some molding, usually along the base of walls and around windows and doors. In those places, molding covers up gaps. Other molding protects corners from dents or protects walls from damage by chair backs. In other places, such as around mantels, along the ceiling, and where paint and wall coverings meet in the middle of a wall, molding serves a decorative function. The molding you choose goes a long way toward defining the look of a room, whether it's minimalist or lushly decorative.

Molding is available in random lengths from 6 to 16 feet. Most is made of softwood, usually pine. Some popular types are available in hardwood, usually oak. These are a little more expensive.

The cost of molding does add up, so make a list of each piece you need, rounding the length up to the nearest foot, then add 5 percent to allow for trimming and fitting. See pages 304–307 for molding installation tips.

Money $ Saver

ALTERNATIVE MATERIALS

■ Finger-jointed molding is made of short pieces joined end to end. It costs less than regular molding, but you may need to sand the joints smooth.
■ Plastic molding is inexpensive, but has wood-grain finishes that may not suit your style. (Some can be painted.)
■ If you plan to paint molding rather than stain it, you may be able to save time and money with a preprimed molding.
■ Paper-covered hardboard molding also costs less, but can be difficult to cut neatly and the paper may tear later.

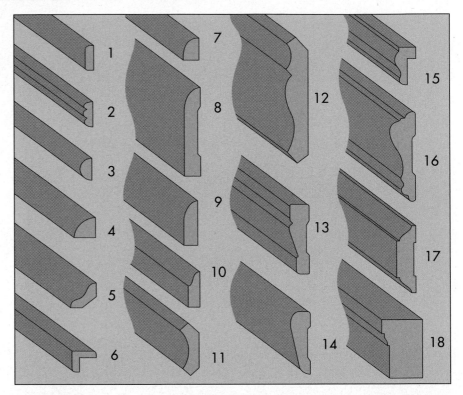

MOLDING SELECTOR

Common Types	Typical Uses
Screen bead; regular (1) and fluted (2)	Both cover seams where screening fastens to frames; finish edges of shelves.
Half round (3)	Serves as screen bead, shelf edging, and lattice.
Quarter round (4)	Serves as base shoe and inside corner guard.
Inside corner (5) and outside corner (6)	Both conceal seams and protect areas where walls meet at corners.
Base shoe (7) and baseboard (8)	Both trim and protect walls at their base.
Stop; ranch (9) and colonial (10)	Both attach to door jambs to limit door swing; hold inside sash of windows in place.
Cove (11) and crown (12)	Both trim and conceal joint between walls and ceilings.
Casing; colonial (13) and ranch (14)	Both trim around interior windows and doors.
Plycap (15)	Conceals plywood edge; tops off wainscoting.
Chair rail (16)	Protects walls from chair backs; hides seams where wall materials meet.
Batten (17)	Conceals vertical and horizontal panel seams.
Brick mold (18)	Used with all types of exterior cladding (not just brick) to trim around doors and windows.

HANDLING AND STORING MATERIALS

One of the joys of having your own shop is the pile of useful materials you collect over time. To ensure a safe, uneventful trip home from your home center, secure materials to your vehicle with rope, bungee cords, or twine. For large purchases or if your vehicle cannot handle the load, pay a little extra and have the materials delivered to your house.

When transporting or unloading sheet goods, have a helper on hand. If that's not possible, lift a panel with one hand near the center of each long edge, as shown in the inset *below.* Pick it up and rest it on your shoulder; avoid carrying it with a bent back. The exception is drywall; because it's thin, heavy, and brittle, it can snap under its own weight. Get help with drywall. Take care not to damage the edges or scratch the surface of the sheets.

Too quickly, however, your pile of material can become a headache and an eyesore. To keep boards and sheet goods easily accessible and prevent warping and other damage, keep these tips in mind:

■ Store materials in a cool, dry place, off the floor. Moisture can distort lumber, delaminate some plywoods, and render drywall useless. If your basement gets wet occasionally, store materials above the high-water line.

■ Ideally, sheet goods should be stored flat. Because most people don't have room to do this, it's best to stand sheet goods on edge, as shown *below,* as vertical as possible to keep them from bowing.

■ Build a storage rack like the one shown *below* to keep lumber at eye level. You want to see the ends of boards clearly and be able to pull out what you need easily.

■ If you don't build a rack, store lumber flat and weight it down at each end and in the center to prevent warping and other distortions. Weighting is especially important if the wood has a high moisture content.

Pick up sheet goods by lifting from knees, not back.

1×3

1×4

Keep materials off floor; add height if moisture is likely.

SELECTING NAILS

Many types and sizes of nails are available, each one engineered for a specific use. The differences may seem small, but they can have a significant effect on the soundness and appearance of your job. Here's a guide to choosing among the standard types of nails:

Use **common** nails and **box** nails for framing jobs. Box nails are a bit thinner for lighter work. **Cement-coated** nails drive in more easily and hold more firmly. Use **roofing** nails for roof shingles and wherever a wide head is needed to hold material that might tear if a smaller head is used. Choose hot-dipped over electroplated **galvanized** nails; they'll last much longer.

Casing and **finishing** nails handle medium- and heavy-duty finishing work. For very fine work, use **wire brads. Ring-shank** and **spiral** nails grab wood more tightly than conventional nails. Specially hardened **masonry** nails penetrate mortar joints, brick, and even concrete. **Corrugated fasteners** are used mainly for strengthening wood joints; they do not hold well by themselves.

You can save money by buying nails in bulk, rather than in the box. However, it is handy to have boxes marked with the nail size.

MEASUREMENTS

PENNIES AND INCHES
In Great Britain in the 1400s, you could buy 100 medium-size nails for 8 pennies. It didn't take long for inflation to destroy that designation, but we use the term penny to this day to size nails. The abbreviation "d" for penny is derived from *denarius,* a small, silver Roman coin used in Britain that, from early times, equated with a penny.

Inch equivalent of nails sizes:

3d=1¼"	10d=3"
4d=1½"	12d=3¼"
6d=2"	16d=3½"
7d=2¼"	20d=4"
8d=2½"	

THE NAIL FOR THE JOB
Use nails three times as long as the thickness of the material you are fastening. For instance, to attach a 1×4 (¾ inch thick), a 6-penny nail (2 inches long) will be a bit short. An 8-penny nail (2½ inches long, a little more than three times the thickness of the 1×4) will do better. Make sure the nail will not poke through the material to which you are fastening.

EXPERTS' INSIGHT

THE TIP OF A NAIL
If you look closely at the tip of a common, box, or finishing nail, you will see that it is not symmetrical. Viewed point-on, the tip is diamond-shaped, not square. Nails are made this way for a reason. If you start the nail so the flatter side of the diamond is parallel to the grain of the board you are nailing it into, there will be less chance of splitting the wood than if the flat side goes against the grain.

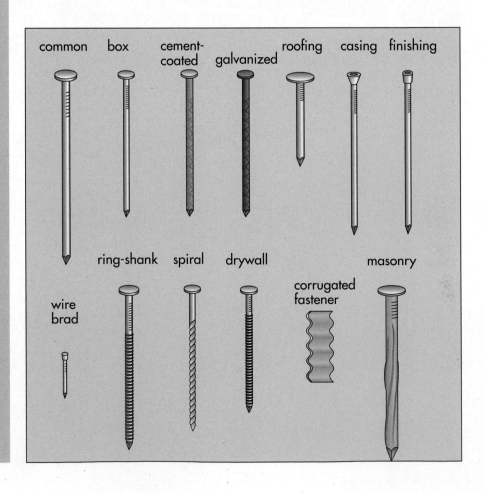

SELECTING SCREWS AND BOLTS

For the few seconds they take to drive in, nails do a remarkable holding job. Yet for the little extra time it takes to drive in a screw, you get a tighter-holding fastener, a neater appearance, and another plus—ease of disassembly. In fact, drywall screws teamed with cordless electric drills have created a mini-revolution in fasteners, including everything from deck screws to general-purpose wood screws.

The most common slot configurations for screws are the **slotted head** and the **Phillips head**, which has an X-shaped slot. **Square-drive** screws are more rare, but are growing in popularity.

There are three head shapes from which to choose. A **flathead** screw can be driven flush with or slightly below the surface of the wood. Use **ovalhead** screws with trim washers for a finished appearance. Install **roundhead** screws when you want the screw head to show.

General-purpose or **drywall** screws offer an inexpensive and easy way to fasten items together. You can buy them by the pound, and they drive easily using a drill with a screwdriver bit. **Trim head** screws use a smaller Phillips or square-drive bit. They hold better than finishing nails, but the countersink hole will be larger.

Use **masonry** screws (often referred to by the brand name Tap-Con) to fasten material to masonry or concrete surfaces. Simply drill the correct-size hole in the masonry surface and drive in the screw. Drive a **hanger** screw into a ceiling joist and fasten the object to be hung using the nut and thread on its lower half.

Use **lag** screws for heavy-duty fastening. Drill a pilot hole and drive in the screw with a wrench.

As with nails, screws should be three times as long as the thickness of the board being fastened. When buying screws, specify the gauge (diameter) you want. The thicker the gauge, the greater its holding power. Make sure you have the correct-size drill bit if drilling pilot holes (see the box at right). For more on driving in screws, see pages 280–281.

Machine bolts have a head that can be turned with a wrench. **Carriage bolts** have round heads for a finished appearance. When buying bolts, be sure to get the correct gauge and length; it must be longer than the materials you are fastening, so you can add the nut and washers. (For more on fastening with bolts, see page 288.) Thin metal can be joined with self-tapping **sheet-metal screws**.

ADHESIVES

Many carpentry jobs call for adhesives, either as the primary or secondary fastener. Purchase a supply of wood glue for general-purpose work, construction adhesive in tubes, two-part epoxy glue for extra-strong holding, panel adhesive for installing drywall or paneling, and perhaps a hot-glue gun with glue sticks.

EXPERTS' INSIGHT

DRILLING PILOT HOLES

To see if a drill bit is the correct size to make your pilot hole, grip both bit and screw together with your fingers. The bit should be slightly thinner than the width of the screw threads.

The thickness of a pilot hole can vary depending on the wood. With softwoods, you can use a smaller hole than you would with hardwoods. Always drill a test hole and make sure the screw will hold tight before you proceed to drill a number of holes in the finished material.

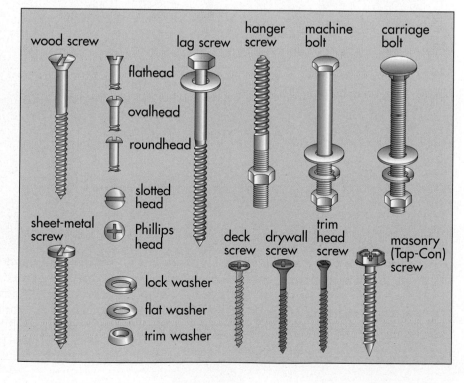

SELECTING HARDWARE

The items shown on these two pages represent just a few of the options available in specialized hardware. At your hardware store or home center, you'll find a product designed for almost every conceivable carpentry need.

When you want to strengthen a weak wood joint, reach for a metal plate or brace, as shown *below left*. **Mending plates** reinforce end-to-end joints; **T-plates** handle end-to-edge joints. **Flat corner irons** strengthen corner joints by attaching to the face of the material; **angle brackets** do the same thing, but attach to the inside or outside edges.

Shelf standards, as shown *below right,* come in a variety of configurations and finishes suitable for utility or more decorative uses. Most standards can be installed on the wall or into supports behind the shelves. Some standards can be installed on either side of the shelves. **Adjustable standards and brackets** come in a variety of colors, sizes, and finishes. Use **utility brackets** for nonadjustable shelving in places where appearance is not important. **Closet rod brackets** let you attach a shelf and a closet rod to the same piece of hardware.

There is a large choice of door and cabinet hardware, as shown on *page 259*. Most full-size doors hang on the classic **butt hinge**, *opposite*. **Piano hinges** mount flush on cabinets and chests, combining great strength with a slim, finished look. **Strap hinges** and **T-hinges** often are used on gates and trunk lids.

There are four basic types of cabinet hinges. **Decorative hinges** work only for doors that are flush with the frame. Use **front- or side-mount offset hinges** for doors that are either flush with the frame or that have lips that overlay the frame. If a door completely overlays the frame, use a **pivot hinge** or a self-closing **European-style hidden hinge**. To open your cabinet doors, fit them with **knobs** or **pulls**, available in many sizes and styles. **Friction, roller, bullet, or magnetic catches** keep cabinet doors closed. (If you are using self-closing hinges, these catches aren't necessary.)

For smooth-operating drawers, choose side-mounted **drawer slides** like the one shown on *page 259*. For extra household security, add a **chain lock** to your door.

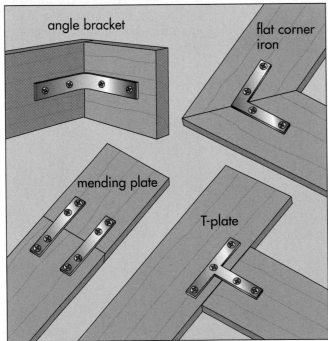

Select appropriate joint and reinforcing hardware.
For a quick and fairly permanent joint or repair, use inexpensive plates like these. For best results, clamp the material together before attaching the plates. Drill pilot holes as centered as possible; otherwise, screws may pull the joint apart as they are driven in.

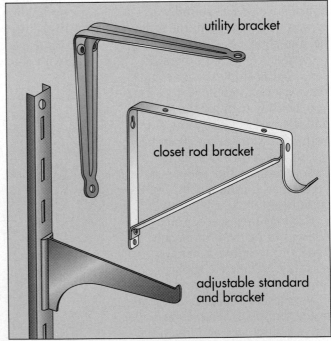

Choose from many types of shelf brackets.
If you've ever tried to make a shelf bracket out of lumber, you'll know how much time and effort is saved by these handy pieces of hardware. For more on installing shelf hardware and shelf construction, see pages 346–361.

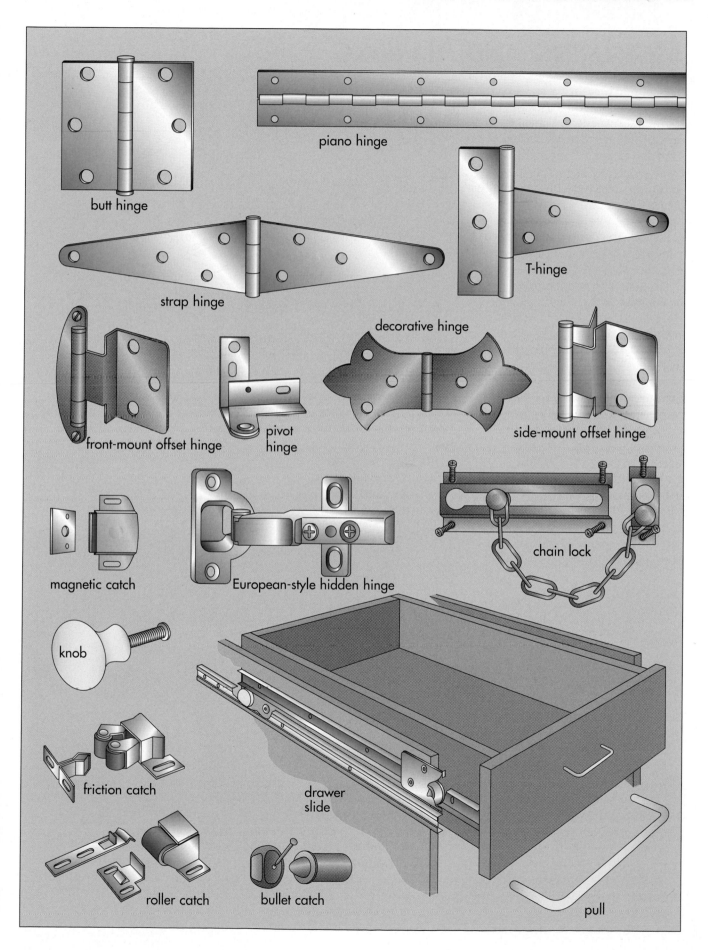

butt hinge

piano hinge

T-hinge

strap hinge

decorative hinge

front-mount offset hinge

pivot hinge

side-mount offset hinge

magnetic catch

European-style hidden hinge

chain lock

knob

friction catch

drawer slide

roller catch

bullet catch

pull

MEASURING AND MARKING

Accurate measuring and marking are the bases of successful carpentry. A mistake in measuring often means wasted time and material. Though it may seem simple, good measuring technique does not come naturally. It takes practice.

Don't rush your measuring. Take your time and double-check your work. Adopt the carpenters' maxim, "Measure twice, cut once."

No matter what measuring device you use, get comfortable with it and learn how to read it accurately. Many a board has met its ruin because someone couldn't distinguish a ¼-inch mark from a ⅛-inch mark. Once you've made a measurement, don't trust your memory. Jot down the figure on a piece of paper or a wood scrap.

Marking, not reading, the measurement is the difficulty. Make a clear mark (see page 261) using a sharp No. 2 pencil, the thin edge of a sharpened carpenter's pencil, a knife, or a scratch awl (especially if working with sheet metal).

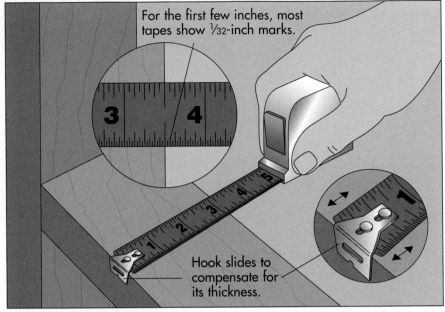

For the first few inches, most tapes show 1/32-inch marks.

Hook slides to compensate for its thickness.

Measure with a steel tape.
A steel tape is the most popular measuring device because it does most jobs with ease. Note that the hook at the end of the tape slides back and forth slightly to compensate for its own thickness. This means that whether you hook the tape on a board end for an outside measurement or push it against a surface for an inside measurement, the result will be accurate. For the first few inches of most tapes, each inch is divided into 1/32-inch increments to facilitate extra-fine measurements.

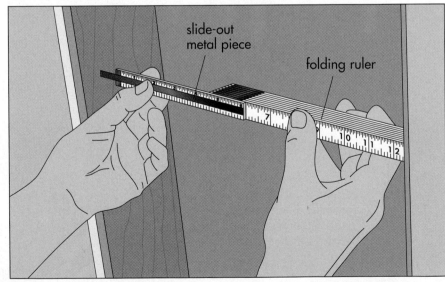

slide-out metal piece

folding ruler

Take an inside measurement.
Where outside measurement is difficult (here the drywall is in the way of measuring between the outside edges of the 2×4s) make an inside-to-inside measurement. A folding ruler with a slide-out metal piece works best. Extend it, measure, and hold the slide with your thumb until the measurement is transferred. You can use a tape measure for such measurements, but it is difficult to be accurate because you have to add an amount to compensate for the length of the tape body.

Make a V mark, not a line.

Marking with a simple line often leads to inaccuracies. By the time you're ready to saw, it's easy to forget which end of the line marks the spot—or where to cut on a thick line from a blunt pencil. For greater accuracy, mark your measurements with a V so you know precisely where to strike the cut line. To ensure pinpoint accuracy, place the point of your pencil at the V, slide the square to it, then make your line.

If you need to extend cut lines across several boards, use a framing square. For longer lines, use a drywall square.

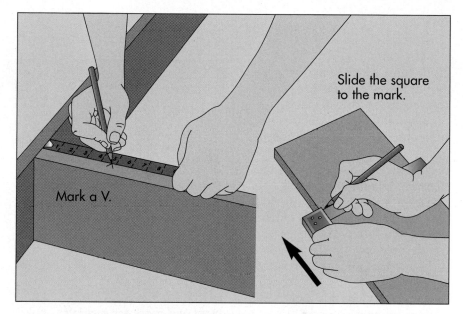

Mark a V.

Slide the square to the mark.

Mark for rip cuts.

Need to mark a cutoff line along the length of a board or a piece of plywood? If the line is parallel to the edge of the board and accuracy isn't critical, use your tape measure as a scribing device. Hold your tape so that a pencil laid against its end will make the correct line. Hold the tape and pencil firmly and pull evenly toward you, letting the tape body or your thumbnail slide along the board edge. For sheet goods, first mark the cutoff line at both ends, then snap a chalk line between the two marks, or clamp a straightedge in place and draw a mark.

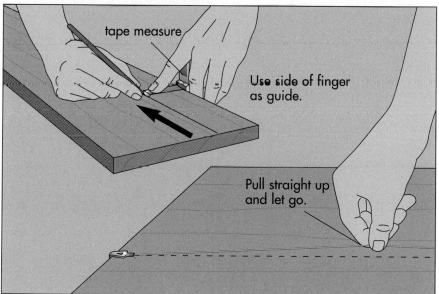

tape measure

Use side of finger as guide.

Pull straight up and let go.

Allow for the saw kerf.

When you cut material, the saw blade reduces some of it to sawdust. So, when measuring, you must allow for the narrow opening left in the blade's wake—called the kerf. Usually, a kerf is about $1/8$ inch wide. If you're making just one cut, account for the kerf by marking the waste side of the cutoff line with an X. There's no confusion then as to the side of the line on which to cut.

If you are cutting multiple pieces out of the same piece of lumber, make double marks to allow for the kerf. Otherwise, you will cut each piece too short.

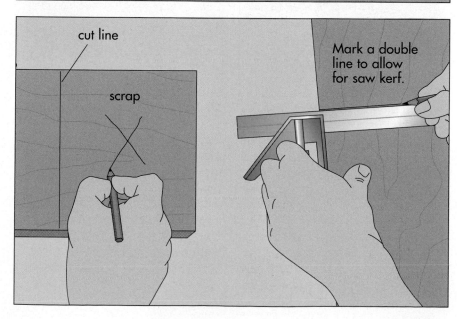

cut line

scrap

Mark a double line to allow for saw kerf.

HOLDING AND MEASURING IN PLACE

The most accurate and mistake-proof way of measuring is not to use a measuring device at all. Simply hold a piece where it needs to fit and mark it. You can do this for a simple cutoff. At other times, such as when you need to cut a board in two directions, use a combination of techniques: Hold and mark, then measure. Often this method isn't feasible, especially where access is limited or when the lumber being cut is too bulky to be held in place. But take advantage of this foolproof approach when you can.

YOU'LL NEED

TIME: Less than a minute for most measurements.
SKILLS: A steady hand and a good eye for accurate marking.
TOOLS: Pencil, speed square.

Hold this end as far out as possible—it should barely touch the board.

Hold and mark for a cutoff.
When you need to cut a board to length, begin by checking one end of the board for square. Press the square-cut end against one side of the opening, and mark the other end for cutting. To avoid distorting the measurement, don't push the square-cut end into the space any more than needed.

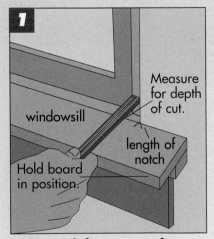
windowsill — Measure for depth of cut. — length of notch — Hold board in position.

1. To mark for a cutout, first measure the depth of the cut.
When you need to cut a board in two or three directions to make it fit around something, begin by holding the board in place. Make a small mark showing where the cutout is to be cut to length. Then measure how deep the cutout must be by measuring the distance between the leading edge of the board and the place where it must end up once it's cut.

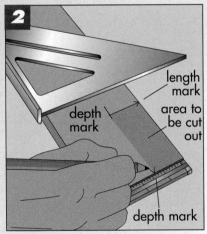
depth mark — length mark — area to be cut out — depth mark

2. Transfer measurement mark.
Use a square to extend the length mark. With a tape measure, transfer the depth measurement to two places on the board—at the length mark and at the end of the cutout. Use a square to draw a line from the length mark to the depth mark. With a straightedge, mark a line between the two depth marks.

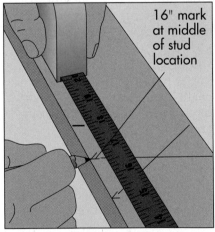
16" mark at middle of stud location

Lay out a plate for a stud wall.
When building a wall, the studs (upright 2×4s) must be 16 inches on center; that is, you want 48- or 96-inch drywall or paneling sheets to end in the middle of a stud. To make marks for studs, mark every 16 inches, minus ¾ inch (15¼ inches, 31¼ inches, and so on). Measure over 1½ inches and make another mark. Draw lines at your marks and an X between to show stud location (see page 261).

SQUARING, PLUMBING, AND LEVELING

Most carpentry projects—from making simple shelves to building walls—require that you square the work. Check for square at every stage of your work: corners, uprights, and board ends.

Making sure that work is plumb and level is equally important. Walls, cabinets, doors—nearly every permanent installation—must be plumb (perpendicular to the earth) and level (parallel to the earth). Don't assume existing walls or floors are square, level, or plumb. Most often they are not because of imperfect construction or settling that has taken place over the years. Techniques shown in this section will help you keep your carpentry projects straight and true.

YOU'LL NEED

TIME: A couple of minutes or less to check that work is square, plumb, or level.
SKILLS: Use of squares and levels.
TOOLS: Combination, speed, framing squares; 2- or 4-foot level; other levels.

TOOLS TO USE

THE MULTIPURPOSE SPEED SQUARE

Almost every carpenter's belt contains a hammer, utility knife, pencil, and the ever-handy speed square. With a speed square, you can quickly mark 45- and 90-degree angles simply by holding the square with its body firmly against a factory edge. Other angles are marked on the body of the square and can be used with a fair degree of accuracy. In addition, the speed square is handy as a guide for cutting square corners (see page 243).

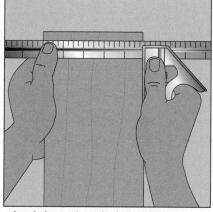

Check board ends for square.
All your careful measuring will be wasted if you start with a piece of lumber that is not square—one edge will be longer than the other. Check the board end by holding a combination square with the body or handle firmly against a factory edge. If the end isn't square, mark a square line and trim the board.

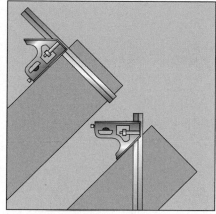

Use a combination square.
With this tool you can easily check for either 45- or 90-degree angles. Also, by sliding the blade, you can check depths. This tool can go out of square if it is dropped, so check it once in a while against a square factory edge (such as the corner of a sheet of plywood).

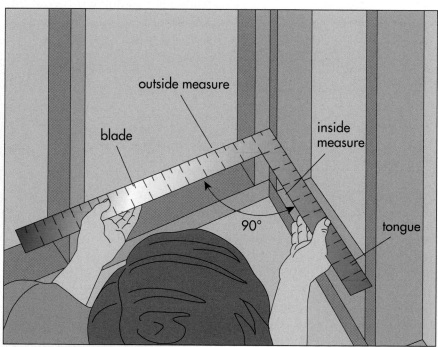

outside measure

blade

inside measure

90°

tongue

Use a framing square.
For larger jobs, use a framing square. Lay the square up against two members where they meet. If the tongue and the blade of the square rest neatly against the members, the sides are perpendicular. Or, place the square on the outside. Again, if the square touches the members at all points, the unit is square. When using a framing square for measuring, be sure to read the correct scale—inside or outside.

TOOLS TO USE

DRYWALL SQUARE

This tool, sometimes called a T-square, helps you cut drywall much faster than other tools. It is well worth its price if you need to cut a lot of drywall. It also is useful for measuring and marking other sheet goods, particularly plywood and particleboard. Because the blade is a full 4 feet long, you need make only one mark rather than two when marking for a cutoff, and you don't have to align straightedges or mess with chalk lines. A drywall square can get out of square if you're not careful with it. Take care to rest it in places where it won't get banged around. Periodically test it for square by holding it against two factory edges of a sheet of drywall or plywood.

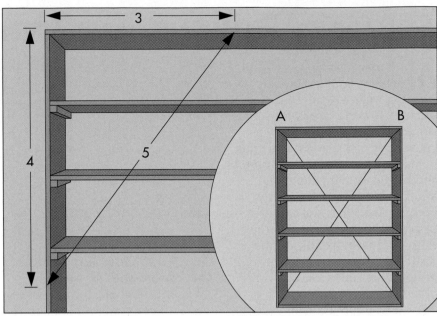

Use the 3-4-5 method.

For large projects, test if a corner is square by using geometry. You don't need to remember the Pythagorean theorem. Just remember "3-4-5." On one side, mark a point 3 feet from the corner. On the other side, mark a point 4 feet from the corner. If the distance between the two marks is exactly 5 feet, it is square. For extra large projects, use multiples such as 6-8-10 or 9-12-15.

As a double check, measure the length of the diagonals. If the project is square, the distance between two opposite corners (marked A in the drawing *above*) will equal the distance between the other two corners (B).

Check for plumb.

To see if a piece is perfectly vertical—plumb—hold a level against one face of the vertical surface and look at the air bubble in the level's lower glass vial. If it rests between the two guide marks, the piece is plumb.

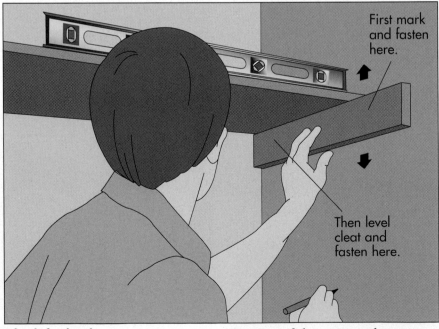

First mark and fasten here.

Then level cleat and fasten here.

Check for level.

In most cases, you can simply set your carpenter's level atop the piece to see if it's level. Raise or lower the piece until the bubble rests between the marks. Mark the position of the piece and remove the level (you don't want to risk knocking it to the floor). Add a fastener to the cleat near the level mark, level the cleat, and finish fastening.

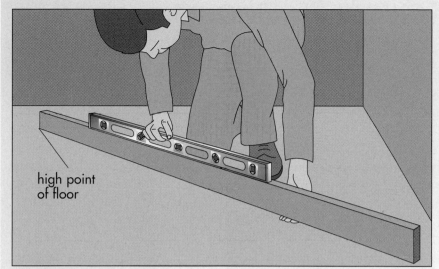

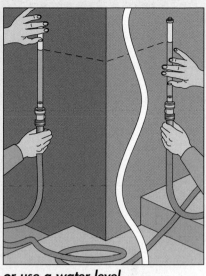

To test for level over long distances, use a board ...
If you need to see if an entire floor is level, select a long, straight board. (Sight down its length to see that it's not bowed.) Place a carpenter's level in the center of the board and raise one end or the other until the bubble is centered between the two lines. Slide the board around until you are sure you have found the high point of the floor. Level the board from this high point and measure the distance from the floor to the bottom of the raised end of the board to see how far out of level the floor is.

or use a water level.
This tool enables you to quickly check for level in awkward situations or over long distances. Basically a long hose and two transparent tubes filled with water, this tool works on the principle that water seeks its own level. Mark at water level.

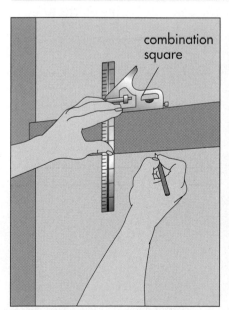

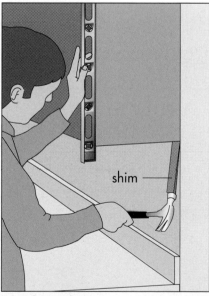

Use small levels in tight spots.
In places where you can't fit in a carpenter's level, use the level that comes on some combination squares or a torpedo level (a short version of a carpenter's level). Or, if you know that an adjoining member or wall is plumb, measure to see that the piece is square to it.

Plumb a cabinet.
When installing cabinets, make sure they are plumb in both directions or the doors will shut or open by themselves. With the cabinet fastened to the wall loosely, hold a level against a vertical framing piece. Tap in shims until the bubble indicates that the cabinet is plumb.

EXPERTS' INSIGHT

TEST YOUR LEVEL

■ Test a new level for accuracy before buying it. If the first one you try isn't accurate, the next one on the shelf may be. If you own a level, test it to see if it has been knocked out of alignment.

■ To make sure your level is accurate, set it on a shelf or table and note the location of the bubble. Then, turn the level around end-for-end on the same surface. It should give exactly the same reading.

■ If it is not accurate, you may be able to adjust it by loosening the four small screws holding the bubble assembly and turning the assembly until it is correct. If the level isn't adjustable, you'll have to buy a new one.

USING SPECIAL MARKING TECHNIQUES

A flexible steel tape measure, a square, and a level usually will equip you to mark your lumber for cutting. But sometimes you'll come across a situation where you'll have to mark around the irregular contours of molding, brick, or stone; mark curved shapes; or mark for angles other than 45 degrees and 90 degrees. These aren't challenges to be left only to master carpenters. The simple techniques in this section are for marking unusual shapes.

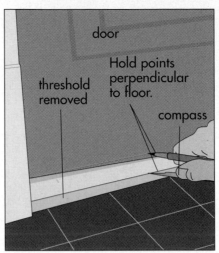

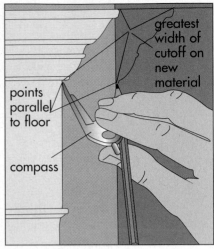

Scribe the bottom of a door.
If the bottom of a door is sticking, close it as far as possible. Set a compass to the correct height above the floor—usually the thickness of the threshold plus ⅛ inch for clearance. Hold the compass point on the floor and the pencil end of the compass on the door. Move the compass along the floor, scribing a parallel cutoff line on the door.

Mark for irregular cuts.
For a complicated contour cut, use a compass that can be tightened firmly so it won't collapse or expand as you trace the contour. Place the new material next to the object it will fit around. Set the compass to the greatest width to be cut off. Take care to hold the two compass points on the same plane (in this case, parallel to the floor) as you make the mark.

EXPERTS' INSIGHT

MAKING AND USING TEMPLATES

■ For material in which you are making multiple or complicated cuts, make a template or pattern before you make the cut. Often, the piece of lumber or sheet goods you are replacing can serve as the template. Carefully remove the old piece, take out any nails or screws that are in it, place it over the new lumber, and trace its outline.

■ At other times, you may need to make a template. Cut a piece of stiff cardboard with a knife or make a pattern out of a piece of scrap wood. Experiment until the template fits exactly, but don't experiment on your final, expensive materials.

■ Whenever you use a template, be sure that it does not slide around as you make your marks—you may need to clamp or tack it in place. Watch your pencil line carefully to see that it is tight against the template at all points.

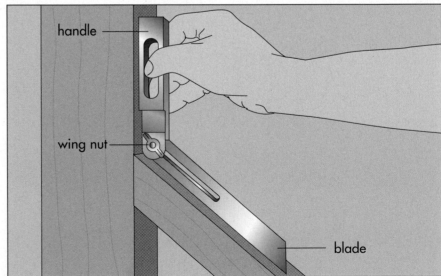

Use a T-bevel for odd angles.
If you want to duplicate an angle that is neither 45 nor 90 degrees, use a sliding T-bevel. Loosen the wing nut so the blade can be moved without difficulty. Hold the handle against one edge and move the blade until it rests firmly against the other edge. Tighten the wing nut firmly. The tool holds the angle you need, allowing you to transfer it to the wood you are cutting. When making an inside measurement, as shown *above*, extend the blade fully to ensure an accurate reading.

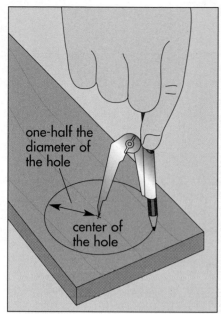

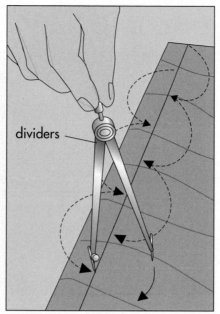

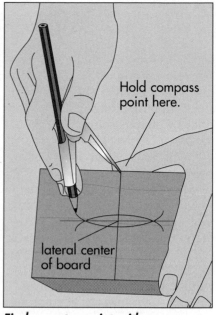

Draw circles with a compass.

To mark small circles—for boards that will be cut to accept pipes, lighting fixtures, etc.—a simple compass will do the job. Mark a spot at the center of the hole and set the compass width to one-half the diameter of the hole. For accuracy, be sure the compass is tightly clamped in position and hold it as perpendicular to the surface as possible.

Step off with dividers.

If you need to mark a series of equidistant points along a straight line, use dividers. Steel pins at the base of each leg grip the surface of the material you're measuring for good control. Use a swiveling motion as you step from one leg to the other leg.

Find a center point with a compass.

If you need to find the exact center point of a board, doing it with math can be confusing—what's half of 9⅜ inches, for instance? To quickly find the center point, open your compass to a bit more than half the board's width and make two arcing marks as shown. The line between the points where the curved lines intersect is the center of the board.

Make a tool for larger circles.

A compass works well for small circles, but if you have to cut out for a sink or another large, round object, you will have to use a little ingenuity. Make your own compass out of a pencil, brad, and string. Be sure to hold the pencil vertical as you draw.

For greater accuracy, make a notch at one end of a small piece of wood. Nail the wood piece in place with a brad at the center of the circle. The notch holds the pencil in place for a smooth, accurate line.

Sometimes, you may be able to find a round household object, such as a can, a bucket, or a wastebasket, that is close enough to the correct size. Place it on the work and trace around it.

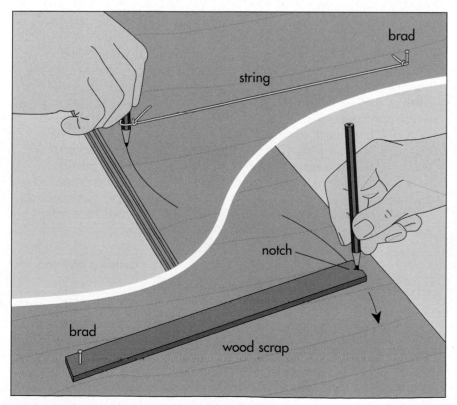

CUTTING WITH A CIRCULAR SAW

Chances are you will do most of your cutting with a circular saw. Whether cross-cutting 1-inch stock, ripping plywood, or cutting bricks with a masonry blade, you'll do the job better if you follow a few basic rules when using this versatile tool.

Whenever you cut, allow the saw to reach full operating speed, then slowly push the blade into the wood. Some carpenters look at the blade as they cut; others rely on the gunsight notch. Choose the method that suits you best. Avoid making slight turns as you cut. Instead, find the right path, and push the saw through the material smoothly. It will take some practice before you can do this consistently. This is a powerful tool with sharp teeth, so take care. It demands your respect.

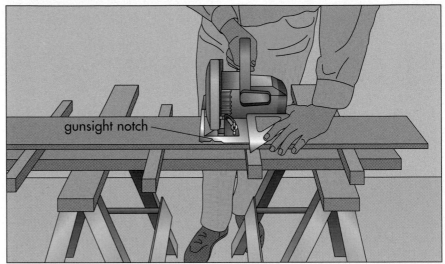

gunsight notch

Support the material properly.
Well-supported work results in clean, safe cuts. If the scrap piece is short, support the board on the nonscrap side. If the scrap is long, it could bind the blade or splinter as it falls away at the end of the cut. To achieve a neat cut and avoid saw kickback, support the lumber in four places. Even with such precautions, you may want to make two cuts: one to cut the work roughly to size, the other for the finish cut.

TOOLS TO USE

CHOOSING A CIRCULAR SAW AND BLADES

■ Choose a circular saw that is comfortable. It should have some heft, but should not be so heavy that it is difficult to maneuver. You should be able to see the blade and gunsight notch easily. Check for ease of depth and angle adjustments. (For more tips, see page 245.)
■ If you buy only one blade for a circular saw, choose a carbide-tipped combination blade that has at least 24 teeth. It works well for rough work and makes cuts clean enough for most finish work. For fine work, buy a plywood blade or a hollow-ground planer blade. For extensive remodeling jobs, get a second carbide-tipped blade that you can use when you may need to cut through nails or other rough materials.

CAUTION!
AVOIDING AND PREPARING FOR KICKBACK

It happens to even the most experienced carpenter: A blade binds, causing a circular saw to jump backward. Kickback can mar the lumber you are working on, and it is dangerous. Unsupported work often is the culprit. But also watch for these situations:
■ A dull blade will bind and cause the saw to kick. Change your blade if you have to push hard to make it cut.
■ Bending or twisting lumber will grab a blade. Sheets of plywood are particularly prone to this. Make sure it is evenly supported, like the 1× above.
■ Kickback also can occur when you back up while cutting or when you try to make a turn. If your cut is going off line, stop the saw, back up, and start again.
■ Occasionally, certain types of wood grain will grab the blade and cause a kickback. There's nothing you can do about this except be prepared.
■ Don't wear long sleeves and don't position your face near the circular saw.

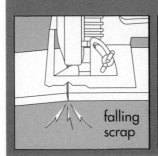

falling scrap

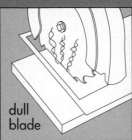

dull blade

bending plywood

EXPERTS' INSIGHT

SET THE BLADE DEPTH CORRECTLY

Before you make any cut, check to see that the blade is set to about ¼ inch deeper than the thickness of the wood. (Be sure to unplug the saw before you do this.) This may seem like a lot of bother, especially if you are constantly switching between 1× and 2× lumber, but here's why it is worth the trouble:

■ A saw blade that extends only slightly below the material will produce a much cleaner cut than a blade that extends way below the material.

■ The deeper the blade is set, the more prone it will be to binding and kickback, jeopardizing the work and your safety.

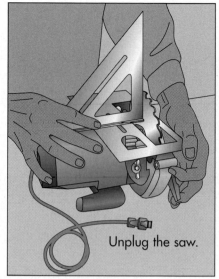

Unplug the saw.

Square the blade.

To square a blade, hold a speed square against the blade and adjust it. (Be sure to position the square between the teeth.) To test if your blade is square to the baseplate, crosscut a piece of 2× lumber. Flip the piece over and press cut edge against cut edge. If you see a gap at the top or the bottom, the blade is not square.

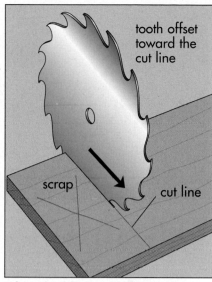

tooth offset toward the cut line

scrap   cut line

Align the blade with the cut line.

Once you have drawn an accurate cutoff line and have properly supported the board, position the saw blade to the scrap side of the line. The teeth on most circular saw blades are offset in an alternating pattern, half to the left and half to the right. When clamping a guide, align a tooth that points toward the cutoff line.

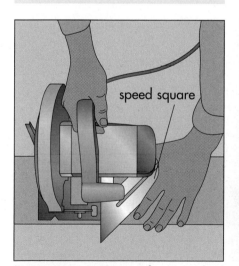

speed square

Use a square as a guide.

With practice, you will learn to cut accurately without using a guide. But for cuts that have to be precise, use a guide. For 90-degree cuts, a speed square works well because it's easy to hold stable. Align the blade, then slide the square into position against the saw's baseplate. Grab the board along with the square, so the square won't slip out of position.

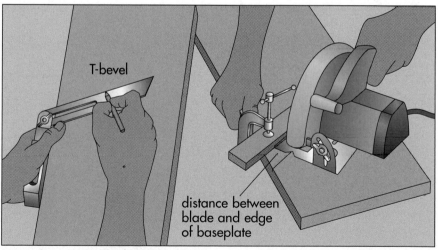

T-bevel

distance between blade and edge of baseplate

Use other guides for angle cuts.

With care, you can improvise a saw guide that will be as accurate as a miter box. Set a T-bevel to the desired angle (see page 266) and transfer the angle to the board.

Select a straight piece of 1× and clamp it along the cutting line as a saw guide. To offset the guide correctly, measure the distance between the blade and the edge of the saw's baseplate and clamp the

guide that distance from the cut line. It may take some experimenting before you get this correct. Be sure to align the blade to the correct side of the line.

You can use the same principle for long rip cuts. Clamp a straightedge—the factory edge of a 1× or a drywall square—onto the material, setting it back from the cut line to allow for the width of the saw's baseplate.

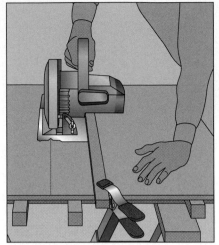

Support sheet goods.

Cut sheet goods with a carbide-tipped combination blade or a plywood-cutting blade for a smoother cut. It is important to support the sheet properly, or the blade will bind. You can do this by setting four 2× support pieces on the floor, a table, or a pair of sawhorses. Arrange two support pieces on either side of the cut line so that when the cut is complete, both pieces of the sheet are stable.

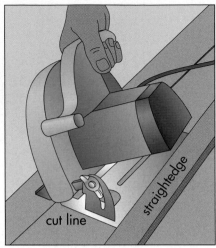

Use a guide.

Use a guide to make a straight, long cut. Get a straightedge that is as long as the material you are cutting—a straight 1×4 or the factory edge of a piece of plywood. Measure the distance from the edge of the saw's baseplate to the blade and clamp the guide that distance away from the cut line. Set the saw in place and check alignment with the cut line. Clamp the opposite end of the guide the same distance from the edge.

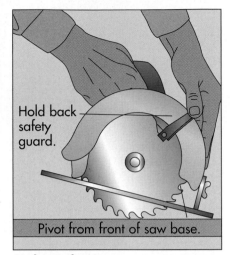

Make a plunge cut.

Use a plunge cut, also called a pocket cut, to make a hole or slit in the middle of a board or sheet. Set the blade to the correct depth. Retract the safety guard and tilt the saw forward, setting the front of the baseplate on your work. Start the saw and lower it slowly into the cut line until the base rests on the stock. Complete the cut.
Note: *Because you will be exposing the blade, any twist could result in a dangerous kickback. Be careful.*

USING A MITER BOX

A miter joint is made when two pieces of wood are angle-cut or bevel-cut at the same angle then joined to form a corner. Most often, two pieces that have been cut at 45 degrees are joined to make a 90-degree corner. Miter cuts must be precise. If they are off even one degree, the corner will be noticeably out of true.

The most inexpensive way to make angle or bevel cuts in narrow stock is to use a miter box—essentially a jig for holding the saw at the proper angle to the work. If you have a lot of joinery to cut, consider buying a power miter saw (see page 247).

Before placing the piece in the miter box, support it on a scrap of 1×4 or some other suitable material. This allows you to saw completely through the work

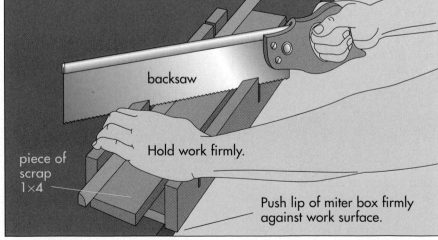

without marring the bottom of the miter box. Place the member against the far side of the miter box, positioned as it will be when in use, and make the cut with a backsaw. Hold the work firmly against the back of the box with your free hand.

If there's any trick to using a miter box, it's not in the cutting technique, but in correctly measuring and marking for the cut. Whenever possible, make your miter cut first, then cut the other end of the piece to the proper length with a straight cut.

CUTTING WITH A HANDSAW

Although you will probably do most of your cutting with power tools, there are times when a handsaw is more convenient. Learn the proper technique, and hand-cutting may turn out to be easier than you expected.

Make a crosscut with a handsaw.

To make a crosscut with a handsaw in narrow goods, set the blade's heel end (nearest the handle) at a 45-degree angle to the work. Set the teeth on the scrap side of the cut line. To make sure the blade doesn't wander, use your thumbnail as a guide. Pull the saw back toward you several times to start the cut. Don't force the blade; use the weight of the saw to start the cut while you guide it. Saw with a rocking motion, using a steeper angle at the beginning of the downstroke and a flatter angle at its completion. Again, don't force it; let the saw do the work.

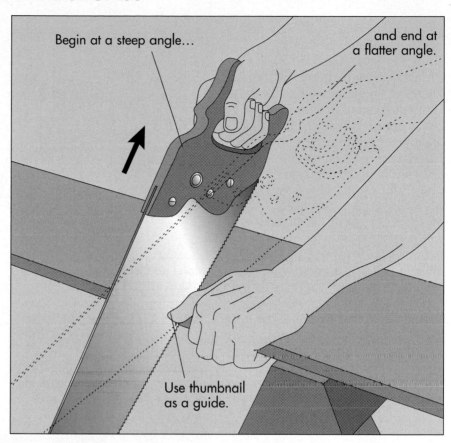

Begin at a steep angle...

and end at a flatter angle.

Use thumbnail as a guide.

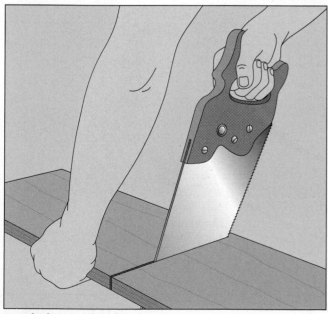

Finish the cut cleanly.

When you near the end of the cut, support the scrap end of the piece of wood. Grasp it firmly with your free hand, exerting a slight upward pressure to keep it from binding. This also will keep the piece from snapping and splintering on the last stroke.

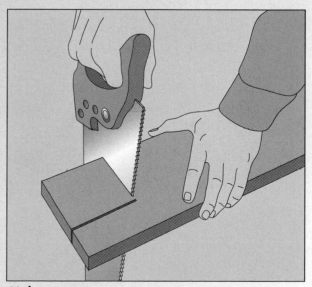

Make a cutout.

To notch the corner of a board, position the blade of the saw so it is perpendicular to the work as you near the end of each cut. In that way, the bottom of the board is cut the same distance as the top. Often it is helpful to reverse the position of the saw, as shown *above*.

MAKING INSIDE AND CONTOUR CUTS

Often you need to make a cut in the center of a piece of lumber or sheet goods or make a curved or irregularly shaped cut. These cuts require two basic steps. First you need to drill or plunge-cut an access hole in the material. Then you need to use a narrow-bladed tool that can handle curved cuts to follow the contours.

To begin an inside cut, you can use a circular saw to make a plunge cut (see page 270). You will need a sabersaw or handsaw to finish the job. If you find it difficult to make a precise plunge cut, use a drill and sabersaw—especially when the finished work will be highly visible.

Note: *Do not attempt to make a curved cut with a circular saw. Such a practice not only can damage your saw and saw blades, but it also can be dangerous.*

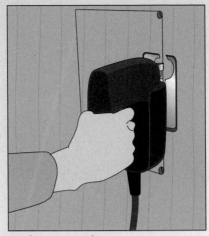

Make an inside cut.
How you start an inside cut depends on the material you're cutting. With lumber and sheet goods, the safest way is to drill a starter hole at each corner of the cutout, as close as possible to the cut lines. Insert the blade of a sabersaw or keyhole saw into one of the holes and complete the cut.

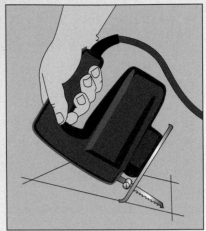

If you are experienced with a sabersaw, make a plunge cut. Tip the saw forward on its baseplate, as shown. Start the saw and slowly lower the blade into the wood along the cut line. A sabersaw blade tends to dance before cutting into the surface, which can badly mar your work. You may want to practice on a scrap of wood first.

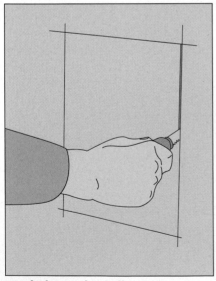

Cut holes in drywall.
For a clean cut, score the paper face of the drywall with a knife before sawing it. Poke the tip of a drywall saw (a type of keyhole saw) into the drywall at a cut line. Either push or punch the saw handle with the heel of your hand.

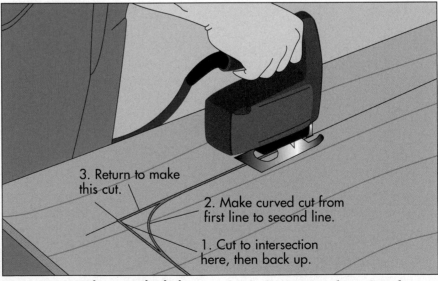

3. Return to make this cut.

2. Make curved cut from first line to second line.

1. Cut to intersection here, then back up.

Cut corners without a pilot hole.
You can maneuver a sabersaw around fairly tight corners, but don't try to make 90-degree turns. Use a three-step procedure to cut such corners. On your first approach to a corner, cut just up to the intersecting line. Carefully back the saw up about 2 inches and cut a gentle curve over to the next cut line. Continue in this direction, supporting the scrap material as you cut, until the scrap piece is free. Then go back and finish trimming the corners with short, straight cuts.

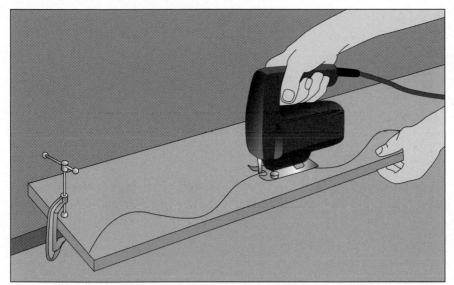

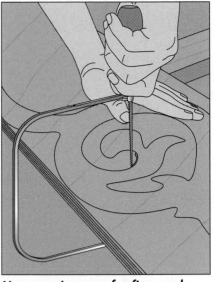

Cut curves with a sabersaw.

For most contour cuts, use a sabersaw. Once you get the knack of using this tool, you can cut curves that are as smooth as any line you can draw. Be sure the piece you are going to cut is stable; clamp it if necessary. Check that nothing is blocking the path of the blade underneath the piece you are cutting.

Turn the saw on, then begin the cut. Guide the saw slowly, without forcing the blade. One sharp turn can break a blade. If the saw begins to bog down or overheat, you're cutting too fast. If you wander from the line, don't try to make a correction with a sharp turn. Instead, back up and start again. Support the scrap material as you reach the end of each cut to prevent it from breaking off.

Use a coping saw for fine work.

For intricate cutting or scrollwork, use a coping saw. This hand tool allows you to set the blade in any direction in relation to its frame. To begin a cut from the inside of a board, remove the blade from the saw frame and reinstall it through a starter hole. For delicate cuts, install the blade with the teeth angled toward the handle so the saw cuts on the backstroke.

Use coping cuts for moldings.

When you're working with moldings, it's difficult to get perfectly matched mitered joints for inside corners, especially because the corners of walls often are not square. That's why professionals usually cope inside corner joints.

Start by cutting the first piece of molding at a 90-degree angle so it butts against the adjacent wall. To cope the overlapping piece, make an inside 45-degree miter cut, as shown. Use a coping saw to cut away the excess wood along the molding profile. Back-cut slightly (cut a little more off the back of the piece than the front) to ensure a neat fit. Whenever possible, make the cut on the coped end first, hold the piece in place, then mark for the cut on the other end.

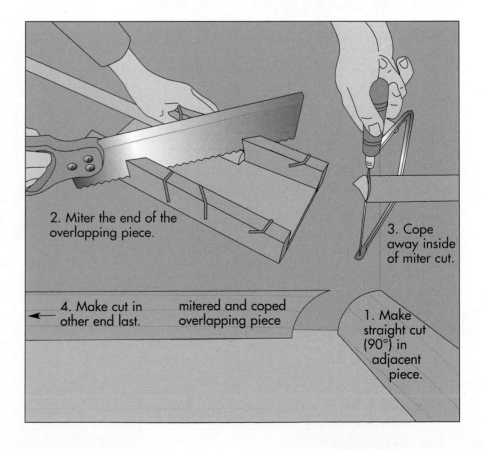

2. Miter the end of the overlapping piece.

3. Cope away inside of miter cut.

4. Make cut in other end last.

mitered and coped overlapping piece

1. Make straight cut (90°) in adjacent piece.

USING CHISELS

Although you may not use a chisel every day, it pays to keep a couple of them on hand. Nothing can replace a chisel for making mortises, dadoes, or notches. An old one often comes in handy for demolition jobs.

Whenever you pick up a chisel, keep both hands behind the cutting face of the blade. As you work, point the chisel away from your body. Because it takes two hands to operate a chisel, always clamp or anchor the material you're working on. Save yourself wasted effort and ruined materials by keeping your chisels sharp. A properly sharpened chisel should slice through paper easily.

TOOLS TO USE

SHARPENING NICKED OR BADLY WORN TOOLS

To sharpen a badly nicked or worn chisel, a single-cut file or a bench grinder works better than a whetstone.

■ To sharpen a chisel with a file, clamp the chisel tightly in a vise with the cutting edge pointing up. Remove nicks by filing nearly perpendicular to the chisel edge. Then hold the file at the same angle as the chisel bevel and file diagonally across the bevel. Work slowly and evenly to obtain a sharp edge. Remove burrs on the flat side with an oiled whetstone.

■ To remove nicks from a chisel's blade with a bench grinder, hold the chisel nearly perpendicular to the wheel and grind until the nicks disappear. Regrind the bevel, using the guide on the grinder to hold the chisel at the bevel angle. Go slowly: Never let the cutting edge blacken or get red hot.

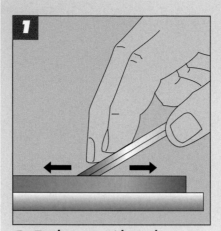

1. To sharpen with a whetstone, grind the cutting edge.
A dull chisel edge will look flat and reflect light. It also may have nicks in it. Drip a pool of oil on a whetstone. Brace the whetstone firmly on a flat surface. Hold the chisel bevel-face-down, at an angle slightly steeper than the bevel, so you are not grinding the entire beveled face. Grind by pressing gently and moving back and forth.

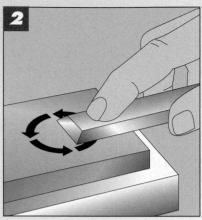

2. Smooth the flat side.
Turn the chisel over and lay its flat side on the whetstone. Add more oil if the stone is dry or if a thick paste has built up. Hone the flat side by pressing gently, moving the chisel with a circular motion. You don't want to grind a new cutting edge on this side; only remove the burrs created after grinding the beveled face.

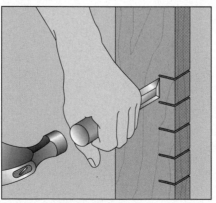

Notch a piece of framing.
Set your circular saw blade to the desired depth of the notch and make cuts at the top and bottom of the notch. If the notch is wide, make one or more cuts in the center of the notch as well. Position the chisel with the bevel outward. Begin cutting at a slight outward angle that gets flatter as you proceed.

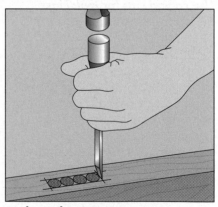

Make a deep mortise cut.
It is difficult to chisel deeply into a narrow board without splintering it. Begin by drilling a series of adjacent holes within the scored outline of the mortise. If possible, use a drill bit that is the same diameter as the width of the mortise. Finish the cut with a chisel, holding the beveled face toward the inside of the mortise as you gently tap.

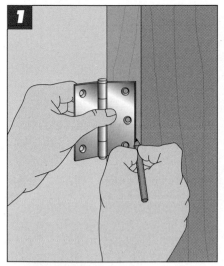

1. Mark to mortise for a hinge.

Do not attempt to mark a mortise for a hinge with a measuring device. Use the actual hinge as a template. Position it correctly on the edge of the door and mark its perimeter with a sharp pencil. Mark for the thickness of the mortise also.

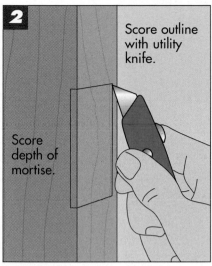

2. Score the lines.

To prevent the wood grain from splintering at the edges of chisel cuts, score the lines you have just marked by gently cutting with a sharp knife. Once the score lines have been established, go over them again with the knife until you have cut to the depth of the mortise. A butt marker also can be used to score lines.

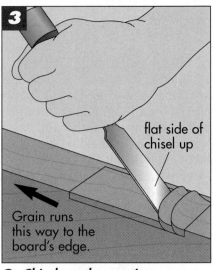

3. Chisel out the mortise.

Hold the chisel with the beveled face down at the angle shown. Whenever possible, cut in the direction in which the wood grain runs to the edge of the board. Otherwise, the chisel will follow the grain deeper down into the board than you intended. Drive the chisel to the depth of the mortise, making several slices across its width.

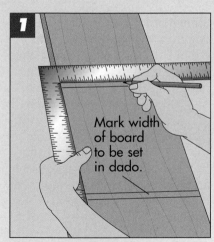

1. To make dado notches, first lay out the lines.

When laying out dado cuts across the width of a board, take extra care to draw lines that are straight and square and that mark the exact thickness of the boards that will be set into them. Use a framing or a smaller square to mark both the top and bottom of the cut.

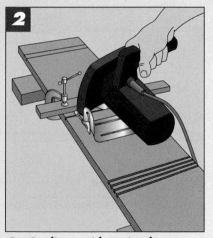

2. Cut lines with a circular saw.

Adjust your circular saw blade to the correct depth—usually one-third of the thickness of the board. Use a speed square (see page 263) or a clamp-on guide to ensure that you stay on the outline marks. After cutting the two outside lines for wide dadoes, make a series of passes through the center of each notch.

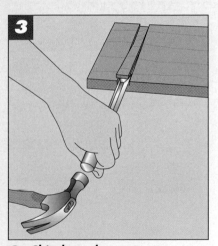

3. Chisel out the waste.

Using a chisel the same width or narrower than your dado notches, tap out the remaining slivers of wood. Start from one edge and work toward the middle, then work from the other side. Smooth the bottom of the notch by scraping it with your chisel, flat side down.

DRILLING

Some carpenters still haul out a brace and expandable auger bit when they can't find a spade bit of the right size. But now the electric drill usually is the tool of choice. Not only can you drill a hole of about any size with a variable-speed power drill, but you also can use a drill to drive screws into wood or metal, buff and grind, and even mix paint or mortar.

Some carpenters keep two drills on hand—one for drilling pilot holes, the other for driving screws. That way, they don't waste time changing bits. A power drill with a keyless chuck speeds up a bit change, although you may find bits slip during heavy-duty tasks.

For perfectly perpendicular holes, you'll need a drill press. But if you learn the techniques here and on the next three pages, you can bore holes that are straight enough for household carpentry.

EXPERTS' INSIGHT

CHOOSING A DRILL

■ Avoid buying a cheap drill with a ¼-inch chuck. It will not have the power you need and will soon burn out. One tipoff to a better-quality tool is the cord. Look for a long cord that flexes more like rubber than plastic.

■ A hammer drill, or a drill with a hammer option, bangs away at the material as it drills. It's useful when boring holes in concrete.

■ A cordless drill can make your work go more easily, but only if it is powerful enough to do most things that a corded drill can do.

■ Some drills are designed specifically for driving in drywall screws. These set the head of the screw at the required depth—deep enough to make an indentation, but not so deep that it damages the drywall.

■ Specialized tasks often require a high-speed drill (one with high revolutions per minute). For example, self-tapping steel stud screws (see page 334) require a drill rated to at least 2,500 rpm.

■ For heavy-duty work, choose a drill with a ½-inch chuck. This will run at fewer revolutions per minute, but will be more powerful than a standard ⅜-inch drill.

For additional information on choosing a drill, see page 245.

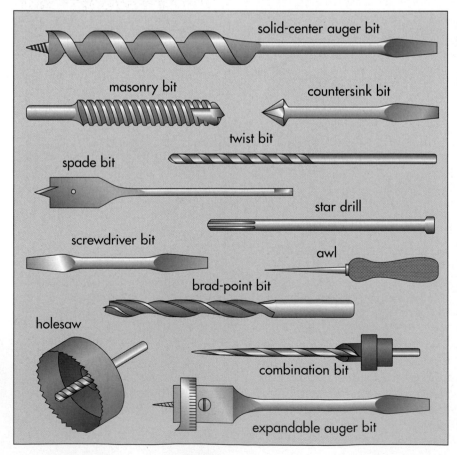

solid-center auger bit
masonry bit
countersink bit
twist bit
spade bit
star drill
screwdriver bit
awl
brad-point bit
holesaw
combination bit
expandable auger bit

Choose the correct bit.
Shown at *left* are some of the more common drill bits. **Auger** bits, either solid-center or expandable, are designed to be used with a hand brace, as is a **screwdriver** bit. For holes ½ inch or smaller in diameter, use **twist** bits. A **brad-point** bit makes a cleaner hole than a twist bit. For holes from ½ to 1¼ inches in diameter, use a **spade** bit. For making holes in masonry or concrete, use a carbide-tipped **masonry** bit or a **star drill**, which you drive with a hammer. A **countersink** bit bores a shallow hole so you can set screw heads flush with or below the surface. A **combination** bit drills both a pilot hole and a countersink hole in one step. Use a simple **awl** to prepare the way for a small screw. For holes larger than 1¼ inches, and/or for drilling precise holes through tough materials, use a **holesaw**.

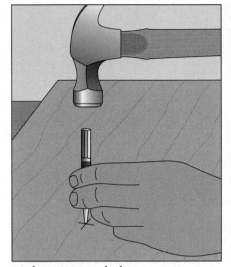

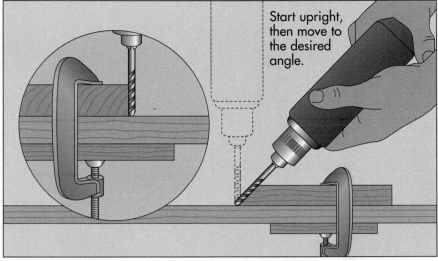

Start upright, then move to the desired angle.

Make a starter hole.
Drill bits tend to skate away when you begin boring holes, so make a shallow starter hole with an awl or a center punch. In softwoods, a gentle tap on an awl with the palm of your hand will do the job. With hardwoods or metal, you may need to tap the center punch or awl with a hammer.

Improvise a guide.
Usually, you'll want to drill holes perpendicular to the board. Check the bit for square as it enters the material by clamping a piece of square-cut scrap lumber in place, as shown. With some drills, you can hold a square on the material and against the body of the drill.

Sometimes you'll want your bit to enter the material at an angle.

Fashion a guide by cutting the edge of a piece of scrap lumber to the desired angle of your hole. Clamp the guide so it aligns the tip of the bit exactly on your center mark. Begin the hole by drilling perpendicular to the surface. Once you have gone deep enough to keep the bit from skating away, shift the drill to the correct angle.

Mark with tape at desired depth.

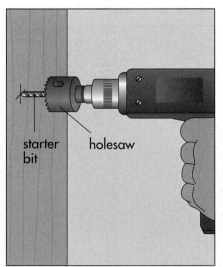

starter bit   holesaw

Mark the bit for depth.
When you want to drill one or more holes to a certain depth, wrap masking or electrical tape around your drill bit so the bottom edge of the tape contacts the surface of the material at the desired depth. Drill with gentle pressure. Back the bit out as soon as the tape touches the surface of the material.

Use a holesaw.
When drilling large-diameter holes with a holesaw, make a starter hole on your center mark to guide the starter bit. To ensure that the other side of the material doesn't splinter when the bit penetrates it, clamp a piece of scrap stock against the other side. Or, drill just far enough so the starter bit pokes through, then drill from the other side.

CAUTION!
AVOID DAMAGING YOUR DRILL BITS AND DRILL
Drilling is a simple procedure, but it's easy to dull or break a drill bit. Be careful not to overheat the bit; an overheated bit will become dull quickly. If you see smoke, stop drilling immediately.
Pause once in a while and test the bit for heat by quickly tapping it with your finger.
If you own a homeowner-type drill rather than a professional model, it is not designed for constant use. If you feel the body of the drill heating up, stop and give it a rest, or you could burn it out.
Hold the drill firmly upright as you work. If you tip the tool while drilling, there's a good chance the bit will break.

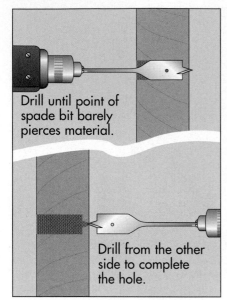

Drill until point of spade bit barely pierces material.

Drill from the other side to complete the hole.

Back up to pull wood particles out.

Clean particles from the flute.

Avoid splinters with a spade bit.

When using a spade bit, drill through the material until the tip of the bit begins to poke out the back side of the material. Carefully reverse the bit out of the hole. Complete the hole by drilling from the other side, using the pilot hole you've just made.

Keep particles from clogging hole.

When you drill deep holes into thick material, wood particles build up in the hole, clogging the bit and causing it to bind. Don't force the bit in farther than it wants to go or you will burn it out. Instead, feed the bit into the wood slowly and back out of the hole frequently with the drill motor still running. This will pull trapped wood particles to the surface. If you're working with sappy or wet wood, shavings may clog the flute of the bit. If this happens, stop the drill, and use the tip of a nail to scrape out the shavings. If the bit jams, reverse the drill rotation. Pull the bit straight up and out.

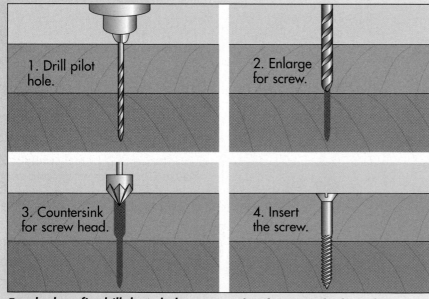

1. Drill pilot hole.

2. Enlarge for screw.

3. Countersink for screw head.

4. Insert the screw.

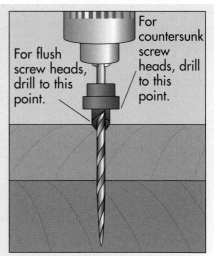

For flush screw heads, drill to this point.

For countersunk screw heads, drill to this point.

For the best fit, drill three holes...

When you use wood screws to fasten two pieces of material together, take the time to provide clearance for the screw to ensure easy driving and to avoid splits. Using a bit that is slightly smaller than the screw, drill through the top and bottom piece. Then select a bit that is as thick as the screw shank and drill through the top board. The screw should slide easily through this top hole and grip tightly as it passes into the smaller hole. Use a countersink bit to bore a space for the screw head. When you drive the screw, it will fit without cracking the wood.

or use a combination bit.

If you're driving a lot of screws, buy a combination countersink-counterbore bit, which drills three holes in one action. Be sure to get the correct bits for the screws you will be driving. If you want the screw head to be flush with the surface, drill until the spot marked on the bit is even with the surface. To counterbore the screw head, drill deeper.

EXPERTS' INSIGHT

DRILLING THROUGH METAL

If you need to make a hole in metal, it is best to use a high-quality titanium bit. But if you work carefully, you can drill through metal with any sharp twist bit. The trick is to keep the bit and the metal lubricated with light oil at all times. If the bit is dry for even a couple of seconds while drilling, it can burn out and become dull.

Before you start, drip motor oil onto the bit and the spot to be drilled. Add oil as you work. Take your time, stopping often to make sure the bit is oiled and not overheating.

If you need to drill a hole larger than ¼ inch in diameter, drill a smaller hole first, then use a bigger bit.

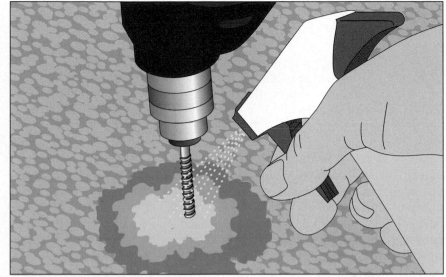

Drill into masonry and concrete.
Use a masonry bit when drilling into brick or concrete surfaces. Usually, brick is easy to drill into and concrete is more difficult. Check the bit often to make sure it's not overheating. If you see smoke, stop immediately.

Here is a trick that works surprisingly well: Spray the bit and the hole with window cleaner as you work. Not only does this keep the bit cool, but the foaming action of the cleaner brings debris up and out of the hole.

Occasionally when drilling into concrete, you will run into an especially hard spot (usually a rock embedded in the concrete). Take the bit out, insert a masonry nail or thin cold chisel, and bang with a hammer to crack the rock and give your bit a place to grab. If you have a lot of masonry drilling to do, buy a hammer drill, which bangs away as you drill.

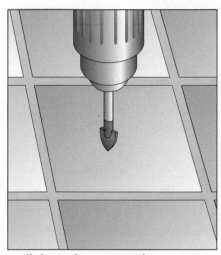

Drill through ceramic tile.
Wall tiles are usually soft, but floor tiles can be very tough. Nick the surface of the tile just enough so the bit will not wander as you drill. Keep the bit and the hole lubricated with a few drops of oil. Use a masonry bit or a special tile bit like the one shown *above*.

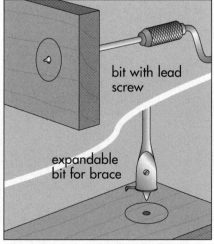

bit with lead screw

expandable bit for brace

Use a brace and expandable bit.
A brace is an old-fashioned tool that works faster than you may expect. To drill large diameter holes, bore until the lead screw of the bit pokes through the material. Then drill through from the other side. To get more pressure on the brace, hold its head against your body and lean into the work.

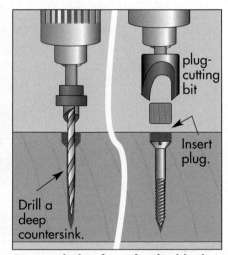

plug-cutting bit

Insert plug.

Drill a deep countersink.

Bore and plug for a finished look.
For a handcrafted appearance, drill pilot holes, then drill a wooden plug using a plug-cutting bit. Drive the screw in, squirt a little white glue into the hole, and tap in the plug. Allow the plug to stick out slightly. After the glue has dried, chisel and sand the plug flush with the surface.

USING A TABLESAW

When shopping for a tablesaw, use a straightedge to check the table; it should be a perfectly flat plane. If the table has extensions, make sure they are flat as well. A small, lightweight tablesaw is handy if you need to move it around often. However, the smaller table area makes it more difficult to use, and you will have a hard time making accurate cuts on large pieces of material.

The fence of a tablesaw should move smoothly along its guide rails and lock firmly and exactly parallel to the blade.

If possible, turn the saw on and watch the blade. There should be no hint of a wobble. A belt-driven tablesaw works more smoothly and lasts longer than one with direct drive.

EXPERTS' INSIGHT

TABLESAW, RADIAL-ARM SAW, OR POWER MITER SAW?

■ A tablesaw and a power miter saw make an ideal combination. With a tablesaw, you can make straight, long cuts with ease. A tablesaw also is superior for cutting dadoes. With a power miter saw, you can crosscut long narrow pieces easily—a task that can be tricky with a tablesaw.

■ A radial-arm saw does the jobs of a tablesaw and power miter saw, but not quite as well. It crosscuts with less precision than the miter saw. Cutting angles other than 90 degrees may be a problem. Making long rip cuts in sheets of plywood also is difficult.

CAUTION!
SAFETY MEASURES FOR A TABLESAW

Because a tablesaw runs so smoothly and seems so stable, it's easy to lose safety-consciousness while working with one. A tablesaw is a tool worthy of respect. Many professionals have had parts of fingers cut off by a tablesaw blade.

Always keep your fingers well away from the blade. Never wear long sleeves or loose clothing. Never reach across the saw blade while it is running. Keep push sticks and an anti-kickback featherboard handy and develop the habit of using them (see page 281). Turn the saw off when you need to free a piece of wood that has become stuck.

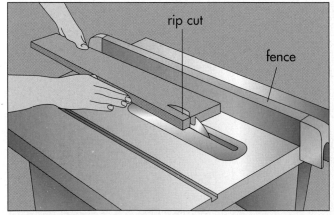

Make a rip cut.
Check that the fence is perfectly parallel to the blade by measuring the space between the blade and the fence at the front and the rear of the blade. Set the blade depth so it is ¼ inch above the top of the board. Start the motor and allow it to reach full speed. Hold the lumber against the fence so the wood glides smoothly and is flush against it at all points as you push it forward. Never allow your fingers to come within 6 inches of the blade; use a push stick when you come to the end of the cut (see page 281).

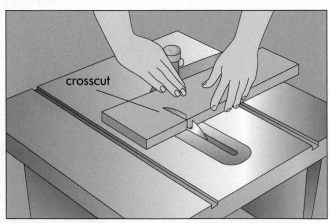

Make a crosscut.
Make sure the miter gauge is exactly perpendicular to the blade; slip it into its channel and square it using the edge of the table as a guide. Set the blade depth ¼ inch above the board and start the motor. Hold the board firmly against the miter guide and slide it toward the blade. Hold the board only at the miter gauge. If you hold the wood on both sides of the cut, the blade may bind, causing a dangerous kickback. Keep your fingers well away from the blade.

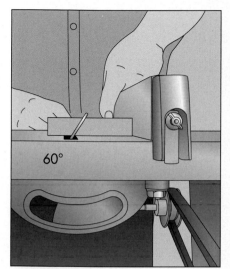

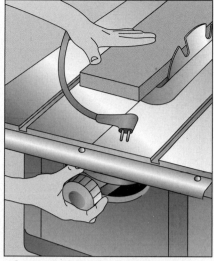

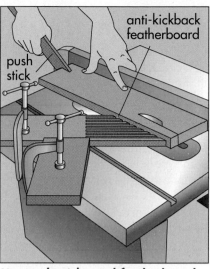

Make a bevel rip cut.

To set the bevel, use the saw gauge or mark the bevel angle on the butt end of the board and tilt the blade until it aligns with the mark. Hold the board against the blade at the correct location, slide the fence against the board, and lock the fence in position. Follow the same procedures as for a rip cut (see page 280).

Always set the height correctly.

Before every cut, adjust the blade depth so it is about ¼ inch above the top of the board you are cutting. This makes a cleaner cut and helps avoid binding and a dangerous kickback. If you are cutting a sheet of plywood that is warped, you may need to raise the blade higher, so it cuts through the sheet completely at all points. Always unplug the tablesaw before making blade adjustments.

Use push sticks and featherboard.

To make an anti-kickback featherboard, cut one end of a 16-inch-long 1×6 at 60 degrees, then cut 8-inch-long slots ¼ inch apart on the angled end. When clamped as shown *above*, it ensures a straight cut and prevents kickback in case the blade binds. Make push sticks out of 1× lumber or ½-inch plywood and use them whenever you need to hold the board within 6 inches of the blade.

Cut dadoes, rabbets, and tenons.

With a dado blade, you can make a variety of groove sizes. With a regular dado blade, sandwich a combination of chippers between the two outside cutter blades to get your desired width. To set the blade to the desired depth, mark the depth on the board and hold it next to the blade as you adjust it. Adjustable dado blades dial to the desired width.

If you need to make a groove wider than the dado blade, make repeated passes, moving the board a little less than the width of the blade for each pass.

On a tablesaw, you will not be able to see the cut as you make it, so test your settings on a scrap piece to make sure the dado is the correct width and depth. Then make the real cut.

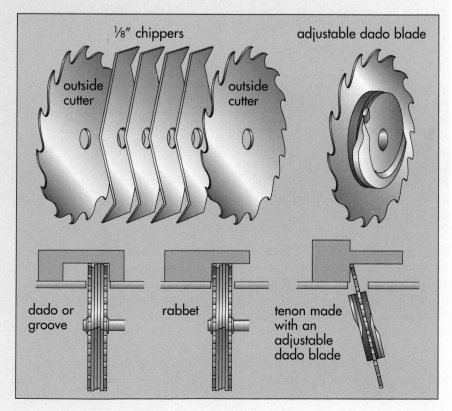

USING A RADIAL-ARM OR POWER MITER SAW

A radial-arm saw works best for crosscutting wood, but you can use it for ripping as well as long as you take it slowly and use precautions (see below right). With attachments available on some models, you can use a radial-arm saw as a router or a sander.

A radial-arm saw table is made of particleboard or plywood rather than metal because the saw blade must cut into the table slightly to cut boards completely. When the tabletop becomes shredded after years of use, you should replace it. The fence, usually a piece of 1×2, needs to be replaced more often.

A power miter saw is designed for two purposes only: miter-cutting and crosscutting small-width boards (usually 1×6 or smaller). Highly portable, a power miter saw sets up easily on a couple of sawhorses. It's ideal for cutting molding on the spot.

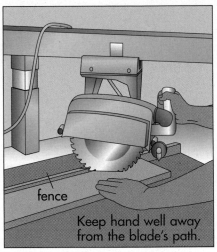

fence · **Keep hand well away from the blade's path.**

Make a miter cut or crosscut.
Test your saw for accuracy by cutting scraps at 45 and 90 degrees and adjust the fence or the saw if necessary. To make the cut, hold the board firmly against the fence. Make sure the board is fully supported and lies flat on the table. Pull the saw toward you, cutting the board so the saw kerf is on the scrap side of the line.

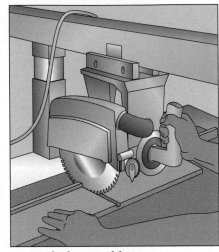

Cut a dado or rabbet.
To cut a notch for a dado or rabbet, raise the blade to the desired height; test the cut depth on a scrap. Check that the board lies flat; any warp will distort the cut. Cut on each side of the notch, then make a series of cuts in the interior. Clean out the notch with a chisel. If you have a lot of notching to do, use dado blades.

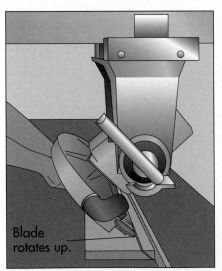

Blade rotates up.

Make a rip cut or beveled rip cut.
Turn the saw so the blade rotates up against the board, the opposite of a crosscut or dado cut. Start the saw with the blade slightly raised above the tabletop, then lower it to the cut line. To avoid kickback, hold the board firmly as you feed it into the blade. Pull the board through the blade to finish the cut.

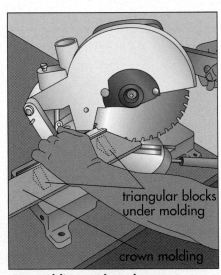

triangular blocks under molding · **crown molding**

Cut molding with a chopsaw.
Hold the piece firmly against the fence, start the saw, and lower the blade to make the cut. In many cases, the cut will not begin at the edge of a board, but in the middle; make your marks accordingly. When cutting crown molding, hold wood at the correct angle with triangular blocks.

CAUTION!
DEVELOP SAFETY HABITS
Radial-arm or power miter saws can be extremely dangerous. Not only can you cut yourself with the blades, but a radial-arm saw almost certainly will kick a board back at bullet-like speed if you are not careful. Develop these safety habits:
■ Never remove the saw guard. Take the time to adjust the guard for maximum safety before making each cut.
■ When ripping boards with a radial-arm saw, use a push stick and featherboard like those for a tablesaw (see page 281). Also, stand to the side of the board, so if it does shoot back, it won't hit you.
■ Keep work well supported so the blade will not bind.

USING A ROUTER

With the versatility and power of a router, you can custom-design and mill lumber to your own specifications. In addition to choosing among a wide variety of bits (shown *below*), you can set your bit to the depth of cut that suits you. Often, it's possible to save money by milling your own lumber rather than buying expensive moldings. For rounding off edges, a router produces a far more professional-looking finish than does a rasp or sander.

> **CAUTION!**
> *BITS ARE SHARP!*
> *Most of the time, you will not even see your router bit as you work. Don't let that lull you into complacency: A router's sharp bit, rotating at tremendous speeds, can do a lot of damage in a millisecond. Keep your hands well away from the work.*

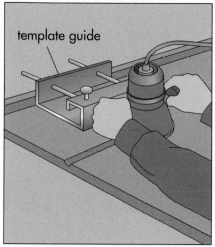

Use a guide.
You can make accurate cuts using a router guide. Sometimes a simple straightedge will suffice; just hold the baseplate tight against it as you cut. A template guide like the one shown allows you to follow a precut template. You may want to purchase a router table, which holds the router in an upside-down position; you can adjust and operate it much as you would a tablesaw.

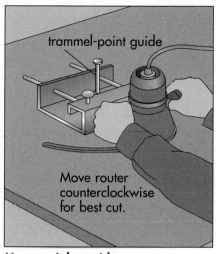

Move router counterclockwise for best cut.

Use specialty guides.
A variety of guides is available for special purposes. To cut smooth circles or curves, use a trammel-point guide like the one shown. A router bit spins clockwise, so you will get the best results if you move the router counterclockwise. You also can buy guides for cutting dovetail joints or hinge mortises.

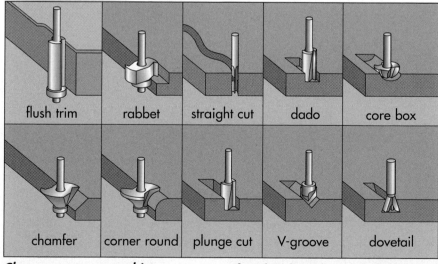

flush trim | rabbet | straight cut | dado | core box
chamfer | corner round | plunge cut | V-groove | dovetail

Choose among many bits.
Piloted bits, such as the **flush trim**, **rabbet**, **chamfer**, and **corner round**, are self-guiding; you don't need to use a guide or template when cutting with them. Use these bits to shape edges of boards or to final-cut laminates after they have been applied. Bits with ball-bearing guides usually work more smoothly.

The other bits shown require a guide or a steady hand. You can use two or more bits in succession to make intricate shapes.

NAILING

The quickest way to make a job look shoddy and amateurish is to make a nailing mistake that mars the wood. All your careful measuring and cutting will be for naught if the wood ends up with "smiles" and "frowns" made by a hammer that missed the nail, or if you bend a nail while driving it.

Professional carpenters make nailing look easy—and for good reason. When properly done, pounding a nail home is not a struggle, but is done with smooth, fluid motions. You may never be as fast at nailing as professionals because they get plenty of practice, but you can learn to drive in nails accurately without damaging the material or yourself.

EXPERTS' INSIGHT

GETTING THE HOLDING POWER YOU NEED

■ How well a nail will hold in wood depends on how much of its surface contacts the wood. The longer and thicker the nail, the better it will hold.

■ When possible, use the Rule of Three: A nail should be three times as long as the thickness of the board being fastened. Two-thirds of the nail then will be in the second board to which you are fastening the first one. If the nail must penetrate through dead space or drywall, increase the nail length by that distance.

■ A thick nail holds better, but not if it splits the wood. In that case, most of its holding power is lost. Special nails, such as ring-shank and cement-coated nails, hold better than standard nails. A headed nail holds better than a finish nail.

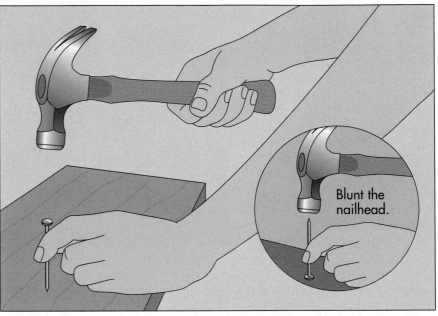

Blunt the nailhead.

Set the nail.
Practice on scrap pieces before you pound nails into finished work. To ensure that the hammer strikes the nail and not your fingers and that the nail will be driven into the board squarely, grasp the nail near its head and the hammer near the end of the handle. Lightly tap the nail until it stands by itself.

If you must drive a nail near the end of a board, drill a pilot hole or turn the nail upside down and blunt its point with a hammer. Either technique will reduce the risk of splitting the wood.

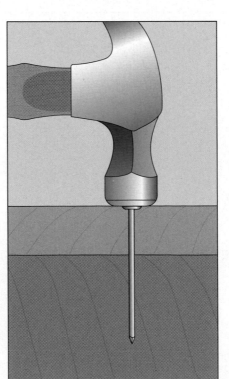

Use proper nailing techniques.
Once the nail is set in place, remove your hand from it. Keep your eye on the nail as you swing the hammer, letting the weight of the hammer head do the driving.

Beginners tend to hold a hammer stiffly and keep their shoulders stiff, swinging from the elbow. This leads to a tired, sore arm and to mistakes. Loosen up. Your whole arm should move as you swing from the shoulder. Keep your wrist loose so the hammer can give a final "snap" at the end of each blow. The entire motion should be relaxed and smooth.

With the last hammer blow, push the head of the nail flush or nearly flush with the surface of the wood. The convex shape of the hammer face allows you to do this without marring the surface.

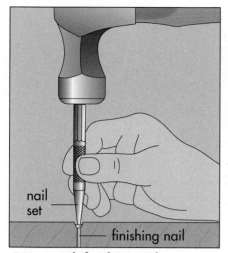

Countersink finishing nails.

In most cases, it's best to drive the heads of finishing or casing nails below the surface. You can fill the hole with wood putty later. This actually doesn't take all that long and leads to a much better-looking finish than nails driven flush. Hold a nail set against the nailhead and tap it in.

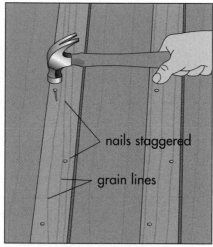

Stagger nails to avoid splits.

When driving several nails along the length of a board, stagger them so you don't split the board. The idea is to avoid pounding neighboring nails through the same grain line; two nails will stress the grain twice as much as one nail. If the work will be visible, stagger the nails in a regular pattern.

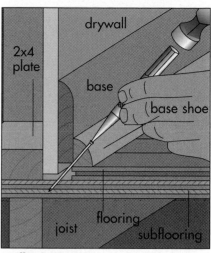

Drill pilot holes.

When you nail within 2 inches of the end of a board or into hardwood, drill pilot holes to avoid splitting the wood. Pilot holes should be slightly smaller than the diameter of the nail. When attaching a base shoe, drive nails into pilot holes so they miss the flooring, which needs room to expand and contract with changes in temperature and humidity.

EXPERTS' INSIGHT

USING MASONRY NAILS

■ Masonry nails offer a quick way to attach materials to concrete, brick, and masonry block. With flat-style masonry nails, be sure to turn the nail in the direction of the grain so it's less likely to split the wood.

■ You can use a standard hammer, but the job is easier with a heavy mallet. Hold the board in place, and drive the masonry nail through it. Once the nail hits the masonry surface, strike it with hard strokes. With subsequent nails, check to see if you have dislodged any nails; you may have to put in more.

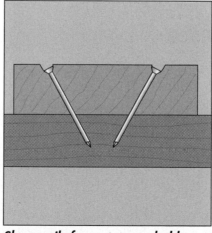

Skew nails for a stronger hold.

In situations where you cannot use as long a nail as you would like, drive nails in at an angle. Drive in one nail at about a 60-degree angle in one direction, then drive in another one in the opposite direction. The skewed nails will work together, making it difficult for the board to pull loose. Set the nailheads into the surface for a finished appearance.

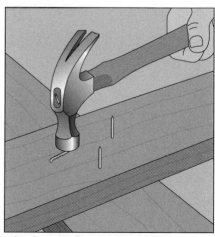

Clinch nails for the best hold.

If looks are not important, but strength is, use nails about 1 inch longer than the thickness of the pieces you're fastening. Drive in the nails, then turn the boards over and bend the exposed portion of the nails so they are nearly flush with the surface and parallel to the wood grain. The resulting joint will be extremely difficult to pull apart.

FASTENING WITH SCREWS

It's not hard to see why screws fasten so well. The threads grip wood fibers in a way that a smooth nail cannot. When the screw is driven home, the threads exert tremendous pressure against the screw head to hold the fastener firmly in place. With the right tools (see box below), driving screws can be almost as quick as nailing. If you make a mistake, it's easy to remove a screw without damaging your work. Screws must be driven with care, however. If you do not start out straight, there is no way to correct the mistake as you continue driving the screw. Without a pilot hole, the screw may split the wood and the screw will not hold securely. If the pilot hole is too large, again, the screw will not grip well.

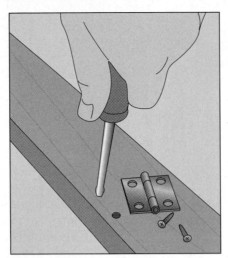

Make a starter hole with an awl.
Small screws seldom require pilot holes (see the box, below right). However, they do need a starter hole. Poke a hole with a scratch awl. Give it a few twists, back it out, and you're ready to drive in the screw.

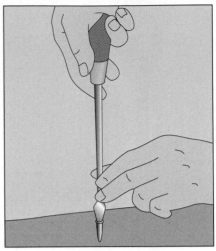

Drive with a hand screwdriver.
Start screws by holding the screwdriver handle with one hand and the screwdriver blade with the other. Don't hold the screw. If the screw is spinning around and not going into the wood, put two hands on the handle to apply more pressure.

TOOLS TO USE

Power-driven screws hold tightly, go in quickly, and are removed easily. Here are some tools that make working with them even more convenient.
■ A variable-speed, reversible drill starts the screws slowly and removes them if necessary.
■ With a magnetic sleeve, screws stick to the bit, making it easy to drive them in hard-to-reach places. Changing bit tips is easy; simply press them into the sleeve.
■ Have on hand a collection of drill bit tips, particularly #1 and #2 Phillips bits and some slotted bits, as well.
■ Consider buying square-headed screws and bits. These bits fit into and grab the screw slot better than Phillips-head and slotted screws.

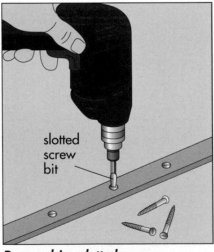

slotted screw bit

Power-drive slotted screws.
Even a few screws can take a long time to drive by hand, so consider using a drill with a screwdriver bit. When driving slotted screws, take care that the bit does not wander partway out of the slot, or you could damage the surface into which you are screwing. Don't drive screws too quickly, or the bit may slip out of the slot. Maintain firm, even pressure as you work.

EXPERTS' INSIGHT

WHEN DO YOU NEED A PILOT HOLE?

If there is a danger of cracking the wood, you should always drill a pilot hole, no matter how small the screw. For instance, if the wood is brittle or if you will be driving a screw near the end of a board, almost any screw can split the wood. But if you are drilling into a sound board at a spot 2 inches or more from its end, it usually will be safe to drive in a No. 6 or thinner screw without a pilot hole. If you are drilling into plywood or framing lumber, you should be able to drive No. 8 screws without pilot holes. For advice on selecting the correct-size bit, see page 276.

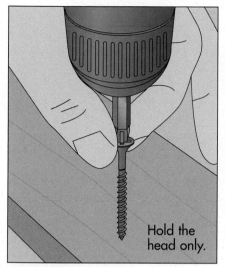

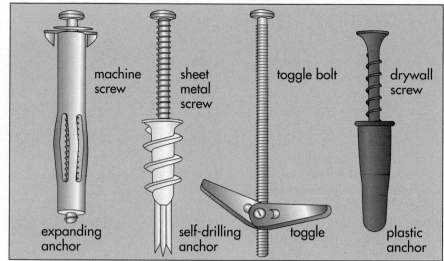

machine screw · sheet metal screw · toggle bolt · drywall screw
expanding anchor · self-drilling anchor · toggle · plastic anchor

Use Phillips-head drywall screws.

You can buy drywall screws by the pound at bargain prices and drive them into most materials in which you would use nails. If you use a magnetic sleeve, place the screw on the bit first, then set the tip of the screw in place on the material. If you need to hold the screw to keep it from wandering, hold the head only, not the sharp threads.

Attach items to walls with special wall fasteners.

If you need to attach something to a wall, the ideal way is to drive a screw into a stud. But often that's not possible. The screws and bolts shown *above* are designed to hold items firmly in drywall or plaster walls. To use **expanding anchors** and **plastic anchors**, drill holes and tap the unit into the wall; the anchor will spread and grip as you tighten the screw. Use **self-drilling anchors** only in drywall. You don't need to drill a hole; just screw them in and insert a screw. To use a **toggle bolt**, drill a hole large enough for the folded-back toggles to fit through. Push the toggles through the hole, and turn the bolt until the toggles snug up to the back side of the wall.

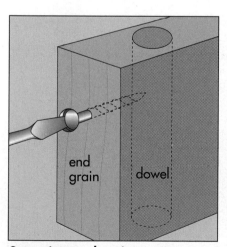

Hold the head only.

Screw into end grain.

When a fastener is driven into the end grain of a board, it will not hold as well as it does across the grain because it runs parallel to the grain rather than at an angle to it. Use a longer screw than you usually would. Where holding power is critical, drill a hole and install a dowel, as shown, into which you can drive the screw.

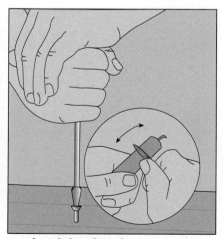

Deal with hard-to-drive screws.

If the going gets tough, the screw may stop turning. Exert pressure on the screwdriver with the palm of one hand and turn it with the other. If you still can't drive it, remove the screw and drill a slightly larger pilot hole. Another solution is to lubricate the threads with candle wax and try again.

EXPERTS' INSIGHT

FASTENING TO METAL WITH SCREWS

■ For fastening thin sheet metal or soft metal, such as brass, you can use one of several types of self-tapping sheet-metal screws (see page 257). Simply drive the screw in; it makes its own path with a metal-cutting point.

■ For heavier metals, drill a pilot hole using the techniques for drilling through metal (see page 279). Then install a sheet-metal screw.

■ For metal ⅛ inch or thicker and where you want an extra-strong joint, buy a drill-and-tap kit. With this, you can make a machine-threaded hole that will accept a machine bolt.

FASTENING WITH BOLTS

Nails and screws depend on friction between the fastener and the wood to do their job. When you tighten a nut on a bolt, however, you're actually clamping adjoining members together, producing the sturdiest of all joints. All types of bolts require a hole bored through both pieces being joined together. Here's information about installing machine and carriage bolts. For help with toggle bolts and other anchors, see page 287.

CAUTION!
Overtightening bolts can strip threads and damage wood, reducing the holding power of the bolt. Tighten the nut and bolt firmly against the wood, give them another half turn, then stop.

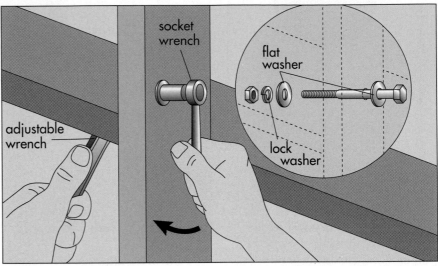

Fasten with machine bolts.
Machine bolts have hexagonal heads and threads running partway or all the way along the shank. When fastening two pieces of wood together, slip a flat washer onto the bolt and slide the bolt through the holes in both pieces of material. Add another flat washer, then a lock washer. Screw the nut on and tighten it. The flat washer keeps the nut and the bolt head from biting into the wood. The lock washer prevents the nut from coming loose. Use two wrenches to draw the nut down onto the bolt: one to steady the nut, the other to turn the bolt head.

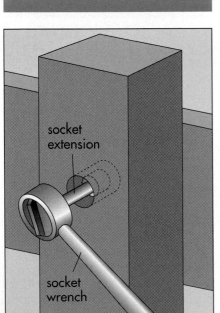

Tighten a countersunk bolt head.
To install a machine bolt in a hard-to-get-at place or when you have to countersink the bolt head, use a socket wrench with a socket extension to reach into the recess. Hold the nut with another wrench.

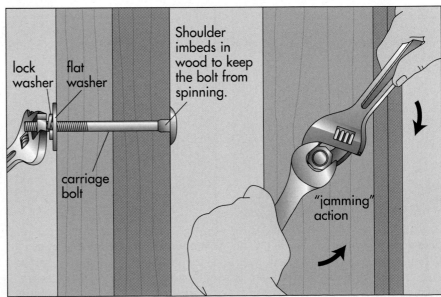

Install a carriage bolt.
A carriage bolt has a plain, round head. Insert it into the hole and tap the head flush with the surface. Slip a flat washer, a lock washer, and a nut onto the bolt. Tighten the nut. The square or hexagonal shoulder under the bolt head keeps the bolt from spinning as the nut is tightened. No washer is needed under the head.

The lock washer should keep the bolt from working loose. As added protection, you can thread another nut onto the bolt, snug it against the first, then "jam" the two together by turning them in opposite directions.

REMOVING NAILS AND SCREWS

Mistakes are a part of every carpenter's day. In fact, knowing how to undo mistakes is one of the hallmarks of an experienced carpenter, and that necessitates a good knowledge of how to remove nails and screws. Whether you're correcting mistakes, disassembling an old structure, or recycling used lumber, you'll find it's worth it to learn how to remove old fasteners quickly and neatly.

Removing screws often is just a matter of reversing your drill and screwing the old fastener out. However, you may be faced with a stripped head or an extra-tight screw (see page 290).

Most commonly, you'll be faced with removing nails. Don't just start whacking away in frustration, or you'll damage the wood. Use these methods and accept that nail removal is a normal part of a carpenter's job.

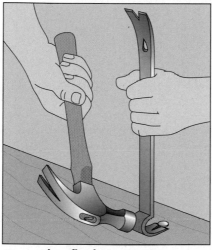

Pry with a flat bar.
If the head of the nail has not been set into the wood, it may be possible to shoehorn a flat bar under it and pry the nail up. Tap the notch of the chisel-like head of the bar under the nailhead and pull back on the bar. Because of its smooth, flat body, a pry bar makes only a slight indentation in the board as you remove the nail.

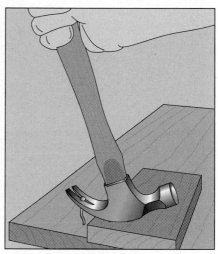

Use a wood block.
There are two good reasons for using a wood block when removing a nail. First, the raised height gives your hammer extra leverage, making it much easier to pull the nail out. Second, the block protects your work. Without it, the head of the hammer would dig in and make an unsightly indentation.

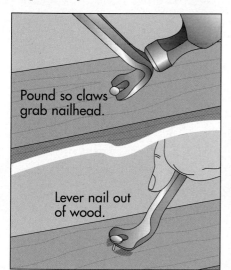

Pound so claws grab nailhead.

Lever nail out of wood.

Dig nails out with a cat's paw.
A cat's paw removes nails that are embedded deeply in lumber. Its drawback is that it also must bite deeply into the wood to grip the nailhead. Place the clawed tip behind the nailhead at a 45-degree angle. Pound the claws under the nailhead, pry the nail partway out, then use a hammer and block.

Tap out to release nails.

Tap in to expose nailheads.

Pound out board to loosen nails.
If you have access to the back side of the joined material, strike the joint from behind, then hammer the members back together from the front. This usually pops the nailheads out far enough for you to get hold of them with your hammer claw.

tight-work hacksaw

Cut the nails.
Where access is tight, sometimes you can disjoin two members by sawing through the nails. If you have a reciprocating saw with a metal-cutting blade, this will be easy. Otherwise, use a tight-work hacksaw. After you break the joint, use a nail set to force the heads out, then remove the nails.

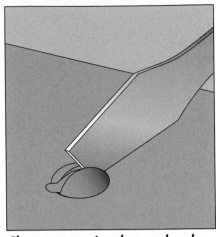

Punch through and pry.

To avoid splitting molding, punch the finishing nails that hold it in place through the molding with a nail set. Try not to make the hole larger; use a small-diameter nail set. Pound the head of the finishing nail deeply into the molding. You'll feel the board come loose. Once the nails are punched through, pry off the molding with a putty knife or chisel, taking care not to mar the wood.

Clean out a painted screw head.

When removing old screws that have been painted, take the time to clean the paint out of the slots. If you don't clean the head, you may strip the screw head, making it even more difficult to remove. Place a screwdriver as shown *above,* and tap with a hammer.

EXPERTS' INSIGHT

REMOVING OLD SCREWS

Here are some tips for removing stubborn old screws:

■ For a slotted screw that has been stripped so much that a screwdriver can't get a good hold, deepen the slot by cutting into it with a hacksaw.

■ Extremely tight screws often can be loosened with heat. Hold the tip of a soldering gun against the screw head for a minute or two, then try it.

■ For stripped Phillips-head screws, it sometimes helps to drill a small hole in the center of the head to give the screwdriver more to grab onto.

■ For an extremely stubborn screw, buy a screw and bolt extracting tool. Drill a small hole in the screw head, insert the tool, turn it with a wrench, and twist the screw out.

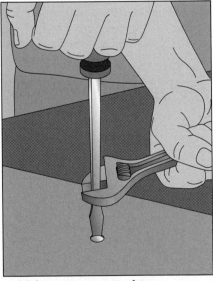

Add force to a screwdriver.

If you need greater turning power, use a screwdriver with a square shank in conjunction with an adjustable wrench. Adjust the wrench so it fits tightly on the screwdriver. Press down on the handle of the screwdriver with the palm of your hand as you turn with the wrench.

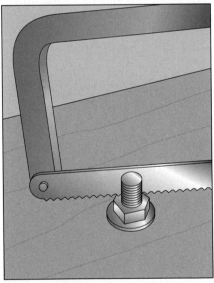

Cut a stubborn nut.

Rusty or damaged bolt threads make it hard to remove a nut. You can solve the problem quickly with a hacksaw. Align the saw blade so it rubs against the threads and cut down through the nut. You will cut off about one-third of the nut. Once you have done this, it will be easy to knock the nut loose or unscrew it.

GLUING AND CLAMPING

A joint will be stronger if you use glue in addition to nails or screws. For some projects that do not require great strength, glue alone will be enough.

Use contact cement to attach wood veneers or plastic laminates to wood surfaces. Apply the cement to both surfaces and let them dry. Align the parts precisely before you join them—the first bond is permanent (see page 293). Use paneling adhesives to attach sheet goods to walls. For interior projects, use carpenter's glue with aliphatic resin. This is superior to standard white glue because it sets up faster, resists heat and moisture better, and is stronger. For the glue to work, however, the pieces must be clamped together firmly until the glue sets.

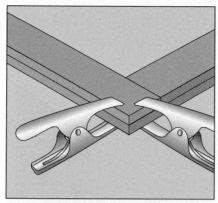

Use speedy squeeze clamps.
For light work, these are the easiest clamps to use. Apply glue to both pieces and place them together in correct alignment. Squeeze the clamp handles to spread the jaws. When you release the handles, the springs will clamp the work together. You may want to have several sizes of these inexpensive clamps on hand.

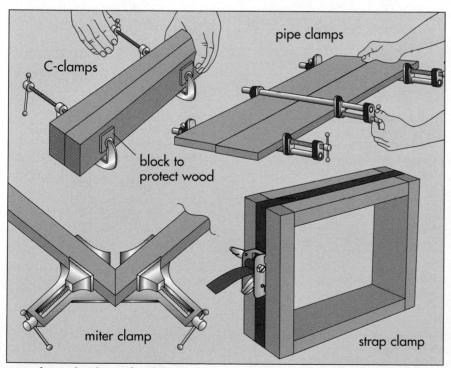

C-clamps
block to protect wood
pipe clamps
miter clamp
strap clamp

Use the right clamp for the job.
C-clamps are inexpensive and work well when the pieces are not too wide. Use blocks of wood to keep the clamps from marring the boards. For miter joints, use **miter clamps** that hold the boards at a

90-degree angle. For large projects, use **pipe clamps**. You should alternate them to prevent buckling. A **strap clamp** works well for cabinetry projects. It will clamp several joints at once and will not mar the wood.

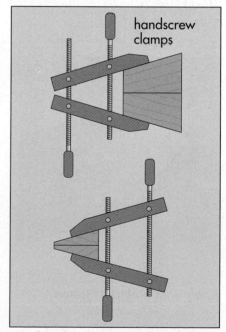

handscrew clamps

Use handscrew clamps for angles.
These clamps work well for cabinetmaking and other woodworking projects. Because their jaws are made of wood, you don't have to worry about marring your project. Adjust the clamp to almost any size or angle by simply turning the two handscrews.

CAULKING AND APPLYING MASTIC

*I*t takes practice before you can lay down a clean-looking bead of caulk. Practice on scrap materials or start in an inconspicuous area before you caulk an area that is highly visible.

Choose among a wide variety of adhesives that are designed for particular jobs (see the chart, *below right*). When working with adhesives, be careful to apply the material smoothly and evenly, so the piece will adhere uniformly. Avoid applying too much adhesive; cleaning up messes can take longer than the actual job.

YOU'LL NEED

TIME: About 20 minutes to caulk around a bathtub or countertop; 10 to 30 minutes to adhere laminate or paneling.
SKILLS: Smooth, steady control.
TOOLS: Utility knife, caulking gun, notched trowel.

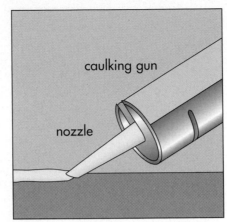

Apply a bead of caulk.
Make sure the joint to be caulked is free of dirt and grease and there are no gaps wider than your bead of caulk. Snip the nozzle of the caulk tube at about a 45-degree angle. The closer to the tip you cut, the smaller the bead will be. You may need to puncture the inside seal with a long nail. Squeeze the handle until caulk starts coming out; move smoothly to apply an even bead.

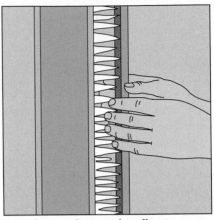

Attach paneling with adhesive.
To attach paneling to walls, apply a bead of adhesive on either the wall or the back of the panel. Use a notched trowel or make a squiggle pattern using a caulking gun. Press the panel against the wall, then pull it out slightly. Wait for a few minutes for the adhesive to get tacky (the manufacturer's instructions will tell you how long), then press the materials together again.

Apply with a notched trowel.
For a smooth, even application, use a notched trowel to apply adhesives. Check the adhesive container for the type and size of notches the trowel should have. Apply the adhesive with the trowel held nearly parallel to the surface to make sure it sticks. Tilt the trowel up at about a 45-degree angle and press firmly as you spread the adhesive.

SELECTING ADHESIVES

Adhesive Type	Primary Use	Holding Power	Moisture-Resistance	Set/Cure Time	Type of Applicator
Contact cement	Applying wood veneer and plastic laminate.	Excellent	Excellent	Must dry first/ 1–2 days	Brush, notched trowel, or paint roller
Epoxy adhesive	Bonding almost any materials. Must mix the parts.	Excellent	Excellent	30 minutes/ 1–10 hours	Throwaway brush or flat stick
Panel adhesive	Attaching drywall or paneling to walls.	Good	Good	1 hour/ 24 hours	Caulk tube or notched trowel
Carpenter's glue	Bonding wood together for small projects.	Good	Fair	30 minutes/ 24 hours	Squeeze-type container
Cyanoacrylate (superglue)	Bonding small items of most any material.	Good	Fair	1–2 minutes/ 24 hours	Squeeze tube

APPLYING LAMINATE

Plastic laminate comes in a variety of colors, patterns, and textures. With practice and the right tools, you can lay down laminate as well, if not as quickly, as a professional.

Be sure that the surface to which you are attaching the laminate is straight, smooth, and supported so it will not flex. New particleboard works best, although laminate also can be applied to plywood and old laminate.

YOU'LL NEED

TIME: About half a day to cover a couple of straightforward countertops.

SKILLS: Accurate measuring and cutting, smooth application of cement, use of a router.

TOOLS: Circular saw or carbide-tipped knife; brush, paint roller, or notched trowel; roller; router, file, or sanding block.

1. Cut the laminate.
Cut the laminate so it is about ½ inch larger than the surface in both directions; you'll trim it exactly after it is installed. Cut it with a circular saw or score its face with a carbide-tipped knife. Cut with the face up if you are using a tablesaw or with the face down if you are using a circular saw.

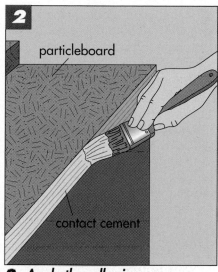

2. Apply the adhesive.
Choose professional-grade contact cement, which costs a bit more than the homeowner-type cement. Spread it evenly on the back of the laminate and the base surface, using a brush, paint roller, or a notched trowel. Allow both surfaces to dry completely before adhering.

3. Attach the laminate.
Cover the surface with brown wrapping paper and position the laminate on top. When the laminate is exactly where you want it, carefully pull out the paper. Roll the entire surface with a rolling pin, starting in the middle and working outward.

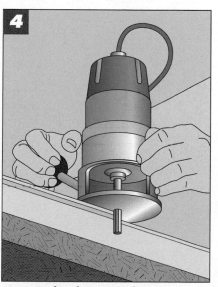

4. Attach edging, and trim.
Attach the edging pieces so they butt tightly against the underside of the top laminate piece. To finish the project, trim the overhanging edges of laminate with a router, file, or sanding block. Take care not to crack the laminate or lift it up as you work.

TOOLS TO USE

■ For the best results, use a router with a special laminate edging bit. This will give you smooth, professional-looking edges that you can't get with a sanding block, rasp, or file. Experiment with the router on scrap pieces to get the depth of the bit set right; if it is too deep, you will cut away too much and ruin the project.

■ For small jobs or for areas where the router can't reach, use a sanding block or a rasp. Work slowly. If you sand away too much laminate, there is no way to fix it.

MAKING SIMPLE, STRONG JOINTS

Strong, good-looking wood joints are essential to all carpentry and woodworking projects. Here are some of the simplest and strongest joinery methods. Each of these joints can be made with hand tools, but if you have shop tools, such as a tablesaw or power miter saw, the job will go faster and the joint will be tighter. None of them requires cabinetmaking expertise.

You'll need to hone your measuring, cutting, and fastening skills to make neat, sturdy joints. See pages 260–277 for a review of the basic techniques.

All of the joints shown on this page are **butt joints**—two square-cut pieces joined together by positioning the end of one member against the face or edge of another member. A butt joint can be fastened with nails or screws only. It will be stronger, however, if reinforced with corner braces, T-plates, angle brackets, dowels, a plywood gusset, or a wood block.

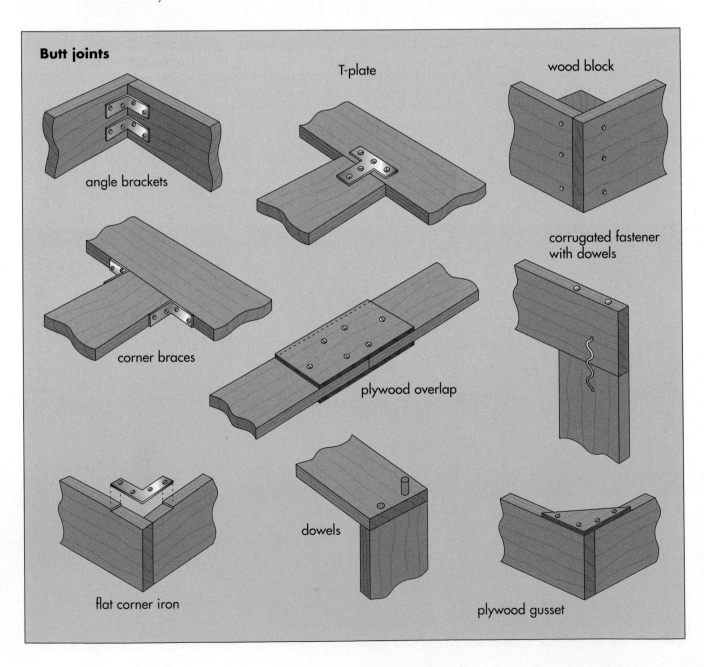

Butt joints

T-plate

wood block

angle brackets

corner braces

plywood overlap

corrugated fastener with dowels

flat corner iron

dowels

plywood gusset

Lap joints are stronger than butt joints and often look better, as well. To make an **overlap joint**, simply lay one of the members on top of the other and nail or screw it in place. For a **full-lap joint**, cut a notch into one member that is as deep as the second piece is thick. Clamp and glue the two pieces together, adding fasteners if you prefer. The **half-lap joint** is the strongest joint (see page 296).

Dado joints are attractive and strong, but are difficult to make.

A **stopped dado** has the strength of a dado and hides the joinery (see page 296).

For a finished-looking corner, make a **miter joint**. Cut the pieces at the same angle (usually 45 degrees), then glue the joint and drive in finishing nails.

A **biscuit joint** also is strong and has the advantage of being completely hidden, To make it, however, requires a biscuit joiner power tool (see page 297).

YOU'LL NEED

TIME About 10 to 30 minutes per joint, depending on complexity.
SKILLS: Ability to make square cuts, drill, use fasteners, and make neat notches.
TOOLS: Square, ruler, pencil, saw, drill and bits, hammer, nail set, screwdriver. The biscuit joint requires a biscuit joiner tool.

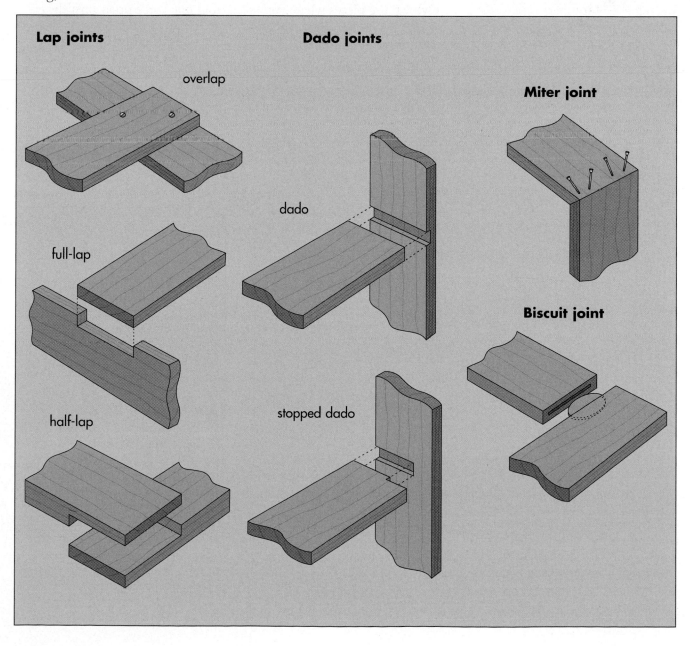

Lap joints

overlap

full-lap

half-lap

Dado joints

dado

stopped dado

Miter joint

Biscuit joint

MAKING A HALF-LAP OR DADO JOINT

Shelves and other wooden structures made with half-lap or dado joints are clearly a cut above those made with butt or even miter joints. Half-laps and dadoes are the stuff of cabinetry rather than carpentry. However, these strong joints don't require a talent for fine woodworking skills, just some skill with basic marking, cutting, and chiseling. Both joints require precise notches. Use sharp saw blades and chisels. To hone your notching skills, practice on a scrap piece of lumber.

YOU'LL NEED
TIME: Allow about 1 hour to make two joints.
SKILLS: Precise marking, cutting, and chiseling skills.
TOOLS: Circular, table, or radial-arm saw; square; chisel.

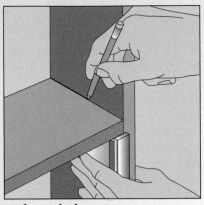

1. Mark for a half-lap joint ...
Overlap the pieces where you want the half-lap joint. You may want to use clamps. Mark for the notches by running a sharp pencil or a knife along the edge of the board. Mark for the notch on the second board using the same method. Or, wait until the first notch has been cut so you can set it over the second board before making your marks.

or for a dado.
Hold one piece up against the piece that will be notched. Mark along both sides with a sharp pencil or a knife. Or, mark a perpendicular line and use a scrap piece as a spacer to mark the second line. If you are sure of your skills, you can use a ruler or tape measure to mark for both sides of the notch.

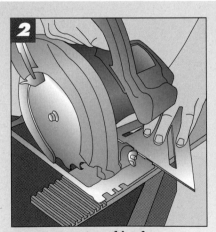

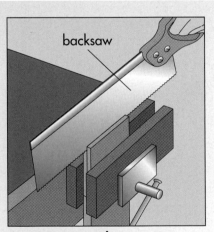

backsaw

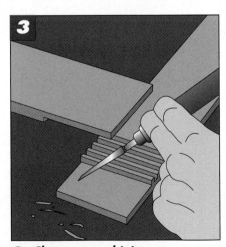

2. Cut a series of kerfs ...
For a half-lap joint, set your saw blade so it cuts exactly halfway through the board. For a dado joint, set the blade to cut one-third of the way through. Keeping the blade on the inside of the notch at all times, make the two outside cuts, then make a series of cuts about ³/₈ inch apart in the area between.

or cut out a notch.
If your cut falls at the end of the board (whether for a half-lap or a dado joint), you simply can cut out a notch. Set your power saw to cut a kerf where the notch will end. Taking care to keep the blade square on both sides, use a backsaw to cut into the end of the board until the blade reaches the first kerf.

3. Clean out and join.
Using a chisel with its beveled surface down, clean remaining wood out of the notch. Make sure the visible edges are straight and there are no bumps in the middle of the notch. Dry-fit the pieces to make sure they are tight. Apply carpenter's glue, clamp, and fasten with nails or screws.

FASTENING WITH DOWELS

A dowel joint is not impressive-looking like a half-lap or dado joint, but it is strong. Making a dowel joint requires no special tools, but there are two difficulties: You must hold the boards square as you work and you must hold the drill as straight as possible to keep from poking a hole through the edge or side of a board. Work on a flat surface to keep the face of the boards even. If possible, clamp the boards together before adding the dowels.

YOU'LL NEED

TIME: 1 hour to make two dowel joints.
SKILLS: Good drilling skills.
TOOLS: Drill with an extra-long bit, backsaw, hammer.

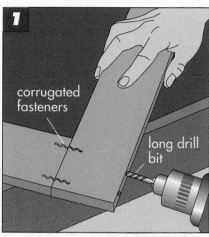

1. Temporarily join and drill.
Position the boards the way you want them and join them temporarily with fasteners or clamps. If you use fasteners, make sure they will not be in the way of the dowels. Square up the corner and drill holes for the dowels.

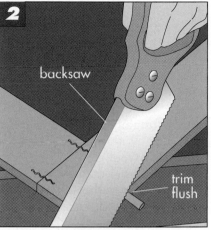

2. Drive the dowels and trim off.
Squirt carpenter's glue into the drill holes and insert the dowels. Tap them all the way in and clean away excess glue. Cut off the dowels as flush to the board as possible without scratching the edge. Sand the remainder smooth.

FASTENING WITH A BISCUIT JOINER

With this tool, you can create neat, sturdy joints with ease. Biscuit fasteners are oval-shaped pieces of plywood that fit invisibly into incisions inside the joint. You can use a biscuit joiner to fasten two boards on edge, join ¾-inch or thicker edging to plywood, or make butt or miter joints. Be sure you hold the tool with its base perfectly flat against the board as you make the cuts. If you will be using more than three or four biscuits on a joint, work fast and have a helper on hand.

YOU'LL NEED

TIME: About 30 minutes to make two joints with eight biscuits.
SKILLS: Use of power tools, ability to align the tool and hold it flat.
TOOLS: Biscuit joiner, hammer, clamps, square.

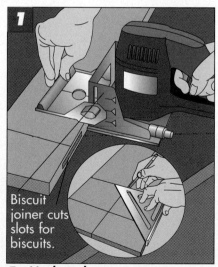

Biscuit joiner cuts slots for biscuits.

1. Mark and cut.
Position the boards as you want them joined. For every place you want to install a biscuit, mark a line running from one board to the other (see inset). Set the tool to the correct depth for the size biscuit you're using. Hold the tool flat against the board as you make each incision.

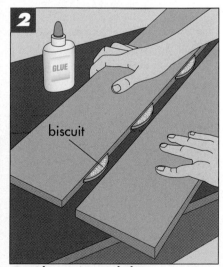

2. Glue, join, and clamp.
After dry-fitting the boards with the biscuits in place, squirt a little carpenter's glue into each incision. Set the biscuits into the incisions and tap the second board into place, sliding the biscuits into their respective slots. Check that the joint is tight and clamp. Wipe away excess glue and allow to dry.

SHAPING AND PLANING

Beveling edges and corners, planing down doors, trueing edges and ends of lumber—most carpentry projects include at least one of these shaping tasks. Three types of tools work best for shaping wood surfaces: planes, surface-forming tools, and rasps or wood files. With practice and a clean, sharp tool, shaping can be a pleasure rather than a chore.

However, even the sharpest shaping tools are no match for a board that's badly twisted, bowed, cupped, or warped (see page 248). Always inspect your material for flaws and select only the stock suitable for the job. Don't assume you can shape it up later.

EXPERTS' INSIGHT

SCRIBING A TRUE LINE

■ To straighten out a piece of lumber or a door, you must first draw the line indicating where the piece should end. This is called a true line. A true line is usually straight, but not always. For instance, a door often must be planed to fit an opening that is not straight. To make a true line, scribe it by holding the piece up against the place into which it must fit. Run your pencil along the opening as you mark the piece for planing.
■ When scribing a line, check the angle at which you are holding the pencil and the thickness of the pencil line. Hold the pencil at the same angle at all points along your scribe line or you will cut off too little or too much wood. Decide if you want to cut off all of the pencil mark or just up to the mark.

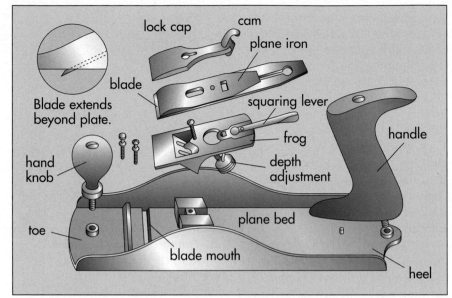

Keep planes in working order.

Various types and sizes of planes are available. Most carpenters use a smoothing plane (shown *above*) or a small block plane (see page 299). To help keep the blade from dulling, lay it on its side when not in use. Retract the blade into the body when storing it. If any parts become rusty, clean them with a little oil and fine steel wool. Adjust the blade so it cuts thin shavings easily; you should not have to fight against the wood.

Use a block of wood to support plane when shaving a narrow edge.

Follow general planing rules.
Follow these tips when using a plane or surface-former:
■ It takes both hands to operate the tool, so clamp your work.
■ Plane with the grain.
■ If you get anything but a continuous, even shaving, the blade is dull or adjusted too thick, or you're planing against the grain.
■ To avoid nicking corners, apply pressure to the knob of the tool at the beginning of your cut and to its heel at the end of the cut.
■ When planing a narrow edge, grip a square-cornered block of wood against the bottom of the plane as you work.

CAUTION!
BEVEL OR SCORE FIRST TO AVOID SPLINTERING

When you shave the end of a door or a sheet of plywood, there's a good chance you will chip the veneer sheet when you cut across its grain, seriously marring its appearance. To avoid what might be an expensive mistake, take the following precautions.

■ Bevel the veneer first. Turn the plane or shaping tool and cut a bevel downward toward the bottom of your work.

■ Use a knife and a straight-edge to score the veneer about ⅛ inch above the scribe line. After shaving the piece, use a sanding block to make an attractive bevel from the bottom of the piece to the scored line.

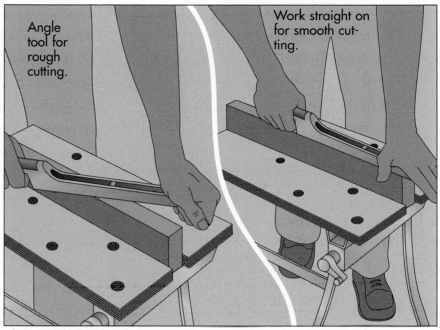

Shape with surface-forming tools.
Surface-forming tools, also known as sure-form tools, come in a variety of sizes and shapes. The one shown, *above,* works much like a plane. You cannot adjust the depth of the cut and it will not produce as smooth a cut as a plane, but it is easy to use.

You can regulate the cut by the way you position the tool against the material. For rough-cutting, hold the tool at a 45-degree angle to the work as you push it. For a smoother result, hold the tool parallel to the board's edge.

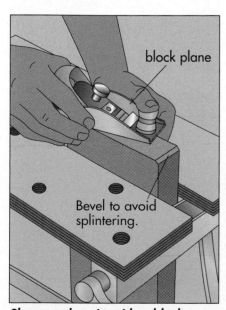

Shape end grain with a block.
As long as you're shaping wood parallel to the grain, planing will go smoothly. But when you need to shape the end grain, you will be working at a 90-degree angle to the grain. A small block plane works best on end grain. Bevel the

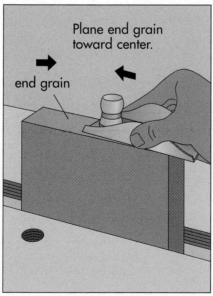

corners first, with the bottom of the bevel at the final cut line. For narrow stock, just plane in one direction. For wider material, shave from each end of the board toward the center. Finish the job by shaving off the hump that remains in the middle.

TOOLS TO USE
POWER PLANER AND BELT SANDER

■ If you have a lot of planing to do, buy a power planer. The depth is easy to adjust, and as long as you hold the base flat against the surface, you will get a smooth cut with little effort. Be sure to use carbide-tipped blades, or you will have to change them often.

■ If you can work carefully, a belt sander shaves material, especially softwoods, with relative ease. Start with a coarse sandpaper. Hold the sanding belt flat to the surface; you'll make gouges if you tip the tool. Once you have taken off almost as much material as you need to, switch to a smoother paper.

SANDING

Once you've taken the time to cut and assemble your project, don't skimp when it comes to the final steps. Do a thorough job of sanding, so the wood will be well prepared for its final finish. Don't expect stain, varnish, or paint to smooth out the surface for you. They will only follow the contours of the wood, and often will accentuate, rather than hide, imperfections. Unless you are using a belt sander with a rough abrasive, don't expect sanding to remove more than ⅛ inch of material; shape or plane instead (see pages 298–299).

CAUTION!
Particularly when sanding with power tools, wear a face mask. To avoid difficult cleanup later, seal the room.

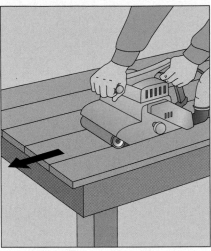

Use a belt sander for rough work.
Use this tool only on rough surfaces and only if you are sure of yourself; it is easy to make gouges if you tip the tool or if you rest it in one spot too long. Always run the sander with the grain, never against it. Don't apply pressure as you work; just let the weight of the sander do the work.

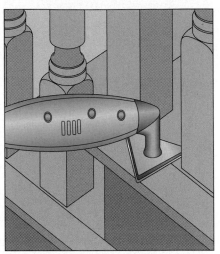

Use a detail sander in tight spots.
For awkward areas, a detail sander can spare you hours of finger-throbbing work. Sanding pads are self-adhesive; just lift one off and put the next one on. Proceed carefully. A detail sander works with an oscillating action. Because it concentrates on such a small area, it takes off material quickly.

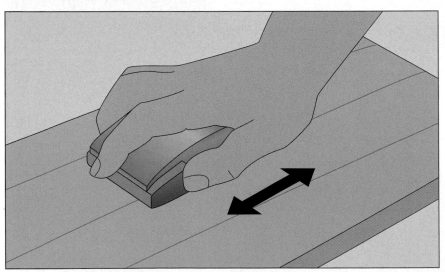

Hand-sand with a block.
Except in hard-to-reach areas, never use abrasive sheets alone—always use some sort of sanding block, either store-bought or improvised. Sanding with a block is less tiring and produces more uniform results.

Tear abrasive sheets to size, rather than cutting them, or you will dull your knife blade quickly.

Check that the bottom of your block is clean and smooth. Any debris can tear the paper and mar your work.

Sand only in the direction of the wood grain. Sanding across the grain or in a circular motion can leave hard-to-remove lines. Don't exert a lot of pressure. If you're using the right grade of paper, light strokes are all you'll need.

EXPERTS' INSIGHT

SAND THREE TIMES
■ Take the time and trouble to sand three times, using progressively finer sandpaper. The wood surface may feel smooth after your first and second sandings, but it will get smoother as you move on to finer-grit sandpapers. A common progression is to start with 80-grit paper, then proceed to 120-, 180-, and possibly even 240-grit abrasives. Clean dust from the wood between sandings.
■ If you can't sand out a stain or discoloration, apply a small amount of laundry bleach to the stain. Try several applications until you get the right color. Dry before sanding it again.

Wrap sandpaper around wood scrap.

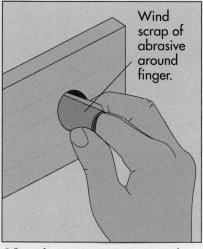

Wind scrap of abrasive around finger.

Roll sandpaper around dowel.

Use ingenuity for tight spots.
When smoothing wood in tight quarters or in unusual situations, special tools can help. Consider buying or renting a detail sander (see page 300) or a contour sanding attachment for your drill.

Often, however, you can get the job done with a sheet of abrasive and a little ingenuity, as these three examples show.

To sand two surfaces where they meet at an inside corner, wrap a creased sheet of abrasive

around a sharp-cornered block. To smooth inside edges of bored holes and small cutouts, wrap abrasive around your finger or a small round object. For sanding outside curves, wrap a sheet of abrasive around a dowel.

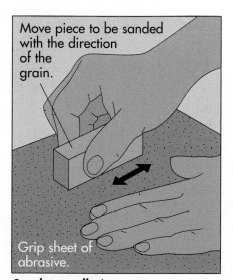

Move piece to be sanded with the direction of the grain.

Grip sheet of abrasive.

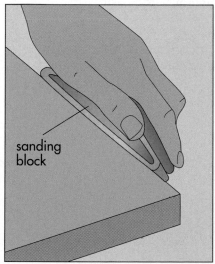

sanding block

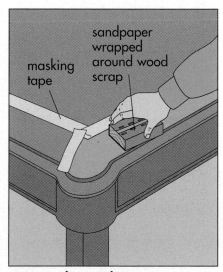

masking tape

sandpaper wrapped around wood scrap

Sand a small piece.
When you need to smooth the surface of a small item, sand it on a full sheet of abrasive held flat with your free hand. This keeps the surface of the piece even and flat. If the abrasive fills with dust, wipe it with a clean cloth or give it a few slaps against your bench.

Round off edges.
Because wood edges are susceptible to nicks and splinters, it is a good idea to blunt them with a light sanding. Hold the sanding block at an angle; use gentle pressure combined with a rocking motion. A molded rubber sanding block like the one shown, *above,* is ideal for this purpose because its base gives slightly.

Protect edges with tape.
Sometimes you'll want to sand one surface without scratching an adjoining surface. To do this, protect the surface you don't want sanded with masking tape. Affix the tape carefully, making sure it is stuck down tightly at all points. Watch closely as you sand and immediately replace any tape that gets ripped or damaged.

FILLING AND FINISHING

Paint, stain, or clear finishes rarely cover up imperfections in wood. Often, they make things look worse rather than better. It pays to prepare your wood carefully before you add a finish.

Fill in holes with wood filler and sand the surface smooth. If you're applying a clear finish, limit your use of putty to small spots; even putty that is made to accept stain never quite looks like real wood. Even if you're going to paint the surface, cover exposed plywood edges. They soak up paint like a sponge and will look rough no matter how many coats of paint you apply to them.

Once the wood surface is prepared, match your paint or clear finish to the intended use of your project. See chart on page 303 for selecting finishes.

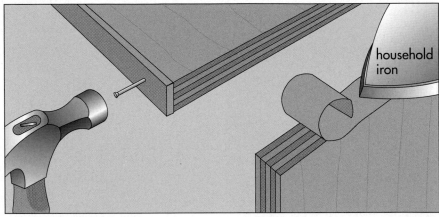

Cover plywood edges.
To conceal a plywood edge, cut a thin piece of molding to fit, apply carpenter's glue to the edge, and fasten the molding with brads (small finishing nails). You also can cover an edge with wood veneer tape. Buy tape that is wider than the thickness of the material and matches its surface. Cut the tape with scissors, leaving at least ¼ inch extra on all edges. Position iron-on tape carefully, so it covers the edge along the entire length. Apply even, steady pressure with a household iron set on high. Use contact cement to apply non-iron-on veneer. Trim the edges with a sharp knife, then sand the corners lightly.

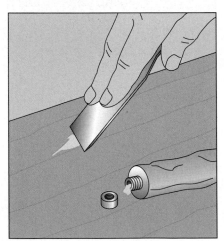

Fill in nail and screw holes.
For small holes, use a dough-type wood filler. Apply filler either before or after staining; experiment to find out which looks best. Begin by tamping a small amount of the filler into the hole with your thumb. Smooth it with a putty knife. Wipe away the excess with a rag dampened with water or mineral spirits, depending on the type of putty (check manufacturer's directions).

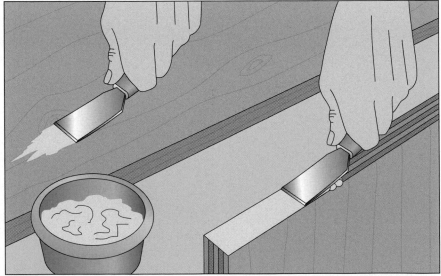

Fill in large areas.
If you're going to paint the entire surface of a project, water-mix putty excels at filling shallow depressions over a large surface area. The putty sets up quickly, so don't mix more than you can use in 10 minutes. To fill cracks around a knot, mix the putty to a pastelike consistency and force it into all the cracks with a putty knife. Feather out the patch to the surrounding wood. To fill edges of plywood or the end grain of boards, mix the putty to a thinner consistency. Sand and apply a second coat if necessary. For deep holes, you may have to apply two layers to allow for any shrinkage of the putty.

SELECTING CLEAR FINISHES

Type	Characteristics	Application and Drying Time
Natural-resin varnish	Resists scratches, scuffs. Spar varnish good outdoors.	Use varnish brush or cheesecloth pad. Dries in 24–36 hours. In humid weather, allow 36 hours.
Polyurethane varnish	Mar-resistant, durable, remains clear.	Use natural-bristle brush, roller, or spray. Let dry 1–2 hours; 12 hours between coats.
Two-part epoxy varnish	High resistance to scuffs and mars. Ideal for floors.	Use brush. Check directions if coating wood filler. First coat dries in 3 hours; second in 5–8 hours.
Shellac	Easily damaged by water. Clear or pigmented.	Use small brush with chiseled tip. Thin with alcohol or recommended solvent. Dries in about 2 hours.
Lacquer	Fast-drying. Ideal for furniture.	Best sprayed in many thin coats. Let last coat dry 48–60 hours, then rub with fine steel wool or hard wax.
Resin oil	Soaks into and hardens grain. Resists scratches.	Usually hand-rubbed in 2–3 coats. Needs 8–12 hours to dry.

Apply penetrating stain.
Apply stain with a brush and wait for a few minutes. The heavier the application and the longer you wait, the deeper the color. Wipe with a clean rag, taking care to make the color even throughout the piece. To make it darker, apply a second coat. If it is too dark, rub with a cloth moistened with the recommended thinner.

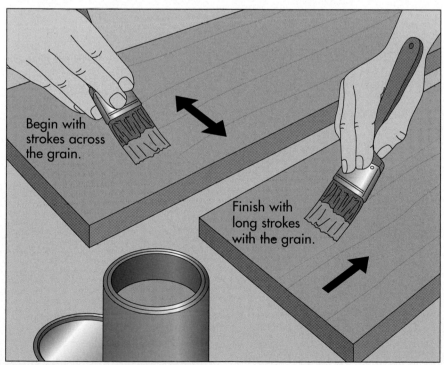

Begin with strokes across the grain.

Finish with long strokes with the grain.

Paint correctly for a smooth look.
Painting with a brush may seem like a simple task, but here are a few tips to keep in mind. Begin applying paint to wood surfaces with short strokes across the wood grain, laying down paint in both directions. Don't bear down too hard on the bristles.

Finish painting with longer, sweeping strokes in one direction only—this time with the wood grain. Use just the tips of the bristles to smooth out the paint.

EXPERTS' INSIGHT

ANTIQUING

■ If you have old furniture or cabinets that are worn or marred, you can avoid all the work of stripping, sanding, and refinishing them by emphasizing the wood's imperfections.

■ If you are new to this process, buy an antiquing kit, which usually includes base and finish coating materials and brushes and applicators. Choose from a variety of finishes: marbleized, distressed, spattered, stippled, crumpled, and others.

■ Remove dirt and wax from the surface, apply the base coat, and let it dry. After sanding, apply a finish coat quickly. Wipe it to achieve the desired finish. Allow it to dry for 48 hours and add a clear, protective finish.

INSTALLING MOLDING

Installing molding to finish off a project can be the most gratifying part of the job. Although it's easier than you might expect, installing molding takes some practice. Start installing molding in an area of the room where it will be the least visible. You'll soon surprise yourself with your speed and neat joinery. The most common mistake is to cut a miter in the wrong direction. Whenever possible, mark pieces clearly, not only for length, but also for the direction of cut.

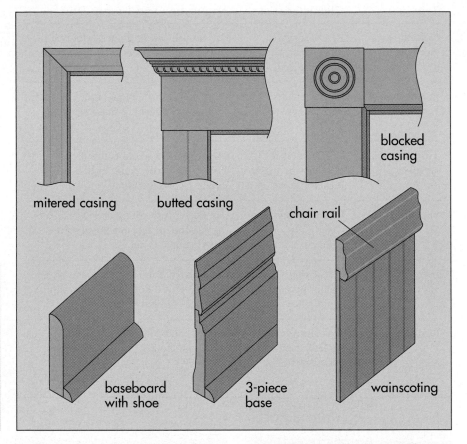

mitered casing   butted casing   blocked casing

chair rail

baseboard with shoe   3-piece base   wainscoting

YOU'LL NEED

TIME: About 10 minutes per piece of molding.
SKILLS: Precise measuring and cutting, figuring out the direction of cuts, nailing.
TOOLS: Tape measure, miter box and backsaw or power miter saw, coping saw, hammer, nail set.

EXPERTS' INSIGHT

BUYING MOLDING

Molding can be expensive, so determine exactly how many pieces of each size you need. On a piece of paper, make columns for each size—8 feet, 10 feet, 12 feet, etc. As you measure for individual pieces, tally how many you need under each column. If you have an old house, you may need moldings that are not made any longer. A lumberyard with a mill or a millwork company can make replicas. If the price is too high or you need only a small piece of molding, you can make a reasonable facsimile using a router, tablesaw, radial-arm saw, and belt sander.

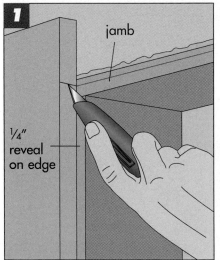

jamb

¼" reveal on edge

1. Measure and mark precisely.
Whenever possible, hold a piece of molding in place and mark it with a knife, rather than using a tape measure. For window and door casings, take into account the ¼-inch reveal on the edge of the jamb. As a guide, use a compass set to ¼ inch to mark the reveal on the jamb.

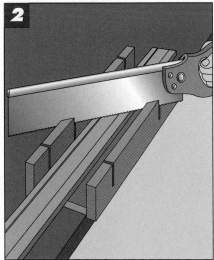

2. Cut the miter.
Sight down the blade of the saw and slide the molding until the saw will cut just to the scrap side of your mark. Hold the molding against the back of the miter box, as shown *above*. Grasp it tightly so it will not slide as you cut it. As an alternative, use a power miter saw or radial-arm saw (see page 282).

INSTALLING BASE MOLDING

Install door and window casing and other vertical molding before you install molding at the bottom of your walls. Choose from ranch or colonial base molding or use a three-piece base for a traditional look (see page 304). It is best to add a quarter round or base shoe as well. These types bend easily with variations in the flooring and buffer scuffs from vacuum cleaners.

You may be tempted simply to miter-cut pieces for inside corners. This often leads to unsightly gaps and misaligned joints because the corners are almost never true 90-degree angles. Instead, cut the first piece to length with a regular 90-degree cut and cope-cut the second piece (see page 273).

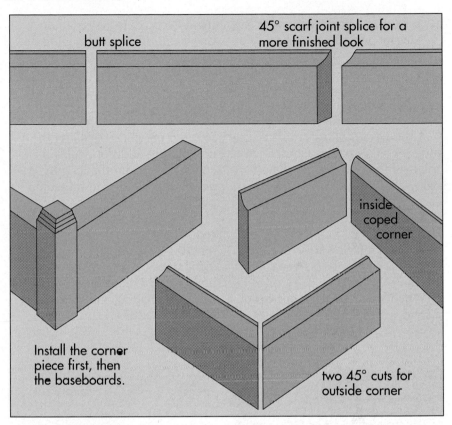

butt splice

45° scarf joint splice for a more finished look

inside coped corner

Install the corner piece first, then the baseboards.

two 45° cuts for outside corner

ACHIEVING THAT PROFESSIONAL LOOK

■ Avoid splits. Thin stock, such as often is used for baseboard molding, is prone to splitting and cracking. Don't take chances. Wherever you will be driving a nail within 3 inches of the edge of a piece, drill a pilot hole. You may be able to simply attach a short piece of molding with construction adhesive.

■ Don't overnail. The most common mistake amateurs make when installing moldings is to put in too many nails. Drive in only as many as you need to hold the piece firmly flush against the wall.

■ Stain first, but paint second. If you will be staining molding, do it before you install it. If you will be painting, install the molding first, then paint.

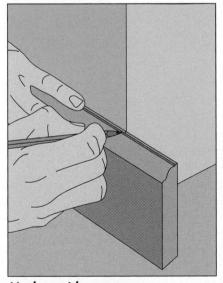

Mark outside corners.
As with all molding, for greater accuracy, hold and mark the pieces in place wherever possible. For an outside corner, butt one end of the molding in place, allowing the other to extend past the corner. Make the mark exactly even with the corner.

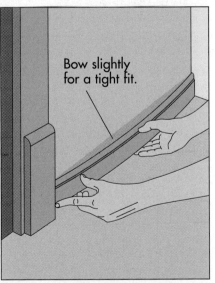

Bow slightly for a tight fit.

Install an inside-to-inside piece.
Mark and cut the piece about 1/16 inch longer than the space. If you are butting against a piece of casing, make sure the casing is well-secured so it does not move when you press against it. Install the baseboard by bending it into position. This will give you a tight fit on both sides.

INSTALLING CROWN MOLDING

Transform a boxy room with the elegant and softening beauty of crown molding. With more and more molding profiles available, you have plenty of options for adding an attractive finishing touch to your home.

Although installing crown molding takes patience and a few tricks of the trade, homeowners who are comfortable with basic carpentry tools and who have coped molding miters before should have few problems. Careful fitting and refitting are crucial to obtaining a close fit between sections of molding.

When working over your head, a solid working platform makes all the difference. Don't try to do the careful fitting and nailing that crown molding requires while working from a stepladder. Make the job easier on yourself by finding a plank and two sturdy sawhorses to make a platform to stand on while installing the molding. In addition, enlist a coworker to hold the lengths of molding while you measure, position, and fasten them.

Before beginning this challenging project, review marking and measuring techniques (pages 260–261), how to use a miter box (page 270), and nailing techniques (pages 284–285).

review marking and measuring techniques (pages 260–261), how to use a miter box (page 270), and nailing techniques (pages 284–285).

YOU'LL NEED

TIME: About 4 hours for a 12×12-foot room
SKILLS: Precise measuring, use of miter box or power miter saw, driving nails.
TOOLS: Deep miter box with backsaw or power miter box, drill, hammer, nail set.

CAUTION!

WHICH SIDE IS UP?
Remember to think upside down as you make miter cuts. Double-check which edge of the crown molding goes up— the difference is subtle.

Money $ Saver

PRACTICE MAKES PERFECT

To avoid expensive mistakes with crown molding, you should hone your mitering and coping skills before you plunge into the job. Ask your local home center or lumber dealer for a 2- or 3-foot scrap of molding similar to the type you plan to use. Practice the steps shown on these pages.

It is particularly important to gain some familiarity with the way molding is cut and coped. The more proficient you are at making overlapping joints, the less likely you are to make costly errors.

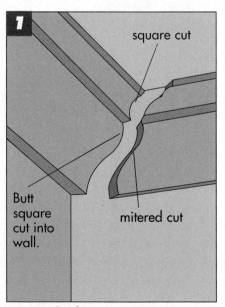

1. Cut the first piece square.
To achieve a mitered look with corners that are seldom perfectly square, run the first piece of crown molding tightly into the corner. Cope-cut the second piece in the shape of the profile of the molding, so it can butt neatly against the face of the first piece.

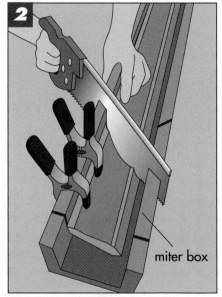

2. Make a miter cut.
Use a deep miter box and a fine-toothed backsaw to make a cut that reveals the profile of the molding. Position the molding so that it is upside down in the miter box. The face of the molding that goes against the ceiling will be on the bottom of the miter box. Remember, for inside corners, the bottom of the crown molding will be the longest edge.

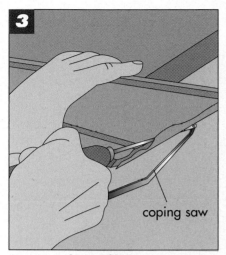

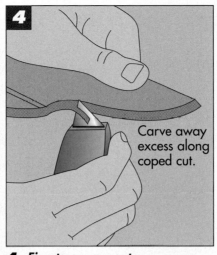

Carve away
excess along
coped cut.

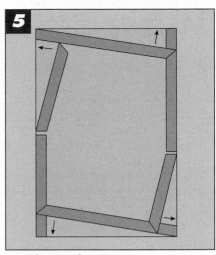

coping saw

3. Cope the profile.

If the mitered cut is correct, you'll be able to see the profile of the molding. Cut away the excess wood along the back side of the molding with a coping saw. Err on the side of removing too much rather than too little; only the outermost edge of the coped molding will be seen.

4. Fine-tune your cut.

Use a utility knife to remove any excess material you missed with the coping saw. Be careful that you do not cut into the exposed face of the molding. Hold the piece in place to test the fit. Take it down and do more carving if necessary.

5. Plan each joint.

Map out the job so that one end of each piece of crown molding always will be cut straight and one end will be mitered and coped. Use butt joints for long runs. Save the most visible parts of the job for last, when you've honed your coping skills.

ceiling joists

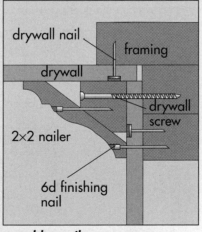

drywall nail

framing

drywall

drywall
screw

2×2 nailer

6d finishing
nail

6. Nail in place ...

If the molding runs perpendicular to the ceiling joists, determine the location of the joists. Drill pilot holes to keep the molding from splitting. As you attach the molding, tack it in place with a few nails. Take a good look at the positioning before completing the nailing.

or add a nailer.

To provide a solid nailing area where the joists run parallel to the crown molding, cut a beveled face on a 2×2, as shown. Cut the 2×2 to length and screw it to the wall so it's in the corner of the ceiling and the wall. The 2×2 provides a surface, at the proper angle, to which you can nail the molding.

TOOLS TO USE

BE SHARP

The right tools—kept clean and sharp—help make a precise job, such as installing crown molding, easier. Here are some tips:

■ Drop off your saw for professional sharpening well before you begin the job. A sharpened saw provides better control and a cleaner cut, and it makes the job go more pleasantly.

■ Buy new coping-saw blades. They break easily, so have half a dozen on hand.

■ Have plenty of clamps to hold the molding while you cut it. The less you rely on your own holding power, the easier and more accurately you'll be able to make the saw cuts.

MAKING STACKABLE SHELVES

These modules are easily moved and restacked. If you need to, you always can build more. Make modules of at least two heights— 10 and 14 inches high are common dimensions—to accommodate your books. For yearbooks, magazines, and photo albums, you may need a module that is even taller. You will need one top piece for each tower of stackable shelves. Choose your lumber carefully: Twisted boards will not line up well. Use a hardwood such as oak and stain it, or build out of pine and give it at least two coats of enamel paint.

YOU'LL NEED

TIME: Three hours per module.
SKILLS: Measuring and marking, squaring, drilling straight holes, cutting dadoes and rabbets.
TOOLS: Power saw, square, drill, drill jig, hammer.

Building with dowels and dadoes.
Use 1×12 for the sides, shelves, and top. Cut the side pieces to the height of the module (the usable shelf space will be 1¾ inches shorter), and the shelf to the width, minus ¾ inch. Cut a ⅜ × ⅜-inch rabbet along the inside back edges of the side pieces and the upper back edge of the shelf. Cut a ¾ × ⅜-inch dado in each side piece, located 1 inch up from the bottom.

Attach the shelf in the dadoes, using wood glue and 4d finish nails, checking for square. Cut a back out of ¼-inch plywood to fit into the rabbets, and attach it with wood glue and 3d finish nails.

Use a drill and jig to drill holes as shown. Also drill holes under the top piece, being careful not to drill too deeply. Insert dowels (but don't glue them) as you stack the modules.

Versatile storage.
If you build carefully, these units will fit together quite snugly. However, if you stack more than three, they may become unstable. If that happens, use angle brackets and screws to attach the top shelf to the wall.

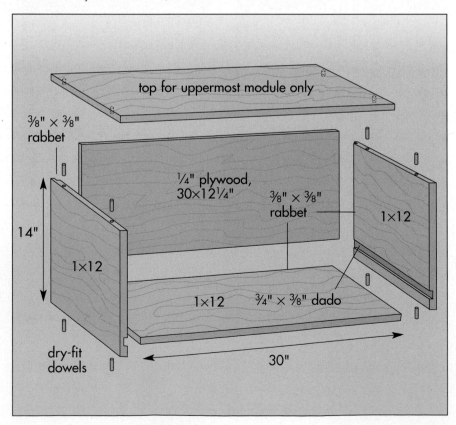

top for uppermost module only

⅜" × ⅜" rabbet

¼" plywood, 30×12¼"

⅜" × ⅜" rabbet

1×12

14"

1×12

1×12   ¾" × ⅜" dado

dry-fit dowels

30"

INDOOR CARPENTRY PROJECTS

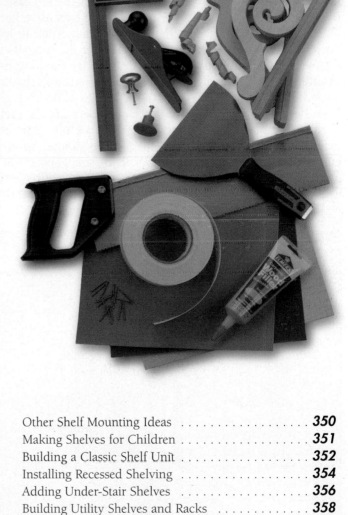

For more ideas and projects involving drywall and surface finishing, see Chapter 16, beginning on page 835.

PLANNING FOR NEW CABINETS

Preparation for installing kitchen cabinets usually is more involved than actually hanging them.

Once you've removed the old cabinets and appliances, install and check plumbing lines, both drain and supply. Run the gas line if needed for a gas cooktop, oven, or range.

Rough in the electrical outlets, switches, and cables for dishwashers. If you will be installing undercabinet lights that are not low-voltage (see page 107, have standard electrical cable sticking out of the walls at points just below the bottom of the wall cabinets. Cut out a vent hole for a range hood.

Smooth and prime all wall and ceiling surfaces, especially those that will show after the cabinets are in place. In most cases, it makes sense to install the flooring before installing the cabinets. Piecing around them is difficult and time-consuming. While you may waste material under the cabinets, a smooth finished floor to work on makes the job easier. If you are using expensive flooring, however, you may want to leave the area under the cabinets uncovered. Overlap the footprint of your base cabinets with the flooring. Add pieces of flooring at all four corners to level each cabinet.

Carefully mark the location of each cabinet on the walls. Allow for small spacers at the corners so you will not have to cram things in too tightly. Mark the location of all the wall studs.

> ## CAUTION!
> DON'T OVERLOAD CIRCUITS
> Make sure that no electrical circuit carries too great a load or you will be resetting breakers or replacing fuses constantly. To figure your circuit loads, total the watts used. Also note the wattage of the light bulbs in fixtures on the circuit. A refrigerator uses 500 watts, a microwave 800 watts, a toaster 1,050 watts. Divide the total by 120, the number of volts. The result tells you how many amperes, or amps, the circuit draws when everything is on—and whether you're overloading the circuit (see pages 39–41 and 78–81).

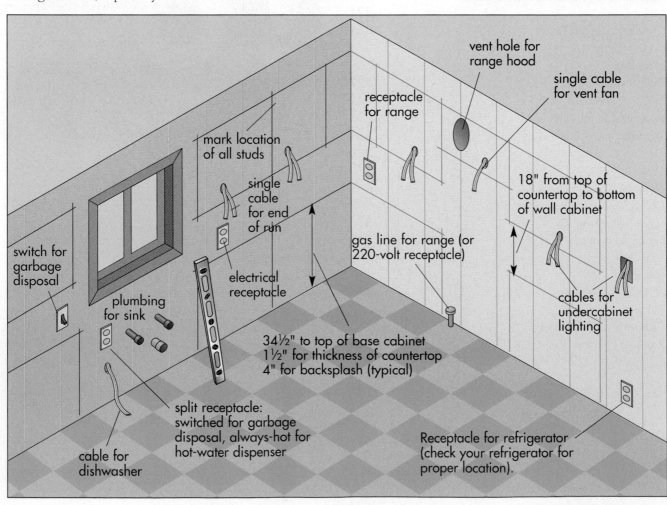

switch for garbage disposal

plumbing for sink

cable for dishwasher

split receptacle: switched for garbage disposal, always-hot for hot-water dispenser

mark location of all studs

single cable for end of run

electrical receptacle

34½" to top of base cabinet
1½" for thickness of countertop
4" for backsplash (typical)

receptacle for range

vent hole for range hood

single cable for vent fan

gas line for range (or 220-volt receptacle)

18" from top of countertop to bottom of wall cabinet

cables for undercabinet lighting

Receptacle for refrigerator (check your refrigerator for proper location).

INSTALLING WALL CABINETS

*T*ake the cabinets out of their boxes and inspect them carefully; you won't be able to return them once you have driven screws into them. If you are installing undercabinet lighting, you may need to drill holes in the back lower lip of the cabinets for the electrical cable to slip through.

If your walls are not plumb or square, you may end up with a cabinet that doesn't fit. Check in advance and reposition your layout accordingly.

Always work with a helper, and have a stable stepladder on hand. If any of the cabinets are heavy, remove the doors to reduce the weight and lessen the chance of damaging the cabinets.

EXPERTS' INSIGHT

FASTEN WALL CABINETS TO WALL STUDS

If you've carried a stack of 10 or 12 dishes, you know how heavy they are. Cabinets holding dishes or canned goods bear a surprisingly heavy load. Because wall cabinets do not rest on anything, the screws attaching them to the wall carry all the weight. Make sure you drive screws into wall studs. If you are attaching to a masonry wall, use metal masonry shields.

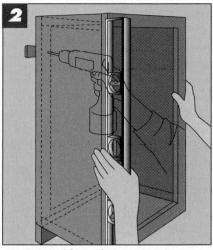

1. Attach a temporary ledger.
Anchor a straight piece of 2×4 lumber to the wall so you can rest the cabinets on it as you work. Level it and attach it with just a few screws or nails, so you won't create a big wall-patching job when you remove it.

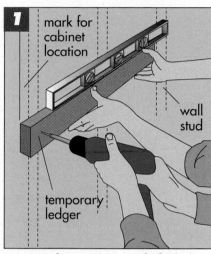

2. Fasten the cabinets.
While a helper holds the cabinet, check for plumb in both directions. Use shims, as shown, if necessary. Once the cabinet is positioned, drive 2½- or 3-inch screws through the cabinet frames and into wall studs. If your cabinet has a lip on top, drive the screws in there so they will not show. Use trim washers for a more finished look on the inside of the cabinet.

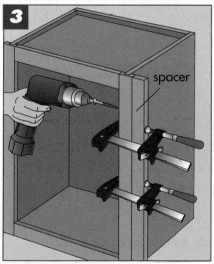

3. Install spacers.
Where the last cabinet meets up against a side wall, hold the cabinet in place and measure for a spacer. Cut it and attach as shown, using clamps to hold it firmly while you drill pilot holes and drive screws from the cabinet into the spacer.

4. Install spacer for inside corner.
If you simply attach two cabinets at an inside corner, usually at least one door will not open fully. Before installing them, attach a spacer to one of the cabinets (see Step 3) and then attach the other cabinet to the spacer. Drill pilot holes and drive in screws.

SETTING BASE CABINETS

Take the time to make sure all the cabinets are level from the beginning. If you give in to the temptation to cheat a little, you will run into frustrating problems, both in installing the other cabinets and in putting on the countertop.

If a baseboard or other piece of molding gets in the way, it is almost always best to take it off the wall and cut it, rather than cutting the cabinet to fit around the trim.

YOU'LL NEED

TIME: Most of a day for an average-size kitchen.
SKILLS: Leveling, driving screws, clamping, cutting.
TOOLS: Drill, level, hammer, chisel, pry bar.

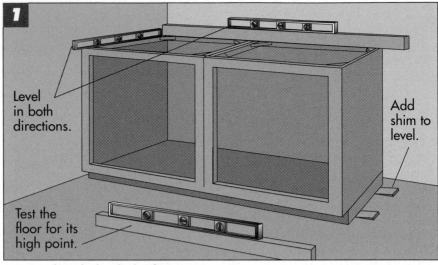

Level in both directions.

Add shim to level.

Test the floor for its high point.

1. Level and plumb the first unit.
Find the highest point on your floor and start there because you can shim up but not down. Set the first cabinet in place and check it for level in both directions. As a further check, make sure the stiles or door faces are plumb. Use shims at the floor to level and solidly support the cabinets. If your wall is out of plumb or wavy, you may need to shim the back of the cabinet as well—make sure when you drive the screws in (see next step) you don't pull the cabinet out of level.

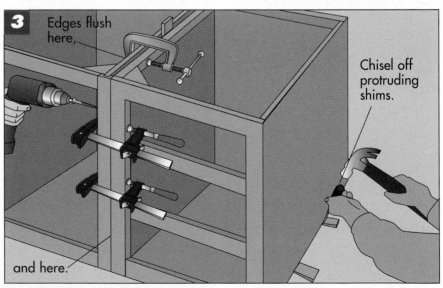

shim

cabinet frame

2. Attach to the walls.
Drive in screws through the back of the cabinet and into the wall studs. When possible, screw through solid framing pieces. After driving in the screws, check to see that the cabinet is still sitting flat on the floor. If not, back out the screws and adjust the shims before driving the screws back in. Check again for level and plumb.

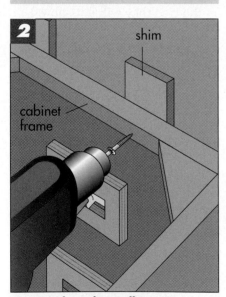

Edges flush here,

and here.

Chisel off protruding shims.

3. Join cabinets together.
After installing the first cabinet, use clamps to hold the next one in alignment as you screw them together. Make sure that their surfaces are flush with each other—not just the face frames, but the top edges as well.

Also make sure the screws are the right length, so they will not poke through the stiles. To keep the surface of the stiles smooth, drill pilot and countersink holes, then drive in the screws.

In most cases, you can use a hammer and chisel to nip off shims that stick out. With layers of shim, use a handsaw.

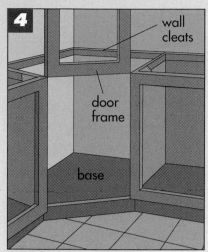

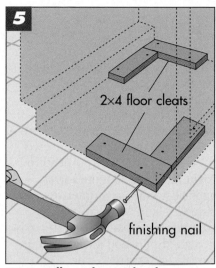

4. Install a corner cabinet...

You may buy a complete corner cabinet with sides or a less-expensive knockdown unit like the one shown above. For this type of corner cabinet, install the base first, then set the two adjoining cabinets in place next to it. Insert the door frame and join it to the adjoining cabinets. Install 1×2 cleats on the walls to support the countertop.

or join two base cabinets.

This method provides you with less usable space, but it may save money. Be sure to install at least one spacer so both doors swing freely. Clamp, drill pilot and countersink holes, and drive in screws.

5. Install a cabinet island.

When there is no wall to attach a cabinet to, as in the case of an island or peninsula, provide strong framing on the floor. Lay the cabinet on its side and measure its inside dimensions. Measure and install 2×4 cleats on the floor carefully so the cabinet slips over the cleats tightly. For exposed areas use finishing nails; otherwise drill pilot holes and use screws.

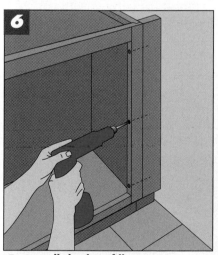

6. Install the last filler piece.

When you come to an inside wall, measure the distance between the cabinet and the wall at both the top and bottom. Rip a filler piece to fit snugly and position it flush with the cabinet face. Drill pilot and countersink holes and drive in screws. Unless the filler piece is more than 4 inches wide, you do not need to attach it to the wall.

7. Install panels.

If your design calls for an exposed edge that is not the side of a cabinet, as is the case when a dishwasher is at the end of a run, purchase an end panel made for the purpose of completing the run. Use clips at the floor, countertop, and wall so the panel can be removed to service the dishwasher.

EXPERTS' INSIGHT

INSTALLATION TIPS

Even durable cabinets made to hold up to decades of normal use can be scratched or dinged easily by carpentry tools. Take special care not to damage cabinets as you work on them. Cover installed cabinets with heavy drop cloths or cardboard from their shipping boxes and keep sharp tools well away from door and drawer faces.

If your floor is out of level or wavy, avoid unsightly gaps at the bottom of your cabinets by installing vinyl cove base. Or remove the kickboard, take out the nails, and reinstall it tight against the floor.

BUILDING AN ISLAND OR PENINSULA

If you purchase custom cabinets, you can design an island or peninsula to suit your needs exactly. If your budget is limited, you can combine standard-sized base cabinets to make your own unit. In both cases, you need to make or have a countertop specialist make a countertop. This simple island, made of two base cabinets, side panels, and a veneered plywood back panel, is simple to construct. The countertop is something most do-it-yourselfers can build. The most difficult part of the project is the installation of electrical cables, gas pipe, plumbing supply and drains, and the vent duct.

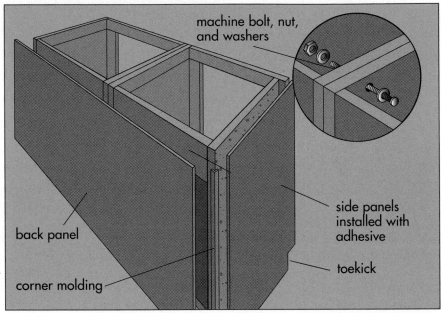

machine bolt, nut, and washers

back panel

corner molding

side panels installed with adhesive

toekick

YOU'LL NEED

TIME: About half a day to build the island.
SKILLS: Basic carpentry, wiring, plumbing.
TOOLS: Screwdriver, drill, adjustable wrench, circular saw, block plane, sandpaper.

Adding a countertop

Plan an island countertop carefully: If it is to be an eating counter, make it wide enough to accommodate seating but not so wide as to hinder traffic flow. Round off exposed corners, to avoid painful encounters.

Countertops usually are made of chipboard, which means they cannot handle much weight if they are not supported from underneath. Make a cantilevered countertop stronger by using plywood attached to a 1×2 frame to thicken the edge. Add bracket supports if you wish to extend the top to make a stool-height informal eating area. Install wood base shoe or vinyl cove base at the bottom. Attach the island to the floor as shown on page 313.

Combining stock cabinets

When using stock base cabinets, you will have access to the shelves from one side only. If you want the countertop to be at a good height for people sitting on stools, trim the cabinets down by cutting off the toekick. To anchor the island to the floor, see page 313.

Join the cabinets together by clamping, drilling pilot holes, and installing bolts. As an alternative, drive general-purpose screws through the frames, being careful not to pierce the other side. Install panels on the sides using construction adhesive. Cover the back with a single panel.

Finish the corners with corner molding. If building a peninsula, vary the design so it butts against your base cabinets.

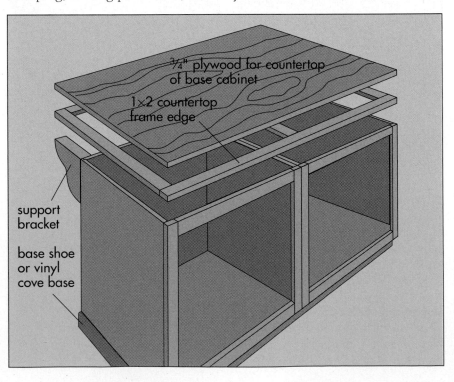

¾" plywood for countertop of base cabinet

1×2 countertop frame edge

support bracket

base shoe or vinyl cove base

ADDING A STAINLESS-STEEL BACKSPLASH

Here's an unusual touch for a household kitchen—a stainless-steel backsplash. It looks stylish and provides a commercial-grade, easy-to-maintain surface between your countertop and the wall cabinets.

The first step is to find a source of the material. If your home center or hardware store can't help you, check in the Yellow Pages under stainless steel or sheet metal. Find a shop that can provide pieces of stainless steel to the exact length you want. Often, stainless steel has to be ordered from a specialty supplier, so schedule accordingly.

Check your measurements or provide a template to be sure you get the correct sizes of pieces. Although it is extremely hard, stainless steel can be damaged during installation. As you work, support the material so it doesn't crimp or get scratched because stainless steel is expensive.

YOU'LL NEED

TIME: A day for several pieces with a few outlet cutouts.
SKILLS: Measuring, checking for square, drilling, cutting metal.
TOOLS: Square, tape measure, drill, sabersaw

TOOLS TO USE

IF YOU MUST CUT STAINLESS STEEL

You can make rough cuts around outlets because the edges will be covered up. But it's hard to make a straight, smooth cut in this amazingly hard material. Use a drill to start the hole, then cut the opening with a sabersaw with a metal-cutting blade designed for cutting stainless steel.

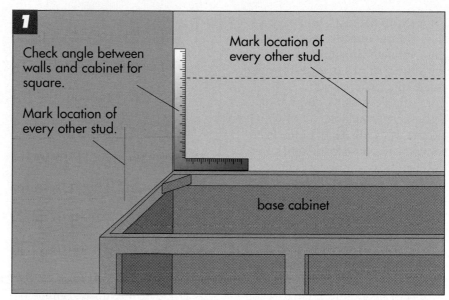

1. Lay out the job.
If possible, do this job before installing the countertop or the wall cabinets. Check the walls for square and measure the lengths you need. Corners are the critical areas; any variation along the length of the piece will be covered by the wall cabinet above and the countertop below. If your walls are plumb, you may be able to get away without the corner trim pieces shown in Step 3. If the walls are out of plumb, you may be able to compensate by cutting a slot in the corner and sliding a bit of one piece of steel into it.

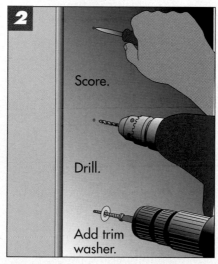

2. Attach with screws, washers.
Set the metal in place and make sure the pieces line up. Drill holes and drive stainless-steel screws, fitted with trim washers, into studs. Because the material is rigid and will be anchored by the cabinets as well, two screws driven in every other stud are adequate.

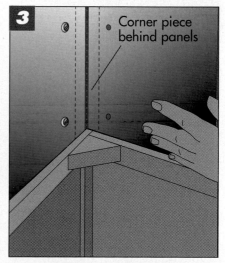

3. Use corner molding pieces.
If you have trouble getting the corners to match up, use a piece of corner molding, attaching it to the wall with clear silicone sealant and butting each panel against it. If one wall is wavy, you can, with patience, scribe and curve-cut one of the pieces using a belt sander.

CHOOSING COUNTERTOPS

Next to cabinets, countertops do the most to set the style of your kitchen. In addition, they are working surfaces that need to be made of a material you are comfortable with. A number of options are available, all of which do the job well. They range from inexpensive post-form laminates you can buy at a home center (only a few colors will be available) to high-priced granite and solid-surface materials.

Wood, such as maple butcher block, is also an option. But such countertops require careful maintenance: Keep them well waxed or give them regular applications of mineral oil. Otherwise, the countertop will discolor and possibly start coming apart at the seams.

Solid-surface
These are durable and can accommodate a seamless sink. They come in a variety of colors and patterns, many of which rival stone. Their cost rivals stone as well; consider this material among the most expensive countertop options. This is not a do-it-yourself material; solid-surface countertops must be fabricated and installed by specialists.

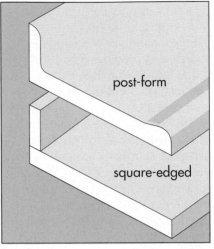

Laminate
Color-core laminates withstand scratches better than laminates on which the color is applied only on the surface. You can buy a ready-made post-form, with either a rolled front edge and a built-in backsplash or a square-edged top. With patience, you can laminate a square-edge top yourself, but the cost of materials may be nearly as much as a factory-made top.

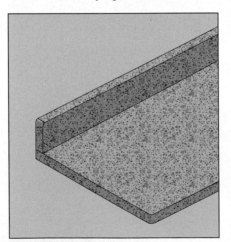

Granite
This beautiful natural product provides decades of use if installed properly. You must hire a contractor to measure and install it for you; they know how to handle this heavy material and have equipment for buffing all the surfaces to a shine. Marble is not recommended as countertop material because it stains easily.

Tile
There are many colors and sizes of tile from which to choose. Be sure the edging and backsplash pieces come in the colors you want. Avoid wall tiles. They are not made to take impact and chip easily. Some people find the grout joints hard to clean; others dislike an uneven surface. But well-installed tile is durable and stylish.

INSTALLING A LAMINATE COUNTERTOP

You can make your own laminate countertop. Unless you are a skilled do-it-yourselfer, however, it may not be worth the time and effort. If your countertop configuration is fairly typical, you can save money by purchasing post-form countertops from your home center. Made with precut corners, these countertops can be trimmed to fit most base cabinets.

But if you don't like the colors available at your home center or if you have an unusual situation, such as a wide counter for an island or a narrow counter for a tight spot, you will need to have a countertop made for you. You may have a wider selection of color and pattern if you choose a square-edge top rather than a post-form (see page 316).

YOU'LL NEED

TIME: Half a day to install several tops carefully.
SKILLS: General carpentry, working carefully to avoid damaging the tops as you work.
TOOLS: Level, carpenter's square, drill, circular saw, compass, belt sander, laundry iron.

CAUTION!

BE SURE THE TOP HUGS YOUR WALLS

If you have a wavy wall or if your walls are more than ⅜ inch out of square, a ready-made top may not fit snugly against your walls. Take measures to straighten out your walls or hire a professional countertop maker to come in and take precise measurements so a custom countertop can be made to fit your space.

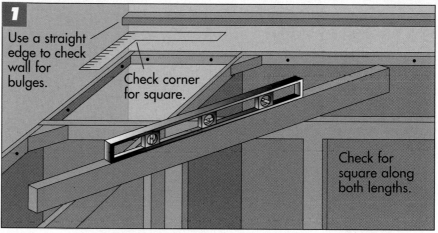

1. Check walls, cabinets for level and square.

Make sure cabinets are level all around so the top will be able to sit flat on them. If necessary, install cleats on walls, as shown, or end panels (see page 313) to support the top firmly. Check walls to ensure they are square with each other and free of major bulges by laying a straightedge down the full length of each. Most post-forms have a "scribe," a lip of laminate that can be trimmed (see below) to compensate for variations of up to ⅜ inch. A square-edged top with a separate backsplash will let you compensate for up to ¾ inch.

2. Cut a top to length.

If you purchase a factory-made top that you must cut yourself, do this with great care. Use a fine-cutting blade and cut it with the face side down to avoid nicks. Check that the blade on your circular saw is square to the base and use a clamp-on guide to make sure your cut is straight. Be sure to support the waste side so it does not fall off before you finish the cut—an easy way to chip laminate.

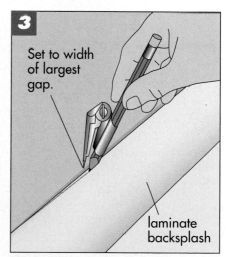

3. Scribe a backsplash line.

The countertop might not fit tight against the wall, either because the walls are out of square or the wall is wavy. If such is the case, push the countertop against the wall, making sure it is aligned correctly with the base cabinets. Use a compass to scribe a line as wide as the largest gap between the countertop and the wall.

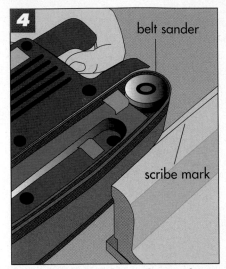

4. Belt-sand to the scribe mark.

Don't attempt to cut to the scribe mark with a sabersaw or circular saw—you'll almost certainly end up chipping the countertop. Use a belt sander with a fairly coarse 36-grit sanding belt. Pressing lightly, slowly sand away material up to the scribed mark.

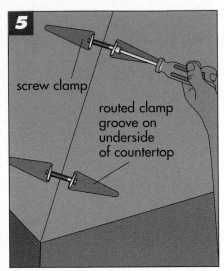

5. Make a splice.

If you need to splice pieces at a corner or in the middle of a run, have a professional make the cuts and rout the grooves for the clamps. Apply waterproof glue to the edges of the pieces, line up the pieces, and start to tighten the clamps. Check the countertop as you work to make sure it doesn't slide out of alignment.

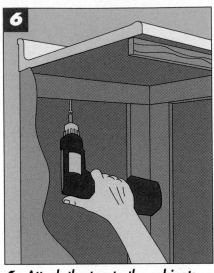

6. Attach the top to the cabinets.

Screws should extend as far into the countertop as possible without poking through it. Drill pilot holes every 2 to 3 feet along the front and rear of the top and drive in screws upward to hold the counter firmly. Screw into structurally sound sections of the cabinet framing. Make sure the countertop does not move as you work.

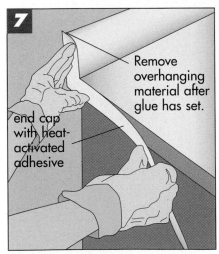

7. Attach end caps.

Buy a precut end cap to cover the end of a post form. If it has heat-activated glue, hold it in place so it overhangs the countertop edge. (You'll remove the excess later.) Slowly run a hot laundry iron along the end cap, being careful not to burn the laminate, until the glue adheres. File, sand, or rout away the excess material.

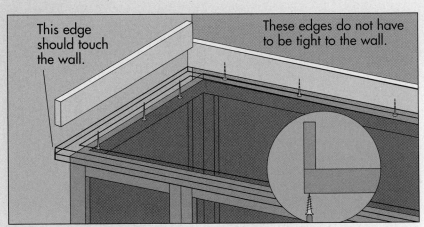

Install a square-edged countertop.

If you buy a square-edged countertop and your walls are not square, this type of edging covers up the gap. Set the top so it overhangs the cabinets evenly. Cut the backsplash pieces to fit and set them in place. Mark their position on the countertop, then pull the top away from the wall. Run a bead of bathtub caulk along the bottom of the edging, set the edging in place, and fasten it with screws from underneath. Attach the top from underneath as shown in Step 6. If your wall bows, fasten the top in place, then glue the edging pieces to the wall with construction adhesive. Brace them with pieces of 1× or heavy objects so the edging conforms to the wall.

ADDING A GARDEN WINDOW

A garden window not only lets in light and makes a room seem more spacious, it gives you a place to nurture flowers or herbs right in your kitchen.

Some units have side windows that open casement-style with a crank; the other glass pieces are fixed in place. Prices vary widely, depending on whether you prefer a vinyl, metal, or wood unit. Some manufacturers offer off-the-shelf units made to standard window dimensions; others produce made-to-measure units only.

YOU'LL NEED

TIME: 1 day to remove a window and add a garden window.
SKILLS: Demolition, measuring, cutting, sealing.
TOOLS: Hammer, flat pry bar, reciprocating saw or metal-cutting keyhole saw, drill, caulking gun, level.

MEASUREMENTS

DETERMINING THE ROUGH OPENING

Garden windows often are not in stock, so you'll need accurate measurements of the rough opening (without removing the old window) to place an order. Here are some hints:

■ If you have old double-hung sash windows with ropes (or chains) attached to weights in the side cavities, measure from jamb to jamb (the surfaces that the sides of the sash slide against) and add 5 inches.

■ For newer-style windows, measure the casing (the molding that is on the wall) from outside edge to outside edge, and subtract 3 inches.

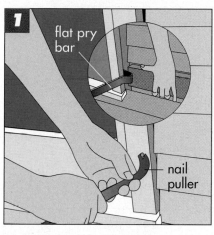

1. Remove the old window.
Use a hammer and flat pry bar to pull off the molding, both inside and outside. On the sides and at the top, you will be able to look through your wall. You'll see a series of nails holding the window in place. Cut the nails with a reciprocating saw or metal-cutting keyhole saw, or chop them in two by chiseling through them with the pry bar and hammer. Remove the window.

2. Measure, fill in.
The directions accompanying your window will tell you what the size of the rough opening should be. Cut away framing pieces only if you know how to reframe the opening in keeping with local codes. Make the opening smaller by filling in the space with 1× or 2× spacers. Allow about ½ inch of wiggle room on all sides of the garden window—you can shim the difference later.

3. Install the window.
Tip the garden window into place, making sure the front edge is flush with the wall surface so the molding will sit flat. Level and plumb, then firmly anchor it to the framing with shims and screws. On the outside, apply generous beads of exterior caulk before covering over the seam with molding. If your new window is a good deal smaller than the old one, you may need to use extra-wide molding (see inset). This is a simpler solution than filling in exterior siding or masonry.

BUILDING A BASE CABINET

Professional cabinetmakers make detailed drawings and figure the dimensions for all of the cabinet components before making the first cut. Follow their example: It's the only way to ensure against costly cutting mistakes, and it will save you time in the long run.

Planning cabinet construction requires three steps. First, make scaled drawings of the project on graph paper. Then make a cut list spelling out the exact dimensions of all the parts. Finally, draw a cutting diagram that shows how you will cut out all the pieces.

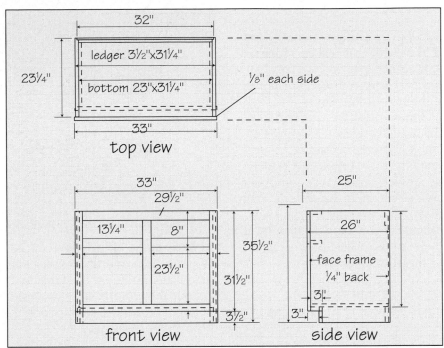

top view

front view   side view

YOU'LL NEED

TIME: Most cabinets can be built in a day.
SKILLS: Accurate measuring and cutting; squaring, fastening.
TOOLS: Power saw, drill, square, hammer, and nail set.

Scaled drawings, cutting diagram. The scaled drawings (*above*) and the cutting diagram (*below*) are for a base cabinet 33 inches wide, 24 inches deep, and 34½ inches high. Be sure the plywood grain runs up and down for the side pieces. You may have to redraw and refigure several times before all of the dimensions come out right.

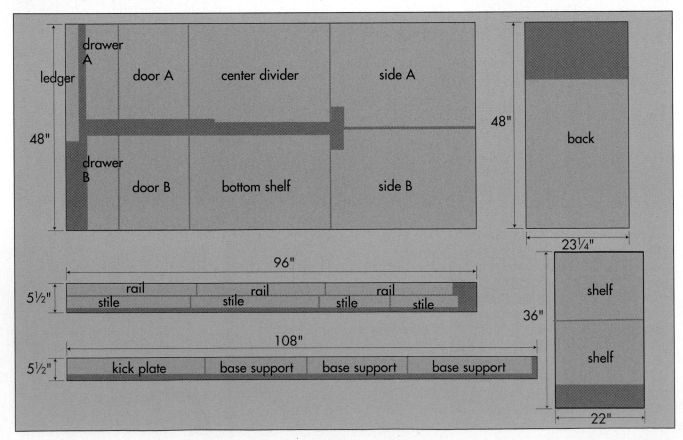

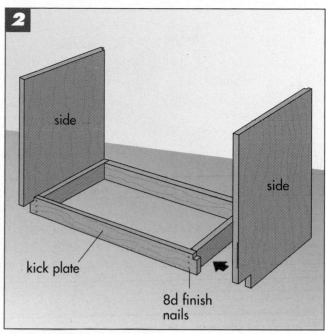

1. Build the base.

Cut the base pieces to the specified sizes. Working on a flat surface, attach the pieces together by drilling pilot holes, applying wood glue, and driving three 8d finish nails at each joint. Periodically check the frame for square as you work. Align the sides with the notched kick plate as shown on the drawing.

2. Cut and attach the sides.

Cut the cabinet sides, then notch the front edge of each to fit over the notch in the kick plate. Rabbet the back edge of each side piece to accommodate the ¼-inch plywood back. Drill pilot holes, glue, and drive 8d finish nails to attach the sides to the base.

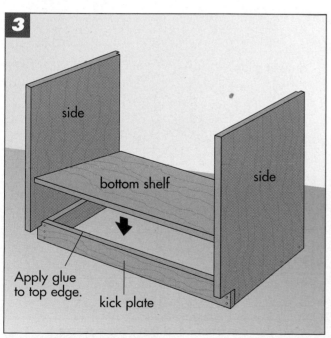

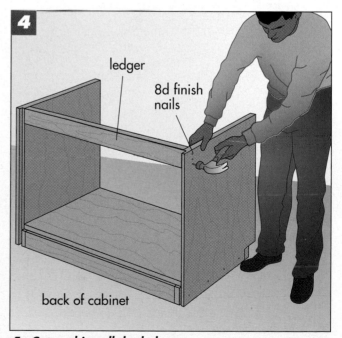

3. Install the bottom shelf.

Cut the bottom shelf to size, and test to see that it fits between the sides. Apply glue to the top edge of the base pieces, and set the shelf in place. Be sure its front edge is flush with the fronts of the sides. Drill pilot holes and drive 6d finish nails through the shelf and into the base.

4. Cut and install the ledger.

Double-check the length of the ledger by measuring the distance between the inside edges of the cabinet sides at the bottom of the cabinet. Cutting to this length will ensure that the cabinet is square. Attach the ledger with 8d finish nails; position it so the back piece can slip into the rabbet.

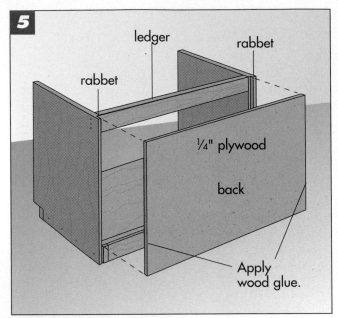

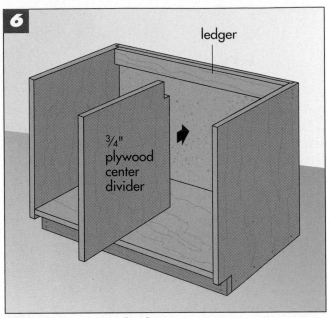

5. Install the plywood back.

Cut a piece of ¼-inch plywood to fit between the rabbets. Take care to cut it perfectly square. It does not need to extend down to the floor, but it must cover the entire back opening. Test fit it, and check that the cabinet is square. Drive several 4d finish nails partway through it near the edges. Lay a bead of wood glue in the rabbet on both sides, and fasten with nails driven every few inches.

6. Fit in the center divider.

Cabinets wider than 24 inches need two doors and two drawers, so there must be a center divider. Cut a piece of ¾-inch plywood so its front aligns with the front edge of the bottom and its top edge aligns with the top. Make a notch to accommodate the ledger. Position the divider in the center of the cabinet, and attach with 8d finish nails and wood glue.

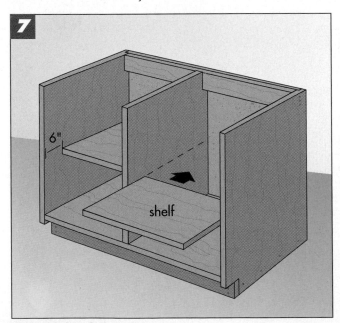

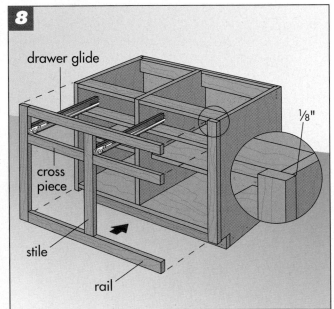

7. Add the shelves.

A base cabinet shelf is usually 6 inches or so shallower than the bottom so that you can reach the pots and pans in the bottom compartment. Cut shelves to fit. Use a framing square to mark the location of the shelves, and attach them with wood glue and 8d finish nails.

8. Add the face frame and front cross pieces.

Cut four plywood front crosspieces, and attach them with glue and 8d finish nails. Cut the vertical stiles, and install them with nails and glue, positioning the outer ones so they extend ⅛ inch past each side of the cabinet. Cut the horizontal rails to fit between the stiles, and fasten them as well. Now you are ready for drawers and doors.

BUILDING A WALL CABINET

Because it has no kick plate or drawers, a wall cabinet is easier to build than a base cabinet. It is essentially a rectangular box with shelves and a face frame. Build a standard wall cabinet 12 inches deep, including the stiles and rails but not including the doors.

Base cabinets usually have one fixed shelf, but wall cabinets work well with two or three adjustable shelves. Make scaled drawings, a cut list, and a cutting diagram (see page 320).

YOU'LL NEED

TIME: Several hours per cabinet.
SKILLS: Accurate planning, measuring, cutting, fastening.
TOOLS: Power saw, drill, framing square, hammer.

Making the cabinet.

Cut the sides to the total height of the cabinet. Install adjustable standards, or drill a grid of holes for shelf pins. For each side piece, cut a $3/4 \times 3/8$-inch rabbet at the top, a $3/4 \times 3/8$-inch dado for the bottom shelf, and a $3/8 \times 3/8$-inch rabbet for the back panel.

Cut the bottom shelf and the top 1 inch shorter than the width of the cabinet, and cut a $3/8 \times 3/8$-inch rabbet in the rear of the top piece. Fasten together the sides, the top piece, and the bottom shelf using wood glue and 8d finish nails. Check for square as you work.

Cut the back from $1/4$-inch plywood, $3/4$ inch narrower than the width of the cabinet and $3/8$ inch shorter than the cabinet's height. Cut carefully so that all corners are square. Cut and fasten the top and bottom cleats. Squeeze wood glue onto the back rabbet, and attach the back by driving 3d finish nails every few inches.

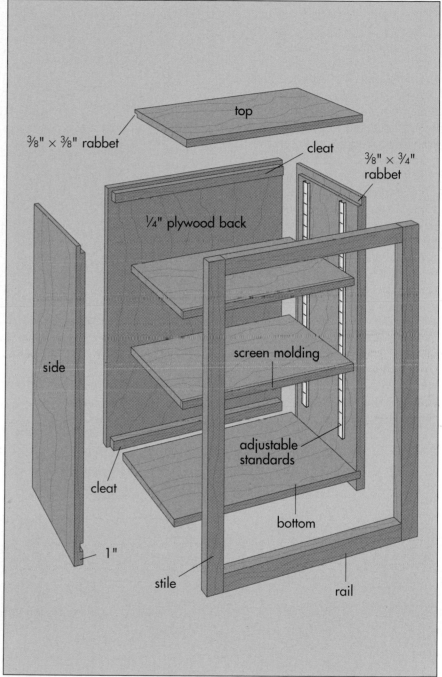

Cut the stiles (the vertical pieces of the face frame) to the height of the cabinet and cut the rails (horizontal pieces) to fit between. Hold in place on the cabinet front to check the cuts; the stiles should extend $1/8$ inch on each side. For the tightest joints, square up and glue the stiles and rails together before fastening them to the cabinet. Attach the completed face frame using wood glue and 8d finishing nails.

Cut shelves to fit inside the cabinet. Make them $1/8$ inch shorter than the opening so you can remove and reposition them easily. Cover the front edges of the shelves with screen molding.

To build and hang a cabinet door, see pages 324-328.

MAKING A CABINET DOOR

*T*here are two basic types of cabinet door: A *panel* door is more complicated to make and requires a table saw; a *slab* door is a single piece of wood, usually plywood. Slab doors are usually edged with trim for a neater appearance and to prevent warping. In addition to selecting a door style, decide how the door will fit in the cabinet (see page 326). A *flush* door fits inside the cabinet frame and must be sized so there is an even ⅛-inch gap all around. An *inset* door has a rabbeted edge around its perimeter that covers the frame. An *overlay* door fits entirely over the frame and is the easiest to make.

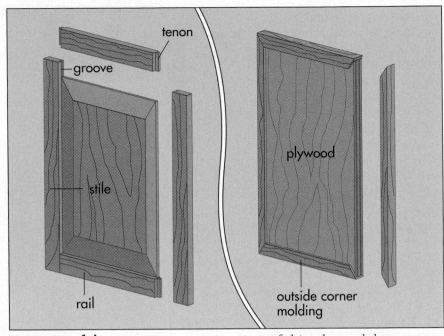

YOU'LL NEED
TIME: 2 hours for a panel door; or a half hour for a trimmed slab.
SKILLS: Measuring and cutting.
TOOLS: Table saw, power or hand miter saw, drill.

Two types of door.

A panel door has two horizontal *rails* and two vertical *stiles*. All four pieces have a groove into which the *panel* fits. Each rail has a tenon on each end that fits into the groove of the rail just as the panel does. The panel could be a flat

piece of thin plywood, but a more attractive option is to bevel the edges of a wide 1-by board.

The slab door shown has been trimmed simply, using outside corner molding on the perimeter. A simple measure like this dresses up a door.

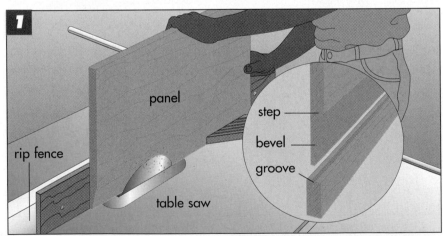

1. Bevel-cut the panel.

If the panel will be wider than 11½ inches (the width of a 1×12), clamp and glue pieces edge-to-edge (see page 291). Fasten a 1×6 or 1×8 to the rip fence to keep the workpiece from wobbling while you work. Adjust the blade so the bottom edge of the bevel will be just thick enough to fit into the

groove you will make in the rails (see step 3 on page 325). To give the panel a "step," adjust so the top edge of the cut will be ⅛ inch below the face of the board. If you don't want a step, raise the blade to cut all the way through. Remove the blade guard, and keep your hands well away from the blade. Bevel-cut all four edges.

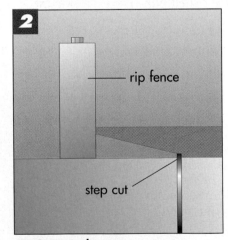

2. Square the step.

If you chose to have a stepped bevel, square the blade and adjust it down so it cuts only ⅛ inch deep. Align the fence so that the blade will cut just the top edge of the bevel and square it up. Test with scraps; this calls for precise adjustment. Run all four sides of the panel through the saw.

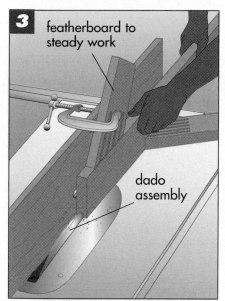

3 featherboard to steady work

dado assembly

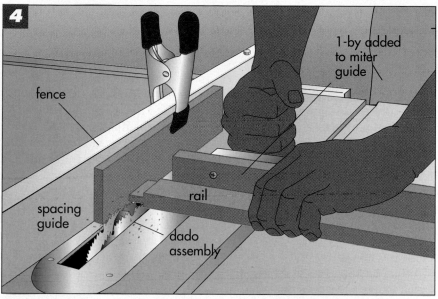

4 1-by added to miter guide

fence

spacing guide

rail

dado assembly

3. Groove the rails and stiles.

Set up to cut a dado (see page 281–283) the same width as the thickness of the door panel at the perimeter. Test cut on a scrap and to make sure the panel will fit the groove snugly. With the 1×6 or 1×8 clamped to the fence, adjust the fence so the blade will cut in the exact center of a board edge. (Test for this by cutting a groove, turning the piece around, and cutting again.) Cut a groove on the inside edge of all rails and stiles.

4. Cut tenons.

Each rail must have a tenon on both ends. A tenon should be ½ inch long and as thick as the door panel. This means that the rail itself should be 1 inch longer than the distance between stiles.

Set a dado assembly to cut half the board's thickness, minus the thickness of the tenon. Attach a straight piece of 1-by to the miter guide so you can hold the rail firmly as you cut. Clamp a scrap piece to the front end of the rip

fence to use as a spacing guide. Adjust the fence so that it positions the rail to cut a tenon ½-inch wide. Cut one side of the tenon, flip the board over, and cut the other.

Experiment on scrap pieces to achieve the precise blade height and the exact width adjustment so that the tenon fits snugly into a stile groove. Take your time, test your setup, and get it right: This is the step that appearances are determined.

5 bar clamp

Glue rail tenons only.

5. Clamp and glue.

Sand any saw marks on the panel. Dry-fit the pieces to make sure they fit tightly. Remove the stiles and apply glue to the rail tenons. (Don't glue the panel into the groove; it must be allowed to expand and contract with changes in humidity without stressing the stiles and rail.) Clamp and let dry.

screen bead

Achieve a raised look.

You can dress up a new or old slab door by installing moldings. Two bands of molding, running either vertically or horizontally, add elegance to any slab door. Or miter-cut four pieces of thin molding, such as fluted screen bead, to form a frame on the door. Even chair rail can be applied for an ornamental look.

Plan all the doors at the same time: Horizontal pieces should all be at the same height, and the distance between molding and door edge should be the same for all doors.

INSTALLING HINGED DOORS

Most cabinet projects call for unobtrusive hinges that, if visible at all, meld with any decor. Of the types commonly available, Euro-style hinges (see page 328) are the most expensive and are entirely concealed. Overlay and offset hinges (*right*) are mostly hidden, with only the smaller hinge leaf visible. If you have flush doors, a concealed wraparound hinge (*right*) will be nearly invisible.

When building new cabinets, install hinges and knobs last, after the doors and drawers are painted or finished. If you want to dress up old cabinets by painting or refinishing, remove the hinges and knobs first. (It is nearly impossible to paint around hinges, and removing them takes surprisingly little time.)

A neat installation of smoothly functioning hinges requires care and patience. All the hinges in a row of cabinets should be at the same height. If a change of height is required, the change should be consistent. Also, cabinet hinges determine the height and angle of doors. If a hinge is installed even 1/16 inch out of alignment, the door will be noticeably out of line with the other doors. If the hinges are not adjustable—and most, except Euro-style hinges, are not—it will be difficult to move one slightly. Work systematically with attention to detail.

You will find yourself often alternating between drilling pilot holes and driving screws. Have two drills on hand, one with a pilot bit and one equipped with a magnetic sleeve and screwdriver bit. Cordless drills make this work much easier. Most hinge screws call for a No. 1 phillips bit; using the more common but too-large No. 2 bit will be frustrating.

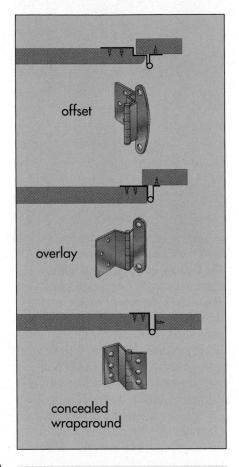

offset

overlay

concealed
wraparound

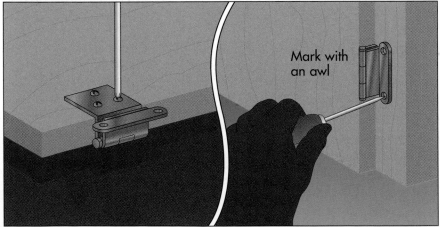

Mark with
an awl

Installing an overlay hinge.
With the door face down, place the hinges about 2 inches from the top and bottom; use a spacer or jig to ensure that all the hinges in a group of cabinets are placed in identical positions. Drill pilot holes in the exact center of each hole, and drive the screws that come with the hinges.

Next, position the door on the cabinet exactly as it will be when hung; using spacers or clamp-on guides. Have a helper hold it while you work. Mark for the pilot holes using an awl, then remove the door to drill the pilot holes. If you feel confident that the door is firmly and correctly in place, drill the pilot holes through the hinge holes and drive the screws in the same operation.

EXPERTS' INSIGHT

ALWAYS DRILL PILOT HOLES

Constantly alternating between drilling pilot holes and driving screws may seem tedious, and you will be tempted to skip an occasional pilot hole and just drive in the screw. Resist that temptation. Though a hinge screw is small, it can easily crack a cabinet stile. A cracked stile must be glued and clamped, a time-consuming process. Also, pilot holes make it much easier to drive the screws straight; screws driven at an angle tend to look unprofessional.

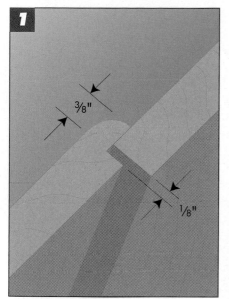

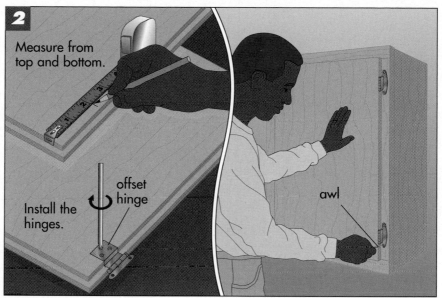

1. Measure for an inset door.

An inset or "lipped" door is ¼ inch larger on all sides than the opening. The rabbet running all around the door is ⅜ inch wide, giving a clearance of ⅛ inch between the inside of the rabbet and the cabinet. You must measure carefully to get a good fit.

2. Install an offset hinge.

Place the door face down, and install the hinges about 2 inches from the top and bottom. Use the same spacing for all the doors.

The key is to center the inset door in the opening. Place ⅛-inch hardboard spacers on the bottom and one side of the opening. Set the door on the spacers (carefully, since you won't be able to see the spacers). Align the door precisely; you may have to pull it away from a spacer slightly. Mark for pilot holes with an awl, or drill pilot holes through the hinge holes, and then drive screws.

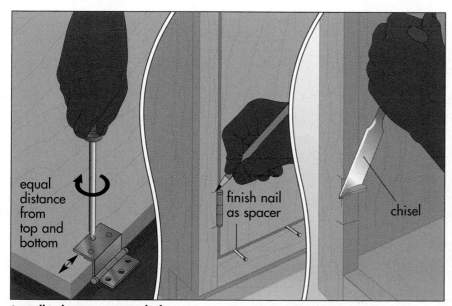

Install a butt or concealed wraparound hinge.

For flush doors, measure an equal distance from top and bottom, as for a concealed wraparound hinge (see page 326). Install a wraparound hinge on the door.

For a butt hinge, use a chisel and knife to cut a mortise, and install one leaf of the hinge in the mortise. Use two finish nails as spacers, and center the door in the opening so that there is a consistent ⅛-inch gap all around. Use a sharp pencil to mark the top and bottom of the hinge. Remove the door, and cut a mortise as thick as the hinge leaf. Position the hinges, mark and drill pilot holes, then drive the screws.

TOOLS TO USE

USE A JIG TO MARK FOR HINGES AND PULLS

Using a tape measure to mark the position for each hinge is not only time-consuming, but could cause inaccuracies. To ensure uniformity, develop a method for spacing all hinges and pulls the same distance from door and drawer face edges and follow it consistently. Here are two ways to do that:

■ Use a small piece of wood as a jig. Hold it against the door edge, press the hinge up against it, and mark for pilot holes.

■ Or use another hinge. It is standard practice to install hinges one hinge length from the door edge. Just hold one hinge against the door edge, slide the other up against it, and mark for pilot holes.

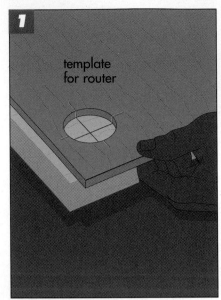

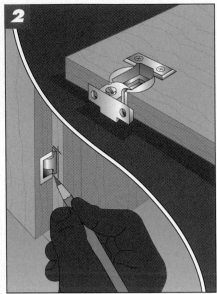

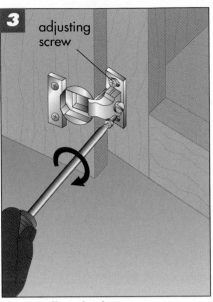

1. To install a concealed hinge, drill a recess hole.

Cut the recess hole with a Forstner bit, shown below, or make a template and cut it with a router. The hole in the template should be the diameter of the recess hole, plus the thickness of the router's bushing (see page 283).

2. Mark the stile.

Insert the hinge in the door, drill pilot holes, and drive the screws. Position the door against the face frame. While a helper holds it in the correct position, mark the location of the hinges on the stile.

3. Install and adjust.

With the door open, have the helper hold the hinges against the marks on the stile. Carefully try the movement of the door until it fits smoothly. Center the adjusting screws in the slots provided. Loosen or tighten the screws to adjust the position of the door.

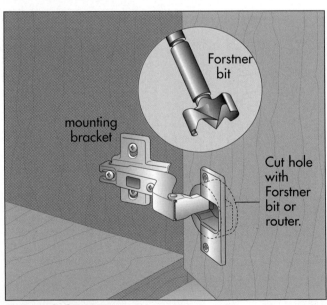

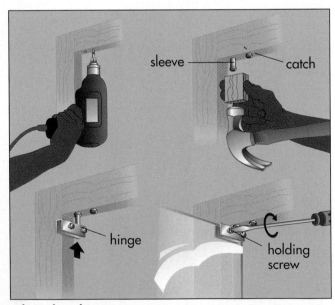

Euro-style hinge.

This type of hinge can be used for an overlay or flush door. It is the easiest hinge to adjust, allowing you to move it up and down, in and out. One side fits into a recess hole in the door, which you can drill with a Forstner bit or cut with a router. The arm slides onto a mounting bracket. To install it, first mount the hinge in the recess hole. Install the mounting bracket onto the inside of the cabinet, then slide the hinge arm onto the mounting bracket.

Glass-door hinge.

Glass doors are always flush, fitting inside the cabinet. To mount the type shown, drill a pair of holes (usually ¼-inch) near the edge of the top rail and another pair near the edge of the bottom rail. Tap a sleeve into the hole nearest the end, and a catch into the other hole. Slip hinges into the sleeves, fit the glass door into the hinges, adjust the door so it fits inside the opening, and tighten the holding screws on the hinges.

BUILDING A WALL

Behind most finished residential walls lies a rather simple construction. Vertical members, called studs, butt at the top and bottom against horizontal members, called plates. Although it looks straightforward, building a wall takes thoughtful planning. When you cover the framing with sheets of drywall or paneling, the seams between sheets must fall in the center of studs. There must be a nailing surface for the sheets at all the corners (see page 332). And, all framing members must be aligned along a flat plane.

If the floor and ceiling are nearly level, it's rather easy to preassemble a stud wall on the floor and then raise it into position. If the floor and ceiling are uneven, or if you're building the wall in tight quarters, it's best to build the wall in place, custom-cutting each stud to fit and toenailing it to the top and bottom plates (see page 331).

Whichever approach you choose, make sure you have a way to attach your wall to the ceiling. If the wall runs perpendicular to the ceiling joists, simply fasten the wall's top plate with two 16-penny nails at every joist. If it runs parallel to the joists, you will have to install cross braces, so you can nail the top plate into solid material (see page 332).

You'll Need

TIME: About 2 hours to build a simple 10-foot wall; longer if you need to build it in place or in awkward situations.
SKILLS: Cutting, measuring, fastening with nails.
TOOLS: Tape measure, chalk line, pencil, framing square, saw, speed or combination square, level, hammer.

Use a framing square to establish a perpendicular line.

Pull the line taut and snap it.

chalk line

1. Mark the wall location.
Begin by deciding exactly where the wall will go. Use a framing square and a chalk line to mark its location on the floor. For long walls, check for square using the 3-4-5 method (see page 264).

Using a level and a straight 2×4 that is as high as your ceiling, mark the wall location on the ceiling, joists, or cross bracing. These marks will help you position the wall before you plumb it. Make sure there is adequate framing in the ceiling to which you can nail the top plate.

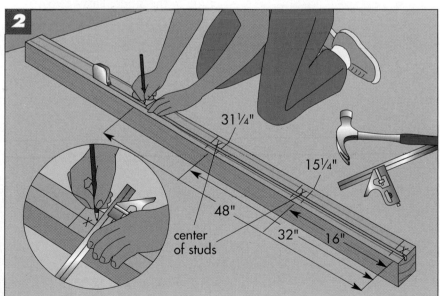

31¼"

15¼"

48"

center of studs

32"   16"

2. Cut and mark the plates.
Using your floor layout as a guide, mark and cut 2×4s for the top and bottom plates (usually the same length). Place them on edge beside each other and mark for the studs. The first stud will be at the end of the wall. The remaining studs should be 16 (or 24) inches on center, meaning that from the edge of the wall to the center of each stud will be a multiple of 16 (or 24). Make a mark every 16 inches; then with a combination or speed square draw lines ¾ inch on each side of your first marks. Draw an X in the middle of the marks to show where to nail the studs.

BUILDING A WALL

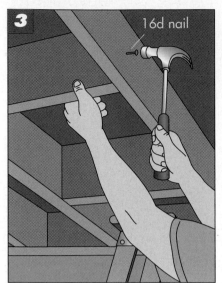

3. Provide nailers, cut studs.

If your new wall runs parallel to the ceiling joists, cut pieces of 2× material to fit tightly between the ceiling joists and install them every 2 feet or so. Measure for your studs (see page 329) and cut them to length.

4. Assemble the wall.

Working on a flat surface, lay the studs on edge between the top and bottom plates. It helps to have something solid, such as a wall, to hold the framing against while you assemble and nail the wall.

For speed, nail one plate at a time to the studs. Drive two 16-penny nails through the plate and into the ends of each stud. Because hammer blows tend to knock studs out of alignment, continually double-check your work while nailing. Keep the edges of the studs flush with the plate edges. If any of the studs are twisted or bowed, replace them.

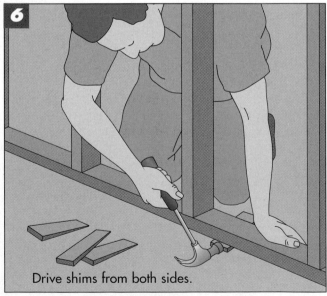

5. Raise the frame.

Framework can be cumbersome, so have a helper on hand. Position the bottom plate about where it needs to go and tip the wall into position. If the wall fits so tightly against the ceiling that you have to hammer it into place, protect the framing with a scrap of 2×4 as you pound. Tap both ends of the frame until it is roughly plumb in both directions.

6. Snug the frame with shims.

If the wall is a bit short in places, drive shims between the bottom plate and the floor or between the top plate and the ceiling joists. Have your helper steady the framework while you drive the pieces in place. Drive shims in from both sides, thin edge to thin edge, to keep the plate from tilting.

7. Fasten frame to wall and floor.
Once the frame is snug, recheck that the wall is plumb in both directions. Check both ends of the wall and every other stud. Fasten the top plate to the ceiling by driving in a 16-penny nail through the plate and into each joist. Fasten the bottom plate to the floor. Use 16-penny nails if the floor is wood; use masonry nails or a power hammer if the floor is concrete.

MEASUREMENTS

GETTING THE STUD LENGTH CORRECT

Few things are more frustrating than building a stud wall only to find that your measurements were off and the wall is ¼ inch too tall. When that happens, the only thing you can do is take the wall down, pull off one plate, remove the nails, cut all the studs, and nail it back together again.

To measure for stud length, nail together two scraps of 2×4 to represent the top and bottom plates. Set this double 2×4 on the floor, measure up to the joist, and subtract ¼ inch for shimming. Take measurements every few feet.

BUILDING A WALL IN PLACE

1. Install top and bottom plates.
If building a wall on the floor and raising it into position are not practical in your situation, begin by cutting the top and bottom plates, and marking them for studs (see page 329). Transfer the marks to the faces of the plates, making sure the marks are clear so you can see them easily to align the studs while toenailing.

Nail the top plate to the joists. Use a level and a straight board to mark the location of the bottom plate or use a chalk line case as a plumb bob. Mark the floor in two places and make an X to indicate on which side of the mark the plate should be positioned.

Use masonry nails or a power hammer to fasten the bottom plate to the floor.

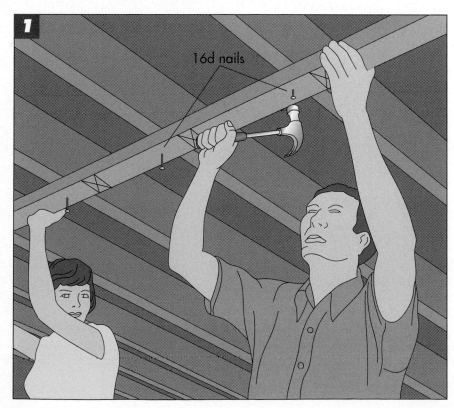

16d nails

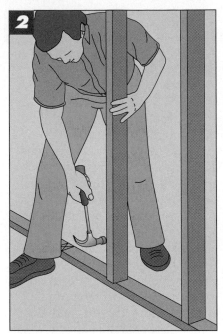

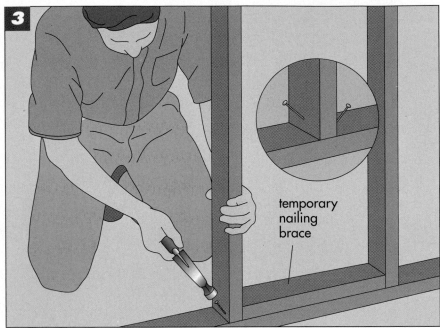

temporary nailing brace

2. Cut and install the studs.

With top and bottom plates installed, measure the required length of each stud individually. Add ¹⁄₁₆ inch for a snug fit and cut. Tap each stud into place. If you really have to whack it to get it into place, it is too long. Don't risk splitting the stud; take it down and trim it a little.

4. Frame at corners.

When framing corners, make sure there is a nailing surface for every piece of drywall or paneling that will be installed. This means adding nonstructural nailers.

In Situation 1, *right,* the extra stud is turned sideways to offer a nailing surface and strengthen the corner. Drive 16-penny nails first through end stud #1 and into the extra stud, then through end stud #2 and into the extra stud and end stud #1.

In Situation 2, *right,* several foot-long 2×4 scraps (usually three in a standard 8-foot wall) serve as spacers between two full-length studs placed at the end of one wall. Tie the wall sections together with 16-penny nails.

Situation 3, *right,* shows two intersecting walls. Nail three studs together and to the plates, then attach to the adjoining wall.

3. Toenail the studs.

To secure the studs, drive 8-penny nails at an angle through the side of studs and into the plate; this is called toenailing. Tap the nail once or twice while holding it parallel to the floor or ceiling. When the nail tip bites into the wood, change the angle to 45 degrees. Drive four to six nails into each joint, two on each side, with an optional one at the front and back. The first nail may move the stud, but the second nail, driven from the other side, will move it back.

If you have difficulty toenailing, drill pilot holes for the nails, using a ³⁄₃₂-inch bit. Or, place a 14¹⁄₂-inch board between studs to serve as a temporary nailing brace.

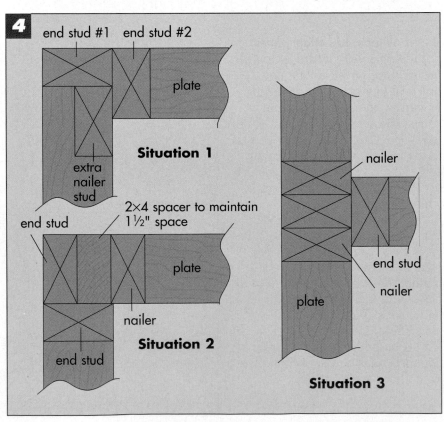

end stud #1   end stud #2

plate

Situation 1

extra nailer stud

end stud

2×4 spacer to maintain 1½" space

plate

nailer

Situation 2

end stud

nailer

end stud

nailer

plate

Situation 3

ROUGHING-IN AN OPENING

If you plan to install a door in your wall, find out the rough opening dimensions you'll need. For a prehung door, measure the outside dimensions of the jamb and add ½ inch for shimming. With a slab door (one that is not prehung), measure the width of the door, add 2½ inches for the side jambs and shims, and add 2 inches to the height for the head jamb, shims, and flooring. Standard door widths are 24, 26, 28, 30, 32, and 36 inches. Door heights usually are 80 inches.

Once you know the opening's size, build the wall as described on pages 329–331, with the addition of the framing members shown below. These framing members have special names and functions.

Jack studs are the vertical 2×4s on each side of the door opening. They are attached to a **king stud** or to another jack stud. This doubling of studs provides solid, unbending support for the door.

The **header** is made of two 2×6s with a ½-inch plywood spacer sandwiched in between. (The plywood is needed to make the header 3½ inches thick, the same thickness as the wall framing.) The header rests on top of the jack studs and spans the top of the opening, supporting overhead loads. For openings that are less than 3 feet wide, you can use 2×4s instead of 2×6s.

Cripples are the short 2×4s added between the header and the top plate. They maintain a 16-inch on-center stud spacing for nailing the drywall and help distribute the weight equally from above.

A window opening is much like a door opening. You install a sill (much like a header) at the bottom height of the window and add more cripples between it and the wall's bottom plate.

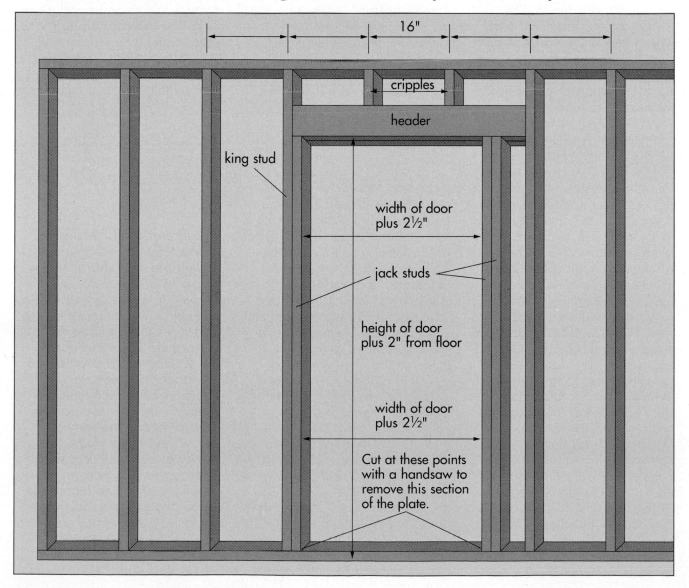

16"

cripples

header

king stud

width of door plus 2½"

jack studs

height of door plus 2" from floor

width of door plus 2½"

Cut at these points with a handsaw to remove this section of the plate.

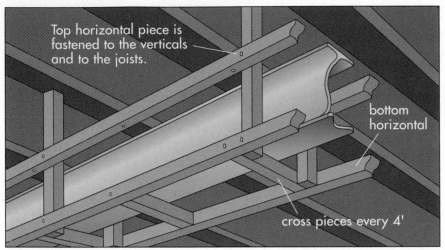

Top horizontal piece is fastened to the verticals and to the joists.

bottom horizontal

cross pieces every 4'

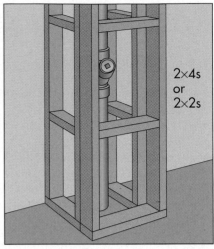

2×4s or 2×2s

Frame around an I-beam.
Use 2×2s to frame around a narrow obstruction, such as a beam. Fasten the frame together with screws rather than nails because the structure will be wobbly as you work. Drill pilot holes whenever you drive a screw near the end of a board.

Make chalk lines on the joists, 1⅝ inches out from either side of the beam. On every other joist, attach a vertical 2×2 to the joists, cutting them to extend 1¾ inches below the bottom of the beam. Fasten horizontal pieces to the bottom ends of the verticals, then fasten horizontal pieces at the top, driving screws into both the vertical supports and the joists. Finish the framing by installing short horizontal cross pieces about every 4 feet between the bottom horizontal frame members.

Frame around a pipe.
You can cover a soil stack or other tall, narrow obstruction with a frame. Mark lines on the floor and measure for top and bottom plates as you would a regular wall. Draw plumb lines on the walls to use as guides. Build three narrow walls of 2×4s or 2×2s; raise them into position; and fasten them to the floor, ceiling, wall, and each other.

WORKING WITH METAL STUDS

Metal framing costs a good deal less than wood 2×4s, and it is lighter. Metal is not susceptible to rot or insect damage, and the factory-made pieces are free from bows, twists, knots, and other imperfections that sometimes make wood hard to work with.

Working with metal studs takes some adjustments. You can't build walls on the floor then raise them up. Instead, you must install the top and floor runners, then insert the studs. Cut metal studs with tin snips or a circular saw and metal-cutting blade. Fasten the pieces together with self-tapping screws.

If you make a mistake, it usually is easier to move a metal stud than a wood one. Running electrical wiring and pipes for plumbing is easy because punchout holes are precut in the studs.

On the downside, once walls are built, you can't attach items to metal stud walls as easily as you can with wood walls. You can fasten items to a metal stud with a screw, but not a nail. If you plan to hang cabinets or shelves on the wall, cross-brace the wall with C-runners. Door jambs and windows can be attached to steel framing, but it's easier to shim and attach the units if you use wood framing, fastened to the metal studs, around these openings.

YOU'LL NEED

TIME: 1 to 2 hours to build a basic 12-foot wall.
SKILLS: Measuring and marking for walls, cutting with tin snips, fastening with a drill or screw gun.
TOOLS: Tape measure, level, tin snips or circular saw with metal-cutting blade, drill or screw gun, plumb bob.

CAUTION!
WATCH OUT FOR METAL
■ *The ends of metal studs, especially those that you cut, often are very sharp. When working with metal, wear gloves. If you're cutting with a circular saw and metal cutting blade, wear long sleeves that are not loose or floppy.*
■ *Cutting metal also can be dangerous because small pieces of metal fly through the air. Be sure to wear eye protection whenever you cut metal studs.*
■ *If you run electrical wiring through metal framing, use sections of plastic foam pipe insulation or specially made plastic grommets to protect wires from damage.*

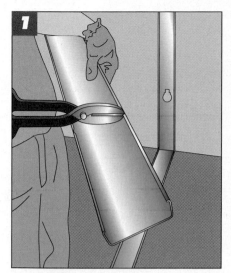

1. Cut the studs.

Lay out framing as you would for a wood wall (see pages 329–332). Cut the runners to be used for top and bottom plates to length with tin snips. Or, use a metal-cutting blade on a circular saw. Using a circular saw is faster, but make sure no one is in the area as you cut, and wear protective eye wear and clothing as you work.

ceiling runner

2. Attach the ceiling runner.

Position the ceiling runner and attach it to each joist with a drywall screw. If joists run parallel to the wall, install cross-bracing so there is something to which you can attach the runner. Position the floor runner directly below the ceiling runner, using a plumb bob. Attach it to the floor with screws or masonry nails.

Twist stud into position.

punchout for wiring and plumbing

3. Cut and insert the studs.

Cut the studs to length with tin snips. Insert them into the runners, starting at a slight angle and twisting them into place. For easier plumbing or electrical installation, make sure all the stud legs are pointed in the same direction and all the predrilled punchouts line up.

4. Attach studs to the runners.

Once studs are placed correctly, drive in $7/16$-inch pan- or wafer-headed screws through the runners and into the studs. Hold the stud flange firmly against the runner as you work. Drive in four screws, one on either side of each runner at the top and bottom.

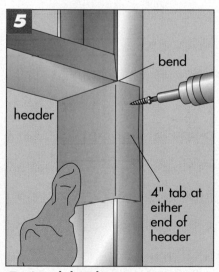

header

bend

4" tab at either end of header

5. Attach headers.

Where you need a door or window header, cut a stud piece 8 inches longer than the width of the opening. Cut the two sides of the stud 4 inches from each end so you can bend back a tab, as shown. Slip the tabs into place and attach with screws.

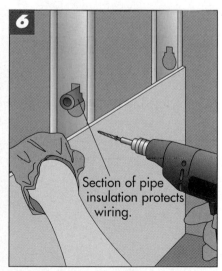

Section of pipe insulation protects wiring.

6. Install the drywall.

Inspect the framing to make sure you have a fastening surface for drywall at all points. Attach the drywall with drywall screws placed 8 to 12 inches apart. Install corner beads with screws or staples. Tape and finish the walls (see pages 342–343).

FURRING BASEMENT WALLS

When finishing basement walls, one option is to build regular stud walls (see pages 329–332), and fasten them to the concrete or masonry walls. A stud wall goes up quickly, gives you room to add plenty of insulation, and ensures that the new walls will be straight, even if the existing walls are not. The disadvantage is you lose some floor space because of the thickness of the walls.

If insulation is not a problem and your basement walls are fairly smooth and straight, you may want to save money in materials and preserve some square footage by building the walls with 1×2, 1×3, or 1×4 furring strips.

The layout is the same as for stud walls. The seams between drywall or paneling sheets must fall on a furring strip, and there must be a nailing surface in all corners and at ends of the sheets.

The construction method, however, is much different. Furring strips are shimmed where necessary, then fastened with glue and masonry nails or with a power hammer, which shoots nails with gunpowder charges (see the "Tools to Use" box, *opposite*).

YOU'LL NEED

TIME: A day for a 12×12 room.
SKILLS: Laying out, measuring, cutting, and hammering.
TOOLS: Hammer, baby sledge, caulking gun, circular saw, tape measure, level, chalk line.

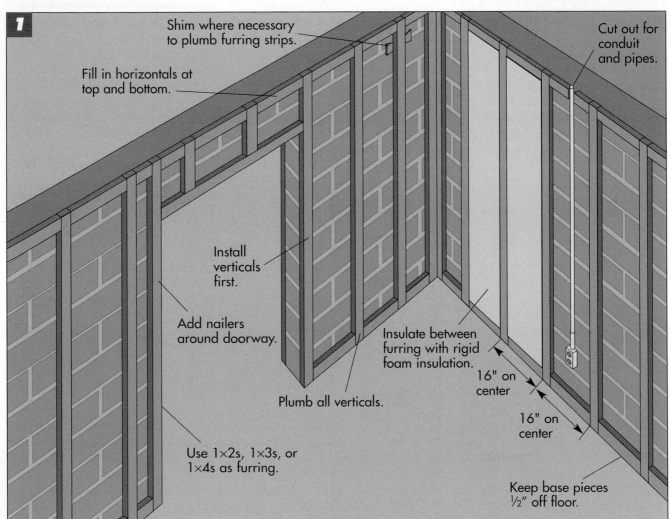

1

Shim where necessary to plumb furring strips.

Fill in horizontals at top and bottom.

Cut out for conduit and pipes.

Install verticals first.

Add nailers around doorway.

Insulate between furring with rigid foam insulation.

Plumb all verticals.

16" on center

16" on center

Use 1×2s, 1×3s, or 1×4s as furring.

Keep base pieces ½" off floor.

1. Plan the furring layout.
Begin the job by marking the locations of the vertical furring strips. One easy way to do this is to position a sheet of your wall material in the corner of the room, plumb it, and strike a chalk line down its outside edge. Using this line as a guide and 16 inches as the center-to-center measurement, mark the locations of the other vertical strips along that wall.

Measure and cut each strip to fit between the floor and ceiling. Cut each piece ½ inch short, so that it will be fastened a bit above the floor as a safeguard against flooding and settling.

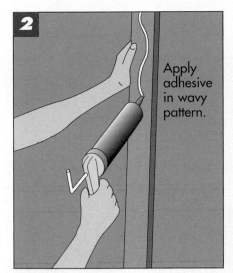

Apply adhesive in wavy pattern.

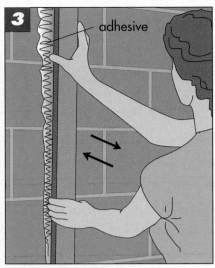

adhesive

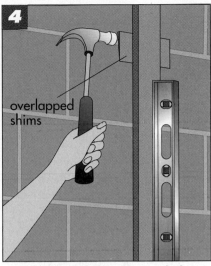

overlapped shims

2. Apply adhesive.

With a caulking gun, squeeze a wavy ¼-inch bead of construction adhesive onto the furring strip. As you finish, turn the gun's handle to ease pressure on the adhesive, discontinuing the flow. Push the strip against the wall in its correct location, pressing firmly to help spread the adhesive.

3. Set adhesive.

Pull the strip off the wall and lean it against another wall to dry and let the adhesive begin to set up. After letting it set for the time specified by the manufacturer, press the strip back into place.

4. Plumb and shim as needed.

Check the strip for plumb. If a dip or bulge is noticeable to the eye, tuck pairs of shims behind the strip and wedge it into line. Double-check your work as the job progresses by holding a straightedge horizontally across four or five vertical pieces. Correct any gaps or bulges.

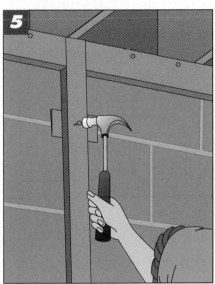

5. Drive in fasteners.

Hammer concrete nails through the strip and the shims and into the masonry wall. On a brick or block wall, it often is easiest to drive the nails into the mortar joints. Use a baby sledge if you have one. Driving nails into concrete walls is extremely difficult; consider a power hammer (see box at *right*).

6. Install the horizontal pieces.

After all the verticals are in place, aligned, and secured, begin work on the top and bottom horizontal pieces. Measure and cut them one at a time. Apply adhesive, shim if necessary, and install them as you did the verticals.

TOOLS TO USE

POWER HAMMER

Choose a power hammer that loads quickly. It usually makes sense to rent a better-quality power tool, rather than buying a cheap one. Experiment with several types of loads to find one powerful enough to drive in the nails completely, but not so powerful as to drive them through the furring strips. **Note:** Follow the manufacturer's directions carefully. A power hammer is literally a firearm, and is dangerous if mishandled.

QUART-SIZE CAULKING GUN

On large jobs, this tool will pay for itself because adhesive purchased in large tubes costs less per ounce. It also will save you time and create less mess because you'll need to change tubes 2½ times less often.

LAYING OUT AND CUTTING DRYWALL

Drywall is inexpensive, and hanging and finishing skills are within the reach of a homeowner. But hanging drywall is difficult work. The sheets are heavy and unwieldy because they are so large. Most rooms are out of square, so cutting is often difficult.

Finishing drywall to a perfectly smooth surface takes three applications of compound and sandings for professionals—four or five for beginners. Finishing success relies in part on careful hanging. So, this is one job you may want to get estimates for hanging and finishing and hire the job out to a professional.

Check framing to make sure you have adequate nailing surfaces (see page 330). Add members that are missing. If you are covering an existing wall, locate all the joists and studs and clearly mark their locations on the walls and ceilings. Draft a strong helper—hanging drywall alone is nearly impossible.

YOU'LL NEED

TIME: With a helper, a day to drywall a 12×12-foot room.
SKILLS: Measuring, physical strength, thoroughness.
TOOLS: Tape measure, drywall square, utility knife, drywall saw, chalk line.

TOOLS TO USE

DRYWALL SQUARE

Don't hesitate to spend the money for a drywall square (see page 242). It quickly pays for itself in time and labor savings. For crosscuts, you simply make one measurement, set the square in place, and run your knife along the square's blade for a square cut. It also simplifies rip cuts (see page 101).

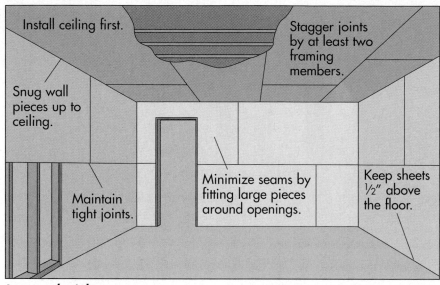

Install ceiling first.

Stagger joints by at least two framing members.

Snug wall pieces up to ceiling.

Maintain tight joints.

Minimize seams by fitting large pieces around openings.

Keep sheets ½″ above the floor.

Lay out the job.
Plan where each sheet will go. Begin by hanging sheets on the ceiling, then butt the wall pieces up against the ceiling. Remember that taping and finishing (see pages 342–343) the drywall takes more time than hanging it (see pages 340–341), so minimize seams wherever possible. Sometimes you can eliminate a butt seam, which is the hardest type of seam to tape, by using 10- or 12-foot sheets instead of standard 8-foot sheets. Installing these big sheets may seem like a lot of trouble, but it will save you time and effort in the long run.

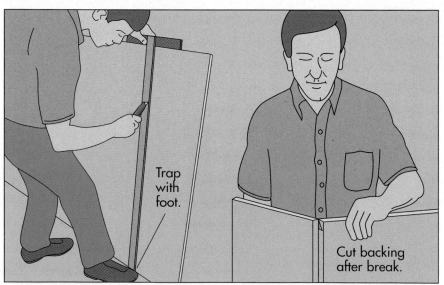

Trap with foot.

Cut backing after break.

Make a crosscut.
Store drywall sheets flat or on edge on pieces of 1× or 2× scrap lumber to hold the sheets off the floor. Before cutting a sheet, make sure the finished surface is facing you. Mark your cut line, stand the sheet on edge, and set your drywall square in place. Clasp the square firmly on top, and brace it at its base with your foot. With the edge of the knife blade against the square, cut downward most of the way, then finish by cutting up from the bottom. Snap the segment back away from your cut line. Finally slice through the backing paper with your knife.

Measure for the last piece.
To determine the correct cutoff length of a corner sheet, measure the distance from the last sheet to the corner at both the top and the bottom. If it is more than ¼ inch out of square, mark both ends of the cut, rather than making a square cut with a drywall square.

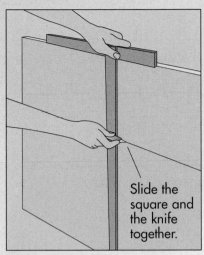

Make a rip cut.
If you need to make a parallel rip cut—one that is the same width all along its length—use your drywall square. Set the square on the edge of the sheet, and hold the knife against it at the measured distance. Slide the square along with the knife in

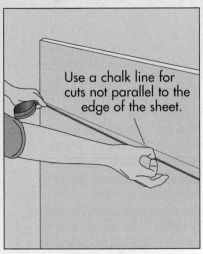

Use a chalk line for cuts not parallel to the edge of the sheet.

position, cutting as you go.
Often a rip cut will not be square; it will be shorter at one end than the other. In this case, make a mark at each end of the sheet and chalk a line between the marks. Cut freehand or use a straightedge as a guide if you need precision.

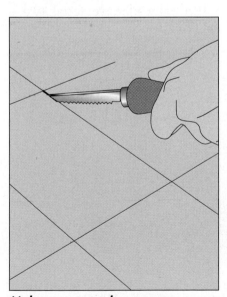

Make a rectangular cutout.
To make a cut for a receptacle box, measure the distance from the box edges to the edge of the last panel. Then measure the distance from the top and bottom of the electrical box to the floor (minus ½ inch) or from the piece above it. Transfer the measurements to the sheet and draw a rectangle. Score the surface with a utility knife, then cut it with a drywall saw.

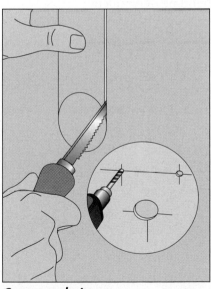

Cut around pipes.
To cut a hole for a pipe, measure and mark the sheet for the center of the pipe. Drill a hole using a holesaw bit that is slightly larger than the pipe diameter. Or, you can draw a circle and cut it out with a drywall saw or a knife.

EXPERTS' INSIGHT

AVOID MOISTURE DAMAGE IN A BASEMENT

■ Wood framing can withstand occasional wetness as long as it is allowed to dry out. But drywall that gets wet once will lose its strength and crumble.

■ If you are drywalling a basement or another place that is subject to chronic dampness or occasional flooding, add nailers to the base of the framing and cut the drywall sheets so they are held off the floor 2 to 3 inches. When you install the baseboard molding, you will need to fur out the gap.

■ To raise drywall even higher, add a 1×6 baseboard directly to the framing and set the drywall on top of it. This will keep the drywall 5½ inches off the floor.

HANGING DRYWALL

Be prepared for strenuous labor when it comes time to hang drywall. The sheets are heavy, you'll be working in awkward positions, and you'll have to hold the sheets in place while you drive in nails or screws. It's tempting to rush the job, but you'll kick yourself later if you do sloppy work. Wide gaps between drywall sheets take a long time to tape, and nobody wants nails popping out later. Here's how to do the job correctly the first time.

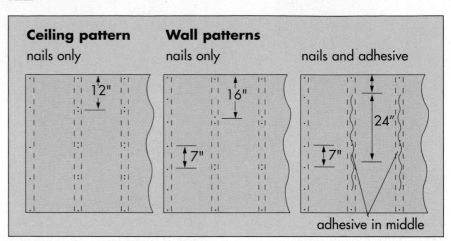

Ceiling pattern
nails only

Wall patterns
nails only

nails and adhesive

adhesive in middle

YOU'LL NEED

TIME: 20 minutes per sheet for walls, 30 minutes per ceiling sheet.
SKILLS: A strong back, fastening in difficult circumstances.
TOOLS: Tape measure, good ladders or scaffolding, hammer or drill with drywall-type screwdriver attachment, drywall taping blades.

Nail or screw according to code.
Local building codes specify how many nails or screws you should use to hang drywall and in what sort of pattern. Codes vary not only from region to region, but from room to room; for example, more fasteners may be required in bathrooms. Check with your building department.

Many professionals don't nail in pairs, but there is good reason to do so: If one nail pops through the paper, the other will hold.

For ceiling panels, the general practice is to pair nails at 12-inch intervals around the perimeter and 12 inches along each joist. Requirements are less stringent for walls. If you don't use adhesive, install two nails into the wall studs at 16-inch intervals and a single nail every 7 inches along edges. When using adhesive, install two nails at 24-inch intervals and one nail at 7 inches along the edge. Keep adhesive 6 inches away from top and bottom of sheet.

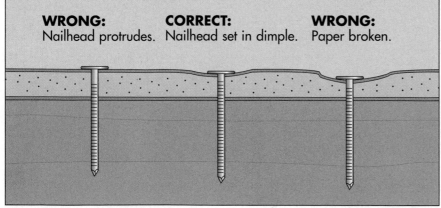

WRONG:
Nailhead protrudes.

CORRECT:
Nailhead set in dimple.

WRONG:
Paper broken.

Set nailheads correctly.
If you simply drive in a nail flush, you will not be able to cover over it with joint compound. If you drive the nail too deeply, you will break the paper on the drywall. When the paper is broken, the nail won't hold; it tears right through the gypsum inner core.

Try to drive the nail so the nailhead is set into a slightly dimpled surface. No portion of the nailhead should protrude above the surface of the drywall.

To test if your nails are driven deeply enough, run a taping blade along the surface of the wall. You should not feel any nailheads click against the blade as you pull it across. Pull out any nails that miss a joist or stud. Swat the hole with your hammer to dimple it.

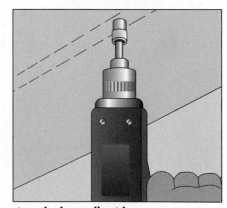

Attach drywall with screws.
If you are using screws, the same principles apply as with nailing: The screw head must be set below the surface, but it must not break the paper. This is difficult to do with a simple screwdriver bit. Use a dimpler bit or a drywall screwdriver (see box on page 341). Always drive in screws perpendicular to the sheet or their heads will tear the paper.

Install the ceiling sheets.

Hang drywall on the ceiling before installing the wall sheets. Start in a corner and against one side of the room and work out from there, keeping the panels perpendicular to the joists. Take time before you start to locate joists and mark their locations on the sheet and the wall. Searching for joists while holding the sheet up with your head is no fun.

The quickest, but most difficult, way to install drywall on a ceiling is to set the panel in place and support it with your head, leaving your hands free to hold and drive nails or screws. Wearing a baseball cap greatly minimizes pulled hair and a sore head.

To make things easier, construct one or two 2×2 T-braces to use as props. Or, rent a drywall hoist. Either solution will make the process easier and result in a much neater job.

TOOLS TO USE

DRYWALL HAMMER

There are hammers made especially for drywall installation. They are light, for easy handling; they have wide heads so it's easier to make a dimple without damaging the paper; and their heads are tilted a bit for access into corners. You may not use one very often, but it will make hanging and, subsequently, taping easier.

DRYWALL SCREWDRIVER OR DIMPLER BIT

A drywall screwdriver has an adjustable bit that, once set correctly, will drive the bit to the correct depth, then stop. A less expensive, and just as good, option is a dimpler bit that you can attach to a drill.

Install the wall sheets.

Once the ceiling panels are up, hang sheets on the walls. If you are installing sheets horizontally, begin with the upper sheets, butting them firmly against the ceiling drywall. Make sure all vertical seams hit studs. Butt the lower panels firmly against the upper panels, tapered edge to tapered edge. Raise up sheets tightly with a wedge or lever.

If you are installing sheets

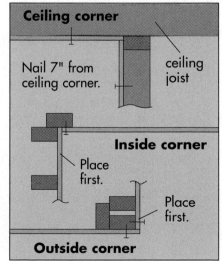

vertically, check the tapered edges to make sure they fall midway across a stud. If they don't, either cut the drywall or attach pieces of lumber to the stud to give yourself a nailing surface for the next piece.

Overlap pieces at corners, as shown *above*. Finish the job by adding the filler pieces, measuring and cutting each piece to size. Make sure each piece has at least two nailing members to support it.

TAPING DRYWALL

Once you've gained some experience, three coats of drywall compound, with sandings, will produce smooth walls. But as a beginner, don't be surprised if it takes you four or five coats. Unless you have large holes that require patching plaster, use ready-mixed drywall joint compound. Dry-mix compounds provide more strength for trouble areas, but you'll need to work fast if you use them. To hide imperfections, apply texture to your walls with a rented texture gun and hopper.

YOU'LL NEED

TIME: For a typical bedroom, 5 hours for the first coat and 2 hours for subsequent coats, plus time for sanding and drying.
SKILLS: Patience and willingness to learn.
TOOLS: Utility knife; 6-, 10-, and 12-inch taping blades; corner taping tool; pole sander or hand sander; tin snips.

EXPERTS' INSIGHT

DRYWALL FINISHING TIPS

■ Use self-sticking mesh tape on the drywall wherever a tapered edge meets a tapered edge, as shown *above*. Use paper tape everywhere else. Mesh tape requires less joint compound, but does not work as well for inside corners.
■ Rusty, gunked-up tools ruin your work. Scrape, wash, and dry blades after every use.
■ When sanding, control the extremely fine dust by using a fan to pull the dust out a window. Seal doorways and wear a breathing mask.

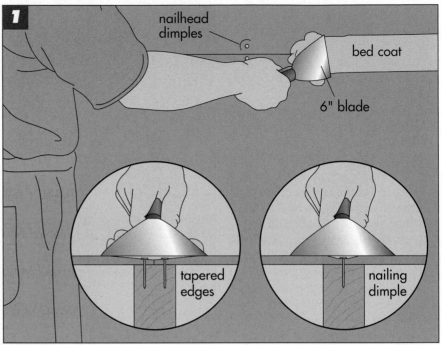

1. Apply a bed coat.
Conceal nailheads by putting compound on a 6-inch taping blade and passing over the spot twice. Make sure you leave compound only in the depression and none on the rest of the sheet. Do this with each coat until the dimple is filled in completely.
   Joints are much more difficult— butt joints especially. If you are using self-sticking mesh tape, simply cut pieces to fit, press them into place, and begin applying joint compound. For paper tape, start by spreading a bed coat over the joint with a 6-inch taping blade. Apply just enough for the paper tape to adhere.

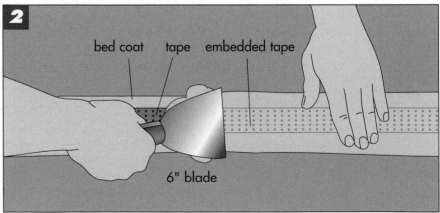

2. Embed the tape in compound.
(Skip this step if you are using mesh tape.) Immediately after applying the bed coat to a joint, center a length of paper tape over the joint and press the tape firmly against the filled joint by running your taping blade along it. If the tape begins to slide, hold it in place with your hand. If bubbles form under the tape, if there are places where the tape is not sticking to the bed coat, or if wrinkles appear, peel the tape back and apply more compound. Then press the tape back again.

3. Apply compound over the tape.
Load a 10-inch taping blade with compound and apply a smooth coat over the tape. Where two tapered joints meet, make sure the blade extends past both tapers. Fill in the tapers only, so you have a flat wall surface. For butt joints, feather out the compound 7 to 9 inches on each side; a small ridge in the middle can be sanded later. After the compound dries, scrape off ridges and bumps, and sand. Apply and sand successive coats until the surface is smooth.

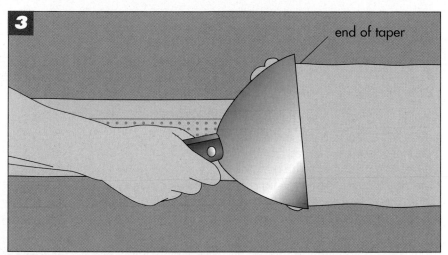

end of taper

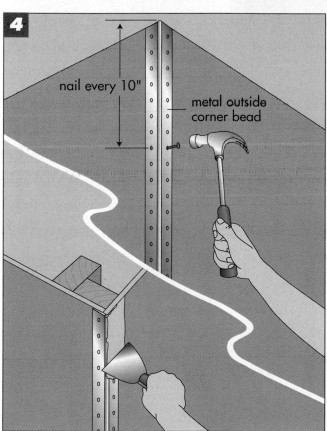

nail every 10"

metal outside corner bead

4. Coat outside corners.
To protect and conceal the drywall edges that meet at an outside corner, cut a piece of metal corner bead using tin snips. Fit the strip over the corner and fasten it to the wall one side at a time. Drive in nails or screws at 10-inch intervals. Check to make sure the flange of the corner bead does not protrude above what will be the finished surface by running a taping blade along the length of the corner bead. Fasten down any areas of flange that protrude. Apply a coat of joint compound with a 6-inch blade angled away from the corner. Allow one side of the blade to ride on the bead, the other side on the wall. For subsequent coats, use 10- and 12-inch blades.

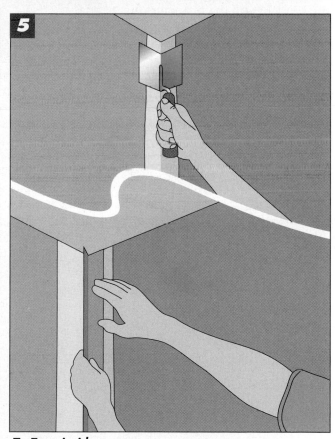

5. Tape inside corners.
Outside corners can be almost fun, but inside corners are more difficult. Apply a bed coat of compound to both sides with a 6-inch blade. Cut a piece of paper tape to the correct length, fold it, and place it in position by hand. Keep it straight to avoid wrinkles. Run a corner taping tool along its length to embed the tape in the compound. Lift and reapply compound wherever the tape has wrinkles, bubbles, or nonadhering spots. Once the tape is embedded, apply some compound to the walls and some to the corner tool. Stroke on a smooth coat. This will take several passes and some practice. You may find it easier to feather out the edges with an 8-inch blade.

INSTALLING PANELING

Sheet paneling needs a solid, plumb backing. Typically, this is a stud wall covered with ½-inch drywall. On the inside of exterior and below-grade walls, sandwich insulation and a vapor barrier between the studs and the drywall to protect panels from moisture.

As you estimate materials, keep in mind that panel seams must hit studs. Lay out the job to avoid thin strips of paneling. It's better to cut 14 inches off the first panel on a wall than end up with a piece 2 inches wide at the end of the wall. Stand the panels up for 48 hours in the room in which they'll be installed to condition them.

YOU'LL NEED

TIME: About a day to panel a medium-size room.
SKILLS: Measuring, scribing, cutting sheets, nailing.
TOOLS: Level, hammer, nail set, caulking gun.

EXPERTS' INSIGHT

CHOOSING PANELING

Sheet paneling is inexpensive and easy to install, but it is also thin and flexible. If your walls are at all wavy, the paneling will accentuate the curves rather than hide them.

If you have problem walls, consider tongue-and-groove planks. They are more expensive and take longer to install, but they'll straighten the walls. Planking requires furring strips and shims every 16 vertical inches for backing.

Be sure to inspect sheet paneling for variations in color, flaws, and splinters.

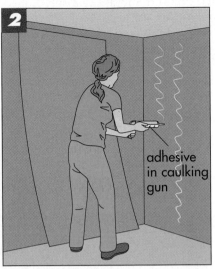

1. Mark the seams.
Mark the location of the studs where the panel edges will meet. Cut the first sheet so its edge falls on the middle of a stud. Set the first piece in place without attaching it. Panels should have a ¹⁄₁₆-inch gap between them to allow for expansion and contraction. To disguise the gap, run a felt marker along the seam.

2. Apply adhesive.
Using a caulking gun, apply a ½-inch bead of panel adhesive on the wall in a wavy pattern so there is no gap larger than 8 inches between adhesive beads. (A large caulking gun that holds quart tubes may be a worthwhile investment.) Press the panel back in place and elevate it above the floor about ½ inch.

3. Tack the sheet in place.
Align the panel so it is plumb and drive three or more finish or color-matched paneling nails halfway in along the top edge of the panel. With the panel dangling, compress the adhesive behind it by hammering on the surface with a block of wood wrapped in cloth.

4. Let adhesive set, attach panel.
Pull out the bottom of the panel and insert a spacer to keep it away from the wall while the adhesive sets up. After the time specified for the adhesive (typically, 3 minutes), press the panel against the wall and drive in nails every 8 inches along the edges and every 12 inches into intermediate studs.

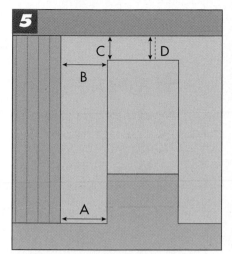

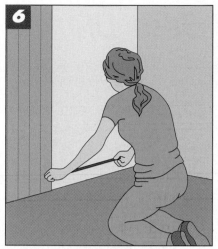

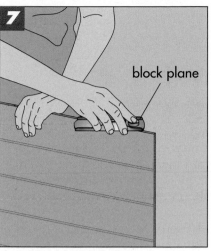

5. Panel around an opening.

To panel around a door or window, measure over from the last panel installed. Measure up from the floor or down from the ceiling to find the height of the opening. Measure in the A, B, C, D sequence shown. If possible, lay out panels so their seams fall over the center of openings. Remember to allow a $^{1}/_{16}$-inch gap between the panels.

6. Fit the last panel on a wall.

For the last piece, you'll need to precision-cut a panel to fit neatly against the inside edge of the wall. Most likely, the corner will not be plumb, so measure from the previous panel to the corner at several points along the panel edge and draw a line with a straightedge. Cut with a circular saw or a sabersaw if the curves are pronounced. When cutting with either of these tools, flip the panel over so the finish side is down.

7. Fine-tune the edge.

It may take several attempts before you get a piece to fit against an irregular corner. Be conservative in your cutting; you can always cut more, but you can't make the sheet bigger. Use a block plane or surface-forming tool to shave off small amounts of material. Hold the tool at an angle so the bulk of the material is cut from the back of the panel, leaving a thin, easily trimmed edge at the surface for final fitting.

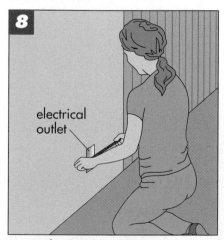

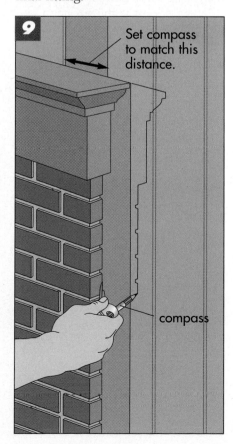

8. Make cutouts.

To cut openings for electrical outlets, measure the distance between the last panel installed and the right and left edges of the outlet. Then measure the distance from the floor to the outlet top and bottom, subtracting the height the panel will be off the floor. Transfer your measurements to the paneling and cut out the hole with a keyhole saw.

9. Cut around complex obstructions.

To cut around such structures as a fireplace and mantel, measure the distance from the last installed sheet to the farthest point along the structure. Measure the height of the structure, allowing for the gap along the floor. Transfer your measurements to the paneling, connect the cut lines with a straightedge, and saw out the bulk of the waste area.

Temporarily nail up the sheet so it is plumb and alongside the structure at the proper elevation. Set a compass (see pages 266–267) to the width the sheet needs to move to meet the last one installed, and scribe the contours onto the sheet.

Make the cut using a sabersaw with a fine-tooth blade or a coping saw. Fit the panel and make fine adjustments with a utility knife. Secure the panel in place.

BUILDING A FIXED-SHELF UNIT

Whether you need a freestanding or wall-mounted shelf, a basic box with fixed shelves is sturdy and can be adapted to most any style. Freestanding units can be stacked and moved into new and different configurations; several wall-mounted units can be combined for ease of installation.

Beginner carpenters can make this unit. Butt-joining the outside corners produces a clean-looking joint with little trouble. If you have some carpentry experience, you may want the cleaner look of mitered joints. Try mitered joints only if you are sure of your ability to make perfectly straight miter cuts; gaps will ruin the project.

To support the shelves, simple butt joints can be strong and stable if fastened with screws. Or reinforce a butt joint by attaching a cleat under the shelf.

A dado joint is the strongest and virtually guarantees that the shelves and the outside pieces will not warp. When you get the hang of dadoes, cutting them is not time-consuming.

The shelves are simple and require precise cutting. Before starting, test your power saw with scrap pieces to make sure you can cut perfectly straight and square without raising splinters. Use a sharp blade. Often it is possible to stack pieces roughly cut to length and make the final cuts on several shelves at once.

The miter-jointed box shown in the steps on page 347 is the most difficult method.

YOU'LL NEED

TIME: Most of a day to build a fixed unit with several shelves and a back.
SKILLS: Accurate measuring and cutting, drilling and driving screws, cutting dadoes.
TOOLS: Power saw, drill, hammer, tape measure, chisel.

The miter-jointed box shown in the steps on page 347 is the most difficult method.

EXPERTS' INSIGHT

FINISHING OR PAINTING A SHELF UNIT

■ Painting a cabinet can be very time-consuming, especially if you need to brush on two coats. Painting boards before they are put together is much easier and faster. Give the boards a primer coat before assembly. (Many primers dry in an hour or less.) If you want two coats of paint over the primer, apply one coat before assembly.

■ If you need to paint a number of units, consider buying an inexpensive paint sprayer or renting an airless sprayer.

■ Staining assembled shelves is difficult; it's hard to get a consistent color in the corners. Stain the pieces, assemble them, and then apply a finish.

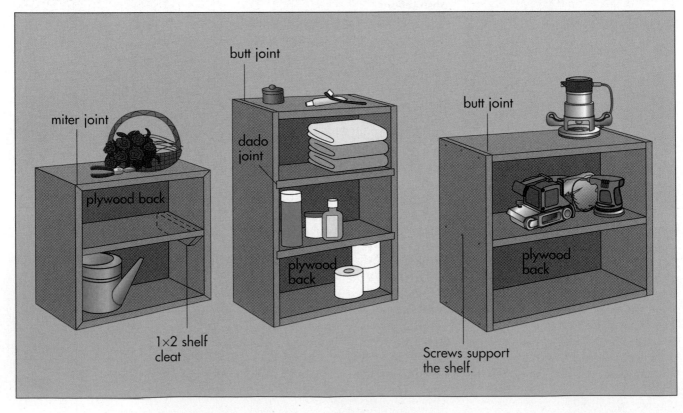

miter joint

plywood back

1×2 shelf cleat

butt joint

dado joint

plywood back

butt joint

plywood back

Screws support the shelf.

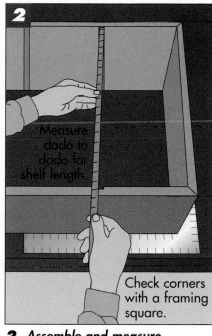

1. Cut outside pieces.

For precise miter cuts, rough cut the outside pieces slightly longer than needed, then cut the miters. Place the two verticals side by side, and clamp them firmly. Draw dado layout lines for each shelf, and use a scrap piece of shelf to make sure you have marked the width correctly. Cut the dadoes ⁵⁄₁₆ inch deep using a circular, radial-arm, or table saw (see pages 245–247). Clean out the dadoes by chiseling out the waste (see inset). Then use the chisel to smooth the bottom of the groove.

2. Assemble and measure.

Join the pieces to form a rectangle by drilling pilot holes and driving 2¼-inch finish screws. Check for square continually as you fasten. Measure from dado to dado for the lengths of the shelves before cutting the shelves to ensure the best fit.

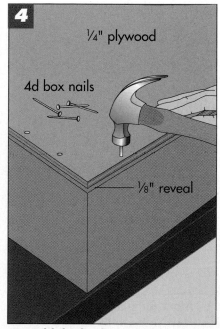

3. Tap shelves into place.

Carefully slip a shelf into both dadoes. Tap it down using a scrap of wood to keep from marring the shelf edge. Avoid tapping one end down farther than the other; alternate between ends every inch or so or gently tap the middle of the shelf to work it into place. When the shelf edges are flush with the edges of the outside pieces, drill pilot holes and drive screws to reinforce and tighten the joints.

4. Add the back.

Cut a piece of ¼-inch plywood ¼ inch smaller than the shelf unit in both directions. Center it on the back so there is a ⅛-inch reveal all around. Drive 4d box nails every 6 inches or so.

INSTALLING ADJUSTABLE SHELVES

Inside a frame, support adjustable shelves near each corner and in the middle of the span if needed. The most common method is to use metal support strips with clips, sometimes called pilasters. Attach them to the inside faces of the side pieces, or cut grooves and set them in. You can also opt for one of the pin methods shown on page 349.

The important thing is to get all four supports level with one another. Work systematically and double-check often—it's easy to misalign the supports.

YOU'LL NEED

TIME: An hour for support strips; several hours for other methods.
SKILLS: Measuring, drilling, attaching with screws.
TOOLS: Drill, hacksaw, tape measure, square, pegboard.

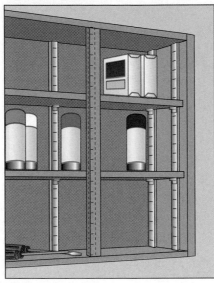

The total system.
Space clips as you would other supports. If the span between vertical outside pieces is too great, install a center stile with a support strip attached. The shelf must be wide enough to fit snugly between the stile and the rear support strip.

EXPERTS' INSIGHT

TALL UNITS NEED A FIXED SHELF

■ Place support strips on side pieces that are stable and strong; if they warp, the clips may no longer support the shelf. Support strips will add some rigidity, but not much.
■ If the vertical pieces are made of 1-by lumber and are longer than 4 feet, install one fixed shelf about halfway up to ensure that the sides do not bow outward. Attach the shelf with a butt joint or a dado joint (see page 296–297). Then install support strips or pins above and below the fixed shelf.

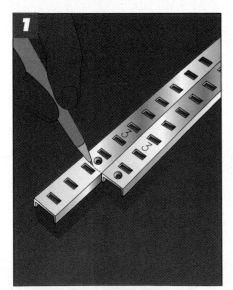

1. Mark for cutting strips.
Cut one piece to the desired height. It doesn't need to extend to the top of the unit, just a notch or two beyond the top shelf. Use the first piece to measure for the others. Line up the slots. To help position the clips later, line up the numbers as well.

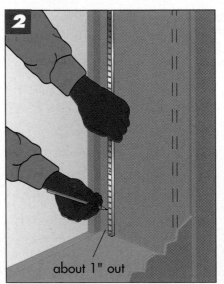

about 1" out

2. Mark and cut dadoes.
Position each strip an inch or so from the edge of the unit, and trace lines. See pages 296 for instructions on cutting dadoes. (If you want to set the support strips into dadoes, remember to cut the dadoes before beginning to assemble the shelf unit.)

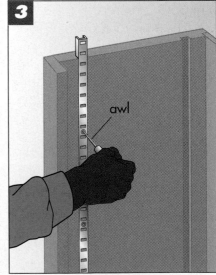

awl

3. Attach with screws.
Position the support strip and use an awl or sharp pencil to mark for the screws. Drill pilot holes with a drill bit and a depth guide so you won't drill through. A piece of tape wrapped around the drill bit will serve this purpose. Drive screws to attach it.

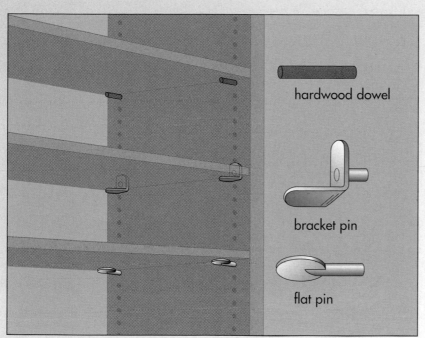

Pin options.

For an inconspicuous support system, drill holes at regular intervals and insert pins. Metal (or plastic) pins come in two types, a flat pin and a bracket pin. Or cut lengths of hardwood dowel to fit into the holes. When using pins, the shelves must fit tightly; if there is more than a ⅛-inch gap between a shelf and the vertical board, the pin could work itself loose and cause the shelf to fall.

MEASUREMENTS

TIPS FOR DRILLING A GRID OF PIN HOLES

■ If the shelf unit has one or more vertical dividers in the middle of the unit, avoid placing holes directly opposite each other on the divider, or else the holes will meet and poke all the way through. To prevent this, offset the vertical lines by ½ inch or so.

■ Save yourself time by drilling only as many holes as you really need. The grid need not extend the length of the vertical board. Start at the lowest possible position for the bottom shelf, and end at the highest possible position for the top shelf.

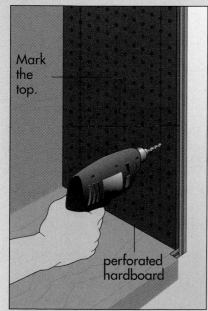

To space holes, use pegboard...

Cut a piece of perforated hardboard (pegboard) to fit into the space, and use it as a guide. Note which end goes up, so you always align it the same way.

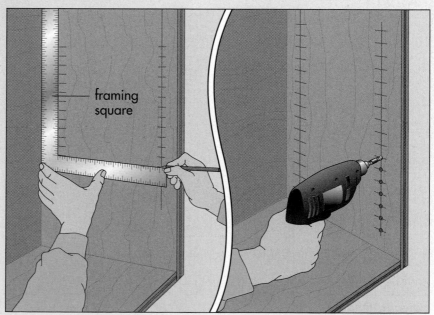

... or use a square.

Draw vertical lines about an inch in from the front and rear edges of the unit. Measure with a framing square or tape measure, and mark evenly spaced horizontal lines at one of the vertical lines. Then use a square to copy the horizontal measurements onto the other vertical line. Use a drill bit depth guide so you don't drill through the standard.

OTHER SHELF MOUNTING OPTIONS

Anything that supports a board and keeps it level and perpendicular to a wall is a shelf support. When using flexible materials like cable or rope as shelf supports, the challenge is to get the spacing between shelves even. (It's very difficult to get knots in a rope evenly spaced.) Chain links are easier to work with. You can finely tune cable brackets by loosening a setscrew.

When hanging a suspended shelf unit, be sure the hook or bracket is strong enough. And always attach it to a framing member (for example, a stud), not just to the wall material.

Sometimes a specialty shelf can be used for other purposes. In the kitchen department of a home center you can find a number of small shelves designed for the back of cabinet doors; these may be suitable for a workshop or in a child's room.

Chains and bolts.
Buy chain with at least 1-inch-long links, and bolts that fit snugly into the links. Drill holes 2 inches in from each shelf edge. Fasten the threaded hooks into studs so each hook is 2 inches from the wall. Insert bolts into links to support the shelves.

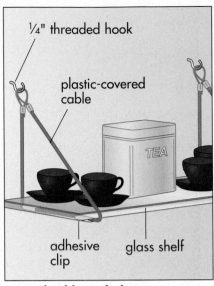

Coated cable and glass.
Sleek plastic covered cables make a modern-style support for a glass shelf. Cable crimps form the loops that attach to a threaded hook. Adhesive clips on the cable hold the shelf horizontal. Glass can be cut to size and edges smoothed at a glass shop.

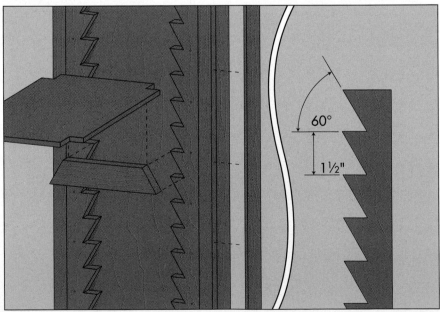

Sawtooth standards.
This traditional support system will take time and much cutting. Make standards by cutting thirty 60-degree triangles in 1×2s as shown. A professional-quality saber saw will help. Make four standards, and attach two to each side piece. Cut two movable cleats for each shelf. Notch the corners of each shelf so it fits between the standards. Install a plywood back for the unit, and attach a fixed shelf near the middle for rigidity.

EXPERTS' INSIGHT

GLASS SHELVES
Sleek and transparent, glass shelves ease the difficulty of lighting knickknacks and collections. Here are some installation tips:
■ Have a glass company cut pieces of extra-thick plate glass. Automobile-type safety glass has a plastic layer laminated in the center to prevent splintering and add strength. The edges must be sanded so they are not sharp; you may choose to pay extra for rounded corners.
■ Supports for glass should have a soft surface. Glue strips of felt wherever the glass will rest on a support.

MAKING SHELVES FOR CHILDREN

Flexibility and durability are the key for children's shelving and storage structures.

Kids grow fast; a shelving system that can adjust in height and function gives the longest service. When possible, make units that can be easily changed, such as the shelf boxes at right. This way, children can make it their own by rearranging it to suit their needs.

Pine 1× is ideal for these shelves. Give it a very durable coat of paint, or stain and finish it so that the inevitable scratches will not be glaring.

YOU'LL NEED

TIME: Several hours for a few boxes; a day for the sports unit.
SKILLS: Measuring and cutting, making dado joints.
TOOLS: Drill, power saw, hammer, tape measure, square.

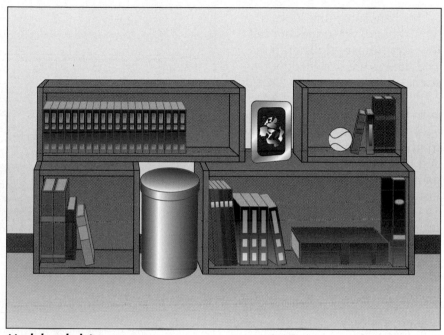

Modular shelving.
Make a variety of sizes—not only different widths and heights, but different depths as well. The spaces between boxes also can be used for storage, so it is not necessary to plan a system precisely. Construct a box with simple butt joints, then reinforce the corners with 3-inch angle brackets. Cut a piece of ¼-inch plywood for the back, and use it to help square up the box.

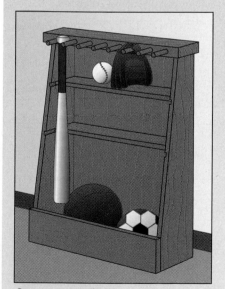

Sports organizer.
This keeps sports equipment from cluttering a room. The pegs are handy for hanging gloves, hats, and baseball bats. Large balls go in the lower bin.

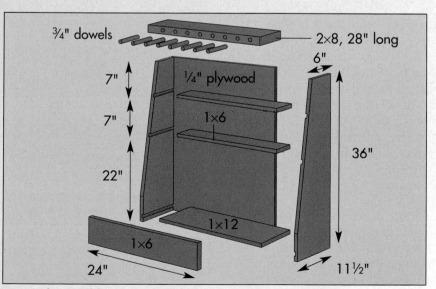

¾" dowels

2×8, 28" long

6"

¼" plywood

7"

7"

1×6

22"

36"

1×12

1×6

24"

11½"

Cut and assemble.
Cut side pieces as shown, and cut ⁵⁄₁₆-inch-deep dadoes (see page 296) for the shelves. Cut the shelves and fasten them in the dadoes with 1⅝-inch trimhead screws. Attach the plywood back with 4d box nails. Use a guide to drill ¾-inch holes, 3 inches deep, into the 2×8; insert the dowels. Attach the 2×8 so it overhangs evenly on both sides.

BUILDING A CLASSIC SHELF UNIT

This handsome unit looks elaborate, yet it does not call for extraordinary skills or tools. The shelves are designed for strength: Reinforced with 1×2s on edge, the shelves can span 4 feet even when loaded with a full set of encyclopedias. Use birch plywood to make the sides and the shelves, and pine moldings if you want to paint the unit. If you choose instead to stain, use hardwood 1×10 for the shelves. Select decorative trim along the top and bottom to suit your decor.

YOU'LL NEED

TIME: 1½ days.
SKILLS: Cutting moldings, drilling a grid of holes, attaching with nails and screws.
TOOLS: Drill, square, miter box, tape measure, hammer.

1. Prepare for construction.

The laminated standards are very rigid, so they won't bow out under the pressure of long shelves full of books. To make them, rip-cut pieces of plywood to 11⅛ inches, or use 1×12s. Cut them to the total height of the unit, or cut them a little short and install moldings that increase the height an inch or so.

If the unit will run all the way to the ceiling, attach 1×2 nailers on the ceiling; you'll attach the standards to these. You can then install crown molding or cove molding at the joint between the shelf and the ceiling.

If the unit will not reach to the ceiling, consider installing a piece of plywood or 1-by lumber fitted into the space between the standards, the top face piece, and the wall.

Attach a piece of ½-inch plywood to the back of the unit, or attach the standards directly to the wall.

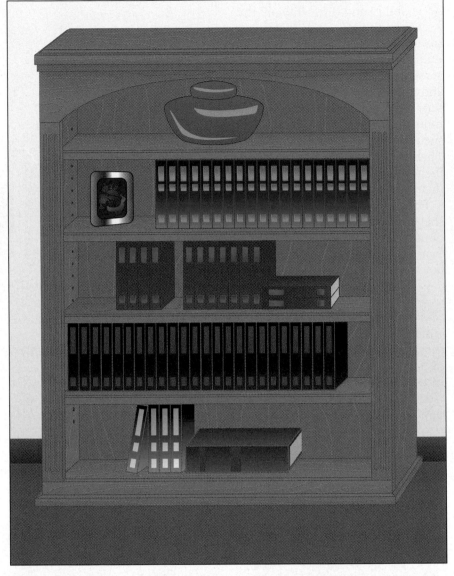

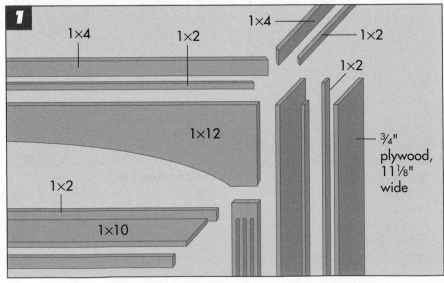

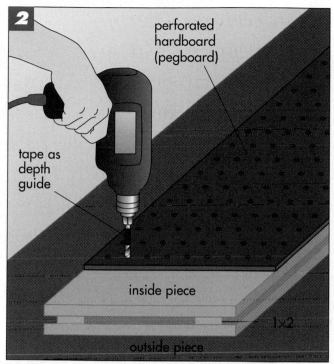

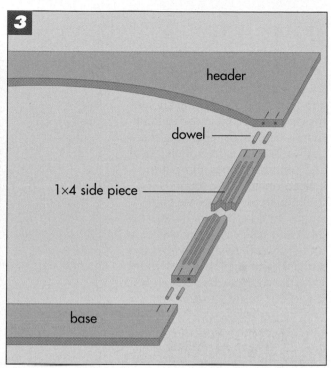

2. Make standards.

Lay the outside piece of each standard on a flat surface, then the 1×2s, then the inside piece. Drill pilot holes, using a depth guide so you don't drill through, and drive 2-inch trim head screws spaced about 4 inches apart. Use perforated hardboard as a template to drill holes for bracket pins (see page 349).

3. Build the face.

Cut the top, bottom, and two side pieces. Draw a long curve along the bottom edge of the top piece, beginning and ending 3½ inches from each end. Cut with a saber saw (see page 273). Working on a large, flat surface, join the side pieces to the top and bottom with blind dowels (see page 297).

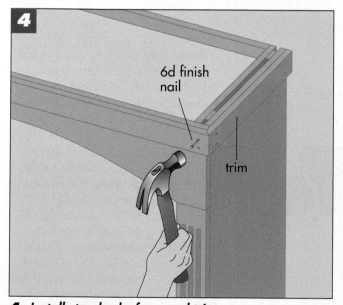

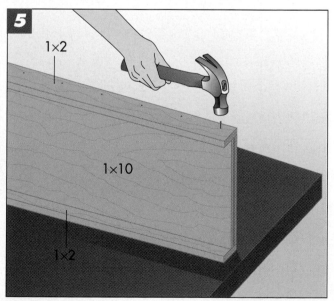

4. Install standards, face, and trim.

Have a helper hold the standards upright while you attach the face. The outside edges of the face should be flush with the outside faces of the standards. Drill pilot holes and drive 1⅝-inch trim head screws every 6 inches. Attach a back piece and anchor the back to the wall, or anchor the standards to the wall with angle brackets. Install trim above and below.

5. Make shelves.

Measure the distance between the standards, and cut 9½-inch-wide pieces of plywood or 1×10s for shelves. For each shelf, cut two 1×2 edging pieces as long as the shelf. Attach them to the front and back edges of the shelf with white glue and 6d finish nails. Insert shelving pins into the holes in the standard, and place the shelves in position.

INSTALLING RECESSED SHELVING

Recessed shelves are real space savers, ideal for collectibles and knickknacks. Setting shelves inside a wall looks more difficult than it actually is; checking that the wall cavity is free of electrical and plumbing lines and cutting a clean opening are the most difficult steps. Otherwise you simply build a box shelf (see page 347) and insert it in the wall. The unit shown here spans across two studs. If a unit 14½ inches wide will suit your needs, you can build it without cutting a stud.

YOU'LL NEED
TIME: A full day.
SKILLS: Cutting walls, basic cabinetmaking.
TOOLS: Saber saw, reciprocating saw or keyhole saw, drill, hammer, tape measure, level.

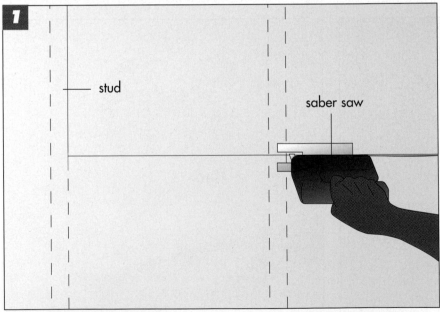

1. Lay out and cut the wall.
Locate studs by rapping on the wall, drilling test holes, or using a stud sensor. Drill holes and insert an unbent coat hanger to explore behind the opening. Do not cut the wall if electrical or plumbing lines are between the studs.

Cut the drywall with a saber saw or keyhole saw. (If the wall is plaster, cutting will be difficult: Score lines deeply with a knife first to prevent cracking the surrounding area.) Cut alongside the studs for vertical lines; mark horizontal cut lines with a level.

CAUTION!
IS IT A LOAD-BEARING WALL?
Some interior walls are simply partitions between rooms. Others are "load-bearing," meaning that they support the roof or a wall on the floor above. Walls that run parallel to joists above are not usually load-bearing. Outside walls are load-bearing, and walls that run perpendicular to overhead joists may be load-bearing as well. Check by taking measurements to see whether a wall above is directly on top of the wall you want to cut into. Do not cut a stud of a load-bearing wall. Consult with a carpenter if you are not sure.

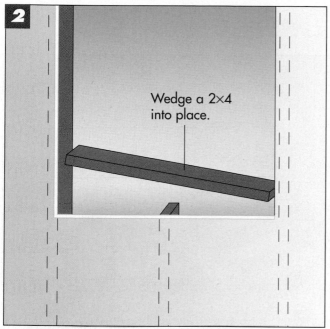

Wedge a 2×4 into place.

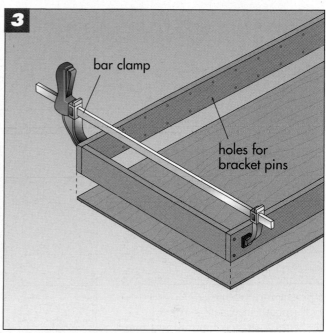

bar clamp

holes for bracket pins

2. Cut the stud and install the sill.

Use a reciprocating saw to cut the center stud at the bottom and the top. Or cut as deeply as you can with a circular saw, then finish the cut with a handsaw. Be careful not to cut through the wall surface on the other side. Cut a 2×4 sill to the width of the opening, and attach it with screws. Make sure it is level.

3. Build the recessed unit.

Build a shelf unit like this butt-jointed frame with adjustable shelves resting on support pins (see pages 349). Rip-cut the boards to the depth of the opening, less ¼ inch for the back piece. Make the unit ½ inch smaller than the opening on all sides. Before assembling, drill holes for bracket pins.

shim

4d finishing nail

6d finishing nail

4. Install shelf unit in the opening.

Set the unit in place. Check for level and plumb, and make sure the front edge is flush with the wall surface. Use shims if necessary. Drill pilot holes and drive 6d finish nails through the sides and bottom; drive one nail through the top into the cut stud.

5. Trim it out.

Install molding around the perimeter. Butt-jointed casing is the simplest, although you may prefer to miter the corners. Drill pilot holes to avoid cracking the wood, and drive 6d nails into studs and 4d nails into the shelf unit.

ADDING UNDER-STAIR SHELVES

The area under a basement stairway often goes to waste; stacking boxes there is awkward because the space is triangular. A shelf system provides a convenient place to store canned goods, bulk purchases, and sports equipment.

Because basement floors may become damp, the bottom shelf should be raised a bit by resting it on pressure-treated 2×4 sleepers, which will not rot even if they get soaked occasionally.

Rather than measuring each upright individually—a complicated process—the technique shown here allows you to quickly cut the outline of the triangle, then make shelves to fit.

YOU'LL NEED

TIME: Most of a day.
SKILLS: Careful measuring, making bevel cuts, fastening with screws.
TOOLS: Power saw, drill, level, framing square, chalk line.

Under-stair shelves.
Basic shelves like these can be quickly assembled with screws. Offset the shelves so they do not line up horizontally; that way, you will be able to drive screws straight through the uprights and into the shelves. For a more finished look and for greater strength, you can set the shelves in dadoes (see pages 269), cut into the uprights.

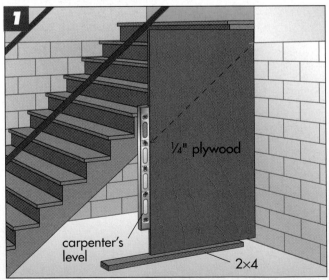

1. Mark and cut backing plywood.
Place a piece of ¼-inch plywood against the stairway, resting it on top of a piece of 2×4, positioned along the stairway where it will be at the back of the shelves. Be sure to check for plumb before measuring and marking. Mark each side, snap a chalk line, and cut. Do the same for the other backing pieces.

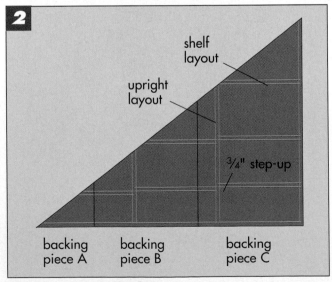

2. Lay out on the backing pieces.
Test to see that the backing pieces fit. Then lay them down and draw layout lines indicating shelves and uprights. Step up each shelf ¾ inch so you can fasten each from the side. Avoid making unusably small triangular shelves. The shelves will be wide; use ¾-inch plywood so they won't sag.

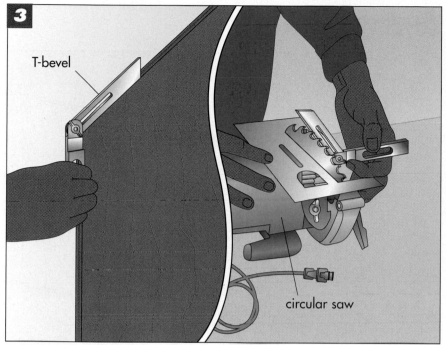

3

T-bevel

circular saw

3. Bevel-cut the pieces.

The uprights should be bevel-cut at an angle, where they meet the stringer, and the shelves at another angle. Hold a T-bevel against the plywood backing pieces to find the correct angle, and transfer that angle to a circular saw, table saw, or radial arm saw. Cut the pieces to width. Measure the layout lines, and cut all shelves and uprights to length. Then cut the bevels.

4

pressure-treated 2×4

4. Attach sleepers to the floor.

Cut two pieces of pressure-treated 2×4 to fit along the bottom of the shelf system. Attach them to a concrete floor with 2-inch masonry nails every foot or so.

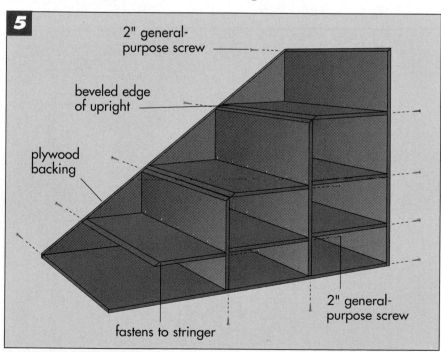

5

2" general-purpose screw

beveled edge of upright

plywood backing

fastens to stringer

2" general-purpose screw

5. Assemble the shelf unit.

Place the shelves and uprights on the backing pieces to make sure they are correctly cut. Use a framing square to line up the shelves. Attach the components by driving 2-inch general-purpose screws every few inches at each joint. Check for square continually, and make sure none of the pieces extends beyond the plywood backing. Slide the assembled unit into place, and fasten the beveled shelf edges to the stringer.

EXPERTS' INSIGHT

BUILDING WIDE PLYWOOD SHELVES

■ Plywood can soak up a lot of paint, making for a costly and time-consuming job. Consider covering the shelf tops with shelf paper, and giving the other surfaces a quick coat of polyurethane. If you choose to paint, birch-veneer plywood soaks up less paint than pine.

■ Whenever cutting across the surface grain of plywood, first score the cut line with a utility knife to prevent splintering. You do not need to do this when cutting with the grain.

■ Give exposed plywood edges a quick sanding with a hand sander to remove burrs and to prevent splinters from developing.

BUILDING UTILITY SHELVES AND RACKS

Utilitarian shelves and racks for a workshop or garage can be made of unfinished plywood and 2-bys. Locate them so lumber and sheet goods can be easily stacked and removed. Make some shelves deep enough for your largest items, and others shallower so cans of paint don't get lost in the back. Before you buy lumber to build your own unit, check the storage options at a home center. Ladder brackets (*right*) and metal shelf units are often more cost-effective than shelves built from scratch.

YOU'LL NEED

TIME: Half a day or less for any of these projects.
SKILLS: Basic measuring, cutting, and fastening skills.
TOOLS: Power saw, drill, square, level, chalk line.

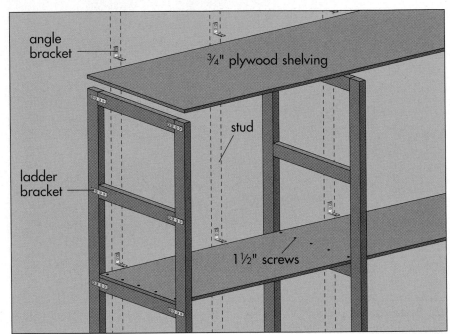

Store-bought ladder brackets.
Ready-made ladder brackets are available at most home centers and will probably cost little more than homemade. Have helpers hold the ladder brackets plumb while you attach ¾-inch plywood shelving with screws. Anchor the unit to the wall with angle brackets and screws driven into studs.

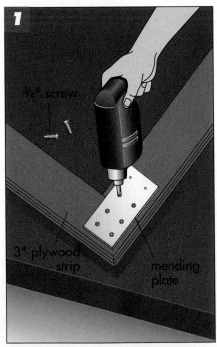

1. Assemble the lumber racks.
Cut 3-inch-wide strips of plywood and assemble them into a U shape, using mending plates and ¾-inch screws to join them.

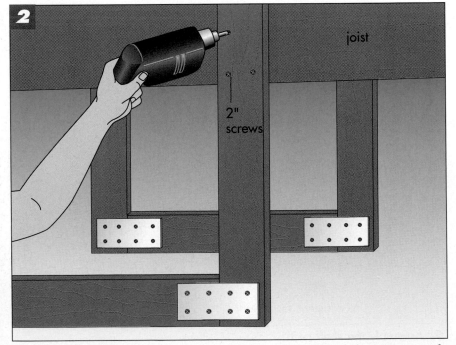

2. Hang the racks.
Chalk a line on the underside of the joists so that the racks will be in line with each other. Attach the the tops of the racks to joists by driving four 2-inch screws through each of the plywood supports and into the joists. Stack the lumber neatly, putting the widest pieces on the bottom to support the other boards and to keep them from warping.

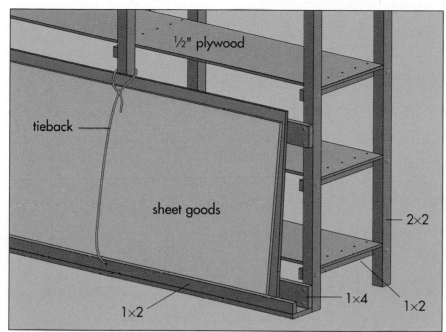

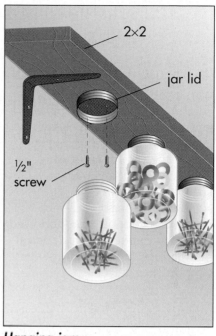

Shelves and plywood storage.

This arrangement will keep sheet goods easily accessible and prevent them from warping. Build standard shelves with 2×2 uprights and 1×2 horizontal supports. Make the bottom plywood channel out of two 1×4s and one 1×2; drill pilot holes and drive screws to fasten them into a U-shape. Drill a hole in the middle of the 1×2 and tie a rope to it. Use the rope to hold sheets of plywood securely in place.

Hanging jars.

Your grandfather may have used this system to organize screws and small items, and it still works. Drive screws to fasten jar lids to the underside of a shelf, and screw the jar onto the lid.

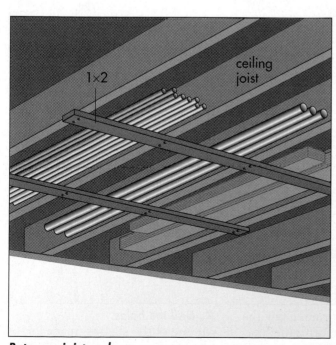

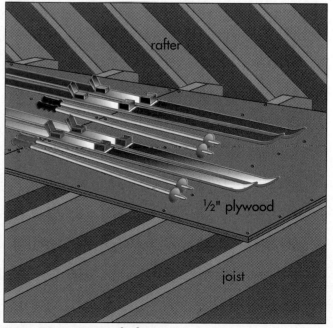

Between-joist rack.

Use the space between open joists in a garage or basement to store lumber, pipes, or other long objects. Attach 1×2s to the underside of the joists for an instant rack. If the stored objects will be heavy, attach 2×4s instead of 1×2s.

Over-joist storage platform.

If your garage or attic has space above the joists, slide pieces of ½-inch plywood up there, and attach them to the joists with 1¼-inch screws. Make the platform roomy, and leave enough empty space on the sides so you can easily get to all the stored objects.

BUILDING ADJUSTABLE ENTERTAINMENT SHELVES

These shelves have an informal look, but if you finish them with a solid covering of enamel paint, or build with oak plywood and stain, they will be classy enough for most living rooms.

The shelves are made of plywood, cut at a gentle curve and edged with veneer tape. The standards are made of 2-inch galvanized conduit, the kind used for heavy-duty outdoor electrical installations. Conduit couplings support the shelves.

YOU'LL NEED

TIME: Several hours, plus time for painting or finishing.
SKILLS: Measuring and cutting curves, cutting metal conduit.
TOOLS: Sabersaw, drill, hammer, framing square, hacksaw.

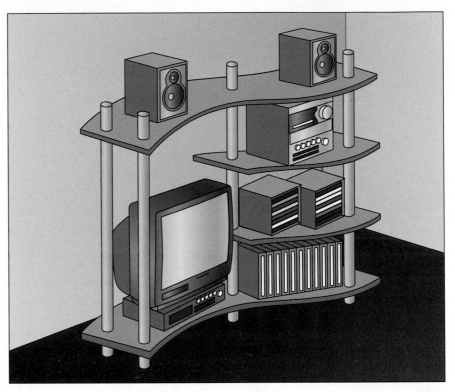

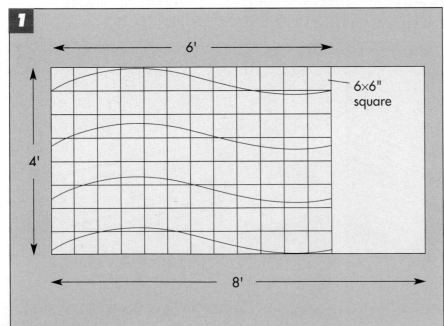

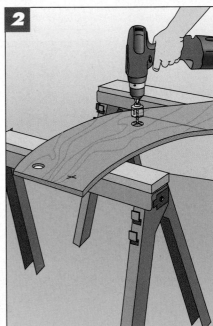

1. Cut the shelves.

On a sheet of plywood, draw lines for a 6-foot-long, 14-inch-wide curved shelf. Use a framing square and pencil to divide part of the plywood sheet into a grid of 6-inch squares. Then draw the top curve, using the illustration *above* as a guide. Experiment until it looks smooth and even. Draw the second line parallel with the first line, and mark for a square cutoff.

Cut the first shelf, and sand the edges smooth. Use the first shelf as a template and draw the next two shelves. Use the framing square to draw a line dividing one of the shelves in half, and cut.

2. Drill the holes.

On one of the shelves, mark for centers of holes 3 inches in from each corner. Mark for another hole in the center of the shelf's width and 33 inches from one end. Drill with a 2-inch hole saw, then use the shelf as a template to mark for holes in the other shelves.

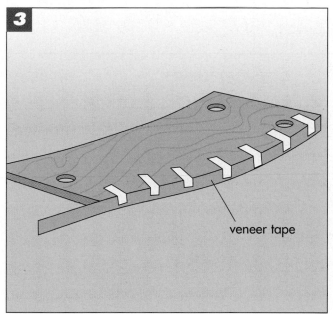

3. Apply edging.

Cover the plywood edges with veneer tape. Attach it by applying glue to the plywood edge and holding the veneer tape in place with masking tape.

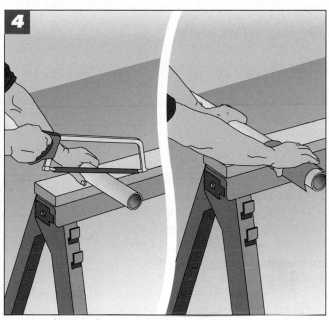

4. Cut the conduit standards.

Cut five pieces of 2-inch conduit (the nonthreaded kind) to 54 inches or so, depending on how tall you want the unit to be. Use a hacksaw or a tubing cutter. To prepare the pipe for painting, first sand the conduit with a loose sheet of medium-grit sandpaper.

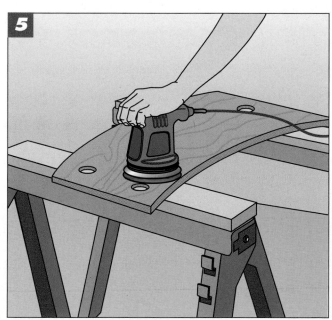

5. Sand and paint standards and shelves.

Sand the shelves smooth. Apply a coat of primer and two coats of enamel paint to conduit, couplings, and shelves. If you like the silvery look of galvanized conduit and couplings, just leave them alone; the finish will last.

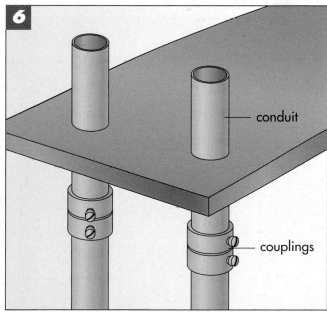

6. Slip on shelves, attach couplings.

At the bottom of each standard, slip on a coupling and tighten the setscrews. Slip the bottom shelf onto all five standards, and slide it down. Slip on couplings for the next shelf, and measure to see that they are all at the same height. Slip on the shelf. Repeat for all the shelves. If the standards fit tightly into the holes, the unit will be stable. If it wobbles, anchor it to a wall with angle brackets and screws.

BUILDING AN ENTERTAINMENT CENTER

This handsome unit hides a TV and a stereo behind cabinet doors, and it includes plenty of shelves for storage and display.

The central cabinet has adjustable shelves 2 feet wide—large enough for standard stereo components and a medium-sized TV. The shallow shelves leave a 3-inch gap at the rear for wires and ventilation. These doors are slabs trimmed with half-round molding, but you could make panel doors instead (see pages 326-327).

YOU'LL NEED

TIME: Two days.
SKILLS: Making doors, measuring and cutting, cutting dadoes.
TOOLS: Power saw, drill, hammer, framing square.

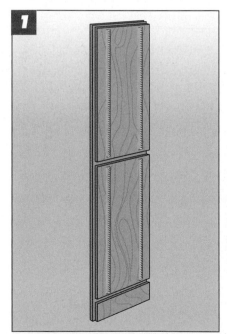

1. Make the side panels.
Cut two pieces of ³/₄-inch plywood to 22×80 inches. Cut a ³/₈ × ³/₄-inch rabbet along the top and side of each (make them mirror images of each other), as well as two ³/₈ × ³/₄-inch dadoes (see page 269). Attach metal shelving standards (see page 348).

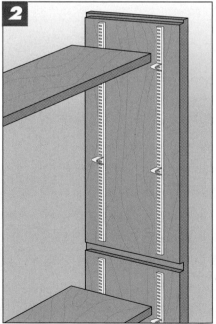

2. Assemble the shelf system.
Cut plywood shelves 18 inches deep and 24 inches wide, and apply common screen molding to the front edges. Working on a flat surface, attach the fixed shelves with glue and 6d finishing nails. Cut ¼-inch plywood for the back; attach it with 3d finishing nails.

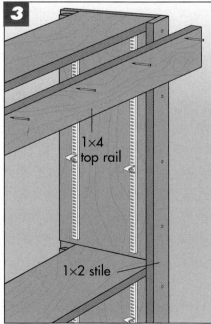

3. Add the stiles and rails.
Cut two 1×2 stiles, and attach them with glue and 6d finish nails, allowing the outside edges to overhang the plywood by ⅛ inch. Cut rails—1×6 for the bottom, 1×2 for the middle, and 1×4 for the top—to fit between the stiles, and attach them the same way.

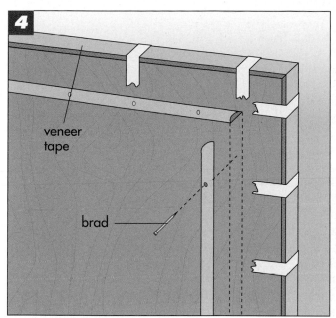

veneer tape

brad

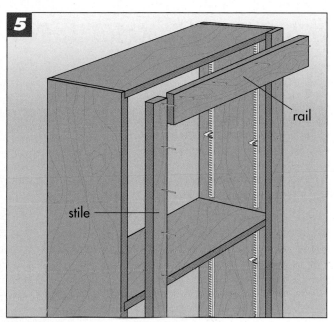

rail

stile

4. Make the doors.

To make trimmed slab doors, start with warp-free plywood. Cut them to size so that there will be a consistent reveal of the stiles and rails when the doors are installed. (Take into account the molding you will use for the bottom and top.) Apply veneer tape to the edges. Trim the door by attaching miter-cut pieces of molding with glue and small brads.

5. Make the open shelf units.

Cut four plywood vertical pieces to the same height as the side panels (Step 1) but only 12 inches deep. Cut rabbets and dadoes and install the metal shelf standards as as in Step 1. Assemble shelves and the back pieces as in Step 2. Add stiles and rails as in Step 3, except install the stiles flush against the edges of the middle unit, as shown.

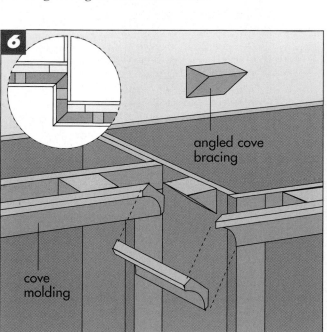

angled cove bracing

cove molding

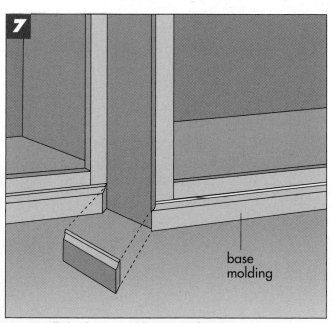

base molding

6. Add the top molding.

Attach the open shelf units to the middle unit with 1¼-inch screws, and attach the entire unit to the wall by driving screws through the back panel and into studs. Trim out the top with cove molding. Rip angled bracing from a 2×2 to back the molding. Make miter cuts for the outside corners (see inset) and coped joints for the inside corners.

7. Install the base molding and finish.

To make the unit appear built-in, purchase molding that matches the base molding in the room. Install it the way you did the top molding (Step 6).

Give all the parts a coat of primer and two coats of enamel paint, or apply stain and then a polyurethane finish if you used hardwood plywood. Then hang the doors with your choice of hinges.

INSTALLING CLOSET ORGANIZERS

A standard closet, with a single rod and shelf, wastes valuable space. Improve your usable storage by dividing it into sections tailored to suit your needs.

Divide hanging clothes into two or three groups according to height. Determine how much width each group requires; make sure the clothes will not be crammed together. Figure how much shelf space you need for sweaters, as well as rack space for shoes. You may want to purchase plastic storage boxes that fit on the shelves. Allow extra room throughout for future purchases.

Draw a diagram of your shelf system on graph paper, and make a materials list that includes ¾-inch plywood and edging for the shelves and upright supports. Use 1×2 for cleats and heel stops, 1¼-inch dowels for hanging rods, metal standards and clips to support the shelves, and hardware to hold rods.

Cut the uprights for the tower of shelves, and install metal standards for adjustable shelves (see page 348). Fasten the fixed shelves with glue and 8d finish nails. Position the shelf unit, check for square, and attach it to the wall with angle brackets and screws.

Cut the top shelf to fit between the side walls and the middle shelf to fit to the shelf tower. Attach 1×2 cleats to the wall, and attach the shelves to the cleats. Cut and install closet rods using special closet-rod hardware. Cut and attach shoe shelves at about a 30-degree angle, and nail 1×2s for heel stops.

YOU'LL NEED

TIME: A full day.
SKILLS: Measuring and cutting, leveling, attaching with nails.
TOOLS: Power saw, level, drill, hacksaw, hammer, square.

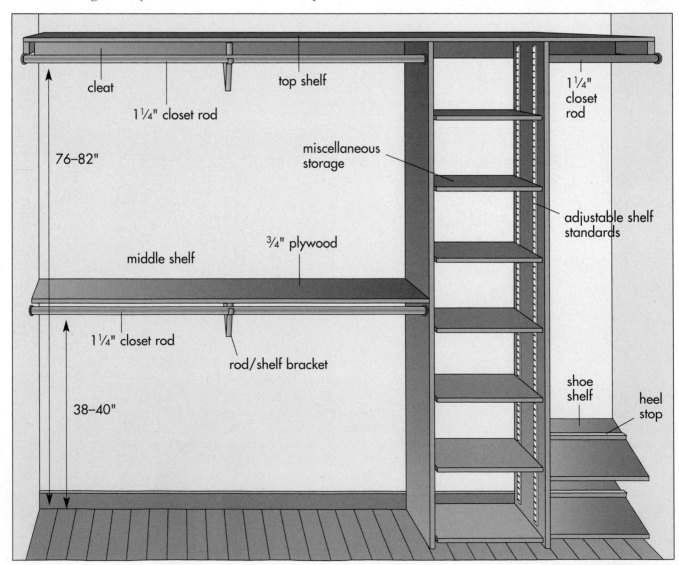

- cleat
- 1¼" closet rod
- top shelf
- 1¼" closet rod
- 76–82"
- miscellaneous storage
- adjustable shelf standards
- middle shelf
- ¾" plywood
- 1¼" closet rod
- rod/shelf bracket
- 38–40"
- shoe shelf
- heel stop

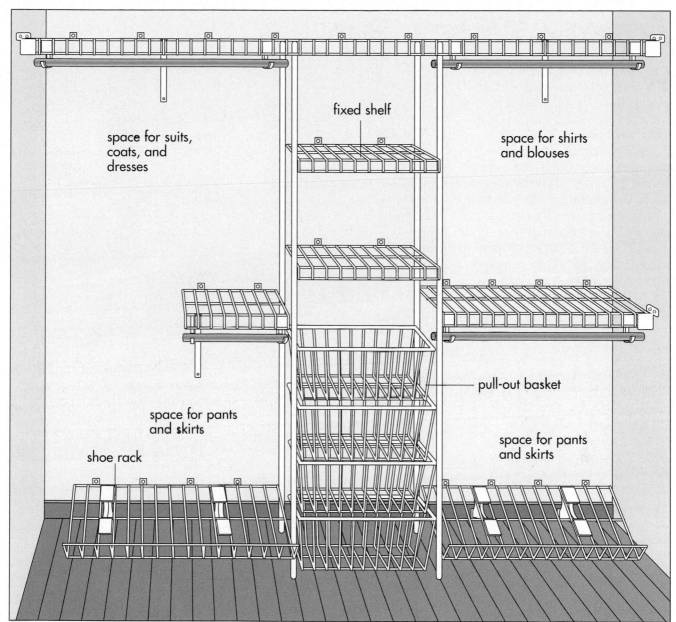

fixed shelf

space for suits, coats, and dresses

space for shirts and blouses

pull-out basket

space for pants and skirts

space for pants and skirts

shoe rack

Wire closet organizers are easy to install, need no painting, and may actually be cheaper than the materials needed to build wood shelves. You may be able to buy a kit that fits your space with little cutting.

Take a drawing with exact dimensions to a home center and ask a salesperson to supply you with all the parts. You'll need shelves with hanger rods, wall-hanging clips, end clips, diagonal supports for shelves over 2 feet, and rubber caps to cover any exposed metal rod ends. You may also want a drawer unit.

Install the drawer tower first; then cut shelves to fit above and on both sides of it. Draw level lines on the walls, install the clips so they are level, and then snap the shelves into the clips.

Install wall-hanging clips at the rear wall. Some types have plastic anchors so you can screw them directly into drywall. Mount hardware to wall studs when possible. Install end wall clips at the side walls.

Cut the shelves with a hacksaw or a pair of bolt cutters. After snapping the shelves in place, install shelf supports.

MEASUREMENTS

COMMON CLOSET SIZES

A closet for hanging clothes is usually 24 inches deep. Make shelves 18 inches deep. Shirts, blouses, and skirts usually require 36 vertical inches. For men's and women's suits and slacks, allow 42 inches. Coats and dresses are usually 54 inches long. Robes and long dresses may require up to 68 inches.

ADDING A WINDOW SEAT

With open shelves on both sides, this seat makes a flat window feel like a bay window. A seat 20 inches deep affords ample room for lounging. Two large drawers underneath are handy for storing linens, and the shelves hold a small collection of books, making this a cozy reading nook.

Begin by removing base molding from the wall; cut and reinstall it on the uncovered wall sections after installing the unit. Mark studs so you can install brackets for holding the shelves and seat in place.

YOU'LL NEED

TIME: A day to build and paint.
SKILLS: Cutting dadoes and rabbets, squaring, attaching with nails and screws.
TOOLS: Power saw, saber saw, drill, hammer, square, level.

1. Build the box and face frame.

From ³⁄₄-inch plywood, cut two side pieces, a top piece, and a back piece to the dimensions shown. Working on a flat surface, fasten the back to the side pieces by driving 2-inch screws through the back and into the sides. Set the top piece in place and drive 2-inch screws through it and into the sides and back.

Cut 1×4 and 1×2 rails and stiles to the dimensions shown. Position the bottom rail so it runs past the box sides ¼ inch on each side, and so the center piece is in its exact middle. Attach by drilling pilot holes, applying wood glue, and driving 6d finishing nails. Attach the stiles and the top rail in the same way; the top rail will be 1½ inches above the plywood pieces. Cut a top piece to fit, and attach it with wood glue and 6d finish nails. Cut four strips for the glide bases, and attach them with 1¼-inch screws.

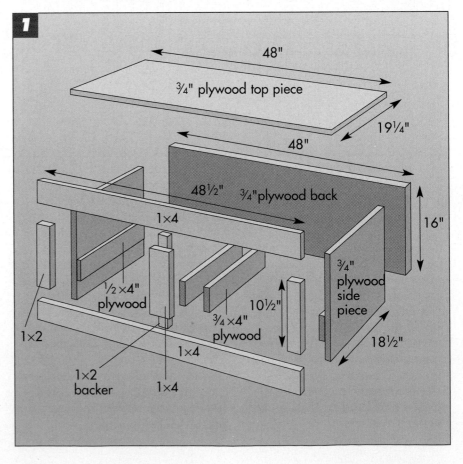

1

48"
³⁄₄" plywood top piece
19¼"
48"
48½" ³⁄₄" plywood back
1×4
16"
1×2
½×4" plywood
¾×4" plywood
10½"
³⁄₄" plywood side piece
1×2 backer
1×4
1×4
18½"

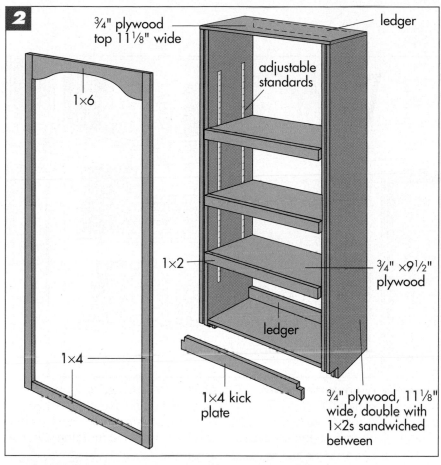

2

¾" plywood
top 11⅛" wide

ledger

adjustable
standards

1×6

1×2

¾" ×9½"
plywood

ledger

1×4

1×4 kick
plate

¾" plywood, 11⅛"
wide, double with
1×2s sandwiched
between

2. Build the shelves.

Decide on the height and width of the shelf units; in a narrow room with a low ceiling, you can run them to the side walls and from floor to ceiling. Make each shelf standard of two pieces of ¾-inch plywood, 11⅛ inches wide, with two 1×2s sandwiched in between (see pages 352–353). If you choose to support the shelves with dowels or pins, bore holes now. (Metal standards can be installed later.) Build each shelf unit by first attaching one standard to the window seat using 3½-inch screws. Plumb it and attach it to the rear wall using angle brackets, then install the second standard. Install the kick plate and bottom shelf. Prefab the face frame, joining the pieces with glue and dowels (see page 353). Install the face frame by drilling pilot holes and driving 1⅝-inch trimhead screws every 6 inches. Build the shelves using 9½-inch plywood with 1×2 edging.

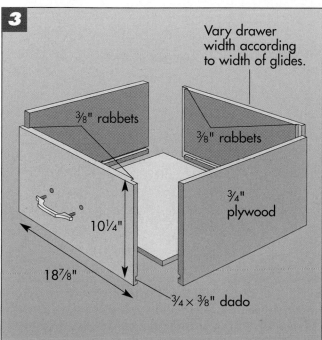

3

Vary drawer
width according
to width of glides.

⅜" rabbets

⅜" rabbets

¾"
plywood

10¼"

18⅞"

¾ × ⅜" dado

3. Build the drawers.

Measure the openings in the base unit, and build drawers to fit. Use ¾-inch plywood for all the pieces. Check the drawer glides to see how much smaller than the opening the drawers should be. Install the drawer pull.

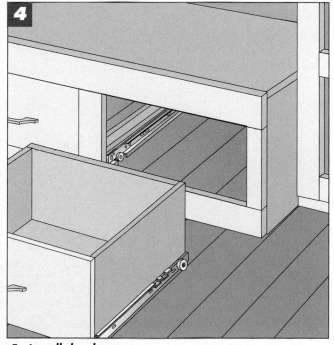

4

4. Install the drawers.

Attach drawer glides to the drawers and to the drawer unit, and slide in the drawers.

Give the entire unit two coats of enamel paint, or stain it and apply a polyurethane finish. Have a cushion (or cushions) made by an upholsterer.

ADDING WRAPAROUND SHELVES

In rooms where every square inch counts, shelves set well above the floor make more sense. Combine them with overhead shelves set around the perimeter of the room, and you can equip a small space with a surprising amount of shelf area. You don't even need generous ceiling height: The most compact ranch home has enough room for one shelf set above the door and window casing.

YOU'LL NEED

TIME: A day to install and trim six or seven shelves.
SKILLS: Measuring and cutting, biscuit-joining, leveling, finding studs, attaching with screws.
TOOLS: Power saw, level, drill, stud finder.

Customize ready-made shelves.
Buy readymade MDF (medium density fiberboard) shelving, ¾-inch thick and 10 inches deep. Finish with gloss or semigloss enamel for crisp good looks and easy cleaning. Give it a finished look by trimming the edges with a stained hardwood molding. Choose shelf brackets to suit your style.

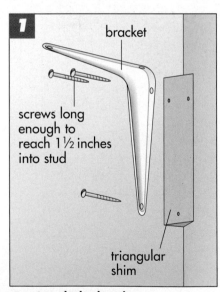

1. Attach the brackets.
Use a level to make horizontal pencil lines indicating the top of each shelf. (So the lines will not be visible.) Use a stud finder to locate studs, and mark for them. Install each bracket ¾ inch below the line, driving screws at least 1½ inches into studs. At the corner, install a triangular shim.

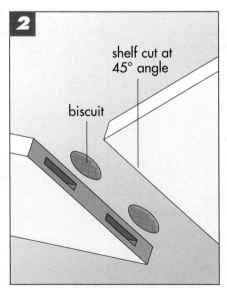

2. Install the shelves.
Cut the shelves to fit, and set them on top of the brackets. If your wall is noticeably wavy, scribe a line at the back of the shelf, and cut with a saber saw so it will fit tightly against the wall. Paint the shelves. At corners, cut both pieces at 45-degree angles and join them with biscuits (see page 297).

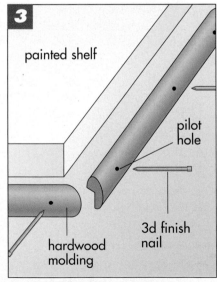

3. Add the trim.
Stain and apply polyurethane finish to the hardwood molding. Cut the molding with a miter saw (see page 270), making 45-degree miters at the corners. Install the molding by drilling pilot holes and driving 3d finish nails. Countersink the nails, and fill the holes with color-matched putty.

FLOORING

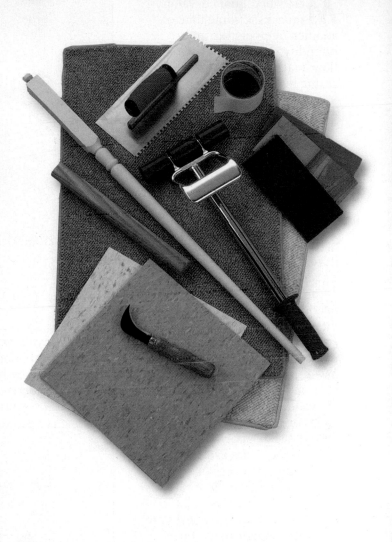

For more tile flooring projects, see Chapter 12, beginning on page 563.

SILENCING SQUEAKS

Most wood floors develop squeaks at some time or another. Temperature and humidity changes cause various floor parts to shrink and swell at different rates. The result: Squeaks develop where loose boards rub against each other or against loose nails.

Modern building codes determine how big the joists must be (typically 2×6 or 2×8), depending on the length they must span. Some older homes, however, were built without benefit of effective codes and may develop sags because the joists are undersized or too widely spaced.

In an older home, the subfloor may be made of 1× planks laid diagonally to the joists; tongue-and-groove softwood strips may be installed over the subfloor. In newer homes, the subflooring may be a single sheet of ¾-inch plywood, or there may be two layers of ⅝-inch plywood.

In other older arrangements, 1×3 "sleepers" are laid across the floor every 12 inches or so. The tongue-and-groove flooring rests on top of the sleepers.

If joists below the squeaks are concealed, repair from above, using the techniques on this page.

If the joists are exposed below, watch while someone walks on the noisy spot. If the subfloor moves, use shims or cleats to support it. Lack of movement may mean that the finished floor is loose and needs to be pulled down with screws. Strengthen any weak joists by installing bridging.

YOU'LL NEED...

TIME: 10 to 15 minutes per squeak.
SKILLS: Basic carpentry skills.
TOOLS: Drill, hammer, and nail set.

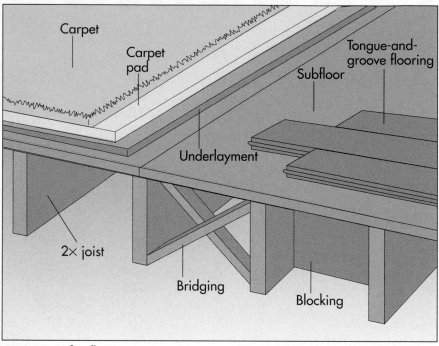

Anatomy of a floor.
Typically a subfloor rests on 2× joists stiffened by bridging or blocking. Underlayment may be used to add rigidity and smoothness for a finished surface, such as carpeting or tile. Tongue-and-groove flooring may rest on a plywood or plank subfloor or on underlayment.

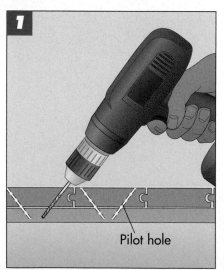

1. To fix a squeak from above, drill pilot holes.
To quiet a loose board from above, nail it to the subfloor. To prevent the wood from splitting, drill pilot holes, angling them as shown.

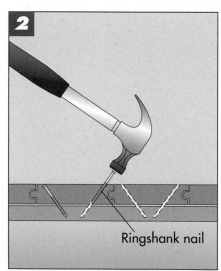

2. Drive in flooring nails.
Drive ringshank nails or finish-head screws. If your flooring was installed with sleepers, there may be a space between the flooring and the subfloor. If so, you must use longer nails. Sink fastener heads below the surface, then fill with wood putty.

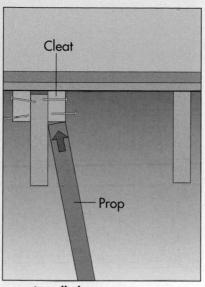

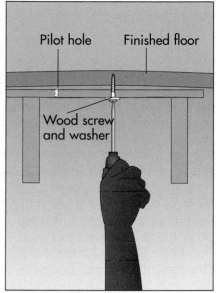

If the subfloor moves and you can work from below, insert a shim...
Use a tapered shim to tighten a loose subfloor board. Dip the tip of the shim in glue and tap it between the joist and subfloor until it's snug.

...or install cleats.
To tighten a series of boards, force a 2×4 up against the subfloor using a temporary prop. Nail or screw the 2×4 to the joist. Repeat on the other side.

Screw upward.
Pull loose finished boards tightly against the subflooring using 1¼-inch roundhead screws. Drill pilot holes (take care not to drill all the way through the flooring), and use washers so the screws won't pull through the subfloor.

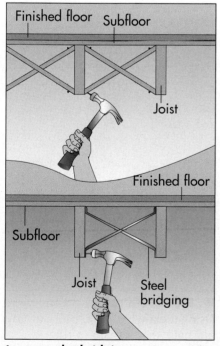

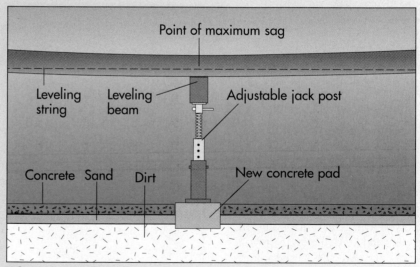

Improve the bridging.
If the bridging isn't tight between joists, drive in new, larger nails or screws at an angle. If squeaks persist, add steel bridging. Push it tight up against the subfloor, then nail it to the bottom inside of the joists.

Lift a sagging floor.
If a floor has a major sag, you may have to add a supporting jack post under it. Break out a section of the basement floor, and pour a 24×24×8-inch concrete pad for the post to sit on. Let the concrete cure for a week. Place the jack post on the pad and set a 4×4 pressure-treated beam, long enough to span several joists, on top of the jack. Jack up the beam until it is snug against the joists, then raise it a quarter turn more. Wait a week and make another quarter turn, continuing this process until the sag is gone. Don't lift faster, or you may cause structural damage.

PATCHING WOOD FLOORS

Replacing a section of a finished floor that is interlocked with tongues and grooves requires patience and hard work. If several boards are damaged, take the time to weave in new boards, rather than cutting straight lines at each end; such a patch is unattractive.

Use the technique shown here for short sections of boards. If the floorboard is very long and most of the board is in good condition, cut out the damaged section of the flooring with a circular saw. Set the saw to a depth exactly equal to the thickness of the finished flooring. Cut as far as possible without piercing adjacent flooring; complete the cut by chiseling, then pry out the damaged section.

YOU'LL NEED...

TIME: About 45 to 60 minutes per area.
SKILLS: Basic carpentry skills.
TOOLS: Drill with spade bit, hammer, chisel, pry bar, nail set, and circular saw.

Money $ Saver

FINDING REPLACEMENT BOARDS

New tongue-and-groove flooring is expensive, and it may not match the old flooring in appearance. Also new flooring strips have to be sanded and stained to match the existing floor—a difficult job.

The solution is to find pieces from elsewhere in the house. Pry out boards from a closet, or from under carpeting. Get more than you need at present so you can have them on hand for later repairs. Fill the resulting voids with plywood.

1. Drill holes in the boards.
Using a spade or Forstner bit, bore holes across the width of the board at the ends and in the middle. Drill only through the flooring board; don't damage the subfloor.

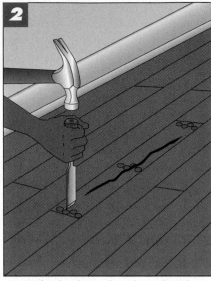

2. Split the board with a chisel.
Use a wood chisel to split the board lengthwise between the drilled holes.

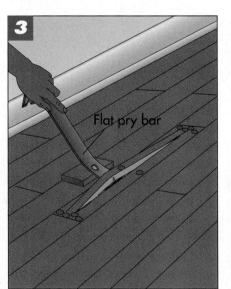

3. Pry out the damaged board.
Slip a flat pry bar into a split. Place a scrap of wood under the bar to protect the good flooring. Pry out the split pieces from the middle, then pry out the rest of the board. Also pry out any little slivers left under the tongue of the adjacent board.

4. Pull out old nails.
Using a claw hammer, pull out any old nails that remain in the subfloor. Use a scrap of wood to protect the flooring.

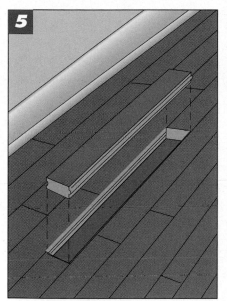

5. Cut new boards.
Use a miter box (see page 270) or a power miter saw (see page 282) to cut new pieces to length. If you are replacing more than one piece, see that adjacent joints are offset at least 2 inches. Cut pieces to fit well but not too tightly.

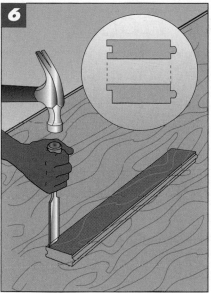

6. Modify the last board.
Prepare the replacement board (or the last board to be placed when repairing a section of flooring) by turning it over and chiseling away part of its groove (see inset). Note how the boards will interlock.

EXPERTS' INSIGHT

WHAT CAUSED THE DAMAGE?
If only a few boards are damaged due to heavy scratching, a simple repair will solve the problem. Other types of damage may be more serious.

If boards have tunnels running through them on the inside, termites or carpenter ants are the likely culprits. Call an exterminator.

If more than a few boards are cracked, the subflooring may be weak. See pages 370–371 for strengthening options.

7. Install replacement board(s).
Test-fit the replacement piece. If you are replacing more than one board, slip the groove of each new piece into the tongue of the adjacent board and tap it in place. Bore pilot holes and angle-nail (see page 370) each piece through the tongue every 12 inches or so before installing the next piece.

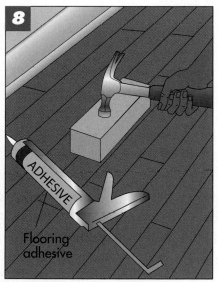

8. Glue the board in place.
Apply flooring adhesive to the subfloor, tongue, and half-groove of the replacement piece (or the last piece when repairing a section), then tap it into place. Use a scrap of wood to protect the flooring surface as you tap.

Removing scratches.
Remove surface cuts or scratches with steel wool and a solvent, such as mineral spirits. Rub with the grain, rinse, and refinish. For deeper cuts, sand with the grain and work in wood filler with a brush. Let the filler set overnight, sand with the grain, and refinish.

REFINISHING WOOD FLOORS

Refinishing a wood floor is a job that takes care and patience. You'll need to rent a random-orbital sander or upright drum sander and a disc-type edge sander. Ask the rental dealer to demonstrate the machines. A sander that uses 220 volts will work much better than a standard 120-volt machine; be sure you plug it into the correct receptacle.

Sanding a floor with a drum sander requires concentration and smooth movements. If you allow the sander to dig into the floor, it will create an unsightly dip. For floors without heavy finish buildup or deep scratches, an upright random-orbital sander (also called a jitterbug sander) is a better choice. It doesn't work as fast as a drum sander but is less likely to damage the floor.

If only the finish is damaged and you do not need to remove deep scratches, consider "screening" rather than sanding. Rent a janitor's buffing machine, and buy circular screens to fit. If a home center does not have this equipment, check with a flooring supply store.

Do this work on a day when you can open doors and windows to let out the dust. Wear a respirator to contend with fine dust, and seal off adjoining rooms with dampened sheets.

1. Remove the base shoe.
After you have removed the furnishings, pry off the baseboard shoe molding—the piece at the very bottom. If there is no shoe, remove the baseboard itself. If the pieces are in good shape, number them on the back so you can reinstall them. Otherwise plan to install new molding.

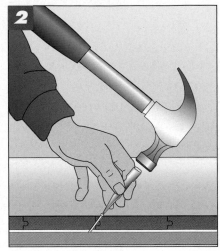

2. Set popped nails.
Any protruding metal will quickly rip up a sanding disc or belt. Use a nail set to drive any popped nails below the surface.

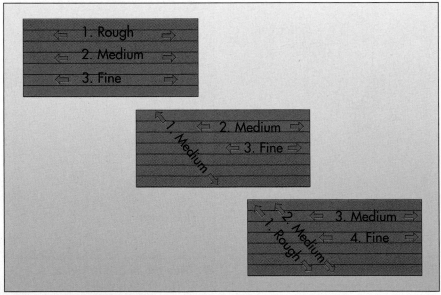

Drum-sanding techniques.
Different situations call for different sanding techniques. For most floors use three sandpaper grits—sanding *with* the grain. It may take several passes with each grit.

Getting nowhere sanding with the grain? Try one diagonal pass, but never sand directly across the grain. Finish up by sanding with the grain.

Badly cupped or warped old floors may require four cuts—two diagonal passes and two with the grain. Be sure to always overlap each pass.

YOU'LL NEED...

TIME: 6 to 8 hours over 2 days for a 10×12-foot room. Allow an additional 2 to 4 days for applying the finish.
SKILLS: Basic carpentry skills.
TOOLS: Hammer, nail set, drum or random-orbital sander, disc-type edge sander, paint scraper or chisel, vacuum, tack cloth, putty knife, and paintbrush or wax applicator.

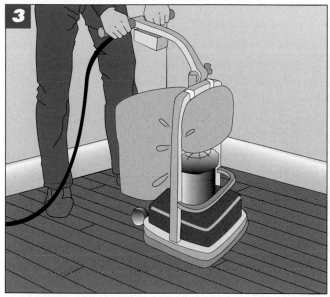

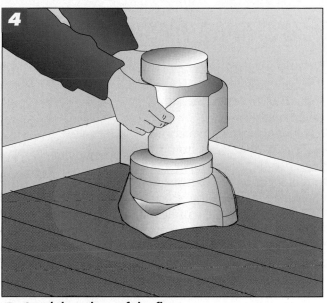

3. Sand the main floor.
Make the first cut with coarse-grit sandpaper. Use coarse grit until you reach bare wood and most of the scratches have disappeared. With a jitterbug sander (as shown above) you don't have to follow the grain of the wood. Use medium- and fine-grit sandpaper for the next two cuts. At each stage expect to use several sheets of sandpaper on each of the four oscillating heads.

4. Sand the edges of the floor.
Use an edge sander for hard-to-reach areas. Work slowly, and finish with a very fine sandpaper so the circular lines will not be visible. In corners that the sander cannot reach, use a sharp paint scraper or chisel, always working with the grain.

5. Remove dust with a tack cloth.
After each sanding pass, vacuum the floor thoroughly. Use a tack cloth after the last vacuuming to pick up the remaining dust.

6. Apply a filler.
Fill in any holes and gaps between the boards using paste wood filler. Apply it first with a putty knife. Always work with the grain. When the filler begins to set, wipe across the grain with an old rag to remove excess. Let the filler dry overnight.

7. Finish with polyurethane.
Apply two to four coats of polyurethane finish with a brush or a wax applicator, sanding with fine sandpaper between coats. Use a tack cloth to pick up all the dust between coats. Do not apply wax over a polyurethane finish.

PATCHING RESILIENT TILE

Most resilient floor tiles will lift out easily once you apply some heat to soften the adhesive underneath.

If you cannot raise a corner, use a chisel, working out from the center to the edges. Once the tile is removed, scrape or sand all remnants of old adhesive off the floor so the new tile will lie flat.

If you cannot find an exact replacement tile, steal a tile from under the refrigerator or another inconspicuous spot, and replace it with a fairly close match.

Different types of tile require different adhesives. To avoid confusion, ask a tile salesperson to recommend a suitable product.

To make the new tile look less conspicuous, rub off the gloss with fine steel wool.

YOU'LL NEED...

TIME: About 15 to 20 minutes, depending on how hard it is to remove the old tile.
SKILLS: Basic skills.
TOOLS: Putty knife, straightedge, utility knife, sanding block, framing square, clothes iron, chisel, and adhesive applicator.

CAUTION!

ASBESTOS TILE

Some older tiles contain asbestos, which is toxic if inhaled. If you are not sure, call in a pro for evaluation. If you must remove asbestos tile yourself, wear a respirator-type dust mask. Keep the area damp while you pry the tile out so fibers cannot fly through the air. Better yet, hire an experienced pro.

1. Soften the tile with an iron.
Lay a towel on top and soften the tile with a medium-hot iron. Take care that the iron doesn't overlap onto adjacent tiles.

2. Pry out the tile.
While the tile is still hot, slip a putty knife under a corner and pry up. Make sure not to pry against the surrounding tiles.

3. Scrape away the adhesive.
Use a putty knife or a paint scraper to remove all of the adhesive. If it does not come up, try heating the area again. You may need to sand away the last remnants of adhesive. Take particular care to remove adhesive from the perimeter of the patch.

Trim line

4. Test the fit of the new tile.
Be sure the new tile will fit and lie flat. If the tile is slightly large and you have to force it in, use a sanding block or plane to shave one or two sides until it fits properly.

5. *Cut the tile to fit.*

If the new tile is too large, use a utility knife and a straightedge to cut it. Slice with several passes, then bend the scrap back to break it off. Smooth any rough edges with sandpaper wrapped around a scrap of wood.

6. *Spread adhesive.*

Apply adhesive with an applicator (as shown above), a notched trowel, or a brush (check the manufacturer's instructions). With some types, you must wait until the adhesive has dried to a tacky feel before setting the tile. With other types, the tile should be set while the adhesive is wet.

7. *Soften the tile with an iron.*

Use the iron to soften the new tile. Protect the tile's surface with a cloth.

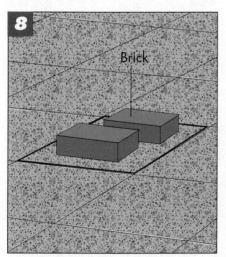

Brick

8. *Weight the tile.*

Set—do not slide—the new tile into position. Wipe away any squeezed-out adhesive using a cloth dampened with water or mineral spirits, depending on the type of adhesive. Weight the tile down for 24 hours before walking on it.

EXPERTS' INSIGHT

SOLVING OTHER TILE PROBLEMS

There are two basic types of resilient tile—commercial tile, which has flecks of color that run through the tile, and surface-printed tile, which has an embossed pattern.

■ **Tears:** Cheaper varieties of surface-printed tiles are easily torn. If this is a recurring problem, remove all the tiles and install tiles of a higher quality.

■ **Lifts:** Surface-printed tiles are often made to be self-sticking, but the self-sticking adhesive is not very strong. When installing a replacement tile, use tile mastic to enhance sticking power.

■ **Scratches:** Scratched commercial tile will often heal itself in time. If you fill a scratch with wax or acrylic finish, the damage will disappear eventually. (See also the Experts' Insight on page 379.)

■ **Burns:** Scouring—plus some careful scraping with a sharp knife—also will remove shallow burns.

■ **Stains:** You can often remove stains by rubbing them with a mild detergent solution. If that doesn't work, try a white appliance wax. As a last resort, scour stains with very fine steel wool and a household cleanser.

PATCHING SHEET FLOORING

Most sheet flooring is glued to the floor in a bed of adhesive. Some newer types of flooring, designed especially for do-it-yourself installation, require adhesive only at seams and edges.

If the entire floor has been laid in adhesive, you usually can work a putty knife underneath and peel up the damaged piece. You may need to apply heat with an iron (see page 376) to loosen it. To make the patch less conspicuous, take time to carefully match its pattern to the surrounding area. To patch the newer types of flooring, cut out the damaged section and cement a patch as you would the seam of a new floor.

Though it is often referred to as "linoleum," most sheet flooring today is made of vinyl with an embossed surface-printed pattern. This product can be durable but if it is deeply scratched or torn, it must be patched or replaced. (Genuine linoleum, which is making a comeback, has color that runs through its body. That means any scratches will conceal themselves.)

A "no-wax" finish will eventually wear away. Rejuvenate the floor using acrylic finish or a product made specifically for no-wax floors.

YOU'LL NEED...

TIME: 20 to 25 minutes, depending on the time needed to clean the underlayment.
SKILLS: Basic skills.
TOOLS: Utility knife, framing square, putty knife, and adhesive spreader.

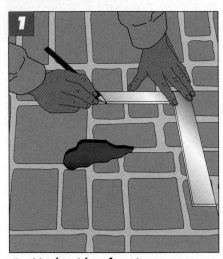

1. Mark with a framing square.
Use a framing square to mark and cut around the damaged area. Cut with a utility knife.

2. Trace the cutout.
Lay the cutout on a piece of matching material so that the pattern lines up precisely. Use a pencil or felt-tipped pen to trace around it. Accuracy is essential for a good fit.

3. Cut with a square.
Either leave the cutout in place and use it as a cutting guide or use a framing square to cut along the trace lines. Place a scrap of plywood under the patching material to prevent damaging the floor.

4. Scrape the underlayment.
Clean the underlayment, making absolutely sure to remove all of the adhesive. Then test-fit the patch. If it is too large, sand the edges.

5. Apply adhesive to the new tile.
If the area around the patch is not set in adhesive, lift up its edges and apply adhesive around the perimeter. Apply adhesive to the patch with a serrated spreader or a brush. Align one edge, matching the pattern, and lower the new section into place.

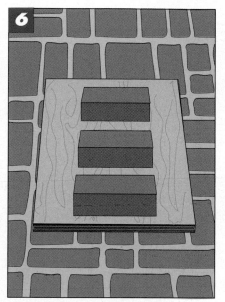

6. Weight down the patch.
Wipe off adhesive that has oozed out from the edges, then weight down the patch evenly for at least 24 hours.

TOOLS TO USE

FLOOR SCRAPERS
■ Vinyl sheet flooring shows even the tiniest imperfection in the underlayment. Use the right tools to make the underlayment perfectly smooth.

■ To remove adhesive or flooring from a large area, buy or rent a floor scraper, which can be operated while standing up. It has removable blades that scrape much more efficiently than a putty knife.

■ Once most of the adhesive has been removed, sand the area. Alternatively, wipe with a solvent-soaked rag to clean up and smooth the adhesive.

EXPERTS' INSIGHT

SOLVING OTHER SHEET FLOORING PROBLEMS
■ **Scratches:** Shallow scratches in wax or a no-wax finish may heal themselves. If you fill shallow scratches with floor wax or acrylic finish, they often seem to disappear. For deeper cuts compress the edges of the torn flooring by dragging a worn coin along—not across—them.

■ **Tears:** If the material has torn all the way through, lift the edges of the wound, scrape away any old adhesive, apply fresh adhesive, and stick the edges down again. For the repair to lie flat, you may need to sand one edge.

■ **Blisters:** If a blister develops in your flooring, flatten it by making a clean cut through its center. Alternating edges, press down on one edge of the cut, work adhesive underneath the other edge, and apply weight.

■ **Holes:** Filling small holes in vinyl flooring is a tougher assignment. The best and quickest way is to fill the void with a special seam-welding product offered by the manufacturer of the flooring. This product dissolves the vinyl, then sets up again to complete the repair.

■ **Patches:** Scrape flakes from a piece of scrap flooring and grind them into a powder. Mix the powder with clear lacquer or nail polish to make a putty-like paste. Work the paste into the hole, packing it well and mounding slightly to compensate for shrinkage. After the paste dries, sand the repair and wax according to the manufacturer's directions.

CLEANING CARPETS

Keeping carpets fresh requires commitment. Once a week—more often in high-traffic areas—use an upright or canister vacuum cleaner with a power (beater) nozzle. This keeps dirt from settling to the bottom and grinding at the fibers. Once a year, shampoo or steam-clean your carpets, depending on how deep the dirt is embedded.

Shampoo comes as either a concentrated liquid detergent you mix with water or an aerosol spray foam. Remember that shampoo is a surface cleaner only. Either remove all of the furniture at once or allow two days, doing half the carpet each day. Whip the detergent into a foam by vigorously scrubbing the carpet. Let the foam dry, then vacuum the dried detergent and loosened dirt. Do not soak the carpet—it might shrink, the colors might run, and mildew might grow.

Steam-cleaning machines actually spray a mix of hot water and detergent deep into the pile, then immediately vacuum up both the solution and dislodged dirt before the carpet becomes soaked. Steaming is much more effective than shampooing. Hardware stores, home centers, and carpet stores usually have steamers for rent. Or purchase an inexpensive steam cleaner.

Oriental and antique rugs require professional cleaning to make sure they don't run or shrink.

In day-to-day life, when a spill occurs, speedy cleanup is of the essence to avoid permanent staining. Remove as much of the spill as possible with a large spoon, a spatula, a putty knife, or a large knife.

Consult the table at right to select a cleaning agent. Apply the first cleaning agent listed for the type of stain. Do not pour the agent directly onto the spill area. Instead pour it onto a sponge and blot—don't rub—the stained area. Remove as much liquid as possible by pressing a paper towel into the stain.

Repeat the pour-into-sponge, blot, and dry sequence with the remaining cleaning agents listed in the table. After all the agents have been applied and removed, rinse the area with fresh water. Dry the area by stepping on a pile of paper towels stacked on the wet area.

If the stain type is not listed, try trichloroethane, a dry-cleaning solution available at many stores, followed by detergent.

CARPET STAIN FIRST AID

Spill	Treatment
Blood	Water, then detergent
Butter	Trichloroethane, then detergent
Chocolate	Detergent, then ammonia
Coffee or wine	Detergent, then vinegar
Crayon	Trichloroethane, then detergent
Egg or fruit juice	Detergent, then ammonia, then vinegar
Furniture polish, grease or oil	Trichloroethane, then detergent
Ice cream	Detergent, then ammonia, then vinegar
Ketchup	Detergent, then ammonia
Lipstick	Trichloroethane, then detergent, then ammonia, then vinegar
Mayonnaise	Trichloroethane, then detergent
Paint (oil)	Trichloroethane
Paint (latex)	Detergent
Shoe polish	Trichloroethane, then detergent, then ammonia, then vinegar
Tea	Detergent, then vinegar, then trichloroethane
Urine	Vinegar, then ammonia, then vinegar again, then detergent
Wax	Scrape, then apply trichloroethane

PATCHING DAMAGED CARPET

Wall-to-wall pile carpeting or machine-made area rugs can be repaired with relative ease. Handmade or Oriental rugs, however, require special care and should be taken to a professional.

To install new carpeting, see pages 392–397.

YOU'LL NEED...

TIME: 1 hour, plus 1 day for the adhesive to set.
SKILLS: No special skills needed.
TOOLS: Hammer, clean can lid, and utility knife.

EXPERTS' INSIGHT

OTHER CARPET REPAIRS

■ If carpeting is pulling up at the edges, press it back into place with a putty knife or tap it with a hammer. If that doesn't do the trick, you may need to stretch it or install a new tackless strip (see page 393).

■ To lift an indentation caused by a furniture leg, lay a damp towel over the area and press with a heated iron for a few seconds. Lift up the towel and rub the indentation with the edge of a coin. Repeat if necessary.

■ To repair a tear or slice, pull back the carpet to reveal the underside. Apply seam tape, and heat it. Or stitch the tear from below, using a heavy needle and carpet thread.

■ To patch a small hole, cut a replacement section of pile and attach it to the padding or flooring using superglue.

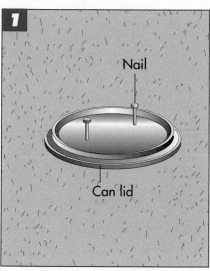

1. Tack a lid over the area.
Partially nail a clean can lid or other template over the damaged area. Leave the heads of the nails projecting.

2. Cut out the damaged area and make a patch.
Using the lid as a guide, cut through the carpet with a sharp utility knife. Repeat Steps 1 and 2 on a piece of scrap carpet to make a matching patch.

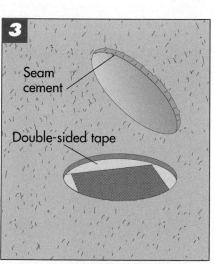

3. Apply tape and seam cement.
Vacuum up loose fibers. Slip double-sided tape halfway under the cutout edges of the old carpet. Apply a thin ribbon of seam cement to the edge of the carpet patch.

4. Weight the patch overnight.
Press the patch into place. Weight the patch overnight with a book or board and a heavy object.

FIXING STAIRS

The staircases in your home have many parts—all of them interlocked with sophisticated joinery that is usually concealed from view.

A pair of stringers (also called carriages) slopes from one level to the next. The stringers support a series of steps, called treads. A simple staircase—such as one that leads to a basement or deck—consists of little more than stringers and treads (see page 383).

The illustration at right shows both "open-" and "closed-stringer" staircases. An open stringer has notches cut out of it; treads rest on the notches. A closed stringer has a series of grooves into which treads and risers fit.

In most interior stairways, risers fill the vertical gaps between the treads. Risers give a more finished appearance, keep dirt and objects from falling to the floor below, and add strength.

Finally, a balustrade—which consists of a handrail, balusters, and a newel post—provides safety along at least one side. Because all the parts are subject to various stresses, they all must fit tightly.

On most interior stairways, the balusters fit into the treads with dado, dowel (see pages 296–297), or dovetail joints. Balusters come in many styles, ranging from simple to ornate. On less-formal and outdoor stairways, the balusters may be attached to a bottom rail, which runs parallel to the railing a few inches above the treads.

You can treat most of the ills that afflict staircases using the techniques shown on pages 383–385. If you want to build a basic, open-riser staircase, see pages 742–745.

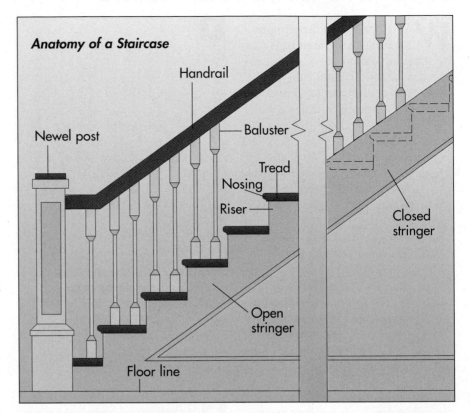

Anatomy of a Staircase

Handrail
Newel post
Baluster
Tread
Nosing
Riser
Closed stringer
Open stringer
Floor line

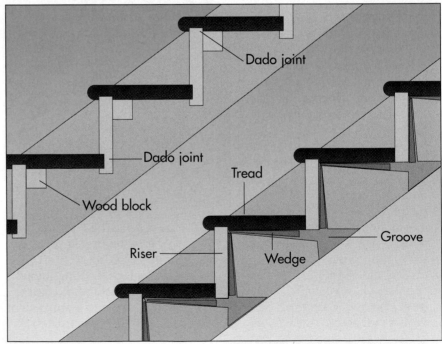

Dado joint
Dado joint
Wood block
Riser
Tread
Wedge
Groove

Treads and risers.
Interior stairway construction typically uses hardwood pieces milled to exact specifications and assembled much like cabinetry. Treads and risers usually fit together with dado joints (above left). In some cases wood blocks provide additional support.

In another arrangement (above right), treads and risers fit into grooves cut in a closed stringer. Wood wedges are tapped in and glued snug to the treads and risers.

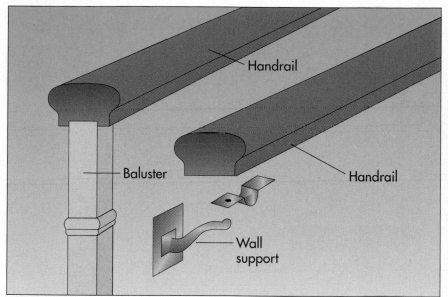

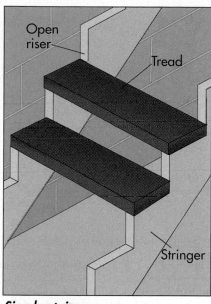

Balusters.
Balusters fit into grooves or holes in the underside of the handrail. At the stairway end, balusters often fit into holes in the stair treads. At the bottom of the stairway, a newel post is firmly anchored to the stair's framing.

If there is a wall on one side of the stairway, it may have a handrail, usually attached to special handrail supports that are anchored to studs in the wall.

Simple stairway.
A stairway for a porch or a basement may consist of stringers and treads. Usually a loose tread can be firmed up by drilling pilot holes and driving new screws. Even the simplest stairway should have a solid handrail.

TIGHTENING RAILS AND BALUSTERS

Wobbly handrails call for detective work. Is the handrail working loose from the balusters, or are the balusters parting company with the treads or bottom rail? If the handrail is pulling away from a newel post, use the technique at right.

A newel post handles a lot of stress. It is usually attached to the stringer, and may be attached to the house's framing as well. Unless you see an obvious solution to a wobbling newel post, call in a pro for help.

YOU'LL NEED...
TIME: About 15 minutes to firm up a baluster.
SKILLS: Basic carpentry skills.
TOOLS: Drill, screwdriver or screwdriver bit, hammer, and utility knife.

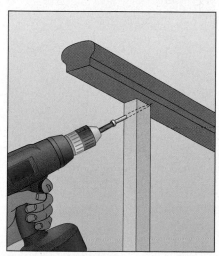

Screw and glue.
Drill a pilot hole at an angle through the baluster into the rail or tread. Countersink a trimhead screw in the hole. Alternatively, drill pilot holes through the railing and into the baluster. Work wood glue into the joint, and drive finishing nails or finishing screws.

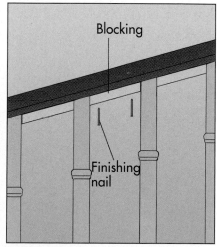

Add blocking.
If the entire railing is loose, add blocking as shown. Use a T-bevel (see page 266) and a miter box (see page 270) or a power miter saw (see page 282) to cut angles for a snug fit. Drill pilot holes, apply wood glue, and drive finishing nails or trimhead screws.

SILENCING STAIR SQUEAKS FROM ABOVE

Most staircase squeaks result from a loose tread rubbing against the top or bottom of a riser or a stringer. To locate the problem, watch as someone rocks back and forth on each tread. If the tread moves, it's time to take corrective action.

You can stop a squeak by forcing the tread either down or up, and wedging it firmly in place.

A small problem can sometimes be solved using finishing nails. However, take care: If you drive a nail near the edge of a tread or riser, continued flexing of the riser could cause the wood to crack.

Work from below if you have access to the underside of the staircase. Otherwise you'll have to attack the situation from above. A few well-placed nails, screws, or hardwood wedges will usually solve the problem.

The directions on these pages enable you to repair several squeaky treads. If the stairway squeaks or groans at many points, however, the problem is likely structural. Go under the stairway and look for a cracked stringer, a closed stringer that is pulling away from the wall, or treads that are pulling away from a closed stringer. To correct a major problem, call in a pro.

YOU'LL NEED...
TIME: About 15 minutes per tread.
SKILLS: Basic carpentry skills.
TOOLS: Backsaw, coping saw, hammer, pry bar, drill, utility knife or chisel, screwdriver bit, and nail set.

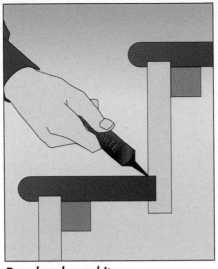

Powdered graphite.
Lubricating squeaks with powdered graphite may quiet them, but only temporarily. Squirt graphite into suspect joints and wipe away any excess graphite.

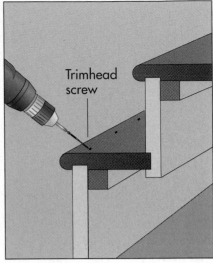

Drive nails or screws.
If the front of a tread is loose and you don't mind the appearance of small holes in the tread, drill pilot holes at opposing angles. Drive in ring-shank flooring nails or trimhead wood screws. Countersink the fastener heads and fill with wood putty.

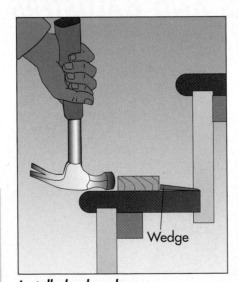

Install glued wedges.
If the tread is loose at the back, coat hardwood wedges (not softwood shims) with glue, tap into place, and let dry. Cut off exposed wedge ends with a utility knife or a chisel.

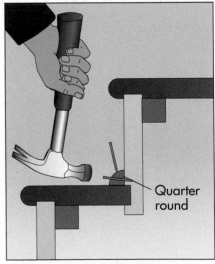

Add quarter-round molding.
For uncarpeted stairs, you can tighten joints with molding. The larger the molding, the better—¾-inch quarter round works well. Apply glue, drill pilot holes, and drive finishing nails into both risers and treads. Use a nail set to sink the nail heads.

SILENCING STAIR SQUEAKS FROM BELOW

Usually repairs made from underneath the stairs will be stronger and more durable than repairs made from above. The problem is getting there. Stairs leading to a basement may be exposed on the underside. Most other interior stairs are not so easy to access.

EXPERTS' INSIGHT

GAINING ACCESS

Removing one or more treads or risers may give you enough room to work. Because one stair part is often set into another part's groove, disassembly is often difficult. But as long as one side of the stairway is open, you should be able to take things apart. Often it helps to cut through nails or screws using a reciprocating saw. When you reassemble the stairs after the repair, the last tread will probably need to be fastened from above.

If the area under the stairway is covered with drywall and extensive repairs are needed, consider removing the drywall, even though replacing and finishing the drywall will be a substantial job.

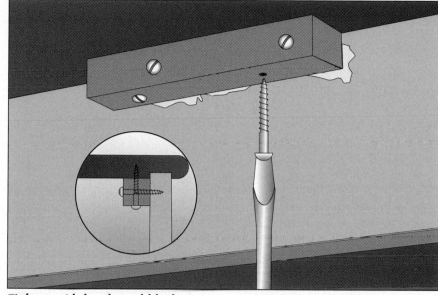

Tighten with hardwood blocks.
Purchase a length of 2×2 oak, birch, or other hardwood, and cut it into pieces about 4 inches long. Drill four pilot holes, running in two directions (see inset).

Where a tread or riser needs support, apply wood glue to the wood block, press it firmly in place, and drive wood screws to fasten it. Make sure the screws are not long enough to poke through the surface of the tread.

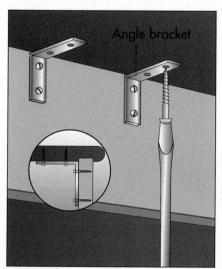

Angle bracket

Use angle brackets for a loose tread.
If the entire tread is loose, use two or three metal angle brackets to tighten it down to the riser. Small brackets act much like wood blocks; larger brackets support the entire tread.

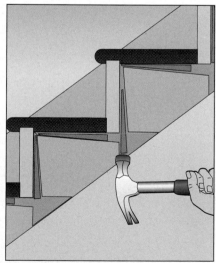

Replace loose wedges.
If old wedges are loose, remove and replace them. If a wedge comes out easily and in one piece, apply wood glue and hammer it back tightly into place. If a wedge is stuck but not supporting the stairway, chisel it out and replace it with a new wedge.

INSTALLING LAMINATE FLOORING

Prefinished plank flooring is as easy to install as hardwood flooring and offers the same appearance. The "planks" consist of medium-density fiberboard (MDF) sandwiched between plastic laminate. The top laminate looks like random-grain wood, but its plastic composition makes it scratch- and stain-resistant.

Precision-milled tongue-and-groove edges make precise installation a snap. The whole assembly is glued together at the edges and floats on a thin, closed-cell polyethylene foam pad.

YOU'LL NEED...

TIME: 6 to 8 hours for a small room.
SKILLS: Basic carpentry skills.
TOOLS: Circular saw, hammer, pry bar, coping saw, and offset handsaw.

1. Lay polyethylene.
Make sure the subfloor is clean, dry, and level. If the subfloor is bare concrete or you suspect that it will become moist, spread a layer of 8-mil polyethylene, and temporarily hold it in place with weights.

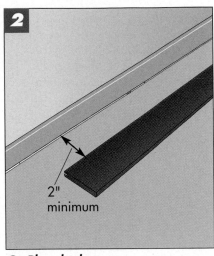

2" minimum

2. Plan the last row.
Show the layout for the room to a flooring dealer and plan the installation so the width of the last row will be at least 2 inches. You may need to rip-cut the first row to achieve this. Also check that the wall where you begin is parallel to the wall where you will end; if not, rip-cut planks at an angle on the wall that will be least visible.

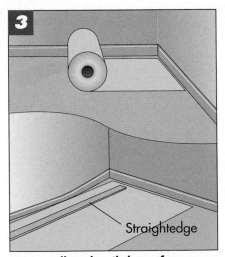

Straightedge

3. Unroll and nail down foam.
Unroll the first strip of foam in the direction the planks will run. Do not overlap the foam edges or adhere the foam to the floor. If you're not starting against a wall or if the wall is uneven, nail a straightedge to the floor to align the first row.

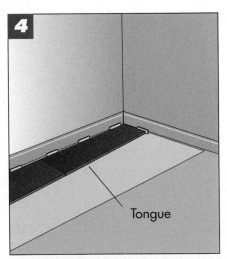

Tongue

4. Lay the first strip.
Lay the first strip with ¼-inch spacers between the grooved end and the wall; the tongue should face outward into the room. Fill end grooves with glue and tap the pieces together. Use a damp towel to wipe up any squeezed-out glue.

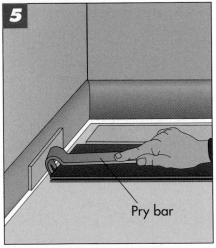

Pry bar

5. Fit planks with a pry bar.
Cut the last piece in the first row, leaving a ¼-inch space at the end. Use a pry bar to push the planks tightly together, then insert spacers and shims to keep them tight. Save the cutoff plank for use elsewhere.

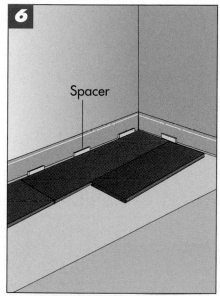

6. Begin the second row.
Cut the first plank of the second row 12 inches shorter; cut the grooved end. Fill all the grooves with glue and tap the pieces tightly together. In some systems you will assemble five or six rows of planks, then use special straps and hardware to hold the pieces tightly together until the glue has dried.

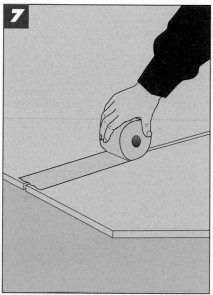

7. Tape foam strips together.
After the first strip of padding is nearly covered, unroll the next strip, butt the edges (do not overlap), and tape them together. Continue gluing planks to the last row.

8. Undercut the door casings.
Undercut door casings with an offset handsaw. Use a piece of scrap flooring as a depth gauge. Hold the blade of the saw flat on top of the scrap as you cut.

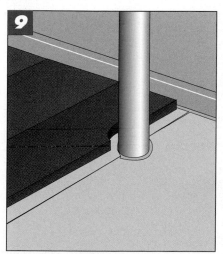

9. Cut around pipes.
Cut planking with a coping saw to fit around pipes, making holes ¼ inch larger than the pipes. The planks should not touch the pipes at any point. See page 266 for hints on how to mark contours.

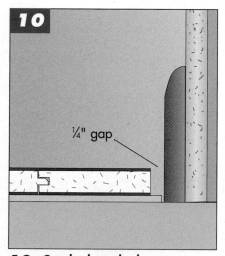

10. Cut the last plank.
Ripsaw the tongued edge of the last plank ¼ inch narrower than the remaining gap. Glue its groove and pry the piece into place. Use spacers and shims to fit the piece snug against its neighbor until the glue has set.

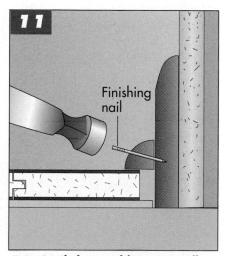

11. Nail shoe moldings to wall.
Once the glue has set, remove the spacers and nail the shoe molding to the wall. Drive nails into the wall, but not into the floor, so the floor can expand and contract with changes in humidity. Wash the floor with clean, warm water.

LAYING A PARQUET FLOOR

Parquet wood flooring, sometimes called woodblock flooring, comes in a variety of materials and stains. A parquet floor has a rich look because it is composed of thousands of little pieces. Yet parquet is easy to install. You don't have to use nails; simply set the pieces in adhesive.

The subfloor should be sound and free of large bumps or dips, but it does not have to be very smooth. You can install parquet over most existing types of flooring, as long as they are secured in place.

Purchase a high-quality adhesive made for parquet flooring. All-purpose or flooring adhesive is not strong enough.

On concrete it's best to include a layer of polyethylene film, sleepers, and a subfloor (see page 391) before laying the tiles.

Cut parquet tiles using a handsaw, circular saw, or saber saw. Because the pieces are small, avoid injury by clamping them to a work table rather than holding them by hand.

YOU'LL NEED...

TIME: 5 to 6 hours for a 12×15-foot room if the subfloor is prepared.
SKILLS: Basic carpentry skills.
TOOLS: Framing square, tape measure, saw, chalk line, notched trowel, and power nailer.

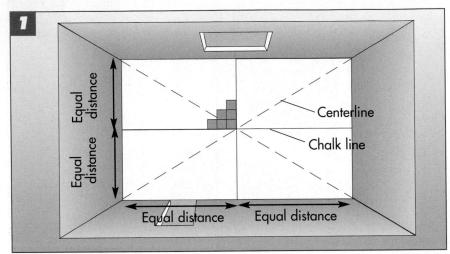

1. Plan the installation.

Plan the installation to avoid having narrow slivers in visible areas. Snap chalk lines between the midpoints of the walls as shown; the lines should be square to each other.

Measure from the lines to the walls to see what will happen at the borders. Most parquet tiles are exactly 12 inches square, so planning is easy. To be sure of your calculations, set tiles in dry-run rows on the floor.

If the layout leads to slivers or awkward pieces at the perimeter, move one or both of the layout lines over approximately 2 inches, and check again.

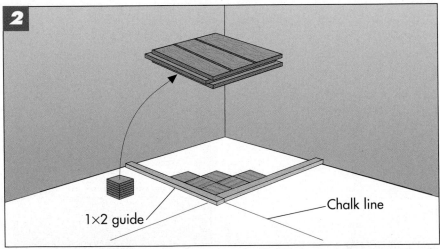

2. Lay the parquet tiles.

Check again that the layout lines are square to each other. Get off to a square start by tacking down a pair of 1×2s along the chalk lines. Tongue-and-groove edges keep the later courses true.

Use a notched trowel (of a style recommended by the flooring manufacturer) to spread adhesive over the floor. The adhesive sets up quickly, so apply small sections at a time. Press each tile carefully into the adhesive, then slide it into its neighbor. Join tiles together with tongues and grooves. Undercut casing molding when you encounter it (see page 387); cut tiles to go around other obstructions.

CHOOSING WOOD FLOORING

Wood flooring comes in strips or planks. Hardwood strip flooring, by far the most common, typically measures 2¼ inches wide and ¾ inch thick; some maple flooring is 1½ inches wide. Strips have tongues and grooves that fit together tightly.

Oak is the most common type of hardwood strip flooring. "Select," which has no knots and is consistent in color, is the most expensive grade. Less-expensive "No. 1 common" has small knots, and the pieces vary in color. Maple, cherry, rainforest woods (sometimes called "cherry"), and fir are also used for making tongue-and-groove flooring.

Nowadays tongue-and-groove strip flooring is usually laid on plywood that has been covered with roofing felt to minimize squeaks. Strips can be installed directly over existing strip flooring

only if the new flooring does not run in the same direction as the old. The strips are installed using a special flooring nailer that ties them tightly together while anchoring them to the subfloor. Once installed the floor must be sanded with three passes using a special floor sander (see pages 374–375). Then the floor may or may not be stained. Finally two or three coats of finish—usually polyurethane—must be applied. The entire process takes a week or more, but produces a floor that is very smooth and durable. If the floor is badly scratched, it can be resanded and refinished as many as three times.

Another option is prefinished tongue-and-groove strip flooring, which is usually a plywood product with a top layer of finished hardwood. The flooring itself costs more, but this option

saves in other materials costs, as well as labor, because it needs no sanding or finishing. However a prefinished floor is not completely smooth; there are slight level differences from one board to the next. Additionally, if scratched, the surface layer of veneer can be sanded only once.

Flooring grades vary depending on the kind of wood. Clear typically is the best, followed by select, No. 1 common, No. 2 common, and 1½-foot shorts, which are the remnants from the other grades.

Before you lay flooring, it is important to let the wood acclimate to the moisture conditions in your house. Have it delivered at least 72 hours in advance, and spread it out in the room where it is to be laid.

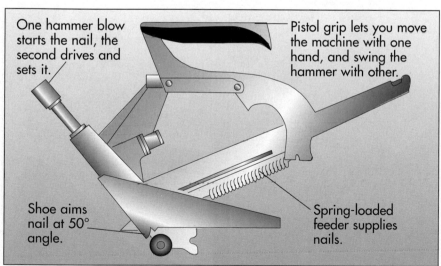

One hammer blow starts the nail, the second drives and sets it.

Pistol grip lets you move the machine with one hand, and swing the hammer with other.

Shoe aims nail at 50° angle.

Spring-loaded feeder supplies nails.

Using a power nailer.
Most wood flooring interlocks with tongues and grooves. Fasteners are driven at a 50-degree angle through the tongue.

A power nailer—available from flooring or rental stores—speeds the job and saves your back. It drives long staples, which are

loaded in clips. Using a heavy hammer, you simply hit the piston drive mechanism to set each nail. The hammer usually has two heads—one for hitting the nailer, and one for tapping boards tightly against each other. Newer nailers are connected to an air compressor by a long hose.

SOFTWOOD FLOORING
Softwood plank flooring is wider than hardwood planks—3 to 8 inches versus 1½ to 2¼ inches—and often is installed in combinations of different widths. Pine and fir are the most common species used. Typically the planks do not have tongues and grooves. The resulting floor is not as smooth as a tongue-and-groove hardwood floor, but many people prefer its casual charm. Planks are face-nailed. Nail heads may be left exposed for a rustic look or covered with wood putty or wood plugs.

INSTALLING TONGUE-AND-GROOVE FLOORING

If you need to firm up a floor, install sheets of plywood. If the new flooring will be too high compared to nearby floors—most people find a height difference of ¾ inch to be a tripping hazard—you may need to remove old flooring before installing the new.

Sweep the floor well, set any popped nails, and remove the baseboard shoes or moldings. If the molding is in good shape, write numbers on the backs so you can remember where the pieces go. Otherwise plan on installing new moldings.

Level any bad dips by pulling up the old flooring, nailing shims to the joists, and renailing the old boards. Staple one or two layers of roofing felt (tar paper) onto the subfloor. This will help prevent squeaks.

Use spacers to create a ⅜-inch gap between the flooring and walls or baseboards. This is important; boards that are installed tight against the wall may buckle. Shoe molding will cover the gap when you're done.

YOU'LL NEED...

TIME: A day for a 12×14-foot room if the subfloor is prepared.
SKILLS: Intermediate carpentry skills.
TOOLS: Square, compass, string line, hammer, pry bar, drill and drill bits, power flooring nailer and mallet, power miter saw, saber saw, and nail set.

⅜" spacer

1. Nail the first board into place.
Place the grooved edge of the first board ⅜ inch from the wall. The power nailer will not be able to reach this close to the wall. Drill pilot holes and drive flooring nails at a 45-degree angle through the tongue every 12 inches.

Driving block

2. Tap the boards together.
To keep the courses parallel, tap the boards together before nailing. Use a wood scrap as a driving block to protect the flooring. Or use the neoprene head of the power nailer mallet. For a professional appearance, offset all neighboring joints by at least 2 inches.

Neoprene head

3. Use the power nailer.
Load the power flooring nailer with staples recommended for your type of floor. Experiment with depth settings; the staple heads should just barely sink below the wood surface. Fit the nailer to a tongue, make sure it rests flat, and hit it with the mallet.

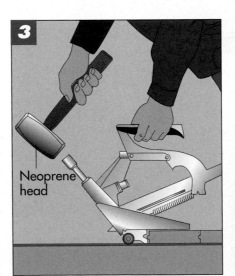

4. Measure for cut pieces.
Measure before cutting the last piece in each course, and cut with a power miter saw or a circular saw. Don't cut off the edge with the tongue or the groove that you'll need. About every six courses , stretch a string line to check for straightness.

5. Scribe around irregularities.

Cut casings at the bottom, using a scrap of flooring as a guide (see page 387, Step 8). To fit around other irregularities, scribe with a compass (see page 266) and cut with a saber saw.

6. Secure the last rows.

You may need to ripsaw the last course. Protecting the wall with a wood scrap, push the last courses tight with a pry bar. Drill pilot holes and drive finishing nails through the face of the boards. Set the nails and fill with wood putty.

EXPERTS' INSIGHT

STRAIGHTENING BOARDS

■ If tapping (Step 2) does not tighten a warped board, pounding the driving block hard with the mallet will probably move it over the last $\frac{1}{4}$ inch or so, but no more.

■ If a board is warped on the side toward the board you are butting against, start nailing at one end and straighten the board by nailing as you go.

■ If the warped edge is away from the board you are butting to, fit the board as tight as possible and drive nails hard into the middle of the board until it is tight.

LAYING WOOD FLOORING OVER CONCRETE

Strip or plank flooring can't be attached directly to concrete. Seal the concrete against moisture with a layer or two of plastic sheeting (see page 114), and then provide a wood surface to attach the flooring to. Laying strip or plank flooring over concrete requires a vapor barrier, sleepers, and a subfloor.

YOU'LL NEED...

TIME: 2 days to install a vapor barrier, sleepers, subfloor, and finished flooring for a 12×14-foot room.
SKILLS: Intermediate carpentry skills.
TOOLS: Hammer, nail set, pry bar, power flooring nailer, power miter saw, and saber saw.

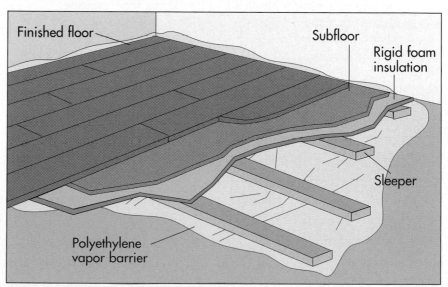

Finished floor — Subfloor — Rigid foam insulation — Sleeper — Polyethylene vapor barrier

Build a subfloor over the concrete.

Lay a polyethylene vapor barrier over the concrete; consult with a carpenter or a building inspector to make sure the barrier will be effective in your conditions.

Install 2×4 sleepers, allowing 14½ inches of space between them. To attach the sleepers, drive masonry nails or screws every 16 inches (see pages 457–458). Lay rigid foam insulation over or between the sleepers. Then screw a ¾-inch plywood subfloor to the sleepers. Install the flooring as shown at on these pages.

Choosing and Buying Carpet

Carpeting offers more colors and textures than anything else you can put underfoot. Compare the fibers to determine the one that best fits your needs and ask your carpet dealer about the density of the fiber or pile. The more fibers per square inch, the longer the carpet life.

Most carpeting sold is tufted or "jute-backed," meaning the yarn is pulled through a woven backing and an additional backing is added for strength and stability.

Carpeting is sold by the square yard in widths of 9, 12, and 15 feet. To compute square yards, divide the square footage by 9. Take a drawing of your room to a carpet salesperson, who can figure the exact yardage requirements.

A good pad prolongs carpet life and insulates against noise and cold. Avoid felt in high-humidity areas and avoid rubber over radiant-heated floors.

Integral-pad carpeting is bonded to a cushioned backing. It's skid-proof, mildew-proof, and ravel-proof, which means you can lay it directly over a concrete basement floor. Installation is easy (see pages 396–397). Indoor/outdoor carpeting also can be laid without a pad.

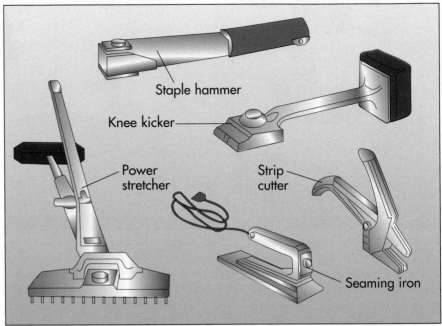

Carpet-laying tools.
No matter what the job, things go more smoothly with the right tools. Carpet laying is no exception. You probably already have some of the basic tools: a utility knife, tape measure, hacksaw, straightedge, chalk line, pliers, and an awl.

With integral-pad carpeting (see page 396), you can get by without all the rented gear. But if you plan to stretch the carpeting, you'll need to rent several other items.

A **strip cutter** makes quick work of cutting tackless strip, which fits around the perimeter of a room. A **staple hammer** fastens padding to wood floors. (Use pad adhesive if the floor is concrete.) Join pieces of carpeting using seam tape and a **seaming iron**. A **knee kicker** and a **power stretcher** help you pull the carpeting taut. In addition a specialty carpet trimmer cuts neatly along walls.

Comparing Carpet Fibers

Fiber	Properties	Relative Cost
Wool	The traditional standard against which other fibers are compared; durable, resilient, and abrasion-resistant; needs mothproofing; fairly easy to clean.	Expensive
Acrylic	Closest to wool of all synthetic fibers; resists abrasion, mildew, insects, and crushing; wide choice of colors; some tendency to pill (form fuzz balls); sheds dirt.	Moderate
Nylon	The strongest synthetic fiber; very durable and resistant to abrasion, mildew, and moths; should be treated for static electricity; hides dirt.	Wide price range
Polyester	Bright, clear colors; cool to the touch; resists mildew and moisture; can be used anywhere; susceptible to oil-based stains; resists soiling	Moderate
Polypropylene olefin	A key fiber in most indoor/outdoor carpeting; extremely durable, moisture-resistant, and nonabsorbent; lower-priced versions tend to crush; the most stain-resistant of all carpets.	Wide price range

INSTALLING A TACKLESS STRIP AND PADDING

Before you start, unroll the carpet and padding in a separate room. Make sure you have the right amount of carpet, and see that it is free of defects.

Prepare the room by removing all the furniture and baseboard shoe moldings. Plane down the high spots in the floor and fill wide cracks or dips with floor-leveling compound. For badly worn floors, install underlayment (see page 399). Then install the tackless strip, carpet pad, and the carpet, using the techniques shown here and on page 394.

A tackless strip creates a framework over which carpeting is stretched and held tight. A standard tackless strip is designed to be installed onto hardwood or softwood; strips for concrete floors are also available.

When abutting a floor covering other than carpeting, nail a metal threshold strip with gripper pins to the floor. Where one carpet section adjoins another, do not use a tackless strip. Later you will seam the pieces together.

Lay the carpet padding within the framework and cut it to size with a utility knife. Make sure the side with the slick membrane faces up. Staple the padding in place, paying special attention to seam lines and edges. If the floor is concrete, roll back one section of padding at a time and spread pad adhesive. Lay the padding back in place.

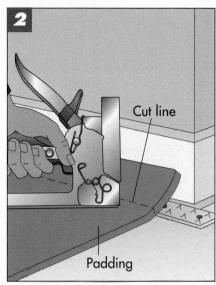

1. Nail a strip to the floor.
Cut a strip to fit and place it ½ inch from the wall, with the pins facing the adjacent wall or opening. The strip has integrated nails; pound them into the floor.

2. Attach the padding.
Staple or nail padding to wood floors; glue it to concrete floors. Do not stretch the padding while you install it. Cut the padding precisely so that it just reaches the strip but does not overlap it.

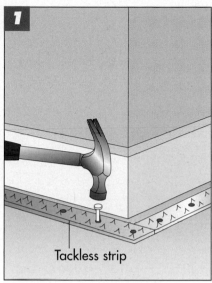

3. Install a threshold.
When abutting a hard surface, such as tile or wood flooring, use a metal threshold. Hammer the lip flat, using a protective board.

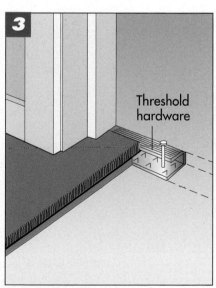

4. Finish the edge.
Another way to finish an edge is to fold the carpeting under itself and tack along the edge. Be sure to stop the padding short if you will use this method.

STRETCHING AND TRIMMING CARPETING

Laying carpeting can be done only with the correct stretching tools; otherwise the carpet will soon develop folds and waves. Rent or buy a knee kicker and a power stretcher (see page 392). A knee kicker is a short tool used near the wall. A power stretcher telescopes out to the length needed. It has teeth at one end and butts against a wall at the other end. To operate, bend it up in the middle, set the teeth, and position the other end against a wall. Then push down in the middle to stretch the carpeting. Rent a power stretcher that's long enough to reach most of the way across the the room.

If the layout requires a carpet seam, position it in a low-traffic or out-of-the-way area. Be sure to run the seam perpendicular to a window or other light source—it will be less visible there.

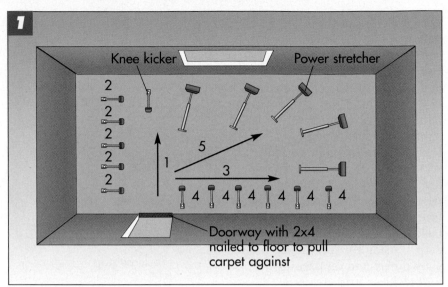

1. Stretch the carpeting.
Use the following sequence:
1. Use a knee kicker to stretch carpeting tight to the wall opposite the doorway.
2. Knee-kick the carpeting tight to the adjacent wall.
3. Power-stretch the carpeting into the adjacent corner.
4. Knee-kick to the adjacent wall.
5. Power-stretch the carpeting diagonally into the opposite corner. After each stretch or kick, push the carpeting down on the tackless strip with the heel of your hand to be sure it grabs.

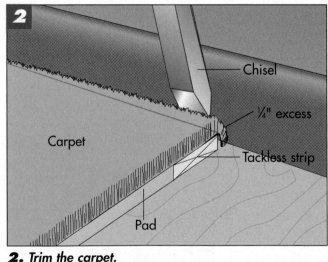

2. Trim the carpet.
Start trimming anywhere and work your way around the edge of the room, using either a utility knife or a carpet trimmer. Leave ¼ inch of excess carpeting as you trim. Use a masonry chisel to tuck this edge between the tackless strip and the baseboard.

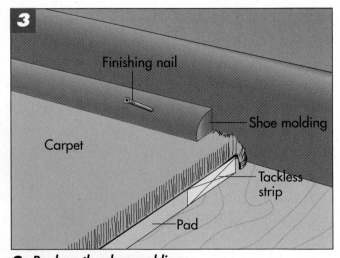

3. Replace the shoe molding.
Finish the job by replacing the shoe moldings. Old molding may look out of place next to new carpeting; if so, replace it with new molding. Nail the molding to the baseboard, not the floor.

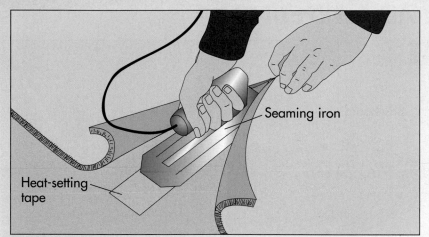

Carpet seaming.
You once needed a heavy-duty needle, some thread, and lots of patience to join two pieces of carpeting. Now most pros bond a special heat-setting tape to the backing, as shown above. Make seams prior to stretching the carpet. Trim the carpet edges straight and butt them carefully.

Fold both edges back and lay the tape along the floor where the seam will fall. Move the heated iron slowly along the tape. As the adhesive melts, press the edges of the carpeting into it with your other hand. Weight down the seam for a few minutes after joining the carpeting.

CARPETING A STAIRWAY

*T*o carpet stairs, you can use a strip left over from carpeting an adjoining room or purchase a runner. If you opt to use a carpeting strip, use tackless stair strips to anchor it. Make sure the pile of the carpet runs down the stairs (that is, it feels smoother when you run your hand in the downstairs direction).

If you decide to use a runner, the best way to secure it is with rods. Stair rods are work to install, but add a decorative touch and are easy to maintain. To install rods, first lay padding in one strip from top to bottom and tack it temporarily at the top. Tack the runner face down to the bottom tread next to the second riser; then stretch the runner under the nosing at the top of the first riser and tack it in place. Then attach the rods as described at far right.

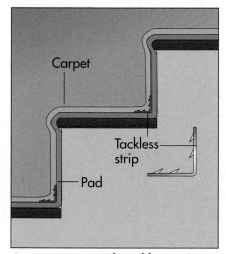

Secure carpet with tackless strips...
You can use special tackless strips to secure carpeting. Lay the pad first, then nail the strips on top of the padding. Cut the carpet several inches wider than needed, and lay it by pressing into the tackless strips as you go. Then trim the sides.

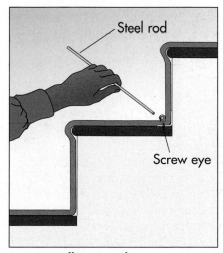

...or install stair rods.
Screw an eye or rod bracket to each side of the tread, ½ inch outside the carpet edge. Slip a rod over the carpeting and through the eye. Pull the carpeting taut. Proceed to the next step. At the top, nail carpet tacks to the end just under the nosing.

LAYING INTEGRAL-PAD CARPETING

Integral-pad (or cushion-backed) carpeting is bonded to its own cushioned backing, thus eliminating the need for a carpet pad. It's especially ideal for applying carpet directly over concrete. Cut-pile, berber, and other styles are available in a good selection of colors.

In small spaces, such as bathrooms and closets, you can cut the carpeting to fit and lay it without carpet tape. Edges have a tendency to curl in time, however, so it's best to anchor big pieces with double-sided tape.

Prepare the room as you would for any other type of carpeting (see page 393). The floor should be structurally sound. Clean the floor well so the tape can adhere.

Buy double-sided carpet tape, which is 2 inches wide. It has a protective paper that covers the top; remove the paper only when you are ready to attach the carpet. If the installation involves seams, buy 5-inch-wide carpet tape and a seam adhesive recommended for your type of carpeting.

YOU'LL NEED...

TIME: 2 to 3 hours for a 12×15-foot room.
SKILLS: Basic carpeting skills.
TOOLS: Tape measure, utility knife, seam roller or kitchen rolling pin, drill and drill bits, hammer, and nail set.

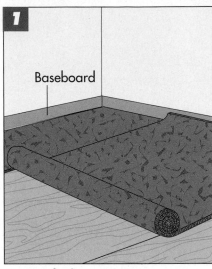

1. Test fit the carpeting.
Cut the carpeting several inches larger than the room and set it in place. Make sure piles fall in the same direction. Allow about 1 inch extra all around the perimeter of the room.

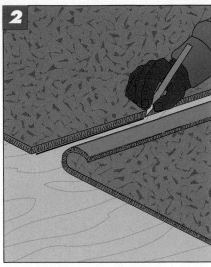

2. Mark for seam locations.
Join any seams by folding back one piece and drawing a line on the floor along the edge of the other piece.

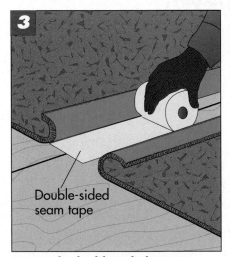

3. Apply double-sided tape.
Center double-sided tape on the line and stick it to the floor. Check to see that the seam runs through the middle of the tape, then peel off the protective paper on top.

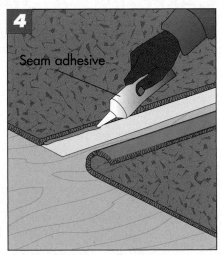

4. Apply seam adhesive.
Press one piece of carpeting into place, taking care not to create folds. Apply seam adhesive along its edge to cement the pieces together.

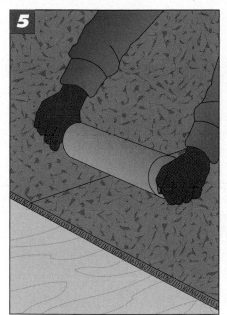

5. Roll a seam.

Use a rolling pin or seam roller to press the carpeting firmly against the tape. Brushing the pile will cause the seam to virtually disappear.

6. Make a tape border.

Without sliding the carpeting out of position, fold it back from two of the walls and apply a tape border. Smooth the tape before removing the paper.

7. Smooth the edges.

Roll the carpeting back so it retains its original position, then drop—don't slide—it onto the tape. Smooth the edges with your hands so the tape adhesive gets a good grip.

EXPERTS' INSIGHT

ADHESIVE INSTALLATION

Integral-pad carpeting can also be installed using a latex adhesive. This holds the carpet more firmly in place, thus reducing wear and helping the carpet last longer. (Of course adhered carpeting is much more difficult to remove.) To install, cut the carpet to fit and set it in place. Fold back half the carpet, and use a notched trowel to spread adhesive onto the floor. Unfold the carpet and press into place. Repeat for the other half of the floor.

8. Trim off excess.

Trim off excess carpeting with a utility knife or a carpet knife. Tamp the edges down by rubbing the carpet with the heel of your hand. The pile will hide minor irregularities.

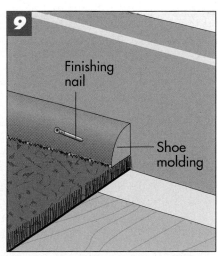

Finishing nail

Shoe molding

9. Finish with base shoe molding.

Finish by installing or replacing the base shoe molding. Nail molding to the baseboard, not the floor. Drill pilot holes and drive in finishing nails. Set the heads of the finishing nails with a nail set.

CHOOSING AND BUYING RESILIENT FLOORING

Resilient flooring—softer underfoot than any other flooring except carpeting—is available in the form of tiles or sheet goods.

Resilient tiles have been a popular do-it-yourself item since World War II, although they have changed considerably in size (from 9 to 12 inches square), appearance (from dull, streaked greens and beiges to vivid colors and patterns), and composition (from asphalt and asbestos to varying blends of vinyl).

Sheet goods have been around awhile also. Because they come in rolls up to 12 feet wide, installing them is more difficult. Installation kits are available, but be aware that a cutting mistake can ruin an entire roll, not just a single tile. (See pages 402–403 for sheet goods installation.)

Choosing the right resilient flooring depends to some extent on the type of use your new floor will get (see chart below).

Cushioned sheet flooring, usually with a pattern printed on the surface, is soft underfoot, has a minimum of dirt-catching seams, and does a decent job of sound-proofing. Some surface-printed tiles are similarly cushioned. "Commercial" tiles are less expensive, easier to install, and much more resistant to dents from items, such as chair legs. Also you should consider whether you want a smooth or a textured surface.

Before you buy, be sure you are clear about the installation directions. Most resilient flooring can be installed on any sound subsurface. Install over existing resilient flooring only if it is firmly stuck at all points.

Beware: Resilient flooring does not cover up imperfections in the subsurface; this is especially true of surface-printed tiles and sheets. If the existing floor cannot be sanded smooth, install subflooring and underlayment above it (see page 399).

Because most of today's tiles are 1-foot square, determining how many you will need requires only simple computations. Estimating the amount of sheet flooring needed is trickier, especially if there's a pattern involved and a seam is needed. It's best to make an accurate plan of the room on graph paper and then take it to a flooring dealer.

CAUTION!
Asbestos Tile
If you need to remove tiles to lay a new floor, be aware that many older tiles contain asbestos. Some states require a licensed asbestos remover to take them out. Ask your flooring dealer how to test old tiles for asbestos and whether you need to hire a licensed firm to remove them.

COMPARING RESILIENT FLOORINGS

Material	Properties	Relative Cost
Linoleum	True linoleum is making a comeback. This is a natural product with color that runs through its thickness. It hides scratches well.	Moderate
Cushioned sheet vinyl	Several grades are available—from moderately durable to very durable. Durability ranges from that of vinyl asbestos tile to about one-half as durable. Resistant to abrasion and discoloration. Vulnerable to burns. Usually contains a vinyl foam layer.	Wide price range
Commercial vinyl or rubber tile	Often used for grocery stores and other commercial spaces, these tiles have random flecks or dots of color that run through the body of the tile. Tiles of different colors can be mixed to form patterns and borders. Rubber tile is a little more expensive, with a similar appearance and even greater durability.	Inexpensive
Surface-printed vinyl tile	Basically the same composition and characteristics as sheet vinyl, but tiles are easier to install.	Wide price range

INSTALLING UNDERLAYMENT

The most common underlayment material is ¼ inch thick and is available in 4×4 sheets. A series of + marks stamped on the surface indicates where to drive nails or screws. Underlayment only smooths a floor. If the floor needs strengthening, see pages 370–371.

To secure the underlayment, you will need lots of ringshank flooring nails or screws. Drive one in every 4 inches around the perimeter and every 8 inches across the sheets into joists. Stagger the sheet joints.

YOU'LL NEED...

TIME: 2 to 3 hours for a simple 12×15-foot room.
SKILLS: Basic carpentry skills.
TOOLS: Tape measure, hammer, straightedge, circular saw, and straight trowel.

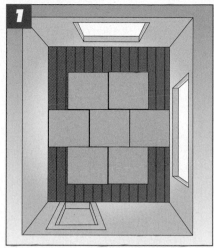

1. Create an underlayment layout.
Begin near the center of the room and arrange 4×4 panels so that four corners never meet at a point. As much as possible, avoid having to install a narrow strip at the perimeter.

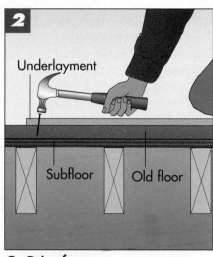

2. Drive fasteners.
Drive nails or ringshank flooring nails through the subfloor. If the subfloor is only a single sheet of plywood, use screws rather than nails to anchor the underlayment surface securely.

3. Mark a sheet for cutting.
Along the edges of the room, slide a sheet of material against the wall, overlapping and squaring it with the previously nailed panel. With a scrap of underlayment or a straightedge as a guide, draw a line along the length of the edge piece. Cut the sheet along the line.

4. Secure the edge pieces.
Fasten the edge pieces into place. Don't worry if the fit isn't exact along the wall. The base shoe will cover a gap of at least ½ inch.

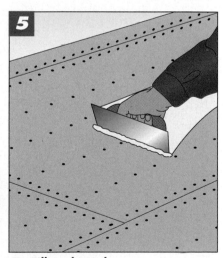

5. Fill and sand.
See that all fastener heads are dimpled slightly below the surface. Using a straight trowel, fill all fastener dimples and joints with flooring patch. Allow the patch to dry, then sand the floor smooth.

LAYING RESILIENT TILE

Because thin surface-printed tiles show even the tiniest imperfections in the subsurface, it is necessary to prepare a floor surface that is very smooth. Thicker surface-printed tiles and commercial tiles can bridge small gaps like fastener dimples, but will show any larger flaws.

Plan the layout first by making a scale drawing of the room, and then by setting out tiles in a dry run. Aim to eliminate any slivers at the perimeter, unless the area will be covered up by furniture.

Self-stick tiles can be installed without adhesive, but they may start to peel after a year or two. Spread adhesive on the floor to ensure a solid installation.

YOU'LL NEED...

TIME: 4 hours for a 12×15-foot room.
SKILLS: Basic skills.
TOOLS: Tape measure, framing square, chalk line, utility knife, and notched trowel.

TOOLS TO USE

CUTTING TOOLS

Cutting resilient tile is not difficult, but it can be time-consuming. To pick up the pace, have a collection of tools ready at hand. Set the tile to be cut on a small sheet of plywood, to prevent damage to the floor. For a square, use a full-sized tile marked with an **X** so you will be sure not to lay it on the floor. Replace knife blades as soon as they start to become dull. If you have plenty of cutting to do, rent a vinyl tile cutter, which makes a straight cut in a couple of seconds.

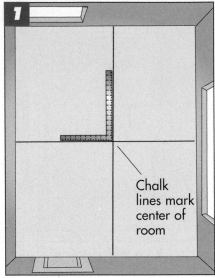

1. Snap layout lines.
Snap chalk lines between the midpoints of the walls. Adjust the lines, if necessary, so that the lines make a right angle.

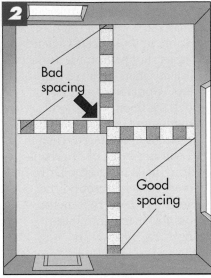

2. Dry-lay rows of tiles.
Dry-lay tiles in an **L**-shape, starting from the center. Check the border tiles. If necessary shift the **L** half a tile over, and snap new chalk lines.

3. Apply mastic.
Use a small notched trowel or a paint roller to spread adhesive over as much of the floor as possible, as long as you can reach the layout lines without walking on adhesive. Allow the adhesive to dry until it is tacky.

4. Lay the tiles.
Apply tiles starting with the **L** corner and building a pyramid. Be certain to keep the tiles square with chalk lines. Don't slide tiles into position: Butt edges against adjacent tiles, fold down into place, and press firmly.

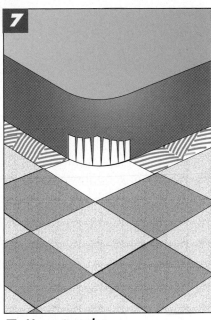

5. Mark for a straight cut.
At the baseboard, tiles need not be cut precisely because the base shoe will cover about ½ inch. To mark for a straight cut, lay a tile on top of the last full one in the row. Put another against the wall, and mark the overlap.

6. Mark for a corner cut.
Corners are not difficult to figure. Mark from one of the walls, just as you would for a border tile. Shift the tiles to the other wall (but don't turn them), and mark again. Mark an **X** on the section to be cut out.

7. Use a template.
For odd shapes, make a cardboard template first; cut with scissors, and transfer the pattern to the tile.

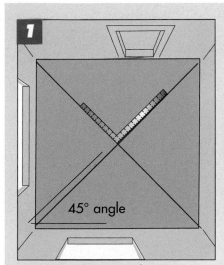

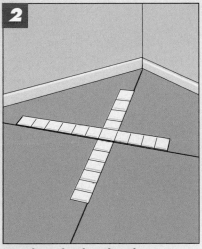

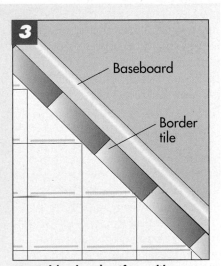

1. To lay a diagonal pattern, begin with chalk lines.
For a diagonal pattern, locate the center of the room and snap chalk lines at 45-degree angles to the wall.

2. Then dry-lay the tiles.
Dry-lay tiles along the lines and adjust for good border spacing. At the walls, you'll need to cut triangles. Cut a tile in half at a 45-degree angle and use it as a guide for the cuts.

3. Add a border if you like.
For an interesting look, border the diagonal field with a row of straight-laid tiles. Install the border first, then cut the diagonals carefully to butt against the border.

LAYING SHEET FLOORING

*E*ven professional carpenters often shy away from installing sheet flooring, for one simple reason: If you make a single cutting mistake, you could blow the whole job and have to buy and install a new piece. Your chances of success are good, however, if you purchase a sheet that comes with a cardboard template and take the time to double-check all your measurements.

It's important to choose a high-quality sheet that is thick and durable. An inexpensive, thin sheet can easily rip while you unroll it.

If possible buy a sheet wide enough so you need not make seams. It is possible to butt two pieces together in the middle of the floor (see page 403). The seam will not be as durable as a continuous sheet, however.

Installing genuine linoleum (rather than vinyl) is a different process. The sheets tend to be narrower, but seams are not much of a problem because this product virtually welds itself together. For the same reason, cutting mistakes are also much less of a problem.

YOU'LL NEED...

TIME: 4 or 5 hours to install in a 12×14-foot room.
SKILLS: Intermediate skills.
TOOLS: Framing square, flooring knife or utility knife, chalk line, notched trowel, long straightedge, pry bar, hammer, nail set, handsaw, compass, and rented flooring roller.

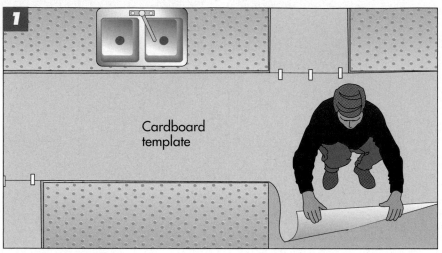

Cardboard template

1. Cut a template.
Remove the base shoe and any other obstructions. Install underlayment (see page 399). Undercut the casings so the sheet can fit beneath them (see page 387).

Find an area larger than the room you will be flooring. If necessary work outdoors. Unroll the vinyl sheet completely and remove the cardboard template that is rolled up inside. Position the cardboard in the room to be floored and cut it to the exact dimensions of the floor. You will probably need to tape cardboard pieces onto the template where the cutting gets difficult. Double-check that the template is the exact shape needed.

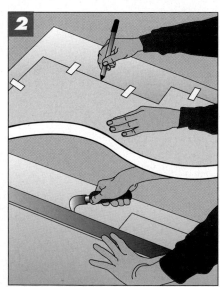

2. Cut the sheet.
Lay the template on top of the vinyl sheet. Tape it down in many places to prevent it from slipping while you are working. Use a flooring knife or utility knife to cut the sheet around the template. Use a straightedge to make long, straight cuts.

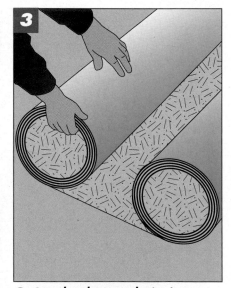

3. Lay the sheet and trim it.
Working with a helper, roll the sheet up from both ends toward the middle, like a scroll. Set the sheet in the middle of the room and unroll it carefully. Avoid creasing the sheet while unrolling or it may rip. Check that the sheet lies flat at all points and make any necessary trim cuts.

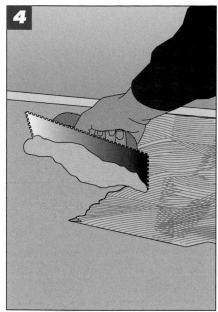

4. Apply mastic.
Weight half the sheet so it cannot move; roll up the other half. Sweep the floor absolutely clean of debris. Following the manufacturer's instructions, spread mastic using a notched trowel.

5. Lay the sheet.
Unroll the sheet onto the mastic. Once you are sure the alignment is correct, roll up the other half of the sheet, apply mastic, and unroll the second half.

6. Roll out bubbles.
Use a rented flooring roller to remove any bubbles under the sheet. Force a bubble out by moving it to the closest edge.

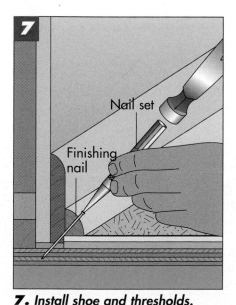

Nail set

Finishing nail

7. Install shoe and thresholds.
Install a new base shoe or reinstall the old shoe; drive nails into the baseboard, not into the flooring. Cover all exposed edges with a threshold.

Tape sheets together

1. To make a seam, cut through two sheets.
Lay both sheets in mastic, with one sheet overlapping the other according to the manufacturer's instructions. Tape both of the sheets together so they won't slip out of place. Use a straightedge and a sharp utility knife to cut through both sheets.

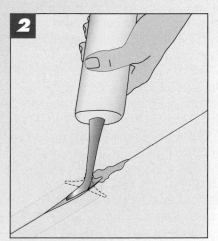

2. Seal the seam.
Lift up the sheet that was on top, and pull out the cutoff strip underneath. Gently smooth the two pieces together and wipe away any squeezed-out mastic. Insert a seam sealer between the sheets and squeeze out glue as you run it along the seam. Wipe away excess sealer and run a roller on the seam.

CHOOSING CERAMIC FLOOR TILE

Ceramic tile is rock-hard, but most types will crack if not installed properly. The subsurface must be firm and inflexible.

A home center typically carries a modest assortment of ceramic and stone tiles. Visit several tile stores to find a much wider selection.

Be sure to buy floor tile; most wall tiles are soft and will crack, even if set in a very firm substrate.

High-gloss glazed tiles have a pleasing glow and are easy to keep clean, but are slippery when wet. Some glazes have bumpy surfaces to make them less hazardous. If you install small tiles, the grout lines will add traction.

Mosaic tile comes in sheets composed of many small tiles held together by a mesh or paper backing. Mosaics may be made of any of the materials in the chart at right. Mosaic sheets are only slightly more difficult to install than standard tiles.

In addition to standard field tiles, you may choose to sprinkle the floor with colorful accent tiles. Field tiles may need to be cut to make room for the accent tiles, or the tiles may come already cut in shapes designed to accommodate the accents.

For a hefty price, you can purchase preassembled decorative groupings. Placed in a prominent location, even a small section of decorative tile can have a big visual impact.

Choose grout along with the tile; a tile store has many colors to choose from. In most cases, floor tile grout should blend with the tile. For a geometric effect, however, you may choose grout of a sharply contrasting color.

COMPARING CERAMIC TILE

Tile	Description	Cutting
Glazed ceramic	Wide selection of colors, glazes, surfaces, and shapes. Durability varies according to type.	Snap cutter or wet saw
Porcelain	Extremely durable. Can mimic the look of glazed ceramic, rough stone, or polished stone.	Wet saw only
Polished stone	Marble is soft and easily scratched; granite is extremely hard. Other types, such as travertine or onyx, are in between.	Wet saw only
Tumbled or honed marble or granite	Pleasingly informal appearance, but very soft and porous; it must be sealed to make it practical.	Wet saw only
Terra cotta	Soft, so it needs to be sealed. Comes in earth tones. Some types, like Mexican saltillos, are handmade and irregular in shape.	Wet saw only
Quarry	Hard and durable, but with a matte rather than glazed surface, so it needs sealing.	Snap cutter or wet saw
Slate	Gray and reddish tones, with a bumpy surface because it is split rather than cut. Some slate is polished, while other slate is rough. Moderately hard.	Wet saw only
Cement-body	Actually small slabs of concrete, covered with vivid colors. Some types are not very durable.	Wet saw only
Glass	Stunningly beautiful but expensive and easily scratched, so it is usually only used for accents.	Not meant to be cut
Metal	Can be brass, copper, steel, or even iron. Used as accents.	Not meant to be cut

DOORS AND WINDOWS

UNDERSTANDING WINDOWS

*I*n addition to providing views of the outside world, windows control the flow of air throughout the interior spaces of your home. Some windows are not intended to be opened, but most windows include one or more movable sashes. Keeping them—and their related coverings—in good working order is the focus of the next 14 pages.

To learn how to replace windowpanes, windowsills, and storm/screen windows, see pages 434–439. Instructions for framing and installing a new window are on pages 445–447.

There is more to a window than meets the eye, especially with the older double-hung type shown at right. Concealed behind the side jambs of the frame are heavy sash weights. Connected with a rope-and-pulley system, the weights counterbalance the sashes—making them easier to open—and hold them in any vertical position you wish.

A series of stops fitted to the jambs provides channels in which the sashes slide. Check the top view (below right) and note that although the outside blind stop is more or less permanently affixed, the parting stop and inside stop can be pried loose if you want to remove the sashes.

In newer double-hung windows the weight-and-pulley mechanisms are replaced with a pair of spring lift devices (see page 409).

With both types of windows, the lower sash comes to rest behind a flat stool. Its outside counterpart, the sill, slopes so that water can run off. Trim—called *casing* at the sides and top and an *apron* below—covers gaps between the jambs and the wall material.

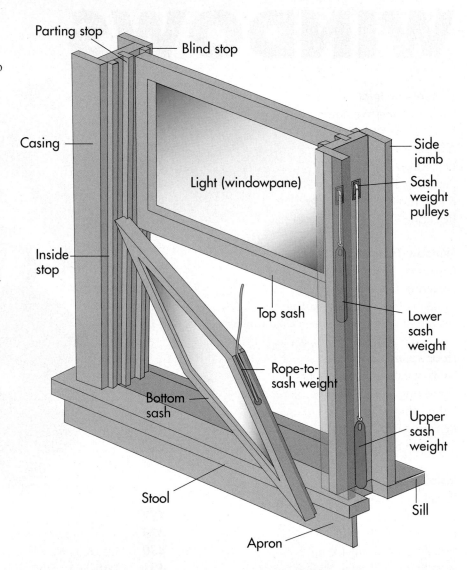

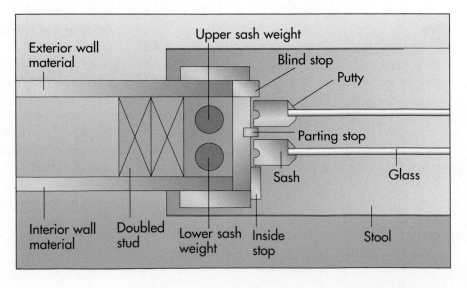

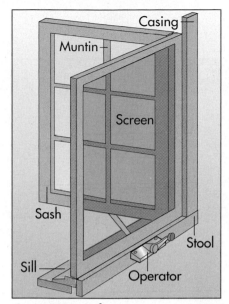

Casement window

Casement windows open and close like a door. In the version shown, muntins separate the panes. However with newer double-glazed casements the muntins—often referred to as grills—snap to the inside of the window to facilitate cleaning or are absent altogether.

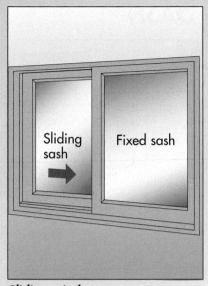

Sliding window

As with double-hung sashes, sliding sashes (also called gliding sashes) open up only 50 percent of the total window area for ventilation. Some sliding windows have one fixed and one sliding sash, as shown. With others, both sashes slide along tracks. Sliding windows can be

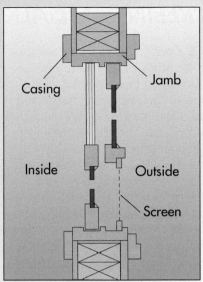

made with wood, metal, or vinyl. In most models, the movable sash slides in the bottom track; in some, it glides on an upper track. An older window's track may be a simple groove made of wood. Newer windows have metal or vinyl tracks, and the sash may have rollers for smooth operation.

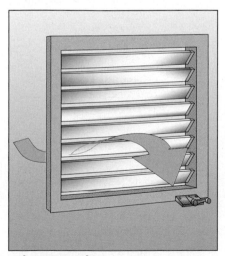

Jalousie window

Turning the crank of a jalousie window pivots a series of glass slats. The frames consist of short metal channels at both ends of the slats. The glass-to-glass joints tend to leak air, so jalousies usually are used only in breezeways, porches, and other unheated zones.

Awning window

An awning window works in the same fashion as a casement window, but the sash tilts outward from the bottom. Some awnings slide downward as they tilt, so that you can open them to a nearly horizontal position

for maximum cooling airflow.

An awning window opens with a side-mounted or two-armed mechanism, operated by a crank, sometimes called a roto-handle. Hinges usually can be disengaged so you can easily remove the sash.

Freeing a Balky Sash

When a double-hung window binds or refuses to open, don't try to force it. Take a look around the sash, both inside and out. Chances are you will find that paint has sealed the sash shut or that a stop molding has warped. The steps shown here will enable you to gently pry and free the sash, preventing damage. If the top sash is painted shut, you may choose to leave it that way, unless you need to move it for cleaning.

You'll Need...

Time: 30 minutes or more, depending on the cause.
Skills: Basic skills.
Tools: Sash knife or utility knife, flat pry bar, and hammer.

1. Break the paint seal.
To break a paint seal, use a sash knife, which is specially designed for this purpose. Or run a sharp utility knife several times between the sash and stop. Be sure to cut through the paint at every point.

2. Pry the window open.
Pry from the outside edges with a pry bar and a protective block of wood. Take your time, using gentle to moderate pressure at several points. Alternating sides, work inward from the edges until the sash pops free.

3. Spread the stops.
If a sash is binding between its stops, try separating the stops slightly by tapping along their length with a hammer and wooden block that fits tightly between the stops. If the binding is severe, you may need to pry the stop off and nail it in a new position.

4. Lubricate the sash.
Once you get the window moving, scrape or chisel any built-up paint off the edges of the sash or between the stops. Lightly sand its jambs; then lubricate with a candle or with paraffin, paste wax, or bar soap.

Experts' Insight

Other Double-Hung Mechanisms

The spring lift shown on page 409 and the weight-and-pulley system shown on pages 410–411 are the most common mechanisms for double-hung windows. Another type uses a tension spring—a flat metal strap that attaches to a spring-loaded drum unit in the sash. Finding replacement drum units may be difficult. A friction sash is made of vinyl or aluminum; it grabs the sash tightly enough that it does not slide down when raised.

ADJUSTING A SPRING LIFT

Tube-type lifting devices house a spring-driven twist rod that helps lift the sash. To improve sash movement, you can adjust the spring devices as shown on this page. But before tampering with these, check to be sure the window has not been painted shut. If it has, follow the procedures on page 408. If the device doesn't seem to work at all, it is probably broken, and you'll need to replace it (see below).

YOU'LL NEED...
TIME: About 30 minutes per window.
SKILLS: No special skills needed.
TOOLS: Screwdriver or drill.

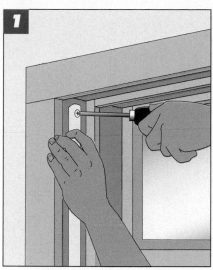

1. Unscrew the lift.
Grip the tube before you remove the screw, holding it in place, or the spring will unwind in a hurry. If the window sails up too easily, hold the screw and let the spring turn a couple of revolutions.

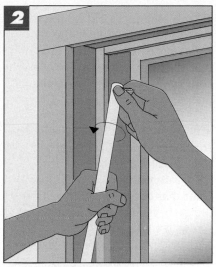

2. Rotate the lift.
If the window is hard to raise, tighten the spring by turning it clockwise. You may need to adjust the lifts on both sides.

REPLACING A SPRING LIFT

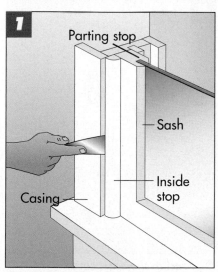

1. Remove the stop.
Using a utility knife, score the paint between the inside stop and the casing. Pry with a putty knife to remove the inside stop on one side of the sash. This should make enough room to remove the sash.

2. Pull out the sash.
Remove the screw that secures the tube, let the spring unwind, and then pull out the sash.

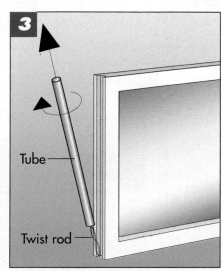

3. Replace the lift rod.
Remove and replace the twist rod/tube unit. Reinstall the sash and adjust the tube (see above).

REPLACING A SASH CORD

Each sash in an old double-hung window is connected to two weights that run through channels in each side of the window. A sash cord or chain is secured to the sash and runs through a pulley near the top of the jamb. Sometimes a window binds because the cord has come out of its groove in the side of the sash; if so, force it back into position. If a cord or chain has become detached from the sash, reattach it with a short screw. If the cord is broken, replace it. A cord will not last as long as a sash chain, which also looks better.

YOU'LL NEED...

TIME: 1 to 2 hours.
SKILLS: Basic carpentry skills.
TOOLS: Putty knife, utility knife, screwdriver or drill, and hammer.

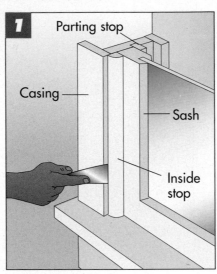

1. Pry out the stop.
Usually you need to remove only one inside stop. Cut through the paint using a utility knife. Using a putty knife, pry carefully at several points to loosen the stop, and then remove the stop with a flat pry bar.

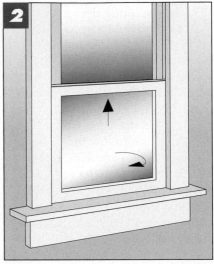

2. Lift out the sash.
Lift the sash and swing it clear from the frame. One or both cords may still be connected. Take care that a cord does not come loose and suddenly fly upward.

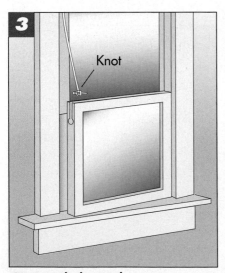

3. Detach the cord.
Hang on to the cord and pull it out of the sash; you may need to pry out a nail or unscrew a screw. **NOTE:** *Be careful never to let go of the cord. Pull it out and slip a nail through the knot so that the cord cannot slip through the pulley.*

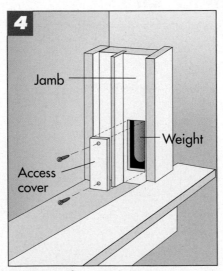

4. Open the access cover.
There will probably be an access cover at the base of the jamb; unscrew the fasteners that hold the cover in place. Gently pry it out to reveal the weights. If there is no access cover, you may have to pry off the jamb.

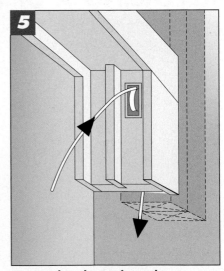

5. Feed in the sash cord.
Untie or cut the cord off of each weight and pull the weight out. Cut new cords or chains longer than they need to be. Feeding new sash cords or chains over pulleys calls for patience. Replace the cords or chains on both sides.

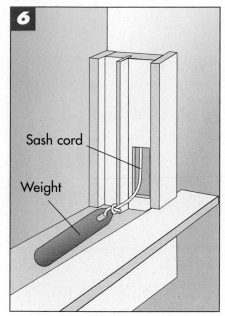

6. Attach the weight.

Once the new cord or chain is visible through the access hole, tie a knot in the other end so that it cannot slip through the pulley. Tie the cord or chain to the weight and tug to make sure the knot is secure. Slip the weight back in place.

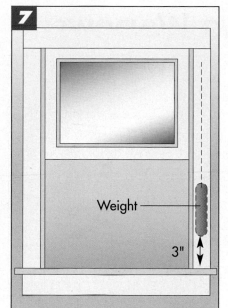

7. Check the weight's position.

Weights should hang 3 inches above the channel bottoms when the lower sash is raised fully. Once you have determined the correct length, knot the other end of the cord or chain and fit it into the groove. Secure the cord or chain with a short screw—don't drive the screw into the windowpane.

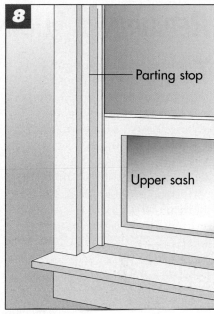

8. Remove the upper sash.

To replace the cords on an upper sash, you have to remove the lower one, then one of the parting stops. Use the same techniques as for the lower sash.

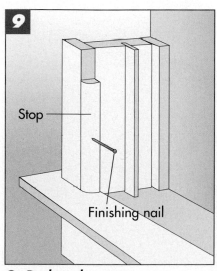

9. Replace the stop.

When you replace stops, partially drive in longer nails, or drive in nails at different points. Raise and lower the sash to check the stop positioning; it should be fairly tight, yet allow for smooth operation.

EXPERTS' INSIGHT

REHABBING AN OLD DOUBLE-HUNG WINDOW?

An old window will probably never insulate as well as a newer window. The cavity that houses the weights (see page 410) cannot be filled with insulation, and the panes are single-glazed. So installing new windows may save money in the long run.

However if you have the time and energy, you can plug most of the leaks and make the window a smooth operator. Remove the sashes and sand their edges smooth. Repair the glazing and paint the glazing so that it is sealed with the glass (see pages 434–435). Caulk around all the casing and apron edges, both inside and outside.

If you install a friction sash channel, you can remove the pulleys and fill in the cavity with insulation. Adding combination storm/screen windows will add a great deal to the insulating ability of a window.

REPAIRING SLIDING WINDOWS

Tracks for sliding (or gliding) windows are notorious collectors of dust and grit, which make for rough opening and closing. Keep tracks clean with regular vacuuming and scrub them when grime starts to build up. Scrape any paint away. To improve performance, spray with a silicone lubricant. If a slider jams, binds, or jumps loose, something may be lodged in the track or the track may be bent. If all seems clear, lift out the sash and check its grooved edges. Clean and lubricate these, too, if needed.

YOU'LL NEED...

TIME: About 30 minutes per window.
SKILLS: Basic skills.
TOOLS: Hammer, screwdriver, and large pliers.

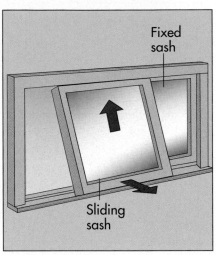

Remove a sash.
To remove a sliding sash, partially open the window, then lift it up and pull its lower edge toward you. The second sash may be fixed in place, or you may need to remove some hold-down hardware before it can be slid over and removed.

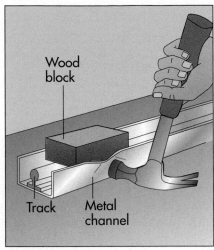

Straighten a track.
To straighten a bent track, cut a wood block to fit snugly in the channel and carefully tap the track against it. Or place a piece of metal on either side of the track and squeeze with a large pair of pliers.

EXPERTS' INSIGHT

HARDWARE REPAIRS FOR SLIDING WINDOWS

■ If a latch does not close readily, remove it and clean it with a brush and vacuum, then spray with silicone lubricant. Also check the strike, where the latch attaches, and clean away any obstructions. If the latch is broken, replace it.

■ To replace a roller or track, look for the manufacturer's name on the window's frame or the sash, and contact them by phone or on the web. A local hardware store may stock hardware for a window that's common in your area.

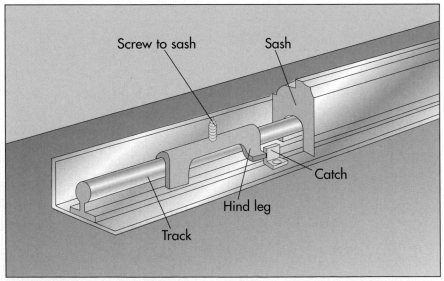

Adjust dogs.
"Catch-and-dog" window latches can get bent. Adjust them so that the dog's "hind leg" hits against the catch. Bigger windows roll on sets of nylon wheels called sheaves, which are self-lubricating and rarely need attention. If a sheave is mangled, remove the assembly and replace it.

FIXING AWNING WINDOWS

Awning windows are repaired much like casements (pages 414–415). If an arm is bent, place a piece of metal on either side and squeeze with a large pair of pliers. If you cannot straighten an arm, you may need to replace it.

Keep operators moving freely. A stiff arm assembly could pull screws loose or even force apart the sash joints. Clean off rust with steel wool and lubricate with graphite or paraffin wax; never use oil because it attracts dust.

YOU'LL NEED...

TIME: About 30 minutes per window.
SKILLS: Basic skills.
TOOLS: Hammer and screwdriver.

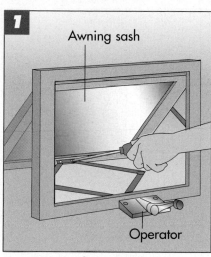

1 Awning sash

Operator

1. Unscrew the arm.
To remove an awning sash, open it as far as you can. Disconnect the operator's side or scissors arm, typically attached with two screws.

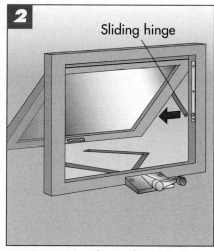

2 Sliding hinge

2. Disengage the sash.
Tilt the sash to a horizontal position. Pry the sliding hinges to the side to disengage the sash. To completely remove a sash, tap out the pins of the upper hinges or unscrew the hinges from the jamb or from the sash.

REPAIRING JALOUSIE WINDOWS

Jalousie window mechanisms depend on a series of gears and levers that may be concealed in the jambs. Keep a jalousie operating smoothly by lubricating all the parts regularly with graphite or silicone—never oil, which will attract dust.

Because they have so many moving parts, jalousies are relatively difficult to repair. Often you must dismantle the entire window to get at the vertical arms. If your unit jams, try freeing it with graphite or another non-oil lubricant.

YOU'LL NEED...

TIME: 30 minutes per window.
SKILLS: Basic skills.
TOOLS: Hammer and screwdriver.

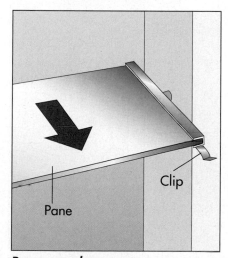

Clip

Pane

Remove a slat.
Simple tab-like clips hold jalousie slats in place. To remove one, just bend open the tab, slide the clip back slightly, and slide out the pane. Replace the slat, then bend each clip holder back to its original shape.

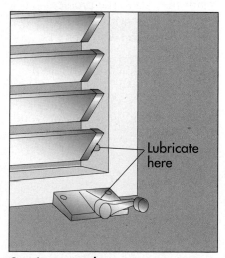

Lubricate here

Service a crank.
If a crank mechanism is stuck or is hard to operate, don't force it. Lubricate the crank shaft and pivot points, and then work the handle back and forth slowly. If the crank turns without opening the slats, purchase and install a replacement crank.

REPAIRING CASEMENT WINDOWS

Accumulations of paint, grease, or dirt cause most casement window difficulties. If your casement is malfunctioning, check all sash and frame edges. A few minutes with a wire brush or scraper may remove the debris that is causing the rub.

Examine the unit's mechanical components. Lubricant may be all you need. Use automobile grease or oil for parts that are encased in a housing (such as the crank operator). Where parts will be exposed to the elements and dust, use graphite, paste wax, or silicone lubricant to avoid attracting dust.

If an arm is bent, remove it and set it on a hard, flat surface. Place a piece of metal on top, and tap with a hammer to straighten the arm. Or use a large pair of pliers.

If a sash binds, partially close it and look for places where the window rubs against the sash. On a metal unit, scraping away excess paint may solve the problem.

Wood casements sometimes suffer the same problems that bedevil doors. Solve these problems by adapting the door-fitting and planing techniques illustrated on pages 420–421. Remove about ¹⁄₁₆ inch extra wood, then apply primer and paint.

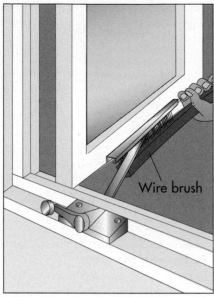

Clean the arm mechanism.
If the sash is difficult to close, try cleaning the sliding arm mechanism with a wire brush. Lubricate with graphite or silicone.

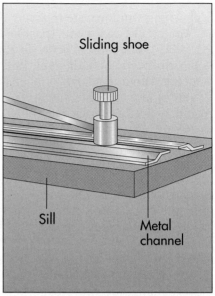

Service the sliding mechanism.
Sill-mounted sliding shoes trap dirt. Unscrew the channel, clean it and the sill, and then lubricate with paste wax.

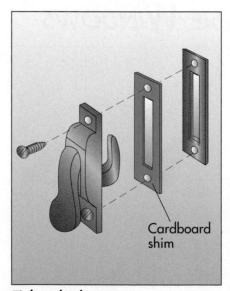

Tighten latch screws.
Tighten any loose latch screws. If a screw won't tighten, tap slivers of wood into the screw holes and drive the screws again. If a handle won't pull its sash snug, shim under it or add weather stripping.

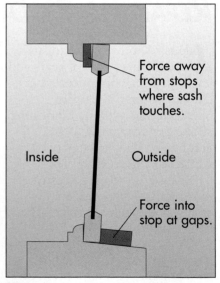

Unwarp.
If a wood sash has warped, counter-warp it with wood strips. Temporarily screw or nail the pieces so they warp the window in the opposite direction. Leave the strips in place for a couple of weeks.

YOU'LL NEED...
TIME: 20 to 30 minutes per window.
SKILLS: Basic skills.
TOOLS: Hammer, screwdriver, wire brush or scraper, pliers, lubricant, and perhaps a plane.

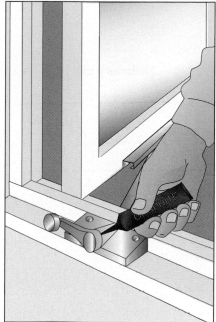

Lubricate a crank.
To keep cranks turning freely, apply graphite or a light oil. With some cranks you may need to take off the handle first.

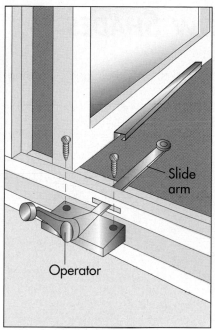

Dismantle an operator.
To dismantle an operator, disconnect the slide arm from the sash, then unscrew it from the frame.

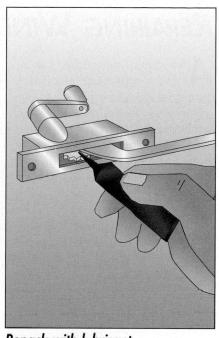

Repack with lubricant.
If the gears are encrusted with old grease, soak the operator mechanism in a solvent, then repack it with a multipurpose lubricant or automobile grease.

INSULATION ABILITY OF WINDOW TREATMENTS

Treatment	Description	Summer Reflective Efficiency	Winter Insulating Efficiency
Venetian blinds	Multiple parallel slats	Effective when closed	Virtually none
Draperies	Tightly woven white fabric	Effective when closed	Fairly effective if tight-fitting
Shades	White shade cloth	Effective when closed	Virtually none
Double-glazing	Insulating glass or single-glazing plus storm window	Not very effective	Cuts heat loss by 50%
Triple- and Low-E glazing	Insulating glass plus storm or coated glass	Low-E is fairly reflective	Cuts heat loss by 70%
Thermal shades	Quilted, fiber-filled material sealed tightly to a window frame	Very effective	Cuts heat loss by 80%

REPAIRING WINDOW SHADES

A window shade (right) has a hollow roller with a coiled spring inside. Drawing down the shade puts tension on the spring; a ratchet and flat pin at one end hold this tension until you release it. A stationary pin at the other end turns freely in its bracket.

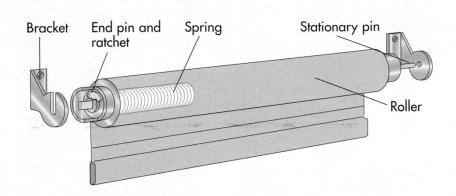

Bracket   End pin and ratchet   Spring   Stationary pin

Roller

YOU'LL NEED...

TIME: 20 to 30 minutes per window.
SKILLS: Basic skills.
TOOLS: Framing square, scissors or utility knife, staple gun, and saw.

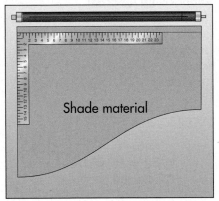

Shade material

Measure shade material.
If you take down an old shade and unroll it, you will see that its shade material has been stapled to the roller. Take off the old material. Then square off the edge of the new material. Carefully align this edge with the guideline on the roller before you drive in the new staples.

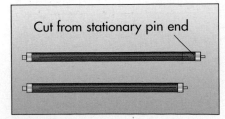

Cut from stationary pin end

Cut roller.
Remove the material, saw the roller to length with a fine-toothed saw, reinsert the stationary pin, cut the material to size, and replace it.

TROUBLESHOOTING WINDOW SHADES

Problem	Cause	Solution
Goes up with a bang	Too much tension on the spring	Take down the shade, unroll a few inches, and replace it in its bracket
Goes up too slowly	Not enough tension on the spring	Increase tension by rerolling
Will not catch	Bent or worn brackets; ratchet not holding	Align brackets; if ratchet is bad, replace roller
Binds	Not enough clearance from brackets	Bend brackets apart or shorten stationary pin
Falls	Excess clearance at brackets; broken spring	Relocate brackets; if spring is shot, replace roller

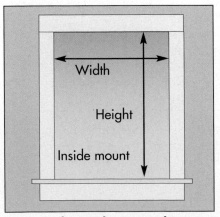

Width

Height

Inside mount

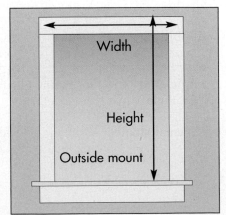

Width

Height

Outside mount

Measure for inside or outside mount.
For inside mounting, measure from jamb to jamb and subtract ⅛ inch for clearance. Measure for length and add 1½ inches. For outside mounting, the width should be at least 1½ inches larger than the opening. The length should be 1½ inches longer than the span from the top of the upper trim to the sill.

REPAIRING VENETIAN BLINDS

Inside the head box of a venetian blind, a tilt tube supports a pair of tape ladders on which the blind's slats rest. To open or close the slats, pull one end of a tilt cord wrapped around the pulley of a worm gear. This gear rotates the tube and changes the pitch of the slats. A lift cord, strung over a series of pulleys and down through the slats to the base piece, raises and lowers the entire slat assembly.

When the tilting mechanism balks, look for cord threads or dirt in the worm gear. If the blind refuses to go up or down, the lift cord has either broken, frayed, or jammed. If so replace both cords and check the tape ladders as well.

YOU'LL NEED...

TIME: 2 hours to replace both cords and ladders.
SKILLS: Basic skills.
TOOLS: Screwdriver, utility knife, and staple gun.

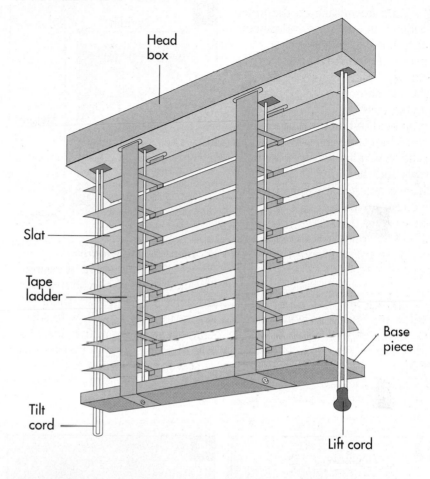

Head box

Slat

Tape ladder

Base piece

Tilt cord

Lift cord

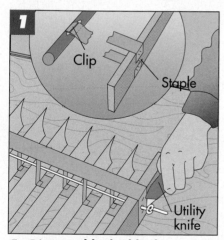
Clip
Staple
Utility knife

1. Disassemble the blind.
Remove any clamps at the bottom of the base. On wood blinds the tapes are stapled. Snip off the lift cord at either side and remove by pulling as if raising the blind. Slide out the slats. In the head box, free the tapes by removing the clips holding the tapes to the tilt tube.

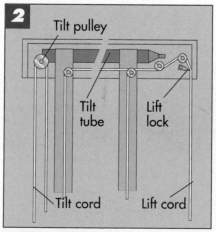
Tilt pulley
Tilt tube
Lift lock
Tilt cord
Lift cord

2. Thread lift cords.
Attach the new tapes to the tilt tube and the base piece, then extend the ladders and slide the slats into place. Thread the lift cords from the base piece on each side up, over the pulleys, and back down through the lift lock.

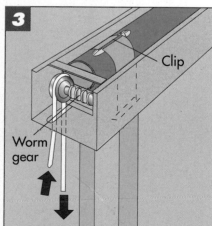
Clip
Worm gear

3. Thread tilt cord.
Note that the ladders' rungs are offset from each other. Weave the lift cord on alternate sides of the rungs. Snip any tassels from the old tilt cord, thread the new cord over the worm gear pulley, and replace the tassels.

INSTALLING INTERIOR STORM SASHES

Fitting a storm sash on the inner side of an existing window cuts heat loss in half without the expense of buying exterior storm windows. You can install kit sashes, as shown on these pages, or make your own from ⅛-inch acrylic held in place with wood picture-frame molding. Fasten acrylic to window casings with screws and then apply self-adhesive weather stripping around the edges so you can remove the pane easily.

If you're considering new exterior storm windows, turn to pages 440–441.

YOU'LL NEED...

TIME: 2 to 3 hours per window.
SKILLS: Basic skills.
TOOLS: Tape measure, framing square, utility knife, sanding block, and hacksaw.

1. Measure the window.
Measure to the outside of casings. Test-fit a piece of acrylic into the trim pieces (see below), then subtract enough to allow for the self-adhesive trim at the sides, top, and sill. Measure and mark a piece of acrylic with a knife at the beginning and end of each cut.

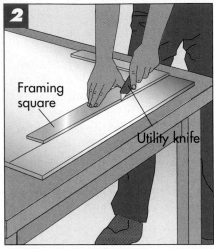

2. Trim the acrylic.
Lay the acrylic piece on a flat surface, protective film–side down. Hold a framing square or drywall square firmly in place and draw a utility knife along the straightedge several times. Place the score on a table edge and push down on both sides to snap the cut. Smooth rough edges with a sanding block.

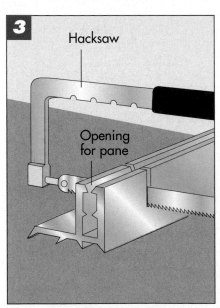

3. Cut the sill.
When you measure for cutting the sill trim, be sure to allow for the strips at the sides. Hold the sill trim firmly in place and cut with a hacksaw. Cut slowly so you do not bend the trim. Snap the sill piece onto the bottom of the pane.

4. Apply self-adhesive trim.
Most side and top trims snap open and have adhesive backings. Cut them to fit using a hacksaw. Snap the pieces onto the perimeter of the pane. After assembly, lift the unit into place and check that it fits; you may need to recut a piece.

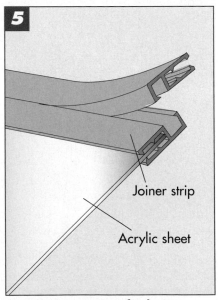

5. Use joiner strips for large windows.
Special joiner strips splice together more than one acrylic sheet for large windows or patio doors. Snap the flexible strips onto a sheet so the joiner strips will fit together as shown, then add the second sheet.

6. Install the sash.
Secure the sill trim. To attach the side and top pieces, remove the adhesive backing's protective paper and press only when you are sure the position is correct; if you reposition it, the adhesive will not be as strong. Make sure there are no air gaps.

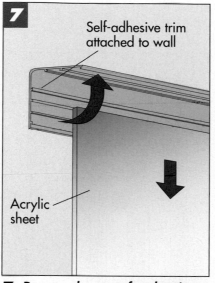

7. Remove the pane for cleaning.
To remove the pane for cleaning or ventilation, snap open the side and top trim and lift out the acrylic.

USING WINDOW TREATMENTS IN COLD CLIMATES

On average, windows comprise only 10 percent of the wall area of a house. Yet they account for as much as 40 percent of a house's heat loss.

R-value measures resistance to heat flow. To determine your window's total R-value, add up the R-values of all your window's features using the chart at right.

A home energy audit—free from many gas and electric utility companies and many state energy agencies—shows you the savings and payback period for new items.

Effective window treatment involves more than simply hanging drapes. The temperature difference between indoors and outdoors creates a convection current between the glass and the insulation. This causes the cold air generated in the airspace to flow out at the bottom, reducing the R-value of the treatment. In addition moisture in the air condenses on the cold glass. The condensate may run down onto the sill right away, or it may accumulate as frost to later melt and run down. Either way the condensate may damage the sill.

WINDOW TREATMENT R-VALUES	
Treatment	**R-Value**
Single-glazed	0.9
Double-glazed (DG)	1.9
Low-E glass	1.3
Interior storm sash	1.8
Exterior storm/screen	1.8
Quilted shade	3.2

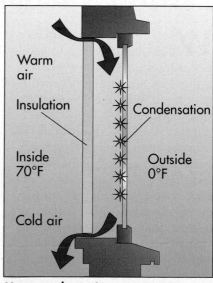

How condensation occurs.
The key to window insulation is a vapor-impervious construction and tight air seals at the sides and bottom. If a storm window—either interior or exterior—is not well sealed, the mix of cold and warm air will create vapor that collects on the windowpane.

UNDERSTANDING INTERIOR DOORS

Almost every modern wood panel door has a vertical-stile and horizontal-rail framework. This construction helps counteract the wood's tendency to shrink, swell, and warp with humidity changes. With a panel door (right), you can see that framing. Spaces between frame members are paneled with wood, louvered slats, or glass.

Smooth-surfaced "flush doors" hide their framing beneath two or three layers of veneer. Alternating the veneer directions minimizes warping. A solid-core flush door has a dense center of hardwood blocks or particleboard; a hollow-core door uses lighter material in the interior, such as ribbons of corrugated cardboard or rigid foam insulation.

For sliding and bifold doors, see pages 424–425.

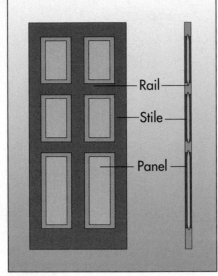

Panel doors.
Made of milled pine components, panel doors are easy to plane and, if necessary, cut down to fit an opening. Cheaper types are made of molded hardboard.

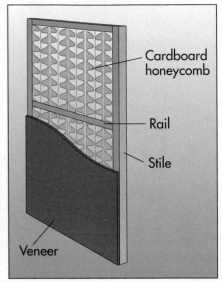

Hollow-core doors.
Covered with oak, birch, or lauan-mahogany veneer, hollow-core doors are inexpensive. They are difficult to cut down, though, because there is only 2 to 3 inches of framing at the top and bottom.

FREEING A BINDING DOOR

When a hinged door sticks, don't be too quick to take it down to plane its edges. Many difficulties are better corrected by making minor adjustments with the door in place.

Most problems result from one or more of the following causes: loose hinge screws, paint that is too thick on the jamb and/or door edge, improperly aligned hinges, an improperly aligned strike plate, a frame that is out of square (usually because the house has settled), or warping of the door.

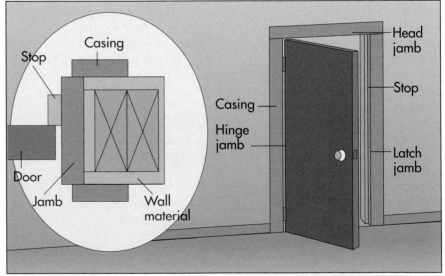

YOU'LL NEED...
TIME: 30 to 90 minutes, depending on whether you have to plane the door
SKILLS: No special skills needed.
TOOLS: Hammer, nail set, chisel, wedge, plane, and screwdriver.

Where's the rub?
If a door sticks or refuses to fit into its frame, open the door and pull up on the handle, then let go. If either hinge is loose, screws need to be tightened. Next close the door as far as it will go without forcing it, and carefully examine the perimeter. Look for an uneven gap along the hinge jamb; this means that the hinges need attention. If the door seems too big for its frame—or out of square with it—mark the tight spots, then sand or plane those spots.

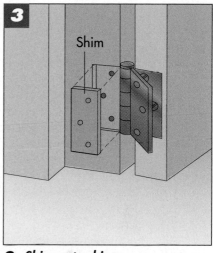

1. Shim the door.
Loose hinge screws can cause sags. To tighten them, first wedge the door open under the latch edge. (Hinges usually come loose for a reason—often because the door binds when it is closed. After tightening the screws, take steps to make sure that the door does not bind.)

2. Plug the screw holes.
Remove the screws and plug their holes with glue-coated golf tees, wood splinters, or dowels. Drive new screws into each plug. If this does not work, try driving longer screws. Make sure the screws are driven straight, so their heads are flat; angled screw heads can cause the door to bind.

3. Shim out a hinge.
If the door binds on the hinge side, scrape and sand away any built-up paint on the edge of the door and the jamb. A hinge leaf should be flush with the surrounding surface. If either leaf is set in, remove the screws, insert a cardboard shim, and rescrew.

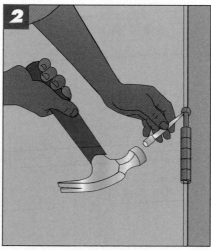

1. Plane the door top in place, if possible.
If the door binds, gently close the door and scribe a cut line at all points where binding occurs, using the jamb as a guide. Usually you won't have to remove the door from its hinges to plane the top or the latch side. First bevel any edges to prevent splintering. For instructions on planing, see pages 298–299.

2. Tap out the hinge pins.
To trim the bottom or an edge you can't reach with the door in place, remove the door. Shim the bottom of the door so it is stable. Use a nail set or screwdriver to hammer out the hinge pins, bottom first, then the top. If the hinge is rusty and the pin is stuck, try squirting with penetrating oil. If that doesn't work, you may need to remove the screws from one hinge leaf.

3. Plane the door.
Brace the door for planing. Avoid planing the hinge side, if possible. If you must do so, first remove the hinges. You may have to reset the hinges afterwards.

CORRECTING STRIKE PROBLEMS

When a door will not latch, or if it rattles when latched, examine the strike plate attached to the jamb. Minor adjustments often will solve the problem.

If the latch does not engage the strike plate, determine if the latch is too far from the strike. Scratches on the strike plate probably mean the latch is hitting the strike but missing the hole.

A door that does not fit snugly against its stop molding almost certainly will rattle. To silence it, move the strike plate or reposition the stop.

> ## YOU'LL NEED...
> **TIME:** About 30 minutes to adjust a strike plate.
> **SKILLS:** Basic carpentry skills.
> **TOOLS:** Screwdriver, file, drill, and chisel.

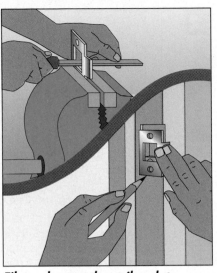

File and move the strike plate.
If the strike plate is off only ⅛ inch or so, remove the strike plate and enlarge its opening with a file. You may need to chisel away some wood when reinstalling. For bigger shifts, relocate the strike. You'll need to extend the mortise (see page 428).

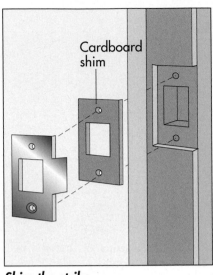

Cardboard shim

Shim the strike.
If the strike is too far away to engage the latch, first check if the hinges need to be shimmed out (see page 421). If the hinges fit properly, shim out the strike using thick cardboard.

SILENCING SQUEAKY HINGES

If a hinge squeaks, it may be under extra pressure because the door is binding (see pages 420–421). Or the hinge may be rusty because of damp conditions. Cleaning and lubricating may solve the problem; but in the case of bad rust, you're better off replacing the hinge.

You might solve the problem by oiling with the pin in place. Spread a cloth on the floor and squirt some penetrating oil into the moving parts. Open and close the door to work the lubricant in.

> ## YOU'LL NEED...
> **TIME:** About 15 minutes per hinge.
> **SKILLS:** Basic carpentry skills.
> **TOOLS:** Hammer, nail set, drill, steel wool, and wire-brush pipe cleaner.

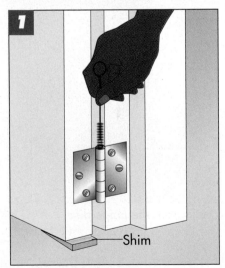

1 Shim

1. Clean the pins.
If oiling does not quiet a rusty hinge, shim the bottom of the door so it is stable. Remove the hinge pin. Clean the pin with steel wool. Poke out the pin hole with a wire-brush pipe cleaner.

2 GRAPHITE

2. Put graphite on moving parts.
Coat moving parts with graphite. When you replace the pin, don't drive it tight; leave space for prying it out again and adding more graphite in the future.

LUBRICATING BALKY LATCHES

Old latches have springs that may break. If lubricating a latch does not free it, remove the unit and take it to a locksmith, who may be able to repair it. Or consider buying and installing a replacement (see pages 428–429).

A latch that has been painted is in danger of binding. Remove all paint by carefully scraping with a chisel or by using a wire-brush attachment on a drill.

If you're going to use powdered graphite to lubricate the lock, place a newspaper under the area to protect carpeting.

YOU'LL NEED...
TIME: 10 to 15 minutes per latch.
SKILLS: Basic skills.
TOOLS: Screwdriver.

Apply graphite to latch.
Turn the handle to retract the latch bolt, then puff powdered graphite into the works. Turn the handle repeatedly to work the bolt back and forth, and apply more graphite if needed. If this does not solve the problem, you may need a new latch.

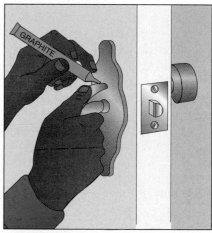

Apply graphite to thumb latch.
Lubricate a thumb-operated latch lever by puffing graphite powder into the lock body. Move the latch up and down to work in the graphite. Wipe away any excess.

DEALING WITH A WARPED DOOR

If a door rattles when closed, or if you have to press hard to get the latch to engage, the door may be warped. Close the door until it just touches the stop, then check to see if the door meets the stop all along its length (see page 420). If there is a gap at either end or in the middle, the simplest solution is to reposition the stop rather than trying to straighten the door.

If a door is badly warped yet valuable, try straightening it out: Remove the door, set it on pieces of wood, and weight it to counter-warp it. Give it at least a week to straighten.

YOU'LL NEED...
TIME: 2 hours to add a hinge; a week if you weight the door.
SKILLS: Basic carpentry skills.
TOOLS: Hammer, nail set, chisel, pry bar, and screwdriver.

1. Move the stop.
To reposition a stop, cut through the paint lines (if any) and gently pry the stop away. Close the door, and scribe a line on the jamb to indicate where the stop should be. Drill pilot holes and drive new finishing nails to reattach the stop.

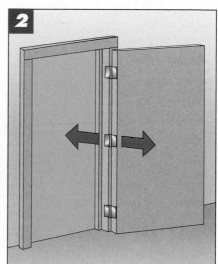

2. Add a hinge.
If a door is warped along the hinge side, you may be able to straighten it by adding a hinge in the middle. Install the jamb side hinge and trace the door hinge. Remove the door and chisel the mortise (see page 426). Rehang and attach the hinge. With a helper, force the door straight and insert the pins.

REPAIRING BIFOLD DOORS

Bifold doors are commonly used for closets. Because they don't swing far outward, they save space in a bedroom.

Most bifold doors are lightweight, with light-duty hardware to match. Roughhousing kids can easily break slats or bend a hinge or a track. Straighten a bent track by placing a strip of wood inside and tapping with a hammer; or use a pair of pliers and two strips of metal.

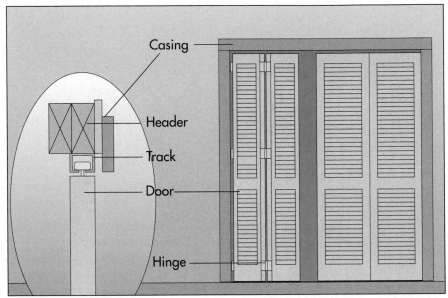

Anatomy of a bifold door.
A bifold door has two halves that are hinged together. One half of the door pivots on fixed pins that attach to holders with slots at the floor and the header jamb. The other half of the door slides along a header track—secured to the header jamb—as the center hinges open or close. The pin that runs in the header track does not support the door; it only guides it.

EXPERTS' INSIGHT

INSTALLING A NEW SET OF BIFOLDS

Installing a new bifold door is straightforward. A unit comes as a kit, with the doors hinged and the hardware supplied. Bifolds typically fit into 24-, 30-, 32-, and 36-inch openings. A typical closet has two bifolds in a 6-foot-wide opening. Flush, panel, and louvered doors are available. Painting can take a long time, especially if the bifold has louvers. Consider buying a prefinished door, or purchase a unit with good-looking wood so that you need only apply a clear finish. More expensive units are available with mirror panels, minimizing the surface area of wood to be finished.

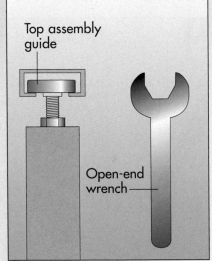

Adjusting the hardware.
Ideally when a bifold door is closed, it should be aligned with the jamb on all three sides. However if the opening is out of square, you may need to compromise on one side. In a typical arrangement, the top assembly guide (above left) fits into a hole and can be adjusted

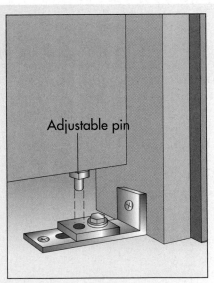

out or in. At the bottom of the door you may find an adjustable pin-and-slot arrangement (above right); loosen the nut to slide the slot. On other models you simply pick the door up, move it over slightly, and set the bottom pin in a different part of the slot. Use an open-end wrench to make adjustments.

REPAIRING SLIDING DOORS

Sliding doors, also called bypass or gliding doors, come in pairs, and slide past each other to open or close. Though flush bypass doors are the most common, paneled and louvered models are also available.

Exterior glass patio doors roll on wheels along a bottom track. Adjust and maintain these as you would a sliding window (see page 412). Be aware, however, that these doors are quite heavy.

Interior bypass doors are usually easy to maintain. However if the door itself is warped, it should be replaced.

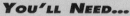

YOU'LL NEED...
TIME: About 15 to 20 minutes per door.
SKILLS: Basic skills.
TOOLS: Slot and phillips screwdrivers, and pliers.

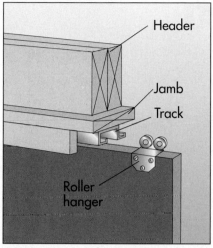

How a bypass door works.
At the top of an interior bypass door, a roller hanger glides through a metal track. Rollers are typically nylon and need no lubrication. The track must be attached firmly to the header because it is the door's sole support. At the bottom of the door opening, a floor guide (see below) provides only guidance.

Removing a bypass door.
To remove a bypass door, lift it above the floor guide and tilt it out slightly. Then pick the door up and guide it out of the track. Be careful; some units are heavy.

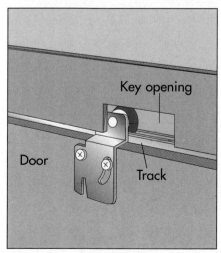

Check for a key opening.
With some models you can free the door only when its wheels are at a key opening in the track.

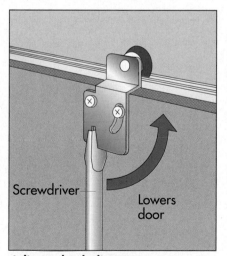

Adjust wheel alignment.
Raise one side or the other by adjusting the roller hanger. In the type shown above, first slightly loosen the two screws. Then insert a screwdriver into the slot and pry the hanger up or down. Tighten the screws.

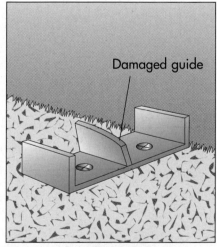

Fix or replace floor guides.
If a floor guide is bent, try bending it back into position with a pair of pliers. If it is broken, or if it is difficult to straighten, replace it.

INSTALLING A DOOR

Replacing a door in an existing jamb (the three pieces that form a doorway) can be challenging, especially if the jamb is out of square. (If you need to install a door with a new jamb, see pages 430–431.)

There should be a gap of ⅛ inch between the door and the jamb on all three sides, and a gap of about ⅜ inch between the door and the finished floor. Never cut more than ¾ inch from either end—this would weaken the door's rail.

Most doors are 80 inches tall but may be taller in older homes.

YOU'LL NEED...

TIME: 2 to 4 hours.
SKILLS: Good carpentry skills, including chiseling a mortise.
TOOLS: Hammer, plane, chisel, drill, screwdriver, center punch, and utility knife or butt marker.

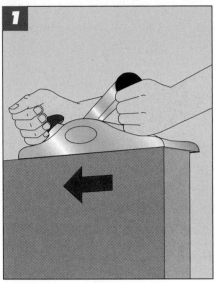

1. Plane or cut the door.
Check the jamb for square. Have a helper hold the door in or against the jamb, and mark for any needed cutting or planing. If you only have to plane, work from the door edge toward the center of the door. (For how to cut the door, see page 427.)

2. Mark for hinges.
Set the door in the jamb and use shims to wedge it in place. Check that the gaps are consistent. Place the top hinge 6 inches from the top, and the bottom hinge about 9 inches from the floor. Use a pencil to mark for the bottom and top of each hinge.

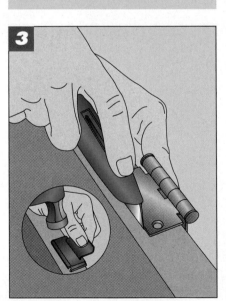

3. Scribe marks for the hinges.
Hold the hinge in place as a template. Use a utility knife to make a light mark around the hinge, then deepen the cut. Or use a butt marker (see inset), which has chisel edges that will make indentations for a perfect cut. Hold it in place and pound on it with a hammer.

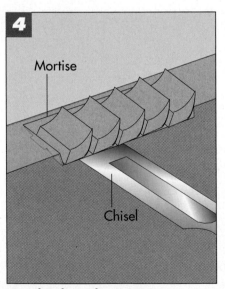

4. Chisel out the mortise.
Using a knife or a chisel, make a cut along the face of the door, as deep as the hinge is thick. Holding the chisel with the beveled edge down, make a series of cuts inside the mortise. Then holding the chisel flat-side down, knock out chips from the side.

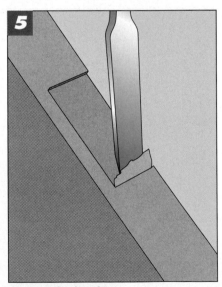

5. Finish chiseling.
Cut away enough material so that, when installed, the hinge leaf sits flush with the surface of the door edge. To shave away a small amount of wood, try using the chisel like a knife, pushing without using a hammer.

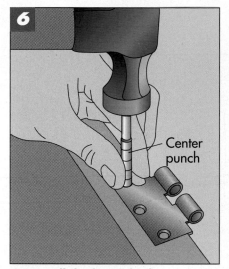

6. Install the hinge leaf.
Install separate hinge leaves on the door and the jamb. Position a leaf in its mortise and mark for drilling with a center punch. Predrill all the holes. Screw the hinge leaves to the mortises.

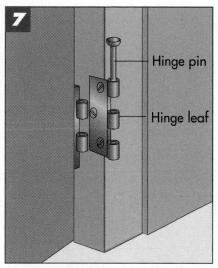

7. Hang the door.
Have a helper hold the door in place and slip the hinge leaves together. Insert the pins. Check that the door swings freely and closes completely against the stop without binding. To make minor adjustments, see pages 420–422; see pages 428–429 for how to install a latch.

TOOLS TO USE

A TOOL KIT FOR DOORS

If you have an older home, chances are good you will need to work on doors from time to time. Gather the right tools and keep them in good working order. In addition to the standard carpentry tools, consider these:
■ A power planer quickly (though messily) trims and smoothes; get one with a carbide blade for longevity.
■ A belt sander equipped with a coarse sanding belt works nearly as quickly as a power planer.
■ Buy a butt marker to match the size of your hinge. It makes it easy to cut a mortise that fits snugly and looks professional.

CUTTING A DOOR

Use a knife to score a line wherever you will be cutting across the grain of solid wood, or whenever you will cut a flush door's plywood surface. To avoid splintering the door face, make your cut below that line.

Newer solid-core doors are filled with a soft type of particleboard material—they have solid wood only for an inch or so around their perimeters. If you have to cut off more than an inch, the particleboard will be exposed; paint it with two coats of sealer.

YOU'LL NEED...

TIME: About 2 hours to cut down a hollow-core door.
SKILLS: Measuring, cutting a straight line, and smoothing.
TOOLS: Knife, circular saw, straightedge, chisel, and hammer.

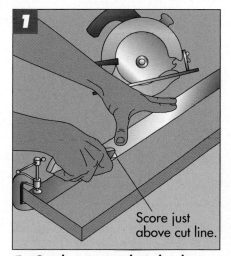

1. Cut the veneer, then the door.
Using a straightedge clamped in position, score the veneer about $^{1}/_{16}$ inch above where you want your cut. It will take several passes with your knife to do this. Move and clamp the straightedge in position for cutting with a circular saw (see page 268). Complete the cut.

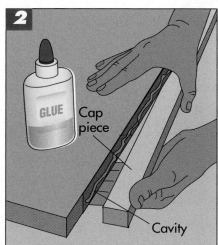

2. Insert a cap piece.
If you cut off more than an inch, the door will be hollow at the place you just cut. (You may need to clear out some cardboard honeycomb with a chisel). Cut a piece of softwood to the needed width and length. Apply wood glue to the upper and lower edges of the cavity, and tap the cap into position. Clamp firmly.

INSTALLING HANDLES AND LOCKS

Once the door has been hung so that it swings freely and closes snugly against the stop, the next step is to install the handle. An entry handle simply opens from either side; a privacy handle can be locked from one side. Purchase drill bits in sizes recommended by the manufacturer. (For instructions on installing other locks, see page 452.)

YOU'LL NEED...

TIME: About 45 minutes.
SKILLS: Measuring precisely, chiseling, drilling, and fastening with screws.
TOOLS: Drill with hole saw and bits (see lockset instructions), utility knife or butt marker, tape measure, center punch, awl, screwdriver, hammer, and chisel.

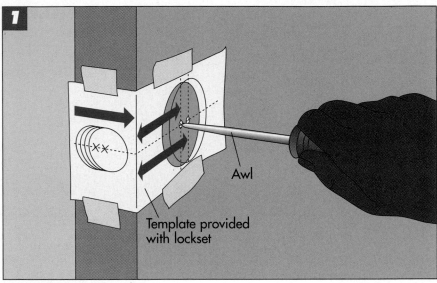

1. Mark for lockset holes.

The handle set or dead bolt will come with a paper or cardboard template. Tape it or hold it against the door. If a strike already exists in the jamb, align the template with it so you won't have to cut a new mortise for the strike. With an awl or the point of a spade bit, mark for the two holes by piercing through the template.

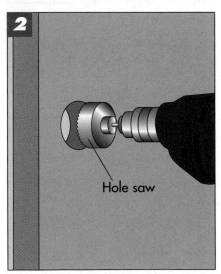

2. Drill the large hole.

Use a hole saw to drill the larger hole through the face of the door first. To avoid splintering the veneer, drill just far enough that the pilot bit of the hole saw pokes through. Then drill from the other side.

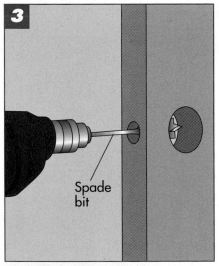

3. Drill the bolt hole.

Use a spade bit to drill through the edge, taking care to hold the bit parallel to the surface of the door. Some types of locksets require that you continue drilling into the rear of the large hole approximately ½ inch.

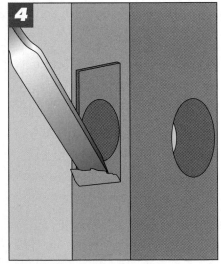

4. Mortise the latch bolt.

Insert the bolt through the smaller hole. Temporarily screw it centered in the door, and mark for its mortise with a sharp pencil or a knife. Cut and chisel a mortise as you did for the hinges (page 426). Depending on the type of bolt, this mortise may be deeper near the center than at the edges.

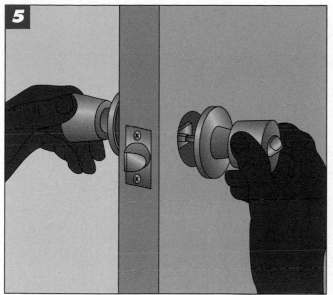

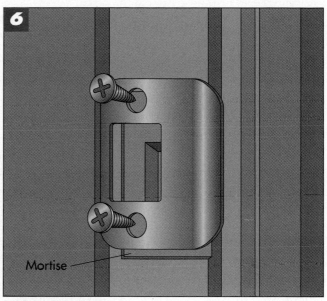

Mortise

5. Install the handle.

Install the bolt by setting it in the mortise, drilling pilot holes, and driving the screws provided. Then install the lockset or handles according to the manufacturer's directions. Tighten all screws. Test the mechanisms from both sides of the door to make sure they operate smoothly; you may need to clean out or widen your holes.

6. Install the strike.

Mark the jamb for the correct location of the strike. The latch or bolt should be vertically centered in the strike opening. Horizontally, make sure the latch or bolt will enter the door while holding it fairly tight against the door stop. Mortise the jamb, drill pilot holes, and install the strike with the screws provided.

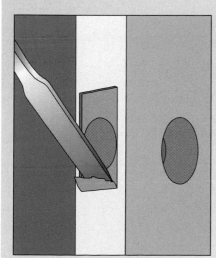

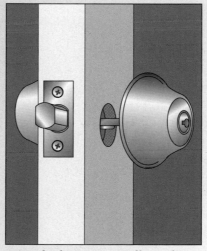

Assembling a dead bolt.

Install a dead bolt much as you would a handle. Mark for the position of the two holes and drill them. Insert the bolt and latch face, mark for the mortise, and cut it with a chisel.

Screw the latch face (above right) into the mortise. For many lock types, you'll need to use a screwdriver to partially extend the bolt. Insert the lock tailpiece through the slot in the bolt. Slip on the interior turn bolt or lock until the two pieces sit flush against the door. Fasten the retaining screws and install the strike plate.

EXPERTS' INSIGHT

CHOOSING A DEAD BOLT

A high-quality dead bolt, properly installed, is usually the most secure lock for a door. For added security, purchase a unit with a metal strike enclosure, which extends deep into the door jamb.

A double-keyed dead bolt, which locks with a key on the inside as well as on the outside, offers the best security in situations where an intruder could reach through a window to the bolt. However it is not safe in case of fire—if you don't have the key handy, you could be trapped inside.

INSTALLING A PREHUNG DOOR

Building a custom door saves money, but takes time and expertise. Prehung units cost more, but you get everything you need—door, hinges, jamb, stop and casing moldings, and even a latch if you want it—all in one accurately made component.

See page 333 if you need to frame for the door. Before you buy a prehung unit, measure the thickness of the wall; plaster and drywall surfaces call for different jamb widths.

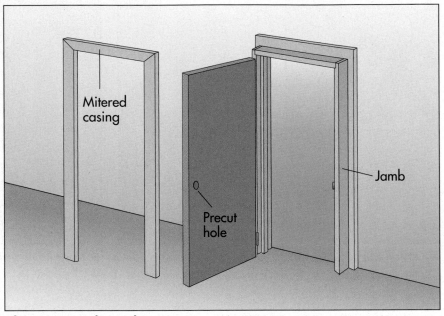

YOU'LL NEED...
TIME: About 2 hours.
SKILLS: Moderate carpentry skills.
TOOLS: Hammer, level, framing square, and saw.

Choosing a prehung door.
A prehung door comes already assembled, with the holes precut for the handle and the strike plate. The casing can be removed from either side of a prehung door. A standard jamb is 3⅝ inches wide to fit into a standard stud-and-drywall wall; in an older home, you may need a wider jamb.

1. Shim a prehung door.
Remove the casing on one side. Set the door into the opening, with the other casing (not visible above) flush against the wall. If necessary shim the hinge side to make it plumb. Check the other two jamb pieces for square by closing the door; the gap should be even all around.

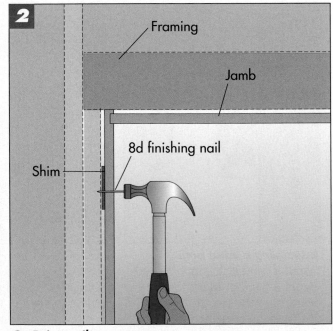

2. Drive nails.
Open the door and shim it at the bottom so it is stable. Anchor the hinge jamb securely with 8d finishing nails that enter the framing. To hide nails, simply remove the stop, drive the nails, then replace the stop. Drive nails to attach the latch jamb, and check again for square.

INSTALLING A SPLIT-JAMB PREHUNG DOOR

With a split-jamb door, the side and top jambs consist of two tongue-and-groove halves that slide together to accommodate variations in wall thickness. This is particularly useful in an old home with plaster walls that may vary in thickness. The door is held in place mainly by finishing nails driven through the casings into the doorway framing.

This works fine for lightweight hollow-core doors. For heavier solid-wood panel doors and even heavier solid-core doors, however, nailing the casings alone is not enough. For these doors, specify solid jambs of a width to match wall thickness.

YOU'LL NEED...

TIME: 1 to 2 hours.
SKILLS: Moderate carpentry skills.
TOOLS: Hammer, level, nail set, screwdriver, and chisel.

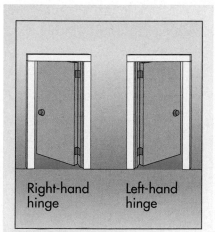

Right/left hand.
A hinge "hand" refers to the side of the door that it is on. A right-hand hinge swings to the right as you push it open.

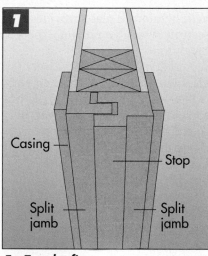

1. Test the fit.
Remove packing materials that hold the two jamb pieces together. Separate the jamb pieces, leaving the door closed inside the stop jambs. With a helper, insert the two pieces into the opening, and make sure they will fit.

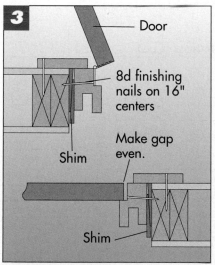

3. Nail the jamb.
Drive 8d finishing nails in the hinge-side casing every 16 inches. Drive 6d finishing nails through the jamb—not the stop—and shims into a stud. Shim the latch-side jamb to make the gap between the door and jamb even, then nail with 8d finishing nails.

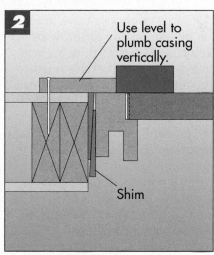

2. Level and nail the casing.
Set aside the non-door part of the casing. With the door centered, drive an 8d finishing nail through the top outside edge of the casing into the stud. With a level held vertically against the inside edge of the side casing, shim the jamb at the hinge locations to plumb the casing.

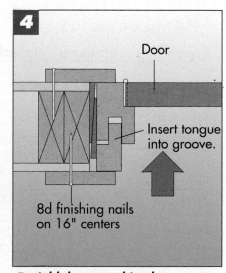

4. Add the second jamb.
Insert the second jamb so that the tongues fit into the grooves. Nail around the casings with 8d finishing nails every 16 inches.

CHOOSING AND BUYING GLASS

You probably don't live in an all-glass house or throw stones. You should, however, know how to buy and install glass for that broken window or storm door that eventually seems to be an affliction for us all.

Standard glass, available at most home centers and hardware stores, is the most common. Unless the pane is very small, spend a little more for double-strength glass; single-strength glass is likely to crack if bumped lightly.

A glass shop carries more types of glass. For a very large older window, or for shelving or a tabletop, purchase plate glass, which is very thick. Tempered glass is recommended for doors because it has extra strength. Safety glass, commonly used for automobiles, breaks into rounded pieces rather than sharp shards.

Wire-reinforced glass provides security where you might expect a break-in.

Acrylic is often chosen over glass in situations where the pane is likely to be bumped. Acrylic has some disadvantages, however. It scratches easily and may look dingy in time. In addition it is flexible, making it easy for a burglar to break.

A variety of tinted, frosted, or patterned glass styles allow light in while obscuring the view; they are sometimes referred to as "obscure glass."

Glass block is several inches thick and comes in several styles. The blocks are mortared together like a brick wall. The result is a decorative wall that admits filtered light, yet is nearly as strong as a masonry wall. You can order a grouping of blocks preassembled

to fit your opening, or you can assemble them yourself using special mortar, spacers, perimeter gaskets, and wire reinforcement.

If a double- or triple-glazed pane is broken, take the sash to a glass shop and have them make up and install the pane. Be sure that the new pane has the same special features of the old one—low-E glazing, for instance.

If a standard pane has broken, first remove all the broken pieces and clean out the opening (see pages 434–435). Measure the opening carefully, then subtract $\frac{1}{8}$ inch from the measurement in each direction. The resulting extra space allows the glass to "float" in the sash and helps prevent it from breaking. Either have a glass dealer cut it for you or buy a large piece and cut it yourself (see page 433).

SELECTING GLASS

Type	Strength	Installation	Cost	Uses
Standard SS	Poor	Easy	Low	Windows, doors, storm doors and windows, cabinet fronts, pictures
Standard DS	Fair	Easy	Low	Same as SS
Plate	Good	Easy	Medium	Tabletops, shelves, high-quality mirrors
Tempered	Excellent	Easy	Medium	Windows, doors, patio doors, skylights, shower doors, and fireplace doors
Safety	Excellent	Difficult	Medium	Storm doors, patio doors, skylights, and tabletops
Wire	Excellent	Difficult	High	Doors, commercial jobs, basement windows, and crime-prevention placement
Insulating	Good	Difficult	High	Windows, patio doors, and large glass areas
Tinted	Good	Moderate	High	Windows, doors, large glass areas, commercial windows, and skylights
Frosted	Good	Moderate	High	Bathroom windows, shower doors, and tub enclosures
Patterned	Fair	Easy	High	Entrance windows, decorative accents, cabinet fronts
Mirror tiles	Poor	Easy	Medium	Accent walls, bathrooms, bedrooms, cabinet liners
Glass block	Excellent	Difficult	High	Translucent windows and interior walls

CUTTING GLASS

A smooth, even score with a glass cutter lets you snap the glass with ease. The trick is to make the right score in a single stroke. If you exert too little pressure on the glass, the cutting wheel will skip; if you exert too much pressure, the edges will crack or chip. Always work on a flat, clean surface. Guide the cutter with a strip of hardwood that's been dampened so it won't slide across the surface, or use a carpenter's square. Don't wait too long after scoring to snap glass—it tends to heal itself. Do not attempt to cut safety glass.

YOU'LL NEED...

TIME: 5 to 10 minutes per pane.
SKILLS: Basic skills.
TOOLS: Glass cutter, square, tape measure, wooden straightedge, and light all-purpose oil.

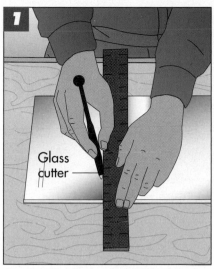

1. Score a line.
Measure and mark each end of the cut with a short score mark. Place the straightedge about ⅛ inch past the marks—the glass cutter does not actually cut right next to the straightedge. Lightly lubricate the line, then draw the cutter along the straightedge in one firm, smooth stroke.

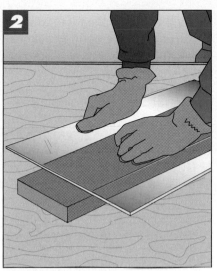

2. Break the glass.
NOTE: *Wear work gloves and safety glasses.* Lay the glass with the scored side up over a board, with the score line directly above the corner of the board. Press down on both sides until the glass snaps. If you need to cut off a sliver that is less than an inch wide, use the glass cutter's teeth.

3. Nip the glass edge.
Nip away irregularities with pliers. Teeth in the glass cutter also are designed for this purpose. Smooth rough edges by rubbing gently with a sanding block. For a very smooth edge (say, for glass that will be used on a tabletop), rub with an oilstone dipped in water.

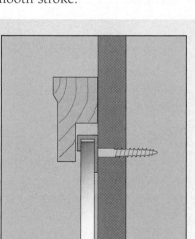

Secure a mirror with clips.
Secure large mirrors with special steel clips or strips sold at glass outlets and home centers. You can cover the clips with molding. To cover a wall with mirror tiles, square them up as you would ceramic tiles (see pages 594–595). Secure with double-sided tape or mastic.

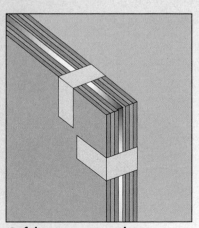

Safely store extra glass.
Secure extra windowpanes by sandwiching each between two pieces of plywood and taping the package together. Store the glass upright rather than laid flat. Mark the package so when you go to the storage area it's not handled roughly.

REPLACING WINDOWPANES

Faced with a broken window, you have three options: Remove the sash and take it to a hardware store or glass shop for reglazing; buy a new pane that is cut to size, and install it yourself; or cut the glass yourself from standard-sized sheets kept on hand for such emergencies.

Dismantling a window (see page 406) is sometimes far more work than simply replacing the glass. Cutting glass (see page 433) isn't difficult, but you might break a pane or two before getting the knack. A hardware store will cut glass to the size you need.

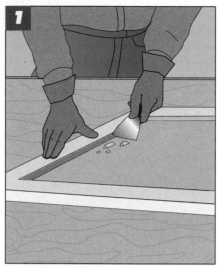

1. Chip off the old glazing.
NOTE: *Wear heavy gloves and long clothing when handling broken glass.* Carefully pull out all the pieces of the old pane. Chipping off old glazing compound can be the hardest part of the job. Use a putty knife or old chisel, or soften old glazing with a soldering iron or heat gun.

2. Roughen the groove.
Scrape away the last of the old compound, then roughen the groove with a scraper so the new glazing compound will adhere properly. Be sure to remove all the old glazier's points, which may be tiny metal triangles instead of the push-type points shown in Step 6.

3. Measure the sash.
Sashes aren't always perfectly square, so measure at several points, then subtract ⅛ inch from each dimension to determine the glass size. Have the glass cut at a hardware store or glass shop, or cut it yourself.

4. Prime the groove and apply a bead of glazing.
Prime the groove with linseed oil, turpentine, or oil-based paint. Untreated wood will draw oil from the glazing compound, shortening its life. Before you insert the new pane, apply a ⅛-inch-thick bead of caulk or glazing compound. This helps seal and cushion the glass.

5. Press the pane into place.
Line up one edge of the pane in the sash, lower it into place, and press gently with your palm or fingertips to seal it into the glazing compound.

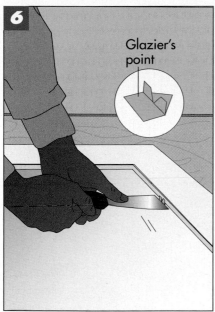

6. Add glazier's points.
Approximately every 12 inches around the perimeter, press a glazier's point (see inset) into the sash with a putty knife. Don't push too hard—you may crack the glass.

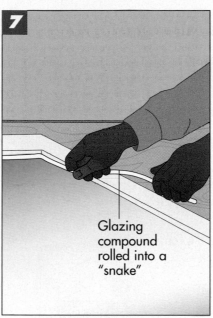

7. Apply glazing compound.
If the glazing compound is in a can, grab a hunk and roll it into a "snake." Alternatively, use glazing compound in a caulk tube. Apply a generous bead of glazing compound. Press it into place to make sure it sticks to both the glass and wood.

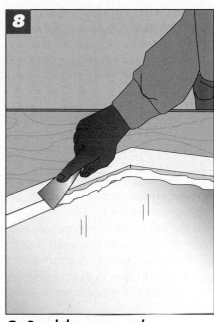

8. Bevel the compound.
Working in only one direction, firmly draw a putty knife all along the bead. If the compound sticks to the knife, wet the knife with turpentine. If small ridges appear, lightly run your finger in the opposite direction to smooth the compound.

9. Paint the compound.
Let the compound dry for a week before painting. Paint should overlap the glass about 1/16 inch for a tight seal.

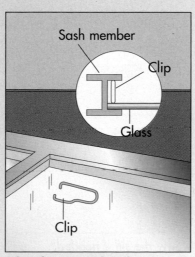

Clips for a metal sash.
Spring clips substitute for glazier's points in steel sashes. Install as shown here. Metal windows needn't be primed before installing the glass.

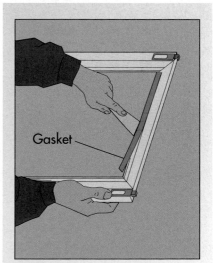

Gasket for storm window.
In an aluminum storm window, a rubber gasket, forced into place with a putty knife, holds the glass. If the gasket is cracked or broken, replace it.

REPLACING SILLS AND SADDLES

Windowsills take a terrific beating from both rain and the sun. Alternate soaking and baking can make them veritable sponges.

The best preventive is a couple of coats of paint applied annually. If a sill is too far gone for that, consider repair options (see the "Experts' Insight" box below).

If the sill is heavily damaged, you may need to install a new sill. Door sills, called saddles or thresholds, also fail over time. Replace either by following the procedures illustrated here.

Determine if the sill or saddle fits under the jambs on either side, then measure, and buy a new piece of sill stock. The drawings at right show how to install a new piece of wood in either situation—but you might opt to replace a saddle with a preformed, predrilled metal or plastic unit.

If you can get the old sill out intact, use it as a template for marking the replacement. If not, measure exactly for a snug fit.

For more about how windows and doors are put together, see pages 406 and 420. To learn about weather-stripping-type thresholds, see page 438.

If the window has problems in addition to the sill, it's probably time to consider installing a replacement window.

YOU'LL NEED...

TIME: 1 to 2 hours per sill.
SKILLS: Basic carpentry skills.
TOOLS: Backsaw, chisel, hammer, nail set, flat pry bar, drill, and caulking gun.

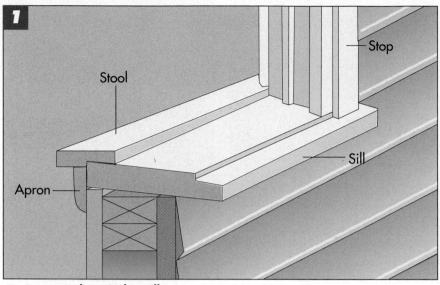

1. Remove the windowsill.
Removing the sill will probably be the most difficult part of the job. You'll have to take off the apron, the stool, and stop molding to remove a sill.

Use a chisel or old screwdriver to probe for nails that may be holding

2. Saw the sill if needed.
If the sill is embedded on either side, saw out a section from the center. Use a handsaw (a backsaw is shown) or a reciprocating saw, taking care not to damage underlying wood. Remove the middle piece, then drive the end pieces inward and pry them out.

the piece in place.

If you can't get the nails out, saw out a section as shown below. You can also demolish it by splitting it along the grain with a hammer and chisel, then pulling out the splintered remains.

EXPERTS' INSIGHT

REPAIRING A SILL

Replacing a sill, though sometimes necessary, is a difficult and demanding task. Before you start removing pieces, consider the possibility of repair. New products make it possible to repair wood pieces that are heavily damaged.

If the wood is cracked and weak, apply liquid hardener, which strengthens the fibers.

If an area is rotted, use a hammer and chisel to carve away the rotted material. Mix and apply two-part epoxy wood filler. Once it dries, the filler can be planed, sanded, and painted like wood.

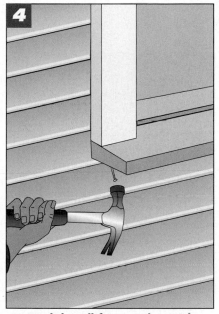

3. Tap the new sill into place.
Gently tap the new sill or saddle into place. Don't force it. If it resists, remove and sand the ends, beveling them slightly.

4. Nail the sill from underneath.
Using rust-resistant nails or deck screws, secure the windowsill from underneath. Countersink the fasteners, then caulk the holes and the ends of the sill.

Nail door saddles onto the framing sill.
Nail or screw a saddle at both ends and in the middle. Countersink fastener heads with a nail set and hide with putty. Caulk both ends of the saddle.

MAINTAINING SCREENING

Even rustproof screening materials (see page 439) require occasional attention. Check the caulking around the frames of combination units, and replace any worn-out gaskets. Vacuum dirt that collects on the screening. Clean oxidized aluminum with car polish.

Older wood-framed screens require careful monitoring and diligent maintenance. Repaint the frames as soon as the old paint starts to fail. Check each unit when you take it down and set aside those that need repair.

Consider how many windows you actually open up during the summer months. Leaving a storm window in place not only saves you some work, it also helps keep an air-conditioned room cool—as long as the window does not receive direct sunlight.

Clean screens.
Remove dust and debris by spraying a screen with a blast from a hose. Scrub metal screens with a stiff brush. Clean the frames as well as the screening.

Paint steel screens.
If older steel screening is heavily rusted, replace it. If the rust is only modest, apply paint that is made to go over rusty metal. A paint pad is the easiest method. Paint one side, let it dry, then paint the other side. To unclog holes, gently rub the back side with a dry pad.

REPAIRING SCREENS AND STORMS

The little parts on an aluminum storm/screen—the splining, gaskets, plastic pins, and sliding clips that hook to the storm's frame—are notoriously fragile. To find replacements, look for the manufacturer's name on the frame, or bring broken parts to a hardware store.

Wood storm or screen frames that have been painted too many times may need to be sanded or planed, then repainted. Installing weather stripping can make wood storms more energy-efficient. Position felt or rubber weather stripping on the window's frame or the frame of the storm to create a tight seal when the storm is attached. You may need to move the closing hardware in order to accommodate the thickness of the weather stripping.

Adjust or replace screen/storm door closers as soon as they begin to malfunction; doors that slam or flap in the breeze wear out quickly. A closer should shut the door slowly but completely. Replacement closers are inexpensive and easy to install.

YOU'LL NEED...

TIME: 10 minutes to 2 hours, depending on the damage.
SKILLS: Basic skills.
TOOLS: Needle-nose pliers, hammer, drill, shears, and screwdriver.

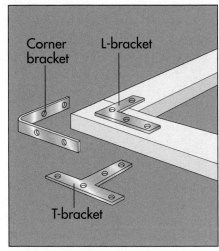

Repair a wooden frame.
Reinforce corner joints in a wooden frame using mending plates. Position a plate, drill pilot holes, and drive screws to fasten the plate. When possible install a plate on both sides; offset the plates so the screws don't run into each other.

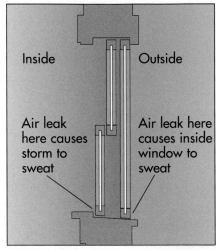

Seal air leaks.
Air leaks around interior sashes or storms cause condensation to form on the sash that's not leaking. The solution is to caulk the air leak.

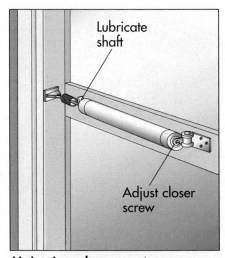

Maintain a closer.
Every autumn, lubricate door closers by wiping the shaft with oil. Check the adjustment for proper operation. Once a closer starts to fail, replace it.

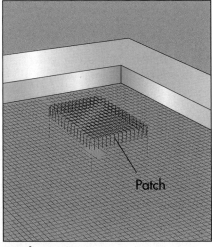

Patch a screen.
Mend a small puncture with a dab of superglue. To patch a hole in a metal screen, cut a patch, unravel a few strands, fit the patch over the hole, and bend the strands toward the hole. Repairing fiberglass screening is difficult; you're better off replacing the entire screen.

REPLACING SCREENING

Install screening much as an artist stretches a canvas—fasten it at one end of the frame, pull the material taut, then secure it at the sides and the other end.

With wood frames, pry screen moldings loose with a putty knife. Work from the center to the ends, applying leverage near the nails. If molding breaks, replace it.

Standard aluminum screening is subject to staining; "charcoal" or "silver-gray" aluminum is easier to maintain. Fiberglass won't stain, but its filaments are thicker, which affects visibility.

YOU'LL NEED...

TIME: 30 minutes per screen.
SKILLS: Basic skills.
TOOLS: Putty knife, shears or scissors, utility knife, staple gun, saw, and spline roller.

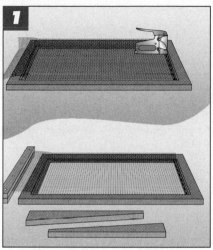

1. Attach the screen at the top.
With shears, cut the screening slightly wider and at least 1 foot longer than the frame, then staple the top edge. Nail a strip of wood to the bench or floor, roll the screen over it, and nail another strip on top of the first.

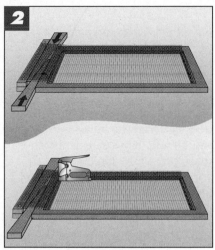

2. Insert wedges and fasten screening.
Rip-cut two wedges and insert them between the cleats and frame on each side. Tap the wedges until the screening is tight. Staple the screening to the bottom edge, then the sides. Trim the excess and refit the screen moldings.

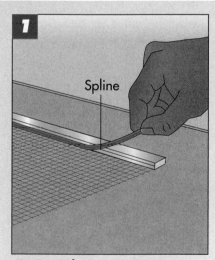
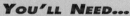

Spline

1. To replace screening in an aluminum frame, pry out the spline.
For aluminum frames, remove the old mesh by prying out the spline. You may need to buy new splining.

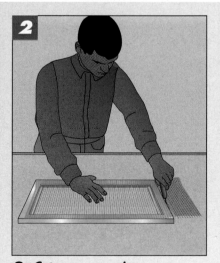

2. Cut new screening.
Square up the frame, lay new screening over it, and cut it the same size as the outside of the frame.

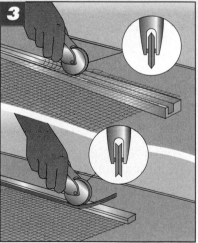

3. Push the screening into place and install the spline.
Bend the screening edges and force them into the channel with the convex wheel of the spline roller. Force the tubular spline into the channel with the concave wheel of the spline roller, tightening the screening.

INSTALLING NEW STORM/SCREEN WINDOWS

Door and window units for new construction arrive with doors or sashes already hung in their frames. Carpenters build "rough" openings, tip the units in place, and add trim.

Combination screen/storm doors and windows also arrive assembled. Because openings for these units are already finished, combinations usually are made-to-order. Installation may be included in the purchase price, but you can save 10 to 15 percent by installing units yourself.

Professional installers are usually paid by the piece, rather than by the hour. This can lead to shoddy installation. If you hire pros, make it clear that you will not write the check unless the windows are installed correctly.

YOU'LL NEED...

Time: 2 to 4 hours for a window.
Skills: Moderate carpentry skills.
Tools: Hammer, drill, screwdriver, and caulking gun.

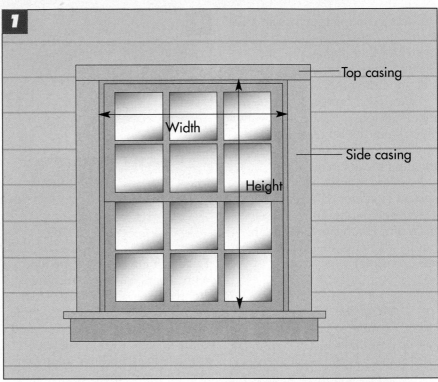

1

Top casing

Width

Side casing

Height

1. Measure window.

A storm/screen unit has a flange that fits over the window casing. This allows some leeway, so the unit does not have to fit precisely. Check the casing for square, and take into account any out-of-squareness. Measure the width between the inside edges of the side casings, and measure the height between the top casing and the sill.

EXPERTS' INSIGHT

BUYING STORM/SCREEN WINDOWS

Combination windows and doors pay for themselves with energy savings, but beware of shoddy products. Poorly made or poorly fitted units can leak air, are difficult to operate, and eventually turn into eyesores.

■ It's worth the extra expense to buy units that are made of thicker-gauge aluminum with an anodized or powdered coating.

■ See that the pins and sliding clips are strong and that replacement parts are available. Consider buying some replacement parts up front; they may be difficult to find later.

■ Better units have warrantees against defects. Choose a company that has been around for a while; a fly-by-night outfit may not be there when you need a part or service.

■ Check the corners of the frames. Lapped joints are stronger and tighter than mitered joints. If you can see light through the joints, you can be sure that they'll admit air.

■ Combinations come in double- or triple-track designs. With double-track units, you must seasonally remove and replace the bottom sash (either storm or screen). Triple-track units have tracks for the top and bottom storm sashes and the screen sash, and are self-storing—you don't have to remove the storm or screen sash you are not using. The deeper the tracks are, the higher a unit's insulation value will be.

2. Trace the outline.
Place the combination unit on the sill; center it between the side casings. The units should be installed square, even if the opening is not square. To check for square, slide a sash nearly all the way up, and see that it aligns with the frame. Sashes should glide smoothly; any binding means the frame is not straight. Trace the outline of the unit with a pencil.

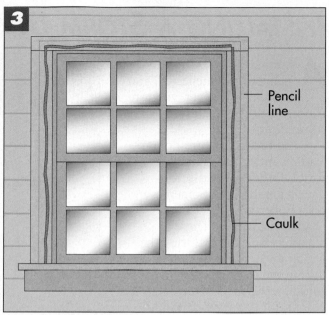

Pencil line

Caulk

3. Caulk the casing.
Scrape and clean away any debris that could inhibit a tight seal between the combination and the casing. Using a caulking gun, run a bead of latex/silicone caulk around the casings about 1 inch inside the pencil lines. Also run a bead along the sill.

4. Drive screws.
Align the frame with the pencil line, press the frame into the caulk, and drive several screws. Test that the sashes operate smoothly and make adjustments if needed. Drive a screw into every available hole. If screws are difficult to drive, or if you are within 2 inches of the end of a piece of casing, drill a pilot hole before driving the screw.

5. Caulk the outside.
Caulk around the outside of the frame where it meets the top and side casings. Also caulk the bottom where it meets the sill.

INSTALLING A STORM DOOR

Assuming your exterior door is a standard 80 inches tall and 3 feet wide or narrower, you can choose standard-size prehung storm doors.

A combination storm door features interchangeable glass panels for winter and screen panels for summer. Some have both upper and lower interchangeable panels. These maximize solar gain during the winter and allow ventilation during the summer. Others have solid lower panels, which are more practical if you have children and/or animals that constantly push against and damage the lower screen unit.

Don't be too frugal when it comes to doors that handle a lot of traffic. Only the highest-quality door will withstand children running in and out, and adults carrying grocery bags in both arms.

A storm/screen security door has an attractive grate and a sturdy lock, so you can leave the door open to summer breezes.

A combination door typically attaches to the brick molding. Measure the inside dimensions of the molding and purchase a door designed to fit.

YOU'LL NEED...

TIME: 2 hours.
SKILLS: Basic carpentry skills.
TOOLS: Hacksaw, drill, screwdriver or screwdriver bit, caulking gun, hammer, level, and tape measure.

1. Temporarily attach the drip cap.
Unpack all the parts and remove the storm and screen panels from the door. Position the drip cap in the center of the top brick molding with the fuzzy gasket pointing out. Drill pilot holes and attach the drip cap with two screws.

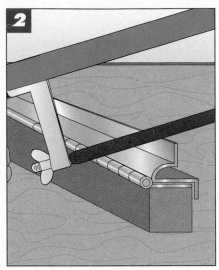

2. Cut the hinge flange.
Make sure you know which side of the hinge flange (also called a Z-bar) is up. Measure the opening height on the hinge side, from the bottom of the drip cap to the door sill. Set the hinge flange on a scrap of wood and cut it to the measured length, minus ⅛ inch.

3. Attach top of the hinge flange.
Apply a bead of caulk to the back of the hinge flange. Have a helper hold the door in position while you work. Align the hinge flange according to the manufacturer's directions. At the top screw hole, drill a pilot hole and drive a screw.

4. Plumb and attach the door.
Check that the hinge flange is plumb. If it is not, loosen the top screw to reposition the flange. Drill pilot holes and drive screws to attach the door.

5. Install the drip cap.
Remove the drip cap. Apply a bead of latex/silicone caulk to its back and reinstall it so that the gap between the top of the door and the cap is even. Drill pilot holes and drive the screws.

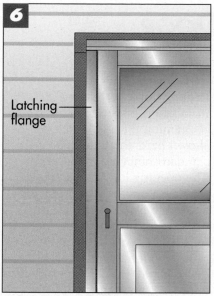

6. Install the latching flange.
Install the storm or screen panels in the door. Check that the door swings freely. Measure, cut, caulk, and install the latching flange (or Z-bar) so that the gap between the door and the flange is even.

7. Install the sweep.
Peel off any protective film from the bottom of the door and the sweep. Slide the rubber gasket onto the bottom of the sweep. Slip the sweep onto the bottom of the door. Slowly close the door and adjust the position of the sweep so it seals at the sill without binding. Drive screws to secure the sweep.

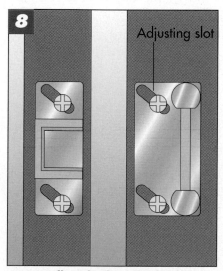

8. Install and adjust the latch.
Assemble and install the latch as instructed by the manufacturer. If the latch does not close easily and latch snugly, loosen the screws and adjust the latching pin.

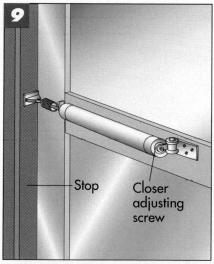

9. Install the closer.
Install and adjust the pneumatic door closer. Hold the closer in place and drill holes in the door (some units will have predrilled holes). Fasten the closer to the door and mark for the bracket that attaches to the stop. Drill holes and fasten the bracket in place.

EXPERTS' INSIGHT

STORM/SCREEN DOOR OPTIONS

Those flimsy aluminum combination doors of yesteryear are still sold, but more substantial units are available. A door with a foam or wood core is difficult to dent. Scratch-resistant surfaces withstand the attentions of pets wanting to come in. Better doors have gaskets that seal storm sashes tight to keep out the cold. Many sweeps have rubber flanges at the bottom that seal just like a standard door threshold.

FRAMING FOR A DOOR

Doors require special framing to provide structural support to the floor or roof above, and a sturdy framework to anchor the door in place.

The door manufacturer will specify the rough opening needed. Measure and assemble carefully so the door will fit.

The framing for a door consists of a header that's supported by king studs and jack studs on both sides of the door. These studs transfer the weight of the home's structure to the sole plate below. Headers are built from two 2×8s, 2×10s, or 2×12s that sandwich a ½-inch-thick piece of plywood. Windows have a similar framing, but they also have cripple studs below to support the windowsill (see page 445).

If you are framing and installing a new exterior door (rather than replacing an existing door),

consult with your local building department. They may require you to apply for a permit and have the installation inspected.

Framing for a sliding door is shown here; the framing for a standard hinged door is similar. The opening for a hinged door may have only one cripple stud above the header because the opening is narrower. (See page 333 for how to frame for a hinged door.)

If you are working on an existing wall (rather than a new addition), first remove the drywall or plaster from the area where the door will go, then remove the exterior siding. If you find any electrical or plumbing lines, hire a pro to have them moved.

Before you remove more than one stud, provide temporary support for the ceiling, or you may damage your home. Build a temporary stud wall and wedge it

under the ceiling, less than 2 feet from the wall that is being demolished (see page 448). Keep the temporary wall in place until the new framing is completed.

Usually, 2×4s are used for framing, but some exterior walls use 2×6s to allow for extra insulation. If you use wood studs, check that the lumber is straight and free of cracks. "Construction-grade" is often good enough, but "No. 2" or better lumber is straighter and stronger, and well worth the small extra cost. Assemble the framing, following instructions on pages 329–333.

Metal studs are economical and perfectly straight. While they are less pleasant to work with than wood, it takes only an hour or so of practice to learn to install them (see pages 334–335).

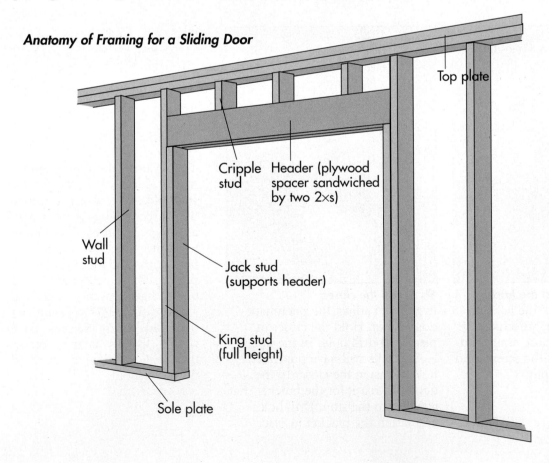

Anatomy of Framing for a Sliding Door

Top plate

Cripple stud

Header (plywood spacer sandwiched by two 2×s)

Wall stud

Jack stud (supports header)

King stud (full height)

Sole plate

FRAMING FOR A WINDOW

Manufacturers of windows specify the size of the rough opening needed. Plan the framing around those dimensions.

If the window is wider than 4 feet, temporarily support the ceiling before you cut the opening (see page 448).

The rough sill must be strong enough to support the window. Typically it is made of doubled 2×s laid flat, supported with cripple studs at each end and at 16-inch centers in the middle.

A header over the window is built in the same way as a door header, using 2×s that sandwich a piece of ½-inch plywood. The wider the opening, the larger the 2×s should be; consult with your building department or the manufacturer's literature.

When framing for a window, first install the king studs. The space between them should be 3 inches wider than the rough opening required for the window. Cut the jack studs so their tops are even with the top of the rough opening, and attach them to the king studs. Make and install a header to span between the king studs, rest it on the jack studs, and fasten in place.

Cut the lower cripple studs 3 inches shorter than the rough opening and attach one to each jack stud. For the rough sill, cut two pieces to span between the jack studs. Set one of the pieces in place, and fasten it to the cripples. Install cripples in the middle and fasten them. Set the second rough sill piece on top of the first and fasten it.

Cut additional cripple studs to fit above the header, and fasten them with angle-driven screws or nails.

Money $ Saver

FRAMING FOR REPLACEMENT WINDOWS

Custom windows can be ordered from several manufacturers, but are frequently more expensive than standard-size windows. If you are replacing an old window, you may be able to save a significant amount of money if you modify the framing to accommodate a standard-size window. Be aware, however, that some modifications in opening size will require patching and repainting the wall, which can be a time-consuming process.

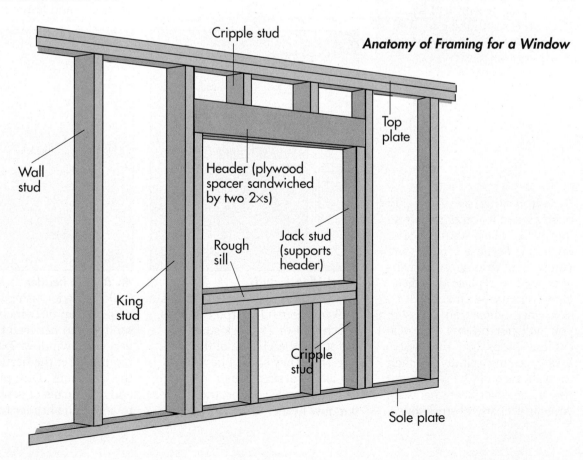

Anatomy of Framing for a Window

Cripple stud

Top plate

Wall stud

Header (plywood spacer sandwiched by two 2×s)

Rough sill

Jack stud (supports header)

King stud

Cripple stud

Sole plate

INSTALLING A WINDOW

Installing windows up to 3½ feet wide can be a do-it-yourself project, but it does require some advanced framing experience. You must know how walls go together (see pages 329–335) and how to keep everything plumb, level, and square.

Carefully plan the window location. Will you run into plumbing, heating, or electrical lines? It's relatively easy to relocate wiring, but difficult to move pipes or ductwork.

Make sure you know the rough-in dimensions of the new window. The exterior opening has to be only slightly larger.

You'll Need...

Time: 6 to 10 hours.
Skills: Advanced carpentry skills.
Tools: Hammer, chisel, pry bar, carpenter's square, keyhole saw or reciprocating saw, nail set, utility knife, caulking gun, drill, carpenter's level, circular saw, and drywall or plaster tools.

TOOLS TO USE

EASE DEMOLITION WITH A RECIPROCATING SAW

A reciprocating saw is mighty handy when it comes to tearing into walls. Have several blades on hand, because chances are you will cut through some nails and need to replace the blade. However use a reciprocating saw only when you are sure you will not hit any electrical cables, pipes, or ductwork. When cutting blindly through drywall, turn off the power and use a keyhole saw; that way, you can feel any obstructions.

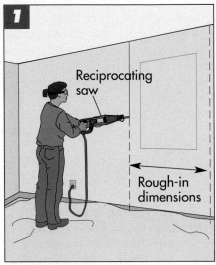

1. Cut the wall.
Mark the opening and cut from ceiling to floor along the adjacent studs; leave the sole plate intact. Make an access hole with a chisel, then a keyhole saw. Or better yet use a reciprocating saw, as shown.

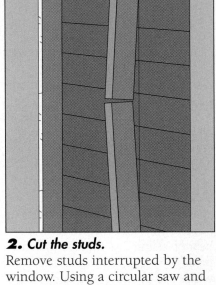

2. Cut the studs.
Remove studs interrupted by the window. Using a circular saw and a handsaw or reciprocating saw, cut through a stud in its center, and pry both pieces away from the sheathing. You may need to install a king stud on each side. Slip it between the drywall and the sheathing and fasten it.

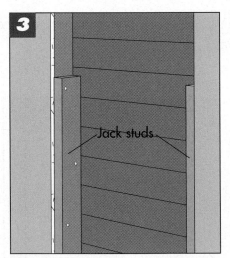

3. Add jack studs.
Using 16d cement-coated sinkers or 3-inch general-purpose screws, attach 2×4 or 2×6 jack studs to the studs at each side of the opening. They should be as tall as the desired rough opening. The jack studs support the window header.

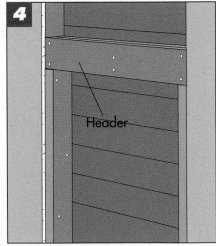

4. Build a header.
Build a header, using two 2×6s with a scrap of ½-inch plywood sandwiched between them. For a very large window, 2×8s may be required. Set the header on top of the jack studs. Drill pilot holes and drive nails or screws at angles to attach the header to the studs.

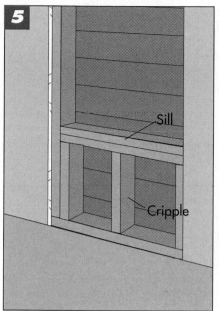

5. Construct a sill.

Construct a 2×4 sill, supported by cripple studs. Set the two outside cripple studs first. Nail 2×4s between the header and the sill to frame side jambs at the rough-in dimension width.

6. Cut the exterior sheathing.

Cut out the exterior sheathing and siding from either the inside or the outside. If you cut from outside, first drill pilot holes to mark corners. Check that the rough opening is the correct size, and that it is level and plumb.

7. Trace and cut the siding.

Windows are heavy, so have a helper assist you. Set the window in place from the outside, level and plumb, then trace around its molding. Use a circular saw, then a chisel to cut away the siding (not the sheathing) to the trace line.

8. Nail the window to the framing.

Cover the exposed sheathing and the inside of the framing with roofing felt (tar paper). Set the window in place and drive galvanized fasteners through the molding. The fasteners should penetrate at least 2 inches into the framing.

9. Nail the jambs to the studs.

Inside, insert shims and check that the window operates smoothly; don't wedge the shims too tightly. Fasten the window jambs to studs. Insulate between the frame and studs, patch and paint the interior wall, attach the inside casing, and caulk the exterior.

EXPERTS' INSIGHT

OTHER INSTALLATIONS

To install a metal window, you may not need to cut the siding (Step 7). Nail the window flange directly to the siding. Then install pieces of exterior trim around the window.

If you have a brick wall, cut the bricks using a circular saw equipped with a masonry cutting blade. Purchase a window with masonry clips, which bend over and are attached using masonry screws. Install molding after the window is in place.

INSTALLING A SLIDING GLASS DOOR

The procedure on pages 446–447 works for rough openings up to 3½ feet wide. For a broader opening, such as a sliding glass door (shown here) or a large bay window, you need larger headers: 2×8s for up to 5 feet of length, 2×10s for up to 6½ feet, and 2×12s for up to 8 feet.

Because an exterior wall bears the weight of an upper floor or the roof, you must devise a temporary support to carry the load while you modify the wall. Install braces, as shown below, and protect flooring with plywood or planks.

Replacing a window with sliding glass doors that open to an outdoor living area will entirely change a home's character. So before you settle on a location, consider privacy, light, ventilation, and the traffic pattern.

Remember that glass loses heat rapidly at night and gains heat rapidly on sunny days. Minimize energy losses by choosing units with insulating glass and by locating them on walls away from prevailing winds.

Sliding glass door units are framed in aluminum, steel, wood, or wood clad with vinyl on the exterior. Standard sizes are 5, 6, and 8 feet wide by 80 inches high. Be sure you can count on good weather the day you cut through the exterior of the house. (Because it's easier to remove framing from a wide opening if you first pull off the sheathing and siding, your home's interior will be exposed throughout most of the project.) Also be sure to have help available to lift the header into position and install the door.

If your sliding glass door will replace an existing window, you can remove the old unit intact, sash and all. Wait until the studs are exposed on both sides before prying them away from the window frame.

Cutting a new opening in a brick-veneer wall calls for quite a bit more work—probably a job for a mason.

> ## YOU'LL NEED...
> **TIME:** 12 to 14 hours.
> **SKILLS:** Advanced carpentry skills.
> **TOOLS:** Hammer, chisel, pry bar, nail puller, carpenter's square, reciprocating saw, nail set, level, drill, circular saw, caulking gun, and tools to repair broken plaster or drywall.

Cut one side along a stud.

1. Remove the drywall or plaster.
Mark cut lines for an opening 3 inches wider than the rough opening, running from floor to ceiling. If possible have at least one of the lines run alongside an existing stud. Cut away the drywall or plaster and remove or relocate any wiring, plumbing, or heating ducts. If necessary slip in and attach a stud on one or both sides.

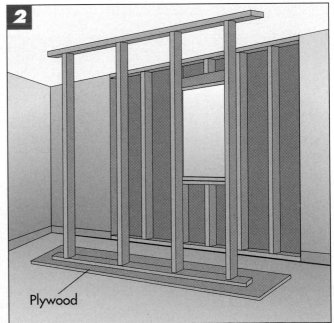

Plywood

2. Install temporary bracing.
Set a piece of plywood on the floor to protect it. Build a stud wall (see pages 329–330) and raise it into position, no more than 2 feet away from the rough opening. Use shims to make the temporary wall snug. Keep this bracing in place until you have finished framing the opening.

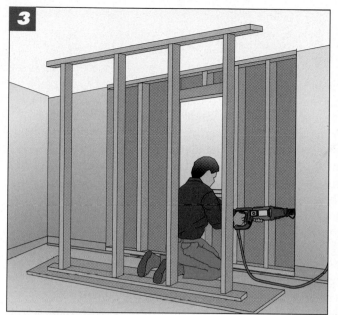

3. Cut the siding.

With a reciprocating saw, cut the siding and sheathing at the top and the sides. Then cut through the toe plate and remove it. Cut through the siding at the bottom of the opening.

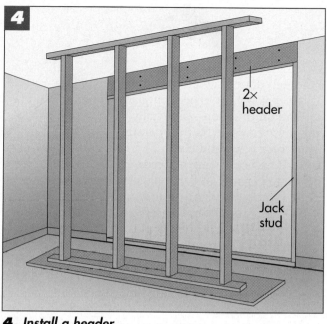

4. Install a header.

Cut jack studs to the height of the rough opening and attach them to the king studs on each side. Check each side for plumb and see that the rough opening is the correct size. Build a header out of 2× lumber and plywood, set it on the jack studs, and attach it with angle-driven fasteners.

5. Mark and cut the siding.

Place the door frame in the opening. Check for level, plumb, and square. Trace around the frame and cut through the siding (but not the sheathing). Cover all bare wood with roofing felt (tar paper) or building wrap and reinsert the door frame. Secure the frame loosely with screws.

6. Plumb the frame.

From the inside use shims to make the door perfectly level at the top and bottom, plumb at the sides, and square at the corners. Make sure that you do not bend the frame as you tap in shims. Fasten the frame and set in the door panels. Insulate between the frame and the opening.

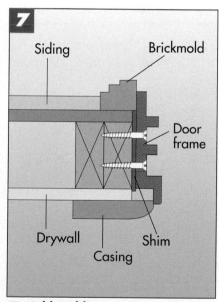

7. Add molding.

Molding bridges the gap between the frame and the siding. Install exterior molding and caulk the joints. Inside, patch the wall and install molding.

SECURING WINDOWS

Intruders usually enter homes through doors, say police. However you can't expect burglars to stand on tradition—especially if you have windows that they easily could force open and climb through without being noticed.

A large expanse of fixed glass is less of a problem than you may think. The clatter from smashing a picture window probably would call attention to a break-in. Most burglars are cautious about being caught, so they don't bother with homes that are secure, opting to move on to easier targets.

If the doors are locked, burglars will concentrate on smaller, operable windows. If the window can't be forced open, a burglar may stick tape to a pane, break it, and quietly pull away the pieces to gain access to the latch.

The solution is to lock your windows in both their closed and open positions. This way no one can reach inside and enlarge the opening. The drawings below and on the next page show a variety of ways to secure windows and sliding doors. Be sure, however, that whatever method you use doesn't block a potential fire exit.

Most homes have many windows. Securing every one can be costly and time-consuming, so start with all sliding glass doors and windows accessible from ground level. Analyze which upper-level windows could be reached from a balcony, garage or porch roof, or tree. Enterprising second-story burglars may bring along a ladder to get at the ones you think are inaccessible.

For an extra measure of protection, hire a security company to install sensing devices in your windows and doors. In a typical setup, when a window is broken, an alarm signal travels to the security company, triggering a call to the police.

Make sure all windows work properly. Sashes that wobble when you crank them, rattle in high winds, or have to be propped open offer only token resistance to break-ins. (For window repairs, see pages 409–415 and 434–435.)

YOU'LL NEED...
TIME: About 20 minutes per window.
SKILLS: Basic carpentry skills.
TOOLS: Drill and bits, screwdriver, pliers, and hammer.

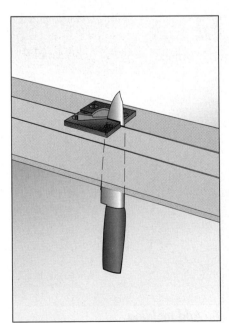

The problem with a sash lock.
Ordinary sash locks offer little security because you can open most of them easily with a knife blade, as shown. A heavy-duty model that clicks shut offers more resistance.

Install a key lock.
Key locks can't be jimmied, even if the glass is broken. Most will also let you lock the window in a partly open position. You'll need to drill a hole in the upper sash for every position you want to be able to lock.

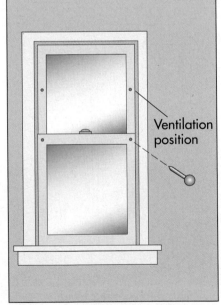

Ventilation position

Using nails as locks.
With the sash closed, drill a hole on each side, as shown above, through the bottom sash and most of the way into the top sash. Open the window halfway, and drill again. To secure the window in either position, insert two nails.

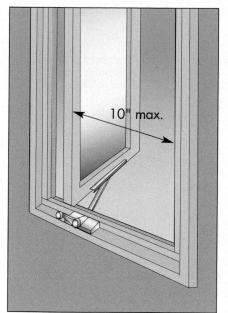

Check a casement window.
Many casement windows won't open enough to admit an adult. To check, open the window and measure from the inside edge of the sash to the jamb.

Remove an operator crank.
If a fully opened window will admit a person, open it partially so the opening is 10 inches or less. Then remove the operator crank and set it out of reach.

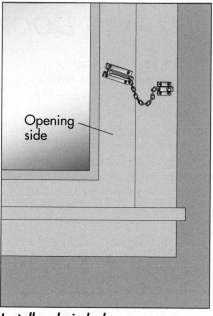

Install a chain lock.
Install a door-type chain lock to keep windows from opening. Fasten it down with the biggest screws possible.

Install a hasp or a stop.
A hasp on a basement window can be secured with a padlock. Use a keyless combination lock or keep the key somewhere that's handy, but not on the sill. If your windows don't have hasps, drive long screws into a stop on each side. Leave a few inches to open the window for ventilation.

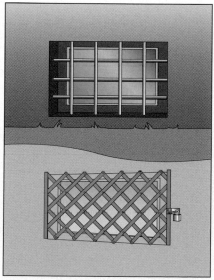

Add a grill or grate.
Custom-made grills mortared into the foundation give basement windows a behind-bars look—but they provide peace of mind in a high-crime area. Scissors-type gates and hinged iron shutters can be padlocked from the inside, yet opened for escape in case of an emergency.

The problem with a sliding window.
Thieves like sliding windows (and sliding glass doors) because some can be jimmied easily from their tracks, even when the door locksets are in the locked position.

SECURING DOORS

The best way to secure a windowless door is with a dead-bolt lock (see page 429). Here are additional security measures you may choose to take.

Double-cylinder dead-bolt locks employ special one-way screws that you can turn in, but not out; otherwise an intruder could simply remove the assembly. Fittings with a double-cylinder lock generally include an extra set of conventional, slotted screws. Mount the lock and strike with these, make any adjustments, then withdraw the slotted screws and replace them with the tamperproof versions.

All surface-mounted hardware depends upon screws for holding power; if the screws that came with your lock don't penetrate at least halfway into the door, discard them and buy longer ones. For added strength, coat the screws with glue before driving them into pilot holes.

Mount any surface lock about 8 to 10 inches higher than the existing knob set so that you can see and operate it easily.

In addition to the devices shown here, a variety of sliding bolts and other locking devices are available in decorative finishes.
NOTE: *Whichever security measures you choose, be sure you install them such that family members can quickly exit the house in case of fire.*

YOU'LL NEED...
TIME: About 30 minutes.
SKILLS: Basic carpentry skills.
TOOLS: Screwdriver, pliers, drill, and hole saw or spade bit for the diameter hole specified for the lock.

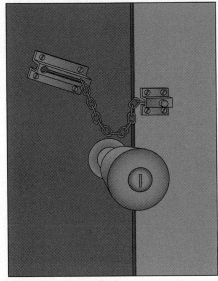

Attach a chain lock.
For extra protection that's quick and simple, install a chain lock. Mount the hardware with screws that penetrate the door frame and the jamb studs.

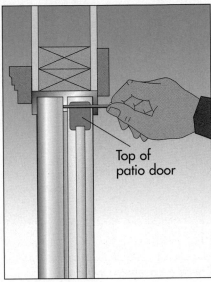

Use a nail as a security pin.
Secure sliding glass patio doors by drilling holes through both the track and the sash frames. Slip nails into the holes to prevent the doors from opening.

Install a bar.
An accessory bar mounts to the door frame to jam the sliding door. It prevents an intruder from forcing the lock, but doesn't protect against jimmying the door up. Alternatively, cut a piece of wood to fit tightly in the bottom track and keep the sliding door from moving.

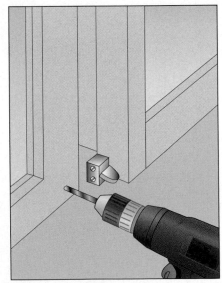

Attach a toe lock.
Toe-operated locks are convenient and the least obtrusive. Mount the lock on the casing and drill a hole in the sash into which a locking rod enters.

ROOFING, SIDING, AND WEATHERIZATION

UNDERSTANDING ROOFS

A pitched roof sheds water much the same way a duck's feathers do. Courses of roofing material—most often some variation of the **shingle**—lie one atop the other and overlap, like a bird's feathers. Shingles on a roof are layered at least two deep, with exposed portions slightly smaller than half the total area of the shingle. At the top, a **ridge vent** or an extra layer of shingles covers the ridge.

Valleys, the places where two slopes meet, direct runoff into gutters, which in turn direct the water into downspouts. For additional protection against leakage, metal or composition flashings are placed under the shingles at the roof's most vulnerable points. Typically these include valleys, dormers, vents, and chimneys, or anywhere the roof's surface is penetrated.

Valleys are notorious problem areas; the flatter the roof, the greater the potential for leaks. Metal **valley flashing** must be wide enough and the pieces must overlap correctly. If no flashing is used, roofing must be woven together seamlessly—a job that's definitely for pros. A valley that does not have metal flashing is vulnerable to damage; avoid walking on it.

Any area with flashing—especially around a chimney—is liable to leak. **Chimney flashing** must be installed correctly and sealed tightly against the vertical surface that it abuts.

Vents, whether they are plumbing pipes or exhaust fans, usually come with integral flashing. Typically, the lower half of the flashing is exposed, and the upper half is covered with roofing.

Beneath the roofing material lies a house's most complex structure, framing (typically **gable** or **hip**). The framing ties together the wall structures and supports not only the weight of the shingles but also other loads, such as snow and ice in colder climates. **Rafters**, rising from the top plate of the wall to the **ridge board**, define the roof's pitch. **Collar ties** in the attic help keep the rafters from spreading; **headers** box in any openings.

Deck sheathing, usually plywood, goes on top of the rafters to give the structure rigidity. A layer of **roofing felt** seals the sheathing against moisture. Rafter ends are trimmed at the eaves with a **fascia board** (to which a **gutter** is fastened) and along the rake with **rake boards**. Once the trim is protected with drip cap, the shingles can go on.

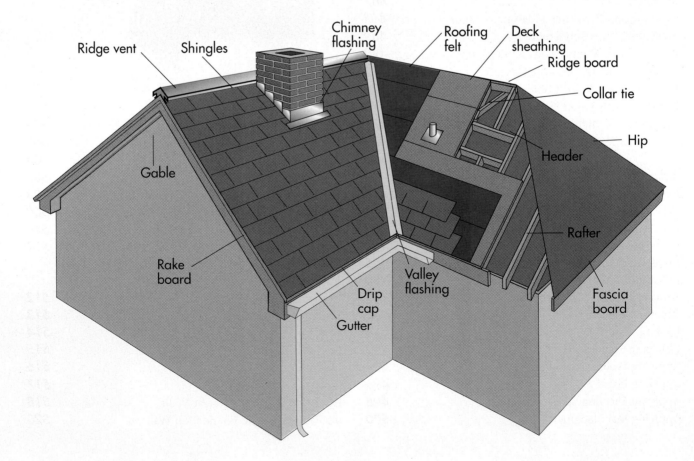

UNDERSTANDING EXTERIOR WALLS

Regardless of your home's exterior skin (siding or brick), its skeleton probably looks like the one shown here. The **sill plate** rests on the masonry foundation. **Rim joists,** collectively called a box sill, rest on the outside perimeter of the sill plate. Floor joists (which also act as ceiling joists for the basement, if there is a basement) attach to the rim joists. In some cases a short framed wall rises from the **foundation,** and the joists rest on this wall. If your basement ceiling is open, periodically check the rim joists, the sill plate, and the **sill seal**.

Attend to any moisture immediately because rot here could cause structural damage. It is also here that termites and other wood-boring insects often enter the house.

Exterior wall framing is made of 2×4 or 2×6 lumber (2×6s are common in newer homes in cold climates because they accommodate thicker insulation). A **sole plate** rests on the joists. Vertical **studs** are usually spaced 16 inches on center (sometimes they are 24 inches on center). The **top plate** is usually doubled to ensure that it can support second-story joists or the roof.

Over a door or window, a header carries the load and must be as strong as the rest of the wall (see page 445).

Insulation between the studs conserves heat (see pages 514–520 for more about insulation). Wood or composition board **sheathing** adds insulation and strength. Then a layer of **building wrap,** either asphalt-saturated building paper or plastic, seals the sheathing. It is essential that the building wrap be installed correctly so that moisture is sealed out rather than trapped inside the wall.

Outside, **siding** faces the elements and gives your home its visual character. Shown here is horizontal lap siding, named because the boards overlap each other. Other types of siding may be vertical or horizontal, but all overlap in some way in order to seal the exterior (see pages 492–493). Vinyl and aluminum siding often give the appearance of wood, but with differing maintenance requirements. Siding made of pressed board needs to be kept well protected or it will disintegrate quickly.

Regardless of its composition, siding deserves a careful semiannual inspection. Scan its surface systematically, using binoculars for closeups of high places if necessary. Look for cracks, splits, peeling paint, and evidence of rot or insect damage. Any breaks in your home's skin— no matter how small—will eventually admit water into wall cavities. If you neglect the repairs explained in this section (see pages 481–489), moisture could wreck insulation, framing, or even **interior wall surfaces.**

If a new paint job is imminent, see pages 844–857. To learn about basic wall-building techniques, turn to pages 329–337.

During your inspection, if you suspect that a wall may be infested with termites or other insects, read the information on pages 490–491 about identifying insects and what to do about them.

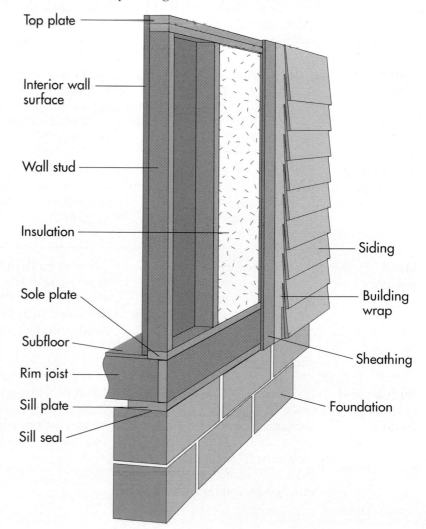

Top plate
Interior wall surface
Wall stud
Insulation
Sole plate
Subfloor
Rim joist
Sill plate
Sill seal
Siding
Building wrap
Sheathing
Foundation

PROTECTING YOUR ROOF

Note that the first five categories in this chart work well on the pitched roofs explained on page 454. But they will not protect a flat or only slightly sloping surface from standing water. Such surfaces require a watertight membrane system (see page 464) and often a contractor's help.

Asphalt shingles and roll roofing are the least expensive options; slate and clay tiles are the most expensive. Most do-it-yourselfers can apply asphalt shingle and wood shingles and shakes. Other types require advanced or pro skills.

ROOF MATERIAL COMPARISON

Material	Features	Maintenance	Life Span
Asphalt shingles	Most popular by far, these are made of roofing felt saturated with asphalt and coated with mineral granules; newer types have a fiberglass base for better weather- and fire-resistance	Little at first, but over the years, shingles curl, crack, and lose surface granules; most cement themselves down in the hot sun; repairs are fairly easy (see page 461)	15 to 30 years under temperate weather conditions; better-quality shingles carry 25-year guarantees
Wood shingles and shakes	Shingles have a uniform, machine-sawn appearance; shakes, a rustic, hand-split look; both have a poor fire rating unless specially treated; both are expensive	Unsealed types sometimes rot, warp, and split—and soon weather to a soft gray; like asphalt shingles, they are not difficult to repair or replace (see page 462)	20 years or more for shingles; up to 50 years for shakes if maintained properly
Slate or clay tiles	Both are heavy, expensive, and absolutely fireproof; tiles are more common in the Southwest, and slate in the East, where the quarries are located	An occasional cracked or chipped tile can be tricky to repair (see page 460); slate is somewhat easier to repair (see page 463)	75 years or more, provided repairs are made before underlayment is damaged
Roll roofing or selvage	Same material as asphalt shingles, but comes in the form of wide strips that are lapped horizontally across the roof's surface	Lightweight, single-layer installations fail frequently—but repairs are easy (see page 465)	5 to 15 years; ask if company will come back for patching
Metal roofing	Older types include terne—a tin/steel alloy—and copper; modern styles include corrugated or ribbed aluminum and galvanized-steel panels. Aluminum, steel, and terne often are painted	All must be flashed and fastened with the same type of metal or electrolytic action will cause deterioration; may need periodic painting.	35 years for aluminum and steel; copper and terne are even more durable
Built-up and "rubber" roofing	Used on flat or low-pitched roofs, fabricated on the job by laminating layers of felt with asphalt or coal tar, then topped with gravel; "rubber" or modified-bitumen roll roofing is installed by torching it down	Leaks due to a poor job are fairly common; fortunately, repairs are not very difficult (see pages 464–465)	5 to 20 years; generally, the more layers, the longer life you can expect it to have; a rubber roof lasts 30 years or more

USING AN EXTENSION LADDER

For strength and rigidity, select a ladder with a duty rating of at least 250 pounds. It should extend 3 feet above the highest eaves on your house. Add another foot to this distance to make up for the propping angle. The extended height of a ladder is about 3 feet less than the total of its sections.

If you have never scaled an extension ladder, ask someone to steady it from below when you make your first few climbs. You will soon gain confidence.

CAUTION!
WATCH OUT FOR POWER LINES
Metal—and even wet wooden or fiberglass—ladders can conduct electricity. Be especially careful when moving or extending a ladder near power lines. In addition, phone and cable lines can be damaged if hit by a ladder.

Always stay clear of power lines, even if your ladder is made of a nonconductive material.

Never allow more than one person on a ladder at a time. Don't use a ladder on a windy day—not only is it hazardous for

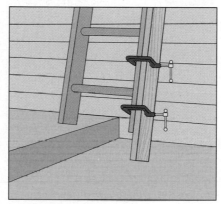

Leg extension.
When the feet of a ladder must span uneven terrain, you can use a sturdy 2×4 to fashion an extension for one foot. Use at least two strong clamps to securely fasten the extension.

you to work in heavy winds, an unattended ladder can blow over, leaving you stranded.

Store ladders indoors, away from moisture and "second-story" burglars. Don't paint a wooden ladder; paint can hide defects.

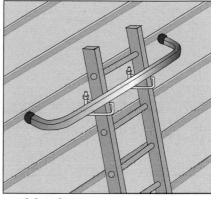

Ladder brace.
The top of a ladder can easily damage a gutter or even siding. A brace improves a ladder's stability, protects siding and gutters, spans obstacles, and keeps the ladder away from the house.

1. Walk the ladder up.
To set up a ladder, place its feet firmly against the foundation. Do not extend it yet; wait until it's vertical. "Walk" the ladder up, hand over hand, keeping your arms straight. It will seem to get lighter as it rises.

2. Pull the rope.
To extend the ladder, brace a rail with your foot and pull the ladder carefully away from the house until you feel you can hold it securely; you may need help. Pull the rope to raise the top section. Go a little higher than you need, then let it slide back down. Make sure both locks catch.

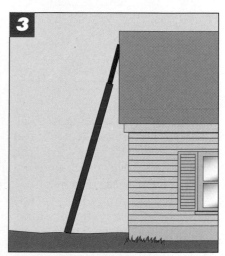

3. Position the ladder.
Position the ladder so that the distance from the base to the wall is about one-fourth of its extended length. Make sure the ladder's feet dig a bit into the ground.

INSPECTING A ROOF

To ensure a tight roof overhead, you should examine it every spring and fall. You don't have to haul out the extension ladder and risk life and limb crawling onto the roof. Just scan it from all sides through binoculars, paying special attention to the problem areas illustrated here.

If you do decide to climb up for a closer look, exercise caution. Also bear in mind that the sun does more damage than the wind and rain combined, so you may want to focus most of your effort on the sunny side of the house. Don't mount a roof on a hot, sunny day. Shingles (especially asphalt shingles) are easily damaged when hot.

If a number of shingles are broken, blistered, or balding and many have lost their luster, prepare for a reroofing job (see pages 474–475).

Clean the gutters.
Keep your hips between the rails, and don't overreach; erect ladders are easily tipped with little motion. For solutions to gutter problems, see pages 470–471.

Use a stabilizer.
For roof work, buy a pair of metal roofing jacks, which are held in place with nails driven under a shingle. Install two jacks and stretch a 2×4 between them. Or secure the ladder with ropes tied to a tree on the other side. Or hook a stabilizer over the ridge.

EXPERTS' INSIGHT

ICE DAMS

In an area with freezing weather, the attic must be kept cold in the winter. If not, snow can melt, flow down near the eaves, and then freeze. The resulting "ice dam" can work its way under shingles and flashing, seriously damaging the roof's sheathing and possibly the framing. If you see signs of ice dams, install attic insulation (pages 512–513). This will keep heat from escaping into the attic space.

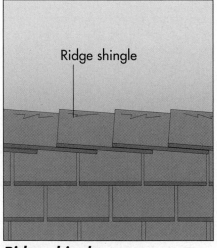

Ridge shingle

Ridge shingle.
Ridge shingles often fail first. Look for cracks and wind damage. In the case of asphalt shingles, the mineral granules may be worn away. A leak here can show up anywhere inside.

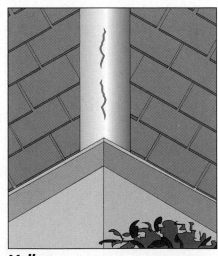

Valley.
Valleys are another place where deterioration causes problems. Make sure any flashing is sound. Shingles should lie flat on top of the flashing. If leaks occur during windy rainstorms, the shingles that lie on the flashing may not be cut correctly; ask a pro.

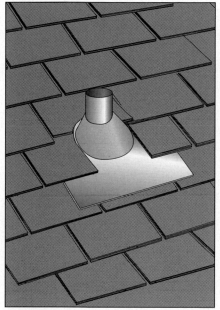

Flashing.

Check other flashing too. It should be tight, rust-free, and sealed with pliable caulking or roofing cement. Installing a new vent like the one shown above is not difficult, but other types of flashing require a pro.

Missing shingle.

Loose, curled, or missing shingles leak moisture that weakens sheathing and harms walls and ceilings. If individual shingles have been damaged by a falling branch, replace them singly. If shingles show general wear and tear, it's time for a reroofing job.

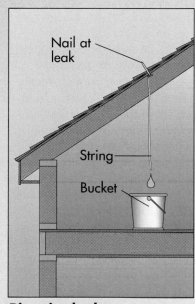

Pinpoint leaks.

Water that gets through a leak in your roof will often follow a meandering, brooklike course. It can travel under sheathing, down a rafter, even along an electrical cable, before showing up as a drip or damp spot on a ceiling or wall.

You may be able to trace the trickle to its source from the attic. Look for water stains on framing and sheathing. Keep in mind that a leak will originate higher than the area where it first appeared. Even then the cause of the leak may be above the point of entry into the attic. Often the culprits are damaged flashing and damaged or mis-applied shingles.

On a sunny day, a leak may appear as a pinhole of light in the attic. If you find one, drive a nail up through it from the attic to mark the spot on the roof itself. Attach a string to guide water to a bucket until you can make the repair.

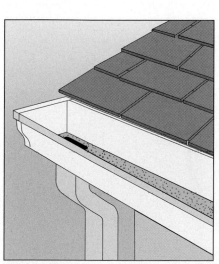

Granules in the gutter.

A large accumulation of granules in the gutter means your roof is losing its surface coating. Expect problems soon.

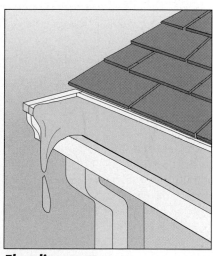

Flooding gutter.

Watch during a heavy rain to see if gutters are free-flowing. Flooding can work up under lower shingle courses.

SOLVING ROOF PROBLEMS

If you are queasy about moving around on high places—especially if your roof is steeply pitched—hire a professional for even small jobs.

If you conquer your fears, however, you will find most repairs are relatively simple. Often the biggest challenges are hoisting up your tools and materials and getting around on the roof.

On gentle slopes wear shoes with rubber soles. Attack steep pitches by hooking or tying an extension ladder over the ridge of the roof. Or use ladder jacks and a length of 2×4 (see page 458). Do not step on gutters or rely on them for support.

With any type of roof, don't walk on it more than necessary. And don't go up at all during hot or cold weather extremes. Try to repair asphalt shingles on medium-warm days (40°–80°F); asphalt roofing turns brittle in cold weather and is too soft to handle when hot.

Wood shingles and shakes are not temperature-sensitive, but they are affected by humidity. Soaking them makes them much more pliable; dry shingles may split when you drive nails in them. Wet wood shingles can be slippery.

Only a few supplies are required for repair work. Roofing cement is available in cans, and you can apply it with a putty knife or a scrap of wood. Butyl caulk and "gutter caulk" are messy to work with, but worth the trouble because they adhere so well. For fastening use galvanized roofing nails that are long enough to penetrate all the way through the sheathing. If you have several layers of roofing, you may need nails as long as 2 inches. Wood shingles and slate tiles require shingle nails, which have thinner shanks. In your garage you may find shingles or roll goods left over from the installation; otherwise take a sample to buy materials of matching color.

Patch cracks, minor splits, and holes with roofing cement. Drive home popped nails and seal them or the shingles that cover them. Make sure that all shingles lie flat. If any are even slightly curled, fasten them down with dabs of cement. Don't be stingy with roofing cement or caulking around the flashing.

REPAIRING SPANISH TILE

Spanish ceramic clay tiles weigh as much as 15 pounds each. And just to make it more difficult, they must be maneuvered on a fragile, slippery surface that may shift underfoot. For your own safety, hire a contractor who specializes in tile roofs for replacement and major repair jobs. If you do venture onto a tile roof, always spread your weight over at least two tiles.

Tiles can last 75 to 100 years if they are exposed only to the elements. However, tiles are brittle and become more so over time. A falling branch or a person walking on the roof can easily break an individual tile. If tiles are failing in several places, even though they have not been bumped, all the tiles probably need to be replaced.

Some clay tiles are rounded, while others are nearly flat. All types are made to interlock, so you probably cannot replace a broken tile with one of a different style.

You can seal small cracks and flashing with roofing cement, though the resulting patch will not be pleasant to look at. Bigger gaps, and especially cap tiles along the ridge, should be mortared by a professional contractor.

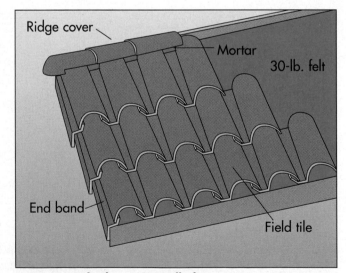

How Spanish tiles are installed.
The roof structure—both the rafters and the sheathing—must be extra-strong to accommodate a tile roof. In a typical installation, thick 30-pound roofing felt is first laid on the sheathing. The tiles themselves interlock and are nailed to the sheathing. Tiles at the ridge are cemented in place and sealed using mortar. Consider installing newer concrete tiles, which last even longer than ceramic tiles.

REPAIRING ASPHALT SHINGLES

Buy roofing cement in caulking tubes to seal minor cracks and holes and to glue down curled shingles. If you have a larger job, buy the roofing cement in larger containers—1-gallon or even 5-gallon buckets.

If the damage is extensive, replace the shingle. When working with asphalt shingles, wait for a warm day when the shingles will be flexible and easier to work with. Avoid ending up with exposed nails as much as possible. If you must leave an exposed nail, cover it well with roofing cement.

YOU'LL NEED...

TIME: About 30 minutes.
SKILLS: Basic roofing skills.
TOOLS: Hammer, pry bar, putty knife, utility knife, flat shovel, caulking gun.

1. Remove the nails.
Loosen the nails in the shingle above by slipping a flat shovel underneath. Lift the shingle above carefully, to avoid cracking it. Pull all four of the nails with a pry bar and slide the bad shingle out.

2. Cut a shingle and slip it in.
Remove 1 inch from the top edge of the new shingle by cutting the nongranular side with a knife. Bend the strip back and forth until it snaps. Slip the new shingle into place under the shingle above. Note the positions of the nails.

3. Drive nails.
If possible, lift the shingle above and drive nails close to the old nail holes. The nailhead should cover the old hole, but be far enough away that the nail bites into the sheathing. It may work to push the nail in place, slip a pry bar over the nailhead, and pound on the pry bar.

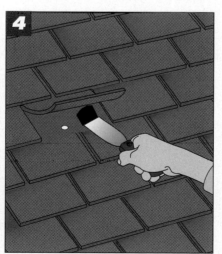

4. Cover heads with cement.
Coat the nailheads with roofing cement, then firmly press the upper course back into place. If necessary, seal the old holes as well. If the shingle curls up, weight it down temporarily.

Repair with flashing.
You also can back up a damaged shingle with a piece of metal flashing. Secure the flashing by setting it in a bed of roofing cement. Then cover the top of the metal with more cement and press the shingle into the cement.

REPAIRING WOOD SHINGLES

A new replacement shingle may differ in color from the surrounding shingles. In time it will weather and look the same.

Choose grade #1 shingles, made of heartwood, which resists insects and fungi. They will last far longer than less expensive shingles made from sapwood.

When replacing shingles, be sure to match the spacing between the existing shingles. Butting the replacement shingle against the old shingles may create a tight joint that traps moisture, which will encourage rot and decay.

You'll Need...

Time: About 30 to 60 minutes per shingle.
Skills: Basic carpentry skills.
Tools: Hammer, chisel, pry bar, utility knife, saw, nail set, drill, caulking gun.

Nail a cracked shingle.
Mend splits by drilling pilot holes and driving shingle or siding nails, which have smaller heads than roofing nails. Seal the gap and the nailheads with roofing cement or butyl caulk (which can be purchased in a color to nearly match the shingles).

Back a hole with flashing.
If a knothole has opened, drive a sheet of aluminum flashing material under the shingle. Be sure that it extends several inches above the hole. If the spot is highly visible, paint the metal to resemble the shingles.

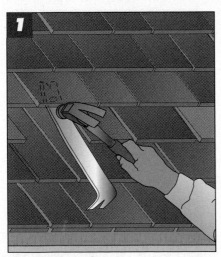

1. Flatten nails.
To remove a damaged shingle, split it along the grain with a chisel and pull the pieces out. The nails that held it in place will remain. Place the flat end of a pry bar over the old nailheads and strike with a hammer to drive the nailheads flush.

2. Tap in a new shingle.
Cut a new shingle to width so that there are appropriate gaps on both sides. With a block of wood and a hammer, drive the new shingle until it is flush with the row and the nailheads are covered.

3. Nail and seal.
Drive two shingle nails into the new shingle at 45 degrees, close to the butt of the shingle above. Use a nail set to drive nailheads flush; seal with caulk.

REPAIRING SLATE SHINGLES

Slate roofs last for decades if installed and maintained properly. In addition to a regular inspection a couple of times each year, inspect a slate roof after violent storms.

Because walking on a slate roof may damage the slate tiles, the easiest, safest method of inspection is to stand on the ground and use a pair of binoculars to look for signs of damage or missing tiles. **NOTE:** *Slate tiles can be extremely slippery, especially if they are damp or wet. Use care when working on a slate roof.*

You'll Need...

TIME: About 1 hour, depending on the extent of the damage.
SKILLS: Moderate carpentry skills.
TOOLS: Hacksaw or slate ripper, glass cutter, drill, hammer, speed square, nail set, tin snips.

1. Cut the concealed nails.
Slip a hacksaw blade under the broken slate, and cut the nails concealed under the course above. (If you live in an area where slate roofs are common, you may be able to buy a slate ripper. This handy tool quickly cuts through the hidden nails.)

2. Cut a slate tile.
Cut a slate tile so there is a gap on either side that matches the gaps in the rest of the roof. To cut slate, score both sides deeply with a glass cutter. Align the score over an edge and snap downward.

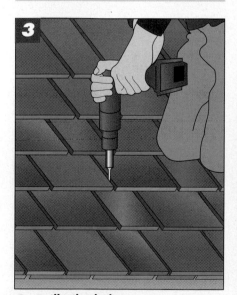

3. Drill pilot holes.
Equip a drill with a masonry bit that is slightly wider than the shank of the nails you will drive. Drill two holes about 3/4 inch above the bottom edge of the course above, in the gaps, as shown.

4. Attach with nails.
Drive in galvanized shingle or siding nails, which have smaller heads than roofing nails, through the holes you just drilled. Drive the nails just flush using a nail set.

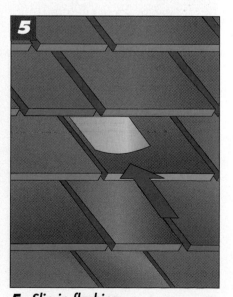

5. Slip in flashing.
Cut a piece of galvanized or copper flashing about 4 inches wide and 6 inches long. Slightly cup it to provide tension and slip it under the slate to cover the nails. (Or use a pre-cupped "bib" made for this purpose.)

Patching Membrane Roofing

One modern way to waterproof large flat roofs is to cap them with gigantic elastomer membrane sheets made from rolls of ethylene propylene diene monomer (EPDM) or other rubber materials. The rolls come in standard sizes: 100 feet long by 10, 15, or 20 feet wide. You may have to hire a roofer licensed by the EPDM manufacturer to repair such a roof. But patching a leak is not difficult.

"Rubber" roofing, or modified-bitumen roofing, comes in 4-foot-wide rolls. Pros weld it in place using a large torch. It also can be applied using roofing cement. Often a roof's life can be extended by brushing on reflective-fibered roof coating with a push broom.

You'll Need...

TIME: About 1 hour, depending on the extent of the damage.
SKILLS: Moderate carpentry skills.
TOOLS: Brush, scissors, putty knife, steel roller, caulking gun.

1. Apply splice adhesive.
Wash the deck around the leak with mild detergent and water. Rinse with fresh water, then wash with "splice wash" to prepare the surface. Using a stiff brush, apply "splice adhesive," which resembles contact cement, to the prepared area of the roof.

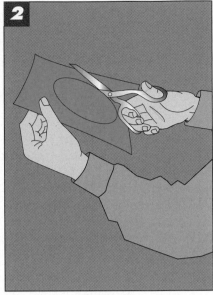

2. Cut a round patch.
Cut a round patch of EPDM rubber 4 inches larger in diameter than the damaged area.

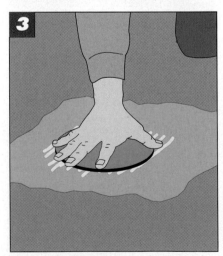

3. Apply the patch.
Apply splice adhesive to the patch and let the adhesive dry to the touch. Once it's dry, place the patch carefully—it cannot be slid—and press it into place.

Steel roller

4. Roll the patch.
Roll the adhered patch with a 2-inch steel roller. If you cannot find a 2-inch roller, rent a linoleum roller or use a piece of steel pipe.

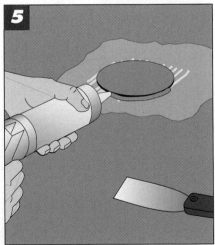

5. Apply lap sealant.
Wait 30 minutes to let the adhesive volatiles escape. Then using a caulking gun, apply lap sealant to seal the edges of the patch. Use a putty knife to flatten the sealant so water cannot collect and puddle.

REPAIRING ROLL AND BUILT-UP ROOFING

Roll and built-up roofing usually are applied to nearly flat roofs, which are easy to work on. (However, avoid walking on them more than you have to.) A smaller roof may be covered with roll roofing, made of essentially the same material as asphalt shingles. Black tar roofs are installed by pros, using a large kettle of hot tar. Sometimes gravel is added. "Rubber" (modified-bitumen) roofing is replacing the hot tar.

After you've slit a blister open, look inside for traces of moisture. Moisture means water has crept under the roofing—usually from defective flashing nearby (see pages 466–467)—or possibly from a hole or a crack in the membrane.

Patch a gravel roof.
If your roof is topped with gravel or crushed stones, carefully brush them away from the damaged area with a whisk broom. Clean out small cracks, pack them with roofing cement, then feather out more cement for about 3 inches on each side. Sprinkle the patch with gravel.

Slice a blister.
Slice open blisters and work the cement inside. Then fasten down the blister edges by driving in roofing nails along each side of the incision. Top off all repairs with a patch that is much larger than the damaged area. Cement it, drive nails, and apply more cement.

YOU'LL NEED...

TIME: About 1 hour, depending on the extent of the damage.
SKILLS: Moderate carpentry skills.
TOOLS: Whisk broom, putty knife, utility knife, hammer.

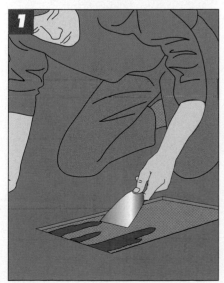

1. To patch a damaged section, cut out the old roofing.
Replace any extensively blistered or buckling sections. Cut out the old roofing with a utility knife and scrape away the old cement.

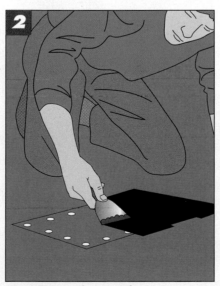

2. Fill in with a patch.
Trim a new piece of roofing for a snug fit, then nail and cement it in place. Apply enough cement to lap all sides by 3 inches.

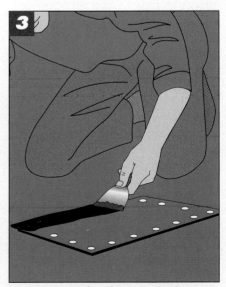

3. Cover with a larger patch.
Press a second, larger patch into the cement; nail and seal it too. Double-patching makes a strong, watertight, long-lasting repair. Regravel as necessary.

REPAIRING AND REPLACING FLASHING

Think of flashing as a special-purpose shingle. Like a shingle, flashing overlaps and interweaves with other roofing materials to shed water.

Flashing is made of thin-gauge metal that is bent and formed to fit angled joints where two or more surfaces abut. Because these intersections are vulnerable to leakage, flashing deserves closer scrutiny than the rest of your roof.

Look for flashing that has pulled away from adjoining surfaces and for roofing cement or caulk that has dried and cracked. Even tiny holes can leak; when in doubt, apply new cement or caulk.

Rusted, cracked, or corroded flashing around chimneys, dormers, and plumbing vents will last for a few more years if you trowel on a coat of fibered asphalt-aluminum roof paint. If there is widespread deterioration or valley-flashing failure, call in a roofer or sheet-metal specialist to replace these sections entirely.

You can replace small flashing pieces as long as you buy precise duplicates and replace them in their exact original positions.

Take care that two types of metal do not come in contact with each other, or corrosion could result. For durability at a reasonable price, choose aluminum flashing. Vent flashing comes as a single molded piece of metal or plastic. Simply fit the piece over the pipe and cover with roofing on the uphill side.

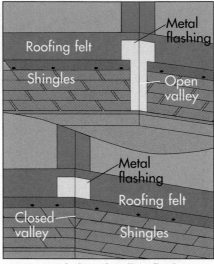

Open- and closed-valley flashing.
Because it is visible, open-valley flashing is easy to inspect. Cement down any shingles that are even slightly curled or loose.

Closed-valley flashing hides beneath the roofing. In some cases shingles are so interlaced on top that it is impossible to check the flashing.

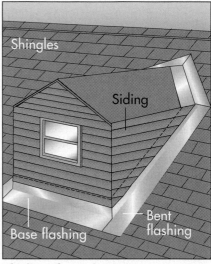

Flashing for a dormer.
To reflash dormers buy pieces of flashing bent at 90 degrees. Using the old flashing as a guide, tuck the flashing under the siding on the dormer. Use valley flashing along the peak. For brick use step flashing capped with counter-flashing let into mortar joints, as shown on page 467.

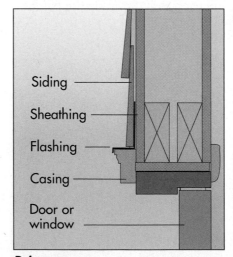

Drip cap.
Drip cap flashing keeps water from seeping under the frames over windows and doors. The drip cap should be several inches high so that water cannot work its way up and around it. Check drip caps periodically for damage.

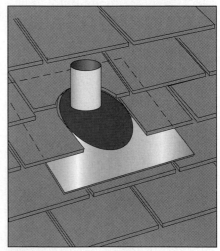

Replace a vent.
Don't bother repairing faulty vent flashing. Just install a new neoprene and aluminum replacement. You'll need to replace only a few shingles (see pages 460–463).

YOU'LL NEED...

TIME: 4 to 6 hours.
SKILLS: Moderate carpentry skills.
TOOLS: Tin snips, putty knife, hammer, cold chisel, trowel, joint strike, caulking gun, ladder, rope.

FLASHING A CHIMNEY

Most chimneys have a two-part flashing system to ride out minor structural shifting. Step flashing and base flashing fit under shingles along the sides of the chimney and lie on top of the shingles below the chimney. Counterflashing is applied over the base and step flashing and serves as a cap to keep water out. Its top edge, bent into an L shape, is mortared into the chimney's mortar joints to hold it securely.

Replacing chimney flashing calls for time and patience. If you are unsure how the old flashing was installed, or if the old flashing leaked because it was not installed properly (rather than because of metal failure), call in a pro. Whenever possible buy flashing pieces already cut and bent to fit. If necessary, form sheet metal by clamping it between two pieces of wood and bending it.

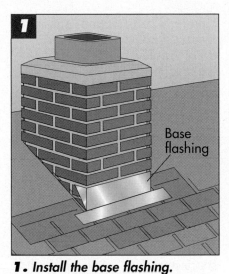

1. Install the base flashing.
To avoid confusion, work by removing one or two pieces and replacing them; then move on to the next pieces. To replace base flashing, apply asphalt primer to the bricks and install the flashing to the front. It should overlap the roof shingles by 4 inches.

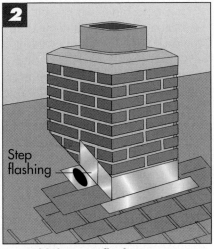

2. Add the step flashing.
To remove a piece of old step flashing, gently pry up a shingle and pry out the nail. Working from the bottom up, slip each piece of new flashing under a shingle, work roofing cement under the flashing, and drive a nail. Also use roofing cement to join the flashing pieces to each other.

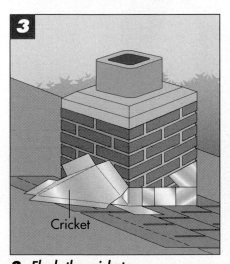

3. Flash the cricket.
If there is a cricket on the up-roof side and it is rotted, build a replacement out of plywood. You may need to cut away some roofing to do so. Use roofing cement to embed the rear corner flashings and base flashing that covers the cricket. Nail the flashing to the deck only.

4. Set the counterflashing.
Set the counterflashing on the front and sides into raked-out mortar joints. Refill the joints with masonry caulk.

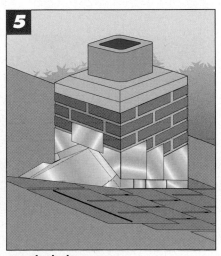

5. Flash the corners.
Make and install counterflashing suitable to the situation on the up-roof corners and side of the chimney. Install it with as few nails as possible; setting metal in a thick layer of roofing cement provides a firm installation. Where you must drive nails, cover the heads with roofing cement.

CLEANING AND REPAIRING A MASONRY CHIMNEY

Chimneys have two enemies: heat and water. The crackling fire you enjoy on winter evenings subjects masonry to temperature extremes that can chip out mortar, especially at the top where the flue penetrates the cap.

Most chimneys have a ceramic flue liner running up through the center. Concrete blocks surround the liner, and bricks cover the blocks. Other chimneys are all brick; a few use firebrick instead of a ceramic tile flue liner. Many also include a chimney cap to keep out rain, nesting birds, and downdrafts. Regardless of your chimney's construction, it pays to inspect it every fall. Examine every visible surface, including the attic. Look for cracks and deteriorated mortar.

Occasionally test for hot spots by feeling with your hand. These may indicate a broken flue—a definite fire hazard that a mason should fix before you use the fireplace again.

How often a fireplace flue needs cleaning depends on how much you use it and the type of wood you burn. Pine and other sappy species produce creosote, which cakes the flue and constricts the opening. The result: smoking and a possible chimney fire. Hire a chimney sweep to clean your chimney, or do the job yourself, as shown here. A faulty firebox design or downdrafts also cause smoking (pages 646–647 offer solutions to these problems).

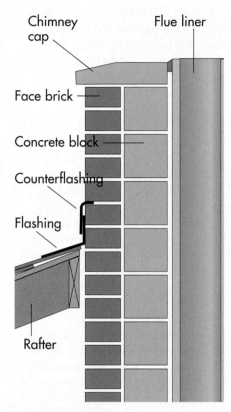

YOU'LL NEED...

TIME: 2 to 8 hours.
SKILLS: Basic masonry skills.
TOOLS: Hammer, cold chisel, caulking gun, sweep tools.

1

1. Seal the fireplace.
Before brushing, open the damper and seal the fireplace opening with a wet sheet, canvas, or poly-ethylene sheeting. Be sure the opening is sealed very tightly and firmly. Measure the diameter and length of your chimney, and buy chimney brushes and extension handles to fit.

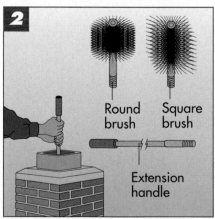

2. Brush the chimney.
From the top, insert the brush, moving it up and down to dislodge debris from the flue liner. Add an extension and repeat until you reach the damper at the bottom. Wait approximately a half hour for the dust to settle. Slowly remove the sheeting. Wet down the soot before you clean out the firebox. Vacuum around the damper before closing it.

3. Repoint and apply caulk.
Rain erodes mortar joints. Chip away loose material, then repoint as explained on pages 642–647. Apply a generous bead of masonry or butyl caulk around the flue for a flexible seal that rides out expansion and contraction. If the area is badly damaged with large, loose pieces, call in a pro.

PREVENTING ATTIC CONDENSATION

An attic that cannot breathe properly has problems. During hot weather, temperatures may reach 150°F, placing a lot of demand on your cooling system. And during cold spells, the temperature difference between the attic and the heated spaces below causes moisture condensation. This can lower the R-value of insulation, rot framing and sheathing, and shorten the life of your roof.

The solution to both problems is to provide adequate airflow through inlets at the eaves (or soffits), then up and out the roof via vents near or at the ridge.

How much ventilation your attic needs depends on whether the insulation includes a vapor barrier (see page 512). If it does, there should be 1 square foot of venting for every 300 square feet of attic floor space. If there is no vapor barrier, double this figure.

Vents do no good if they are clogged. Make sure that insulation does not lap over a soffit vent; you may have to section off the area with wood blocking. Also check that gable and ridge vents are free of caked-on dust.

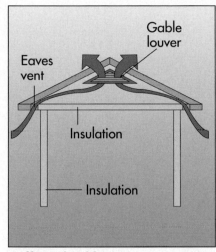

Soffit and gable vents.
In an unfinished attic, you might get by with gable louver vents at both ends. The larger and higher the vents, the more effective they will be. A gable fan, controlled by a heat-sensitive switch, can keep your attic cool, reducing energy costs. Better yet, add eaves vents as well.

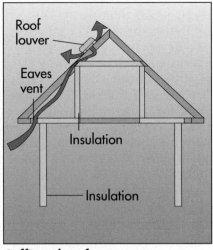

Soffit and roof vents.
Finished attics need both eaves vents and roof louvers. Inlets and outlets should be about equal in area. A ridge vent (see below) may run continuously along a ridge. If the roof is insulated, special channels may be needed to allow air to flow from the eaves up to the ridge vent.

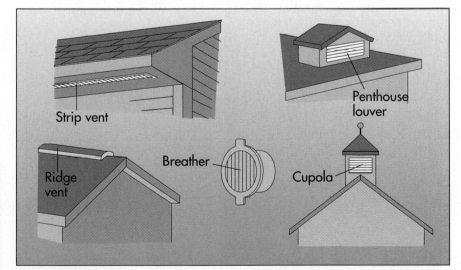

Choosing vents.
There are ventilation components for almost any roof. Breathers are easy to install, but you need many of them. Soffit strip vents provide greater airflow. Up top, you can choose gable or roof-mounted louvers (shown above). A ridge vent is an unobtrusive answer, but a professional roofer must install it. Add design interest with a cupola. Penthouse louvers work well on big, flat roofs. Many of these projects are big jobs best left to a contractor.

CAUTION!
WORKING IN AN ATTIC
If the floor of an attic is unfinished so that insulation is visible, one misstep could put your foot through the ceiling of the room below, causing damage that is a pain to fix. Maneuver strips of plywood, as wide as possible, into the attic. Either screw them to the joists permanently or move them around as you work.

REPAIRING AND MAINTAINING GUTTER SYSTEMS

Your roof's drainage system diverts thousands of gallons of water away from your house annually, so you can see why it merits a semiannual inspection.

Here's how the drainage system works: All gutters slope slightly toward their outlets. From there two elbows connect to the downspout; at the bottom a third elbow directs the spout outlet away from the wall.

Check gutters and downspouts every spring before heavy rains begin and late in the fall after leaves have fallen. Remove all debris logging the system, look for rust or corrosion, and be vigilant in looking for low spots where water may pool.

Standing water is the cause of most gutter problems, so check that gutters slope down toward their outlets. Pour or spray water into a gutter and watch what happens. Eliminate sags by lifting the gutter section slightly. Look for and repair loose hangers, or bend up the hanger with a pair of pliers. If this doesn't do the trick, install an additional hanger.

If you have widespread drainage problems, see pages 472–473 for installing a new system. Or call gutter companies for prices on replacing the entire system. They can install seamless aluminum gutters with leaf protectors for virtually maintenance-free operation.

YOU'LL NEED...

TIME: 4 to 6 hours for a medium-size house.
SKILLS: Basic carpentry skills and comfort working on heights.
TOOLS: Hose and sprayer, wire brush, putty knife, ladder, hammer, hacksaw, pliers, drill.

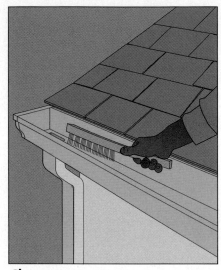

Clean a gutter.
Debris clogs up gutters and downspouts and holds moisture that causes rust, rot, and corrosion. Clear away debris by hand (wear gloves). Finish up by using a wire brush to scrape away caked-on debris.

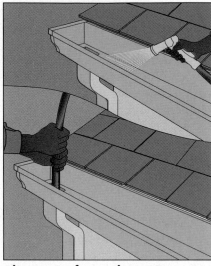

Blast water from a hose.
Hose your gutters clean, beginning at the high end of each run—or in the middle of runs having spouts at both ends. Often you can blast out spout blockage with water pressure or a plumber's snake. Otherwise you may have to dismantle the downspouts.

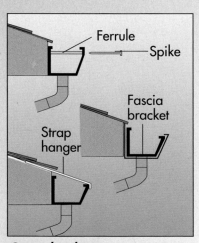

Gutter hardware.
There are three forms of gutter hangers: a spike and a ferrule driven through the gutter into rafter ends (see page 473), a strap nailed to the roof sheathing, or a fascia bracket attached to the fascia. If a gutter sags, add a strap hanger.

Ferrule
Spike
Fascia bracket
Strap hanger

Make minor repairs.
If the inside of a gutter is rusting, scrape and wire-brush it clean, then apply a thin coat of roofing cement. Seal any cracks or gaps at joints using gutter caulk. If sections of a downspout are coming loose, drill pilot holes and drive short sheetmetal screws.

Patch a gutter.
Patch a rusted-out gutter with metal flashing. Bend a piece of sheet metal so it can rest in the opening. Spread a layer of roofing cement and set the patch into the cement. Then coat the patch with more roofing cement.

Install a screen guard.
Screen guards keep out leaves. Buy guards made to fit your size of gutter. Slip the inner edge under the first course of shingles and bend the screen into place.

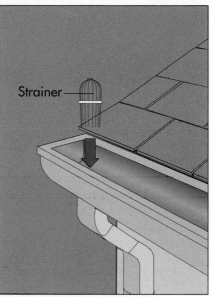

Add a wire-cage strainer.
Wire-cage strainers eliminate downspout clogging. However, you will still have to clear debris from around the cages.

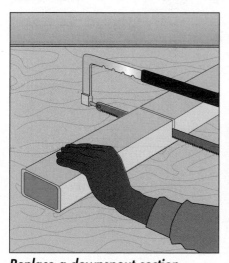

Replace a downspout section.
Cut downspouts with a fine-tooth hacksaw. Mark a line around the circumference so the edges will be square. Use a file or sandpaper to remove any burrs.

Redirect water with a splash block.
Splash blocks must be pitched away from the foundation walls. Use gravel to raise and shim a splash block.

Or use an extension.
If water puddles near the house, or if your basement leaks during rainfalls, take steps to move the water at least 8 feet away from the house. A corrugated plastic extension stays in place; a perforated roll-up hose extends like a party noisemaker when the water comes down.

INSTALLING GUTTERS

Gutter downspout systems consist of a series of modular pieces assembled to suit your situation. If your entire gutter system needs replacing, get a quote from a gutter contractor. A pro may be able to do a seamless job for little more than what it would cost you for components.

Make a list of the components shown below, then inspect your house and write down how many of each you'll need. The chart below will help you choose the material that best suits your needs. Don't mix metal parts or fasteners: Different metals contacting each other can cause rapid corrosion.

Most gutters come in 10-foot lengths and require a downspout every 35 feet. Longer runs should be pitched toward an outlet at either end. Gutters should always be pitched away from valleys and toward corners. Installing even a short run of gutter calls for two ladders and an extra pair of hands.

If you're repairing part of an existing system, dismantle it as little as possible and measure for the new parts. Don't pass up a chance to paint exposed fascia boards—or install one of the many prefinished fascia products offered by gutter manufacturers.

Cut most metal gutters with tin snips. For heavier-gauge metal or vinyl, use a hacksaw. Assemble the sections with slip-joint connectors, and caulk all joints and nailheads with manufacturer-recommended caulk. Newer gutter types with neoprene-gasketed slip connectors don't need any caulk.

You have a choice of gutter hangers. Strap hangers work only with flexible roofing, such as asphalt shingles, that you can lift up to put the hanger under. If your roof has rigid wood shingles or slate, use fascia brackets or spike-and-ferrule hangers. Spikes are easiest to install, but they may sag under heavy loads.

> ### YOU'LL NEED...
> **TIME:** 1 day for new gutters for a medium-size house.
> **SKILLS:** Basic carpentry and ladder skills.
> **TOOLS:** Hammer, hacksaw, level, caulking gun, two ladders, pliers, tin snips or metal shears.

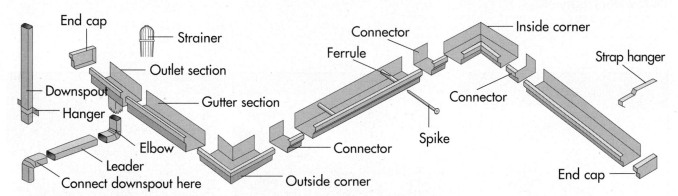

CHOOSING GUTTER MATERIALS

Material	Features	Maintenance	Life Span; Cost
Steel	Plain galvanized or enamel finish	Prone to rusting; should be painted	15 years; inexpensive
Aluminum	Enamel or plastic-clad finish; easy to install, but fragile	Resistant to corrosion, but may need occasional repainting; easily dented	15 to 20 years; moderate
Vinyl	Sturdy and durable; can be tricky to install; available in white or brown	Immune to rot and rust; cannot be painted	50 years; expensive
Copper	Durable; not widely used; joints must be soldered	Does not rust or corrode, but leaky joints require soldering	50 years; most expensive

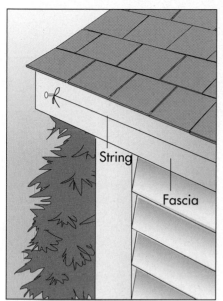

Plan the slope.

If the old system drained efficiently, follow the path of the old gutters. Gutters slope toward the spouts. Check the manufacturer's recommendations for the rate of slope. Don't assume that your eaves are level: Tape a level to a long, straight 2×4 to check for the correct slope, and tack up a string for a guide.

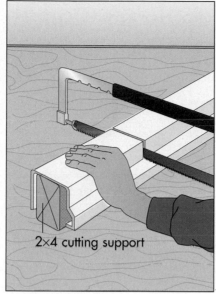

Cut the gutters.

For stability insert a 2×4 when sawing gutter sections. Always file cut edges to smooth off sharp burrs. Assemble gutter runs on the ground first, caulking and screwing or riveting all joints, except those at the corners.

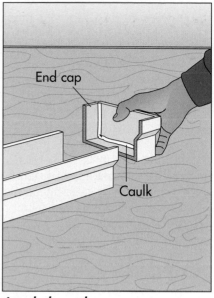

Attach the end caps.

Most end caps simply snap onto gutter sections. Test-fit each joint to make sure it will go together. Apply a bead of gutter caulk or joint sealer to prevent leaking. Push the pieces together and drive any recommended fasteners.

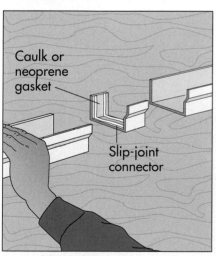

Assemble end-to-end connectors.

Unless they come with gaskets, caulk slip-joint connectors just prior to assembly. These important components are the most susceptible to leaking. Take care when lifting a long run made up of two or more gutter sections; if you bend the run, the parts may disassemble.

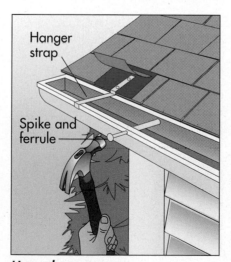

Hang the gutters.

Have a helper hold the pieces while you drive fasteners. Continually double-check with a level to see that the gutter slopes toward the downspout. Space hangers 24 or 32 inches apart. Spikes must go into rafter ends, and not just into the fascia board.

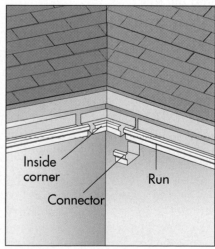

Connect at a corner.

Connect two runs with corner sections. Caulk, then fasten with rivets or sheetmetal screws. Once the system is installed, go back and check all the joints. Apply gutter caulk at every joint you are not sure of, smoothing it with a finger. Run a hose on the roof to test the system.

REROOFING WITH ASPHALT SHINGLES

Check your local codes to see how many layers of roofing your roof can handle. In most cases, if a roof has only one or two layers of roofing, it can be reroofed simply by installing new shingles on top of the old ones.

If your roof already has multiple layers of shingles, a "tear-off" job is needed: All the roofing and felt (and perhaps the flashing) must be removed. This is a demanding and very messy job. Buy a roofing spade for removing shingles.

Asphalt shingles come in many colors, shapes, textures, and qualities. They are sold by the square—the amount of material needed to cover 100 square feet. In the long run, it is well worth the extra cost to buy shingles that are guaranteed for 30 years.

You'll save plenty of back-breaking work if you pay extra for the roofing materials to be delivered via a conveyor belt up onto the roof.

Use nails long enough to penetrate the sheathing; the length will depend on the thickness of the old and new roofing.

Use your old shingles as guides and you'll find that a reshingling project can go quickly. Before you begin, nail all loose or curled shingles, and replace any that are missing. Reset any popped nails.

A roofing hammer has a guide that allows you to quickly position shingles at the right height above the course below.

> ### YOU'LL NEED...
> **TIME:** 3 hours per 100 square feet.
> **SKILLS:** Basic roofing skills.
> **TOOLS:** Regular or roofing hammer, utility or roofing knife, chalk line, speed square, pry bar, ladder.

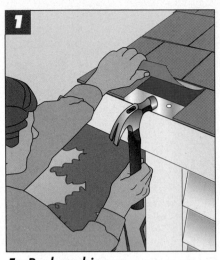

1. Replace drip cap.
Check drip-edge flashing at the eaves and rakes. If it is failing, replace as you would any other flashing (see pages 466–467). Also check fascia boards and replace any rotted pieces.

Chalk line

2. Set flashing in valleys.
Use sheet-metal flashing for valleys. Position the flashing so it rests firmly on the roof, then attach with nails near the edges. Valley flashing should project about 1 inch beyond the eaves. Snap chalk lines on both sides of the center, angled outward at a rate of 1 inch per 8 feet.

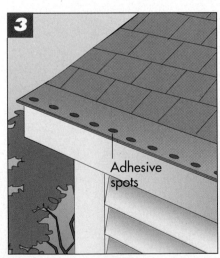

Adhesive spots

3. Lay a starter course.
Purchase a starter strip, which is a continuous roll about half the width of shingles. Or make starter strips by trimming shingles to the width of the old exposure— usually 5 inches. Nail the starter strip at the eaves.

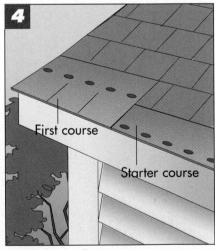

First course

Starter course

4. Start the first course.
Shingles measure 1×3 feet, with cutouts that divide the shingle into three tabs. Simply butt each new shingle against the bottom edge of an old one, staggering the tabs. Always stagger end joints from one course to the next.

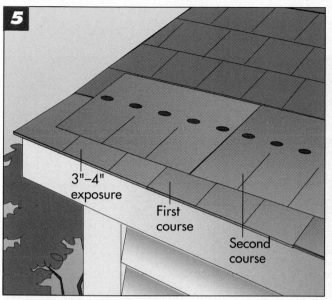

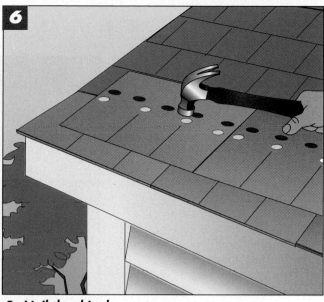

5. Position the shingles.

Build courses stair-step fashion. The first course will have only a 3- or 4-inch exposure, but a gutter will conceal this. Small slits in the top of the shingles will help you align the courses to produce a consistent-looking pattern. At the gable end, cut each piece to overhang by about an inch. Or let the pieces "run wild"; later, snap a chalk line along the vertical edge and cut the line with a utility knife.

6. Nail the shingles.

After the first course, the exposure will be about 5 inches. Each shingle requires four nails, placed about ½ inch above the cutouts. Do not sink the nailheads so far that they bite into the surface of the shingle. When the sun heats the roof, it will melt the adhesive spots in the shingles and adhere them together.

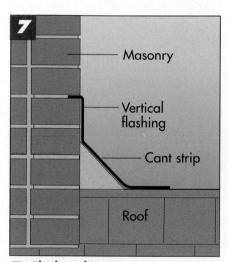

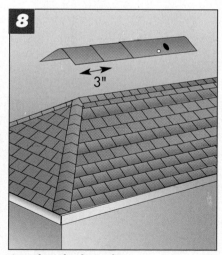

7. Flash a chimney.

Add new chimney flashing as you apply the roof; some pieces are installed on top of the shingles, while others rest on top of one shingle and under another. A cant strip at the base of a vertical surface improves runoff. For more about chimney flashing, see pages 466–467.

8. Shingle the ridge.

Cover the ridge of the roof with special ridge shingles, or cut ordinary shingles into three separate tabs to fit. Overlap the ridge shingles to conceal the nails, leaving about a 5-inch exposure. The last nails will be exposed; cover them with dabs of roofing cement.

EXPERTS' INSIGHT

ROOFING TIPS

■ If your area is subjected to high winds, make sure that the starter strip and first course are nailed down well.

■ When installing shingles on top of valley flashing, snip a 2-inch triangle out of the upper corner of the shingle (which will be covered). This helps ensure that wind-driven rain cannot sneak up and under the protective flashing.

■ Work when the weather is warm so that the shingles can adhere to each other. Do not work in very hot weather or you could damage the shingles.

REROOFING WITH WOOD SHINGLES AND SHAKES

Wood shingles and shakes are often installed on spaced sheathing—that is, 1×4s or 1×6s that are laid across rafters with 2- to 4-inch spaces between them. This arrangement provides air circulation that allows the wood to dry out. Building codes in some climates may permit installing wood shingles on top of solid sheathing, or even directly over asphalt shingles. Check with your local building department.

Wood roofing works best if the roof has at least a 6-in-12 pitch (a 6-inch rise in the slope of the roof for every 12 inches of horizontal run). It may not provide adequate protection for a flatter roof.

To lay wood shingles and shakes, use many of the same basic techniques as for asphalt shingles (pages 474–475). You'll need a couple more tools and a little more preparation work, though. Additional tools include a multipurpose roofer's hammer for nailing, trimming, and gauging courses, and a lightweight power saw for more precise cutting.

Purchase the best shingles or shakes you can afford. Buy flashings made for use with wood shingles or shakes. Use nails made for wood roofing and long enough to penetrate the total thickness of the roof plus the sheathing. If you pay extra for delivery of materials to your rooftop, you will save your energy for the actual roofing work.

YOU'LL NEED...

TIME: 4 to 6 hours per 100 square feet.
SKILLS: Basic carpentry and roofing skills.
TOOLS: Roofer's hammer, utility knife, lightweight power saw, pry bar, ladder.

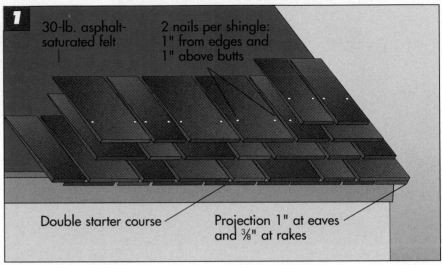

1 30-lb. asphalt-saturated felt — 2 nails per shingle: 1" from edges and 1" above butts

Double starter course — Projection 1" at eaves and ⅜" at rakes

1. Install the shingles.
Apply roofing felt as recommended by your local building department. Start a wood shingle roof with a double starter course, projecting over the edges by an inch. This will ensure that rainwater flows into a gutter rather than behind it.

Stagger the joints of succeeding courses. There should be a ½-inch gap between shingles or shakes on each side. It is important that the gaps of succeeding courses be offset by at least an inch. Drive two nails per shingle, about 1 inch from each edge. Make sure that all the nailheads are covered by the shingles of the next course.

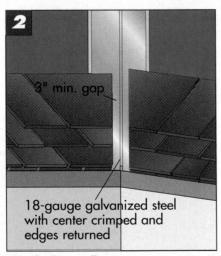

2 3" min. gap

18-gauge galvanized steel with center crimped and edges returned

2. Flash a valley.
Flash valleys with 18-gauge W-metal galvanized flashing made for shingle or shake roofing. Cut the shingles or shakes so their edges are about 3 inches away from the center of the flashing. Avoid having any roofing pieces narrower than 4 inches.

EXPERTS' INSIGHT

SHAKE AND SHINGLE EXPOSURE

In a typical installation, shakes 18 inches long are overlapped 10 inches, leaving an exposure of 8 inches. Shakes 24 inches long are often overlapped 14 inches, for an exposure of 10 inches. These arrangements ensure that the roof is covered by at least two layers of roofing at all points. If you overlap 18-inch shakes by 12 inches or 24-inch shakes by 16 inches, you will have three-layer protection, which may be recommended in areas with severe weather.

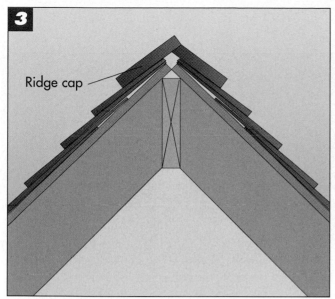

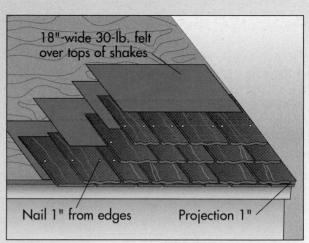

18"-wide 30-lb. felt over tops of shakes

Nail 1" from edges   Projection 1"

3. Roof the ridge.
Cover the ridge with overlapped 1×4 or 1×6 boards. Caulk the overlap to prevent leakage. Alternatively, purchase hip shakes, which are about 12 inches long and have beveled edges for a more finished look. Attach the ridge caps with extra-long nails that penetrate the sheathing.

Roof with shakes.
Install shakes the same way as wood shingles but interweave 18-inch-wide strips of 30-pound roofing felt as shown above. Install a layer of roofing felt, then a course of shakes, then another layer of felt, and so on. The bottom of each row of felt should be positioned so it is just covered by the two courses of shakes above (otherwise, it would show in the gaps between shakes).

CHOOSING A SKYLIGHT

A skylight brightens interior rooms in a way no artificial source can match. Even on cloudy days, a skylight provides a surprising amount of light—and the operating cost is nil.

Prefabricated kits—available in various domed, rectangular, and square shapes—include an acrylic window (or "light") and a flanged metal frame that you nail to your roof deck.

Unless your roof line is exposed inside, you will have to figure out how to make the light reach down through the attic space into the ceiling below. Often the greater part of a skylight installation is building the shaft through which the light shines. You may need to build a frame and cover it with drywall. Some newer models have a flexible shaft that can be snaked down into a room below; this eliminates the need for framing.

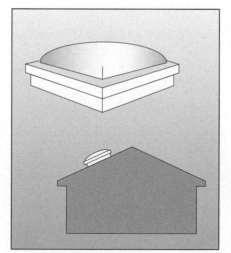

Domed skylight.
Domed skylights are suitable for installation on flat or pitched roofs. Some also include a cranking system so you can open them for ventilation. Some types allow you to see clouds and stars, but most are opaque and only allow light.

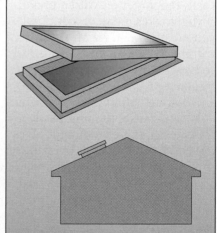

Dormer skylight.
Dormer skylights make sense only for pitched roofs. Good skylights are double-glazed, with an airspace to reduce heat loss. An automatic opener raises the lid when things get hot and helps keep a room cool.

INSTALLING A SKYLIGHT

Cutting a hole in the roof for a skylight requires only modest framing and flashing ability. You will need to construct a light shaft through your attic, unless your home has a flat roof or a ceiling that follows the slope of the roof.

Plan the location of your skylight, then work from the inside out, framing the ceiling opening and building the shaft before you cut into the roof. Skylights are designed to span two or three rafters on typical 24-inch spacings; often it is necessary to cut and tie off rafters and ceiling joists to accommodate the shaft. **NOTE:** *Be sure that you shore up the ceiling with temporary bracing before cutting into the ceiling.*

For a flat-roof installation, frame the opening, paint the rafters and headers around it, then install the skylight. You may also need to raise the unit with nailers, as shown on page 479.

Once you have built a skylight shaft, topping it off with a prefab skylight takes a day or less. First, you must cut and tie off the rafters with headers, as you did with the ceiling joists. Locate the opening by sliding the shaft into position and marking around its perimeter.

When you set the unit in place, fit its flange under roofing at the top and sides, but let it overlap the shingles on the down-roof side.

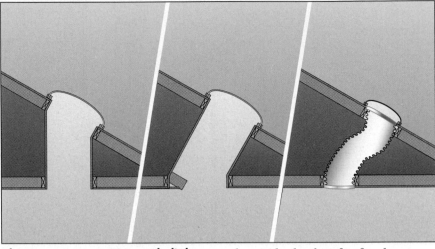

Three ways to position a skylight. If you locate a skylight directly above the ceiling opening, you can get by with a simple straight shaft (above, left). A tilted shaft (middle) lets you offset the roof and ceiling openings. These are trickier to construct. The ceiling opening can be bigger than the skylight. To build a shaft, construct a sleeve with ½-inch plywood, check it for fit, then paint the inside white to ensure maximum reflective value. Alternatively, build 2×4 framing and cover it with drywall.

A "sun tunnel" (right) is a flexible shaft that comes with the skylight. To install one, cut a hole in the ceiling and follow the manufacturer's instructions.

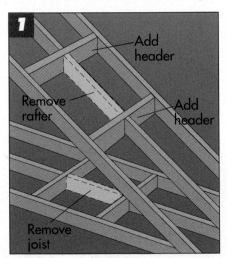

1. Frame the ceiling and the roof. Work in the attic space. Use a level to reference down from the roof to the ceiling. When planning the opening, be sure to include the thickness of framing members as well as the thickness of the plywood or drywall. Install headers before cutting the roof sheathing or the ceiling drywall.

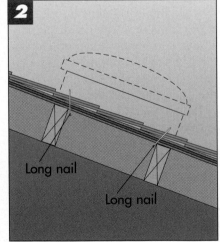

2. Mark the opening. To mark the opening, drive long nails through the roof at each corner, then chalk an outline on the top side.

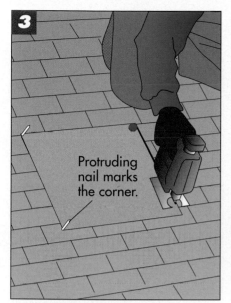

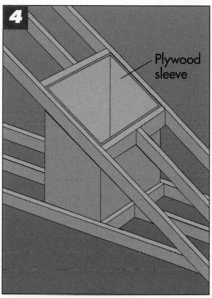

3. Cut the opening.

You may need to cut away an opening in the roofing larger than the hole in the sheathing. Cut through shingles and building felt with a utility knife and pry away the roofing. Cut the sheathing using a saber saw, a circular saw, or a reciprocating saw. When you saw the sheathing, don't let it fall—it might damage the ceiling.

4. Install the shaft.

Use nails to mark the ceiling below for the opening and cut the drywall with a saber saw. Carefully measure for the size of each plywood piece. Slide each piece up from below and nail it to the framing.

5. Roof around the skylight.

Follow the manufacturer's instructions carefully to prevent future leaks. Slide the top flange under the roofing and allow the bottom portion to rest on the roofing. Seal under the flange before you nail it, then cement the shingles to it with roofing cement.

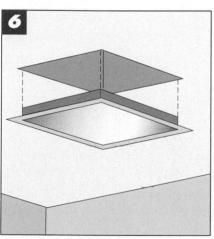

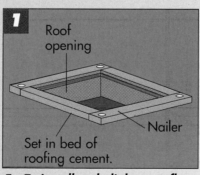

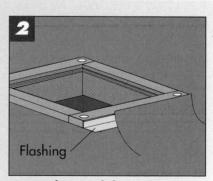

6. Install a diffuser.

A diffuser makes it easy to finish the opening and hides flaws in the shaft. If you have no diffuser, trim the opening neatly. Caulk the corners where pieces of plywood abut, then paint. (To finish a drywall shaft, see pages 342–343.)

1. To install a skylight on a flat roof, add nailers.

On flat roofs take steps to ensure that water cannot work its way up and under the skylight during heavy rain. Install nailers around the opening. Set them in roofing cement before driving nails or screws; otherwise standing water may overflow the frame.

2. Roof around the opening.

Seal around the nailers with roofing cement, then slip flashing under the roofing and up the sides of the nailer. The skylight should fit tightly around the roofing material.

UNDERSTANDING BRICK WALLS

Most "brick" or "stone" houses built after World War II do not have solid masonry walls. Instead, builders faced conventional framing with a masonry veneer—combining the weather resistance of brick or stone with the superior insulating qualities of wood stud construction. An older home may have two thicknesses of brick instead of a wood frame.

Check the section view at right. Studs, not bricks, bear the load. A single tier of brick connects to the studs with short metal strips called ties. Between the brick and the sheathing is an airspace, which drains away moisture that might penetrate the brick surface. Weep holes near the bottom allow condensed moisture to drip away;

never block up a weep hole.

The foundation must support the heavy masonry skin as well as the framing system. If veneer is added to a wall, an inspector must make sure the foundation is strong enough to carry the load.

Although masonry-veneer walls are relatively impervious to weather and time, inspect them periodically. Pay particular attention to mortar joints that may need to be repointed (see pages 642–643). Solid masonry walls—usually used today only for garages, garden walls, and commercial structures—may consist of several tiers of brick or stone or of concrete blocks that have been veneered. To learn more about these materials, see pages 632–635.

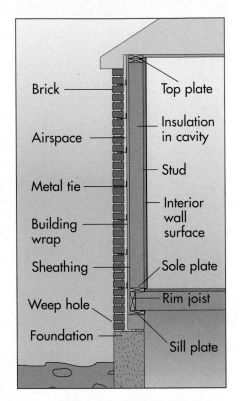

Brick
Airspace
Metal tie
Building wrap
Sheathing
Weep hole
Foundation

Top plate
Insulation in cavity
Stud
Interior wall surface
Sole plate
Rim joist
Sill plate

UNDERSTANDING STUCCO WALLS

Stucco walls usually begin with wood-stud framing, although stucco can be applied directly to masonry surfaces. Often, as the drawing at right shows, spacer strips are nailed to the sheathing, and metal lath resembling chicken wire is attached to the spacers. In some installations the spacer strips are omitted. In such a case, stucco—a cement-based plaster—is troweled onto the metal lath.

As with interior plasterwork, it takes two or three layers of stucco to build up a smooth surface. A scratch coat oozes through the lath for a good grip; the brown coat (which is omitted in some installations) smoothes out major irregularities in the surface. The finish coat completes the job.

As with concrete (see pages 672–677), you can trowel, scrape, stipple, and spatter stucco for textures ranging from glassy smooth to rugged rustic. Many

textures reflect the personality of a certain installer and may be difficult to reproduce; others are simple to mimic once you know which tools to use. You also can add coloring pigments to the finish coat of both cement and vinyl stucco for an exterior that will never need painting.

Properly applied, stucco lasts for decades with little attention. Watch, though, for cracks that may develop around windows, doors, and chimneys. If not sealed, these may admit moisture that could eventually rot framing. As with masonry-veneer walls, keep your eye on long, running cracks that might indicate settlement.

For information on patching cracks and holes, see pages 488–489. If you are planning to paint stucco, be sure to apply a coating formulated for use on stucco (see pages 836–837).

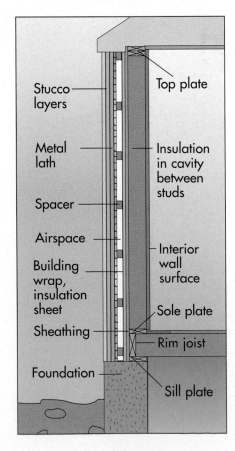

Stucco layers
Metal lath
Spacer
Airspace
Building wrap, insulation sheet
Sheathing
Foundation

Top plate
Insulation in cavity between studs
Interior wall surface
Sole plate
Rim joist
Sill plate

WHERE SEALING IS NEEDED

Different building materials swell and shrink at different rates. This results in cracks where siding meets masonry, where siding butts trim, and where flashing contacts roofing. Use caulk wherever unlike materials meet. The illustration below shows typical spots to check.

Caulking material falls into two categories—rubber-derived formulations, such as latex and butyl, and synthetic-based, high-performance materials. The type you select depends upon the job you want it to do.

Before buying, read the product data for preparation requirements, materials the caulk will adhere to, and paintability. The chart below compares the common sealants.

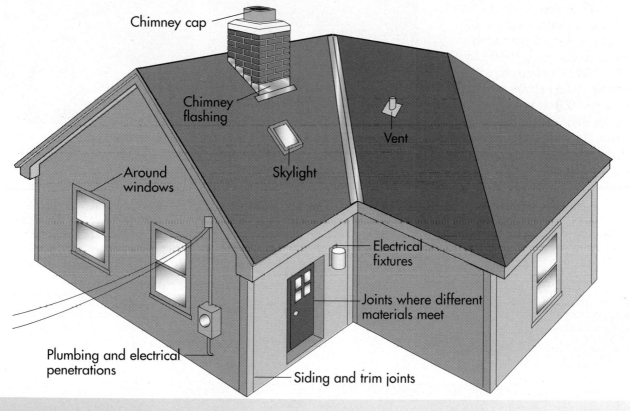

Chimney cap

Chimney flashing

Vent

Around windows

Skylight

Electrical fixtures

Joints where different materials meet

Plumbing and electrical penetrations

Siding and trim joints

CHOOSING SEALANTS

Type	Characteristics	Cost
Latex	Inexpensive and easy to work with; liable to shrink and crack in time	Inexpensive
Latex/silicone or latex/acrylic	Good general-purpose, fast-drying sealant; remains flexible for years; ideal for filling small cracks and joints; paintable	Moderate
"Tub and tile" caulk	Highly adhesive and waterproof; good for wet areas, such as tubs and showers	Moderate
Butyl or "gutter"	Excellent exterior caulk for gutter seams, flashings, storm windows, and large joints; paintable	Moderate
Silicone	The most durable caulk; remains flexible, but many types do not stick well; water-based products perform better and are paintable	Most expensive
Foam	Quickly fills wide cracks and openings; remains flexible; paintable, but impossible to smooth out; "non-expanding" type is easier to control	Moderate

REPAIRING WOOD SIDING AND SHINGLES

Damaged siding permits moisture to enter exterior walls, where it can rot the sheathing and even the framing. It needs quick attention.

Keep exterior walls well covered with quality paint (see pages 848–859). Make repairs as soon as you spot damage. Pack small cracks, splits, and open seams with latex/silicone or butyl caulk.

You may be able to repair splits and holes using epoxy wood filler (see page 486). If not, you'll have to replace the damaged board or shingle. If more than a few boards or shingles are failing, consider re-siding the entire wall (see pages 492–501).

YOU'LL NEED...

TIME: 1 to 3 hours for one course.
SKILLS: Moderate carpentry skills.
TOOLS: Chisel, hammer, pry bar, close-work hacksaw, square, putty knife, utility knife, plane, backsaw, drill, caulking gun.

1. Loosen the board.

To remove a length of siding, cut through the paint along its bottom edge. Work a chisel under its lower edge, then switch to a flat pry bar. To keep from damaging the surrounding siding, pry by pulling away from the house rather than pushing toward it.

2. Pry it away.

Each course of lapped siding is held in place by nails driven through the course above it. First deal with the lower nails. If the nails begin to come out with the board, jam the nail with a pry bar and tap the board down. This may cause the heads to pop out, making them easy to pry away. The same can be done for the nails in the course above.

3. Cut nails that won't pop out.

If the nails aren't cooperating, or if they are not accessible from the surface, slip a hacksaw blade underneath the siding and cut them. A close-work hacksaw works well for this. Be careful not to scrape the siding beneath the damage.

4. Prepare to cut out the damaged area.

To cut a piece to length, tap wedges under the course above and use a square to mark the cut lines. Cut first with a utility knife to diminish splintering.

5. Saw the siding.
Use a backsaw or fine-toothed handsaw to cut the face of the siding. Use short strokes, holding the top of the blade to keep it from buckling. As you finish each cut, be careful not to cut siding below the damaged area.

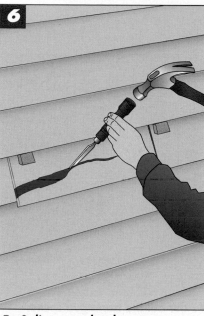

6. Split away the damage.
Split the damaged area along the grain and remove a piece at a time. Carefully pry away all remnants under the board above. Pry away or pound down all nails. Check that the replacement piece can slide all the way up into position.

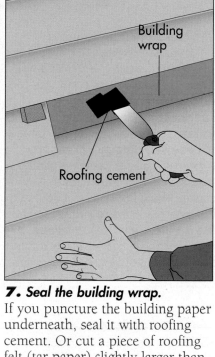

7. Seal the building wrap.
If you puncture the building paper underneath, seal it with roofing cement. Or cut a piece of roofing felt (tar paper) slightly larger than the opening and shoehorn it in. Fasten any loose paper with roofing nails or staples.

Building wrap

Roofing cement

8. Slip in the patch.
Cut the replacement for a snug fit, then slide it under the board above, tap it into place, and remove the wedges. Avoid too tight a fit, however. Use a block plane to skim off one edge if you have to force the patch.

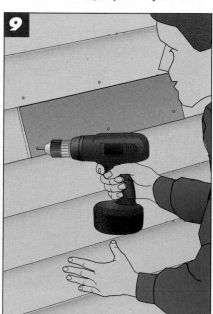

9. Drill pilot holes.
Wherever you will drive a nail less than 3 inches from the end or edge of a board, drill a pilot hole first to prevent splitting the board.

10. Nail, and caulk the seams.
Finally nail the new board at the top and bottom. Use siding nails, which have thin shanks. Fill nail holes and the vertical seams with caulk, then prime and paint.

REPLACING A SECTION OF ALUMINUM SIDING

Most aluminum siding is shaped like beveled wood siding and installed horizontally, as shown here. The less common vertical aluminum siding interlocks in much the same way, so repairs are essentially the same.

Because siding pieces are very long, it usually is easier to patch a damaged spot rather than replace the whole piece. The patch fits over the existing siding, so the cut does not have to be precise. A repair like this will result in joints that look nearly the same as other joints.

You'll Need...

Time: An hour to cut and replace a section.
Skills: Basic cutting skills.
Tools: Square, utility knife, perhaps a circular saw, tin snips, flat pry bar, pliers, caulking gun.

1. Cut out the damaged section.
Using a square as a guide, cut a rectangle around the damaged area. It will take several passes with a utility knife to cut through the siding; you may need to change blades partway through.

2. Finish the cut.
You may find it easier to finish the cut using a pair of tin snips. A circular saw with the blade installed backwards makes cutting easy, but take care not to damage nearby pieces. Pull the cutout away and unsnap it from the wall.

3. Cut the patch.
Cut a patch of matching siding at least 3 inches wider than the cut-out area. Cut off its nailing strip along the top. Test to see that the piece will fit. Its top should slip at least ¼ inch up under the piece above, and its bottom should be able to snap into place.

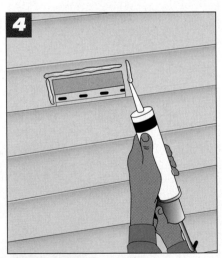

4. Apply caulk.
Clean the area of all residue. Use a caulking gun to apply clear silicone sealant to the perimeter of the hole.

5. Lock the patch in place.
Slip the patch into place and slide it up until it locks in place. Press the sides flat and wipe away any squeezed-out caulk.

REPLACING ALUMINUM END CAPS

Corners of a house often get bumped, so it's common to see aluminum end caps that are dented. Replacing them is not difficult.

The original installer may have left some end caps in your garage or basement. If not, bring an old end cap to your supply source to find an exact replacement.

Chances are that the old siding has faded, so you may not be able to get an exact color match. If so, paint the pieces to match the siding before installing them.

YOU'LL NEED...

TIME: About an hour to replace six or seven end caps.
SKILLS: Basic cutting, fastening, and caulking skills.
TOOLS: Hacksaw, hammer, flat pry bar, drill, blind pop riveter.

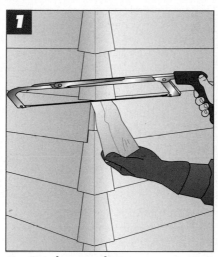

1. Cut damaged caps.
In some cases broken or dented corner caps will pull out easily. However, you may need to pry out the siding above to get at the nails. If you cannot pull out the nails without damaging the siding, cut through them with a hacksaw. If you can't get to the nails, cut through the corner piece itself.

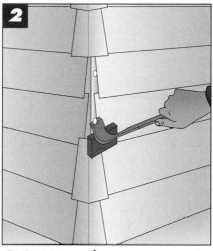

2. Remove nails.
Remove the damaged corner caps, then take out the remaining nails with a flat pry bar. Use a scrap of wood to prevent denting the siding as you pry.

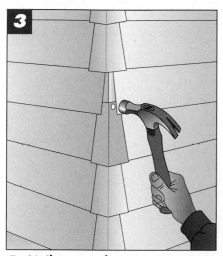

3. Nail new end caps.
Starting at the bottom, slide each replacement cap under the bottom lip of the course above, and slide it up until it snaps into place. Taking care not to dent the siding, attach each cap with one or two nails or screws. You may need to angle the fastener in order to hit solid wood.

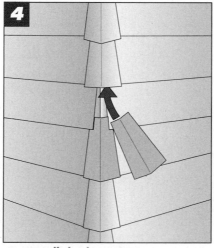

4. Install the last piece.
Cut the nailing strip off of the top replacement cap so it can slip under the course above by about ¼ inch. Test to see that it fits snugly and can snap into place at the bottom. Apply silicone caulk to the back side of the cap, slide the cap into place, and wipe away any excess caulk.

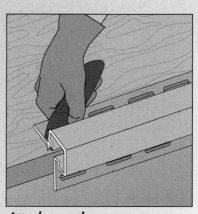

Attach a replacement post.
If you have to replace a dented corner post (a problem common to aluminum and vinyl siding), cut through the sides with a knife; it will take several passes. Cut the flange off a replacement piece and test to see that it fits. Apply clear silicone caulk to the flanges and attach using screws or blind pop rivets.

REPAIRING DENTED ALUMINUM SIDING

This technique is more time-consuming than patching with a replacement piece (page 484), but it's useful if you have a hard time finding siding to match.

Automobile-body filler is available at an auto parts store. It comes as a two-part epoxy; add a bit of hardener and mix with a small scrap of plastic or wood. It quickly hardens to the point where it can be planed or sanded. An hour or two later, it can be painted.

You'll Need...

TIME: Several hours, including time for the material to harden.
SKILLS: Basic patching skills, spraying paint.
TOOLS: Lock-joint pliers, drill, wide putty knife, sanding block, spray paint can, painting tools.

TOOLS TO USE

BODY REPAIR TOOLS

If you have a number of dents to patch, invest in some tools that will enable you to quickly make and smooth the patches.
■ Self-tapping screws with large heads can be quickly driven into the soft aluminum and pulled out.
■ A pull-style paint scraper (with removable blades) makes it easy to scrape away excess body filler when it is partially hardened.
■ To grind down the patch after it has fully hardened, use a vibrating or random-orbit power sander.

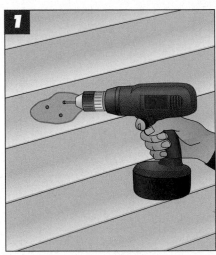

1. Drill a series of holes.
Equip a drill with a ⅛-inch bit, and drill several holes in the middle of the dented area. One or two of these will be pilot holes for the pull-out screw (Step 2), and the others will help the body filler to grab tightly onto the siding.

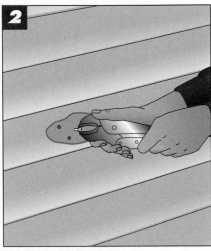

2. Pull out the dent.
Drive a No. 8 screw slightly into the deepest point of the dent. Grab the screw head with lock-joint pliers, and pull the dent partway out. Do not pull the siding out beyond the surrounding surface. If the dent is large, repeat this process with other screws in other locations.

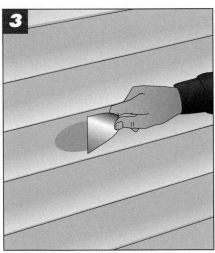

3. Apply auto-body filler.
Sand the dented area until it is bare of paint. Mix and apply two-part auto-body filler using a wide putty knife or the plastic scraper that comes with the filler. Smooth the patch so it is slightly higher than the surrounding siding. Once it has started to harden, scrape it down further.

Foam painting pad

4. Finish the patch.
Sand the area with 120-grit paper until it is smooth and level with the surrounding surface. Spray on metal primer, then apply color-matched paint suited for aluminum siding.

REPLACING A VINYL SIDING STRIP

In some cases you can repair a section of vinyl by slipping a patch over the damaged area, in much the same way as shown for aluminum siding on page 484. However, many types of vinyl siding do not allow you to slip the top edge of the patch securely under the course above. Fortunately vinyl bends without denting, so you can pry out the top course far enough to remove existing nails and fasten the top of the repair piece.

YOU'LL NEED...

TIME: An hour for most repairs.
SKILLS: Basic carpentry skills.
TOOLS: Zip tool (made especially for vinyl siding), pry bar, utility knife, square hammer.

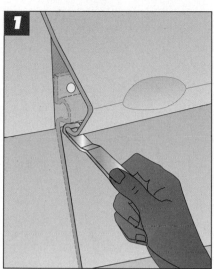

1. Pry out the damaged strip.
Unless you want to replace the entire strip, use a utility knife to cut it in place (see page 484). To remove a strip, insert a Zip tool under the lower lip, pull down, and slide the tool to the left or right. Also pull out the bottom of the course above.

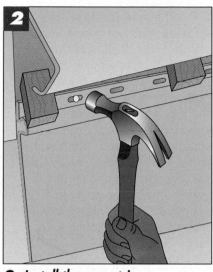

2. Install the new strip.
Carefully pry the upper course back, and use blocks to hold it away from the house so you can get at the nails. Remove the nails and the damaged piece. Fasten the new strip by nailing through the centers of the nail slots. Do not drive the nails tightly.

EXPERTS' INSIGHT

PAINTING VINYL SIDING

Vinyl siding is advertised as eliminating the need for painting. But some types (especially older and less expensive vinyl siding) may fade significantly in the sun. If you prepare carefully, you can apply paint to vinyl. First rough the vinyl with a hand or power sander and 60-grit sandpaper. Then apply a coat of alcohol-based primer, followed by exterior paint.

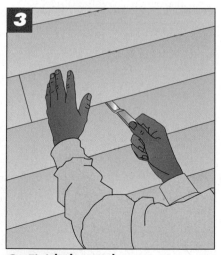

3. Finish the patch.
Relock the new strip by pulling down and sliding the Zip tool while pressing in along the bottom edge.

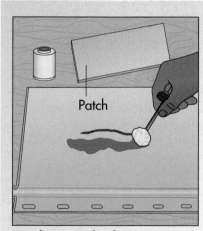

Patch

Patching vinyl siding.
To fix a tear, you needn't replace the piece. Cut a piece of plastic slightly larger than the damaged area. On the back side of the siding, apply PVC pipe primer, then cement. Press the patch into the cement and hold it for a few seconds.

REPAIRING STUCCO WALLS

Small cracks in stucco can be filled with butyl or silicone/latex caulk and then painted. But if there are many cracks or if a section is coming loose, you must chip away the old material down to the lath or masonry underneath, then build up a new surface in two or three layers. Problem areas larger than 8 feet square usually require restuccoing of the entire wall. This is a major job that you may want to leave to a professional (see pages 706–708).

Make repairs during mild weather when there's no danger of freezing. Plan on the project taking at least three days. Wait at least six weeks before painting, then prime and apply paint recommended for concrete and stucco.

Colored stucco is difficult to match. Experiment with pigments, keeping in mind that colors will fade as much as 70 percent by the time the stucco dries. Never let the coloring pigment exceed 3 percent of the batch's total volume.

Blending the patch's final surface with the surrounding area can be difficult. Consult with a pro to find out (or guess at) the technique and tool used by the original installer.

YOU'LL NEED...

TIME: 3 working days for a large patch, extended over 10 to 12 days to cover drying time.
SKILLS: Moderate to advanced masonry skills; knowledge of the special technique used by the original stucco contractor.
TOOLS: Cold chisel, pry bar, hammer, stapler, trowel, hawk, improvised rake, spray hose, metal straightedge.

1. Prepare the area.

Chip away loose stucco using a cold chisel, pry bar, and hammer. You may need to use wire cutters or tin snips to cut the metal lath. Staple new roofing felt and metal lath onto the sheathing (see page 706). Make sure the surrounding stucco is firmly attached to the wall; if not, chip away some more.

3. Scarify.

When the stucco begins to firm up, scratch it with a scarifying tool, or an improvised rake made by driving nails through a piece of wood every inch. The scratches should be about ⅛ inch deep.

2. Trowel the first coat.

Mix a batch of stucco base coat, following directions on the bag. Place a dollop of stucco on a hawk or a piece of plywood, and push the stucco into the metal lath using a straight trowel. Apply the first coat to a depth of about ¼ inch below the surrounding surfaces. Smooth the area.

TOOLS TO USE

FINISHING STUCCO

Stuccoers use a variety of tools to achieve the final surface. If you are unsure how to mimic the surrounding area, spread stucco on a plywood scrap and practice using these methods:

■ Dab at the stucco with your palm or a trowel and pull straight back to achieve peaks. Perhaps "knock down" the peaks by lightly passing over the surface with a trowel.

■ Produce a basically smooth surface. Dip a whisk broom in a bucket of stucco and dash it at the wall to produce hills. Perhaps knock them down.

■ Make a swirled surface by brushing with a whisk broom using wavy or arcing strokes.

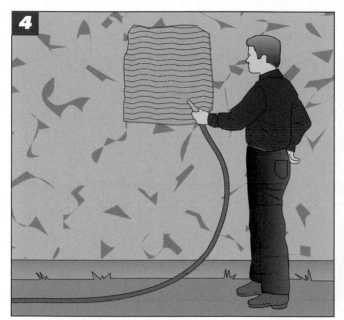

4. Cure the base coat slowly.

The more slowly the stucco cures (dries out), the stronger it will be. Mist the scratch coat with a fine spray as often as necessary to keep it damp for two days. In windy or sunny weather, repeat several times a day. If the air is dry, tape a piece of plastic over the patch while it cures.

5. Add the brown coat.

Some installations omit this step and go straight to the finish coat (Step 7). Mix a batch of stucco for the second or "brown" coat. Apply this coat to within about ⅛ inch of the surface, and level it off with a metal straightedge or a large trowel.

6. Float the surface.

"Float" the brown coat by working it with a trowel until bleed water comes to the surface. (See page 675 for more about floating.) Avoid overworking; stop once the water has appeared.

7. Texture the finish coat.

Mist the brown coat for two days and wait a week. While you are waiting, practice applying finish stucco to a scrap of plywood until you can achieve a texture that blends in with the rest of the wall. Moisten the brown coat and mix a batch of finish stucco. Smooth on the finish coat. Texture it within a half hour.

DEALING WITH WOOD-BORING INSECTS

Wood-eating insects fall into two groups—subterranean (those that eat wood but nest underground) and nonsubterranean (those that live in the wood itself).

Watch for subterranean insects in early spring and fall. This is when the reproductive members of termite colonies sprout wings, take off on mating flights, discard the wings, and establish nesting places. If you find a pile of wings, suspect a colony nearby.

Nonsubterranean wood-boring insects, including powder-post beetles and carpenter ants, as well as several termite species, remain above ground. Sometimes you can spot their entrance holes in the wood's surface; a pile of sawdust pellets is another telltale sign.

If you suspect termites, call a licensed pest exterminator. Don't panic—although these pests can demolish a house, it would take years to do so.

Exterminators surround the house with what amounts to an underground moat of insecticide, usually by injecting chemicals into the soil with special equipment. Isolated from the earth, worker termites in the house soon die of thirst; the remainder of the colony starves or moves on.

Nonsubterranean termites confine their activities to limited areas, such as the inside of a porch column, a window, or a door frame. If the wood has not been weakened structurally, the extermination process will consist of boring holes into the wood and injecting a liquid or powdered chemical. If the damage is more extensive, the wood member must be cut away and replaced with new treated lumber.

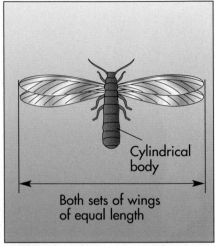

Termites.
Termites resemble ants but have cylindrical bodies and are light gray in color. During the mating season, workers have two pairs of equal-sized wings; otherwise they are wingless. Most termites live in the ground outside the house and make daily forays into the house to retrieve wood fibers.

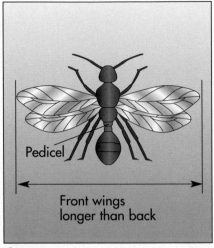

Carpenter ants.
Winged carpenter ants have a very thin waist called a pedicel, and the back pair of wings is shorter than the front. Carpenter ants make their homes in moist wood. If you take steps to keep out moisture, they will die off.

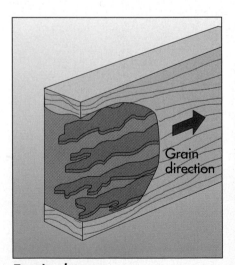

Termite damage.
Subterranean termites form tunnels in the direction of the wood grain, sometimes leaving nothing but a shell. By the time the damage is visible, the board is typically too far gone to save.

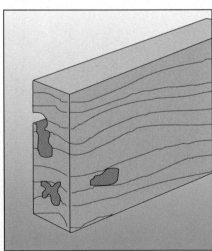

Carpenter ant damage.
Nonsubterranean insects burrow across the grain. Occasionally their tunnels break through the surface. This type of damage often becomes evident in time to save the board.

How they get in.

Most termites live in the forest, where they have an abundant supply of food in the form of dead and fallen trees. Unfortunately they don't distinguish between wood in its natural state and wood that has been through a sawmill. To discourage termites from picnicking in your home, clear away any firewood or construction debris near your house. Because they can gain access through even tiny holes, you will probably not be able to fence them out. Call in an exterminator if they have already invaded your home.

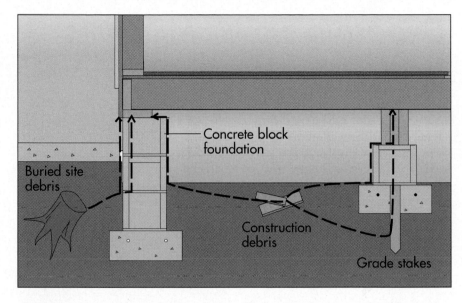

Apply insecticide in a crawlspace.

Many homes in termite-infested areas are built on crawlspace foundations. Termiticide should be applied around the bases of all rigid structures that are between the soil and the sill or floor framing. These structures include masonry walls, masonry piers, and plumbing pipes. As a second line of defense, foundation walls and piers should be capped with sheetmetal termite shields. Know the effective life of your shields and replace them before your house is reinfested.

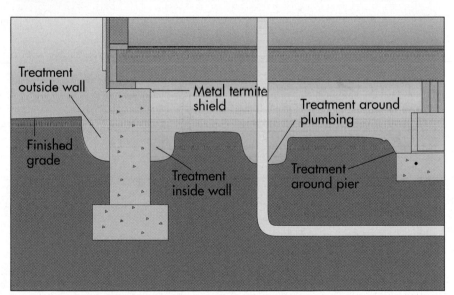

Treating a basement.

Professionals treat full-basement foundations as if they were boats floating in a sea of termites. The soil outside the wall is treated all the way to the footing, and termiticide is applied to the entire soil surface before the basement floor slab is poured. If the foundation wall consists of hollow masonry blocks, the wall is capped with solid concrete and a sheet-metal shield. If termites are found after the home is built, holes are typically drilled and filled with termiticide all around the foundation.

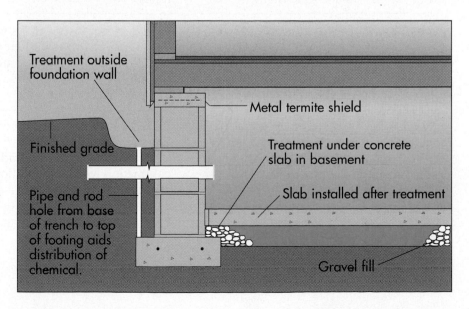

CHOOSING SIDING MATERIALS

No other improvement can do as much for your home's appearance and livability as a new exterior surface. Add new siding to create an entirely different appearance, or duplicate the old look using a low-maintenance product that won't need repainting for decades. For a guide to the range of siding materials and styles available, see the chart below.

Before you choose a siding for your house, examine what's underneath. Tightly interlocked new siding greatly reduces air infiltration through exterior walls. It won't make up for lack of insulation and sheathing, however. If you're looking for energy savings, you might be wise to strip walls to their sheathing or studs and upgrade the R-value with insulation (see pages 512–519). Or perhaps the answer is to beef up existing insulation with a polystyrene backing that's available with some manufactured sidings (see page 500).

Carefully plan how the new siding will be covered with moldings. Adding a layer to the exterior may mean that window and door frames need to be extended outward by the thickness of the new siding. Of course, if you remove the old siding and install new siding of the same thickness, you won't have that problem.

CHOOSING SIDING

Material	Appearance	Features/Price	Durability
Wood, plywood	Widest range of styles, textures, and finishes; available preprimed or presealed	Difficult to apply over existing siding; prices vary according to the material; many types are naturally insulating	Depends upon species and pretreatment; plywood and sapwood must be well sealed
Hardboard	Lap and vertical panel styles with a variety of textures and prefinished colors; also available in preprimed form	No problems with grain, splitting, or knots; large panels mean fewer joints for easier installation and greater weather resistance; color selection limited; moderate price	Vinyl-clad types guaranteed up to 30 years; other types must be kept covered with paint or they will swell
Shingles and shakes	Shingles are smooth and can be cut into designs; shakes are rustic	Of some insulation value; pieces often get damaged but are easy to replace	Guaranteed up to 20 years, but appearance deteriorates
Aluminum	Mostly available as horizontal lap siding; vertical, shingle, and shake styles also available; broad selection of colors	Choice of finishes at prices ranging from moderate to high; lightweight, unaffected by fire and termites; drawbacks are that it dents easily, is noisy, conducts electricity	Guaranteed up to 35 years, easily cleaned; many types need to be repainted
Vinyl	Choice of lap and vertical styles; large selection of colors and textures	Impervious to most perils; color is impregnated all the way through; higher rate of expansion and contraction makes application critical; fairly expensive	Lifetime guarantees; cannot be repainted

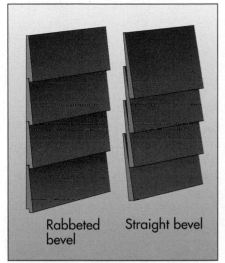

Lap siding.

Rabbeted bevel   Straight bevel

Lap siding, also called clapboard, is applied horizontally, with boards lapped at least 1 inch. Rabbeted-bevel siding has a predetermined exposure. Straight-bevel siding can have an exposure of between 4 and 8 inches—the narrower the exposure, the classier the look and the thicker the coverage.

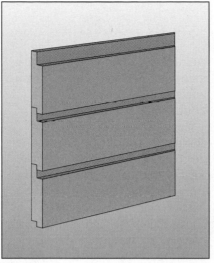

Shiplap.

Shiplap or channel-groove siding has rabbeted edges to interlock the boards. It can be installed either horizontally or vertically.

Wood shingles.

Shingles have a smooth appearance, adapt readily to misshapen walls, and are easy to apply. Creative carpenters can create an intricate "gingerbread" look by cutting shingles to various shapes and forming patterns.

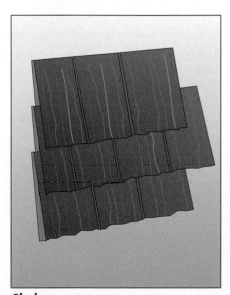

Shakes.

Shakes are like shingles but are thicker and have an irregular, hand-split look. They're more expensive than wood shingles.

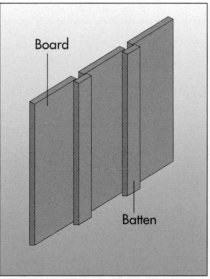

Board

Batten

Board-and-batten.

Board-and-batten siding is installed vertically, with gaps between the boards that are covered by the battens. With reverse board and batten, the battens are applied first.

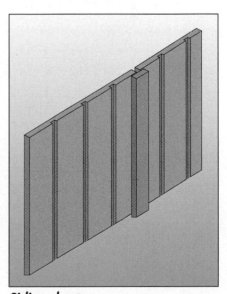

Siding sheets.

Often referred to as "T1-11," grooves give plywood siding sheets the appearance of boards. Various spacings of grooves are available. Joints may be shiplapped or covered with battens. All exposed edges must be well-covered and protected from the elements.

APPLYING WOOD SHINGLES AND SHAKES

Of all siding materials, shingles and shakes are the easiest to install. The job is repetitive but requires only basic carpentry skills. Nail up a batten guide strip for each course, fit each piece ⅛ inch from its neighbor, and drive in two or three nails.

You can apply shingles and shakes directly over old wood siding. If your house has wood or plywood sheathing, you could remove the old siding, repair defects, and staple on some new building wrap first.

Shingle grades run from 1 to 4, in a variety of sizes and textures. Choose No. 1 or No. 2 grade material for exterior walls. No. 3 and No. 4 grade are structurally sound but not good-looking; use them only where appearance isn't a factor, as in the first layer in double-course shingling.

To apply double-course shingles, nail up two layers, one on top of the other (see Step 1). This lets you expose more of the shingle surface and creates a deeper shadow line between courses. Expose slightly less than one-half of the shingle for single coursing, about two-thirds for double-course applications.

For a neat, uniform look, carefully plot exposures so they'll line up with window tops and sills, and then hold the courses exactly level. If you want to add design interest, you can nail them so the bottom butt edges are random lengths.

Shingles up to 8 inches wide need two rustproof shingle nails each; with wider shingles, use a third nail.

Soak bundles of shingles for several hours before you begin or the wood may expand and pull away during the first heavy rain.

YOU'LL NEED...

TIME: 6 to 8 hours for a 10×25-foot wall.
SKILLS: Basic carpentry skills.
TOOLS: Saw, level, hammer, tape measure, chalk line, square, pry bar, water level, block plane.

EXPERTS' INSIGHT

MAKING IT ALL THE WAY AROUND

With siding that has horizontal sight lines, it is important that the siding courses meet at exactly the same height at the corners. Start the job by marking level lines indicating the bottoms of the bottom course and several upper courses, all around the house. It is easy to do this if you use a water level or a laser level.

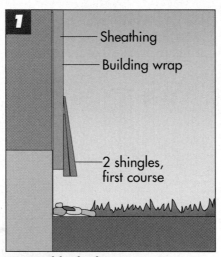

1. Double the bottom course.
Use two shingles for the first course, three if you'll be double-coursing. Overhang below the sheathing about 1 inch.

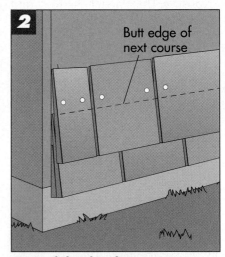

2. Nail the shingles.
Drive nails ¾ inch from each edge and at least an inch above where the butt edges of the next course will fall.

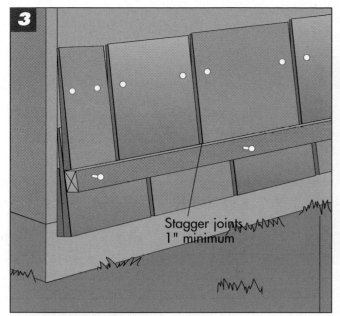

3. Use a horizontal guide.

To keep butts perfectly level, tack up a guide strip as shown. Once you are sure that the guide is level and at the correct height, installing the shingles is quick and easy. Always stagger edge joints by at least an inch from course to course.

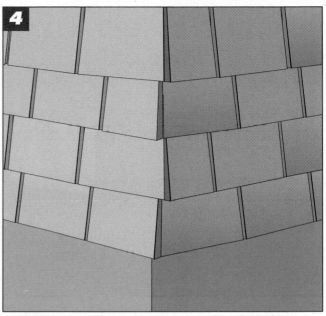

4. Alternate courses at a corner.

As each course arrives at a corner, butt the corner shingles alternately as shown, using a block plane to fine-tune the fit. Alternatively, miter the edges, cover them with wood or metal molding, or install vertical edge molding pieces and butt the shingles tight up to the moldings.

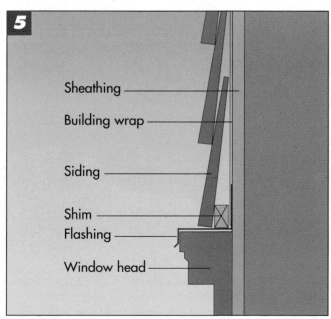

5. Flash around a window.

Carefully fit building wrap around window and door moldings. Install drip-edge flashing at the top so that water is sure to run away from the house. Add a shim piece onto the flashing so the bottom shingles slope away from the house to shed rain. Cut the shingles carefully and install them tightly to the moldings.

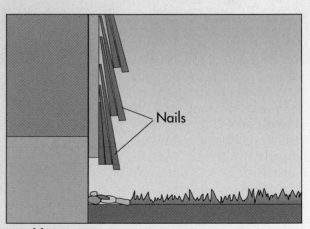

Double-coursing.

There are two basic ways to install shingles, each of which guarantees that the sheathing will be covered at all points. With a single-course installation (see Step 2, page 494), less than half the length of a shingle is exposed; and the nails are hidden. With double-course installation, each course is doubled, and the nails are driven near the bottom of the shingles, so they are exposed. For double-coursing, use longer nails. Edges of the outer course should be ½ inch below the undercourse.

APPLYING BOARD SIDING

Install horizontal wood siding in much the same way as you would install wood shingles and shakes (pages 494–495). Keep in mind that this work calls for much more precise measurements and careful carpentry.

Ensure that boards will remain perfectly level from course to course, and that courses will line up with the tops and bottoms of door and window frames. Use a water level or laser level to make marks all round the house so the siding will meet at the same height at all corners.

Usually it is easiest to install vertical corner trim boards first, and then butt the horizontal siding to them. One alternative is to bevel-cut siding pieces and make hundreds of exact corner joints. This looks great, but calls for excellent carpentry skills. Or purchase metal caps to finish off the corner of each course.

Vertical siding—especially with random-width boards—requires fewer painstaking calculations. Plan for openings and corners before you get to them, though, and be sure to plumb each board.

Handle all siding lumber carefully, especially prefinished and preprimed types. These relatively soft woods often split when nailed near an edge. To keep this from happening, drill pilot holes first or use special preblunted siding nails.

YOU'LL NEED...

TIME: Several days to side an entire house, with a helper.
SKILLS: Intermediate to advanced carpentry skills.
TOOLS: Hammer, drill, handsaw, miter saw, level, chalk line.

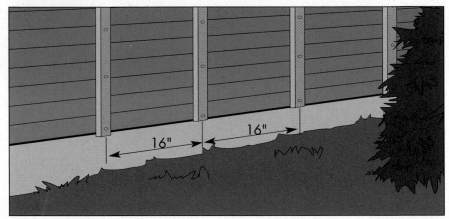

Prepare for horizontal siding.
Check with local codes or consult with a siding expert to see if you should apply roofing felt or building wrap before siding.

If the old siding is plywood or shiplap, you can nail siding directly over it. The new siding will make your walls thicker, so you may need to extend door and window trim by the same amount.

For the easiest installation, if the existing siding is horizontal, you may choose to tear it off.

Alternatively, nail vertical 1×3s every 16 inches, as shown above. Drive nails through the old siding into the studs beneath. You will need to extend the window and door trim quite a bit. Nailers, however, give you the option of installing rigid ¾-inch insulation (shown below) between the strips, increasing your home's energy efficiency.

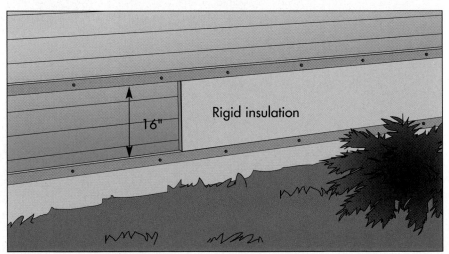

Prepare for vertical siding.
If you have existing horizontal siding and want to install vertical siding, you may choose to remove the old siding first. Alternatively, attach horizontal nailing strips. Space them about 16 inches from center to center; make sure that they are all installed onto the horizontal siding at the same thickness (that is, at the same distance away from the wall). Fill the gaps with rigid ¾-inch insulation.

If the existing siding is uniform (check it with a long, straight board) and you do not need additional insulation, you can install vertical or plywood siding directly onto the horizontal siding.

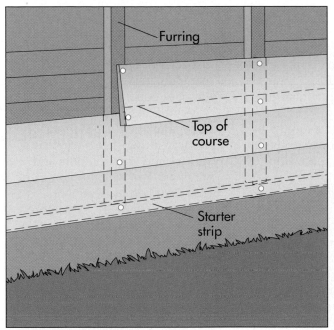

Adding lap siding.

Decide how wide a reveal you want—the distance from the bottom edge of each piece of siding to the course above. (This is mostly a style decision, but the narrower, the greater the insulation value.) A siding reveal that's 10 inches wide or less requires two nails driven into each stud. Wider siding needs three nails.

Installing shiplap.

Channel-groove siding gets two nails across the width of each board. Nail about 1 inch from the board's edges. Be sure to drill a pilot hole wherever you drive a nail less than 3 inches from a board's edge.

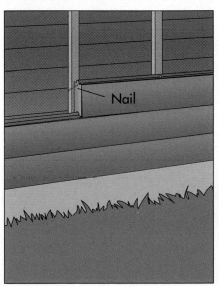

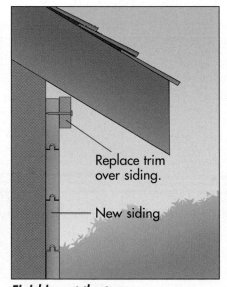

Installing tongue-and-groove.

Tongue-and-groove siding is nailed through the tongue of each course. Wide boards may need a second nail midway up the board.

Finishing at the top.

Siding should extend up under trim boards. If the trim is in good shape, number the trim boards as you remove them, remove the old nails, and reuse the trim. Often it is easier to install new pieces.

EXPERTS' INSIGHT

ATTACHING SIDING FIRMLY

Ideally, any siding should be attached with nails driven into wall studs—not just the sheathing or the old siding. However, if the sheathing is wood planks or plywood in good shape (rather than a fibrous or Styrofoam-like material), siding can be firmly installed with ringshank nails driven into the sheathing alone.

Purchase siding nails recommended for the siding you will install. You may want two lengths, one for driving all the way into studs and one for attaching to sheathing only. Wherever you will drive a nail less than 3 inches from a board's edge, drill pilot holes first.

APPLYING SHEET SIDING

Large hardboard and plywood sheets cover a wall rapidly. Most sheets are only 7/16 inch thick, minimizing trim problems around doors and windows. To install sheet siding yourself, you'll need to know basic measuring and cutting techniques, and you'll need an assistant to help handle the sheets.

Some sheets come with rabbeted edges that interlock to make a vertical shiplap joint. Others simply butt together, and their seams are covered by a batten strip (see page 499) or special T-shaped molding (below).

Ideally, sheets should be nailed to studs, spacing nails 6 inches apart on edges and 12 inches apart on intermediate studs. If the sheathing is wood and in good condition, it's all right to nail the edges of the sheets to the sheathing only. Use rust-resistant ringshank siding nails or the color-matching nails available from the manufacturers of prefinished siding materials.

Never drive sheets tightly together; allow for expansion by leaving a 1/16-inch space and caulking the gap.

Cut sheet siding with the good face down if you're using a circular saw or with the good face up if you're using a saber saw or a handsaw. An inaccurate cut will spoil an entire sheet, so plot dimensions on graph paper and double-check them before you begin sawing. It sometimes helps avoid confusion to hold the piece up, oriented as it will be installed, after marking and before cutting. This enables you to envision how the cuts should be made. Remember to seal the raw edges of cuts made to preprimed and prefinished sheets before installation (check the manufacturer's specifications for the right sealer).

Metal accessories, similar to those shown on pages 500–501, simplify fitting sheets together at corners and around doors and windows. You can also fabricate your own corner treatments, as shown on page 499. (For more about working with plywood and hardboard, see pages 260–263.)

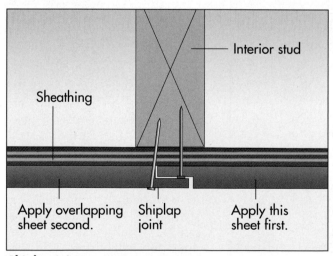

Sheathing

Interior stud

Apply overlapping sheet second. Shiplap joint Apply this sheet first.

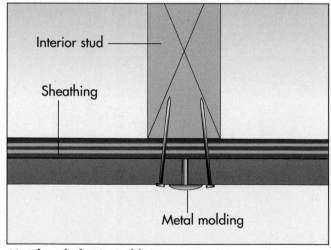

Interior stud

Sheathing

Metal molding

Shiplap joints.
To attach sheets with shiplap joints, nail up the first sheet, with its shiplap flush against the sheathing, and test-fit the next sheet (whose shiplap fits over the shiplap of the first sheet). Apply a bead of caulk along the edge of the first sheet, then install the next. Don't try to drive a nail through both laps.

Metal and plastic moldings.
Metal moldings offer an inconspicuous way to finish butt joints. Some types must be installed as you install the first sheet. Others can be driven in between the sheets. Drive fasteners as recommended by the manufacturer. On a vertical installation, when the wall is taller than the length of a sheet, use metal moldings at the horizontal butt joints as well.

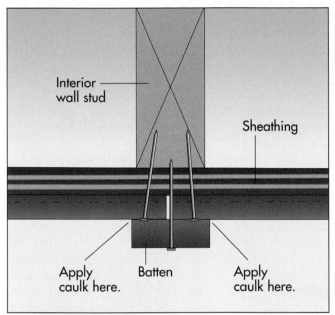

Wood battens.

You also can cover butt joints with wood battens. Fasten the battens tightly with nails driven every 2 feet or so, then apply butyl or latex/silicone caulk to each side of the batten. For a board-and-batten effect (see page 493), space more vertical strips across the sheet's width.

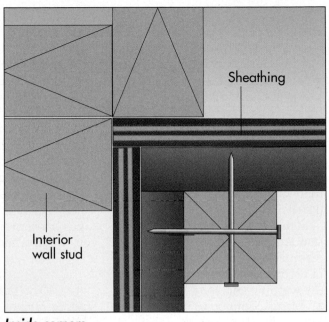

Inside corners.

Finish inside corners with 2×2 trim, as shown. You can also select from a variety of cove moldings milled for this purpose.

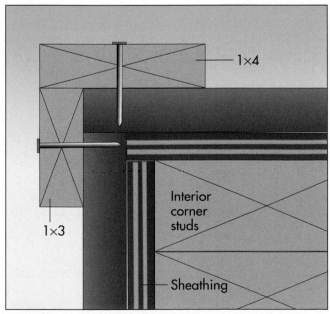

Outside corners.

At the outside corners, lap one 1×4 with one 1×3, as shown above. (If you use two 1x4s, one side will be wider than the other.) It is sometimes easiest to nail the two pieces together first, and then cut the assembled corner to length. Attach the corner with siding nails.

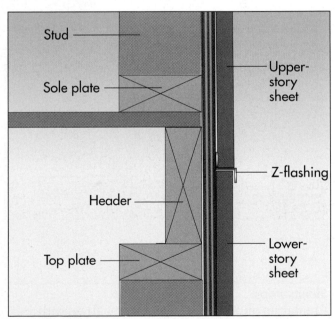

Horizontal joints.

On taller walls, such as the sides of two-story houses, you'll encounter horizontal joints. Nail the bottom sheet down, apply a bead of caulk, lay special Z-flashing in place, and nail the top sheet.

APPLYING MANUFACTURED SIDING

Aluminum and vinyl sidings are designed especially for re-siding applications and are relatively easy to install. Check the warranty, though, to see whether you risk voiding it by doing the work yourself. The integrity of the installation depends on closely following the manufacturer's instructions.

Manufactured siding uses standardized, lightweight components that go up fast and fit together snugly, with none of the warping and splitting problems common to wood. Metal siding must be grounded because it conducts electricity.

Aluminum and vinyl sidings expand and contract considerably with temperature changes. That's why they come with slots, instead of holes, for nailing. Locate nails near the center of these slots—and make sure you don't drive the nails so tightly that they impede the inevitable movement.

Beware of siding companies with hard-sell presentations and attractive financing arrangements. Many siding contractors are reputable, but there are plenty of fast-buck operators.

Hardboard siding will swell if it absorbs condensation from within walls—install it with an adequate vapor barrier. Cut and attach it as you would wood siding.

YOU'LL NEED...

TIME: Several days, but manufactured siding can be applied more quickly than wooden lap siding.

SKILLS: Basic carpentry and sheet-metal skills.

TOOLS: Hammer, drill, measuring tape, square, saw, Zip tool (often provided by the manufacturer), tin snips, caulking gun.

EXPERTS' INSIGHT

VINYL SHAKES

Also available are vinyl components made to look like painted wood shakes. They come in various widths for a random appearance. They must be installed on smooth, wood sheathing. Like vinyl and aluminum siding, the trim pieces are installed first. The pieces interlock for quick installation; once the first course is established level, there is no need to periodically check the courses for level or the proper reveal.

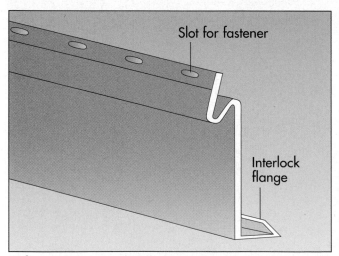

Siding strips.
Aluminum and vinyl sidings come in strips with interlocking top and bottom flanges for tight joints between strips. Nail one course through the prepunched holes in the top lip, then interlock the bottom of the next piece with the top of the one just installed.

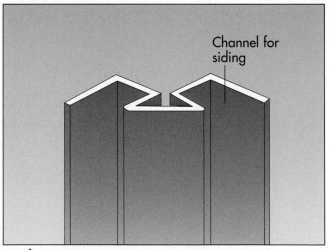

Inside corners.
Inside corner pieces have flanges on each side where the siding strips fit. Test that the corner is plumb in both directions before you install it. If not, draw a plumb line and shim the inside corner so it is plumb and firmly attached. Apply caulk to the back of the corner piece just prior to attaching it.

UNDERSTANDING WEATHERIZATION AND VENTILATION

Chapter 11 (pages 521–562) deals with heating and cooling equipment, the biggest energy consumers in most homes. The rest of this chapter describes their silent partners—the weather stripping, insulation, and ventilation systems that help you make the most of that precious energy.

These three components work to control the heat that your home loses in the winter and gains in the summer. Weather stripping seals outside walls, windows, and doors, keeping outside air out and inside air in. Insulation retards heat transfer through solid surfaces. Ventilation exhausts excess heat, as well as stale air and humidity. Older homes often suffer from too little weather stripping and insulation, while some newer homes lack sufficient ventilation.

Chances are your home could stand some upgrading on all of these counts (see the drawing below for points you should check). Start with weather stripping. It's the easiest and least expensive component to deal with. You need a tight seal at all doors, windows, and anything else that opens. Caulk, a form of weather stripping, fills gaps between immovable elements where air could penetrate. For caulking basics, see page 481. Window putty, also called glazing compound, seals joints between glass and wood (see pages 434–435).

Once your home is snugly weather-stripped, you can assess the effectiveness of its insulation. You need the most insulation up top, either above your topmost ceilings or between the rafters. Next in line are the exterior walls. If your home sits atop a crawl-space or unheated basement, there should be insulation around ducts and pipes, as well as under the first-level floor or around the space's perimeter.

After you've tightened up your home's weather stripping and insulation, take a fresh look at its ventilation. Roof, soffit, and gable vents let an attic breathe (see page 469). Vent fans do the same for other areas (see pages 131–133).

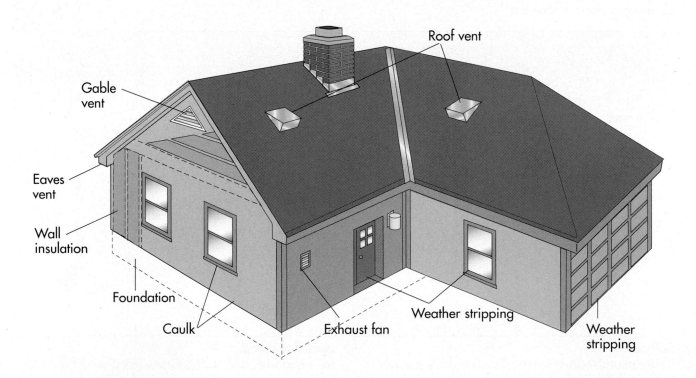

A house that's efficiently tight, yet able to breathe.
In an energy-efficient home, insulation—either fiberglass batts or blown-in—completely fills the spaces between wall studs and ceiling joists of the top floor. Caulk seals exterior door and window moldings tightly against the siding. Flexible weather stripping makes a tight seal when a window or door is closed. Attic vents allow moisture to exit the house.

IDENTIFYING HIDDEN AIR LEAKS

You would never think of leaving a window open in the winter—unless someone else was paying the heating bill. Yet the total of all the little cracks and holes in the floors, walls, and ceilings of an average older home is often equivalent to an area of 2 square feet.

House doctors—technicians who specialize in finding and sealing such cracks—call these "hidden" heat leaks, because we never seem to see them.

The illustration at right points out the leaks that you can uncover if you give your house a good once-over. The chart below shows the square-inch area of these leaks, both before and after treatment. After you've pinpointed the problem areas, use the techniques on pages 504–511 to plug these leaks.

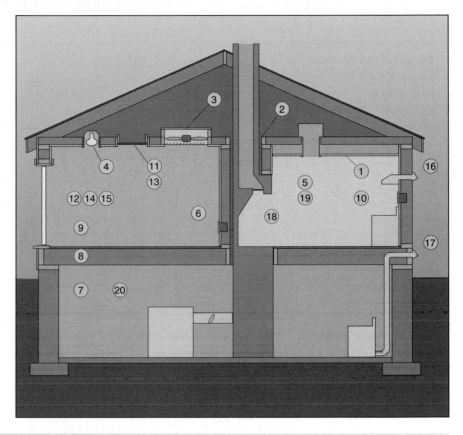

SIZING UP TYPICAL RESIDENTIAL AIR LEAKS

Leak	Square Inches	Leak	Square Inches	Leak	Square Inches
Ceiling		**Exterior Wall, continued**		**Vents**	
1 Dropped/100 square feet		9 Floor/wall joint:		16 Range, damper open	9
no vapor barrier	78	uncaulked	27	damper closed	2
with vapor barrier	8	baseboard caulked	7	17 Dryer, damper open	4
2 Chimney, framing gap	12	10 Electric outlet or switch	0.2	damper closed	1
gap weather-stripped	1	with cover gasket	0.05	**Fireplace**	
3 Whole-house fan, closed	8	**Doors**		18 Damper open	54
covered with tight box	0.6	11 Attic fold-down	17	average damper	
4 Lighting fixture, recessed	4	weather-stripped	8	closed	9
surface-mount	0.3	12 Entrance	8	clean, tight damper	5
5 Pipe or duct, uncaulked	1	weather-stripped	6	with stove insert	2
caulked at ceiling	0.2	with magnetic seal	4	**Heating System**	
Interior Wall		13 Attic hatch	6	19 Ducts	
6 Electrical outlet or switch	0.2	weather-stripped	3	in unheated space	56
with cover gasket	0.03	**Door and Window Frames**		caulked and taped	28
Exterior Wall		14 Brick wall:		20 Furnace with flame-	
7 Sill on masonry:		uncaulked frame	2	retention head	
uncaulked	65	caulked	0.4	burner	12
caulked	13	15 Wood wall:		add stack damper	9
8 Band or box sill:		uncaulked frame	0.6		
uncaulked	65	caulked	0.1		
caulked	13				

APPLYING CAULK

If you have never used caulk, start in an inconspicuous area until you can hone your skills. Some types stick more readily to fingers and tools than to the surfaces that they're sealing. It takes a tube or two to learn how hard to squeeze and how fast to move the nozzle for a smooth, unbroken bead.

For most jobs you can use an inexpensive caulk gun. Its squeeze handle pushes a plunger against the bottom of a caulk tube, forcing caulk through the nozzle. See page 481 to choose the right type of caulk for the job.

Before applying caulk, first scrape out the old, cracked caulk and flaked paint. Be sure the surfaces are dry. Even high-quality caulk may crack or come loose in time, so if the gap to be caulked is wider than ⅛ inch, consider covering the area with molding or use foam sealant.

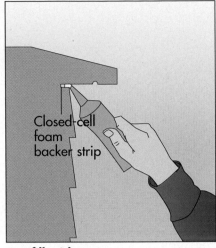

Pre-fill wide gaps.
Pack ¾-inch or wider gaps with closed-cell foam backer strips, then complete the seal by caulking. For a big job, save money by buying a full-barrel gun and loading it with compound sold in bulk.

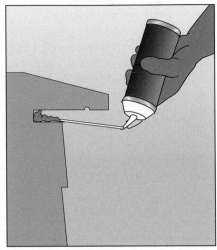

Use foam sealant.
Alternatively, apply foam sealant. Purchase the "non-expanding" type, which actually does expand some. Shake the can, hold it upside down, insert the tip into the opening, and squeeze.

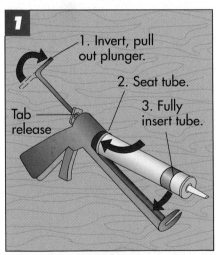

1. Load a caulking gun.
To load a caulking gun, invert its plunger handle and pull the plunger all the way back. Some guns have a tab that you push before you can pull the plunger back. Insert the caulk tube, then push the plunger forward until it stops.

2. Cut the nozzle.
Snip off the nozzle's tip. The closer the cut is to the tip, the narrower the bead will be. With some tubes, you need to puncture the inside seal with a wire or a long nail.

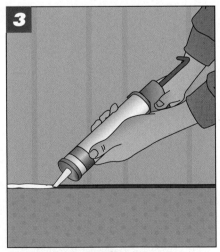

3. Caulk an inside corner.
Between perpendicular surfaces, bisect the angle with the gun's nozzle to make a smooth concave bead. Hold the gun at a 45-degree angle and pull it toward you in a smooth, steady stroke, maintaining an even pressure on the trigger. You should not apply caulk at temperatures below 50°F.

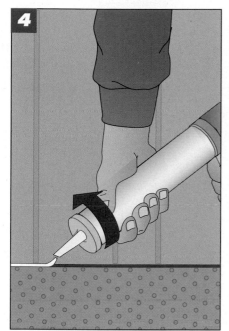

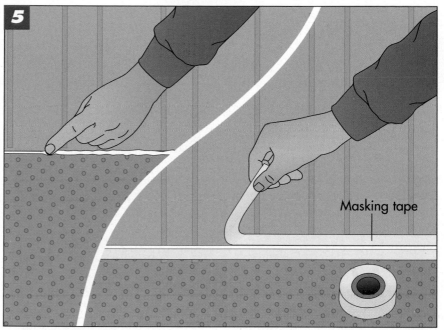

4. Finish the line.
At the end of a stroke, lift the tip with a twist to catch caulk oozing from the nozzle, then quickly release the plunger. Remove any excess from the nozzle.

5. Smooth...
Smooth the bead of caulk using a moist fingertip or a moist, tightly wadded rag. Try to smooth it in one stroke, applying even pressure. This takes some practice.

...or, tape and caulk.
For a nearly perfect line, first press masking tape on each side of the joint. Caulk, wipe with your finger, and pull away the tape.

Masking tape

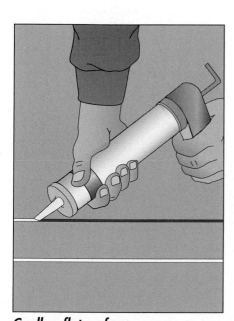

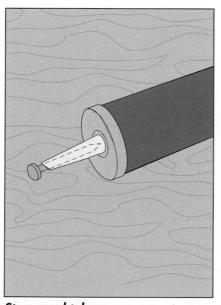

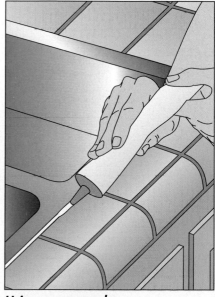

Caulk a flat surface.
Between flat surfaces, straddle the joint with the nozzle and pack it so that the caulk bulges out slightly.

Store used tubes.
Save partial tubes by sealing them with a nail or screw. Or invert the cut-off tip of the nozzle and stuff it into the opening.

Using squeeze tubes.
Toothpaste-style tubes are handy for tub and sink caulking and for minor touch-up jobs. Snip the tube's tip with a utility knife and squeeze. If you replace the tip's cap, you can likely reuse the tube several times.

PLUGGING AIR LEAKS

Usually you can feel any heat leaks that are caused by inadequate weather stripping or caulking. On a cool, windy day, systematically pass your hand around the perimeter of a door, window, or any openable part of your home. Do you feel a draft? If so you've located an air gap that needs to be sealed. Continue searching and you may find others.

Note that some types of heat loss, such as radiation through single-pane windows, seem to produce a draft but actually don't. If you have doubts about whether you've found a leak or the effects of radiation, hold a sheet of plastic food wrap over the opening. If the plastic moves, there's an air leak around the opening and you need weather stripping or caulk.

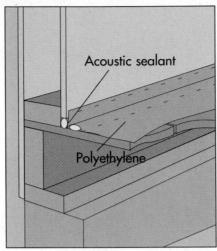

Seal a floor/wall joint.
Prior to installing finish flooring and baseboard, staple polyethylene sheeting over non-hardening sealant to close the joint between a floor and a wall.

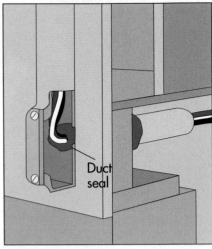

Seal cable entrances.
Seal service-entrance cable penetrations with moldable non-hardening duct-sealing compound. Alternatively, use foam sealant.

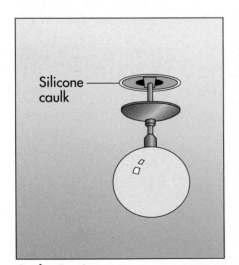

Seal canopies.
Use silicone caulk (which resists hardening even when it gets hot) to seal fixture canopies up against the ceiling. This is necessary only on a ceiling directly below an attic.

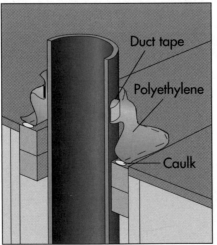

Fill around a vent pipe.
In the attic, seal around vent pipes. First lay a generous bead of latex/silicone caulk. Cut a piece of plastic 4 or 5 inches wide and embed its bottom in the caulk as you wrap it around the pipe. Secure the top of the plastic with duct tape.

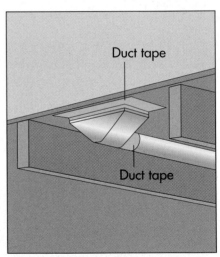

Use duct tape for ducts.
Believe it or not, duct tape has an official function—to seal ducts. Purchase professional-quality duct tape, which will last far longer than the cheaper variety. Clean and dry the area before application. Press the duct tape into place carefully so there are no folds and few wrinkles.

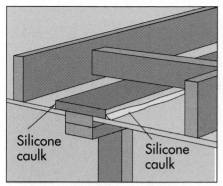

Caulk the ceiling drywall.
Up in the attic, you may need to push aside insulation to see the ceiling's drywall or plaster. Close the joint between the drywall and the wall's top plate with latex/silicone caulk.

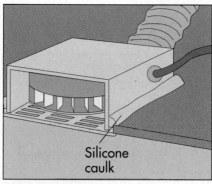

Caulk vent fans.
Working from the attic above, seal a bathroom vent with silicone caulk. Where the fan's ductwork exits the house, check that the louvers are working smoothly so the opening shuts when the fan is not operating.

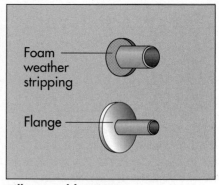

Fill around large pipes.
Another solution for large pipe gaps is foam weather stripping. Find a type of foam that just fills the gap, without too much cramming. Complete the seal and give it a finished look by installing a pipe flange; fill the back of the flange with latex/silicone caulk.

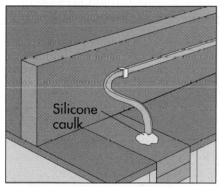

Caulk around electrical cable.
Seal all electrical penetrations with butyl, silicone, or latex/silicone caulk.

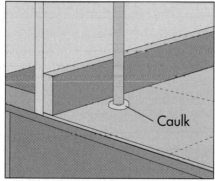

Caulk around pipes.
Smaller gaps around pipes can be filled with either silicone or latex/silicone caulk.

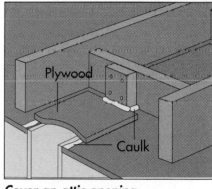

Cover an attic opening.
If an interior wall opens to the attic, cut pieces of 1× lumber or plywood to fit snugly. Caulk the pieces in place over the openings.

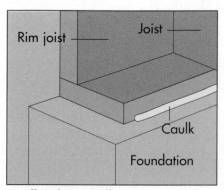

Caulk a house sill.
Although the weight of the house rests on it, a sill can leak air. Seal the wood sill/masonry foundation joint with long-lasting butyl, silicone, or latex/silicone caulk.

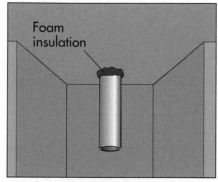

Use foam for large gaps.
Large gaps around pipes can be filled with foam sealant. To add further protection, cover the sealant with plastic, using staples and duct tape.

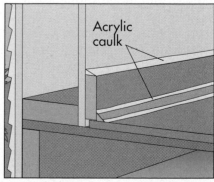

Seal moldings.
If there is a baseboard on an exterior wall, seal it with latex/silicone caulk. Smooth the caulk with a wet finger, then paint.

WEATHER-STRIPPING WINDOWS WITH SPRING METAL

Although not as easy to install as other types of weather stripping, bronze or aluminum spring metal makes the best seal, especially where the sash slides against the frame. Designed to fit inside window channels or frames, its out-of-harm's-way location helps it survive years of openings and closings. Plus, it is all but invisible. Press-in-place plastic V-strip seals just as well but is likely to pull away after repeated slidings of the sash.

Spring metal comes in kit form—with enough strips and nails to treat a typical window. Or you can buy it by the running foot in coil form. Get the type with predrilled holes.

This page show how to fit spring metal around double-hung and casement sashes, but you can easily adapt these techniques to suit other window types (see page 407). To provide a tight seal, be sure the metal compresses when the window shuts.

Many older double-hung windows have the top sash painted or even nailed shut. This seals it tightly but may make it difficult to clean the window. You may choose to loosen the top sash and install spring metal weather stripping.

Spring metal cuts easily with tin snips. Unroll it carefully to avoid kinking.

YOU'LL NEED...
TIME: 30 to 60 minutes per double-hung window.
SKILLS: Basic carpentry skills.
TOOLS: Screwdriver, utility knife, tin snips, hammer.

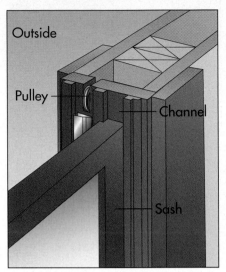

Sash channels.
Before cutting and fitting the new weather stripping, fully open the sash. For double-hung windows, fit strips to completely fill the sash when it is fully closed. Nail the strips with the open side facing the exterior. Drive all the nails, then pry the leaves apart to obtain a tight seal.

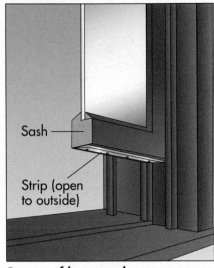

Bottom of lower sash.
Fasten a strip to the underside of the lower sash bottom rail. If the upper sash is not fixed in place, do the same to the top rail of the upper sash.

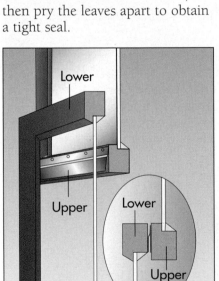

Where the sashes meet.
Where the sashes meet when closed, nail a strip to the bottom rail of the upper sash with the open side facing down. You may need to flatten the strip in order to make it fit.

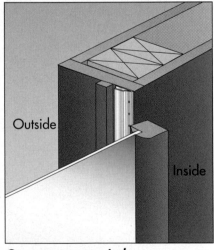

On a casement window.
On casement windows, nail strips to the frame. Install strips spring-side-in so sashes open freely.

WEATHER-STRIPPING WINDOWS WITH GASKETS

Rolled vinyl, foam, and other gasket-type weather stripping products work well for two surfaces that meet, rather than slide against, each other. When the window closes, they compress to seal air leaks. Some types are attached to metal strips. Bulbous types provide better seals. Stretch the gasket material slightly as you attach it and make sure there are no gaps at the corners. Some types are nailed or screwed in place, while others are self-adhesive.

Exterior installation provides a tighter seal and is less noticeable. Work carefully if you are on an upper floor (see page 457).

(see page 457)

YOU'LL NEED...
TIME: 30 minutes per window.
SKILLS: None required.
TOOLS: Scissors or utility knife, hammer.

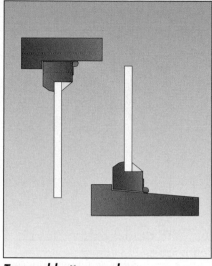

Top and bottom sashes.
Seal the top and bottom sashes by attaching a strip to the outside of the upper sash top rail and the outside of the lower sash bottom rail. Make sure that the weather stripping seals completely at all points—but not so tightly as to make it difficult to close the sash.

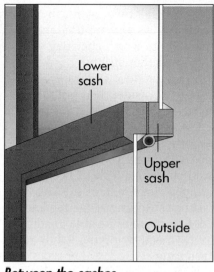

Between the sashes.
Create a tight seal between two sashes by attaching a strip to the bottom of the upper sash. The strip should completely cover the gap, yet allow the window to close fully.

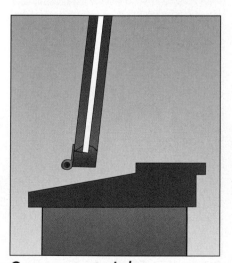

On a casement window.
On casement windows, attach strips to the sash or to the casing and the sill, whichever provides a tighter squeeze.

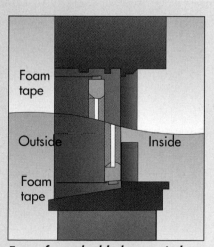

Foam for a double-hung window.
For double-hung windows, use foam only on the top and bottom of the sashes, or attach it to the frame at the top and bottom. Foam can't handle friction.

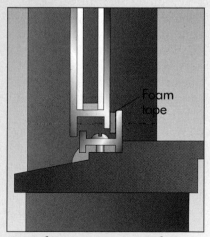

Foam for a casement window.
On metal casement or awning windows, stick press-in-place foam tape onto the frame. You will probably need to use the thinnest material available. Apply the foam to all four sides of the opening.

WEATHER-STRIPPING DOORS

Doors leak twice as much air as windows and are used more often, so it's worth checking your doors' weather stripping.

Close the door and look—first from the outside, then from the inside—for gaps in the weather stripping. When the wind is blowing, hold a sheet of plastic food wrap near the door on the inside to detect leaks. Check for crimped, flattened, or missing weather stripping at the top and sides. You might be able to adjust spring metal by prying lightly on the spring section. Other types probably will have to be replaced.

Feel along the threshold. Air infiltration means you need one of the bottom-of-the-door devices shown on page 511. And how's the door itself? Warping, an out-of-square frame, or deteriorated caulk around the edges give air a chance to make an end-run around even the tightest weather stripping. (See pages 420–423 for repairing doors.) Examine storm doors too. The felt gasket around the frame and the sweep or gasket at the bottom of the door may need replacement.

Check any interior doors that open to an attic, garage, basement, or other unheated space. Builders often don't bother to seal these big heat-losers at all. Worse yet, some contractors cut costs by installing hollow-core doors that have little insulation value. If that's the case at your house, your best bet would be to invest in the far greater thermal efficiency of a solid- or foam-core door.

YOU'LL NEED...

TIME: 30 minutes per door.
SKILLS: Basic skills.
TOOLS: Scissors, utility knife, tin snips, hacksaw, hammer.

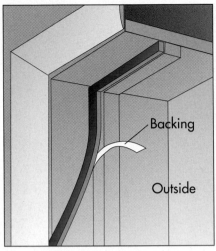

Foam tape.
Foam tape installs easily but does not always do the trick. If the door closes tightly, the foam may tear off or prevent the door from latching. Use it when there is a gap between the door and the stop. Cut strips to length, peel off the backing, and press the foam in place on the inside of the stops.

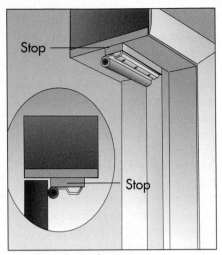

Metal-and-vinyl strips.
This material is effective and durable, and can be used in conjunction with spring metal. Close the door. Cut pieces to fit using tin snips or a hacksaw. Press each piece so it just touches the door. Drive the screws provided into the center of each slot so you can adjust the position if needed.

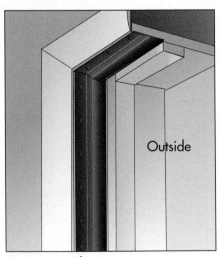

Spring metal.
Cut spring metal carefully to fit, using tin snips. Nail each strip to the jamb inside the stop, with the open end facing the exterior. On the latch side, notch-cut the piece to fit tightly around the strike plate.

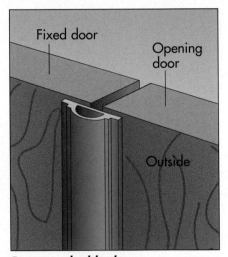

Between double doors.
If you have an older set of double (French) doors, apply foam tape to the inside of the half-round molding. If the molding is damaged, replace it. Alternatively, use insulated molding like the type shown above. Nail the molding to the face of the door that's usually the closed door.

SEALING UNDERNEATH DOORS

A door's bottom edge poses two weather-stripping problems. First the threshold has to withstand lots of traffic. Second any seal attached to the door must clear carpeting or other uneven floor spots within the arc that the door traverses.

The devices shown here solve these difficulties with varying degrees of effectiveness. If your door has a badly worn threshold, consider replacing it with a metal or wood threshold that has a replaceable gasket.

YOU'LL NEED...

TIME: 45 minutes to replace a threshold, 20 minutes to install a door sweep.
SKILLS: Basic carpentry skills.
TOOLS: Drill, screwdriver, tin snips, hammer, hacksaw, handsaw.

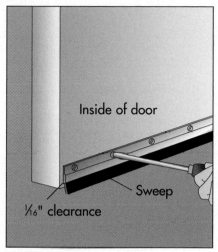

Door sweep.
This is the easiest solution, as long as the threshold is above the level of the carpeting or flooring. Close the door. Cut the sweep carefully to fit using tin snips or a hacksaw. Position the sweep so its gasket just touches the threshold. Drive screws into the centers of the slots so you can adjust the sweep up or down as needed.

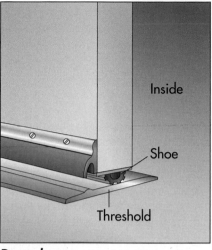

Door shoe.
A shoe makes a durable seal and has a drip cap that sheds water away from the door. If there is not enough clearance under the door, you will have to remove the door and cut or plane its bottom (see pages 426–427).

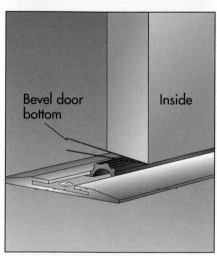

Threshold with gasket.
A bulb threshold works like a door shoe (above right). It provides an excellent seal, but the door bottom must be cut accurately. Bevel the door bottom as shown, so it seals tighter as it closes. Replace the rubber bulb periodically.

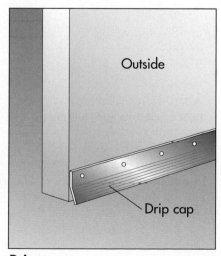

Drip cap.
If water seeps under your door and into the house, nail a drip cap to its outside face.

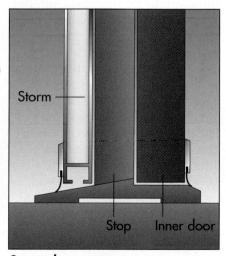

Storm door sweep.
Don't forget storm doors. You can buy replacement rubber or plastic sweeps for these that install on the outside. You may need to drill pilot holes through the metal door before driving screws.

INSULATING AN ATTIC FLOOR

A poorly insulated attic sends heat right through the roof in cold weather and serves as a solar collector on hot, sunny days. The solution is to insulate the attic floor. If the space will be used only for storage, insulate the floor as shown on this page. If the space is finished or you intend to finish it later, insulate the ceiling and walls as shown on page 513.

First look for leaks that might damage insulation, and make sure you have adequate ventilation (see page 469). You may choose to cut summer heat buildup with an attic fan or whole-house fan (see pages 130–133).

If your attic has a floor, you have two options: pull up sections and work the insulation under, or hire a contractor to blow in loose-fill through holes bored into the floor. If the attic lacks a floor, bring up planks or plywood panels to set atop the joists. This will allow you to move around without stepping through the ceiling.

If there already is a vapor barrier, use unfaced materials so moisture doesn't get trapped between the two barriers. Be sure not to cover recessed light fixtures or exhaust fans; doing so could cause a fire. Instead, install baffles that keep the insulation about 3 inches away on all sides.
NOTE: *Some insulating materials, such as fiberglass and mineral wool, are harmful to lungs and skin. Be sure to wear a painter's mask, gloves, and long sleeves.*

YOU'LL NEED...
TIME: 4 to 6 hours for an attic.
SKILLS: Basic skills for batts and blankets; intermediate skills for blowing in loose-fill insulation.
TOOLS: Utility knife, staple gun, rented blower for loose-fill.

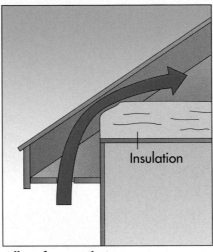

Allow for ventilation.
When placing batts or blankets, take care not to jam them against the roof; leave space at the eaves for airflow.

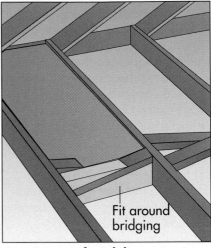

Cut pieces to fit tightly.
To cut a blanket or batt, place it on a piece of plywood with the facing side up. Use a piece of 2×4 as a guide and to compress the insulation. Cut with a utility knife. When you encounter bridging or other obstacles, cut for a snug fit.

EXPERTS' INSIGHT

VAPOR BARRIERS
When warm air meets a cold surface, condensation results, producing moisture that can damage insulation as well as a house's structure. A properly installed vapor barrier—which may be the paper, foil, or plastic facing of the insulation or a sheet of plastic—keeps moisture from collecting.

In most areas, the vapor barrier should be placed on the side of the insulation that faces inside. In the Southeast, however, the vapor barrier should face the outside. Check with your building department if you are not sure.

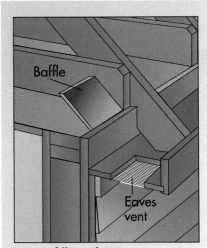

Loose-fill insulation.
For loose-fill, nail baffles at the eaves. Or buy special plastic baffles that will fit between joists and ensure airflow. Insulation should cover the wall top plate but not obstruct airflow. Pour some insulation between joists, then level it with a board. Be sure you don't leave low spots or voids.

INSULATING A FINISHED ATTIC

In a finished attic, the space above collar ties, coupled with gable louvers at the ends (see page 469), gets rid of winter condensation as well as summer heat. If you don't have collar ties, install them.

If your attic already is finished, you'll have to cut holes in the knee walls and the ceiling to gain access to insulate these areas. For patching walls and ceilings, see pages 862–869.

YOU'LL NEED...

TIME: 6 to 8 hours for an unfinished attic; additional time if you have to cut into and repair finished walls.
SKILLS: Basic skills.
TOOLS: Utility knife, chalk line, hammer or screwdriver, stapler. More tools may be needed to add collars or to refinish walls.

Install collar ties.
Add collar ties if your attic has none. Use 2×4s for spans of 6 feet or less; use 2×6s or larger for longer spans. Plan the height, and use a chalk line to mark the locations on the joists. Cut the ties to fit, then nail or screw them to the rafters. You may also choose to install knee walls (see below).

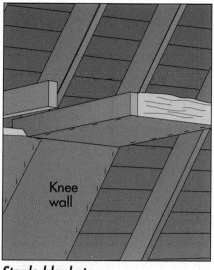

Staple blankets.
Staple insulation blankets to the collar ties, with the vapor barrier side facing correctly (see page 512). Continue down the roof and the knee wall to the floor.

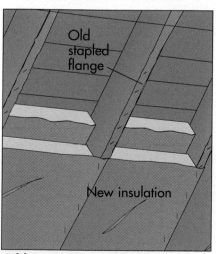

Add to existing insulation.
If you're adding to existing insulation, cut away its stapled flange and push it to the back of the cavity. Slash the old vapor barrier. Place the new insulation over the old. Staple flanges to the rafters, with the vapor barrier facing correctly. Lap the insulation joints (as shown above) as you go.

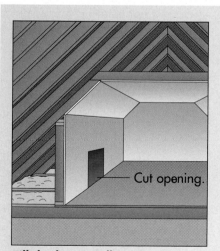

Fill the knee-wall space.
In a finished attic, make openings to get at spaces above collar ties and behind knee and end walls. Lay loose-fill or blanket material between joists in the knee-wall space. Use a broom handle to push into "unreachable" spots.

Fill the ceiling.
Don't insulate between the roof rafters in the knee-wall space. Place material between the wall studs, with the vapor barrier facing correctly. Pour loose-fill material between the rafters in the sloping part of the ceiling. Finish off with batts in the attic above the collar ties.

INSULATING A CRAWLSPACE

After attics, unheated crawlspaces are the next vital places to insulate. You have two options: drape batts or blankets around the perimeter walls, or suspend material between floor joists.

Draping the walls creates a sealed air chamber, which gains further insulation value. With some houses, however, you have no choice but to insulate between the floor joists.

Wrapping a crawlspace is a dirty but straightforward task—as long as you have enough space to move around. You'll need unfaced batts or blankets, 6-mil polyethylene sheeting to cover the ground, 1×2s and nails, and rocks or bricks. Wear goggles, gloves, knee pads, and protective clothing.

Close off unnecessary openings, but don't seal vents permanently; a crawlspace needs these for "breathing" in hot, muggy weather. A crawlspace must have at least two vents, located at opposite corners, that can be opened in the summer. A crawlspace that can't breathe turns into a giant moisture chamber in hot, humid weather.

WARNING: *If you live in an extremely cold region, such as Alaska, the Northern Plains, or northern Maine, don't use the technique explained on this page; it could cause frost heaving that might damage your foundation. Check with local contractors or your building code department for techniques used in your area.*

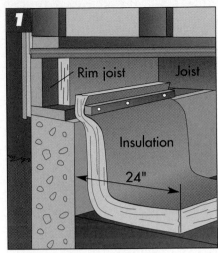

1. Insulate between joists.
For walls perpendicular to joists, place insulation against the rim joist. Cut pieces oversize so they fit snugly. Next unroll enough insulation to overlap the sill plate and cascade down, covering the earth at the wall's base. Secure the insulation by nailing or screwing on a 1×2.

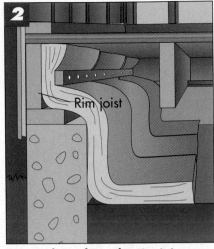

2. Insulate along the rim joists.
Where a wall is parallel to the joists, let the material drape over the rim joist, down the wall, and over 2 feet of the ground. Secure the insulation with a 1×2.

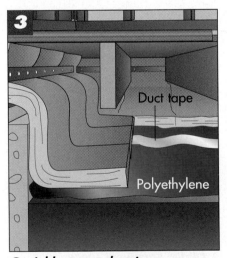

3. Add a vapor barrier.
After insulating the walls, roll up the batts and lay a polyethylene vapor barrier on the floor. Lap the joints by 6 inches. Attach the vapor barrier to the foundation with duct tape. Also tape the joints between the strips. Make sure you don't puncture the plastic.

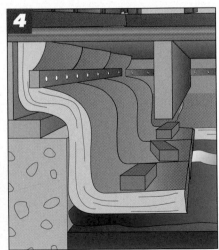

4. Weight the insulation.
Weight the polyethylene and insulation with rocks or bricks. Don't use wood—it could rot or attract termites.

INSULATING A FLOOR

Floors built over crawlspaces, enclosed porches, or other unheated areas need insulation too. If the joists are covered underneath, your best bet is to have a contractor blow in loose-fill insulation (see pages 518–519). If you have open joists, install batts, blankets, or rigid planks, using one of the methods shown here.

Rigid insulation planks can be easily and quickly attached to the underside of joists if no obstacles, such as pipes or ducting, get in the way. However they don't provide as great an R-value. It's usually worthwhile to cut blankets or batts to fit around obstacles.

Unless you're simply adding another layer to existing insulation, get faced material and install it with the vapor barrier side facing the heated area. Foil facing works well here because it reflects heat back into living areas. Pay special attention to achieving good coverage at joists and headers around the floor's edges.

Cold slab floors present a special problem because you can't get material under them where it would do the most good. It may help to hire a contractor to wrap the outside of your foundation. Keep in mind you'll probably end up with a higher R-value by insulating the floor itself. To do this, glue down wood sleepers (see page 391), place rigid insulation planks between the sleepers, then lay new subflooring and finish flooring.

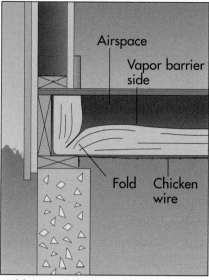

Fold to seal the joist.
Start each insulation strip by folding it so that the insulation covers the rim joist. You can staple chicken wire to the joists to support the batts.

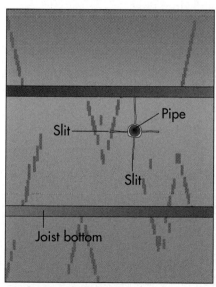

Seal around obstacles.
If you encounter a pipe or other obstacle, cut one or two slits in the insulation at the opening. Slip the insulation in place, then cut the insulation to fit snugly around the obstacle. Seal the slits with duct tape.

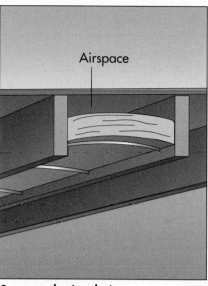

Support the insulation.
Or you can support the insulation with friction-fit rods that slip between the joists. Leave some airspace between the insulation and the floor.

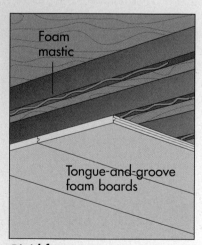

Rigid foam.
To install rigid planks, apply adhesive to the bottoms of the joists and press the lightweight foam strips in place.

INSULATING DUCTWORK AND PIPES

As much as 20 percent of your heating and cooling energy can escape via ducts. If you insulate the ducts that run through your attic, garage, and other unheated areas, you can prevent most of this loss.

Purchase 2-inch-thick duct blankets or standard insulation, which cuts heat loss by about one-third more than 1-inch material. You'll also need several rolls of duct tape to seal all duct joints before you insulate. If your ducts don't have dampers to balance airflow, consider adding some prior to insulating (see page 547).

YOU'LL NEED...

TIME: 2 to 4 hours, depending on access to the ducts or pipes.
SKILLS: Basic skills.
TOOLS: Utility knife or hacksaw.

EXPERTS' INSIGHT

INSULATING A PARTIALLY FINISHED ROOM

In a partially finished space, you may be depending on radiated heat from the ducts to keep things warm. In this situation, you would be better off to insulate the walls and forget about the ducts.

If the area receives only occasional use, consider installing a couple of basement registers (see page 546) and insulating the ducts and floor above.

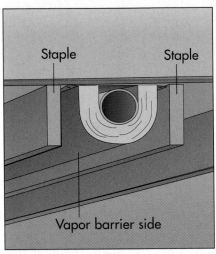

Insulate around ducts.
For ducts that run between joists, cut blankets to fit and staple them to the floor, as shown. Install the insulation with the vapor barrier facing out. Avoid compressing the insulation—the fluffier it is, the better it works. Seal any joints with duct tape.

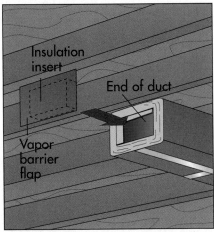

Seal the end.
Take special care to seal the end of a duct. Extend the wrapped insulation several inches beyond the end of the duct. Cut an insert with a flap, as shown above, so the insulation fits snugly into the opening and the flaps extend several inches in all directions. Fold and tape the flap as you would a package.

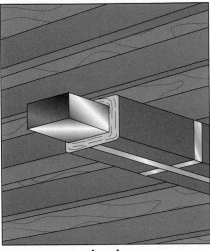

Wrap rectangular ducts.
For other ducts, wrap insulation around all sides, and seal the joints with tape. Install with the vapor barrier facing out and avoid compressing the insulation. Take the time to cut carefully around obstacles so the insulation seals tightly without compressing.

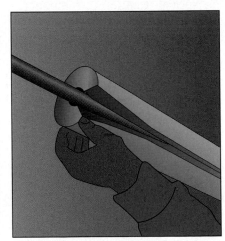

Insulate hot-water pipes.
Foam pipe insulation comes in various lengths. A lengthwise slit lets you fit the sleeve on the pipe. Cut pieces to length using a utility knife. Wrapping hot-water pipes saves energy costs. You can wrap cold-water pipes, too, to reduce condensation and prevent water damage to structures. At elbows, cut the pieces at 45 degrees for a mitered joint.

INSULATING BASEMENT WALLS

Basement walls are made of solid masonry, which readily transfers heat and cold from the outside. This makes adding insulation a standard part of a typical basement renovation. If your winters are mild, you can get by with an R-value of 7; in colder areas, aim for at least R-11.

To achieve these R-values with batts or blankets, frame out 2×3 or 2×4 stud walls over the masonry walls (see pages 329–335). Then staple the insulation between the studs of your new built-out walls. Cover the wall surface with drywall or paneling.

Rigid foam insulation planks allow you keep a new wall's thickness to a minimum by furring out the walls with 1× lumber (see pages 336–337).

Solve moisture problems before you begin. Seepage or leaks render insulating materials useless—even if your basement leaks or floods only once every 10 years. Don't worry about mild condensation; insulation and a vapor barrier will eliminate this.

Wall spaces above ground level are more in need of insulation, so pay particular attention there. You may choose to replace a window with glass block.

As with crawlspace walls, these insulating techniques could cause frost-heave problems in extremely cold regions. Check your local building codes for approved insulation procedures.

You'll Need...

Time: 8 hours or more to insulate an entire basement.
Skills: Basic skills.
Tools: Hammer, saw, utility knife, caulking gun, stapler.

1. Staple insulation to studs.
If you choose fiberglass batt or blanket insulation, frame up new stud walls. Staple insulation between the studs. Don't skimp on the staples: Drive one every 10 or 12 inches.

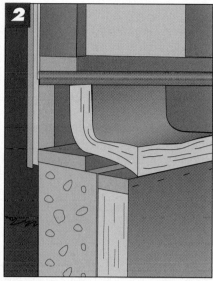

2. Insulate the sill.
Above the sill, fit in small pieces of insulation. Allow the pieces to drape over the top of the stud wall for complete coverage. Secure the insulation with tape, staples, or wood strips (see page 514).

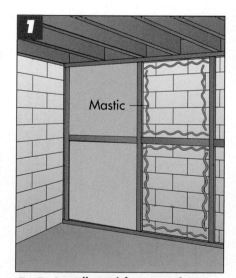

Mastic

1. To install rigid foam, make a grid and glue pieces to the wall.
For rigid foam insulation, attach a grid of 1×2s or 1×3s to the basement wall. Use construction adhesive to cement the planks to the walls between the furring strips. Measure as you go to ensure tight fits. Cover the framing and insulation with drywall.

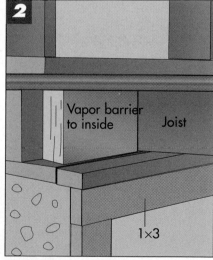

Vapor barrier to inside   Joist

1×3

2. Insulate the sill.
Cut pieces of batts or blankets to fit snugly in the spaces over the top of the sill. Have the vapor barrier face inside.

INSULATING EXISTING EXTERIOR WALLS

An older wood-frame home may lack insulation in some or all of its exterior walls. The solution is to have a pro blow in insulation. This is a tedious and expensive process, but usually pays off in the long run. (However, adding insulation to a home with double-brick construction is seldom cost-effective.) Unless you choose liquid foam, you'll need a vapor barrier to protect the new insulation from condensation (see box, below right).

YOU'LL NEED...

TIME: Several days for an entire house.
SKILLS: Advanced insulation skills (often a job for a professional contractor).
TOOLS: Drill, tape measure, wall-refinishing tools, and specialized tools for blowing insulation into wall cavities.

1. Check the wall cavity.
Determine whether the wall cavities run unimpeded from the attic to the basement by dropping down a weighted string. If they do, you can pour in loose-fill insulation from the attic.

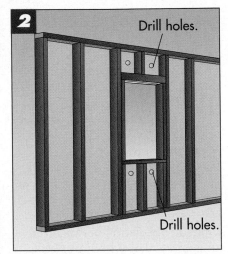

2. Identify the framing members.
Most wall cavities have headers, sills, and blocking, so you can remove exterior siding and bore a series of holes to gain access. To insulate an entire wall, all the framing members must be identified, and a hole must be drilled into every cavity.

EXPERTS' INSIGHT

IMPROVING EXISTING INSULATION

Existing insulation in an older home may have compressed to the point where it does little good. If the walls still feel cold after weather-stripping and sealing your home (pages 502–511), it may make economic sense to upgrade their R-value. Get several written bids that specify the R-values as well as the amounts of material needed. A properly insulated 2×4 wall should have a value of at least R-10.

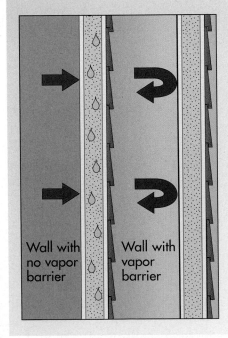

Provide a vapor barrier.
Without a vapor barrier, all insulation, except foam, will quickly turn into a soggy mess.

Unfortunately, it isn't feasible to get a continuous waterproof membrane into a finished wall. However, you can seal the wall's interior surface for the same effect. Caulk any cracks you find at the floor and ceiling and around doors or windows (see pages 504–505). Then apply at least two coats of waterproof oil- or alkyd-base paint, or use a paint especially formulated for this purpose.

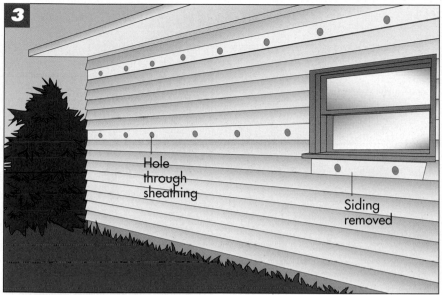

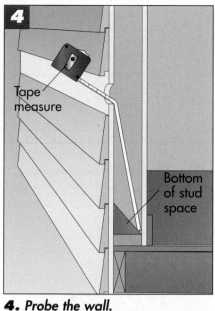

3. Remove siding and drill holes.
If the siding is horizontal, remove strips at the top, under windows, and possibly at the 4-foot level, just under fire blocking. After peeling back the building paper, use a hole saw to bore holes into each cavity.

If the house has shingle siding, individual shingles can be easily removed and replaced. With other types of siding, it is common to drill holes with a hole saw and fill them later with the circular plug that was cut out by the hole saw.

4. Probe the wall.
Probe with a steel tape or a plumb bob to see if there are obstructions that might create uninsulated pockets. For a complete job, this probing should be done in every wall cavity.

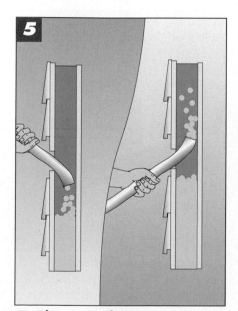

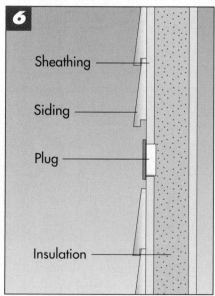

5. Blow in insulation.
First blow material into the cavity to the level of the inlet hole, then flip the nozzle up to fill the space above.

6. Plug the holes.
After filling each cavity, insert a snap-in plug to seal the hole. Then apply building wrap or paper over the sheathing.

7. Replace the siding.
Finally replace siding materials. Use the same installation techniques described for siding repairs on pages 482–489.

INSULATING OUTSIDE FOUNDATION WALLS

Surprisingly the average basement accounts for 20 percent of a home's heat loss.

The best location for foundation insulation is along the outside of a masonry wall, where it can protect the masonry from damaging frost. The mass of the masonry acts to moderate the temperature swings of the outdoor air. The insulation keeps the wall warmer in summer, reducing condensation and basement humidity.

YOU'LL NEED...

TIME: 2 days for an entire house.
SKILLS: Basic excavating and carpentry skills.
TOOLS: Shovel, wire brush, hammer, pry bar, utility knife, square, wide putty knife, paintbrush, roller.

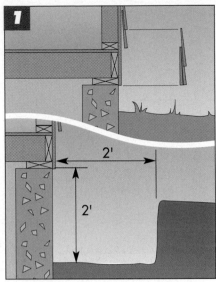

1. Remove siding and excavate.
Remove several bottom courses of siding (see pages 482 and 496). Save the siding for reinstallation. Excavate a trench around the foundation 2 feet below the sill and 2 feet wide. Place the excavated soil onto sheets of polyethylene.

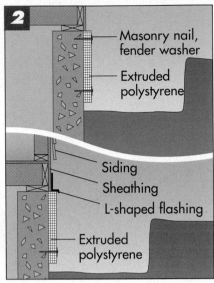

2. Attach polystyrene insulation.
Fasten 1-inch-thick sheets of foam insulation to the foundation, using fender washers and masonry nails. Install L-shaped aluminum window flashing against the building sheathing and over the top edge of the foam.

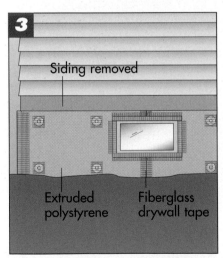

3. Tape the joints.
Scratch the surface of the foam with a wire brush to give the protective coating a "tooth" to adhere to. Apply self-adhesive fiberglass drywall tape to all the joints and corners.

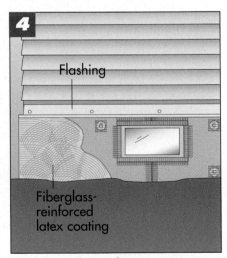

4. Stucco the surface.
Brush on fiberglass-reinforced latex coating or surface bonding cement. Cover an area from the flashing to several inches below the final ground level.

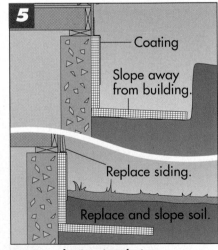

5. Lay sloping insulation.
Lay horizontal 2×8-foot sheets of foam so they slope away from the foundation at the rate of 1 inch per foot minimum. Replace the soil and grade the area so it slopes away from the building. Replace the bottom courses of siding. Plant grass seed or lay sod.

HEATING AND COOLING

GETTING TO KNOW YOUR HVAC SYSTEM

How's the climate in your home? Whether you feel too hot, too cold, or just right depends on the temperature and humidity of the air around you. Your home's air circulation system—whether it be forced-air, piped, or radiant—adds or removes heat. It may also control the humidity level by adding or removing moisture.

This chapter shows how heating and cooling systems work, how you can maintain and improve their efficiency, and what your choices are in new equipment. It also offers tips about what you can do to lower your expenses for gas, oil, or electricity.

As a homeowner, you should have a basic understanding of your system. Leafing through this chapter will help; however, because system technology varies, there is no substitute for consulting a pro.

These two pages identify and explain the three most common HVAC (heating, venting, and air-conditioning) systems. You may also have a heat pump (pages 532–533) or central air-conditioning (pages 542–543). Your heating plant may be a furnace (which heats air) or a boiler (which produces hot water or steam). Either is usually fired by gas or oil, but wood is also still used; see pages 528–539. Or you may have smaller, room units; see pages 552–555.

Though heating and cooling components vary enormously, all take advantage of heat's inherent tendency to move from a warmer object or space to a cooler one. This means you can couple a heat source, such as a burner, electric resistance element, or heat pump, with a heating plant, usually a furnace or boiler, to send heated air, water, or steam via a distribution network to a home's various rooms. After the medium gives off its heat, it then recirculates to the heating plant. A control unit, almost always a thermostat, maintains a preset temperature by switching the heating plant on and off (see pages 540–541).

FORCED-AIR SYSTEM

Ducted systems circulate air from a furnace to registers in each room via a network of ducts. Modern forced-air versions have a blower that pushes treated air through supply ducts and pulls it back through return ducts.

An older home may have a less-efficient gravity system, which works the same way but without a blower. Warm air rises from the furnace to the rooms, and cool air falls through the returns. Supply and return registers may be on the floors or in the walls.

Blower-driven forced-air heating systems have two advantages over steam and radiant systems: They can be easily adapted to centrally cool a home, and the system can be easily adapted to humidify the home (see pages 548–549).

Troubleshooting and maintenance tips for air furnace systems can be found on pages 524–527. To add to or modify a forced-air system, see pages 546–549.

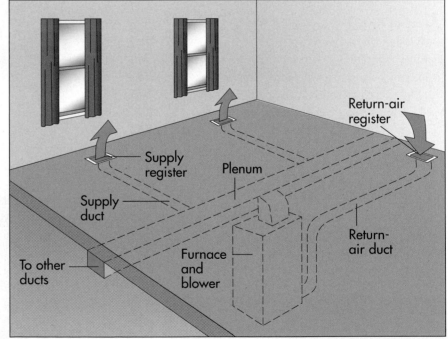

How the air moves.
In a typical forced-air system, a furnace, usually fired by gas or oil, heats the air inside. A blower, powered by an electric motor, sends air out of the furnace and into the main duct, called the plenum. Smaller supply ducts tap into the plenum and carry warm air to individual rooms via supply registers, which usually can be controlled by simple levers. A separate system of return ducts carries cool air back to the furnace.

Hot-Water or Steam Heat

In a piped system, water or steam distributes the heat. The heating plant, called a boiler, sends hot water or steam through supply lines to radiators in each room of the house.

In a hot-water system, warm water circulates up to the radiators, often (but not always) helped by a circulating pump. Cooler water flows back to the boiler via return lines. Heat rises and falls slowly, so the radiators maintain fairly even temperatures.

Most steam systems have only one pipe running to each radiator. Because steam rises, no circulation pump is needed. Steam radiators are usually either very hot or completely cold.

If your home has hot-water or steam heat, check pages 534–539 for more detailed information.

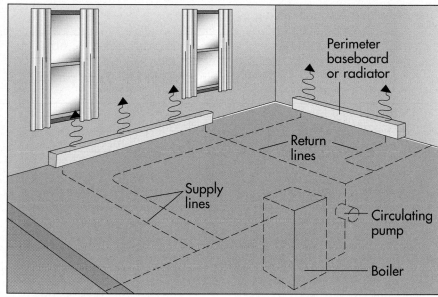

How the water circulates.
A hot-water system is "closed," meaning that the same water keeps circulating through the pipes, often without being changed for years. A steam boiler must have water added regularly, because steam dissipates into the rooms during heating.

Radiant Heat

Radiant heating warms the floor or ceiling in a room, silently providing even heat. Some systems use electrical cables; others circulate hot water through small-diameter tubing.

In most areas, electric radiant heat is expensive, and usually used only for added-on powder rooms and other small spaces.

Older hot-water radiant heat often consists of copper pipes run through concrete floors. This type tends to corrode and often needs to be completely replaced after a number of decades. Newer tubing is made of extremely durable polystyrene and can be attached under a wood floor or run under ceramic tiles.

If you have radiant heat, do not bore holes or break into the floor unless you are certain where the lines run.

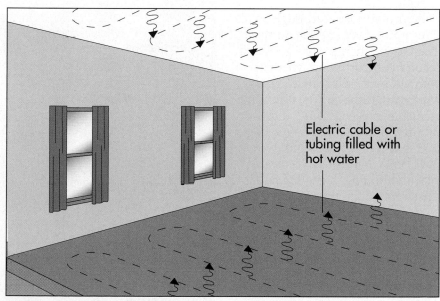

Maintaining radiant heat.
In a radiant system, pipes or tubes usually run through or under the floor, so the heating takes up no wall or floor space in a room. The heat is wonderfully even and gentle; many people love the feel of a warm floor in the winter.

Radiant heat is easiest to install in the ceiling, but because this is less efficient, it should be done only in areas with mild winters.

Because the tubing or cables are buried, fixable problems are either at the electrical circuit panel or at the connections to the boiler.

MAINTAINING A FORCED-AIR SYSTEM

A forced-air heating/cooling system completely recirculates the air in your home as many as three times every hour—a big job. Fortunately most components of a forced-air system are easy to take care of—once you know what they are and where they're located.

Begin by noting which registers supply treated hot air and which ones return cold air to the furnace (see anatomy drawing on page 522). Most rooms have at least one hot-air supply register. Supply registers usually have adjustable dampers that let you modulate the airflow or shut it off entirely.

Cold-air return registers typically are larger and less numerous. Many homes have only one per floor, located in a hallway or other central spot. Returns never have dampers, because shutting one off would partially suffocate the system.

Make sure registers aren't blocked by furniture, draperies, or carpeting. Supply registers must have unobstructed space above. You may choose to equip some registers with plastic diverters that channel air horizontally for more even heating distribution. Return registers must be open to air currents from all directions.

To trace the entire duct network, take a trip to your crawlspace or basement. The drawing below shows how ducts eventually connect to the furnace and how air moves within it.

While the blower is operating, feel the joints of all accessible ducts. Any leaks will decrease your system's efficiency. Seal joints using professional-quality duct tape, which remains durable even when exposed to heat. If a joint is widely parted, drill pilot holes and drive sheetmetal screws before taping.

In an older home, the ducts may be clogged with debris, or may contain mold or mildew that disperses into the air when the blower operates. Have a heating pro check for these possibilities.

KEEPING AIR MOVING

Sizes and shapes may differ, but all forced-air furnaces work essentially like the one illustrated at right.

Return air passes through an air filter into a blower compartment. The blower then pushes air into a second compartment, where it's warmed by a heat source. This source might be electrical heating elements (see page 527), a gas- or oil-fired heat exchanger (see pages 528, 530), or a heat pump (see page 532). If you have central air-conditioning, a cooling coil in the supply duct above the heat source extracts heat from the moving air during hot months (see pages 542–543).

The heated or cooled air then moves into a plenum from which the supply ducts radiate to carry air to the various rooms.

Air enters this particular furnace at the bottom and exits at the top. Known as an upflow type, it's best suited to basement installations. Other types send the heated air downward or to the side.

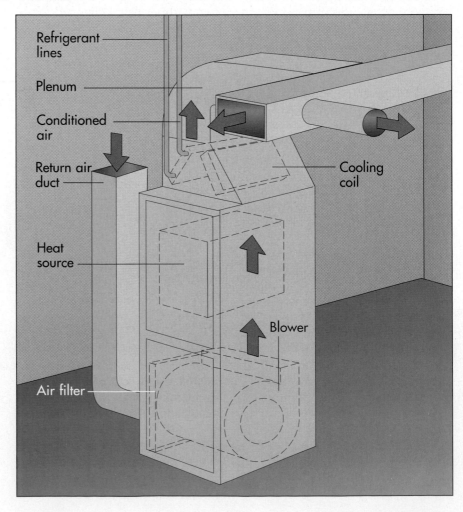

Refrigerant lines

Plenum

Conditioned air

Return air duct

Heat source

Air filter

Cooling coil

Blower

REPLACING A FILTER

Blowing air from a furnace stirs up dust and perhaps pollen. A high-quality filter catches nearly all of these particles.

A neglected filter chokes airflow and makes the unit work harder, thus wasting energy. A severely clogged filter can cause a furnace to overheat and shut down.

Some filters can be cleaned, while others must be replaced. Inexpensive filters trap only larger particles. To keep your air even cleaner, purchase the highest-quality filter available for your furnace. Some types trap some mold and bacteria as well.

To effectively remove pollen, mold, and bacteria as well as nearly all dust, have a contractor install an electrostatic filter, which is typically attached near the plenum.

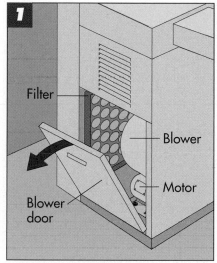

Filter
Blower
Motor
Blower door

1. Open the door.
Most blower doors lift or swing open. On counterflow models, the door will be at the top of the furnace. Purchase an exact replacement filter made for your furnace make and model.

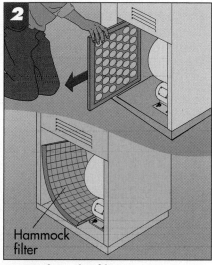

Hammock filter

2. Replace the filter.
Many filters slide out. Look for dirt on or around the blower, too. Vacuum, if necessary. A hammock-type filter wraps around the base of the blower; it is also easy to replace.

OILING AND ADJUSTING BLOWERS

Make blower maintenance part of your seasonal tune-up schedule—and check out the unit whenever air seems to be moving faster or slower than usual.

Some blowers have direct-drive motors; others operate with an adjustable V-belt-and-pulley setup (shown at right). You needn't adjust the direct-drive type, but the V-belt type may need oil; check the manufacturer's instructions.

With either model, look for lubrication ports on the motor and on the blower pulley on belt-drive units, as shown at right. Lubricate at the beginning of each heating and cooling season.

An adjustable motor pulley lets you change the speed of a belt-drive model by loosening a setscrew and adjusting the distance between pulley faces.

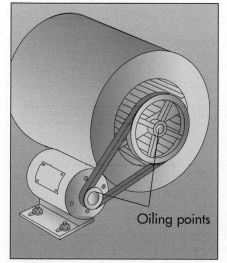

Oiling points

Oil the ports.
If a motor has oil ports, they'll be at each end of the shaft. Also, check for lubrication points on the blower fan. With an oil can, squirt a few drops of SAE-10 nondetergent oil into these ports.

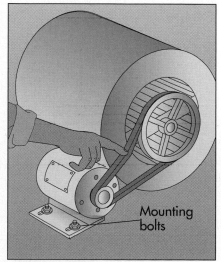

Mounting bolts

Adjust the belt.
Adjust the belt so it's loose without slipping; it should depress about 1 inch. Keep mounting bolts tight. Check the belt for fraying, cracks, and signs of wear. Keep a spare belt on hand.

BALANCING AN AIR SYSTEM

If some rooms in your home are consistently too hot or cold, a simple balancing project may solve the problem. A forced-air system can be balanced by reducing the airflow to a room that is too warm. Warm air can then reach colder areas, typically those farthest from the furnace.

Partially closing registers in a hot room will cool the room off, but won't redirect the air. Instead, adjust dampers in the ductwork. Dampers are controlled by a handle or a locknut arrangement. You may find one at the point where each duct takes off from the furnace plenum. If your system lacks dampers, consider installing them (see page 547).

Wait for a cold day to begin the procedure. If only one or two rooms have airflow problems, you might be tempted to adjust only one or two dampers. However you'll get better results by tuning the entire system.

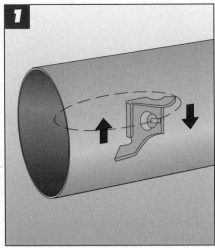

1. Open the dampers.
To open a damper, loosen the locknut and turn the handle parallel to the duct. To identify which ducts serve each room, close them one at a time to determine which room isn't getting air. Label the dampers.

Open the registers in all the rooms, and open all the dampers in the ducts.

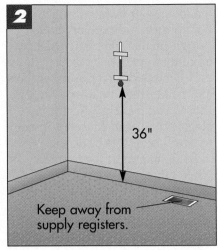

Keep away from supply registers.

2. Tape thermometers in rooms.
Synchronize several thermometers by laying them together for 30 minutes and then noting any differences. Tape a thermometer on a wall in each room, 3 feet above the floor but not above a supply register.

Summer and winter settings.
If you have central cooling, you may have to rebalance the ducts every summer and winter. Mark seasonal settings on the ducts.

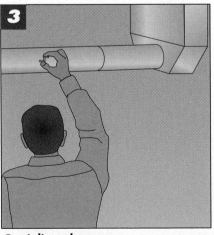

3. Adjust dampers.
Adjust dampers to the rooms, starting with the one where your home's thermostat is located.

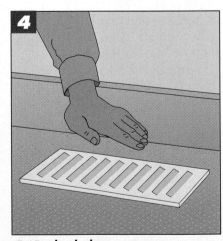

4. Recheck the temperatures.
Note any increase in air delivery to other rooms. Recheck the temperatures and continue adjusting dampers until you achieve the balance you desire.

MAINTAINING AN ELECTRIC RESISTANCE FURNACE

To envision an electric-resistance furnace, think of a giant toaster with a fan blowing through it. As air pushed by the blower moves through the heating elements, it picks up warmth, then continues into the plenum and ducts to registers in each room.

Because no combustion occurs in an electric furnace, it doesn't require the flue or heat exchanger needed for gas and oil furnaces. Therefore maintenance is almost nil. Operating costs, however, usually run substantially higher for electric units.

Check the anatomy drawing at right. An air-circulation switch, often on the house thermostat but sometimes on the furnace, lets you run the blower continuously. Underneath, accessible through a removable cover, there may be fuses or breakers for each of the heating elements. A transformer steps up amperage to the high levels needed for heating. Relays turn the elements on or off according to signals from the thermostat.

The chart below lists the few things that can go wrong with electric-resistance furnaces and what you can do about them. Always shut off the furnace's main circuit breaker before removing the control or access panels. You'll find the breaker located next to the furnace or in your home's main service panel. Don't attempt to work on the heat elements— that's a job for a professional.

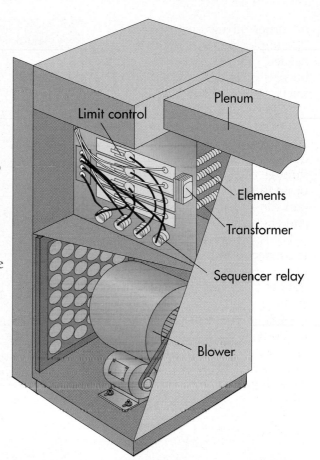

Limit control

Plenum

Elements

Transformer

Sequencer relay

Blower

TROUBLESHOOTING AN ELECTRIC FURNACE

Problem	Causes	Solutions
No heat	Furnace switch or main breaker open; thermostat set too low	Check the switch, the fuse or breakers, and the thermostat. If the blower runs but there's no heat, check the fuse or breaker block.
Cycles on and off too often	Clogged filter or failing blower, causing unit to overheat	Replace the filter. Oil and adjust the blower (see page 525).
Not enough heat	Improper thermostat setting; defective heating element; clogged filter or duct	Check the thermostat, then the fuse or breaker; replace a blown fuse or flip on the breaker. If the fuse blows or the breaker trips when you turn on the power, call a professional. Replace the filter.

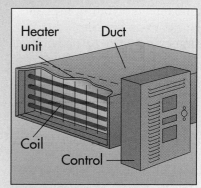

Heater unit

Duct

Coil

Control

Heat pump.
If your home has a heat pump, it may have resistance-type duct heaters, like the one shown here. These mini-furnaces automatically pitch in when the temperature drops below what a heat pump can handle by itself. See pages 532–533 for more about heat pumps.

UNDERSTANDING A GAS FURNACE

Burners in a gas furnace are simple, but the controls needed to automatically turn the burners on and off and to provide safety are more complex.

A set of tubes called a manifold feeds the burners a mixture of gas and air, which is ignited by the pilot. The blower pushes air through the heat exchanger and up to the plenum. Flue gases exit past the exchanger up the flue and chimney.

For safety, a combination valve is connected to the pilot. If the pilot goes out, the valve shuts off the gas. A second safety—the limit switch in the plenum—turns off the gas if the plenum gets too hot; it also stops the blower when the temperature in the plenum drops to a certain level after the burners have shut down.

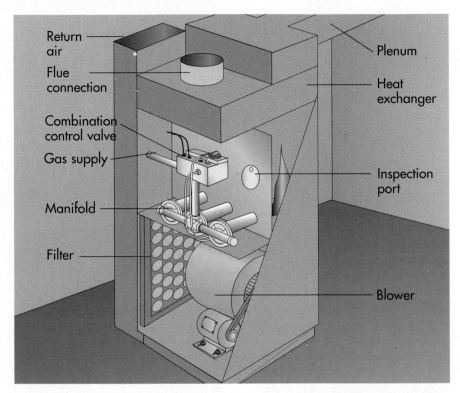

Return air
Flue connection
Combination control valve
Gas supply
Manifold
Filter
Plenum
Heat exchanger
Inspection port
Blower

CHECKING THE FLUE AND CHIMNEY

Flues can develop leaks, releasing highly lethal carbon monoxide into your home's air. The same can happen if the chimney becomes partially clogged with debris or animal nests.

These dangers warrant an annual checkup. Inspect all the points illustrated at far right, paying special attention to the pipe between the furnace flue and the chimney. For more about chimneys and flues, see page 468.

For no charge, the gas company will probably inspect your flue and test for carbon monoxide. If they find a problem, they may shut off your furnace. Ask for an exact description of the problem, as well as the steps you should take to make your flue safe. If the problem cannot be solved by a simple step like sealing joints in the flue, call in a professional.

Test the draft.
Hold a candle to the opening in the top access panel with the furnace running. A flue leak will blow out the flame.

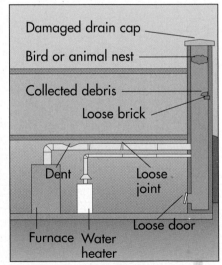

Damaged drain cap
Bird or animal nest
Collected debris
Loose brick
Dent
Loose joint
Loose door
Furnace Water heater

Possible sources of leaks.
Any of these problems may cause a carbon monoxide leak. If you suspect a damaged flue pipe, replace the pipe. An improperly installed flue pipe can also be the culprit. The flue must be the correct size; the slope and number of bends of the pipe are also factors.

LIGHTING A PILOT, REPLACING A THERMOCOUPLE

Some gas furnaces, boilers, and water heaters ignite with an electrical spark system. Most, however, depend on a gas pilot light for firing. When the unit fails to operate, it's usually because the pilot has gone out; you may need to replace the thermocouple or make adjustments.

To relight a pilot, follow the steps on the instruction plate attached to the furnace. With most, you'll find a gas cock with three settings—off, pilot, and on. Turn the cock to "off," wait a few minutes for residual gas to clear, then switch to the "pilot" setting. Hold a long lighted match or stick to the pilot, depress a reset button, and hold it down for a minute.

If the pilot stays lit, turn the cock to "on" and the burners will fire. If the pilot goes out again after you release the reset, repeat the entire procedure, holding the reset down a little longer.

If you can't get the pilot lighted after two or three tries, most likely you'll need to replace the thermocouple, a copper tube with a bulbous end that gets heated by the pilot flame.

To replace a thermocouple, shut off the gas inlet valve and remove the access cover so you can see the burners. Disconnect the thermocouple from the control by unscrewing a hold-down nut. At the other end, it may be held in place with a nut or it may simply pull out. Purchase two replacements of the same length (so you can have one on hand for the next replacement). When you install the replacement, take care not to kink the tube and make sure the bulbous end is touched by the pilot flame.

A weak or wavering pilot flame also may shut everything down. The flame should be blue, with the tip barely flecked by yellow. If the pilot flame doesn't fit this description, make sure that it isn't being buffeted by a draft. Then try cleaning out the opening of the pilot tube with a needle or nail.

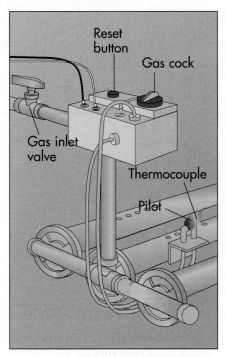

YOU'LL NEED...
TIME: 10 to 15 minutes.
SKILLS: Basic gas-plumbing skills.
TOOLS: Flashlight, adjustable wrench, long matches.

TROUBLESHOOTING A GAS FURNACE

Problem	Causes	Solutions
No heat	Thermostat too low; switch, fuse, or circuit breaker open; gas shut off; pilot out	Check thermostat, switch, and fuse or breaker. Relight pilot.
Cycles too often	Usually a clogged filter or a blower problem	Replace filter. Oil and adjust blower (see page 525).
Not enough heat	A clogged filter; burners may need cleaning	Replace filter. Have burners cleaned by a professional.
Blower runs constantly	Fan switch set for continuous circulation; limit control out of adjustment	Reset fan switch on furnace or adjust limit control (page 527).
Furnace squeaks or rumbles	Squealing: blower belt slipping or bearings need lubrication Rumbling with burners off: misadjusted pilot Rumbling with burners on: dirty burners	Oil blower and adjust belt (page 525). Adjust pilot (see above). Have burners cleaned by a professional.

UNDERSTANDING AN OIL FURNACE

Compared to gas and electric furnaces, an oil-fired forced-air heating plant has more components. It has the same filter-and-blower unit common to the other furnace types, but the heat producer in an oil furnace—its burner—includes a second motor/blower setup. This one combines oil with air, ignites the mixture with an electric spark, then blasts a torchlike flame into a fireproof compartment just below the heat exchanger.

Examine the drawing at right. The combustion air blower pulls in air through an adjustable shutter, mixes it with oil in an air tube, sets it afire with a pair of electrodes, and then forces it through a nozzle into the combustion chamber. A transformer steps up voltage to the electrodes. In some models, a primary safety control keeps an electric eye on the flame; if it fails to light, the safety shuts down the burner. Other types do the same job with a heat sensor in the flue pipe.

The motor on the combustion air blower also drives an oil pump. This pulls oil through lines from the fuel-oil tank. An automotive-type filter strains the fuel.

Despite this complexity, modern oil burners are reliable. They do, however, require annual tune-ups, which, if neglected, will add to your fuel-oil bills. The box at right lists the jobs that generally need to be completed before each heating season.

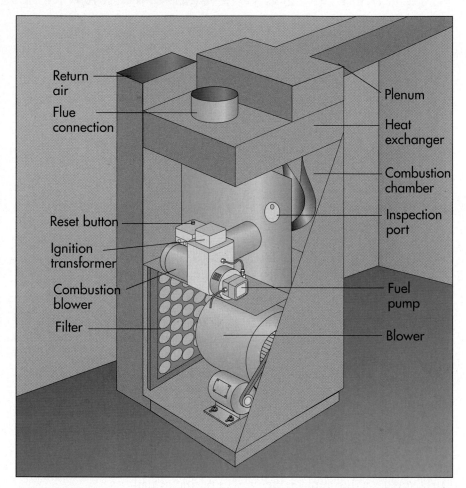

Return air
Flue connection
Reset button
Ignition transformer
Combustion blower
Filter
Plenum
Heat exchanger
Combustion chamber
Inspection port
Fuel pump
Blower

EXPERTS' INSIGHT

REGULAR MAINTENANCE FOR AN OIL BURNER

■ Clean or change the oil filter in the fuel line at least once a year. Some oil filters have a replaceable cartridge; basket types must be washed with kerosene. With either, make sure to install a new gasket when you reassemble the filter.

■ If your unit has a pump strainer, you should clean it annually. Soak it in kerosene and replace the gasket.

■ Clean the fan blades monthly with a long-handled brush.

■ Lubricate the burner motor every month or two, unless it's permanently lubricated (in which case you won't find lubrication ports, or the instruction plate will so indicate). Most require light oil. Look for instructions on the housing.

■ Check all flue connections annually (see page 528).

■ Get a professional tune-up at the start of the heating season. Insist that the service technician take instrument readings for combustion efficiency, smoke density, and draft. The technician also should check the firing system, clean the ignition electrodes, and clean or replace the combustion nozzle.

CHECKING SAFETY CONTROLS

If an oil burner shuts down, reset the safety switch and try again. If the burner kicks off again, shut off all power—the burner motor and ignition may be protected by separate fuses or breakers.

If your burner has an electric-eye primary safety, look for an access cover that lets you get to its photocell. Wipe the photocell with a clean rag or tissue to remove soot. Reassemble it, turn on the burner, and see if the furnace fires.

The second type of safety—a stack switch—mounts on the flue. Remove the screw holding the unit to the stack, slide it out, and wipe off the sensor.

Don't continually try to restart a balky oil burner. Unburned oil could accumulate in the combustion chamber and "flash back." If the furnace won't fire after three attempts, call for professional service.

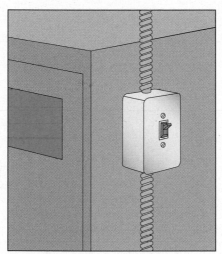

Disconnect switches.
There may be one burner disconnect switch on the side of the furnace and another outside the furnace room. Switch them off before attempting any repairs.

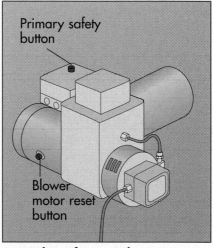

Primary safety button

Blower motor reset button

Reset the safety switch.
If the primary safety or stack switch shuts off, wait 5 minutes, then press the reset lever or button. Combustion air blowers usually are protected by an overload device. Restart by pressing the reset button.

TROUBLESHOOTING BEFORE CALLING FOR SERVICE

Problem	Causes	Solutions
Burner doesn't run	Thermostat setting is too low; main switch, a circuit breaker, or fuse is open; motor may be overheated	Set the thermostat 5°F higher than usual. Check switches, breakers, and fuses. Oil motor. Press reset.
Burner runs but won't fire	Oil or spark is not getting to the unit; safeties are sooty	Make sure oil valves are open and there's oil in the tank—don't trust the gauge: dip a rod into it. Clean safeties.
Burner cycles too often	Clogged blower filter or other blower problems; improperly set limit control	Replace filter. Oil and adjust blower (see page 525). Check and adjust limit control.
Burner smokes or squeals	Combustion air blower motor needs oiling	Shut off the unit, let it cool, and fill the oil cups; check them again after the motor has run for an hour or so.
Chimney smokes	A cold flue causes this when the burner first fires; but if smoking persists, it's a sign of incomplete combustion, which means the unit is wasting fuel.	Call for service and request the instrument tests listed in the box on page 530. Don't attempt to adjust a burner yourself.

UNDERSTANDING A HEAT PUMP

Of all heating components, a heat pump is the most complex. It is best understood as a reversible air-conditioner. Like an air-conditioner, it can lower indoor temperatures by removing heat from the air and expelling it outside; it's also capable of extracting heat from outside air and pumping it indoors.

To do its job, a heat pump—like all refrigeration devices—takes advantage of liquid's tendency to absorb heat as it expands and turns into a gas, giving off heat as it's compressed into a liquid (see anatomy diagrams at right).

A split-system heat pump (shown at right in the heating mode) uses two units, one outdoors and one indoors. In the outdoor unit, a fan moves air through a coil that absorbs heat. A compressor then superheats the vapor and sends it through refrigerant lines to a second coil in the furnace. There a blower pushes return air through the coil, warming the air and forcing it into the ducts. Meanwhile refrigerant travels back to the outdoor unit to begin another full cycle through the pump.

An automatic reversing valve reverses these flows. It has to be automatic because when outside air temperatures approach the freezing mark, heat pumps tend to freeze up. When this happens, a sensor activates the reversing valve and the unit defrosts itself.

In some heat pumps, the compressor, fan, coils, reversing valve, and blower are enclosed in a single outdoor cabinet, as shown at right. Only the system's main supply and return ducts penetrate exterior walls; there is no separate furnace.

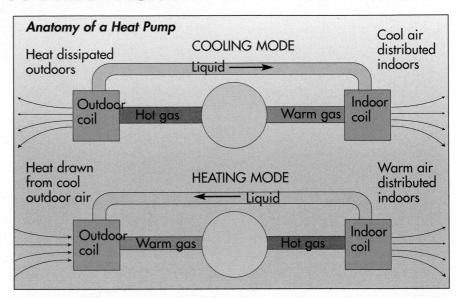

Anatomy of a Heat Pump

COOLING MODE
Heat dissipated outdoors — Liquid → — Cool air distributed indoors
Outdoor coil — Hot gas — Warm gas — Indoor coil

HEATING MODE
Heat drawn from cool outdoor air — ← Liquid — Warm air distributed indoors
Outdoor coil — Warm gas — Hot gas — Indoor coil

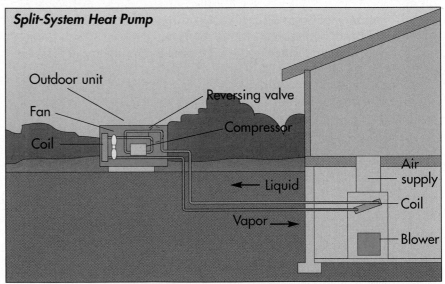

Split-System Heat Pump

Outdoor unit
Reversing valve
Fan
Compressor
Coil
Air supply
← Liquid
Coil
Vapor →
Blower

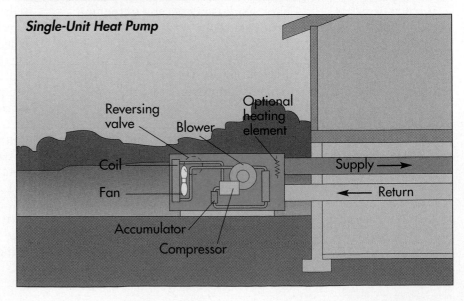

Single-Unit Heat Pump

Reversing valve
Optional heating element
Blower
Coil
Supply →
Fan
← Return
Accumulator
Compressor

OPERATING A HEAT PUMP

Heat pumps work well down to temperatures of about 15°F. If temps go below that, most units require a backup heating source, usually electric-resistance elements installed in the furnace, the ducts, or the pump cabinet. These units also take over for the pump while it's defrosting.

When a heat pump's defrost cycle runs continuously—or not at all—the backup system takes over, a shift you might not notice until your electric bill arrives. That's why it pays to familiarize yourself with what happens during a normal defrost cycle.

When the temperature hovers around freezing, frost forms on the outdoor coil. When this occurs, the reversing valve should activate to melt the ice. You may hear gurgling or even see steam rising from the outdoor unit.

Heavy ice accumulation means the unit isn't defrosting. No ice, or defrost cycles that last longer than 15 minutes, indicate that the pump is stuck in cooling mode.

For either condition, check the outdoor coil. Leaves, snow, or other matter may be cutting off airflow through the coil. Clear the obstruction and the system should return to normal operation.

If it doesn't return to normal and the coil remains coated with ice, the reversing switch may be stuck. Try freeing it by switching your house thermostat to the cooling mode. If the ice remains on the coil after an hour, flip the system selector switch to the "emergency heat" setting and call a heating contractor for service.

If all electrical power has been off for more than an hour at temperatures lower than 50°F, because of either a power outage or a tripped circuit breaker, do not attempt to restart a heat pump for at least 6 hours after the power has been restored. Instead, turn the system selector switch to "emergency heat," wait 6 hours, then return to the normal heat setting; turning the system switch to "off" doesn't shut off the heater. This time-delay gives the heating element in the compressor's oil crankcase time to warm up the system's lubricant and prevent valve damage.

The chart below identifies the most common maladies of heat pumps and what to do about them. As with other heating units, it's good to have a heat pump serviced annually.

TROUBLESHOOTING A HEAT PUMP SYSTEM

Problem	Causes	Solution
Pump does not run	No power to the unit or the thermostat is not calling for heat	Check the thermostat setting, the electrical disconnect switch, and the fuses or breakers in the circuit panel. Most pumps have a "reset" switch in the outdoor cabinet.
Short cycles	An obstruction blocking the outdoor coil; malfunctioning blower unit; clogged filter	Clear the outdoor coil (see above). Check the filter and blower unit (see page 525).
Long or frequent defrost cycles	A blocked outdoor coil could cause defrosting that lasts longer than 15 minutes or that occurs more than twice an hour.	See text above for symptoms and what to do.
Uneven heating	Heat pumps deliver a cooler flow of air than you may be used to. Also, indoor temperatures normally will drop 2° to 3°F when the outside temperature reaches the system's balance point differential. This is the point at which the backup heating kicks in.	Minimize airflow discomfort by carefully balancing the duct system (see page 526). To offset the balance point differential, you may have to raise the thermostat setting in colder weather.

MAINTAINING PIPED SYSTEMS

*I*n many hot-water heating systems, the water temperature reaches 240°F, far above the 212°F needed to produce steam. Yet because the water travels slowly through pipes and loses heat along the way, hot-water radiators are less hot than steam radiators when the heat is on.

The main difference between the two is that hot-water systems are sealed, and contain only carefully controlled amounts of air in the radiation units, piping, and boiler. Steam systems, on the other hand, are open-ended and must "breathe."

This explains why you can often hear hissing radiators and banging pipes with a steam system. The steam has to push the air ahead of it up the riser (vertical) pipes and out the vents on each radiator.

Conversely, hot water has little air to impede its progress and circulates smoothly through the system, generally with nothing more than a few muffled thumps to let you know it's operating. You may also hear a circulating pump come on from time to time.

A hot-water system may have heavy radiators or more-compact convectors (see page 550). However, because steam heat is so hot, it always uses heavy cast-iron radiators.

Steam boilers require regular monitoring because they must be continually filled to the proper level. Hot-water boilers call for less maintenance.

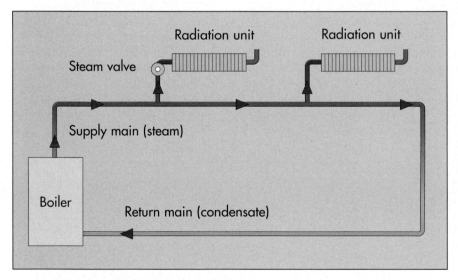

Steam system.
Most steam-heat piping systems employ a one-pipe distribution network like the one at left. A single pipe serves as both supply and return for each radiator. Steam rises from the boiler to the radiators, gives off its heat, and condenses to water. Then the condensate drops back down the same pipe to a return main. This feeds the boiler with water to be boiled for the next steam cycle. Some steam radiators have a second pipe for the returning condensed water.

Hot-water system.
Most hot-water systems use the two-pipe network shown at left. Water flows through radiation units and returns through separate pipes. An expansion tank serves as a cushion, allowing water pressure to increase and circulate more readily. Unlike steam radiators, hot-water units can be partially closed down to regulate the amount of water flowing through them, and therefore the heat.

In a "series loop" system (not shown), water flows from one radiation unit to the next in a chain; there are no mains. Turning off one radiator stops the flow of water to the other units.

TROUBLESHOOTING RADIATORS

Steam and water radiation units—old-fashioned upright radiators or newer upright or baseboard convectors—are simply pipes that dissipate heat. Their maintenance consists of making sure water or steam can flow through the pipes.

If a steam unit doesn't heat well, check its air vent. Liquids and gases can't get into a pipe that's full of air. See that it slopes toward the pipe (toward the return pipe in a two-pipe system); trapped water will keep it from heating up.

Steam radiators are difficult to regulate. Turning a valve to an in-between position won't modulate the heat; it just causes the unit to bang. What you need is an adjustable air vent, available from some plumbing suppliers. Decreasing the size of the vent's aperture slows the rate at which steam enters the radiator.

Hot-water radiators—especially the ones farthest from the boiler—should be bled every fall. You can adjust for heat simply by turning the inlet valve.

EXPERTS' INSIGHT

BALANCING A SYSTEM

Balance a steam or hot-water system much as you would with forced air (see page 526). With some piping, flow valves near the main pipes serve the same function as duct dampers. If your system doesn't have these, you use the inlet valves (for hot water) or adjustable vents (for steam) on each radiator. When you get the balance you want, remove their handles so the settings can't be altered by someone else.

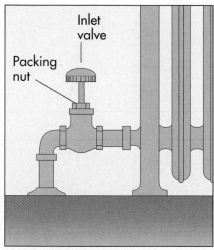

Stopping leaks.
If an inlet valve leaks, try tightening its packing nut. Then try tightening the nuts on either side of the valve. If that doesn't work, drain the system if you have hot water, or turn off the heat if you have steam. Disassemble and repack it as you would a faucet (page 148). Or replace the valve.

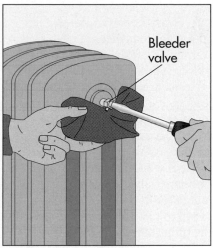

Bleed a hot-water unit.
If the upper portion of a hot-water radiator does not warm up, bleed it. Hold a rag or a small cup under the bleeder valve, and open it using a screwdriver, pliers, or a special key. Air or spluttering water will probably come out. When only water squirts out, close the valve.

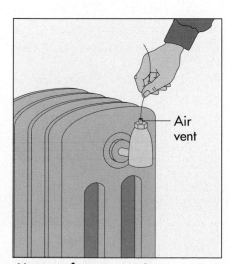

Air vents for steam units.
If a radiator warms only slightly, but evenly, water may be trapped inside. Poke the airhole with a wire to clear it or replace the vent.

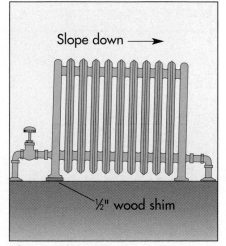

Slope and position.
Make sure a radiator is pitched toward the return pipe. In addition, remove obstructions like draperies or furniture. Radiators depend on air circulating freely around them. Use only radiator covers designed to aid circulation.

MAINTAINING A STEAM BOILER

A steam boiler works like a giant tea kettle. A gas or oil burner heats water to the boiling point, sending steam to radiators.

Some boilers have an automatic feed, usually combined with the low-water cutoff, that supplies fresh "makeup" water when needed. With others, you must manually open and close an ordinary valve. Preventive maintenance includes checking controls monthly and occasionally flushing the boiler (see page 538).

To prolong boiler life and maximize efficiency, schedule an annual checkup in the spring just before you shut down the heating system. Rust thrives when the unit is idle. Ask about chemically treating the boiler water to reduce its oxygen content to prevent rusting.

If a gas pilot light won't stay lit, see page 529 for relighting it and replacing a thermocouple.

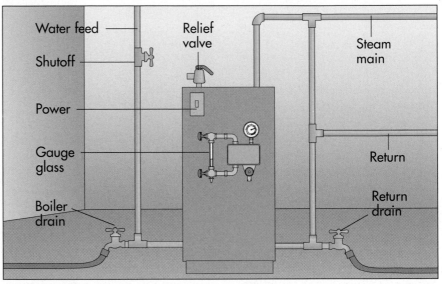

How it works.
Modern-day boilers are complex. The water doesn't simply rest inside a big kettle—that would take hours to heat up. Rather, water circulates around the heat source through a series of passages or tubes. Boilers also require controls to monitor and regulate their operation. These include a pressure gauge and regulator that shuts down the heat source when steam reaches a preset level, a pressure-relief valve that releases steam if the regulator fails, and a low-water cutoff that shuts down the system if the water level gets too low.

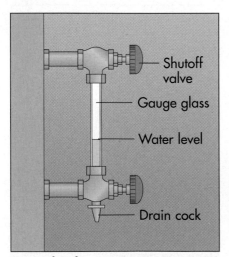

Water level.
Check the glass water-level gauge every 10 to 14 days during the heating season. If you have an automatic feed, inspect it monthly. Check when the boiler cycle is not firing. If the level is low, open the supply valve (not shown) until you reach the correct level.

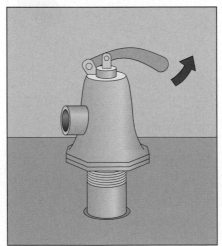

Relief valve.
This is a safety device that protects against overheating. Test it once a year. With the boiler running, lift the lever for less than a second. It should release steam, then reseat tightly when you let go. If not, have it replaced.

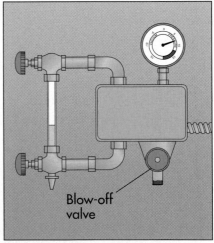

Blow-off valve.
Open the blow-off valve (also called the low-water cutoff) once a month during heating season—more often if your water has lots of sediment. Turn down the thermostat, open the valve, and allow water to run until it's clear of sediment and debris. Be careful because the water will be hot.

TROUBLESHOOTING A STEAM BOILER

If a boiler goes cold, check to be sure its main switch hasn't been inadvertently turned off, then look for a blown fuse or tripped circuit breaker at the electrical circuit panel. Also try raising the thermostat setting and see that the thermostat is working (see pages 540–541).

If the boiler's burner unit is getting power, check the gauge glass to see if the boiler has enough water. When the water level drops below a certain point, the low-water cutoff turns off the burner or the electric heating elements; otherwise heat would "cook" the tank.

You can easily add water to a boiler—but first examine the return lines for leakage. Most steam systems gradually lose water through evaporation, but a big return leak will trip the low-water cutoff after just a couple of heating cycles. (Because supply lines carry only steam under relatively low pressure, they rarely develop leaks.)

If you have a leak in a supply or return, call a plumber, not a heating contractor. One of the techniques on page 146 might allow you to run the system until help arrives.

When you do add water to a boiler, be certain that you don't overfill it. Steam systems depend on an airspace above the water line, called a chest, where steam builds up a head. If you flood the chest, water could back up the return lines or trip the relief valve—both messy situations.

If your boiler has an automatic water-feeding device, you won't notice any problems with the water level; the automatic feed will make up any shortage with each heating cycle. This means that a leak could go unnoticed for quite some time. Also constantly introducing fresh, cold water to the system will add to fuel and water bills. This is why you should shut off the feed every so often—most systems have valves or bypass piping for that purpose—and keep an eye on the water level for a few days.

Remember to flush the automatic feed at the intervals recommended by the manufacturer. A feed that gets stuck open could flood the boiler.

TROUBLESHOOTING BEFORE CALLING FOR SERVICE

Problem	Causes	Solutions
No heat	No power to the unit; no water; burner problems	Check the thermostat, switches, fuses or breakers, and the water level. Boiler burners differ little from those on furnaces (see pages 528–531).
Poor heat	Rust and scale in a boiler, constricting passages and reducing efficiency; buildup on heating surfaces of soot from combustion	Flush the boiler (see page 538). Cleaning the heating surfaces is a job for a professional.
Chronically low water level	Leaking return lines or, more serious, a leak within the boiler itself	For return-line leaks, see the main text above. Boiler leaks require major repairs or may mean you need to buy a new unit.
Clouded gauge glass	Usually the boiler needs flushing, but sometimes the glass itself needs cleaning	Flush boiler (see page 538). To clean gauge glass, turn off boiler, close valves, loosen nuts above and below glass, lift up the glass, pull it out, and clean it with a bottle brush.
Noisy pipes	Probably water trapped in return lines or in the return main	Check the pitch of all returns—they must slope back toward the boiler. Adjust the slant, if necessary, with new pipe hangers.

MAINTAINING A HOT-WATER BOILER

Hot-water controls typically include a combination gauge, often called an altitude gauge, that lets you keep an eye on both water temperature and pressure. It also lets you know when the boiler needs water or is malfunctioning. With some systems, a pressure-reducing valve takes care of the water problem automatically.

Hot-water systems depend on an expansion tank that must be properly charged with air to prevent the water from boiling. With newer installations you'll find this tank hung from the ceiling near the boiler, as in the drawing at right. In older homes it may be located in the attic.

Newer expansion tanks include a purge valve that simultaneously releases water and lets in air. Older versions have a gauge glass, like the one on a steam boiler.

If your system is a forced-water (hydronic) system, look for one or more motor-driven pumps—called circulators—on return lines near the boiler. Some circulator motors are lubricated permanently and do not need maintenance. Others require a few drops of light oil annually. Read the instruction plate attached to the motor, however, because overboiling also causes problems.

Systems that have more than one circulator may be zoned to independently control the temperatures in different areas of your house. Zoned systems have low-voltage, motor-driven zone valves on the supply lines. Each valve obeys orders from its own thermostat. These require no regular maintenance, but they can fail occasionally (see the chart on page 539).

If the pilot light won't stay lit, see page 529 for relighting it and for replacing a thermocouple.

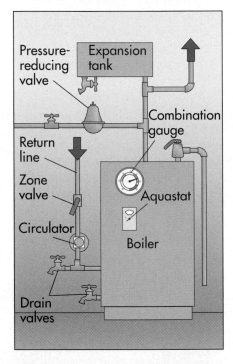

EXPERTS' INSIGHT

FLUSHING THE SYSTEM

Flush a steam boiler if the water in the gauge glass is rusty and flushing through the blow-off valve doesn't clear it. Flush a hot-water boiler if you need to work on a radiator or a pipe.

To do this, shut off the power and automatic feed, if you have one. Open vents or bleeder valves in the highest radiators. Attach hoses to the boiler drain and the return drain, open them, and let the water run out. Shut the drains, refill the boiler, and drain it again. Repeat the process until the water in the gauge is clear. For a hot-water system, you'll need to bleed all the radiators.

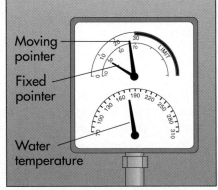

Combination gauge.
A combination gauge on the boiler has three indicators. The moving pointer shows actual pressure; the fixed pointer, the minimum pressure. If the moving pointer drops below the minimum, the system needs water. The lower temperature gauge shows water temperature. Maximum boiler water temperature is set by moving a pointer along the sliding scale of an aquastat (shown above right). Don't tamper with an aquastat setting.

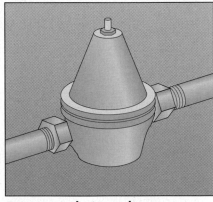

Pressure-reducing valve.
This safety device automatically maintains the correct water pressure. To be sure it's doing its job, check the combination gauge and call for repairs, if necessary. If there's no pressure-reducing valve, you can manually feed the boiler by opening the feed water valve and closing it again when pressure reaches 12 pounds per square inch (psi). High water consumption means there's a leak in the supply or return piping or in the boiler itself.

TROUBLESHOOTING A HOT-WATER BOILER

Despite their complexity, hot-water boilers provide trouble-free service for years. When a problem does develop, it is usually with the expansion tank or a circulator, not the boiler itself.

Get to know your boiler and all the controls and valves. Especially in an older home, these may be complicated. If necessary call in a heating expert to explain it, and label all the valves.

Water spurting from a pressure-relief valve means that there's not enough air in the tank. The tank has filled with water, which expands as it heats up and trips the safety. Check this by touching the tank when the system is heating. Normally the bottom half will feel hotter than the top; if the top seems hot also, it means the tank has filled with water and must be bled.

With most tanks, you'll need to first let the system cool. Then attach a hose to the tank's purge valve and run off two or three buckets of water. The valve lets in air at the same time. An older tank might have an ordinary valve rather than the purge type. With these, first close a second valve in the line between the tank and boiler, and then completely drain the tank.

After bleeding the tank, return all valves to their normal settings and start the boiler. Let it run for about an hour, then check the system's pressure on the combination gauge.

When a circulator fails, its motor may continue to run. This happens because the motor and pump are connected by a spring-loaded coupling designed to break if the pump jams. However, the system will not heat properly. Usually the broken coupling makes a racket. A leaking circulator means the pump seal must be replaced. Call a service technician for all repairs to a circulator.

TROUBLESHOOTING BEFORE CALLING FOR SERVICE

Problem	Causes	Solutions
No heat	No power to the boiler; low water level; burner problems	Raise the thermostat. Check the switches, fuses, circuit breakers, and water level. Troubleshoot the burner's safety controls.
Poor heat	A sudden change usually means too much or too little water; a gradual change results from deposits in the boiler or on the heat exchanger	Check the combination gauge, then the expansion tank. If the problem developed slowly, try flushing the boiler, then call a professional for a tune-up.
Leaks	The circulator; pressure-relief valve; piping; or, more rarely, boiler tank	Is water coming from the pressure-reducing valve, underside of a circulator, or supply or return pipes? Water may travel quite a distance from a leak, but always in a downward direction. Consider repairing pipes yourself (see pages 146–147), or call a plumber for service.
Only some radiators heat up	Suspect trapped air, especially in units far from the boiler. If an entire zone is cold, the problem lies with a zone valve or its circulator.	Bleed air from the cool units. Check the circulator. If a zone valve is stuck, you'll feel heat in the pipe up to the valve but not beyond.
Clanging pipes	A sudden racket usually means a circulator has gone bad. Chronic banging noises may be the result of improperly pitched return lines.	Check the circulator. For banging, use a level to check the slope of all return lines (see page 535).

TROUBLESHOOTING A THERMOSTAT

Pop the cover from a standard thermostat and you'll discover that your heating system's "brain" has remarkably few components. That's because it amounts to nothing more than a temperature-sensitive on/off switching device. A programmable thermostat, on the other hand, adds high-tech circuitry.

The sensing is done by a coil, or a strip, of two metals that expand and contract at different rates. As room temperature drops below the setting you've selected, this bimetal coil or strip closes a set of electrical contacts, sending a low-voltage signal to a transformer that turns on the furnace or boiler. When air warms above the thermostat setting, the bimetal opens the contacts again, shutting off the heat. Switching to the cooling mode simply reverses these cycles.

The switch is typically a sealed tube filled with mercury. When the coil tips the tube, the mercury tips over to complete an electrical circuit.

A thermostat for a piped system should have a heat anticipator. This shuts off the boiler a little early since pipes will continue to heat after the boiler has turned off.

Thermostats are as reliable as any other switch. When a heating or cooling problem comes up, first make sure the temperature setting is at the right level—sometimes turning the dial up or down a few degrees will get things going again. Troubleshoot the system's other components, as shown on the preceding pages. If they're all in working order, shut off the main power switch, return to the thermostat, and try the procedures shown below. (For information about installing new energy-saving thermostats, see page 556.)

The wires that lead to a thermostat carry very low voltage, so there is no need to shut off power before working on one.

A thermostat should be positioned to measure the temperature of an average airspace in your home. If it is near a heat source or in the path of drafts, it may not provide comfortable heat levels for the rest of the house. Keep lamps and other heat-producing appliances away from the thermostat.

YOU'LL NEED...

TIME: 10 to 20 minutes to clean a thermostat; 30 minutes to check the thermostat's accuracy.
SKILLS: Basic maintenance skills.
TOOLS: Screwdriver, paper or a dollar bill, fine brush, level, thermometer.

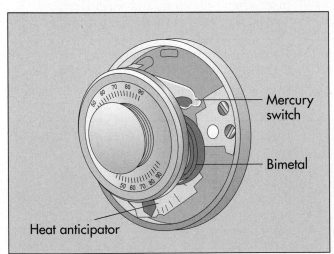

What's under the cover?
Remove the outside cover by simply pulling it off. To gain further access to parts underneath, remove two or more screws and detach the dial. The mercury-filled contact for the switch does not need to be cleaned. If your system turns on and off too often for your liking, turn the heat anticipator toward a longer setting. If you experience wide temperature swings, turn the anticipator to a lower setting.

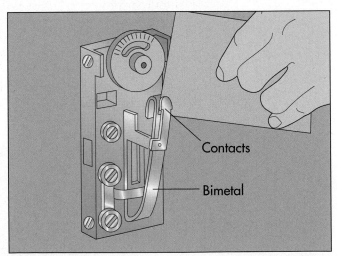

Cleaning the contacts.
In older units, clean dirt from exposed contacts by drawing a new dollar bill or other piece of paper between them. Or you can use a cotton swab dipped in alcohol.

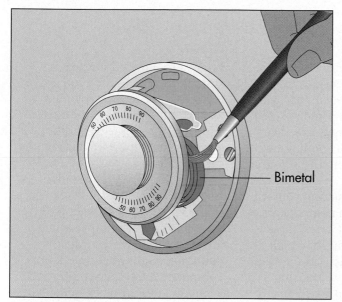

Dust the bimetal.
Dust on the bimetal will impair a thermostat's efficiency. With a small brush, clean the bimetal and any place you find dust. Or blow out dust using "canned air" designed for cleaning electronic devices.

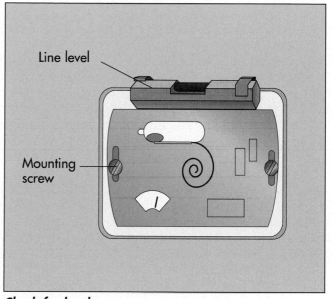

Check for level.
Thermostats with mercury switches must be level. To reposition a thermostat, first remove the cover. Loosen the mounting screws, level the thermostat, and retighten the screws. If screws were driven into drywall only, they may come loose. Install plastic anchors (see page 287). To level a round thermostat, hold a level or a weighted piece of string up to the vertical alignment lines.

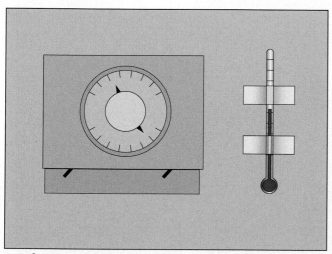

Test for accuracy.
To check the accuracy of a thermostat, tape a thermometer to the wall. If your thermostat delivers the wrong level of heat, you could simply scratch a mark on the cover indicating the desired temperature. Or replace the thermostat.

EXPERTS' INSIGHT

REPLACING A THERMOSTAT

Installing a new thermostat is an easy project, but you must work methodically. Shut off power—the voltage is not dangerous, but crossing live wires could cause damage to the controls at the heater. Remove the mounting screws, and gently pull the old thermostat out. Loosen screws to remove the wires, and label each wire with a marked piece of tape so there will be no confusion. Wrap the wires around a pencil or a small stick, making certain they cannot slip back through the hole and into the wall cavity.

To ensure good contacts, cut the bare wire ends and restrip the insulation (see pages 56–57). Bend the wire ends to wrap around the terminals of the new thermostat, and screw them down tight. Check for level as you anchor the new unit.

MAINTAINING A CENTRAL AIR-CONDITIONER

You've probably noticed that degree for degree, cooling consumes far more energy than heating. Why?

The answer lies in the nature of the cooling process. The cooling unit must absorb heat from the air—a big task in itself. It also has to reduce humidity to a more comfortable level. It does this by overchilling the air, then pushing controlled amounts of warm, humid air through the cooling coil, causing moisture to form on the coil. This moisture is carried away through a condensate drain.

What's more, cool air weighs more than warm air, so, unlike heat, it doesn't tend to rise of its own accord. The result: First you pay dearly to lower the temperature and humidity of the air, then you need additional energy to move the air around.

Any inefficiency in a room air-conditioner or a central system just compounds the already heavy electrical load that it pulls. To minimize this energy draw, keep your home's cooling equipment in top operating order. These pages show you how.

Begin by familiarizing yourself with the two main components of a cooling system. One of these is the condensing unit, in which refrigerant is condensed into a liquid. You'll always find this component located outdoors, where it can release heat (and most of the system's noise) to the outdoor air.

The condensing unit sends the now-cool refrigerant to an evaporator coil inside the house. Here, a blower moves air through the coil to cool and dehumidify it. If your home has a central system

hooked to a forced-air heating system, the evaporator coil is located in the furnace plenum, as illustrated below and on page 524. In this case, the conditioned air is moved into the house by the furnace blower.

Room air-conditioning units house all their parts in a single, two-compartment cabinet (see page 544). Heat pumps, which are essentially two-way air-conditioners, have additional components (see pages 532–533).

If you have an older home with piped or radiant heating, some new techniques allow installers to add central air by snaking small-diameter ducts through walls and ceilings. The resulting system is a little noisy but cools effectively.

How it works.

To trace the circuits of heat and cold through a whole-house air-conditioning system, study the drawing at right. Outdoors a compressor and condenser coil "make cold" by pressurizing refrigerant gas, which loses heat as it turns into a liquid. The coil, a network of tubing and fins, transfers the heat to the outdoor air pulled through it by a fan. Cool refrigerant flows through tubing to the evaporator coil, where the refrigerant absorbs heat from air pushed through it by the furnace blower. Cool, dry air then moves into the plenum. Meanwhile water that condensed from the air in the plenum runs down a condensate drain. Finally the refrigerant, a hot gas once again, returns through another line to the condensing unit.

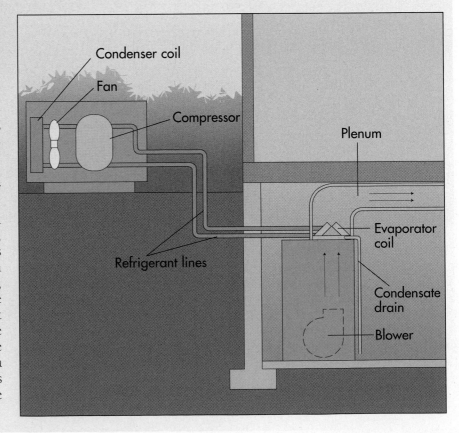

Condenser coil

Fan

Compressor

Plenum

Evaporator coil

Refrigerant lines

Condensate drain

Blower

TROUBLESHOOTING A CENTRAL AIR-CONDITIONER

It's cost-effective to schedule a tune-up at the start of every cooling season. For example, some of the refrigerant may have leaked out, which can gradually diminish your system's efficiency. When anything goes wrong with a central air-conditioner, call a service contractor.

You can forestall repairs by following these maintenance procedures once a month during the cooling season. The condenser coils resemble an automobile radiator, with loops of tubing laced through a honeycomb of aluminum fins. Leaves, debris, or even a heavy accumulation of household dust on these fins chokes off the airflow upon which cooling systems depend.

When you clean the fins, treat them gingerly; they bend easily. Sharp tools may puncture the relatively soft copper tubing.

Don't neglect your furnace blower unit, either. Moving cool, heavy air strains the belts and bearings. To learn about keeping blowers working, see page 525.

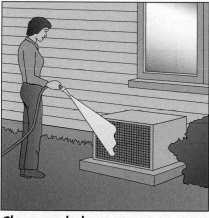

Clean regularly.
Keep the condensing unit clear so air can flow freely. First shut off power and turn up the thermostat. Remove the grille and any housing, and brush away leaves and dust. Cover the fan and electrical parts with plastic to keep them dry. Hose the coils and fins clean. Keep shrubs pruned back.

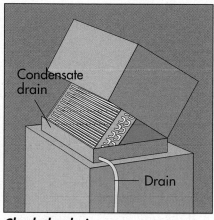

Condensate drain

Drain

Check the drain.
During humid weather, check the condensate drain to be sure that it's carrying off excess moisture. If water puddles under the coils, the drain line is probably clogged. If it is clogged, disconnect the line and flush it with a hose. Then pour in a little household bleach, and reattach the line.

Change the filter.
A clogged filter can shut down a unit. Change filters several times per season. Never run a system without a filter.

TROUBLESHOOTING BEFORE CALLING FOR SERVICE

Problem	Causes	Solutions
System not running	Incorrect thermostat setting; no power to the unit	Be sure the room temperature is above the thermostat setting. Check circuit breakers and main power switch.
System runs but doesn't cool	May need refrigerant; airflow problems	Check for a clogged filter or malfunctioning blower. Look for blockages at the condensing unit. Low refrigerant must be recharged (replenished) by a professional.
System cycles too often	May indicate airflow problems; defective thermostat	Check the condensing unit's airflow, then the filter and blower. Check the thermostat.
Uneven cooling	If some rooms are too cool and others too warm, the duct system needs balancing.	To balance an air system, see pages 526 and 547. If the house doesn't cool sufficiently, the unit may be undersized.

MAINTAINING A ROOM AIR-CONDITIONER

Most room air-conditioners are permanently lubricated. Routine upkeep consists only of keeping filters and coils clean.

When a unit refuses to run, make sure its filter is clean and that the power cord is plugged in. Check the main service panel for a blown fuse or tripped circuit breaker. Wait 5 minutes before you restart a room air-conditioner after it turns off, so that built-up heat can dissipate first.

If the unit cycles on or off too often or otherwise runs erratically, suspect thermostat problems. Often this means that the thermostat sensor has been knocked out of position. The sensor should be near the coil, but not touching it. Adjust it by carefully bending the wire.

If you hear a gurgling noise, or if water drips from the front panel, shut off the power and check with a level to make sure the cabinet's outer section slopes toward its condensate drain.

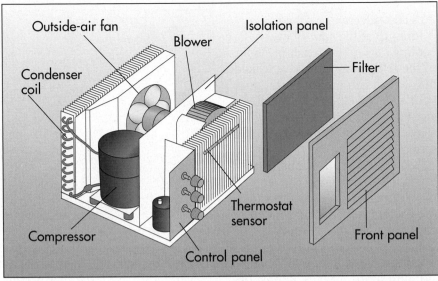

How it works.
A window-installed room air-conditioner has all the same components of a central system, but it's scaled down to fit into a two-section enclosure.

The unit's smaller inside cell includes a blower, evaporator coil, and thermostat sensor that reads the temperature of air coming into the evaporator coil. The thermostat is located behind the control panel. A removable front panel covers everything and often holds the filter as well.

An isolation panel separates the components that are inside and those that are outside the window. The panel may have a shutter you adjust from the control panel to bring in outside air.

In the outside portion of the unit, a fan moves air through a condenser coil, where the refrigerant is liquefied and sent to the evaporator coil.

Clean or replace the filter.
Turn off the unit and remove or tilt back the cover to get at the filter. Some types of filters need to be vacuumed; others should be washed or replaced. Clean or change the filter every two to three weeks during the cooling season.

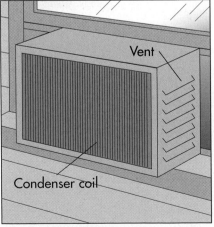

Check the condenser coil.
Every month, check the condenser coil and the intake vents for obstructions, such as leaves or dirt. Hose out this part of the unit every spring.

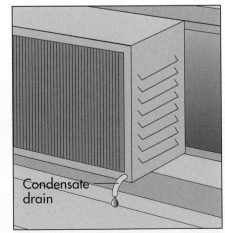

Check the drain outlet.
Also check the condensate drain outlet. If it's plugged up or the unit is not properly pitched away from the house, condensation can't run out.

USING AN EVAPORATIVE COOLER

In many areas summer heat is associated with high humidity. The usual solution is a refrigerant-charged air-conditioner that wrings both heat and humidity from the air—at a high cost in electricity.

Some regions suffer from too-low humidity. In these areas, humidity can be traded for cooling through the simple phenomenon of evaporative cooling, and at much lower cost.

Nature's equivalent to a man-made evaporative cooler is a thunderstorm on a hot day. We all have felt the dramatic drop in temperature that occurs after the rain stops. The cooling is due not to the rain itself but to water evaporation after the storm is over.

An evaporative cooler consists of a water reservoir, a water-soaked fibrous pad, and a blower that pulls air through the wet pad.

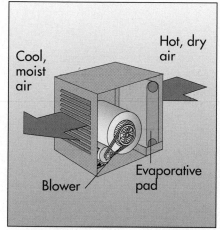

The blower draws in hot, dry air from outside and discharges the cooled air into the house. Leaving a window open in the room to be cooled allows the cooled air to flow through the room on its way outside.

Depending on the size required, evaporative coolers can be installed on the roof, on the ground, in a wall, or in a window.

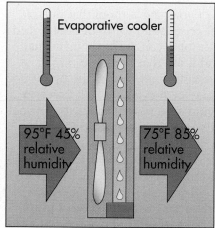

When the water evaporates from the cooling pad, any mineral content in the water is left behind on the pad. These mineral deposits build up rapidly in regions that have hard water. Check the pads once each month. Some pads can be demineralized by soaking them in a commercial lime remover; others must be replaced.

EXPERTS' INSIGHT

WHAT'S THE RIGHT SIZE?

Evaporative coolers are sized by cubic feet of air they move per minute (cfm). Here's how to find the size unit you need.

Compute the volume of your home's conditioned space in cubic feet; for example, 8×24×40 feet equals 7,680 cubic feet. In the chart at right, find the location nearest you and the recommended minutes per air change. For example, Phoenix, AZ—2 minutes. Divide volume by minutes to find cooler cfm; for example: 7,680 cubic feet ÷ 2 minutes equals 3,840 cfm unit. For an uninsulated home, multiply by 2; highly insulated, divide by 2.

RECOMMENDED MINUTES PER AIR CHANGE

State, City	Temp. Drop (°F)	Minutes per Air Change
AL, Birmingham	18	NR
AZ, Phoenix	30	2
AR, Little Rock	18	NR
CA, Los Angeles	18	2
CO, Denver	27	4
GA, Atlanta	16	NR
ID, Boise	25	4
KS, Topeka	20	3
MT, Great Falls	25	NR
NE, North Platte	22	3
NV, Las Vegas	34	3
NM, Albuquerque	28	3
ND, Bismarck	22	3
OK, Tulsa	22	1.3
SD, Rapid City	23	3
TX, Dallas	22	2
UT, Salt Lake City	28	4
WY, Casper	27	4

NR = not recommended due to high ambient air humidity.

ADDING A WARM-AIR SUPPLY

If you have a room that doesn't get enough warm or cool forced air, or if you are building a small addition that needs heating, adding a new warm-air supply may be the solution. If, however, your system is already working at its capacity, consider solving the problem by installing one of the independent space heaters shown on pages 551–555.

Before going to a sheet metal shop for materials, draw a rough sketch of what you're trying to do. Measure the length of the proposed run and also the diameter of the pipe that's used for existing runs.

YOU'LL NEED...
TIME: 2 to 3 hours to run a new warm-air outlet.
SKILLS: Intermediate sheet-metal and carpentry skills.
TOOLS: Tin snips, screwdriver, pliers, hammer, drill, saw.

1. Install a register.
When planning the installation, consider two facts: First the shorter the supply run, the more efficiently it will heat. Second registers located on outside walls are the most effective at keeping a room comfortable. Drill locator holes up from the space below, then work from above. Drill holes in the corners, and then cut the opening with a keyhole saw, reciprocating saw, or saber saw.

Saber saw with metal-cutting blade

2. Tap into the ductwork.
The simplest solution is to tap into a nearby supply line run. If that won't work, tap directly into the plenum. Cut the opening in either its bottom or side. To cut a round opening in the middle of a duct, first drill a hole large enough to accommodate the metal-cutting blade of a saber saw, then cut with the saber saw. If the metal is too wobbly to cut with a power saw, use tin snips.

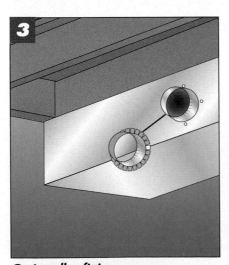

3. Install a fitting.
"Take-off" fittings come with flanges inserted into the plenum, then folded flat. Insert the fitting into the hole so it lies flat. Drill pilot holes and drive sheetmetal screws to secure the fitting.

4. Attach a boot.
Most registers connect to their ducts with a "boot" fitting, which has a flange that fits into the opening. Nail or screw the boot securely to the underside of the subfloor. Make sure the register fits snugly into the boot.

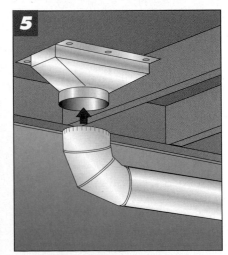

5. Hook up the run.
Fit an elbow to the boot and assemble the rest of the run. Secure all connections with screws, then wrap them with professional-quality duct tape.

INSTALLING AN IN-LINE DAMPER

Dampers—essentially doors located inside supply ducts—control the flow of heated or cooled air to room registers. Dampers let you cut down the flow to a spot that's getting too much air and redirect it to one that's not getting enough. This balancing process lets you adjust temperatures to make up for differences in exposures, length of duct runs, heat-producing appliances, or other anomalies (see page 526).

If your ducts don't already have dampers, installing them is straightforward and requires few materials. Dampers for round ducts come preassembled in a section of duct that fits into existing runs. When buying them, you'll need to know the diameter of your ducts—5, 6, or 7 inches.

Rectangular supply ducts vary in size and cross-section, so you may need to have these made to order by a sheetmetal fabricator (find one in the Yellow Pages) or a heating contractor. They also can show you how to install them.

For most systems the best way to gain control is to install a damper in each supply line, just past the point where it exits the plenum (see pages 524–526). To get at these, you may have to work in cramped quarters.

Most duct runs dismantle more easily than you might think. They are secured with just one or two screws at each joint. Unscrew either end of a section, and maybe the boot as well, and you usually can wrestle the section loose.

1. Open up the duct.
Take off any duct tape from both ends of a duct section and remove the screws. Pull a section away from the end toward the furnace to disengage its plain (female) end. Then slide the crimped (male) end free.

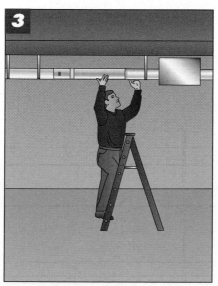

2. Attach the damper.
From the noncrimped end of the duct section, cut a piece that is 4 inches shorter than the new damper section. Slip the plain end of the damper section over the other duct's crimped end. Secure the joint with sheetmetal screws and duct tape.

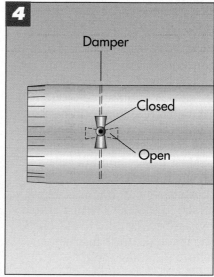

3. Install the ductwork.
Reassemble the run with the new damper section. Crimped ends of the sections always point away from the furnace.

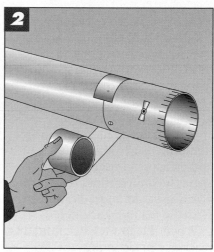

4. Use the damper.
In the open position, the damper lever will be parallel to the duct; when it's fully closed, it will be perpendicular. For instructions on balancing a system, see page 526.

YOU'LL NEED...
TIME: 1 to 2 hours.
SKILLS: Basic sheet-metal skills.
TOOLS: Hacksaw, screwdriver, ladder.

INSTALLING A POWER HUMIDIFIER

If your furnace isn't equipped with a humidifier, or if it has only a passive, evaporative plate humidifier, you need something that can cope with the big volumes of dry air that pass through a heating system.

Many older evaporative humidifiers are difficult to clean and can spread bacteria. Newer types, including those that spray a warm mist, are more healthful and virtually maintenance-free.

When the air's relative humidity reaches a preset point, the unit's humidistat turns off the humidifier until the moisture level drops again. (Most people are comfortable in the 30- to 50-percent humidity range.) The unit also cycles on and off with the furnace blower.

If your home has copper or plastic plumbing, you can easily tap into an existing water line with a saddle tee. Most humidifier kits come with a self-tapping shutoff valve that connects into copper pipe. With steel pipes, use a conventional tee-and-union connection. (See page 180–181 for these plumbing connections.) Your electrical connection can come from any nearby junction box (see page 125).

Most power humidifiers mount on the furnace plenum, as illustrated here. A few, however, attach to the main return or to a bypass between the two. Consult the manufacturer's instructions before installing these.

YOU'LL NEED...

TIME: 2 to 3 hours.
SKILLS: Basic sheet-metal, plumbing, and electrical skills.
TOOLS: Tin snips or saber saw, drill, screwdriver, wrench, wire stripper, pliers, caulking gun.

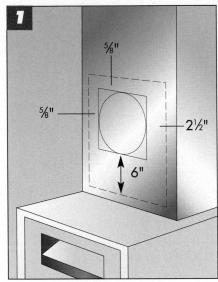

1. Plan the cutout.
Your installation may look different from that shown on this page; consult the manufacturer's directions. Most humidifiers come with a template. Tape it onto the plenum and mark for cutting the opening.

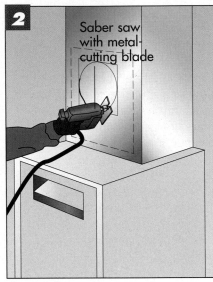

2. Cut the opening.
Drill pilot holes, then cut an opening with a saber saw that's equipped with a metal-cutting blade. Or you may be able to use tin snips. Drill pilot holes for the mounting screws.

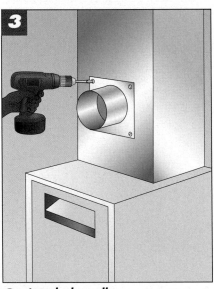

3. Attach the collar.
Slip the mounting collar in place, caulk the joint, and secure it by drilling pilot holes and driving sheetmetal screws.

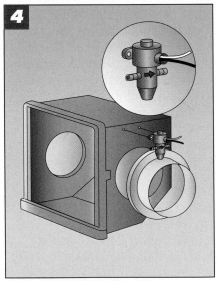

4. Position the unit.
Anchor the humidifying unit to the collar. Make sure the arrow on the solenoid valve points in the same direction as the water flow.

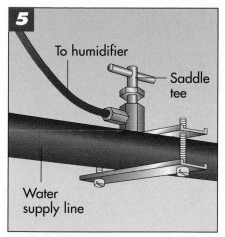

5. Supply water.

Install a flexible copper or plastic supply line. In most cases you can tap into a cold-water line with a saddle tee, which can be installed without shutting off the water.

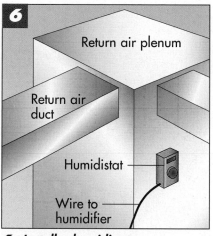

6. Install a humidistat.

Position the humidistat on the main return duct. Follow the manufacturer's directions for the electrical hookups.

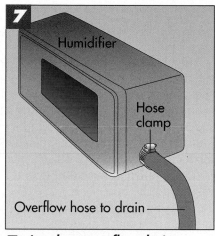

7. Attach an overflow drain.

For the overflow drain, attach a length of flexible rubber tubing to the humidifier outlet with a hose clamp. The drain should run into a utility sink or a floor drain.

ADDING A HIGH-WALL RETURN

In the heating mode, it makes sense to locate both supply and return registers at or near floor level. Heated air rises from the suppliers, while heavier, cool air settles back to the returns. However, in the cooling mode it is more efficient to have the return near the top, where it can suck the rising warm air.

You don't need to rip open an entire wall to install a return register near the ceiling. The space between two studs in an interior wall can function as a return duct. You may be able to use the space between floor joists in the same way.

Avoid a spot that has other heating or plumbing runs. Wiring will not impede airflow.

If the wall you're working on includes fire blocking, you'll need to make a third opening in the wall to remove it.

A high-wall return will make a big improvement in a room's comfort level. Your cooling system will run more efficiently, too. If you need to rebalance the system, see page 526.

1. Cut grille openings.

For the greatest benefit, locate the return on an interior wall opposite a supply register, about 6 inches from the ceiling. Locate studs, drill pilot holes, then cut out the grille opening. Make another opening directly below at the floor level. Saw out the sole plate and cut a hole in the subflooring.

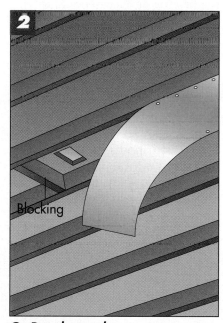

2. Run ductwork.

If a joist cavity below runs in the right direction, turn it into a duct by adding blocking as needed and covering the bottom with sheet metal. If that is not feasible, run ductwork as shown on page 547. Connect the new duct to the existing return system.

REPLACING RADIATORS WITH CONVECTORS

Radiation is a hot surface's tendency to "throw" heat into the air around it. Radiation accounts for only part of the way a radiator works. Hold your hand above one and you can feel heated air rising from the top. This process, called convection, helps distribute the heat.

Whether a charming antique radiator or a more modern baseboard type, the shape of the unit may be more important than physical size. Longer, lower types don't put out any more heat than upright units, but they spread it over a broader area.

A large unit may or may not radiate more heat than a smaller one. The square-inch area of the heating surface exposed to air passing through, as well as around it, is the critical factor. So radiation units are sized according to the square inches of radiation that a unit offers. With help from your heating contractor, you can calculate the number of square inches you'll need to warm a given area of your home.

In selecting a replacement or new unit, also consider the type of metal from which it is made. Cast-iron gains heat and dissipates heat slowly, stretching the cooling-off period between heating cycles. Units made of steel, copper, aluminum, or combinations of these metals heat up rapidly and cool quickly. This means that a single fin-type convector in an otherwise iron system could result in a room that is alternately too hot and too cool.

All radiation units need room around them in order to function efficiently. A modern fin-type convector has a cover that is precisely sized to effectively move cool air up and out.

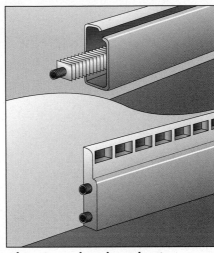

Choosing a baseboard unit.
Fin-tube units (top) rely on convection, and heat and cool rapidly. Use them for hot-water—not steam—systems. Cast-iron baseboard units (bottom) also save space but maintain a more even heat. They are a good choice if used in conjunction with existing cast-iron radiators.

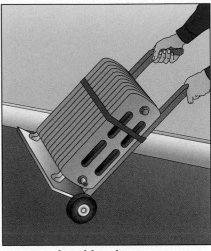

Remove the old radiator.
Preparing to replace a radiator with a newer unit is a job best left to the pros. The boiler should be turned off and the system allowed to cool. If it's a hot-water system, the pipes must be drained. Then the old radiator can be disconnected and, with the help of a two-wheeled cart, removed.

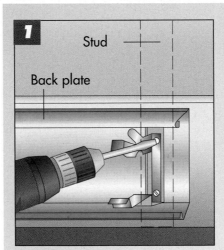

Installing convectors.
A new convector (for hot water heat only) is easy to install. First the plate gets attached to studs in the wall. Then fin-covered copper pipes are hooked to the system using the same techniques as for standard copper pipe (see pages 184–187). In some cases valves are installed.

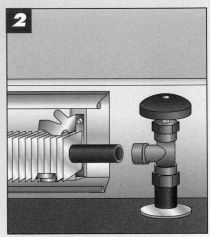

Make the pipe connection.
Connecting a new convector to existing piping is often a challenge even for a professional plumber. In some cases the pipe can be joined directly to the old valve using a reducer fitting, as shown above. Often, however, the pipes need to be snaked around and perhaps connected beneath the floor.

CHOOSING SPACE HEATERS

Many furnaces and boilers are bigger than they need to be, which means you easily can add more registers or radiation units, as shown on the preceding pages. If, however, you want to warm a sizable space, and especially if you need only part-time heat, an independent space heater might be a better alternative.

The drawings on this page illustrate the main types of space heaters. There are dozens of variations on these types.

To narrow the field, ask yourself exactly what job the heater needs to do. Will it be used only occasionally or briefly for backup or auxiliary heating? If so, an electric wall, ceiling, or baseboard unit might be the answer. These are inexpensive, easy to install, and use little or no floor space. Running one for extended periods, however, will add significantly to your electricity bill. The "oil-filled" electrical units (which are actually filled with a sort of antifreeze) are comparatively efficient energy users.

Advances in wood-burning technology have turned the wood-burning stove into an efficient modern heater. Unless you cut your own wood, however, check on wood prices before you buy one. Remember that cutting wood, stacking and carrying it into the house, and removing ashes demand large expenditures of human energy. Storing wood near your home may also attract termites and other insects.

Fireplaces are not included here because most do not do a good job of space-heating. Many actually rob heated air from your home through the chimney.

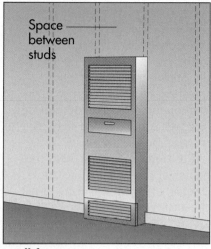

Wall furnace.
For providing ample heat while taking up only a small amount of horizontal space, it's hard to beat a wall furnace. Because it's natural gas, it's economical. Installation requires a power line, a gas line, and a vent that runs outdoors (see pages 552–553).

Electric wall unit.
Electric heaters install anywhere and come in many different models. They are often a good choice for a small area or as a supplemental heat source to boost heat in a room that's a little cold. To install one, see page 554.

Wood stove.
Modern wood stoves are virtually airtight; they use catalytic converters and special drafting systems to extract maximum heat from each load of logs. Some wood-burning heaters have thermostatic controls. One of these can warm a small house. For installation, see page 555.

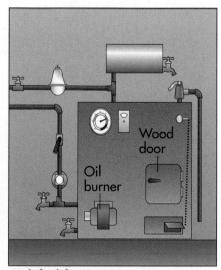

Multifuel furnace.
Multifuel furnaces burn wood, coal, gas, or oil, producing heat even when you're gone for long periods. These tend to be efficient when burning wood, and less so when burning oil or gas.

INSTALLING A GAS WALL FURNACE

A wall furnace packs all the elements of a forced-air heating system into a compact cabinet that mounts in or on an exterior wall.

With direct-venting models, a pair of metal pipes—one inside the other—penetrates the wall. One pipe supplies fresh air for combustion; the other exhausts fumes. With direct venting, you don't need to run a chimney to the roof. And because the fire is fed with outside air rather than house air, the system conserves indoor heat and runs more efficiently.

Check local community and building codes before buying a direct-vent furnace. Some codes restrict the type you can use and also may require professional installation. After installation, have the gas company come out to inspect it for safety; they will probably do so for free.

Except for the gas line, there is nothing tricky about the installation. You'll need to make a wall opening, and if you choose a horizontal model, you may have to install a header (see page 332).

Position the furnace near the center of the wall, where doors, drapes, or furniture won't block the airflow. The outside vent should be at least 24 inches below the eaves or other overhead projections and 12 inches above the ground.

The drawings on these pages show installing a typical upright unit. Unless you have experience running pipes for gas hookups, this is a job best left to gas-line professionals. You'll also need to run 120-volt power from a nearby wall outlet, a junction box, or the service panel; see pages 108–109. If you can cut the drywall or plaster accurately, the heater's flange should neatly cover the hole and you won't need to patch the wall.

YOU'LL NEED...

TIME: 6 to 8 hours, including running the electrical and gas lines.
SKILLS: Intermediate carpentry, plumbing, and electrical skills.
TOOLS: Hammer, drill, saber saw or reciprocating saw, screwdriver, pliers, wire stripper, tubing cutter, pipe wrench, caulking gun.

Flush-mounted units.
You can hang some units directly on the wall with brackets supplied by the manufacturer. This reduces carpentry and saves plenty of installation time, but the furnace will protrude out into the room.

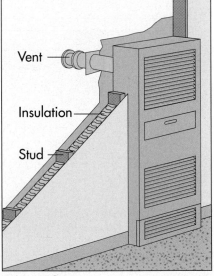

Recessed units.
Many units are recessed into the wall. Many can fit in the standard 14½-inch space between studs; wider units call for extensive carpentry. To prepare for a recessed installation, locate studs, cut away drywall or lath and plaster, and remove any insulation.

EXPERTS' INSIGHT

AVOIDING AND TESTING FOR GAS LEAKS

Before working on a gas line, turn off the gas at the nearest shutoff valve. Open a window before opening the line, because a small amount of gas will be in the pipes.

After making the connections, turn on the valve and test for leaks. Brush a mixture of dishwashing detergent and water onto all the fittings. Bubbles indicate a leak.

All gas leaks call for immediate action. If you ever detect the unmistakable aroma of escaping gas, open some doors and windows, extinguish all cigarettes and open flames, close the main gas shutoff valve, and call your gas utility company.

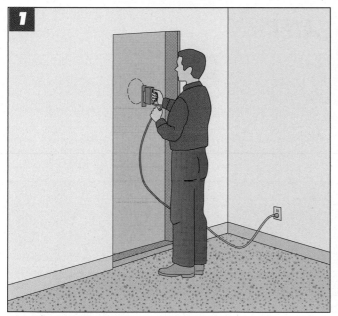

1. Cut the opening.

Remove drywall or plaster if you are installing a recessed unit. Determine where the flue will exit the house. Use a long bit to drill a hole through the drywall or plaster and out the exterior wall. Enlarge the hole using a saber saw (shown). When installing a flush unit, use an extra-long bit to drill the hole and cut from both the inside and the outside.

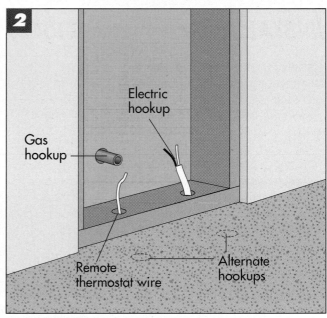

Gas hookup

Electric hookup

Remote thermostat wire

Alternate hookups

2. Run the lines.

Drill holes and run three lines—code-approved gas pipe, cable for 120-volt electrical power, and low-voltage cable for the thermostat (Step 4). These can come through either the wall or the floor.

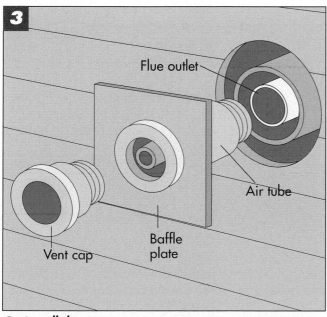

Flue outlet

Air tube

Vent cap

Baffle plate

3. Install the vent.

After you've installed the furnace, assemble the vent, making connections airtight by caulking the baffle plate. Be careful not to crack the connections where the vent pipes attach to the furnace and where the door opens for access to the burner and pilot. Leaks here will blow out the pilot.

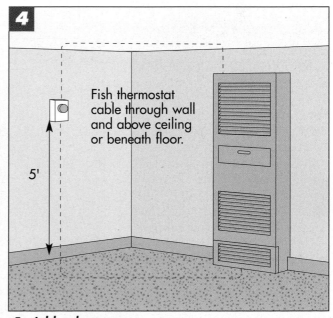

Fish thermostat cable through wall and above ceiling or beneath floor.

5'

4. Add a thermostat.

Some units come with an integral thermostat, but a remote thermostat gives a more accurate reading and makes for more comfortable heating. Run the thermostat cable through the ceiling or the floor, or behind the baseboard.

Installing an Electric Heater

*E*lectric heaters put out quiet, almost instantaneous heat— just what you need to take the nip from chilly bathroom air, warm a basement shop, or boost the temperature in a chronically cool room. Because electric heaters needn't be vented, you can tuck one almost anywhere.

Although these heaters use expensive electric power, using one strategically could cut the cost of running your central heating system. Consider, for instance, installing a baseboard unit in a room that's used only occasionally.

Electric heaters require lots of power. With small 500- to 1,000-watt models, you may be able to tap into a 120-volt receptacle on a lightly used circuit. If a unit draws more than 1,000 watts, however, it should have its own 20-amp circuit. High-output heaters require a 240-volt current—a job for a professional electrician. See pages 76–77 for calculating electrical loads.

An electrician also might install a remote switch next to a door or in another convenient location. Timer switches save energy by shutting off a unit after it has operated for a preset time period.

For safety reasons, don't place the heater or the switch near a bathtub or other wet place. And make sure the heater's grille can't be penetrated by a child's fingers.

The instructions here show how to recess a fan-powered model into a wall. A ceiling fixture with lamp-type heaters also may include an exhaust fan.

You'll Need...

TIME: 3 to 4 hours.
SKILLS: Basic carpentry and electrical skills.
TOOLS: Drill, keyhole or saber saw, wire stripper, screwdriver.

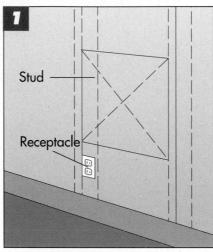

Stud

Receptacle

1. Prepare installation site.
Most wall heaters are made to fit between studs. Locate studs, drill a starter hole, then carefully cut out the opening with a keyhole saw or saber saw. In outside walls you'll probably find insulation in the cavity. Cut it off above and below the opening.

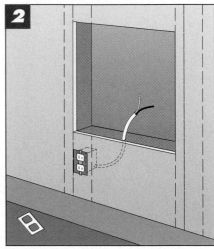

2. Tap into an electrical source.
Shut off power to any electrical circuit being worked on. For small units, tap electricity from a nearby outlet box. For larger units, you'll have to run a new, separate circuit from the main service panel.

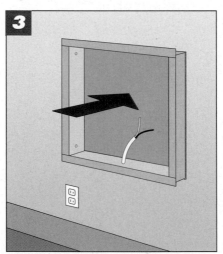

3. Run electrical cable through the heater housing.
Most units come with a housing that has mounting flanges for attaching to plaster or drywall. Run the electrical cable through the housing before installing it.

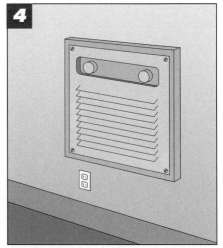

4. Complete the electrical connections.
Complete the wiring connections; the unit has a built-in junction box. Slip the heater into its housing and screw on the grille to make it tamper-resistant.

INSTALLING A WOOD-BURNING STOVE

Newer wood-burning heaters can keep a load of logs glowing for 12 hours or more. They burn so completely you need to shut down the heater only once a week to clean out the ashes.

To maintain this long-burning fire, wood heaters carefully control combustion. Most feature airtight construction and an automatically regulated draft. A catalytic converter may be located inside the stove or in the flue. As a result, wood-burning heaters draw little air and lose a minimum of heat.

You do pay a price for this efficiency, however. Slow-burning fires produce creosote, which can build up in a chimney and ignite. Because of this, you need to follow strict installation and maintenance procedures. Use only a masonry chimney or a metal chimney with a Class-A rating from Underwriters Laboratories. Follow the heater and chimney manufacturers' requirements to the letter, and check local building codes too.

Flue sections fit together with their crimped ends facing toward the heater. This allows any condensation in the vent to flow back to the fire. For an airtight assembly, seal each joint with furnace cement and secure it with three metal screws.

To break in a new wood heater, light small fires the first few times you use it. Otherwise heat could crack a casting. Proper maintenance is important too. Remove ashes at recommended intervals to prevent warping and burnouts, and clean the flue annually (see page 468).

When a wood-burning heater smokes or won't draw properly, make sure it's getting enough combustion air. If that's not the problem, your chimney might not be tall enough. A chimney contractor can help you evaluate and correct this situation.

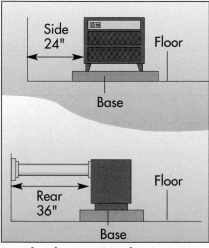

Get the clearances right.
Check installation instructions and local fire codes for minimum distances to a combustible wall. Most units must rest on a masonry or other noncombustible base. Even if a flue is rated "zero clearance," be extra safe and keep it several inches away from wood.

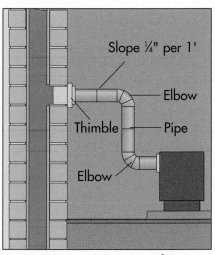

Connecting to a masonry chimney.
If location permits, it's easiest to connect to a masonry chimney, as shown. Keep the flue pipe runs short, with no more than two elbows. Have the chimney inspected and cleaned at least once a year.

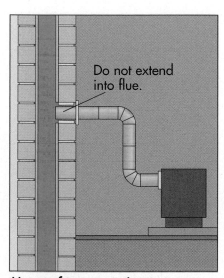

More safety precautions.
Make sure the flue pipe doesn't extend into the flue to create an obstruction. Make the connection at least 18 inches below the ceiling.

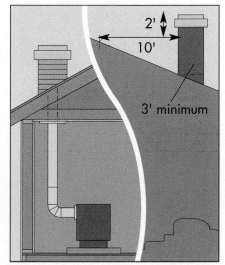

Alternatives to a masonry flue.
If you don't have a masonry flue, you'll have to run a class-A metal flue through the ceiling and roof. For a proper draw, the chimney should extend above the roof peak. If that would make it unwieldy, consult local codes for minimum clearances from the roof.

INSTALLING A PROGRAMMABLE THERMOSTAT

Programming a heating and cooling system often results in a sizable reduction in energy bills. Generally the greater the spread in degrees between the "home" and "away" (or day and night) settings—called the setback—the more energy savings you'll realize. The exception is the water heater. Water heats slowly and may require an hour or more to raise the temperature back up again.

Timed thermostats include a 24-hour clock. You select the beginning and ending times for the setback period, then forget about it. Another type uses a photocell to switch from one setting to another at dusk and dawn.

See pages 540–541 for general instructions on locating and wiring a thermostat. Keep the thermostat away from drafts or heat sources such as lamps, and locate it well away from any heat ducts.

Adjusting the setback may require experimentation. Begin by trying a setting 10°F lower or higher than your normal heating and cooling levels. If the house cools down or warms up too much, decrease the setback to 8°F. Also adjust the timings on the setback cycle to accommodate your schedule.

If your home has a heat pump, consult your heating contractor before buying a timed thermostat. Using a programmable thermostat with a heat pump may actually add to your utility bills.

You'll Need...
Time: 20 to 30 minutes.
Skills: Basic skills.
Tools: Level, screwdriver, wire stripper.

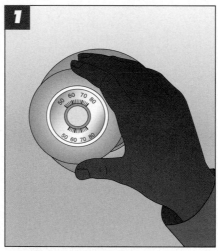

1. Detach the old thermostat.
Shut off the furnace or boiler and the electricity. Remove the cover plate and the dial, unscrew the mounting screws, and pull out the thermostat. Wrap the wires around a pencil so they can't fall back into the wall. Label the wires and sketch a diagram as to which terminals they were connected to.

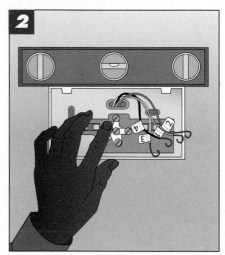

2. Level and mount the plate.
Thread the wires through the access hole in the new unit's mounting plate, and make sure that the unit can press flush against the wall. Check for level and drive mounting screws. If the screws encounter only drywall, install plastic anchors.

3. Connect the wires.
Hook the wires to the appropriate terminals, using your labels as guides; wires generally are color-coded. After the wires are connected, gently push any excess wire back into the wall.

4. Attach the cover and operate.
Attach the cover to the back plate. Turn on the electricity and the furnace; then program the unit. Fine-tune settings over a period of a few weeks.

ZONING A FORCED-AIR SYSTEM

*I*n a typical heating, ventilation, and air-conditioning (HVAC) system, a single thermostat placed in a central location calls for warm or cool air. The blower comes on to circulate the conditioned air throughout the home. In the case of a piped system, the boiler sends heat through all the pipes until the thermostat tells it to stop.

In large homes especially, having only one thermostat may cause unequal distribution of heat and cooling because different rooms have different needs. Balancing the system (see page 526) may solve the problem. A more reliable solution is to establish two or more zones, each with its own thermostat. Zoning provides several benefits:

■ The temperature can be tailored to the activity in a zone.

■ Energy is saved by neither overheating nor overcooling.

■ Because each zone calls for heating or cooling at different times, you generally can get by with a smaller system.

Installation of a zoned system is definitely a job for a qualified heating and cooling contractor. Ducts must be precisely sized. Calculations get complex. The installer takes into account the size and type of boiler or furnace, the distance the ducts travel, and how efficiently the home is insulated.

When air ducts are zoned, some may be shut off, which leads to increased pressure, higher velocity in the open ducts, and a possible freeze-up of air-conditioning coils. The system may require a static-pressure regulating damper to automatically regulate air pressure and airflow at the blower.

Calculating pipe runs for a zoned hot-water system isn't as complicated because radiators or convectors can be controlled individually. But it is still a job for a professional.

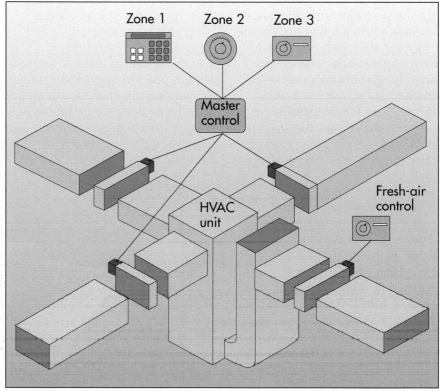

A typical system.
With a zoned system, as shown in the anatomy drawing above, individual thermostats call for warm or cool air for different zones. These zones—a single room, a floor, or a whole wing of the house—allow for different temperatures in these different areas of the home. You also have control over the fresh air that is fed into the blower unit.

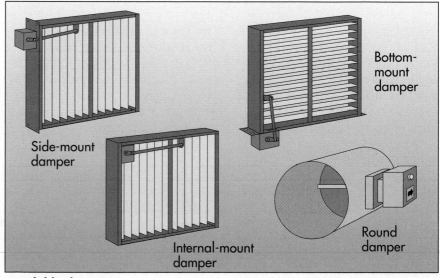

Available dampers.
Zone-control dampers come in a variety of configurations and sizes. This allows a contractor to retrofit a damper to nearly any existing duct configuration that might be found in a particular zone.

EVALUATING HEATING NEEDS

*I*n the past a heating contractor would guess a house's needs and order a system with considerably more capacity than needed. Such seat-of-the-pants engineering guarantees warmth but wastes energy. Now knowledgeable contractors calculate the exact heat load based on the house's design. They measure total heat losses, then compute the load for the geographic region, using design temperatures. The result, expressed in Btus (British Thermal Units), provides a guide for sizing the heating plant. If, for example, your home has a total heat load of 93,000 Btus, you'll need a furnace or boiler with perhaps up to 100,000 Btus.

If you're replacing a furnace, make sure that it wasn't oversize to begin with. Properly sized units run almost all the time in cold weather; oversize units often cycle on and off. Insulation, storm windows, and weather stripping substantially reduce heat losses. See pages 502–520 for ways to make your home more snug.

CALCULATING HEAT LOSS

*E*very part of a house loses heat to the outdoors, but at different rates, calculated as an R-value. To assess your home's heating needs, a contractor computes the volume of air and its exchange rate, then the heat loss value for each exterior surface—each surface's area divided by its R-value. The main areas of heat loss are the roof, chimney, walls, windows, doors, and foundation. For more about heat losses, see page 503.

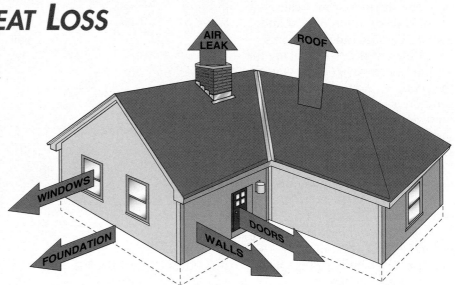

SHOPPING FOR ENERGY

*W*hat are the relative costs of heating with oil, natural gas, liquid propane (LP) gas, fuel oil, or electricity? To find out which would be the most economical, determine the unit cost of each form of energy from each utility, and then get out the calculator and do some math.

Electricity is priced by the kilowatt hour (kwh); natural gas by 100 cubic feet (ccf); and oil and LP gas by gallons. Rating these might seem like comparing apples and oranges. But each unit yields a predictable number of Btus. It's Btus—millions of them—that you need to heat your home.

The table shows the Btu yields for different energy units and the coefficients of performance (COP) for types of equipment. To figure the cost of each Btu generated by a new heating plant, divide the cost of each energy unit by its Btu yield. Energy forms are not equally efficient, so divide the cost per Btu you just obtained by the COP for the equipment you're considering. Because a single Btu doesn't amount to much, multiply by 1 million. Your final computation for each choice should look like this:

Cost per million Btu = Cost of the energy unit ÷ its Btu yield ÷ COP × 1 million.

CALCULATING ENERGY YIELDS			
Energy Form	**Unit of Measurement**	**Btu Yield**	**COP**
Electricity	1kwh	3,412 Btus	
Electric-resistance			1.0
Heat pump			1.5
Natural gas	1 ccf	103,000 Btus	0.70
Fuel oil	1 gallon #2 oil	139,000 Btus	0.70
LP gas	1 gallon	91,600 Btus	0.70

SELECTING A HEAT PLANT

Once your home's heating load has been calculated (see the top of page 558), a knowledgeable contractor can go one step further. Using the energy-yield data (see the table on page 558) and heating degree days from the U.S. Weather Service, a contractor can predict with surprising accuracy what you'd actually pay per year to operate a particular system.

Make sure to get this estimate. It enables you to predict the payback period for equipment that might be costly to begin with, but economical in the long run. If, for example, heating unit A is priced at $500 more than unit B, but would save $100 a year in energy bills, the payback period for unit A would be five years.

Estimating payback periods calls for some guesswork, of course. Experts can't say exactly what will happen to relative energy costs in the years to come. It's also hard to make allowances for auxiliary equipment that adds to your comfort by cooling, humidifying, or cleaning the air, as well as heating it. Imprecise as they may be, payback calculations offer the best way to make sure you're getting your money's worth when you purchase a new heating unit.

The drawings below show the different ways to install a forced-air furnace and its ductwork in a house that doesn't already have them. At the bottom of the page, you'll find information about three devices that improve the efficiency of a gas or oil furnace or boiler.

The payback period is even more important when you investigate more sophisticated (and expensive) equipment, such as solar units and heat pumps. Payback periods for these units can be lengthy.

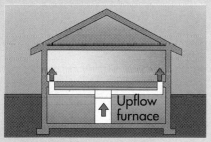

Selecting a furnace style.
Upflow furnaces make sense for basement installations. Most ductwork is usually down there, where it's easy to run.

A downflow furnace can be concealed in a closet. Ducts run through a crawlspace or in the floor.

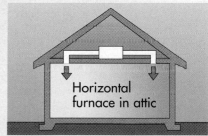

Horizontal furnaces and their ductwork can be installed in either an open crawlspace or (if the climate is warm) in an attic.

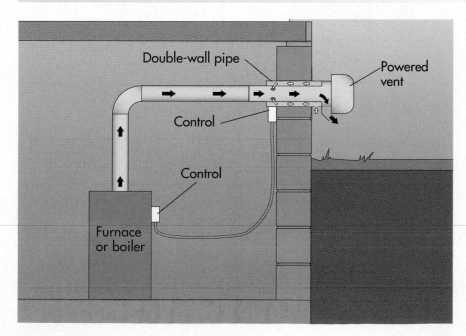

Energy-Saving Devices.

■ Gas and oil furnaces lose about 20 percent of their heat up the flue. A motorized flue damper (shown at left) stops flue heat loss by closing the vent after a unit has cycled off.

■ Gas pilots that constantly burn are wasting fuel. Electric ignitions usually are coupled with the damper control. When heat is called for, the control opens a valve and lights the pilot, which ignites the burners.

■ A newer, tightly sealed home may benefit from installing a heat recovery ventilator (HRV). It provides ventilation without letting in cold air.

EVALUATING COOLING NEEDS

An undersize air-conditioner just can't keep up on those really hot days. An oversize unit can make a room even more uncomfortable, however, because it cools in short, energy-wasting bursts, and then shuts down. Meanwhile, the indoor humidity level climbs and the air begins to feel clammy. Properly conditioned summer air, remember, is drier, as well as cooler.

Whether it's a room or central air-conditioner, a cooling unit should be just large enough to cope with prolonged hot spells. At those times, you can expect it to run almost constantly, controlling humidity as well as temperature.

This means that the unit's output, in Btus, must roughly equal the sum of the heat gains of your house or room. If you're shopping for a central system, get bids from several installers and let them compute the gains, as explained below. For a room unit, you can do the figuring yourself without too much trouble (see below right).

Some manufacturers size their equipment's output in tons rather than Btus. To convert tons to Btus, multiply the tonnage by 12,000.

Chances are you won't be able to get an exact Btu-for-Btu match between a model's capacity and your home's heat gains. Generally it's safer to go to the next smaller size. With a slightly undersize unit, indoor temperatures might rise somewhat on really hot days, but continuous dehumidification will maintain a tolerable level of comfort.

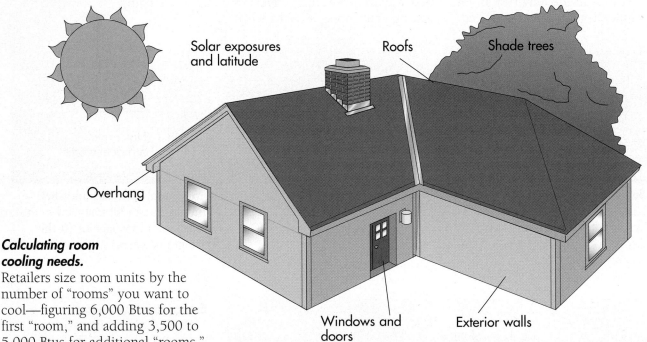

Solar exposures and latitude

Roofs

Shade trees

Overhang

Windows and doors

Exterior walls

Calculating room cooling needs.

Retailers size room units by the number of "rooms" you want to cool—figuring 6,000 Btus for the first "room," and adding 3,500 to 5,000 Btus for additional "rooms." Other factors come into play, too. How big is a typical room? And what about exposure, insulation, the number of windows and doors, heat gains from appliances, and the number of people who will use the space?

Use the chart at right to calculate your Btu needs. Move up to the next larger size for hot spots and for spaces with ceilings over 8 feet high. If you want an exact computation, ask a contractor for a cooling-load estimate form, along with the Btu factors they normally use.

Calculating heat gains.

To calculate peak cooling demand, expect contractors to go through an even more lengthy and detailed process than that for heat losses (see page 558). Besides assigning Btu gains to the exterior factors illustrated above, they also need to know about hot or cold spots inside, how many appliances you have, and even how many people are in the family.

COOLING NEEDS

Cooling Area/ square feet	Capacity/ Btus
265–300	6,000
300–350	7,500
350–450	9,000
450–520	10,000
520–600	11,000
600–750	12,500
750–900	15,000
900–1,050	16,500

BUYING A CENTRAL AIR-CONDITIONER

Once a contractor knows what your home's heat gains are, an installer will check the furnace blower and ductwork to determine whether they can handle the heavier cooled air. While the plenum is being checked, ask whether it can be modified easily to accept an electronic air cleaner, a power humidifier, or both. Even if you can't afford these items now, planning for them will save on installation costs later. (For more about humidifiers and air cleaners, see pages 548–549.)

You also may want to consider installing a zoned system. Establishing zones could save on energy costs by keeping daytime temperatures higher in empty bedrooms (see page 557).

A two-speed condensing unit minimizes operating costs because it matches a system's capacity to its needs. Lights on the thermostat let you know whether a two-speed unit is running at high or low speed, giving you a chance to raise the temperature setting and reduce demand when you choose.

Natural-gas–powered systems are also available. Installation costs will be greater than for an electric air-conditioner, but you may recover the difference, and more, in lower operating costs, reduced maintenance, and longer life. This depends on your energy costs.

Finally don't be surprised to find a wide range of prices for equipment with similar Btu capacities. Quality differences account for most of this variance. Some components are guaranteed for five years, others for ten.

BUYING A ROOM AIR-CONDITIONER

Central cooling is more efficient than a series of room air-conditioners. If you only want to cool a few rooms, however, you might come out ahead by using room units.

The initial investment will be less, especially if you don't have forced-air heating to which you can add central air-conditioning. If you turn room units off or to a higher temperature setting when not using the spaces they cool, you'll save even more money.

When shopping for a room unit, consider how it will be used. A unit opposite a doorway may cool several rooms, but you may need

to set up a fan to help circulate air.

Room units are designed to fit into a double-hung window. If you have narrow windows or casement windows, special units are made to fit; you may need to remove the sash during the summer.

Or consider a through-the-wall installation. Wall-mounted units don't obstruct views and run more quietly than window units.

Calculate the capacity you need, as explained on page 560, then find a unit with a Btu rating within 10 percent of that figure.

Compare energy efficiency ratings carefully The higher the rating, the less electricity a unit

will draw. High-efficiency models often also feature sophisticated controls, such as timers and switches that let you choose whether or not the fan will run when the compressor is off.

Most room units come with installation instructions. Mounting one in a window will take a couple of hours. You'll need help to set the heavy, awkwardly balanced chassis in place.

Check for air leaks around the housing or sashes, and seal gaps with an air-conditioner gasket or weather stripping.

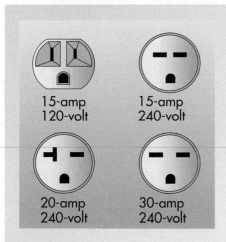

15-amp
120-volt

15-amp
240-volt

20-amp
240-volt

30-amp
240-volt

Getting power to a unit.
If your room unit is a small 120-volt model, you probably can plug it into an existing circuit. Make sure that the connection is properly grounded and that it will not overload the circuit (see pages 34–41).

Larger model 120-volt room air-conditioners and all 240-volt models need to have their own individual circuits. If you have a choice between 120- and 240-

volt units, select the 240-volt equipment because it operates more efficiently.

Plug and receptacle styles for 240-volt appliances vary according to amperage. (See typical receptacle styles at left.) Don't change receptacles unless the circuit wiring can handle the new load.

To learn about adding new circuits and installing major appliances, see pages 76–81.

CONSERVING ENERGY

Energy conservation starts with efficient equipment that's conscientiously maintained. See pages 502–520 for ways to weatherize your home and minimize the load on your heating and cooling equipment.

In the end, the way you operate your climate-control systems is as vital to fuel bills as your driving habits are to your car's fuel economy. Rushing to adjust the thermostat every time you feel too hot or too cold wastes energy, just as a lead foot on your car's accelerator does.

The chart below lists how to control heating and cooling components with the same light and steady touch you use when you're behind the wheel.

FINE-TUNING YOUR HEATING AND COOLING HABITS

	Item	Tactic	How You Save
HEATING	Thermostat	Set back 8 to 10 degrees at night; set to 55°F (or 58°F if you have a heat pump) when you're away for more than a day or two.	Savings of 8 to 15 percent are not unusual.
	Fireplace	Ordinary fireplaces will not reduce your heating bill; many draw off more heated air for combustion than they add. Most dampers leak heat even when closed; consider a glass fire screen (more about fireplaces on page 468).	Tightly sealed glass screens definitely cut heating bills; close before retiring, and the fire will burn itself out.
	Ventilation	A range hood or bathroom fan can exhaust all the heated air in your home in about an hour. Control bath units with timers; use range hoods sparingly in cold weather (more about fans on pages 130–133).	Indiscriminate use of fans could be adding to your heating costs.
	Water heater	Lower setting 5 or 10 degrees, but not below 120°F. Add an insulation blanket, which you can buy in kit form, around the tank, especially if the unit is in an unheated space (more about water heaters on pages 202–210).	Depends on where you live; lowering the setting saves more with electric units than with gas.
COOLING	Thermostat	Keep setting no lower than 78°F. On really hot days, turn it up even further. Regardless of the temperature outside, you'll feel comfortable if indoor levels are 15°F lower than outside.	Dropping settings from 78° to 77°F costs 8 percent more; dropping to 72°F costs 60 percent more.
	Appliances	Operate heat-producing appliances, such as washers, dryers, and dishwashers, at night or early morning so heat and humidity don't add to the cooling load.	Energy savings will be greater if your utility has off-peak rates; comfort levels will be greater too.
	Ventilation	An attic fan, coupled with attic insulation, can make a big difference in cooling load. If you don't have them, add power ventilators to dispel excess humidity in the kitchen or bath (see pages 130–132 for both).	An attic or whole-house fan uses only about a tenth of the energy consumed by a central air-conditioner.

TILING

PLANNING YOUR TILING PROJECT

Good architectural design often goes unnoticed. A well-proportioned house or intelligently laid-out kitchen simply has a natural rightness about it. In the same way, instead of shouting for attention, a well-designed tile installation should just fit in. When a surfacing material jumps out at you, the design probably has failed.

The age of your house, the decorating style you seek to capture, and your budget all affect the design you choose. Books, magazines, and tile brochures are probably the best sources of ideas. However be sure the types and patterns of tile that you find attractive suit your space.

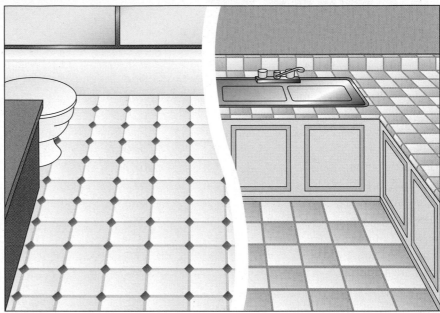

Proportion tile to room size.
As a general rule, tile size should be proportional to the size of the room. That is, small tiles generally work best in small rooms and large tiles look better in large rooms. Larger tiles seem less large when used on horizontal surfaces. Use larger tiles on lower surfaces; wall tiles or countertop tiles that are bigger than the floor tiles tend to make a room top-heavy.

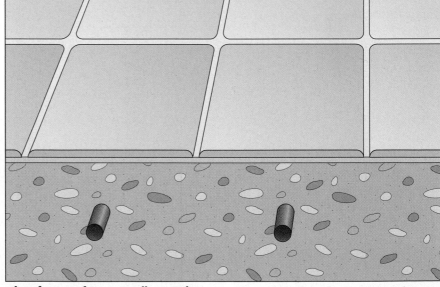

Plan for comfort as well as style.
Radiant heating systems in which heated water passes through tubing embedded in or under the floor surface are becoming increasingly popular. Tile is a great choice for the finish surface on a radiant floor. Because the tubing usually is embedded in concrete, the concrete pad can be used as an ideal setting bed for tile. Also tile is a highly conductive material that transmits heat quickly and efficiently. If you are tiling a new addition or need to improve heating in a room, consider incorporating a radiant heating system into the design.

EXPERTS' INSIGHT

DESIGNING WITH COLOR

With so many stunning tile colors readily available, it's tempting to wield a broad brush and let the color fly. But because today's fashionable color is often tomorrow's eyesore, white and almond tend to be the tones of choice for most homeowners. These light neutral tones help brighten up rooms and can coexist with almost any other colors as your decorating schemes change. But many people think too much white or off-white is monotonous. Accent and border colors often cancel out this impression. In rooms with plenty of windows, consider using darker tiles to offset the ambient lighting.

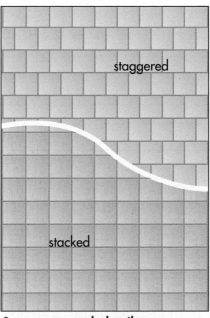

Stagger or stack the tile.

Area tiles usually are installed in a grid pattern or a staggered pattern. A stacked pattern is the easiest to install, and the clean straight lines appeal to many people. Although they require careful alignment, staggered joints have a pleasingly retro look.

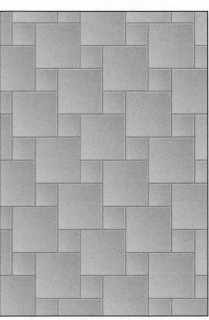

Make the most of one color.

Using only one color of tile does not have to result in a plain-looking installation. Use tiles of different sizes to add a level of contrast. Consider different grout colors and grout joint sizes. Or, use tiles with only small variations in color.

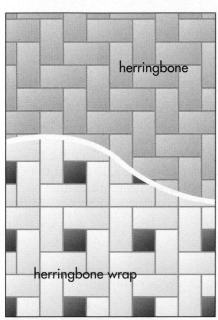

Consider herringbone.

Plain rectangular tiles gain a new dimension when installed in a herringbone pattern. As a variation, wrap a small square tile with rectangular tiles.

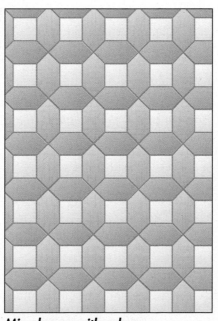

Mix shapes with colors.

Manufacturers offer tiles purposely sized to allow for mixing different shapes into a coherent whole. You can add further interest with this approach by using two or more colors as well.

Define your space.

Borders help define the perimeters of a tile installation and can add a whole new level of interest to the surface. Here, variously colored and sized tiles create a border surrounding a field of tiles installed diagonally.

SELECTING THE RIGHT TILE FOR THE JOB

Although simplicity is part of the universal appeal of ceramic tile (it is essentially a thin a slab of baked clay), don't assume that just any tile will suit your project. You'll have to consider several factors as you select the right tile for the job: The material from which the tile is made (ceramic tile is made from clay; some tiles do not use clay at all but are actually slabs of stone milled into regular shapes), the degree of firing, the type of glaze, and the shape of the tile.

If you are planning several tiling projects for your home, you may want to contact one of the associations created by tile manufacturers, designers, retailers, and installation contractors. These groups have developed standards and acceptable practices relating to tile and tile installations.

The American National Standards Institute (ANSI) has prepared a list of minimal standards that are followed by all professionals in the industry. The Tile Council of America (TCA) publishes the inexpensive annual *Handbook for Ceramic Tile Installation,* which sets forth the ANSI standards. Contact the TCA at P.O. Box 1787, Clemson, SC 29633 or at www.tileusa.com/publication_main.htm.

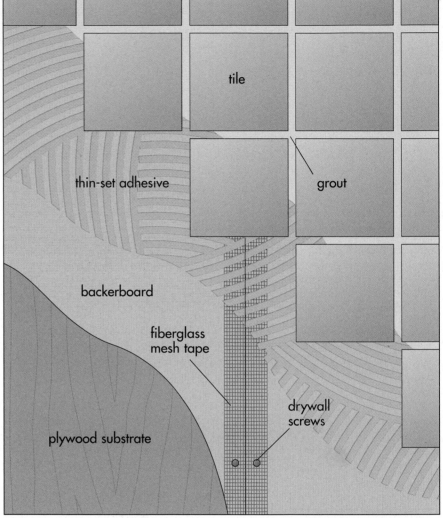

Plan out a typical installation. Installing tile is a bit like making a sandwich: You proceed one layer at a time. The substrate, often plywood, is the layer in direct contact with the framing (studs for a wall installation or joists for a floor installation). Backerboard serves as the setting bed for the tiles themselves. Tiles form the outer layer. Adhesive is used to bond each layer.

TILE INSTALLATION CHECKLIST

The ANSI standards cover proper materials and installations for just about any type of tile job you can imagine. Use this simple checklist as a design and shopping guide.

Type of Tile
- ☐ glazed wall tile
- ☐ glazed floor tile
- ☐ ceramic mosaic tile
- ☐ paver or quarry tile
- ☐ natural stone

Location of Installation
- ☐ always dry or limited water exposure
- ☐ frequently wet
- ☐ interior
- ☐ exterior
- ☐ subject to freezing

Special Requirements
- ☐ fire resistant
- ☐ stain resistant
- ☐ crack resistant
- ☐ color
- ☐ heavy use

WATER ABSORPTION

Clay absorbs water, and water can cause cracks in tiles and create damage beneath the surface. Ceramic tiles that have been kiln-dried longer and at higher temperatures absorb less water, but they also cost more. So it makes sense to choose tiles precisely rated for the protection you need.

Tile Rating	Best Uses
Nonvitreous	This tile typically is used for decorative purposes only. It is intended for use indoors, in dry locations, such as a fireplace surround or a decorative frieze in a dining room
Semivitreous	This type of tile is used indoors in dry to occasionally wet locations, such as a kitchen wall or behind a serving area in a dining room.
Vitreous	This multipurpose tile is used indoors or outdoors or in wet or dry locations for anything from bathroom floors or walls to a patio surface.
Impervious	Such tile generally is used only in hospitals, restaurants, and other commercial locations where the ability to thoroughly clean is important.

Choose a glaze.
A glaze is a protective and decorative coating, often colored, that is fired onto the surface of tiles. Glazes can be glossy, matte, or textured. Glazing is not related directly to the water-absorption categories listed above. Although glazing does keep moisture from penetrating the top surface, the unglazed sides and bottoms of the tile don't have the same protection.

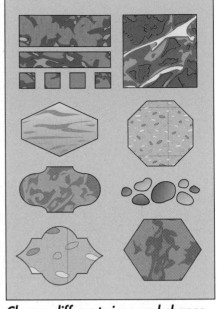

Select the type of ceramic tile.
Modern ceramic tile is made from refined clay, usually mixed with additives and water. It then is hardened in a kiln. Several different types of tile are created through that process. Quarry tiles are unglazed and vitreous tiles, usually ½ inch thick and used for flooring. Pavers are ⅜-inch-thick vitreous floor tiles and are available glazed or unglazed.

Choose different sizes and shapes.
Square tiles are the most common and the easiest to install. But rectangles, hexagons, and other shapes are readily available. An easy and inexpensive way to add interest to a tile installation is to mix shapes, sizes, and colors; tile retailers and home centers offer a wide range of options.

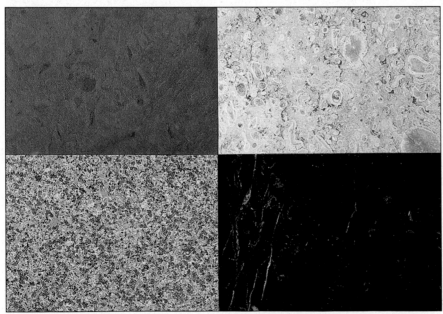

Consider stone tile.
Use natural stone tile on floors, walls, and countertops. Marble, granite, flagstone, and slate are widely available; other types of stone may be available in your area. Dimensioned (or gauged) stone is cut to a uniform size and thickness and can be installed much like ceramic tile. Hand-split (or cleft) stone tiles vary in size and thickness.

EXPERTS' INSIGHT

OTHER TILING CHOICES
Cement-bodied tiles are made with a concrete mix that is extruded or cast, then cured to form a strong, dense tile. They usually are stained to look like pavers, quarry tile, stone, or brick. Often you can buy them with a factory-applied sealer. Brick-veneer tile is made like ceramic tile, but with a coarser body that simulates brick. Terrazzo is manufactured with small pieces of granite or marble set in mortar, then polished. Precast terrazzo tiles are available for floors and walls.

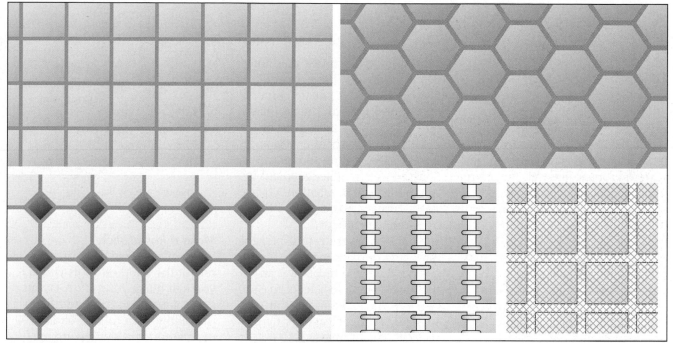

Use mosaic tile.
Mosaic tiles are 1- or 2-inch squares or similarly sized hexagons or pentagons mounted together as a larger unit. Most commercially available mosaics are vitreous and freeze-thaw stable and can be used on most tiling projects. Mosaic tiles are sold almost exclusively mounted on sheets or joined with adhesive strips. Back-mounted mosaic tiles are much easier to install than individual tiles. They can be mounted with standard thin-set adhesive and grout.

MEASUREMENTS

NOMINAL VS. ACTUAL SIZE

Most do-it-yourselfers learn quickly that when buying lumber, a 2×4 doesn't measure 2 inches by 4 inches. The tile trade has a similar discrepancy. Individual ceramic tiles are often sold with dimensional names that describe their installed size, that is, the size of the tile plus a standard grout joint. Thus, 6×6-inch tiles measure $\frac{1}{8}$ inch shorter in each direction. The actual size will be $5\frac{7}{8}\times5\frac{7}{8}$ inches. Only when installed with a $\frac{1}{8}$-inch grout joint will the installed size of the tile be about 6×6. Always check the actual size of the tiles before you buy them.

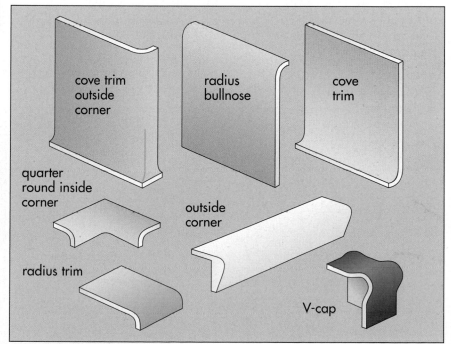

Determine the right trim tiles.
In general, tiles are divided into field tiles, which are flat, and trim tiles, which are shaped irregularly to turn corners or define the edges of an installation. There are dozens of trim-tile profiles, and the names of each can be confusing. When choosing tiles, be sure to check the availability of these specialty tiles and select a style with trim tiles suitable for your project.

SELECTING LAYOUT TOOLS

Layout involves little more than measuring and marking. The tools required are inexpensive hand tools. You probably own most, if not all, of them already.

For making scale drawings, **graph paper** is often the best material to use. You can buy graph paper with various sizes of grids; ¼ inch is the most common. Measure the area to be tiled and sketch it so each ¼-inch grid represents 1 linear foot. The only accessories you will need are a **ruler, pencil,** and **eraser.** Graph paper also comes in handy when sketching tile designs; just let each grid represent a tile.

An **architect's rule** can be used in place of graph paper. An architect's rule has three sides, with different scales marked along each edge. It allows you to quickly convert measured distances to scale, or to count the grids on graph paper. The trick is to choose a scale that will fit on the paper.

A **combination square** or a **framing square** can be used for measuring short distances and precisely marking square corners. You can get by with one or the other, but chances are that you will use both of them if they are available. A framing square can double as a straightedge to aid in layout and tile installation. Or use short, straight boards called layout sticks, shown at *right*.

A **tape measure** is indispensible for laying out and marking tiles for cutting. You also must have an accurate 2- or 4-foot **level** to check horizontal and vertical surfaces for plumb and to mark accurate layout lines.

An inexpensive **plumb bob** is necessary for finding plumb, and a **chalk line** allows you to quickly mark layout lines. Most chalk lines will perform double duty as plumb bobs. So that you'll be able to clearly see your mark, buy yellow chalk for dark tile and blue chalk for light-colored tile.

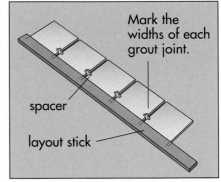

Mark the widths of each grout joint.

spacer

layout stick

Make a layout stick.
When tiling large, flat surfaces, one of the handiest tools is one you can make yourself. A layout stick is just a homemade ruler that allows you to lay out an installation without having to measure and mark for each tile location. Line up a row of tiles on a flat surface, with spacers between. Set a straight piece of pine alongside the tiles. Start at one end of the stick and mark the width of the grout joint between each tile. You will need a new layout stick if you change tiles or grout widths on a new installation.

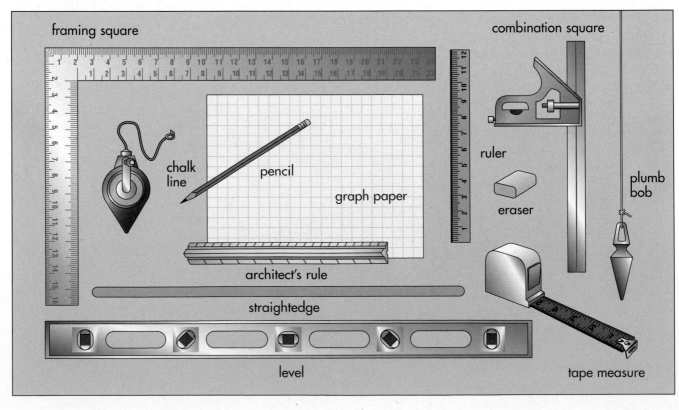

framing square

combination square

chalk line

pencil

graph paper

ruler

eraser

plumb bob

architect's rule

straightedge

level

tape measure

CHOOSING CUTTING TOOLS

One of the goals of setting tile is to lay out the job in a way that minimizes the need to cut tile. But at the very least you will need to cut tiles for corners and around fixtures.

Tile-cutting tools range from the slow and tedious to the fast and furious. Deciding on which tools you need is largely a matter of the size of your project and the number of cuts required.

A **snap cutter** is similar to a handheld glass cutter except that it is mounted on a guide bar. Various models operate differently, but all follow a basic two-step approach. First the tile is set in the cutter and scored along the snap line. Then the handle is pressed down to snap the tile along the line.

Tile nippers resemble pliers, but they are equipped with carbide-tipped edges. They are indispensable for making small notches and curves in tile. They can also be used for breaking off pieces of tile that have been scored with a snap cutter. Nippers usually leave a rough edge. Use a **rubbing stone** to smooth sharp edges. A **rod saw** is a strip of tungsten carbide that fits into a standard **hacksaw** body. It's a slow but handy way to cut tight curves. Another faster option for making small cuts is a power **diamond-tipped cutter.**

A **wet saw** is a power tool that quickly makes smooth, straight cuts in tile and other masonry. Wet saws are equipped with a pump that sprays water to cool the blade and remove chips. They are messy, but not particularly dangerous or difficult to use. If fact you might enjoy watching just how easily the blade cuts its way through a piece of tile, marble, or granite.

For drilling holes, use a **carbide-tipped hole saw** mounted on an **electric** or a **cordless power drill.**

> **CAUTION!**
> *DON'T BUY WHEN YOU CAN RENT*
> New home improvement projects offer the perfect excuse to add new tools to your collection. However, some tiling tools are so specialized that you won't use them again until your next tiling job. Too many tools can quickly destroy your project budget. Tool-rental stores offer a variety of tools, many specifically chosen for do-it-yourselfers needing special tools for a short period of time. For tiling projects, it's especially smart to rent power tools, such as a wet saw or a diamond-tipped cutter. Also, check with your tile supplier. Often the store will lend customers tools at no charge if the tiles were purchased there.

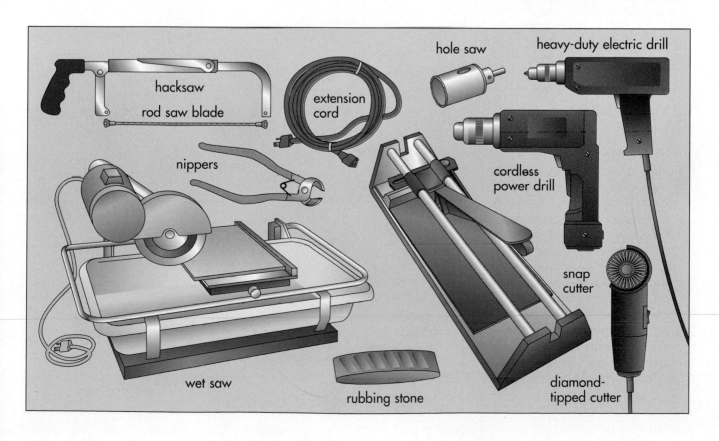

hacksaw
rod saw blade
extension cord
hole saw
heavy-duty electric drill
nippers
cordless power drill
snap cutter
wet saw
rubbing stone
diamond-tipped cutter

SELECTING INSTALLATION TOOLS

For mixing thin-set mortar and grout, you need a sturdy bucket. An empty, clean **drywall-compound bucket** will suffice for relatively small jobs, but a **mortar-mixing box** is better for larger jobs. A **mortar mixer** is a great time saver for mixing two or more gallons of thin-set mortar or grout. The mixer is mounted, like a drill bit, on an electric drill.

Notched trowels have two smooth sides for spreading adhesive and two notched sides for combing the adhesive to the right depth. Check the tile and adhesive manufacturers' recommendations for the proper notch size.

You'll need a **beating block** to press the tiles evenly into the adhesive. Use a piece of 2× lumber covered with terrycloth or buy a rubber-faced model. With Mexican pavers and other irregular tiles, use a **rubber mallet** instead.

A canvas **drop cloth** readily absorbs moisture and has enough heft to protect surfaces from dropped tiles. Use **masking tape** to cover plumbing fixtures.

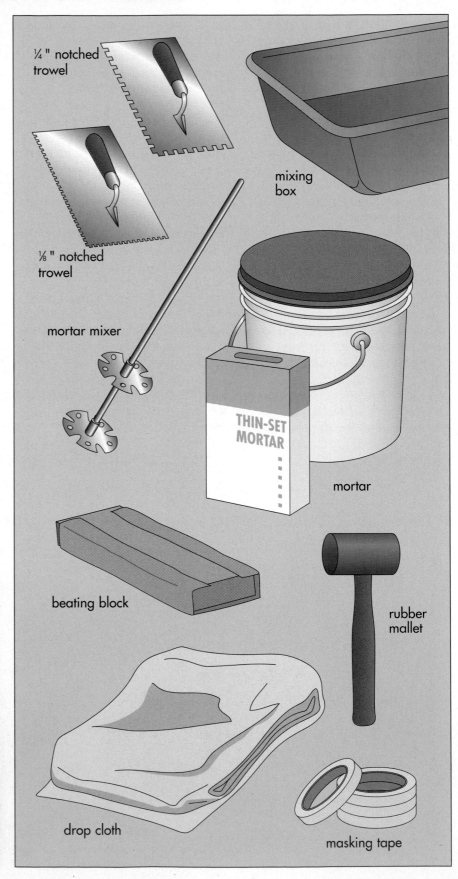

¼ " notched trowel

⅛ " notched trowel

mortar mixer

mixing box

THIN-SET MORTAR

mortar

beating block

rubber mallet

drop cloth

masking tape

CAUTION!

SAFETY EQUIPMENT

Installing tile is not a particularly dangerous project, especially if you exercise common sense and follow a few basic safety practices. When using power tools or cutting tile with hand tools, protect your eyes with safety goggles. Plug power tools into an outlet or extension cord equipped with a ground-fault circuit interrupter (GFCI). When mixing and handling adhesive and grout, wear a charcoal-filter mask and rubber gloves.

CHOOSING GROUTING TOOLS

Many of the tools used for applying thin-set mortar also can be used for spreading grout. A **grouting float** is a rubber-backed trowel used for pressing the grout into the joints. It also removes excess grout from the tiling surface, although a **squeegee** may be more thorough. A **mason's trowel** is handy for finishing grout joints, although you also can use a **putty knife** or the handle of an **old toothbrush.** A **margin trowel** is used to mix small batches and for scooping adhesive or grout onto the setting surface. A **grout bag** is useful when you need to force grout into joints that can't be reached easily with a grout float.

Good-quality **sponges** are best for cleaning grout off the tile surface. Look for sponges made especially for tiling work. Use **cheesecloth** to remove the haze left on the tile after the grout has set for a while. For applying caulk and sealant around edges, you will need a **caulking gun.**

EXPERTS' INSIGHT

DRESS FOR SUCCESS
Tile setting is a messy business, so wear clothes that you won't mind ruining. When working with adhesive or grout, wear short sleeves because long or baggy sleeves tend to fall into the muddy mix. Protect your hands with rubber gloves when using any product with concrete. When you are installing a tile floor, wear knee pads. They cushion your knees and protect them from sharp objects.

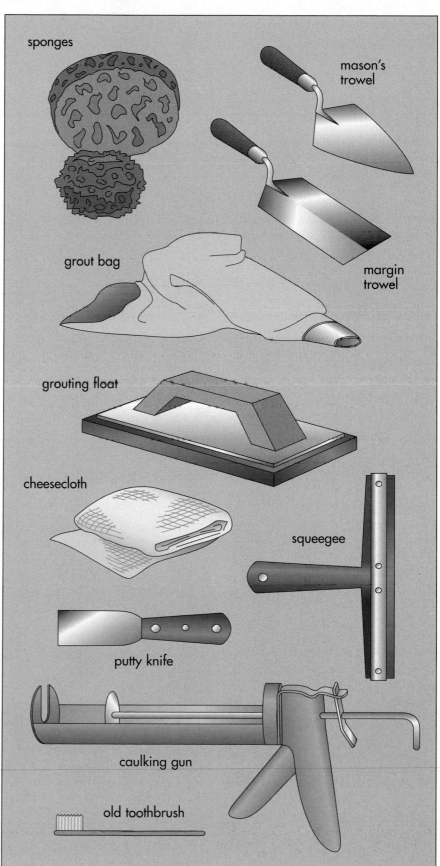

sponges

mason's trowel

margin trowel

grout bag

grouting float

cheesecloth

squeegee

putty knife

caulking gun

old toothbrush

USING TILE SPACERS

The space between tiles serves two important functions: It provides room for the grout essential to any tile job, and it allows for some creativity in your design. You can change the look of a finished tile installation significantly by changing the width of the grout joint or by altering the color of the grout.

Tile spacers are small pieces of plastic used to ensure consistent width of the grout joints. They come in a variety of sizes and shapes to match different types of tile and tile installations. Many types of ceramic tile today are self-spacing, that is, they have small lugs along their sides that ensure proper spacing. If you use self-spacing tiles, you need not use tile spacers unless you prefer a wider grout joint than the lugs allow.

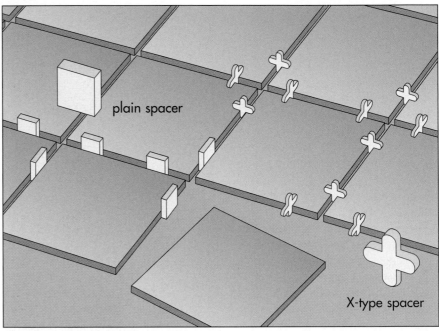

Purchase manufactured spacers.
Buy plastic tile spacers from your tile supplier. They are available in sizes from 1/16 inch to 1/2 inch. X-shaped spacers are the most common. They are placed at each corner. Though less common, plain spacers often are preferred for spacing and holding wall tiles firmly in place.

CAUTION!
REMOVE SPACERS
Spacers should be left in place until the adhesive has set enough to prevent the tiles from slipping out of alignment. They should then be removed—even if the package they came in says otherwise. If spacers are left in place, they prevent grout from completely filling the joints and can result in a weak installation. If the spacers are difficult to remove, use needle-nose pliers to form a hook from a length of clothes hanger wire. Then use the hook to pry out the spacers.

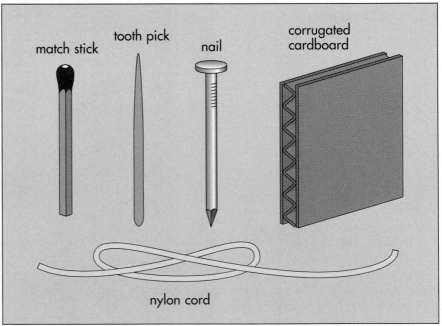

Make your own spacers.
Plastic spacers are one of the least expensive materials used for tile installation. But for a small job or in a pinch, you may use an alternative. Look for objects that have a consistent size, such as wooden matchsticks, toothpicks, or nails. Nylon cord can be used over a long run. Remember to remove the spacers before grouting.

SELECTING ADHESIVES

The setting adhesive bonds the bottom of the tile with the setting bed. Recent improvements in setting adhesives make it easy for do-it-yourselfers to set tile with professional results. Although adhesives fall into the broad categories of organic mastic and thin-set mortar, in reality there are many types of products and manufacturers. The first step in choosing an adhesive is to determine what kind of installation you are doing (wet or dry? indoor or outdoor? floor or wall?) and to what substrate the tile will be applied.

Organic mastics are popular because they require no mixing. However, they are not suitable for areas exposed to heat or for exterior installations. Thin-set mortars usually are mixed by the installer. A variety of thin-set additives are available to create an adhesive best suited to specific installations. The chart below offers general guidelines.

Buy ready-mixed organic mastic.
Organic mastic is a premixed adhesive that is easy to use. It is especially popular for use on walls because tiles will not slip when set in place.

Mix your own thin-set mortar.
Thin-set mortar requires more work than does organic mastic, but offers superior bonding strength and flexibility.

CHOOSING THIN-SET MORTARS

Type	Description and Uses
Water-mixed mortar	Also referred to as *dry-set mortar,* this is a blend of Portland cement, sand, and additives. Mix with water.
Latex- and acrylic-mixed mortar	Also referred to as *latex mortar,* this mortar is similar to water-mixed mortar, but has latex or acrylic added to it. The additives improve adhesion and reduce water absorption; they may be premixed with the mortar in dry form or added as a liquid by the installer. It's an excellent choice for wet and dry installations.
Epoxy mortar	This is a mixture of sand, cement, and liquid resins and hardeners. It's costly, but effective with any setting material and is good choice when the substrate is incompatible with other adhesives.
Medium-bed mortar	This adhesive remains stronger than regular thin-set mortar when applied in layers of more than $1/4$ inch. It's useful with tiles that do not have uniform backs, such as handmade tiles.

CHOOSING SETTING BEDS

A tile installation is only as good as the surface to which it is applied. Investing in adequate materials for the setting bed is as important as buying the right tile for your project. Tiled floors, in particular, require an extremely stiff setting bed; any imperfection in the subfloor can crack tiles and ruin your project.

You may be able to set the tile over an existing subfloor or wall surface, or you may want to add a layer or two of setting material to ensure a stiff and durable installation. The introduction of cement-based and gypsum-based backerboard has dramatically simplified tile installations without compromising strength and durability. Previously tile was applied over thick beds of mortar, almost exclusively by trained professionals. The process was time consuming and required skill and experience.

EXPERTS' INSIGHT

MORTAR-BED INSTALLATIONS

Modern thin-set mortars are typically applied in a layer only ⅛ to ¼ inch thick; that's how they get their name. Traditional (mudset) tile installations use thick mortar as the setting bed. Mortar, with wire-mesh reinforcement, is poured over tar paper to a thickness of 1 to 2 inches. Then the tiles are set on the mortar before it cures. Mortar-bed installations are strong and particularly useful on shower floors.

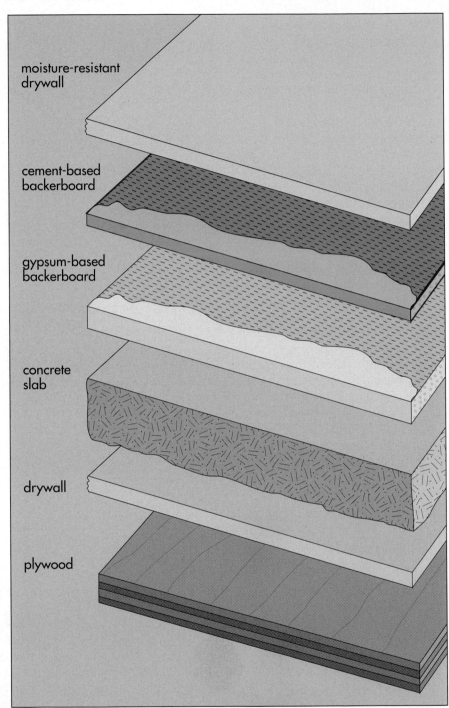

Choose a setting bed.

Backerboard often is called cement board, although some products contain no cement. Sold in varying thicknesses and sizes, backerboard is easy to install and provides a ready-made surface for setting tile. Cement-based backerboard has a mesh coat and is cut using a carbide-tipped scoring tool.

Gypsum-based backerboard can be cut with a utility knife.

Concrete slabs (old or newly poured) are ideal setting beds for tile floors. With suitable adhesives, tile can be installed over plywood. A double layer of drywall (regular or moisture-resistant) is a suitable setting bed only in dry areas.

SELECTING GROUT

Grout is a mortar used to fill the joints between tiles. It stiffens the tile installation and helps prevent moisture from penetrating the joint. Grout usually is sold with all of the dry ingredients mixed together; the installer adds the liquid. It also is available in caulking-gun tubes with all of the wet and dry ingredients already mixed and ready for application.

Grout not only seal joints, it plays an important role in the overall design. The width and color of the grout joint can radically alter the finished look of a tile installation. Choose a grout color to complement, match, or contrast with the tile. Increase or decrease the joint size to provide the most appropriate balance for that size room.

CHOOSING GROUT

Type	Description and Uses
Plain grout	Also referred to as unsanded grout, this is a mixture of Portland cement and additives chosen to achieve specific characteristics. It is used for grout joints of $\frac{1}{16}$ inch or less. It's also recommended for absorptive tile and marble.
Sanded grout	This is similar to plain grout but has sand added. It is used for grout joints greater than $\frac{1}{16}$ inch. The ratio between sand and cement varies, depending on the size of the joint.
Epoxy grout	This grout contains epoxy resin and hardener. It's used when chemical and stain resistance are required or where high temperatures are likely.
Colored grout	Offered in premixed packages in a wide assortment of colors and formulations, you can usually find a colored grout to match any need and fill any typical grout joint. Natural grout can be used if you prefer the look of cement.
Mortar	This is similar to sanded grout, but is used for joints between brick pavers, slate, or other masonry materials.
Premixed grout	Some grouts are available premixed and ready to use out of the container. Choices are smaller, and the cost is high, but it may be a good choice for small jobs.

Know your grout.
Grout and tile are the two visible materials on a tiled surface. A good tile installation requires a good grouting job. Use the best ingredients, mix them right, and apply the grout so it completely fills the joints between tiles. Although tile is completely inflexible, you can achieve some flexibility in the grout joints by adding latex or acrylic additives to the grout. Additives also can increase water and stain resistance. When grout joints begin to fail, they should be repaired immediately or water damage could occur behind the tile.

SELECTING MEMBRANES

In addition to backerboard or other setting bed materials (page 576), some installations call for use of a membrane. The two types are waterproofing membranes and isolation membranes.

Waterproofing membranes are used to prevent moisture from penetrating through the surface (usually the grout joint). If water will often sit on your floor tiles, or if your wall tiles will be in a room that often becomes very humid, moisture can seep through grout or unglazed tiles and cause serious damage to the substrate and even the structural wood. A sealer (page 579) may solve the problem for wall tiles, but floor tiles that will get soaked need a membrane.

Tar paper (that is, felt paper saturated with tar) has long been the standard waterproofing membrane. Polyethylene sheeting is another inexpensive option. The most effective waterproofing membrane is chlorinated

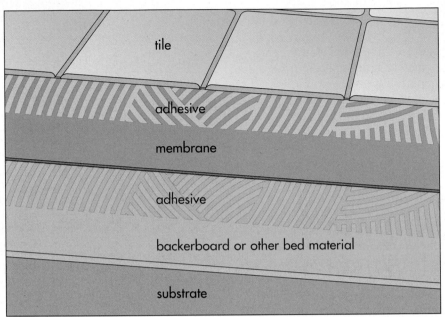

polyethylene (CPE), a strong and thick sheet that is joined to the substrate with adhesive. Liquid membranes are applied with trowel or brush.

The function of an isolation membrane is to protect the tiled surface from damage due to

movement in the underlying surface. Use one when you tile over an existing floor that shows signs of movement from seasonal changes or settling of the house. Chlorinated polyethylene sheets are often used as isolation membranes.

Tar paper waterproofing.
Tar paper is an inexpensive and easy-to-install membrane. It is sold in rolls of varying widths and lengths and can be stapled or nailed to studs or drywall.

CPE waterproofing.
Chlorinated polyethylene is a durable and flexible product that offers the best water resistance of any available membrane. It is particularly effective on floors that will be wet on a regular basis.

Liquid waterproofing.
Single-component liquid membranes are spread on the setting bed. Once cured, they form a reasonably waterproof layer. Multicomponent membranes require liquid and fabric installed in layers.

CHOOSING CAULK AND SEALERS

Tiles may last centuries, but a tile installation has no chance of reaching such a ripe age unless it is maintained regularly. Some components of the installation need to be replaced or renewed every few years. *Caulk* refers to a variety of flexible products used to fill joints that should not be grouted for one reason or another. *Sealers* are protective coatings applied over the entire tiled surface or all the grout lines; they prevent staining and protect tile and grout from water infiltration.

The best choice for a long-lasting, mildew-free joint in high-moisture installations is silicone caulk. Latex caulk is not suitable for tile jobs. Use siliconized acrylic caulk in areas exposed to only minimal moisture. Tub-and-tile caulk contains a mildewcide, but it is not always effective.

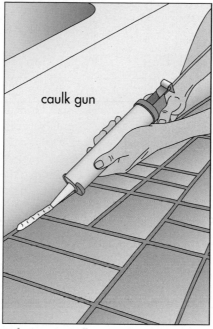

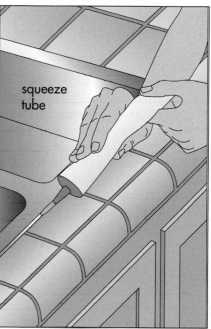

Where to caulk.
Use caulk instead of grout in expansion joints (see box below), between dissimilar materials, and around penetrations in the tiled surface such as between tiles and a sink. Like grout, caulk is available in sanded and plain formulations, and in colors that match the grout. Caulk tubes used with a caulk gun are the easiest to use. Buy a squeeze tube for small jobs.

TILE AND GROUT SEALERS

Sealers are used on unglazed tile and stone products. They are also applied to grout. *Penetrating sealers* are intended to be absorbed beneath the surface of the tile and grout. They reduce the absorbency of the surface without necessarily adding a sheen. *Coating sealers* are formulated to remain on the surface, where they generally add a glossy or semiglossy sheen. Use a *grout sealer* on a wall with glazed tile. It will keep your grout watertight and make it easier to clean. Usually, you must wait two weeks after tile installation before applying grout sealer.

EXPERTS' INSIGHT

EXPANSION JOINTS

■ Tile and grout generally don't expand and contract with seasonal and temperature changes, but the materials beneath and around them may. Expansion joints are safety features that anticipate that movement and prevent the tile and grout from being damaged by it. On most installations, expansion joints are intended to look like grout joints, but they are filled with a flexible material such as silicone caulk.

■ Use expansion joints around the perimeters of all tile installations, especially where the tile edges meet a different material. Use them where floors meet walls, countertops meet backsplashes, and where tile meets wood or another material. Any runs of tile on a floor that exceed 24 feet must be interrupted with an expansion joint.

■ The most typical method of creating an expansion gap is to leave a ¼-inch joint between the tile and the adjoining surface, then fill the joint with caulk. The setting bed should also be designed with expansion joints.

ASSESSING SUBSTRATES

The *substrate* of a floor or wall includes the setting bed (page 576) and any other layers beneath the tile surface. Even if tile adheres firmly to its setting bed, it won't last long if that setting bed isn't part of a completely sound and sturdy substrate.

The structural needs of your substrate may change when you add a new type of surface. For example, if you are planning to install ceramic tile on a floor that currently is covered with resilient sheet flooring, you will be adding a lot of weight to the underlying framing. If you doubt that the joists and subfloor are strong enough, consult a professional.

A quick way to tell if a floor is firm enough to handle ceramic tile: Jump on it. If it feels springy, there's a good chance that your tiles or grout lines will crack in time. Add a layer of plywood or backerboard to strengthen it, or consult a professional.

Walls should be firm to the touch. New tiles will not add significant strength.

SUBSTRATE RECOMMENDATIONS

Substrate	Preparation
Exposed joists	■ Verify that the framing will support the new floor. ■ Install ¾-inch CDX plywood. ■ Install backerboard or underlayment-grade plywood.
Concrete slab	■ Repair cracks or low spots in the concrete. ■ Ensure that the slab is flat, clean, and dry. ■ Roughen the surface to improve adhesion.
Finished floor	■ Verify that the framing will support the new floor. ■ If necessary, remove the finish flooring. ■ Install backerboard or underlayment-grade plywood over suitable subfloor, or over the old finish flooring.
Wall paneling	■ Remove thin sheet paneling. ■ Install backerboard, plywood, or drywall.
Drywall	■ Scrape away any loose paint and roughen the surface with sandpaper. ■ Clean the surface or apply deglosser. ■ Add a second layer of drywall for added strength.
Masonry or plaster walls	■ Repair cracks and level indentations. ■ Ensure that the surface is sound, not soft and crumbling or springy when pressed. ■ Clean the surface or apply deglosser.

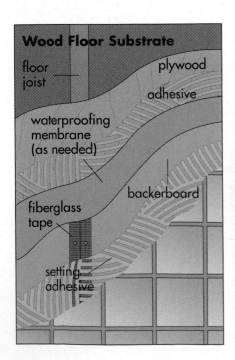

Wood Floor Substrate

floor joist
plywood
adhesive
waterproofing membrane (as needed)
backerboard
fiberglass tape
setting adhesive

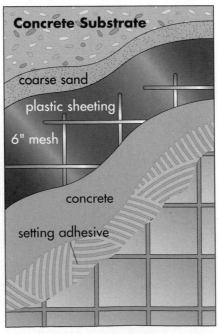

Concrete Substrate

coarse sand
plastic sheeting
6" mesh
concrete
setting adhesive

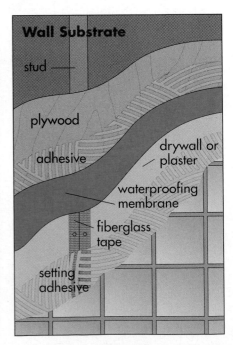

Wall Substrate

stud
plywood
adhesive
drywall or plaster
waterproofing membrane
fiberglass tape
setting adhesive

CALCULATING MATERIALS

Before you go shopping for tile and setting materials, determine how much of each material you need. Fortunately that doesn't mean that you have to count every last tile you intend to install. Tiling materials are usually sold by the square foot, so for most jobs, all you have to do is measure the surface to be tiled, then take that number to the store with you.

Buy more tile than you plan to use. Expect to break a few tiles, and to need a few more than anticipated. It's handy to have a few extra tiles should you need any replacements someday. So get an extra 5 to 10 percent more than your estimate.

Where to Buy

Tile and setting materials are widely available. Small lumber yards and hardware stores may carry a limited selection, while home centers and tile outlets offer a much wider choice. It pays to shop around, because prices and selection can vary significantly. Of course you should shop for a good price, but also look for a retailer who is knowledgeable and willing to answer questions. A little good advice might save you plenty of time and money. Be sure to ask about the store's policy on returns. In the event that you buy considerably more than you need, you should be able to return unopened boxes and packages for a refund.

Metrics

Tiles are manufactured and sold all over the world. So the tiles you choose may have been manufactured to a metric size, which was then rounded off to inches. So, for example, you may have a "13-inch" Italian tile that actually measures $13^3/_{16}$ inches.

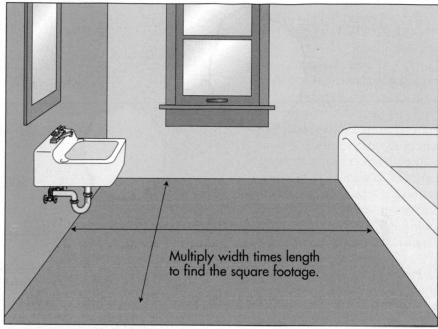

Multiply width times length to find the square footage.

Determine square footage.
If you are tiling a single rectangular surface, simply measure the width and the length (in feet), and multiply the two numbers to determine the square footage. For multiple surfaces, calculate each one separately, then add the results. When a door or a window interferes, include it in your initial calculation, then find the square footage of the obstruction and subtract it from the overall total.

If you will be installing large, expensive tiles, make a drawing of your space, with exact dimensions, and bring it to your dealer, who can help you to determine the most economical layout.

ESTIMATING GROUT AND ADHESIVES

The amount of grout you need depends on the size of the tiles and on the width and depth of the grout joint. Packages of grout often include tables for estimating the amount needed. This chart gives you a rough idea of how many square feet can be covered with one pound of grout. The figures should be treated only as estimates, but they do show how much the coverage changes depending on tile size.

Tile Size	Joint Width	Coverage per Pound of Grout
2"×2"×$^1/_4$"	$^1/_{16}$"	24 square feet
$4^1/_4$"×$4^1/_4$"×$^5/_{16}$"	$^1/_{16}$"	16 square feet
$4^1/_4$"×$4^1/_4$"×$^5/_{16}$"	$^1/_8$"	8 square feet
6"×6"×$^1/_4$"	$^1/_{16}$"	28 square feet
6"×6"×$^1/_4$"	$^1/_8$"	14 square feet
12"×12"×$^3/_8$"	$^1/_{16}$"	37 square feet

When applied with the trowel notch size recommended by the manufacturer, one gallon of adhesive will cover 30 to 50 square feet of wall and 20 to 40 square feet of floor.

PREPARING THE SITE

When tiling floors or installing wall tiles down to the floor line, remove baseboard trim. If the baseboard is trimmed with shoe molding (a thin rounded strip attached to the floor), you probably need only remove the shoe, leaving the baseboard in place, in order to tile the floor. If you plan to reuse the trim, take care not to damage it as you remove it. Insert a thin pry bar or stiff putty knife to lift the shoe or pull the baseboard from the wall. Gradually work your way along the molding until it comes off. Write numbers on the backs of the pieces to help you remember where they go. Remove as many obstacles as possible so you will not have to make many precise tile cuts. When preparing to tile a floor, set a tile on the floor and use it as a guide for cutting the bottoms of casing molding.

If you are tiling a bathroom, remember that removing and replacing a toilet is easier than tiling around it, and will lead to a much cleaner-looking job. (Be sure to stuff a rag in the soil pipe to prevent sewer gas from backing up

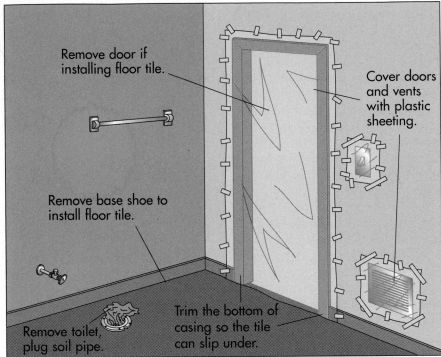

Remove door if installing floor tile.

Cover doors and vents with plastic sheeting.

Remove base shoe to install floor tile.

Remove toilet, plug soil pipe.

Trim the bottom of casing so the tile can slip under.

into the bathroom.) You may want to remove the vanity as well as doors. (You may also need to trim the doors after the tile is installed.)

When preparing to tile walls, remove electrical outlet covers (the outlet box may have to be adjusted before replacing the covers), and fixtures. Sinks and appliances may have to be

removed, depending on your installation. Because the tiles add thickness to the wall, it is usually best to leave window and door casings in place. Keep dust and odors from spreading throughout the house by taping plastic sheeting over doorways. Cover vents with plastic as well.

PREPARING SURFACES TO BE TILED

Floors
■ Remove the original flooring, if it is not firmly stuck to the sub-floor, if it is uneven, or if the thin-set mortar will not adhere to it.
■ Make sure that the subfloor is at least $1\frac{1}{8}$ inch thick and composed of suitable materials (usually a combination of plywood, backerboard, or concrete).
■ If a plywood floor seems loose in spots, drive nails or screws through it into floor joists.
■ Fill low spots in the subfloor, then smooth the surface and clean it thoroughly.

Walls
■ Remove wallpaper, thin panel-ing, or anything else that flexes when you press it.
■ When tiling over new drywall, don't bother taping the joints but do seal the surface with a thin coat of adhesive applied with the flat side of a trowel.
■ Scrape away loose paint.
■ Lightly sand glossy surfaces to remove the sheen.
■ Patch holes and cracks, and sand smooth.
■ Thoroughly clean the wall and allow it to dry.

Countertops
■ Remove sink or faucets, and other obstacles.
■ Remove old tile if it exists.
■ To tile over a square-edged lam-inated countertop that is sound, give it a thorough sanding and remove the backsplash.
■ If you have a post-form coun-tertop with curved edges, remove it and install a new substrate of plywood and backerboard.
■ Make sure the substrate is thick enough for trim pieces and that the trim won't prevent drawers from opening.

LAYING OUT THE JOB

Tile looks best when it is set in a straight line and at least appears to be square and level with adjacent surfaces. Laying out the installation is the most important step for ensuring such an outcome. Tile is an unforgiving material, and floors and walls are rarely as square and level as you might think—or hope. One of the secrets to a successful layout, therefore, is learning how to fudge the installation so the fudging isn't apparent. The other secret is to plan for as few cut tiles as possible. Adjust the layout to minimize cuts and hide those cut tiles along less conspicuous walls and under baseboard trim. Don't be surprised if your house exceeds some of the tolerances recommended here. Tile setters have had to deal with such irregularities for centuries, and cures are plentiful.

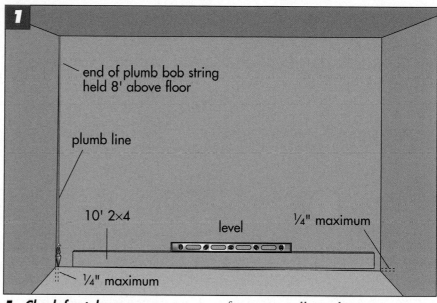

end of plumb bob string held 8' above floor

plumb line

10' 2×4

level

¼" maximum

¼" maximum

1. Check for tolerances.
Check tiling surfaces for square, level, and plumb using the techniques shown below. If a surface is out of alignment in excess of the amounts shown above, the best solution is to change the surfaces—for instance, fur out a wall, or shim up a subfloor. If this is not feasible, make the unevenness less visible by avoiding narrow tile pieces at the corner. You might be able to split the difference, making two edges slightly out of line instead of having one edge that is way off.

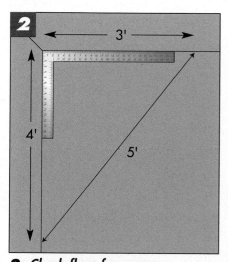

3'

4'

5'

2. Check floor for square.
For small rooms, check the squareness of the floor by setting a framing square at inside and outside corners. For larger rooms, use the 3-4-5 method: Measure along one wall exactly three feet from the corner, and along the other wall four feet. If the distance between those points is exactly five feet, the floor is square.

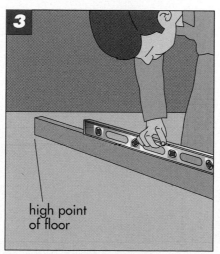

high point of floor

3. Check floor for level.
Use a 2- or 4-foot level to check along each wall. To check for level over a longer span, place the level on the edge of a straight 6- or 8-foot board. If the floor is only slightly out of level, and you are not planning to run tile up the wall, this should not affect your installation.

Bubble indicates level.

4. Check walls for plumb.
Place a level vertically on the wall at various spots, or use a plumb bob. Set the level horizontally on the wall to see how flat it is (you can also stretch a string tightly along the wall). A wavy wall, even if it is plumb, should be corrected before tiling.

EXPERTS' INSIGHT

PLANNING FOR FOCAL POINTS

When you walk into a room for the first time, chances are there is something there that catches your eye immediately. As you stand in the room, other areas may become more noticeable. It might be another doorway, a fireplace, a window, counters, or appliance groupings. Plan your layout so that the installation looks best in these focal areas. For example, cut tiles placed around a sink should all be of equal size. If your floor is out of square so that you must have a line of cut tiles that grow progressively smaller, plan so it will be behind a couch or in an area that is not a focal point. Use perpendicular lines and full tiles at focal points.

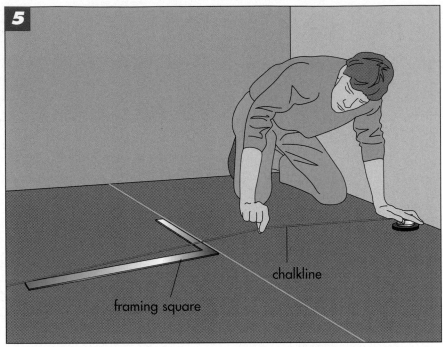

chalkline

framing square

5. Establish reference lines.
Accurate reference lines are critical to the success of a tile installation. Trace around a piece of plywood with two factory edges, or chalk two lines that are perfectly perpendicular. You will place the first tile at the intersection; this tile establishes the alignment and position of the rest of the tiles. (For instructions on your specific tiling project and more information on how to plot reference lines see pages 609, 615, and 618.)

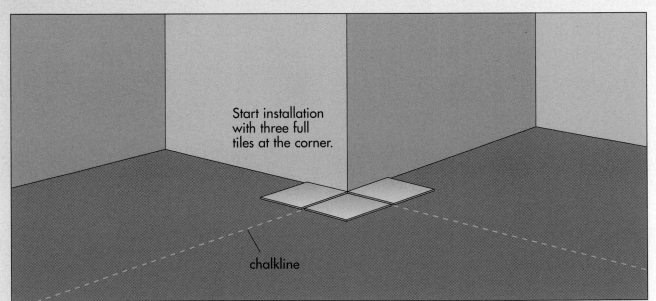

Start installation with three full tiles at the corner.

chalkline

Laying out an L-shaped room.
Often, the outside corner of an L-shaped room will be a focal point, so start there. Here's the simplest way to lay it out: From the corner, extend two straight lines along the floor to the opposing wall. Plan to set three full tiles at the corner, then extend the layout. This will not work, however, if the outside corner is seriously out of square. Also if this method results in very small pieces along a wall, it may be best to modify it.

6.

6. Do a dry run.
With reference lines drawn, you can measure from the lines to the walls and calculate how the tiles will be arranged. However, the safest method is to set tiles in place along the reference lines.

For this dry run, don't use any adhesive, but be sure to space the tiles properly. Take your time, and find out how each edge will look. Don't hesitate to change the entire layout if it will make for a more attractive appearance.

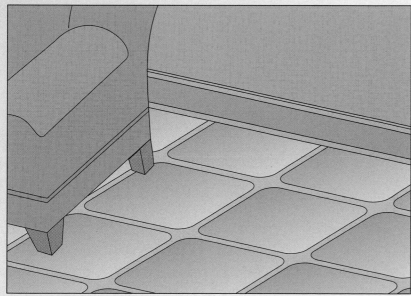

Hiding cut tiles.
One big advantage of a careful and thorough layout is that you can plan where cut tiles will go. A simple rule of thumb is to place cut tiles in the least visible areas. On a floor installation, for example, one wall may be largely covered with furniture. If you place cut tiles under or behind the furniture, they are not likely to be seen. On other installations, you may prefer to adjust the layout so that it has evenly sized cut tiles along the opposite edges.

CUTTING WITH A CIRCULAR SAW

Whether crosscutting 2×4s, ripping plywood, or cutting tiles or bricks with a masonry blade, you'll do the job better if you follow a few basic rules for using a circular saw.

Whenever you cut, allow the saw to reach full operating speed, then slowly push the blade into the wood. Some carpenters look at the blade as they cut; others rely on the gunsight notch. Choose the method that suits you best. Avoid making slight turns as you cut. Instead, find the right path, and push the saw through the material smoothly. It will take some practice before you can do this consistently. This is a powerful tool with sharp teeth, so take care; it demands your respect. Support the material to avoid having the saw bind and possibly kick back at you. Don't wear looose sleeves or position your face near the blade.

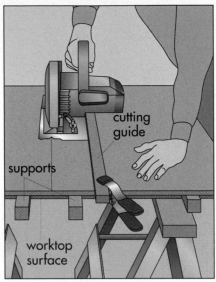

Support the material properly.
A well-supported board results in clean, safe cuts. If the scrap piece is short, support the board on the nonscrap side. If the scrap is long, it could bind the blade or splinter as it falls away at the end of the cut, so support it in four places.

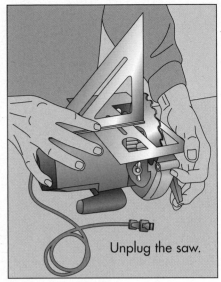

Square the blade.
Turn the saw upside-down, hold a square against the blade, and adjust it. (Be sure to position the square between the teeth.) Cut some scrap pieces and check to make sure the saw cuts squarely through the thickness of the board.

TOOLS TO USE

CIRCULAR SAW AND BLADES

■ Choose a circular saw that is comfortable. It should have some heft, but should not be so heavy that it is difficult to maneuver. You should be able to see the blade and gunsight notch easily. Check for ease of depth and angle adjustments.

■ If you buy only one blade for cutting lumber and plywood, chose a carbide-tipped combination blade that has at least 24 teeth. It works well for rough work and makes cuts clean enough for most finish work. For more specialized uses, buy a plywood blade, a finishing blade, or a masonry blade.

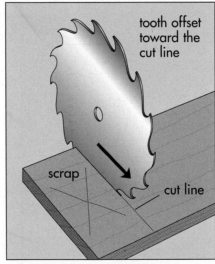

Align the blade with the cut line.
Once you have drawn an accurate cutoff line and have properly supported the board, position the saw blade on the scrap side of the line. The teeth on most blades are offset in an alternating pattern. When preparing to cut, look at a tooth that points toward the cutoff line.

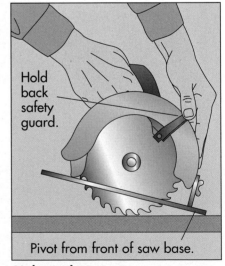

Make a plunge cut.
Use a plunge cut, also called a pocket cut, to make a hole or slit in the middle of a board or sheet. Set the blade to the correct depth. Retract the safety guard and tilt the saw forward, setting the front of the baseplate on the stock. Start the saw and lower it slowly into the cut line until the base rests on the stock. Complete the cut.

DRILLING

An electric drill enables you not only to drill a hole of about any size with ease, but also to drive screws into wood or metal, buff and grind, and even mix mortar or paint.

Experts keep two drills on hand—one for drilling pilot holes and the other for driving screws. That way, they don't waste time changing bits. A drill with a keyless chuck speeds up a bit change, although you may find bits slip during heavy-duty tasks.

In addition to the bits shown at right, purchase a magnetic sleeve that holds inexpensive screwdriver bits. This simple tool will make driving screws nearly as easy as pounding nails.

EXPERTS' INSIGHT

CHOOSING A DRILL

■ Avoid buying a cheap drill with a ¼-inch chuck. It will not have the power you need and will soon burn out. A good drill will be variable-speed and reversing (VSR), will have a ³⁄₈-inch chuck, and will pull at least 3 amps. One tipoff to a better-quality tool is the cord. Look for a long cord that flexes more like rubber than plastic.

■ Choose a heavy-duty, ½-inch drill if you will be using it to mix mortar. A smaller drill can burn out quickly while churning this thick substance.

■ A cordless drill can make your work go more easily, but only if it is powerful enough to do most things that a corded drill can do.

■ A hammer drill is useful if you need to drill a number of holes in concrete.

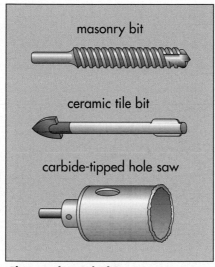

Choose the right bit.
Use standard twist or spade bits for boring through wood. A carbide-tipped masonry bit drills through concrete or brick. Use a carbide-tipped hole saw for larger holes. A ceramic tile bit will make a hole in tile without cracking it.

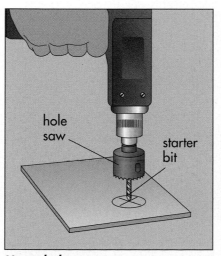

Use a hole saw.
Cutting a hole in the middle of a tile is easy to do with a carbide-tipped hole saw. Measure to the center of the hole (you will need to make two measurements), and place the tile on a flat surface that you don't mind damaging. Nick the center point to keep the starter bit from wandering. Keep the drill perpendicular in both directions as you drill, and don't press too hard.

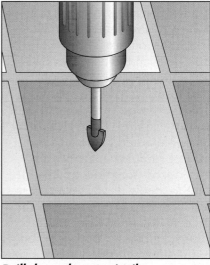

Drill through ceramic tile.
Wall tiles are usually soft, but floor tiles can be very tough. Nick the surface of the tile just enough so the bit will not wander as you drill. Keep the bit and the hole lubricated with a few drops of oil. Use a masonry bit or ceramic tile bit like the one shown above.

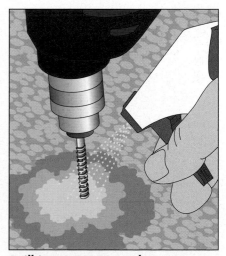

Drill into masonry and concrete.
Use a masonry bit when drilling masonry surfaces. Usually brick is easy to drill into and concrete is more difficult. Check the bit often to make sure it's not overheating. Stop if you see smoke. Spraying the bit with window cleaner as you work keeps the bit cool, and the foaming action brings debris up and out of the hole.

CUTTING BACKERBOARD

Backerboard usually has to be cut to size before it can be installed. You may also have to drill holes in the board so that it will slide into place. If you have ever installed drywall, you will find the score-and-snap method to be very familiar. There are several types of backerboard on the market, and new materials are introduced from time to time. Be sure to follow the manufacturer's instructions if they vary from the process described here. You can cut backerboard with power tools, but it will be messier, not any faster, and may damage your blade or motor.

YOU'LL NEED

SKILLS: Measuring, cutting.
TIME: Each cut requires no more than 5 to 10 minutes.
TOOLS: Drywall square or straightedge, utility knife or scoring tool, and rubbing stone.

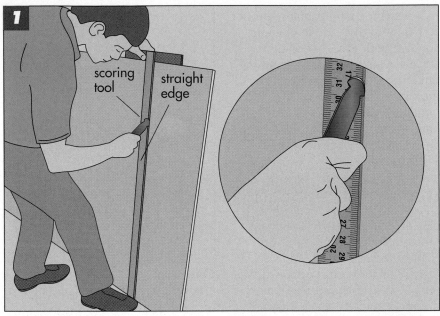

1. Score the board.
For cement-based board, measure carefully and mark cut off lines on both sides of the backerboard. Align a straight edge with the line on one side. Pull the scoring tool along the straight edge; make as many passes as are necessary to break through the mesh on the surface. Place the straight edge on the other side and repeat the process. The mesh must be completely severed on each side. (A faster but somewhat riskier method: Proceed as you would for drywall, cutting one side, snapping the cut edge over, then cutting the other side.)

2. Snap.
Place the backerboard on a flat surface. Press down with your hand on one side of the cut line. With the other hand, lift up just enough to snap the board along the scored edges. Some types of backerboard may break easier if you elevate the board on one side of scoring line, then press down.

3. Smooth edges.
Be careful when handling the cut board. Some types of backerboard may leave a sharp edge along the cut line. The best way to smooth the edge is to use a rubbing stone.

TOOLS TO USE

A HOLE SAW
Cement-based backerboard is often used under tiled surfaces in wet areas. That means you may have to fit it over plumbing protrusions in the wall, countertop, or floor. Most holes can be drilled quickly and effectively using a power drill equipped with a carbide-tip hole saw. The hole saw should be available where you buy your tile or at any large home center. Another method is to mark and score a circle on both sides of the board, then tap through with a hammer.

INSTALLING BACKERBOARD

If it has been cut correctly, backerboard is fairly easy to install. Each type is installed with screws or nails, then the seams are joined with fiberglass tape and mortar. If you are planning to tile in a wet area, remember to take proper waterproofing steps. Cement-based backerboard itself is not damaged by moisture, but it is not waterproof. Water can permeate the board and the underlying framing, causing serious damage. For best results, install a waterproofing membrane behind the backerboard (page 578). Use the type of fasteners recommended by the manufacturer. Roofing nails work, but corrosion-resistant screws offer superior holding power. Edges of backerboard must by supported by studs or joists, or glued with construction adhesive to a sound wall surface.

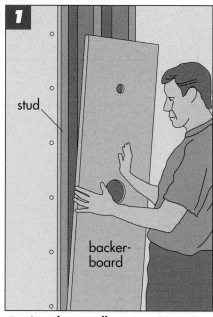

1. Attach to walls.
Attach backerboard directly to bare studs or over an existing layer of drywall. In either case, make sure the drywall screws or nails are long enough to penetrate the framing at least ¾ inch.

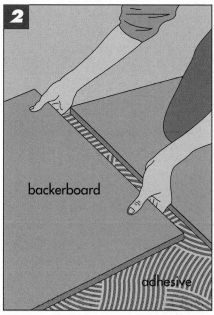

2. Attach to floors.
Coat the clean subfloor with adhesive applied with a notched trowel. Set the boards so that all joints fall over floor joists. Press the board into the adhesive before fastening with screws.

EXPERTS' INSIGHT

EXPANSION GAPS BETWEEN BOARDS

One of the most important steps you can take to ensure a long-lasting tile installation is to plan for some movement on and below the finished surface. Expansion gaps, filled with a flexible material, allow for normal movement without jeopardizing the integrity of the tile and grout. Each manufacturer has specific recommendations for expansion gaps around board edges. As a general rule, you should leave a ⅛-inch gap between boards and a ¼-inch gap around bathtubs and shower pans.

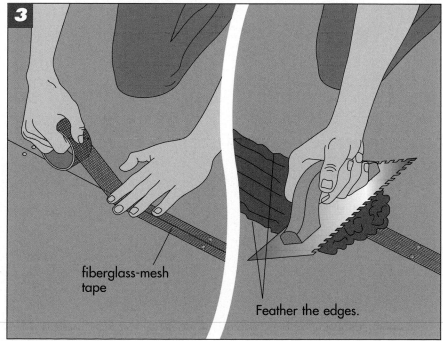

fiberglass-mesh tape

Feather the edges.

3. Finish the joints.
With all boards fastened, apply adhesive-backed fiberglass-mesh tape to the joints. Holding a trowel nearly flat, spread adhesive over the tape, pressing it into the mesh. Feather the edges of the adhesive for a smooth finish. Make sure there are no high spots; shallow low spots are not a problem.

MIXING THIN-SET MORTAR

With the setting bed in place—cleaned, and marked for the layout—it is time to prepare the adhesive. For tiling walls, you will probably use an adhesive that does not have to be mixed. For tiling floors, you can use premixed thin-set or floor tile adhesive, but the thin-set mortar that you mix yourself will be the strongest (see page 575).

Mixing will be easier if all the ingredients are at room temperature; buy the powder and any additives in advance and store them overnight in a heated part of the house. Mixing can get sloppy, especially if you are using a power mixer. Place the bucket in the middle of the area to be tiled, or on top of a drop cloth.

Use a heavy-duty, ½-inch drill for power mixing, as a smaller drill may burn out. Keep a second bucket on hand, about half full of water, for cleaning your mixer.

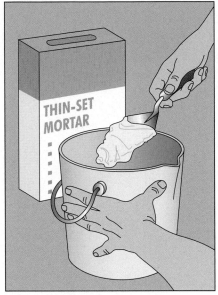

Mixing by hand.
Mix small batches of thin-set mortar (less than two gallons) by hand. Use a trowel or a stiff piece of wood, and make sure you scrape the bottom of the bucket as you stir.

Using a mortar mixer.
Mix larger batches with a mortar mixer mounted on a powerful drill. Clamp the bucket with your feet to keep it from spinning. Set the mixer in and start mixing with short bursts of power to keep the mixture from spilling.

EXPERTS' INSIGHT

HOW MUCH TO MIX?

Like other cement-based adhesives, thin-set mortar begins to cure almost as quickly as it is mixed. If you mix too much at once, it may be unusable when you reach the bottom of the bucket. On the other hand, it is a waste of time to mix batches that are too small. Professional tile setters mix enough adhesive to last them somewhere between 30 and 60 minutes. However, if you are working in a room with dry air, you may need to mix less mortar. Experiment with progressively larger batches.

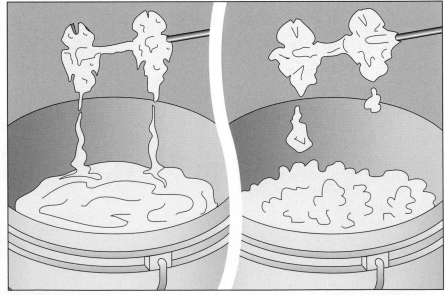

Proper consistency.
It takes some practice and experience to know when the mortar has just the right amount of ingredients. The mix is too loose if it runs off the mixing tool. Add more dry ingredients and mix some more. Lift the mixer again.

The mortar is ready when it falls off, but no longer runs off, the mixing tool. If the mortar starts drying out before you've used it up, discard the batch and mix a new one. Adding more liquid at that point will make the mortar less adherent.

SPREADING THIN-SET MORTAR

After mixing the mortar, let it rest for 10 minutes before applying. Scoop a small amount onto the setting surface and comb it with a notched trowel. If the ridges hold their shape and do not flatten out, the batch is ready to spread. Begin spreading mortar at the intersection of your reference lines. Take care not to cover up the lines. Work in small areas. If you've never tiled before, spread only enough to cover 2 or 3 square feet. As you gain experience, you can expand the size of the working area. Packages of thin-set mortar refer to the *open time*—the amount of time you have to set tiles on combed adhesive. Use a margin trowel (see page 573) to scoop adhesive onto the bottom of your notched trowel, or drop dollops of mortar onto the floor and then spread them out. Give the thin-set mortar a quick stir from time to time.

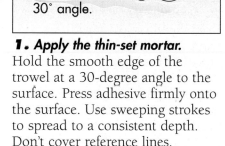

Hold at 30° angle.

1. Apply the thin-set mortar.
Hold the smooth edge of the trowel at a 30-degree angle to the surface. Press adhesive firmly onto the surface. Use sweeping strokes to spread to a consistent depth. Don't cover reference lines.

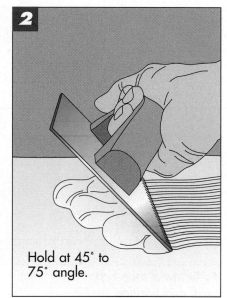

Hold at 45° to 75° angle.

2. Comb the thinset mortar.
Turn the trowel to the notched edge. Hold the trowel at a 45- to 75-degree angle to form the proper depth of ridge. Comb over the entire surface to produce equally sized ridges.

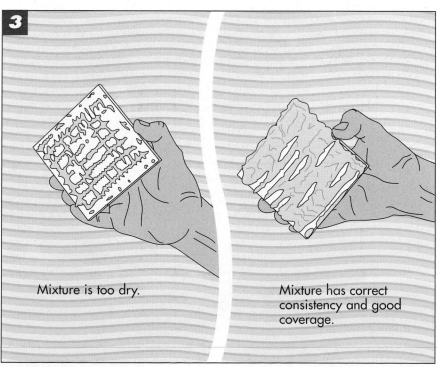

Mixture is too dry.

Mixture has correct consistency and good coverage.

3. Check the coverage.
After spreading and combing a small amount of the mortar, press a tile in place. Twist it a bit so that it is set in the adhesive, then pry it up and look at the bottom. About 75 percent of the surface should be covered. If too little adhesive has stuck to the tile bottom, the mixture is probably too dry.

CAUTION!

WORKING WITH EPOXY ADHESIVE

Epoxy-based adhesives are expensive and tricky to use. Fortunately, they are usually not needed for residential tile jobs. But if you have a setting bed that is incompatible with other adhesives, or are installing tile in an area likely to receive extreme heat, epoxies may be necessary. Read all instructions carefully. Wear a charcoal-filter mask, work in a well-ventilated area, and avoid skin contact with the mixed solution. Mix epoxy adhesive by hand and carefully follow the manufacturer's instructions about the proportion of wet and dry ingredients.

CUTTING TILE

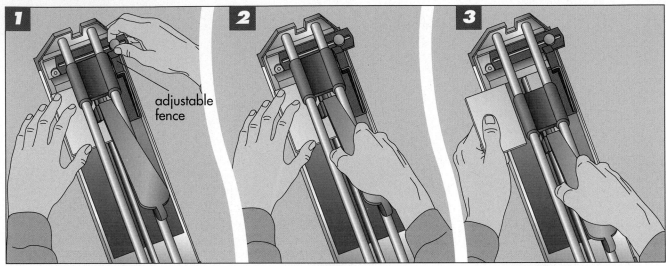

1. To use a snap cutter, mark and position the tile.

Mark a cut line on the tile with a pencil or felt-tipped pen. Place a tile in the cutter, glazed side up, aligning the cut line with the cutting wheel. Set and lock the fence on the cutter to hold the tile in place.

2. Score the tile.

Hold the tile in place with one hand and the handle with the other. Set the cutting wheel on the top of the tile. Pull or push (depending on your model) the handle while maintaining steady pressure on the tile. Try to score the tile evenly on the first pass.

3. Snap the tile.

When the tile has been scored, press back on the handle just enough to snap the tile along the score line. If the tile will not break, the score line was probably incomplete or not deep enough.

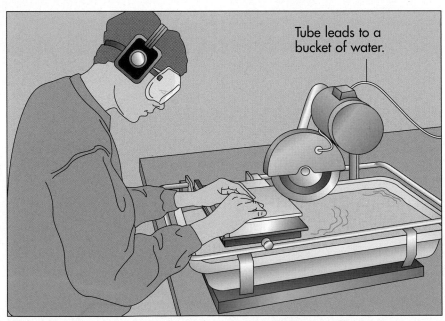

Tube leads to a bucket of water.

Use a wet saw.

Wear safety glasses and hearing protection. See that the blade is in good condition and that the water bucket is full. Place the tile on the sliding table and lock the fence to hold the tile in place. Turn the saw on, and make sure water is running onto the blade. Press down on the tile as you slide it through, taking care to keep your fingers out of the way. When the water runs out, refill the bucket; do not cut with the saw for even a few seconds unless water is running onto the blade.

CAUTION!

BEWARE OF EDGES

One of the advantages of a wet saw is that it makes very smooth cuts. When using a snap cutter or tile nippers, however, the resulting edges can be razor sharp. After cutting the tile, immediately smooth those edges. Grasp the tile on an uncut edge. Move a rubbing stone back and forth over the cut side, smoothing and rounding over the edge as you go. If you do not have a rubbing stone, you can achieve the same result with carbide-grit sandpaper. Use a sanding block, or wrap the sandpaper around a block of wood.

TRIMMING TILE

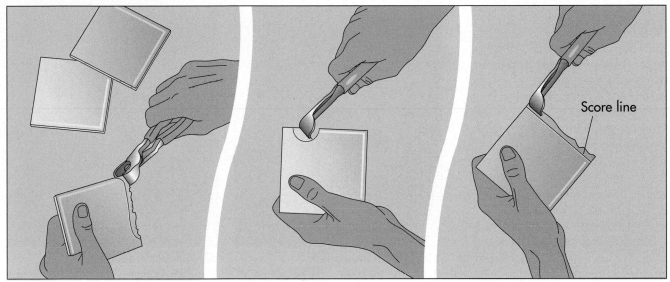

Score line

Use tile nippers for a curved cut...

For cuts that are not straight, use a rod saw (see below right) or tile nippers. (Most floor tiles cannot be cut with a rod saw, so you will need to use nippers.) Practice on scrap pieces of tile to get the hang of it. Hold the nippers roughly parallel to the cut line, and bite away small chunks.

...for a notch...

If the notch will have square corners, use a snap cutter to score at least some of the lines; this will make it a bit easier to nibble precisely up to the lines. Nibbling a notch requires patience. Bite away only a little at a time or you may break the whole piece.

...or for a sliver.

Nippers are also useful for very narrow straight cuts when you do not have a wet saw. Use the snap cutter or a glass cutter to score the glaze on the tile. Place the jaws close to, and parallel with, the score line. Take a series of bites along the cut line.

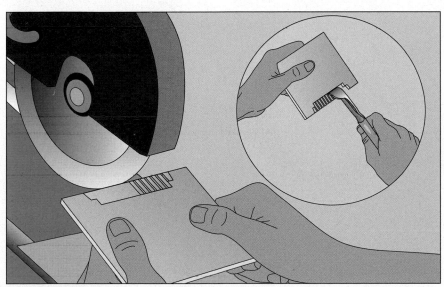

Make irregular cuts.

Use a wet saw to make irregular cuts that would take a long time to accomplish with nippers. To make a series of closely spaced, parallel cuts with the wet saw, hold the tile in your hands. Rest your hands on the sliding table as you move the tile into the blade. By holding the tile at the correct angle, you can produce a series of cuts that all end at the cut line. Break off the tile pieces with your fingers or nippers, then clean up the cut edge with a rubbing stone.

TOOLS TO USE

THE ROD SAW

A rod saw (shown on page 571) is a cylindrical hacksaw blade made of tungsten carbide. If you are on a tight budget or do not have very many odd-shaped cuts to make, this tool can be a handy accessory. Set the rod saw snugly in the hacksaw body, firmly support the tile, and cut using a sawing motion. With a rod saw you can fairly quickly through wall tiles, but it will be rough going—and perhaps impossible—with floor tiles. A rod saw is useful for cutting tight curves.

SETTING TILE

When the adhesive has been combed to the right thickness, immediately begin setting tiles. The most important tile is the first one you set; make sure that it is aligned perfectly with your layout so that the rest of the tiles will fall into place nicely. You will be rewarded at this stage for having spent all that time on the layout. Your reference lines will help to guide you through the entire process; take care not to cover them over with adhesive.

Work in sections small enough to set the tiles before the adhesive begins to dry out. Start by spreading adhesive in a 2- to 3-square-foot area; set the tiles and remove excess adhesive before moving on to the next section. With practice, you can work in larger sections. If the adhesive has begun to skin over, do not set tiles in it. Rather, scoop up and discard the adhesive and apply a fresh layer.

Whenever possible, set all full tiles first, then set the cut tiles. But also avoid kneeling on top of just-set tiles in order to lay the cut ones. On a large job, you might want to set all of the full tiles one day, then handle the cut tiles the next day.

Take care not to tile yourself into a corner. Set tiles so that you can leave the room without walking on them. Don't disturb floor tiles until the adhesive has cured—preferably overnight.

YOU'LL NEED

TIME: About one hour for every 3 to 5 square feet of field tiles; small, complex installations take two to three times as long.
SKILLS: Setting tiles into the adhesive and cutting tiles to fit.
TOOLS: Beating block and hammer, putty knife or trowel, sponge, and tile cutter.

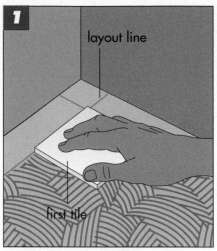

1. Begin at the corner.
With the adhesive spread, place the first tile at the intersection of the reference lines. Press and twist it slightly into place, aligning the tile with both lines. Do not slide the tile through the adhesive.

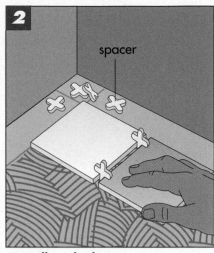

2. Follow the layout.
Place another tile next to the first. Use spacers unless the tiles are self-spacing. Press and twist the tile to ensure that it is fully embedded in the adhesive. Accurate placement of the first few tiles is critical.

3. Fill in the field.
Continue setting tiles along the layout lines in the section. Then set the tiles in the field, working out from the corner. Insert spacers as shown. (Spacers can also be laid flat at the intersection of the grout lines, but must be removed before grouting.) If the tiles are self-spacing, keep an eye on the gaps between tiles to make sure that they remain uniform. Avoid sliding the tiles once they have been set in the adhesive. Check the backs of the tiles from time to time to see that they are adhering properly.

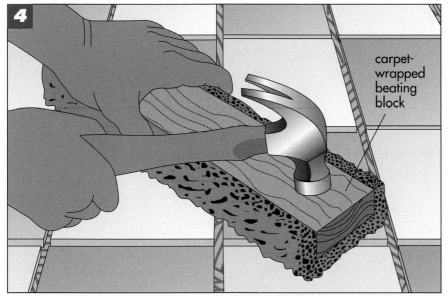

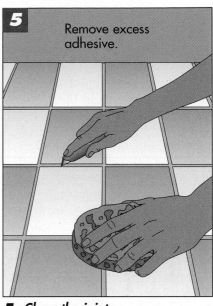

4. Use a beating block.

After setting tiles in one section, use a beating block (see page 572 for tips on making a beating block) to ensure a level surface and full adhesion. Place the beating block so that it spans several tiles, and give it a few light taps with a hammer. Make sure each tile gets tapped this way.

5. Clean the joint.

Immediately after setting tiles in each section, remove excess adhesive before it starts to dry. Clean the tile with a damp sponge, and use a putty knife, utility knife, or margin trowel to remove excess from between tiles.

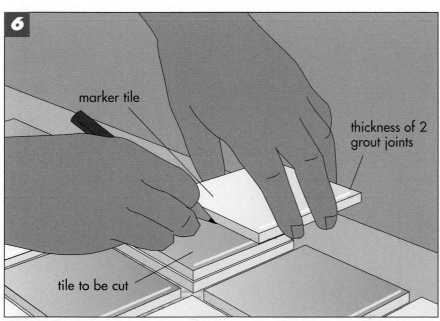

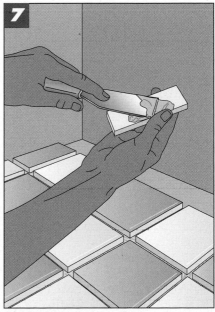

6. Cut tiles last.

When all of the full tiles have been set in the field, begin setting cut tiles around the perimeter. Because walls are rarely square, it is usually best to cut one tile at a time. The safest method is to measure each tile "in place." Set the tile to be cut directly on top of the adjacent tile. Then set another full tile on top, two grout joints away from the wall. Use the top tile to mark the cut line.

7. Back-buttering tiles.

When you are unable to use a trowel to apply the adhesive on the setting surface, *back-butter* individual tiles: Use a notched trowel or a putty knife, depending on the size of the tile, and spread adhesive on the back. Use enough adhesive so that the tile will be level with other tiles.

SETTING MOSAIC TILE

Historically tile mosaic has been an elaborate decorative technique using small pieces of tile, stone, and shells set one by one to produce unique patterns. Today mosaic tiles are almost always sold in sheets, with small tiles held together by a mesh or paper backing or with small adhesive dots. These sheets make installation much quicker than setting tiles individually. You can find mosaic tiles in a variety of patterns, glazed and unglazed. Glass mosaic tiles are available in 1-inch squares. Mosaic tiles are particularly suitable for use on floors, but are also popular for walls and countertops.

EXPERTS' INSIGHT

ARRANGING PATTERNS

Sheets of mosaic tiles are sometimes composed of randomly arranged tiles in a variety of colors. This randomness looks best when it has a balance to it; colors should be scattered around the surface, not clumped together. You can control the balance somewhat by planning the arrangement of the tile sheets. Before you start spreading adhesive and setting the tiles, take time to study the patterns on individual sheets. You may find that some sheets look better than others when placed next to each other. Some mosaic sheets are set according to a pattern. In that case, install the tiles so that you continue, rather than disrupt, the pattern.

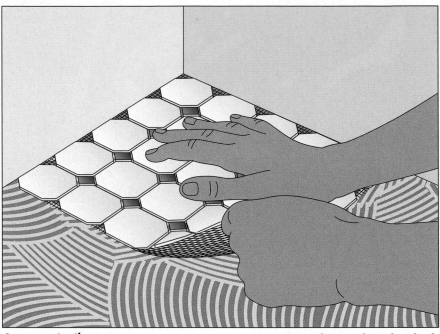

Set mosaic tiles.
Back-mounted mosaic tiles should be set in thin-set adhesive. Because various backing materials perform differently, check with the supplier for any special instructions. Take care to ensure that each individual tile on a sheet is fully embedded in the adhesive. Move a beating block (see page 572) slowly across the whole sheet, lightly tapping it as you go.

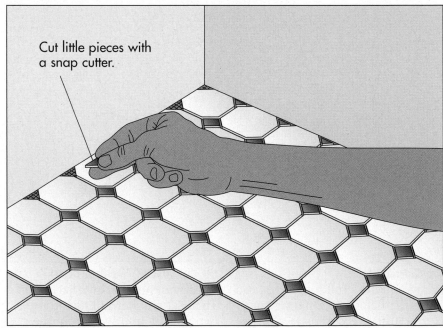

Cut little pieces with a snap cutter.

Cut mosaics.
One advantage of small mosaic tiles is that you can often manage an installation without having to cut individual tiles. Use a utility knife to cut strips of tiles away from the sheet. If you do need to fill in spaces with small, cut tiles, remove the tiles from the backing and cut them with a snap cutter or nippers. Back-butter the tiles with adhesive before setting.

WORKING WITH IRREGULARLY SHAPED TILE

Handmade paver tiles lend a pleasing informality to a room. Mexican tiles, *saltillos,* are one common choice; they have the added benefit of being very inexpensive. Handmade tiles will not be uniformly shaped; they can vary widely in shape, thickness, size, and color from tile to tile. Choose the tiles by inspecting each one and discarding those with severe blemishes.

Irregularly shaped tiles present several installation challenges. Not only are sizes unpredictable, but some of them may be significantly warped. Tiles of different thicknesses can create a tripping hazard if not installed with care. Because the backs are often not flat, back-butter each tile with adhesive. Handmade tiles cannot be cut easily with a snap cutter; a wet saw is much more effective. Some types require application of a sealer before grouting.

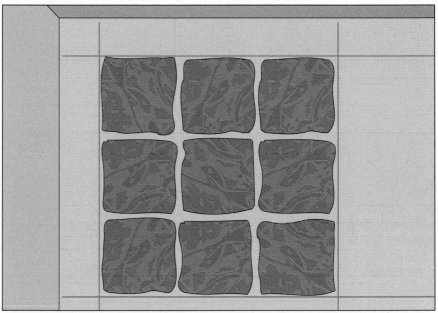

Floor layout for irregular pavers.
When the tiles are not of predictably uniform size, layout becomes less precise. Rather than using plastic spacers, break the layout into a grid. For tiles that are approximately 12 inches square, use chalk lines to make 3-foot squares; each square will hold nine tiles. Dry-fit the tiles first, adjusting the spaces between them by sight. Then set the tiles one square at a time.

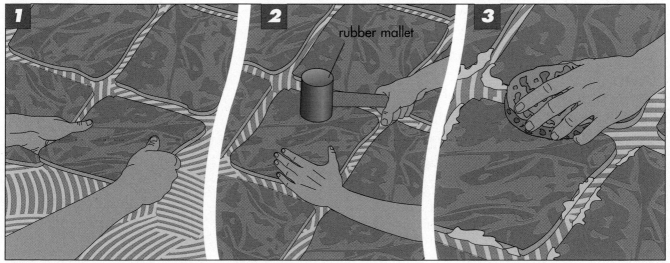

rubber mallet

1. Set the tile.
Comb on thin-set mortar (page 591). For tiles with irregular backs, apply adhesive on the backs as well to ensure an adequate bond. To make sure you can compensate for warped tiles and varying thicknesses, use a trowel with ½-inch notches to spread the adhesive.

2. Tap with a mallet.
With uniform, machine-made pavers, you can use a beating block as described on page 595. With handmade pavers, however, tap on each tile individually. Use a soft mallet, not a hammer. You can set a rag on the paver to protect the surface further.

3. Clean the tiles.
Remove mortar that oozes up between the tiles. Take care to keep mortar off the surface of the tiles. Before grouting, clean the tiles with a sponge and water. Apply sealer to unsealed tiles before grouting.

WORKING WITH STONE TILE

Stone tiles are made from stone that is quarried all over the world. Many types are available, and they vary widely in color and price. Polished stone has a shiny, almost glazelike finish that looks best on walls and interior floors. Honed stone has a smooth, matte finish that does not show wear as much as does polished stone. If properly sealed, honed tiles can be used in wet areas where polished stone would be too slippery. Flamed stone has a rough finish that is most useful on heavily traveled floors. Most stone is brittle, so the the substrate must be strong— at a minimum, backerboard over ¾-inch plywood. Because stone is heavy, be sure your floor joists are strong enough to hold it. Check with an engineer or architect if you are not sure. Cut stone tile with a wet saw, and use a blade suitable for the type of stone you are cutting.

TYPES OF STONE

Type	Description	Pros	Cons
Marble	A limestone that has been changed deep beneath the earth's surface into a hard composition of crystals. Characterized by varied patterns and colors of veins.	Elegant appearance, used in many of the world's most famous buildings; beautiful and long-lasting.	Veins add to appeal, but weaken the marble. Dark-colored marble can fade in sunlight. Easily scratched and stained.
Granite	Quartz-based stone with a tough, glossy appearance. Colors range from light to dark, with varying patterns and graining.	Harder than marble; resists scratching. Easy to care for; resists acids. Excellent choice for kitchen countertops. Generally very dense and capable of withstanding freeze-thaw cycles.	Quarried all over the world, with varying characteristics from each region. Softer granites can sometimes show wear.
Slate	A rough-surfaced tile that is split, rather than sliced, from quarried stone. Available in slabs or as cut tiles, usually 12 inches square. Gauged slate is ground smooth on the bottom, while ungauged (or cleft) slate is rough on both sides.	Widely available and reasonably priced.	Somewhat brittle, with less range of colors than other stones. Dark slate may fade in sunlight. Irregular surface can produce undesirable flooring. Ungauged slate needs to be set in a thick mortar bed.

Materials to Use with Stone Tile

Be sure to get the right materials for setting, grouting, and sealing your stone tiles.

■ Latex-modified thin-set mortar works for most installations, but epoxy thin-set may be needed. Do not use organic mastics. Marble is somewhat transparent, so use white thin-set rather than gray.

■ With ceramic tile, a contrasting grout color is often used as part of the design. With stone tile, and especially with marble and granite, the objective is usually to minimize or eliminate the visual impact of the grout joints, so the surface resembles a solid whole. Choose a grout color that closely matches the stone. Use unsanded grout with marble and slate tiles, and epoxy adhesive as grout with closely spaced granite tiles.

■ Clear sealers can improve the appearance of stone tile and protect it from dirt, water, and stains. Use a low-sheen penetrating sealer on a floor; glossy sealers work well with other surfaces. Choose a sealer recommended for your type of stone. Test on a scrap tile to make sure it won't discolor your tiles. Granite usually needs no sealer.

EXPERTS' INSIGHT

SHOPPING FOR STONE

Often the most attractive stones are the weakest because of their deep veins. Stone tiles are often sorted according to their background color, but variations within the sorted colors can be substantial. Look through each box of tiles before you buy. Get extras so you can return tiles that are unsatisfactory. Buy only from a knowledgeable and reputable dealer.

SETTING GRANITE AND MARBLE TILE

Granite and marble are usually quarried and then manufactured to uniform sizes and thicknesses. Standard tiles are 12 inches square and 3/8-inch thick with one side polished smooth. To minimize chipping, the exposed edges of granite and marble tiles are beveled. In fact, the edges are usually so smooth and straight that the grout joint between tiles can be very thin; sometimes the tiles are installed without any grout joints at all. Do a complete dry run before applying adhesive and laying tiles.

YOU'LL NEED

TIME: About a day for a 12-foot-long countertop.
SKILLS: Cutting and setting tiles and carefully aligning tiles.
TOOLS: Wet saw or grinder with a diamond blade.

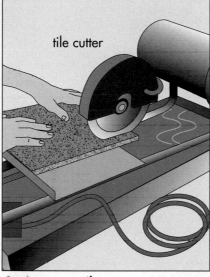

Cutting stone tiles.
Use a wet saw. Natural stone sometimes breaks along existing fissure lines when you try to cut it. If this becomes a problem, cut the tile through only two-thirds of its thickness, then flip it over and finish the cut from the other side.

TOOLS TO USE

STONE CUTTER
The best tool for making neat rectangular cutouts is a small stone cutter equipped with a diamond blade. Rent or borrow one from the tile dealer or a rental store. (Tile setters often mount a diamond blade on an electric grinder.) After cutting in each direction, knock the cutout free and use tile nippers and a rubbing stone to clean up the corners.

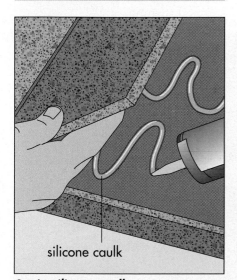

Set in silicone caulk.
It may not look professional, but many tile setters use this technique. After you have done a complete dry run and know exactly where each tile will go. Lift up one or two tiles at a time and make squiggles of clear silicone caulk on the substrate. Set the tiles in it quickly but carefully.

Seal it first.
Manufacturers recommend that some types of stone tiles be set with an expensive epoxy mortar. An alternative technique is to coat the back of the tiles with nonpourous epoxy. Once the coating has dried, the tiles can be set with regular thin-set mortar.

Finish the edge.
You can buy special edging tiles for some types of stone. Or install narrow strips on the edge, and set the tiles on top of them, to produce the illusion of a massive slab. Have the exposed edges polished by the dealer, or polish them with a rubbing stone, and perhaps brush on several coats of clear lacquer.

GROUTING TILE

Grout is a thin mortar mixture that is used to fill the joints between tiles. It protects tile edges from nicks and cracks, and it helps keep water from working its way below the tile surface. The size and color of the grout joint can be as important to the finished appearance of a floor as the tile itself. So it pays to choose and apply the grout carefully. (See page 577 for more on grout selection.) Do not apply grout until the adhesive has set, which normally takes up to 24 hours. If you are tiling more than one surface, such as a bathroom floor and walls, set the tiles on all the surfaces before you begin grouting. Then grout the walls before the floor. For stronger and less permeable grout, mix the powder with latex additive rather than water.

YOU'LL NEED

TIME: Several hours for a typical bathroom floor.
SKILLS: Mixing and spreading grout, shaping grout joints, and careful cleanup.
TOOLS: Bucket, trowel or mortar mixer; awl; rubber gloves; grout float; sponge; and joint shaper.

CAUTION!
USING COLORED GROUT
If you are using colored grout, mix a small test batch. Let it dry so you can see the finished color. Also spread some of the grout on a scrap tile to see if it stains the tile surface. When adding color additive to grout, mix it in before adding the liquid. And make note of the exact quantities of ingredients used so that you can mix consistent colors from one batch to the next.

1. Mix by hand...
Measure the liquid and pour it into the bucket. Add the dry ingredients a little at a time. Stir cautiously with a clean trowel or piece of wood. Add more dry ingredients as needed.

...or use a mortar mixer.
For preparing large amounts, use a mortar mixer attached to an electric drill. Set the blade in the mixture, then mix at a slow speed. Don't lift the blade out until it has stopped turning.

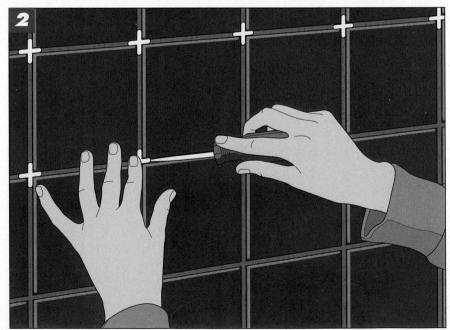

2. Remove spacers, clean joints.
Before you begin spreading grout, remove all of the spacers between tiles. An awl or some other thin tool will make removal easier. Also remove any adhesive that was squeezed into the joints between tiles. A razor blade or grout saw will speed this process. Vacuum the joints and put masking tape over all expansion joints, which will be caulked later.

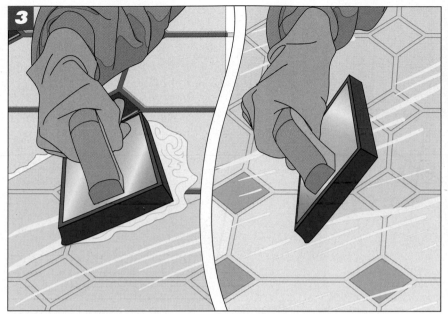

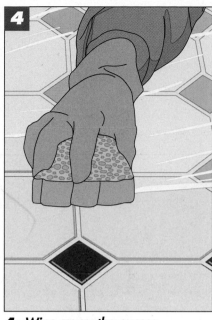

3. Apply the grout.

For a floor, dump enough grout on the tiles to cover about 3 square feet. For a wall, scoop a good-sized dollop up with the float. Hold the grout float at about a 35-degree angle, and spread the grout diagonally across the tiles. Press the grout firmly and completely into the joints. Make two or three passes, working in a different direction for each pass.

Tilt the float up so it is nearly perpendicular to the surface, and wipe away excess grout. Move diagonally to the joints, to avoid digging into them with the float.

4. Wipe away the excess.

When you have finished grouting one area, use a dampened sponge to wipe the tiles. Use a circular motion. If the grout is hard to wipe from the tiles, don't wait so long next time. Take care that the joints are consistent in depth. Rinse the sponge often.

TOOLS TO USE

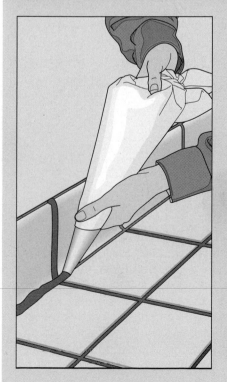

A GROUT BAG

A grout (or mortar) bag looks a bit like a pastry bag used for decorating cakes. It is useful for grouting joints that can't be reached with a trowel, or for particularly porous tiles that soak up grout quicker than you can clean it off the surface. Use a tip on the grout bag no wider than the width of the joint. Fill the bag with grout, then place the tip in the joint. Move the bag as you squeeze grout into the joint. Grout the full length of joints rather than grouting around each tile. Let the grout harden a little, then shape the joints (see page 602). Once the grout has set for 30 minutes or more, sweep the joints with a broom or stiff brush to remove the excess.

EXPERTS' INSIGHT

WATCH THE GAPS

Don't forget about the expansion joints. These joints at corners and edges must be filled with expandable caulk, which allows the surfaces to expand and contract without cracking or damaging the tiles. Use masking tape to keep grout out of the expansion joints. Some grout will still seep under the tape and into the joint. So when you have finished grouting, remove the tape and clean out the grout. Or wait for it to dry, and cut it out with a grout saw or utility knife. Let the joint dry completely, and vacuum before caulking.

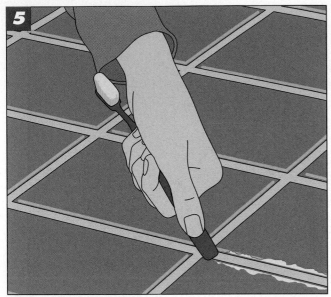

5. *Shape the joints.*

After wiping the tiles, clean and shape the joints. Pull a barely dampened sponge along grout lines, removing high spots as you go. Some people like thick grout lines that are nearly flush with the surface of the tile, while others prefer grout lines that recede. The important thing is that they be consistent. Buy an adjustable grout shaper, or use a toothbrush handle or a wood dowel. The shaper should be a bit wider than the joint.

6. *Fill the gaps.*

If you notice a gap or inadvertently pull grout out from a joint, fill it right away with grout. Wearing rubber gloves, press a small amount into the void, filling it completely. Then shape the joint and remove any excess grout.

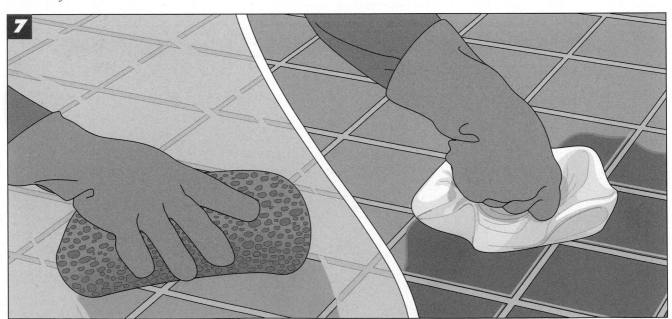

7. *Remove the grout film.*

Once you have cleaned the tile surfaces of grout and shaped the joints, let the grout set up for another 15 or 20 minutes. With your sponge and a bucket of clean water, and wearing a rubber glove, start the final cleaning of the tiles. Timing is critical: The grout should be dry enough to not be affected by the sponge, yet haze on the tile surface should be not so dry that it is difficult to remove. Rinse the sponge and wring it out. Pass the sponge slowly over a line of tiles. Flip the sponge over and make another straight run. Rinse the sponge and continue. With proper timing and careful execution, this process should remove nearly all of the grout residue from the tile surface. After another 15 minutes, polish the tiles with a dry piece of cheesecloth or a clean rag.

CAULKING AND SEALING

Caulk fills expansion joints around the perimeter of a tiled surface. Its flexibility allows adjacent surfaces to expand and contract without damaging tile; and it won't crack, as grout would. Many fine tile jobs have been marred by ugly caulking, so take the time to do it right. (See page 579 for information on choosing caulk.) Practice on scrap pieces until you feel you've got the knack. Place the tube in the gun, cut the tip, and puncture the seal with a long nail. Some people like to cut the tip at a severe angle, while others like to cut it nearly straight across. Have a damp rag handy, soaked with water or mineral spirits, depending on the type of caulk you are using.

YOU'LL NEED

TIME: Less than an hour for most projects.
SKILLS: Applying and smoothing caulk, and using a paint roller.
TOOLS: Caulk gun, paint roller and tray or paintbrush, and rag.

EXPERTS' INSIGHT

GROUT SEALERS

You can significantly improve the durability of grout joints by sealing them. Wait until the grout has fully cured—a week or two—before applying grout sealer. Use a disposable foam-rubber paintbrush, which allows you to cover the grout without getting sealer on the tile. Allow the first coat to dry, then apply a second. Renew the grout sealer from time to time.

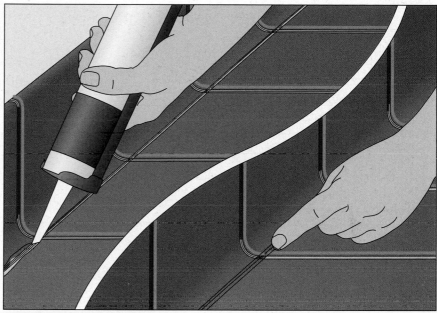

Apply and smooth caulk.
Position the tip of the tube on the surface to be caulked, and get yourself into a comfortable position. Squeeze the trigger carefully until caulk begins to flow. Continue squeezing as you pull the gun along. Either leave the bead of caulk as it is, or use a wet finger or damp rag to smooth it. Strive for a consistent-looking line.

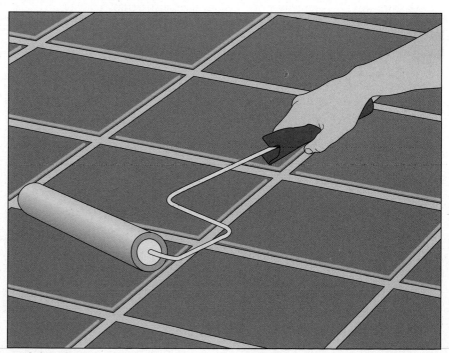

Seal the tile.
Some tiles must be sealed when they are installed; others must have a sealer reapplied every few years. Check with the tile manufacturer for specific instructions. If you are installing unsealed tiles, you may have to apply the sealer before grouting. Renew the sealer as needed. A foam-rubber paint roller works well for most types of tile sealer.

TILING FLOORS

Unless your home was seriously underbuilt, your floors are strong enough so that you can install carpeting or another type of resilient flooring with confidence. But ceramic tile has much more demanding requirements. The weight of the tiles is not usually the problem; deflection is. If a ceramic tile floor flexes, grout and even tiles can crack. If you have any doubts about the strength of the floor, ask a contractor to inspect it before you begin tiling.

Sometimes a bouncy floor can be firmed up by driving screws through the subflooring and into joists. Or, you may have to add another subfloor layer, or even beef up the joists. However, if you build up the floor so much that the new tile surface will be a half inch or more higher than an adjacent floor surface, it will look and feel awkward. That's why in some situations it is simply not practical to lay a ceramic tile floor.

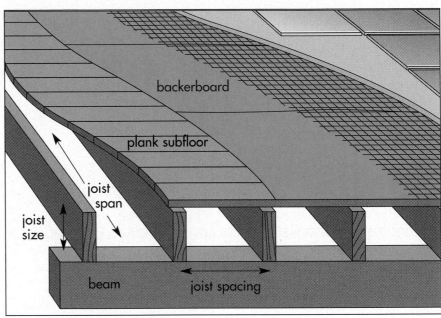

Anatomy of a floor.
Floor joist strength is determined by the size of the joist, the length of the joist's span between supports, and the amount of space between joists. If your joists have spaces larger than 16 inches between them, for instance, then you will need an extra strong subfloor. Plywood is the best subfloor material, but many older homes have strong subfloors made with planks of 1× lumber.

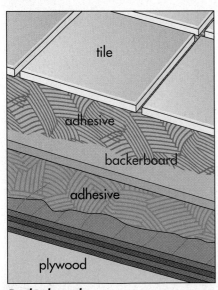

Backerboard
Older installations set tiles on a thick bed of mortar. Backerboard is an excellent modern day substitute. Use as thick a board as possible, installed over a plywood subfloor. See pages 588–589 for cutting and installation help.

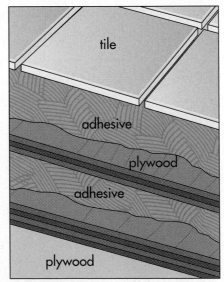

Plywood
Although plywood is somewhat soft and flexible, it also has great strength. When two sheets are laminated together, the result is a very firm surface.

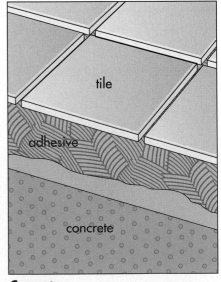

Concrete
Concrete is the best subsurface and works well for straightening out-of-level floors. Do not use curing or acceleration chemicals if you pour a concrete floor. An older concrete surface must be sound; tiling will not strengthen it.

Preparing a wood floor for tile.

If you will be tiling directly over plywood, it is best to install two layers of ⅜-inch-minimum plywood, rather than one thick sheet. Use exterior-grade plywood for the top layer. The edges should always fall over a joist, but stagger the sheets so that the joints do not fall directly over each other. Coat the bottom sheet with construction adhesive before setting the top sheet in place. Leave a gap of ⅛ inch or more around all edges of the top sheets, including at the joints. Fasten the plywood with screws or ring-shank nails. If an existing plywood subfloor is strong enough, sand the surface thoroughly, then vacuum. Talk to your tile dealer about the best adhesive to use.

If the existing floor is composed of 1× or 2× planking in good condition, drive screws into joists wherever it seems at all loose, and perhaps install a layer of plywood over it. If it has cracks and does not feel strong, remove the planking and install plywood.

Preparing a concrete floor for tile.

Concrete is a great base for tile, as long as it is structurally sound and flat. Some slabs may actually be too smooth, and should be scruffed up a bit by grinding with an abrasive wheel. Do not install tile over concrete that was treated with a curing or acceleration chemical when it was poured. These additives will prevent adhesive from bonding properly. If you are uncertain about whether or not such additives were used, try to locate the builder of the house or the concrete contractor. They may have a record. You can also test the slab yourself by sprinkling water on it. If the water isn't absorbed, the concrete was probably treated. Apply a latex bonding agent or add a subfloor.

Install plywood.
For the top layer of plywood, leave ⅛-inch gaps between the sheets. Fasten with screws or ring-shank nails in a 6-inch grid in the field, and every 4 inches at the joints and around the perimeter.

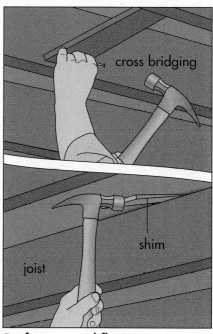

Beef up a wood floor.
Strengthen a weak subfloor by installing wood or metal cross bridging between joists. Close small gaps between joists and the existing subfloor with shims, or drive screws from above.

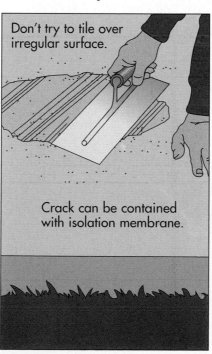

Fill in low spots.
Clean out low spots in a concrete slab and fill with thinset mortar. Use a trowel or straightedge to level the surface.

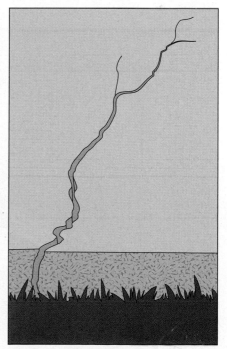

Dealing with cracks.
Cover small cracks in concrete with an isolation membrane (see page 578). Cracks that result in uneven surfaces indicate underlying structural problems; do not tile over such a surface.

EXPERTS' INSIGHT

REPLACING BASEBOARD

■ As long as you're tiling your floor, you may want to update your baseboards as well. New tile may well emphasize your old baseboard's imperfections.

■ Old vinyl cove base can get pretty ratty-looking. Install new cove base after the tile job is done. Make sure that the new material is as wide as the original stuff or you will have an ugly line on the wall. Apply with cove base adhesive or latex silicone caulk.

■ The base shoe gets banged up in time, too, so go ahead and replace it as well. Use stain or paint on it, then cut it with a miter box and fasten it with finishing nails.

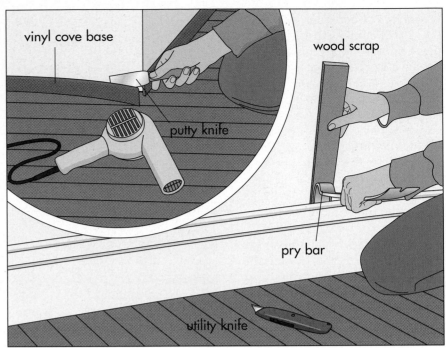

Remove the baseboard.

Before tiling a floor, remove the baseboard from the surrounding walls. If the joint between the baseboard and wall is sealed with paint, score it with a utility knife first. Pull vinyl cove base away with a putty knife. If it resists removal, try heating the vinyl with a hair dryer to loosen the adhesive. Use a pry bar to remove wood baseboard. Protect the wall with a thin piece of wood. If your baseboard has a *shoe*—a small rounded molding at the bottom—remove that piece.

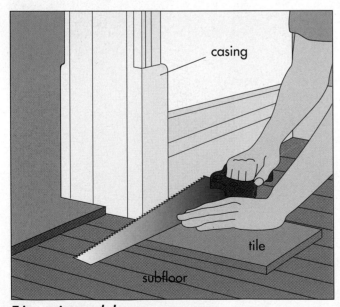

Trim casing and doors.

It is usually not a good idea to remove door casings. But cutting tile to fit around casing is difficult, and usually leads to a sloppy-looking job. So trim the bottom of the casing, and fit the tiles beneath it. With the subfloor installed, place a tile up against the casing. Lay a handsaw on the tile as you cut through the casing.

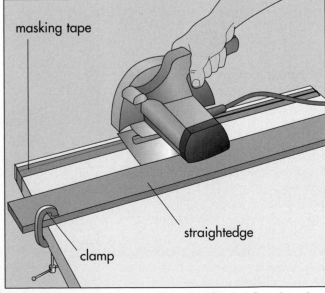

To make sure a door will swing freely after the tiles are installed, place tiles on the floor nearby. If not, use the tiles and a pencil to scribe a cut line at the door's bottom. Allow for a gap of at least ¼ inch. Remove the door by popping out the hinge pins. Place masking tape along the bottom of the most visible side of the door, and mark a cut line. Cut through the tape using a circular saw with a clamped straightedge as a guide.

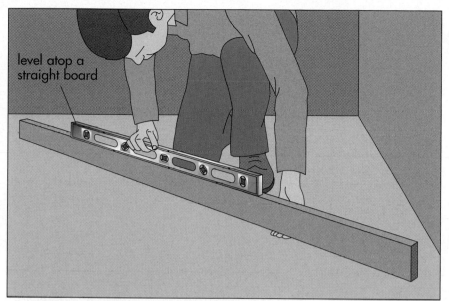

level atop a
straight board

Check floors for level.
Use a carpenter's level and a straight board to check the floor for level and to find any spots that are not flat. If the entire floor is out of level with the wall, it can still be tiled. If you plan to extend tile up the wall, however, you should consider leveling the floor or using tapered baseboard to make the transition attractive.

EXPERTS' INSIGHT

PLANNING TRANSITIONS
A newly tiled floor may be higher than the adjoining floor. Plan your approach to these transitions before you begin any work. The most common technique is to install a transitional piece called a threshold. You can buy metal or wood thresholds that are sloped to ease the transition. Some are designed to be installed after the tile is laid and grouted, and others should be installed at the same time as you lay the tile. Using a table saw, you can make your own threshold out of oak or another hardwood.

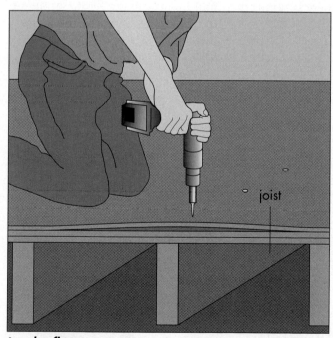

joist

Level a floor.
Small bumps in the floor must be dealt with before you begin tiling. If the wood subfloor comes up in places, try driving screws through the flooring and into a joist to level it out. You may be able to take out small high spots with a belt sander.

To straighten out dips and low areas, or to level out an entire floor, use a self-leveling floor patch. These are made by manufacturers of tile adhesive.

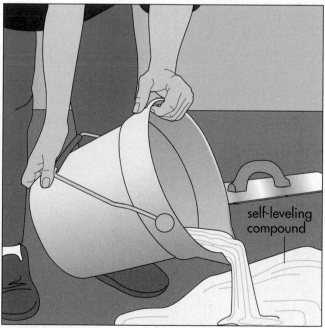

self-leveling
compound

Place barriers where necessary to keep the compound where it belongs. Mix the dry ingredients with water, then pour it on the floor. The mixture will level itself out to a certain degree, but use a long flat trowel to help things along. The compound should be cured and ready for tiling within a few hours. Most self-leveling compounds are intended to function at depths no greater than 1 inch. If the work seems intimidating, talk to a contractor about preparing a level subfloor for you.

TILING A KITCHEN FLOOR

*T*iling a kitchen floor can be a major disruption to any household. This project may affect access to food, meal preparation, and upset traffic patterns through the kitchen. Some preparation can be done well in advance of the tiling; some cabinets can be removed, new subflooring applied, and doors removed. For the tiling itself, set aside a long weekend so that the kitchen can be back in operation as quickly as possible.

YOU'LL NEED

TIME: 3–4 days to prepare, lay out, and tile an average-size kitchen.
SKILLS: Disconnecting and removing appliances, removing base cabinets, preparing a subfloor, and tiling the floor.
TOOLS: Screwdriver, hammer, pry bar, and putty knife.

TOOLS TO USE

KNEE PADS

Tiling floors is hard on your knees. In addition to the stress of kneeling much of the time, your knees are vulnerable to injury from tools and pieces of material left around the work area. That's why contractors who spend a lot of time working at floor level consider knee pads essential. For occasional use on wood or tile floors, non-marring foam, rubber, or rubber-capped pads are a good choice. (You'll find these useful for gardening as well.) For heavy-duty protection, but less comfort, buy the skateboarder-type knee pads that have a hard nylon shield on the front.

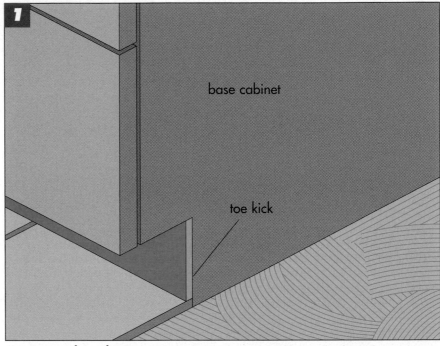

base cabinet

toe kick

1. Assess the cabinets.
As a general rule, there is no need to install tile where it will be covered by cabinet bases or other permanent fixtures. Instead, use a thin pry bar and stiff putty knife to remove the toe kick and any molding along the floor. Set tile up to the cabinet. After all the tile is installed and grouted, trim the upper edge of toe kick to fit and reinstall it and the molding

Remove fastener joining cabinets.

Remove toe kick where it overlaps a joint.

2. Remove cabinets where needed.
Sometimes cabinets must be removed to take out the old flooring or to replace the subfloor. Remove fasteners holding the countertop in place, and the screws that join cabinets to each other and to the wall. In addition, remove overlapping pieces of toe kick and other molding.

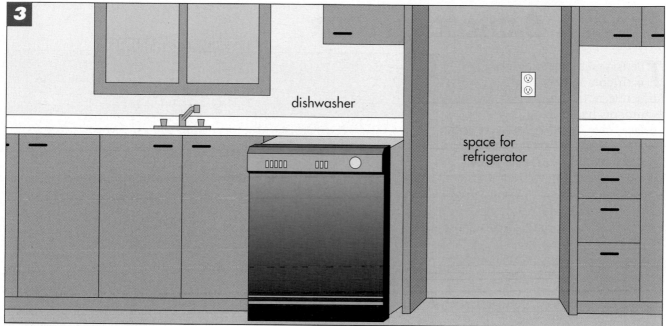

3. Consider the appliances.

One of the issues you will have to address is whether or not to tile beneath appliances. Think of how your kitchen floor would look if your home were empty and up for sale. Untiled spaces where appliances usually sit would be unattractive to potential buyers.

Freestanding appliances, such as refrigerators, ranges, and dishwashers, should be removed from the kitchen to install tile underneath the appliance location. It is also best to tile beneath built-in appliances, although the work can be trickier. Often, when you tile beneath a built-in dishwasher,

for example, you raise the floor level such that the dishwasher will no longer fit under the countertop. You can raise or notch out the countertop a bit to accommodate the appliance. Adjustments may also have to be made in the plumbing connections.

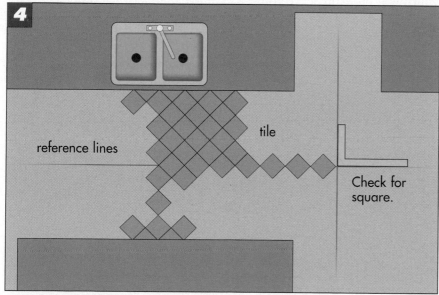

4. Lay out the job.

At the center of the floor, mark perpendicular reference lines with a pencil or chalk line. (In odd-shape rooms you may want to center the layout on the most visible section of the floor rather than in the center of the room.) Check to make

sure that the lines are square (see pages 583–585). Using appropriate spacers if needed with your tile, dry set tiles along the reference lines to check the layout. Adjust the layout to minimize the number of cut tiles and to avoid creating any extremely small pieces.

5. Set the tiles.

Begin at the intersecting reference lines and spread thin-set mortar over a small area. Do not cover the lines. Set properly spaced tiles. Use a beating block (see page 572) after setting each section of tiles. Check alignment as you go.

TILING A BATHROOM FLOOR

Tile is a great material for bathroom floors: tough, attractive, and easy to clean. Many bathrooms have tile on every surface; plan ahead if you want to resurface your walls, countertops, or tub and shower areas. One of the great joys of tiling a bathroom is the chance to experiment with bold colors and unusual designs.

A typical bathroom floor does not require a waterproof installation, although you should choose tiles and setting materials that are suitable for a surface that will get wet from time to time.

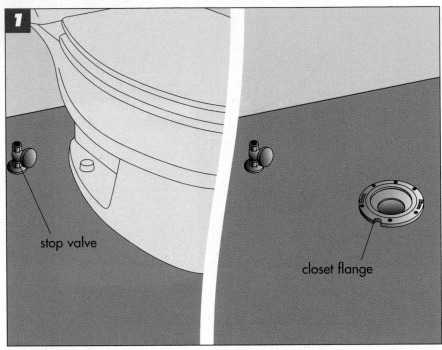

1. Assess the toilet.
When tiling over a finished bathroom floor, the toilet can be left in place. But you will have to cut tiles to fit all around the base, which will probably leave you with an unprofessional-looking job. It is easier in the long run to remove the toilet and tile up to the closet flange. With fewer cut tiles, the job will look better and pose fewer maintenance problems.

YOU'LL NEED

TIME: A full weekend for an average bathroom floor.
SKILLS: Removing and resetting a toilet, preparing a subfloor, and laying out and tiling a floor.
TOOLS: Wrench, hacksaw, and tiling and grouting tools.

EXPERTS' INSIGHT

REMOVING SINKS

If you have a pedestal or wall-mounted sink with legs sink, remove it before you start to tile. Shut off the water supply and disconnect the supply lines. Remove the trap with a pipe wrench. Unbolt and remove the top of a pedestal sink, then unbolt and remove the pedestal. (One-piece pedestal sinks are bolted to the floor and wall.) Remove the legs of a wall-mounted sink and pull the sink up and off of the mounting bracket. You may also want to remove a vanity, depending on its position.

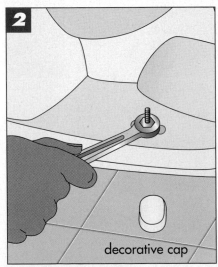

2. Remove the toilet.
Shut off the water supply and disconnect the supply line. Flush the toilet, then sponge the remaining water from the tank. Pry off the decorative caps, then unscrew the flange nuts. If the nut is rusted tight, cut through it with a hacksaw; the easiest way is to

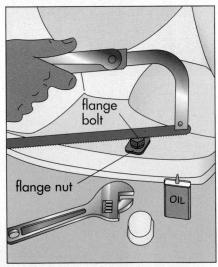

cut down, as shown, and then unscrew it. With a helper, lift the toilet off the flange, and carry it to another room. Stuff a rag in the closet flange (make sure it's large enough so it won't fall down the hole) to contain sewer gases, and scrape off any wax, putty, or caulk.

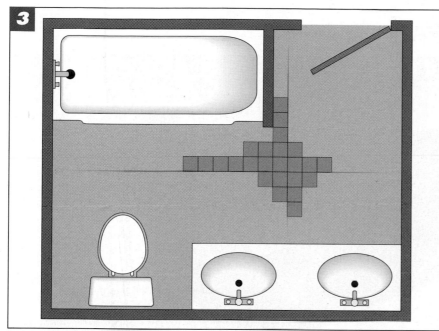

3. Lay out the job.

Small, rectangular bathroom floors are relatively easy to lay out. Arrange grout joints so that they are parallel to the most visible straight edges in the room, such as along counters and tubs. Hide cut tiles in less exposed spots. In such a small area, it is worth your while to check the layout by dry-setting all of the tiles before you begin the installation. See pages 583–585.

4. Set the tiles.

Set full tiles as close as possible to the closet flange. Use nippers to cut tiles to fit around the flange. You don't have to worry about precision here, since the toilet will cover the area.

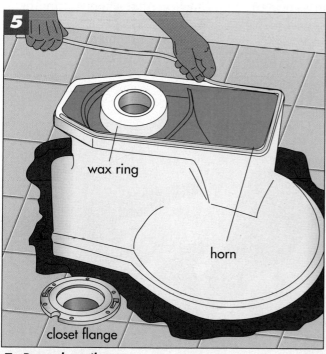

wax ring

horn

closet flange

5. Reset the toilet.

After the tile has been grouted, reset the toilet. Install new bolts in the flange; they may need to be longer than the old ones to compensate for the height of the tiles. Clean the horn of the bowl and install a new wax ring. If the flange is well below the tile surface, you may need a second wax ring to seal the gap. Set the toilet over the bolts, then tighten the nuts.

EXPERTS' INSIGHT

TILING OVER TILE

■ When remodeling a bathroom, you may want to replace an old tiled floor with new tiling. Removing the old tile can be a major headache, and it may not be necessary. Instead, you can use the existing floor as a setting bed for the new tile.

■ First, make certain that there are no structural problems with the floor—if the grout is significantly cracked and tiles are loose, it could signal underlying problems that need to be addressed before proceeding. Talk to your tile dealer about the best products and techniques to use over a tiled floor. Normally, the old tiles will need to be sanded heavily, to rough up the glazed surface. You may also need to fill in old grout joints if they aren't level with the tile surface.

■ Keep in mind that the new tile will add to the height of your bathroom floor. Place tiles on top of your existing floor to find out whether this new height will make it awkward to move from the hall into the bathroom. Usually, a threshold will smooth the transition.

TILING AN ENTRYWAY

Most professional tilesetters agree that the best substrate for tile is an old-fashioned mortar bed. But laying it smooth is a job for the pros. Backerboard has made it easier for do-it-yourselfers to install their own tile. There are times, though, when backerboard won't work. This is often the case when you cannot afford to raise the height of the finish floor too much. Entryways frequently pose this dilemma, because the floor connects with several rooms and often a stairway as well. In those situations, a modified mortar-bed installation is best.

YOU'LL NEED

TIME: 2–4 days, depending on the size of the entryway and the amount of preparation needed. Allow time for cement to cure.
SKILLS: Troweling cement to a consistent thickness; preparing a subfloor; and tiling a floor.
TOOLS: Steel trowel, stapler, utility knife, and paint roller.

EXPERTS' INSIGHT

BRINGING THE OUTDOORS IN

Often the best types of tile to use for an entryway are those that are commonly used on exterior applications, such as unglazed pavers, (machine- or handmade), slate, and half brick. If you also plan to tile an adjacent patio, porch, or other entrance to the house, use matching tiles inside and out to unify the spaces. Be sure the tiles you choose won't become slippery when wet.

Measure felt paper, cut with a utility knife 2–4 inches longer than needed. Roll it loosely, then unroll in position.

1. Prepare floor.
Stabilize any spongy areas of the floor using drywall screws twice as long as the thickness of your flooring. If necessary, add plywood so your subfloor totals at least 1⅛-inch in thickness. Install 15-pound felt roofing paper overlapping the edges 2 to 3 inches, and staple the paper to the subfloor every 6 to 8 inches. After stapling, trim the edges with a utility knife so the felt doesn't ride up any adjacent molding or stairs.

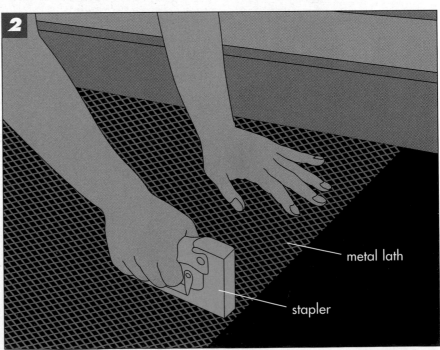

metal lath

stapler

2. Attach metal lath.
Staple galvanized metal lath (mesh) over the felt paper. Available at masonry-supply stores and large home centers in 2-foot-wide strips, the lath can be cut with tin snips. Butt the pieces together; don't overlap them.

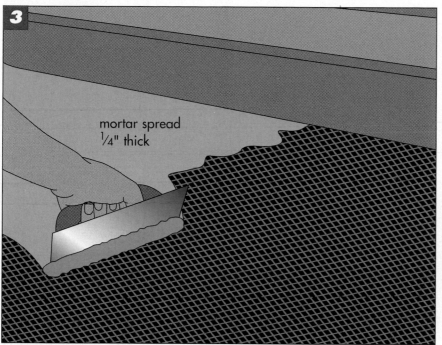

3. Spread the mortar.

Prepare a cement mixture of half portland cement and half fine (builders) sand. The fine sand should not contain stones that would make the surface bumpy.

Spread cement with a steel trowel to a depth of ¼ inch, smoothing all ridges. Avoid smearing mortar on stair riser or adjacent molding.

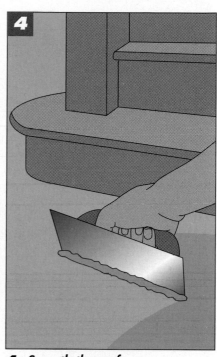

4. Smooth the surface.

Let the mortar cure over night. Then carefully go over the cement with a trowel to scrape away any high spots. Sweep it to remove any loose material.

5. Lay out and set tiles.

An entryway can be difficult to lay out because different parts of the floor are visible from different directions. Choose the most public point of view and plan your layout around it. Dry fit the tiles to ensure there won't be any slivers of tile.

6. Grout and seal.

If the tiles were not sealed when you bought them, apply the sealer recommended by the tile maker before grouting. After the tiles are grouted (see pages 600–602), wait about a week before applying a liquid top coat, which should be renewed once or twice a year.

CHOOSING SEALERS AND FINISHES

Grout lines, unglazed tile, and unpolished natural stone are vulnerable to stains, dirt, grease, and mildew. For protection of porous surfaces apply a sealer or finish (the terms are interchangeable). Product types vary according to porosity of the material being covered and the degree of sheen you want. All require that the surface is clean, dry, and free of any other coatings or wax before application. Typically sealers and finishes can be applied in one coat but for very porous surfaces like brick, two coats are needed. Confirm that the sealer or finish you choose is rated for outdoor use; some are rated for indoor use only. Use a small paint brush when sealing the grout alone; apply it with a roller when sealing tile and grout.

TILING WALLS

Walls often are not very flat. Flexible drywall can be installed over bowed and twisted studs; once it is covered with paint or wallpaper, most people will never notice. But if you try to install tile on an irregular wall, the underlying problem will be magnified. It is very difficult to correct carpentry errors with tile. So check the walls carefully—and make necessary corrections—before you begin tiling.

YOU'LL NEED

TIME: About one hour per 5 square feet to set and grout tile, plus time for wall preparation.
SKILLS: Checking walls for straightness and squareness, preparing a substrate, installing tile, and grouting.
TOOLS: Level, straightedge, and tiling and grouting tools.

1. Assess the walls.
Use a carpenter's level to check walls for plumb. Set a long level or straightedge against the wall at various points to determine if the wall is flat. An out-of-plumb wall can be tiled, but it may affect the appearance of adjoining surfaces. If the wall is not reasonably flat, repair it first.

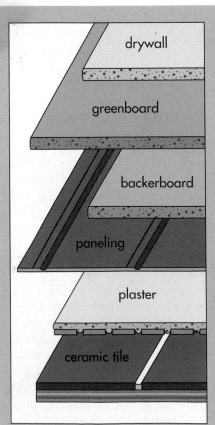

drywall

greenboard

backerboard

paneling

plaster

ceramic tile

WALL SUBSTRATES

Tile can be installed over most existing wall surfaces as long as the wall is flat and in sound condition.

Drywall: The most common wall surface, and a good substrate for tile in dry locations. Can also be used in moderately wet areas if you brush on liquid waterproofing before tiling. Repair holes or cracks with patching compound. Remove wall paper and loose paint. Lightly sand painted surfaces. Perhaps add a second layer of drywall for added strength or to cover damaged areas.

Moisture-resistant drywall: Commonly known as greenboard or blueboard, it is similar to standard drywall, but is water-resistant—though not waterproof. It can be used in fairly wet areas, but should receive the same waterproofing installation as regular drywall.

Backerboard: An ideal substrate for tile, especially as part of a waterproof installation on shower walls or bathtub surrounds. When installing backerboard over an existing wall surface, use corrosion-resistant nails or screws that are long enough to penetrate the wall studs.

Wall paneling: Most sheet paneling is too thin and fragile to be used as a substrate for tile. Remove the paneling and cover the wall with backerboard or drywall before tiling.

Plaster: Install tile over plaster that is hard, flat, and in good condition. If the plaster crumbles when you poke it with a knife, it is too weak and should be replaced with backerboard or drywall. Repair cracks and indentations.

Ceramic tile: You can tile directly over a previously tiled surface as long as it is in good condition. Remove loose or broken tile and fill the cavity with mortar. Aggressively sand the surface to remove the glaze.

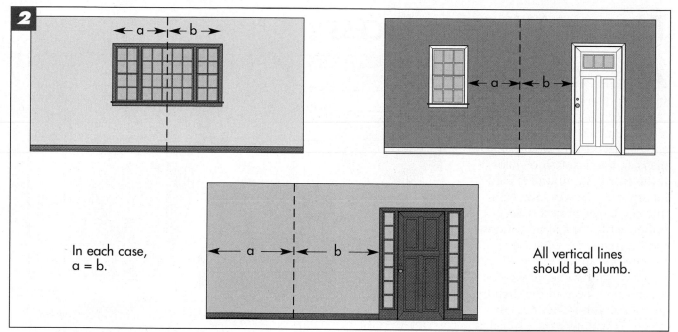

In each case, a = b.

All vertical lines should be plumb.

2. Establish a center line and lay out.

On a large wall, it is usually best to start the layout with a vertical line somewhere near the middle. If a single obstruction, such as a wall or a window, is reasonably centered in the room, then draw a line through its center. With two obstructions, make your center line at the middle of the distance between their inside edges. If you have a single offset obstruction, divide the unobstructed portion of the wall in half.

Then add a horizontal line to divide the wall into four quadrants. Add reference lines to separate the field tiles from any trim tiles. Use a carpenter's level to establish vertical and horizontal reference lines.

On a wall that is less than 8 feet wide, you may want to make sure that the cut tiles on either side are close to the same size. The only way to ensure this is to make a complete dry run of one horizontal course.

EXPERTS' INSIGHT

EXTENDING ELECTRICAL BOXES

When tiling around electrical outlets and switches, remove the cover plates and set tile right up to the cutout in the wall. This may mean that you will have to move the electrical box forward, so that it will be flush with the finished tile surface. Extension rings are available at electrical supply outlets; mount them on the existing boxes. Before you begin tiling, make sure that you can find extension rings in the size you need, or talk to an electrician about other options.

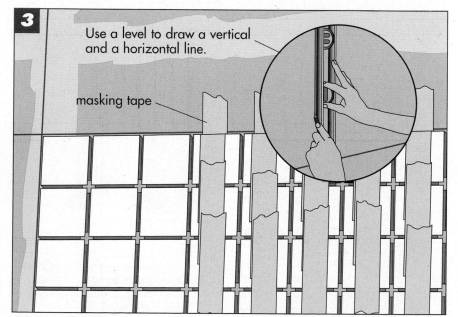

Use a level to draw a vertical and a horizontal line.

masking tape

3. Hold the tiles.

Gravity works against you when installing wall tiles. Wall tile adhesive usually is sticky enough to prevent tiles from falling off, and most wall tiles are self-spaced so they will not slide down. In a more difficult installation, you may have to use spacers to keep the tiles from slipping, and masking tape to hold them on the wall. On each column of tiles, affix tape that is taut and well-adhered to the wall tile while the adhesive cures.

TILING A WINDOW RECESS

A tiled window recess won't rot, will prevent and resist water stains, and won't get scratched by cats seeking a sunny refuge. Plain terra cotta tiles are an attractive choice; decorative, hand-painted tiles can add a splash of color. If the surrounding wall is tiled, incorporate the window recess into the larger project. Use bullnose tiles or special windowsill tiles to round the edges. It is usually best to tile the recess after the wall, so that the recess tiles can overlap the wall tile. In a tub surround with a window, cut down on maintenance problems by replacing sashes with glass block and then tiling the recess.

YOU'LL NEED

TIME: Less than a day of labor, but allow a day for the adhesive to cure before grouting.
SKILLS: Careful removal of molding and setting wall tile.
TOOLS: Flat pry bar, and tiling and grouting tools.

EXPERTS' INSIGHT

TILE AS TRIM

Tile is most often used to cover fairly broad areas; it makes for a wall that is low in maintenance as well as attractive. Sometimes, however, tile can make a stunning impact when it is used for small accents. One excellent example: Wood casing trim around doors and windows serves to hide an unattractive gap between materials. Tile can perform that function just as well, and with a good deal more pizzazz, especially if you choose decorative trim tiles.

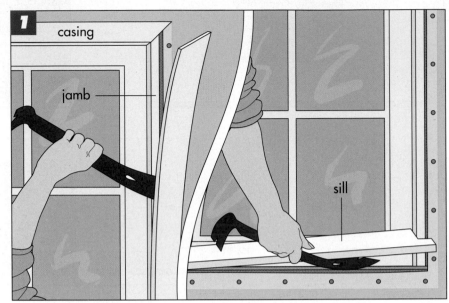

1. Remove molding and sill.
Remove the window casing, then pry off the sill. You may need to cut the sill to get it out. Now examine the jamb and decide how far inward toward the window the tile will extend. If the window has stop molding, decide whether to leave it in place or remove it. You can tile directly on top of the jamb or install backerboard first.

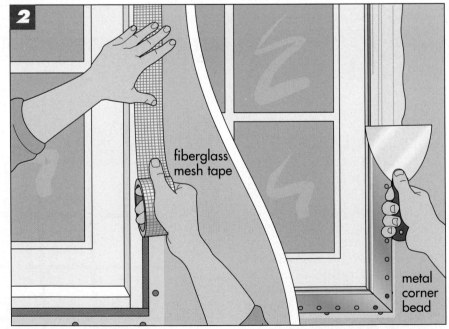

2. Prepare the wall.
Stuff the gap with fiberglass insulation if none exists; take care on an old window not to hinder the movement of the weights that are attached by ropes to the sashes. If you will be tiling the wall, apply fiberglass mesh joint tape, and fill in with joint compound. Allow to dry, apply a second coat, and sand smooth. If you will be painting the wall, carefully install metal outside corner bead, apply joint compound, and sand. Sand the jamb as well.

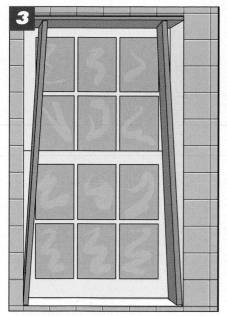

3. Support top pieces.
Install any wall tiles flush to the jamb so you will have a consistent grout line at the corners (see *right*). Make a support system using three boards to hold the ceiling tiles in place. Allow them to set before continuing.

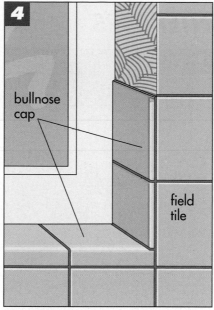

4. Set the tiles.
Set tiles in adhesive and grout the same as for a standard wall installation. Use bullnose caps for a tiled wall (as shown) or for a painted wall. Or, use one of the other options pictured *below*.

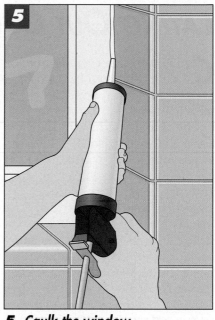

5. Caulk the window.
Take special care to completely caulk the joint between the tile and the window; you don't want all your work to be destroyed in a few years by water damage.

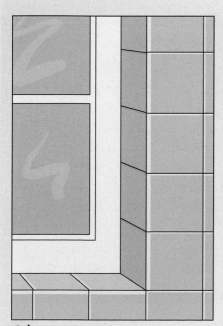

Other corner options.
The arrangement shown in the steps above, with bullnose caps used on the recessed surfaces, is the most common. You may prefer to use bullnose on the

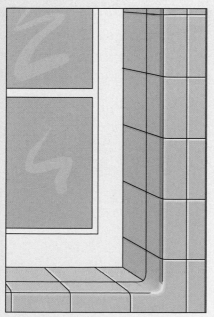

wall (*above, left*). Or use corner edging tiles similar to V-cap tiles used on countertops, but without the raised lip (*center*); install the edging pieces before tiling the recess. For a decorative touch,

apply a border trim around the recess (*above, right*). Install bullnose pieces in the recess so they cap the border trim, or butt field tiles up to the border pieces if they have a finished edge.

LAYING OUT COUNTERTOPS

Countertops are everyday work surfaces and are often subject to up-close scrutiny. Small misalignments can grow in importance if you have to stare at them all the time, so take the time to get your layout perfect. Most countertops are small enough that you can do a full dry run with loose tiles before starting the installation. Try to place equal-sized cut tiles along the sides and back. If the back wall is uneven, make the adjustment with the cut tiles at the back.

YOU'LL NEED

TIME: A day and a half to install substrate and tile.
SKILLS: Measuring and marking a layout; cutting and fastening plywood.
TOOLS: Drill, level, square, and circular saw or saber saw.

1. Install a plywood surface.
The countertop substrate should be at least one layer of ¾-inch exterior plywood. Take care that the front edges are square, and parallel to the walls. Level the whole top. Attach the top with construction adhesive and screws.

EXPERTS' INSIGHT

USING AN EXISTING COUNTERTOP AS THE SUBSTRATE

■ If conditions are right, you can tile over an existing laminated (such as Formica) countertop. The top must be square edged; a post-form countertop (with rounded edges) will not work. And it must be in sound condition, level, and firmly connected to the cabinets.
■ Remove the backsplash. Sand the entire surface thoroughly—use an electric vibrating sander, or spend a good deal of time hand-sanding with a sanding block and 60-grit sandpaper.

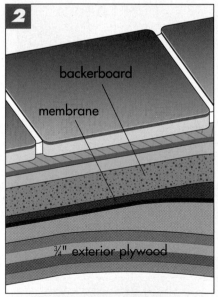

backerboard

membrane

¾" exterior plywood

2. Waterproof the substrate.
For a fully waterproofed installation, add a waterproofing membrane (15-pound felt paper or 4-mil polyethylene), followed by backerboard. Seal the joints of the backerboard with fiberglass-mesh tape, filled with thin-set mortar.

3. Lay the job out.
When laying out an L-shaped countertop, start at the inside corner and plan to use full tiles there. Align field tiles with the edge of the substrate unless you plan to use edging trim tiles, in which case draw a reference line separating trim from field tiles.

(See page 621 for edging possibilities.) If possible, plan so that grout lines will be evenly spaced from the sides of the sink. Run cut tiles around the back edges along the backsplash.

4

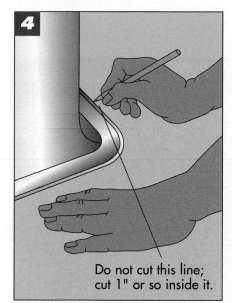

Do not cut this line; cut 1" or so inside it.

5

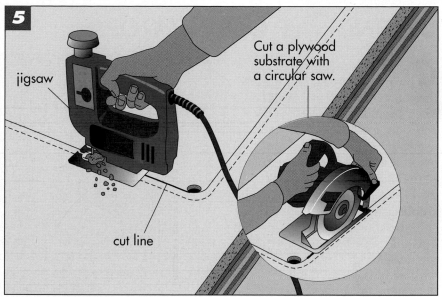

jigsaw

cut line

Cut a plywood substrate with a circular saw.

4. Mark the sink cutout.

Determine where the sink can fit into your sink base cabinet. Flip the sink upside down and trace the outline. Remove the sink and draw a cut line an inch or so inside the outline. Some new sinks come with a paper cutting template that can be used instead.

5. Cut the hole.

You could simply cut the opening with a circular saw, starting with a plunge cut, but cutting through backerboard with a circular saw will make a huge cloud of dust. So use a saber saw instead. Drill holes just inside the cut line at each corner. Use a drill bit large enough

to match the radius of the sink corners. Use a saber saw equipped with a rough-cutting blade to cut the sink opening. Have extra blades on hand; you'll probably need them. Install the sink before or after tiling, depending on the type (see *below*).

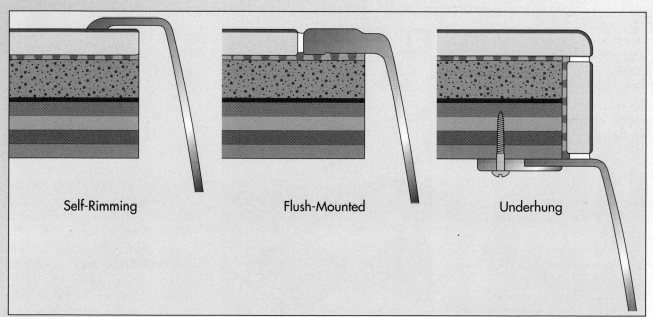

Self-Rimming

Flush-Mounted

Underhung

Sink Options

If your countertop tiling project involves a sink, be sure to buy the sink and learn how it is installed before you set any tile. The most common type of kitchen sink is "self-rimming."

Install it after the countertop has been tiled; the edges of the sink rest on top of the tile. Install a flush-mounted sink before tiling, and run the tile up to the edge of the sink. Underhung sinks are difficult to install, but perform

well. Neither a flush-mounted nor an underhung sinks has a lip, so messes and water from the countertop can be wiped directly into the sink. (See page 579 for tips on caulking around a sink.)

SETTING TILE COUNTERTOPS

Choose tiles made for the purpose. That usually means that they will be ½ inch thick. They should be glazed, or they will stain easily. It is usually best to use either a light-colored grout or one that comes close to the color of the tile, rather than a dark, starkly contrasting color that will emphasize any imperfections.

To be sure the tile color and finish is consistent, work with a tile dealer who can supply you with all of the field tiles, decorative or bullnose tiles for the front edge, and radius bullnose for the backsplash. Every tile whose edge will be exposed must have a rounded edge on one side called a bullnose or cap. Don't use a field tile and then attempt to give it a finished edge with grout; it will look ugly and wear poorly.

Use the adhesive recommended by your dealer. Thin-set mortar is usually the best choice. If you want to make the installation waterproof, be sure to choose all materials with that end in mind.

Work slowly and systematically. Setting a tile countertop is an ideal weekend project and provides good training for tackling more complex tiling jobs later on.

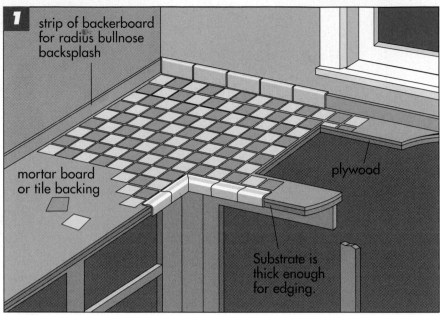

strip of backerboard for radius bullnose backsplash

mortar board or tile backing

plywood

Substrate is thick enough for edging.

1. Plan the job.
Prepare a firm, level, and flat surface for the tiles. Be sure that the total thickness of the substrate will be covered by the edging you choose (see next page). Check the substrate for level and square. If you are using backsplash edging tile with a large radius, provide backing for it by fastening a strip of backerboard to the wall (see page 622). Check the layout for the backsplash to find out if you will encounter any obstructions.

tile to be cut

Leave a gap.

2. Lay out a dry run.
Set the tiles in place, positioning them exactly as you want the finished surface to look. Use plastic spacers, and check that all lines are straight. To mark lines for cutting, hold each tile in place rather than measuring (page 595).

YOU'LL NEED

TIME: A full day to install about 12 feet of countertop, plus 2–3 hours the following day for grouting and cleaning.
SKILLS: Laying out, spreading adhesive, cutting, installing, and grouting tile.
TOOLS: Tape measure, level, square, tile cutter, notched trowel, grout float.

EXPERTS' INSIGHT

THE RIGHT GROUT
Because grout joints on countertops are visible and subjected to spills, it is important to use the best grout mixture possible. Use sanded grout for grout joints wider than $\frac{1}{16}$ inch. Mix the grout with a liquid latex additive rather than water for added protection against liquid penetration. If mildew is likely to be a problem, use an additive that inhibits the growth of mildew. Plan to seal the grout a week or two after installation.

3

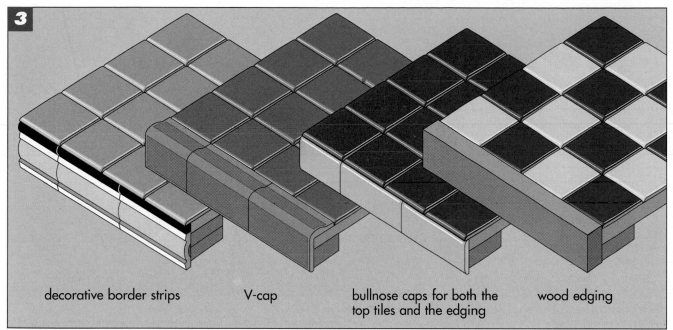

decorative border strips   V-cap   bullnose caps for both the top tiles and the edging   wood edging

3. Choose the edging.

The edging on a countertop is not just a decorative element added on at the end of the job. As an integral part of the counter, it must figure in your planing at each step of the way. Your choice of edge treatment will affect preparation and thickness of the substrate as well as the placement of reference lines.

You can add color and interest to a countertop by edging it with a combination of decorative border strips overlapped by bullnose tiles. A V-cap provides a slight lip that keeps water from dripping down the edge of the counter. Another alternative involves two bullnose edging pieces, one on the counter surface, one on the edging. Install the edge pieces and the surface tiles at the same time to keep them aligned.

EDGING WITH WOOD

Wood looks great as an edging material on kitchen countertops, and it is easy to install. It does create some additional maintenance concerns, however. Wood expands and contracts with temperature and humidity changes, but tiles and grout do not. So keep the wood separated from the tile with caulk. Set the edging flush with the top of the tile, or a little higher to create a drip-proof lip. Position the tiles about ⅛ inch shy of the edge of the substrate, to allow space for caulk. Attach the edging to the plywood substrate with countersunk screws every 6–8 inches, then hide the screw heads with plugs or filler. Or attach the edging with a biscuit joiner, for a surface free of screw holes.

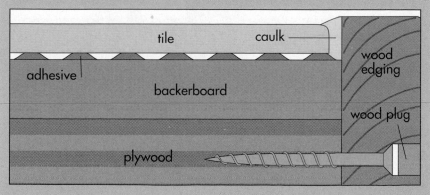

tile   caulk

adhesive

backerboard

wood edging

wood plug

plywood

CAUTION!

SEAL THE WOOD

One of the biggest challenges posed by wood edging on a countertop is keeping the wood looking as good as new years after it was installed. Use a tough hardwood, such as maple or oak, to help minimize dents and scrapes. Before installing the edging, coat all sides with a durable clear wood finish such as polyurethane. Apply more finish to any penetrations made in the wood while it is being installed. In the years to come, watch for dark stains on the wood, which could indicate that water has found its way into the wood. In that case, sand away the stain and apply another coat of finish.

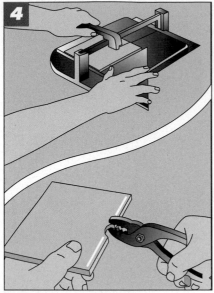

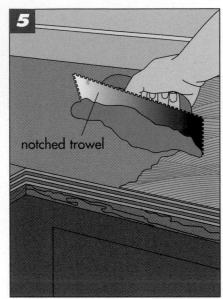

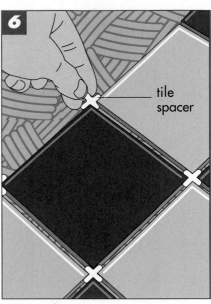

4. Cut tiles.

For the straight cuts, use a snap cutter. If you have many cuts to make, a wet saw may make the job go faster. Many of the cuts will be for the same size, so you can set the guide and cut them factory-style. For small curved or irregular cuts, use nippers or a rod saw. See pages 592–593 for instructions.

5. Spread adhesive.

Mix the thin-set mortar as directed on the label. If the powder does not contain a latex additive, use a liquid latex additive instead of water to mix with the powder. Let the mixture rest for ten minutes, then mix it again. Spread the adhesive with a notched trowel.

6. Set tiles.

Set the tiles along the reference lines, pressing each one into the adhesive with a slight twist. Avoid sliding the tiles. Use plastic spacers to keep all of the joints even. Check the alignment of set tiles regularly.

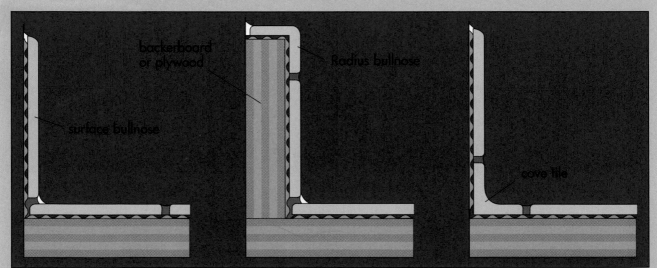

BACKSPLASH OPTIONS

Integrate the backsplash with the countertop, using the same tile patterns on both surfaces, with grout joints that line up. Or, treat the backsplash as an element all its own, using colors and sizes of tile that are unrelated to those on

the countertop. Make colorful backsplashes by using a variety of tiles. If you are creating a backsplash of surface bullnose tiles directly on the wall, it must be reasonably flat and in sound condition. A built-up backsplash

mimics the look of a traditional mortar-bed installation. Use plywood or backerboard to fill in the space behind a radius bullnose. A cove tile in the corner makes cleanup easier. Each material requires a different layout.

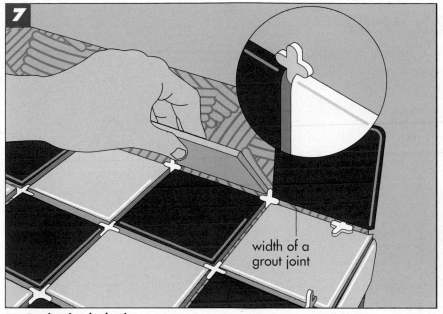

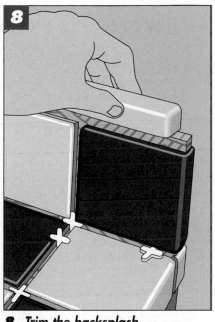

width of a
grout joint

7. Set backsplash tiles.

If you are using backsplash tiles that are the same width as the tiles on the countertop, install them so that the grout joints line up. Because these tiles are not subject to much wear and tear, it is possible to set them directly on the wall. Set backsplash tiles above the countertop tiles by the width of a grout joint.

8. Trim the backsplash.

If you use bullnose tiles set directly on the wall, you will not need to add trim tiles to the backsplash. If the backsplash is built out away from the wall, add radius bullnose trim tiles.

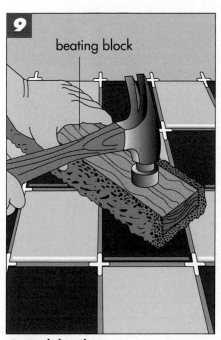

beating block

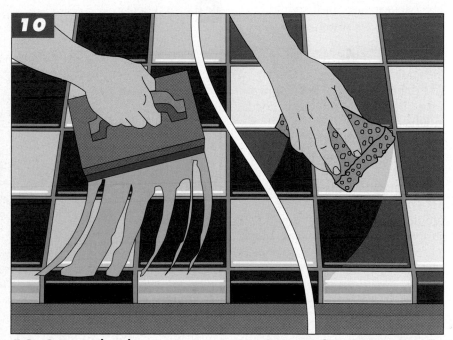

9. Bed the tiles.

After setting tiles in one section, bed them into the adhesive with a beating block. Move the beating block over the tiles while tapping lightly with a hammer. Clean out any excess adhesive that squeezes into grout joints.

10. Grout and seal.

Let the set tiles rest for 24 hours. Mix grout with a latex additive. Apply with a grout float, pushing the mixture into the joints. When the joints are filled, hold the float at nearly a right angle to the countertop and wipe away the excess. Do not use grout in the joint between the countertop and backsplash tiles; this joint and the space between the backsplash tile and the wall should be filled with caulk or sealant.

Wipe away excess grout with a sponge, then remove the grout haze once it appears. Apply grout sealer after the grout has cured.

TILING A TUB SURROUND

*I*n a tub that also contains a shower, plan to install tile from the top of the tub to about 6 inches above the shower head. If the tub doesn't have a shower, tile at least one foot above the tub (more if you anticipate a lot of splashing). If you want to tile the ceiling as well, use a fast-setting adhesive; it will hold the tiles in place without support. (Install ceiling tile so that it doesn't have to line up with the wall tiles—say, diagonally—because getting it to fit will be very difficult. If an end wall continues out past the tub, continue the tiles at least one full vertical row beyond the tub, and run it down to the floor. Use bullnose cap tiles for the edges.

Set the tile on a backerboard substrate (see pages 588–589 for information on backerboard). The backerboard itself should be installed over a waterproofing membrane of 15-lb. felt paper or 4-mil polyethylene. Overlay the edges of the membrane and seal the seams of the backerboard with fiberglass mesh tape bedded in adhesive.

If you have a window with wood casing and jambs, consider tearing it out or cutting back the casing and tiling the recess (pages 616–617). You can eliminate the problems of a wood window altogether by installing glass block.

YOU'LL NEED

TIME: A day to prepare the substrate, most of a day to tile, and a few hours to grout.
SKILLS: Cutting and installing backerboard, patching walls, cutting and installing tile.
TOOLS: Drill, hole saw, scraping tool, wall patching tools, level, a straight board, notched trowel, snap cutter, nibbler, hacksaw with rod saw, grouting float.

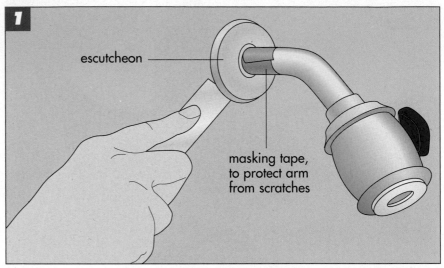

escutcheon

masking tape, to protect arm from scratches

1. Remove the hardware.
You don't want to cut tiles to fit precisely around hardware. Pry the shower-arm escutcheon away from the wall, and perhaps remove the shower arm as well. Remove the tub spout; most can be unscrewed by sticking the handle of a screwdriver or hammer in the spout and turning counterclockwise. Remove the faucet handles and escutcheons.

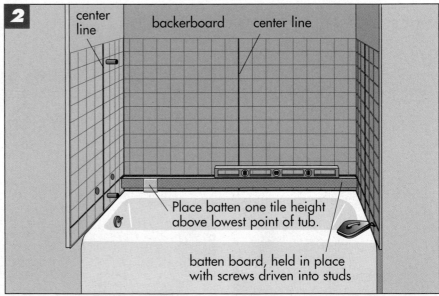

center line   backerboard   center line

Place batten one tile height above lowest point of tub.

batten board, held in place with screws driven into studs

2. Prepare and lay out.
The walls must be solid, and at least close to plumb and square (see page 583). If necessary, remove the existing substrate and install a waterproofing membrane and backerboard. Be sure that the new surface is flush with any adjoining surface.

Establish a vertical reference line by laying the tiles in a row on the tub and making sure you will either have the same size tile on each end, or that you will not have any very narrow pieces. If the end walls are out of square with the rear wall, factor in how the pieces will change size as you move upward. Measuring from the low point of the tub if it is not level, establish a horizontal reference line and tack a very straight batten board along its length.

CAUTION!

PROTECT YOUR TUB AND DRAIN
This kind of job creates abrasive debris. Sharp chips from cut tile, as well as grit from backerboard and dripping adhesive, will fall into the tub. Without protection, the tub will be scratched and the drain will clog. Refinished tubs or drains that already run slowly are particularly vulnerable. To provide minimal protection for the tub, throw down a dropcloth. A better solution is to buy a special tub cover, or to tape red rosin paper (the pink protective paper that contractors use) to cover the tub. To prevent clogs, stick a rag firmly in the drain hole.

3. Cut the tile.

Use a snap cutter for the straight cuts. Hold the tile in place and mark it for cutting. Align it on the cutter, score the surface by pushing down while sliding the cutter once across the tile, then push down on the handle. For a series of cuts of the same size, use the adjustable guide. Smooth the ragged cut edges with a rubbing stone or file.

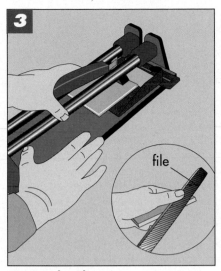

4. Set the tile.

Apply adhesive with a notched trowel, taking care not to cover your layout lines. Set the tiles, giving each a little twist and pushing to make sure it sticks. Start with the row sitting on the batten. Most wall tiles are self-spacing. Once you have several rows installed, remove the batten and install the bottom row.

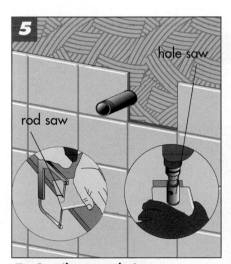

5. Cut tile around pipes.

Cuts around pipes usually do not have to be precise because the opening is covered with an escutcheon. Use a nibbler to eat away at a curved cut, or a hacksaw equipped with a rod-saw blade. To cut a hole, use a tile-cutting hole saw. Or, set the tile on a piece of scrap wood, drill a series of closely spaced holes with a masonry bit, and tap out the hole.

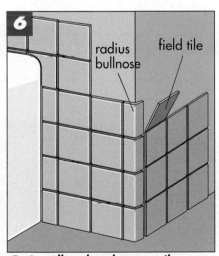

6. Install end and corner tiles.

Cut the curved piece at the corner of the tub with a hacksaw fitted with a rod-saw blade; it may take several attempts to get it just right. Use radius bullnose tiles everywhere there is an exposed edge. (Do not use a field tile edged with grout—it will look very sloppy.)

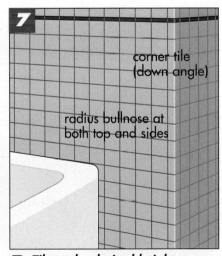

7. Tile to the desired height.

When you reach your top row, wipe away excess adhesive from the wall as you install bullnose caps, as shown on page 621. Use outside corner pieces ("down angles"), which have two cap edges, at all outside corners.

8. *Attach ceramic accessories.*

Apply adhesive and use masking tape to hold soap dishes and other accessories in place until they are set. Take the tape off after a day or two and apply grout, but wait a week or so before using.

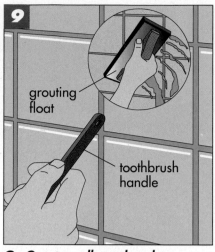

grouting float

toothbrush handle

9. *Grout, caulk, and seal.*

Mix the grout with latex additive, and push it into the joints with a grouting float held nearly flat. Tip the float up and wipe away the excess. Carefully wipe the surface to produce consistent grout lines. Use a toothbrush handle or other tool to shape the joints. Caulk the corners and edges. Wipe and dry-buff the haze.

10. *Reattach the hardware.*

Reattach the plumbing hardware. If you need to install a shower arm, use a thin tool handle to tighten it. If the new tile has caused valves or nipples to be recessed too far and you can't install a faucet or spout, visit a plumbing supplier and pick up suitable extensions. Once the grout has cured, apply sealer.

TILING AN ACCESS PANEL

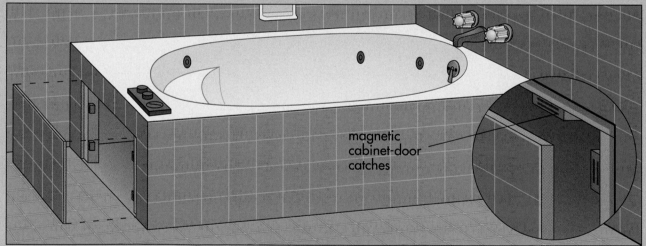

magnetic cabinet-door catches

Plumbing access panels are usually located in an adjoining room, but yours might be in the bathroom. The panel may have been installed when the bathroom was built, or it might have been built out of necessity when a plumber needed to gain access to the pipes and valves supplying the tub. Don't just tile over the panel; a plumber may need to get in there again someday. The easiest solution is to cover the panel with a piece of plastic, well-painted plywood, or a plastic access panel made for the purpose (available at home centers).

Or, make a tiled access panel. Cut a piece of plywood sized to hold full tiles. Install tiles on it so they will align with the surrounding tiles, and trim the edges with painted wood molding; drive screws through the molding to hold the panel in place. Or skip the molding, and attach with magnetic cabinet door catches, as shown *above*.

MASONRY

GETTING TO KNOW YOUR STRUCTURES

Garage floors.

To withstand the weight of cars and small trucks, a garage floor slab should be at least 4 inches thick. It should be strengthened with reinforcing wire mesh and be poured on top of at least 4 inches of solidly tamped gravel or sand.

A footing running around the perimeter of the slab adds extra support for the garage walls. It can be shallow if there is no significant frost danger in your area or if local building codes permit a "floating" slab—one that can rise or fall an inch or so with frost heave. Otherwise, the footing should extend below the frost line. Anchor bolts in the footing allow you to firmly attach the bottom plate of the wall framing.

To handle condensation, blown-in rain or snow, and moisture from vehicles, the slab should slope toward the floor drain or garage door at a rate of ¼ inch per foot.

Footings.

Before building a masonry wall, you must pour a solid footing or the wall will crack. (The exception is a dry stone wall, which has no mortar joints.) How extensive the footing should be depends on how much weight it must carry. For a low garden wall you need only a small pad. A tall masonry or concrete wall, however, requires a substantial footing that extends below the frost line.

To support posts for a deck, gazebo, or similar project, you need to set post footings below the frost line in areas with frost or your structure will move up and down with the changing seasons. Simply dig holes and pour in the concrete footings. Or, insert cylindrical concrete tube forms into the holes before pouring the concrete.

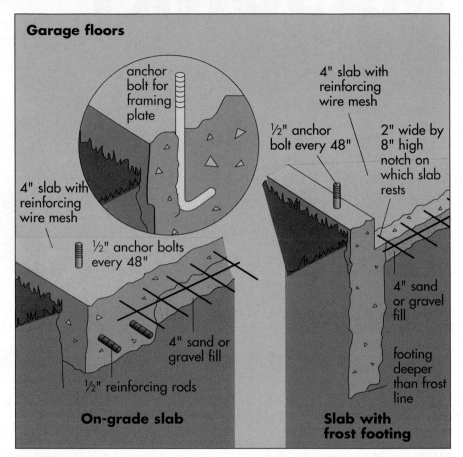

Garage floors

anchor bolt for framing plate

4" slab with reinforcing wire mesh

½" anchor bolt every 48"

2" wide by 8" high notch on which slab rests

4" slab with reinforcing wire mesh

½" anchor bolts every 48"

4" sand or gravel fill

4" sand or gravel fill

footing deeper than frost line

½" reinforcing rods

On-grade slab

Slab with frost footing

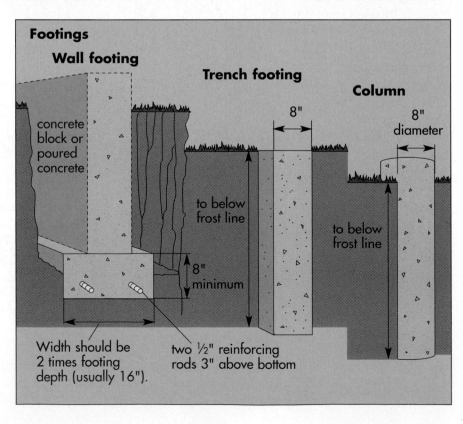

Footings

Wall footing

Trench footing

Column

concrete block or poured concrete

8"

8" diameter

to below frost line

to below frost line

8" minimum

Width should be 2 times footing depth (usually 16").

two ½" reinforcing rods 3" above bottom

Patio surfaces.

If you want to lay a patio of bricks, concrete pavers, or tiles that are ¾ inch or more thick, the most common way is to set them in a bed of sand that rests on a stable surface. If your soil is stable, 2 to 4 inches of sand alone may be enough of a base. But to be sure that your patio does not develop waves and splits, excavate deeper and start with a bed of gravel. Either way, it is important to thoroughly tamp down both the soil and the substrate, using a vibrating tamper, which you can rent. Once the sand is level, install the finish material and fill in the joints between the pavers with fine sand (see pages 756-759).

Other techniques can be used for patio construction. You can set tiles designed for outdoor use in mortar on a solid concrete base or set flagstone directly on firmly tamped soil.

Below-grade walls.

To hold back the weight of soil, a wall built below grade must be strong. But even the strongest wall cannot withstand the hydraulic pressure that builds up behind it when soil becomes saturated with rainwater. So, in addition to being built solidly, the wall must have a way for water to escape. Weep holes, small in diameter and spaced 4 to 10 feet apart, allow water to pass through the wall. Or, in the case of a foundation wall, you can direct water along one or both sides of a wall. The most common way to do this is with perforated drainpipe set in a bed of gravel and sloped slightly.

A landscaping retaining wall commonly is battered, that is, sloped toward the soil it retains. This gives the wall strength. Structural walls cannot be battered, so build them strong, with plenty of reinforcement.

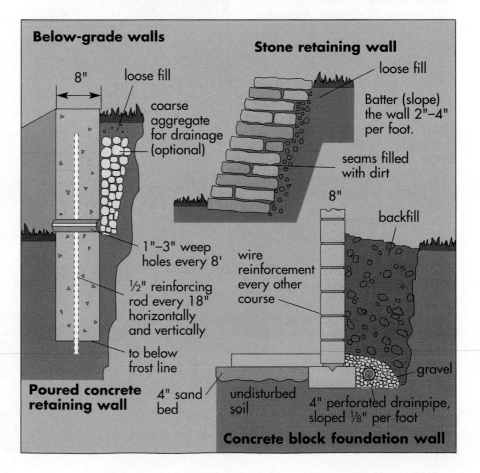

Patios

bricks or pavers

Joints between bricks are filled with fine sand.

sand

gravel

Soil should be free of organic material and well tamped.

Below-grade walls

8"

loose fill

coarse aggregate for drainage (optional)

1"–3" weep holes every 8'

½" reinforcing rod every 18" horizontally and vertically

to below frost line

Poured concrete retaining wall

4" sand bed

Stone retaining wall

loose fill

Batter (slope) the wall 2"–4" per foot.

seams filled with dirt

8"

backfill

wire reinforcement every other course

undisturbed soil

4" perforated drainpipe, sloped ⅛" per foot

gravel

Concrete block foundation wall

Selecting Masonry and Concrete Tools

Successful masonry and concrete work requires special techniques. Having the correct tool is essential if you want to end up with straight mortar lines and smooth surfaces. Compared with carpentry tools, masonry tools are not expensive, so don't hesitate to buy top-quality tools. Cheap tools can make the job more difficult and lead to shoddy-looking work that you'll have to live with a long time. If your budget is tight, consider renting professional-quality tools rather than buying something from the bargain bin.

A **circular saw, framing square, tape measure, chalk line, line level**, and **4-foot level** are general-purpose tools you'll need. For mixing and transporting masonry materials and concrete, get a sturdy contractor-quality **wheelbarrow** with a capacity of at least 3 cubic feet. Make sure the tire is an air-filled type. A **mortar box** is handy for mixing a lot of material, and a **mortar hoe** allows you to mix materials more easily than a garden hoe or a shovel.

To prepare the site and move concrete and mortar ingredients you'll need a **round-point shovel** for general digging, a **square-blade shovel** for moving sand and wet concrete, and a **spade** for squaring up a slab excavation or a footing trench.

Use a **tamper** to prepare soil for masonry surfaces. The beginning steps in finishing concrete require a **darby**, a **wood float**, and a **bull float**. For final finishing, use a magnesium or steel **finishing trowel** (usually it's best to have both). An **edger** is necessary to round off and strengthen edges of slabs. Make control joints with a **jointer** while the material is still wet. Or, cut joints after concrete is set using a circular saw equipped with a **masonry blade**.

Cutting bricks, blocks, or stones will be much easier if you have a **bricklayer's hammer, a brick set** or **masonry chisel**, and a 2-pound **baby sledgehammer**.

When building concrete or masonry walls, you'll need **line blocks, line clips, mason's line**, a modular **spacing rule**, and a **plumb bob** (a chalk line can be used in place of a plumb bob).

For placing mortar, use a well-balanced pointed **brick trowel**. Use a **pointing trowel, ⅜-inch back filler**, or a **sled jointer** to tuckpoint, or force, mortar into joints being repaired. Finish the joints with a **joint strike**; these are available in different shapes and help you strike (finish) mortar joints between bricks, blocks, or stones. A good stiff **hand brush** is necessary for finishing the job, along with a variety of stiff brushes for cleanup.

If you finish the concrete with a nonskid surface, have handy a stiff-bristled push broom. To cure concrete, you need a garden hose with an adjustable nozzle or an oscillating lawn sprinkler.

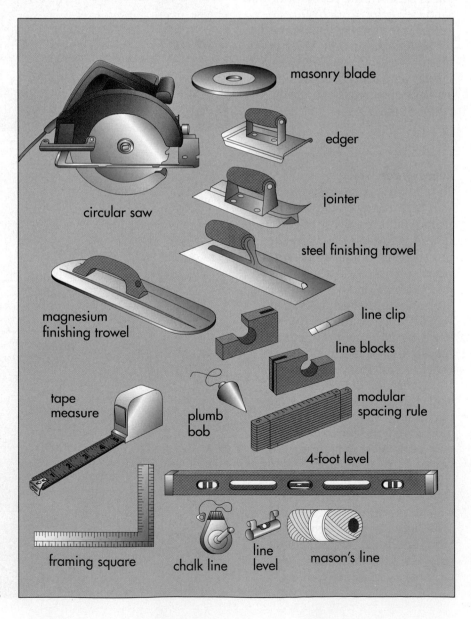

masonry blade

edger

jointer

steel finishing trowel

circular saw

magnesium finishing trowel

line clip

line blocks

modular spacing rule

tape measure

plumb bob

4-foot level

framing square

chalk line

line level

mason's line

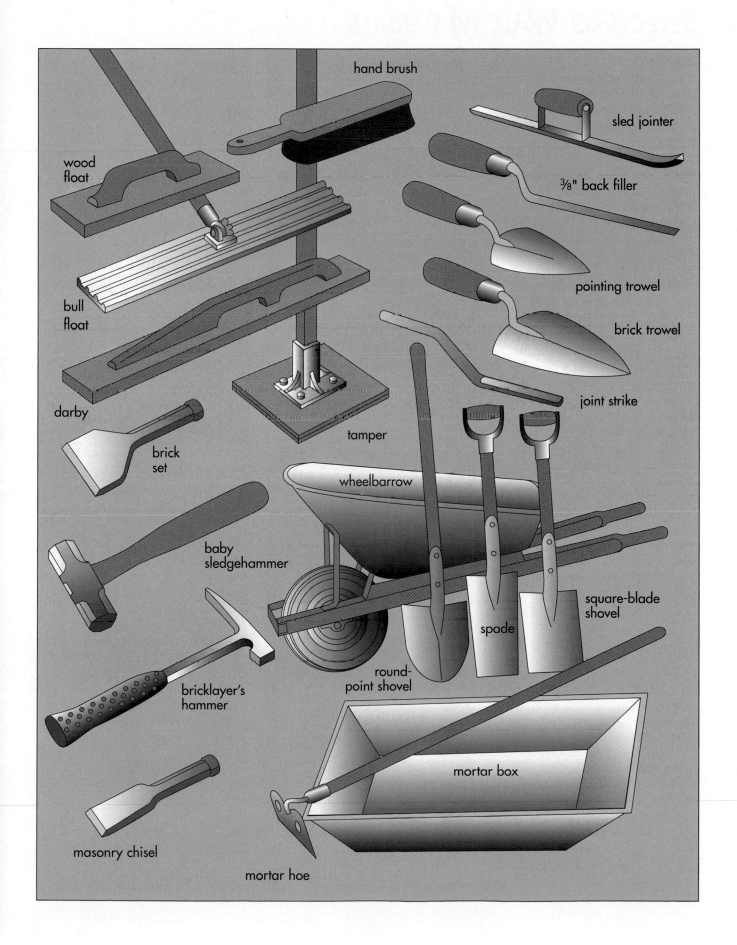

hand brush

sled jointer

⅜" back filler

wood float

pointing trowel

brick trowel

bull float

joint strike

darby

tamper

wheelbarrow

brick set

baby sledgehammer

square-blade shovel

spade

round-point shovel

bricklayer's hammer

masonry chisel

mortar box

mortar hoe

SELECTING WALL MATERIALS

Concrete.

Concrete is a mixture of sand, coarse aggregate, Portland cement, and water. The **sand** used in concrete should be blank-run sand, which is fairly round in shape and of various sizes. The **coarse aggregate** is gravel or crushed stone. Concrete should have aggregate pieces no larger than one-quarter the thickness of the pour. For example, if the pour is less than 4 inches thick, the aggregate should be less than 1 inch in size. **Portland cement** is made of clay, lime, and other ingredients that have been heated in a kiln and ground into a fine powder. Choose Type 1 cement. (See pages 652–679 for how to work with concrete.)

Brick.

Manufactured by firing molded clay or shale, bricks vary widely in color, texture, and dimensions. Despite these variations, they fall into four main categories: common or building, patio, fire, and facing.

Bricks are modular, meaning that they are either one-half or one-third as wide as they are long. The most common nominal modular unit size is 4 inches. Like lumber, bricks are described according to nominal rather than actual sizes. For instance, the actual size of a 4×8 brick is 3⅝×7⅝ inches. The nominal size is the actual size plus a normal mortar joint of ⅜ to ½ inch on the bottom and at one end.

For outdoor projects that must withstand moisture and freeze-thaw cycles, ask for SW (severe-weathering grade) bricks. For indoor uses, such as facing a fireplace or a planter, you can use MW (moderate weathering) or NW (no weathering). (See pages 686–687 for bricklaying techniques.)

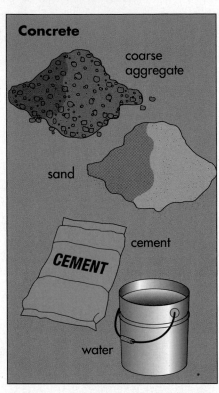

Concrete

coarse aggregate

sand

cement

CEMENT

water

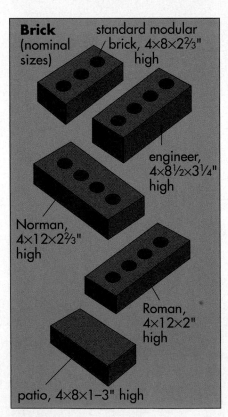

Brick (nominal sizes)

standard modular brick, 4×8×2⅔" high

engineer, 4×8½×3¼" high

Norman, 4×12×2⅔" high

Roman, 4×12×2" high

patio, 4×8×1–3" high

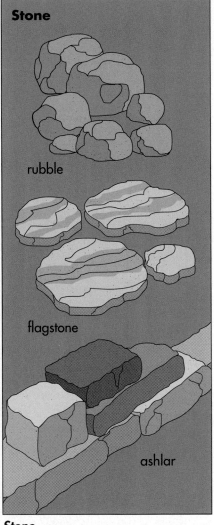

Stone

rubble

flagstone

ashlar

Stone.

Building stone is divided into three basic types: rubble, flagstone, and ashlar.

Rubble is round rocks of various sizes. **Flagstone** consists of flat pieces, 2 to 4 inches thick, of irregular shapes. **Ashlar**, or dimensioned stone, is cut into pieces of uniform thickness for laying in coursed or noncoursed patterns.

Quarried stone is cut from a mountainside or a pit; fieldstone is rock that has been found lying in fields or along rivers. (See pages 682–685 and 688–689 for how to build stone walls.)

Mortar

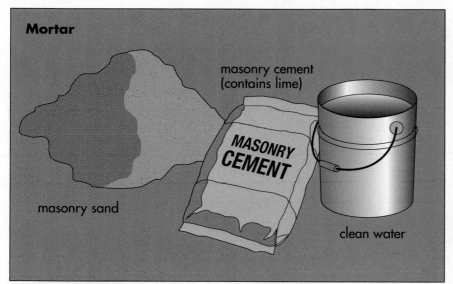

masonry cement
(contains lime)

MASONRY CEMENT

clean water

masonry sand

Lightweight veneers

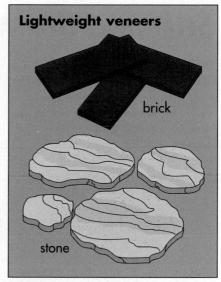

brick

stone

Mortar ingredients.

Essential to all brick and block construction, mortar is a paste made of **water, cement, lime,** and **sand**. Lime slows the setting speed, making the mortar easier to work. Mortar by itself is not as strong as concrete, but it has strong adhesive properties. In combination with stone, brick, or block, it creates extra-strong walls. In addition, mortar serves as an attractive spacer between materials and helps hide their imperfections. It also has a decorative function. Joints can be tooled to various finishes (see page 643). Mortar also can be pigmented.

Masonry veneers.

Lightweight veneers are made of **brick,** natural or artificial **stone,** and terra-cotta (unglazed, fired clay). Except in very dry climates, their use should be restricted to interior projects, such as covering concrete or masonry walls or as a decorative finish over drywall or plaster walls (see pages 702–703).

Concrete blocks
(nominal sizes)

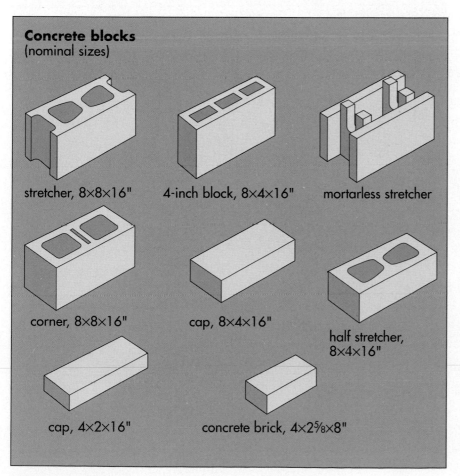

stretcher, 8×8×16"

4-inch block, 8×4×16"

mortarless stretcher

corner, 8×8×16"

cap, 8×4×16"

half stretcher, 8×4×16"

cap, 4×2×16"

concrete brick, 4×2⅝×8"

Concrete blocks and bricks.

Concrete blocks and bricks are cast from a stiff concrete mix and are heavy. ("Cinder" blocks, made of light-weight clay or pumice, are not as strong.) Hollow cores in the block help conserve material, make the blocks easier to grip and place, add insulation value, and provide channels for utilities. Use N-grade blocks for places where a wall will be exposed to freezing and S-grade blocks where the wall will be shielded from the weather.

A typical **stretcher** concrete block—the most commonly used block—has a nominal size of 8×8×16 inches and weighs about 45 pounds. **Corner** blocks have finished edges. A bundle of blocks usually has a mixture of stretchers and corners. Use **caps** to finish off exposed tops of block walls. **Mortarless** blocks are laid on top of each other without mortar joints. Once the wall is stacked in place, you reinforce it and grout it.

SELECTING SURFACING MATERIALS

Stone.

Use stone materials where you want a rugged look in exterior walls, borders, and patio surfaces. Most of the cost of stone is in transporting it.

If you live near a field or river that has large, attractive stones, you can find, rather than buy, your own fieldstone. Be sure to get permission from the landowner to take stones, and protect your back when you lift them.

Flagstone (see page 632) and **stone tile** are the most commonly used stones for patio surfaces. Stone tile is cut as precisely as regular tile. **Slate** is suitable for interior floors. Use it for exterior surfaces only in mild climates. Slate can be purchased randomly cut or as "Vermont tile," which comes in boxes containing the exact tiles for a certain patchwork-style pattern.

Tile and block.

A wide variety of tiles is available for exterior use. **Adobe,** once strictly limited to use in the Southwest and subject to rapid decay, is now reinforced with asphalt and is suitable for use in all types of climates.

Tile comes in a huge variety of shapes, colors, and surfaces. To avoid a slippery surface, choose unglazed tiles for exterior use. Tiles that are ¾ inch or more thick can be set in sand for exterior surfaces (see pages 756–759). Thinner tiles should be set in mortar on a solid concrete base for patios or used only on interior floors (see pages 680–681).

Turf block, made of strong cast concrete, can be set directly on top of smooth, well-tamped soil. Grass grows right through turf block. Its grid configuration provides excellent drainage.

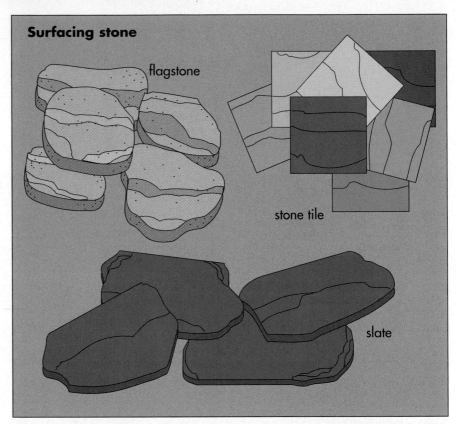

Surfacing stone

flagstone

stone tile

slate

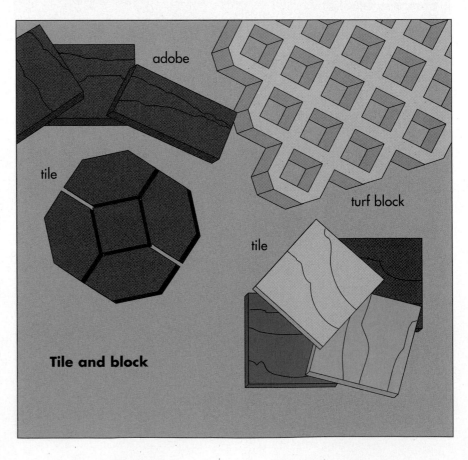

adobe

tile

turf block

tile

Tile and block

Concrete pavers.

Concrete pavers are extremely popular because of their low cost and durability; they will outlast any patio material except stone. However, some people feel they lack the warmth of stone or tile and that they look too much like imitation brick.

Pavers are relatively easy to install. They can be set to allow for some drainage between their joints. Several interlocking patterns are available. Colors include pink, gray, and a reddish brown color. Some have exposed aggregate surfaces. Higher-priced pavers come close to the color of stone or adobe, often by slightly varying the colors from stone to stone. Pavers also can be custom-pigmented.

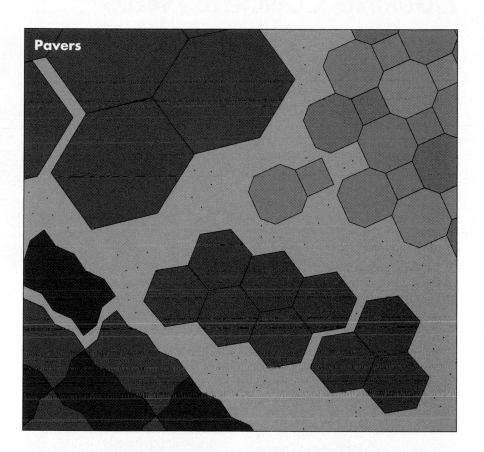

Pavers

Loose materials.

Small stones and pebbles can be used for borders or patio areas that do not receive much traffic. They are easy to install; just excavate, add synthetic weed block material and edging, pour the material in, and rake it smooth. Once tamped down, these materials make a stable surface with just enough give for comfortable walking.

Choose materials that complement your patio, deck, or yard. Landscaping material suppliers usually have large bins of different materials from which to choose. **Crushed granite, redrock,** and **quartz pebbles** compact well, but usually have sharp edges that can hurt bare feet. **River rocks** are smooth and handsome-looking, but make an uncomfortable walking surface and are slippery when wet.

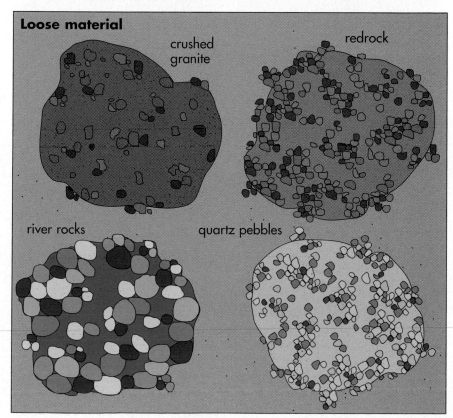

Loose material

crushed granite

redrock

river rocks

quartz pebbles

FIGURING CONCRETE NEEDS

With the help of a simple calculator, you can determine accurately how much concrete you need. Suppliers measure and sell concrete by the yard, which means cubic yard (3×3×3 feet or 27 cubic feet).

Measure the project accurately, especially the depth of slabs and any variations in the excavation. A large slab that is only ½ inch thicker than you think it is will need a lot more concrete than your calculation. Double-check the figures with a concrete supplier—you both have an interest in getting the measurement right.

CAUTION!

Don't underestimate. Nothing is worse than finding out that you are just a few cubic feet short of having enough concrete. Aim at having a little too much concrete; adding more after the first batch has set will weaken the final product.

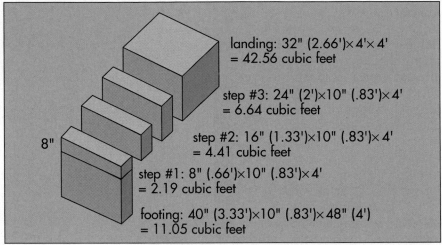

landing: 32" (2.66')×4'×4'
= 42.56 cubic feet

step #3: 24" (2')×10" (.83')×4'
= 6.64 cubic feet

step #2: 16" (1.33')×10" (.83')×4'
= 4.41 cubic feet

step #1: 8" (.66')×10" (.83')×4'
= 2.19 cubic feet

footing: 40" (3.33')×10" (.83')×48" (4')
= 11.05 cubic feet

8"

Calculate for steps and footings.
To estimate concrete needs, divide odd-shaped jobs into easy-to-figure sections. Add the results to get total volume. In this example, the steps have 8-inch (.66-foot) risers and 10-inch (.83-foot) treads, and the landing is 4×4 feet. (To get the measurement in feet, divide inches by 12.) Use this formula: Length × width × depth equals volume. The sum of the volumes of this footing, landing, and steps is about 67

cubic feet. Assuming you'll fill the forms about two-thirds full of rubble (see page 670), you need about 22 cubic feet of concrete. If you add in a 10-percent cushion, you get around 25 cubic feet. Divide that by 27 (the cubic feet in a cubic yard), and your estimate is a bit less than 1 cubic yard.

To find the area of a cylindrical pier, square the radius and multiply by 3.14, then multiply by the depth of the pier.

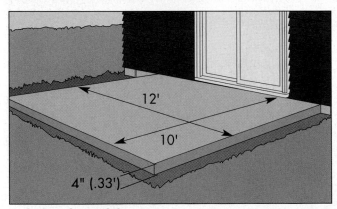

12'

10'

4" (.33')

Calculate for a slab.
To estimate concrete for a rectangular slab, multiply width times length times depth. In the slab shown, this is 10×12×.33 feet = 39.6, which rounds up to 40 cubic feet. Add 10 percent for a cushion and divide by 27, and you find that you need 1⅔ cubic yards. For a circular slab, determine the area in square feet by squaring the radius of the circle (half the diameter) and multiplying by 3.14. Then multiply by the depth of the slab to determine the volume in cubic feet. Divide by 27 and add 10 percent for excavation variation.

CONCRETE ESTIMATOR

Slab Thickness	Concrete required in yards or cubic feet by surface area of job in square feet				
	20	50	100	200	500
4 inches	.2	.6	1.2	2.5	6.2
	(6.7)	(16.7)	(33.3)	(66.7)	(166.7)
6 inches	.4	.9	1.9	3.7	9.3
	(10)	(25)	(50)	(100)	(250)
8 inches	.5	1.3	2.5	5.9	12.5
	(13.3)	(33.3)	(66.6)	(133.3)	(333.3)

One yard of concrete equals 27 cubic feet.

BUYING CONCRETE

You can buy concrete three different ways. For small jobs, such as setting a few fence posts, buy bags of premixed concrete that you simply mix with water. Premix comes in bags weighing up to 80 pounds that contain cement, sand, and aggregate mixed together. Each sack contains enough mixture to make from ⅓ to ⅔ cubic foot.

For jobs that require half a cubic yard or more of concrete, it's best to order ready-mix concrete delivered in a concrete truck. This is not only much easier than mixing your own, but you will be assured of a reliable mix.

If you have a large job that requires you to work in small stages, it makes sense to buy cement, sand, and aggregate and mix your own concrete. In a mortar box or a machine mixer, combine 10 shovelfuls of Portland cement, 22 shovelfuls of sand, and 30 shovelfuls of aggregate for each cubic foot of concrete. Making small batches allows you to place and finish one section at a time.

The ideal temperature for working concrete is 70 degrees. Warmer or colder temperatures hasten or retard the rate of setting and curing. Avoid severe cold because freezing can ruin concrete.

Money $ Saver

ON-SITE MIXING TRUCKS

Standard concrete trucks carry concrete that has been mixed at the company's site; thus, the supplier will be reluctant to sell less than a yard of concrete. A new innovation is a delivery truck that mixes the concrete right at the site. Usually, this is more economical for smaller amounts of concrete.

CONCRETE MIXING PROPORTIONS

Coarse Aggregate
Use ¾- to 1-inch gravel 50–60 percent*

Sand
40–50 percent

+

Cement
Use five, 94-pound bags of Portland cement for concrete strong enough to withstand 3,000 pounds per square inch (PSI) or six bags to withstand 3,500 psi***

⎱ 1½ tons**

= 1 cubic yard of concrete

* The more aggregate, the stronger the mix.

** These ingredients can be purchased separately or together in a mixture commonly known as con-mix.

*** For projects requiring extra lateral strength, such as a driveway.

1. To mix your own concrete, layer the ingredients and combine.
Shovel the gravel, sand, and cement in the order shown to achieve a consistent mix in the shortest time. This way, it is less likely that the finer ingredients will settle to the bottom. Mix together the dry ingredients with a mortar hoe before adding water.

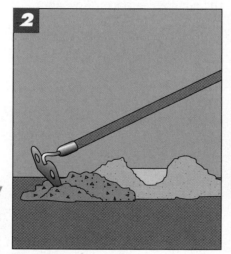

2. Mix in the water.
Add small amounts of water to the dry mix, and stir it thoroughly with a mortar hoe. Eventually, the mixture will take on the consistency of mud. When it turns a uniform shiny gray color, the mixture is close to the correct consistency; test it using the procedure in Step 3.

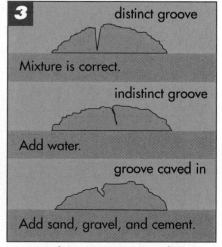

3. Test the consistency or slump.
Smack the top of the concrete with the back of your shovel to make a smooth surface. Chop it to create a groove about 2 inches deep. If the surface stays smooth and the groove maintains its shape, you have the right mixture. If the groove is indistinct, add water. If the groove caves in, add more dry ingredients.

PATCHING HOLES IN CONCRETE

For spalled (flaking) surfaces or for hairline cracks and small broken areas, use the patch materials discussed in the chart on page 639. If your concrete surface is badly settled and cracked, however, remove the damaged section and pour new concrete. Concrete patches rarely blend in, so if you are concerned with appearance, you may want to replace entire sections regardless of the extent of the damage.

YOU'LL NEED

TIME: 1 to 2 hours for several small patches; a full day to remove and repour a section.
SKILLS: Chiseling, mixing concrete, finishing concrete.
TOOLS: Cold chisel, baby sledge, brush, finishing trowel, mixing trough or wheelbarrow.

EXPERTS' INSIGHT

CHECK OUT CRACKING

■ Spalling or cracking in an old slab may be caused by freezing and thawing cycles or by settling of the ground under the slab.

■ If a slab is less than three years old and it's spalling, the concrete probably was mixed incorrectly. More flaking likely will occur in the future. Serious cracks also can result from a weak mix, the failure to install reinforcing metal where it should have been, or unstable ground beneath the slab. Your best bet is to tear up the concrete and begin again.

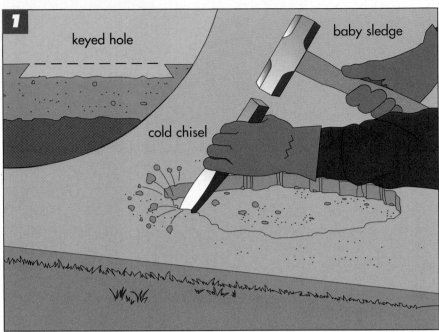

1. To repair a spalled area, "key" the hole with a chisel.
All around the damaged area, hold a cold chisel at an angle and pound with a baby sledgehammer to remove the top ½ to 1 inch of the concrete surface. "Key" the hole by undercutting the edges so the bottom of the hole is larger than the top. This keying effect helps lock the new patching material into the old concrete, making a permanent bond.

2. Clean and dampen the hole.
Brush out dust and small particles. If any of the area surrounding the hole appears loose, remove it as well. Wet the hole with water, but don't leave any standing water. You may want to apply a latex bonding agent to the area to ensure that the new material adheres to the old surface.

3. Pour and finish the patch.
Mix the patching compound and pour it in. Tamp it firmly in place to make sure all areas are firmly in contact and there are no air bubbles in the material. To allow for shrinkage, mound the patching compound slightly higher than the surrounding surface. Finish with a steel trowel.

CONCRETE PATCH SELECTOR

Type	Uses	Description and Mixing Instructions
Latex, vinyl, and epoxy patch	Use for general-purpose repair jobs, such as filling hairline cracks, repairing small breaks and patches, and tuckpointing small areas. Latex and epoxy are best for patio surfaces.	Sold in powdered form with or without a liquid binder. Mix with the appropriate binder, usually a sticky white liquid, to a whipped-cream consistency. Mixing any product with a latex reinforcer makes it stronger, as will adding extra Portland cement to concrete.
Hydraulic cement	Use to plug water leaks in masonry walls and floor surfaces. This fast-drying formulation allows you to make the repair even while the water is leaking in.	Available in powdered form. Mix a small amount with water or a commercial binder, then work quickly.
Dry, premixed concrete	Use wherever you need to replace whole sections of concrete.	Mix with water. The thicker the consistency, the faster it sets up.

TOOLS TO USE

RENT AN ELECTRIC HAMMER

If you're faced with demolishing a 2- or 3-inch-thick concrete slab, try breaking it up with a sledgehammer. If the slab is thick or if the going gets rough, how-ever, don't take the chance of straining your back.

Call a rental center for an electric hammer that will help you break up the slab without much back-breaking strain. (You won't need a pneumatic jackhammer unless you have an extra-large job.) Wear safety goggles and gloves to protect your eyes and hands from flying concrete fragments.

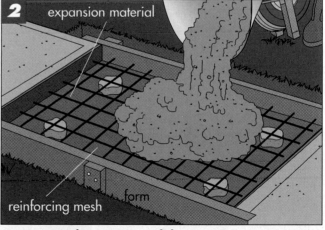

1. For a larger section, remove damaged concrete.
Score the bottom of the control joints (grooves) that separate the damaged section from adjacent ones. Use a brick set or cold chisel and a baby sledge to chisel a line of white marks along the control joints. This will produce a row of hairline cracks that prevent random cracking beyond the expansion joint as you work.

Break out pieces by hammering at the same spot with an 8- or 10-inch maul until the concrete fractures. Using a sledgehammer, break it into pieces small enough to lift without straining your back. Use pieces of rubble, as shown in the inset, to break large pieces apart. Carefully chip away final areas along the control joints. Then clear away the waste.

2. Form and pour a new slab.
Chop out any roots; they may have been the cause of your problem to begin with. Build forms and expansion material, as shown above and described on pages 660–661. Spread sand or crushed rock to fill in low spots in the subgrade. Tamp the whole area firmly. Lay in reinforcing wire mesh to within 2 inches of the form's edges. Position the mesh midway, vertically, in the slab by laying it on pieces of small debris or rubble. Pour concrete mix in the form and finish it (see pages 670–675). Duplicate the finish texture and color of the existing concrete as closely as possible.

REPAIRING BASEMENT LEAKS

asement leaks not only make life miserable, but they can weaken the foundation of your home. Basement walls should seal out a moderate amount of water, but few will withstand a great deal of water pressure. If the wall leaks only during heavy rains, you may be able to solve the problem by adding extensions to your gutter downspouts to direct rainwater away from the basement walls. You may find that your yard slopes in a way that causes rainwater to flow toward your home. If so, some corrective landscaping may be needed to solve your problem.

YOU'LL NEED

TIME: Several hours for most small patching jobs; several days or more if you need to seal the outside of the wall.
SKILLS: No special skills needed.
TOOLS: Stiff brush, cold chisel, baby sledgehammer.

1. For slow seepage or damp walls, brush on interior sealer.
Clean away dirt, grease, and dust from the wall. If you are using a cement-based sealing product, wet the wall thoroughly with a fine mist from a garden hose. Mix the liquid and powder components of the sealer thoroughly and apply with a stiff brush.

2. Fill any cracks.
As you brush, be sure to fill in all the pores in the wall. Go over cracks several times to fill them. If a crack is too large to fill in with sealer, use hydraulic cement (see below). With some sealers, you must keep the sealant wet for several days to ensure bonding. Apply a second coat if necessary.

1. To plug leaking holes or cracks, widen and "key" the spot.
Enlarge the hole or crack with a cold chisel and hammer. Undercut it to make a "key," so the plug won't come loose. Make the hole at least ½ inch deep. Whisk out fragments of concrete.

2. Mix the cement.
In a bucket, add water to the dry hydraulic cement mix until it has a puttylike consistency. Then work it by hand. For a hole, roll it into the shape of a plug. Roll a long snake shape for a crack.

3. Apply the cement.
Squeeze the material into the opening. Keep pushing and pushing to make sure it fills every tiny crevice. Any water leaking through the wall at the time of the repair should stop running. Hold the cement in place for several minutes to allow the patch to set.

SOLVING BASEMENT WATER PROBLEMS

Problem	Symptoms/Tests	Causes	Solution
Condensation	Damp walls, dripping pipes, rusty hardware, mildew. To identify condensation, tape a mirror in the dampest spot and wait 24 hours. If it's foggy or beaded with water, suspect condensation.	Excess humidity in the air, usually from an internal source, such as a basement shower, washing machine, unvented dryer, or from a significant difference between the wall temperature and inside air temperature.	Install a dehumidifier, improve ventilation, and seal interior walls.
Seepage	Dampness on a section of a wall or floor, most often on a wall near floor level. As with condensation, tape a mirror to the wall. If moisture condenses behind it, seepage is the culprit.	Surface water is forcing its way through pores in the foundation or an expansion joint. The source may be poor drainage or a leaky window well.	Improve exterior drainage. If problem is minor, an interior sealer may work. If not, waterproof the outside of the foundation.
Leaks	Localized wetness that seems to be oozing or even trickling from a wall or floor. It usually appears during heavy rain. Test by running a hose outside near the leak. Pay particular attention to mortar joints between blocks.	Cracks that may result from normal settling or improperly poured concrete. (If you see a cracklike line running horizontally around your basement wall, it may be that the builders poured part of the wall and allowed it to harden before pouring the rest.) Faulty roof drainage or a grade that slopes toward the wall exacerbates the problem.	Improve exterior drainage. You may be able to plug several holes. For widespread leakage, waterproof the entire foundation and install drain tile.
Subterranean water	A thin, barely noticeable film of water on the basement floor is often the first sign. Test by laying down plastic sheeting for two days. Penetrating moisture will dampen the concrete underneath.	Usually a spring or a high water table forces water up from below under high pressure, turning your basement into a well. This may happen only during rainy periods.	Install a sump pump. Drainage tile around the perimeter of the foundation may help, but only if it drains to a low spot or a storm sewer.

Remove the dirt close to the house by hand.

1. To seal a wall from the outside, excavate to the trouble area.
If the problem is fairly high up on the foundation wall, you may be able to do the digging yourself. Otherwise, hire an excavating contractor to backhoe a trench wide enough for you to work in. Remove the dirt close to the wall by hand. Brush the wall clean.

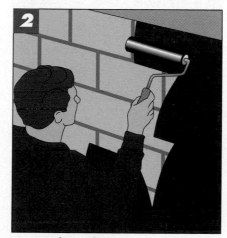

2. Apply sealer.
You can hire contractors who specialize in this type of coating. To do it yourself, wash the wall clean, allow it to dry, and apply two coats of tarlike bituminous sealer. Or, backplaster the wall with two coats of mortar (like the stucco process shown on page 695) and apply the sealer.

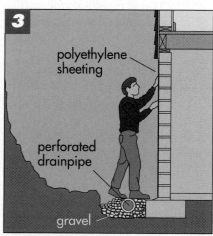

polyethylene sheeting

perforated drainpipe

gravel

3. Install perforated drainpipe and a polyethylene barrier.
Dig a trench along the footing and install a sloping, perforated drainpipe embedded in gravel (see page 683). Stick heavy-gauge polyethylene sheeting to the wall sealer. Drape it over the footing, but not the gravel drain. Overlap all seams at least 6 inches.

PATCHING CRACKS AND TUCKPOINTING

Even well-built masonry walls require occasional repairs. Mortar joints that are exposed to the weather typically need to be tuckpointed every 30 years or so.

Cracking, the most common masonry malady, results from uneven settling of footings or from expansion and contraction due to temperature changes. Expansion cracks usually occur with uniform width and often follow joints between bricks or blocks. Settling cracks taper along a mostly vertical path, are widest at the top, and end as hairline cracks near the bottom of the wall.

Horizontal cracking may appear in basement walls made of concrete blocks. Usually the cause is pressure from backfill soil and water pushing in from the outside. If the wall bulges noticeably, you have a serious problem. You may need to dig out the backfill and re-lay the blocks—a job most suited to a professional contractor.

The same procedures are used to repair a cracked mortar line and for tuckpointing. For a long-lasting tuckpointing job, chisel or grind out all the joints. If your grout lines generally are worn and cracking, you need to tuckpoint the entire area or the problem will worsen rapidly.

Tuckpointing is painstaking, slow work. It can be done from a ladder, but you'll find the work easier, and you'll do a better job, if you set up scaffolding.

YOU'LL NEED

TIME: 2 hours to tuckpoint 25 square feet of wall.
SKILLS: Working with mortar.
TOOLS: Joint strike or sled jointer, pointing trowel, ⅜-inch back filler, cold chisel, baby sledgehammer, stiff brush, whisk broom.

1. Chisel out the joints...
With a baby sledge and a cold chisel, remove mortar from joints to a depth of ⅜ to 1 inch. It is possible to tuckpoint without chiseling out old mortar, but the tuckpointing will not last as long. Because chips will fly as you work, wear safety goggles and heavy gloves.

or use a grinder.
If you need to work on a large area, rent or purchase a 4-inch grinder to efficiently remove old mortar. Whichever method you use, if the joint crumbles easily all the way through the wall, tear down the whole section and re-lay the bricks with new mortar. Tuckpointing by itself will not add strength to weak masonry joints.

2. Scrape and brush out debris.
Use the point of a cold chisel or the tip of a pointed trowel to scrape away patches of mortar that remain after chiseling or grinding. Briskly sweep away debris with a stiff whisk broom. Mix the mortar using 1 part Portland cement to 2 parts masonry sand and enough water to form a puttylike consistency (see page 686).

EXPERTS' INSIGHT

WAIT FOR WALL MOVEMENT TO STOP

■ To repair wall cracks caused by settling, you must wait until the movement stops before patching or tuckpointing. This may be as long as a year after the first signs of cracking appear.

■ To determine if settling still is occurring, bridge the crack with a piece of duct tape and check it occasionally for twists, tears, or pulling loose.

3. Place the mortar.

Load an upside-down trowel with mortar and hold it against the wall. With a ⅜-inch back filler, force the mortar into the joints. Fill the head (vertical) joints first, then the bed (horizontal) joints. It will take practice before you can tuckpoint without dropping mortar or smearing bricks.

4. Strike the joints.

Use a damp sponge to wipe away excess mortar while it is still wet. Brush the joints to remove mortar crumbs. Correct timing is essential for striking the joints. The mortar should be stiff, but not hard. Choose the appearance of your joint from those shown *below*.

5. Restrike and brush.

To ensure that your joints are watertight, strike them a second time, making sure they seal tightly against the bricks. Let the mortar set up somewhat, then brush away crumbs with a stiff brush. Scrub mortar stains off the wall within 24 hours.

Choosing a Mortar Joint

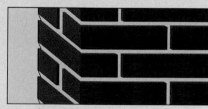

Struck joint

Make a struck joint with the edge of a pointed trowel, angling the joint from top to bottom. This is an attractive joint, but will collect water on the lower edge.

V-joint

Use a V-shaped strike or a bent piece of metal to make a V-joint. Strike it quickly after the bricks are laid or the mortar will bunch up. This joint sheds water well.

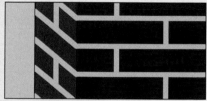

Flush joint

Cut the excess mortar from the face of bricks as you lay them. Every two courses, check to see if joints are tight.

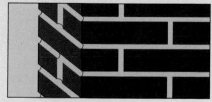

Concave joint

This is the most common brick joint. Strike it using a piece of pipe or a jointer made for this purpose. It sheds water well and is the easiest to make watertight.

Weathered joint

Use a pointed trowel, as with a struck joint, but hold it in the opposite way, angling from bottom to top. It's difficult to make this joint look consistent.

Raked joint

A raked joint looks great, but it is the weakest and the least water-resistant joint. To strike it, use a trimmed piece of wood or a special jointer.

REPLACING BRICKS AND BLOCKS

A few damaged or deteriorated bricks don't spell doom for a wall. They can be replaced with relative ease. Begin by examining your wall carefully. If the damaged bricks or concrete blocks are directly over or under a door or window, there is a chance the wall could sag if you remove several bricks or blocks at once. To avoid collapsing a section of wall, replace one brick at a time, rather than removing several at once. Call in a professional mason if you are not sure of yourself.

YOU'LL NEED

TIME: About 1 hour to replace a brick or a concrete block.
SKILLS: Careful chiseling, mixing mortar, pointing mortar lines.
TOOLS: Baby sledgehammer, cold chisel, drill with masonry bit, pointed trowel, pointing tool.

1. Chip out the old brick.
Use a baby sledgehammer and cold chisel to chip away the old mortar and brick. Drill a series of holes with a masonry bit to make it easy to break the brick apart, remove the pieces, and ensure that you do not damage surrounding bricks. Brush away debris and dampen all surfaces of the cavity.

2. Slide the new brick in.
Lay a ½- to 1-inch-deep bed of mortar on the bottom of the cavity. Butter the top and ends of the new brick. Slip the brick in without compressing the bed of mortar. Or, use an upside-down trowel to help slide the brick in (see Step 2 *below*). Adjust the brick so all the joints are even. Strike the joints to match the rest of the wall.

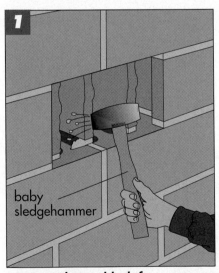

baby sledgehammer

1. To replace a block face, remove the old block face.
Unless the entire concrete block is fractured, remove only the damaged face and leave the rest of it. Use a baby sledge and a cold chisel. It may help to bore a series of holes in the block using a drill with a masonry bit.

Rest block on trowel.

2. Set a new block face in place.
Use a circular saw with a masonry blade to notch the webbing of a new block. Then use a chisel to release one face of the block. Dry-fit the new block face to make sure it is flush with the wall surface. Lay a bed of mortar and butter the block face on three sides. Slip the block in using a pointed trowel.

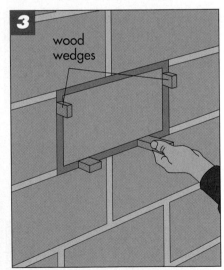

wood wedges

3. Hold in place with wedges.
The new block face will not stay in place as easily as a new brick, so use wedges to hold it firmly in the correct position. Once the mortar stiffens, remove the wedges, fill in the holes left by the wedges, and strike the joints.

REMOVING EFFLORESCENCE AND STAINS

Efflorescence is a white powder that results when mineral salts in mortar are dissolved by water. These deposits usually disappear after a few years. If you want to get rid of them now or if you have other stains or problems, try the techniques listed in the chart below. As a general rule, try common household cleaners first; use acid only if necessary. Do not use acid on limestone or marble. **CAUTION:** *Always pour acid slowly into water; never poor water into acid.*

YOU'LL NEED
TIME: 1 to 2 hours to scrub away most stains.
SKILLS: Basic skills.
TOOLS: Protective eyewear, gloves, heavy clothing, stiff brush, water bucket.

REMOVING STAINS FROM BRICK WALLS AND PATIOS

Type of Stain	Remedy
Efflorescence	Try water and a brush and wait a few days. If something stronger is needed, scrub the wall with a solution of 1 part muriatic acid to 15 parts clean water. Rinse with water when finished.
Mortar smears	Remove with a muriatic acid solution as strong as 1 part acid to 10 parts water if your bricks are dark; 1-to-15 solution for lighter bricks. Let stand for 10 to 15 minutes, then rinse thoroughly.
Mildew	Scrub gently with a solution of 1 part bleach to 3 parts water, with a little laundry detergent or trisodium phosphate mixed in. Let stand for 15 minutes, then rinse.
Hardened paint	Scrape off as much as possible with a putty knife. Scrub with a metal-bristled brush and cold water. If this doesn't work, try a commercial paint remover, but test it on a small spot first to make sure it does not stain the brick.
Graffiti	Purchase a spray-paint remover and follow directions.
Iron rust	Try scrubbing with household bleach; let it stand for 15 minutes, then rinse. If that doesn't work, scrub with a solution of 1 pound oxalic acid to 1 gallon of water. Let stand for 5 minutes, then rinse thoroughly. Test on a small area first to make sure it will not stain the brick.

REPAIRING CHIMNEYS

A chimney is susceptible to a number of problems, ranging from the buildup of flammable deposits in the flue to damaged and leaking masonry. Serious damage requires repair by a professional mason. Homeowners willing to get up on the roof can handle basic inspection, repairs, and minor improvements. This section shows the basic steps for inspecting your chimney to keep it in safe working order and some improvements to make future maintenance procedures simple.

YOU'LL NEED

TIME: 1 to 2 hours to make a yearly inspection; several hours to clean out a chimney.
SKILLS: For most jobs, no special skills are needed.
TOOLS: Rope, tuckpointing tools, mason's trowel.

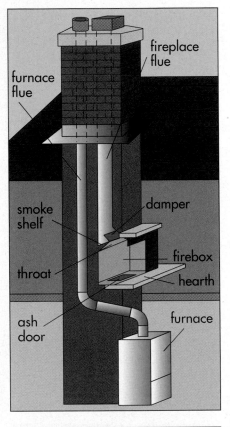

CAUTION!

AN OUNCE OF PREVENTION
■ *If your fireplace chimney becomes caked with flammable deposits, you could have a flue fire. This is extremely dangerous; the heat is intense, and the fire is difficult to put out. A flue fire can possibly even lead to a house fire. So be sure your chimney is clean before you light a fire.*
■ *If your fireplace has not been used for a while, have it examined by a professional who specializes in chimneys.*
■ *Your chimney often is connected to the framing of your house. The weight of a damaged chimney can lead to serious structural problems. If you suspect severe damage, call in a professional.*

Understand chimney anatomy.
The **firebox** has splayed sides that serve to pull air across the **hearth** to the base of the fire. The sloping upper rear wall of the firebox deflects heat back into the room. At the top of the firebox, the **throat** pulls smoke up into the flue. A **damper** there allows you to control the draft and close the flue when the fireplace is not in use.

Higher up the chimney, a **smoke shelf** stops cold air from coming down the flue and diverts it back up the **flue**. Without the smoke shelf, cold air from the outside would drop down and push smoke into the living area.

Many fireplaces have an **ash door**, plus an ash pit and a clean-out door, allowing you to remove your ashes from the outside of the house. Some ash pits have an air vent to create a better draft.

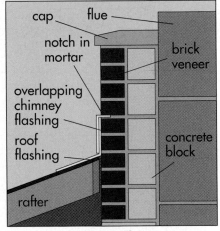

Inspect your upper chimney.
The part of your chimney that is exposed to weather is the most likely to fail. Inspect it thoroughly for crumbling bricks and mortar. (Your chimney may not look quite like the drawing above; it may be all brick, for instance.) Replace broken bricks and tuckpoint them if necessary (see pages 642–644). Make sure the chimney cap overhangs the brick. Check for loose or missing flashing.

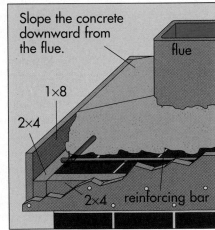

Make a new chimney cap.
Chimney caps often are constructed incorrectly so they don't protect the bricks from water damage. Shown here is a design for a cap you can pour in place. Hold the form in place with a few masonry nails and remove it after the concrete has set. When finishing the concrete, be sure to slope it away from the flue so water can run off easily.

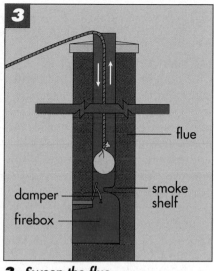

1. To clean a fireplace chimney, seal off the inside opening.

Cleaning produces a great deal of hard-to-vacuum soot, so make sure it cannot enter your home. Firmly tape a wet sheet or a piece of heavy polyethylene sheeting to the opening. Check that there are no cracks for soot to seep through.

2. Make a "brush."

You can rent or buy a regular chimney brush with extensions for reaching down your chimney. Or, make a cleaning tool out of a piece of canvas and a rope. Wrap chains or pieces of broken bricks in the canvas, tie a rope to it, and lower it into the flue.

3. Sweep the flue.

Move your "brush" vigorously up and down in the flue, slowly moving downward as you work. Lower the brush all the way down to the damper, pull it up, and repeat the process until you no longer hear caked deposits being dislodged from the flue.

EXPERTS' INSIGHT

AN ANNUAL CHECKUP

Every year, make a quick inspection of your chimney. Look at the following:

■ See if any tree branches are within 10 feet of the chimney. Trim off the branches if they are; they can cause draw problems and create fire hazards.

■ Check to see that the damper and its controls work smoothly. Use a flashlight to see if it opens and closes completely.

■ Check the draw. When you light a fire, the smoke should rise easily and not flow into your living area.

■ Clean out ashes that have accumulated in the ash pit.

■ On the roof and in the attic, check the chimney bricks and repair any damaged areas.

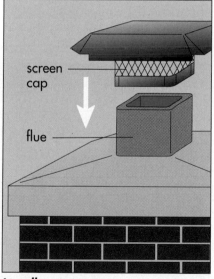

Install a screen cap.

Here is an easy way to keep birds and squirrels out of your chimney, and protect the inside from water damage. Measure the outside dimensions of your flue and purchase a screen cap to fit it. Installation is simple—place it on top of the flue and tighten the hold-down screws.

Money $ Saver

GAS FIRED UNITS

■ If your old chimney is not safe for wood-burning fires, before you install a gas unit make sure it poses no structural dangers. Make any needed repairs to ensure it will not collapse and will not compromise the framing.

■ If you want to have a fire in your fireplace without replacing the entire chimney, consider installing a gas-fired unit. This needs little or no venting, so it does not matter if your chimney draws poorly. Though it's not a wood-burning fireplace, it does have advantages: You don't have to haul and store logs, it's easy to start, and many slide-in models have heat-circulating systems that efficiently heat your home.

REPAIRING CONCRETE STEPS

Once a crack develops in concrete, water seeps in and causes further damage, especially in regions that have freezing temperatures. Fix small cracks and chips in your stairs right away or you may have to replace the whole stairway. If your steps are made partially of brick, see pages 642–644 for brick repairs.

Buy patching concrete or concrete sand mix and add extra Portland cement. Mix in only enough water to make the material doughlike. If the chipped-out area is large, drive masonry screws partially into the damaged area to help anchor the patch in place.

YOU'LL NEED

TIME: 2 hours for most repairs.
SKILLS: No special skills needed.
TOOLS: Hammer and cold chisel, pointed trowel.

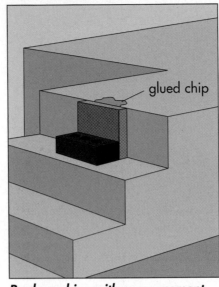

glued chip

Replace chips with epoxy cement.
If a piece or two has broken out in such a way that it will fit back in place, you can glue it back on. Clean both pieces and make sure they are dry. Mix epoxy cement, apply it to the chipped-out spot, and brace the chip in place with a brick and a piece of wood.

EXPERTS' INSIGHT

WHERE THE STEPS MEET THE HOUSE

If you have a crack where your concrete steps butt against the house, any patch you make probably will crack again within a year or two. The steps and the house rest on different foundations, so they shift and settle in different directions. If you don't seal the crack, the problem will get worse. Here's how to seal out moisture and debris.
■ If the crack is small, seal it with silicone, butyl rubber, or siliconized acrylic caulk.
■ If the crack is large, insert expansion joint material into it for the best seal, or use oakum.

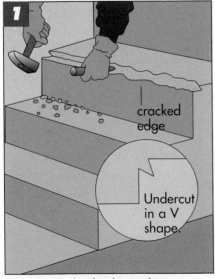

cracked edge

Undercut in a V shape.

1. To mend a broken edge, chip out the edge.
If an edge is broken or cracked, remove all loose material so no cracks remain. With a hammer and cold chisel, cut the edge back to make a V-shaped groove (see inset). Clean the area thoroughly and moisten it.

2x8

2. Make a form and fill.
Use bricks to hold a board against the riser to act as a form for the concrete. Mix the patch material and pack it into the groove. Smooth the top of the patch. As the material begins to set up, remove the form and smooth the edges of the patch.

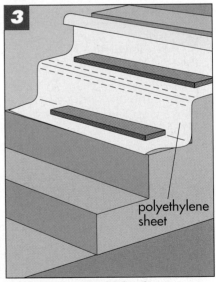

polyethylene sheet

3. Cure the patch slowly.
To ensure that the patch will stick, make sure it cures slowly. Cover the repair with polyethylene sheeting and hold it in place with scraps of lumber. Keep the patched area damp for about a week by spraying it with water.

REPAIRING RAILINGS

Here's a common and pesky problem: The metal railing on a concrete stairway comes loose, either at its base where it connects to the step or at the top where it connects to the house.

Often the problem is rusty metal. If only screws are rusty, you can replace them. If the bottom of the railing itself is rusted away, it may be time for a new railing.

Just as often, the screws or anchors were not large enough for the job and have come loose and cracked the concrete. To make these repairs, you can use epoxy putty, anchoring cement, masonry screws, or masonry anchors.

YOU'LL NEED

TIME: 2 hours for most repairs.
SKILLS: No special skills needed.
TOOLS: Hammer and cold chisel, drill with masonry bit, trowel.

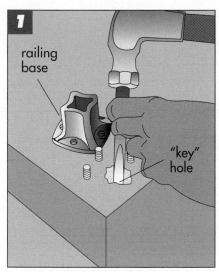

1. To re-install a bolt on a stair, chip away a hole.
Remove loose material. Enlarge the hole, if necessary, so it will be deep enough for the new bolt and so the epoxy putty or anchoring cement has plenty of area to grab onto. "Key" the hole by making it larger at the bottom than at the top; this provides a greater area for the patch to stick to.

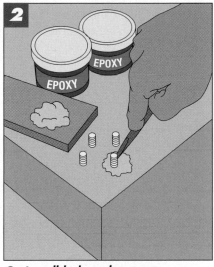

2. Install bolt and cement.
Hold the bolt in position and fill the hole with epoxy putty or anchoring cement. Make sure the bolt sticks up at the correct height, is plumb, and is in the correct position. Tamp the epoxy putty or cement firmly and meld it with the concrete surface.

Anchor the top of the rail.
At the point where the rail meets the house, you need some serious fastening power. Small screws with plastic anchors will not do the trick.

If the concrete has broken away, you will need to set bolts

in cement or epoxy putty. Or, fill the old hole and use a masonry screw or anchor. Masonry screws can be driven directly into pilot holes. Simply drill the hole and drive in the screw.

You also can use masonry anchors, also called lag shields.

Drill the correct-size hole (in some cases you can simply enlarge the old hole) and tap the anchor in until it is flush with the wall surface. Then hold the bracket in position and drive the screw in place.

REPAIRING ASPHALT SURFACES

Asphalt, also called blacktop, is an inexpensive material with which to pave a driveway or a walk. Because asphalt is made of gravel and petroleum rather than Portland cement, it is flexible. It also is soft and requires regular maintenance. Every couple of years, you should seal asphalt surfaces with an emulsified sealer, sold in large buckets. Spread the sealer with a long-handled roller or squeegee made for the purpose. This seals small cracks before they get larger. If your asphalt is badly in need of maintenance, follow the steps here and on page 651 to fill potholes and cracks before applying sealer. If your driveway is too far gone for repair, contact a professional contractor for a new drive; laying asphalt is not a do-it-yourself job.

YOU'LL NEED

TIME: A couple of hours for most patching jobs.
SKILLS: No special skills needed.
TOOLS: Baby sledgehammer, cold chisel, putty knife or trowel, shovel, tamper or piece of 4×4, roller or squeegee.

EXPERTS' INSIGHT

KEEP IT WARM

Asphalt is flexible when warm and brittle when cold. If possible, wait for the temperature to reach at least 70°F before patching. If you must patch asphalt during cold weather, keep the materials and tools in a warm place until you use them.

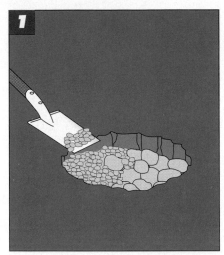

1. To patch a pothole, dig out the hole and add gravel.
For a large damaged area, chip away loose asphalt and dig down about 12 inches or until you reach a solid base. Shovel in rocks and gravel to conserve patching material. Tamp the gravel down.

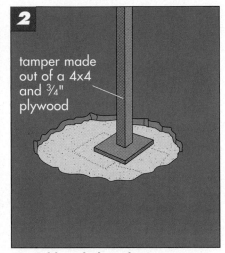

tamper made out of a 4x4 and ¾" plywood

2. Add asphalt and tamp.
Purchase bags of cold-mix asphalt patching compound and apply it in 1- to 2-inch layers. Slice the patching compound with your shovel to open any air pockets. Tamp down each layer firmly with a tamper like the one shown or use the end of a 4×4.

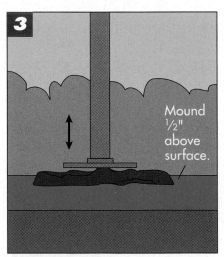

Mound ½" above surface.

3. Mound and tamp.
Keep adding and tamping patching compound until it is mounded about ½ inch above the surrounding surface. Tamp it firmly with a tamper. Sprinkle the patch with sand to prevent tracking, then drive a car back and forth over the patch to compact it until it's level.

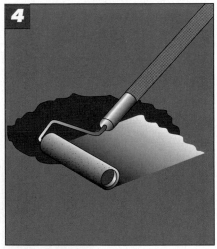

4. Seal the area.
Seal the patch by pouring a generous amount of sealer on it and working it into the patch and the surrounding area. For the best results, use a roller or a squeegee designed for sealing driveways. For small areas, you can use a throwaway paint roller. To achieve a uniform appearance, seal the whole driveway.

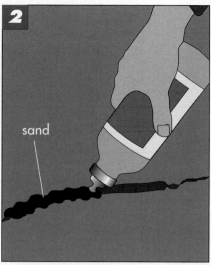

1. To patch a large crack, "key" the hole.
For cracks wider than ⅛ inch, chisel away crumbling asphalt and "key" the hole, making the bottom wider than the top (see page 640). Scrape and brush away loose matter. (Cracks narrower than ⅛ inch can be filled just with sealer.)

2. Fill with liquid sealer.
Partially fill the crack with sand. Pour in liquid sealer or squeeze asphalt sealer that comes in a caulking-type tube into the crack. Smooth out the patch with an old putty knife or trowel.

3. Mix and apply patching paste.
Mix sand with liquid sealer until you get a pastelike consistency. Push the paste into the crack with a trowel or putty knife, making sure to cram it into every corner. Smooth the patch so it is slightly higher than the surrounding surface.

REPLACING BRICKS IN A PATIO

Patio bricks set in sand are simple to replace. The most difficult part of the job is removing a broken brick without damaging its neighbors. If the patio bricks are mortared or set in concrete, use a cold chisel and baby sledgehammer to chisel out the damaged brick carefully, breaking off and removing small pieces so you do not crack the surrounding bricks or mortar. Chisel away the mortar joints and concrete bed too. Brush latex bonding agent into the cavity and set the new brick in a bed of mortar.

YOU'LL NEED
TIME: 1 to 2 hours to remove and replace several bricks.
SKILLS: Care in removing damaged bricks.
TOOLS: Flat pry bar, hammer, cold chisel, 4×4 for tamping.

1. Remove the damaged brick.
Use a flat pry bar to pry out the old brick. You may need to crack the brick and take it out in pieces. If it is a tight fit, try using two putty knives or trowels, one on each end, to shoehorn the brick straight up.

2. Tamp and replace.
Add sand and tamp the area well, making sure the sand level is not too high. Replace the brick and tap it level with a hammer and a piece of scrap wood. Fill the joints with fine sand, brush, and spray with water. Repeat until the sand remains at the level of the bricks.

PLANNING DRIVEWAYS AND WALKS

Walkways and driveways should be both practical and good-looking. Begin your designing process by determining the natural paths people take to doors and any high-use areas. Avoid building a walk that will be bypassed in favor of walking on the lawn. Concrete is not a beautiful material, so use it as a frame to outline your lot. Add variety by combining other paving materials with concrete.

Once you have a general plan, visit your building department to find out about the zoning regulations and building codes governing your project. Codes typically dictate the dimensions and type of concrete you must use for footings and slabs. They tell you how much and what type of metal reinforcement to use and if you need a sand or gravel base under the material. Building codes also spell out setbacks—how far from the property line your building must be set. Once your plans are approved, you can get a building permit. Plan the work schedule so you will be ready for each inspection.

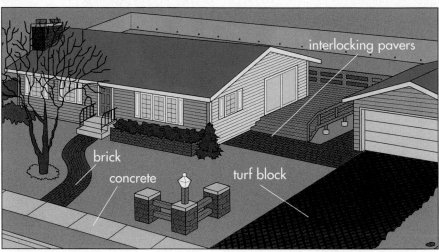

Make a total plan.
Planning starts with knowing what you want. Short of hiring an architect, the best way to get ideas and a sense of style is to drive around town and look at other people's drives and walkways.

Use concrete in places where you need solid strength. But large concrete slabs can pose a drainage problem. You may need to install a drain in the middle of the slab, make sure the slab drains into the street, or provide drainage around the edge of slabs (see page 654).

For patios and walkways, you usually can install a surfacing material, such as bricks, pavers, or loose material for about the same price as a concrete slab. If built well, many such surfaces hold up as long as concrete.

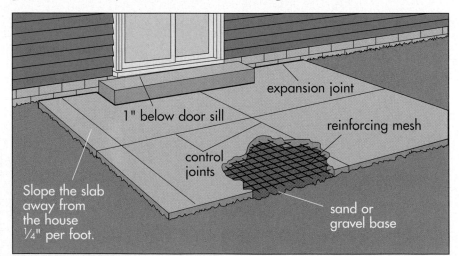

Plan a patio slab.
As you plan for and design a patio slab, be sure to locate it away from large trees whose roots may crack it. You may need to remove roots as you grade the excavation and before you add the **sand** or **gravel base.** Slabs collect a lot of precipitation, so slope the slab away from the house. Also, it should be no closer than 1 inch below a door sill or threshold. Because concrete does not flex without cracking, you'll need to add **reinforcing mesh. Control joints** allow the slab to flex without creating unsightly cracks. **Expansion joints** provide a buffer between the house foundation and the slab. Select a finish (see pages 674–677) and plan on having an experienced finisher on hand.

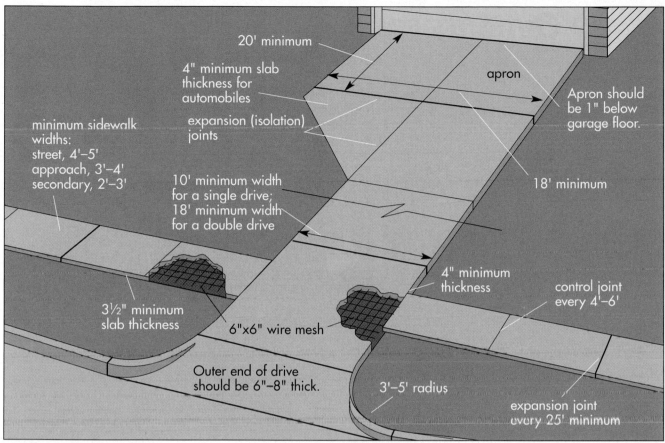

20' minimum

4" minimum slab thickness for automobiles

apron

Apron should be 1" below garage floor.

minimum sidewalk widths:
street, 4'–5'
approach, 3'–4'
secondary, 2'–3'

expansion (isolation) joints

10' minimum width for a single drive;
18' minimum width for a double drive

18' minimum

4" minimum thickness

control joint every 4'–6'

3½" minimum slab thickness

6"x6" wire mesh

Outer end of drive should be 6"–8" thick.

3'–5' radius

expansion joint every 25' minimum

Plan driveways and walks.

Whenever possible, slope a driveway toward the street and make sure water entering the street can drain away easily. If you cannot do this, slope or crown the driveway slightly so water can drain to the edges. Or, plan for a drain in the middle of the slab.

The large slab just outside the garage door is called the **apron**. Make sure it provides enough room for cars to maneuver, especially in the case of a two-car garage. The apron should be 1 inch below the garage floor to keep water out of the garage.

Use **expansion joints** (also called isolation joints) wherever new concrete butts up against old concrete or another material. This allows the two to move separately. It is also a good idea to install an expansion joint every 15 feet or so in large slabs. Cut or strike **control joints** every 4 to 6 feet in walks or small slabs (see page 674).

EXPERTS' INSIGHT

ADDITIVES FOR CONCRETE

Often, concrete lasts longer if you have it modified with an additive. Ask your building inspector and your concrete supplier if they recommend any of the following for your situation:

■ If you live in an area subject to severe freezing, consider using air-entrained concrete. This type of concrete is full of tiny bubbles that remain in the concrete after it has set. They enable the concrete to withstand the expansion and contraction that occurs during freeze-thaw cycles. You can order air-entrained concrete delivered in a truck or you can add an air-entraining agent when you mix it in a concrete mixer. But you cannot add the agent if you mix concrete by hand. When you add the agent, you will need to cut down on the amount of sand; check the instructions to find out what the ratio should be.

■ If you are pouring concrete on a cold day, consider adding calcium chloride to the mix. This will make the concrete set faster, which reduces the danger of cracking due to freezing. Be prepared to work fast.

■ If the weather is hot, it may make sense to add a retarding agent to keep the concrete from setting up too quickly.

■ In some areas and in some situations, you can eliminate the need for metal reinforcement by ordering fiberglass-reinforced concrete. Compare the price with the cost of wire mesh or reinforcing bar to see if this makes sense for your situation.

LAYING OUT SITES FOR SLABS

Although concrete is very strong in many respects, it has limited tensile (lateral) strength. A slab without a firm, uniform base almost certainly will crack and heave unevenly, leaving you with a difficult repair job. This happens with driveways, for example, where the sand base underneath washes away, allowing the weight of vehicles to crack the slab.

If possible, place concrete slabs on undisturbed soil—soil that has never been dug up. In many areas, this means digging down until you reach clay. If you must pour a slab on top of recently dug soil, as would be the case with backfill from a foundation dig, pack the soil by watering it for several days and giving it time to settle. Then compact the earth, using a hand tamper for small areas or a rented vibrating tamper for larger areas.

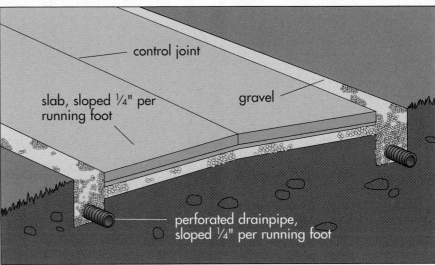

Install perimeter drainage systems.
When rain falls on a large concrete slab, the low ends of sloped sections receive a lot of water quickly. In many cases, this can be solved simply by digging a border and planting flowers or shrubs in a bed covered with wood chips. For more severe puddling, dig a trench and fill it with gravel. For even more drainage, dig a trench at least 12 inches deep and install sloping perforated drainage tile in gravel, as shown. Each of these options can be installed after the slab is poured.

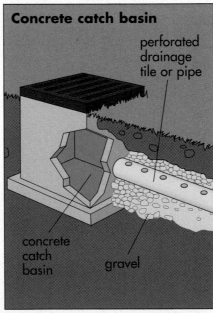

Install a catch basin and dry well for severe drainage problems.
For large areas where you anticipate a lot of water that has no place to go, consider sloping the ground toward a catch basin located in the center of the area.

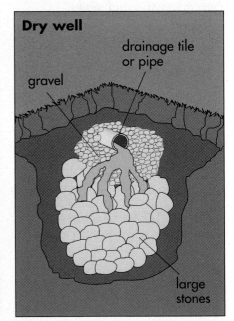

The water caught there can be piped out, either into a city sewer system or into a dry well.

A dry well is a large hole filled with stones and topped with a layer of gravel. It holds water until it can percolate into the ground.

Mark with a piece of tape.

Move measuring tape and line until 4' and 5' points line up.

Check for square using the 3-4-5 method.

Drive in a stake at one corner of the slab, such as against the foundation. Working from that fixed point, check for square as you drive stakes for the other corners. Use the 3-4-5 method. Measure 3 feet along one side and make a mark or drive a stake. Then measure 4 feet along the line and mark the spot with a piece of tape. Make sure both measurements begin at exactly the same point. Measure between the 3- and 4-foot marks, moving the line until this distance is exactly 5 feet. You'll then have a square corner. If you have room or have a large slab, use multiples of 3-4-5: 6-8-10 or 9-12-15.

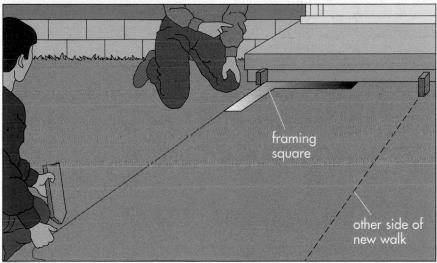

framing square

other side of new walk

Use a square for walks.

To square one side of a long, narrow slab, such as a walk, use a carpenter's framing square. Square the line from a step, slab, or foundation. Position the second line by measuring off the desired width so the two lines are parallel.

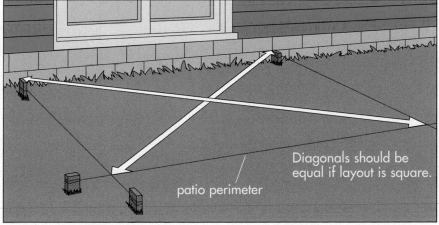

Diagonals should be equal if layout is square.

patio perimeter

Check by measuring diagonals.

As a final check that the slab perimeter is square, measure from corner to corner in each direction. The two measurements should be the same. Make sure you line up the same edge of the tape measure when you do this. Don't use this method in place of the 3-4-5 method, only as a double-check.

EXCAVATING FOR SLABS

If your soil is soft, your back is strong, and you have plenty of time, you can dig the hole for a small slab by hand (or you can hire young and willing laborers).

For large jobs or in places where the digging is tough, rent a small digging machine or hire an excavating contractor.

The process is easy; the digging often is not. You'll need to remove all organic matter—not only the sod, but also roots ½ inch or more in diameter. Many building codes require you to dig down to undisturbed soil (subsoil that has never been dug up).

YOU'LL NEED

TIME: A day for a person to dig 100 square feet 6 inches deep.
SKILLS: Accurate digging, laying out, and leveling.
TOOLS: Shovels, spade, baby sledgehammer, mason's line, line level, chalk line.

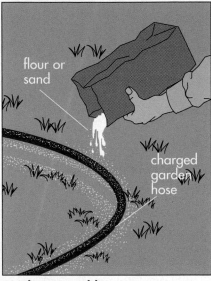

Mark a curved line.
Where your plan calls for a curve in the slab, lay a charged garden hose (turn on the water with the nozzle shut) in position to mark the slab perimeter. Take into account the width of the stakes and forms. Pour flour or sand over the hose. Lift it up and you'll have an easy-to-follow curved line.

Spare your back as you dig.
You'll spare yourself a lot of pain and fatigue by using your knee, not your back, to push the shovel into the soil. As you dig, simply position your knee against your lower hand and push forward with your knee. You'll be surprised how much extra force it provides.

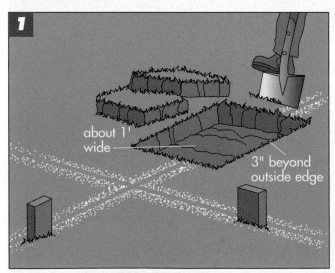

1. Mark and trench the perimeter.
Mark the location of the slab edges by sprinkling flour or sand over the mason's lines strung when you laid out the project (see page 655). Remove the line, but leave your stakes in place. Use the marks as a guide for digging a shallow trench about 1 foot wide. Dig the trench so it extends about 3 inches beyond the outside edge of the slab.

2. Mark slab height on the house.
If the new slab butts against an existing structure, snap a chalk line on it to establish where the surface of the slab will meet the structure. Patio surfaces should be about 1 inch below door thresholds to keep rain and snow out of your house. Outdoor slabs should be about 1 inch above the lawn surface. If the slab does not abutt the house, make a mark on one of the corner boards indicating the top of the slab.

3. Set lines and drive stakes.

Reattach the mason's lines. Where they meet the house, set them level with the chalk line that marks the slab top. Pull the line taut and level it using a line level (see page 659). Mark that spot on one of the outside corner stakes. Measure down from that mark ¼ inch per running foot of slab (the distance from the house to an outside corner) and make a second mark. Tie the line securely to the second mark. Repeat this procedure on the other side.

Drive in form stakes at a point outside of the line at a distance from the line equal to the thickness of the forming lumber (see inset). Be sure the tops of the form stakes are a little below the level of the line.

> ### CAUTION!
> When reattaching the mason's lines, be careful not to wrap the lines the wrong way around the stake. If you have any doubts, recheck for square (see page 655).

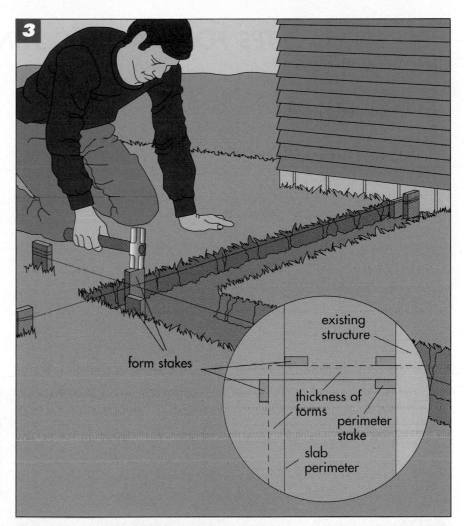

form stakes

existing structure

thickness of forms

perimeter stake

slab perimeter

4. Excavate the interior.

Remove the sod and topsoil to reach the desired depth. You may want to use the sod elsewhere in your yard. If so, undercut it horizontally about 2 inches beneath the surface and cut it into easy-to-handle 8×16-inch sections. Save enough to resod around the edges of the new slab.

If you plan to place sand or gravel beneath the slab, excavate at least 5 inches deep. Check the bottom from time to time as you dig by laying a straight 2×4 or 2×6 on edge so its top barely touches the mason's line. If you remove too much soil in some spots, fill them with sand or gravel—not loose soil. Use a flat spade or square shovel to shave away the final inch of soil from the bottom and sides of the excavation.

PREPARING SITES FOR WALL FOOTINGS

Because the weight of a concrete slab is distributed over many square feet, it usually does not need footings. Slabs "float" (ride up and down) 1 to 2 inches as the ground freezes and thaws.

But a footing is required to support a wall of any sort (a dry stone wall is one of the few exceptions). A footing spreads the weight so the wall doesn't sink, so it's usually twice the width of the structure it supports. The footing must extend below the frost line to avoid damage from frost heave. Check local codes to see how deep the footing must be.

To do its job without sinking or shifting, a footing must rest on stable, undisturbed soil. A footing beneath a foundation wall also must have adequate drainage to avoid damage from hydraulic pressure (see page 629). To be sure you've planned for the demands of your particular climate and soil conditions, consult with your local building department.

YOU'LL NEED

TIME: A day or two for a medium-size project.
SKILLS: Excavating, squaring, leveling.
TOOLS: Shovel or digging machinery, screwdriver, mason's line, line level, carpenter's level, plumb bob, hammer.

EXPERTS' INSIGHT

FOOTING REQUIREMENTS

■ In most situations, a footing 22 inches wide and 12 inches deep, with two pieces of ½-inch reinforcing bar running through it, is strong enough to support a one-story wall. But if the soil in your area is soft, your local building codes may require a larger footing.

■ Formed or unformed, a footing must rest on undisturbed soil. If the soil is black, it almost certainly is topsoil and you must dig deeper. In most areas, undisturbed soil will be clay. In some areas, you'll hit bedrock only a few feet below grade. A building inspector should approve pouring directly on top of bedrock, even if you haven't dug below the frost line.

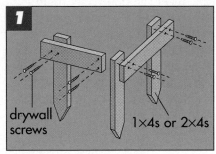

drywall screws   1×4s or 2×4s

1. Install batter boards.
Lay out the job as shown on pages 654–655, driving in stakes to mark the wall's outside corners. Place batter boards about 3 feet beyond these stakes by driving in 1×4 or 2×4 stakes and attaching 3- to 5-foot-long horizontal pieces to them. Fasten with drywall screws. (Nailing will loosen the stakes.)

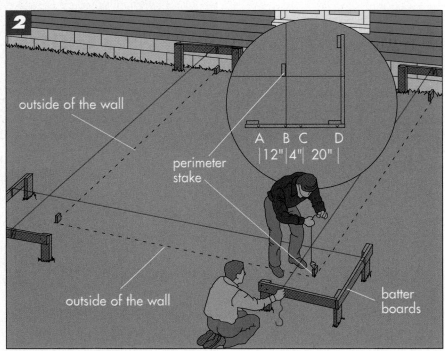

outside of the wall

perimeter stake

outside of the wall

A B C D
|12"|4"|20"|

batter boards

2. Lay out the site.
Attach mason's lines to the batter boards and the house. Transfer the line marking the outside of the wall (B in inset) to the batter boards by having someone dangle a plumb bob over the outer edge of each perimeter stake while you stretch the mason's line. When the lines intersect over the stake, mark the points where the mason's lines cross the batter boards.

Now that you have marked for the outside of the wall (B), measure over on the batter board and mark for the inside edge of the footing (A), the outside edge of the footing (C), and the outer excavation line (D). The dimensions shown in the inset above are for an 8-inch-wide wall and, thus, a 16-inch-wide footing. See page 665 for instructions on building forms for footings.

3. *Dig trench and lay out footing.*
It may not be necessary to build forms for your footings. Depending on your local codes and the nature of your project, simply digging a trench for the footing may suffice. Check with your local building department.

Digging a hole as big and as deep as needed for a wall footing can be a slow, back-breaking job, so consider hiring an excavator or renting a small backhoe or trench digger. Dig the trench to the top of the footing or to about 3 inches below the top of the footing if you will be building a form (see pages 665–666).

Use a plumb bob to locate the outside corners of the footing. Partially drive in the stakes that line up with the outside edges of your forming lumber (see inset). Follow the same procedure to position the form stakes for the inside edge of the footing form.

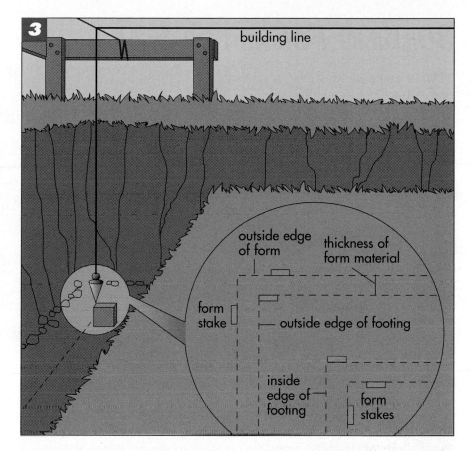

4. *Level tops of stakes.*
If there is a footing on the existing structure, drive in form stakes so the tops of the stakes are at the same level as that footing. Or, drive a stake so its top is at the correct depth for the footing top. Then drive the outside corner stakes so they are level with those next to the building. Check for level with a line level or carpenter's level resting on a straight board.

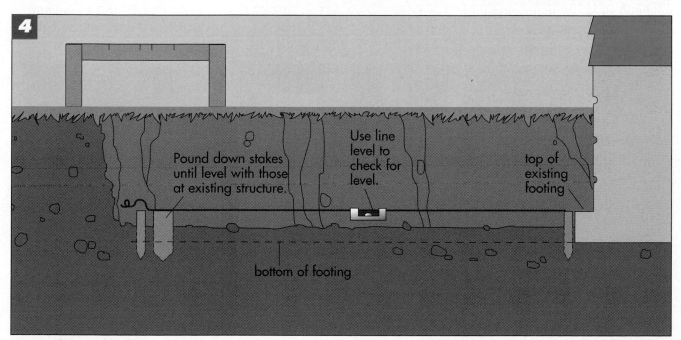

BUILDING FORMS FOR SLABS

Once you pour concrete, your slab will be impossible to change. As wet concrete flows into a form, it fills the niches and faithfully reproduces every detail of the mold you provide.

If you build strong forms that are straight where they should be and curved correctly according to your plan, the final product will look professional. But if you put up forms that bulge, tilt, or have loose-fitting joints, the finished product will have embarrassing flaws for years to come. Take the time to be fussy when building forms. If the formed surfaces will be visible, inspect your forming lumber for knotholes, cracks, and other defects that would show in the poured concrete.

Concrete forms must be sturdy, straight, and plumb. If you're in doubt about whether the forms are rigid enough, drive in an extra stake or two and add braces.

Stake forms every 3'–4'.

Install straight forms.
Because most concrete slabs are about 4 inches thick, smooth, straight 2×4s make ideal forming materials. When anchoring the forms, drive two double-headed nails through the stakes and into the 2×4s. Place your foot (inset above) or hold a sledgehammer (shown *below left*) against the opposite side of the forms to make nailing easier. Be sure the tops of the forms are level with or above the tops of the stakes, or you will have trouble screeding later (see page 673). Buttress each form with foot-long 1×4, 2×2, or 2×4 stakes every 3 to 4 feet. Use a string to make sure the forms are straight and level.

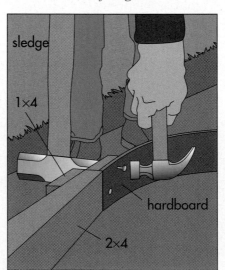

sledge

1×4

hardboard

2×4

Form a curve.
Where your plans call for a curve, substitute 3½-inch-wide strips of ¼-inch hardboard or plywood instead of lumber. For strength, use 2 or 3 plies of hardboard. If you use plywood, cut the strips perpendicular to the wood grain of the surface plies so the curved strips will be easier to bend.

Don't try to measure the length of the pieces to be bent. Tack one end temporarily with two 4-penny nails through the thin material and into the stake. Spring the material into the shape you want, mark the point where you'll cut it, and make the cut. Then nail it in place.

Add extra support where needed.

Don't skimp on bracing your forms. Nothing is quite so disastrous as having forms collapse in the middle of a concrete pour. If that happens, all you can do is frantically pound the forms back together, brace them, and shovel the concrete back in place.

When bracing the forms, pay particular attention to the places where two forms meet. If the forms butt end to end, drive in stakes to lap the joint. At corners, drive stakes near the end of each form. To strengthen curved forms, drive stakes every 1 to 2 feet along the outside radius. Fill gaps beneath the forms with rubble or scraps of wood. Resulting irregularities will be buried later.

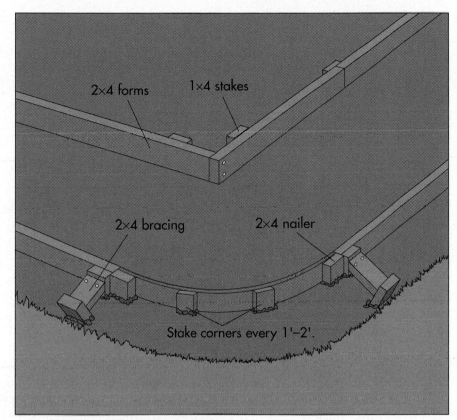

Divide a large slab.

Adding dividers on a large project allows you to pour a manageable amount of concrete at one time. If the dividers will be temporary, use any straight length of lumber. If you plan to leave the divider in as part of the slab, however, use redwood or pressure-treated lumber. Use 2×2s to sandwich the reinforcing mesh, keeping it at the right level for maximum effectiveness.

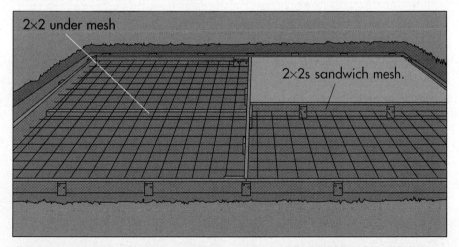

Protect permanent dividers.

Brush on a coat of wood sealer to enhance rot resistance of any wood forms that will remain a permanent part of the slab. Put masking tape on the top surfaces to keep wet concrete from staining the wood and to avoid scratching the forms when you screed. Drive interior stakes 1 inch below the top of the permanent dividers so they will not be visible once the concrete is poured.

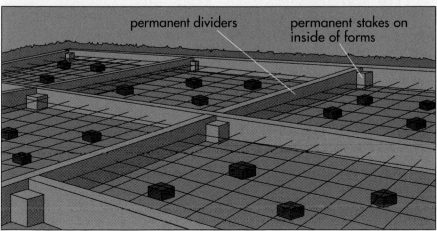

FORMING STAIRWAYS

It takes careful planning to build a stairway that is comfortable to walk on. If one step is an inch or so different from the rest, climbing the stairway will be awkward and possibly dangerous.

Each step consists of a horizontal run (tread) and a vertical rise (riser). For adults, a riser height of about 7 inches and a tread width of 10 to 12 inches makes for a stairway that is comfortable and safe.

Steps leading to a house should be at least 3½ feet wide, preferably wider. For flights rising more than 5 feet, a landing with at least a 3-foot run is desirable. However, a landing beneath an exterior doorway should extend 1 foot on each side of the opening and have a run of 5 feet.

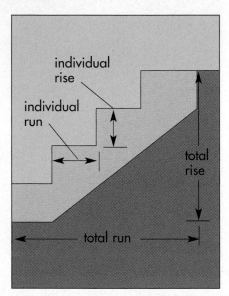

You'll Need

TIME: 2 days to figure, form, pour, and finish a small stairway.
SKILLS: Good carpentry skills, ability to figure accurately.
TOOLS: Tape measure, level, hammer, circular saw, framing square, baby sledgehammer.

CAUTION!

CHECK LOCAL CODES
The building codes for your area may dictate such dimensions as the size of risers and treads and the relationship between rises and runs, width, height of sets of steps, landing size, and footing requirements. Check with your local building department to ensure your plans conform—before they are set in concrete.

Calculate rise and run.

Total rise is the total distance that the stairway rises from the ground to the landing. Total run is the horizontal distance covered by the stairway. Individual rises and runs refer to the height and depth, respectively, of each step. The sum of each run and rise should equal about 18 inches. If you want a series of steps with a gentle rise of 5 inches, you should provide runs that are 13 inches deep.

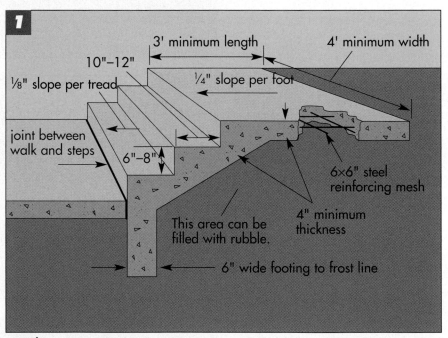

1. Plan your stairway.

To decide how many steps you need, measure the total rise and divide by 7 inches (or whatever individual rise you use). Round off the result to the nearest whole number to get the number of steps. Divide total rise by the number of steps to get the exact dimension of each individual rise.

Decide on how deep you want each tread to be (the individual run). Multiply that run by the number of steps to find the total run and, thus, where the stairway will end.

The footing at the base of the stairway should be 6 inches thick and extend beneath the frost line. (Check your local codes for the exact requirement.) Construct the forms so there is an expansion joint between the stairway and the walk. To keep rain and ice from gathering on the steps, slope each one ¼ inch per running foot for the landing and ⅛ inch per tread.

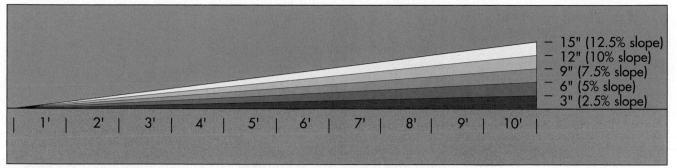

- 15" (12.5% slope)
- 12" (10% slope)
- 9" (7.5% slope)
- 6" (5% slope)
- 3" (2.5% slope)

| 1' | 2' | 3' | 4' | 5' | 6' | 7' | 8' | 9' | 10' |

Calculate ramp dimensions.

Ramps are useful if you have someone in a wheelchair or if you need to move wheeled equipment regularly. Otherwise, steps are a better choice; walking down a ramp feels awkward.

To frame a ramp, simply construct braced forms for the sides. Maintain a constant concrete depth of at least 4 inches, even at the bottom of the ramp. Do not try to feather out the concrete to nothing. For most purposes, it's best if a ramp does not rise more than 1 foot in 10 feet, a 10 percent slope.

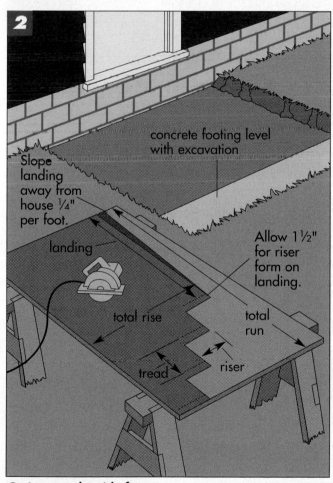

Slope landing away from house ¼" per foot.

concrete footing level with excavation

Allow 1½" for riser form on landing.

landing

total rise

total run

tread

riser

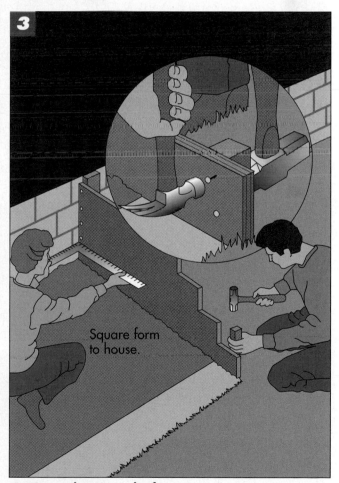

Square form to house.

2. Lay out the side forms.

On a sheet of ¾-inch plywood, lay out the side forms by drawing lines showing total rise and total run. When laying out the length of the landing, be sure to allow 1½ inches for the riser forms at the end of the landing. Mark the end of the landing and draw lines establishing the location of the finished treads and risers. For adequate drainage, the landing should slope away from the house at a rate of ¼ inch per running foot.

3. Cut and position the forms.

Cut both side forms and set them in place at the entry. Use a framing square to make sure they are perpendicular to the building foundation. Check the forms for proper slope and plumb and make sure they are level with each other. Drive supporting stakes into the ground and against the house. Use a baby sledgehammer to support the stakes as you nail the forms to them (see inset).

4. Cut and install riser forms.

Cut 2× lumber to the correct height and length for your risers (see page 662). With a circular saw or tablesaw, bevel the outside bottom of each riser, except for the lowest one. Leave about ⅛ inch of each bottom unbeveled for strength. This bevel makes it easier to use trowels to finish the tread after concrete is poured. Install the top riser first and the bottom one last, using at least three double-headed nails or screws.

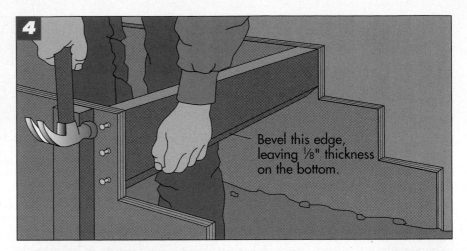

Bevel this edge, leaving ⅛" thickness on the bottom.

5. Brace the form.

Wet concrete is heavy and exerts a great deal of outward pressure on your form. Support the form at all points where it may bulge out when the concrete is poured. Make sure none of the braces will get in the way when it comes time to trowel the treads or the landing. For stairs wider than 4 feet, add a riser support by attaching a 2×6 or 2×8 to a 2×4 stake driven deep into the ground near the center of the bottom form. Anchor pointed cleats to the support and to the riser pieces. To shore up the sidewall forms, drive 2×4 stakes into the ground, then nail 1×4 braces to the 2×4s and to the stakes that anchor the sidewall forms. Nail on a 1×4 cross-tie to support the sidewalls.

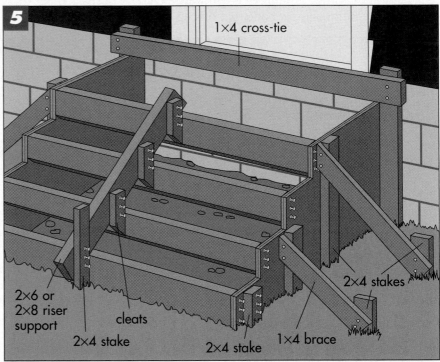

1×4 cross-tie

2×6 or 2×8 riser support

cleats

2×4 stake

2×4 stake

1×4 brace

2×4 stakes

Build form for a parallel stairway.

To build a form for concrete steps that run parallel to the building, strike a level line on the building wall to establish the landing height. Measure from this line to position the plywood forms for the front and side. For deeper stairs (a greater distance between risers), factor in a ¼-inch slope per foot. Brace the plywood pieces with stakes. Cut the beveled riser pieces. Have a helper hold the top and bottom risers level to determine the location of the diagonal brace. Attach it to the house, then attach the risers, cleats, and braces.

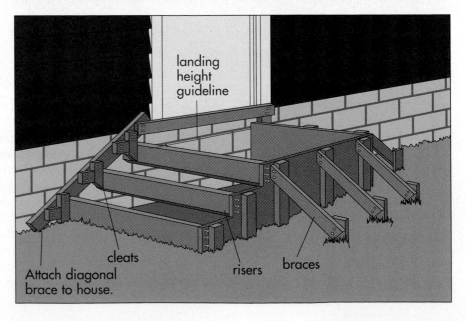

landing height guideline

Attach diagonal brace to house.

cleats

risers

braces

BUILDING FORMS FOR WALL FOOTINGS

Footings must be located on undisturbed soil below the frost line. Check your local building codes for requirements regarding size, depth, and metal reinforcement. (See pages 658–659 for how to lay out and excavate for wall footings.) You may not need to build forms; in some situations a simple trench is enough.

Make footings wide enough to distribute the weight of the wall adequately. Usually this means making the footing twice as wide as the wall is thick. A footing also must be thick enough so it will not crack. As a rule, the thickness of a footing should equal the width of the wall, but it should be no less than 8 inches thick.

To protect against structural damage that could result when a footing cracks and shifts because of unstable soil conditions, install two or three ½-inch reinforcing rods the full length of the footing (see page 671). Also, be sure to provide for drainage (see pages 629 and 641). For more information on building forms, see pages 660–661.

Brace foot or sledgehammer behind form while nailing.

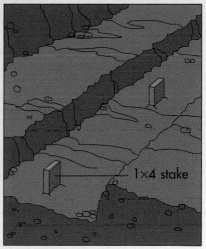

1×4 stake

1. Build and install forms...
Except for stepped footings (see page 666), the only forming materials you'll need are 2×4s for the footing rails and 1×4s for stakes. Position the stakes (see page 660), then secure the rails to them, making sure the top of each rail is even with or slightly above the top of the stakes.

or trench and stake.
If the soil is firm enough to hold its shape when filled with wet concrete, simply dig a trench footing. Keep the sides of the trench even to avoid wasting concrete. For screeding guides, center a row of stakes about 4 feet apart; check the height of the stakes with a line level.

2. Secure and level the forms.
Every few feet along the length of the form, use a carpenter's level to make sure parallel forms are the same height. Also, check to see that the forms are level lengthwise. Drive stakes every 4 feet to anchor the forms securely. Make sure the stakes penetrate at least 6 inches below the bottom of the footing trench that you dig (see page 666) to ensure that the form boards will be secure.

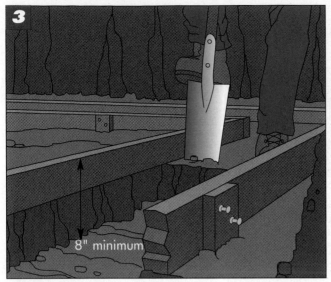

3. Dig the trench.

Once you are satisfied that the forms are level and secure, excavate an additional 5 to 6 inches of earth; the total depth of the footing should be no less than 8 inches. Keep the sides of the trench even with the form as you dig. Check the forms again to see that they are level and aligned properly.

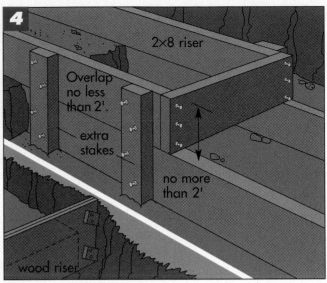

Step down with footings.

If your site is sloped, you can step the footings down to save concrete. If you have wood forms, use 2×8s and extra stakes. For an earth form (above), make a wood riser that wedges securely between the two levels. Stepped forms should rise no more than 2 feet per step; the upper and lower forms should overlap by at least 2 feet.

BUILDING FORMS FOR POURED WALLS

Forms for poured walls must be stronger than those for most other concrete projects. This is because they must contend with two substantial forces: the weight of the material itself and the hydrostatic pressure created as wet concrete pours into the wall.

If you mix your own concrete, you can pour it into the form slowly and use somewhat less massive forms. But for ready-mix concrete poured directly down the chute of a truck, use ¾-inch plywood backed by 2×4 studs at least every 24 inches.

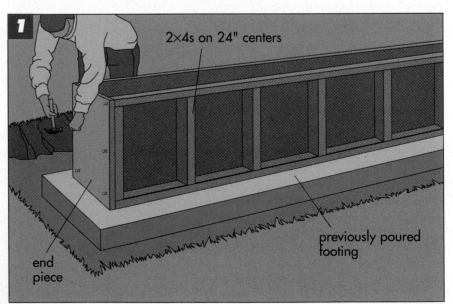

You'll Need

TIME: 3 hours, with a helper, to build a form for a 4-foot-high, 25-foot-long wall.
SKILLS: General carpentry skills.
TOOLS: Circular saw, tape measure, square, hammer or drill with screwdriver bit.

1. Construct the forms.

Sidewall forms are basically plywood-faced 2×4 stud walls. Working on a flat surface, nail the 2×4 frame together with two 16d common nails or 3-inch screws at each joint. Fasten the plywood sheathing around the perimeter with a few 8d nails or 2-inch screws. Coat the inside form surface with new or used motor oil before setting the form in place. Nail or screw the end pieces securely.

BUILDING COLUMN AND PAD FORMS

Column and pad forms are among the simplest concrete projects. They warrant careful planning, however, because these small pieces of concrete provide essential support for decks, wood stairways, and outbuildings.

Any outdoor structure that connects to your house should have footings that extend below the frost line. Otherwise, frost heave will stress the junction between the house and the structure and lead to serious damage. Where frost is not a problem, you usually are safe excavating to a depth of 24 inches.

YOU'LL NEED

TIME: 1 to 2 hours for most column and pad forms.
SKILLS: No special skills needed.
TOOLS: Posthole digger, round-point shovel, hammer or drill.

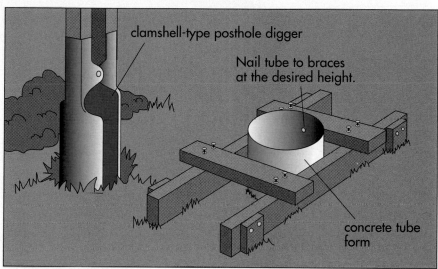

clamshell-type posthole digger

Nail tube to braces at the desired height.

concrete tube form

Install column forms.

A column form simply can be a hole in the ground. Use a clamshell-type posthole digger or rent a power auger if you have a lot of holes to dig. To save on concrete, try to be precise with your digging. Make the bottom of the hole a bit larger in diameter than the top to "key" it into the ground. Shovel in a few inches of gravel before pouring the concrete.

Concrete tube forms save on concrete because they are precisely dimensioned. If you want to continue the column footing above grade, brace the form as shown. Otherwise, shovel in a couple of inches of gravel and set the form in the hole.

2×4

1×4 stake

Make a small concrete pad.

To make a pad to support heavy items, such as air-conditioners, transformers, and hot tub spas, dig out all organic material and build a form of 2×4s. Dig postholes that extend below the frost line to keep the pad from rising and falling with temperature changes.

Before finishing the pad, check manufacturer's recommendations regarding the slope required for a particular appliance.

ADDING REINFORCEMENT

Once the forms are securely in place, double-check them for plumb and level. Prepare the slab area by filling low spots and installing metal reinforcement.

Reinforcement, in the form of 6×6-inch-grid metal mesh or ribbed steel reinforcing rods (rebar), is necessary because concrete is fragile under tension. A concrete structure that is larger than a few square feet will crack without such support.

To prevent the forms from absorbing too much water from the concrete and becoming glued to it, brush used motor oil on the the inside of the forms.

YOU'LL NEED

TIME: 1 to 2 hours for a medium-size slab.
SKILLS: Basic skills.
TOOLS: Shovel, rake, lineman's pliers or hacksaw.

Grade for a slab.
Fill in low areas within the forms with gravel or sand, then use a piece of 2×4 to level the area. The 2×4 also acts as a rough depth gauge to show you if you graded deeply enough. Tamp the area firmly, then grade again. If there

are gaps between the earth and the bottom of the forms, backfill along the outside edge of the forms with dirt or sand to fill those voids. Otherwise, some of the concrete will leak out, wasting material and making it difficult for plants to grow near the edge of the slab.

Fill in a step form.
To save concrete when pouring a deep structure, such as a stairway, fill some of the space with large stones, chunks of broken concrete, or other nonorganic filler material. One way to do this is to lay a low

U-shape stone wall about 6 inches from the inside of the sidewall forms and the top riser form. Fill this space with rubble or well-compacted soil. Make sure the concrete will be the correct thickness at every point.

Unroll and place wire mesh.
Position the roll of reinforcing mesh as shown, so that you unroll it upside down. This helps keep it from rolling back into its original shape. Place the wire so its edges reach within 1 to 2 inches of the edge of the finished slab. Place bricks or rocks 2 or 3 feet apart under the mesh so the wire is supported roughly in the vertical center of the slab.

Reinforce footings with rebar.

To strengthen footings, place rebar one-third of the way up from the base of the form. Overlap the rod ends by at least 12 inches and tie them together tightly with wire. The arrangement shown satisfies most building codes, but check with your local building department to be sure.

For small jobs, you can use a hacksaw to cut rebar. Cut it about two-thirds of the way through and bend it until it parts. For large jobs, use a circular saw with a Carborundum blade.

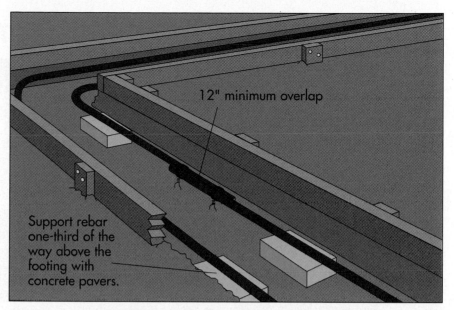

12" minimum overlap

Support rebar one-third of the way above the footing with concrete pavers.

Reinforce steps.

To prevent steps from cracking or pulling away from the house, attach them solidly to the foundation with rebar. For a concrete foundation, drill holes slightly downward at least 4 inches into the foundation wall. Drive a length of rebar into each hole and bend the rod down to lock it in place. Grout the hole if the rod is not tight. For a hollow concrete block foundation, chisel a hole big enough to stuff paper inside to seal the block's holes at the bottom. Fill the whole cavity with concrete and insert a bent rod. Once the connection to the foundation is made, fashion a grid by tying intersecting rods to those tied to the wall.

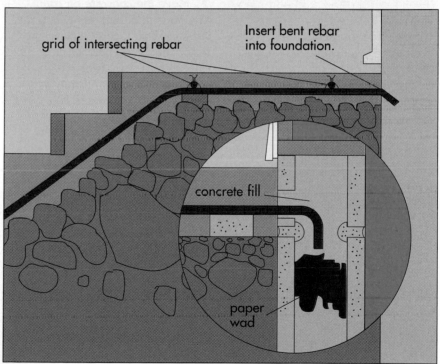

grid of intersecting rebar

Insert bent rebar into foundation.

concrete fill

paper wad

Add expansion joints.

Whenever new concrete butts up against an existing structure, separate the two with expansion joint material. The gap created allows for expansion of both surfaces and thus prevents cracking. Temporarily hold the expansion joint material with bricks or blocks, which you can remove while pouring the concrete. Or, you can nail the joint material in place.

Bricks will be removed during the pour.

expansion joint material

POURING, SCREEDING, AND FLOATING

Once concrete starts to flow, it's too late to alter forms, run for tools, or look for more help. So before you start mixing concrete or before the ready-mix truck arrives, be sure you are ready.

If the compacted base is not still damp from an earlier wetting, sprinkle it and the forms with water to prevent the new concrete from losing moisture too rapidly. This is especially important on a warm, windy day.

YOU'LL NEED

TIME: 4 to 8 hours, depending on the size of the slab.
SKILLS: Screeding, concrete finishing (a specialized skill that takes a lot of practice to learn).
TOOLS: Shovels, wheelbarrows, rake, screeding straightedge, bull float or darby.

CAUTION!

ARE YOU REALLY READY?
■ *On all but the smallest jobs, have at least two helpers. For a large job, have enough help on hand so some can rest occasionally while others keep the wheelbarrows in motion.*
■ *Enlist a bona fide concrete finisher; it's not possible to learn while you try to smooth out the concrete. If you don't have a willing helper who has finished a slab successfully before, hire someone.*
■ *Be sure all reinforcing rods or mesh are in place.*
■ *Have the site inspected the day before the pour, so you will have time to make required changes.*

Position ramp to clear form.

1. Move the concrete on ramps.
Mix your materials as near to the job site as you can. Or have the ready-mix truck park as close as is safe. (A concrete truck weighs an immense amount and may crack sidewalks or driveways.)

Wet concrete weighs 150 pounds per cubic foot. When wheeling it, keep loads small enough to handle. To cross soft soil or lawns, lay a walkway of 2×10 or 2×12 planks. Build ramps over the forms so you do not disturb them. Use two or more wheelbarrows to keep the job moving; the ready-mix company may charge you for waiting time.

2. Dump and move the concrete.
Start placing fresh material in the farthest corner of the forms. Dump it in mounds that reach ½ inch or so above the top of the form. It helps to have one person working a shovel while two or more others run the wheelbarrows. The shoveler directs the wheelbarrow handlers and tells them where to dump the concrete. Wear heavy boots that fit snugly; you will be slogging around in concrete part of the time. Pace your efforts because you'll be moving a lot of concrete before the pour is completed.

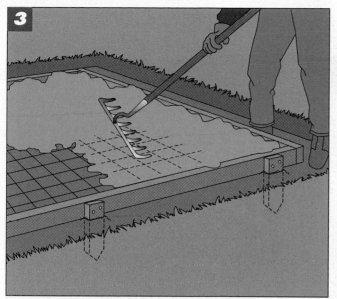

3. Pull reinforcing mesh up.

While pouring the concrete, use a hoe, rake, or shovel to pull the wire mesh up into the concrete. For the greatest strength, keep the mesh positioned halfway between the bottom of the excavation and the finished surface of the slab. Watch that the mesh doesn't get pushed against the form at any point. Keep it 1 to 2 inches away from all forms.

4. Tamp concrete to remove air pockets.

Whether you're pouring a slab, steps, or another project, take precautions to ensure the concrete adheres at every point and there are no air pockets in the concrete, especially at places where a formed edge will be exposed. To do this, run a shovel up and down along the inside edge of all forms and tap the sides of the forms with a hammer. Be sure to check that all corners are filled in and tamped adequately.

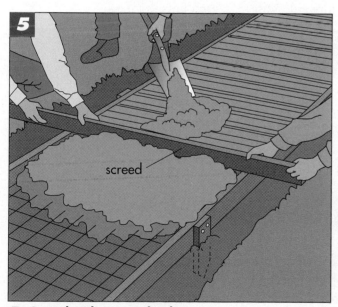

5. Screed with a straightedge.

Begin screeding (leveling) as soon as you've filled the first 3 or 4 feet of the length of the form. Keep both ends of the screed—a straight 2×4—pressed down on the top of the form while moving it back and forth in a sawing motion and drawing it toward the unleveled concrete. If depressions occur in the screeded surface, throw on a shovel or two of new material, then go back and screed the area again.

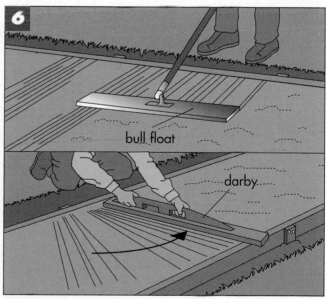

6. Float the surface.

Screed the surface again if necessary to level the surface a final time. Then use a bull float or a darby to begin smoothing the surface and to imbed the aggregate pieces in the concrete below the surface. Run a bull float in long, back-and-forth motions, slightly raising its leading edge so it does not dig into the concrete. If you are using a darby, work in large, sweeping arcs.

FINISHING CONCRETE

Finishing concrete is a specialized skill that you can't learn quickly. If the project is large, have someone on hand who knows finishing. If it's a small project and appearance isn't important, however, it's a good time to learn a new skill.

Timing is critical. If you start too soon, you'll weaken the surface. Start too late and the concrete will be unworkable. The waiting period depends on the weather and type of concrete. Start when the water sheen is gone from the surface and the concrete will carry foot pressure without sinking more than ¼ inch.

YOU'LL NEED

TIME: 1 hour per 50 square feet.
SKILLS: This is a specialized skill learned only with practice.
TOOLS: Steel trowel, edger, jointer, plywood for kneelers, circular saw with masonry blade, wood float, broom.

EXPERTS' INSIGHT

HIRING A PROFESSIONAL

■ If your project is larger than 250 square feet, you may need to hire a professional even if you or a friend have finishing experience. Choose someone who is reliable; if your finisher doesn't show up, you're sunk.
■ Check the Yellow Pages or go to job sites and ask for a finisher. Even if finishers work regularly for a company, many will work for others after-hours. Tell them how many square feet the job is and if there are steps or other complications. They may charge by the area or the hour.

1. Edge the corners.
Edging creates rounded edges that prevent damage from chipping and add an attractive finish. Edging also compacts and hardens the concrete along the form.

Hold the edger against the form and flat on the concrete surface. Tilt the front edge up slightly while you push it forward. Raise the rear slightly when drawing the edger backward.

Use short back-and-forth strokes to shape the edge and to work larger pieces of gravel deeper into the concrete. Complete the edging by holding the tool level and using long, smooth strokes. Repeat the edging process after each finishing task.

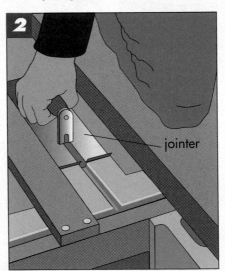

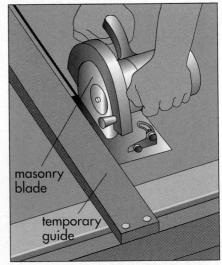

2. Make control joints.
Jointing results in a series of grooves that prevent concrete slabs from cracking randomly. To be effective, a control joint should be one-fourth as deep as the thickness of the slab.

Create control joints by finishing them into the wet concrete with a jointer or by sawing grooves in the surface after the concrete has hardened. Work the jointer as you would an edger, using a straight 2×4 as a guide. To cut concrete with a circular saw, use a masonry cutting blade. Cut the concrete as soon as it is hard, but not set—usually a few hours after Step 5 on page 675.

3. Float with a hand tool.

Floating pushes aggregate deeper into the concrete, smooths the surface, and draws a wet mixture of sand and cement to the surface, making further finishing possible. A wood float produces a coarse-textured surface; a magnesium float makes a smoother surface.

If water begins to surface when you begin floating, stop floating and wait a while before trying again. Hold the float nearly flat and sweep it in wide arcs to fill low spots and flatten lumps. Smooth the marks left by edging and jointing.

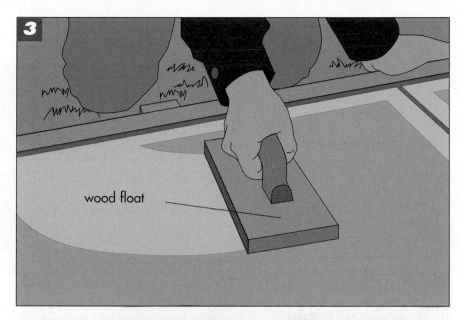

wood float

4. Finish with a steel trowel.

To achieve a smooth, dense surface, switch to a steel trowel after floating. Hold the trowel blade nearly flat against the surface, with the leading edge raised slightly. Overlap each pass by one-half of the tool's length so you end up troweling all the surface twice in the first operation. For an even smoother surface, trowel the surface a second or even third time. On the final troweling, the trowel should make a ringing sound as you move it over the concrete.

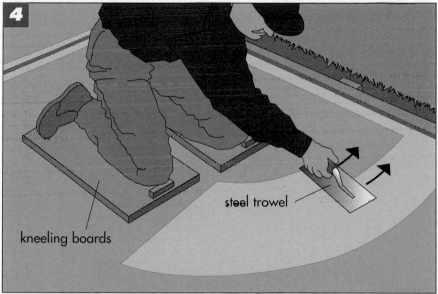

kneeling boards

steel trowel

5. Make a broom finish.

For a nice-looking, slip-resistant surface on steps, walks, and drives, pull a damp broom across the surface of the just-troweled concrete. The stiffer the bristle, the coarser will be the texture. Only pull the broom—do not push.

Have a brick or a piece of 2×4 handy on which you can knock the broom now and then to keep it clear of concrete buildup.

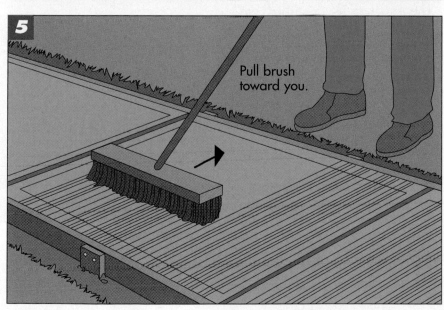

Pull brush toward you.

ADDING CUSTOM FINISHES

Most custom finishes end up with a rough surface. But you will still need someone with good concrete finishing skills to bring the concrete to the correct level and smoothness to take the custom finish. One exception is the brick pattern shown on page 677. In that case, most do-it-yourselfers can start with a tamped sand or gravel bed, mix and pour small amounts of concrete at a time, and proceed from one form to the next.

YOU'LL NEED:

TIME: 1 to 2 additional hours of work for a medium-size slab. Be sure to limit the size of the job so the concrete will not set up before you finish.
SKILLS: Concrete finishing.
TOOLS: Garden hose, trowels, brushes, joint strike.

EXPERTS' INSIGHT

FINISHING OPTIONS

■ For a broom finish, trowel the concrete as described on page 675. Then use a straw broom to make swirling patterns on the surface of the concrete. Use either wide arcs or squiggly strokes.

■ To create patterns, you can rent concrete embossing stampers in many patterns. They work best if your concrete contains gravel no larger than 1/4 inch. To move the job along, rent at least two stampers. When the surface has begun to set, but is still soft, press the stamper in place firmly by stepping on it. Work quickly, alternating stampers.

1. To make an aggregate surface, sprinkle stones on the surface. Pour the concrete and screed it to about 1/2 inch below the top of the forms. As soon as the water evaporates from the surface (watch carefully), sprinkle stones in a uniform layer over the concrete.

2. Push the stones in. With a wooden float, carefully press the stones into the concrete until the surface is smooth, even, and as free of stroke marks as a floated slab. If the slab is a large one, apply a curing retarder to give you extra working time.

3. Expose the stones. When the concrete becomes firm (after about an hour), gently brush away excess concrete with a stiff broom. If the stones come out, stop working and wait for the concrete to harden further. Spray a fine mist on the surface. Continue sweeping until runoff water is clear and the stones are exposed.

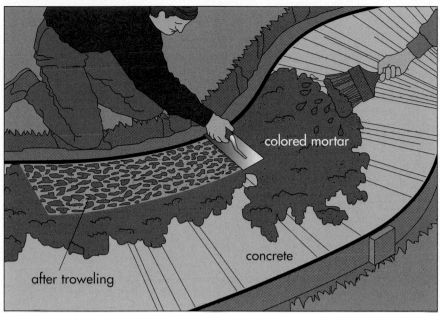

colored mortar

concrete

after troweling

Make a travertine finish.

This finish should be used only in areas not subject to freezing (see box, right). Pour, screed, and float the concrete. As soon as the water evaporates from the surface, use a brush to spatter on pigmented mortar the consistency of thick paint. After the mortar has stiffened slightly, use a steel trowel to smooth the high spots to make the distinctive travertine pattern.

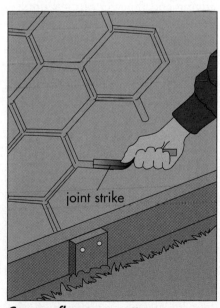

joint strike

Carve a flagstone pattern.

To make your surface look like flagstones or geometric shapes, score the concrete soon after you finish it with a bull float or darby and after water has evaporated from the surface. A joint strike works well for this technique. Go over the marks each time you do other finishing operations.

1. To make a brick pattern, pour concrete into a form.

This method is ideal for small jobs. These brick-shaped forms are available at home centers. Set the form on top of the gravel or sand bed and shovel concrete into it. Make sure each section is filled to the top of the form but no higher.

2. Remove form and finish with a trowel.

After water has evaporated from the concrete surface water, wiggle the form out carefully so clean-looking lines remain. Flick away crumbs and carefully give the surface a trowel finish. Once the concrete is cured, fill the gaps with mortar.

Adding Color to Concrete

White and various shades of tan concrete can be ordered ready-made from some suppliers; they simply adjust the mix of raw materials to achieve the color. For more intense colors, you can add pigment to the concrete as it is mixed. This makes sense only if you need color throughout the slab, as you might for a rough broom-finish or aggregate surfaces or on steps, walks, or patios where the edges of the slab show. If you mix several batches of concrete, it's difficult to keep the color consistent. Most often, however, you'll need or want to add pigment only to the surface, where the color shows.

You'll Need:

TIME: About 2 hours per 100 square feet of concrete.
SKILLS: Careful, even spreading of the pigment powder.
TOOLS: Concrete finishing tools.

Experts' Insight

Paint and Stain For Concrete

The safest coloring method is to wait for the concrete to cure then apply special concrete stain or paint.

■ Chemical stains yield better results. These are applied when the concrete is cured completely and are designed to seep into the concrete and bond with it, producing a color that lasts longer than paint.

■ Paint adheres to surface only. Some paints are durable, but with heavy use even the best paints wear away and require another coat every few years.

Apply tint to the concrete surface. The most economical way to apply pigment to a walkway or slab is to spread it on the surface before the concrete has set. The greatest challenge with this approach is spreading the color evenly.

After edging and floating, spread about two-thirds of the required amount of powdered color pigment over the area to be tinted. As soon as the powder becomes wet, edge and float the surface again to spread the pigment evenly. Spread out the rest of the powder and repeat the edging and floating process until the surface is finished. In this way, you can work the pigment in twice, giving you even coverage.

Apply pigment-curing compound. Curing pigmented concrete is tricky. The normal curing techniques (see page 679) are not recommended because they can cause the color to become uneven. Check the pigment manufacturer's recommendations, which often involve spraying the concrete with a special curing compound designed for colored concrete. Mix this compound and spray it on. After curing and drying, seal the surface with a nonwax, polymeric sealer to accentuate the color and make cleaning easy.

CURING CONCRETE

Proper curing can make or break a concrete project. Hydration, the chemical process that hardens cement, stops after the concrete first sets, unless you keep it moist and fairly warm. Without adequate hydration, the concrete will be weak.

Whether you choose to cover or periodically spray the concrete, keep it damp or wet for several days after pouring it. If the weather is cold, insulate the concrete during curing by spreading straw over the top of it.

YOU'LL NEED

TIME: Periodic attention over several days.
SKILLS: No special skills needed.
TOOLS: Garden hose, sprinkler.

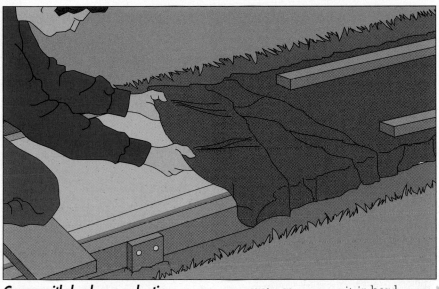

Cover with burlap or plastic.
The most effective curing method is to cover the concrete surface with burlap or old blankets and keep these wet with frequent waterings. Be sure the fabric is clean so you won't stain the concrete. Place the covering on the concrete as soon as it is hard enough to resist surface damage. Weight down the covering with scraps of lumber.

If you cannot wet the surface periodically, cover it with plastic sheeting. This traps moisture and works as well as wet cloth.

Keep a sprinkler running.
Frequent wetting with a lawn sprinkler, especially during daylight hours in the summer, also provides the moisture concrete needs to cure slowly. Before spraying the water, make sure the concrete is set hard enough so the spray will not damage the surface. If you apply too much water before the concrete is set, it could cause spalling or chipping at a later date, which can ruin the job.

Cover with straw if it gets cold.
If cold weather strikes after the pour, spread 6 to 12 inches of dry straw or hay over the concrete, then cover the straw with canvas or plastic sheeting. Be especially careful to cover the edges and corners of slabs, the places most likely to freeze.

APPLYING STONE OR TILE VENEERS ON SLABS

A mortared stone or tile veneer surface is beautiful, long-lasting, and needs almost no maintenance. With this approach, a garden-variety walk or patio slab can be improved dramatically at relatively low cost. Any stone or tile veneer ¾ inch thick or less must be installed on a solid concrete surface. If the slab is not smooth, level it with concrete patch first because it is difficult to level a veneer surface as you apply it. (If you need to lay a slab, see pages 654–661 and 670–675.)

YOU'LL NEED

TIME: About 1 day to install 100 square feet of veneer; a few hours the next day to grout it.
SKILLS: Cutting stone or tile.
TOOLS: Straightedge, large-notched trowel, tile cutter, rented wet saw, hammer, cold chisel, rubber mallet, grout float, towels, sponges.

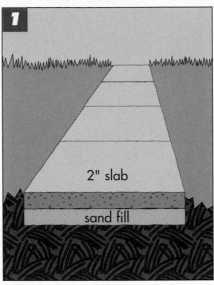

1. Install or patch concrete base.
The base for your stone or tile veneer surface must be solid. If it shifts or buckles, the veneer will crack. The slab should be at least 2 inches of concrete over a sand base. Use a straightedge to make sure it is level. Fill in low spots with patching concrete. Knock off high spots with a hammer and cold chisel.

2. Dry-lay the pieces.
If you are using irregular-shaped stones, dry-lay the pieces on the surface in the pattern you want before you mix mortar. Maintain consistent joint spacing and avoid placing small pieces along the edge. Once you've laid out about a 16-square-foot section, set aside the pieces, being careful to preserve the pattern.

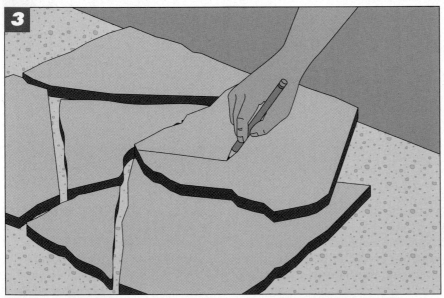

3. Mark and cut.
When you need to cut an irregular piece for a clean fit or come to the end of a tile veneer run, mark the cut line on the stone or tile by holding it on top of the adjacent piece. See page 684 for cutting stone. An inexpensive tile cutter works well for straight cuts on most types of tile. It has a guide that can be screwed in place to cut a series of tiles the same size.

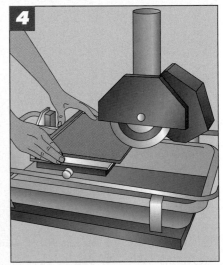

4. Use a wet saw.
For thicker tile or stone or to cut inside corners accurately, rent a wet saw. It quickly and cleanly slices through the hardest of materials, even granite. To keep the blade from getting dull, keep water running on it.

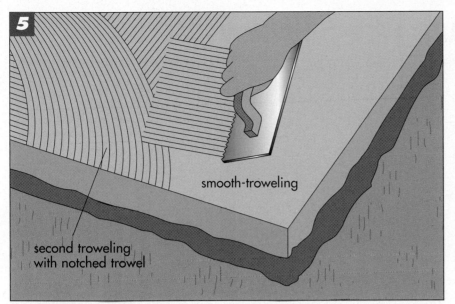

smooth-troweling

second troweling
with notched trowel

5. Apply the mortar.

Unless you are applying thick, uneven stones that require a thick mortar to help even the surface, use a thin-set mortar with a latex additive. These are available in liquid or powder form. Mix the mortar, allow it to "slake" for 10 minutes, then mix it again.

Apply the mortar in two steps. Trowel on a smooth base coating about ½ inch thick. Then go over the surface with a large-notched trowel, taking care that the notches do not penetrate through to the concrete base. Use long, sweeping strokes as you apply this second coat.

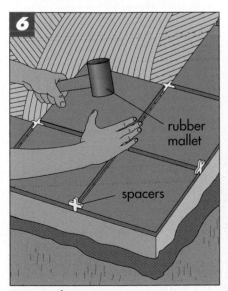

rubber mallet

spacers

6. Lay the veneer.

Lay stone in the pattern you dry-laid. If applying tile, as shown, place each piece straight down so you do not have to slide it into position. Use spacers or eyeball the joints every few tiles to make sure they're even. If tiles are not flush, use a flat piece of lumber and a rubber mallet to gently tap them into alignment.

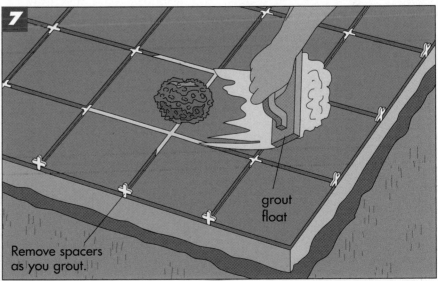

grout float

Remove spacers as you grout.

7. Grout the joints.

Allow time for the mortar to set (usually one or two days). Mix the grout of your choice, using a latex additive to keep it from cracking later on. Push the grout into the joints with a grout float, making sure you move the float in at least two directions at all points. Once you are sure the joints in a small section are packed fully, scrape

with the float held nearly perpendicular to the tiles to remove as much waste as possible. Clean the grout from the veneer surface and make smooth grout lines, first by laying a wet towel on the surface and pulling it toward you, then by wiping carefully with a damp sponge. Sponge-clean the surface several times.

BUILDING DRY-LAID, FREE-STANDING WALLS

Building a wall of natural stone is hard work, and stone can be expensive. But the results are enduring and strikingly beautiful. Dry-laid stone walls rely on gravity, rather than mortar, to hold them together. As a result, they are more difficult to build than mortared walls because you spend more time getting stones to fit well and rest solidly on each other. Don't try to build a dry stone wall more than 3 feet high; it is difficult to keep it stable.

YOU'LL NEED

TIME: With stones at the site, about a day to build a wall 3 feet high and 10 feet long.
SKILLS: Patience to keep trying for the right fit.
TOOLS: Round-point shovel, brick hammer, mason's line.

EXPERTS' INSIGHT

USING A FOOTING

If your area is subject to frost, a stone wall will rise and fall an inch or so every year because of frost heave. Even in warm climates, the weight of the stones will make a wall settle. As long as the wall is not cemented together with mortar, this is not a problem. The stones will move a bit in relation to each other, and you may have to refit a stone or two over the years. But if the stones are placed well to begin with, the wall should remain solid. You can cement the stones together with mortar; however, that requires a footing, dug below the frost line, to keep the mortar from cracking.

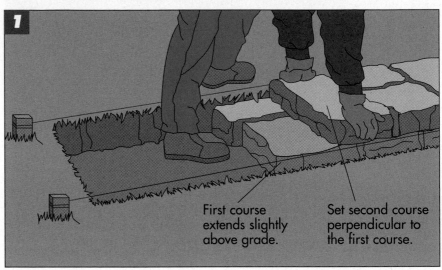

First course extends slightly above grade.

Set second course perpendicular to the first course.

1. Dig a trench and begin laying the stones.
Drive stakes and stretch mason's lines to establish the two outside edges of the bottom of the wall. Remove sod, any roots larger than ½ inch in diameter, and 2 or 3 inches of soil to provide a smooth, level base. Dig the trench deep enough so the top of the first course is slightly above grade.

Begin placing stones by setting them securely into the soil. Lay the stones in each course perpendicular to those in the course below them. This helps tie the courses together and strengthen the wall.

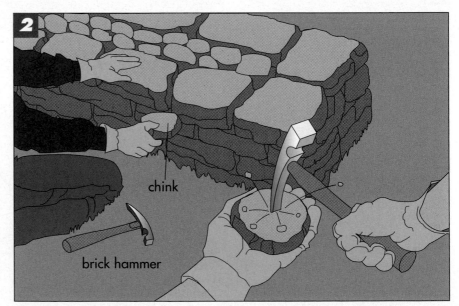

chink

brick hammer

2. Fill in voids with small stones.
Fill voids in the center of the wall with small stones and plug vertical gaps between stones by tapping chinks (small pieces of stone) into place. Cut these chinks and any other small stones you need with a brick hammer. Wear eye and hand protection when breaking stones. Always avoid placing stones of the same size directly on top of each other.

3. **Batter, top off with capstones.**
Batter the wall as you work; that is, build the wall so it becomes slightly narrower as it rises. This makes the wall more stable. Notice in this wall how the stones form bonds both across the width and along the length of the wall. Select large, flat stones for the top course. Some masons spread mortar over the stones in the next-to-top course, then set the capstones into the mortar. This helps seal the top of the wall from moisture, which otherwise may freeze and weaken the wall.

CAUTION!
WATCH YOUR BACK
Working with stone can be, almost literally, backbreaking work. Have a strong-backed helper on hand and lift the heavy stones together. Lift with your legs, keeping your back straight and upright to avoid strain. Take frequent breaks and do not work more than a few hours a day if you are not used to this kind of labor.

CHECK LOCAL CODES
In many localities, building codes also apply to stone walls, especially if they are used as retaining walls. Before you begin, check with your building department and follow their instructions.

BUILDING DRY-LAID RETAINING WALLS

The basics of building a retaining wall are the same as for a free-standing wall. The main difference is you need to excavate the hillside and provide drainage.

Before building the wall, you need to cut and fill the grade (see page 685). Wrap the gravel and drainpipe in landscaping fabric to filter out loose soil that might clog the system.

If the soil you want to retain is more than 4 feet high, do not attempt to hold it all back with one dry stone wall. Build steplike terraces instead.

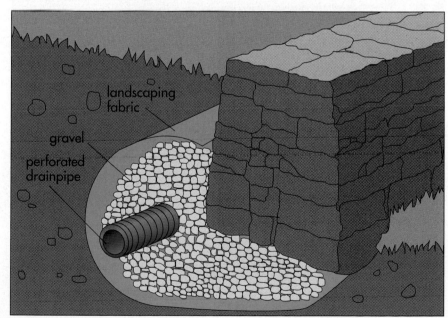

Excavate and provide drainage.
Dig into the hill you want to retain to excavate a base for the wall. On the hill side of the wall, dig a drainage ditch. Lay down landscaping fabric and gravel and set perforated drainpipe on the gravel, making sure the pipe slopes slightly toward a spot where you want excess water to flow. Cover the drainpipe with gravel and landscaping fabric.

Build the wall as you would a dry stone wall. Be sure, however, to slope it slightly toward the hill that is being retained.

YOU'LL NEED
TIME: For a 10-foot-long and 3-foot-high wall, about a day to excavate and provide drainage and a day to build the wall.
SKILLS: Good digging skills.
TOOLS: Round-point shovel, brick hammer, brick set, baby sledgehammer, mason's line.

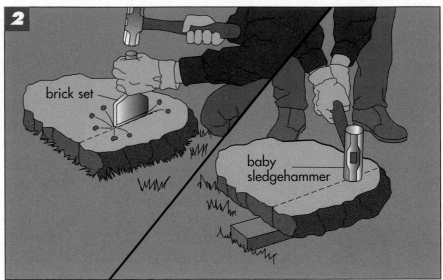

1. Excavate and lay first course.

After staking and laying out the front perimeter, dig away the soil so you have enough room to lay the stones and install the drainpipe (see page 683). Dig a level area for the wall and lay the first course. If a stone is loose as you place it, trowel some soil under and around it to stabilize it.

2. Cut stones to fit.

Lay subsequent courses carefully, experimenting with different stones and making adjustments so they sit solidly on each other. See page 682 for how to mark and cut stones with a brick hammer. To cut large stones to fit, score a line all the way around, about ⅛ inch

deep, with a brick set. Be sure to wear gloves and safety goggles as you work. Place the stone on a solid support along the score line and hit the unsupported part with firm strokes from a baby sledgehammer until the stone splits in two.

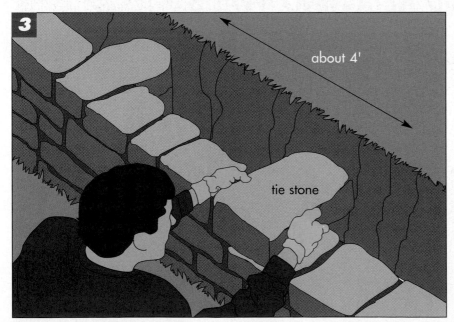

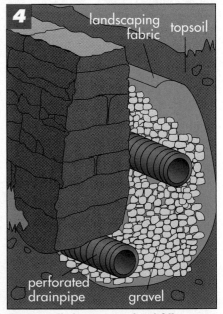

3. Batter the wall and install tie stones.

As you build the wall, avoid placing stones such that joints line up vertically. Use long stones that span two or more joints whenever possible. Be sure every stone rests solidly in place or it may work its way loose later.

Slope the face of the retaining wall 10 to 20 degrees from vertical so it leans toward the backfill it is to retain. Use a batter guide (see pages 688–689). To keep the middle of the wall from bulging out, install long tie stones about every 4 feet, halfway up the wall.

4. Install drainpipe, backfill.

Behind the wall, lay gravel on the landscaping fabric, place drainpipe on gravel bed, and cover it with more gravel. Use two pipes for severe drainage problems. Wrap the fabric around the gravel bed and cover it with more gravel. Top off with 5 to 6 inches of topsoil.

BUILDING SHORT FLAGSTONE WALLS

A short flagstone wall is easy to build because it does not require a drainage system or a footing and can be constructed with light flagstones. This type of wall can be used for flower beds or small walls that do not have to retain large amounts of soil. Usually it is best if such a wall is no more than 3 feet high. During a heavy rain, water will seep out of the face of the wall.

YOU'LL NEED

TIME: About 1 day to build a wall 3 feet high by 15 feet long.
SKILLS: Laying stone.
TOOLS: Round-point shovel, rake, brick set, baby sledgehammer, brick trowel.

1. Cut and fill.
Dig a trench about 10 inches deep and 1 foot wider than the wall. Either cut away or add dirt to the hill you will be retaining so it slopes back about 1 inch per rising foot. Maintain the same slope across the length of the wall. Fill the trench with gravel and rake it smooth and level with the adjoining ground surface.

direction of batter

2. Lay the stones.
Lay the first course using large stones so they span the gravel bed. As you lay succeeding courses, stagger the joints and be sure each stone rests solidly, without wobbling. Save smaller stones for the upper courses, but keep some large flagstones for the top course.

Batter the wall toward the hill.
You may leave the joints in the wall bare. Or, you can mix soil with a small amount of water to achieve a mortar-like consistency. Press the soil into gaps in the wall. In time, small plants or grass will grow there, lending a rustic, mature appearance to the wall.

3. Mortar the top course.
This is an optional step, but it will make a wall stronger. Dry-fit the top course in a pleasing pattern, then remove the stones and place them adjacent to the wall so you can remember where they go. Mix and apply a 2-inch layer of mortar on the next-to-last course and lay the top stones. You may need to fill in some gaps with small stones.

WORKING WITH MORTAR

Laying bricks in mortar is a skill that requires practice before you become proficient. You probably will never be able to throw mortar and lay bricks as quickly as a journeyman, but with patience you can learn to make straight walls with clean joints.

Professional masons take their mortar seriously. Mortar must be just the right consistency, neither soupy nor dry. It must have the correct ratio of sand, lime, and cement. Otherwise, laying bricks will be a struggle and it will be difficult to keep the courses even.

For small jobs and repair work, use premixed mortar that contains sand. For larger jobs, you may be able to save money by buying the sand and the cement separately and mixing them yourself.

YOU'LL NEED

TIME: A beginner will move slowly, but after 1 or 2 days you can learn to move at a fairly good pace.
SKILLS: Leveling, laying mortar.
TOOLS: Mason's hoe, mortar box or wheelbarrow, brick trowel, mortarboard.

CAUTION!

AVOID COLD WEATHER
Mortar loses its strength if the temperature drops below 40 degrees. Don't risk ruining your work. Hold off on the project and wait for warmer weather.

mason's hoe

1. Mix the mortar.
Consult your supplier for the best mix for your area and your project. In most cases, a good ratio is 4 parts sand, ½ part lime, and 1 part mason's cement. Adding lime and sand weakens the mortar. Measure by shovelfuls.

Mix small batches in a wheelbarrow; for larger jobs use a mortar box. Shovel in half the sand, then all the mortar and lime, then the rest of the sand. Mix the dry materials thoroughly, then carefully mix in clean water a little bit at a time.

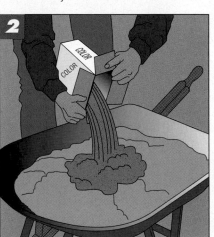

2. Add color pigment.
If you want to color the mortar, add the pigment to your dry mix. Follow label instructions carefully. Keep accurate track of your proportions so if you mix another batch you can achieve the same color. If you retemper (remoisten) colored mortar, you will change its color, so don't mix too large a batch and don't let it dry out.

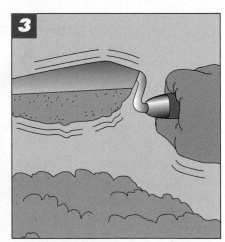

3. Test the mortar.
Pick up a small amount of mortar with your trowel and quickly turn the trowel upside down. If the mortar sticks to the trowel, it is the correct consistency. If the mortar stiffens before you use it all, add water and remix. (Don't do this with colored mortar.) But if it stiffens a second time, throw it out and make a new batch.

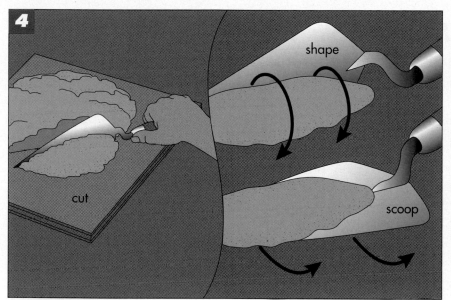

4. Pick up the mortar.

Drop a shovelful of mortar onto the mortarboard. Place the mortarboard close to your work and keep it at a comfortable height so it will be easy to move mortar onto the wall.

Simply getting the mortar on your brick trowel in the correct position takes some practice. Slice off a gob and shape it so it is about the size and shape of your trowel. Scoop it up with a smooth sweep, giving a slight upward jerk with your wrist to make the mortar stick firmly to the trowel. Take the time to practice this essential technique.

5. Throw the mortar.

Bricklayers talk of "throwing" mortar for a reason. Don't try to carefully place it. In one motion, flick your wrist and pull the trowel toward you. Plopping the mortar onto the bricks helps it adhere better. Using a standard-size brick trowel with the correct amount of mortar, you can throw enough mortar for two bricks.

6. Furrow the mortar.

Spread the mortar to an even thickness if necessary. Lightly draw the point of the trowel across the length of the mortar to make a furrow down its middle. Don't make the furrow too deep or you may form an air pocket.

7. Butter the brick end.

Some bricks stick better if they are dampened. Ask your supplier if this is recommended. After the corner brick is laid, butter one end of the other bricks using a scraping motion with the trowel.

8. Place the brick, remove excess.

Place each brick so you have to slide it only slightly into place. Push it firmly up against the preceding brick. Immediately slice off the excess mortar oozing from the sides; use this excess as part of your next trowel load.

BUILDING MORTARED STONE WALLS

Choose stones that blend well together, both in color and texture. A good variety of sizes not only looks better, but it also makes it easier to find the correct size of stones without having to cut them to fit. Ashlar is best to work with, but semidressed stones or rubble work well also. Have the stones delivered as close to your work site as possible to minimize lifting. Be prepared for some difficult physical labor. You'll have to lift, shift, and try different stones to get the best fit.

YOU'LL NEED

TIME: 1 day to pour the footing and 2 days to build a wall 4 feet high and 10 feet long.
SKILLS: A willingness to keep trying for the best fit, making clean mortar lines.
TOOLS: Round-point shovel, tamper, mortar box and hoe, drill or hammer, mason's line, brick trowel, wedges, brush.

EXPERTS' INSIGHT

WORKING WITH MORTAR

Don't allow excess or smeared mortar to dry and set on the stones. Every stone or two, take the time to wipe the stones clean with a wet rag. It is much harder to remove excess mortar once it sets.

Because stones are not as porous as bricks or blocks, they do not absorb much moisture and mortar sets up more slowly. If mortar squeezes out quickly, sprinkle on a bit more mortar mix or Portland cement to absorb water and stiffen the mortar before setting on a stone.

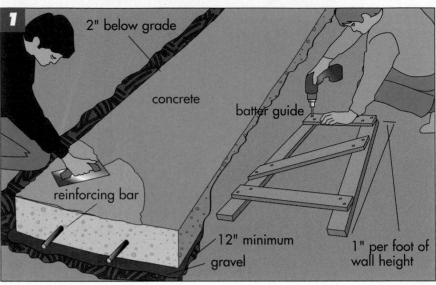

1. Lay a concrete foundation.
Unlike a dry-laid stone wall, a mortared wall develops ugly cracks if it settles unevenly. Dig a trench about 6 inches wider than the wall and 6 inches deeper than the frost line or at least 12 inches deep. Tamp at least 2 inches of gravel at the bottom, position two pieces of reinforcing bar, and pour at least 8 inches of concrete. Finish the concrete footing so it's 2 inches below grade.

Make two batter guides out of 1×4 lumber; use these to make sure your wall batters, or slopes inward, about 1 inch per rising foot on both sides.

2. Lay the first course.
Allow the concrete foundation to set and cure for several days. Spread a 2-inch-thick bed of mortar. Start on the end with a tie stone—a stone that spans the width of the wall. Use large stones along the visible face of the wall and fill in the middle with smaller stones and mortar. Tap the stones with the handle of your trowel to force air pockets out of the mortar.

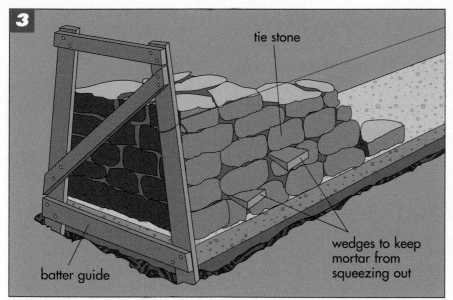

tie stone

wedges to keep mortar from squeezing out

batter guide

shim or wood scrap

3. Lay the stones.

Position the batter guides at each end of the wall and use mason's lines to make sure you maintain a uniform slope and line up the stones straight.

Dry-fit several stones, remove them, throw the mortar, then set the stones in position. Place tie stones about every 4 feet in alternating positions for each succeeding course. If a heavy stone squeezes out too much mortar, use wood wedges to support the stones until the mortar sets. Maintain uniform joint spacing.

4. Rake the joints.

As you complete a section of wall, use a piece of shim or a scrap of wood to scrape away mortar to a depth of about 1 inch. Follow with a stiff brush and a wet rag if necessary to make sure stones are clean and the joints are uniform.

5. Build second lead, fill in the middle, and top with capstones.

Use flat, smooth stones for the visible ends of the wall. Build up the ends, called leads, first. Lay no more than three courses of stones in a day because the weight of the stones will squeeze mortar out of the bottom courses.

Fill in the middle section, again dry-fitting the stones, removing them, laying on plenty of mortar, and carefully setting the stones in the mortar. Remember to include tie stones every 4 feet or so.

Cap off the wall with a row of large, flat stones. When you mortar these stones on top of the wall, do not rake the joints. Leave them flush with the surface of the capstones to keep water from sitting in the joints, freezing, and damaging the wall.

BUILDING CONCRETE BLOCK WALLS

Laying concrete blocks is hard, physical labor. Not only will you be lifting 40-pound blocks all day long, but often you'll be handling them in awkward positions. There's mortar to be mixed and transported, which involves plenty of heavy lifting as well. So have plenty of strong-backed help. Professionals work in fairly large crews, so don't expect to do this project alone.

YOU'LL NEED

TIME: With a helper, at least a full day for a 10×8-foot wall.
SKILLS: Laying straight courses, checking for plumb, throwing mortar, checking course height.
TOOLS: Chalk line, mason's string, plumb bob, story pole or modular spacing rule, carpenter's level, pointed trowel, brick set, baby sledge, joint set or sled jointer, circular saw with masonry blade, pointing trowel.

EXPERTS' INSIGHT

TIPS FOR BUILDING A SOLID BLOCK WALL

■ A solid footing or foundation is essential to building a solid block wall. Check local building codes, and follow the instructions on pages 658–661.

■ Choose a Type "S" or "M" mortar. Both have good strength and are resistant to damage from freezing.

■ Use true concrete blocks, which weigh 40 pounds or more, rather than lightweight cinder blocks. Concrete block is stronger and more moisture-resistant; it's worth the expense.

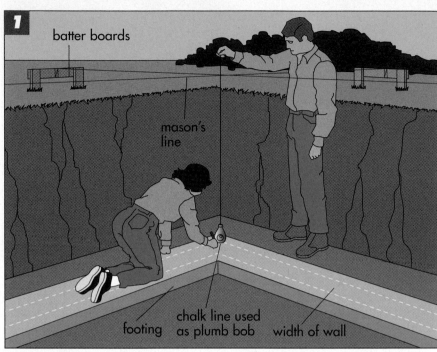

1. Establish the corners.
Mark the locations of the corners. Stretch a mason's line between the batter boards you set up before excavating for the footing, placing the line on the mark for the outside of the wall (see pages 658–659). Have a helper dangle a plumb bob from the point at which the mason's lines intersect at each corner, taking care not to disturb their alignment. Mark the locations on the footings with a thick pencil.

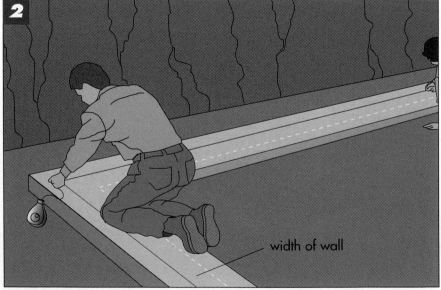

2. Mark for the walls.
Sweep the footings clean and snap chalk lines between the corner marks. Check the lines for square, using the 3-4-5 method described on page 655.

If your project involves just one wall, skip Steps 1 and 2. Simply determine the two end points of the wall and snap a chalk line on the footing to designate the edge of the wall. Go on to Step 3.

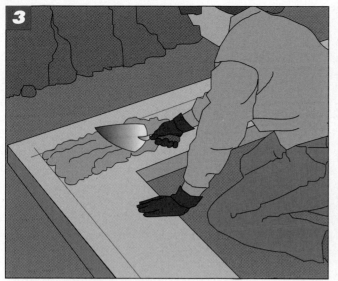

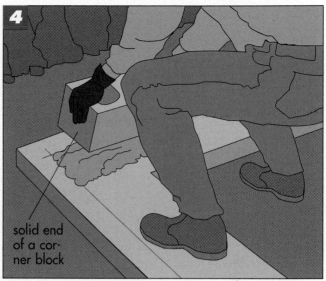

solid end
of a cor-
ner block

3. Lay the bottom mortar.

Make sure the footing is still clean and lay a 1-inch bed of mortar for the first course of block. Start at one corner, running the length of three or four blocks. Make the bed of mortar about 1 inch wider than the block you'll be placing.

4. Set the corner block.

Carefully place a corner block in position, with the smaller holes in its cores facing up and its smooth-faced, solid end on the corner. Gently press the block into place in the mortar.

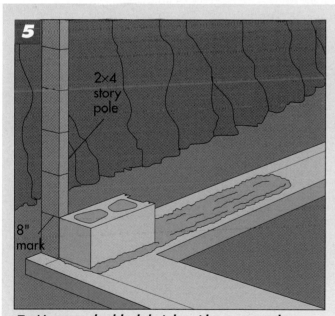

2×4
story
pole

8"
mark

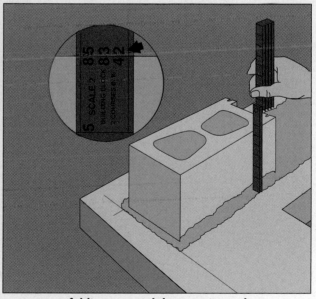

5. Measure the block height with a story pole...

Use a story pole to check for proper course height. To make a story pole, choose a straight 2×4 and make clear perpendicular marks every 8 inches. As you add the courses, the top of each concrete block should align with one of the marks. If the block is too high, tap it down into the mortar with the trowel handle. If it's too low, pull the block out, place more mortar on the bed, and re-lay the block.

...or use a folding or modular spacing rule.

If you use a conventional folding rule or tape measure, the top of the block should be 8 inches above the footing. Confirm that the mortar joint under the block is exactly $3/8$ inch thick. On a modular spacing rule (see inset) the top of the block should match the line at the "2."

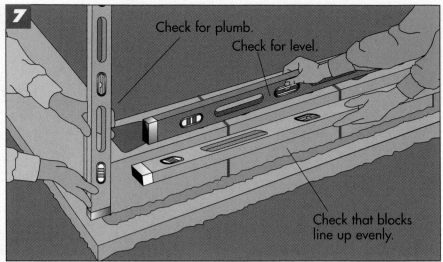

Check for plumb.

Check for level.

Check that blocks line up evenly.

6. Butter and lay the next blocks.
Before laying the second block, butter its flanges (or ears) while it is standing on end. Butter it well because this mortar forms the vertical joint between the first and second blocks. Set the block in place, making sure you have a ⅜-inch joint spacing. Repeat with subsequent blocks.

7. Check for level and plumb.
Place a level along the length of the first three blocks. If they are not perfectly level or if their tops do not form a straight line, press or tap down on the high points until they are level.

Check for plumb by holding the level against the side of each block. If any block is not plumb,

press with the heel of your hand or tap with the handle of your trowel to adjust it.

Every three or four blocks, check for level and plumb and make adjustments. Periodically use your level or a long straightedge to make sure the faces of the blocks align.

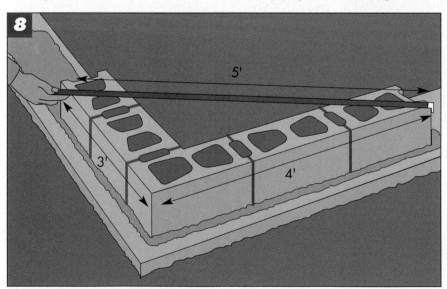

5'

3'

4'

8. Check for square, build lead.
Check corners for square first by holding a framing square against the outside edges of each side. Then use the 3-4-5 method as a double-check (see page 655).

Apply a 1-inch-deep layer of mortar along the top edges of the blocks of the first course. As you

place the second corner block, align its outside corner with the corner below it. Press the block into the mortar just enough so its weight compresses the mortar to a ⅜-inch joint. Continue laying blocks until you have built up a corner lead.

9. Install spacers if necessary.
Spacers made of cut blocks can be used to extend leads if you cannot make the number of blocks come out even by slightly enlarging the mortar lines. Cut spacer blocks and install them early, rather than trying to cut the closure block in the middle to fit.

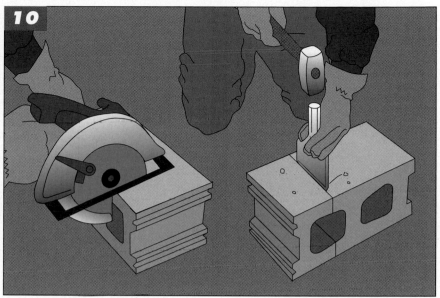

10. Cut concrete blocks.
If you need to cut blocks to fit, be sure to take into account the $\frac{3}{8}$-inch width of mortar lines when measuring. To cut by hand, place the block on sand or loose soil and use a brick set and hammer to make a line about $\frac{1}{8}$ inch deep on both sides of the

block. Then work along the line again, hammering harder and moving the brick set each time you rap it. Continue until the block breaks along the cut line.

For precision cuts, use a circular saw with a diamond or masonry cutting blade. Be sure the block is dry when you cut it.

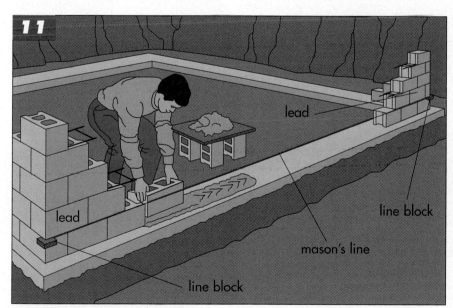

lead

line block

mason's line

lead

line block

11. Fill in between the leads.
Once you have two corner leads in place, hook line blocks around the corners and stretch a mason's line between them. Align the mason's line with the top of the blocks in the course being worked on and hold it about $\frac{1}{16}$ inch away

from the blocks' outer edges.

With the mason's line stretched in place, begin setting the blocks between the leads. Check the line often to make sure no blocks or mortar are touching it because they might otherwise push the line out of alignment.

12. Install the closure block.
Butter both ends of the closure, or final, block and lay it to complete the course. If some of the mortar falls off the flanges, lay the block anyway. Fill gaps in the joints by tucking mortar in place from the sides with your trowel.

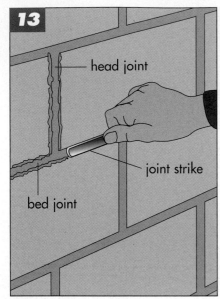

13

head joint

joint strike

bed joint

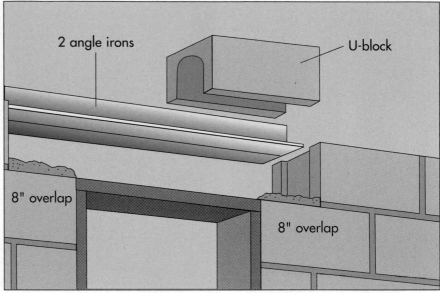

2 angle irons

U-block

8" overlap

8" overlap

13. Strike the joints.
Use a joint strike or a sled jointer to finish each joint after you have laid two courses above it. Tool the head (vertical) joints first then the bed (horizontal) joints. Brush off loose mortar, then restrike. For blocks below grade, simply strike off excess mortar with your trowel.

Install window or door lintels.
Plan door and window openings so you'll have to do minimal cutting of blocks to fit around them. For doors, it's best to use metal units designed for use in masonry walls, but you can build wood frames as well. You can make your own lintel with two

angle irons and U-blocks. Cut or purchase angle irons 16 inches longer than the opening is wide, allowing for an 8-inch overlap on either side of the opening. Set them back to back and place U-blocks on top. Place windows as the wall reaches the appropriate height for the opening.

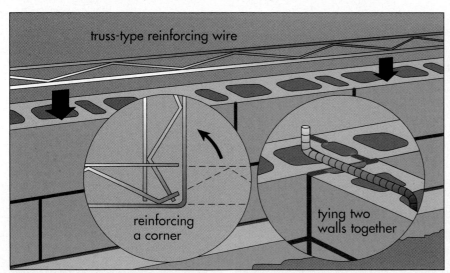

truss-type reinforcing wire

reinforcing a corner

tying two walls together

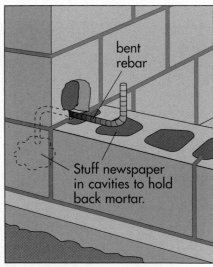

bent rebar

Stuff newspaper in cavities to hold back mortar.

Add reinforcing wire when needed.
For retaining walls and foundation walls on which there will be considerable lateral pressure, beef up the wall with truss-type or ladder-type reinforcing wire. Embed the wire in the mortar of every other horizontal joint. As you imbed it, overlay the ends of the sections by at least 6 inches.

The left inset shows how to

position the wire when reinforcing a corner. Simply cut two of the wires in the truss and bend the remaining one to form the corner.

The right inset shows how to tie intersecting walls together with an S-shaped, 3/8-inch rebar. Once covered with mortar and the next course of blocks, the rebar is secured firmly to the webbing of the blocks.

Tie a new wall to an old one.
If you're building a new wall adjacent to an old one, tie the two together. Every other course, knock a hole through the existing wall, stuff newspaper into the cavity, and place an S-shaped piece of rebar in the hole. Fill the hole with mortar. Stuff newspaper in the cavity under the other end of the rebar, lay the second course, and fill the cavity with mortar.

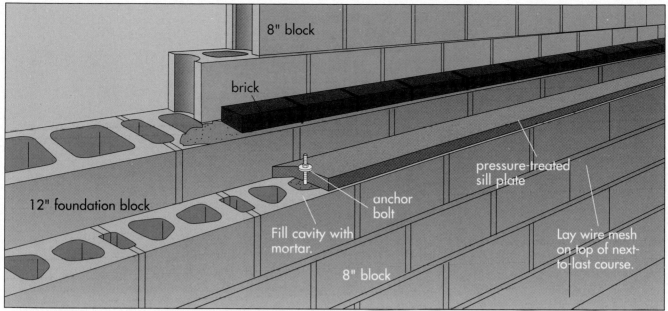

8" block

brick

12" foundation block

Fill cavity with mortar.

anchor bolt

pressure-treated sill plate

Lay wire mesh on top of next-to-last course.

8" block

Cap the wall.
If the foundation wall supports brick or stone veneer, use a combination of brick and smaller-size block as the cap, as shown here in the top example. For example, if the foundation blocks are 8 inches, stack 4-inch block and bricks on top.

If the wall serves as a foundation for a wood frame building, lay wire mesh on top of the next-to-last course of blocks. Embed anchor bolts in the mortar in the cores of the top course of blocks. Once the mortar sets, drill holes in a pressure-treated sill plate, set the sill plate over the anchor bolts, and fasten it in place with washers and nuts.

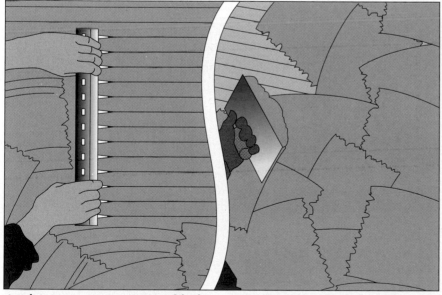

Applying stucco on concrete block.
To apply a stucco finish on concrete blocks, first paint the blocks with latex concrete bonding agent. Apply the scratch coat with a finishing trowel and scratch it with a plasterer's rake or a scratching tool made of a piece of 2×2 and 4d nails. Keep the scratch coat moist for two days, then apply a finish coat. (See pages 706–708 for instructions on applying stucco.)

Money $ Saver

SURFACE-BONDED BLOCK
Special mortarless concrete blocks can form a strong wall when simply stacked on top of one another, reinforced, and grouted. This type of block, however, is expensive.

A more practical solution is to build a surface-bonded wall, which uses standard concrete blocks. With this process, you only mortar the first course of blocks. Then you simply stack the rest of the blocks on top of one another. Once all the blocks are stacked, apply a coat of ready-made bonding agent made of Portland cement mixed with pieces of fiberglass. The bonding material is available in many colors. The resulting wall actually is stronger than a standard mortared wall.

PLANNING BRICK WALLS

Several brick projects are included on pages 697–702: brick veneer walls, single-tier walls, garden walls, and lightweight veneers. All involve the same basic bricklaying techniques. The procedures used with bricks are similar to those used with concrete block walls, only the scale is different (see pages 690–694). Both types of masonry walls require you to learn the art of working with mortar (see pages 686–687).

When planning a brick wall, check with your local building department for requirements regarding the type and size of materials you can use. There usually are standards as well for how the new wall should be attached to your house.

Make sure that a new wall rests on a solid foundation. Footings must be reinforced and extend below the frost line. Generally, a footing should be twice as wide as the wall it supports and its vertical thickness should equal the thickness of the finished wall. (See pages 658–659 and 665–666 for concrete footings and pages 690–695 for block foundation walls.) A brick veneer wall on a house, however, doesn't necessarily need a new foundation; a solid ledge will suffice (see page 697).

Shown are some of the most common brick patterns—what masons refer to as bonds. Select a pattern, as well as a top cap if your project requires it. In addition, choose the type of mortar joint that best suits your needs (see page 643).

Brick bond patterns

Running: all stretcher courses, with staggered joints

Common: a header course every sixth course

Flemish: alternating stretchers and headers in each course

Garden: headers separated by three stretchers in each course

English: alternating header and stretcher courses

Stack: all stretcher courses with stacked joints

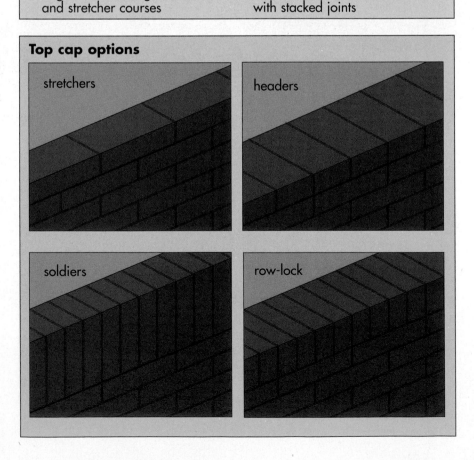

Top cap options

stretchers

headers

soldiers

row-lock

PREPARING WALLS FOR BRICK VENEER

Older homes often were built with double brick walls: two separate brick walls with a 1- or 2-inch air space between them. More common today is a single-width, or brick veneer, wall covering the face of a frame building. Although the brick wall is tied to the frame wall at various points (see page 699), there is an air space between the two. This space can be filled with insulation. Such a wall is cladding only, not a structural element of the house.

YOU'LL NEED

TIME: Varies considerably depending on the composition, complexity, and condition of the wall being covered.
SKILLS: Excavating and carpentry.
TOOLS: Spacing rule, shovel, hammer, level, drill with masonry bit, pry bar or other demolition tools, circular saw.

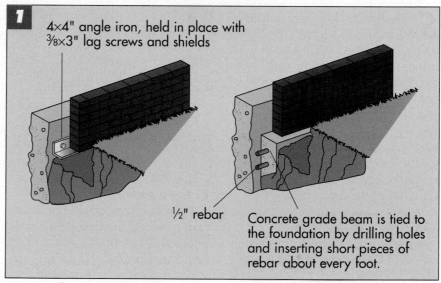

4×4" angle iron, held in place with ⅜×3" lag screws and shields

½" rebar

Concrete grade beam is tied to the foundation by drilling holes and inserting short pieces of rebar about every foot.

1. Provide support for the bricks.
Excavate a trench about 1 foot deep and at least 18 inches wide along the original foundation. To support the brick veneer, use one of the methods shown, either an angle iron or a concrete grade beam. Or you can use a wide concrete slab or concrete block foundation (see pages 690–695).

If you'll be bricking around any windows or doors, use a spacing rule to determine at what level the first course should be so a row-lock course of bricks can be positioned conveniently beneath the opening (see page 700).

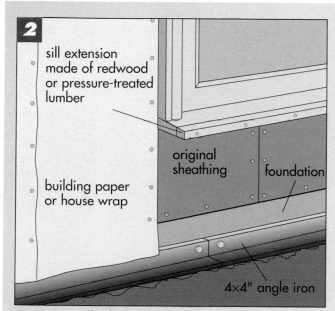

sill extension made of redwood or pressure-treated lumber

building paper or house wrap

original sheathing

foundation

4×4" angle iron

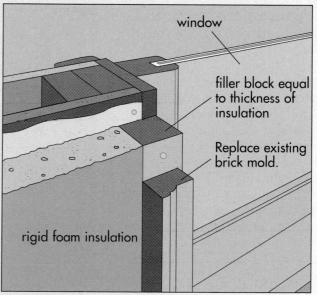

window

filler block equal to thickness of insulation

Replace existing brick mold.

rigid foam insulation

2. Prepare the house wall.
Remove siding on the wall with a pry bar and cover the wall with construction paper or house wrap. The paper or wrap should overlap the edge of the steel angle or grade beam. To facilitate drainage, nail redwood or pressure-treated extensions to windowsills so they reach at least ⅜ inch beyond the new veneer. If possible, add 1 to 2 inches of rigid foam insulation between the existing wall and the new veneer. Remove window and door moldings, trim out with redwood or pressure-treated filler blocks, and reattach the molding. You may need to replace the existing molding with brick mold.

LAYING SINGLE-TIER BRICK VENEER

Single-tier brick veneer is much like siding. It serves only as an outer finished shell whose functions are protection and decoration. A single-tier veneer wall supports only itself. It requires an air space between the bricks and the structure to vent moisture that builds up in the cavity. You also need a means of tying the veneer to the structure. Otherwise, the bricklaying techniques are essentially the same as for any brick structure.

YOU'LL NEED

TIME: A day for an 8×10-foot wall.
SKILLS: Mixing and applying mortar, measuring and leveling, cutting bricks, striking joints.
TOOLS: Trowel, level, story pole or modular spacing rule, brick set for cutting bricks, baby sledge, hammer, jointer, brush.

3. Measure and align as you go.

After you lay three or four bricks, measure the thickness of both the head and bed joints. They should all be ⅜ inch thick. If they aren't thick enough, pull out the bricks, spread more mortar, and lay them again. Use a carpenter's level to make sure the tops are level and even with each other. Check the face of each brick to make sure it is plumb. Finally, lay the level horizontally along the face of the bricks to make sure you are building a straight wall.

CAUTION!

Check alignment immediately after laying the first few bricks. If you wait too long, the bricks will absorb too much of the mortar's moisture to allow you to move bricks without the mortar crumbling.

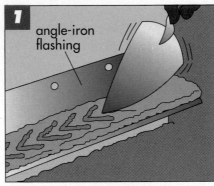
angle-iron flashing

1. Lay a bed of mortar.

Install galvanized or aluminum flashing along the base of the wall. Before you mix the mortar, dry-lay a course of bricks and make required position adjustments. Mix the mortar and sprinkle or soak several bricks with water. On one end of the flashing, throw a 1-inch-deep bed of mortar long enough to lay two or three bricks. Furrow the mortar bed with the tip of the trowel, as shown. (See pages 686–687 for more directions on how to handle mortar.)

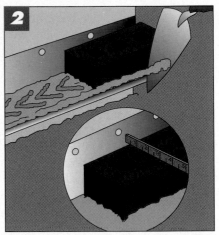

2. Lay the first brick.

Press the first brick into place, keeping a ½-inch air space between the brick and the wall surface and a ⅜-inch mortar joint beneath it. The air space helps insulate the wall and allows condensation to drain away. Trim excess mortar, returning it to your mortarboard or placing it farther down on the flashing.

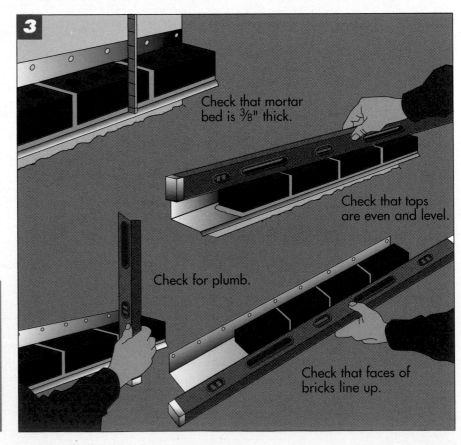

Check that mortar bed is ⅜" thick.

Check that tops are even and level.

Check for plumb.

Check that faces of bricks line up.

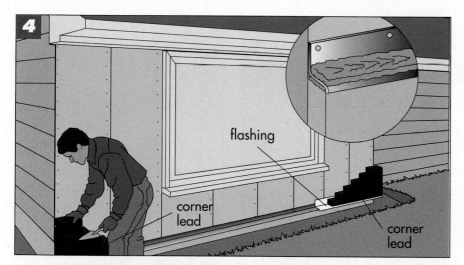

flashing

corner lead

corner lead

4. Build up the leads.
Lay a bed of mortar and continue laying brick until you have built a five- or six-course lead at each end of the wall (for more on building leads, see below and page 692). Check your work often to make sure all the units are level, plumb, and aligned. Also check that you are maintaining a ⅜-inch-thick mortar bed.

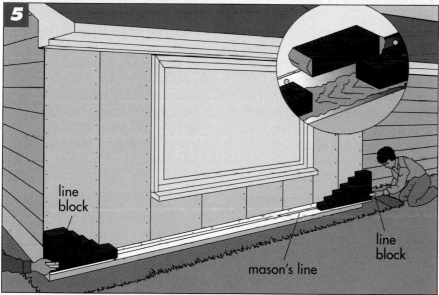

line block

line block

mason's line

5. Fill in the middle.
Stretch a mason's line between the corner leads. Position line blocks (see page 693) so the mason's line aligns with and is about ¹⁄₁₆ inch out from the top of the first course of bricks. Lay the remainder of the bricks in the first course. Mortar both ends of the last brick in the course (see inset) before setting it in the mortar bed. Move the line blocks and mason's line up one course and continue laying bricks up to the mason's line.

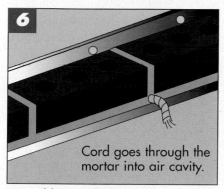

Cord goes through the mortar into air cavity.

brick tie

6. Add weep holes.
As you lay bricks on top of the flashing, lay short pieces of ¼-inch cord on the flashing about every 2 feet. Make sure the cords extend all the way through to the flashing. Once the mortar stiffens, pull out the cords to create weep holes. These weep holes vent moisture that builds up behind the brick.

7. Anchor the brick veneer.
To tie the brick veneer to the existing wall, nail brick ties every 32 inches horizontally and 16 inches vertically. Stagger the rows across the wall so the ties are no more than 24 inches apart. Use 8d or 10d ring-shank nails or galvanized deck screws. Embed the ties completely in the mortar.

EXPERTS' INSIGHT

BUILDING CORNER LEADS
When building a corner lead, you need to lay bricks going in two directions in an alternating pattern so the bricks will lock together.

Keep this simple rule in mind: The number of bricks you lay in the first course should equal the number of courses in your lead. For example, if you want your lead to be nine courses high, lay five bricks in one direction and four bricks in the other. That will give you a base for a lead with nine courses.

8. Strike the joints.
Using the jointer needed to produce the mortar joint of your choice (see page 643), strike the head (vertical) joints first, then the bed (horizontal) joints. Strike the joints soon after laying the bricks. If you wait too long, the mortar will stiffen and be unworkable.

9. Clean with a brush.
After striking the joints, let the mortar set up for a while, then remove the burrs and crumbs of mortar left along the joints. Use a stiff brush for smaller pieces and a trowel for larger ones. Clean off mortar smears with a dampened rag and a brush, taking care not to soak any mortar joints.

flashing

Cut row-lock headers with brick set.

10. Install row-lock header bricks.
To brick up the bottom of a windowsill or to cap off a veneer that extends only partway up a wall, set row-lock headers, as shown here, or headers that are laid flat. Install flashing and weep holes (see page 699). You may have to cut the bricks or adjust the joints to make the headers fit.

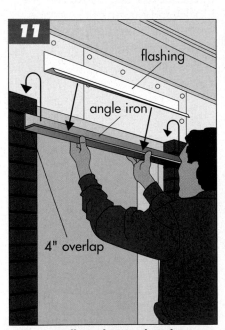

flashing

angle iron

4" overlap

11. Install angle-iron headers.
To support bricks that go over doorways and windows, secure a 3½×3½×¼-inch angle-iron header across the opening. Ends should rest on the course, even with the top of the opening. At least 4 inches of the angle should rest on the brick walls at both ends.

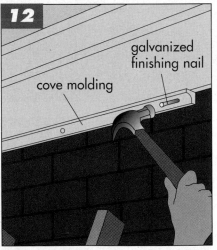

galvanized finishing nail

cove molding

12. Cover top gaps with molding.
If you brick all the way up to a soffit, cover the gap between the soffit and the top course of brick with molding. This not only gives the job a finished look, it also keeps out moisture and insects. Nailing can be tricky. Angle galvanized finishing nails into the framing behind the fascia or straight up into the fascia itself. Caulk the seam between the molding and the brick.

EXPERTS' INSIGHT

EXPANSION JOINTS

■ Wherever a new masonry wall butts up against an existing wood, brick, or concrete surface, avoid bonding the two surfaces together firmly. Over the years, settling and expansion and contraction resulting from weather changes causes the two surfaces to move in different directions. Seal the joint between them with a material that is flexible.

■ Expansion joint material is made for this purpose. Secure it to the existing wall before you begin work, and butt your new wall against it.

■ Or, after the new wall is built, cram oakum (a plumbing material) into the gap. Finish with a thick bead of high-quality silicone, acrylic with silicone, or butyl caulk.

BUILDING A GARDEN WALL

In addition to being an attractive landscape feature, a simple garden wall is an ideal way to learn bricklaying, particularly if you are planning a more ambitious project and want to hone your skills. For more about techniques, see pages 698–700. See page 696 for pattern options.

YOU'LL NEED

TIME: 4 hours for the footing and a full day to lay bricks for a 16-foot-long, 3-foot-high wall.
SKILLS: Excavating, building forms, laying and finishing concrete, beginner skills in laying brick.
TOOLS: Concrete tools for footing, pointed trowel, mason's hoe, wheelbarrow, stiff brush, mason's line, line blocks.

corrugated brick tie

1. Set the footing and lay bricks.
Dig a footing that is 2 inches longer than the wall, twice the width of the wall, and as deep as the frost line in your area. Form the edge of the footing with 2×4s (see pages 665–666) or let your hole act as the form. Pour concrete to just below grade. Allow the concrete to cure for several days.

Snap chalk lines along the footing to define the perimeter of the wall, which should be centered on the footing. Lay the bricks, using the same techniques as for a veneer wall (see pages 698–700), checking for plumb, level, and alignment as you work.

As you set the bricks in two rows together, embed corrugated metal brick ties in the mortar about every 12 inches in every third or fourth course.

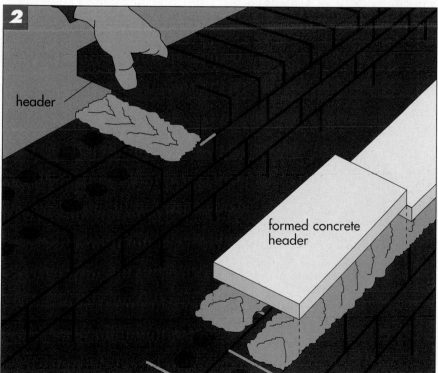

header

formed concrete header

2. Top off the wall with headers.
Once the wall reaches the desired height, cap it off with a header. You can use header bricks laid flat or formed concrete headers, as shown here, or row-lock headers (see page 700), flagstones, or limestone block. Slope the headers slightly to allow for drainage.

EXPERTS' INSIGHT

DRAINAGE FOR A RETAINING WALL

If your wall is a free-standing one, there is no need to worry about drainage, other than sloping the headers slightly. But if your wall is more than 2 feet high and is cut into a slope or holds back a terraced planting area, it will have to bear substantial water pressure when the ground becomes wet. In such a case, be sure to provide drainage in the form of a sloped perforated drainpipe set in a bed of gravel (see pages 654–655).

INSTALLING LIGHTWEIGHT BRICK VENEER

It's seldom possible to install a single-tier brick wall on an interior wall; floors simply will not support the weight. Even a basement floor can't bear the weight; footings undergird only the foundation walls, not the slab.

However, lightweight veneers can be applied to interior walls, and they look nearly as attractive as real brick. Because they are fire-retardant, you can often use them for firewalls behind wood-burning stoves. Check local codes.

You'll Need

Time: A day for an 8×10-foot wall.

Skills: Applying adhesive, measuring, leveling, cutting.

Tools: Trowel recommended by manufacturer, hammer, mason's line, line level, hacksaw with masonry blade, brush, jointer.

1. Apply the adhesive.
Start in an upper corner of a wall. Spread a ⅛-inch layer of mortar adhesive over a 2×4-foot area.

For outside walls, use roofing nails to nail a moisture barrier of 15-pound roofer's felt and a layer of metal lath to the walls. Then trowel on a coating of mortar, working in 2×3-foot sections.

MEASUREMENTS

To determine if you must start with a full or a partial brick, divide the length of each brick, plus the width of the mortar joint, into the width of your wall. This will tell you how many full bricks you'll need for each course. If the answer contains a remainder, you'll need to start with a partial brick.

The length of the first and last bricks should be the same, so divide any fraction of a brick by two to determine how long the starting brick should be. Avoid narrow fragments of brick. If the remainder is less than 4 inches, divide the remainder in half and trim that amount from the first and last brick in each course.

2. Install the bricks.
Start at the top of the wall to ensure there will be a full course of brick where appearance counts. Attach a string running the length of the wall, held out from the wall about ½ inch, exactly one course down from the ceiling. Use a line level to make sure the string is level. If your ceiling is wavy or out of level, you may need to bring the line down a bit to make room for every brick. Press each brick into the adhesive, twisting it slightly to ensure a good bond. Align the bricks to the string. Leave ⅜ inch between bricks for normal-looking joints. To cut the bricks, use a hacksaw with a masonry cutting blade or rod.

3. Strike the joints.
Fill the joints between the bricks with more mortar adhesive or use a colored mortar of your choice after the adhesive has dried. Use either a pencil-type brush or a grout bag with the correct tip. Avoid smearing mortar adhesive on the face of the bricks; wipe up spills immediately. Once the joints have dried, coat the wall with a sealer recommended by the dealer.

INSTALLING STONE VENEER

Lightweight stone veneers may be made of natural stone or cast from concrete and given natural-looking colors and textures. Stone veneer pieces range from ½ inch to 2 inches in thickness. With some lighter products, you can use an adhesive to attach the pieces directly on a finished interior wall (see page 702). With heavier material, you'll need to apply expanded metal lath and attach the pieces with mortar.

YOU'LL NEED

TIME: Two days to cover an 8×10-foot wall.
SKILLS: Arranging stone in a pleasing pattern, cutting stone, applying metal lath and mortar.
TOOLS: Hammer, tin snips, flat finishing trowel, plasterer's rake or a homemade scratcher (see page 707), brick set for cutting stone, jointer, brush.

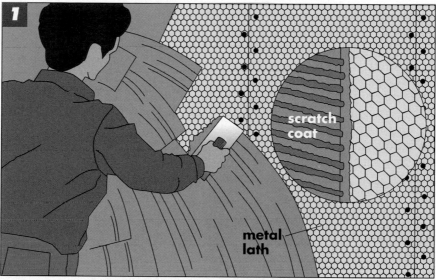

scratch coat

metal lath

1. Apply lath, first mortar coat.
For interior walls, nail expanded metal lath directly onto the wall. For exterior walls, nail on 15-pound roofing felt, then metal lath. Trowel on a ¼-inch coat of mortar over the lath. After the mortar has just begun to set up, roughen the surface with a rakelike tool (see page 707), scratching it to a depth of ⅛ inch. Let this coat dry and cure for 48 hours before applying the next layer of mortar and the stone. Meanwhile, lay the stones out on the floor as they will be positioned on the wall. As you arrange them, keep the joint spaces consistent.

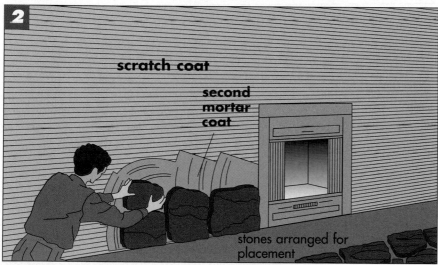

scratch coat

second mortar coat

stones arranged for placement

2. Apply stone veneer.
Cover the scratch coat of mortar with a ½-inch layer of mortar, working with an 8-square-foot area at a time. Just before positioning each stone, also apply a thin layer of mortar to the back of the stone veneer. Press the stone into the mortar bed, moving it back and forth and rocking it slightly to create a thorough bond. Place the bottom corner stones first. Then, working upward, add pieces toward the center of the area you are veneering, keeping the joint space you established in your plan. (See page 684 for instructions for cutting stone.)

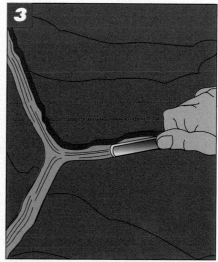

3. Strike the joints.
As soon as the mortar has stiffened, but before it has set, use a jointer to strike the joints. Brush away the crumbs and burrs at the joint edges. Immediately clean any mortar off the face of stones with a damp rag and brush. Avoid soaking the mortar joints.

BUILDING A CURVED-WALL PLANTER

The serpentine lines of this brick planter do more than lend it an elegant appearance. The curves actually add significant strength and vertical stability to the wall.

If you have some experience laying straight brick walls, you'll be surprised by how easy it is to build this graceful planter. The biggest challenge is laying out the plywood template; the bricklaying is straightforward.

As with other mortared brick walls, this project requires a footing. To avoid having your project ruined by frost heaving and cracking, check with your local building department about the frost line and footing depth required in your area.

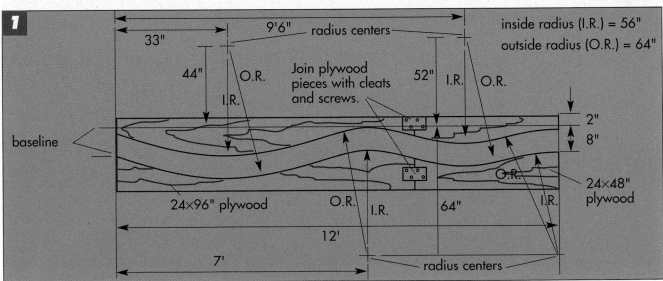

1

inside radius (I.R.) = 56"
outside radius (O.R.) = 64"

9'6" — radius centers

33"

44"   O.R.

I.R.

baseline

24×96" plywood   O.R.   I.R.   64"   I.R.

12'

7'   radius centers

52"   I.R.   O.R.

2"
8"

Join plywood pieces with cleats and screws.

O.R.

24×48" plywood

1. Cut the template.

From a full sheet of ½-inch plywood, cut 24×48-inch and 24×96-inch pieces. Fasten them together end to end with cleats and screws, as shown. Lay the plywood panel on a flat surface (a lawn or a driveway will do) and draw a straight baseline 2 inches from the long edge.

Measure from the baseline and the end of the sheet to locate the four radius centers shown (mark these on the lawn or driveway). Use a drywall square or a framing square to help you find the spots.

From each radius center, draw two curved lines using a compass made out of a pencil and string. Have a helper hold the string at the radius center while you draw the lines. Draw all eight radii on the board. Use a saber saw to cut out the curves.

2. Dig and pour the footing.

Set the two template pieces on the ground at the wall site. Separate them so there is a consistent 8-inch gap between them (use lengthwise bricks as spacers). Drive in stakes and nail them to the template pieces to anchor the template firmly so it will not shift if you step on it while you dig.

With a square shovel, dig a trench for the footing. Dig several inches below the frost line or at least 12 inches deep if frost is not a problem in your area. Dig along the template and the straight areas of the wall. Tamp the soil and shovel in 2 to 3 inches of gravel. Pour concrete to within a couple inches of grade. Allow the footing to cure for a few days.

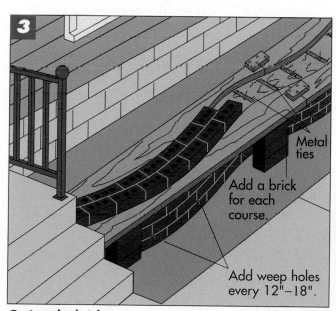

3. Lay the bricks.

Use the template as a guide for laying the bricks. Make a one-course dry run to see how well full bricks fit and to adjust the width of vertical joints between them. Stagger the two tiers of bricks, as shown. (For more on building brick walls, see pages 696–699.) On the first course and every two courses thereafter, place metal ties across the tiers at 24-inch intervals. As you lay the course just above final grade, make weep holes (see page 699) every 12 to 18 inches. As you work, check the wall for plumb. Hold the outer template up against it every other course.

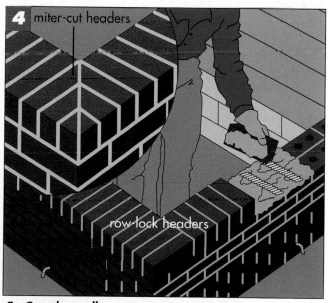

4. Cap the wall.

Top off the wall with row-lock headers. At the corners, position the bricks as shown in the lower portion of the drawing. Or, for a more finished look, miter-cut the bricks using a circular saw with a masonry blade (see inset). Strike the joints and allow the mortar to cure for a few days. Coat the inside of the wall with a masonry waterproofing compound. In the planting area, place 6 inches of sand or pea gravel for drainage. Cover with topsoil and add your plants.

APPLYING STUCCO

Stucco makes an excellent exterior surface. It is durable and weather-resistant, has a pleasing texture, and can be painted. Even in severe climates, you'll find older stucco houses still in mint condition.

A stucco finish is nothing more than two or three thin coats of a mortar that is 1 part masonry cement to 3 parts sand, with a small amount of lime and water added. Stucco requires a solid backing. Never apply stucco over fiberboard sheathing or foam insulation. Both of these materials give enough that a well-thrown baseball can dent or puncture the stucco wall.

There are infinite possibilities for the final textures. The examples shown above right represent some of the standard textures, but you can experiment with different trowels and techniques to create different textures. Just be sure you can reproduce the texture consistently over a broad area.

If left untinted, stucco dries to a medium-gray color. You can add an oxide pigment to the finish coat or stain or paint the surface after the top coat has cured. If you mix in pigment, carefully measure and mix each batch exactly the same way to obtain a consistent color. You can make a bright white stucco by mixing together white Portland cement, lime, and white silica sand for the finish coat.

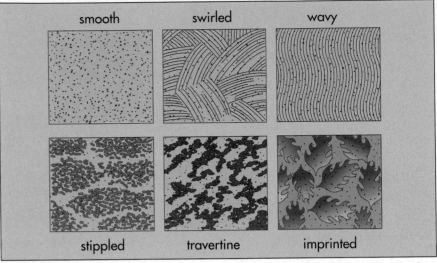

smooth   swirled   wavy

stippled   travertine   imprinted

You'll Need

TIME: A day for preparation and each coat on an 8×20-foot wall.
SKILLS: Troweling with smooth, even strokes.
TOOLS: Brush, hammer, tin snips, flat trowel, hock, plasterer's rake or homemade scratcher, hose. (For scratched finish texture, a brush or whisk broom.)

Select a texture.
The wide range of finish textures available makes stucco a versatile wall covering. To achieve a **smooth**, plasterlike appearance, trowel the final coat several times as it becomes progressively stiffer. For a **swirled** texture, trowel the mortar just once, using an arcing motion, and allow the resulting pattern to remain. For a **wavy**, scratched surface, trowel the mortar smooth, allow it to harden slightly, then draw a brush across

it lightly. The stiffer the brush, the coarser the pattern.

To **stipple** the top coat, hold a whisk broom at an angle to the wall and pat the surface with the ends of the bristles in an irregular pattern. For a **travertine** finish, spatter on a coat of thin mortar in a contrasting color and trowel it slightly after it has stiffened. To make an **imprint**, use leaves or other patterns to make imprints in the soft mortar and trowel the surface lightly.

1. Prepare wall, apply first coat.
For a concrete, brick, or block wall, simply brush on concrete bonding agent and allow it to dry. Apply stucco directly to the wall.

To apply stucco over a wood wall, nail on 15-pound roofing felt, then cover it with 17-gauge metal netting (buy 150-foot rolls

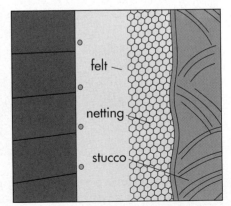

felt —

netting

stucco

to minimize seams). Cut the netting with tin snips and attach it with galvanized roofing nails.

Apply the scratch coat with a flat finishing trowel. Trowel on a ¼- to ½-inch layer of mortar, forcing it into the netting so some extrudes through the netting to "key" the coating in place.

2. Scratch the first coat.

3. Keep the mortar wet.

2. Scratch the first coat.
Once you start one wall, always complete it to avoid start-and-stop lines. Allow the scratch coat to harden only slightly, then scratch it with a plasterer's rake or a homemade tool like the one shown. (To make it, simply drive 4d galvanized nails through a piece of 2×2 at 1-inch intervals.) Scratch the entire mortar surface to a depth of about ⅛ inch, running the tool in long lines along the surface.

3. Keep the mortar wet.
As with all concrete or mortar products, slow, damp curing provides the greatest strength. Allow the scratch coat to cure for 36 to 48 hours; keep it damp by periodically misting it with water from a garden hose. Watch the weather; you'll need to mist more often on a hot, dry day than on a cool, damp day.

EXPERTS' INSIGHT

THE BROWN COAT

■ For an extra-strong stucco wall, you can apply a coat of mortar between the scratch and the finish coats. This is called the brown coat.

■ Apply the brown coat soon after you scratch the scratch coat. If you must wait before applying the brown coat, keep the scratch coat wet after scratching it to keep it from curing. Mix, apply, and scratch the brown coat in the same way as you did the scratch coat. Allow it to set for a few hours, then keep it moist for two days for a slow cure.

4. Apply the finish coat.
With a flat finishing trowel, apply a ⅛- to ¼-inch-thick finish coat onto the dampened scratch or brown coat (see box at left). If you add powdered pigment, add water to the pigment and mix it completely before adding it to the stucco. Finish to the texture of your choice (see page 706). Allow the stucco to cure for several days, misting the surface occasionally to slow the curing process. Complete the project by caulking around doors and windows. If you paint the stucco, wait at least six weeks before you paint and use a paint formulated to cover concrete.

USING NEW STUCCO PRODUCTS

The stucco technique on pages 706–707 is the least expensive way to cover a wall with stucco, but it takes a long time. It can be especially tedious to keep the various coats moist for several days. New products and techniques are now available. The materials are more expensive, but installation is easier.

Flashing and a water barrier are installed in such a way that water that comes into the wall (through small openings around windows, for example) can escape, keeping studs and insulation dry. Instead of a scratch coat of stucco, sheets of cement board form the substrate. This provides a straight, even surface, something not easy to achieve with standard stucco methods. The cement board is covered with a thin coat of Portland cement, then with a coat of aggregated polymer, which is applied without special troweling techniques. Available in many colors, the polymer surface resists dirt and cleans more easily than a standard stucco finish.

YOU'LL NEED
TIME: A day to cover about 200 square feet.
SKILLS: Carpentry, smoothly applying polymer.
TOOLS: Hammer, chalk line, level, stapler, trowel, knife, drywall square.

CAUTION!
BEWARE OF INSULATION-BASED SYSTEMS
Some polymer systems use sheets of soft insulating material, such as polystyrene, as the base for the polymer instead of cement board. Such systems have two serious problems: They trap moisture inside walls and dent easily.

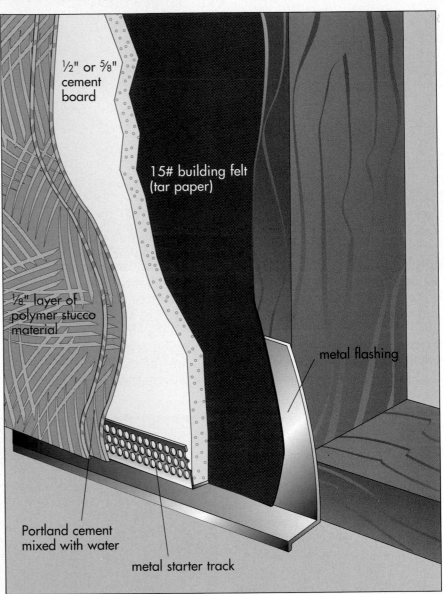

½" or ⅝" cement board

15# building felt (tar paper)

⅛" layer of polymer stucco material

metal flashing

Portland cement mixed with water

metal starter track

Install a polymer stucco wall.
Remove window and door moldings and trim out with filler blocks that are the same thickness as the new stucco wall (see page 697). Along the bottom of the wall, use a level and chalk line to mark a line, then install flashing along the line. Staple 15-pound building felt (tar paper) to the wall, taking care not to rip it. Overlap joints about 3 inches. Install a metal starter track on the flashing.

Attach the cement board sheets by slipping them into the starter track and fastening them with 2-inch roofing nails or screws designed for cement board. To cut cement board, use a drywall square and a utility knife. Cut into the board and through the mesh on one side, break back the board, and cut through the mesh on the other side. Fill in joints between cement boards with a mixture of Portland cement and water.

Once that sets, cover the entire surface with a thin coat of the Portland cement mixture. After that layer dries, trowel on the polymer texture to a thickness of about ⅛ inch.

DECKS AND PATIOS

UNDERSTANDING DECK TERMINOLOGY

At first glance, a deck looks like a simple tablelike structure. In fact, decks involve layers of construction, each with its own name and specific function. By taking the time to learn the anatomy of a deck, you will be well on your way to understanding the steps required to construct one. The illustration below and the following text identify the important components of a typical deck. Specific types of decks may differ a bit; such variations are discussed later in the book.

A deck's foundation provides the critical base of the entire structure and ties it to the earth. The exact size and composition of the foundation depends on your climate, the size of the deck, and other considerations, but it normally consists of **concrete piers.** The foundation must be stationary and strong enough to transfer the load on the deck safely to the ground.

Posts are used on all but the shortest decks. They establish the height of the finished structure. Most decks are built with 4×4 posts. The posts can be cut off below the deck surface or may rise above the surface to provide support for a railing or overhead structure. Posts rest on top of concrete piers.

Beams typically are the first horizontal members of the deck, and they usually are the largest members. Beams are attached to the posts. Most decks are connected to houses by a **ledger.** The ledger functions as another beam, connecting the frame of the deck to the solid foundation of the house.

Joists are the series of boards spanning the distance from beam to beam or beam to ledger. Joists are connected to the ledger with joist hangers; they can overlap, or cantilever, the beams. Joists are spaced 16 or 24 inches on center; that is, they are centered on lines marked every 16 or 24 inches.

A **rim joist,** or fascia board, hides the edges of the joists.

The surface layer of the deck is called the **decking,** or deck boards. Decking is fastened to the joists with nails or screws.

If the deck is more than 2 feet above the ground, it should have a railing. While railing designs vary, a standard version consists of **rail posts,** which tie it to the deck frame; **balusters,** usually small, vertical pieces that provide the infill; a **top rail** and **bottom rail,** to which the balusters are attached; and a **cap rail,** which sits atop the entire railing.

Stairs are composed of **treads** (the part you step on), which are fastened to **stringers,** which are the boards that span the distance from the deck surface to the ground. **Risers** are the vertical boards that fill in the space between treads. Risers often are not used on deck stairs.

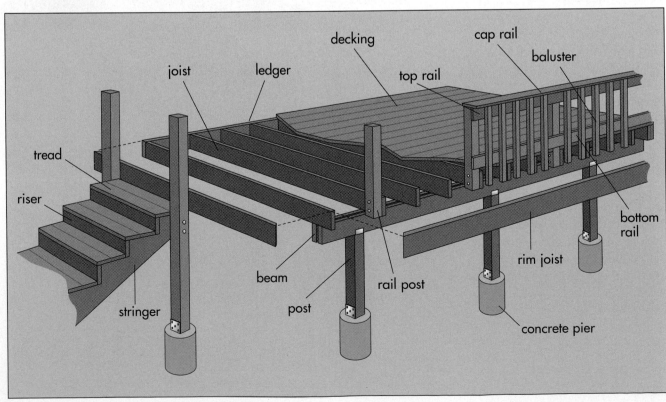

multilevel deck

elevated deck

wraparound deck

Choose a deck configuration.

A well-designed deck should meet your needs and suit the style of your house. Sometimes a simple rectangular deck off the kitchen or family room meets both criteria perfectly. Often, however, circumstances may call for a deck with more drama and variety.

Using the same basic techniques, you can design a deck that wraps around two or more sides of the house. A deck constructed at two or more elevations can be functionally versatile and visually appealing. Decks can serve the ground floor, an upper floor, or both.

A single deck can serve simultaneously as a balcony, porch, stairway, patio, and walkway. And remember, a deck doesn't have to be connected to the house at all; it can stand alone. Budget limitations and construction requirements may limit your dreams, but don't let them stand in the way of a creative design that could also solve problems.

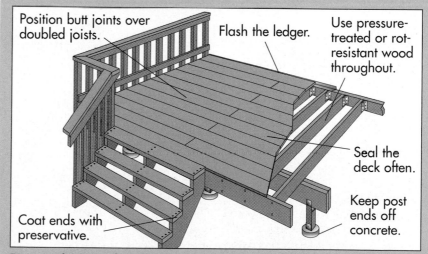

AVOIDING ROT AND WATER DAMAGE

Position butt joints over doubled joists.

Flash the ledger.

Use pressure-treated or rot-resistant wood throughout.

Seal the deck often.

Keep post ends off concrete.

Coat ends with preservative.

Rot-producing fungus is the biggest enemy of wooden decks. To thrive, the fungus requires permanently moist wood. Here are tips on moisture defense:

■ Set posts in metal brackets, away from contact with concrete.
■ A built-up beam (a beam using two separate boards) lasts longer if you use moisture-draining spacers (see page 733).

■ Use butt joints in the decking so water can drain. Position the joints over doubled joists, with spacers between the joists to provide a path for water.
■ Pay careful attention to flashing around the ledger.
■ Brush extra preservative on all cut ends of pressure-treated lumber, especially those surfaces that are horizontal, such as post ends.

CHOOSING A SITE

The best site for your deck may seem obvious, but give the site some careful thought before you plunge in. A deck most often is a transitional structure between your house's interior and exterior. The site you have in mind might solve one problem, only to create another. It can affect traffic patterns through the house and in the yard. The correct site makes such movement seem natural and unobtrusive. A poorly chosen site, however, can block an enjoyable view from inside the house. Or it could unintentionally congregate people near a child's room where you want quiet or a bathroom where you would prefer privacy. A site that is too sunny or too shady may result in an underused deck. Take time as you pick the site to write down your thoughts. List your preferences and draw a site plan to help evaluate the tradeoffs.

EXPERTS' INSIGHT

DECKS AND LANDSCAPING

A deck changes the look of your house and your yard. Most people want to soften the presence of the deck as much as possible. One good way to do that is with a thoughtful landscaping plan. A border garden of perennials, for example, relieves the transition from yard to deck, while shrubs can help camouflage the framing beneath the deck surface. Be sure to keep plantings trimmed so they are not in contact with the deck.

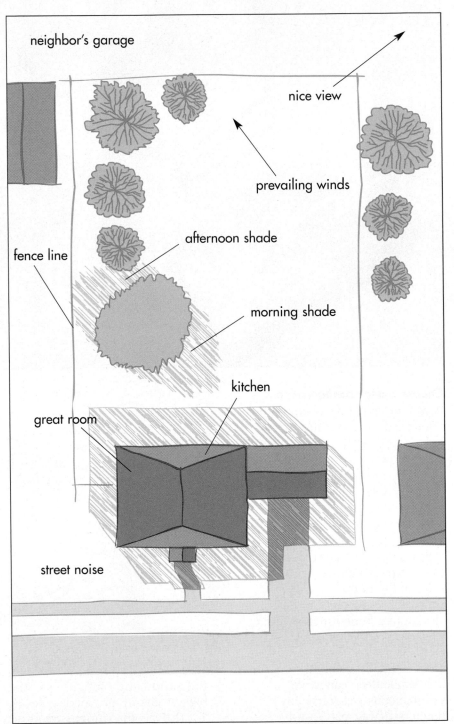

Draw a site plan.
Draw a site plan of your house and yard. Include all doors and windows, as well as utility hookups, walkways, shrubs and trees, and views that you wish to maintain or block out. Note the movement of the sun and how it affects shading and sunlight; be sure to account for seasonal changes. Add every detail that could affect the deck location, such as prevailing winds, buried septic tanks and utility lines, setback requirements, and downspouts. Use tracing paper over the site plan to sketch possible shapes and locations.

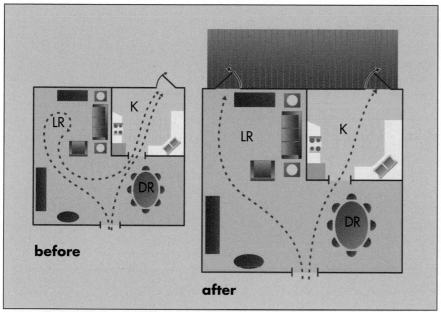

before

after

Use a deck to control traffic.

Sometimes a little remodeling can provide the best access to your deck. By adding a door, as shown here, some traffic to the deck is routed through the living room so work in the kitchen isn't interrupted. Retaining the door from the kitchen to the deck allows food and dishes to be carried back and forth with little interference. Conversely, an existing door may be a hindrance to the deck, in which case you may want to consider removing it or replacing it with a window.

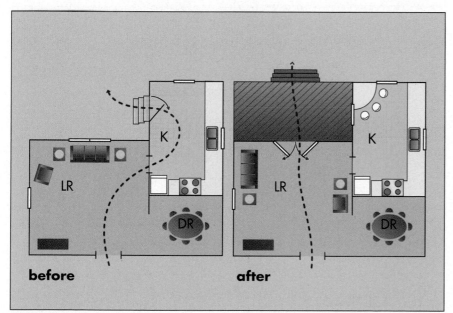

before

after

Relocate a doorway.

In this example, moving the back door redirected traffic and significantly improved the kitchen space. A double window in the family room was replaced with a patio door so traffic to the deck and yard was routed away from the kitchen. Replacing the door in the kitchen with a window allowed room for a bright eating area, or the space could have been used for cabinet and counter storage. If the kitchen is large enough, you could also keep the existing door in place.

MEASUREMENTS

ADDING A DOOR

If you're considering installing a new door, think about what kind of door will maximize your view of and access to the deck. For example, you could expand a 32-inch half-window door to at least a 36-inch-wide, full-window door.

If you have room, consider installing a double-wide door, sliding glass door, or a hinged door with a fixed all-glass side-light. Installing doors is within the capabilities of most do-it-yourselfers, but you may be able to get it installed affordably and more quickly by an experienced contractor.

CAUTION!

WATCH FOR UNDERGROUND PIPES AND LINES

If you have a septic system, make sure you know the location of the tank and drainage field. Locate buried gas, electric, or telephone lines. You can call your utility companies to mark these locations. Check with your municipality for the location of water and sewer lines. Ask them how deep the lines are buried. They may be willing to come to your home and mark the locations of the lines.

PREPARING FOR THE PROJECT

The transition from theory to practice can be the most difficult phase of a deck-building project. This is the point where doubts may start to plague you.
■ Will the deck be big enough?
■ Can I really afford to build it?
■ Do I have the skills needed to build a deck?

Listen carefully to the doubts and try to answer them thoroughly before proceeding. Don't rush into the project. Think through all of the procedures and consequences. If you've recently moved into the house, it might be too soon to build a deck. By waiting a full year, you'll have time to observe the house and yard through a full course of seasonal changes and weather conditions.

Budgeting is a tricky—and highly personal—part of the project. With thorough planning, however, you can avoid surprises. As long as you supply all of the labor, you can determine your out-of-pocket expenses by preparing a detailed list of materials (drawn from your equally detailed plans), which you can take to several suppliers for estimates. If your budget is tight, only you can decide if you want to borrow the money and build today or save your money and build tomorrow.

Deck building is straightforward work, but parts of it are physically demanding. And all of it requires close attention to detail. If you remain concerned about your ability to build the deck you want, narrow down those parts of the job that trouble you the most.

Perhaps you worry about getting the ledger installed correctly or the posts set plumb and in a straight line. If so, take on the role of general contractor and subcontract parts of the job. You may be able to hire an experienced carpenter to do those segments of the job that you feel uncomfortable about. This mini-apprenticeship may be all you need to boost your confidence for tackling your next remodeling project.

No matter how long it takes, resolve your doubts before ordering lumber. Once that delivery truck backs into your driveway, you want to have a building permit in hand, a clear idea of what your deck will look like, and a plan for who's going to handle the work.

CAUTION

WHOSE PROPERTY IS IT?
Property owners often are surprised to learn about the many restrictions placed upon their building projects. Just because you know where your property lines are and plan to stay within them, don't assume you've covered all the bases.
You may be required to observe setback stipulations. Some locales insist that you keep all parts of a new deck a specified number of feet away from adjoining property lines. You may even have to have your lot surveyed to verify property lines. Historic districts and subdivisions may limit the size or style of the deck you can build. You may be able to challenge the restrictions by requesting a variance, but the time to do that is before you build, not after you've started the project.

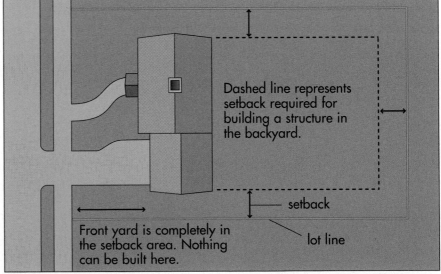

Dashed line represents setback required for building a structure in the backyard.

setback

lot line

Front yard is completely in the setback area. Nothing can be built here.

Keep it legal.
Like most major home improvements, a deck addition must be done in compliance with local building codes and zoning laws. Submit plans to your town or county building department for approval and to obtain a building permit. Depending on its policies, the building department also may require inspections to make sure you're following the approved plans. This legal supervision ensures that your design will be built properly. Remember, building codes prevent your neighbors from doing things you might not like. Failing to comply with codes could result in having to remove what you've built.

Not everyone is covered by zoning laws or required to get a building permit. But it's up to you, not the authorities, to find out what laws cover your project.

Play it safe.
The elements that make decks useful, fun, and good-looking, such as stairways, railings, multiple levels, hot tubs, or high elevations, also create safety hazards, especially for children. Complying with local building codes doesn't guarantee a safe deck. Legal requirements represent minimum standards; your situation may demand more. Minimize risks by observing these precautions:

■ When building a deck railing, space the balusters no more than 4 inches apart, even if your local code allows wider spacing.

■ Treat deck stairs the same as indoor stairs; if young children are around, put a gate at the top and bottom.

■ If you install built-in benches, make the railings behind them at least 24 inches above the seat to prevent a child from climbing or tipping over the side.

■ Hot tubs should be fenced off with a childproof gate. If that's not practical, use a secured cover.

Space balusters no more than 4 inches apart

Add gate to stairs.

Place outdoor furniture as you plan to use it on the deck.

Mark levels.

Flour marks outline of deck.

Make a trial run.
Mark the perimeter of your deck and its various levels with flour. Place your lawn furniture inside the perimeter to get a feel for how much space you need. Use strings to indicate railing heights. Set the string lines at the height of the proposed deck to give you a sense of its profile.

Money $ Saver

TAKE A SHORTCUT
■ You may be surprised at the time- and money-saving services available at your local home center or lumberyard. They may offer ready-made plans, either sold individually or collected in book form. If you find a plan you like and your building site presents no unusual problems, the cost of printed plans can be money well spent.

■ If you want a simple deck that's neither large nor fitted with many custom features, consider buying a precut deck kit. Some larger home centers and lumberyards offer these complete deck packages at attractive prices.

CALCULATING SPANS

Posts, beams, joists, and decking comprise the structural members of a deck. Their spacing and sizing are critical to ensuring a deck is safe and secure. Building codes vary, and it is up to you to contact your local building department for guidance in designing your deck.

When calculating allowable spans, be aware that specifications vary depending on the type of wood you use. Also, spans often change for a deck that is higher than 12 feet. And when you change the size or spacing of one structural member, it can affect the size and spacing of others. For example, you could use fewer posts, spaced farther apart, if you use a larger beam.

The table at *right* lists spans typically allowed for pressure-treated (pt) Southern yellow pine. The calculations that produce these spans assume that the deck must support a load of 50 pounds per square foot. That figure breaks down into 10 pounds per square foot of "dead weight" (the weight of the construction materials) and 40 pounds per square foot of "live weight" (the weight of people and objects on the deck).

WOOD STRENGTH VARIES

Species and grades of wood vary in strength. Design your framing with the strength of the wood in mind. Southern yellow pine and Douglas fir have the same allowable spans and are the most common types of pressure-treated framing lumber. Redwood and Western red cedar are weaker and so need shorter spans. Check with your local lumberyard or home center for the types of lumber available and suitable for use in your area.

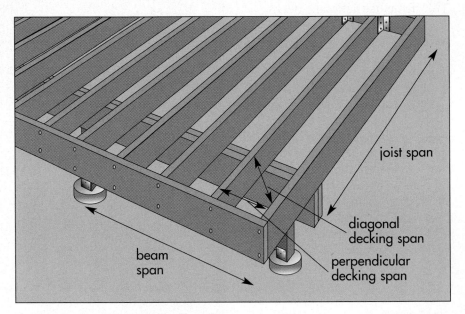

joist span

diagonal decking span

beam span

perpendicular decking span

DECK LUMBER SPANS

BEAM SPANS FOR PT SOUTHERN YELLOW PINE
Maximum Beam Span Between Posts Based on Beam Spacing

Nominal Beam Size	On-center distance between beams (or ledger to beam)								
	4'	5'	6'	7'	8'	9'	10'	11'	12'
(2) 2×6	7'	6'							
4×6	7'	7'	6'						
(2) 2×8	9'	8'	7'	7'	6'	6'			
4×8	10'	9'	8'	7'	7'	6'	6'	6'	
(2) 2×10	11'	10'	9'	8'	8'	7'	7'	6'	6'
(2) 2×12	13'	12'	10'	10'	9'	8'	8'	7'	7'

JOIST SPANS FOR PT SOUTHERN YELLOW PINE
Maximum Joist Spans Based on Joist Spacing

Nominal Joist Size	12" Joist Spacing	16" Joist Spacing	24" Joist Spacing
2×6	10'4"	9'5"	7'10"
2×8	13'8"	12'5"	10'2"
2×10	17'5"	15'5"	12'7"

DECKING SPANS

Species	Nominal Decking Size	Recommended Span
Redwood, Western red cedar, pressure-treated Southern yellow pine or Douglas fir	5/4×4, 5/4×6 (radius edge, except Southern yellow pine)	16"
	5/4×4, 5/4×6 (radius edge, Southern yellow pine)	24"
	2×4, 2×6	24"

CHOOSING HARDWARE

Using the right fasteners is important. This is no place to save a few dollars. Fasteners and connectors must withstand years of exposure without rusting or otherwise weakening their grip. Every fastener should be suitable for long-term exterior use.

Galvanizing is the most common treatment for metal fasteners used outdoors. But there are differences in the methods and materials used in galvanizing. The best process is hot-dip galvanizing, in which the fastener is dipped in molten zinc. The thickest coating of zinc is found on fasteners that meet that standard—ASTM A153.

Stainless steel fasteners cost considerably more, but they are extremely resistant to degradation. Use them near saltwater or other regularly wet or corrosive conditions. Aluminum fasteners are not recommended.

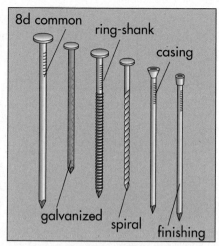

Use galvanized nails.
When nailing on the decking boards, ring- or spiral-shank nails provide a much better grip than common wood nails. On the other hand, they can be difficult to remove if you need to replace decking. Hot-dipped galvanized nails are best for most decks. Use stainless steel for extremely wet or corrosive applications.

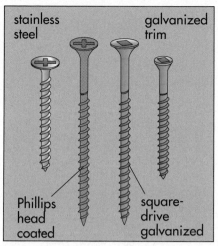

Screws hold well.
Stainless steel, anodized, or hot-dipped galvanized screws are excellent choices for fastening decking. Screws for this purpose often are referred to as decking screws. They are available in 2- to 3-inch lengths, with either Phillips or square-drive heads. Do not use regular black-coated screws intended for wallboard or other interior purposes.

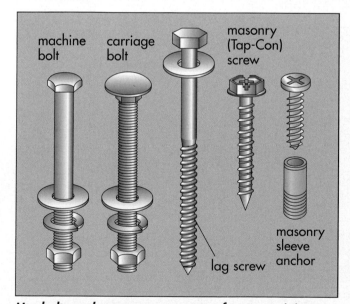

Use bolts and masonry connectors for strong joints.
The strongest fasteners for joining structural members are machine and carriage bolts. Machine bolts require a washer on both ends; carriage bolts require a washer only on the nut end. Carriage bolts have a rounded head. Use ½-inch bolts unless directed otherwise. Lag screws are necessary when access is restricted. Use anchors when fastening ledger boards to masonry or concrete foundations.

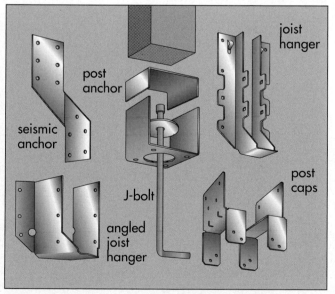

Post and joist connectors simplify joint work.
Ready-made lumber connectors have simplified many aspects of deck construction. Seismic (or hurricane) anchors help secure joists to beams. Post anchors tie posts to the concrete piers via a J-bolt, eliminating the need to embed posts in concrete. Joist hangers offer a secure pocket for joists, while post caps allow a quick means of supporting beams on posts.

PLANNING FOUNDATIONS

The foundation is designed to support the entire load of the deck. All of the construction above the foundation is intended to direct that load into the ground. In most cases, decks are supported by concrete piers set far enough in the ground to remain stable through every season. In some cases, however, posts can be sunk into a small concrete pad at the bottom of the posthole.

Check your local building codes to see what is required. Code requirements are based on local climate and soil conditions and should ensure that your deck will not move with time, twisting away from the house and ruining the integrity of the framing.

Although it requires digging more footings, a freestanding deck (see page 750) is supported next to the house rather than by a ledger on the house. It offers the greatest strength, security, and protection from moisture.

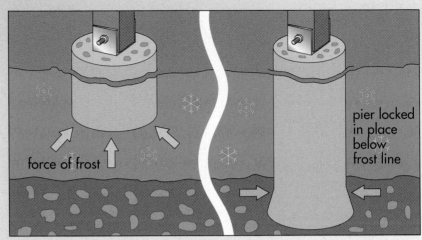

Prevent frost heave.

The foundation must be strong and stable. In cold climates, the effects of frost penetration must be considered in the design of the foundation. If frost is allowed to form beneath a concrete footing or pier, it can push the entire deck up with so much force that it weakens the entire structure. To guard against frost heave, building codes require that the bottom of the foundation rest below the frostline, which is the maximum depth the frost will penetrate. In some parts of the country, this requires foundations to be dug 4 to 5 feet deep. Your local building department can tell you what size and depth your foundation must be.

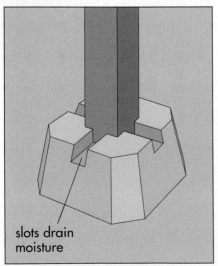

Use precast concrete footings in frost-free areas.

In areas where frost heave isn't a problem, precast concrete footings are the simplest foundation. The footing should sit on compacted or undisturbed soil.

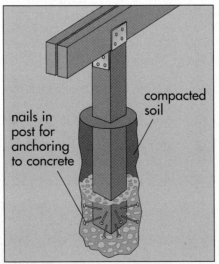

Place post in concrete footing.

This foundation uses only a small amount of concrete to form a footing entirely below the frostline. The post material must be rated for ground contact. Nails in each side hold the post in the concrete. Backfill the remainder of the hole with compacted layers of soil.

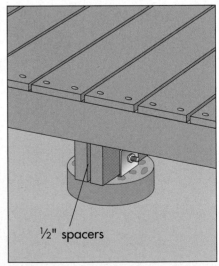

Sit beams for low decks on footing.

Posts are necessary only to raise the deck to the desired height. For low decks, posts can be eliminated. Just set the beams directly in the post anchor. A beam of 2× lumber must be widened with ½-inch spacers to fill a 4×4 post anchor.

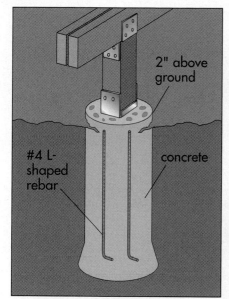

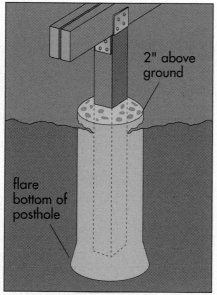

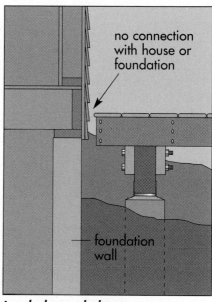

Reinforce footings with rebar.
Reinforcing steel bars, or rebar, add strength to concrete structures. Building codes generally stipulate the number and size of rebar needed. Deck piers typically need one or two pieces of rebar set in the concrete.

Embed the post in concrete.
Pressure-treated posts can be embedded in concrete piers, eliminating the need for metal post anchors. This technique creates a stronger foundation than other methods, but aligning the posts is trickier. Also, moisture may accumulate between the post and the concrete, creating a place that may eventually weaken with rot.

Let deck stand alone.
A freestanding deck has no connection with the house. Instead of a ledger, which is bolted to the house, this deck has an extra row of posts and another beam. This method eliminates the danger of weather-induced damage to the house due to improper flashing.

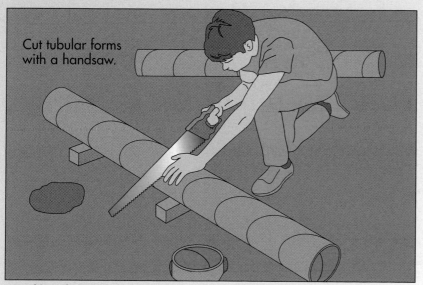

Use fiber-form tubes.
Fiber-form tubes are an easy way to make concrete piers. They may be required by codes in areas where loose or sandy soils are common. The tubes are sold in 12-foot lengths, in various widths. The tubes should be cut as square as possible with a handsaw, then suspended above the bottom of the hole (see page 729) to allow concrete to spread out and form a wider footing.

DRAWING PLANS

You don't need a drafting or architectural degree to produce accurate plan drawings of your deck. But you may need drawn plans to obtain a building permit. Don't be surprised if you are required to have an architect's stamped approval on the plans. Use graph paper to draw elevation and overhead views of your deck to scale (typically ¼ inch to the foot). Drawing working plans can be tedious, but the work pays off by eliminating all of the guesswork from construction. Add enlarged detail or section drawings of railings, stairs, and other complex components that can't be presented in specific detail on the main drawings.

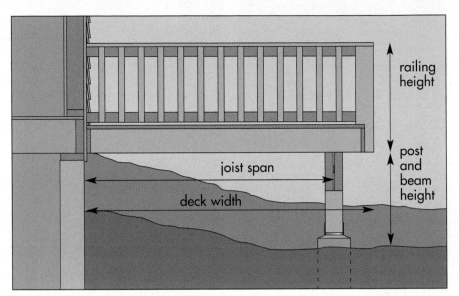

Draw elevation (side or front) view.
An elevation drawing is a vertical view of the deck. It should include each layer of the deck, from footings to railings, with appropriate dimensions given for each. In addition to a side elevation view, you might find it helpful to draw a front elevation, which would be the view if you were looking directly at the house.

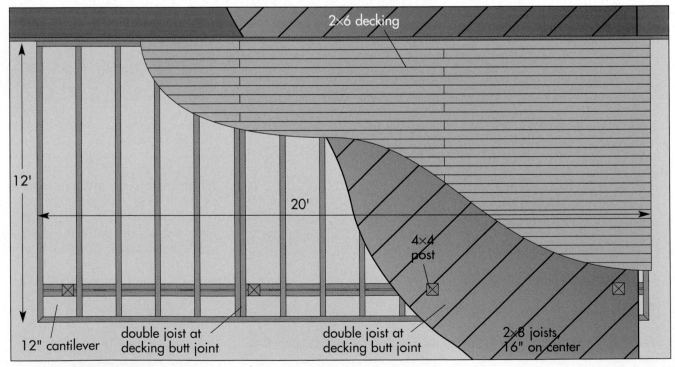

Complete a plan view.
Also called a bird's-eye or overhead view, a plan view shows the footprint of the deck. It is particularly important in establishing exact locations for piers, beams, and joists. An accurately scaled plan view not only helps guide the framing of the deck, it allows you to estimate the amount of lumber to buy. The drawing above combines a view of the finished deck with the decking installed and the foundation and framing. On more complex decks, these two perspectives can be drawn separately. Draw the foundation and framing plan first, then use tracing paper to produce the finished view.

ORDERING AND STORING LUMBER

With your plans drawn, you can write up a list of the lumber and other materials you'll need to complete the project. The list at right shows the required lengths for most of the lumber for a typical 12×20-foot deck. Because lumber generally is sold in lengths of even-numbered feet (beginning with 8 feet), however, your final lumber order will be different.

Plan your order for the most efficient use of lumber. For example, the decking requires two boards to complete each run. You could buy a 14–foot board and an 8–foot board for each run, but you'll have less waste if you buy all 14-foot boards and cut some of them in half. Allow at least 10 percent for waste.

With the lumber and materials list, shop around for the best prices and delivery fees. Be sure to find out if you will be able to return unused, uncut lumber.

Plan for outside lumber storage
Store wood outside by "stickering" it with strips of wood in between layers to create air spaces. Use scrap pieces of 2×4s or 4×4s to keep the stack off the ground. Weights on top of the stack help prevent warping. Cover the stack with a tarp.

LUMBER AND MATERIALS LIST FOR 12×20-FOOT BASIC DECK

Foundation (for 3-foot frost line)

Premixed concrete		4⅔ cubic feet
Fiber-form tubes	4	8×38"
Gravel or sand		as needed for drainage
Rebar	8	No.4 L-shaped pieces

Framing

Ledger board	1	2×8×10'
	1	2×8×9'9"
Metal flashing		as needed
Posts	4	4×4× needed deck height
Beams	2	2×10×13'
	2	2×10×7'
Plywood spacers (for beams)	11	½×3×8"
Joists	16	2×8×11'9"
End joists	2	2×8×12'
Header joists	1	2×8×6'6"
	1	2×8×13'3"

Decking

Decking boards	39	2×6×14'

Nails and Fasteners

Joist hangers	12	2×8
	2	3½×8
Post anchors	4	4×4
Post caps	4	4×4
Bolts or anchors for ledger		as needed
16d common nails or 3-inch decking screws @1,000/lb		about 14 pounds

Optional

Stairs
Railings
Sealer/stain

INSTALLING THE LEDGER

The ledger attaches to the house framing or a masonry wall. It serves the same function as a beam, except that the load carried by the ledger is transferred to the house foundation. Installing a ledger first creates a reference point for the rest of your deck. Using a ledger reduces costs and labor by cutting the number of postholes that must be dug and filled with concrete.

However, attaching the ledger can be a time-consuming chore—one of the most difficult steps in building a deck. On houses with beveled siding, you may need to cut away some siding to create a flat surface for the ledger. This opening must then be flashed carefully to keep water out of the wall. The ledger should be of the same dimension lumber as the joists and 3 inches shorter than the width of the deck to allow room for the overlapping end joists.

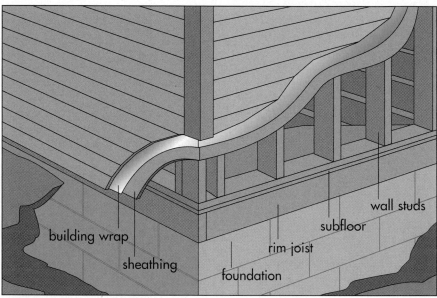

Locate the ledger on the house.
The finished deck surface should sit about 1 inch below the bottom of any door threshold. Add this figure to the thickness of the decking material to determine the location for the top of the ledger.

Thus, if you are using 2×6 decking (1½ inches thick), measure 2½ inches below the bottom of the threshold, then draw a level line at this height to represent the top of the ledger.

EXPERTS' INSIGHT

HIRE A PRO?

The ledger is just a board (or series of boards), but on some houses it can be a tricky component of a deck. It must be level, safely beneath the doorway threshold, and attached firmly to the house's framing or a masonry wall. If you need to remove siding to create a flat surface for the ledger, flashing must be installed carefully around the opening. If this job seems too intimidating, consider hiring an experienced carpenter to get you started.

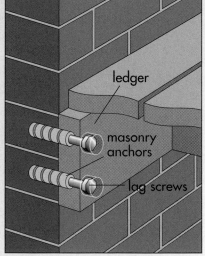

Attach ledger to masonry wall, ...
Cut the ledger to size and have a helper hold it in place against the wall. Make sure the ledger is level, then drill bolt holes through the ledger every 16 inches. Insert a pencil through the holes to mark their

location on the wall. Remove the ledger and drill holes for expansion anchors at the marked locations. Insert the anchors, then attach the ledger by inserting lag screws with washers through the ledger and tightening them.

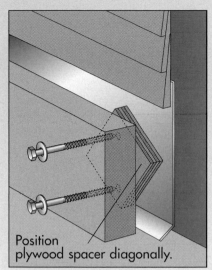

Position plywood spacer diagonally.

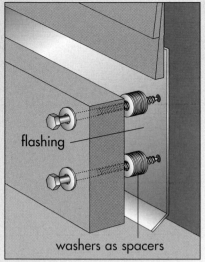

flashing

washers as spacers

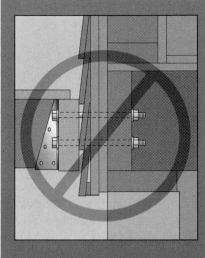

...attach with spacers, ...
An air space between the ledger and the wall helps keep both dry. Your building supplier may stock plastic or aluminum spacers manufactured for deck use, but you easily can cut your own out of pressure-treated plywood. Position the spacer

diagonally so it sheds water. Other choices for spacers include galvanized or stainless steel washers or sections of plastic or metal pipe cut to length. If you use pipe, add washers on either end to keep the pipe from digging into the ledger and flashing.

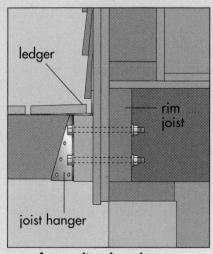

ledger

rim joist

joist hanger

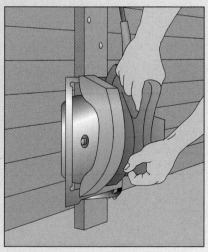

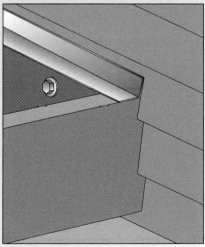

...or fasten directly to house.
This section view shows a ledger properly installed on a clapboard wall. The siding has been removed and flashing added to keep water out of the house. The ledger is bolted through the rim joist.

To make even, vertical cuts through uneven siding, use a 2×4 as a flat surface for the saw. Set the blade just deep enough to remove the siding without cutting into the sheathing.

Slide the flashing under the siding an inch or more (cut a notch around the door threshold if necessary). After the ledger and joists have been installed, bend the flashing over the ledger edge to allow water to drip off.

PREPARING THE SITE

*E*liminate drainage problems around your proposed deck before you build it. Some of the ground beneath the deck will be wet from time to time, but you want the areas around the foundation to be firm. If you have standing water or chronic soggy areas near the site, consult a landscaping contractor for advice on improving the drainage. If a downspout empties close to the deck, reroute it. If necessary, add a drainage ditch to divert water away from the house and deck. Be sure water drains into a dry well or municipal sewer and not into a neighbor's yard.

YOU'LL NEED

TIME: Several hours to remove the sod; about 2 hours for simple grading and spreading gravel.
SKILLS: No special skills, although removing sod can be hard work.
TOOLS: Garden rake, flat garden spade.

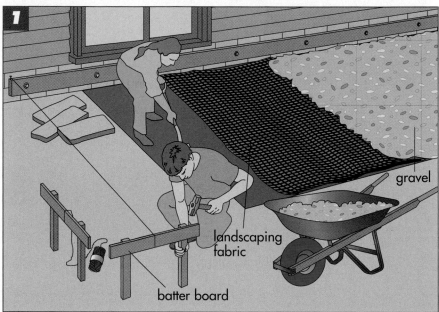

1. Level the grade.
Install batter boards and pound stakes in place for tying guidelines to aid you in grading the site. (You'll set guidelines for the deck structure later.) Remove the sod. If the deck will be close to the ground, check for high spots in the grade that could interfere with joist placement. Smooth high spots with a rake or shovel. To ensure grass and weeds won't grow under the deck, cover the area with landscaping fabric. In addition to controlling weeds, landscaping fabric allows water to drain through it while keeping the gravel from sinking into the soil. Fasten the fabric in place with landscaping fabric staples and cover the surface with a 2- to 3-inch layer of gravel.

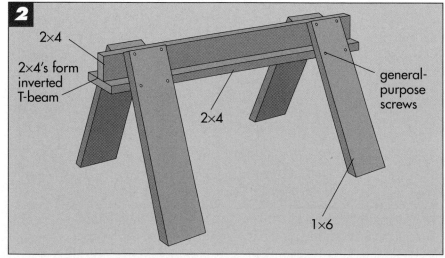

2. Build sawhorses.
You'll need a stable work platform on which to cut your deck material. This sawhorse design is easy to build and far more sturdy than the metal-bracket and scrap-lumber types you can buy at home centers. Cut one 8-foot 2×4 in half to make the T-beam. Make the 30-inch legs from a single 10-foot 1×6. Put it together with 2½-inch general-purpose screws.

EXPERTS' INSIGHT

PLAN FOR LUMBER
Give some thought to where to unload and store the lumber. Store the lumber close enough to the deck site to save you from moving it again, but not so close that it interferes with construction. A garage near the deck site is ideal for keeping lumber dry and secure. If you store lumber outdoors for any length of time, see the recommendations on page 721.

LAYING OUT A DECK

After installing the ledger and preparing the ground, lay out the structural elements of your deck. Layout is the process of marking the perimeter of the deck with mason's lines so you can establish the location of postholes. It is not physically demanding work, but the success of your project depends on locating the lines accurately.

The main reason for installing the ledger on the house first (see pages 722–723) is to create a solid and level reference point for creating an accurate layout. The mason's lines marking the perimeter of the deck should be level. If you are building a deck on a sloped site, make the stakes for the batter boards long enough to allow for a level line. If you allow the mason's line to run parallel with the slope, the dimensions for your deck will be thrown off, perhaps by a significant margin.

The illustration below shows both the site layout and the relationship of the layout to the finished deck itself. The mason's lines running perpendicular to the ledger mark the outside faces of the end joists. The line running parallel with the ledger helps locate the centers of the foundation piers.

On a more complicated deck, you might want to set up one set of mason's lines to mark the perimeter of the deck and another to locate postholes. (Use different colored string to identify each.)

Finally, decide where you want to set up a work site and where you will pile lumber scraps. Create a temporary worktable by laying a couple of 2×4s and a piece of plywood on sawhorses. Make sure you have outdoor extension cords long enough to reach your work site from the nearest outlet.

CAUTION

WATCH OUT FOR UTILITY LINES
Before you dig postholes, check for the location of buried electrical cables, natural gas or water pipes, or underground telecommunications cables. Your telephone, water, electric, and gas companies and cable television supplier can give you explicit instructions about where and where not to dig. In many states, utility companies have combined to set up a clearinghouse so you can make a single phone call. The clearinghouse then will mark the location of all the underground utility lines on your property.

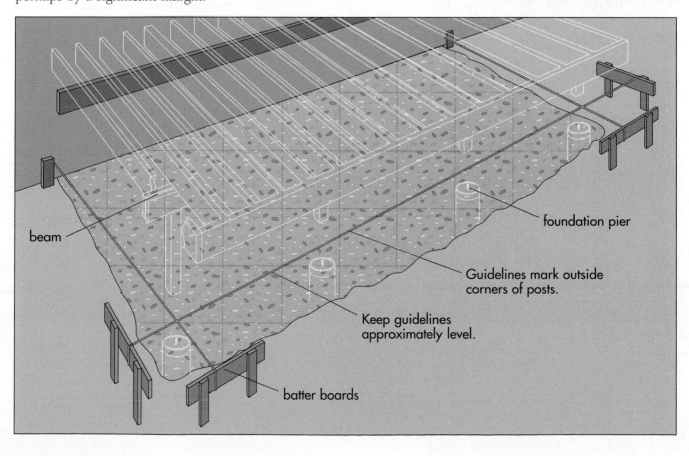

beam

foundation pier

Guidelines mark outside corners of posts.

Keep guidelines approximately level.

batter boards

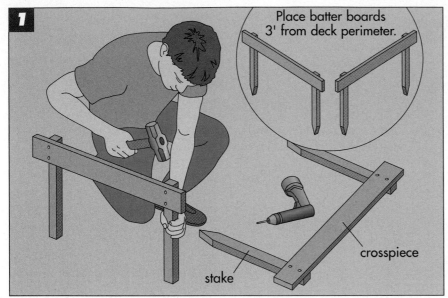

Place batter boards
3' from deck perimeter.

crosspiece

stake

1. Build batter boards.

To lay out a basic rectangular deck, build two pairs of batter boards. Use 1×4s or 2×4s for the stakes and crosspieces. Stakes should be 3- to 4-feet long if the site is level, longer if it's sloping. You can buy pointed stakes at the lumberyard or cut points on the bottoms of the stakes yourself. Cut the crosspiece to length and attach it to the stakes with screws or nails. Locate the stakes about 3 feet away from where the mason's lines will intersect and drive the stakes straight into the ground with a baby sledgehammer. Drive the stakes deep enough to support tightly stretched lines. You'll position the top of the crosspiece level with the top of the ledger when you level the mason's lines.

SQUARING UP WITH THE 3–4–5 METHOD

If you don't get your deck layout square, it will create problems at every succeeding step. Mason's lines that are out of square result in postholes in the wrong spots. Misaligned postholes lead to sloppy post configurations and cockeyed beams. To ensure that your layout is square, use the 3–4–5 method, illustrated below. Multiples of these dimensions, such as 6–8–10 or 9–12–15, are even more accurate. From a corner, measure 3 feet along the back edge and 4 feet along the other edge, marking the spots with a piece of tape. Make sure both of these measurements begin at exactly the same point. If the layout is square, the diagonal measurement between the marks will be 5 feet. If it isn't, adjust the mason's line until the diagonal measures up.

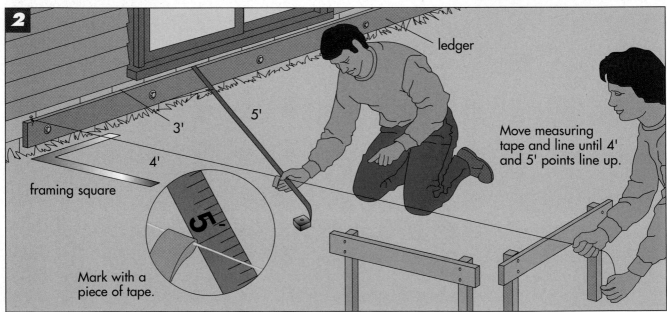

ledger

3'

5'

4'

framing square

Mark with a piece of tape.

Move measuring tape and line until 4' and 5' points line up.

2. Position string lines.

Adjusting the mason's lines is best done with two people. Drive a nail into the top side of the ledger, 1½ inches in from the edge. Tie a line to the nailhead and stretch it past the batter board. Use a framing square to roughly position the line perpendicular with the face of the ledger. Then tape the line to the batter board crosspiece. Repeat the process at the other end of the ledger. Next, measure along each mason's line to locate the centerline of the footings. For our 12×20-foot deck this will be 11 feet from the back of the ledger. Mark the location on the line with tape, then run another line parallel to the ledger, intersecting the 11-foot marks.

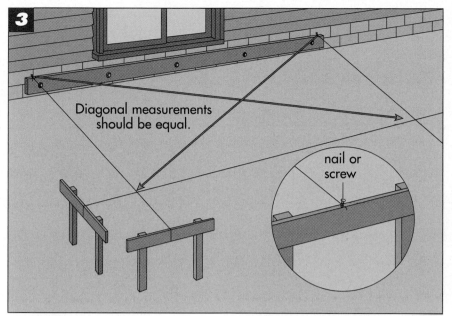

3. Check your layout.
With a helper, carefully measure the diagonals inside the mason's lines. If they are equal, the layout is square. If they are not equal, adjust the taped line ends until they are. Once you are sure the lines are square, drive nails or

screws into the tops of the crosspieces at the proper location. Leave the nail or screw sticking out about an inch and tie the line around it snugly. If you bump the batter boards at any point, check for square again and readjust the mason's lines as needed.

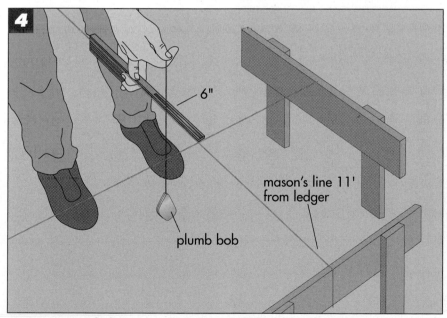

4. Locate postholes.
This is another job that may be done more easily with two people. On our basic deck, the outside footings will be centered 6 inches from the sides of the deck. On the 11-foot mason's line, measure in 6 inches from each side string line. Using a dark permanent marker,

mark the mason's line. From each of those marks, measure in another 6 feet 4 inches to locate the two intermediate postholes and mark the mason's line again. To transfer the marks on the mason's line to the ground, use a plumb bob.

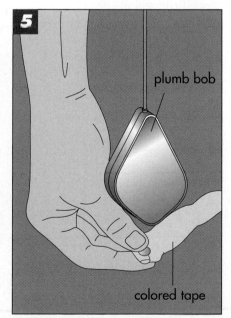

5. Mark posthole locations.
Dangle the plumb bob just above ground level. When it is perfectly still, mark the location by sticking a large nail directly under it. For added visibility, first pierce the nail through a piece of colored tape or paper. The nail marks the center of each posthole.

DIGGING POSTHOLES

Before you dig postholes, check with your local building department for specific code requirements for the type, depth, and strength of deck posts and footings. These codes are based on local climate and terrain. Footings must be stable in soft soil, withstand frost heave, and provide a base to keep posts or beams above decay-causing moisture.

The depth for post footings should be below the frostline (the depth to which frost permeates the soil) to prevent movement caused by freezing and thawing. This depth varies with local climate. You may be required to place a precast pier pad on gravel below the frostline.

A posthole normally is between 24 and 42 inches deep, depending upon the soil type, the depth to the frostline, and the height of the post. If the soil at the base of the hole seems loose, compact it with a tamper. Don't try to dig postholes with a shovel; at the least you should borrow, rent, or buy a posthole digger. If your design requires a large number of holes, rent a power auger or hire a contractor to handle the job. If you rent a power auger, be sure to get thorough instructions on its use.

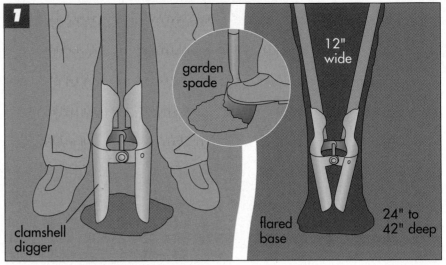

1. Use a posthole digger.
If needed, use a garden spade to remove sod. With the handles squeezed together, jam the posthole digger into the ground. Spread the handles apart and lift the dirt out. If you hit large rocks, rent or buy a digging bar (basically an elongated crowbar). Roots can be cut with a tree saw. Do your best to keep the hole as plumb as possible and the bottom level. Flare the bottom of the hole to widen the footing base. Holes should be about 12 inches wide for a typical 4×4 post.

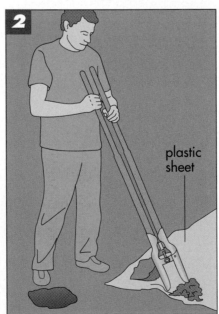

2. Keep dirt away from hole.
If you have never dug a posthole, you may be surprised at how much dirt is removed. Don't make the mistake of piling dirt too close to the hole. Set it several feet away, preferably on a sheet of plywood or plastic to make your clean-up job simple.

YOU'LL NEED

TIME: 1 to 4 hours, depending on the type of tool used to dig the holes, the type of soil, and the number and depth of the holes.
SKILLS: Using a manual posthole digger requires no special skills, but get complete instructions before using a power auger.
TOOLS: Garden spade, clamshell posthole digger, digging bar, sheet of plywood or plastic.

CAUTION!

TAKE YOUR TIME
Digging postholes is demanding labor. If you need to dig holes that are 3 to 4 feet deep, do not be surprised if you spend up to an hour on some holes. You may spend a good bit of this time coaxing out rocks and cutting through roots.
This work can be tough on the arms and shoulders and even tougher on the back. Even if you are in relatively good physical shape, it makes sense to take your time and take frequent breaks. As hard as the digging is, don't cheat on the required depth. Rest assured that once this task is finished the rest of the job will seem easy.

PREPARING THE FOUNDATION

If you removed the mason's lines to dig the postholes, carefully replace them. Make sure the postholes are deep and wide enough for the footings required for your deck. Remember, the base of the footings must be below the frostline. If the site gets lots of moisture, place gravel in the holes to aid drainage. Cut fiber-form tubes with a handsaw, taking care to make square cuts. These forms should be long enough so they are at least 2 inches above grade and about 6 inches above the bottom of the hole.

YOU'LL NEED

TIME: 1 to 2 hours for each posthole, including building the forms, mixing and pouring the concrete, and inserting the post base.
SKILLS: Basic masonry skills; follow instructions on the bag to mix concrete.
TOOLS: Mixing tub, mason's hoe, shovel, water hose.

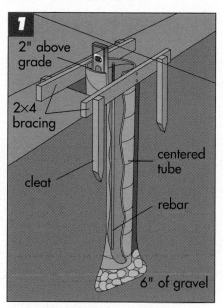

1. Build the forms.

Set a fiber-form tube into each hole and fasten 2×4 braces to the sides with decking screws. Center the tube under the mason's line and check for plumb. Drive short cleats into the ground and attach them to the braces. Cut a piece of rebar to length and place it in each tube. Fill each tube with a foot of concrete. After a few minutes, lift the rebar 4 inches off the bottom.

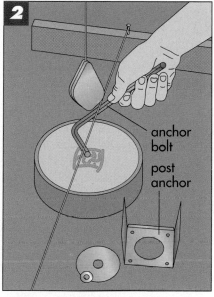

2. Pour the footings.

Fill the remainder of the tube with concrete. Before the concrete sets, insert an anchor bolt into the center of the footing. Leave the threaded end protruding upward with the shank perpendicular to the footing surface. Smooth the surface of the concrete. After the concrete is set, the post anchor can be positioned on the bolt.

ESTIMATING CONCRETE NEEDS

■ Whether you mix concrete yourself or have ready-mix concrete delivered by truck, you need to know in advance how much you will need. Most ready-mix companies require a minimum order, which you may be able to meet only if you are building a large deck requiring many postholes.

■ To make your own concrete, you can buy premixed bags weighing up to 90 pounds each. These generally make from 1/3 to 2/3 cubic foot per bag, but check the label to determine how much mixed concrete can be made from each bag.

■ To calculate how much concrete you need, determine how much is required for each hole, then multiply that amount by the number of holes. Calculate the total volume of each hole using this formula: 3.14 times the squared radius (one-half the diameter) times the height (total depth of the posthole). A 1-foot diameter hole, 3.5 feet deep, would require 2.75 square feet of concrete. $(3.14 \times .5^2 \times 3.5 = 2.75)$

■ If you set the posts in the concrete footing, subtract the space that the post will fill in each hole to determine accurately the amount of concrete needed.

Money $ Saver

PREPARE STAIR LANDING

If you plan to rest stairs on a concrete pad, you may be able to save time and energy by preparing the pad now so you can complete your concrete work at one time.

The trick is determining exactly where the pad will be placed, which is difficult to gauge when the deck hasn't been built yet. To position the pad accurately you have to trust your plans and know where you want the stairs located. See page 742 for positioning and building a form for pouring a concrete stair landing.

INSTALLING POSTS

Before installing the posts, you'll need to remove the mason's line centered over the footings. Before doing so, however, you might want to add another line to help you to align the posts. For 4×4 posts, set this line 1¾ inches (half the actual width of a 4×4) from the existing line. Then set the posts in place with the face of the post just touching the newly placed line.

You'll Need

TIME: About 20 to 30 minutes to install each post.
SKILLS: The ability to establish plumb using a level.
TOOLS: Hammer, cordless drill or screwdriver, level.

EXPERTS' INSIGHT

CUT YOUR POSTS DOWN TO SIZE

Always rough-cut posts longer than actually needed. With the post braced in place, the extra length allows you to plumb it easily. This is important if you are building a low deck whose posts might finally be only 1 or 2 feet high. Also, the extra length provides you with some working space for transferring the ledger height to the post and measuring down the post to the proper post height. Once you have double-checked your marks, detach the post from the bracing and cut it to the proper length, or cut in place.

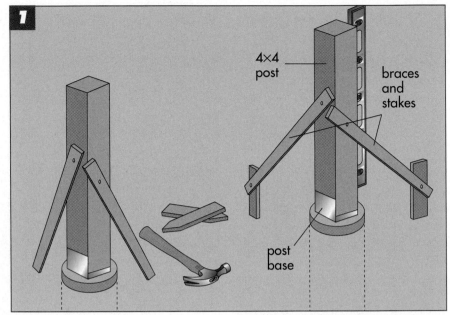

1. Set and brace the posts.
Measure and cut the posts so they are higher than the bottom of the ledger. For each post, you'll need two stakes and two braces. Insert the post into the post anchor. Hold it as straight as possible and attach the braces with one screw so they pivot. Drive the stakes into the ground next to each brace. Using a level, plumb two adjacent sides of each post. Holding the post plumb, have a helper attach the braces to the stakes.

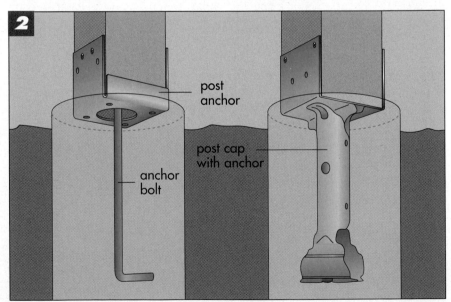

2. Fasten the posts.
Before attaching the post to the post anchor, recheck the post for plumb. When the post is plumb, drive nails or screws through the anchor into the post. Post anchors and caps vary, so be sure to use the type and number of fasteners specified by the manufacturer. Take care when driving fasteners that you don't move the post out of alignment. When finished, recheck the post for plumb. Finally, use a utility knife to cut away any of the fiber-form tube that remains above ground level.

MARKING AND CUTTING POSTS

Marking and cutting posts is a relatively delicate operation. If you get it right, your deck will be level and the rest of the job will be easier. Get it wrong, and you'll mar the appearance and actually complicate later steps. So don't rush this step. Enlist an assistant if possible to help with transferring level marks. If time has passed since you set your posts, check them for plumb. Often, posts get bumped or bracing gets kicked, knocking your supports out of plumb. Readjust if necessary.

YOU'LL NEED

TIME: About 15 minutes per post.
SKILLS: Ability to use a level, cut upright posts with a circular saw.
TOOLS: A long straight board, carpenter's level or water level, pencil, tape measure tape, circular saw, chisel.

CAUTION!

TREATING CUT POSTS

If you are using pressure-treated lumber for your deck, have a supply of wood preservative on hand. Although the treated wood absorbs a good dose of the chemicals used in preserving the wood, the coverage is most thorough on the outer surfaces. When you cut a treated post or board, you expose wood that is less-thoroughly treated. To avoid future maintenance problems with your deck, brush some preservative on the cut ends. Because they'll be most exposed to weather, horizontal surfaces, such as posts ends, particularly need this treatment.

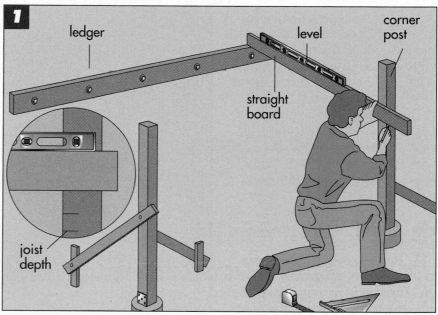

1. Establish post height.
Rest one end of a long straight board on top of the ledger. Hold the other end against a corner post. Place a level on top of the board and level it. Mark where the bottom of the board touches the post. Next, measure down from that mark the depth of a joist (For a 2×8 joist, measure down 7¼ inches). Measure down from this second mark the depth of the beam (for a 10-inch beam, this would be 9¼ inches). Make a level mark at this location around the post. This is the post cutoff line.

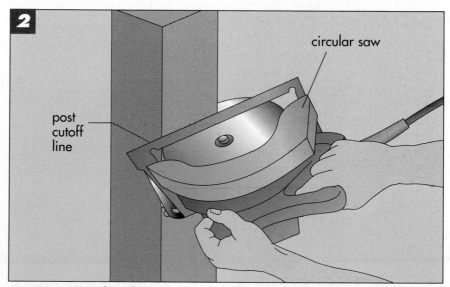

2. Cut posts to length.
After the cutoff lines are marked on each post, double-check your measurements by placing a long board and level along the line of posts. Make sure the cutoff lines are level with each other. Set your circular saw for a maximum depth of cut, then cut from opposite sides of each post, taking care to follow the lines. If you have trouble making level cuts, tack a board across the posts to rest the baseplate of the saw on. If necessary, use a sharp chisel to clean off the post top.

INSTALLING THE BEAM

On our basic deck design, the beam sits on top of the posts, and joists sit on top of the beam. Joists also can be set on the same plane as the beam by installing them with joist hangers.

The beam should be pressure-treated unless you are using a naturally rot-resistant wood. Sometimes it is difficult to find a solid 4× beam in the width you need, and a 4×10 or 4×12 beam can be heavy. For these reasons, a built-up beam made of two 2×s can be more convenient.

To ensure that the outside edges of the beam align squarely with the ledger, reattach the mason's lines, marking the sides of the deck before installing the beam. This is far more important than having the ends of the beam overhang the outside posts by the same distance. Check for square and measure the diagonals from beam to ledger before fastening the beam to the posts.

Generally, beams should be installed with the crown side up. To find the crown, sight down the narrow edges of a board (see page 735). If one edge seems to have a high spot (crown) on it, place a mark on this edge to remind you to set this edge up. In constructing a built-up beam, make sure the crowns of both boards are on the same side of the beam.

YOU'LL NEED

TIME: About 1 hour for a solid beam; longer if installing a built-up beam.
SKILLS: Cutting large-dimension lumber, fastening.
TOOLS: Hammer, circular saw, drill and bits, wrench, level.

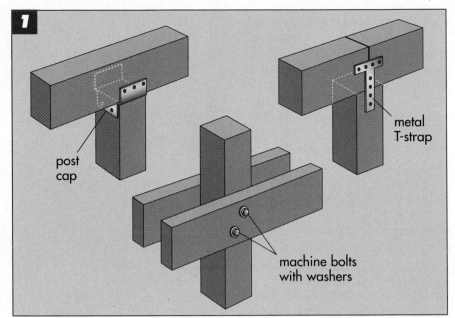

post cap

metal T-strap

machine bolts with washers

1. Join beam to posts.
The beam-to-post connection is critical to the integrity of your deck. The strongest connections are formed when the beam rests fully on top of the posts, as with two of the examples above. Metal brackets, straps, or ties add additional stability. You'll be able to select from a wide variety of these fasteners at your home center or lumberyard. Your building supplier should be able to help you choose the right ones for your deck. With these connectors, always use the type and number of nails or screws recommended by the manufacturer.

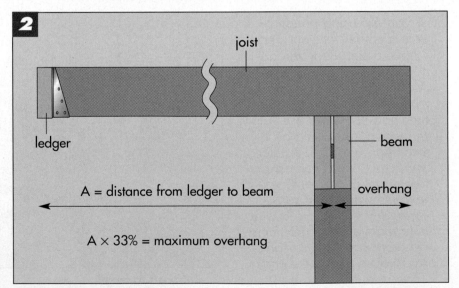

joist

ledger

beam

overhang

A = distance from ledger to beam

A × 33% = maximum overhang

2. Calculate joist overhang.
On our basic deck design, the posts are centered 11 feet from the house, while the deck surface extends to 12 feet. This overhang, or cantilever, creates a more attractive deck because the beam is set back out of view. In general, joists can overhang the beam one-third, or about 33 percent, of the distance between the ledger and the beam. However, your local building code may dictate different requirements: Be sure to check on cantilever limits.

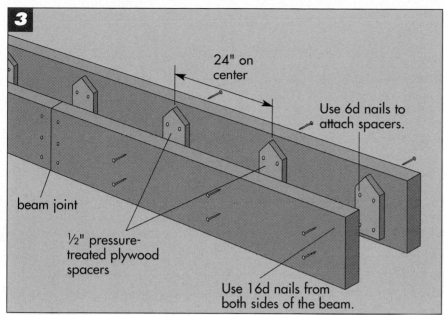

24" on center

Use 6d nails to attach spacers.

beam joint

½" pressure-treated plywood spacers

Use 16d nails from both sides of the beam.

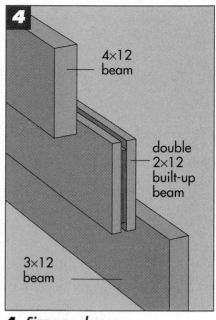

4×12 beam

double 2×12 built-up beam

3×12 beam

3. Construct a built-up beam.

A beam composed of two 2× boards separated by ½-inch spacers will match the width of 4×4 posts. The spacers also allow water to drain through the boards, ensuring a longer life than if they were nailed together. Use pressure-treated plywood to make the spacers, and point the tips to encourage water runoff. Use a spacer every 24 inches on center. Attach the spacers with 6d galvanized nails and drive 16d galvanized nails through the beam and spacers from both sides of the beam. Stagger joints and place them over posts.

4. Size up a beam.

If you make a built-up beam using two 2× boards, keep in mind that the structural strength of the beam is not equal to a 4× beam. It is only equal to the width of the two boards (3 inches), not its finished width (3½ inches). Spacers don't add strength.

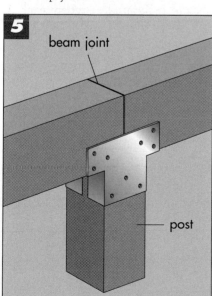

beam joint

post

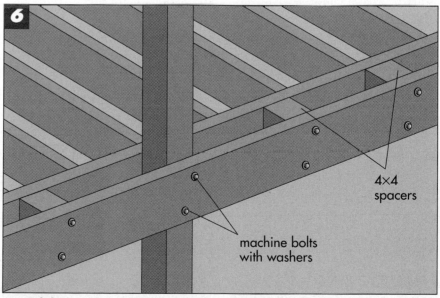

4×4 spacers

machine bolts with washers

5. Place joints over posts.

For a built-up beam, it is smart to locate even staggered joints over a post. If you are using a solid beam, however, you must center all joints over posts. Cut the beam squarely so as much of the beam as possible contacts the post.

6. Bolt beams to continuous posts.

If your deck has posts running through the framing for railings, you should bolt a double beam to the posts as shown above. Use short pieces of 4×4 as spacers and use ½-inch machine bolts with washers on both sides. To reduce the chance of splitting a post, offset the bolts horizontally. Note that this technique relies on the fasteners for much of its strength and integrity. It is not as strong as when the beam sits on top of the posts. It is a good idea to consult with a building professional before using this approach.

HANGING JOISTS

If properly installed, joist hangers are a more secure method of attaching joists to the ledger than the old technique of toenailing joists. In fact, most building codes require hangers for deck joists. Take care to buy joist hangers that match the size of joist you are installing. A 2×6 joist requires a different hanger than a 2×8 joist. Make sure the hangers are intended for exterior use. For built-up or 4× joists, use 3½-inch-wide hangers. For end joists, use a heavy-duty right-angle bracket that attaches on the inside corner so no hardware is visible.

YOU'LL NEED

TIME: 15 to 20 minutes to mark and fasten each joist.
SKILLS: Measuring, cutting, installing joist hangers.
TOOLS: Hammer, tape measure, pencil, framing square, speed square, circular saw.

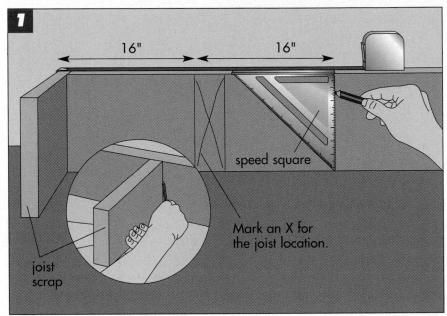

speed square

Mark an X for the joist location.

joist scrap

1. Lay out joists on the ledger.
Temporarily tack a scrap piece of 2× joist stock to the end of the ledger to represent the end joist you will install later. Hook your tape over the edge of this scrap and make a mark every 16 inches on the front edge of the ledger.

Then go back with a square and extend each mark down the face of the ledger. Use a scrap of joist stock set on the joist side of each line to mark the width of each joist. Mark an X between the two lines to make it clear where each joist should go.

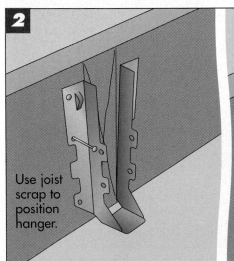

Use joist scrap to position hanger.

2. Attach joist hangers.
Attaching a joist hanger can be trickier than it looks. Use the fasteners recommended by the joist manufacturer. Hold the hanger with one side aligned with the layout mark on the ledger.

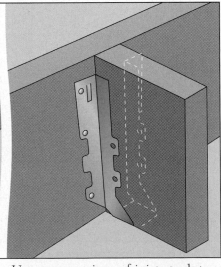

Use a scrap piece of joist stock to make sure the hanger is positioned so the joist top and ledger top are flush. Nail one side of the hanger to the ledger, leaving the other side loose.

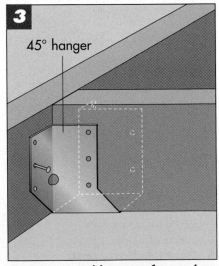

45° hanger

3. Use special hangers for angles.
Some deck designs have joists that meet the ledger at an angle. Forty-five degree hangers usually can handle a 40- to 50-degree angle. Use bendable seismic anchors for other angles. Cut joist ends at the appropriate angle for full bearing.

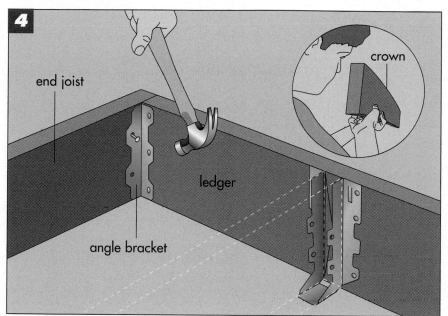

4. Install the joists.

Measure and cut the joists to length. Both ends should be square and free of splits. The end joists will be 1½ inches longer than the others to overlap the ledger. Apply preservative to the cut ends. Set each joist in place with the crown up (see inset). Make sure joists are straight and parallel. Nail in the other side of the hanger, then nail joists to the hangers. Overlap the end joists on the ledger ends, then attach angle brackets to the inside corner.

EXPERTS' INSIGHT

KEEP IT SQUARE

The more care you take to install the joists square with the ledger, the easier the rest of the construction will be. Don't assume you can square up things later. Use a framing square to align each joist at the ledger. Along the beam, use a spacer to test the position of each joist. To make the spacer, cut a perfectly square piece of joist stock exactly 14½ inches long. Have a helper use the scrap to space and align the joists along the beam.

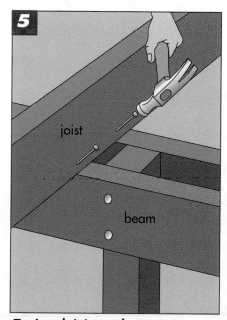

5. Attach joists to beam.

With the joists straight and square with the ledger, fasten each with a 16d nail driven at an angle into the beam just deep enough to hold it in place. (After installing the header joist, you can remove these nails to allow the frame to be squared up.)

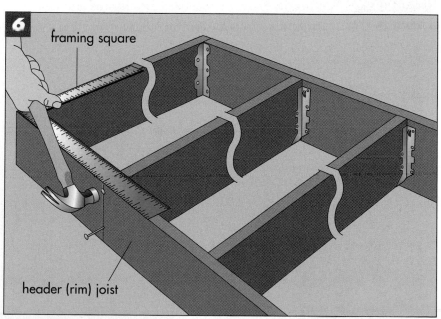

6. Install header joist.

The header, or rim, joist is fastened to the ends of the joists. It's helpful to mark a layout on the header similar to that on the ledger. While a helper aligns the tops, drive three 16d nails through the header into the joist. With the header installed, check the frame for square by measuring the diagonals. If necessary, remove the toenails at the beam to make minor adjustments. Finally, fasten joists to the beam permanently with two 16d nails toenailed through each side of the joist.

INSTALLING DECK BOARDS

Don't cut corners when it comes to choosing your decking material. This surface is the business side of your deck. It gets the most use and takes the most abuse. If your lumber and decking were not pretreated, consider applying a water repellent now. At this point, you can coat the tops of the joists and reach other parts of the deck that may be inaccessible later. It's also a good idea to coat both sides of the deck boards before installing them.

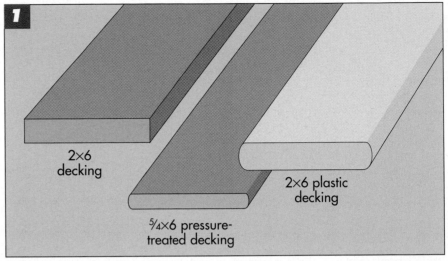

2×6 decking

⁵⁄₄×6 pressure-treated decking

2×6 plastic decking

YOU'LL NEED

TIME: One-half to a full day for a basic deck, depending on material and design.
SKILLS: Cutting and fastening boards straight and secure.
TOOLS: Circular saw, hammer or screw gun or drill equipped to drive screws, chalk line or mason's line.

1. Choose your decking.

Building centers generally carry several choices of material for decking. Nominal 6-inch boards are the most popular width. Boards wider than 6 inches tend to warp too much, while narrower boards take longer to install. Standard 2×6 boards are 1½ inches thick and are the least expensive. Five quarter (⁵⁄₄ inch) boards are about 1 inch thick and cost a little more. However, they are often a better grade of wood and are available with a radius edge (rounded edge). Decking also is available in plastic and wood-plastic composites. The process for installation is the same as wood decking. These products cost more, but they require little long-term maintenance.

2. Select deck board fasteners.

Several products now are available to fasten deck boards to joists without nailing or screwing through the surface of the decking. These fasteners are concealed between boards. That means a better-looking deck and less rotting around fasteners. These fasteners, however, make it more difficult to remove and replace individual boards at a later date. They also cost more than nails or screws and installation is more time-consuming. You may not be able to find all the options shown here at your home center, but one or two should be available.

Galvanized or anodized deck screws (see page 717) hold the best and are relatively quick to install. Galvanized nails are faster to install, particularly if you use a power nailer, but can pop out over time.

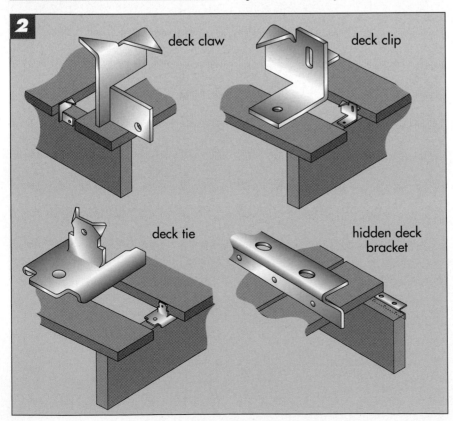

deck claw

deck clip

deck tie

hidden deck bracket

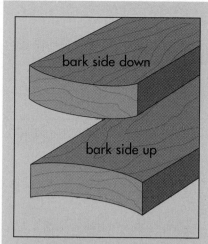

WHICH SIDE UP?

A rule of thumb is to install decking boards with the bark side up. It is thought this allows water to drain off if the board cups. However, studies show decking installed with the bark side down is less likely to develop splits in the surface. The best advice is to make sure the wood is dry and install the best looking side up. For added prevention, apply water repellent every year.

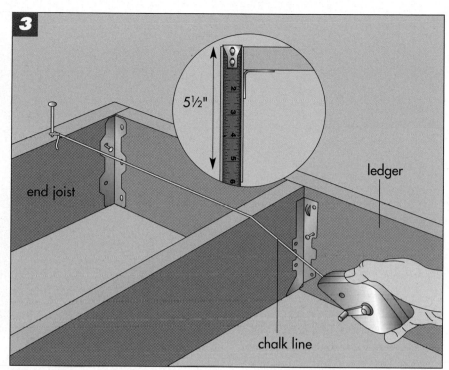

3. Install starter board.
Your job will proceed much easier if you install the first board as straight and as square as possible. On both end joists, measure out from the house the width of one decking board (5½ inches) plus ¼ inch for a drainage gap. Mark the joists, then snap a chalk line or run a mason's line between them. Set the first decking board along this line. For best results, use the straightest board you can find for the starter board.

EXPERTS' INSIGHT

SCATTER THE BOARDS

Making a trip to your lumber pile every time you need another decking board wastes time and energy. Instead, carry a number of decking boards to the deck and scatter them across the joists.

As you begin laying the decking, you can use the loose boards as a working platform, particularly when you are right up against the house. Later you can position your reserve boards so each can be pulled quickly into place for fastening.

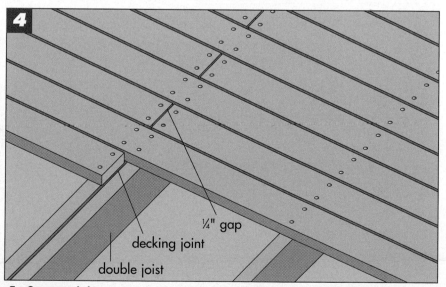

4. Stagger joints.
On a narrow deck, you may not have any butt joints between decking boards. However, on our 20-foot-wide basic deck, we planned for the joints by installing two sets of double joists. This requires the use of one long and one short board in each row of decking, with the joints staggered on the double joists. Leave a ¼-inch gap between board ends to allow for water drainage through the decking and the double joist.

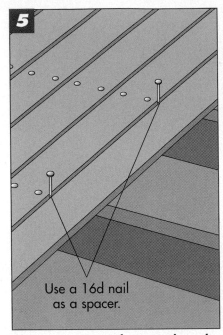

5. Leave a space between boards.
Deck boards need to have a gap between them to allow water and dirt to fall through. Bear in mind that the wood shrinks over time as it continues to dry. Use a 16d common nail as a spacer.

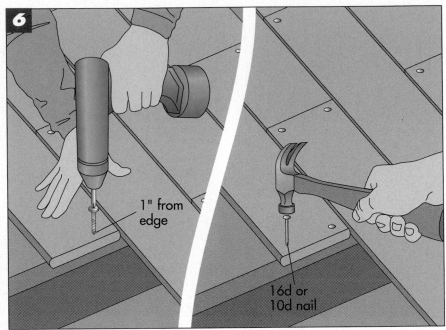

6. Use proper fastening methods.
Decking can be installed with decking screws, nails (16d nails for 2× decking, 10d nails for ⁵/₄ decking), or special concealed fasteners. Use two nails or screws at each joist crossing, about 1 inch from each side of the board.

Whether using nails or screws, drill angled pilot holes at the ends of boards to prevent splits. Drive heads of nails flush with the decking. As the wood dries, drive them deeper. If you use a power nailer, adjust the depth so the nail heads are slightly below the surface of the decking board.

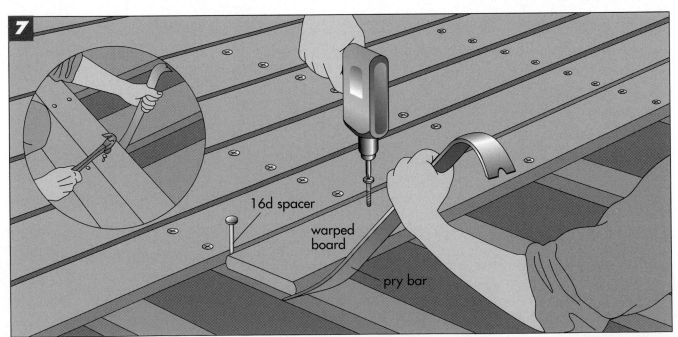

7. Keep it straight.
Straighten crooked boards as you fasten them. Use a utility-grade chisel or a pry bar to force warped boards into alignment. You can do this by yourself (see inset), but the process is much simpler if you lever the decking while a helper drives in the fasteners. On severely warped boards, you may have to repeat this from one joist to the next. Check for straightness every few rows by measuring from the header joist. If you're significantly out of true, hide the mistake by making small adjustments in the spacing gap over several of the next rows rather than all at once.

EXPERTS' INSIGHT

PLANNING AN OVERHANG

Give some thought to the amount of overhang you want on your finished deck. An overhang isn't necessary. You can cut the decking flush with the joists. However, you may be happier with the appearance of your deck if you let the decking extend beyond the edges on each side.

A 1- to 2-inch overhang is most common and gives a finished appearance to your deck. As you install your decking, let the boards overhang the end joists (see below). They will be cut to length after the entire decking surface is installed.

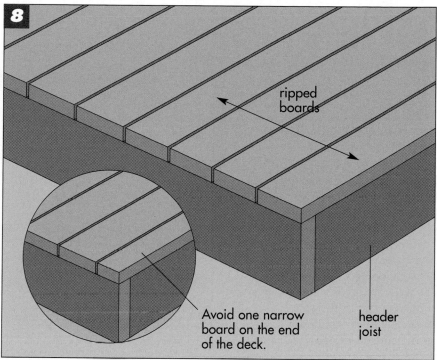

ripped boards

Avoid one narrow board on the end of the deck.

header joist

8. Plan ahead.

When you get down to the last three or four rows of decking, start planning ahead for the last row. Chances are that full-width boards won't fit perfectly, and you should avoid installing one narrow board at the end. Instead, rip small amounts off the last several rows of boards while maintaining the same gap between boards. Let the end row overhang the header joist by the same amount as the overhang on the sides.

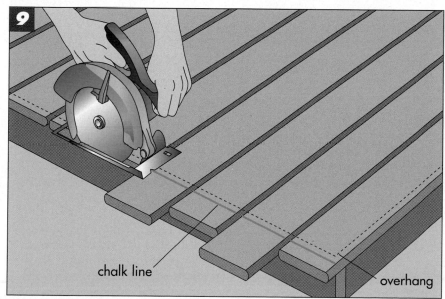

chalk line

overhang

9. Trim the edges.

When you've installed all the decking, snap a chalk line along the edges to mark the intended cutoff line. Check that the overhang is the same on all three sides. Set the blade of the circular saw so it just clears the bottom of the decking. Carefully cut the decking by following the chalk line. If you are concerned about cutting a straight line, tack a long, straight board on the decking as a saw guide.

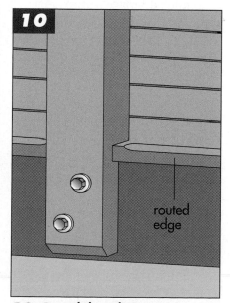

routed edge

10. Round the edges.

To prevent the wood from splintering and to enhance the beauty of your deck, round the sharp edges of the decking. Use a router equipped with a round-over bit.

INSTALLING RAILINGS

Railings are intended to prevent falls, but this basic function doesn't preclude the desire for a creative design. To the deck user, the decking surface may seem the most important and visible part of a deck. To neighbors and passersby, however, the railing is the most obvious feature. Legal code requirements dictate what constitutes a safe deck (see right). Beyond that there are an endless number of design choices and construction techniques.

The most common railings are similar to the traditional picket fence. A typical framework consists of 4×4 posts spanned by a 2×4 or 2×6 cap rail and a 2×4 bottom rail. Balusters attached to these rails provide the style.

The illustrations on these two pages show one simple, attractive design. Another option is a completely enclosed railing. Faced with siding and open only at the bottom for drainage, it provides more privacy and blocks wind.

To prevent sagging railings, keep the spans between posts less than 6 feet. The posts should be bolted to the frame of the deck; use two $7/16$-inch bolts for each connection. Notched posts are the best-looking choice. Cut a notch $1\frac{1}{2}$ inches deep on the bottom of the post and about 8 inches long. Using this technique, you can use shorter bolts and the posts won't protrude so much from the side of the deck. If your decking overhangs the edge of the deck, cut an opening for the post.

YOU'LL NEED

TIME: 1 to 2 days, depending on the size and complexity of the railing.
SKILLS: Basic carpentry skills.
TOOLS: Circular saw, chisel, tape measure, pencil, hammer, power miter saw (optional).

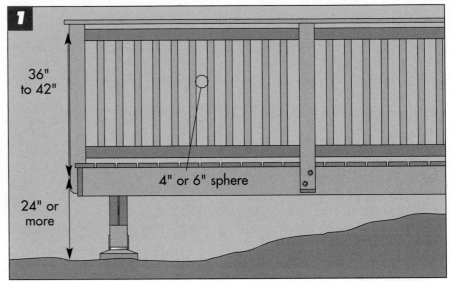

1. Check your code.
When a deck is 24 inches or more above ground, most building codes require a railing. Usually the railing must be between 36 and 42 inches high and must have balusters spaced close enough to prevent a 4- or 6-inch-diameter sphere from passing through them. (The sphere is intended to represent a child's head.) Before you begin railing construction check with your local building department to review codes.

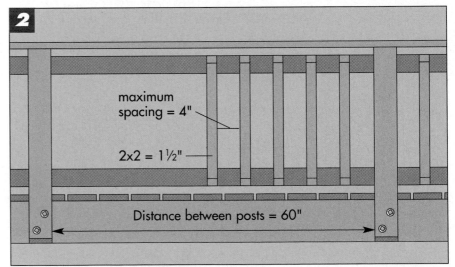

2. Calculate baluster spacing.
Local building codes define the maximum gap between balusters. Getting evenly spaced balusters requires some math (numbers here refer to the above drawing). Add the width of a baluster to that of the maximum spacing and divide this figure into the total distance between posts [(60÷(1.5+4)=10.9]. Round up the result to find the number of required balusters (11). Then to find the actual spacing between balusters, multiply the number of balusters by the width of one (11×1.5=16.5). Subtract that result from the total distance between posts (60-16.5=43.5). Divide the remainder by the number of spacings (always one more than the number of balusters) to determine the final spacing between balusters (43.5÷12=3.625 or $3\frac{5}{8}$ inches).

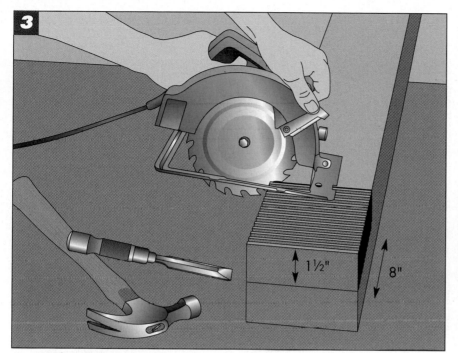

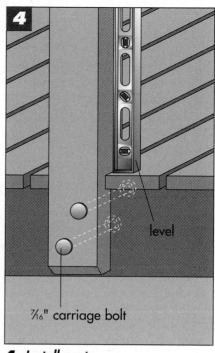

3. Notch railing posts.

Measure a distance equal to the joist depth, less ½ inch, and mark the inside face. Use a circular saw or a tablesaw to make a series of closely spaced cuts 1½ inches deep up to the line. Knock out the pieces with a hammer, then use a chisel to clean out the notch. Cut a 45-degree bevel on the bottom outside corner. If decking will overhang the deck, notch the decking for the post, leaving an ⅛-inch gap on each side of the post.

4. Install posts.

Set the post on top of the decking, flush against the joist. Use a level to keep it plumb and drill two holes through the post and joist. Secure each post with 5-inch-long, ⁷⁄₁₆-inch carriage bolts.

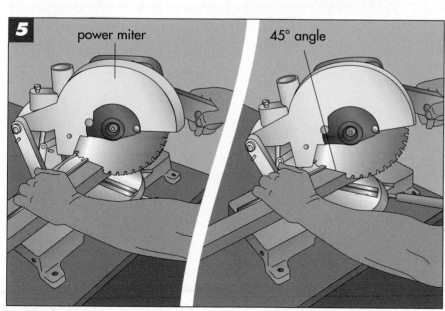

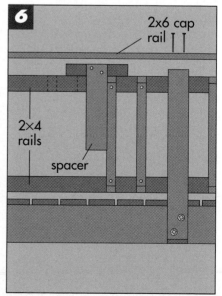

5. Cut balusters.

Cut the balusters from 2×2 stock. Clamp four to six pieces together and cut them all at once with a circular saw. For a large number of repetitive cuts you may want to rent or buy a power miter saw. When cutting pieces with square and beveled ends, cut each baluster roughly to size with square ends. Then add a stop block (a simple jig fastened to the saw base) at the intended baluster length. Finish the baluster with the 45-degree bevel cut.

6. Install rails and balusters.

Install 2×4 top and bottom rails equally spaced from the top of the post and the deck surface. Attach a 2×6 cap rail to the posts. Measure and mark a layout for the balusters or make a spacer as shown. Attach balusters with 8d nails.

BUILDING STAIRS

Unless your deck is within a step of the ground, you will need to build stairs. Building codes usually are quite strict about stair dimensions, although exterior stairs are often afforded more latitude than interior stairs.

Stair building lingo can be confusing at first. Rise is the vertical distance from one tread to the next; run is the horizontal depth of the tread. The total rise and total run are the overall vertical and horizontal measurements of the stairs.

For greatest stepping comfort, try to build deck stairs with a 6- to 7-inch rise and an 11- to 16-inch run. The large range in run distances is because you can use either two or three 2×6s for each tread. The deeper treads can be a safety feature when stairs are wet or covered with snow and ice.

Stairs that are 3 feet wide are comfortable and safe, and may be mandated by your local code. Use three stringers on 3-foot-wide stairs. Although you can get by with two stringers on narrower stairs, the time and cost of making that extra stringer are minimal. If you build wider stairs, add an additional stringer for every 2 feet of stair width.

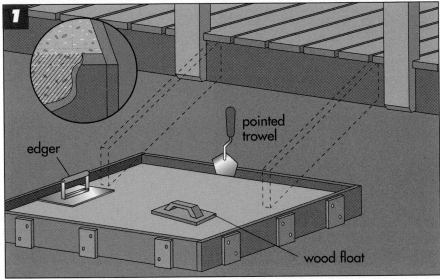

1. Prepare the concrete pad.
Excavate and build forms for a 4-inch concrete pad set on 6 inches of gravel. Mix and pour concrete. Screed the surface with a 2×4, then smooth it with a wood float. Run a pointed trowel between the concrete and form boards; follow with an edger. After an hour, smooth the concrete with a steel trowel. Or, prepare a bed of tamped gravel at least 6 inches deep. See page 744 for how to attach stringers to the footings.

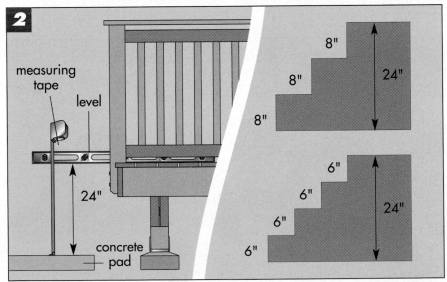

2. Find the rise.
Use a level to extend the deck to the spot where the stairs will land (usually the pad or gravel bed). Measure the total rise and divide by 7 (the height of an ideal rise). The result, rounded to the nearest whole number, is the ideal number of risers for the stairs. Now divide the total rise by the number of risers to determine the actual rise for each step. For example, assume the total rise is 24 inches; 24 divided by 7 is 3.4. Round 3.4 down to 3 and divide this into 24. The result (8 inches) is the rise for each step. An 8-inch rise is on the high side so you can take the option of rounding 3.4 up to 4, then dividing 4 into 24, for a more comfortable rise of 6 inches (with 4 risers rather than 3).

3

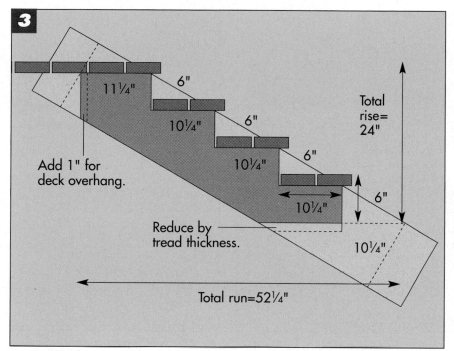

11¼"   6"

10¼"   6"

Add 1" for
deck overhang.

10¼"   6"

10¼"   6"

Total
rise=
24"

Reduce by
tread thickness.

10¼"   6"

10¼"

Total run=52¼"

3. Find the run.

If you're not constrained by space, choose a convenient, comfortable tread depth: Two 2×6s for each tread, with gaps between them for drainage, and a 1-inch overhang.

The resulting run is 10¼ inches. Estimate the length of a 2×10 or 2×12 stringer you'll need by measuring from where the stringer connects with the deck to the ground-level riser.

EXPERTS' INSIGHT

CHOOSING THE RIGHT LUMBER FOR STRINGERS

Stringers carry the weight of the stairs, so they need to be large and solid enough to perform their job. You may be able to get by with 2×10s for deck stringers, but 2×12s are always the safer choice.

Look for boards that are straight and relatively free of splits and knots. If the ends are split, cut away the split section before laying out the stringer. Check that no knots are loose. If they fall out after you build the stairs, they will not only be unsightly but may weaken the stringer significantly.

4

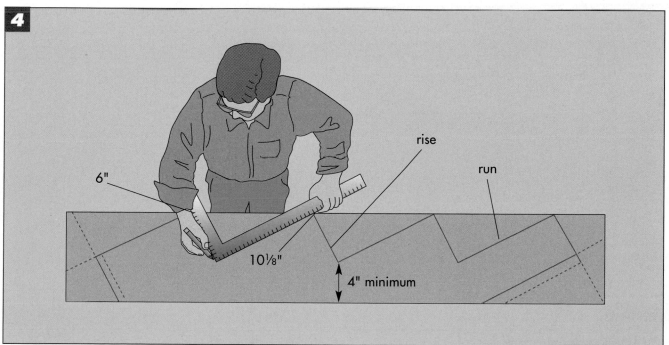

6"

rise

run

10⅛"

4" minimum

4. Make the stringers.

For 3-foot-wide stairs, cut three identical stringers. Lay out and cut the first one, then use it as a template to lay out the other two.

To lay out the stringer, place a framing square on a stringer so the 6-inch mark on the outside of the square's tongue and the 10⅛-inch mark on the outside of the square's blade both align with the top edge of the stringer. Mark the rise and run along the outside of the square. Move the square and repeat. Mark an additional cutoff of 1½ inches off the bottom and add the amount of the decking overhang at the top.

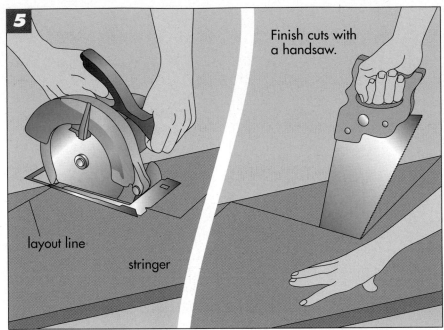

Finish cuts with
a handsaw.

layout line

stringer

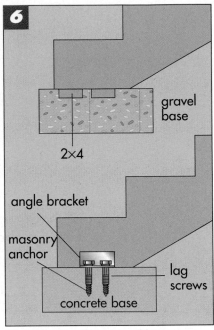

gravel
base

2×4

angle bracket

masonry
anchor

lag
screws

concrete base

5. Cut the stringers.

With the layout completely marked on the first stringer, carefully cut it out with a circular saw. Cut only up to the layout marks. Where the tread and riser meet, the circular saw blade won't cut all the way through. Finish the cuts with a handsaw. Set the stringer in place and check the accuracy of your layout. Once you're assured all the markings are correct, use the cut stringer as a template for cutting the others.

6. Attach stringers to footing.

On a gravel pad, attach two 36-inch 2×4s to the bottoms of the stringers and embed the 2×4s in the gravel. On a concrete pad, space outside stringers 36 inches apart, center the middle stringer, and attach with masonry anchors.

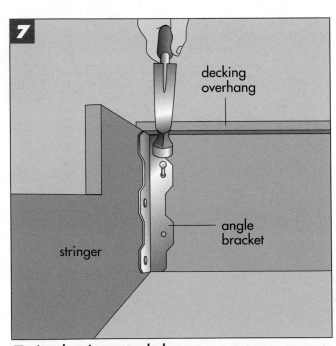

decking
overhang

angle
bracket

stringer

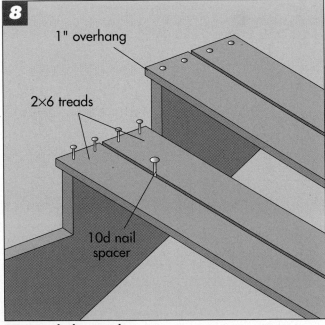

1" overhang

2×6 treads

10d nail
spacer

7. Attach stringers to deck.

Stringers must be installed straight and square. The top should be level with the top of the joist, slipping directly under the overhanging deck boards. Use angle brackets or framing anchors to attach stringers to the joist. As with any structural bracket, use only the fasteners recommended by the manufacturer.

8. Attach the treads.

Each tread is made of two pieces of 2×6 decking. Cut each 38 inches long to provide a 1-inch overhang on each of the outer stringers. Use a 10d nail to measure the gap between treads and between the back tread and the stringer. The treads should overhang the front of the stringers by 1 inch as well.

9

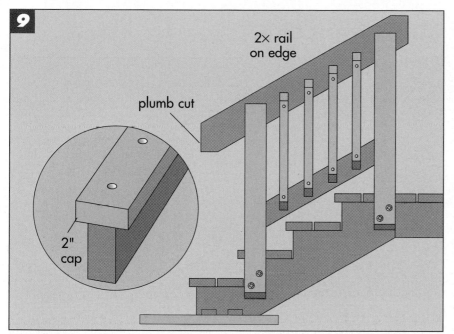

2× rail
on edge

plumb cut

2"
cap

9. Build the railing.

The stair railing should match the style of your deck's railing as much as possible. Use similar balusters, spaced the same distance apart. One important difference, however, is that the handrail must be easy to grasp. This can be accomplished by setting a 2× top rail on edge so it can be grasped. Even better, place a 2-inch-wide cap on the top rail for optimum safety. Prepare and fasten posts and balusters as you did for the deck railing. Make plumb cuts on the top rail.

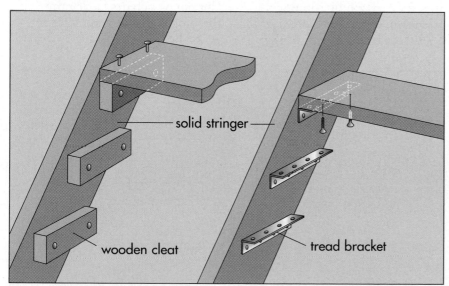

solid stringer

wooden cleat

tread bracket

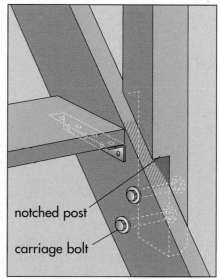

notched post

carriage bolt

Use a solid stringer alternative.

The strongest stairs are made with treads sitting on top of notched stringers. But some people don't care for the appearance, preferring to mask the tread ends with solid stringers. You still need to lay out stringers, but instead of cutting them, you install wooden cleats or tread brackets to the inside of the stringers. Once the stringers are attached to the deck, treads are cut to fit between the stringers and are fastened to the brackets or cleats. If you use this method on a wide stair, you should still prepare a notched middle stringer.

Notched posts on solid stringers.

Posts on solid-stringer stairs must be prepared differently as well. Notch the post if you like. Set it in place, checking for plumb, then mark an angled line where it touches the stringer (top and bottom). Cut the notch and fasten it with carriage bolts.

FRAMING A WRAPAROUND DECK

On a wraparound deck you should decide on your decking pattern before you begin framing. The most common solutions are shown here. Each one requires a different framing and foundation plan.

Decking run in two sections perpendicular to each other, offers a straightforward bit of visual interest and is usually the easiest to build. Decking that turns a corner (page 747) may be the most attractive, but it is trickier to frame. And laying the decking can be tricky as well, especially if you choose mitered decking. Decking that runs in the same direction (page 747) makes the entire deck look and feel like a unified whole. The framing is a bit unconventional, with joists running parallel to the house on one side and perpendicular to it on the other side. The construction, however, is no more complex than for a basic deck.

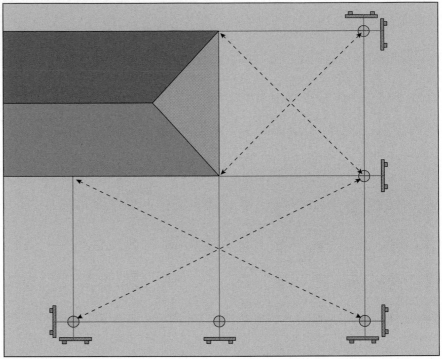

Lay out the deck.
Approach the layout for a wraparound deck as though you were building two separate decks. Split the L shape by running a mason's line from the corner of the house to a batter board. In this way, you can ensure each section is square by measuring the diagonals. For this layout, mason's lines mark the centers of posts. Check span charts to determine the proper spacing and sizes for posts, beams, and joists.

Run perpendicular decking.
This wraparound design is essentially two decks set next to each other. The ledger for one section continues beyond the house out to a post, and the parallel beam extends the same distance. At the point where the two sections meet, make sure there is an adequate nailing surface for all decking pieces. Avoid a situation where you need to drive a nail or screw closer than 1 inch from the end of a decking board. Beyond that, framing requirements, such as size and spacing of posts, beams, and joists, can be calculated separately for each section of the deck. This approach works especially well when you want to add a section to an existing deck.

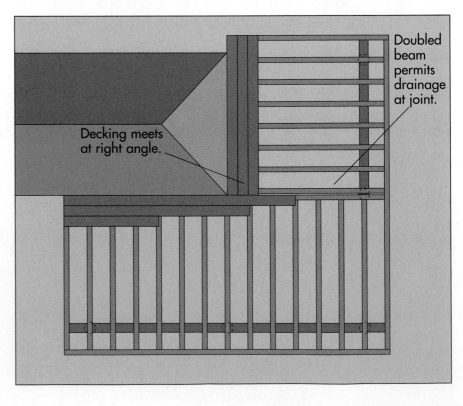

Decking meets at right angle.

Doubled beam permits drainage at joint.

Turn a corner in three ways.

Turning the corner with decking gives a deck a more handcrafted look. But plan carefully, or the point where the decking makes the turn may become a problem spot. Mitered decking is difficult to install because it's hard to keep every joint aligned perfectly. If you first install a decking spacer board along the miter angle, joints won't have to be perfect. A herringbone pattern is the easiest to install and creates a distinctive look.

It is critical that all decking pieces be supported adequately at each end. Doubled joists, with spacer blocks between them, solve this problem. You may not need to use this much lumber, however. For instance, instead of doubling the joists, you might add a 2×4 to each one to increase the nailing surface. You will need to cut many of the joists at a 45-degree angle and use angled joist hangers.

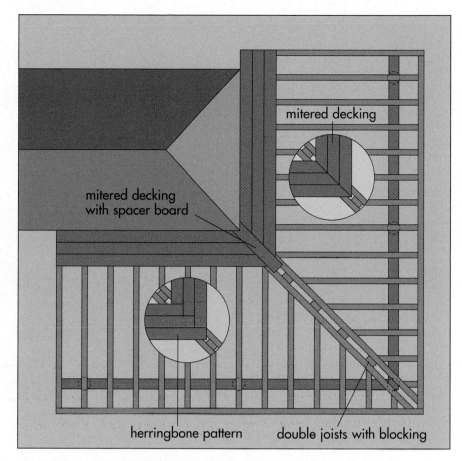

Use a continuous decking pattern.

Another attractive option is to run the decking on both sides of the house in the same direction. This continuity, however, requires a major adjustment in the underlying framing. Install conventional ledgers on both sides of the house. On one side, install a beam that runs the length of the deck. On the other side of the house, install shorter beams, running parallel with the first beam. You can attach these to the house with a second ledger. (Remember, beams must sit below the ledger.) But it may be easier to install footings and posts near the house. Lap the joists over the short beams. Plan ahead for how best to install the decking so joints between boards don't create an irregular pattern at the corner section. Usually, it is best to start with a piece that runs along the house for part of its length.

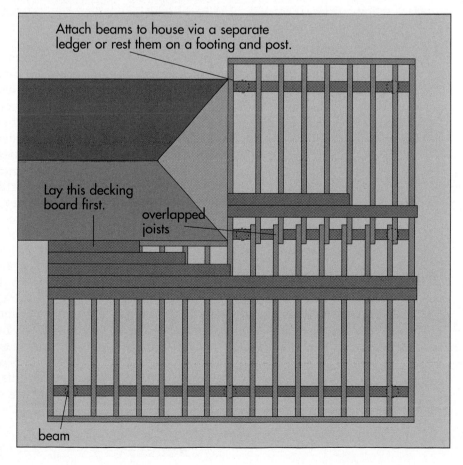

Let layout serve all deck levels.

Multilevel decks can be built as a series of independent decks set next to each other. Often, however, a more efficient approach is to let parts of the foundation and framing serve both levels simultaneously. In the example at right, the upper level is constructed as an individual deck. Posts supporting the upper-level beam also support the ledger for the lower level. When building the framing, it often works out well to step levels down by the width of one joist. If you are using 2×8s, that will give you a standard step rise; if you are using 2×6s, you will get a gentle step. The lower level could be expanded or offset by shifting post locations. In this example, the lower level doesn't require a railing, which adds to the distinctiveness of each level.

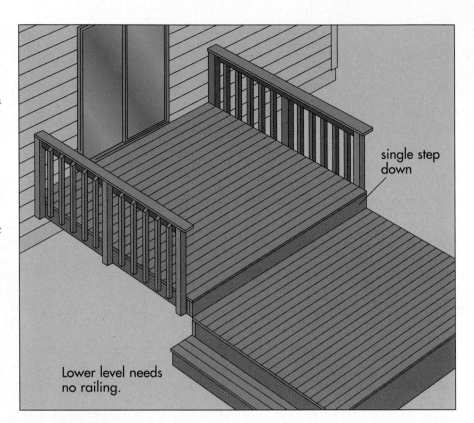

single step down

Lower level needs no railing.

EXPERTS' INSIGHT

ADDING OUTDOOR LIVING AREAS

Your family's lifestyle can change dramatically with the addition of a deck or patio. You'll find that a well-planned outdoor living area can take pressure off interior spaces by providing alternative spots for cooking, eating, and relaxing.

Thoughtful planning is well worthwhile; a master plan will preclude later regrets. Before you build, consider carefully whether you have adequately provided for three key components: outdoor living space, storage area, and a service area. Add a play area if children are involved.

Start with the outdoor living space. The slope of your lot will help you decide whether a deck is your best option. On flat lots, you have a complete range of choices among styles of decks and patios. If you must work on a slope, you may find that an elevated deck is the only practical idea. Study the area's relationship to the interior floor plan. You'll want convenient access, so take advantage of existing doors or consider installing a sliding glass door.

With these generalities in mind, plan the location of storage units to hold your yard and garden or recreational equipment.

The third ingredient is a service area. Make it large enough for garbage cans, firewood, potting benches, or whatever your family requires.

This bears repeating: Check with local zoning or building departments for restrictions before you get too attached to any potential plan. Many zoning regulations require outbuildings and decks to be a specified distance from lot lines. Be sure you don't build on a part of your lot where there's an easement or over an underground utility, such as a septic system.

Finally, plan for privacy and screening. Consider the plantings you have, those you want to add, and fences you might want to build.

With goals established, you're ready to work out details such as the size of your deck or patio, the materials to use, and the budget. With the know-how in this chapter, doing it yourself will yield worthwhile results you can enjoy for years.

Create framing level changes by using stacked boxes, ...

Stacked boxes are an easy way to change levels, but usually are cost efficient only for smaller levels. If the decking runs in the same direction, build the frame so each member rests directly above the underlying frame, as shown. Use toenailed deck screws or mending plates to hold the joists together. If the decking runs in different directions, build a framing box with the joists running in the opposite direction. You can build two modest-sized steps at the doorway with this approach by setting a small box (2×3 feet) on top of a larger box (4×6 feet).

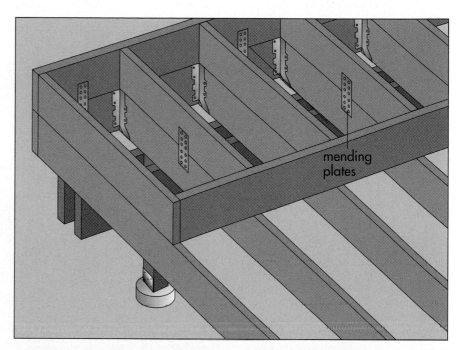

...using a beam as ledger, ...

To create a one-step level change, often the most efficient technique is to build the upper level so the joists and header joist rest on the beam with no overlap. Attach joist hangers to the beam to carry joists for the lower level. This method can be used to frame a succession of gradual level changes. For a larger height differential between levels, attach a ledger on the outside of the posts and proceed to frame the lower level. Add steps as necessary, perhaps using the stacked boxes method above.

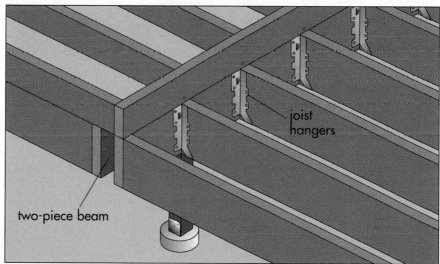

...or building individual decks.

Sometimes it makes the most sense to create level changes by building two or more individual decks. One level could be attached on one end to a ledger on the house, while the other could be freestanding. Each level has its own foundation and framing and is built to the standards required of a single deck. Typically, it's best not to tie the decks together with screws or bolts: Boards will crack and split if one footing settles differently from the other. The best approach often is to build two separate deck levels, then join them together with a set of stairs.

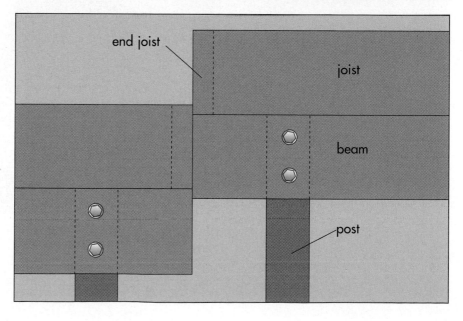

BUILDING FREESTANDING DECKS

A freestanding deck has no connection to the house and, therefore, can be constructed just about anywhere. You can build a freestanding deck adjoining the house, of course, if you don't mind adding a row of footings instead of a ledger board. Or you can install the deck in a remote part of the yard to take advantage of a great view or to add to its privacy. Use a series of freestanding decks built at different levels to create a gradual stairway.

A modular deck (pages 751–753) is the simplest of freestanding decks and needs no foundation. In fact, a freestanding deck may not need the substantial footings required for attached decks. If the footings for an attached deck do not extend below the frostline, boards could crack in the winter because the footings will rise up and the ledger will not. But a freestanding deck with footings above the frostline is in no such danger—all the footings will rise and fall together.

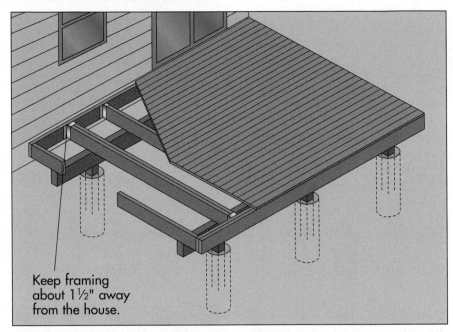

Keep framing about 1½" away from the house.

Create an independent foundation.
An elevated freestanding deck can be built following standard deck-building procedures. Instead of tying into the house's foundation through a ledger, however, a freestanding deck requires its own independent foundation. On a simple rectangular design, this requires that you double the number of footings and attach a beam on each row of posts.

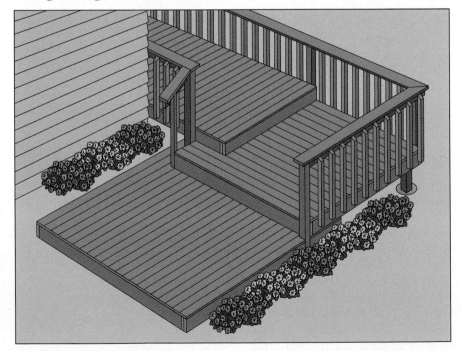

Combine attached and freestanding deck areas.
By setting a substantial part of a deck so it is separated clearly from the house, the transition from house to yard becomes more graceful. The lower portion of the above deck is separated from the house just enough to leave room for an attractive flower bed.

CREATING MODULAR DECKING

These simple structures, often called duckboards, are easy to build, and they can be combined into a myriad of shapes with an attractive parquet design. If you have a level yard and soil that is not soggy, they can last a long time. If you lay them on a firmly tamped bed of gravel, they will remain fairly stable.

If you are going to use modular decking in high-traffic areas or find the modules have more spring to the step than you'd prefer, add a 2×4 cleat to the center of each module as reinforcement.

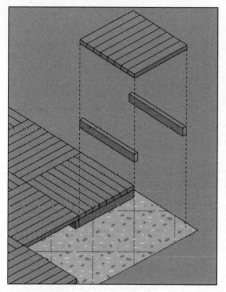

Combine basic modules.
A modular deck can be constructed in a weekend and installed on any level surface in your yard. It requires no connection to the house and no foundation. Add or subtract modules to suit your needs.

Mix and match modules.
With a bit of creativity, you may be able to think of several ways to combine modular construction with standard deck-building techniques. For example, here the modules form a path from the garage to the deck. If your needs or traffic patterns change over the years, it is a simple matter to pick up and rearrange the modules. You can even stack them to make low steps. Alternate the direction of the decking for a parquet effect, as shown, or lay them so the decking lines are continuous.

Add units to form any pattern.
Modular construction, by its nature, is versatile and adaptable. You can use the modular approach, for example, to build a large border around a flower bed. A larger deck could encompass several individual beds. The modular approach works particularly well for raised gardening beds. For noninvasive plants, simply arrange the modules around an open space. For larger plants or for a raised bed, build a simple planter box and butt the modules up to it.

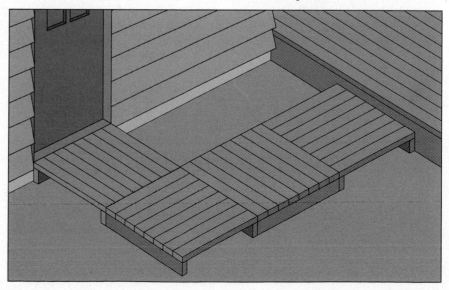

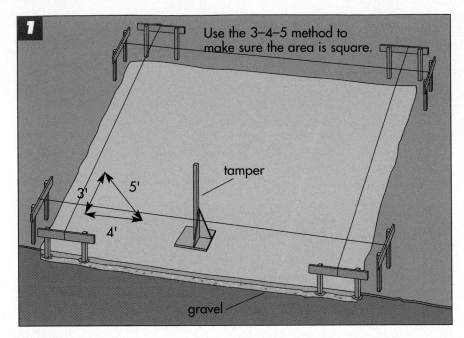

Use the 3–4–5 method to make sure the area is square.

tamper

3'   5'

4'

gravel

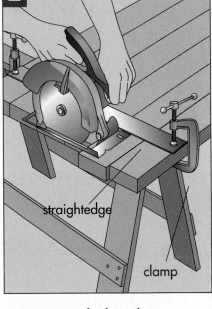

straightedge

clamp

1. Prepare the site.
Use batter boards and mason's lines to mark the outline of the area. Allow for a 3-inch border of sand around the perimeter of the deck. Use the 3–4–5 method (see page 726) to ensure a square layout. Remove the sod and soil to a depth of 5 inches (or more or less, depending on how high you want the deck to sit). Spread 3 inches of gravel on the ground, level and tamp it, then add 1½ inches of sand. Level and tamp again. For an extra-firm surface, rent a vibrating tamper.

2. Gang cut the boards.
For each module, you need ten 29-inch pieces of pressure-treated 2×4s. Make the job go faster by setting several 2×4s edge to edge on sawhorses, then cutting them in one pass with a circular saw. Use a straightedge to clamp the boards and guide the saw.

Money $ Saver

SAVE THE SOD
The sod and topsoil you remove to make room for your deck can be added to your compost pile. Be sure to place the grass side down to stop the grass from growing.

Before you do so, however, think about some other uses you may have for it. Perhaps part of your yard would benefit from transplanted sod—an out-of-use garden bed might need just such a boost. Use a straight-bladed shovel and cut the sod in careful rectangles to pull up sections of sod that can be laid out easily in another location. Be sure to pull up as many of the roots as possible as you work.

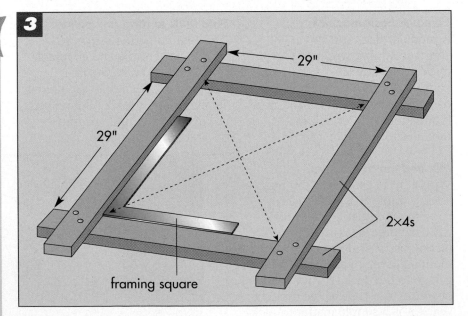

29"

29"

2×4s

framing square

3. Build a jig.
To ensure each module is identical and perfectly square, make this jig out of 2×4s. Use four boards, each about 3 to 4 feet long. Make sure the inside edges are straight and measure 29×29 inches. Align the corners with a framing square before nailing the boards together. Use several nails at each corner. The jig doesn't have cross bracing, so be sure to check it for square from time to time.

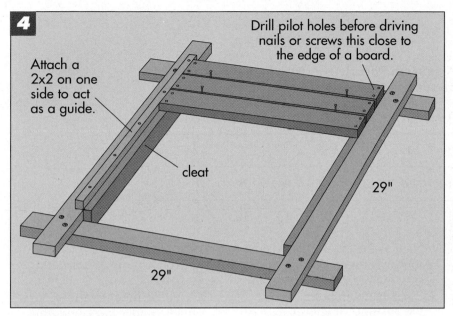

4

Attach a 2x2 on one side to act as a guide.

Drill pilot holes before driving nails or screws this close to the edge of a board.

cleat

29"

29"

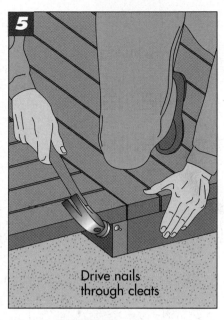

5

Drive nails through cleats

4. Build the modules.

Set the jig on a solid, flat surface, such as a concrete driveway. Each module requires eight decking pieces and two bottom cleats. Set two boards on end at opposite sides of the jig, as shown, to act as nailing cleats. Attach the rest of the boards with 12d galvanized nails or 2½-inch decking screws. Space the boards with the 12d nails, making a ⅛-inch gap between boards. You may need to adjust the spacing to make the last piece come out even with the end of the cleats.

5. Set the modules.

Lay the modules in place, alternating the direction of the boards if you want a parquet effect. Attach the modules to each other by drilling pilot holes and driving in galvanized nails or decking screws at an angle.

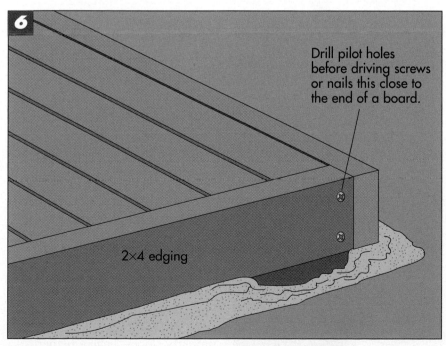

6

Drill pilot holes before driving screws or nails this close to the end of a board.

2×4 edging

6. Add the edging.

Once you have assembled the modules in a pattern, you may want to install 2×4s around the edges of the deck to add a finishing touch. Cut two 2×4s to fit flush with the decking and install them on opposite ends. Remove enough sand to allow the edging to rest flush with the deck surface. Then cut two more 2×4s long enough to overlap the ends of the installed edging. Replace the sand and tamp around the edges.

EXPERTS' INSIGHT

WOOD PATH

These simple modules can serve another function. Set them end to end to form a wood path or sidewalk. The modules are considerably easier to build and install than a concrete walkway or a brick sidewalk. Use the wood path to connect the house to the garage, or the house to a freestanding deck. Use the jig shown in steps 3 and 4 to build 29-inch-wide units, or adjust the size of the jig for a narrower version. With a bit of excavation, the modules could be set to rest at grade. In areas with cold climates, it may make sense to store the modules in the garage during the winter.

HOW HIGH CAN YOU GO?

**Maximum Post Height, Based on Load Area
(beam spacing × post spacing, in square feet)**

Post Size	36	48	60	72	84	96	108	120
4×4	10'	9'	8'	7'	6'	5'		
4×6	14'	12'	11'	10'	9'	8'	7'	
6×6	17'	16'	15'	14'	13'	12'		

This table presents standard height limitations for Southern pine and Douglas fir (graded #2 and better), the most commonly available species in pressure-treated lumber. To determine an acceptable post length for your deck, figure the "load area." Multiply the joist span (in feet) by the beam span (in feet) to determine the load area (in square feet). The joist span is defined as the spacing between beams or between the beam and ledger; the beam span equals the distance between posts.

For example, if your deck has joists spanning 8 feet and a beam spanning 6 feet, the load area on the deck equals 48. Look under the appropriate column in the table and you will find you can use 4×4 posts up to 9 feet long. If your deck has a higher elevation, use bigger posts. (See page 716 for more on joist and beam spans.)

The above figures will be acceptable under most building codes, but always check your local codes before starting work. Of course, you can always use larger posts than are required. On elevated decks, 6×6 posts often look better than 4×4s, even if they aren't needed.

EXPERTS' INSIGHT

SAFE HEIGHTS

■ The maximum acceptable length of posts that you can use on a given deck depends on several factors, including the size of the post, wood species and quality, the sizes and spans of joists and beams, and local building codes and regulations.

■ Higher decks require larger posts spaced closer together and resting on larger foundations.

■ If the posts on your deck also will support a substantial overhead structure, check with a professional or your local building department officials about the best size to use.

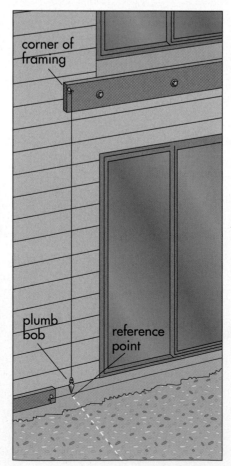

Locate the footings.
It's crucial to locate footings correctly so the posts they support will be exactly plumb as they reach far upward to support an elevated deck. Begin by accurately locating a reference point for the entire framing structure.

The easiest way is to install the ledger board, then hang a plumb bob from the corner. This identifies the location of the corner of the framing, so make the correct calculations to figure the true reference point for the footings.

To lay out the actual location of the first footing, use the 3–4–5 method (see page 726) to extend a mason's line out from the house at exactly 90 degrees. If your property slopes, have a helper hold a board with a level on it, with its end resting on the ground where the footing will be. When the outward measurement is correct and the board is plumb in both directions, you will have the correct location.

BRACING TALL POSTS

Building codes often require decks with posts taller than 6 feet to have lateral bracing. Your local code will dictate if deck posts must be braced. Most bracing can be made with 2×4s; but for braces more than 8 feet long, use 2×6s. Secure braces with ⅜-inch lag screws with washers, or carriage bolts with nuts and washers.

Freestanding decks should be braced if they are more than 3 feet above ground. Decks that may be exposed to earthquakes, high winds, or especially heavy loads have stricter bracing requirements. Although it may not be required, bracing strengthens any deck and takes little extra time or expense. Solid skirting or a high-quality lattice may take the place of bracing under some codes.

EXPERTS' INSIGHT

BRACING FOR DISASTER

Bracing is one construction practice that nonprofessionals sometimes don't understand and, thus, too often overlook. The posts on elevated decks, just like the walls of most framed houses, must be secured laterally to resist climatic and load forces. Without bracing, excessive winds against the side of a house could cause the walls to sag. On most houses, the bracing is provided by sheathing. But most decks don't have sheathing, so additional bracing is necessary to keep the posts from swaying. The taller the posts, the more important the bracing is to the structure.

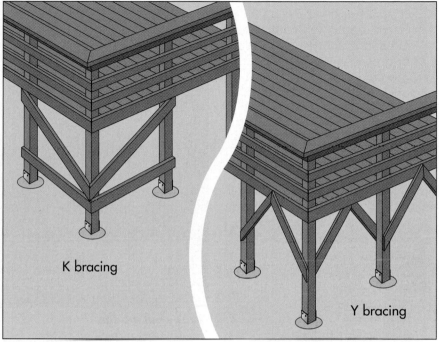

K bracing

Y bracing

Brace decks between posts.
Bracing styles are often named after the letters they form. The most common types are K and Y, above, and X and W, below. The strongest bracing ties posts to beams. Post-to-post braces usually must be longer because they must span from one post to the next. The style of bracing you use may depend on how accessible you want the space beneath the deck to be.

To prevent rot and give the braces a neater appearance, angle the end cuts so each end is vertical when the brace is installed. When two braces meet on a post, leave a small gap between them to allow for drainage.

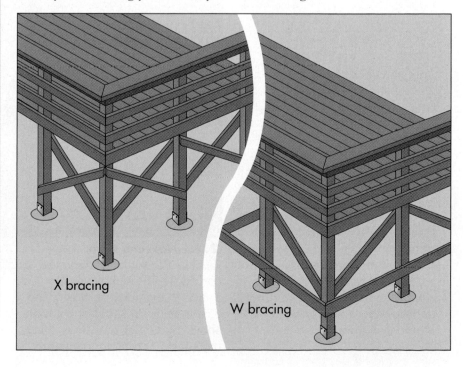

X bracing

W bracing

LAYING BRICK PATIOS IN SAND

Set bricks or other paving materials in a well-tamped bed of sand and you'll have a flexible but firm patio surface that will stand up to years of use, even in areas subject to frost. A brick-in-sand patio is an ideal do-it-yourself project. But carrying the bricks and digging, smoothing, and tamping the patio surface involves hard work that will put a strain on your back. Don't tackle it by yourself; have helpers on hand.

YOU'LL NEED

TIME: Several days to dig and lay an 80-square-foot patio.
SKILLS: Measuring, leveling, laying out square lines, cutting bricks, setting bricks.
TOOLS: Round-point shovel, spade, line or water level, hose, carpenter's level, hammer, brick set, baby sledgehammer, screed, circular saw with masonry blade, broom, rubber mallet.

EXPERTS' INSIGHT

HOW MUCH BEDDING?

Adequate bedding is essential for a patio to remain smooth and level for years to come. If you live in an area with periods of heavy rain or winters with below-freezing temperatures, a brick-in-sand patio should rest on a bed of 1 to 2 inches of tamped sand that, in turn, rests on 4 to 6 inches of tamped gravel. In dry climates with soils that have a heavy clay, sand, or rock content, a sand base alone may be sufficient. Check with your building department to see what is required in your area.

1

For a square corner, rest bricks on a concrete foundation.

Use upright soldiers to make a curved corner.

Use 2×4 lumber for edging and section dividers.

1. Lay out the site.
Use the techniques on pages 726–727 to lay out the site. Select the style of edging and the brick pattern you want. Use the 3-4-5 method to establish square corners and use a line level or water level to establish the correct slope, about ¼ inch per running foot. If your yard already slopes a bit, but not more than ½ inch per foot, you can follow its contour so you will not have to fill in and resod the lawn after building the patio.

2

Use hose or a line-and-stake compass to make curved edges.

2. Excavate and tamp.
Remove the sod and dig to the correct depth. Remove roots 1 inch in diameter or larger. The paving material should be 1 inch above grade. Dig out the soil for the edging and patio to a depth that leaves room for adequate bedding material. Adjust the surface height by using more or less bedding material. Tamp the ground firmly, especially if you have not reached undisturbed claylike soil.

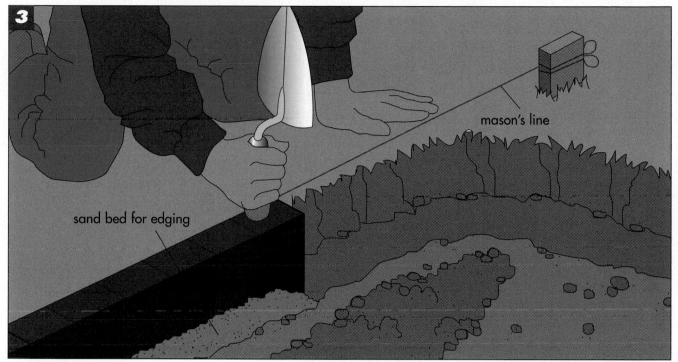

3. Install the edging.
Stretch a mason's line to serve as a guide for the height and alignment of the edging. For the brick soldiers shown here, place a small amount of sand in the bottom of the excavation and tap the bricks with the handle of your trowel to set them at the height you want. Fill around the sides of each brick with sand as you work. At this point, backfill with just enough soil to keep the bricks from leaning outward.

TOOLS TO USE

PREPARING THE GROUND WITH A TAMPER

It is important that the ground under the sand and gravel bed be firm. In most cases, that means tamping each layer. For small areas, you can use a scrap piece of 4×4 or a fence post for tamping. Or, make a tamper from plywood and 2× lumber like the one shown on page 631. Small hand tampers can be rented, also.

For large patios, consider renting a vibrating power tamper. It's a challenge to transport a large vibrating tamper to the work site, but once you get one there, it speeds up the tamping process dramatically.

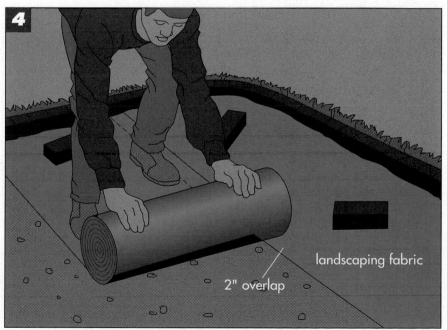

4. Cover with landscaping fabric.
If your bedding is only sand, cover the tamped soil with landscaping fabric before adding the sand. The fabric reduces weed growth, but allows water to filter through into the soil. For a sand and gravel bed, lay the fabric on top of the tamped gravel. Overlap the sheets about 2 inches. Then spread, smooth, and tamp the sand.

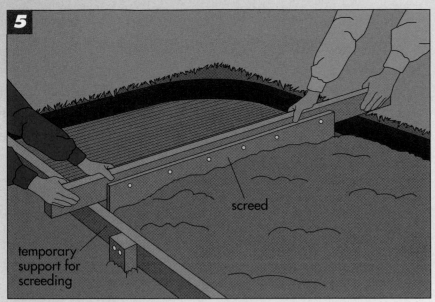

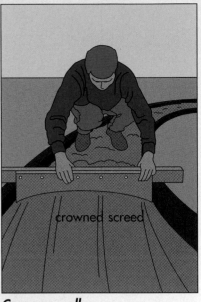

5. Screed the sand.

Shovel in the sand to roughly the correct height. Dampen it and tamp it down. Draw a straightedge across the sand to smooth it out. For this purpose, make a screed out of a straight 2×4 with a length of 1×4 or 1×6 nailed to it. If the patio is wider than 8 feet, you will need to install temporary supports for screeding. With a helper, work the screed back and forth as you move it sideways to achieve a level surface.

Crown a walk.

When screeding a walkway, give it a slight crown, so water will run off easily. Make a screed with a curved cut, as shown. Pull it across the edging or forms as you would with a flat screed.

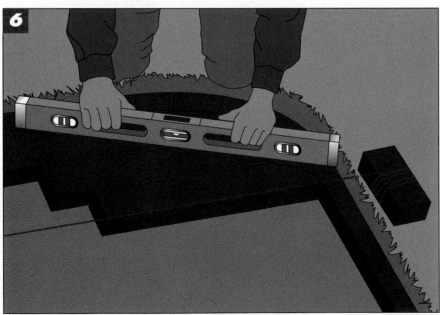

6. Lay the bricks.

Start in one corner and begin laying the bricks or pavers. Set them straight down rather than sliding them into place so as not to disturb the level sand surface. Set each brick snugly against its neighbors and tap each one gently with a rubber mallet or block of wood. Use a level to check for proper slope and to make sure the bricks are all at the same height. If a brick is too low, pick it up, trowel in more sand, and tap it into place until it rests at the correct height.

7. Check for straightness.

Every third or fourth course, use a taut string line as a guide to make sure you are laying the bricks in straight lines and at the proper elevation. Do not step or kneel on the bricks as you work: Use a piece of plywood as a kneeler.

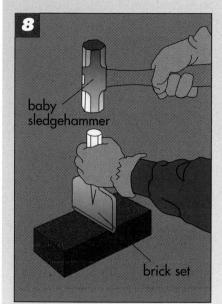

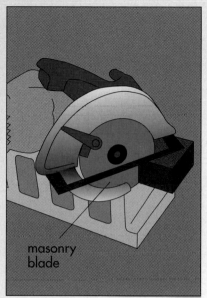

8. Cut bricks to fit.

To cut a brick or paver by hand, score it all the way around by tapping a brick set with a baby sledgehammer. Place the brick on a bed of sand or loose soil several inches deep and give it a sharp blow with the brick set.

For a cleaner-looking cut, use a circular saw with a masonry cutting blade. Be sure to wear gloves and eye protection.

9. Fill the joints.

Spread a thin layer of fine sand over the patio surface and gently sweep it back and forth so the sand fills the joints. Be especially careful at first not to dislodge the bricks. Once the joints are full of sand, hose off the entire surface with a fine spray to wash away the remaining sand particles. This compacts the sand and forces it into the joints. Repeat this process, sweeping in more sand and spraying, until the sand is level with the top of the bricks.

EXPERTS' INSIGHT

FILLING JOINTS WITH THE DRY MORTAR METHOD

You can make your patio more permanent by using dry mortar mix rather than plain sand in the joints. For this method, leave $\frac{1}{2}$-inch spaces between the bricks when you set them in place. Sweep the dry mortar mix into the joints, remove excess mortar, and sprinkle the surface gently with water until the mix is wet. Repeat the sprinkling process twice at 15-minute intervals to ensure you have enough water in the mortar. The mortar will harden within a few hours and cure in a week. If your ground heaves with the frost, the mortar lines will crack.

INSTALLING A SEMICIRCULAR BRICK PATIO

A semicircular patio looks complicated, but actually it requires little more skill than installing a rectangular patio. In fact, because only the central core requires cut brick, you may need to cut fewer bricks than you would for other designs.

As with all masonry work, have the bricks or pavers delivered close to the site to minimize lifting and hauling.

YOU'LL NEED

TIME: 2 days to install a 200-square-foot patio.
SKILLS: Ability to lay out a semicircular pattern, cutting brick.
TOOLS: Round-point shovel, rake, tamper, mason's line, rebar, carpenter's level, hammer, screed, brick set, baby sledgehammer, broom, hose.

Cut brick needed here.

EXPERTS' INSIGHT

OTHER OPTIONS FOR CURVED EDGINGS

This project uses ¼-inch hardboard as a temporary edging for the patio. For a permanent edging, you may be able to find redwood bender board, which is about ¼ inch thick and 3½ inches wide. Or ask your lumberyard to rip clear 1×4 redwood along its thickness, leaving you with two pieces about ⁵⁄₁₆ inch thick. If you soak the redwood in water for a couple of hours, it will bend easily without cracking. Other permanent edgings include steel ribbon, plastic, flagstone, poured concrete, and bricks.

1. Install the edging.
Rig up a compass using a stake and a piece of rebar tied to a mason's line. Using the compass as a guide, and keeping the rebar vertical, pound in stakes evenly spaced about every 2 feet. Excavate to a 4-inch depth, removing all organic material.

Set the hardboard edging in place, bending it and leveling it as you go. Attach it to the stakes with screws so it is 1 inch above grade. Check for a smooth curve. Because stakes are difficult to install accurately, you may need to unscrew the edging at some points and use shims to correct the curve.

2. Screed the site.

Tamp the soil, then cover the site with landscaping fabric. Fill the area with crushed gravel and sand, or sand alone, until it is 1 to 2 inches below the edging. Rake it as smooth and level as you can.

Notch one end of a straight 2×4 screed so that it rides along the edging as you smooth the base. The depth of the notch should equal the thickness of the bricks or pavers. Install a 2×4 pivot base for the screed, taking care to stake it so the top edge of the screed will be level. Screed the sand, tamp it down with a hand or power vibrating tamper, then screed again.

Refer to pages 756–759 for detailed instructions on laying a patio surface.

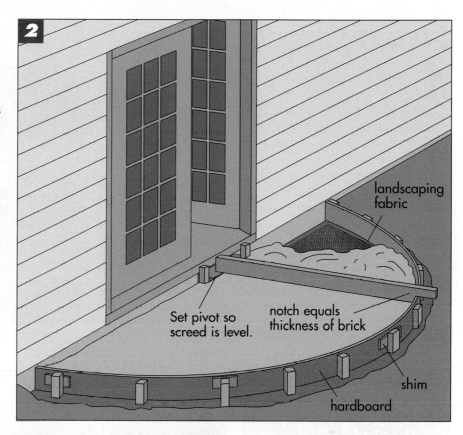

landscaping fabric

Set pivot so screed is level.

notch equals thickness of brick

shim

hardboard

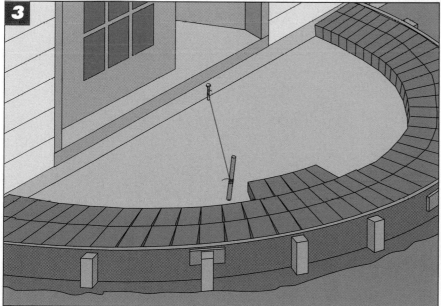

3. Install the bricks or pavers.
Start at the outside of the form and lay all the border bricks. Then work inward, completing each course before moving on to the next. Once you've laid several courses, use pieces of plywood on the bricks as kneelers; avoid kneeling or standing directly on the bricks. Every few courses, check your work by scribing an arc with your homemade compass. The joints between the bricks or pavers will be slightly pie-shaped and larger at the end nearest the edging. After the bricks are laid, sweep extra-fine sand into the joints, moisten with a mist or fine spray, and sweep in more sand where needed. Remove the hardboard edging and fill in soil firmly around the perimeter.

CAUTION!
MAKE THE BASE FIRM
■ Take extra care when installing and tamping down the subsurface of your patio. The curved edge of a patio like this one is especially prone to sinking and buckling over the years because it is not held firmly in place. Even the permanent edgings described on page 760 are not extremely strong.
■ You may want to dig a little deeper near the perimeter and install some gravel as well as sand. If you use a hand tamper, do a thorough job; take turns with a helper so you don't get tired. The best way to ensure a solid subsurface is to rent a power vibrating tamper.

LAYING FLAGSTONE SURFACES

The simplest method of installing a flagstone patio is to place the stones on well-tamped soil. Such a patio surface is quick to install; however, you'll need to readjust settled stones every year.

The flagstones should be at least ¾ inch thick or they will crack. Purchase stones of a fairly uniform thickness so they will be easy to lay evenly. If you choose a combination of large, medium, and small stones, you'll be able to make creative patterns more easily.

YOU'LL NEED

TIME: 1 day to excavate and lay a 100-square-foot patio.
SKILLS: A willingness to keep trying stones for the right fit.
TOOLS: Shovel, tamper, rake, brick set, baby sledge, hose.

EXPERTS' INSIGHT

OTHER METHODS OF LAYING FLAGSTONE

You can lay flagstones in a sand bed, as you would a brick or paver surface (see pages 756–759), by simply filling the joints with sand or soil, tamping it in gently, and allowing grass or moss to grow in the joints.

Or, you can cover a concrete slab with flagstone, laying it in mortar as you would stone or tile veneer (see pages 680–681). If you use this method, be sure to dry-lay the stones before mixing the mortar so you can set them in place quickly. Otherwise, you'll have a mess on your hands as you try various stones to see if they fit.

1. Lay out the perimeter.
Flagstone patio surfaces look best if they don't have sharp edges. One way to create graceful curves is with a water hose. "Charge" the hose by closing the nozzle and turning on the water. This makes the hose less flexible so you can form it into curves easily. Lay out the hose in the shape you choose and pour flour or sand all along its length. When you remove the hose, you'll have a clear line marking the excavation area.

2. Excavate and tamp.
Dig up the sod. Remove all significant organic material, including tree roots ½ inch thick or larger. If you don't, the patio will settle unevenly as the roots rot. If this means you have to dig deeper than the thickness of the stones, fill in low spots with sand or soil.

Rake the area level and tamp the soil firmly with a hand tamper or use a power vibrating tamper for larger areas. Fill in and retamp low spots. Install edging, if desired, before you lay the stones.

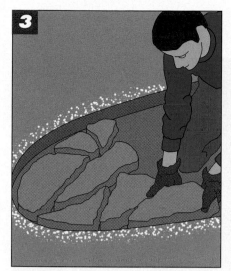

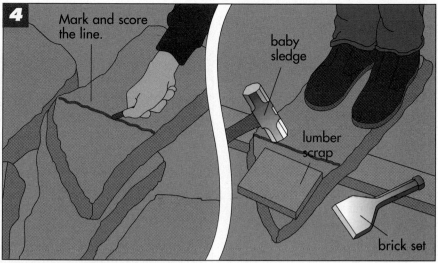

3. Lay the stones in a pattern.
Start with large stones around the perimeter. If a stone is too high, pick it up and dig out some soil; if it's too low, add some soil or sand beneath it. Test each stone to make sure it does not rock. Work slowly and take breaks; this kind of labor can harm your back even if you do not feel a strain.

4. Cut stones where necessary.
Wherever possible, use uncut stones. When you have to cut a stone, lay one stone over the one it will adjoin and trace its outline with chalk, a pencil, or a scratching tool.

Use a brick set and baby sledgehammer to score the line, making a groove about ⅛ inch

deep. Set the stone on top of a scrap piece of wood. For large stones, have someone stand on the other end. Split the stone with a single blow from the sledge. If the scrap piece is large enough to use elsewhere, protect it with a lumber scrap. You may have to make more than one split if you need to make a curved edge on a stone.

MEASUREMENTS

PLEASING PATTERNS

■ The trick to a professional-looking flagstone surface is keeping the gaps between stones consistent. Test your gaps with a scrap piece of wood; a piece of ½-inch plywood works well.

■ Mix the sizes of the flagstones evenly. Make separate piles of small, medium, and large stones. Select from the piles alternately so you won't end up with a lot of small stones in one corner of the patio and big ones in another.

■ Keep trying; there's no shortcut to making a pleasing pattern. You'll have to keep trying different configurations and occasionally cut a stone to maintain good-looking gaps.

5. Fill the joints.
Shovel dirt into the gaps between the stones, taking care not to get too much on the stones. Wet the patio surface with a fine spray, cleaning the stones while thoroughly wetting the soil. Fill in

low spots, spray again, and repeat until you have level-looking joints that are about ⅛ inch below the surface of the stones. Plant the gaps with grass seed, moss, or a low-growing groundcover to discourage weeds from growing.

LAYING A CONCRETE PATIO SUBSTRATE

Patios made of bricks or concrete pavers can be installed dry, on a bed of well-tamped sand. In areas with warm climates, you can set thick tiles the same way. But in most places, an outdoor tile surface needs to rest on a solid substrate of concrete.

Installing a new concrete slab is a major undertaking. Talk with your building inspector and find out the requirements for your area; these regulations are there to ensure that a slab will survive in your climate. In areas with severe winters, it is important to lay a well-tamped bed of gravel before pouring the concrete, so that water can drain away before it has a chance to freeze and crack your concrete surface.

Here we show you how to install a surface that is smooth enough to receive tile. If you want smooth, finished concrete, hire a concrete finisher; this is a skill that takes time to learn. If the prospect of building forms and pouring concrete is daunting, hire a contractor to handle that part of the job for you. Do not tile over an existing concrete patio without first examining it,then preparing it (see page 767).

YOU'LL NEED

TIME: With two helpers, one day to excavate, half a day to build forms, and a day to pour and finish the concrete.
SKILLS: Measuring and cutting wood, testing for square, driving stakes, fastening with nails or screws, screeding, finishing concrete (a special skill—have an experienced finisher at least give you advice).
TOOLS: Hammer, circular saw, carpenter's level, shovels, wheelbarrows, rake, screed, bull float or darby, broom, concrete finishing trowels.

1. Excavate the site.
Use mason's line and stakes to mark the perimeter and height of the new slab. Allow for the slab to slope down away from the house ¼ inch every running foot. Remove the sod and topsoil to reach the desired depth. If you want to use the sod elsewhere, undercut it horizontally about 2 inches beneath the surface and cut it into easy-to-handle sections. Save enough to resod around the edges of the new slab. If you plan to place gravel or sand beneath the slab, excavate at least 5 inches deep. Check the depth from time to time as you dig by laying a straight 2×4 on edge so its top barely touches the mason's line.

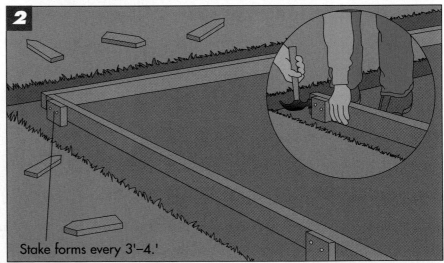

Stake forms every 3'–4.'

2. Install the forms.
Use straight 2×4s or 2×6s for the forms (depending on the desired slab thickness). Anchor the forms by driving 2×4 stakes, and pounding two double-headed nails through the stakes and into the form. Place your foot against the opposite side of the forms to make nailing easier. Be sure the tops of the forms are level with or above the tops of the stakes. Support each board with foot-long stakes every 3 to 4 feet. Make sure that the forms are square and properly sloped away from the house.

Divide a large slab.

Roll reinforcing mesh out, and cut it to fit. Adding dividers on a large patio allows you to pour and finish manageable amounts of concrete. If the dividers will be temporary, use any straight length of lumber. If you plan to leave the divider in as part of the slab, use pressure-treated lumber or redwood. At right, two 2×2s sandwich the mesh, keeping it at the right height for maximum effectiveness.

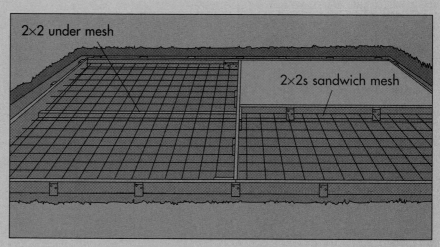

2×2 under mesh

2×2s sandwich mesh

Protect permanent dividers.

Install permanent dividers every 12 feet. Brush on a coat of wood sealer to enhance rot resistance. Put masking tape on the top edges to keep wet concrete from staining the wood and to avoid scratching the forms when you screed. Drive interior stakes 1 inch below the top of the permanent dividers so they will not be visible once the concrete is poured.

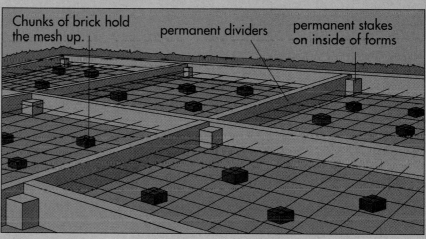

Chunks of brick hold the mesh up.

permanent dividers

permanent stakes on inside of forms

Position the ramp to clear the form.

3. Transport the concrete on ramps.
Mix your concrete as near to the site as possible; do not use curing compounds. Or have the ready-mix truck park as close as is safe. (A concrete truck weighs enough to crack sidewalks and driveways.) Wet concrete is heavy; keep wheelbarrow loads small enough to handle. To cross soft soil or lawns, lay a walkway of 2×10 or 2×12 planks. Build ramps over the forms so you do not disturb them. Use two or more wheelbarrows to keep the job moving.

4. Dump and move the concrete.
Start dumping concrete in the farthest corner of the forms. Dump it in mounds that reach ½ inch or so above the top of the form. It helps to have one person working a shovel while others run the wheelbarrows. The shoveler directs the wheelbarrow handlers and tells them where to dump the concrete. Wear gloves and heavy boots that fit snugly. Pace your efforts because you'll be moving a lot of concrete before the pour is completed.

5. Pull up reinforcing mesh.

While pouring the concrete, use a hoe, rake, or shovel to pull the wire mesh up into the concrete. For the greatest strength, keep the mesh positioned halfway between the bottom of the excavation and the finished surface of the slab. Watch that the mesh doesn't get pushed against the form at any point. Keep it 1 to 2 inches away from all forms.

6. Tamp concrete to remove air pockets.

For best results, the concrete should adhere to the forms and dividers and contain no air pockets. Run a shovel or rebar up and down along the inside edge of all forms and tap the sides of the forms with a hammer. Be sure to check that all corners are filled in and tamped adequately.

7. Screed with a straightedge.

Begin screeding (leveling) as soon as you've filled the first 3 or 4 feet of the length of the form. Keep both ends of the screed—a straight 2×4—pressed down on the top of the form while moving it back and forth in a sawing motion and drawing it toward the unleveled concrete. If depressions occur, fill in with concrete and screed again.

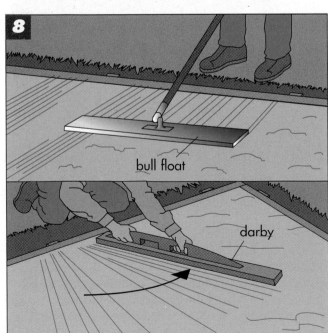

8. Float the surface.

Screed a second time, to make sure the surface is level. To smooth the surface, run a bull float in long, back-and-forth motions, slightly raising its leading edge so it does not dig into the concrete. If you use a darby, work in large, sweeping arcs.

9. Broom the finish.

For a smooth finish, professionals use a steel trowel. For a tiling finish, a broom finish is fine. Dampen the broom, and pull it only—do not push it. Have a brick or piece of 2×4 handy so you can knock the broom now and then to keep it clean.

PREPARING A CONCRETE SURFACE

You can tile over an existing concrete patio that's in good condition as long as it is at least 3 inches thick, sloped to allow water to drain off, and free of serious cracks. If the patio has a crack that keeps growing every year, or if one side of the crack is higher than the other, then it has structural problems. Don't tile over a slab in such a condition. Also, see that the slab is sitting slightly above ground level and is cleaned of any oil, dirt, and curing compounds.

YOU'LL NEED

TIME: An hour for most patches.
SKILLS: Spreading patching compound smoothly.
TOOLS: Concrete trowel, mason's trowel, 2×4, grinding tool, hose, stiff brush.

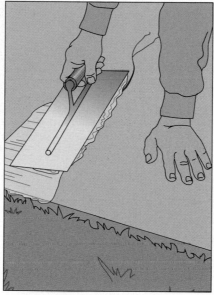

Patch cracks.
Fill small cracks or other irregularities with a concrete patching compound. Latex and epoxy compounds work well. Or use sand-mix concrete mixed with latex additive.

Fill in low spots.
Use a straightedge to locate low spots on a patio. Screed a patching or self-leveling compound over the low spots to create a flat surface. Finish with a trowel and/or broom to match the surrounding surface.

Repair edges.
If concrete is broken along the edges of the patio, chip away any loose concrete, clean, and wet the area. Braced a board along the damaged area, then fill with patching compound or fresh mortar. Smooth with a trowel and allow to set.

Roughen the surface.
If the patio has a smooth, steel-troweled finish, you will have to roughen the surface before tiling. Use a grinding tool with an abrasive wheel; or a tool-rental store may have a special tool for the job.

Clean the surface.
Scrub the surface with water and a stiff brush. Use a degreaser to remove oil and grease stains. If the patio is smooth and dirty, rent a power washer with at least 4,000 psi to clean and roughen the surface simultaneously.

LAYING PATIO TILE

An outdoor tile surface comes under a good deal of stress, so use the best-quality materials available for each step. Talk with your tile dealer about specific products that will perform best outdoors. Don't give water any chance to enter or hide beneath your tiled surface. Pack the grout joints as tightly as possible, then seal them carefully. Renew the grout sealer and caulk or sealant in expansion joints regularly.

YOU'LL NEED

TIME: About a day to install 100 square feet of tile; a few hours 1 to 2 days later to grout it.
SKILLS: Cutting and installing tile.
TOOLS: Notched trowel, snap cutter or wet saw, rubber mallet, grouting float, sponge.

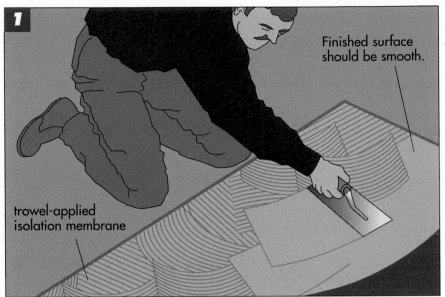

1. Apply an isolation membrane.

A trowel-applied isolation membrane is a caulklike substance that never fully hardens. It forms a layer that separates the tile from the patio, making it less likely that cracks in the concrete will translate to the grout and tile. Apply it with the notched side of the trowel, then smooth it with the flat side.

2. Dry-set the tiles.

Allow the isolation membrane to cure. Lay the tiles in a dry run (see pages 680–681) over at least part of the surface before mixing any adhesive; this is particularly important if you will be setting tiles in a pattern. If the patio is slightly out-of-square, dry-setting gives you a chance to judge how best to arrange and cut tiles.

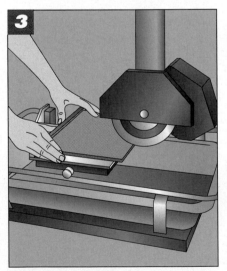

3. Use a wet saw.

For thick tile or stone, or to cut inside corners accurately, rent a wet saw. It quickly and cleanly slices through the hardest of materials, even granite. To keep the blade from getting dull, keep water running on it at all times.

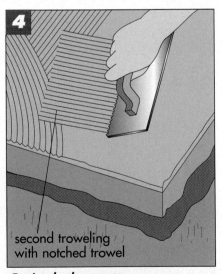

4. Apply the mortar.

Use thin-set mortar mixed with a liquid latex additive. Apply the mortar in two steps. Trowel on a smooth base coat, about ½ inch thick. Then comb the surface with the notched side of the trowel, taking care that the notches do not penetrate through to the concrete base. Use long, sweeping strokes.

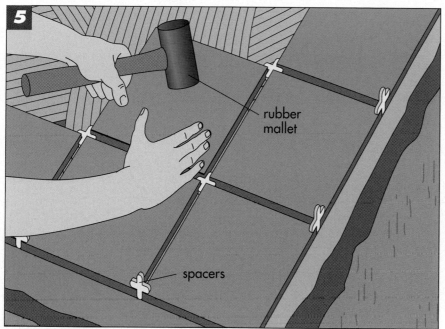

5. Set the tile.
Give each tile a twist as you push it into the adhesive. Take care not to slide the tile into position. Use spacers to keep the tiles aligned.

If the tiles are not flush, use a beating block and hammer or a rubber mallet to gently tap them into alignment.

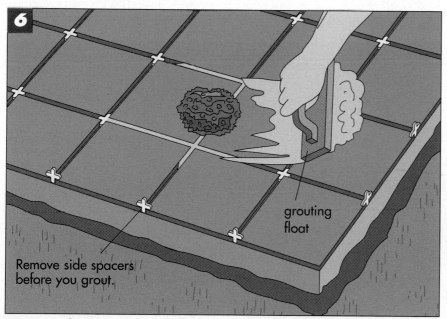

Remove side spacers before you grout.

6. Grout the joints.
Allow time for the adhesive to set (usually one or two days). Mix the grout of your choice, using latex additive to keep it from cracking later on. Push the grout into the joints with a grouting float, making sure you move the float in at least two directions at all points. Once the joints in a small section are fully packed, scrape with the float held nearly perpendicular to the tiles to remove as much waste as possible. Clean the grout from the tile surface and make smooth grout lines, first by laying a wet towel on the surface and pulling it toward you, then by wiping carefully with a damp sponge. Sponge-clean the surface several times. After the surface has dried, buff with a dry towel.

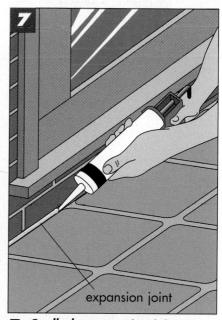

expansion joint

7. Caulk the expansion joints
Choose a caulk or sealant that closely matches the grout in color. Clean the joints of any adhesive that may have been squeezed up, then clean and vacuum the joint. Run a neat bead of caulk or sealant along the expansion joints. Shape the joints, if you like, with the back side of a spoon, a dampened rag, or your finger.

TILING OUTDOOR STEPS

Although not often seen today in new construction, tiled stairs have a long and rich history. You can add tile to both the risers and the treads of a concrete stairway. On a wood stairway, a popular choice is to install tiles on the risers only. Risers are not stepped on, so they can be covered with thin wall tiles if you prefer. Cover the entire riser, or use a few decorative tiles to accent. Large, unglazed paver or quarry tiles are attractive for exterior treads. The tiles should be at least ½ inch thick and slip resistant. Special bullnose tiles are available that can extend over the riser. Install riser tiles before you install the tread tiles.

YOU'LL NEED

TIME: About one day to install tiles on a typical front entry, plus an hour or two to grout.
SKILLS: Installing floor tile, cutting, and installing plywood or backerboard.
TOOLS: Tape measure, saw, hammer, drill, tiling and grouting tools.

CAUTION!
SAFE STAIR DIMENSIONS
Before tiling over stairs, make sure they are safe. The treads, the surface you step on, should be about 11 inches deep, although for exterior stairs it is often recommended that they be deeper. The riser, the vertical element between treads, should be about 7 inches high. Check with your building department if you are not sure about your stair dimensions.

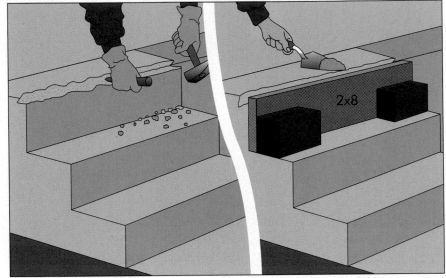

Prepare concrete stairs.
Concrete stairs are the best surface for tile. But the concrete must be in solid condition, with no major cracks or other structural damage. Seal small cracks with a concrete patching compound. Repair damaged edges by chipping away any loose concrete, then sweeping and wetting the area. Place a board along the damaged area, then fill it with patching compound or fresh mortar. Smooth with a trowel and allow to set.

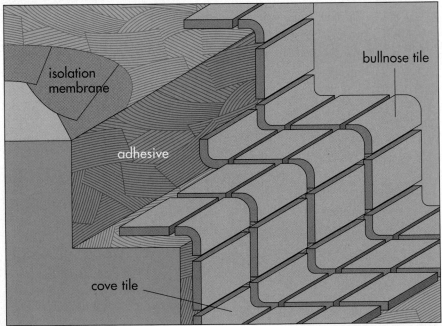

Tiling concrete stairs.
The most professional installation calls for a new mortar setting bed applied over the entire surface. But you can also tile over concrete stairs following the general guidelines for a concrete patio (see pages 767–769). Remove oily stains and make sure that the concrete does not contain curing compounds. Spread a trowel-applied isolation membrane before setting tiles. Use bullnose and cove tiles as shown to strengthen the edges and make cleanup easier.

OUTDOOR PROJECTS

CHOOSING HARDWARE

A large number of hardware options are available for outdoor projects. If you have an unusual fastening problem, check with your local home center or hardware store; chances are good they will have the solution.

Gates are usually heavy and need large hinges fastened with long screws. Before choosing either a **strap hinge** or a **T-hinge**, make sure the hinge fits your situation—you want to be able to drive all the screws into solid wood. A **screw-hook hinge** is a good solution when you don't need the hinge to be showy. Install a **gate spring** if you want the gate to close automatically.

If your structure calls for posts that are not sunk in the ground, choose a fastening method that raises them off the concrete a bit to prevent rot. Often, you will need to set a **J-bolt** in the wet concrete of a footing before you can attach a **post anchor**. To attach a beam to a post, use a **post cap**. **Joist hangers** enable you to attach ends of joists to a ledger board firmly.

Choose fasteners that will hold firmly and not rust. Galvanized-and-coated **deck screws** make great all-purpose fasteners. (If you're working with redwood or cedar, use stainless steel screws to prevent discoloring the wood.) To attach wood to concrete, use **lag shields** with screws for the strongest connection. **Masonry screws** are easier to install and almost as strong. Use **lag screws** for heavy-duty fastening. **Machine bolts** have a head that can be turned with a wrench. (Always use washers when installing lag screws or machine bolts, or their heads will get buried in the wood.) Use a **carriage bolt** when you want a dressier look on one side.

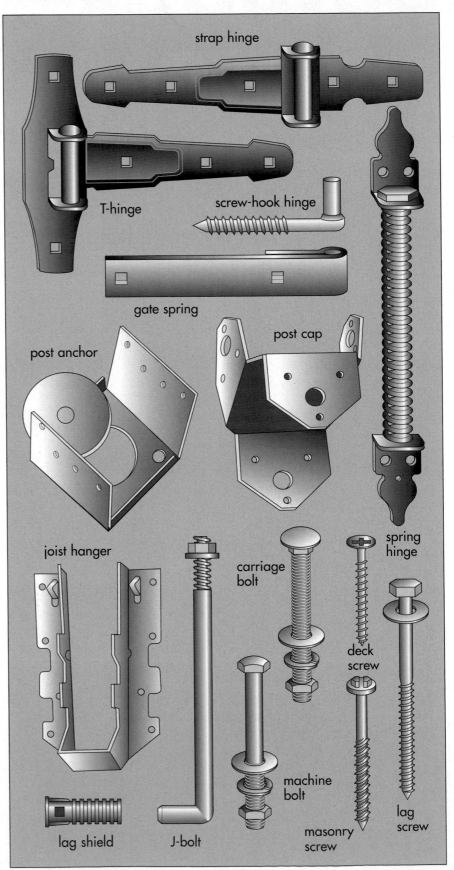

strap hinge

T-hinge

screw-hook hinge

gate spring

post anchor

post cap

spring hinge

joist hanger

carriage bolt

deck screw

machine bolt

lag shield

J-bolt

masonry screw

lag screw

INSTALLING POSTS AND FOUNDATIONS

Many outdoor projects call for installing posts. If the structure is attached to the house, or if it is fairly large, there is no need to sink the posts into the ground. You can rest them on top of footings, thereby ensuring against rot. But if the structure needs posts with lateral strength, you must set them in holes and then fill the holes with concrete, gravel, or tamped soil. Use pressure-treated posts with a preservative retention level of at least .40 or soak redwood or cedar in preservative.

When possible, set the posts in holes and build some of the structure before pouring concrete. That way, you can correct mistakes, and you will not be in danger of loosening the posts from their footings as you pound on them or lean ladders against them.

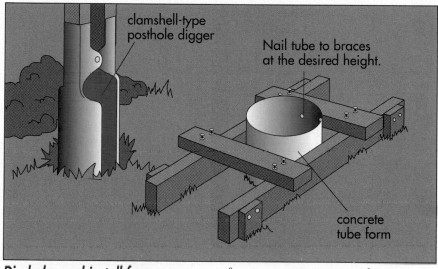

clamshell-type posthole digger

Nail tube to braces at the desired height.

concrete tube form

Dig holes and install forms.
A column form simply can be a long hole in the ground. To make the best use of concrete, try to be precise about your digging. Make the bottom of the hole a bit larger in diameter than the top to "key" it into the ground. Concrete tube forms save on concrete because they are dimensioned precisely. If you want to continue the column footing above grade, brace the form. If you live in an area subject to freezing, you will need to dig below the frost line if you are building a major structure.

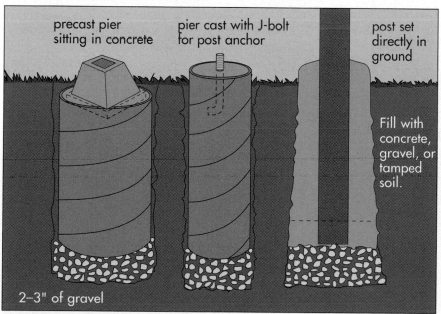

precast pier sitting in concrete

pier cast with J-bolt for post anchor

post set directly in ground

Fill with concrete, gravel, or tamped soil.

2–3" of gravel

Select a type of footing.
Set a precast concrete pier into concrete. Choose one that is designed to hold a 4×4 post. For posts sunk in the ground, add a few inches of gravel to the bottom of the hole, so moisture can drain away from the post. When you fill the hole (with concrete, gravel, or tamped soil), mound it up a bit above grade, so water will run away from the post. For posts that set atop a footing, sink a J-bolt in wet concrete and choose among several types of post anchors that attach to it. Some are adjustable so you can compensate for small mistakes (see page 772).

(see page 772)

EXPERTS' INSIGHT

HELP WITH DIGGING POSTHOLES

■ Power augers should be handled by two people—even those designed for use by one person can wrench your back seriously if the blade runs into a rock or root. The easiest types of augers to handle are those mounted on a vehicle or those that are self-supporting.

■ Fencing and landscaping contractors may have small, truck-mounted power augers for drilling holes. Save your back by hiring them to do it; the price may be reasonable. Be sure to have your holes clearly marked before the crew arrives.

INSTALLING A FENCED ENTRYWAY

Not only will a fenced entryway be an attractive addition to your home, it will keep bike riders and walkers from taking a shortcut across your lawn. In addition, it will create an ideal setting for ornamental plantings.

Most of the basic principles and techniques of building a fence are involved in this project. Fences have three basic components: Posts provide lateral strength, top and bottom rails span the distance between the posts, and pickets (or sometimes, latticework) attach to the rails. If you choose to add a gate, see pages 778–781.

Begin by checking local setback requirements. Then lay out the posthole locations using mason's lines and stakes to establish straight lines. Use the 3-4-5 method (see page 726) when you need to establish a square corner.

Panelized sections of fencing are the easiest to work with. To ensure the distance between panels is correct, set one post, position the panel, and then set the second post (see page 773).

Apply extra preservative to the parts of the posts to be inserted into the ground. Shovel 2 to 3 inches of gravel into the bottom of each hole, set the post in, and plumb it in both directions. You may need to stake it in place temporarily. Install all the posts a little taller than they need to be so you can trim them to the correct height later. Fill the holes with tamped soil or concrete (allow the concrete to cure for a few days before proceeding).

If your yard is fairly level, you may want to cut all the posts at the same level for a neat appearance. Use a line or water level to mark them. If you have a sloping yard, use a chalk line to mark for a straight slope, or just cut each post to the same height above grade; the fence sections will be at various heights. Cut each post by marking a line all the way around its perimeter with a square, then cutting with a circular saw.

Build a picket entryway.
Build an entryway like this right next to the sidewalk, or set it back 2 to 3 feet to leave room for plantings. Though it is low and mostly decorative, it does need to be built strongly in case people lean or bump against it. If you have a corner lot, it may make sense to have one side longer than the other, but in most cases it will look best if it is symmetrical. The post caps and newels shown are just two examples of the many types available at lumberyards and home centers. You can use a saber saw to create your own picket designs.

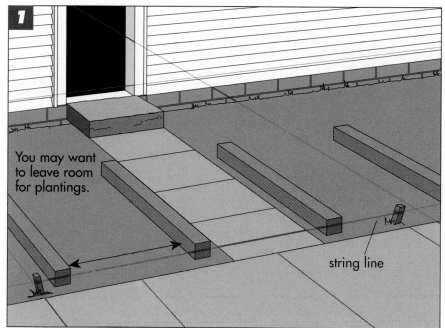

You may want to leave room for plantings.

string line

1. Lay out the posts.

Establish a straight line for your fence by pounding two small stakes into the ground beyond both ends of the fence. Choose the locations of your posts along the mason's line. For most designs, the posts should be no more than 6 feet apart.

When purchasing posts, take into account the depth of the hole (see Step 3) and make sure they are longer than they need to be—you will cut them to height later.

Prepare for digging the postholes by cutting out the sod so your auger won't go astray as you dig.

2. Dig the postholes.

Use a clamshell-type digger for a few easy holes or rent a power auger (the type shown here can be used by one person), or hire someone to dig the holes for you. For most situations, a hole that is 30 inches deep will give you enough stability.

3. Set the inside posts, tamp soil.

Shovel a few inches of gravel into the bottom of each posthole; this will allow water to drain away from the post bottoms to prevent rot. Set the two inside posts in the holes. As your helper holds the post plumb in both directions,

shovel in 8 inches or so of soil and tamp it firm with a long 2×2 or a piece of metal reinforcing bar—do a thorough job. Repeat until the hole is filled and mounded up a bit to help water drain away from the post.

EXPERTS' INSIGHT

LONG-LASTING POSTS

Do things right to avoid having to replace posts in a few years. Select pressure-treated lumber with a preservative retention level of at least .40 or that has been treated for ground contact. Or get dark-colored heartwood of cedar or redwood, if possible, and thoroughly soak the ends in a sealer/preservative.

To really hold posts in place, set them in concrete rather than in tamped soil. Also, pound at least eight nails part way into the base of the post to ensure a tight bond between post and concrete.

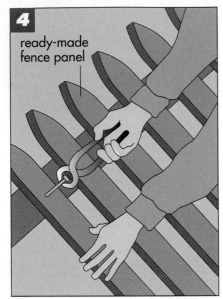

4
ready-made
fence panel

4. Make or purchase pickets.
You can make pickets out of 1×
by cutting one picket to the design
of your choice and using it as a
template to cut others with a
saber saw. Using pickets removed
from a ready-made fence panel is
a faster and more economical
method.

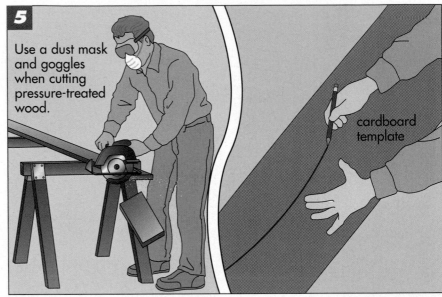

5
Use a dust mask
and goggles
when cutting
pressure-treated
wood.

cardboard
template

5. Cut rails and make template.
Have a helper hold the outside
posts plumb (you'll set them later),
while you measure for the length
of the top and bottom rails. Cut
the rails so they will fit between
the two posts. If you choose to
position the pickets so their tops
are arched rather than inclined as

shown on page 777, make a
template. It must be as long as a
fence section and it should have
a smooth, sweeping arch. Cut it
wide enough so it can rest on the
top rail as you use it. Draw it
freehand, or use a compass made
of pencil and string or a scrap of
wood (see page 267).

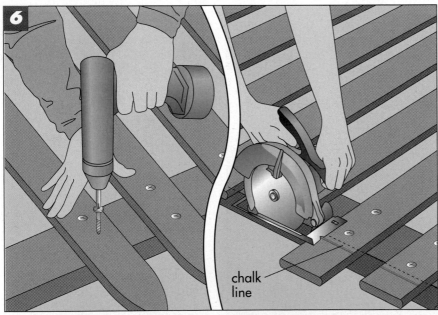

6

chalk
line

6. Fasten the pickets.
Lay the top and bottom rails on a
flat surface, such as a well-swept
garage floor. Measure to make
sure rails are the correct distance
apart on both ends, and square to
each other. Use a board as a guide
for an inclined effect or a
cardboard template on the floor

with its bottom resting against the
top rail. Set the pickets on top of
the rails so their tops follow the
guide. Set them all out before
fastening so you can stand back
and check that you've achieved the
desired effect. Attach to the rails
with nails or screws. Make a
chalkline cut at the bottom.

7
Set outside post
after section is
positioned.

7. Set the outside posts.
Put the fence section in place
against the inside post. Put
temporary blocks under it to hold
it off the ground at least an inch.
Have a helper hold it while you
set the outside post in the hole.
Adjust the post so it fits snugly
against both rails. Set the post.

NOTCHING FENCE RAILS INTO POSTS

Attaching the rails to your fence posts by toenailing will work in most circumstances, but if the fence is likely to be leaned on or in the path of prevailing winds, consider setting the rails in notches cut in the posts.

First determine the location of the rail. Use a square to draw a top cut line and a scrap of rail to strike a bottom cut line. (For a 2×4 rail, this would be 3½ inches.) Set your circular saw to a depth equal to the thickness of the rail (1½ inches for a 2×4). Make four or five cuts between the lines. Chisel out the excess and fasten the rail in place.

8. Attach the panel.
Hold the rails tightly against the post. Drill pilot holes to prevent splitting, and drive toenails or angled screws through the rails and into the post. Finish driving with a nail set to prevent marring the wood. For extra strength, add metal angle brackets, or small wood cleats.

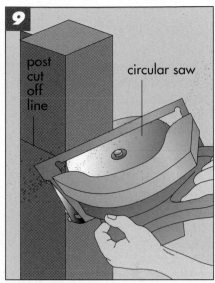

9. Trim the posts.
After you have attached both rail sections, mark the posts for cutting by using a square to mark a line on all four sides of the post. Set your circular saw to its full depth and make a cut, taking care not to damage the pickets. Finish the cut with a handsaw

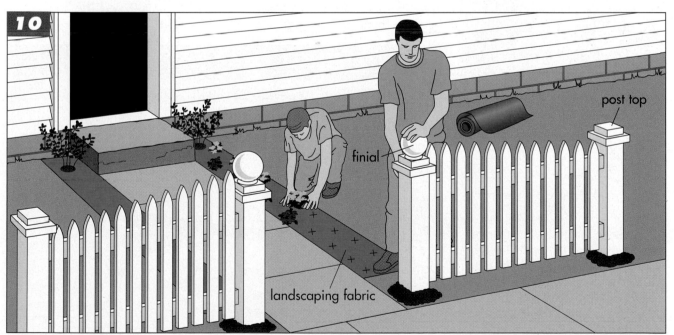

10. Add post caps, finials.
Post tops are not just decorative. If you simply leave the posts cut flat, rain water will seep into the wood through the end grain. Even high-quality pressure-treated lumber will develop cracks if the ends are exposed. You can make a post top by cutting a piece of 2×6 square (so it is 5½ by 5½ inches). Chamfer the edges with a plane, circular saw, or belt sander. Attach the caps with casing nails, countersink the nails, and fill with caulk. Purchase manufactured finials at your home center or lumber yard. Bore holes and attach the finials using the double-threaded screws provided. Paint the fence with two coats of exterior paint, or apply a generous coat of sealer with UV protection. Finally, complete your decorative plantings. Landscaping fabric covered with mulch limits weeds.

BUILDING A Z-FRAME GATE

This gate is sturdy and easy to make. The more closely spaced the pickets, the stronger the gate. You will probably want to use the same pickets on your gate as are on the fence. But don't be afraid to mix up designs a bit. A gate with a curved top adds visual interest to a straightforward fence.

Choose your hardware along with the gate design. Any of the three types shown on page 772 will work well; they simply attach to the post differently. A T-hinge is stronger than a strap hinge, but a screw-hook hinge is the strongest, and makes it easy to remove the gate—simply lift it up.

YOU'LL NEED

TIME: Half a day to build and hang a gate.
SKILLS: Measuring, checking for square, cutting, fastening with screws or nails.
TOOLS: Drill, framing square, circular saw, sabersaw, hammer.

EXPERTS' INSIGHT

WEIGHT VS. STRENGTH

A massive gate may be stronger in itself, but its extra weight requires heavy-duty hinges and may strain your posts. A lighter gate is easier to use, can be installed with lighter hardware, and looks less forbidding. Consider the use and abuse the gate will get. If kids will be hanging on it, you may want to build a stronger box-frame or sandwich gate. In addition, make sure the post is strong, and install heavy-duty hinges.

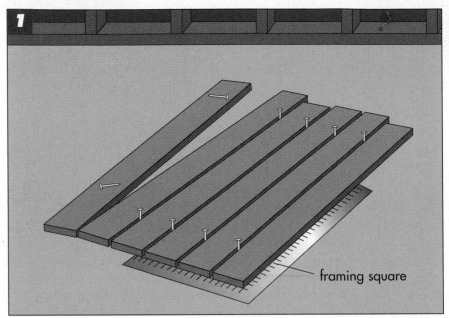

framing square

1. Lay out the pickets.
Cut the pickets roughly to length (you will cut the tops off later) and lay them on a well-swept, flat surface. Space them evenly apart, with at least ⅛-inch space between them so the wood can expand and contract. If possible, space them so they come out to the exact width you want. If not, cut the pieces on either side. Avoid narrow pieces. Use a framing square to make sure the bottom corners are square.

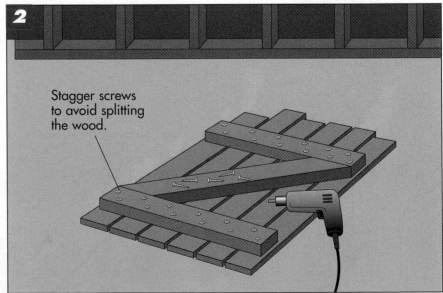

Stagger screws to avoid splitting the wood.

2. Add bracing.
Cut two 2×4s to the width of the gate, minus ¼ inch. Taking care not to bump the pickets out of alignment, set the 2×4s on top of the pickets parallel to each other and about 4 inches from the bottom and the top of the gate. At each joint, drive in two 2-inch decking screws. Drill pilot holes using an alternating pattern to avoid splitting the wood. Hold a 2×4 diagonally from the top of the hinge side to the bottom of the latch side and mark for cutting. Cut and install it in the same way.

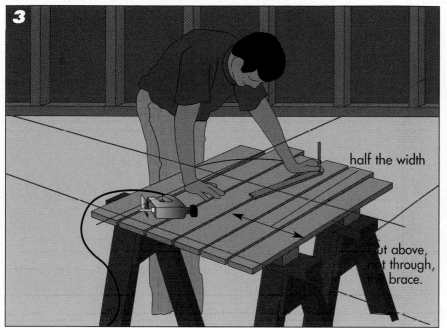

half the width

...ut above, ...ot through, ...brace.

3. *Mark a curve and cut.*
Turn the gate over and place it on a set of horses or a table so you can cut it. Make a compass out of a pencil and string (see page 267) to draw a curve on the top. Take care that the cut won't go below the top brace on the sides. Cut along your guideline with a sabersaw and lightly sand all the edges. Paint the gate or apply sealer. (See page 781 for how to hang the gate and install a latch.)

4. *Prepare the posts.*
Plumb and brace your posts carefully. If the hinge post is not plumb in both directions, the gate will either close or open by itself and you'll need to install a gate-closing spring. Firmly tamp soil around the base of each post or set the post in concrete.

MATERIAL MATTERS

APPLYING FINISHES BEFORE ASSEMBLY

Tom Sawyer discovered that it takes a lot of time to work a brush into all the nooks and crannies of a fence. Even a short fence soaks up a surprising amount of paint or stain.

Unless you are like Tom and have gullible friends, your best bet is to finish the fence pieces before you assemble them. So, after the posts are set, cut the rails and screening, lay them out on sawhorses or another support system, and apply the finish of your choice with a roller or brush.

Use good exterior paint or stain. Both wood and metal must be primed first; this properly seals the surface so the top coating will hold up longer under exposure to severe weather.

Spraying paint makes this job even faster, but the overspray wastes a lot of finish and may kill nearby vegetation if you're not careful. You also must be careful to spray on calm days or you risk getting windblown paint on houses and cars parked in the area.

Once your prefinished fence is assembled, you'll have to go back and touch up spots that have been marred by hammer tracks, saw cuts, and other knocks and dings of assembly. Just to be on the safe side, apply a third coat to the tops of the posts and to the joints between the rails and posts.

MAKING A BOX-FRAME GATE

This gate is a bit sturdier than a Z-frame and takes a good deal longer to build. But don't be afraid to tackle it if it is the look you want. This simple square or rectangular frame is braced by a diagonal member. The tricky part is the half-lap joint. A tablesaw or radial-arm saw will make this easier, but you can make a good-looking joint with a circular saw if you work carefully. As with all gates, start by making sure your opening is flanked by firmly set and plumb posts (see page 779).

YOU'LL NEED

TIME: Most of a day to build and hang a gate.
SKILLS: Measuring and squaring, cutting, making a half-lap joint, fastening with nails or screws.
TOOLS: Circular, table-, or radial-arm saw; drill; hammer; carpenter's square; tape measure.

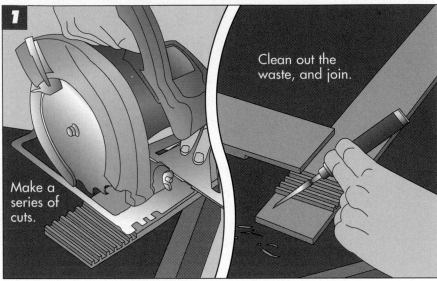

Make a series of cuts.

Clean out the waste, and join.

1. Make a frame with lap joints.
Cut the frame pieces. Set your saw to cut to a depth exactly one-half the thickness of the framing pieces. Experiment with scrap pieces to make sure this is precise. Hold one board on top of the other to mark for the joints. Cut to the inside of the line; make a series of closely spaced cuts in the area of the joint. Chisel out the remaining wood. Cut the other piece the same way. Dry-fit to make sure the pieces fit tightly. Apply exterior carpenter's glue, clamp, drill pilot holes, and drive two 1¼-inch screws. Check for square as you work.

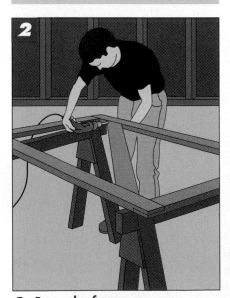

2. Brace the frame.
Hold a piece of 2×4 in place, running diagonally, and mark for cutting. After cutting carefully, set it inside and fasten it to the frame by drilling pilot holes and driving 3-inch screws. The tighter this joint, the stronger the gate.

Use an alternating pattern to avoid splits.

3. Attach pickets and hardware.
Evenly space the pickets on the frame, or plan to cut the outside pickets a bit—avoid narrow pieces on the ends. Attach to the frame by drilling pilot holes and driving 2-inch screws, taking care that they don't poke through. See page 781 for how to hang the gate.

Williamsburg-style closer
Here's a disarmingly simple closing mechanism. Install a short post near the hinge post of the gate, attach a chain to both posts, and add a weight to the chain. The classic design uses a cannonball but you can use any object weighing 5 pounds or so—the heavier the weight, the more firmly the gate will close. Kits include faux cannonballs.

BUILDING A SANDWICHED GATE

Because the solid boards on this gate are placed diagonally, they help brace the gate. For the strongest design, use tongue-and-groove boards, but regular 1× pieces with spaces between them work well. With a sandwich design, the gate will look the same from both sides. You may want to place a 2×3 or 2×4 cap on top of the gate for protection against rainwater. If not, apply plenty of sealer or paint to the exposed end grain on top. Prepare a working area for this project by sweeping debris from a driveway or walk.

YOU'LL NEED

TIME: About a half day to build and hang the gate.
SKILLS: Measuring and squaring, cutting, driving screws or nails.
TOOLS: Drill, carpenter's square, circular saw, chalk line.

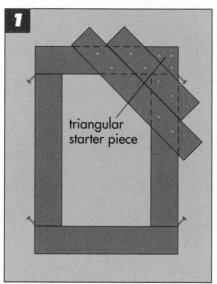

triangular starter piece

1. Build a frame and lay out.

Lay out one set of 1×6 frame pieces. Nail or screw them together so they won't come apart as you work. Set the diagonals on the frame starting with a 45-degree-cut triangle in the corner, and allowing the other pieces to hang over the edge. Drill pilot holes and drive 1¼-inch screws for all joints.

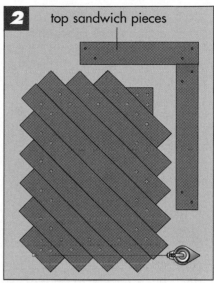

top sandwich pieces

2. Cut edges, finish the sandwich.

Drill pilot holes and use an alternating pattern for the screws, to avoid splitting boards. Chalk lines for all four edges. Set the circular saw blade so it barely cuts through the diagonals (not the frame), and cut carefully. Add the top sandwich pieces, drilling pilot holes and driving 2-inch screws.

3. Hinge the gate.

Set the gate on blocks so the top of the gate lines up with the top of the fence post and the side is flush against the post. For a strap or T-hinge, hold the hinge in place, drill pilot holes, and drive the screws. For a screw-hook hinge, drill a pilot hole at a 45-degree angle into the post, screw in the hook, slip on the hinge strap, and fasten it to the gate.

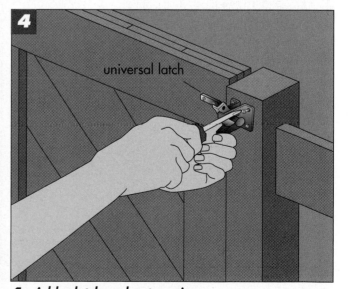

universal latch

4. Add a latch and gate spring.

A universal latch clicks shut automatically. Put the gate in its fully closed position and attach the pieces with screws. If the gate needs to be openable from the outside, drill a hole and run a string through it. Install a gate spring if you want the gate to close automatically.

BUILDING A BASIC ARBOR

This design has a solid look and feel with a touch of whimsy on the top. Designing and cutting the wing-like joists will be challenging, but can be fun as well. Install 6×6 posts for a massive look, or use 4×4s to save money and make the structure look lighter. A suggested size for the arbor is 4 feet by 4 feet. Use rot-resistant lumber, such as cedar, or lumber that has been pressure-treated to resist rot. Set the posts in concrete and wait a few days before completing the arbor. Or build the entire structure and pour the concrete afterwards.

YOU'LL NEED

TIME: Two days, plus time for the concrete to cure.
SKILLS: Basic carpentry.
TOOLS: Posthole digger, circular saw, high-quality sabersaw, handsaw, level, drill.

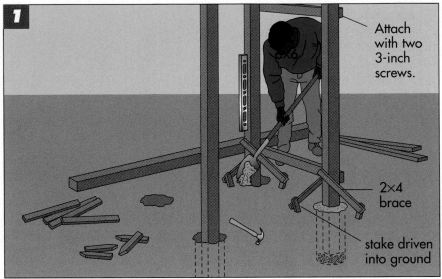

Attach with two 3-inch screws.

6×6

2×4 brace

stake driven into ground

1. Lay out, dig holes, plumb posts. Lay the arbor out, using the 3-4-5 method to make sure it is square (see page 655). Dig postholes at least 30 inches deep, shovel in 3 inches of gravel, and set in the posts. Cut four 2×4 braces to the desired width of the arbor and attach them to the posts as shown.

Temporarily brace the posts so they are plumb in both directions. Check again for square; try to be within a half inch of perfection. Shovel in concrete to fill the hole, mounding it up a bit at the top so water will run away from the posts. Or tamp soil firmly into the hole.

Cut line is level with the other 3 posts.

2. Cut the post tops.
Cut all the posts level with each other 9 feet above the ground. Use a level sitting on top of a straight board to mark for this. To cut a 6×6, cut all four sides with a circular saw and finish cutting the middle with a handsaw.

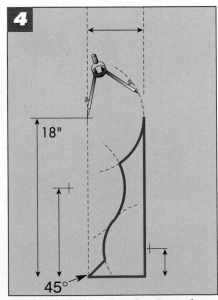

lattice panel

1×2 nailer

3. Attach lattice and nailers.
For each side, cut a lattice panel so it slightly overhangs the 2×4 braces evenly on bottom and top, and attach it with 1¼-inch screws. On the inside of the arbor, attach 1×2 nailers and screw the lattice to the nailers.

18"

45°

4. Make a template for the rafters.
On a piece of cardboard, draw a rectangle 5½ inches wide to represent the end of a 2×6 rafter. With a compass, draw arcs as shown or make up your own design. Cut out the template with a utility knife.

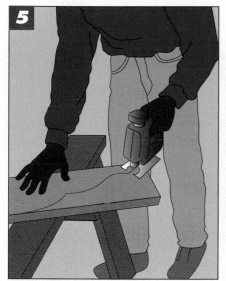

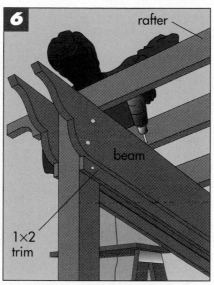

5. Cut rafters and beam pieces.

Cut 2×6s to the length you want for rafters and beam pieces—about 30 inches longer than the width or length of the arbor. Mark the ends with the template and cut. Cutting is easy using a high-quality sabersaw. Consider renting a professional model for this job to ensure you get good, clean cuts.

6. Attach beams and rafters.

To make the beams, attach four pieces, one on each side of the posts, their tops flush with the tops of the posts, and attach using 3-inch deck screws. Wrap posts with 1×2 trim; drill pilot holes for 6d casing nails. Space the rafters evenly, and attach by angle-driving 3-inch deck screws.

7. Add the top pieces.

Lay out for regularly spaced 1×2 top pieces. These are not just for appearances; they keep the rafters from warping. Attach them by drilling pilot holes and driving 1⅛-inch deck screws.

Finish the structure by giving it a couple of good coats of paint or sealer/preservative.

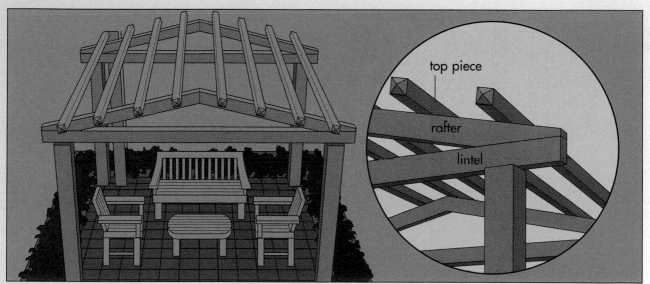

Variation: peaked arbor.

If you want a larger width or a different look, consider a peaked arbor. Install the posts and, if desired, the lattice sections as you would for the square arbor. For the lintel and rafters, use 4×6s as shown for a very solid look, or use 2×6s.

Cut the lintel 3 inches longer than the opening. With a helper, lift it into place on top of the posts, so it overhangs each post 1½ inches on each side and is flush in front. To determine the angles for the cuts on the rafters, have a couple of helpers hold pieces in place while you mark.

All four rafter pieces must be identical. Install them with 3-inch deck screws. Working carefully because the rafters will be unstable, add the top pieces— either 4×4s or 2×4s—by drilling pilot holes and angle-driving 3-inch screws.

BUILDING AN ARCHED ARBOR

Do-it-yourselfers often are leery of building curved structures. But you can build this one if you have basic skills and some patience. For the arbor, use rot-resistant lumber; and for the arch pieces, choose 1×8s that have no large knots.

This arbor has a simple lattice made of horizontal 1×3s. The arched top supplies the visual interest. If you want further variation, simply add vertical 1×3s, evenly spaced, about 6 feet tall on either side.

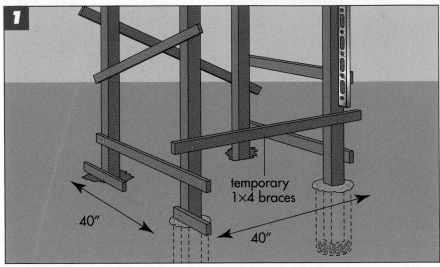

temporary 1×4 braces

40"

40"

YOU'LL NEED

TIME: Two days to build the arbor and finish it.
SKILLS: Basic carpentry, cutting curves with a sabersaw.
TOOLS: Posthole digger, level, circular saw, drill, sabersaw, and 9 or 10 clamps.

1. Set the posts in concrete.
Mark the ground for four posts square to each other. A recommended size is 40 inches square. Dig holes, 30 inches deep or more, and shovel in 3 inches or more of gravel. Temporarily brace the posts so they are plumb in both directions. Recheck for square. You can pour the concrete now and wait for a few days for it to cure before building the arbor; or firmly brace temporarily, build the arbor, and pour the concrete at the end of the job. Or shovel in soil and firmly tamp it down. Make sure the concrete or tamped soil is mounded up so water will run away from the posts.

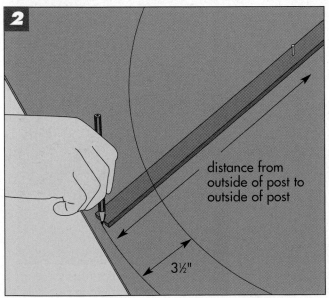

distance from outside of post to outside of post

3½"

2. Draw a template.
Measure the distances between posts to make sure you have the exact dimension that your arches must span (outside to outside). On a large piece of cardboard or paper, make a pattern for your arches, using a string or scrap of wood as a compass (see page 267). The arch will form exactly half of a circle, and will be 3½ inches wide. Cut out the template.

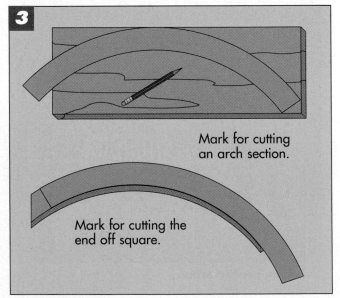

Mark for cutting an arch section.

Mark for cutting the end off square.

3. Cut arch pieces.
Cut the template in half to make it easier to use. Cut the ends square. Lay the template on pieces of 1×8 and mark for 12 curved pieces, all of them as long as possible. Cut out the pieces with a jigsaw, working carefully for smooth cuts. Don't worry about making all the pieces the same length; you will cut them off later.

4

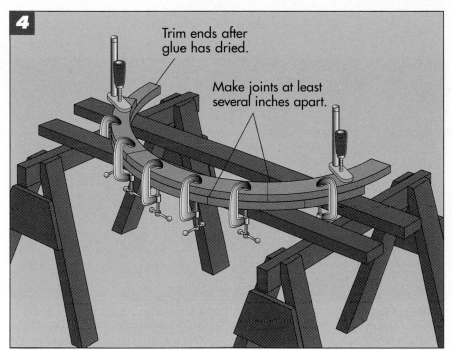

Trim ends after glue has dried.

Make joints at least several inches apart.

4. Laminate and trim the arches.
You will use six pieces for each arch. Lay them out so that the joints are offset, as shown; if the joint of a top piece is within 2 inches of a bottom joint, the arch will be weakened. Apply squiggles of a strong glue to one full arch and clamp the pieces together as shown. Allow the glue to dry completely.

5

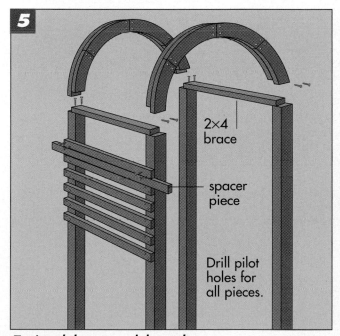

2×4 brace

spacer piece

Drill pilot holes for all pieces.

5. Attach braces and the arch.
Using 3-inch deck screws, attach two 2×4 horizontal braces to the top of the posts, leaving 1½ inches of space at each end for the inner arch pieces. With a helper, set the arches in place and attach them to the braces, drilling pilot holes and driving 3-inch screws. The arches will be wobbly, so work carefully.

6

6. Attach the lattice pieces.
Use a spacer piece (step 5) to make sure all the lattice pieces form a regular pattern. Drill pilot holes for all the screws. As you add the top pieces, you will feel the arch growing more stable. Paint the structure or apply stain and sealer. Because plants will grow on it, it is important to apply plenty of finish—it will be hard to reapply later.

ADDING AN ATTACHED SUNSHADE

Adding a sunshade that attaches to your house offers advantages over building a freestanding structure. The ledger provides a solid starting point, reducing wobble while you're building, and it eliminates two posts, making the space underneath more open.

To prevent wood warping and materials pulling apart over time, be sure to use the right-sized lumber and to fasten it securely. Use lumber that is rot resistant.

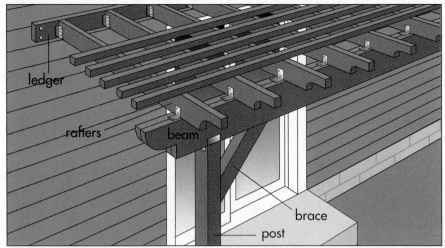

ledger

rafters   beam

brace

post

YOU'LL NEED

TIME: Two days with a helper for a sunshade like the one shown.
SKILLS: Basic carpentry skills.
TOOLS: Ladders, circular saw, drill, saber saw, hammer, level, chalk line, square, tape measure.

Putting it together.

For the ledger and the rafters, use 2×6 boards for spans up to 12 feet, 2×8s for spans up to 16 feet, and 2×10s for spans up to 20 feet. This assumes only light materials sitting on top of the rafters; if you will be adding significant weight, you'll need sturdier rafters. Local codes also may call for different dimensions.

The top pieces are important not only for creating shade, but also to keep the rafters from warping. You may want to change the configuration depending on which direction the sunshade is facing and how much shade you want.

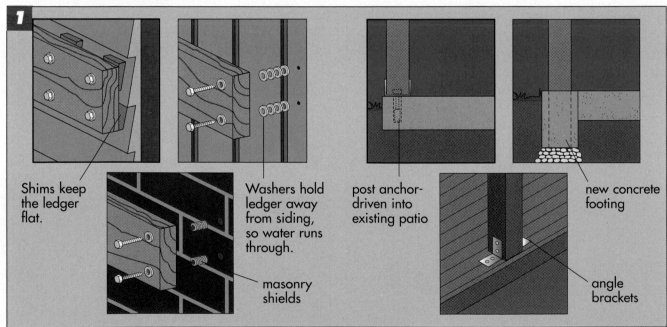

1

Shims keep the ledger flat.

Washers hold ledger away from siding, so water runs through.

masonry shields

post anchor-driven into existing patio

new concrete footing

angle brackets

1. Install ledger and anchor posts.

Cut a ledger board to the length of your sunshade and attach it firmly to your house, making sure it is level. For a frame house, attach to the studs or to the floor framing for the second story. Use shims to make the ledger sit flat and then flash or caulk the top. Or use washers to hold the ledger away from the house so water can run through and the wood can dry out. To attach to a masonry wall, use masonry screws or shields as shown (see page 722).

Cut the posts longer than they need to be. On a patio surface, use a post anchor, or dig a posthole and set the post in concrete. If the posts will rest on a deck, crawl under the deck (if possible) and drive screws up into the posts. Otherwise, use angle brackets.

2. Plumb posts, mark for cutting.

Temporarily brace the posts so they will be firm while you work on them. Check the posts for plumb in both directions.

The beam will rest on top of the posts, so you will cut them as high as the bottom of the ledger, minus the width of the beam. With a helper, use a level sitting atop a straight board or a line level to mark the corner post for cutting to exact height. If you will have an interior (noncorner) post, run a tight chalkline from corner post to corner post to mark for cutting it.

Another option: Cut the post to the height of the bottom of the ledger, and make a beam by attaching boards on either side of the posts, flush to the top of the post (see page 782).

3. Cut posts and install post caps.

Draw a line all the way around each post using a square, and cut two sides with a circular saw. Attach a post cap on top.

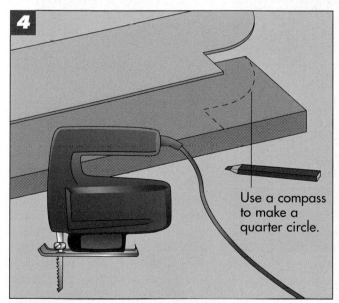

Use a compass to make a quarter circle.

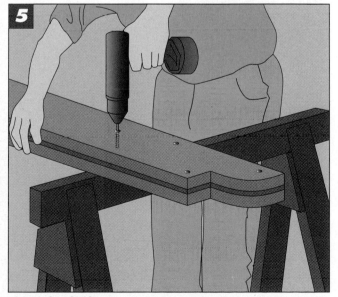

4. Cut the beam pieces.

Make a template for the beam and rafter ends on a piece of cardboard that is the same width as the lumber. Use the scallop design shown above, or make up your own (see page 782). Cut the first beam piece to length (remember, it will overhang the posts), and then cut out the decorative ends on both sides with a saber saw. Use it as a template for the other piece.

5. Make the beam.

Cut pieces of ½-inch pressure-treated plywood into strips the same width as the beam pieces. Sandwich the boards together, and fasten them with 3-inch deck screws driven in an alternating pattern every 4 to 6 inches. This will make a very strong beam that is 3½ inches thick—just right for placing on top of a 4×4 post.

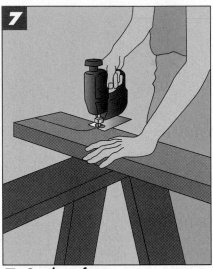

6. Attach and brace the beam.
With a helper, set the beam into the post caps, making sure it overhangs the posts the same length on both sides. Drive 1¼-inch screws or 6d galvanized nails to hold the beam in place.

To make a brace, cut a 4×4 at a 45-degree angle on both sides. Check your circular saw to make sure its blade is square (see page 258). Mark for the cut as shown, and cut the two angle-marked sides. To install the brace, have a helper hold it in place, so both ends are tight and flush to the beam and the post. Drill pilot holes and drive two 3-inch screws at each joint.

7. Cut the rafters.
Cut a rafter to length, taking into account the overhang. The design shown above is the reverse of the beam design; use the template that you used for the beam, and hold it backwards. Cut both ends of one rafter, and use it as a template for the others.

8. Attach the rafters.
Lay out the rafters first so they will be evenly spaced. For extra strength, use hurricane ties as shown. Or drill pilot holes and angle-drive deck screws if you don't like the look of the ties.

9. Add the top pieces.
Cut the 2×2 top pieces to length. Experiment with different spacings to see how much shade you want. One attractive option is to "self-space," that is, to use a scrap piece of 2×2 as a spacer. Attach to the rafters by driving a 3-inch decking screw at each joint.

EXPERTS' INSIGHT

OTHER CANOPY MATERIALS

For a richly textured look, install several layers of criss-crossed materials on top; for instance, a layer of 1×2s on top of the 2×2s in this design.

Other canopy options include rolls of reed, bamboo, and shade cloth. If winters are harsh where you live, store your canopy during winter to prolong its life. Ready-made sheets of lattice can work, but use a heavy-duty material that is a full ¾-inch thick, and support it every 12 inches.

For protection against rain, the roof must slope away from the house at least ½ inch per running foot. Install stretched canvas or corrugated fiberglass panels on top.

PLANNING AN OUTDOOR ROOM

By combining several of the projects described in this book, you can create an outdoor living area that has the feeling of an enclosed space while preserving the pleasure of being outdoors. Often you can transform an area marred by street noise or an unpleasant view into an enjoyable outdoor room.

The base for the room can be a deck or patio—any smooth surface suitable for outdoor furniture. If you need a new surface, prefab modular wooden squares are the quickest to install, followed by pavers or flagstones set in a bed of sand. You'll also want to install a permanent flagstone or paver walkway to the room.

Once you've settled on the location of your outdoor room, decide how much privacy and wind or sound buffering you want. Often installing a grillwork screen, fence, or a dense hedge on one or two sides will provide the needed protection. For the side facing your house, a bench, planters, or a flower bed can clearly mark the boundaries of the room without limiting access.

Too much sun can be more bane than blessing. The best solution may be to cover the southern half of the room with an overhead structure (see pages 786–788) so that about two-thirds of the area will be shaded. Space the overhead rafters to produce more or less filtered light depending on your climate and the number of nearby shade trees in your yard.

For seating, a stationary bench or two can be combined with movable furniture to give you maximum flexibility. A nearby fire pit can be a focal point for evening entertaining. As a final touch, low-voltage lighting can give you just enough illumination. Hang lanterns or string lights to creative a festive atmosphere for parties or other gatherings.

BUILDING A GRILLWORK SCREEN

Here's a project that can add privacy to an outdoor living area, buffer a prevailing wind, or hide an unsightly view. In addition, it will be an ideal place to plant climbing flowers or vines. This project uses readily available lumber and is easy to build.

This simple design can be modified to suit your needs. Once the posts and 1×6s are in place, you can hold up 2×2 pieces in various configurations until you find an attractive pattern. Move the pieces closer together or further apart, depending on how much privacy you want and what type of climbing plants you will be using. Or, use ready-made lattice panels instead of 2×2s.

The overall size of the project is flexible as well: Post-to-post width can be 6 to 10 feet; height can be 5 to 8 feet.

Choose rot-resistant lumber, such as brown pressure-treated or the heartwood of cedar or redwood. If you plan on painting your trellis, you'll have an easier time of it and get better results if you paint the pieces before installing them; it's hard to avoid drips when painting all those intersecting pieces. With a less drip-prone product like stain or sealer, you can apply your finish after the screen is constructed.

YOU'LL NEED
TIME: About a day.
SKILLS: Measuring and cutting, plumbing posts, digging post holes, attaching with galvanized screws or nails.
TOOLS: Circular saw, drill, hammer, posthole digger, level.

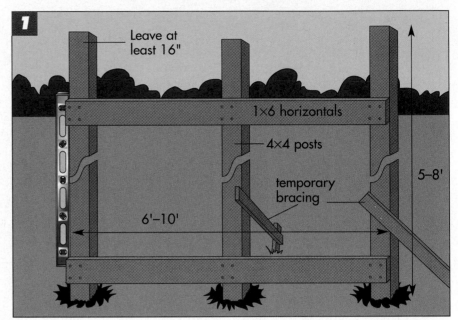

1. Set posts and horizontals.
Dig all three postholes, at least 30 inches deep. Shovel in several inches of gravel, and set the two outside posts in the holes. Check the posts for plumb in both directions, and make sure they line up. Temporarily brace them, using stakes driven into the ground. Fasten two 1×6s, one a couple of inches above the ground and the other near the top (leave at least 16 inches for the overhead structure). Drive four screws into each joint. Center the middle post and attach it to the 1×6s as well. If you will be setting the posts in soil only, tamp them in place now. If you will be using concrete, wait until the structure is built.

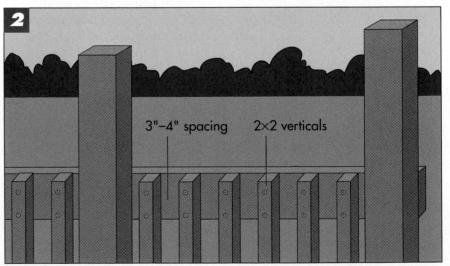

2. Install verticals.
Plan the spacing so that there are about 3 to 4 inches between pieces. Be sure the spacing between the outermost 2×2 vertical and its adjacent post is also 3 to 4 inches. Install the verticals by drilling pilot holes and driving two 2-inch deck screws into each joint, through the 2×2 and into the 1×6. The structure will be a little wobbly now, but will firm up later.

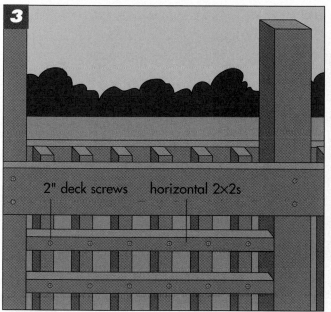

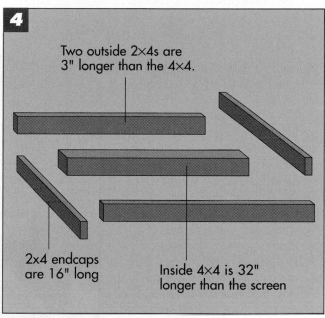

Two outside 2×4s are
3" longer than the 4×4.

2×4 endcaps
are 16" long

Inside 4×4 is 32"
longer than the screen

2" deck screws   horizontal 2×2s

3. Add horizontals.

Lay out for the horizontal 2×2s; usually it is best to use the same spacing as for the verticals so that the holes are square. Cut 2×2s to fit snugly between the posts, up against the inside faces of the posts. Install them by driving a 2-inch deck screw into each joint. Add the other 1×6 pieces with 2-inch screws.

4. Build the top section.

Measure up from the top 1×6s about 16 inches. Level across and cut off the tops of all three posts. Cut a 4×4 about 32 inches longer than the width of the screen, two 2×4s 3 inches longer than the 4×4, and two 2×4s at 16 inches. Assemble them in a simple box. Attach all the joints with 3-inch deck screws, drilling pilot holes near the edges of boards.

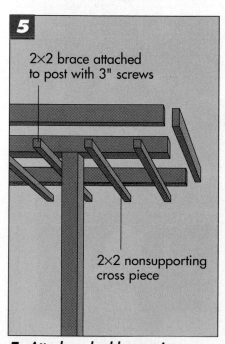

2×2 brace attached
to post with 3" screws

2×2 nonsupporting
cross piece

5. Attach and add crosspieces.

Set the top section on top of the posts, overhanging the same distance on both ends. At each post, add a 2×2 brace, attaching with 3-inch screws. Attach additional 2×2s, evenly spaced.

6. Finish or paint, plant vines.

Give the whole structure a coat or two of paint, stain, or sealer. Do a thorough job; you won't want to have to remove vines to refinish the grillwork screen later.

Planting is the final step. For a screen with widely spaced lattice pieces, choose climbing plants that either are bushy or that cling well, such as roses or clematis.

BUILDING BASIC TRELLISES

A trellis is any structure that contains lattice; lattice is any combination of materials that allows light to filter through and provides a place for plants to climb. Thousands of trellis designs are possible, using a wide variety of materials. Usually the lattice of a trellis is made up of thin, evenly criss-crossed material, often wood strips. But large or patterned pieces can also make a trellis.

The design shown at right can be built in a few hours using commonly available materials. Use rot-resistant lumber, and soak the 2×4 ends that go into the soil with a sealer/preservative. Use 1⅝-inch deck screws to fasten the horizontal 1×2s to the 2×4 posts, then to the three verticals. Drill pilot holes if there is any danger of cracking the wood.

Set the 2×4 posts in holes 20 to 30 inches deep, and firmly tamp soil back in the hole, keeping the posts fairly plumb as you work. Or support the posts with fence stakes: Set the structure in place, pound the stakes into the ground, and tie the posts to the stakes with copper wire. With this arrangement, you can remove the structure at the end of the summer and store it until spring.

YOU'LL NEED

TIME: For any of these three designs, just a few hours.
SKILLS: Basic carpentry.
TOOLS: Post-hole digger, drill, saw, wire cutters.

2×4 posts

1×2 lattice pieces

Use fence stakes if posts aren't set at least 20 inches in the ground.

A-frame with chicken wire.

Because the triangular design of this garden trellis makes it very stable, it doesn't need to be anchored to the ground unless you have exceptionally high winds in your area. Build each side on a flat surface, spacing the horizontal pieces evenly and attaching them to 6-foot vertical supports that are spaced 4 feet apart. Use two 3-inch deck screws at each joint. Lean the two sides against each other at the top; keep them about 5 feet apart at the bottom, and drape chicken wire over the whole structure. Attach the wire with a staple every foot or so on all the 2×4s.

With the chicken wire acting as a hinge, you can fold this structure up and move it easily.

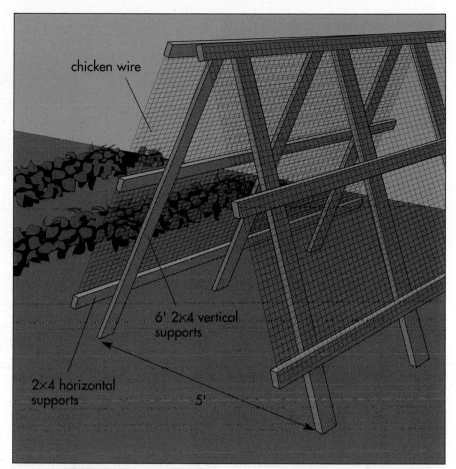

chicken wire

6' 2×4 vertical supports

2×4 horizontal supports

5'

Wire mesh planting bed.

This project is ideal for squash and other climbing vegetables. The timbers can be permanent parts of your garden, while the wire mesh may need to be replaced every few years. For the border of the planting bed, use at least 1× pressure-treated lumber supported with 2×2 stakes.

Use landscaping timbers for a more permanent but less space-conserving border. A surprising amount of square footage in a small garden will be eaten up by the width of the timbers. Keep them in place by boring holes every 3 feet and pounding in 2-foot-long pieces of rebar.

For the climbing lattice, purchase 4-inch wire mesh—the type that is used for reinforcing concrete. Fasten it to the insides of the planting bed with U-shape wire fasteners, taking care not to crimp the wire as you bend it over.

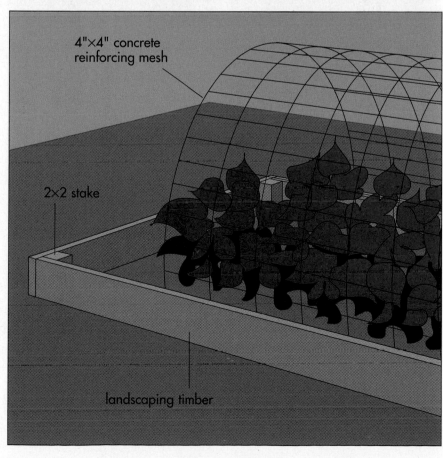

4"×4" concrete reinforcing mesh

2×2 stake

landscaping timber

MAKING BENTWOOD TRELLISES

Bentwood furniture has been an American tradition for hundreds of years. Using only branches of various thicknesses and working quickly, artisans fashioned chairs and tables that have lasted for years. Most of us will never learn how to make a rocking chair, but with a little patience we can make a homey-looking trellis or two. And it will cost next to nothing in materials.

The first step is to find the materials. Choose branches that are still green, so they will bend easily. You will need to scavenge. Check with tree trimmers or nurseries; look in swampy areas or along rivers; pick up fallen branches after a storm; or just look around your own property. When a tree has been cut down, often its stump will send up shoots that are easily worked.

Cedar, cypress, and willow are all easy to work with and long-lasting. Oak, maple, hickory, and apple also work well. Other woods, such as elm, sycamore, mulberry, peach, and grape vines, are easy to work with but will only last for a year or two. Just about any wood that is easily bent will be good enough to practice on. After you get good at it, you can look for higher-quality materials.

The greener the wood, the better. Plan to start building your trellis within a day of cutting the wood from its live source. Soaking wood in water does not usually do much good.

To tie the pieces together, a skilled builder may be able to use thin branches, but beginners should use wire and nails. Copper wire will turn an attractive green with time.

Here are some classic bentwood trellis designs, all of them 6 to 8 feet tall. If you want a smaller version, scale back the number of pieces, so you don't end up trying to twist branches into impossibly tight curves.

Make ready an open area in which to work. A driveway or garage floor will do, but you will have a more pleasant time with a picnic table or large work bench.

YOU'LL NEED

TIME: After the materials are gathered, several hours to make one trellis.
SKILLS: This is a special skill that you learn as you go.
TOOLS: Branch cutters or pruning saw, pliers, hammer.

1. Lay out a basic frame.
On a convenient working surface, lay out two long vertical pieces, about 2 feet apart for a 6 to 8-foot-high trellis. Lay the bottom and top horizontals on top, and stand back to see that everything looks square and symmetrical.

2. Join with wire and a nail.
Pound a single nail into each joint. If a nail pokes through, bend its tip over with a hammer. Eyeball the structure again for square, and wrap each joint with wire. Begin by wrapping by hand, looping the wire around in a crossing pattern. Twist tight with lineman's pliers.

3. Join the curved top pieces.
This may be a bit difficult until you get the knack. You may need a helper. Bend the top of one vertical piece, then the other, and hold them together in a smooth arch. Make adjustments until it looks right. Attach each piece with wire wrapped around both of its ends and twisted tight with pliers.

4. Fill in the design.

Once you have made a rectangle with a curved top, you can proceed to make any of a great number of designs (see below). Start with the verticals. Many designs call for a center vertical, and others require two outside pieces. Then add horizontal or angle pieces. Attach all joints with a nail and wire where possible, and with wire only elsewhere.

5. Add braces where needed.

Diagonal pieces can be added for strength, but do so in a symmetrical pattern, so they are part of the design. Bentwood trellises are very informal, so no one expects anything close to precision. But attempt to balance materials—use pieces of the same width on either side, for instance.

6. Anchor to the ground.

Metal fence stakes are the easiest to use and are unobtrusive, but wooden stakes will work, too. A 4½-foot metal stake, driven 2 feet into the ground, will probably be strong enough. Drive the stakes into the ground the same distance apart as your main vertical pieces. Wire the verticals to the stakes in at least two places

Try these designs.

For the design above, the six short curved pieces in the middle must be bent and allowed to harden before attaching. Curved ends that are not attached to another piece (see the heart inside the middle trellis) are difficult; you will have to tie them in place for a few days until they harden into position. A design with mostly straight pieces, such as the one above, will be easier to make than one with lots of curves.

CONSTRUCTING A BASIC BENCH

Regardless of how simple the bench design is, rigidity must be built in to prevent the piece from wiggling. If the bench will be stationary, you might be able to attach it to a deck railing, or sink posts into the ground. But for a stand-alone bench, either use a series of massive supports (as in the design on page 797), or supply angled braces, as in this design.

YOU'LL NEED

TIME: Most of a day.
SKILLS: Measuring and squaring, accurate cutting, attaching with screws or bolts.
TOOLS: Circular saw, drill, tape measure, square.

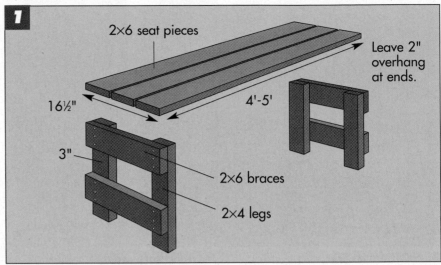

1. Make supports and add seat.
Cut four legs to the height of your bench, minus 1½ inches (a bench height of 17 inches is standard). Cut four 2×6 braces, 16 inches long. Construct the two supports by attaching the braces to the legs as shown. Drill pilot holes and drive three 2½-inch deck screws into each joint.

Cut three 2×6 seat pieces, no more than 5 feet long, and set them on top of the supports, allowing a 1½-inch overhang on each end. Drive two 3-inch deck screws into each joint. The structure will be a bit wobbly at this point.

2. Make the long braces.
Check to see that the legs are square to the seat pieces. Hold a piece of 2×4 against a leg and the seat, as shown, so that it extends 6 inches or so past the middle of the bench. Mark the two ends for angle cuts. Cut, check to see it will fit, and use it as a template for a second brace.

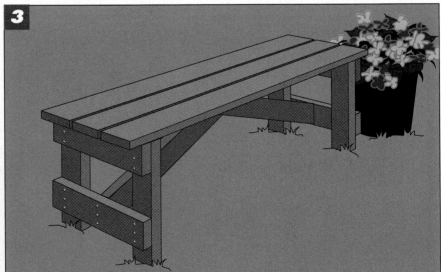

3. Add the long braces.
Position the long braces so that they run past each other in the center of the bench. Attach them to the cross-braces with 3-inch deck screws, and to the middle seat piece by drilling pilot holes and driving screws upward through the brace and into the seat piece, taking care that they do not poke up through the seat.

Sand all the edges of the bench smooth, taking special care with the ends of the seat pieces. Brush on sealer/preservative, or give it at least two coats of paint.

BUILDING A SLATTED BENCH

This sturdy bench has massive supports. It can be attached to a deck, or used as a movable piece of furniture. The seat, made of eight 2×2s, is more complicated to build than one made with a few 2×6s, but has a pleasingly hand-crafted look.

Take extra care when choosing the 4×4s. They need to be nearly free of cracks because you will be using very short pieces. A high grade of redwood will cost more, but will probably perform much better than standard pressure-treated lumber.

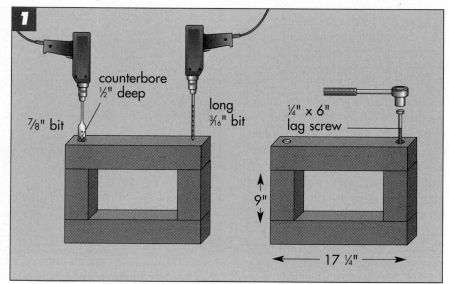

YOU'LL NEED

TIME: Most of a day.
SKILLS: Measuring and squaring, cutting, boring long holes.
TOOLS: Circular saw, drill with long bit, socket wrench, square.

1. Make the supports.
For each support, cut two 4×4s to 9 inches and two to 17¼ inches. Assemble the pieces building-block style. At each joint, drill a pilot hole for a lag screw. Take care that the pieces remain flush with each other as you work. To ensure that the screw heads do not protrude above the surface of the wood, drill a second counterbore hole, about ½ inch deep, using a ⅞-inch bit.

Place washers on the screws and ratchet them tight. Set the supports on a flat surface with the screw heads on top and bottom, so they will not show.

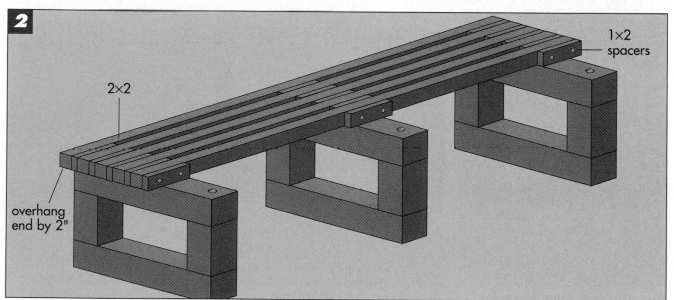

2. Assemble and attach the seat.
Cut eight 2×2s to the length of the bench minus 1½ inches, and 21 pieces of 1×2 to 6 inches. Attach a 2×2, so its face is flush with the sides of the supports and it overhangs the ends by 1½ inches, by drilling pilot holes and angle-driving 2-inch decking screws. Then sandwich pieces as shown, alternating 2×2s with 1×2 spacers. On every other piece, drive an angled screw into the support or a 3-inch screw horizontally, to tie several seat pieces together. By the time you've attached the eighth 2×2, the seat should be very close to exactly the width of the supports. If the seat is a little narrower, add a piece of cedar shim to the last spacer, so it comes out right. Sand the seat thoroughly, and apply a good coat or two of sealer/preservative.

BUILDING A WRAPAROUND TREE BENCH

A feature like this can turn a secluded spot in your backyard into a relaxing place to sit and read, putting to good use a shady area.

Construction will take some patience and unusual methods, but it is not difficult if you follow the steps in order. The method is to build the bench in two sections, and then determine where to place the postholes by holding the bench temporarily in place.

YOU'LL NEED

TIME: One or two days.
SKILLS: Measuring and marking for odd angles, precise cutting, digging postholes, fastening with screws and bolts.
TOOLS: Circular saw and power miter saw or radial-arm saw (you can rent one), speed square, posthole digger, drill.

The length of this side equals the diameter of your tree.

30°

18"

1. Measure tree and cut 6 pieces.
Choose a tree that is not leaning heavily and has no visible roots.

Measure the tree's diameter 18 inches from the ground. Wrap a string around the tree and measure the string; this is the circumference. Divide by 3 (or pi, 3.14) to get the diameter.

Cut six pieces of 2×4 to be used as the seat pieces closest to the tree. For each, make the longest side as long as the diameter of your tree; this will produce a tree bench that leaves room for the tree to grow. (If you have a fast-growing tree, add an inch or two.) Cut each end to exactly 30 degrees. Use a power miter saw or radial-arm saw to make the cuts; test with scrap pieces to make sure the angle is precisely correct.

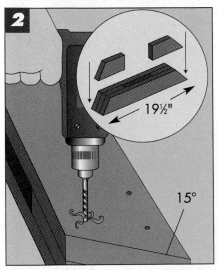

19½"

15°

2. Assemble the seat supports
Construct six supports out of 2×4s. Sandwich two 6-inch-long pieces between two 19½-inch-long pieces. Some faces of these will show, so make sure the ends are evenly cut and all three pieces are flush. Drill pilot holes and drive 3-inch screws from either side.

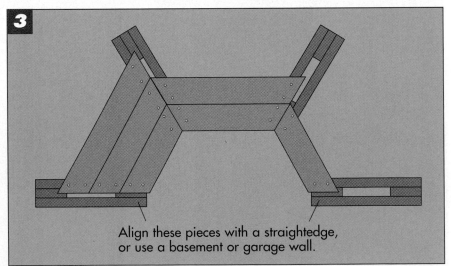

Align these pieces with a straightedge, or use a basement or garage wall.

3. Build the first half-section.
On a large flat surface, lay out the first seat section, using four seat supports and three of the inside seat pieces. Adjust so they fit together tightly, and the two outer supports line up in a straight line.

Cut the rest of the boards to fit, all with 30-degree cuts on each end. You may need to hold and measure in place for some. Work carefully, testing as you go. After positioning the pieces tightly, attach them to the supports by drilling pilot holes and driving 3-inch deck screws.

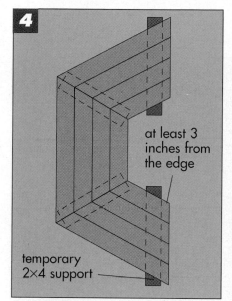

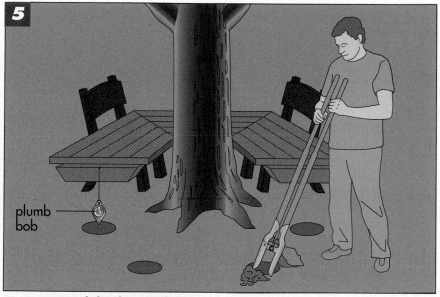

4. Build the second half-section.
The second section will have only two seat supports, so screw a piece of 2×4 onto the bottom of each end to temporarily hold it together while you assemble the bench; you will take these pieces out after the bench is built.

5. Locate and dig the post holes.
Set the two sections in place by resting them on chairs. To determine the location of each post hole, hang a plumb bob (you can use a chalkline) from the center of each seat support, and dig up a little turf or mark the spot directly below the plumb bob. You may need to shift the whole assembly to avoid roots.

Dig the post holes, about 24 inches deep. Do not cut any roots that are larger than 1 inch in diameter. If necessary, leave some post holes shallow. Shovel 2 inches of gravel into the bottom of each hole to promote drainage.

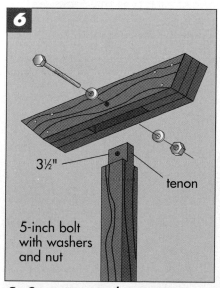

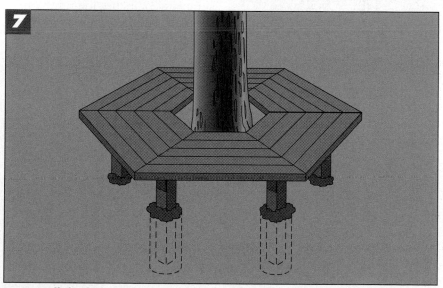

6. Cut posts, attach to supports.
Cut six 4×4 pressure-treated posts to the depth of each hole, plus 16 inches. Cut a tenon on one end, as shown, so the post will fit tightly into the seat support. (To do this, set your circular saw blade 1 inch deep, cut a series of lines on each end, and clean out with a chisel.) Install each post with a bolt.

7. Install the bench.
With a helper, set the section with the four seat supports in place, inserting the posts into the holes. Then lower the other section into place. You will need to spend some time making adjustments—adding or removing dirt here and there—until the bench is reasonably level in all directions. Drill pilot holes and drive screws to connect the second section to the first. Remove the temporary 2×4 braces. Into each hole, shovel in 8 inches of dirt, tamp firmly with a pole or 2×4, then repeat until the dirt is mounded up so water will run away from the post.

Sand all edges smooth, so there will be no danger of splinters. Brush on a coat or two of sealer/preservative, or apply paint.

MAKING AN ARBOR BENCH

With the addition of some climbing plants, this arbored bench can make a delightful retreat. Cutting the rafters so the resulting arch is smooth is the most difficult part of this project.

Once the curved pieces are cut, building this structure is no more difficult than making a straightforward arbor. Use high-quality, rot-resistant lumber, such as the heartwood of redwood or cedar. Avoid any rough pieces or pieces with large knots.

YOU'LL NEED

TIME: About a day and a half.
SKILLS: Measuring and squaring, cutting smooth curves, digging postholes, fastening with screws.
TOOLS: High-quality sabersaw, circular saw or power miter box, level, posthole digger, drill.

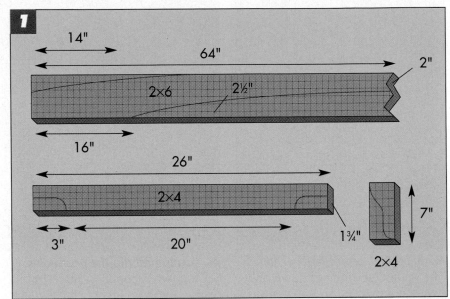

1. Cut the curved pieces.

To make the templates for these pieces, use large pieces of cardboard or paper; you may have to tape some pieces together. For the rafters, you will need a template 32 inches long, so you can use it on both halves. For the top pieces, you need only a template for one end cut. Mark a grid, draw freehand, and cut out carefully with a utility knife. Cut the 2×6s and 2×4s to length. For the curved cuts, use a professional-quality saber saw. Once you have one of each type that looks good, use it as a template for the others. Sand the pieces smooth.

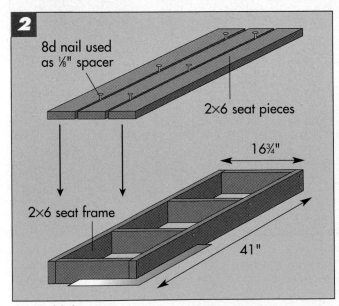

2. Build the seat.

Construct a 2×6 frame 41 inches by 16¾ inches. Check it for square. Drive two 3-inch screws at each joint. Cut three 2×6 boards to 41 inches for the seat. Using 8d nails as spacers between the seat pieces, attach the pieces so their ends are flush with the frame and their sides overhang the frame evenly.

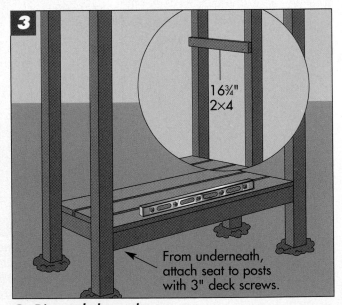

3. Dig postholes and set posts.

Set the bench on the ground and mark for four postholes. Dig the holes at least 30 inches deep. Plumb the posts and brace them until you level and attach the seat piece to the four posts with 3-inch deck screws. Fasten the top 2×4 braces about 76 inches above the ground with 3-inch deck screws.

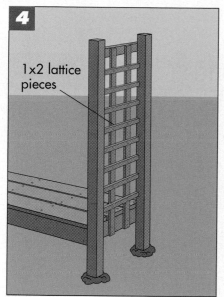

1×2 lattice pieces

4. Build the lattice.

Cut the posts to a level height (see page 782). On each side, evenly space two 1×2 vertical pieces that run flush to the top of the 2×4 brace and the bottom of the bench frame. Fill in with horizontal 1×2s, cut to fit between the posts. Space them consistently. Attach them to the vertical 1×2s (not to the posts) with a 1⅝-inch screw at each joint.

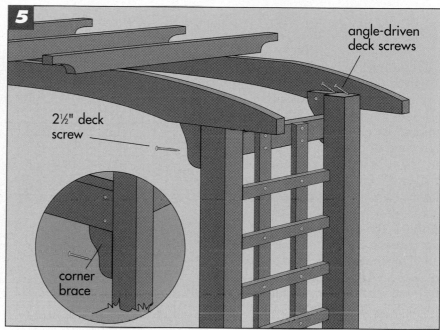

angle-driven deck screws

2½" deck screw

corner brace

5. Add rafters and corner braces.

Set the front rafter in place, withthe bottom edge about 2 inches below the top of the posts. Attach it to the posts from behind by drilling pilot holes and angle-driving 2½-inch deck screws. Take care that the screws do not poke through the front of the rafter. Work carefully to avoid splitting the rafters. Add the decorative corner braces beneath the seat frame and the rafters. For each, drill pilot holes, hold the braces in place, and drive 3-inch deck screws into the posts and bench frame pieces.

Position top pieces at regular intervals.

6. Finish with the top pieces.

Lay out the top pieces on the rafters so they are at regular intervals. Attach them to the rafters with angle-driven screws. Sand the seat and the inside face of the posts smooth. Finish the arbored bench with a couple of coats of paint, or use a sealer/preservative. Plant climbing vines at either end so they crawl up the lattice.

EXPERTS' INSIGHT

MAINTAINING A TRELLIS

Moisture trapped on the lattice pieces can rot your trellis. Give it two coats of long-lasting finish before adding plants. Inspect it once a year a day or two after a rainfall. If water has soaked into the wood rather than beading on the surface, it's time to recoat. Delicately remove the vines from the trellis in order to get it out of the way for refinishing. Your plants will probably survive if you work carefully. Inspect your posts as well. If a puddle forms around the post, mound well-tamped soil up so that water will run away.

MAKING A SCALLOP-BACK BENCH

This attractive bench project gives you the chance to do some basic furniture making without having to execute fancy joints. Use clear or nearly clear redwood or cedar. You may have to ask your lumberyard to mill a ¾×8 (1×7½ inch actual dimension) for the back and 3×3s (2½×2½ inch actual dimension) for the legs. If this is too difficult, you can substitute a 2×8 for the back and 4×4s for the legs. Decking boards of ¾×6 are easily available in cedar, but you may have to special-order for redwood.

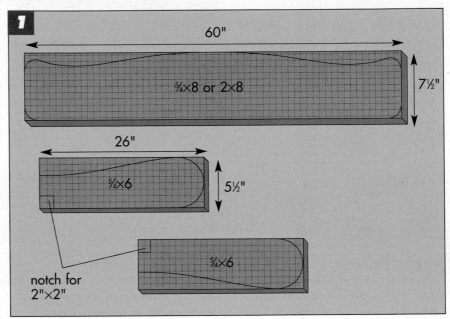

1. Cut the back and armrests.
Make cardboard templates of the patterns shown above, and transfer them to the lumber. If ¾×8 is difficult to find, use 2×8. Trace the patterns and cut carefully with a saber saw. Use coarse (50–60 grit) sandpaper to round the edges (except the post notch) of these pieces, then finish them with medium (80–100) and then fine (120–150) sandpaper.

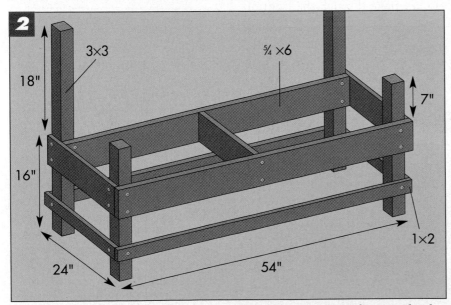

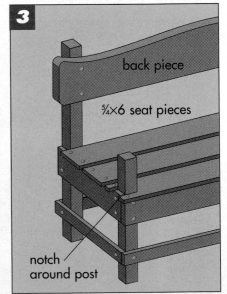

2. Construct the frame.
Using ¾×6, 3×3, and 1×2 lumber, build a frame as shown. You may want to make the notches for the rear posts (Step 4) before you build the frame. Note that the front (shorter) posts are inside the frame, while the rear (taller) posts sit behind the main frame. Check for square as you work. Attach all the pieces with 2-inch decking screws; drill pilot holes wherever you will drive a screw near the end of a board. Cut three ¾×6 pieces to 56 inches for the seat.

3. Add seat and back pieces.
Arrange the seat pieces so they overhang the frame by an inch on the sides and front. Notch around the front posts. Attach the pieces to the frame with 2½-inch screws. Install the back piece so that it overhangs the same distance on both posts.

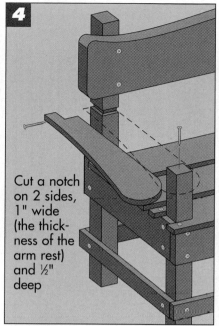

Cut a notch on 2 sides, 1" wide (the thick-ness of the arm rest) and ½" deep

4. Add armrests.

Make a ½-inch-deep notch on two sides of each rear post. Carefully cut several passes with a circular saw and clean out with a chisel. Slip the armrest into the notch, and rest it on top of the front post. Fasten with 2-inch deck screws, drilling pilot holes to eliminate splits.

5. Sand and finish.

Complete sanding all of the edges so the bench will be free of potential splinters. To retain the natural look of the wood, brush on a sealer/preservative with a light stain. For a more formal garden setting, give the the bench a couple coats of exterior enamel. This bench is ideal for a secluded area just off a flagstone path or graveled walkway.

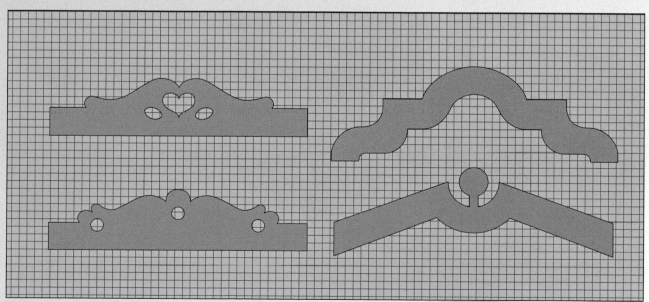

Alternative back designs

The back piece gives the bench its distinctive look, so you may want to come up with your own design. It should be symmetrical, so that the right half mirrors the left half. Don't be afraid to use your imagination, but avoid overly ornate designs; having a few simple curves usually makes the best statement. To ensure that the back piece will be strong enough, be careful not to cut away more than half of the board's width.

BUILDING A BENCH SWING

A bench like this will be one of your family's favorite spots in your yard or porch. The procedures for building it are not difficult, but you must do each of them precisely. A bench that hangs suspended from four points and gets pushed around a lot needs to be built well. Make sure every screw is attached firmly and without splitting the wood. Cut the pieces accurately, so they fit together tightly, and use a strong wood, like clear fir.

YOU'LL NEED

TIME: About a day and a half.
SKILLS: Precise measuring, squaring, cutting (especially lap joints), fastening with screws.
TOOLS: Power miter or radial-arm saw, drill, square, socket wrench.

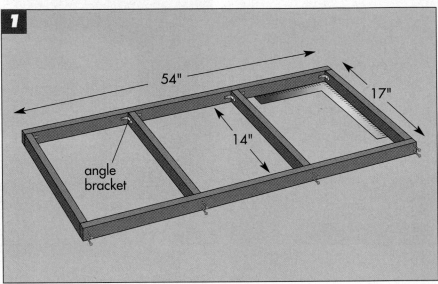

1. Build the seat frame.
Cut two 2×3s to 54 inches, and four to 14 inches. Carefully assemble the pieces to form a strong frame. Use a square as you work, and make sure the whole structure lies flat. Drill pilot holes before driving two 3-inch deck screws into each joint. On the insides of the joints, reinforce with angle brackets.

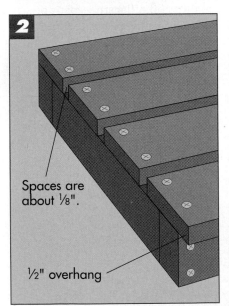

2. Attach the seat pieces.
Cut four 1×4s to 54 inches, space them evenly on the frame so that the ends are flush and the front piece overhangs ½ inch. Attach by drilling pilot holes and driving two 2-inch deck screws into each joint, so their heads are just slightly sunk below the surface of the wood. (You don't want water to puddle over the screw heads.)

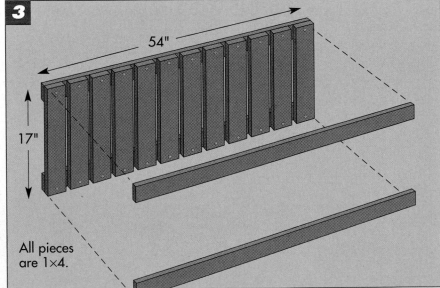

3. Build the back.
Make the back by sandwiching vertical 1×4s between horizontal 1x4s. Cut four 1×4s to 54 inches, and twelve 1×4s to 19 inches. Lay two of the long pieces on a flat, well-swept surface, parallel to each other and square. Lay the 12 short pieces on the long pieces, flush at the top and bottom with the edges of the long pieces. Make the two outside pieces flush to the ends of the long pieces and see that all the pieces are consistently spaced, with about ½-inch gaps. Attach with one 1¼-inch deck screw per joint. Recheck for square. Add the top pieces, flush at the edges. Drill pilot holes and drive two 2-inch deck screws per joint.

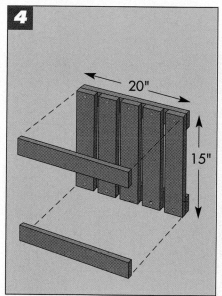

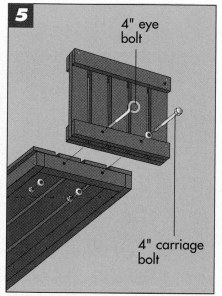

4" eye bolt

4" carriage bolt

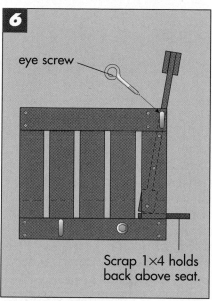

eye screw

Scrap 1×4 holds back above seat.

4. Build the arms.

For each arm, cut four 1×4s to 20 inches and five more to 15 inches. Sandwich the pieces together as you did for the back (step 3). Here, the gaps between the verticals will be about ⅝ inch.

Give the back and the arms a thorough sanding. Round off all the corners so there will be no sharp edges.

5. Attach the arms.

Lay the seat on a flat surface, and position one arm against it, so its front edge runs an inch past the front of the seat frame. Fasten the arm to the seat frame with a 4-inch carriage bolt in the rear and a 4-inch eye bolt in front. Flip the seat up and drive several 3-inch deck screws. Repeat on the other side.

6. Attach the back.

With a helper or two, slip the back in place. Use scrap pieces of 1×4 to hold the back ¾ inch above the seat surface. Tilt the back for comfort, as shown. Attach the back to the arms by drilling pilot holes and driving 3-inch deck screws. At the point where the top of the arm meets the back, drive a 4-inch eye screw.

7. Attach the hooks and hang.

Sand the bench so no one will get splinters, and apply finish or paint. Attach chain to the eye screws and bolts, and suspend from two eye hooks driven into very solid material overhead. Position the overhead hooks so that the chain angles slightly away from the swing on both sides so it doesn't rub against the swing. You will need to adjust the chain until you get just the right angle. Squeeze the hooks tight with pliers, to ensure that the chain cannot pop out.

EXPERTS' INSIGHT

WHERE TO HANG A SWINGING BENCH

If kids will play on the swing, provide plenty of room for swinging back and forth. How far they can swing will depend on the length of the chain. Don't position the swing near a window or breakable objects.

When locating a swing on a porch that has a ceiling, you will need to find the joists; simply attaching the bench to 1x bead board or other ceiling materials is a recipe for disaster. Use a stud finder, or tap with a hammer to find joists. Drive the hooks into the center of the joists.

MAKING AN ADIRONDACK CHAIR

Here's a classic design that's relatively easy to build. The contoured seat makes it far more comfortable than a straight bench.

Use wood that is resistant to rot and free of large knots and blemishes. The dark heartwood of redwood or cedar is an excellent choice; it will look great stained and sealed. Or use Select pressure-treated wood that has been kiln-dried after treatment (KDAT), then paint it. Choose boards clear of knots, checks, and cracks.

YOU'LL NEED

TIME: A day to cut the pieces and assemble the chair.
SKILLS: Accurate measuring and cutting, drilling pilot holes and driving screws.
TOOLS: Circular or table saw, saber saw, drill, square, compass, C-clamp.

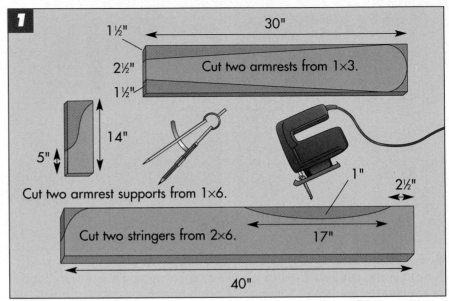

1. Cut the curved pieces.
Wherever you need two pieces that are the same, use the first piece as a template for the other. Use a compass to mark for the rounded end of the first arm piece. Draw the curved line of the stringer freehand, pressing lightly with the pencil and erasing and starting again until you get a smooth curve. The armrest supports do not have to be this exact shape; draw a design that pleases you.

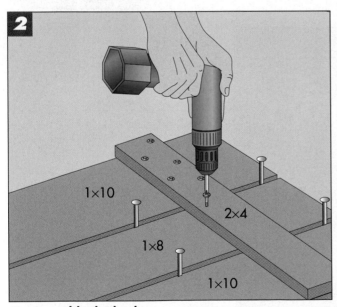

2. Assemble the back.
Cut two pieces of 1×10 and one 1×8 to 30 inches. Lay them next to each other on a flat surface with the 1×8 in the middle. Use spacers to maintain ¼-inch gaps between the boards, and make sure they are square to each other. Lay two 2×4 braces on top. They can overhang; you will cut them later. Attach the braces with polyurethane glue and 2-inch screws. Take care that the screws do not poke through.

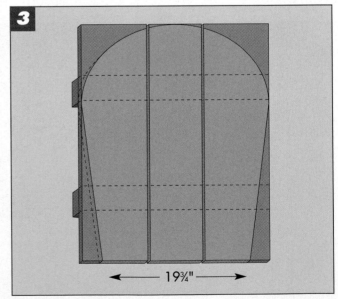

3. Cut the Back
Turn the back assembly upside-down. Mark for the arching upper cut using a notched wood compass (see page 267). Draw the two lower cut lines with a straightedge, taking care that the bottom width is 19¾ inches. Cut the straight lines with a circular saw, and use a saber saw for the curved cut. Before cutting, make sure you will not be cutting through any screws; remove some if necessary.

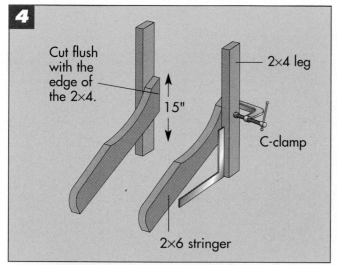

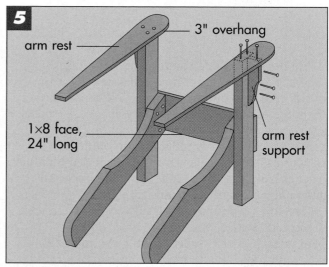

4. Assemble the legs and stringers.

Cut two 2×4s to 24 inches. Make a mark 15 inches from the bottom of one 2×4, and hold it next to a framing square on a level surface. Position one of the stringers that you cut in Step One so that its upper corner is at the 15-inch mark, and clamp it. Drill pilot holes and drive several 2½-inch decking screws. Cut the leading edge of the stringer flush with the edge of the 2×4. Repeat for the other leg; remember to make one left and one right leg.

5. Add arm rests, face piece.

Attach an arm rest support to the side of each leg. Clamp in place so that the top edge is flush with the top of the leg, carefully drive pilot and counterbore holes, and drive screws. Cut a piece of 1×8 to 26 inches, and attach it with screws to the front of the leg-and-stringer assemblies, so that the top edge is flush with the top of the stringer. Attach the arms to the top of the posts, so their front edges overhang the posts by 3 inches.

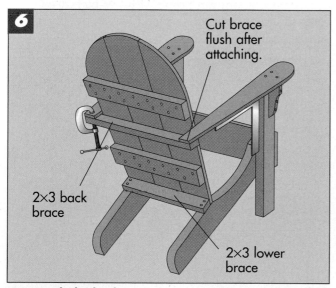

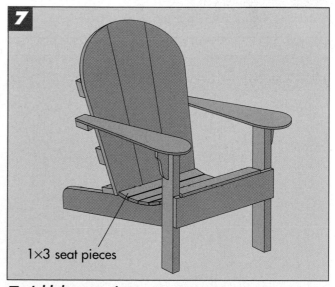

6. Attach the back.

Cut a 2×3 lower brace to 23 inches, and attach it to the stringers just at the end of the curved cuts. Have a helper hold the back in position while you drive screws to attach its bottom edge to the brace. Use a framing square to true up the arm rests, and mark for the position of the 2×3 back brace. Cut it longer than needed, and attach it with screws driven through the 1× lumber. Attach the arm rests to the back brace with two screws at each joint. It may help to use clamps while working. Cut the back brace flush on both sides.

7. Add the seat pieces.

If you would like to change the angle of the back, back out the screws, then move the bottom brace. Cut six 1×3s to 23 inches, and position them on the seat so they are evenly spaced. Drill pilot holes and drive two 2-inch screws at each joint.

Fill any countersunk holes with wood filler or dowels. Sand so there is no possibility of splinters; round off any sharp corners. Apply paint or finish.

BUILDING A RAISED PLANTER

Choose or design a planter that harmonizes with your deck, patio, or house. If you want it to blend in so that only the flowers will be noticed, use the same materials and finish as your house or deck surfaces. Create visual interest by adding simple bands of 1×2 or other molding. On outdoor structures like planters, simple butt-jointed moldings usually look better than mitered joints, especially after a few years of wear and tear.

Develop a planting strategy. If you live in an area with mild winters, you may be able to plant perennials in a box—check with local nurseries. If you want to be able to move things around, build light planters, or use planters as holders for flower pots. Protect your deck or patio surface from the water that seeps out the bottom of a planter—it can cause ugly stains. Provide a pathway for the water to seep through the patio or deck, or place a water-holding trivet under the planter.

YOU'LL NEED

TIME: About two thirds of a day.
SKILLS: Basic carpentry.
TOOLS: Circular saw, drill, tape measure.

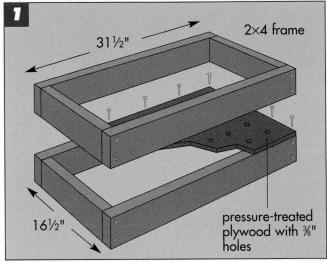

1. Build the frames, add plywood.
Use pressure-treated lumber and plywood that has a CCA rating of .40 or more or the label says "ground contact." Construct two simple frames out of 2×4s, both the same size. Check for square, and drive two 3-inch deck screws into each joint.

Cut a piece of pressure-treated plywood to fit, and fasten it to the bottom frame with 1⅝-inch deck screws. Drill a series of ⅜-inch holes in the plywood, so that water will be able to seep through easily.

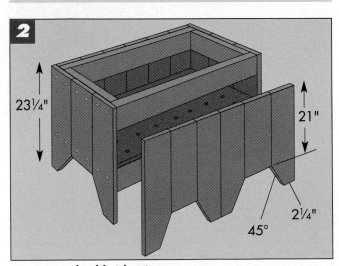

2. Cut and add side pieces.
Cut 12 legs with 45-degree cuts on one corner. The top of the miter cut will meet the bottom of the six straight-cut shorter pieces. Cut one piece, and use it as a template for the others. Cut shorter pieces to fill in. The dimensions shown will give you a planter that is 24 inches high. Attach legs and fillers to the frames with 1⅝-inch decking screws at each joint.

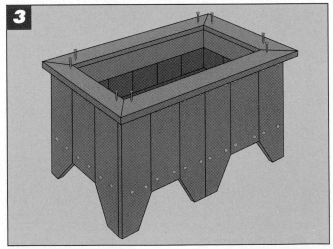

3. Add the top pieces.
Use 1×4s that are straight, dry, and have few knots. Hold in place, with the boards overhanging the front by an inch, and mark for mitered cuts, as shown, or cut the ends square and simply butt them together.

These top pieces come under a good deal of stress, so fasten them securely. Drill pilot holes and drive 2-inch deck screws, most of them into the frame and some into the side pieces.

Shovel in 4 to 6 inches of gravel, then fill with light soil that has plenty of organic matter.

MAKING A BENCH PLANTER

*B*enches and planters often sit side by side on a deck or patio, so why not build them together? This design uses stacked 2×4s for a solid, building-block sort of look. Here is a simple arrangement with two planters and one bench. You can easily modify this design to turn a corner and have three planters with two benches; the center planter will have both benches tied into it at 90-degree angles. Use rot-resistant lumber and choose smooth sides for the top of the bench.

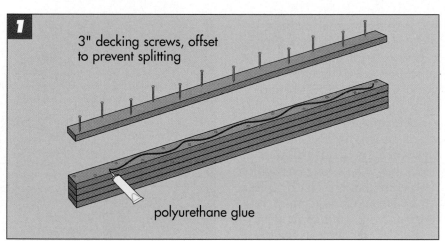

3" decking screws, offset to prevent splitting

polyurethane glue

1. Make the bench.

Laminate eight or more 2×4s, each no more than 8 feet long. Cut them all to the same length (the ends do not have to match exactly because they will not show). Stack them, apply a squiggle of polyurethane glue, and drive 3-inch deck screws every 6 inches in an alternating pattern to avoid splitting the wood. Use 2½-inch screws for the first piece, then use 3-inch screws. Glue and clamp the last piece rather than driving screws, so there will be no visible screw heads.

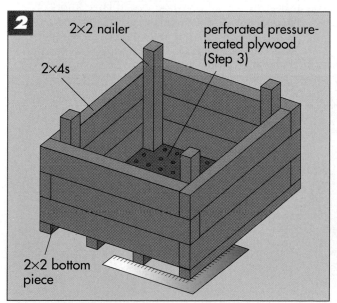

2×2 nailer

perforated pressure-treated plywood (Step 3)

2×4s

2×2 bottom piece

filler piece

2. Start building the boxes.

For a box 24 inches square and 21 inches tall, cut nineteen 2×4s to 22½ inches, four 2×2s to 24 inches, and four 2×2 nailers to 19½ inches.

Set the bottom 2×2s on a flat surface, evenly spaced to form a 24-inch square. With a helper or two, stack the first two courses of 2×4s in the pattern shown. Hold the pieces flush at their ends and tie them together by driving screws from the inside, through the nailers and into the 2×4s. To make the work easier, you can drive screws from the outside. Stack and attach three courses of 2×4s.

3. Fasten them together.

After you have built the boxes three courses tall, set them in place and set the bench on top. Continue stacking and attaching the 2×4 planter pieces. Install filler pieces next to the bench.

Build the box five courses tall. Cut a piece of pressure-treated plywood to fit inside each planter, drill a series of ⅜-inch holes in it, and screw it to the bottom pieces. If you like, protect the sides of your 2×4s by stapling thick plastic sheeting to the inside of the planters. Fill with 4 to 6 inches of gravel, a sheet of weed blocking fabric, and then light soil rich in organic material.

CONSTRUCTING A SEMICIRCULAR PLANTER

With its unusual shape, this planter will be a focal point in your backyard or patio. It's not difficult to build, though you will spend some time marking and cutting the curved pieces.

There are no 2× framing pieces in this design; the 1×4s and plywood cutouts carry all the stress. It will be strong enough for a structure that is 3 feet by 3 feet, but no larger. Choose highly rot-resistant wood, and apply plenty of sealer-preservative to the inside, bottom, and the 1×4 pieces because they will get wet.

YOU'LL NEED

TIME: Most of a day.
SKILLS: Measuring and squaring, marking and cutting smooth curves, fastening with screws.
TOOLS: Circular saw, sabersaw, square, drill.

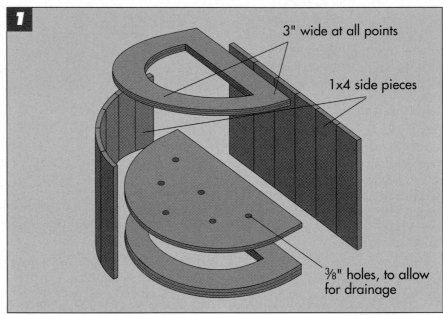

1

3" wide at all points

1×4 side pieces

⅜" holes, to allow for drainage

1. Cut plywood, side pieces.
Use a notched-wood or string-and-pencil compass (page 267) to mark the planter's contours on a sheet of ¾-inch pressure-treated plywood. Cut the plywood bottom piece and drill a series of ⅜-inch drainage holes. Use it as a template for the top and bottom D-shaped pieces. Cut the top piece carefully using a piece of plywood free of large knots or other weak spots. Cut all the 1×4 side pieces to the same length; 18 inches is the recommended height.

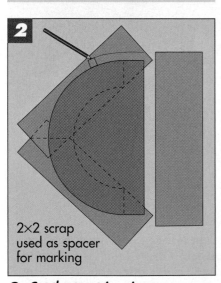

2

2×2 scrap used as spacer for marking

2. Cut the top trim pieces.
Depending on the size of your planter, use 2×10 or 2×12 to make the curve with two pieces. Use the top plywood piece and a scrap piece of 2×2 to mark for trim pieces that will overhang the sides by at least ½ inch. Cut with a saber saw and sand smooth. Cut the straight trim piece as well.

3

3. Assemble the box.
Attach the top plywood piece to the underside of the trim pieces, using 2-inch deck screws. Set the bottom piece on 2× scraps, to hold it off the ground while you work. With a helper, attach side pieces to it with 2-inch deck screws.

Once you have most of them attached, carefully slip the top piece over the structure, so the trim overhangs the side pieces. Fasten the tops of the side pieces to the plywood and the top trim by drilling pilot holes and driving 3-inch screws at an upward angle.

Sand and finish. Place 6 inches of gravel in the bottom of the planter, then fill with light soil that is rich in organic material.

BUILDING A PLANTER WITH A SITTING LEDGE

Gardening is easy if you can sit right next to your flower bed. And sometimes it's pleasant to just sit near the foliage. This solid structure can easily provide a place for plants and the gardener alike.

This easy-to-build planter box can accommodate anything from flowers to a small vegetable patch. Bottom pieces facilitate air circulation to protect the base of the planter and—if the box is on a deck—the deck planking itself.

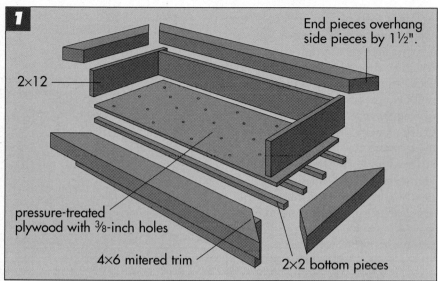

End pieces overhang side pieces by 1½".

2×12

pressure-treated plywood with ⅜-inch holes

4×6 mitered trim

2×2 bottom pieces

You'll Need

Time: Several hours.
Skills: Measuring and squaring, cutting with a circular saw, attaching with screws.
Tools: Circular saw, drill, square.

1. Cut the pieces.
Choose rot-resistant lumber for all pieces. Cut 2×2 bottom pieces and a sheet of pressure-treated plywood to form the base. The 2×12 end and side pieces will wrap around the plywood and sit on the 2×2s. Cut the end pieces

6 inches longer than the width of the plywood, so they run past the side pieces 1½ inches on each side. The box is capped with mitered 4×6 top trim. Use a speed square to mark for the 45-degree cuts; you will need to cut both sides with a circular saw.

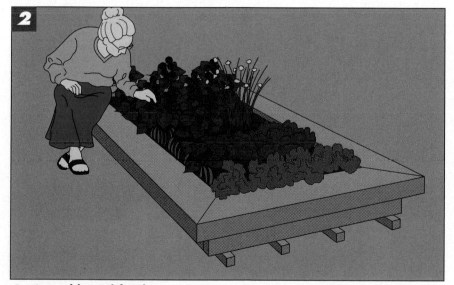

2. Assemble and finish.
Drill a grid of ⅜-inch holes in the plywood. Place it on evenly spaced 2×2s, and attach with 1⅝-inch deck screws. Assemble the sides and ends, attaching to each other and to the 2×2 bottom pieces with 3-inch deck screws. Attach the mitered trim pieces together by drilling pilot holes and horizontally

driving 3-inch deck screws. Drill pilot holes and drive 3-inch deck screws at an upward angle, from inside the box, through the 2×12s and into the 4×6s.

Sand all corners and edges smooth. Apply paint or sealer. Fill with several inches of gravel, followed by light soil that is rich in organic material.

EXPERTS' INSIGHT

GALVANIZED AND PLASTIC LINERS
Pressure-treated lumber and the heartwood of redwood or cedar will last a long time, especially if you allow for proper drainage and coat the wood with a sealer/preservative. But there are no guarantees that the wood will not become discolored or rot.

A custom-made galvanized liner placed in the finished planter will protect it. Build the planter, then have a sheet-metal company custom-make a liner with a drainage spout. Add holes for water to run out the bottom.

Or buy a piece of pond liner fabric to fit your planter. This material is available at gardening shops and home centers.

MAKING WINDOW BOXES

*T*his is a quick way to add charm to your home's exterior. Choose a spot that gets enough sun, but watch out for places that bake in the summer sun—a shallow box will need to be watered every day during the hot months. Use rot-resistant wood, and seal it well so it can stand the heat.

Determine the best height for your box. If the flowers will be tall, or if the view out of the window is important, you may want to lower it a foot or more below the windowsill.

YOU'LL NEED

TIME: Most of a day to build and hang a window box.
SKILLS: Basic carpentry.
TOOLS: Circular saw or power miter saw, saber saw, drill, square, sanding block, hammer.

EXPERTS' INSIGHT

WAYS OF ATTACHING WINDOW BOXES

■ Though small, a window box can get quite heavy when it rains, so anchor it well. It will tend to pull away at the top of the box, so anchor the top directly, and support it with well-anchored brackets.

■ On a frame house, drive long screws through the top portion of the box into framing members of the house, which are usually easy to find under a window. Attach brackets in the same way.

■ On a masonry house, things get a bit tougher. You will need to use masonry screws or lag bolts with lag shields driven into the masonry surface.

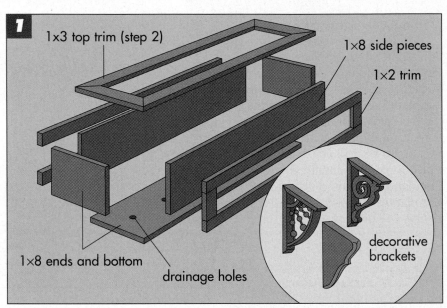

1x3 top trim (step 2)
1x8 side pieces
1x2 trim
1x8 ends and bottom
drainage holes
decorative brackets

1. Cut the pieces.

Cut the 1x8 bottom and sides to the length you want for your box—you may want to match the width of your window, including trim. Drill ⅜-inch drainage holes in the center, every 6 inches or so.

Cut the end pieces 1½ inches longer than the width of the bottom piece. The long 1x2 trim pieces are 1½ inches longer than the side pieces, and the short 1x2s are 4¼ inches long.

2. Build and brace.

Assemble the bottom and sides, drilling pilot holes and driving 2-inch deck screws to form a strong box. Add the 1x2 trim, which covers up the edges of the end and bottom pieces, flush to the bottom and top of the box. Fasten the trim with 4d galvanized nails. Cap the box off with 1x3 top trim, mitered at the corners and attached with 6d galvanized nails.

Apply paint or sealer. Anchor the box as described at left. Choose a decorative bracket like the one shown, or use a miter-cut 2x2 in the same way as the 4x4 angle brace is used on page 813. Fill with 2 inches of gravel, followed by light soil.

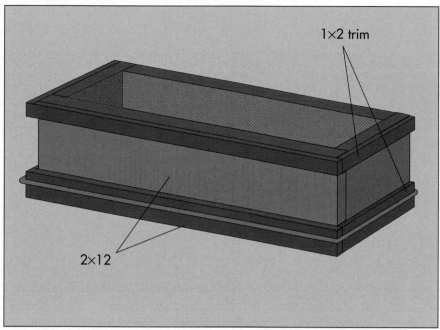

Building a large window box.

You can do some serious gardening outside your window with a massive box like this. Build it simply, using materials like pressure-treated 2×12 and painting it the color of the house. If you want, you can cover it with siding to match your house, or add a few pieces of trim.

Decide whether you will be gardening from inside your home or outside, and position the box for easy access. You don't want to have to climb a ladder every time you water or weed.

Make a wood support.

Support a heavy box at three points. Anchor a ledger for the rear of the box to rest on; attach angled braces to support the front of the box; and anchor the top of the box directly to the house, adding washers as spacers to allow room for airflow.

Add decorative touches.

Whether your window box is large or small, consider adding some ornamental touches. Make an apron like the one shown above, or come up with your own design, perhaps mirroring some other decorative element from your home's siding or trim.

You can make a cardboard template of half the design. Trace it onto a piece of 1× lumber, then flip it over for the other half. Cut out carefully with a saber saw. Sand all the curves so they look smooth. Attach the apron by drilling pilot and counterbore holes and driving screws upward.

Even if the box is otherwise supported, consider adding decorative end braces as well. Trace and cut them out of 1× lumber.

BUILDING A LEAN-TO SHED

A small shed like this has an advantage over a large garage: It's not big enough to become a hopeless mess with tools buried out of sight. You can build a larger structure than shown on these pages, but make it longer, and not much wider, so that it will be easy to keep organized. If you do make it wider by a foot or more, use 2×4s instead of 2×4s for the rafters and the floor joists.

Plan the size according to your needs. You may want to install a workbench or a potting bench. Be sure all your tools can be hung within easy reach, so you don't have to pile them up in a corner. If you want to do some carpentry work out of the shed, plan to store sawhorses in it, so you can quickly bring them outside. You may want to have an electrician install a receptacle.

If you live in an area with severe winters, frost heave will cause shallow footings to rise and fall, perhaps as much as an inch. If your shed will be attached to the house, it is important that it not rise and fall while the house stays still. So either leave it unattached, or check with local regulations, and be sure to dig and pour footings that extend below your frostline—the depth to which your ground freezes during the winter.

Because the structure will be exposed to the weather, use pressure-treated lumber and plywood throughout.

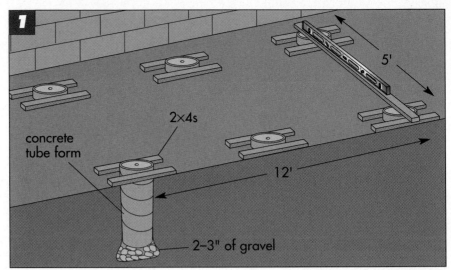

1. Install footings.
Mark the outline of your shed with stakes and string lines, and check for square (see page 655). Because the footing of a house is usually wider than its walls, you will probably not be able to dig right next to the house. Dig post holes at least 24 inches deep, or below your frostline. Shovel a few inches of gravel into each hole.

All the footings must be level with each other. Use a level and a straight board to find the highest spot, and start there. Insert a tube form and anchor it as shown, or use the arrangement shown on page 773. Then anchor all the other tube forms at the same level.

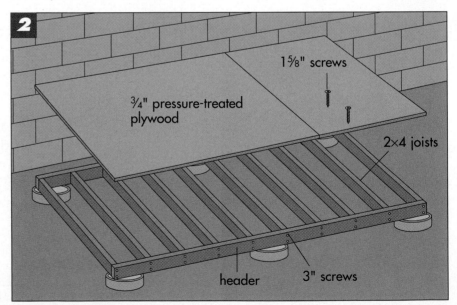

2. Build the floor.
Cut two 2×4 headers to the exact length of the shed, and cut the joists to its width, minus 3 inches. Work on a large, flat surface. Lay the headers side by side and mark them for joists every 16 inches (see page 817). Set all the pieces in place, and attach with two 3-inch deck screws at each joint. Set the floor frame on the concrete footings, and check for square.

Cut pieces of ¾-inch pressure-treated plywood to fit. Attach the plywood to the joists with 1⅝-inch deck screws.

ledger

8'

window rough
opening (see
instructions with
your window)

7'

door
opening

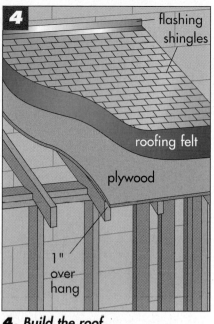

flashing

shingles

roofing felt

plywood

1"
over
hang

3. Frame the shed.

Attach a ledger board to the house, 8 feet above the floor. Make sure it is level, and that its ends are plumb with the ends of the floor. Build the 7-foot-high front wall by laying it out on the floor. Raise it into position and temporarily brace it so it is plumb. To make the first rafter, have a helper hold a 2×4 in place while you mark it. Use it as a template for the others. Attach the rafters with angle-driven 2-inch decking screws. For the side walls, measure each stud individually, by holding it in place with a level to make sure it is plumb while you mark it.

4. Build the roof.

Cut ½-inch plywood to fit, so it overhangs the rafters by 2 inches on all three sides. Attach with 1⅝-inch deck screws. Staple on roofing felt, and lay the shingles. Where the roof meets the house, install flashing; consult with your supplier or inspector for the right installation on your house.

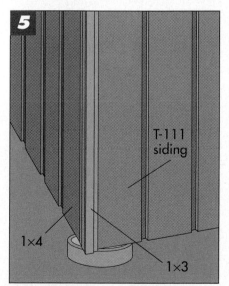

T-111
siding

1×4

1×3

5. Attach siding and trim.

Cover the exterior of the shed with siding. Make it snug against the house, and keep it about 2 inches above the ground. Caulk the joint where the plywood meets the house, and trim the outside corners with pieces of 1×3 and 1×4 lumber.

6. Add window and door, paint.

To build a simple door, use the instructions for a Z-frame gate, pages 778–779. Make the door out of a piece of sheet siding, or use 1×6s with no spaces between them. Attach to the shed with T-hinges; add a door spring if you want it to close automatically.

Add a gate latch, or install a hasp with a padlock for security (see page 772). Install your window, and trim it with butt-jointed 1×3s.

Apply two heavy coats of exterior paint to the siding, taking care that the bottom of each piece of lumber gets plenty of coverage.

BUILDING A SHED ON SKIDS

This shed is about as simple to buid as a free-standing roofed structure can be. It is completely enclosed to keep things dry inside. Building on skids saves you the work of installing a foundation. The weight of the shed keeps it stable. You'll need to know the size of the rough openings so you'll be able to purchase your window and prehung door before you build. A suggested size for the shed is 8 feet by 12 feet.

YOU'LL NEED
TIME: Several weekends, with a skilled helper.
SKILLS: Basic carpentry.
TOOLS: Circular saw, handsaw, drill, shovel, level, T-bevel.

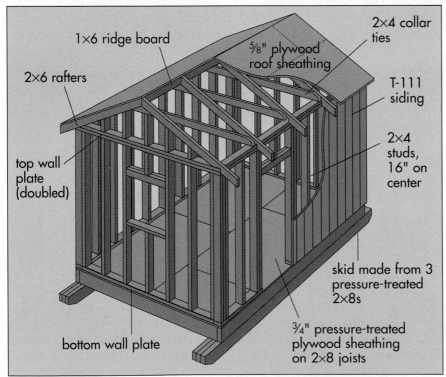

1×6 ridge board

2×6 rafters

⅝" plywood roof sheathing

2×4 collar ties

T-111 siding

2×4 studs, 16" on center

top wall plate (doubled)

skid made from 3 pressure-treated 2×8s

bottom wall plate

¾" pressure-treated plywood sheathing on 2×8 joists

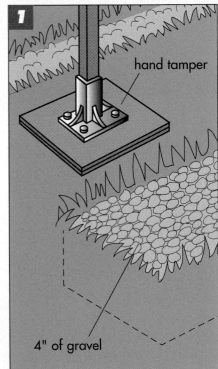

1

hand tamper

4" of gravel

View the project.
The structure rests on massive skids made of triple 2×8s. The floor framing is made of 2×8 joists, 16 inches on center.

The shed uses standard stud construction, with 2×4 studs 16 inches on center. The roof is supported by 2×6 rafters, 24 inches on center, that meet on a 1×6 ridge board at the peak. Collar ties on every other rafter ensure that the walls will not bow outward (see page 819).

1. Provide a foundation.
The skids must be level with each other. Dig parallel trenches, 3 feet longer than the shed's length, and fill the trenches with 4 inches of well-tamped gravel. Check that the tamped gravel is level.

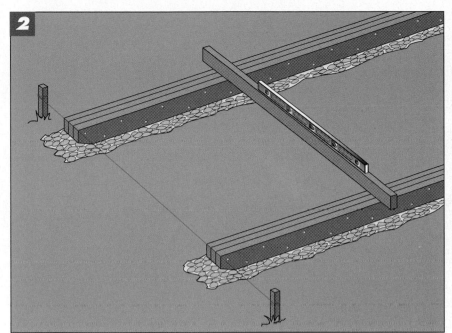

2

2. Build and set the skids.

Make the skids out of three pressure-treated 2×8s; be sure they have a CCA retention level of at least .40 or have a label that says *ground contact.*

Cut the first piece 32 inches longer than the length of the shed, giving it a decorative cut like the one shown. Use it as a template for the other five pieces. Laminate the pieces together by driving 3-inch deck screws in an alternating pattern every 6 inches.

Set the skids on the gravel. Run a string line that touches both ends, and use the 3-4-5 method to check for square (see page 726). Make sure the skids are level, and level with each other.

EXPERTS' INSIGHT

OTHER FOUNDATION POSSIBILITIES

This shed will float in areas subject to hard frosts—it will rise up a bit in the winter and settle back down when the ground thaws. Many garages also float, so this is not a problem unless your local building department demands footings that extend below the frostline.

Because the skids distribute the weight of the shed over a large area, the foundations under them do not have to be very deep. A standard concrete patio slab, in good condition, will be strong enough.

If you live in a dry area with soil that never stays wet for long, you may be able to simply tamp the ground firm and set the skids on top of it.

3

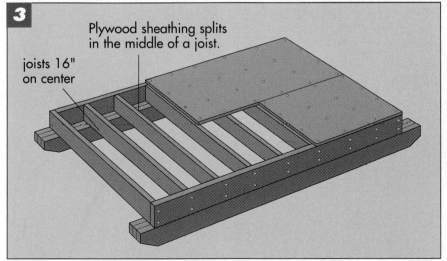

Plywood sheathing splits in the middle of a joist.

joists 16" on center

3. Frame and sheath the floor.

Use pressure-treated 2×8s and plywood. Cut two 2×8s to the length of your shed, set them next to each other, and mark for joists that are 16 inches on center. (This means that you must subtract ¾ inch from each multiple of 16 before making your line; see the illustration for Step 4.)

Cut joists to the width of the shed, minus 3 inches, and assemble the framing box with 3-inch deck screws. Use the plywood to make sure the frame is square. Attach plywood to the joists with 1⅝-inch deck screws.

4

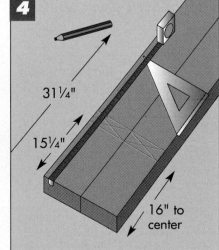

31¼"

15¼"

16" to center

4. Cut and lay out wall plates.

For each wall, begin by cutting the bottom and top plates. Set them next to each other, and lay them out as you did the floor joists. Study the framing drawing on page 818 before laying out for the window and door.

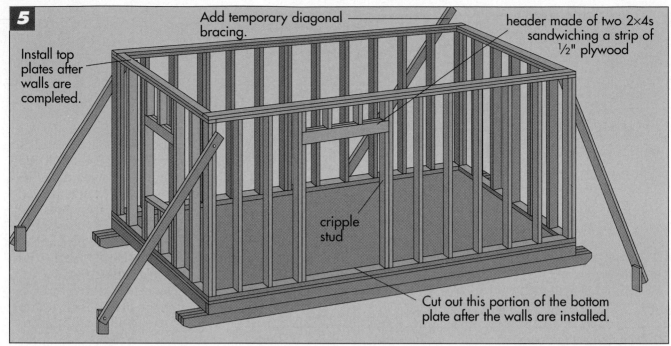

5 Install top plates after walls are completed.

Add temporary diagonal bracing.

header made of two 2×4s sandwiching a strip of ½" plywood

cripple stud

Cut out this portion of the bottom plate after the walls are installed.

5. Frame the walls.

Have your prehung door and your window on hand, so you know the rough openings for each. Buy pre-cut studs, or cut them to the height of the wall, minus 4½ inches. Note that on either side of the window and the door, cripple studs are used. Assemble the walls on the shed floor or another flat surface. Position the studs on the layout lines, and drive two 3-inch deck screws or 16d nails for each joint. With two or more helpers, raise each wall into position and temporarily brace it so it is plumb in both directions. Fasten the walls together and add the top plate.

EXPERTS' INSIGHT

FIGURING ROOF PITCH

The horizontal distance traveled by a rafter is called the roof's run. The vertical distance, from the top of the wall to the top of the roof, is the rise. The slope of a roof is inches of rise per inches of run. A 6–12 pitch, for instance, means that the roof rises 6 inches for every 12 inches of run.

Your building department will probably have pitch requirements, so check with the folks there before building. You may want to duplicate the pitch of your house roof on your shed's roof. To figure the pitch of an existing roof, use two levels, one held plumb and the other held level, and measure the rise and run.

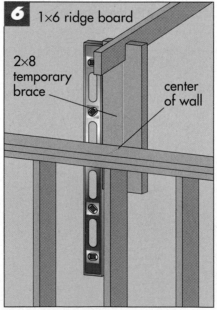

6 1×6 ridge board

2×8 temporary brace

center of wall

6. Temporarily prop the ridge.

Determine how high your ridge board should be. At each end, firmly anchor a notched piece of 2×8 to the inside of the wall framing. Use a level to make sure the board is plumb. Cut a 1×6 ridge board to the length of the shed and set it in place.

7 ridge cut

birds-mouth cut

7. Mark for the rafters.

Have two helpers hold a 2×6 in place against the ridge board and the top plate while you mark with a pencil. Mark the top cut at the ridge and the birds-mouth cut where the rafter will sit on the top wall plate. You may have to experiment before getting it right.

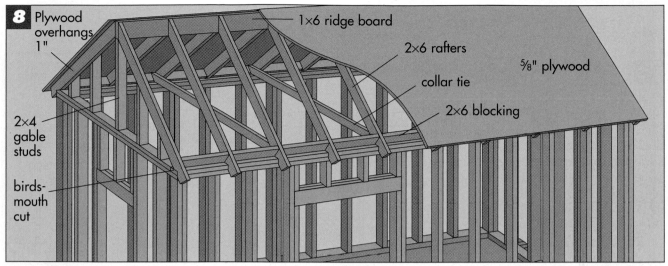

8 Plywood overhangs 1"
1×6 ridge board
2×6 rafters
collar tie
⅝" plywood
2×6 blocking
2×4 gable studs
birds-mouth cut

8. Build the roof.

This will be the most time-consuming part of the job. Cut two rafters and test them by holding them in place; joints at the ridge and at the top plate should be tight. Use the first rafter as a template for making the others. Cut 2×6 blocking to 22½ inches so that you will end up with rafters spaced 24 inches on center.

Work with at least two helpers, because your structure will be very wobbly at first. Mark layout lines on the top plates and both sides of the ridge. Have the helpers hold the rafters in place as you attach. Drive nails through the ridge and into the rafters, and toenail at the birds-mouth cut. Install the blocking as you go. Every other rafter, install a collar tie linking rafters from one sidewall to the other. Cut and notch 2×4 gable studs to fit.

Attach the plywood sheathing with 8d nails. Let it overhang the gable ends by 1½ inches. Immediately cover the sheathing with roofing material.

9 ⅛" gap

9. Install window and siding

Attach the window to the framing; check for plumb and square before driving screws. Attach ⅝-inch T-111 siding directly to the studs with 8d siding nails, 6 inches apart on the edges, and 12 inches apart elsewhere. Leave a ⅛-inch gap between the siding and the window frame, and caulk it. Trim the corners with 1×3 and 1×4 (see page 815).

10 Plumb and attach hinge side first.
jamb

10. Install a prehung door.

Buy a solid-core, exterior door with a lockset that will withstand weather. Attach the hinge side of the jamb first, checking for plumb and driving 8d casing nails. Make the front edge of the jamb flush with the siding. Shim and attach the other side of the jamb so the door closes easily. Add Z flashing above the door and attach brick molding over the jamb and siding.

11 ledger
2×4 frame

11. Add a landing.

Start with a ledger board attached to the shed, and support the front of the 2×4 frame with posts sunk in concrete or tamped soil. To keep rain and snow out of the shed, make sure that the top of the finished landing will be an inch or so below the interior floor.

BUILDING A SIMPLE PLAYHOUSE

Some playhouses are grand productions that use the same construction techniques you would expect in a full-size house, including stud walls, rafters, and real windows and doors—sometimes even electrical wiring. However, given that kids typically outgrow a playhouse in a few years, it makes sense to keep things simple. This project can be built in a weekend. Because it uses plywood reinforced with minimal framing, the only difficult steps involve plunge cutting the windows and doors.

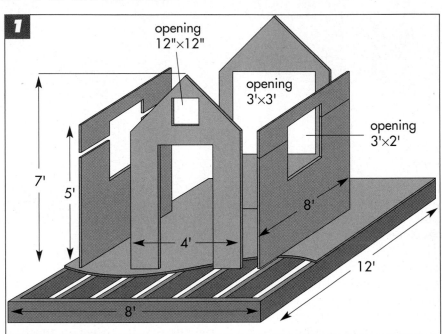

1. Make the base.
Using pressure-treated 2×4s, build a framing box for the floor. Make it larger than the house will be (see Step 6), with joists 16 or 24 inches on center. Sheath the frame with ½-inch pressure-treated plywood. (See pages 814 and 819 for instructions on laying out joists and building a base.)

YOU'LL NEED

TIME: Two days, with a helper.
SKILLS: Basic carpentry, applying roof shingles.
TOOLS: Circular saw, level, hammer, handsaw, tape measure, drill, chalkline.

Support the plywood well so ends of cuts do not crack.

2. Cut the pieces.
Out of a sheet of ¾-inch plywood, mark with a chalk line and cut the perimeter of the front piece as shown in step one. Use it as a template for the rear piece. For each of the sides, use one full sheet and one sheet rip-cut to 12 inches wide.

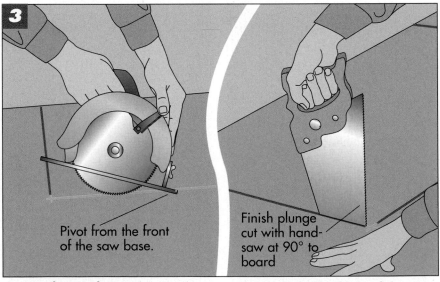

Pivot from the front of the saw base.

Finish plunge cut with hand-saw at 90° to board

3. Cut the windows.
Place the top and bottom wall pieces together and mark the window opening. Measure and mark the end windows. Cut out with a circular saw. You will need to make some plunge cuts. Set the blade to the correct depth. Retract the safety guard and tilt the saw forward, with the front of the baseplate resting on the plywood. Start the saw and lower it slowly into the cut line.

Finish the cuts with a handsaw, held at a 90-degree angle to the plywood so it cuts the same distance on both sides.

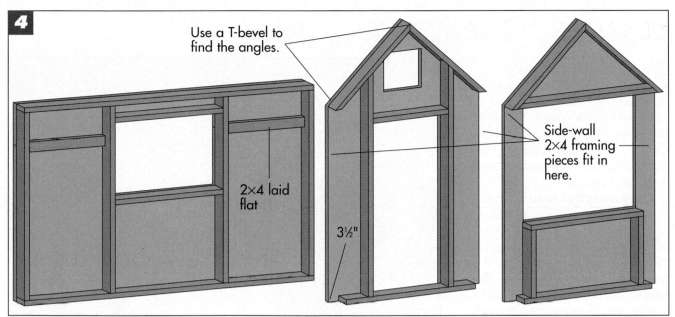

4

Use a T-bevel to find the angles.

2×4 laid flat

3½"

Side-wall 2×4 framing pieces fit in here.

4. Add framing and assemble.
Reinforce the plywood walls with 2×4 frames. For each of the side walls, build a rectangular box, the same size as the wall, out of four 2×4s fastened together with 3-inch deck screws. Lay the plywood on top, and fasten with 2-inch deck screws. Turn the wall over and add 2×4s to frame around the window, and flat-laid 2×4s to secure the plywood splice.

With two helpers, raise one end wall and one side wall, and attach them at each corner with 2-inch screws driven through the end wall and into the framing of the side wall.

Add framing for the end walls as shown. Use a T-bevel to find the angles, and cut the pieces with a circular saw. Attach the end walls to the side walls with 3-inch screws tying 2×4s together and 2-inch screws driven through the plywood.

Center the structure on the base and attach it with 3-inch screws driven into joists.

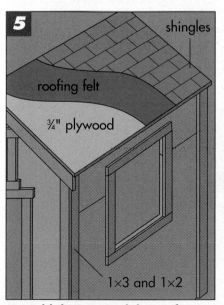

5

shingles

roofing felt

¾" plywood

1×3 and 1×2

5. Add the trim and the roof.
Trim is not necessary, but it will make the structure look more like a real house. For something easy to install yet charming, use butt-jointed 1×3s as shown. Install ¾-inch plywood for the roof, and lay roofing felt and shingles.

6

6. Decorate and paint.
Trim and decorate to suit your kids' taste. Adding a simple 2×4 fence around the "deck" like the one shown here is a nice finishing touch and makes your kids feel like real homeowners.

Sand all the edges well so there will be no splinters. Brush on two coats of high-quality exterior paint—bright, primary colors are a good choice.

INSTALLING A PLAYGROUND AREA

If a playground kit suits your kids' requirements and you're satisfied with the quality of its materials, that's your best option. However, you may decide a better choice is to buy the components your kids enjoy most, and create your own design.

Use lumber that won't rot and is unlikely to splinter. Heartwood of redwood or cedar is a good choice. Modern pressure-treated lumber is not dangerous after it is installed, but may crack. Kiln-dried pressure-treated wood (KDAT) is less likely to splinter and is worth the expense.

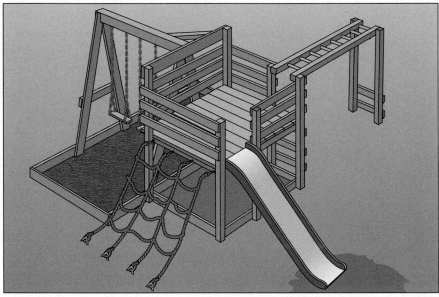

YOU'LL NEED

TIME: Two days, with a helper.
SKILLS: Measuring, plumbing and leveling, cutting.
TOOLS: Level, circular saw, wrenches, post-hole digger, drill.

The play center shown here will amuse children of many ages. A semi-sheltered sandbox provides a safe place for toddlers to play for hours at a time. Swings, a slide, a net ladder, and a fort will keep young children happy and active as they grow older. Monkey bars and a tire swing add more challenging and rambunctious activities for older kids up to 10 or 11 years of age.

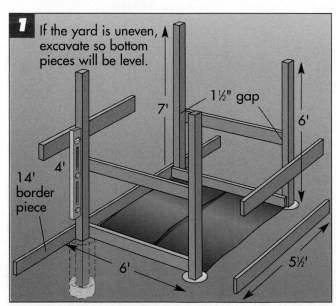

1 If the yard is uneven, excavate so bottom pieces will be level.

7'
1½" gap
6'
4'
14' border piece
6'
5½'

1. Build the basic frame.

Lay out for four postholes that form a square, dig them at least 30 inches deep, and shovel in a few inches of gravel. Excavate away all the sod from the area inside the square, and cover the area with landscaping fabric.

Place the posts and temporarily brace two of them so they are plumb in both directions. Construct the frame as shown out of 4×4s and 2×6s. Drive two 3-inch screws at each joint. Cut the posts to height.

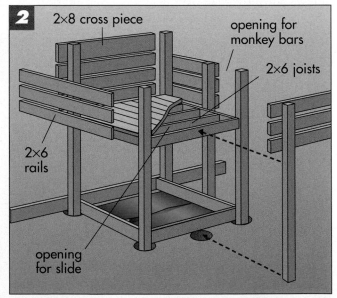

2 2×8 cross piece
opening for monkey bars
2×6 joists
2×6 rails
opening for slide

2. Add the platform and rails.

Install three evenly spaced 2×6 interior joists. Cut and fasten decking boards (either 2×6s or ⁵⁄₄×6 decking), leaving a ¼-inch gap between the boards. Install two more posts, leaving room for the monkey bars on one side and the slide on another. Cut and install 2×6 rails and one 2×8 crosspiece, spacing them evenly and checking for level.

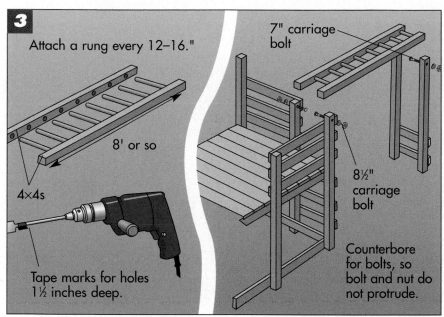

3

Attach a rung every 12–16."

8' or so

4×4s

Tape marks for holes 1½ inches deep.

7" carriage bolt

8½" carriage bolt

Counterbore for bolts, so bolt and nut do not protrude.

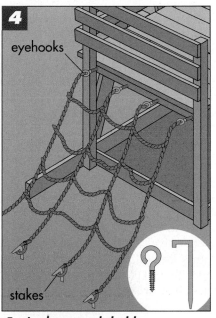

4

eyehooks

stakes

3. Make the monkey bars.

Place a piece of tape on a 1¼-inch drill bit as a depth gauge for boring holes 1½ inches deep. Cut two 4×4s to the length of the monkey bars, lay them side by side, and mark them both for evenly spaced holes. Drill the holes. Cut 1¼-inch dowel pieces

that are 4 inches shorter than the total width of the monkey bars. Dry-fit the pieces to make sure the unit will fit snugly in your opening. Disassemble, squirt polyurethane glue into each hole, reassemble, and clamp together. Install two posts at the other end of the monkey bars.

4. Anchor a web ladder.

Where the ladder will attach to the platform, drill holes and install eyehooks. At the bottom, attach the webbing by driving stakes. To reduce risk of injury, bury the hooks or shield them with blocks of rubber.

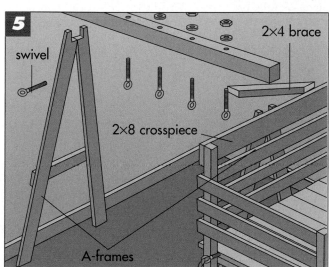

5

swivel

2×4 brace

2×8 crosspiece

A-frames

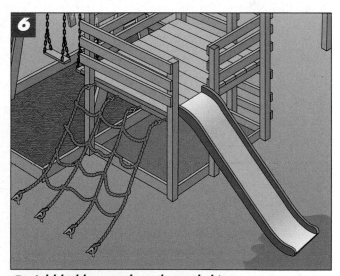

6

5. Build the swing set.

On a 12-foot-long 4×6 or 4×8 beam, mark for holes, depending on the width of your swing seats. Drill with a long bit and install eyehooks for the swings and a swivel eyehook for the tire swing. Construct A-frames out of 2×6s, with notches at the top so the beam will fit snugly. Attach one A-frame to the 2×8 cross piece, set the beam in its notch, and have a helper hold the other A-frame while you set the beam into its notch. Add the 2×4 angle support, driving 3-inch screws to secure the beam.

6. Add ladder, sand, and wood chips.

Add the three remaining wood-chip area framing pieces, excavate the area, and install landscaping fabric. Fill this area with wood chips, and fill the area under the platform with sand. Attach the ladder and the swings according to manufacturer's directions. Sand the structure carefully, and paint or apply a sealer/preservative.

BUILDING BIRDHOUSES

Birds are not only fun to have around, they help keep your yard free of insects. In urban and suburban areas, however, birds have a difficult time finding a place to nest. A birdhouse may be the key to making your area suitable habitat for certain types of birds. A bird feeder (pages 826–827) also might help.

Some birdhouses are purely decorative. If you want to attract birds, design your project with specific inhabitants in mind (see the chart at lower right). Once it is built, don't paint it with bright colors; most birds prefer to blend in with their surroundings, so green or brown tones are best—or apply a light stain to cedar or redwood.

Place a birdhouse where squirrels and cats can't get at it. To keep the inside dry, face the hole away from prevailing winds. If you hang the birdhouse, use two wires, so it will not spin. Many birds are comfortable living fairly close to humans, but will get skittish when people approach. So place the house within easy viewing distance while keeping it away from often-used footpaths. Often the best option is to place the birdhouse on top of a pole made of pipe.

Clean your birdhouse thoroughly once a year. Use a mildewcide if there is evidence of lice or other pests. Some birds will not move into a house that has not been cleaned.

YOU'LL NEED

TIME: A couple of hours.
SKILLS: Moderate carpentry skills.
TOOLS: Drill, hammer, speed square, any type of saw.

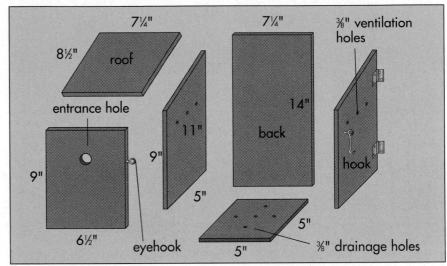

Plan a basic birdhouse.
Use this plan for a general-purpose birdhouse. Or decide which species of bird you want to attract, and build the house to the dimensions shown in the chart below. As you measure for cutting individual pieces, keep in mind how the pieces will overlap. For instance, the front piece should be 1½ inches wider than the floor.

Use cedar or redwood 1×8 lumber that is completely dry. Cut the pieces, and drill the holes. Attach the nonhinged side, the floor, and the front together, drilling pilot holes and driving 1⅝-inch deck screws or 6d galvanized nails. Attach the other side with hinges only, and add the roof. Drill pilot holes and screw in the eye and the hook.

MATCHING THE HOUSE TO THE BIRD

Species	Floor Size	Height	Hole Diameter	Distance Above Ground
Bluebird	5" × 5"	8"	1½"	5' to 10'
Chickadee	4" × 4"	8" to 10"	1⅛"	6' to 15'
Finch	6" × 6"	6"	2"	8' to 12'
Flicker	7" × 7"	16" to 18"	2½"	6' to 20'
Kestrel or Screech-Owl	8" × 8"	12" to 15"	3"	10' to 20'
Nuthatch	4" × 4"	8" to 10"	1¼"	12' to 20'
Starling	6" × 6"	16" to 18"	2"	10' to 25'
Tree Swallow	5" × 5"	6"	1½"	10' to 15'
Titmouse	4" × 4"	8" to 10"	1¼"	6' to 15'
Downy Woodpecker	4" × 4"	8" to 10"	1¼"	6' to 20'
Red-Bellied and Red-Headed Woodpecker	6" × 6"	12" to 15"	2½"	12' to 20'
Carolina Wren	4" × 4"	6" to 8"	1½"	6' to 10'
House Wren or Winter Wren	4" × 4"	6" to 8"	1" to 1¼"	6' to 10'

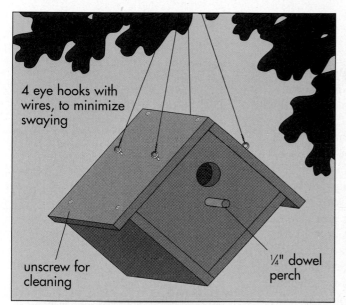

4 eye hooks with wires, to minimize swaying

unscrew for cleaning

¼" dowel perch

Build a diamond-shaped house with perch.

To build this simple project, cut front and back pieces about 8 inches square. Cut the side pieces to fit. The roof pieces should overhang the sides by about an inch. Use screws for at least one of the roof pieces, so you can remove it for cleaning. For the perch, drill a ¾-inch hole, squirt in a little polyurethane glue, and tap in a piece of ¼-inch hardwood dowel.

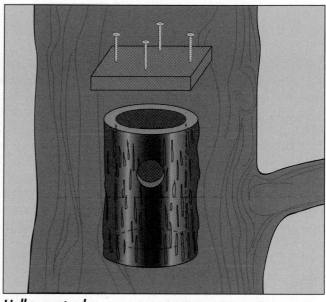

Hollow out a log.

This may last only a few years, but it is attractive and easy to build. Cut a piece of log that is about 4 inches wider than the floor dimension you want (see the chart, page 824). Drilling from the top, make a series of holes with a 1-inch bit. (Mark the bit with a piece of tape to make sure you don't drill too deeply.) Clean out the center with a chisel, and drill the opening hole. Attach the cover with screws.

Construct an open-ended house.

Robins, phoebes and barn swallows will be attracted to a house with an open front. Place it 8 to 15 feet above the ground, securely anchored to a bough or trunk that will not sway in the wind. Position the house so it is at least partially protected from prevailing wind.

There's no need for a hinged or removable section because you can clean this one easily.

Cut the sides, roof pieces, and floor out of 1×8 (which is actually 7¼ inches wide). You will need to bevel-cut the top edges of the side pieces at 45 degrees. Attach the pieces together with 2-inch deck screws or 6d galvanized nails. Add the 1×2 threshold and the mounting board, which doubles as the back of the house.

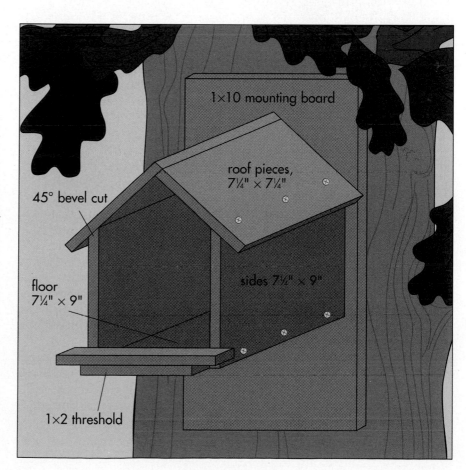

1×10 mounting board

roof pieces, 7¼" × 7¼"

45° bevel cut

floor 7¼" × 9"

sides 7½" × 9"

1×2 threshold

CONSTRUCTING BIRD FEEDERS

Because some birds are more sensitive than others to the presence of people, you may want to place two or three feeders at varying distances from the house. Experiment with different kinds of seed to find the type that attracts the birds you most want to see. If a feeder is close to a tree or some other form of cover, rather than being out in the open, you will be more likely to attract shy birds. Make and place the feeder so it will be easy to fill.

YOU'LL NEED

TIME: Several hours.
SKILLS: Measuring, squaring, and cutting, driving nails or screws.
TOOLS: Saw, drill, square, hammer, posthole digger.

1. To make a hopper feeder, cut and assemble the pieces.
Use cedar or redwood 1×10 with very few knots. Cut the pieces to the dimensions shown. To make the cleats that hold the glass, rip-cut 1× stock to ¾ inch wide; the length does not have to be exact. Attach the cleats with small brads and polyurethane glue. Note the small piece at the bottom that keeps the glass from sliding down.

For all joints, drill pilot holes before driving 1⅝-inch decking screws or 6d galvanized nails. Assemble the back, sides, and floor. Add the 1×2 trim pieces, flush with the bottom so they form a lip for the tray. Attach the roof with hinges that allow you to open it all the way for easy filling.

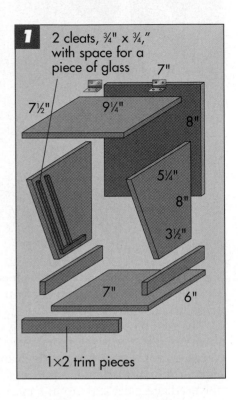

1 2 cleats, ¾" x ¾," with space for a piece of glass
7"
7½"   9¼"
8"
5¼"
8"
3½"
7"   6"
1×2 trim pieces

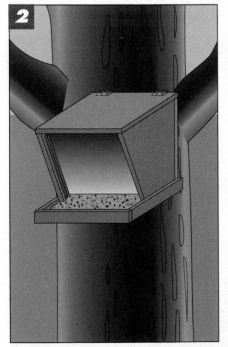

2. Add glass and mount.
Measure the opening and have a piece of glass cut to fit. Slide it into place; there's no need to caulk it. Attach the feeder to a pole or the side of a tree. Drill pilot holes and drive screws through the back or the bottom.

EXPERTS' INSIGHT

KEEPING THE SQUIRRELS AWAY

Squirrels are remarkably ingenious creatures. If there is a way for them to get at a feeder or a birdhouse, they will figure it out. So make a serious effort to outsmart them.

If you can hang a feeder by 2 feet or so of wire, that will probably keep them away. Or, put the feeder on a pole, and wrap the pole with 3 feet of galvanized or aluminum sheet metal; they will have a hard time climbing up it (especially if you spray it with a lubricant such as WD40).

You can buy ready-made baffles designed to keep squirrels from climbing a pole. Or make your own, using galvanized or aluminum sheet metal as shown.

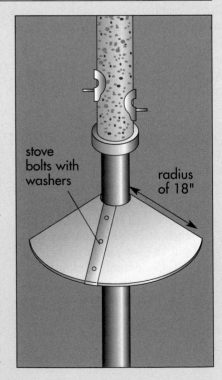

stove bolts with washers
radius of 18"

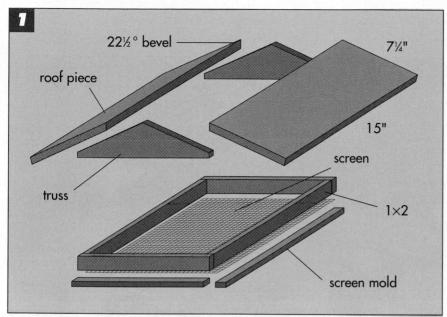

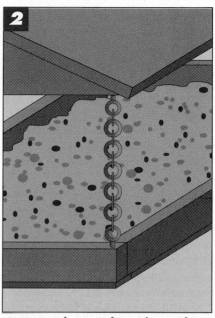

1. To make an open-air feeder, build the roof and the tray.

Use heartwood of redwood or cedar, clear or with only tiny knots. For all joints, drill pilot holes and drive 1⅜-inch screws or 6d galvanized nails.

Bevel-cut the top edge of the roof pieces at 22½ degrees. Temporarily join the roof pieces at the peak with small brads, and use the roof as a template to mark for the trusses. Cut the trusses and attach the roof to them.

Construct a 1×2 frame that will hang directly below the trusses. Cut aluminum screen to fit, and attach it to the underside with pieces of screen molding; attach the molding with small brads.

2. Hang the tray from the roof.

Insert four eye hooks into the trusses and four into the tray; position them so that the tray will hang directly below the roof. Cut four sections of chain, all with the same number of links, about 6 inches long. Use pliers to open the chain links, insert them into the eye hooks, and close them again.

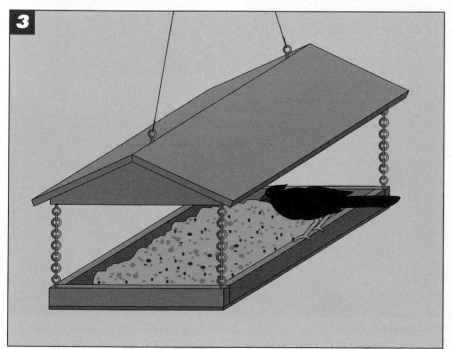

3. Finish and hang the feeder.

A coat of sealer/preservative will hold the natural color of your wood; otherwise it will turn gray. Insert two eye hooks through the peak of the roof and into the trusses. Hang the feeder with chain or wire. This feeder will be easy to load with seed, and the screen will help seeds to dry out after rains.

Make a suet feeder.

Some birds need suet to survive the winter. Although you can buy a hanging wire basket designed to hold suet, a section of log with holes bored in it works as well and blends better into the surroundings.

ADDING A WATER GARDEN

Once an extravagance available only to the wealthy, garden pools are now affordable and buildable for almost any homeowner. A pool will enable you to bring exciting new species of plants and animals into your back yard.

You can make a simple and small reflecting pond by digging a hole and setting a galvanized horse trough in it. (Troughs are available at farm supply stores and some home centers.) Add a recycling pump to keep the water aerated. The project presented here is more elaborate, and allows you to choose your own shape and size.

This is a big project. To save your back, you may want to hire some high school kids to do most of the digging.

If possible, choose a flat spot for the pool—remember that the rim of the pool must be level. A spot in the sun rather than under a tree will keep the water warmer, and you won't have to clean out all those leaves.

The right mix of plants and fish can work to keep the pool clean and healthy. But maintaining a pond only in this way is tricky. If you add a pump with a fountain, your job will be made easier, because the fountain adds a bit of oxygen to the water, and keeping the water moving helps prevent insects (including mosquitoes) from breeding. Have an electrician install an outside receptacle with a GFCI outlet, so you can plug in the pump.

YOU'LL NEED

TIME: Several days, with a helper.
SKILLS: Digging, leveling, laying stones, connecting a pump.
TOOLS: Shovels, rake, hand tamper, wheelbarrow, garden hose, level, scissors.

1. Dig the hole.
Contact your utility companies to make sure you will not damage electrical, gas, phone, or water lines. Lay a garden hose on the lawn in the shape of your future pool. Keep the shape fairly simple.

Dig a hole that is at least 2 feet deep. (In areas with cold winters, dig at least 3 feet deep if you want fish to survive.) Completely remove any organic material, roots, and sharp stones.

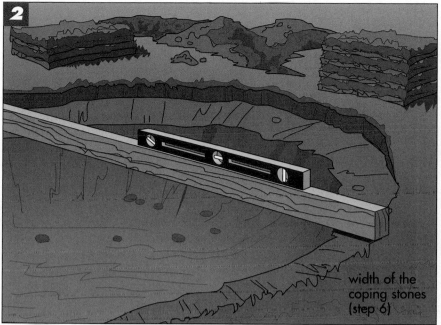

width of the coping stones (step 6)

2. Cut sod and level the rim.

Around the edge of the pool, use a square-edged shovel or an edge cutter to neatly remove the sod in a path that is wide enough for the paving materials you will be using (see Step 6).

Use a level set on top of a straight board to see that the pool rim is level all the way around. If needed, remove soil from the high spots or add soil to the low spots, and tamp firmly.

3. Pack the sides, then add sand.

Use a hand tamper to compact the soil on the sides and bottom of the pool. Make sure there is nothing that could tear the plastic liner (Step 4). Shovel sand onto the bottom of the pool, and spread it out with a rake, so it is about 2 inches thick.

4. Lay the liner and bricks.

Use pool liner made of PVC plastic or synthetic rubber, at least 45 mils thick. Place it in the middle of the pool bottom and unfold it,

molding it to the shape of the pool as you go. Make sure there is plenty of liner all around the perimeter; it may pull down when you fill the pool.

Use a garden hose to fill the pool with water, and edge the pool with bricks. Cut the liner along the sod line with a pair of scissors.

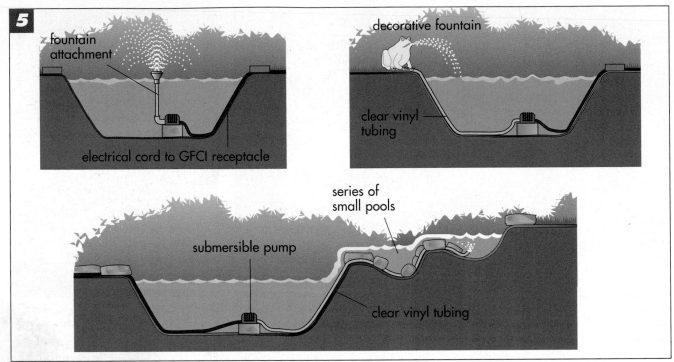

5 fountain attachment

electrical cord to GFCI receptacle

decorative fountain

clear vinyl tubing

series of small pools

submersible pump

clear vinyl tubing

5. Install a water pump.

You have three options: A fountain in the middle of the pond (upper left) can either spray up into the air, or it can be set lower so it just bubbles up and keeps the water in motion. A variety of fountain heads are available.

A decorative fountain placed outside the pool (upper right) recirculates water through a statue of your choice. Use a statue made for the purpose, or think up your own playful design.

A waterfall (bottom) is not as hard to make as you may think. Use the soil that you took out of the pool to create an elevated area with dips. Line the area with pool liner, and lay smooth rocks over it, taking care not to rip the liner.

6 brick

gravel and sand

pavers used for coping (flagstones also can be used)

6. Add pavers and pebbles.

Behind the bricks, lay a base of gravel and sand; tamp and smooth it. Set the coping stones or pavers so they overhang the bricks by an inch or so. Shovel fine sand into the gaps between the coping stones, and brush with a broom. Wet the surface with a fine mist from a hose and let it dry. Repeat these two steps until the joints stay filled with sand. You may choose to layer the bottom of the pool with smooth decorative stones.

7. Add the right plants and fish.
Home centers and nurseries now carry a variety of plants designed for use in pools. Consult with a knowledgeable salesperson to find the best plants and animals for your area and your type of pool.

It is possible to have plants grow in mud that you add to the bottom of the pool, but keeping the plants in containers is much easier, and allows you to move plants around at will. Plant in the late spring or later. Begin with underwater oxygenating plants, such as milfoil and waterweed. Then add surface plants, such as water lily and water chestnut. You may also want some plants for the edge of the pool; Japanese iris and arrowhead are good choices.

Surprisingly large fish will survive in a garden pond. Goldfish are a good, reasonably priced choice; there are many types, some of which aren't at all golden in color. A few minnows or other small fish can help keep a pool clear of algae and insects. Game fish—catfish, bluegills, and trout, for instance—may work in your area. If you have the time and are sure raccoons cannot reach them, you may want to spend the money for Japanese koi, a kind of carp that lives as long as humans and often behaves like a family pet.

Consult with a dealer and come up with a master plan for your pond's fish and plants. Certain fish will not get along with other types, and some fish will destroy certain types of plants.

CAUTION!
PROTECT YOUR FLORA AND FAUNA

■ *Wait a few days before adding plants or fish to your pond, so the chlorine can leach out of the water.*
■ *Slowly acclimate your fish to the water's temperature before you put them in. If you have trouble with raccoons or other predators, provide a place for the fish to hide, such as overhanging flagstones around the edge.*
■ *Every three to four years, remove all the plants and fish, and drain the pond. Clean the liner thoroughly, and perhaps replace the pump.*

INSTALLING TIMBER-AND-BRICK STEPS

Steps like these take only about as long to build as concrete steps (see pages 662–664). The result, however, is more stylish and inviting. If the timbers are fastened firmly with rebar and spikes and the sand bed is well tamped, the steps will be nearly as solid as concrete and much easier to repair should settling occur.

Choose timbers that will withstand the climate in your region. Pressure-treated landscaping timbers are readily available; choose from 5×6s, 6×6s, and 6×8s. Pave the steps with severe weather (SW) brick.

YOU'LL NEED

TIME: A day to build a landing with two or three steps.
SKILLS: Laying out stairs, cutting timbers, laying brick in sand.
TOOLS: Baby sledgehammer, brick set, circular saw, tamper, mason's line, line or carpenter's level, tape measure, story pole or modular spacing rule, drill with long bit or bit extension, rubber mallet, broom, hose.

EXPERTS' INSIGHT

STAIR HEIGHT AND DEPTH

It's important for an entry stairway to be comfortable for walking because it's used so often. By laying 6×8 timbers narrow side up, you will get 7½-inch step rises, a comfortable height for most people. For elderly people and children, 6×6 timbers will make a shallower than normal step. For the depth, 11 to 12 inches is suitable for a single step. Add 1-foot increments for deeper steps.

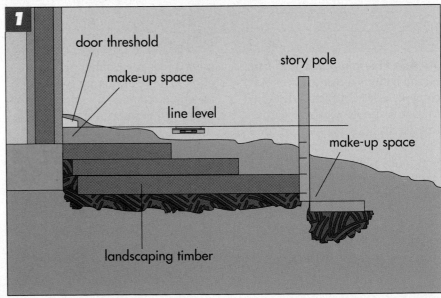

door threshold
make-up space
line level
story pole
make-up space
landscaping timber

1. Lay out the stairs.

The rise of each step is determined by the thickness of the timber you use. If the total rise is not evenly divisible by that thickness, make up the distance at the lowest step and at the door sill. Avoid making the bottom step more than 1 inch higher than the rest. (See page 662 for how to figure rise and run for a stairway.) Use a line level and a homemade story pole (or modular spacing rule) to determine your layout. For a short stairway, use a straight 2×4 and carpenter's level instead of the line level.

12" spike

rebar driven through timbers into ground

2. Build the frame.

Excavate the site according to your plan layout. But when you dig, allow an extra 6 inches of working space on each side. Lay a 2-inch bed of well-tamped gravel for the bottom timbers. Make sure the steps slope away from the house ¼ inch per running foot.

Where the tops of the timbers will not show, drill ⅜-inch holes about every 2 feet and drive 3-foot rebars through the timbers and into the ground to anchor the steps. Where the tops will show, drill long pilot holes with a ³⁄₁₆-inch bit and fasten the timbers together with 12-inch spikes.

TOOLS TO USE

DEALING WITH TIMBERS

■ You will need high-quality, long-shank ⅜- and ³⁄₁₆-inch drill bits to bore holes through the landscaping timbers for the spikes and rebar. A normal-length bit attached to a bit extension also will work but tends to come loose with use.

■ Drilling through the timbers will put a strain on 3.0- or 3.2-amp drills. Don't force the bit; allow the drill to cool down frequently. Or, rent or buy a 3.5-amp drill that will handle the job with ease.

■ Cut the timbers by sawing all four sides with a circular saw, then sawing the middle with a handsaw. If you have many to cut, rent an oversize circular saw, which will cut all the way through the timber.

3. Screed and tamp.

Starting with the bottom step, tamp the gravel firm, then spread 2 to 3 inches of sand. Notch a screed board the thickness of the bricks or pavers and screed the sand to that level. Tamp, add more sand if needed, then screed again. Once you install the bricks, move to the next higher step and prepare it in the same way. (See pages 760–761 for more on screeding and laying bricks in sand.)

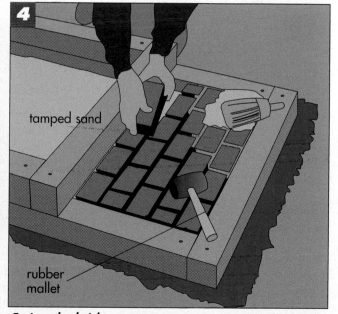

tamped sand

rubber mallet

4. Lay the bricks or pavers.

Choose a pattern (see page 696) and install the step surface. Cut the pavers or bricks with a brick set and baby sledgehammer or use a masonry cutoff saw or a circular saw with a masonry blade. Use a rubber mallet to pound in hard-to-fit bricks. Once each section is finished, spread fine sand on the surface and sweep it into the joints. Gently spray with water, add more sand, and repeat until the joints are filled.

INSTALLING A FLAGSTONE WALKWAY

For a casual walkway that looks as if it has been in place for years, consider a flagstone path. The seasoned look is achieved by leaving sod between the stones. As with any masonry materials set directly into the soil, these stones will settle with time and have to be reset every few years.

Begin by laying out the path. Lay a charged hose (close the nozzle and turn on the water) in the pattern you want. Pour flour or sand on it to establish outlines. (See pages 762–763 for more about laying flagstones.)

YOU'LL NEED

TIME: Several hours to install about 50 square feet of flagstone.
SKILLS: No special skills needed.
TOOLS: Hose, shovel, garden trowel, baby sledgehammer, brick set.

EXPERTS' INSIGHT

ESTABLISHING A WALKABLE SURFACE

■ Although a flagstone walkway should look casual and pleasantly free-form when you are done, try for as even a surface as possible when laying the stones. Use a straight 2×4 to check that you don't have radical rises or valleys.

■ Unless you have extremely firm or claylike soil, it usually is best to set the flagstones so they are ¾ inch or so higher than you want them. In time, they will settle.

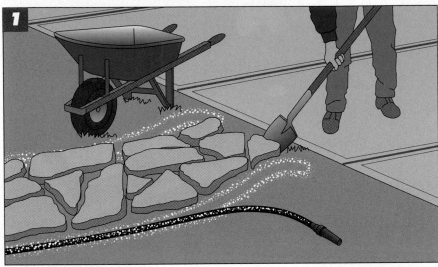

1. Lay out the flagstones.
Following the outline for your path, lay the stones directly on the ground. Turn them in different directions and try different stones, until you come up with a pattern with fairly consistent joint lines that are about 1½ inches wide. Combine large and small stones as you lay out the pattern. If you need to cut a stone, use a baby sledgehammer and brick set to etch a ⅛-inch-deep line on both sides of the stone. Support the stone along the cut line and strike the waste side until it breaks (see page 763). Slice the sod around the first stone.

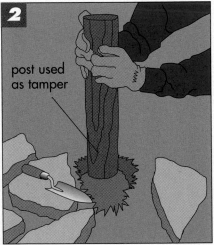

post used as tamper

2. Excavate and tamp.
Move the stone away. Dig out the sod, being careful to preserve the sod between the stones. Remove roots or stones that might make it difficult to set the stone level. Fill the hole with soil or sand as necessary and tamp it firmly.

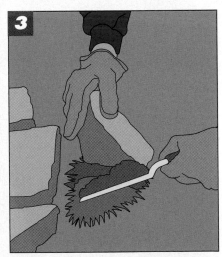

3. Place the stone.
If a stone rocks or wobbles when you step on it, take it out and note the pattern of indentations made in the ground. Add soil to the places where the stone did not rest on the soil or dig away places where the stone made a heavy indentation mark. Replace the stone. After all the stones are in place, give the path a good soaking with a fine spray of water.

SURFACE FINISHING

CHOOSING EXTERIOR PAINT

House paints made to cover siding and exterior trim tend to be more durable and more expensive than interior paint. That's because exterior paints contain additional resins and other ingredients that make them last longer and resist moisture. Also many have a larger amount of pigmenting, which gives them a deeper, more vivid color.

Like interior paint, exterior paint comes in two basic varieties: water-thinned (latex) and solvent-thinned (oil- or alkyd-based). Those with oil and alkyd bases dry slowly, making them susceptible during application to being marred by insects and sudden rainstorms. Once they set up, they develop a hard surface that is resistant to water. However, unless the surface is very well prepared, they are prone to flaking.

Properly applied, modern latex exterior paint (though not porch and deck paint) is more durable than solvent-based paint. Latex paints are easier to work with, dry quickly, and have a porous, "breathing" quality that makes them less likely to flake. They will likely peel, however, if applied over an improperly prepared oil- or alkyd-based finish.

Chalking-type latex paints shed dirt by gradually eroding with each rainfall. Usually you can see the "chalk" on foundation walls, shrubbery, and your coat sleeve if you brush against a painted surface. Newer formulations achieve durability without this chalking feature.

Latex paints tend to show brush marks, while solvent-based paints "level" to a more even surface. If a surface will be often handled or walked on (as is the case with a porch), solvent-based paint provides a more durable surface.

Do not use latex paint over a surface covered with solvent-based paint, unless you first apply a primer or thoroughly sand the surface. To find out which type of paint is present, remove a flake or chip and see whether it is flexible. Latex paint will bend slightly before cracking; a flake of solvent-based paint will snap readily. If you bring in a chip, a paint dealer can tell you for sure. If you're not certain what type of paint was used before, it's safest to apply a solvent-thinned paint.

Most people prefer a flat, eggshell, or satin finish for large exterior expanses. Reserve semigloss and gloss for areas subject to hard use or for trim.

What about one-coat house paints? If you plan to match or approximate the present color, any paint will cover in one coat. However, products sold with a one-coat guarantee are thicker, with more resins and pigments. Most guarantees specify that the paint must be applied over sound existing surfaces or primed new wood. You will pay more for a one-coat paint, but the extra money spent might pay off handsomely, especially in terms of time saved.

The chart on the opposite page will help you sort through the often-confusing array of products found in paint stores. As a general rule, the more expensive the paint, the more durable it will be.

ESTIMATING PAINT NEEDS

How much paint you need depends upon the type and condition of the surfaces that you'll be covering, the method of application, and the paint itself. Conditions vary considerably, so read the manufacturer's coverage figures, then buy a little more than you need.

If your home has narrow lap siding, add another 10 percent to your estimate. For textured materials, such as shingles or shakes, add 20 percent. Masonry and stucco—both porous surfaces that soak up lots of paint—can take up to 50 percent more.

To compute surface area, measure from the foundation to the eaves and multiply by the distance around the house. For each gable end, measure the distance from eaves to the peak, measure the width of the wall, and multiply the two. Then divide the result by two.

If you buy paint of a standard color, most stores will let you return unopened cans. Check with your retailer about return policies for custom-mixed paint.

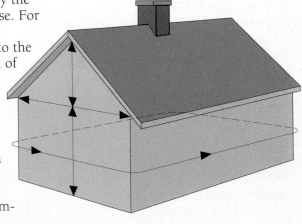

COMPARING EXTERIOR PAINTS

Type	Characteristics/Uses	Application
Vinyl latex	Easy cleanup, durability, and fast drying make latex the choice for amateurs. It can be applied over damp surfaces. Latex is naturally mildew-proof but is incompatible with a previous solvent-based finish.	Don't thin latex. Apply with one stroke of the brush or roller; if you work it out too far, you'll get thin spots.
Acrylic latex	The highest-quality latex paints contain 100 percent acrylic resins; vinyl resins are not as durable. It dries faster than most and will cover just about any building material, including masonry and properly primed metal.	Application technique is about the same as vinyl latex paint.
Alkyd	Alkyd, the most common type of solvent-thinned paint, has most of the same properties as oil-based types, but dries more rapidly; good over old oil- or alkyd-based coatings; excellent hiding power.	Thicker consistency makes alkyd more tiring to apply, but it levels smoother than latex.
Oil	Slow drying times (12 to 48 hours), strong odors, and messy cleanup make oil a less popular choice for amateurs, though some pros swear by its durability.	Drying time makes marring by bugs and rain real perils.
Primers	Use a recommended primer to seal new wood or metal, to kill stains, or prior to applying latex paint over existing solvent-based paint. Alcohol-based primer is the most effective, but solvent and latex types also work.	Priming usually is easier than finishing, but porous surfaces can soak up a lot of primer.
Stains	Solvent- or latex-type stains provide transparent, semi-transparent, or opaque finishes for natural wood siding and trim; some include preservatives or offer a weathered look.	Brush, roll, or spray on almost any way you prefer.
Porch and deck	Alkyd and polyurethane types are the most durable because they produce a hard, washable surface. Some types are formulated for concrete floors. Surface preparation varies; colors are limited.	With most types, you just pour the paint on the floor, then work it outward with a long-handled roller or applicator.
Metal	Solvent- or water-thinned types include rust-resisting priming ingredients so you needn't worry about small bare spots. All-bare metal should be primed separately. Rusty-metal primer seals a rusty spot.	Brush, roll, or spray on for a broad range of finish effects.
Marine	Formulated especially for boats, marine paint provides a super-durable finish on wood and some metal trim. It's expensive, so it's generally inappropriate for large areas.	A gooey consistency makes it difficult to apply.
Masonry	This category includes latex, epoxy, Portland cement, rubber, and alkyd. Some serve as their own primers. Seal masonry with clear silicone. For basement waterproofing techniques, see pages 649–651.	Latex is easy to apply; other types can be a lot of work.

CHOOSING INTERIOR PAINT

Many people consider interior painting an easy chore requiring no particular skill. As a result, they may plunge in unprepared and produce a botched job that haunts them for years. While it is true that almost any handy person can learn to paint well, it takes practice and attention to detail to produce smooth walls with evenly distributed color. This section will help you learn the correct way to paint or wallpaper a room, seal wood grain, and apply special finishing treatments.

Start by choosing the right paint. A well-informed salesperson can answer your questions, as long as you give the necessary information—the type and color of paint that's on the wall, the condition of the wall, and what sort of wear you expect the wall to endure. If a salesperson is not helpful, go to a different store.

A close reading of the paint can will tell you a few key things. The chart on the opposite page compares paints you're most likely to use.

Whichever type you choose, it's wise to spend more for high-quality paint. Cheaper paint may not cover in one coat, may be more likely to peel in time, and could fade, especially in direct sunlight. Given the amount of time you will spend preparing and painting your walls, it even makes sense to throw out a can of paint if you are displeased with the color.

The most common choice for interior painting is latex. High-quality latex paints are nearly as durable as solvent-thinned products. Latex cleans up with water, has less of an odor than solvent-thinned paint, is environmentally friendly, and dries to the touch quickly, so you can usually put furniture back in the room in an hour or so. However, dried latex paint takes weeks to completely cure. Handle it with care during that time because it can be easily stained or damaged.

If latex paint is applied over solvent-thinned paint, it will likely peel off in time—a disastrous result that will require hours of tedious scraping to remedy. If you suspect that the existing paint may not be latex, take a chip to a salesperson for testing. A latex paint chip will bend a bit before breaking; a solvent-based chip will be more brittle. If you have solvent-thinned paint on the wall, either cover it with a new coat of solvent-thinned paint or apply primer first (see box below).

Solvent-thinned paints, usually alkyd-based, require a solvent, such as mineral spirits (paint thinner), for cleanup. Spend more for odorless thinner; smelly products are unpleasant to breathe. Solvent-based paints generally are more durable than water-thinned paints.

Interior paints come in different sheens. From dullest to shiniest, the most common designations are: ceiling paint, flat, eggshell, satin (or low-luster), semigloss, and high-gloss. The glossier a finish, the harder and more durable it will be—and the more imperfections it will show.

Flat paint is generally considered "washable" but not "scrubbable." Eggshell or satin finishes have a low sheen but can be scrubbed occasionally. Semi- and high-gloss paints are popular for woodwork, kitchens, baths, and other areas that endure hard wear or in which there is high humidity. Again, higher-quality paint is more washable than cheap paint, no matter what the sheen.

Colors are notoriously tricky to choose. They react to each other and cast reflections that may change the appearance of everything in a room. Colors vary under different lighting, and large areas might become far more intense than you imagine when you are looking at small paint-sample chips. Consider buying a quart of the hue that catches your eye and trying it out on a sizable area before you invest in several gallons of paint that may not be returnable.

EXPERTS' INSIGHT

TO PRIME OR NOT TO PRIME

If the wall to be painted is in sound condition, if the new color is close to the existing color, and if you are sure the new paint will stick, then no primer is needed. However, you will need primer for the following conditions:

■ Stains—either localized or spread throughout the room because of smoke—may bleed through repeated coats of paint. The solution is to apply a stain-killing primer. For small spots, you can use a spray-on primer.

■ If the existing paint is solvent-thinned and you want to apply latex paint, apply an appropriate primer first. Solvent-thinned or alcohol-based primers work best.
■ If a wall has been patched, or if new drywall needs to be covered, apply latex primer first.
■ If your paint will not easily cover the existing color, purchase primer and have it tinted to approximate the paint color.

COMPARING INTERIOR PAINTS

Paint	Uses	Features/Characteristics	Thinner/Primer
Latex	The choice for most interior paint jobs; don't use it over unprimed wood, metal, or wallpaper.	Glosses vary from flat to high. It adheres to all but slick surfaces. Latex usually dries fast enough to apply two coats in one day. It is less durable than alkyd-base paints.	Latex is easy to clean up with water and soap. Prepare raw surfaces with a latex or alkyd primer.
Alkyd	Use alkyd for a rough surface or super hiding power. Don't apply over unprimed drywall—it will roughen the surface.	Dries somewhat more slowly than latex and has a slightly stronger odor. Alkyd might be banned in some areas.	For thinning and cleanup, use solvents. Coat unfinished surfaces with alkyd primer.
Oil	Natural-resin oil paints have all but disappeared.	Oil dries slowly, gives off flammable fumes, and doesn't stand up as well as alkyds.	Thin and clean up with mineral spirits, low-odor thinner, or turpentine.
Oil-based primer	Good all-purpose primer	Oil-based primer dries slowly and gives off fumes.	Thin and clean up with mineral spirits.
Latex primer	Prepares patched areas and new drywall	Inexpensive, dries quickly	Easy to clean up with water and soap
Alcohol-based primer	Best primer for most purposes	Kills almost any stain and gives tooth to slick surfaces	Thin and clean up with denatured alcohol.
One-coat	Use it only if surface is sealed, is of a similar color, and doesn't have a lot of patchwork that needs to be covered.	One-coats are ordinary latex or alkyd paints with additional pigment to increase hiding power and are therefore more expensive.	Thinning lessens paint's ability to hide flaws. Clean up with water or solvent, depending on whether latex or alkyd.
Texture paint	Designed to cover up imperfections and give the look of stucco-finish plaster	Some premixed; with others, you must stir in "sand." Application is moderately difficult; paint a section at a time, and keep the desired effect consistent.	Thinning defeats the purpose; stirring can be arduous. Check label for compatible primers.
Acoustic	Coats acoustic tiles without affecting their sound-deadening qualities	Apply acoustic paint by spraying or use a special roller. Color choice is limited.	Thin and clean up with water; no primer is necessary.
Metal	Use over primed or bare metal surfaces; "rusty-metal primer" can be applied over rust.	Self-primers are designed to adhere to bare surfaces. Preparation depends on the type and condition of metal (see pages 856–857).	Some are thinned with water, others need solvent or mineral spirits. Primer depends on the metal being covered.

CHOOSING BRUSHES

Selecting the right brush for a paint job isn't difficult. Except for foam types, all brushes fall into one of two categories: natural-bristle brushes and synthetic-bristle brushes. Natural-bristle brushes are made with animal hairs and formerly were considered the finest type available. However, some of today's synthetic varieties perform just as well.

If you're using an oil-based paint, choose a natural-bristle or a quality synthetic-bristle brush. Never use a natural-bristle brush with water-thinned finishes. The bristles will become mop-like, resulting in a streaked finish. Many paintbrush manufacturers label the brush package or handle with the type of finish for which the brush is designed.

Disposable brushes come in a wide range of widths and sizes and are suitable for many painting projects. Because they are inexpensive, they can be tossed when the job's done, saving considerable cleanup time. However, painting with a disposable brush may mean you have to apply two coats of paint, where a high-quality brush would cover with one coat. Also a cheaper brush may shed some bristle hairs, which are tedious to remove.

Should you spend extra for a quality brush, or are the inexpensive ones the better buy? If you're willing to take the time to clean your brush after using it, buy better quality. It will serve you well for years. However, if you paint only occasionally and don't like cleaning up, a less-expensive brush is the wiser investment.

To test a brush for quality, spread the bristles and inspect their tips. Quality natural-bristle brushes will have little "flags," like split ends, on the bristle ends. The more the better. On better-quality synthetic brushes, you'll see fuzzy-looking tips.

Check the brush's ferrule, the aluminum or stainless-steel band near the handle. It should be wrapped tightly and neatly around the brush and solidly secured to the handle.

Among your first buys should be a 4-inch wall brush, a 2-inch trim brush, and a 2-inch sash-trim brush. Later you might want to add a 6-inch wall brush for masonry paint jobs and a round brush for delicate work. A brush spinner speeds cleanup jobs.

The four handle styles shown below serve different functions. A beaver-tail handle lets you grip a wider brush in the palm of your hand; pencil and flat handles allow greater fingertip control; the kaiser handle also offers good control, plus a grip that's comfortable to your hand.

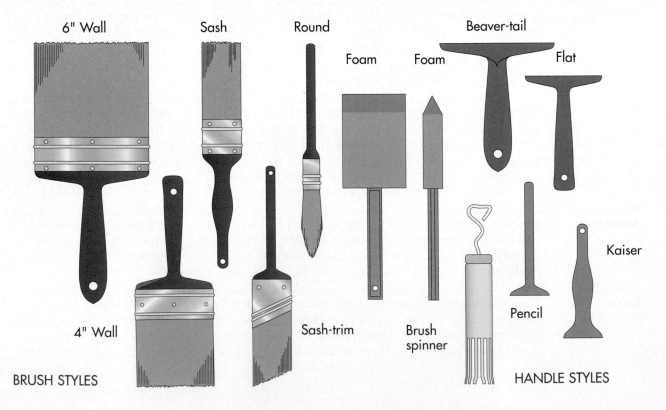

6" Wall Sash Round Foam Foam Beaver-tail Flat Kaiser

4" Wall Sash-trim Brush spinner Pencil

BRUSH STYLES HANDLE STYLES

USING AND CARING FOR BRUSHES

Your brush will be a pleasure to use as long as you pay attention to proper loading, cleaning, and storing recommendations.

Before you use a new paintbrush for the first time, spin it by the handle between your hands, then slap it against the edge of a table to remove loose bristles. Work the bristles against a rough surface, such as a concrete wall, to soften the ends. To condition a natural-bristle brush, soak it 24 hours in linseed oil.

When you start painting, you may find more loose bristles and stray ones that stick out from the sides of the ferrule. Pick out loose bristles. Remove stray bristles by using a putty knife to force them against the ferrule so you can snap them off.

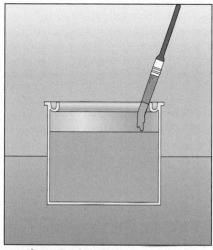

Loading the brush.
Dip the brush into the paint to only one-third the length of its bristles. If you go deeper, you'll waste paint and create a mess. Squeeze the excess paint from the bristles by scraping them lightly against the side of the container as you remove the brush.

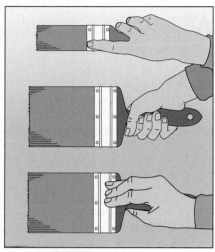

How to hold it.
Hold small brushes between your thumb and your index finger. For larger brushes, use a palm grip or lay your fingers on the ferrule. Some people prefer to hold a large brush with three or four fingers on the ferrule.

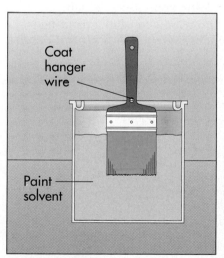

Coat hanger wire

Paint solvent

Temporary storage.
If your work is interrupted for an hour or less, leave the brush in the paint. Position it so the paint covers the bristle tips only. For longer interruptions, wrap the brush in foil or plastic. If you'll use the brush within a day or two, immerse it in solvent or water, as shown above. Drill a hole in the handle for hanging.

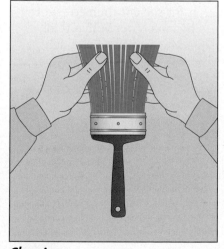

Cleaning.
To clean a brush, work out the remaining paint by firmly stroking the brush back and forth on newspaper. Work until the brush is dry. Before storing a brush for an extended period, remove all the paint you can with the appropriate thinner. Work the bristles, as shown.

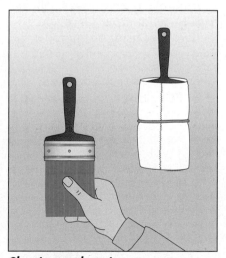

Shaping and storing.
Wash the brush in soap and water, shape the bristles, and let them dry. Then wrap the brush in the cardboard cover it was sold in. Or wrap it with several layers of paper toweling. The bristles should be held in shape but not squeezed.

CHOOSING ROLLERS AND PADS

Most people find it efficient to paint trim and edges (such as where the ceiling meets the wall or where the wall meets the trim) with a brush, and then paint the large expanses of walls and ceilings using a roller. But don't hesitate to try different tools and techniques.

Rollers range in width from 4 to 18 inches. They have a plastic or wooden handle (often machined to accept an extension handle) and a metal frame on which the roller cover is inserted.

Spend more for a professional-quality roller frame that rolls smoothly. A cheaper model may make it difficult to load the roller cover. Buy an extension handle that allows you to easily reach the ceiling—it will save you plenty of time and energy. Some extension handles are adjustable for length.

Trim rollers reach into small and hard-to-get-at areas. Once you get the knack of using a trim roller, they're as easy to control as trim brushes. Trim rollers come in varying widths and configurations. The 3-inch-wide version gets into areas too tight for a full-size roller. Cone-shaped types are used for inside corners, around door and window casings, and almost any point where two surfaces intersect. Doughnut-style rollers paint moldings and other fine work.

A high-quality roller cover (also called a roller sleeve) has a lint-free pile that is uniform in texture and securely fastened. Cheaper covers tend to apply paint unevenly or shed fibers onto the wall. Buy a cover made for the type of paint you will apply.

Mohair covers are designed for gloss finishes and varnishes; they produce a smooth finish because the nap is short and tightly woven. Dynel, acetate, and polyurethane foam covers can be used with all paints. Use a lamb's-wool roller cover for solvent-thinned paint.

Choose a cover with a thick nap—say, ¾-inch—for rough surfaces and to achieve one-coat coverage. A thick nap will produce a slight pebbly stipple. Use a short-nap cover, either ⅜- or ¼-inch, to produce a smoother surface. If you're using water-thinned paint, buy a cover with a plastic sleeve. For solvent-thinned paint, use a cardboard sleeve.

Pad painters are also handy. The pads may be a carpetlike material or plastic foam inserted in a plastic mop-like applicator or a paint-brush handle. Although excellent for applying paint to almost any surface, they really earn their keep when you have to paint shakes, fencing, screening, and shutters.

A paint tray, either metal or plastic, completes the system. If you'll be working on a stepladder, buy a paint tray that has ladder hooks to keep the tray secure. To save on cleanup time, purchase plastic tray inserts, which you throw away once the painting is done. With these, the paint never touches your tray.

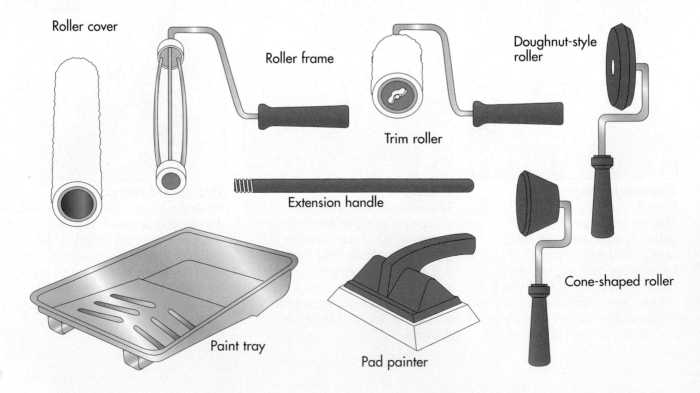

Roller cover

Roller frame

Doughnut-style roller

Trim roller

Extension handle

Cone-shaped roller

Paint tray

Pad painter

Using a Roller

Anyone who has ever painted with rollers or pads will vouch for the ease with which these lay down paint.

However, an even application does not come automatically. Keep your eyes peeled for skid marks on the painted surface. Rollers tend to slide as they move, causing small tracks in the finish, which will show when the finish has dried.

Most surfaces are irregular to some extent. To achieve the best coverage when using a roller or pad, lay on the paint from several different directions. In this way, you won't miss shallow depressions, such as joints between drywall panels. After applying paint to an area, go over it again with light vertical passes, taking care to even out thick spots.

Cover the floor and any furniture with a heavy drop cloth. Even when used carefully, rollers do scatter paint speckles.

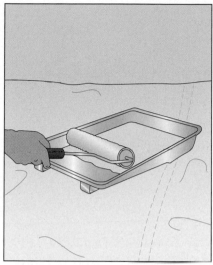

Loading a roller.
Fill the well of the tray, but not the slanted portion. Push the roller into the paint, pull it back a bit, then repeat until paint covers the entire roller. Even out the paint on the slanted part of the tray.

Rolling a wall.
For the best coverage, apply the paint in two or more directions. Minimize dripping by starting the roller on the upstroke. Don't work a roller too quickly, especially when the roller cover is loaded with paint: You'll splatter, which wastes paint and makes a mess.

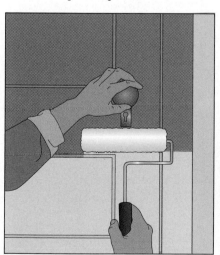

Rolling woodwork.
Rollers work well on wide, flat woodwork, such as raised-panel doors. Paint the recesses first, then finish the flush surfaces. If you do not like the pebbly stipple that the roller produces, run a brush over the paint immediately after using the roller.

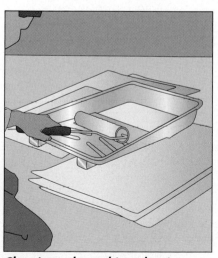

Cleaning solvent-thinned paint.
To clean a roller cover, work out all the excess paint you can on newspaper. Turn to fresh pages as needed. With solvent-thinned paint, pour solvent into the tray and work the roller back and forth. Repeat until the solvent remains clear.

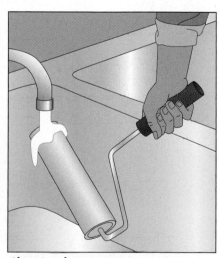

Cleaning latex paint.
Wash out water-based paints in a sink. Let water run over the roller until it is clear. Squeezing the roller speeds things. Wring the cover dry by squeezing it between your hands. Wrap clean, dry roller covers in aluminum foil or plastic bags. Clean pad painters as you would roller covers.

Using a Power Roller

If you have ever painted a room with a roller, you know that most of your time is spent loading just the right amount of paint onto the roller. After about every 50 to 100 square feet, you have to pour more paint into the paint tray.

Power paint rollers and pads eliminate both of these steps and more than double your speed. The power equipment will pump from a 1-gallon can or a 5-gallon can.

Before purchasing a power roller, see that it will be reasonably easy to clean; most are designed for latex paint and water cleanup. Choose a model with few parts to disassemble.

Before painting, practice on a large scrap of cardboard. Turn on the paint control for a few seconds at a time until you get a sense of how much on-time is required. Rollers generally require on-times of about 5 seconds; pads require 1 to 2 seconds.

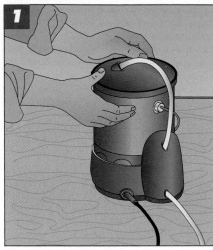

1. Prepare the can.
After opening the paint container and stirring the paint, put the special cover on the paint can. Set the can into the base of the paint pumping unit and then lock it securely in place. Insert the suction tube into the hole in the cover. Push it to the bottom, then raise it ½ inch.

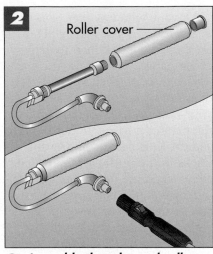

Roller cover

2. Assemble the tube and roller.
Hook up the parts according to the manufacturer's directions. Especially if the parts are all plastic, take care not to cross-thread when screwing the pieces together. Some types have a long handle that fills with paint and makes it easy to reach the ceiling.

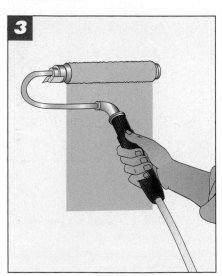

3. Apply paint.
Turn the flow on and off with the switch on the handle. Don't overload the roller or it will leak and spatter.

4. Clean the parts.
When you're finished painting, run the roller or pad dry, remove the arm, and purge the paint from the hose, letting it run into the paint can.

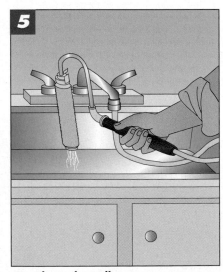

5. Clean the roller.
Attach the paint hose to a faucet adapter—if there is one—and run water through the roller until it is clean. Squeeze the excess water from the roller and stand it on end to dry. Clean the seals on the roller arm.

USING A STEPLADDER

To avoid breaking into a cold sweat every time you get above the third rung of a stepladder, select a ladder you can trust, then learn a few safety habits.

Aluminum ladders are lightweight and easy to transport, but they tend to flex, making them unstable. Wooden ladders are more stable when new, but they become wobbly after repeated use. Fiberglass stepladders are the most reliable.

A label on the ladder provides its strength rating. Type III household-grade ladders are rated at 200 pounds; Type II commercial-grade, 225 pounds; and Type I industrial-grade, 250 pounds. Each type has been tested at 4 times these loads. For security and durability, buy at least a Type II ladder.

Lengths range from 2 to 16 feet; 6-footers are suitable for most indoor needs (see page 457 for choosing outdoor extension ladders).

If you follow these simple safety rules, you needn't worry about stepladder accidents.

■ If possible, lean a stepladder against a wall. Make sure that the legs rest solidly on the floor.

■ When you open the ladder, double-check that you've opened it fully and that you've locked the bucket tray and braces in position.

■ Work from a ladder that is tall enough for the job. Don't climb higher than one step below the top, and never stand on the bucket tray.

■ Never paint a wooden ladder. Paint hides defects in the wood, preventing you from discovering possible problems.

■ Never climb a stepladder that has loose or broken rungs or a split or broken side rail.

■ Rather than leaning way over to the side to reach a spot, take a few seconds to move the ladder.

Testing for stability.
Open the ladder and test it by lifting one side and pulling it toward you. Keep the braces fully open and locked. If a ladder feels wobbly, throw it out and buy a new one.

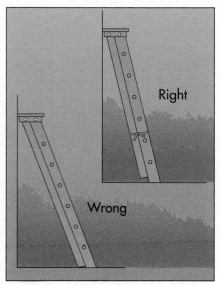

Leaning a stepladder.
Prop a stepladder against a wall at a fairly steep angle so that the back legs don't catch on the floor. To make sure that the back legs do not destabilize the ladder, tie the legs shut.

Making a scaffold.
Two stepladders and a 2×12 make a convenient scaffold. If you don't have two stepladders, you can use a sawhorse to support one end of a scaffold plank.

Working on stairs.
In a high stairwell, use an extension ladder, a sawhorse, and a plank. To protect the wall, pad the ladder rails.

IDENTIFYING AND SOLVING PAINT PROBLEMS

Perennial paint and surface problems (see page 847) will pop right through a new paint job. If your house suffers from any of these, get to the root of the problem and correct the condition. Only then is it time to scrape the surface, prime, and proceed with painting the final coat.

Most paint problems are the result of moisture attacking from underneath the paint. New energy-efficient construction methods can contribute to these problems by sealing a house so tight that it cannot breathe. The solution is adequate ventilation; see page 502. This is particularly true in moist areas like the kitchen, bathroom, and laundry. Ducted ventilation fans provide the best way to remove excess moisture vapor. Good vapor barriers on inside walls also help control moisture problems (see page 512).

Control moisture.
Lessen the effects of moisture by installing ducted ventilation fans (see pages 130–133). If you don't have fans, opening a window helps. If exterior walls don't have a vapor barrier, painting the interior wall with nonpermeable paint will prevent vapor penetration.

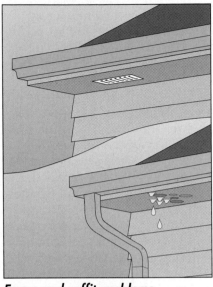

Eaves and soffit problems.
Poor ventilation in the attic may cause soffits to peel. Before you repaint, correct this by adding soffit vents (see page 469). Leaky gutters drip water onto eaves and then onto the house siding, so maintain or replace gutters (see pages 470–473).

Cut back foliage.
Leaves hold moisture after a rain. Trim trees and shrubs often, especially those along the house's foundation.

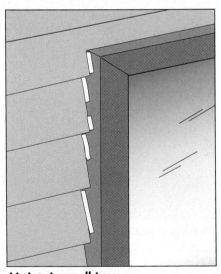

Maintain caulking.
Remove old, cracked caulking material with a putty knife, then apply new caulk (see page 481).

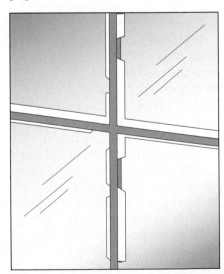

Window glazing.
Replace any loose and missing glazing compound on windows. Let the glazing dry for a week before you paint it.

REMEDIES FOR COMMON PAINT PROBLEMS

Problem		Causes	Remedy
Peeling		Moisture from inside or prolonged contact with rain or other moisture; finish coat applied over wet surface	Improve ventilation by installing siding, gable, or soffit vents.
Alligatoring		Usually a finish coat applied over a wet primer, or too much oil in the thinner	Sand and scrape down to bare wood, apply primer, and let dry thoroughly.
Checking		Shrinking and swelling of the building material over a period of time	Remove paint to bare wood, prime the area, and let dry.
Blistering		Finish coat applied over surfaces that are not completely dry	Remove paint to bare wood, prime the area, and let dry.
Bleeding		Sap and pitch working out of the wood	Apply stain-killing sealer to all knots and pitch pockets to prepare the surface for a coat of finish.
Nail stains		Using nails that are not rust-resistant	Sand the surface and seal with alcohol-based primer, then repaint.
Mildew		Usually a combination of moisture, high humidity, and inadequate ventilation	Scrub off the mildew with a bleach solution, let the wood dry thoroughly, then paint with mildew-resistant paint.
Chalking		Formulation of paint used	Before painting, wash thoroughly; some older paints are made to chalk (see page 836).

REMOVING OLD EXTERIOR PAINT

Many of the problems described on the preceding pages require you to strip down the defective areas to bare wood and prime them before painting. Unfortunately, there's no easy way to do this tedious job. A variety of stripping techniques are shown on these pages. Often it takes a combination of techniques to tackle a job. Experiment to find the mix that works best.

If paint is peeling from very large areas, get advice from a local painter. Preparation of old wood can be tricky, and sometimes homeowners spend tons of time stripping and repainting, only to have the new paint peel. If possible, strip and paint a small area and wait a year to see how well the paint sticks.

Old paint comes off most readily when it's dry. Start in the worst spot, work a scraper underneath, and lift off as much of the old finish as you can. You'll have better luck chipping from the edges of bad spots, rather than trying to wear through an unbroken surface.

Once you master a pull scraper, it's possible to get down to bare wood with a single stroke. Hold the blade at an angle and apply firm pressure as you drag it along. When a blade stops cutting well, either change it or sharpen it as you would a knife or chisel (see page 274).

When you reach tight-sticking paint, feather the edges by sanding. Then spot-prime all bare areas, slightly overlapping the sound paint.

Remove paint from metal surfaces with a wire brush attachment on an electric drill. Don't worry about baring the metal; just remove rust, as well as the loose or caked paint, then prime it (see pages 856–857).

Chemical paint strippers should be your last alternative. Although effective, you risk dripping the remover on sound paint, creating more problems.

If you have large areas of masonry to strip, consider hiring a professional contractor to sandblast them. Make it clear that the contractor will clean away all dust and sand when finished.

YOU'LL NEED...

TIME: Several days for an entire house.
SKILLS: Basic skills.
TOOLS: Putty knife, scraper, pull scraper, electric paint softener, wire brush, drill with wire brush attachment, propane torch or heat gun, and power sander.

Removing loose paint with a putty knife.
Remove what paint you can by scraping with a putty knife. Scrape in at least two directions at all spots to make sure you're getting all the loose stuff. Then go over the area with a wire brush. This combination works well for small areas or places where the paint is very loose.

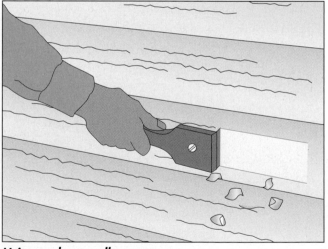

Using a sharp pull scraper.
Most jobs call for harder work. Purchase a pull scraper with multiple replacement blades. Experiment to find which angle works best; you want to remove the paint without digging into the wood. Press down hard as you scrape; it sometimes helps to push on the tool with one hand while you pull with the other hand.

Removing paint with a power sander.
Power-sand large areas with an orbital sander equipped with fairly rough sandpaper—60- or 80-grit. Change the paper once it stops being effective. If you are skillful, you may want to try a belt sander, which removes paint more quickly. Be careful: It is easy to dig into the wood when using a belt sander.

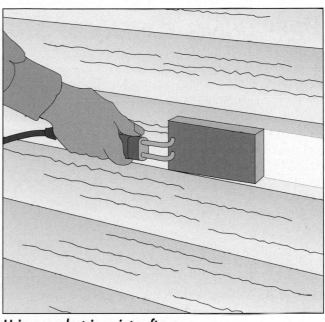

Using an electric paint softener.
For heavy paint deposits, use an electric paint softener. Hold the tool on the paint until it starts to bubble or wrinkle, then scrape off the paint. A paint-removing heat gun, shaped much like a blow dryer for hair, works similarly.

Using chemical paint removers.
Chemical paint removers are best for heavy paint deposits on small areas. Follow the manufacturer's directions to the letter (see page 892–893).

Using a propane torch to soften paint.
A propane torch with a spreader tip "cooks" paint fast so you can scrape it off. Be careful not to start a fire, and have an extinguisher handy. The resulting surface may be slightly charred in places. Be sure to seal it with a high-quality primer before painting or the paint may peel from the charred areas.

PREPARING EXTERIOR SURFACES

If your siding and trim is in good shape, you can happily sidestep the most maddening part of an exterior paint job—removing chipped or peeling paint (see pages 848–849). But don't get out your paint clothes and brushes quite yet.

Go around the house and take off all screens, storm windows, and hardware that can be removed. Inspect the exterior and replace damaged siding materials (see pages 482–486). Use a nail set to drive protruding nails below the surface.

Give your house a bath. You'll need a garden hose and a car-wash brush attachment, a scrub brush or sponge for stubborn dirt, and a mixture of water and trisodium phosphate (TSP) to remove dirt and reduce the gloss of existing oil- or alkyd-based paints.

Remove loose and cracked glazing from the windows and reglaze them (see pages 434–435). Glazing should dry a week before painting. Also caulk all cracks and gaps in the siding; around porch columns; and under, over, and around windows and doors (see page 481).

If you're using an oil- or alkyd-based paint, wait at least a week after the bath before you paint the house. You can paint with latex the next day. When the siding is dry, spot-prime all bare areas. Don't miss exposed metal surfaces on gutters, downspouts, and windows.

YOU'LL NEED...

TIME: 5 to 6 hours to thoroughly wash and rinse a house.
SKILLS: Basic skills.
TOOLS: Whisk broom, hose, scrub brushes, car-wash brush, hammer, nail set, screwdriver, and a caulking gun.

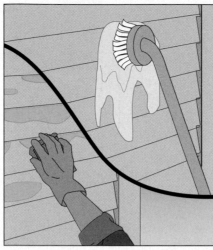

Clean the siding.
Wash the house from the top down, using a mixture of trisodium phosphate (TSP) and water. Rinse well. Let dry one day for latex or one week for oil paint. For mildewed areas, scrub with household bleach and water or a commercial cleaner. Repaint with mildewcide paint.

Make needed repairs.
Set popped nails and spot-prime them. Also caulk cracks, replace damaged siding, and prime bare metal spots.

Brush away dust.
With a whisk broom or a paintbrush, flick off the dust you missed with the hose. Keep this brush handy as you paint, to clear away other debris.

Remove obstacles.
Take off fixtures or cover them the day you paint. Remember to take down other accessories, such as house numbers and the mailbox. To speed up the job, remove, clean, and paint screens, storm windows, shutters, and other detachable components separately.

PREPARING AND PLANNING TO PAINT

Begin exterior painting when the sun has dried off the prepared surfaces. Follow the sun so you're working in the shade; this gives the paint a chance to cure slowly and adhere better.

Work from the top to the bottom of the house to avoid the mess caused by spilled or splattered paint. For a one-story house, do the siding first, then go back and paint the windows, doors, railings, steps, and so forth. If you're painting a two-story structure, do the trim as you go to avoid leaning your ladder against fresh paint.

Always paint above the top of the ladder. Don't try to paint under it, or you'll have ladder tracks where the rails touched the siding.

Protect nearby foliage.
A little paint spattered on grass will disappear with the next mowing, but it will remain on mulch and taller plants. Protect shrubs, flowers, patios, and walks with drop cloths. Use rope and canvas or old sheets to tie tall bushes back out of the way.

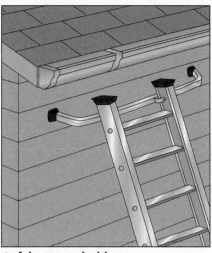

Safely set up ladders.
Set ladders on sure footing—never a plastic drop cloth. If the ground is uneven, dig a small hole for one of the legs, or place a wide board under a leg, positioned so that the ladder does not wobble. Use a ladder brace for stability and to hold the ladder away from the side wall for more painting room.

Hang the paint with a bucket hook.
To keep the paint bucket from spilling, hang it from a ladder rung with a bucket hook, which you can buy or make from heavy-gauge wire.

Bucket hook

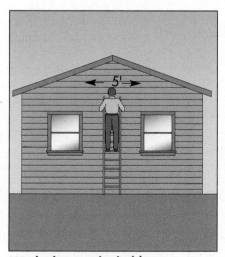

Work close to the ladder.
For safety's sake, don't stretch more than an arm's length on either side of the ladder—it's just not worth the risk. Move the ladder instead.

5'

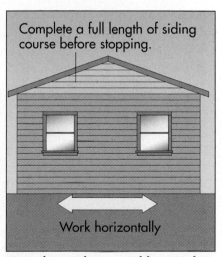

Complete a full length of siding course before stopping.

Work horizontally

Time the work to avoid lap marks.
Plan the work so that sundown does not catch you in the middle of several courses of siding. Otherwise you will get lap marks.

PAINTING SIDING

Horizontal or vertical siding can be covered quickly, especially if it has a smooth surface. It is usually most efficient to paint siding first, then trim.

If you're applying primer, follow the same procedures as for the finish paint. You may notice lap marks with the primer as it sinks into the wood or other material to seal it. These won't show after you've applied the finish coat.

Remove lighting fixtures and turn off electricity so you can safely paint behind and below them. Let the paint dry before replacing the fixtures.

YOU'LL NEED...

TIME: 4 to 6 days for a small house.
SKILLS: Basic painting skills.
TOOLS: Brushes, ladder, screwdriver, and drop cloths.

Hit the siding bottoms.
Start by painting the underside of a horizontal siding course. If you do the faces first, you'll be touching up continually. Coat the undersides of three or four courses, using plenty of paint so the wood seals properly. Level out the paint with the tip of the paintbrush.

Stab into corners.
When painting next to a casing, paint the corner first, then the underside of the siding. Stab the bristles up into the corner.

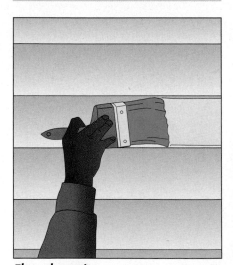

Flow the paint.
Apply plenty of paint to the surface of the course and don't worry about lap marks yet. Just cover and seal the surface thoroughly. Fill in the face of the siding courses, flowing the paint onto the surface with fairly short horizontal strokes. You needn't exert much pressure on the brush.

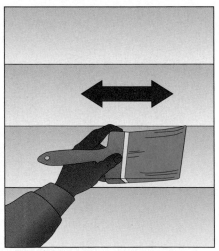

Level the paint.
When the surface is covered with paint, level and smooth it with a horizontal stroke. Make sure tiny cracks are filled. Don't try to save money by brushing the paint thin; even it out on the surface, using fairly long brushstrokes.

Take care at the edges.
Tip the bristles downward as you cut in along the bottom of the last course of siding. This keeps paint off the foundation.

FINISHING SHINGLES AND SHAKES

Because shingles and shakes are porous, painting or staining them can take longer than you think, and it may use up more paint than is commonly estimated.

If the wood is new, you can give it a natural look simply by sealing it with a clear sealer. Because there is no pigment in the sealer, you can slop it onto the wood without worrying about lap marks.

Semitransparent and solid stains (see pages 836–837) require more care because they contain a pigment that must be smoothed to prevent lap marks. Also, because the pigment in stain settles fairly quickly, you'll need to give the liquid a few good stirs with a paint paddle every so often to keep the finish color consistent.

If you're planning to paint new shingles, test the paint on several that have dark brown stains. If the stains bleed through, apply a stain-killing primer first.

Both paint and stain will dry quickly. Always work into a wet edge and finish out a course of siding before you leave for any length of time.

Keep the ferrule and handle of your brush wiped clean; that can be difficult if you're working with stain. Follow the leveling-out technique described on page 852. If you can, rent a power paint sprayer (see page 860). After spraying, touch up with a brush. If you use a roller or pad painter, use covers with medium to long nap length.

YOU'LL NEED...
TIME: 4 to 6 days for a small house.
SKILLS: Basic painting skills.
TOOLS: Brushes, ladder, drop cloths, screwdriver, power sprayer, corner roller, and pad applicator.

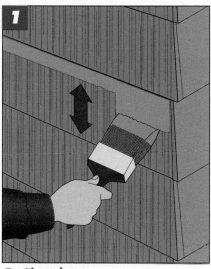

1. Flow the paint.
Do the underside of shingles first, as you would with lap siding. Brush out any runs down the striations. Apply paints and stains in the direction of the grain or striations. Check the area often for missed spots.

2. Erase drips.
Check frequently for drips and runs. Smooth them out with a fairly dry brush while the finish is still tacky.

Using pads and rollers
Pad applicators make finishing shingles and shakes easier. Most are designed for edges as well as faces.

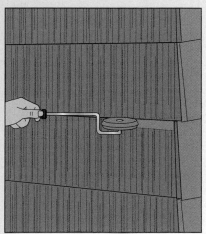

Corner rollers work well for undersides. Use a medium- or long-nap roller or a wide brush for the faces.

PAINTING TRIM

If someone gives you the choice of painting the siding on a house or the trim, choose the siding. Although it doesn't consume much paint, trimming out a house takes an inordinate amount of time. Using the same paint color for the trim as the siding helps some, but the job is tedious, nonetheless.

Before you get out your sash brush and begin work, study the illustrations on this page for some of the situations you'll encounter.

YOU'LL NEED...

TIME: 45 minutes to an hour for a window.
SKILLS: Intermediate painting skills.
TOOLS: Sash brush, screwdriver, masking tape.

EXPERTS' INSIGHT

USING MASKING TAPE

Applying masking tape can make for clean paint lines at joints between two different surfaces. However, because slight flaws in exterior painting will not be as noticeable as they would be in interior painting, most house painters do not use it. After a few hours of practice, you can learn to cut a clean line using a brush alone. You may, however, choose to use masking tape on windowpanes and to cover hardware.

Seal the joints between trim and siding.
Paint a tight seal between the trim and siding material, especially over the tops of doors and windows. This seal is best made by slightly overlapping the siding paint (see page 852). That allows you to cut a clean line between the trim and the siding.

Protect windowsills.
Windowsills take a beating from the elements. If they're weather-worn, give them several coats of paint. Stop applying coats only after the paint has stopped soaking into the wood.

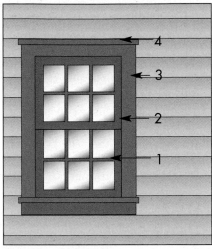

Paint a window.
Paint the outside of windows in the order indicated above, starting with the muntins and then working outward.

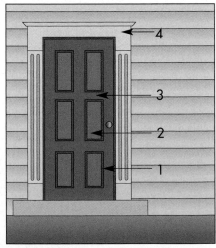

Paint a door.
Mask or remove the knob set and other hardware before painting doors. Paint the door in the order shown above.

Spray hardware.
To save time and create a professional appearance, remove hardware that is to be painted or covered with clear finish, and position it on a sheet of newspaper. Spray-paint it using a can. Keep the nozzle moving at all times and use light applications to prevent buildup and drips (see page 861).

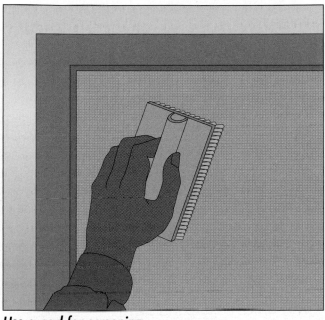

Use a pad for screening.
Paint or varnish screening first, then the frame. Use a special applicator pad to paint the screening—it is designed to apply paint without filling in the screen. (Spray-painting is another option for painting screening; see page 859.)

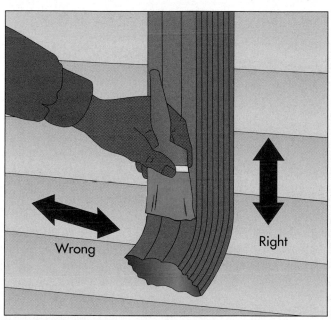

Avoid paint runs.
It takes concentration and a methodical approach to erase all paint drips and runs. Every few minutes, when your brush is fairly dry, look back at your work and brush away imperfections using light, even strokes. When painting a downspout, be sure to paint parallel to the flutes. If you don't, you risk messy drips and sags.

Finish with the railings.
Do ornamental metal and wood last. Prepare the surfaces properly and use the correct primer (see pages 856–857). It's difficult to paint small intersecting members (like those of a railing) without creating drips. If possible, use spray paint for these.

PREPARING AND PRIMING METAL

All metals oxidize if they're not properly coated, and paint can't adhere to the oxide coating. To stop the oxidation process, strip away grease, dirt, and rust, then apply a primer that is chemically formulated to neutralize oxidation. This primer also provides a surface to which the finish coat can adhere.

Primer made for automobile bodies is usually a good choice, but consult with your paint dealer to make sure. You also can buy special metal paints that combine the primer with a finish coating. Use these over surfaces that are in at least fairly good condition. Aluminized paint includes aluminum dust as a pigment and also works as a combination primer-finish on metals not exposed to severe weathering.

The finish paint must protect against weather and abrasion. Once the surface has been adequately primed, you can use almost any paint—exterior-grade for outdoors, indoor types for inside jobs. However, don't apply a lacquer over anything but a lacquer-based finish paint or primer.

Even polished decorative metals, such as brass, copper, and bronze, need protection if you want them to keep their shine. Buff tarnished hardware items with fine steel wool, metal polish, or a felt wheel and abrasive compound, then coat them with clear lacquer or polyurethane.

Remove paint.
Paint remover works better on metal than on wood. Use it to take off multiple layers (see pages 892–893).

Wash and wire-brush surface.
Wash the surface with a commercial degreaser, then wire-brush away any rust or peeling paint. A brush wheel attachment on a power drill makes short work of this task.

Feather edges of well-stuck paint.
Use a loose piece of sandpaper or a hand sanding block to feather the edges of the remaining sound paint. Otherwise, the repaired area will show through. Finally, wash or brush any paint flakes and dust away from the work area.

EXPERTS' INSIGHT

RUSTY-METAL PRIMER
Standard metal primer works only when all the rust has first been removed and the surface is completely dry. Rusty-metal primer, on the other hand, can be applied directly on top of rust. It will not smooth the bumpy surface of the rust, but it will stop the rust from spreading and will provide "tooth" for the finish paint to adhere to.

YOU'LL NEED...
TIME: 4 to 6 hours to prep and paint a metal railing.
SKILLS: Basic painting skills.
TOOLS: Paintbrushes, wire brush, drill with wire-brush attachment, sandpaper, and steel wool.

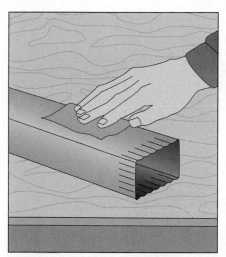

Prepare gutters and downspouts.
Clean and paint the inside of metal gutters first. Gutters and downspouts (shown) often need only spot-sanding and priming.

Apply primer or sander.
Treat sound paint with liquid sander. This product produces a "tooth" to which the new paint can adhere. Alternatively, sand the old paint thoroughly or apply alcohol-based primer.

Sand the primer.
Lightly sand primed surfaces with very fine sandpaper or steel wool. Don't sand through the primer.

PAINTING METAL

Spray, brush, or roll paint onto metal finishes. Whichever application you choose, bear in mind that several thin coats will hold up better than one or two thick layers. Let each coat dry before applying the next. Brushed or rolled-on paint should dry at least overnight (36 hours is better) before you apply another coat.

A good job calls for patience and good lighting so you can correct problems before the paint dries. Work the paint in one direction and move from dry to wet areas. Don't lap brushstrokes by painting over a dry edge. Smooth corners, too, so they don't dry with accumulations of paint.

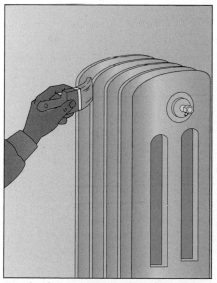

Apply the paint.
Flow the paint on with smooth, even strokes. After a few minutes, check the freshly painted areas for drips, runs, and sags. When you're painting a complicated piece such as a radiator or chair, be sure to look from several different angles so you can spot places you missed.

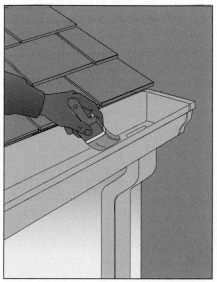

Seal gutters.
To make galvanized gutters really last, paint the inside surfaces with an asphalt-based paint. Besides protecting the metal, it seals tiny leaks. After using the appropriate metal primer, the top coat of paint can be almost any outdoor type. (Aluminum or plastic gutters never need to be painted.)

PAINTING MASONRY

Several types of paint will adhere to masonry. A paint dealer will carry paints designed for many types of surfaces and situations. Because they dry to a very hard finish, epoxy paints are probably the best all-around choice for floors, walls that are washed frequently, and exterior applications. Portland cement paint is another good choice; it works well on all walls except those previously painted with another type of finish. Latex paint, probably the easiest to apply, also adheres to foundation walls. Check with your paint dealer for other types suitable for specific applications.

Before painting a masonry surface—especially basement walls and floors—be sure to correct any existing moisture problems (see pages 640–641). If you don't, no paint will adhere. Also, remove peeling paint with a wire brush, and make necessary masonry repairs (see pages 642–645).

To finish the prep work, degrease the surface using detergent and water. Then etch the surface with a mixture of 1 part muriatic acid to 3 parts water. This removes and neutralizes alkaline material in the mortar joints. (Be sure to wear rubber gloves and a long-sleeved shirt to protect your skin from the acid.) Finally, rinse the surface with clear water.

After the surface has dried thoroughly, apply the finish with a wide short-bristled brush or a roller cover with a long nap.

YOU'LL NEED...

TIME: 6 to 8 hours to paint a basement.
SKILLS: Basic painting skills.
TOOLS: Scrub brush, paintbrush, roller with an extension handle.

Painting a floor.
Apply a degreasing solution to an oily garage or basement floor. Some products spray on; others require a scrub brush. Use a roller with an extension handle to paint a floor—to prevent backache from bending over. Paint one section at a time.

Fill in a pitted surface.
Smooth a rough-textured wall (but not a floor) with a 1:1 Portland cement and tile-grout mix, scrubbing it into depressions. To smooth a light texture, use an abrasive tool.

Apply the paint.
Apply paint with an old or cheap stiff-bristle brush. You'll have to push hard on the brush and even scrub it into very porous surfaces. If you want a rough texture, use a long-nap roller to apply the finish.

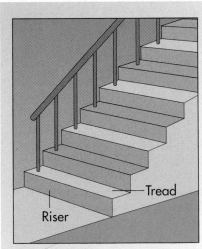

Painting stairs.
To paint steps that are used daily, paint the risers and every other tread. When the finish is dry on those, paint the treads you skipped.

Tread
Riser

SPRAY-PAINTING

Spray-painting is by far the fastest means of applying paint, stain, or other finishes. When done carefully, spraying yields professional-looking results that are hard to match with a brush or roller.

Spray-painting does have its drawbacks. It consumes much more finish than painting with a brush or roller. It's also messy. Overspray makes spraying impractical in many situations, such as in finished rooms or outside where a neighbor's car or house will be affected. Some communities even prohibit outdoor spraying.

You'll need plenty of ventilation if you spray-paint inside. Open nearby windows and, if there's an exhaust fan close by, turn it on. Always wear a painter's mask to keep from inhaling airborne paint particles, and wear a hat and protective clothing. Painting outside is less hazardous in terms of ventilation, but wear your mask nonetheless.

Here are some spray-painting pointers to keep in mind:
■ Prepare all surfaces the same way you would if you were to paint them with a brush or roller.
■ Tightly cover anything you don't want painted. For smaller areas, use newspaper and masking tape; for large areas, use drop cloths sealed at the edges with masking tape.
■ When spraying solvent-thinned paint indoors, make sure there is no open flame in the workshop area—the evaporating solvent is extremely flammable.
■ Never spray outdoors on a windy day. The air must be fairly calm or you won't get a nice finish—and you risk overspraying your neighbor's car. Even on calm days, make sure no valuable items are nearby.
■ Paint mixtures must be specially prepared for a spray gun. If the paint is too thick, it will clog the gun. If it's too thin, the paint will run on the surface. Even with the right mixture, have a brush handy to catch runs and drips.
■ When painting fencing with a spray gun, have a helper hold a wide piece of cardboard behind the fence to catch the overspray.
■ Don't spray gutters, corner trim, or siding material that joins the foundation of your home unless you have the roof, corner, or foundation covered properly.
■ Don't spray-paint windows; instead, use a sash brush. The same rule applies for other trim—doors, basement sashes, and storm windows. However, a spray gun is excellent for painting screens.

Setting up a spray booth.
If you can't take your work outside, set up a paint booth inside. For small projects, your booth can be as simple as newspaper pages taped together and positioned behind and below the item to be sprayed. Use a cardboard panel as a shield to absorb overspray.

If you're painting a large piece or have a lot of spraying to do, fabricate a booth from 4-mil polyethylene plastic film and fasten it to the walls and floor in a corner of your workshop, basement, or garage.

How large a booth you need depends on the scale of the project being painted, of course. Be sure to give yourself plenty of

working room. Overspray carries a surprising distance, and cleaning it off masonry is a chore you want to avoid.

Keep the top of the booth open to allow paint fumes to escape. For safety reasons and skin protection, wear a spray mask, hat, rubber gloves, and long sleeves.

USING A SPRAY GUN

The first rule of spray-painting is to keep the equipment clean. If you don't, you'll spend most of your time dealing with equipment malfunctions and cleaning up spatters and runs. You'll also end up with a shoddy-looking job.

Also crucial is the thickness of paint being sprayed. If it's too thin, it will not cover and will drip and run. If it's too thick, it will clog your equipment and produce a finish that looks spattered. For the best results, read the container label and follow the paint and sprayer manufacturers' advice.

Your spray technique also deserves consideration. When you spray, keep a stiff wrist and hold the spray gun nozzle 8 to 10 inches away from the surface, parallel to the ground. And don't start spraying from a still position. Begin your movement, then pull the trigger and start spraying.

Fan the spray on the surface, using several light coats instead of one heavy coat. The paint will be thick at the center and feathered out at the edges. So, as you paint, overlap your spray pattern by about one third so the thickness of the paint will be uniform.

On gutters, point the gun away from the roof. Along foundations, paint the bottom two courses of siding with a brush, or mask off the foundation to at least a foot below the last siding course.

Strain the paint.
Before putting paint into the gun's reservoir, run the paint through a strainer to rid the mixture of impurities that may clog the gun.

Test the machine.
Experiment on scrap material to gauge the proper distance between the gun and the surface. Also, you can adjust most guns for different spray patterns.

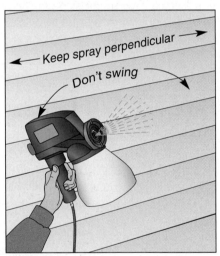

Keep spray perpendicular
Don't swing

Apply the paint.
Hold the gun perpendicular to the surface—don't swing it in an arc. Keep your wrist stiff to deter this temptation. For lap siding, angle the gun to spray the undersides. Apply a thin coating, and then let overspray fill it in.

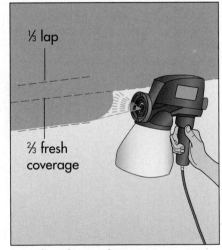

⅓ lap

⅔ fresh coverage

Overlap the strokes.
Lap successive strokes by about one-third of the spray width to achieve even paint coverage.

YOU'LL NEED...
TIME: 6 hours to paint the exterior of a small house.
SKILLS: Intermediate painting skills and basic mechanical skills.
TOOLS: Spray gun, filter for paint, brushes, drop cloths.

USING A SPRAY CAN

Painting with spray cans is expensive, but the time you save compensates for the added expense. This is especially true when dealing with hard-to-paint items, such as wicker furniture, radiators, and small cabinets.

First shake the can. When you hear the rattle of the metal ball that mixes the paint, shake the can for another minute or so.

To prevent the nozzle from clogging, after each use invert the can and depress the button until only propellant comes out. Then wipe the nozzle clean. If the nozzle clogs, often you can open it by using a needle to puncture the paint seal over the spray hole. If this doesn't work, buy a low-cost replacement nozzle.

NOTE: *Aerosol paint is flammable, so don't spray-paint near flames.*

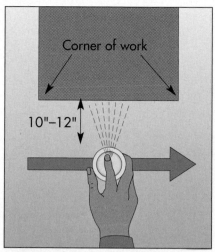

Apply with even strokes.
Hold the can 10 to 12 inches from the surface. Apply smooth, even strokes, moving the can parallel to the surface, rather than just pointing it in different directions. Don't try to cover the surface completely in the first stroke, or the thick paint may sag or drip. Apply several thin coats instead.

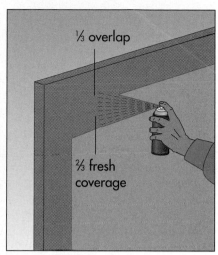

Lap the strokes.
Overlap the strokes by about one-third. After you've made several passes, stop and check to make sure the surface is covered.

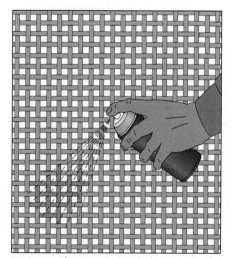

Painting lattice.
On openwork like lattice, tilt the can at an angle to minimize the paint flowing through the openings. Crisscross your spray patterns to catch all the edges.

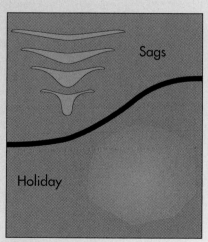

Problems to avoid.
Sags and runs are caused by too much paint. Wipe away the excess, then spot-spray with short bursts to blend in the touch-up.

Holidays occur when there's not enough paint on the surface. Spot-in these areas, as you would a sag or run.

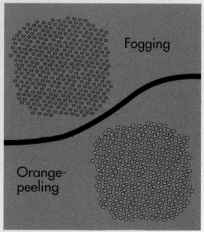

Fogging is the dull, pebbled effect produced when the spray can is held too far away. Spot-spray these areas as well.

Orange-peeling results from too thick a covering of paint or from too much air pressure. Wipe and spot-paint these areas.

REPAIRING DRYWALL

Drywall—also known as plasterboard and by trade names such as Sheetrock®—consists of big sheets of pressed gypsum faced with heavy paper on both sides. After the sheets have been nailed, screwed, or glued to studs, the joints are covered with a perforated paper or fiberglass mesh tape. Joints are then filled and smoothed over with joint compound, often referred to as mud, to create a smooth surface.

Drywall repairs are easy once you get the knack of working with the material, especially the joint compound. See pages 338–343 for more about working with drywall.

YOU'LL NEED...

TIME: 10 to 20 minutes, depending on the size of the repair.
SKILLS: Basic skills.
TOOLS: Drywall taping knives, sanding block, sponge, putty knife, paintbrush, hammer, drill.

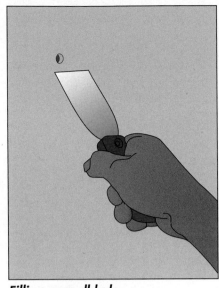

Filling a small hole.
For very small holes, apply joint compound to the void with a putty knife. Allow the compound to dry. If it shrinks, you may need to apply a second coat. To smooth the patch, either sand it or wipe it gently with a damp sponge.

EXPERTS' INSIGHT

JOINT COMPOUND

Ready-mixed joint compound comes in buckets; just scoop it out and apply it. Ready-mix is easy to sand, but it dries slowly and is not strong.

Dry-mix joint compound comes in bags of powder that you mix with water. Bags are typically labeled 90, 45, or 20; the compound will harden (though not dry) in roughly that many minutes. Regular dry-mix is stronger than ready-mix; "easy-sand" dry-mix is not.

Use ready-mix for small repairs. For substantial patches, or to speed up the drying time, apply one coat of dry-mix and use ready-mix for the top coats.

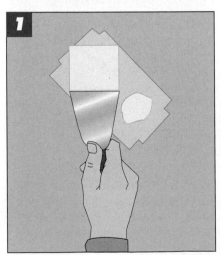

1. To fill a dent, apply joint compound.
Brush away any loose material. Use a taping blade to first pack the dent with joint compound and then to level it off. If the patch shrinks after drying, apply a second and perhaps a third coat.

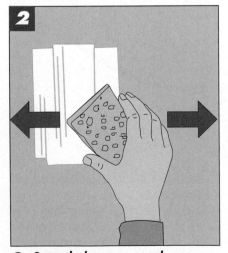

2. Smooth the compound.
Sand the surface very lightly—or smooth it by wiping with a damp sponge.

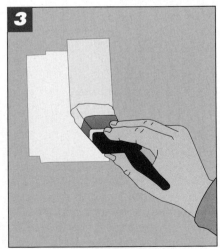

3. Prime and paint.
Joint compound must be primed before you paint. Just about any type of primer, including latex, will do the job. Some paints are self-priming.

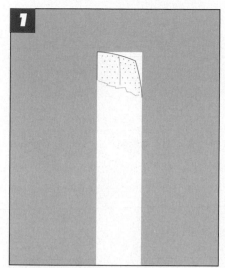

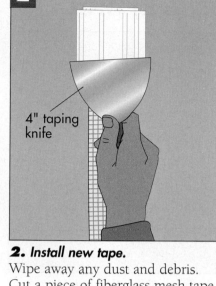

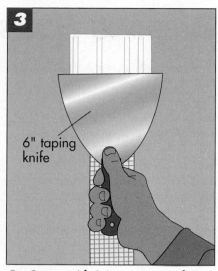

1. To repair loose tape, remove the tape.

If drywall tape is peeling, pull it gently off; you may need to pry it up with a putty knife first. Use a sharp knife to make a clean break at the point where the tape becomes firmly embedded. If the tape has a bubble, cut around the area with a utility knife, and pry out the damaged tape.

2. Install new tape.

Wipe away any dust and debris. Cut a piece of fiberglass mesh tape to roughly fit; it's all right if it is a bit short at either end. Press the tape into place. Apply joint compound over the tape and use gentle strokes of a 4-inch taping knife to cover the tape.

3. Cover with joint compound.

If you are applying ready-mix, or "easy-sand" compound, mound the compound up a bit. If you re-apply regular dry-mix compound, level it with the knife. Let it dry, then apply one and perhaps two more coats, feathering the edges. The patch should look and feel even with the surrounding wall. Sand, prime, and paint.

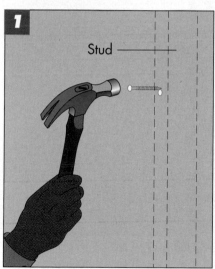

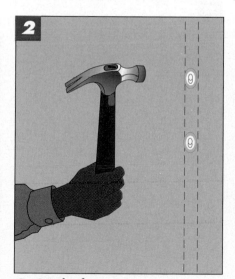

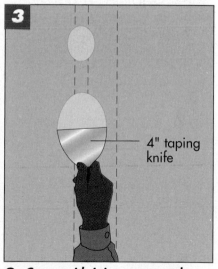

1. If nails have popped out, secure them with new fasteners.

If a nail is very loose, it may have missed the stud entirely; pull it out and drive a nail or screws into the stud. If it feels pretty firm, it either wasn't driven all the way or it barely caught the stud. Drive new ringshank nails or drywall screws just above and below the popped nail.

2. Set the fasteners.

If using nails, "dimple" the nails below the surface by tapping with a hammer. Take care not to break the paper. Drive screws slightly below the surface. Run a taping knife over the area to make sure that the fastener heads are recessed. Fill the dimples or screw holes with joint compound.

3. Cover with joint compound.

After the compound has dried, apply a second and perhaps third coat, until the hole is filled to the same level as the surrounding wall. Sand, prime, and paint.

PATCHING HOLES IN DRYWALL

Usually the space between studs is 14½ inches. If a hole or damaged area is fairly large, cut out a section that spans from stud to stud so the patch can be solidly attached to nailers fastened to the studs, as shown on page 865. Smaller holes can be patched without attaching to framing, but they will not be as strong.

Most drywall is ½ inch thick, but some walls have ³⁄₈- or ⁵⁄₈-inch-thick drywall. Purchase patching drywall to match your existing material.

If a wall is damaged due to a doorknob that knocks against it, install a stop at the bottom of the door to prevent further damage.

EXPERTS' INSIGHT

OTHER PATCHING MATERIALS

Special drywall patching kits save time and hassle. Some kits use a screen that adheres to the front of the drywall; just apply joint compound over the screen. Other kits have clips that clasp a patch firmly to the surrounding drywall. You cut the patch, clip it, apply mesh tape, and cover with joint compound.

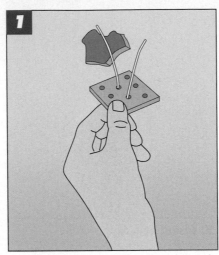

1. To repair a small hole, prepare the backing.
Cut a piece of pegboard that is slightly larger than the damaged area, but small enough to slip through the hole. Or use a piece of wood through which you have drilled two holes.

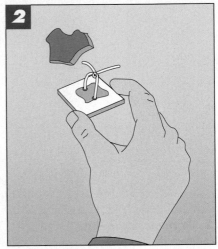

3. Tighten.
Tie the wire on the patch to a pencil or small stick, and twist it tight. After the patch dries, cut the wire off and use a taping knife to fill the recess with joint compound. (See page 862 for how to choose joint compound.)

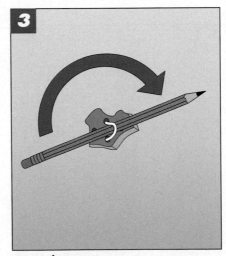

2. Insert the backing.
Tie a wire to the pegboard, smear joint compound on the inside perimeter of the pegboard, and slip the patch into the wall. When you pull back on the wire, the patch should cling to the back of the wall.

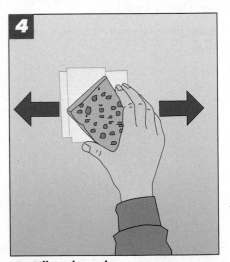

4. Fill and patch.
Allow the joint compound to dry. Apply two or three more coats, until the patch looks and feels level with the surrounding wall. Sand smooth or use a damp sponge to level the repair. Prime and paint.

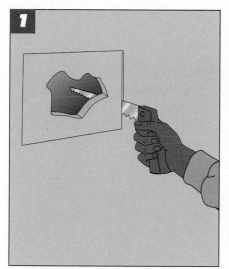

1. For a medium-size hole, cut out a rectangle.
For holes up to 8 inches wide, mark a rectangle and cut it with a keyhole saw or a drywall saw.

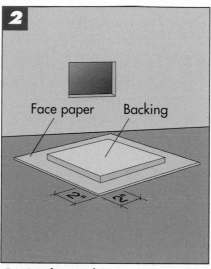

Face paper   Backing

2. Cut the patch.
Cut a drywall rectangle 2 inches larger than the hole on all sides. Turn the patch upside down and carefully use a utility knife to remove the 2-inch perimeter, but leave the face paper intact. Test to see that the patch fits comfortably into the hole.

3. Prepare for the patch.
Use a taping knife to spread a medium-thick bed of joint compound around the perimeter of the damaged area.

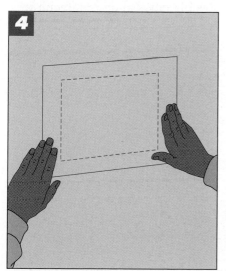

4. Install the patch.
Insert the patch and smooth the face paper against the wall all around. (The face paper takes the place of drywall tape.) Blend the patch with the surrounding surface by feathering the edges with coats of joint compound. Sand or smooth with a damp sponge, then prime and paint.

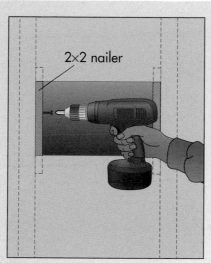

2×2 nailer

To repair a large area, frame the sides.
For larger holes, cut a rectangle that spans from stud to stud. Cut 2×2 nailers slightly longer than the opening's height. Position the nailers as shown, and attach them by driving nails or screws.

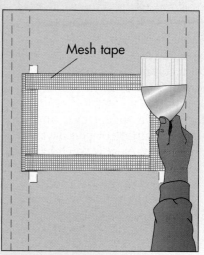

Mesh tape

Patch and tape.
Nail or screw the drywall patch into place. Apply fiberglass mesh tape to the perimeter, then cover it with three coats of joint compound. Allow each coat to dry and feather the edges to blend the patch with the wall. Sand it smooth or wipe it with a damp sponge. Prime and paint.

REPAIRING CRACKED PLASTER

Examine plaster walls and ceilings before patching to make sure that repairs will last. Press hard with your hand on the surface all around any cracks. Here's what you may find:

■ If the plaster is solid and there are only a few hairline cracks, fill them with caulk or an aerosol crack sealer.

■ If the plaster is solid but there is a web of hairline cracks, the plaster itself is failing, perhaps because it was mixed incorrectly when installed. Usually the problem is cosmetic only, but could return after painting. Aerosol crack sealer may help, as may painting with latex semigloss paint, which remains flexible. Otherwise, either hire a plasterer or cover the surface with drywall.

■ If the area feels spongy, the plaster and perhaps the lath has come loose from the wall. Either remove all loose material and patch, or hire a plasterer. In extreme cases, or in the case of a loose ceiling, consider applying new drywall over the surface and taping it.

■ If a crack widens over time, the house is settling or you have a structural problem. You'll have to update repairs every so often. Seal the crack with flexible caulk.

The repairs shown here and on the next three pages are homeowner-friendly. For a new plaster surface that is rock-hard, you'll need to hire a plasterer.

YOU'LL NEED...

TIME: 1 hour of work, but allow for 2 overnight periods of drying.

SKILLS: Basic skills.

TOOLS: Hammer, chisel or old screwdriver, putty knife, taping knife, old toothbrush, sanding block, and a sponge.

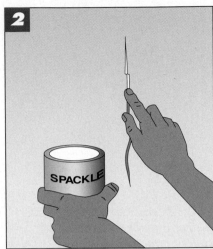

1. Enlarge the crack.
Widen a medium-size crack to at least ¼ inch with a chisel or old screwdriver, and blow out any loose plaster. Press on the area of the wall surrounding the crack. If any part is spongy, chip away the plaster until you come to solid material, then patch as shown on pages 868–869.

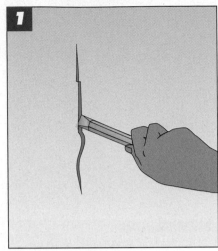

3. Seal the patch.
Seal patches with primer before painting or the patch may "bleed" through and change the color of the paint.

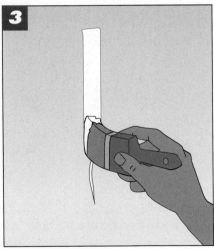

2. Fill with caulk or spackle.
Apply vinyl spackling compound, which retains some flexibility. Work it into the crack, and let it mound up a little. When it has dried, sand or sponge it smooth. Alternatively, fill the crack with latex/silicone caulk, which is more flexible but also more difficult to level with the surrounding wall.

EXPERTS' INSIGHT

PLASTER PATCHING MATERIALS

■ Dry-mix joint compound is strong, making it a good choice for wide cracks and holes.

■ Vinyl surfacing compound is soft and flexible. Use it for narrow cracks or holes.

■ Patching plaster or gauging plaster creates a genuine plaster surface, but it takes time to learn how to apply it correctly.

■ Latex/silicone caulk stays flexible and so can accommodate shifting cracks.

■ Aerosol crack seal is ideal for small cracks. Spray it just before priming.

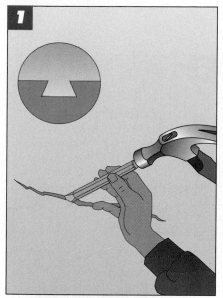

1. For a wide crack, use a chisel to "key" it.
Undercut wide cracks, making them broader at the bottom than the surface to lock in the filler material (see inset). Sometimes you can do this by scraping with a chisel or screwdriver; some people prefer to use an old-fashioned "church-key" type of can opener.

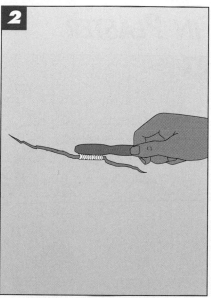

2. Remove loose material.
Clean the debris and crumbly material out of the crack with an old toothbrush or a wire brush. It helps to vacuum out the hole.

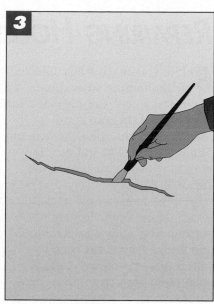

3. Wet the area.
Use a small brush to wet the crack before patching.

For a patch that is less likely to crack, apply fiberglass mesh tape over the crack. This will make the repaired area bulge a bit, so you will need to feather the compound out on each side (see page 869).

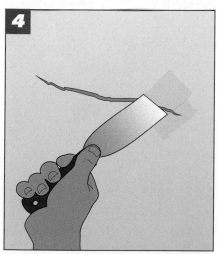

4. Force compound into the crack.
Pack joint compound, surfacing compound, or patching plaster into the crack with a putty knife or a wide-blade taping knife. First force the material into the crack, and then level it off.

5. Apply additional coats.
Let the compound harden, then level off the repair with a second and perhaps a third application. If you are using soft compound, mound the patch up a bit because it's easy to sand or sponge it down.

6. Smooth and seal.
Allow the patch to dry thoroughly, then either sand it smooth or rub it with a damp sponge. If you have not embedded mesh tape in the patch, spray the area with aerosol crack sealer. Seal it with primer, then paint it.

REPAIRING HOLES IN PLASTER

Before you attack a big hole or bulge, find out what caused the plaster to fail. See page 866 for some tips. If the wall is water-stained or damp, solve the leak or plumbing problem and wait a month or two to make sure the area will stay dry.

In most cases, a hole in plaster is just the tip of the iceberg; the surrounding surface is likely loose and weak. Always cut back to sound plaster; you won't get a solid bond with crumbling edges. If most or all of a wall is loose and weak, consider removing all the plaster and installing drywall over the lath. You could also cover the plaster with drywall, but that will necessitate modifying your moldings to accommodate the thicker wall. See pages 338–343 for hanging and taping drywall. Usually you can remove the plaster only and leave the wood or metal lath in place. If the lath is rotted or badly rusted, replace it.

You may be able to fill a medium-size hole with dry-mix joint compound only, but make a stiff mix of the compound to ward off sags. Patching plaster is less likely to sag.

Once you have chipped away the loose plaster, carefully measure its thickness, which can vary considerably from area to area even on a single wall. The patching drywall may be thinner, but should not be thicker than the plaster. Usually, either 3/8- or 1/2-inch drywall will work.

YOU'LL NEED...

TIME: An hour of work and a day of drying time.
SKILLS: Basic skills.
TOOLS: Hammer, drill, masonry chisel or old screwdriver, utility knife, taping knife, sanding block, sponge, painting tools.

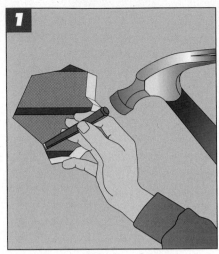

1. Remove all loose plaster.
Dig back with a masonry chisel, flat pry bar, or old screwdriver until you encounter solid plaster. Brush out any remaining debris.

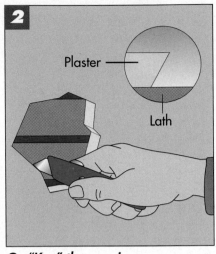

2. "Key" the opening.
Though not as important as with cracks, undercutting the edges makes a stronger repair. Scrape with a utility knife, chisel, screwdriver, or "church-key" type of can opener.

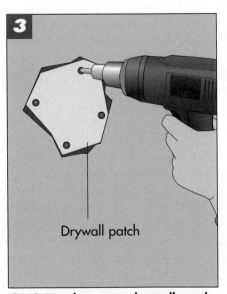

Drywall patch

3. Cut and screw a drywall patch.
If there is wood lath behind the hole, cut a piece of drywall—the same thickness or thinner than the plaster—to roughly fit in the hole. Make sure it does not stick out past the plaster. Attach it to the lath with 1 1/4-inch drywall screws driven into the lath.

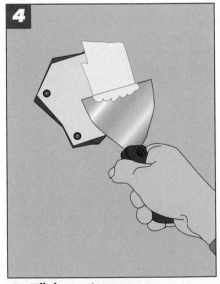

4. Fill the perimeter.
Blend a stiff batch of dry-mix joint compound, and use a taping knife to press it into the spaces between the patch and the wall. Then smooth the surface.

5

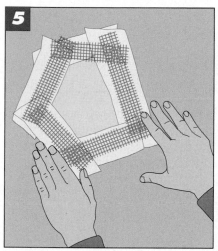

5. Add mesh tape.

While the compound is wet, cut pieces of fiberglass mesh tape and embed them in the compound. This will bond the compound with the surrounding wall and protect against cracks.

6

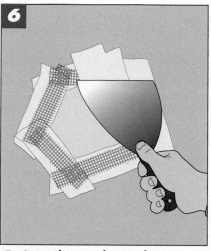

6. Smooth over the mesh.

Apply more joint compound and spread it over the mesh. The idea is to cover the mesh, but not build up the compound too thick. After it has dried, apply two more coats of ready-mix compound or surfacing compound.

7

7. Sand and finish.

Once the compound has dried, sand it smooth or rub lightly with a damp sponge to level the area. Apply primer and paint.

REPAIRING PANELING

If you scratch or mar paneling, you usually can make a cosmetic repair in a few minutes with paste wax or a crayonlike touch-up stick. Don't try to spot-sand and refinish your prefinished paneling; you risk doing more harm than good.

If a panel has suffered serious damage, you'll have to replace it entirely. Finding a match may be your biggest challenge.

If your paneling was glued directly to drywall, you may have to replace the drywall before reinstalling the paneling. If electrical wiring runs in the wall you're working on, shut off the power to the circuit before doing any cutting, sawing, or nailing.

YOU'LL NEED...

TIME: An hour of work per panel.
SKILLS: Basic skills.
TOOLS: Hammer, pry bar, pliers, taping knives, chisel, caulking gun, and nail set.

1

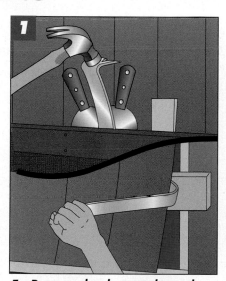

1. Remove the damaged panel.

Identify and mark the edges of the damaged panel. Pry off the baseboard and top molding by inserting a taping or putty knife, then a pry bar. Pull out the nails with pliers, then pull the panel off. Start at the bottom, where there's usually no adhesive. Pull out nails as they pop. Finish prying the panel away, working from the bottom to the top. Use a wood block to protect adjacent panels.

2

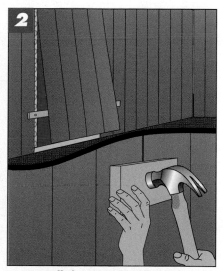

2. Install the new panel.

Remove all old adhesive with a scraper or chisel. Apply panel adhesive to studs with a caulking gun. Nail the panel loosely at the top and wedge it out, as shown, until the adhesive gets tacky. Press the panel into place, then use a wood block to tap it against the studs, as shown. Nail the edges with color-matched brads.

PREPARING INTERIOR SURFACES FOR PAINT

Paint works wonders for a room's appearance, but it can't perform miracles. Paint will not heal cracked walls, smooth rough textures, or fill any but the tiniest nail holes. In fact, paint applied to a wall that is not well prepared may peel, causing you major headaches later.

After you've cleared the room, but before you've opened the first paint can, give every surface careful scrutiny. Start with the walls, checking for cracks, runs, or ridges in the old paint. All of these can be treated easily with a scraper and sandpaper; then use a primer for bare spots. Use a paint remover (see page 892) to strip cracked or gloppy paint from woodwork. If the old paint is peeling, suspect moisture or poor preparation. Both problems

require removing the old paint and priming the surface. Of course, any moisture leaks should be immediately corrected at the source.

Mend superficial plaster or drywall blemishes with surfacing or joint compound. Bigger repairs (see pages 862–869) require more time, not only for patching, but also for curing and priming. (On textured walls, you may have trouble blending the patched area completely with its surroundings.)

You can paint over clean, sound wallpaper, but in most cases you're better off stripping it (see page 880). If you decide to paint over wallpaper, paint a small test spot in an inconspicuous area and wait a few days. If the pattern bleeds through, apply stain-killing primer. If the paper begins to

peel, strip all of the wallpaper.

After you've made repairs, give the ceiling, walls, and woodwork a thorough bath with household detergent, and rinse well. Prime exposed spots with a compatible primer. At this point, you've completed at least 50 percent of your painting project.

Use heavy-duty drop cloths that will stay in place to protect floors and rugs. If you step on a drip, you will likely track paint around the room, so cover a broad area.

YOU'LL NEED...

TIME: 2 to 4 hours per room.
SKILLS: Basic skills.
TOOLS: Portable light, screwdriver, putty knife, sandpaper, sponge or mop.

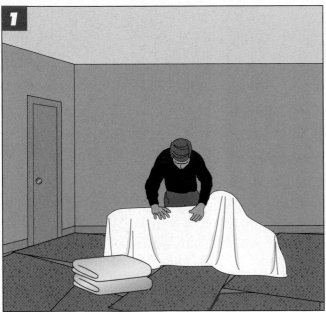

1. Clear and protect the room.
If practical, remove all furniture from the room. You may choose to group heavy items in the middle and protect them with drop cloths. Cover the floor carefully. Ideally, you should tape down a layer of heavy cardboard or plastic, and cover that with a heavy-duty drop cloth.

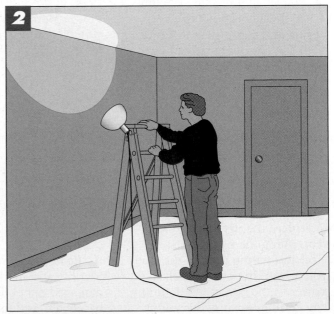

2. Provide lighting.
Set up strong lights so you can see what you're painting. Provide general lighting. Also, aim other lights at angles to highlight minor imperfections. If there is a ceiling light, disconnect it and let it hang (see page 872). Cover the globe to protect against spatters. Alternatively, disconnect the light entirely and replace it with a simple work light.

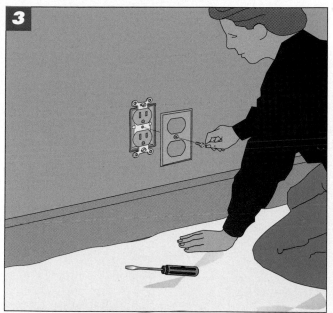

3. Remove coverplates.

It always saves time to remove obstacles rather than paint around them. Even if you plan to paint switch and receptacle plates, remove them and paint them separately.

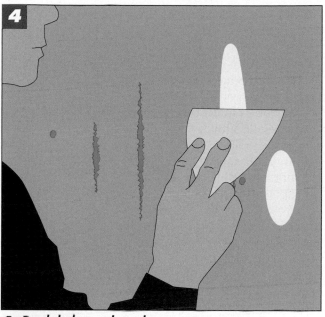

4. Patch holes and cracks.

Regardless of the size, fill every hole and crack with vinyl surfacing compound. Allow it to dry, then sand it smooth. Prime all patches before painting.

5. Ensure the paint will stick.

Sand rough spots smooth, and sand any runs from previous paint jobs. To ensure that the new paint will stick, you have three options: (1) Sand all the walls and trim using 80- or 100-grit sandpaper on a drywall-type sanding pole; (2) apply liquid sander, which removes the sheen from glossy and semigloss paints; (3) paint the room with primer. If you will apply latex paint over existing solvent-thinned paint, perform at least two of these operations.

6. Clean the surfaces.

Wash the ceiling and walls with a sponge or mop, paying special attention to the tops of baseboards and moldings. Any dust will cling to your brush or roller and mar the paint job.

PAINTING CEILINGS

To succeed at painting a room, start at the top and work your way down. In other words, the ceiling comes first.

Unless the surface is brand new, you usually can get by with one coat of paint on a ceiling. Even stubborn stains will disappear if you spot-prime them first.

If you're planning a one-coat application, let the paint lap onto the walls. If you will apply two coats to the ceiling, cut in (trim up to the ceiling/wall line) with a trim brush. Otherwise, the paint will build up on the wall and leave a ridge.

Paint across the ceiling at the room's narrow dimension, especially if you're using a fast-drying paint. Otherwise, the paint may lose its wet edge.

A roller frame with an extension handle greatly speeds up the job, although you still need a trim brush to cut in the ceiling paint where it meets the walls. A doughnut-style roller makes quick work of painting the corner between a wall and the ceiling.

Rollers emit a fine spray of paint that settles over the room like dust. Cover furniture in the room, as well as the floor, carpeting, and woodwork. Canvas drop cloths work best because they absorb spills and are easy to walk on, but plastic drop cloths or newspapers will do the job too.

Buy ceiling paint—it is flatter than flat wall paint and hides imperfections very well. It is not scrubbable, but ceilings are not prone to handprints and smudges.

YOU'LL NEED...

TIME: 3 to 4 hours.
SKILLS: Basic painting skills.
TOOLS: Drop cloths, brushes, ladder, and a roller with an extension handle.

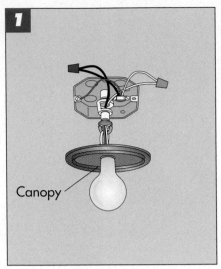

1. Protect lights.
Usually you can remove a light fixture's canopy. Remove the canopy's mounting screws and allow the fixture to hang down, as long as it is not a heavy chandelier. (See page 98 for how to dismantle fixtures.) Wrap the fixture in plastic, or cover the finish parts with masking tape.

2. Paint the corners.
Start a ceiling job by cutting in a strip along the walls, as shown. If you'll be applying only one coat, lap the paint onto the wall as well.

3. Roll and cross-roll.
Start rolling the paint with a series of diagonal swaths. Don't worry about spreading the paint evenly; just get it on the ceiling. Then even out the paint and fill in any open areas by cross-rolling.

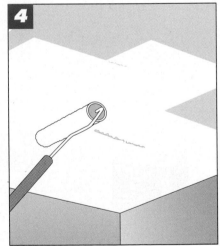

4. Level the paint.
Continue working, spreading the paint from dry areas into the wet paint. Rollers slip on smooth surfaces, so check for skips. After you've finished a section, check to see whether you've created thick lap marks. If so, even them out by going over them lightly with a fairly dry roller.

PAINTING WALLS

Once the walls have been patched, perhaps primed, and cleaned thoroughly, the ceiling has been painted, and all of the switch and receptacle plates have been removed, you're ready to paint walls. Do all the edging first. This includes cutting in the ceiling and around moldings and trims. Once these details are done, it's payback time: You can paint the big, flat surfaces quickly.

A neat job requires concentration and a methodical approach. Take care to keep the edges wet to prevent lap marks. Keep the roller from slipping to the side and causing skid marks. Avoid the temptation to make a roller load last too long, or you will end up with places that are not fully covered.

When painting with semigloss or high-gloss finish, make the final brush strokes away from light sources, including windows. This way, the tiny ridges that a brush leaves won't be as noticeable.

Always give paint a brisk stirring before starting, even if the paint was just shaken at the store. As you work, stir the paint occasionally. Keep an eye on the paint in the roller tray. As long as you're filling the roller, the paint will remain properly blended. If you leave the tray for an hour or so, cover it with plastic wrap. When you're ready to get back to work, stir the paint lightly with a paint paddle. When left untouched, paint skins over.

YOU'LL NEED...

TIME: 5 to 6 hours for a 14×16-foot room.
SKILLS: Basic painting skills.
TOOLS: Drop cloths, ladder, brushes, specialty paint applicators for painting around trim, roller, extension handle.

1. Brush the corners.
Begin painting walls by cutting in the corners and around all of the woodwork. With practice, you can cut neat lines without the use of masking tape. If you will paint the trim later, lap the wall paint onto the trim slightly. Paint about 3 inches out from the edges.

2. Apply paint.
For large surfaces, load the roller and apply the paint in a large "M" shape. Start the roller going up, then pull it down.

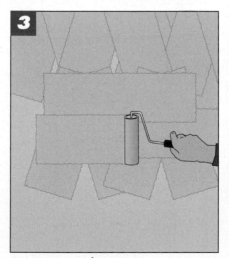

3. Even out the paint.
Level and fill in the M shapes by cross-rolling. You can work horizontally, as shown, or vertically. By working the paint this way, you get an even paint surface. Watch for roller skids.

4. Paint in planned sections.
Determine how much area a loaded roller can fully cover. Do not attempt to "stretch" the paint, or you will probably need to apply another coat. (You can see the coverage clearly only after the paint has dried.) Plan to work in sections that are similar in size.

PAINTING WOODWORK

Painting woodwork is hard work. Next to prepping, it's the most time-consuming painting job. If you master the tricks shown here, however, you'll minimize the tedium and speed your progress.

If at all possible, learn to paint freehand. With practice, anyone with a fairly steady hand and good brushes can master freehand techniques and save a tremendous amount of time compared to applying masking tape.

A coat of paint will probably emphasize rather than cover imperfections. Before you begin painting, patch holes with wood filler. Let the material dry overnight, then apply primer.

If you'll be using the same paint on the woodwork as on the walls, paint the woodwork as you come to it. Generally, however, you should use a higher gloss on woodwork. If you do, or if the woodwork will be another color, paint the walls first.

Windows and raised-panel doors are the toughest assignments because of the amount of cutting in and the fact that you can't use full brush strokes. If you can't paint freehand, cover the glass with masking tape or use a painter's shield. Some people find it efficient to paint windows somewhat sloppily and then scrape the excess afterwards. Use a razor blade scraping tool to clean off smeared paint.

YOU'LL NEED...

TIME: 1 to 2 hours for a standard window.
SKILLS: Moderate painting skills.
TOOLS: Sash brush, masking tape, painter's shield, putty knife, and a drop cloth.

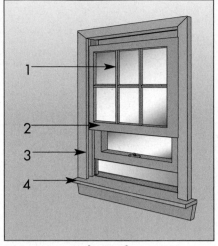

Painting a sash window.
Paint double-hung windows in the sequence shown, starting with the muntins, then working outward. Move the sashes several times while the paint is drying to make sure the sashes do not dry shut.

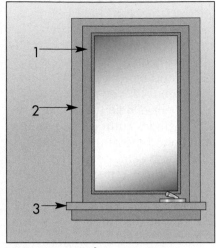

Casement window sequence.
Use the same sequence shown at left for casement windows. Keep the window slightly open until the paint is dry.

Mask window panes ...
Painter's masking tape protects windowpanes from paint. Peel off the tape immediately after you finish painting; if you wait until the paint is fully dry, you could crack it as you remove the tape.

Painter's shield

... or use a shield.
A painter's shield keeps paint off the glass, too. Keep a damp cloth handy to frequently clean the shield's edge as you work around the muntins.

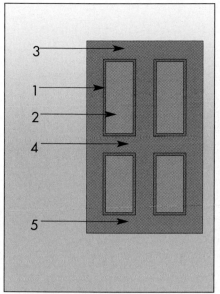

Panel door sequence.
Start painting panel doors at the molding edges. Then fill in the panels, the hinge stile, the rails, and the latch stile. To apply a gloss finish, use a cross-brush method: Apply paint on the door horizontally, then make vertical finishing strokes. Always finish a door once you've started it. If you don't, the lap marks may show.

Roll flush doors.
Flush doors are easier and quicker to paint. Either a brush or a roller will give good results. If you use a roller, be sure to roll the entire surface, because any brush marks will look very different.

Painting baseboards.
Paint the top edge of a baseboard first. Next cut in along the floor, and then fill in between. Painter's masking tape helps if you don't have a steady hand.

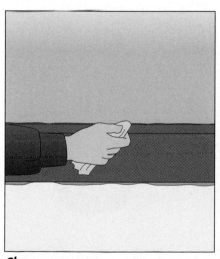

Clean as you go.
Have on hand a rag dampened with water or mineral spirits, depending on the type of paint. Clean up overlapping paint smudges as soon as they occur. If you don't, the paint will set up and be much tougher to remove.

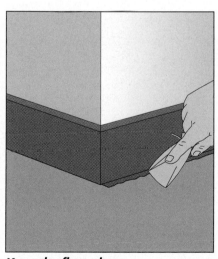

Keep the floor clean.
A cloth wrapped around a putty knife works well to clean up paint drippings on hardwood and resilient flooring along baseboards.

Seal a stain.
If a woodwork stain bleeds through the paint, spray or brush on a stain-killing primer, let dry, then repaint.

PAINTING CABINETS

This is an inexpensive way to make a dramatic improvement in the appearance of a kitchen. It requires painstaking, methodical work, but it is well worth the effort.

Purchase paint made especially for cabinets. Alkyd paint generally outperforms latex, but many types of latex paint are durable and washable. For two weeks after application, handle latex painted cabinets carefully and certainly do not scrub them.

While you're at it, you may choose to install new shelf paper on shelves and drawer bottoms.

YOU'LL NEED...
TIME: 2 days to paint cabinets in a medium-size kitchen.
SKILLS: Basic painting skills.
TOOLS: Screwdriver, putty knife, drop cloth, and a trim brush.

Remove doors and drawers.
Before painting cabinets, dismantle them as much as possible. Unscrew and remove all hinges and knobs or pulls. Lay a drop cloth or newspapers on the floor; you may need to use an adjacent room as well. Stand the drawers upright, or prop them so no edge touches the drop cloth.

Paint the drawer faces and doors with a roller or a brush. Aim to make the roller stipple or brush strokes consistent for all the drawers and doors.

Place doors on small scraps of wood. Paint the insides first, wait a day, then flip and paint the outsides. Paint the edges of doors first, then the faces. Check all around each piece to make sure there are no drips or sags.

Work from inside to outside.
Begin painting cabinets at their least accessible points and work outward. Do the inside edges first, then move toward outer surfaces. You may be able to use a roller for the faces, as long as you can roll all the surfaces; any brush strokes will be noticeable.

Prop a piece to paint both sides.
To paint both sides and the edges of a shelf in one session, drive in four small nails to serve as legs. Paint the underside, then the top.

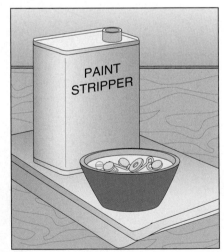

Strip the hardware.
Clean previously painted cabinet, door, or window hardware by soaking it overnight in paint stripper. Rinse with mineral spirits. Buff the surfaces lightly with steel wool. Alternatively, buy and install new hardware.

CLEANING UP AFTER PAINTING

Even if you've thoroughly covered and masked the surfaces you don't want to paint, there will likely be splatters to clean. For water-thinned finishes, use dishwashing detergent in warm water with a soft cloth to remove stray paint. If the paint is solvent-thinned, use thinner on a soft cloth. Where thinner has been applied, follow up with water and household detergent.

If you happen to scuff freshly painted walls or woodwork, don't attempt to wash the scuff mark until the paint has had time to cure—at least 30 days.

Store paint in a cool, dry place. If you don't use the paint within a two-year period, dispose of it properly (see page 21).

Take canvas and plastic drop cloths outdoors and thoroughly shake them. You can wash a canvas drop cloth in the washing machine.

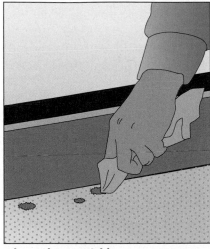

Clean drips quickly.
Wipe away splatters with soap and water or the solvent used to thin the paint. It's best to catch these splatters as you work, rather than hours or days later.

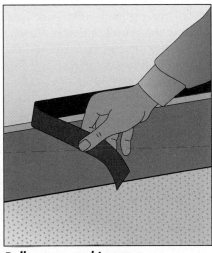

Pull away masking tape.
Remove masking tape as soon as you have completed a line, while the paint is still wet. Otherwise the paint will tear and you'll end up with a ragged and crumbling edge.

Scrape up dried paint.
Use a razor-blade scraper to chip off big paint droplets that have already set. A putty knife will work, too. Acetone or latex paint remover will clean away dried latex paint; use paint stripper sparingly to remove dried solvent-thinned paint.

Razor-blade window panes.
Use a razor-blade scraper to trim around windowpanes. Try not to break the seal between the glass and the paint.

Reseal paint cans.
If more than a quart of material remains, seal it in the original paint can. Tap the lid with a hammer and block of wood to shut it tightly. Store paint cans upside down to prevent a skin from forming. If you end up with less than a quart, pour the paint into a glass jar that seals tightly. The paint will keep better in this small container.

APPLYING FAUX FINISHES

Most faux (look-alike) finishes involve adding a tinted and diluted wash or glaze to an already painted surface to create a textured, layered effect. A **wash** is water-base paint that has been diluted with water. A **glaze** is an oil-base product that has been diluted with solvent. Usually several splotchy layers in varying colors or shades—sometimes subtle, sometimes bold—are applied over a base coat that is still visible in the background. Both the application technique and the choice of colors determine the final outcome. Generally, faux finishes add depth, texture, and interest to walls.

Some techniques involve selective removal of color. For these, the glaze or wash is applied over the entire base-coat surface, and then some of it is removed to achieve the desired effect.

If you use a fast-drying latex wash, you'll have to work quickly to avoid lap marks caused by edges drying before you can blur or feather them. To slow the wash's drying time, add a little commercial glaze to it. Working with a partner will speed the process, too.

Because the background color is meant to be visible, evaluate the condition of the base coat before you begin. You may need to repaint if the walls are damaged (see pages 862–869) or if the base coat is dingy or the wrong color.

If your base coat is oil-base or acrylic paint, you will need to use an oil-based glaze that has been thinned with solvent. You can use oil glaze over a glossy finish if you sand first. (Water-based products will not adhere well to a glossy finish, even if it has been sanded.)

If your base coat is latex or alkyd paint with an eggshell, satin, or semigloss finish, you can apply either a water-base wash or an oil-base glaze.

If your faux finish involves adding layers (rather than taking away layers), it's generally best to work with an eggshell base coat. If your faux finish involves taking away paint, it's best to work with a semigloss base coat.

Generally, your first layer of wash or glaze will be more diluted—as much as 9 parts water to 1 part paint for a wash—than subsequent layers. The final layer of wash or glaze will be the most visually noticeable, so it's important to think through the color scheme before you begin applying layers. Note: Give special attention to keeping the coverage consistent in corners.

The simplest faux finish techniques—colorwashing, sponging, and ragging on—also work well for walls that have imperfections, because the layers tend to conceal flaws.

■ Before you begin, set up the space and cover the floor and furniture as you would for any interior paint job (see page 870).

■ For **colorwashing**, start with a thin solution of glaze or latex wash. If you apply a light wash or glaze over a darker paint, the effect will be chalky or antiqued-looking. A darker wash or glaze over lighter paint will lend a translucent quality.

To colorwash with a glaze, apply the glaze, diluted 70 to 90 percent with solvent, with a brush. Blend it out with a dry paintbrush or rag, wiping off glaze until you achieve the effect that you like. You can apply additional layers in the same way; just be sure each preceding layer has fully dried.

To colorwash with latex washes, mix 9 parts water to 1 part paint. In a hurried and slapdash manner, apply this very thin wash. Let the layer dry, then in the same way, apply two or three more layers. Next apply a thin layer of wash, diluted with 4 parts water to 1 part paint. Then, using a damp sponge or paintbrush, blur the edges to blend the wash with the background color.

■ **Sponging** is similar to color-washing, but it involves applying diluted paint in successive layers with a large, damp sponge. A sea sponge (a natural sponge) with medium-size pores is a popular choice.

Start with a damp sponge, moistened with water if you will apply a latex wash, or with solvent if you will add a diluted glaze. Dab the wall gently, and rotate the sponge while you lift it off. Use smaller sponge segments for corners. In the hardest-to-reach corners, use a fine artist's paintbrush to create dots that mimic the sponge effect. Let each layer dry before applying the next.

■ **Ragging on** is like sponging, but it involves using a damp cotton rag instead of a sponge. The effect is a mottled appearance. This works well with colors that are similar to the base coat or variations on the same color.

■ **Ragging off** involves covering the entire base coat with a wash or glaze, then selectively, and quickly, removing paint using a moist rag. This technique requires fast work. Using an alkyd glaze gives you a little more time because it remains wet longer.

■ **Dragging** is another removal technique that creates a uniform striped effect. The technique involves covering the entire base coat with a wash or glaze, then dragging a brush or rag across the surface to create parallel stripes. This technique works best with a semigloss base coat and with walls in excellent condition.

CHOOSING WALLPAPER

Wallpapering a room—once a messy, tricky task best left to professionals—is now almost as easy as painting. Improved wall coverings deserve part of the credit; they don't rip, shrink, or wrinkle as easily as older papers.

New slower-acting adhesives help, too, by giving you more time to hang the materials correctly.

On the following pages, every step of the job is covered—from removing old wallpaper to the advanced techniques needed for

doing ceiling work. Because prepasted and vinyl coverings are easiest for beginners, there are sections devoted to hanging these time and effort savers (see pages 889 and 891).

SELECTING WALLCOVERINGS

Type	Use	Application Tips	Cost
Solid paper	The least-expensive type of wall covering. Can be damaged if scrubbed, so use only in a low-traffic areas.	Difficult to strip. Hang with wheat-based paste. Work carefully because this material is easy to tear. Butt edges and roll seams; clean immediately, using a damp (not wet) sponge.	Low
Vinyl-coated paper	Most any situation, except where there's high humidity. More durable than solid paper.	Paste and hang one strip at a time; roll the seams and immediately clean the adhesive from each seam.	Wide range
Paper-backed vinyl	Excellent for high-traffic or high-humidity areas	May be stripped. Hand-printed vinyls must be trimmed. Use plenty of adhesive; do not stretch as you hang. If the seams curl, paste them down with vinyl-to-vinyl adhesive; remove excess adhesive immediately.	Wide range
Cloth-backed vinyl	Excellent for high-traffic and high-humidity areas.	May be stripped. Stiff and difficult to shape to wall or ceiling surfaces. If the paper is lightweight, use a wheat-paste adhesive; if heavy, use a vinyl adhesive.	High
Wet-look vinyl	Kitchens, bathrooms, laundry areas, and mudrooms	You may need to apply a lining paper first; surface imperfections will show.	Medium
Flocked	Avoid in high-traffic or difficult-to-clean areas.	Keep adhesive off the face; if adhesive does get on the face, remove it immediately with clear water and blot, don't rub. If flocking mats, gently go over it with a suede brush.	High
Foil	Kitchens, bathrooms, and laundry areas, because it is easy to clean	Consider hiring a pro; this is difficult to hang. Don't crease paper as you paste and hang it. Be careful around electrical switches and outlets.	High
Burlap/ grass cloth	Anywhere except in hard-use areas where there's lots of grease, dampness, and dirt	Lining paper required. Butt edges and roll seams. Mix vinyl adhesive with ½ pint less water than instructed; apply two coats of adhesive with a mohair paint roller cover.	High
Hand-screened paper	To achieve a stylish effect	Because it is expensive and often made of paper that is easily torn, consider hiring a professional.	Very high

REMOVING OLD WALLPAPER

Unless you're working with a strippable-type paper, stripping old paper is a messy, time-consuming task. Before you decide to take on the job, ask yourself if you really need to take the old paper off before applying the new. If the old wallpaper is on the wall nice and tight, leave it there. You can eradicate a small blemish by cutting away the damaged section and piecing-in a patch to level the surface. Bubbles can be slit, reglued, and flattened.

If the old paper is loose or in bad shape, you have no choice but to remove it.

YOU'LL NEED...

TIME: 6 to 8 hours for a room.
SKILLS: Basic skills.
TOOLS: Taping knife, scoring tool, sponge, spray bottle, scraper, and a wallpaper steamer.

Scrape and peel loose paper.
Some heavier wall coverings—especially vinyl types—can be peeled off in strips. Loosen an edge with a taping knife and pull it down or up. A wallpaper scraper with a replaceable blade is the best tool, though a paint scraper can work. Slip it under the paper with one hand and peel with the other.

Use a scoring tool.
If the paper won't peel off in one continuous strip, make slits just deep enough to cut the paper. A wallpaper scoring tool (shown) does this quickly. Use it like a computer mouse to make a random pattern of curved cuts.

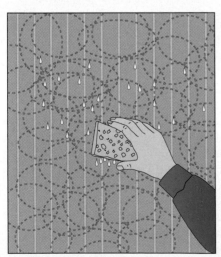

Scrub with wallpaper remover.
After scoring the paper, soak the slits with a liquid wallpaper remover. If the wall covering has a light vinyl coating, it may help to sand the coating first. Scrape off the old paper.

Use a sprayer.
If the wall is plaster, soak the paper thoroughly with mist from a plant sprayer or a pump sprayer. When wet enough, use a scraper to remove the paper. Avoid soaking drywall, which can be damaged by excess moisture.

Use a wallpaper steamer.
A wallpaper steamer works well for removing lots of paper. It has a small boiler that furnishes steam to a plate that you hold against the wall. Especially if you're dealing with nonstrippable wallpaper, you can remove more old paper in an hour with a steamer than you previously could in a day of soaking and hard work.

PREPARING WALLS FOR PAPERING

For sheer dramatic impact, few interior wall treatments rival wallpaper. For a clean-looking job, take the time to prepare the walls meticulously. Most coverings will show rather than hide every nick, hole, and ridge.

You're in luck if the wall you want to paper is painted and in good repair. If the paint is glossy, simply dull the gloss with an abrasive so the adhesive will stick properly. Wash down the area with a strong household detergent, let it dry, and then hang the paper.

If the paint is peeling from the surface, remove it with a scraper, wash down the walls, then seal the surface with a sealer or wallpaper sizing. For walls with a sand or textured finish, first scrape and lightly sand the surface, then cover it with lining paper.

Lining paper is a plain, lightweight wallpaper with no pattern. You apply it with presized wheat paste, butting the edges and rolling the seams. The edges do not need to be butted tightly. A liner can solve minor but not major wall problems.

Nicked, cracked, and crumbling walls or ceilings call for corrective action. See pages 862–869 for ways to repair drywall and plaster.

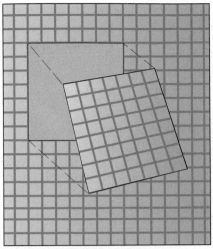

Patch a damaged area.
If the old paper is loose in just a few spots and you plan to paper over it, temporarily tape a piece of wallpaper over the damaged area. Use a straightedge and utility knife to double-cut a rectangle; slice through both the patch and the old paper. This will produce a patch that fits precisely.

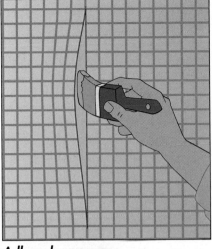

Adhere loose paper.
Lightly sand any seam overlaps. If you don't, the seams will show through the new wallpaper. Remove grease and dirt by washing the entire surface. Glue down curled edges with wallpaper adhesive. Vinyl-to-vinyl adhesive is the strongest; coat both the paper and the wall surface.

Remove coverplates.
Remove all hardware and turn off electrical circuits before you hang paper. If you don't, your trimming task will be more difficult—and dangerous.

Apply sizing.
Use sizing to seal new walls or those covered with wallpaper. The sizing keeps the porous surfaces from absorbing the adhesive. Consult with your wall covering dealer if you are unsure whether you need sizing.

HANGING WALLPAPER

One key to a visually successful papering job is finding the point in the room where a pattern mismatch will not be noticed. You can count on a mismatch, because the last strip you put up will have to be trimmed lengthwise to butt up against the first strip.

One such point is adjacent to a door or window frame. This gives only a few inches of discord above or below the opening. The ideal location is often above the entry door into a room, because the mismatch is hidden behind you as you enter the room. Other spots are an inconspicuous corner or a location that will be covered by draperies or furniture.

The first strip is very important because it "locks in position" all the strips that follow. Unless the first one is plumb, all the other strips will be out of alignment, and the error will compound itself as you apply each successive strip to the walls.

Because wallpapering is a messy job, take special pains to "work clean." Wash your hands often. Use clean water and a sponge to wipe away paste after hanging each strip of paper. Keep the pasting table free of adhesive, and clean your tools if they have paste on them.

If you're using prepasted paper, disregard Step 3 and simply soak the strip in your water trough (see page 889).

EXPERTS' INSIGHT

FIGURING WALLCOVERING NEEDS

■ First determine how much material you need. Measure the height of each wall, then measure the distance around the room, including door and window openings. Multiply these two figures, and you'll have the area of the wall surface. You may need extra to match patterns (see page 884). A wallpaper dealer will translate these figures into the number of rolls needed.

■ After selecting the type of wallpaper (see page 879), ask the salesperson to recommend the right adhesive and the quantity you need. Foils, paper-backed burlap, vinyls, backed flocks, hand prints, murals, and borders require vinyl adhesive. Prepasted wallpaper requires no adhesive, just a shallow trough wide enough to soak each rolled-up strip before you hang it.

■ Standard tools include a paint roller and tray (if you don't use a paste brush), a utility knife with plenty of sharp blades, a tape measure, an 8-foot straightedge, a plumb bob, a chalk line, long-bladed scissors, a stepladder, drop cloths, a wall scraper, and sponges. You'll need a pasting table unless you're using prepasted paper. Rent one or use two card tables or sawhorses covered with a sheet of hardboard.

■ Special tools include a paste brush, a water tray for prepasted paper, a seam roller, and a smoothing brush.

■ Once you have the paper, go around the room and lightly mark lines where the seams will go. This will help you plan the location of the mismatch.

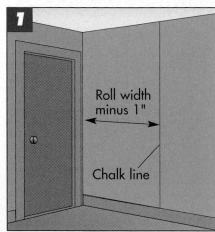

1. Chalk a reference line.
Hang a chalk line from a tacked nail near the top of the wall to near the bottom. Snap the line, and double-check with a level to see that it is plumb.

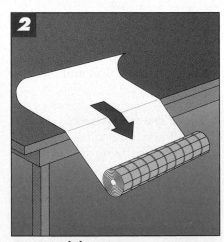

2. Uncurl the paper.
Uncurl the paper by unrolling it against the edge of a table. Cut the first strip several inches longer than needed.

3

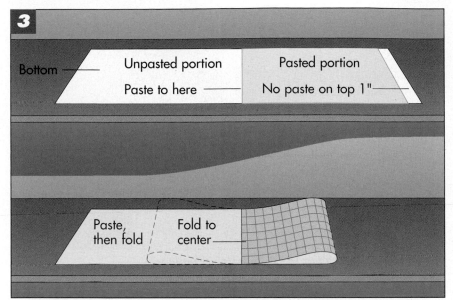

Bottom —

| Unpasted portion | Pasted portion |
| Paste to here | No paste on top 1" —

Paste, then fold | Fold to center —

4

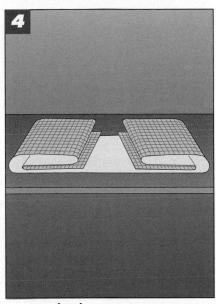

3. Apply paste.

You'll need a worktable large enough to accommodate at least one full-length wallpaper strip, plus one booked strip (see Step 4). A simple sheet of plywood on a set of sawhorses or a worktable works well. Keep the table clean; wipe up spilled paste immediately.

Consult with your dealer and read the manufacturer's

instructions for the best type of adhesive. Premixed paste is the easiest to use and is worth the extra cost. Wheat-based adhesive is strong enough for most coverings. Clay-based adhesive is stronger but difficult to work with. Apply the paste to half of the strip, leaving an inch at the end to grasp. Fold it over and paste the other half.

4. "Book" the paper.

"Book" the pasted paper by folding it over twice. Let the pasted paper rest in this fashion for a few minutes, or according to the manufacturer's directions. Resting time is critical; it allows the covering to absorb the adhesive.

5

Mismatch will occur above entry door.

6

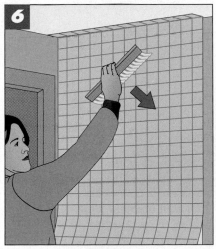

7

5. Apply at the top.

Unfold the top half of the pasted paper. Align the paper with the plumb chalk line you snapped, and overlap the paper slightly onto the ceiling. Check that the side of the paper aligns precisely with the plumb line; make any adjustments sooner rather than later.

6. Remove bubbles.

Smooth the paper onto the surface with the wall brush or a clean sponge. Work from the center to the edges of the paper to remove all air bubbles. Continue to check the plumb line, because brushing may cause the covering to slide.

7. Apply the lower half.

Reach behind the strip and unfold the bottom half. Slip it into place against the plumb mark. You can pull and reposition it as needed.

8. Finish applying the first strip.
Smooth the lower section of paper. With a level, check for plumb. If the strip is not plumb, start again. Smooth with vertical strokes.

Straight pattern   Drop pattern

Measuring and cutting strips to match a pattern

Each strip must not only span from ceiling to baseboard with a few inches to spare; it must be long enough to do so while matching the pattern of the strip it butts against. Place the strip to be cut next to the one it will butt against in order to measure.

A paper with a vertical pattern does not need to be matched. A pattern with a straight horizontal design is easy to match. If the pattern has diagonal lines, you may need to waste a good deal of material. With a drop pattern, the design element of one strip is repeated lower than the strip it abuts. The larger the pattern, or the "repeat," the more material is likely to be wasted.

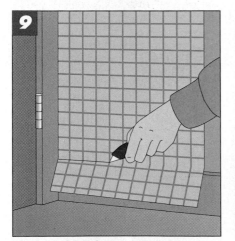

9. Trim the edges.
Tap the paper into the corners with the brush. Gently press the paper into the corner at the ceiling and against the top of the base molding. Using a utility knife, cut it carefully to avoid tearing. Be sure to use a very sharp blade, and change blades often to ensure a razor-sharp edge. A metal straightedge can help.

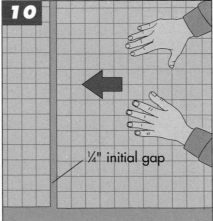

¼" initial gap

10. Butt the next strip.
Cut the next strip following the guidelines presented above. Double-check that it will span from ceiling to floor while matching the pattern of its neighbor. Butt seams by aligning the new strip about ¼ inch from the adjoining one. Slide it over so that the edges buckle slightly. Smooth the new strip as in Step 8.

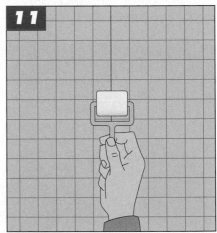

11. Roll the seams.
About 15 minutes after you've hung each strip, roll the seams with a seam roller to ensure good adhesion. Do not roll flocked papers. If a seam refuses to lie flat, apply vinyl-to-vinyl adhesive and re-roll the seam.

PAPERING AROUND CORNERS

Consider yourself lucky if you find a corner in an older house that's plumb. To negotiate problem corners, you'll need to master "double-cutting."

As you hang adjacent strips, overlap them by at least ½ inch, making sure the pattern matches. With a straightedge as a guide, use a razor-sharp utility knife to cut through both layers of paper. Make the cut while the paste on the paper is still soft.

Carefully pull both selvages—the scrap pieces—from the surface, as shown in the box below. With a smoothing brush, smooth the seam created when you removed the selvages.

At either an inside or outside corner, be sure you firmly tap the paper against the surface with the brush. After you've finished the corner, stick a series of thin straight pins near the edge of the corner—not in it—to "clamp" the paper until the adhesive dries. Arrange the pins in such a way in the pattern that holes won't show once the pins have been removed.

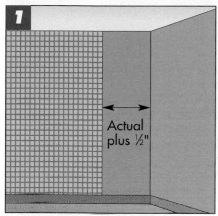

1. Measure for the corner strip.
Measure the distance from the corner to the near edge of the last strip of paper you applied, both top and bottom. Add 1 inch to the measurements.

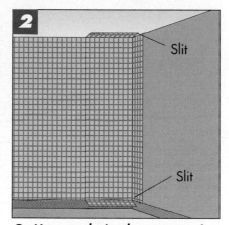

2. Hang and trim the corner strip.
Cut, paste, and hang this strip so it butts the previous strip. Tap it firmly into the corner. Cut slits at the top and bottom corners as shown. Trim the strip at the top and bottom.

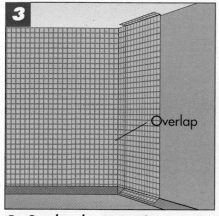

3. Overlap the next strip.
Snap a new plumb line on the wall, allowing for at least a 1-inch overlap, or more if the pattern necessitates it, on top of the previous strip. Hang the next strip with its edge on the plumb line. Tap the paper into the corner.

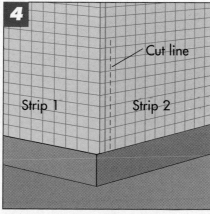

4. Wrap an outside corner.
On outside corners, wrap the paper approximately 1 inch around the corner. Apply the next strip, overlapping it, and double-cut with a utility knife.

Double-cut

Remove over-lapping scrap selvage

Remove underlying scrap

Smooth and roll seam

Make a double-cut seam.
Double-cut through both thicknesses of wallpaper. Peel off the waste from the outer paper. Slightly lift the edge of that strip, and peel out the waste edge from the inner strip. Smooth both strips, then roll the seam.

PAPERING AROUND OPENINGS

One of the more demanding tasks in a wallpapering project is cutting around moldings and openings. Mistakes here will be embarrassingly noticeable. So take the time necessary to achieve straight lines and tight fits.

Always work with a knife that has a sharp blade to avoid pulling or tearing the covering. Before making your cuts around casings, be sure that the covering is snug against it. Otherwise, you may find to your dismay that the line you've cut falls short of covering the wall. If you don't feel comfortable making the cuts freehand, slip a metal straightedge into the joint and then make the cut using it as a guide.

YOU'LL NEED...

TIME: 30 minutes per opening.
SKILLS: Intermediate skills.
TOOLS: Smoothing brush, utility knife or razor blade, paste brush, straightedge, seam roller.

EXPERTS' INSIGHT

REPAIRING TORN PAPER

If you do make a mistake and tear the paper, deal with the problem immediately. If you cannot repair the tear to your satisfaction, remove and replace the entire strip of wallpaper.

To repair a tear, lift the two sides, apply extra adhesive, and press the sides back in place. Wipe the surface clean of excess adhesive. If you need extra holding power, apply vinyl-to-vinyl adhesive.

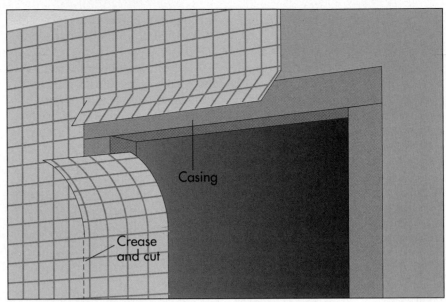

Cutting around casings.
Let the strip adjoining the opening overlap the casings. Begin to smooth the covering, but don't come too close to the casing or you may tear the covering. Once the strip is correctly aligned and the paper is partially smoothed, make a cut at the corner of the casing to allow you to smooth the covering all the way up to the casing. Use a taping blade or a straightedge to create a crease at the point where the casing meets the wall. Cut the crease along the side of the casing with a sharp utility knife.

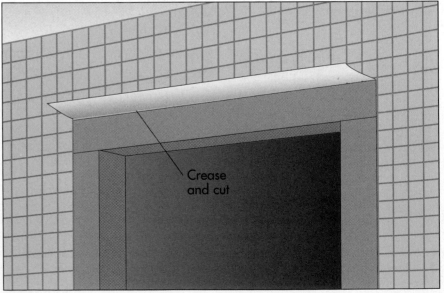

Cutting the top of casings.
At the top of the casing, crease the paper and cut it where the molding joins the wall. Then smooth the edge of the wallpaper. If the casing is thick, a minor cutting mistake here might not be noticeable.

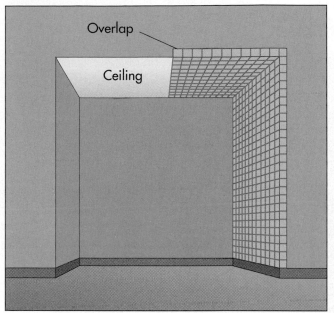

At a wall opening.

When you encounter a recess or an entryway without a door, first hang the covering on the interior walls of the opening. Allow at least 1 inch of overhang along the sides and the top. Make diagonal slits at the two corners, and wrap the paper around the outside corners. Paper the outside wall, letting the pieces "go wild" for a couple of inches before trimming.

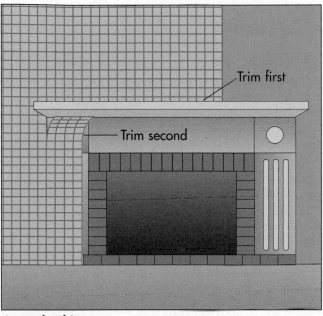

Around cabinetry.

Trim along the top of fireplace mantels or bookcases before you do the sides. This allows you to wrap the paper around the sides and make truer cuts.

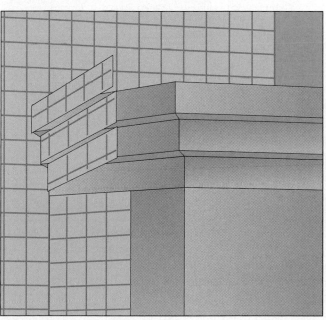

Improvise for complicated cuts.

To fit around tricky corners and moldings, you will need to cut slits so the paper will lie flat. Use plenty of adhesive.

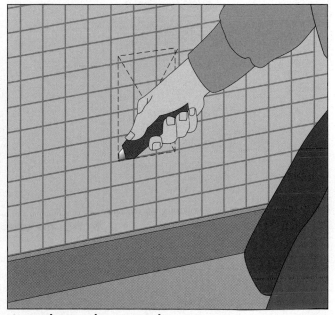

Around an outlet or switch.

Shut off the electricity to circuits before you work around switches and outlets. Apply paper right over the outlet or switch, then trim away the overlap. Make sure the opening is small enough that the coverplate will conceal it but large enough that no paper protrudes into the electrical box. If you make a mistake, an oversize coverplate may hide it.

PAPERING OVER A COVERPLATE

To add a professional touch to your wallpapering job, paper over the switch and receptacle cover plates.

Some fanatics paint the switch toggles and receptacles with matching background paint. Before you go that far, however, consider the possibility that anyone with failing eyesight might not be able to find the camouflaged switch or outlet.

YOU'LL NEED...

TIME: About 15 minutes per coverplate.
SKILLS: Basic wallpapering skills.
TOOLS: Pin, pencil, masking tape, brush, scissors, and a utility knife.

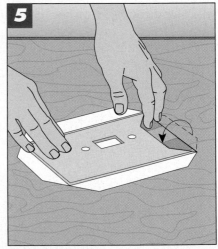

1. Cut a rectangle.
Install the coverplate where it will go. Cut a rectangular section of matching wallpaper, line it up over the coverplate so the pattern matches, and temporarily tape it to the wall.

2. Mark the corners.
Gently feel the outline of the coverplate under the paper and prick a tiny hole at each corner of the plate, using a straight pin.

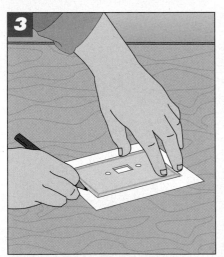

3. Trace the outline.
Remove both the paper and the coverplate. Lay the paper face-down on a worktable, and place the coverplate face-up on top. Line up the plate corners with the pin holes and trace the outline on the back side of the paper.

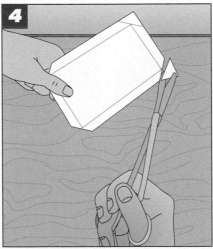

4. Trim the cover.
Cut the paper so there is a ½-inch border around the outline of the coverplate. Trim the corners at 45-degree angles down to the outline.

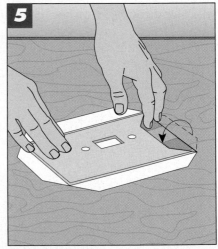

5. Glue the cover.
Brush vinyl-to-vinyl adhesive primer onto the front of the plate. Allow it to dry, then apply vinyl-to-vinyl adhesive over the primer. Place the plate face-down on the paper and press firmly. Smooth out any bubbles. Line up the corners and fold the edges of the paper around the plate.

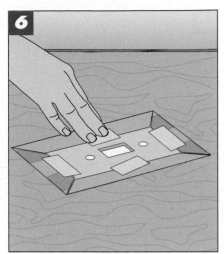

6. Secure with tape.
Tape the edges of the paper to the back side of the plate with masking tape. Let the adhesive dry before proceeding further.

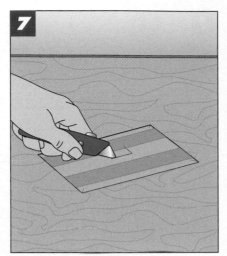

7. Cut the opening.
Using a sharp utility knife, carefully cut out the openings in the plate. If the cut paper edges are loose, apply more adhesive under the paper.

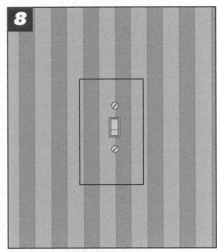

8. Fasten the plate.
Punch through the paper with an awl or nail at the locations of the coverplate screw holes. Fasten the plate with the coverplate screws.

HANGING PREPASTED WALLCOVERINGS

Prepasted wallcoverings are the no-fuss, little-muss way to a beautifully papered room. There are some secrets to success, however, including wall preparation, adhesive soaking time, and careful attention to smoothing and trimming.

Soaking time is critical. Be sure to follow the manufacturer's directions to the letter so that the tackiness of the adhesive will be just right.

Occasionally, depending on the porosity of the wall surface, there won't be enough adhesive on the covering to hold it to the wall. If this occurs, mix a small amount of the proper adhesive for the paper (or use premixed adhesive) and apply it to the edges and ends of the strips after the strips have been cut to length and soaked. Or apply the adhesive directly to the wall.

YOU'LL NEED...
TIME: 10 to 15 minutes per strip.
SKILLS: Basic wallpapering skills.
TOOLS: Water trough plus other wallpapering tools listed earlier.

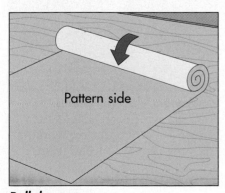

Roll the paper.
Cut the strips to length. Loosely reroll the paper with the pattern side in. This will permit the water to activate the paste.

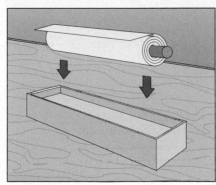

Soak the paper.
Fill the trough with enough water to cover the roll. Submerge the paper in the water, weighting it with a rod.

Unroll and apply.
After soaking, remove the paper by letting it unroll gradually as you make your way up the ladder. Smooth, roll, and trim the paper.

PAPERING CEILINGS

Ever wonder why more ceilings aren't wallpapered? The law of gravity makes it difficult. It's physically taxing to maneuver wallpaper strips up onto a ceiling that's 8 feet (or more) high. However, if you're determined to paper a ceiling, it can be done.

If you plan to paper both the ceiling and walls, paper the ceiling first. Consider applying a border at the top of the wall so you don't have to match the pattern where the ceiling meets the wall.

Prepare the ceiling as you would the walls (see page 881). Patch all cracks and cover any stains with a primer. Drop the canopies on light fixtures and, after shutting off the power supply, disconnect the fixtures to get them out of the way.

To get up to a comfortable working level, use two stepladders or two sawhorses and a length of 2×12 or a scaffolding plank. The scaffolding must span the width of the ceiling so that you can apply the wall covering without constantly moving the ladders and the scaffolding. A helper will come in handy—the long lengths of wall covering are just too awkward for one person.

To start, snap a chalk line across the narrow width of the ceiling, allowing for a slight overlap onto the wall. If the paper is especially heavy, as some vinyls are, pin it in place until the adhesive dries.

YOU'LL NEED...

TIME: 2 to 4 hours for a small room.
SKILLS: Advanced wallpapering skills.
TOOLS: Chalk line, smoothing brush, utility knife, paste brush and pasting table (unless you're using prepasted paper), roller with an extension handle, and a seam roller.

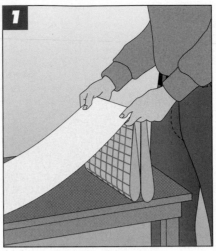

1. Handle with extra care.
Cut the first sheet several inches longer than the width of the ceiling. Apply paste, and "book" the paper accordion-style (see page 883). Don't crease the paper or touch the pattern side to the paste when you fold it.

V-notch

3. Trim the edges.
At each corner, cut out a V-notch to permit the trim edges to lie flat against the walls. Add paste, if needed. If you will not be papering the walls, trim the edges using a straightedge.

2. Apply the first strip.
Align the first strip with the chalk line and pat the paper in place with your hand. Overlap the paper onto the adjacent walls. After you've stuck up a portion of the first strip by patting it, brush it smooth. Cut succeeding pieces so that the pattern will match (see page 884).

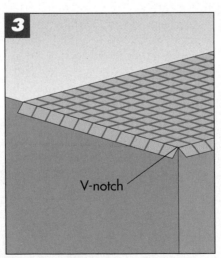

4. Smooth, then roll seams.
After applying each strip, flatten with a smoothing brush, working from the center. Roll the seams using a seam roller.

HANGING VINYL WALLCOVERING

Vinyl wallcovering is heavier than most standard coverings. You can buy it in wide widths, which reduces the number of seams to fit and roll. Also, the material usually is easy to strip from a wall or ceiling surface.

The heavy vinyls have another important advantage. The strips hide defects in a drywall or plaster wall that is in poor condition.

You can use regular wallpaper adhesive to apply lightweight vinyl papers, but special vinyl adhesive is best. Because vinyl won't stick to itself without special adhesive, all seams that are not butted should be double-cut (see page 885).

If you apply untrimmed vinyl with butted seams, be sure the adhesive is soft on both the strips. Lap the seams about 1 inch. Make a freehand cut through both layers of paper, pull loose the selvages, and smooth the seam. If lapping is necessary, be sure to use vinyl-to-vinyl adhesive at the joint. Apply the adhesive just as you would regular wallpaper paste.

YOU'LL NEED...

TIME: 10 to 15 minutes per strip.
SKILLS: Basic wallpapering skills.
TOOLS: Paint roller, utility knife, wood straightedge, seam roller, vinyl wallpaper paste, vinyl-to-vinyl adhesive, razor blade.

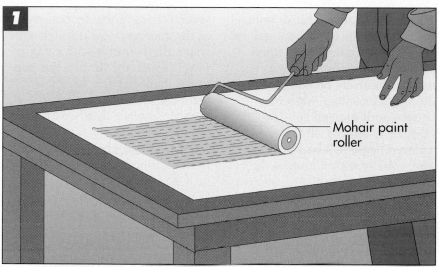

Mohair paint roller

1. Apply adhesive.
Cut the first strip several inches longer than the height of the wall. Cut the subsequent strips so they match the pattern (see page 884). Spread the vinyl adhesive that the manufacturer has recommended, using a mohair paint roller. Fold and book the strip as you would a standard covering (see page 883). With pure vinyl wall covering, there is no need to wait for the adhesive to soak in.

2. Smooth the strips.
Apply strips following the instructions on pages 882–889. Smoothing vinyl is more demanding work than smoothing other types of coverings. Use a wood straightedge (shown). Don't use a steel straightedge unless its edges have been rounded.

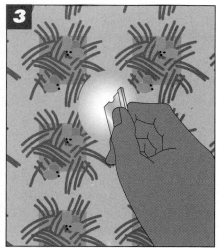

3. Eliminate any bubbles.
After 20 minutes, hold a bright light against the wall to check for bubbles. Puncture each bubble with a razor, and roll the covering flat using a seam roller or a wood straightedge. If you spot a bubble after the adhesive has dried, use a syringe to squirt adhesive into the space behind the bubble.

RESTORING AN OLD FINISH

Before you strip a finish from furniture or woodwork, take a closer look. Sometimes a wood surface that appears to need refinishing really only needs a thorough cleaning. Wash the surface with mineral spirits or an oil soap to remove all the surface grime. Then you'll be able to assess the true condition of the wood and the finish.

If the finish is lightly distressed, treating it with a wood restorer may be the solution. First you'll need to repair the blemished areas. Some shallow dents and scratches can be treated with a simple application of water. When the wood absorbs the water, it expands, and may restore the damaged area to its original shape. Prick the finish with a straight pin

several times in the deepest section of the damage. Coat the area with water, then cover it with a damp towel. Touch the tip of a hot iron to the damaged area for a few seconds. After the wood is dry, sand the surface lightly with 180-grit sandpaper.

If the damage to the finish is more significant, such as a burn, or if it covers a larger area, try filling in the area with a shellac stick (also called a burn-in stick) or wood putty.

Shellac sticks come in a variety of colors. Choose one that will match the final color of the finish. First, scrape the area clean. Then, with the shellac stick positioned over the damaged area, melt the tip of it with a hot palette knife. Let the melted shellac overfill the

area slightly, then level the area with a utility knife. To add rigidity, spray the area with a clear finish.

Wood putty also comes in a variety of colors. You can adjust the color by adding a universal tinting color (UTC) before you apply it. First scrape the area clean. Then mound the wood putty into the damaged area, taking care to wipe away any excess from the surrounding area. After it has hardened, sand it smooth. Disguise the repair by painting a simulated wood grain with an artist's brush and oil colors. Protect the repair by spray-painting it with a clear finish.

Once the damaged areas have been repaired, apply the wood restoring product of your choice.

USING PAINT REMOVER

Paint removers (strippers) soften paint and most other brush-on finishes so that you can lift them off with a scraper. They are messy, however, so be sure to cover work surfaces with several layers of newspaper or plastic sheeting.

Apply paint remover with an old or inexpensive brush. Throw away the brushes when you're finished.

Fumes from paint removers cause eye irritation and headaches. If you can't work outside, ventilate the room where you're working and take a fresh-air break every 15 minutes or so.

Procedures vary from product to product, so be sure you read the label directions thoroughly before opening the container. Remember, you're dealing with powerful ingredients that deserve respect. Wear a long-sleeved shirt, long pants, gloves, eye protection, and perhaps a respirator.

1. Prepare, and pour the stripper.
Prepare your work area with adequate ventilation and protection for your surroundings. Pour stripper on horizontal surfaces and spread it with a brush. Use plenty of the stripper.

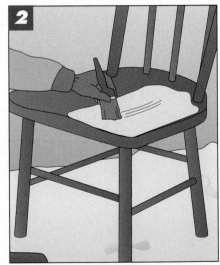

2. Spread with a brush.
Brush remover in one direction only. Don't attempt to "rub" it into the old finish—float it over the surface.

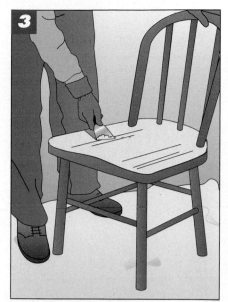

3. Scrape the sludge.
After an hour or so (check the instructions), the remover will bond with the paint or varnish to make a bubbly sludge. Use a wide scraper or putty knife to scrape and remove the sludge. Keep the blade at a low angle to avoid scratching bare wood. Use tools of various widths to remove as much sludge as possible.

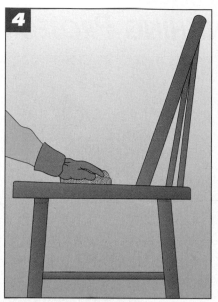

4. Rub with steel wool.
Remove more sludge using a flexible scraper or wadded-up pieces of wallpaper. Clean off the remaining residue with a pad of steel wool. Lift the pad often as you work, and dip it in water or mineral spirits to clean it.

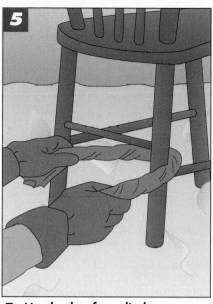

5. Use burlap for cylinders.
Make a rope by twisting burlap or heavy, coarse cloth, and use it to clean round turnings. Dip the rope in remover, wrap it around the turning, and pull it back and forth like a shoe-shine rag.

6. Brush crevices.
For carvings or around moldings, use a wire or fiber brush. Don't use too much pressure because the brush can mar the surface.

7. Dig into tight spots.
Remove paint in recesses with an old toothbrush or other small brush. To strip hardware, soak it in remover, clean with steel wool, and then rinse with clean water.

8. Wash away the residue.
If you use a water-soluble stripper, you can wash down the piece with water. Don't use water on veneered surfaces or glued joints. With other strippers, you will need to clean the piece with mineral spirits or lacquer thinner.

SANDING A REFINISHING PROJECT

Sanding is the most important phase of every refinishing project. The amount of sanding required depends on the condition of the surface. Start with the finest sandpaper that will smooth the wood and remove defects. If the piece is in good shape, you may be able to use 80- or 100-grit paper for the first sanding. If there are significant dents, however, you may need to start with 60- or even 36-grit paper.

The instructions on these pages show how to use several types of power sanders, which can save time and effort. However, if you have the time and energy, hand-sanding works just as well—in fact, some pros prefer it because they get a better feel for the progress. Use a drywall-type hand sander, and several smaller sanding blocks.

Whether you use power tools or sand by hand, wipe away sawdust after every sanding, then clean the surface with a tack cloth.

You may be tempted to stop after the second sanding because the wood will feel quite smooth. Don't neglect the third and the final sandings however—you'll be amazed at how much smoother wood can get.

Later, as you're applying the finish, sand lightly between coats with very fine sandpaper. This roughens the surface enough so that the next coat can adhere to the previous one.

YOU'LL NEED...

TIME: 4 hours for a moderate-size dining room table.
SKILLS: Basic sanding skills.
TOOLS: Hand-sanding blocks, tack cloth, belt sander, orbital sander, sandpaper, steel wool, and a drill with counter-sanding attachment or abrasive-coated nylon pads.

1. Rough sanding.
If the wood is really banged up, start out by belt-sanding with a coarse- to medium-grit abrasive (see page 300). Be careful because a belt sander cuts quickly and the edges of the abrasive can groove the wood surface. Alternatively, use coarse-grit sandpaper with a hand sander or an orbital sander.

2. Clean the surface.
Remove all dust and other residue after each sanding. Wipe with a tack cloth or a cheesecloth rag dampened with mineral spirits. Be sure that the cloth you use is clean and lint-free.

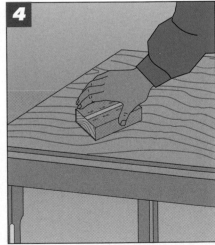

3. Second sanding.
Make the second cut with an orbital sander using medium or fine sandpaper. Don't apply much pressure; let the machine do the work. If your sander doesn't have a dust pickup and the dust particles become bothersome, vacuum or brush them off, then continue sanding.

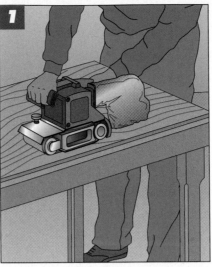

4. Third sanding.
Unless you plan to bleach or water-stain the wood, dampen the surface to raise the grain. Use very fine sandpaper on a sanding block to finish. Do this step and the final smoothing by hand. Sand in one direction only.

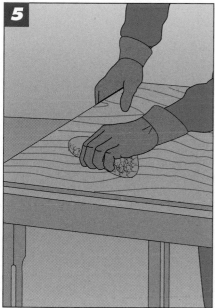

5

5. Final smoothing.
Extra-fine (000) steel wool does an excellent final smoothing job. Wear gloves when using steel wool and vacuum up metal particles. Apply only enough pressure to take the "tooth" off the grain.

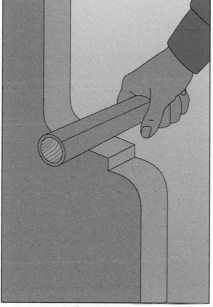

Improvising for curves.
Sanding curved surfaces calls for ingenuity. A sanding "block" fashioned from a dowel rod makes a handy tool.

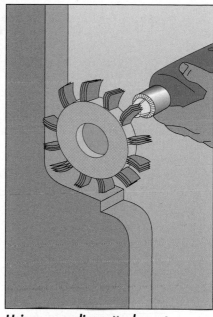

Using a sanding attachment.
A contour sanding attachment for a power drill smooths almost any curve. Use it for removing finishes as well.

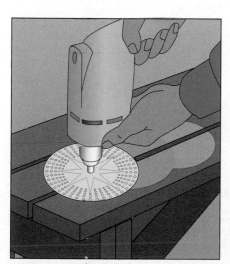

Using a sanding disk.
A perforated disk takes off lots of wood or old paint quickly. Smooth the surface with an orbital sander.

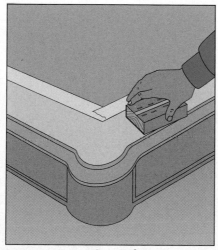

Protecting nearby surfaces.
Use strips of masking tape to protect edges of areas that you don't want to sand. Make sure the tape is pressed tightly in position.

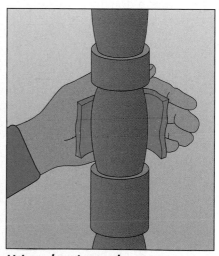

Using abrasive pads.
Coarse nylon pads smooth difficult items, such as turnings, legs, and moldings, with ease. These pads are washable.

FILLING AND SEALING

Some woods, such as fir and oak, have a prominent grain pattern that no amount of sanding will smooth. If you want a glassy-smooth finish for these surfaces, use pore filler. To fill nail holes or other imperfections, use wood filler or water putty. All three are shown on these pages.

After filling and sanding a wood surface, you may have to seal it prior to staining to lock in the filler. Sealers also keep stains from bleeding up through the top coat. Some sealers are applied before stains and slow down the rate at which wood absorbs pigment, giving a lighter, less grainy appearance. Other sealers are best applied after staining.

Fillers and sealers differ widely, so read labels carefully before you buy. Terms such as "wood filler," "dough," and "putty" vary in meaning from product to product. Some fillers are hole pluggers. These have a doughy consistency that makes it easy to pack them into depressions. If you want to stain a piece of wood, be warned that many fillers aren't very absorbent, which means the filled areas could show up as whitish spots after you apply the stain. The solution is to buy a filler that has been tinted to match the stain you've selected. Or you can tint the filler yourself with the stain you'll be using, as long as they are compatible.

Other fillers, available in both paste and liquid forms, level the pores in open-grain wood. These also can be colored.

YOU'LL NEED...

TIME: 3 to 5 hours to fill and seal the surface of a table.
SKILLS: Intermediate sanding and painting skills.
TOOLS: Putty knife, sandpaper, and brushes.

EXPERTS' INSIGHT

USING SEALER

Sealers amount to nothing more than a clear coating. They prevent the finish coats from causing the stain or filler to bleed through or soften. Thinned shellac makes an excellent sealer, as do some varnishes. Penetrating oils (see page 903) serve as their own sealers. Be sure that the sealer you select won't react adversely with the stain or filler you'll be using underneath, or with the finish you'll be applying last.

1. To plug holes with wood filler, mound up the filler.
Press hole-filling wood dough into the hole or depression with your finger. Use a putty knife to level it. Press lightly so the mixture ends up slightly above the level of the surrounding wood. For a small hole, you may find it easier to use your finger for both tamping and leveling.

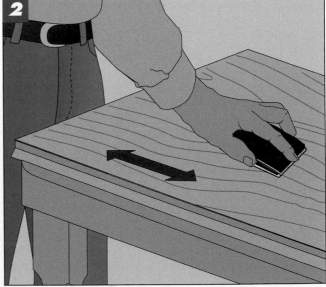

2. Sand it smooth.
Once the filler has dried, sand it lightly with a sanding block equipped with very fine sandpaper. Sand with the grain, and take care to avoid marring the surrounding wood surface.

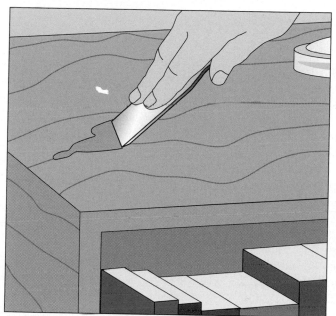

To fill larger areas, apply water putty.
Water putty, also called painter's putty, is a good choice if you will be painting. Use it on plywood edges or wood end grain, as well as for patching.

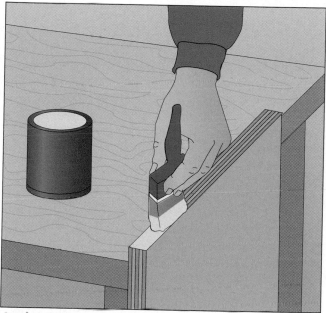

Apply to end grain.
To fill particularly porous end or edge grain, thin the water putty to a fairly thick brushing consistency. Apply it with a brush or a putty knife. Once it has dried, sand it smooth. If the wood needs to be strengthened as well as filled, apply a two-part epoxy paint filler. If the end grain will come in for heavy use, consider covering it with screen molding.

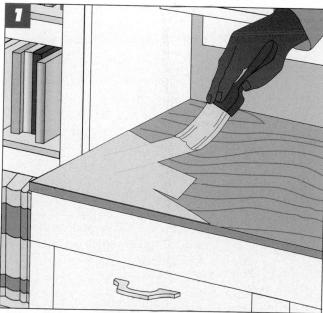

1. To fill pores, brush on pore filler.
Liquid or paste pore filler, often called paste wood filler, makes open-grain wood glassy smooth. It is available in a range of colors, and can be custom-tinted to any color you choose. Once dry, however, tinted filler does not absorb stain. Apply it by brushing in all directions. Work it into the grain; let it dry 10 to 15 minutes.

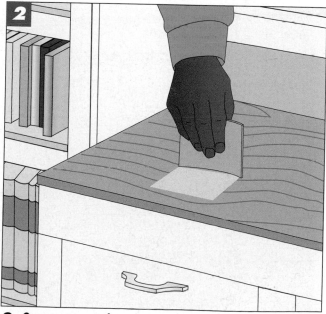

2. Scrape away the excess.
Level the filler with a piece of cardboard across the grain. When it loses its sheen and turns dull, firmly wipe a rag across the grain. Rub until the filler has been removed from the surface, yet fills the grain. Let it dry completely before applying stain or clear finish.

STAINING WOOD

If you're not satisfied with a wood's hue, you can either stain or bleach it. Stain colors wood; bleach lightens it. Except for certain varnish- or sealer-types, stains and bleaches do not protect the surface. For that, you need a coat of shellac, varnish, lacquer, or polyurethane.

When you select a stain, make sure that it's compatible with the finish you'll be applying. Lacquer and some polyurethanes react adversely to the pigments in some stains.

Don't let showroom samples determine your final color choice. They give only a general idea of the end result. Most dealers offer small samplers so you can make tests (see page 899). Note, too, if the manufacturer recommends sealing the grain before or after you stain it (see page 896).

Most stains dry a shade or two darker than the color you see. You control the color by the length of time you let the stain penetrate the wood. If it gets too dark, moisten a cloth with the recommended thinner and wipe again to dilute and wash away some of the pigment.

A few stains contain white pigment for a blond or "pickled" look, but a better way to lighten wood is to bleach it. Wood that has been bleached will render the stain a more vivid color. Bleaching wood is typically a two-step process that involves an overnight wait for the chemicals to work their magic.

Laundry bleach or oxalic acid also can be used, but must be neutralized after application with white vinegar or ammonia. Mix 1 part vinegar or ammonia with 10 parts water. Provide plenty of ventilation; bleach and ammonia give off toxic fumes that can irritate your sinuses and eyes (wear a mask and goggles).

CHOOSING A STAIN

There are many stains from which to choose. Some are designed for ease of use; in turn, you give up control over the result. Others are for the perfectionist who doesn't mind the numerous steps required to achieve the deepest, clearest finish. Consider the end result desired, then decide on the product for the job. Always follow the directions.

Type	Description	Best at	Pros	Cons
Oil-based stains	Traditional stains; concerns now about environmental effects of petroleum vapors	Touching up; restaining	Permanent; doesn't fade; doesn't raise grain; additional coats darken	Difficult to clean up; unpleasant odor; flammable
Water-based stains	Replacing oil-based stains because they are easy to use and safe for the environment	Floors and other woodwork, children's toys	Easy to clean up; safe to use; additional coats darken	Raises wood grain; doesn't penetrate deeply; requires finish coat
Penetrating oil stains	Also called Danish oils and rubbing oils; these protect wood as well as stain it	High-traffic floors; woods with attractive grain	Doesn't require finish coat; wipes on with a rag; doesn't hide grain	Flammable, limited choice of colors
Gel stains	Simplest for the amateur to use; gel adheres to vertical surfaces and does not run	Complicated or vertical surfaces	Simple to apply; doesn't raise grain; additional coats darken	Expensive; difficult to clean up; limited choice of colors
One-step stain and finish	Quickest way to finish wood if you are not too critical about exact color achieved	Door and window casings	Uniform results; doesn't raise grain; quick to use	Cannot build up color; color is not deep or clear

Seal porous areas.
End grain absorbs stain too quickly. Seal end grain with a product made for the purpose, which will likely be called a sanding sealer. Sand the sealer lightly before staining.

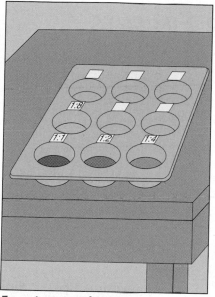

Experiment with mixes.
Mix stain and thinner in ratios of 1:0, 1:1, 1:2, 1:4, and 1:8 in a cupcake tin. Label each sample with the ratio.

Test the stains.
To evaluate colors, test your mixes on an inconspicuous area of the piece to be stained. For an accurate idea of the final appearance, apply whichever clear sealer you will be using; clear sealer can significantly change the color of a stain.

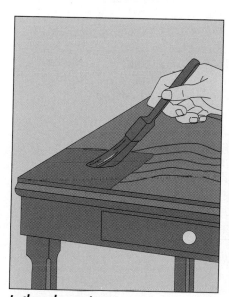

Lather the stain on.
Apply the stain by liberally brushing or wiping (as recommended) it on in the direction of the grain.

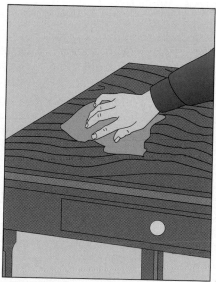

Wipe it off.
Let the stain stand for a while, then wipe it off. The longer the stain remains on the wood, the darker the color. Wipe with long strokes, taking care to maintain even color coverage.

Applying gel stain
Gel stain is virtually mistake-proof, but it takes a bit more time to apply. Work the stain in with a cloth. Apply at least three coats, wiping each. Let the stain dry, buff with an abrasive pad, then add the clear finish of your choice.

CHOOSING CLEAR FINISHES

For many do-it-yourselfers, clear finish automatically means polyurethane. Formulated for easy brushing or spraying, polyurethane dries rapidly; needs no rubbing or polishing, as oils and lacquers do; and makes a surface far more resistant to water, scratching, alcohol, grease, and everyday wear.

However, many professional furniture finishers tend to sneer at polyurethane because it looks like what it is—a plastic coating. Even a satin-finish polyurethane, they maintain, detracts from the look of fine furniture.

For a mellow, antique look, consider more natural products. Varnish and shellac form a hard, old-world coating. Danish and tung oil finishes penetrate the wood and produce a subtle, natural-looking coating. These natural products are not as durable as polyurethane, but they usually protect the wood well as long as they are occasionally reapplied.

The chart below summarizes the properties and characteristics of today's commonly available finishes.

SELECTING CLEAR FINISHES

Type	Characteristics	Application Tips	Finish	Drying Time	Cost
Natural-resin varnish	Resists scuffs and scratches; available in colors, as well as clear; spar varnish for outdoor applications	Apply with a varnish brush, artist's brush, or cheesecloth; thin with recommended solvent.	From high-gloss to satin to low-gloss	24 to 36 hours; if humid, 36 hours	Low to medium; marine-type, high
Oil-based polyurethane	Mar-resistant; durable; yellows over time; if used with a fairly dark stain, the yellow tinge is not apparent	Use a natural-bristle brush with chisel point or lamb's-wool applicator.	From high-gloss to dull sheen	1 to 2 hours; 12 hours between coats	Medium to high
Water-based polyurethane	Not as durable as oil poly, but does not yellow; needs regular reapplication	Apply with brush or lamb's-wool applicator.	From high-gloss to satin	First coat, 3 hours; second coat, 5 to 8 hours	Medium to high
Shellac	Forms a hard film, but is dissolved by alcohol and easily damaged by water; available clear or pigmented	Use small brush with chisel tip; thin with alcohol solvent; protect with a top coat of paste wax.	High-gloss; finish may be dulled with steel wool.	About 2½ hours to the touch; 3 to 4 hours between coats	Low
Lacquer	Fast-drying; produces a smooth finish; used mostly for furniture	Spray many thin coats; allow last coat to dry 48 to 60 hours; rub with fine steel wool.	Wide variety	Fast	Medium
Danish or tung oil	Penetrates wood and hardens the grain; moderate resistance to stains, scratches, and burns; good resistance to water and alcohol	Usually hand-rubbed; most often needs two or three applications	Deep, rich look	8 to 12 hours	Medium to high

APPLYING VARNISH AND SHELLAC

Surface preparation is the foundation for a beautifully varnished or shellacked finish. However, be aware that the finish will emphasize, rather than cover, any problem areas.

Dust is varnish's mortal enemy. If you're not careful, dust will collect on the newly applied finish and ruin your efforts. To keep this from happening, shut off forced-air heating and cooling ducts in the area and remove all dust from the room before starting.

Thin the varnish according to the instructions on the container label, using the solvent that's recommended. One sign of poor application technique is the emergence of tiny air bubbles on the surface of the piece. To avoid this, don't shake the can, bear down too hard on the bristles, or wipe the brush's bristles across the rim of the can. To get rid of bubbles after they form, apply more varnish and brush lightly until you work them out.

Applying shellac isn't different from laying on varnish, but it usually requires more coats. Always use a pristine brush to minimize imperfections. Shellac is available in various cuts, or thicknesses. Have your paint dealer advise you on the proper cut for the project at hand. Orange or amber shellac adds a charming color as it protects.

You'll need to apply from five to eight coats of shellac. After letting each coat dry for the time specified, lightly buff the surface with very fine steel wool. Vacuum up all particles and wipe the surface with a tack cloth between coats. Finish the job with hard paste wax, buffing the wax with a cloth to a high-gloss finish. Let it dry 24 hours, then wax the surface a second time, buffing it to a brilliant shine.

1. Spread the varnish.
Apply varnish or shellac in several directions, but always finish brushing with the grain. Don't bear down on the brush or you'll produce bubbles.

2. Minimize bubbles.
Varnish or shellac can easily get infiltrated with tiny bubbles that appear in the finish. To eliminate these bubbles, don't shake the can. Remove excess varnish from the bristles by gently tapping, not wiping them, against the can rim.

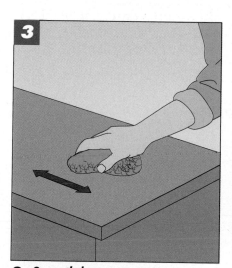

3. Smooth between coats.
Allow the varnish or shellac to harden. Use very fine sandpaper or steel wool to level the surface between coats. This slightly roughens the surface to help the next coat adhere. Be sure to wipe away all dust and debris, using a tack cloth, before each application.

4. Apply the finish coat.
Level the final coat of varnish or shellac with short, light strokes. Use the tip of the brush to achieve the smoothest surface.

Applying Polyurethane Finish

When you apply polyurethane varnish to a surface, you're actually sealing it in plastic—a plastic so tough that hardly anything can penetrate it. In addition to this exceptional durability, polyurethane is easy to put on; fairly fast-drying; super-resistant to chemicals and water; and available in low-gloss, satin, and high-gloss finishes.

Before applying polyurethane, complete the preparation steps discussed on pages 892–897. If you've applied a stain or wood filler to the surface, make sure it is absolutely dry before adding the polyurethane.

Apply either oil-based or water-based polyurethane with a brush, lamb's-wool applicator, or lint-free cloth. Latex poly is easy to use with a sprayer; oil-based poly tends to clog up the works, so you're better off doing this by hand.

All types of wood require at least two coats of oil-based polyurethane. The first coat works as a primer and sealer; the second serves as a finish coat. With water-based polyurethane, a third coat is recommended, because the finish wears away fairly quickly. Sand between coats if dust or lint gets into the wet finish. Sanding also makes it easier to tell where you applied the subsequent coat.

When you add the finish—both coats—keep the work between you and a light. In this way, you will see missed spots as the finish is applied. Missed spots are caused by poor penetration into the wood or inadequate application. They leave little dimples in the finish, and they're almost impossible to touch up after the material has dried.

Not all polyurethanes are clear. Some are colored to resemble pigmented shellac. With these, you'll usually need to apply several coats of the finish to reach the color tone that you want. Each coat will produce a deeper tone, so try a test run on a scrap of the same material to determine how many coats you will need.

If you reach the color tone before achieving the sheen you want, let the surface dry thoroughly, and then apply clear polyurethane finish to complete the project. However, the clear finish will slightly change the color tone underneath.

You can apply a clear polyurethane finish over paint. Don't expect the polyurethane to hide any defects in the material.

Low-gloss polyurethanes are less durable than high-gloss products. Use low-gloss finishes as top coats to cut the shine off high-gloss coatings underneath.

As with varnish and shellac finishes, dust and dirt control is critical with polyurethane. Work in a room with no air currents blowing from heating and cooling ducts. Avoid doing anything that would cause dust to become airborne, especially sweeping the floor just before the finish is applied. Use a tack cloth to remove dust from the work.

Applying Lacquer

Lacquer produces a very smooth, quality finish. It dries super-fast, making it a dust-dodger. After lacquer dries, you can rub away dust and brush marks from its surface. It's also inexpensive and available in clear finishes and a variety of colors.

Lacquer's fast drying time also is one of its disadvantages. It dries so quickly that you must correct mistakes immediately. Also, you can't apply lacquer over a painted finish; it will lift off the paint.

Again, proper preparation is a key. Prepare the surface as you would for any other clear wood finish (see pages 892–897).

Lacquer may sag and run. It's best to use many thin coats with a spray gun. If you spot a sag or run, let it dry, then remove the defect using wet/dry sandpaper. Or wipe the run or sag immediately with a soft, lint-free cloth saturated with lacquer thinner. Spot-fill the area you wiped, and continue on with the work. The blemish will show after the lacquer has dried, but it won't be noticeable after the surface has been rubbed properly with steel wool or rubbing compound, then waxed.

Generally, for lacquer to look and perform its best, you'll need to apply at least three coats. Unlike most clear finishes, you don't have to smooth the surface with sandpaper or steel wool between coats because the material "dissolves" and blends into the preceding coats.

After the lacquer has dried for 48 hours, finish by rubbing the surface with very fine steel wool and hard wax or rubbing compound. As you do this, work in a small area. Completely rub out this area before you move on to other areas. Otherwise, the compound will dry and be hard to buff off.

USING OIL FINISH

That deep, rich patina you see on old gun stocks and some antique furniture probably consists of nothing more than boiled linseed oil and turpentine—coat upon coat, laboriously rubbed into the wood's grain. You can do the same yourself. Just combine 2 parts oil with 1 part turpentine, pour it on, rub off the excess, and let it dry completely. Repeat and repeat and repeat until you've totally saturated the grain, a process that may take six to 10 applications and dozens of hours of tiresome rubbing.

Or you can achieve much the same effect with a couple of coats of Danish oil or tung oil. Like ordinary oil, these penetrate into the wood for a surface that's more than skin deep. They also contain a synthetic or natural resin that hardens inside the wood grain. The result: a finish that actually toughens the wood, yet doesn't call for nearly as much rubbing.

Usually you need only two or three applications of resin oil to get a deep, lasting finish. Unlike linseed oil, it dries overnight, doesn't gum up in warm weather, and rarely needs to be renewed—yet it's just as resistant to stains, scratches, minor burns, water, and alcohol. If damage does occur, you can just rub it out with sandpaper or steel wool and then apply more penetrating oil. Unlike polyurethane varnish, oil lends itself to spot repairs.

Penetrating resin oils vary somewhat. Some include varnish; others, plastics; and still others are combined with wax. A few also come in different weights to suit open- or closed-pore woods. Many come in various colors, or you can tint them for staining effects.

Read the manufacturer's instructions before applying a resin oil. Most go on with the easy steps illustrated here.

1. Pour and spread the first coat.
Flood the surface with oil and spread it with a brush or cloth. The first coat will soak in quickly.

2. Wipe and sand.
Wait a few minutes, then test the surface. If dry, apply more oil. Wait a few minutes and wipe off the excess. Sand lightly before the second coat to remove any raised grain. After this, don't sand again.

3. Rub in more coats.
Add subsequent coats with the grain, rubbing hard. Allow 24 hours' drying time between coats. Apply additional coats until you're satisfied with the finish.

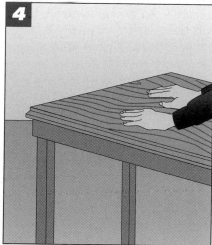

4. Hand-rub the final coat.
Rub in the final coat with your palms; your hands supply heat. If desired, finish with a hard wax.

ANTIQUING AND DISTRESSING WOOD

Antiquing and distressing are refinishing techniques that offer an appealing alternative to the traditional clear, shiny finish. These methods work well with worn or badly outdated pieces of furniture or woodwork, adding a rustic dignity.

There are various methods of antiquing that produce different effects. One of the fun things about antiquing is that you don't have to be painstakingly careful. You may even want to "distress" the surface more by smacking it a few times with nails driven into a board or with the claws of a hammer. Before you get carried away, however, make sure the piece you're working with wouldn't be better refinished in the traditional manner. Sometimes, hidden under an old finish or a crust of dirt is a real treasure worthy of proper restoration. Refinishing a valuable antique finish can radically reduce its appeal to collectors.

When antiquing an item, you can either strip it to bare wood or apply a new base coat over the existing surface. Most people choose the latter. Either way, make sure the surface is free of dirt and wax. Remove any drawers and hardware. If a mirror is involved, remove it if you can; if not, mask it with newspaper.

Most people buy the materials and tools needed for their project in kit form. Usually included are base and finish coats of antiquing finishes, brushes, and special design applicators. The tools you'll need, if the kit doesn't supply them, include a 3-inch brush, 150-grit sandpaper, a mixing bucket and paddle, thinning solvent, and wiping cloths.

Once you've readied the surface to your satisfaction (be sure to dull a glossy surface), brush on the base coat. You may need two coats to hide dark surfaces. Apply the material in even strokes. If you spot runs or sags, catch them with the tip of the brush stroked across the grain. Look for spots you may have missed; if you find any spots, coat them now, because the base coat must completely cover the surface. Let the finish dry. Check the can label for drying time—usually 2 to 4 hours.

The next step is to sand the base coat, using a 150-grit open-coat abrasive or fine steel wool. Remove all sanding residue with a vacuum cleaner or tack cloth.

Next comes the glaze. Working in a small area, brush on a thin coat of glaze; don't apply too much. Wipe the surface or apply the design you want (see below for ideas and techniques to create some effects). Then move on to the next area. The glaze dries fast, so you need to work quickly.

To simulate wear, wipe corners and edges through to the base coat. Wipe gently over carvings and grooves to produce an antique look.

Allow the glaze to dry for 48 hours. Finish the project by applying a clear finish or hard wax to the surface.

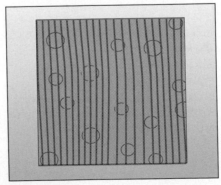

Distressed wood.
Poke the glaze with an ice pick, then rub raw umber into scratches and dents.

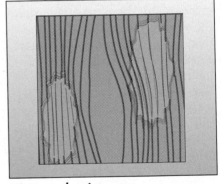

Distressed paint.
Let the glaze dry, then sand to expose the undercoat.

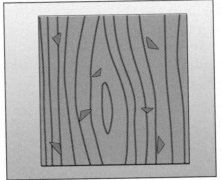

Splattering.
Wipe on glaze; dip a small, stiff brush in thinner; shake it out; stroke the bristles to spray droplets on the glaze.

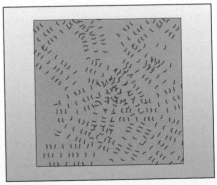

Stippling.
With a dry brush, jab straight down into wet glaze. Rotate the brush between jabs.

HOME IMPROVEMENT GLOSSARY

For words not listed here or for more about those that are, refer to the index, pages 916–928.

A

Access panel. A removable panel in a tub surround, wall, or ceiling that permits repair or replacement of concealed items, such as whirlpool pumps or faucet bodies.

Actual dimension. True size of a piece of lumber, after milling and drying. See also Nominal dimension.

Adapter. A fitting that makes it possible to go from male endings to female endings or vice-versa. Transition adapters allow for joining different kinds of pipe together in the same run. Trap adapters help connect drain lines to sink traps.

Aerator. A device screwed into the spout outlet of most sink faucets that mixes air with the water to achieve less water splash and smoother flow.

Aggregate. Gravel or crushed rock; when mixed with sand, Portland cement, and water, it forms concrete.

Air chamber. A short, enclosed tube on water lines that provides a cushion of air to control sudden surges in water pressure that sometimes result in noisy pipes.

Amp (A). A measurement of the electrical current in a circuit at any moment. See also Volt and Watt.

Armored cable. Two or more insulated wires wrapped in a protective metal sheathing.

Ashlar. Rectangular blocks of stone of uniform thickness used mainly to build dry-laid walls.

Auger. A flexible metal cable fished into traps and drain lines to dislodge obstructions.

Awl. A sharp-pointed tool used to make small starter holes for screws or to scribe lines.

B

Backerboard. A ready-made surface for setting tile. Also called cement board. Can be cement-based or gypsum-based.

Backfill. Soil used to fill in an excavation next to a wall. It adds stability to the wall and keeps water away from it.

Backsplash. Typicall, a 3- to 4-inch-high length of material at the back edge of a countertop extending the full length.

Ballast. Transformer that steps up the voltage in a fluorescent lamp.

Ballcock. The assembly inside a toilet tank that, when activated, releases water into the bowl to start the flushing action. It also prepares the toilet for subsequent flushes.

Balusters. Spindles that help support a staircase handrail.

Bat. A half-brick. Bats are used when whole bricks won't fit into the allotted space.

Batt. A section of fiberglass or rock-wool insulation measuring 15 or 23 inches wide by 4 to 8 feet long.

Batten. A narrow strip used to cover joints between boards or panels.

Batter. The practice of tapering the sides of a stone wall to give it added stability.

Batter board. A board frame supported by stakes set back from the corners of a structure. Saw kerfs or marks on the boards indicate the location of the edges of the footings and the structure, which can be used to reposition those points on the site following its excavation.

Beam. In framing, a horizontal support member.

Bearing wall. An interior or exterior wall that helps support the roof or the floor joists above.

Beating block. Used to press tiles evenly into adhesive. Can be a store-bought rubber-faced model or a piece of plywood that you've covered with terry cloth.

Bed joint. The layer of mortar between two courses of masonry units. See also Course.

Bell wire. A thin wire used for doorbells. Typically 18-gauge.

Bevel cut. A cut through the thickness of a piece of wood at other than a 90° angle.

Bimetal. Part of a switch composed of two layered metals that heat and cool at different rates to open or close a circuit automatically. They are commonly used in circuit breakers and thermostats.

Biscuit joiner. A power tool used to cut incisions in lumber into which flat wooden biscuits are glued.

Blanket. Fiberglass or rock-wool insulation in a long roll 15 or 23 inches wide.

Blind dado. A channel cut across the grain that stops short of one or both edges of the workpiece.

Blind-nail. To nail so that the head of the nail is not visible on the surface of the wood.

Board. Any piece of lumber that is less than 2 inches thick and more than 3 inches wide.

Board foot. The standard unit of measurement for wood. One board foot is equal to a piece 12×12×1 inches (nominal size).

Bond. (1) Any of several patterns in which masonry units can be arranged. (2) To join two or more masonry units with mortar. (3) The cementing action of an adhesive.

Box. To mix the same kind and color of paint from small containers before painting to ensure the color is the same throughout the painting job.

Brick set. A wide-bladed chisel used to cut bricks and concrete blocks.

Bridging. Boards nailed between joists to add rigidity and keep the joists from warping. Often used to quiet squeaking floors.

Btu (British thermal unit). The amount of heat needed to raise 1 pound of water 1 degree Fahrenheit. Heating and cooling equipment commonly is rated by the Btu it can deliver or absorb.

Building code. Local ordinance governing the manner in which a home may be constructed or modified. Most codes are concerned with fire and health, with separate sections relating to electrical, plumbing, and structural work.

Bullnose tile. Also called cap tile shaped to define an edge of a surface.

Bus bar. A main power terminal to which circuits are attached in a fuse or breaker box. One bus bar serves the circuit's hot side, the other the neutral side.

Butt joint. The joint formed by two pieces of material when fastened end to end, end to face, or end to edge.

Butter. To apply mortar on bricks or blocks with a trowel.

BX. A trade name for flexible armored cable. See Armored cable.

C

Cable. Two or more insulated conductors wrapped in metal or plastic sheathing.

Cantilever. A beam or beams projecting beyond a support member.

Capillary action. The action that occurs when a liquid is drawn into a thin space between two surfaces, such as when molten solder is drawn into and around a copper pipe joint.

Carcass. The box-like outer body or framework of a cabinet or shelf.

Casing. Trimming around a door, window, or other opening.

Caulk. Any compound used to seal seams and joints against infiltration of water and air.

Cement. A powder that serves as the binding element in concrete and mortar.

Cement board. A backerboard with a mesh coat that acts as a surface for setting tile.

Ceramic tile. Made from refined clay usually mixed with additives and water and hardened in a kiln. Can be glazed or unglazed.

CFM (cubic feet per minute). A rating that expresses the amount of air a blower or fan can move.

Chalk line. A reel of string coated with colored chalk, used to mark straight lines by pulling the string taut and snapping it, leaving a line.

Chalking. The tendency of some exterior paints to gradually erode over a period of time.

Chamfer. A bevel cut made along the length of a board edge.

Chink. A narrow piece or sliver of stone driven into cracks or voids in a stone wall to achieve added stability.

Circuit. The path of electrical flow from a power source through an outlet and back to ground.

Circuit breaker. A safety switch that automatically interrupts electrical flow in a circuit in the event of an overload or a short.

Clean-out. A removable plug in a trap or a drainpipe that allows easier access to blockages inside.

Cleat. A board attached to strengthen or add support to a structure.

Clinch. To hammer the exposed tip of a nail at an angle, bending its point into the surrounding wood for added joint strength.

Closet bend. The elbow-shaped fitting beneath toilets that carries waste to the main drain.

Closure brick (or block). The final unit laid in a course of bricks or blocks. See also Course.

Code. See Building code.

Common. A terminal on a three-way switch, usually with a dark-colored screw and marked COM.

Compressor. The part of a cooling unit or heat pump that compresses refrigerant gas so it absorbs heat.

Concrete. A building and paving material made by mixing water with sand, gravel, and cement. See also Cement; Mortar.

Concrete nails. Hardened steel nails that can be driven into concrete.

Condensing unit. The outdoor segment of a cooling system. It includes a compressor and condensing coil designed to give off heat. See also Evaporator coil.

Conductor. A wire or anything else that carries electricity.

Conduit. Rigid or flexible tubing through which wires are run.

Contact. The point where two electrical conductors touch.

Continuity tester. A device that tells whether a circuit is capable of carrying electricity.

Control joint. A groove tooled into a concrete slab during finishing to prevent uncontrolled cracking later on. To be effective, these joints should be one-fourth the thickness of the slab.

Coped cut. A profile cut made in the face of a piece of molding that allows for butting it against another piece at an inside corner.

Corner bead. Lightweight, perforated metal angle used to reinforce outside corners in drywall construction.

Corner lead. The first few courses of masonry laid in stair-step fashion at a corner to establish levels for the remaining units in those courses.

Counterbore. To drive in a screw below the surface of the surrounding wood. The void created is filled later with putty or a wooden plug.

Countersink. To drive the head of a nail or screw so that the top is flush with the surrounding surface.

Coupling. A fitting used to connect two lengths of pipe in a straight run.

Course. A row of masonry units. Most projects consist of several courses laid on top of each other and separated by mortar.

Cove. A concave form, as in the face of a style of molding.

Cripple. A short stud above or below a door or window opening.

Crosscut. To saw a piece of lumber perpendicular to its length or its grain.

Crown. (1) Paving that is slightly humped so water will run off. (2) A contoured molding sometimes installed at the top of a wall.

Cupping. A type of warping that causes the edges of a board to curl up along its grain.

D

Dado joint. A joint formed when the end of one member fits into a groove cut partway through the face of another.

Damper. A valve inside a duct or flue that can be used to slow or stop the flow of air or smoke.

Darby. A long-bladed wood float commonly used to smooth the surface of freshly poured concrete in situations where using a smaller float isn't practical.

Deadbolt. A locking device activated only with a key or thumb turn. Unlike a latch's beveled tongue, deadbolts have squared-off ends.

Delayed-start tube. A type of fluorescent tube that takes a few seconds to warm up.

De-rate. To lower the rating of total service capacity used because not all the appliances and fixtures on a circuit are in use at the same time.

Dimension lumber. A piece of lumber that is at least 2 inches thick and at least 2 inches wide.

Dimmer. A switch that lets you vary the intensity of a light.

Double cylinder. A type of lock that must be operated with a key from inside, as well as outside.

Dowel. A piece of small-diameter wood rod used to reinforce joints.

Doweling jig. A metal device that clamps onto a workpiece edge or end and aids in accurately locating and drilling holes for dowels.

Drain-waste-vent (DWV) system. The network of pipes and fittings that carries liquid and solid wastes out of a building to a public sewer, a septic tank, or a cesspool. It also allows for the passage of sewer gases up through the roof.

Drywall. A basic interior building material consisting of sheets of pressed gypsum faced with heavy paper on both sides. Also known as wallboard, gypsum board, plasterboard, and Sheetrock®.

Dry-laid wall. A wall of masonry units laid without mortar.

Duplex receptacle. A device that includes two plug outlets. Most receptacles in homes are duplexes.

E

Easement. A legal right for restricted use of someone's property. Easements often are granted to utility companies so they may service the utility lines running through a property.

Eaves. The lower edge of a roof that projects beyond the wall.

Edging. Strips of wood or veneer used to cover the edges of plywood or boards.

Edger. A concrete finishing tool for rounding and smoothing edges to strengthen them.

Efflorescence. A powdery stain, usually white, on the surface of or between masonry units. It is caused by the leaching of salts to the surface.

Elbow. A fitting used to change the direction of a water supply line. Also known as an ell. Bends do the same thing with drain-waste-vent lines.

Electrical metallic tubing (EMT). Thin-walled, rigid conduit suitable for indoor use.

Electrons. Invisible particles of charged matter moving at the speed of light through an electrical circuit.

End grain. The ends of wood fibers that are exposed at the ends of boards.

Evaporator coil. The part of a cooling system that absorbs heat from air in your home. See also Condensing unit.

Expansion joint. A space between structures, filled with a flexible material, to allow for expansion and contraction during temperature changes without damage.

Exposed aggregate surface. A concrete finish achieved by embedding aggregate into a concrete surface.

F

Face brick. A type of brick made for covering (veneering) walls.

Face frame. The front structure of a cabinet or chest of drawers made of stiles and rails; it surrounds the door panels or drawers.

Fall. Used to express the slope at which drain lines are installed to ensure proper waste drainage. Minimum fall per foot is $\frac{1}{4}$ inch.

Fascia board. Horizontal trim attached to the outside ends of rafters or to the top of an exterior wall.

Female. Any part, such as a nut or fitting, into which another (male) part can be inserted. Internal threads are female.

Field tiles. Flat tiles, in contrast to trim tiles that are shaped to turn corners or define surface edges.

Filler. A pastelike compound used to hide surface imperfections in wood. One type, pore filler, levels a surface that has a coarse grain.

Finish coat. The final coat of mortar or plaster in a stucco finish. (See also Stucco.)

Finishing. The final smoothing stage in concrete work.

Fire blocking. Short horizontal members sometimes nailed between framing studs, usually about halfway up the wall. They serve to slow a fire from moving up the framing space.

Firebrick. Heat-resistant brick for lining fireplaces and boilers.

Fishing. Getting cables through finished walls and ceilings.

Fish tape. A long strip of spring steel used for fishing cables and for pulling wires through conduit.

Fitting. Any connector (except a valve) that allows you to join pipes of similar or dissimilar size or material in a straight run or at an angle.

Fixture. (1) Any electrical device permanently attached to a home's wiring. (2) Any of several plumbing

devices that provide either a supply of water or sanitary disposal of liquid or solid wastes.

Fixture drain. The drainpipe and trap leading from a plumbing fixture to the main drain.

Flashing. A layer of material, usually metal, inserted in masonry joints and attached to adjoining surfaces to seal out moisture.

Flexible metal conduit. Tubing that can be bent easily by hand, through which wires are pulled. Also known as Greenfield.

Float. A rectangular hand tool used to smooth and compress wet concrete. Also, the first process of finishing a concrete surface.

Fluorescent tube. A light source that uses an ionization process to produce ultraviolet radiation. This becomes visible light when it hits the coated inner surface of the tube.

Flush. On the same plane as, or level with, a surrounding surface.

Flue. A pipe or other channel that carries off smoke and combustion gases to the outside air.

Flux. A stiff jelly brushed or smeared on the surfaces of copper and brass pipes and fittings before soldering them to assist in the cleaning and bonding processes.

Footing. A thick concrete support for walls and other heavy structures built on firm soil and extending below the frost line.

Force cup. *See* Plunger.

Framing. The skeletal or structural support of a home. Sometimes called framework.

Frost line. The maximum depth frost normally penetrates the soil during the winter. This depth varies with the climate from area to area.

Four-way switch. A type of switch used to control a light from three or more locations.

Furring. Lightweight strips of wood applied to walls to provide a plumb nailing surface for paneling or drywall.

Fuse. A safety device designed to stop electrical flow if a circuit shorts or is overloaded. Like a circuit breaker, a fuse protects against fire from overheated wiring.

G

Gable. The triangular area on the end of a house's external wall located beneath the sloping parts of a roof and the line that runs between the roof's eaves.

Galvanized. Coated with a zinc outer covering to protect against oxidation. Nails and screws used in exterior applications often are galvanized to prevent them from rusting.

Ganging. Assembling two or more electrical components into a single unit. Boxes, switches, and receptacles often are ganged.

Gate valve. A valve that lets you completely stop—but not modulate—the flow of water within a pipe. See also Globe valve.

General-purpose circuit. Serves several light and/or receptacle outlets. See also Heavy-duty circuit and Small-appliance circuit.

Glazing. (1) A protective and decorative coating that is fired onto the surface of some tiles. (2) The process of installing glass by securing it with glazier's points and glazing compound.

Globe valve. A valve that lets you adjust the flow of water to any rate between fully on and fully off. See also Gate valve.

Grain. The direction of fibers in a piece of wood; also refers to the pattern of the fibers.

Granite. A quartz-based stone with a tough, glossy appearance; granite is harder than marble.

Graphite. A soft, black carbon powder used to lubricate working metal parts such as those found in a doorknob or lock.

Green board. Similar to regular drywall, this material is moisture resistant, though not waterproof. Also referred to as blue board.

Greenfield. See Flexible metal conduit.

Grit. The abrasive material bonded to sandpaper. Grit is designated by numbers, such as 120-grit. The higher the number, the finer the abrasive.

Ground. Refers to the fact that electricity always seeks the shortest possible path to the earth. Neutral wires carry electricity to ground in all circuits. An additional grounding wire, or the sheathing of metal-clad cable or conduit, protects against shock from a malfunctioning device.

Ground-fault circuit interrupter (GFCI). A safety device that senses any shock hazard and shuts down a circuit or receptacle.

Grout. A thin mortar mixture. Also, the process of applying grout. See also Mortar.

Grouting float. A rubber backed trowel used for pressing the grout into the joints.

Gusset. A piece of wood nailed or screwed over a joint to give it added strength.

Gypsum board. See Drywall.

H

Hardwood. Lumber derived from deciduous trees, such as oaks, maples, and walnuts.

Head joint. The layer of mortar used to tie the ends of adjoining masonry units together.

Header. The framing component spanning a door or window opening in a wall and supporting the weight above it.

Heavy-duty circuit. Serves just one 120- to 240-volt appliance. See also General-purpose circuit and Small-appliance circuit.

Heat gain. Heat coming into a home from sources other than its heating/cooling system. Most gains come from the sun.

Heat loss. Heat escaping from a home. Heat gains and losses are expressed in Btu per hour.

Heat pump. A reversible air-conditioner that extracts heat from outside or inside air.

HID (high-intensity-discharge) lamp. A lamp that works in the same way as a fluorescent tube, but that has a bulb like an incandescent lamp.

Hip. The outside angle of a roof formed by the intersection of two sloped sides of the roof.

Hot wire. The conductor that carries current to a receptacle or other outlet. See Ground and Neutral wire.

I

Impervious tile. Tiles least likely to absorb water; they are generally used only in commercial locations.

Incandescent bulb. Light source with an electrically charged metal filament that burns at white heat.

Increaser. A fitting used to enlarge a vent stack as it passes through the roof.

Inside diameter (ID). Almost all plumbing pipes are sized according to their inside diameter. See also Nominal size and Outside Diameter.

Insulation. A nonconductive covering that protects wires and other electricity carriers.

Inside corner. The point at which two walls form an internal angle, as in the corner of a room.

Isolation membrane. A sub-surface layer for tile installations. Chlorinated polyethylene (CPE) sheets are used for an isolation membrane.

J

Jack studs. Studs at both sides of a door, window, or other opening that help support the header. Sometimes called trimmers.

Jamb. The top and side frames of a door or window opening.

Joint compound. A formula used with paper tape to conceal joints between drywall panels.

Joint strike. A tool used to finish the joints between masonry units. Joints are struck for aesthetic reasons as well as to compress the mortar into the joints.

Jointer. A tool used for making control joints, or grooves, in concrete surfaces to control cracking. *See also* Control joint.

Joists. Horizontal framing members that support a floor or ceiling.

Junction box. An enclosure used for splitting circuits into different branches. In a junction box, wires connect only to each other, never to a switch, receptacle, or fixture.

K

Kerf. The void created by the blade of a saw as it cuts through a piece of material.

Kilowatt (kw). One thousand watts. A kilowatt hour is the standard measure of electrical consumption.

King studs. Studs on both ends of a header that help support the header and run from the wall's sole plate to its top plate.

Knockouts. Tabs that can be removed to make openings in an electrical box. They accommodate cable and conduit connectors.

L

Lag screw. A screw, usually at least $\frac{1}{4}$ inch in diameter, with a hexagonal head that can be screwed in with an adjustable or socket wrench.

Laminate. A hard plastic decorative veneer applied to cabinets and shelves. Can refer to a material formed by building up layers, as with plywood, or to the process of applying a veneer to a surface, such as a countertop.

Lap joint. The joint formed when one member overlaps another.

Layout. A plan, often sketched on the wall or floor, showing where cabinets or shelves will be located.

LB connector or fitting. Elbow for conduit with access for pulling wires.

Lead. See Corner lead.

Leads. Short wires.

Ledger. A horizontal support (usually lumber) that holds up the ends or edges of other members.

Level. The condition that exists when a surface is at true horizontal. Also, a tool used to determine level.

Linear foot. A term used to refer to the length of a board or piece of molding, in contrast to board foot.

Load-bearing wall. A wall that supports a wall or roof section on the floor above. Do not cut or remove a stud in a load-bearing wall without proper alternative support. See also Partition wall.

M

MDF (Medium Density Fiberboard). Made of very fine wood chips, this material is available in 12- and 16-inch-wide pieces often used for shelving.

Main drain. That portion of the drainage system between the fixture drains and the sewer drain. See also Fixture drain and Sewer drain.

Marble. A hard and durable limestone characterized by varied patterns and colors of veins.

Masonry cement. A special mix of portland cement and hydrated lime used for preparing mortar. The lime adds to the workability of the mortar.

Membrane. A subsurface layer for tile installations. Tar paper is used for a waterproof membrane. Chlorinated polyethylene (CPE) sheets are used for an isolation membrane.

Mexican paver. Unglazed tile used most often on floors.

Miter joint. The joint formed when two members meet that have been cut at the same angle.

Modular spacing rule. A measuring device used to verify that a course of masonry units is at the proper height.

Molding. A strip of wood, usually small-dimensioned, used to cover exposed edges or as decoration.

Mortar. A mixture of masonry cement, masonry sand, and water. For most jobs, the proportion of cement to sand is 1 to 3. Also, the process of applying mortar.

Mortise. A shallow cutout in a board usually used to recess hardware.

Mosaic tile. Small (1- or 2-inch) vitreous tiles, mounted on sheets or joined with adhesive strips.

N

National Electrical Code (NEC). A set of rules governing safe wiring methods drafted by the National Fire Protection Association. Local codes sometimes differ from and take precedence over the NEC.

Neon tester. A device with two leads and a small bulb that determines whether a circuit is carrying current.

Neutral wire. A conductor that carries current from an outlet back to ground. It is clad in white insulation. See Ground and Hot wire.

Nipple. A short pipe that has threads on both ends, used to join fittings. A close nipple has threads that run from both ends to the center.

No-hub pipe. A type of cast-iron pipe designed for use by do-it-yourselfers. Pipes and fittings are joined using stainless-steel clamps with rubber gaskets.

Nominal dimension. The stated size of a tile (usually including a standard grout joint) or a piece of lumber, such as a 2×4 or a 1×12. The actual dimension is somewhat smaller.

Nominal size. The designated dimension of a pipe or fitting. It is slightly larger than the actual size. See also Inside diameter.

Nonmetallic sheathed cable. Two or more insulated conductors clad in a plastic covering.

Nonvitreous tile. Porous ceramic tiles for use indoors in dry locations.

O

O-ring. A round rubber washer used to create a watertight seal, chiefly around valve stems.

On-center (OC). The distance from the center of one regularly spaced framing member or hole to the center of the next.

1-by (2-by). Refers to nominal one- or two-inch thick lumber of any width, length, or type of wood. Actual thickness are ¾ inch and 1½ inch, respectively.

Organic mastic. A premixed setting adhesive for tiles. Used often on walls because it holds tiles in place.

Outlet. Any potential point of use in a circuit, including receptacles, switches, and light fixtures.

Outside corner. The point at which two walls form an external angle, the corner you can usually walk around.

Outside diameter (OD). Plumbing parts are rarely measured by their outside diameter, with flexible copper tubing being the primary exception. See also Inside diameter and Nominal size.

Overload. When a circuit is carrying more amperage than it was designed to handle. Overloading causes wires to heat up, which in turn blows fuses or trips circuit breakers.

P-Q

Packing. An asbestos material (used mainly around faucet stems) that, when compressed, results in a watertight seal.

Particleboard. Panels made from compressed wood chips and glue.

Partition wall. Unlike a load-bearing wall, a partition supports no structure above it and can therefore be removed.

Pavers. Vitreous floor tiles, usually ⅜-inch thick and glazed or unglazed.

Pilot hole. A small hole drilled into a board to avoid splitting the wood when driving a screw or nail.

Pipe joint compound. A material applied to pipe threads to ensure a watertight seal. Also called pipe dope. See also Teflon tape.

Plumb. The condition that exists when a surface is at true vertical.

Plumb bob. Tool used to align vertical points.

Plumber's putty. A doughlike material used as a sealant. Often a bead of it is around the underside of toilets and sinks.

Plunger. A suction-action tool used to dislodge obstructions from drain lines. Also called a force cup and a plumber's friend.

Pointing. *See* Tuckpointing.

Polarized plugs. Electric plugs designed with asymmetrical prongs so the hot and neutral prongs cannot be inserted into a receptacle incorrectly.

Primer. A first coating formulated to seal raw surfaces and hold succeeding finish coats.

Premix. Any of several packaged mixtures of ingredients used for preparing concrete or mortar.

PSI. Pounds per square inch. Water pressure is rated in PSI.

Pressure-treated wood. Lumber and sheet goods impregnated with one of several solutions to make the wood more impervious to moisture and weather.

PVC (polyvinyl chloride). A type of plastic pipe that's suitable for cold water only.

Quarry tile. Unglazed, vitreous tiles, usually ½ inch thick, used on floors.

R

R-value. A measure of the resistance to heat transfer that an insulating material provides. The higher the R-value, the more effective the insulation.

Rabbet. A step-shaped cut made along the edge of a piece of wood used to join boards tightly.

Raceway wiring. Surface-mounted channels for extending circuits.

Radiation. Energy transmitted from a heat source through the air. So-called home-heating "radiators" actually depend more on convection than radiation.

Rafters. Parallel framing members that support a roof.

Rails. Horizontal pieces of a cabinet facing.

Rake. The inclined edge of the roof of a home.

Rapid-start tubes. Fluorescent tubes that light up almost instantly.

Ready-mix. Concrete that is mixed in a truck as it is being delivered.

Rebar (reinforcing rod). Steel rod used to reinforce concrete and masonry structures.

Receptacle. An outlet that supplies power for lamps and other plug-in devices.

Reducer. A fitting with different-size openings at either end used to go from a larger to a smaller pipe.

Reinforcing wire mesh. A steel screening used to reinforce certain types of concrete projects, such as walks, drives, and patios.

Relief valve. A device designed to open if it senses excess temperature or pressure.

Retaining wall. A wall constructed to hold soil in place.

Ridgeboard. Topmost beam at a roof's peak to which rafters tie.

Rigid conduit. Wire-carrying metal tubing that can be bent only with a special tool.

Rip. To saw lumber or sheet goods parallel to the grain pattern.

Rise. The vertical distance from one point to another above it; a measurement you need in planning a stairway or ramp. *See also* Run.

Riser. The upright piece between two stairsteps. *See also* Tread.

Rod saw. A strip of tungsten carbide that fits into a standard hacksaw body. It is used for cutting tight curves in tile.

Romex. A trade name for nonmetallic-sheathed cable.

Roofing cement. Asphalt- or plastic-based compound used as an adhesive and to seal flashings and minor leaks.

Roughing in. The process of preparing the initial stage of a plumbing, electrical, carpentry, or other project. These components won't be seen after the drywall or other finishing is in place.

Rout. To shape edges or cut grooves, using a router.

Row-lock course. Several bricks laid side by side on their faces and pitched slightly (when used outdoors) to shed moisture; used below windows and as wall caps.

Rubble. Uncut stone found in fields or as it comes from a quarry. Often used for dry-laid walls.

Run. (1) Any length of pipe or pipes and fittings going in a straight line. (2) Any length of wiring between fixtures.

S

Saddle. See Threshold.

Saddle tee. A fitting used to tap into a water line without having to break the line apart. Some local codes prohibit its use.

Sanitary fitting. Any of several connectors used to join drain-waste-vent lines. Their design helps direct waste downward.

Sanitary sewer. Underground drainage network that carries liquid and solid waste to a treatment plant. See also Storm sewer.

Sash. The part of a window that can be opened, consisting of a frame and glass.

Scratch coat. The first coat of mortar or plaster, roughened (scratched) so the next coat will stick to it.

Scratch sealer. A protective, usually clear, coating on wood or metal.

Screed. A straightedge, often a 2×4 or 2×6, used to level concrete as it is poured into a form or to level the sand base in a form. Also, the process of leveling concrete or a sand base.

Scribe. To use a geometry compass or scrap of wood to transfer the shape or dimension of an object to a piece of wood to be cut.

Sealant. Coatings used to protect tile and grout from water infiltration.

Semivitreous tile. Semiporous ceramic tiles that can be used indoors, in dry to occasionally wet locations.

Septic tank. A reservoir that collects and separates liquid and solid wastes, diverting the liquid waste onto a drainage field.

Service entrance. The point where power enters a home.

Service panel. The main fuse or breaker box in a home.

Set. The process during which mortar or concrete hardens.

Setback. The distance a home must be built from property lines (dictated by local zoning ordinances). Also, a temporary change in a thermostat's setting.

Setting nails. Driving the heads of nails slightly below the surface of the wood.

Settlement. Shifts in a structure, usually caused by freeze-thaw cycles underground.

Sewer drain. That part of the drainage system that carries liquid and solid waste from a dwelling to a sanitary sewer, septic tank, or cesspool.

Shake. A shingle that has been split, rather than cut, from wood.

Consequently, shakes often have a rougher, more natural appearance than standard wooden shingles.

Sheathing. The first covering on a roof or exterior wall, usually fastened directly to rafters or studs.

Shim. A thin strip or wedge of wood or other material used to fill a gap between two adjoining components or to help establish level or plumb.

Shoe molding. Strips of molding commonly used where a baseboard meets the floor. Sometimes known as base shoe.

Short circuit. A condition that occurs when hot and neutral wires contact each other. Fuses and breakers protect against fire, which can result from a short.

Shower pan. The floor of a shower stall that houses the drain. Can be a prefabricated unit made of fiberglass, acrylic, terrazzo, or other materials.

Siding. Planks, boards, or shingles used as an external covering of the walls of a home. Typically nailed to the sheathing.

Sill. The lowest horizontal piece of a window, door, or wall framework.

Sill cock. The valve of an outdoor faucet. Building codes frequently require sill cocks to be frost-proof so that they are not damaged by ice produced by cold weather.

Slate. A rough-surfaced tile that has been split, rather than sliced, from quarried stone.

Sleepers. Boards laid directly over a masonry floor to serve as nailers for plywood, or strip or plank flooring.

Slump. The wetness of a concrete or mortar mix; the wetter the mix, the more it spreads out, or slumps.

Small-appliance circuit. Usually has only two or three 20-amp receptacle outlets.

Snap cutter. Cutting tool for tile. Resembles a glass cutter, except that it is mounted on a guide bar.

Soffit. Covering attached to the underside of eaves or a staircase.

Softwood. Lumber derived from coniferous trees, such as pines, firs, cedars, or redwoods.

Soil stack. A vertical drainpipe that carries waste toward the sewer drain. The main soil stack is the largest drain line of a building into which liquid and solid waste from branch drains flow. See also Vent stack.

Soldering. A technique used to produce watertight joints between various types of metal pipes and fittings. Solder, when heated to molten form, joins two metal surfaces together.

Solderless connectors. Screw-on or crimp-type devices to join two wires.

Sole plate. Bottommost horizontal part of a stud-framed partition. When a plate rests on a foundation, it's called a sill plate.

Solvent-welding. A technique used to produce watertight joints between plastic pipes and fittings. Chemical "cement" softens mating surfaces temporarily and enables them to meld into one.

Spacers. Bits of finished wood or particleboard used to fill in the space at the end of a run of cabinets. Also small pieces of plastic that are used to ensure consistent grout-joint width between tiles.

Spalling. Cracking or flaking that develops on a concrete surface.

Span. A distance between supports.

Spline. A thin piece of wood fitted into slots on the edges of two joined boards to strengthen the joint.

Square. The condition that exists when two surfaces are at 90 degrees to each other. Also, a tool used to determine square.

Stack. The main drain pipe that runs vertically through a house. The stack carries away sewage and waste water to the sewage system and vents gases above the roofline.

Stiles. Vertical members of a door assembly or cabinet facing.

Stone tile. Marble, granite, slate and flagstone. Dimensioned (or gauged) stone is cut to uniform size. Hand-split (or cleft stone) varies in size.

Stop valve. A device installed in a water supply line, usually near a fixture, that lets you shut off the flow to one fixture without interrupting service to the rest of the system.

Storm sewer. An underground drainage network that collects and carries away water coming into it from storm drains. See also Sanitary sewer.

Story pole. A measuring device, often a straight 2×4, with a series of marks set at regular intervals, used to verify that a course of masonry units is spaced at the proper height.

Straightedge. An improvised tool, usually a 1×4 or 2×4 with a straight edge, used to mark a line on material or to determine if a surface is even.

Stretcher. A brick or block laid between corner units.

Strike. The process of finishing a mortar joint. See also Joint strike.

Stringer. The main structural member of a stairway.

Stripping. Removing insulation from wire or sheathing from cable.

Stucco. A finish composed of two or more layers of mortar applied to either indoor or outdoor walls.

Stud. Vertical 2×4 or 2×6 framing members spaced at regular intervals within a wall.

Stud finder. Electronic or magnetic tool that locates studs within a finished wall.

Subfloor. Usually plywood or another sheet material covering the floor joists.

Subpanel. A smaller, subsidiary fuse or breaker box.

Substrate. The setting bed and any other layers beneath a tile surface.

Sweep. A flexible strip placed on the bottom edge of a door for insulation and to prevent drafts.

System ground. A wire connecting a service panel to the earth. It may be attached to a main water pipe or to a rod driven into the ground.

T

Tailpiece. That part of a fixture drain that bridges the gap between the drain outlet and the trap.

Taping. The process of covering drywall joints with tape and joint compound.

Tee. A T-shaped fitting used to tap into a length of pipe at a 90-degree angle for the purposes of beginning a branch line.

Teflon tape. A synthetic material wrapped around pipe threads to seal a joint. Often called pipe tape. See also Pipe joint compound.

Template. A pattern to follow when re-creating a precise shape.

Terrazzo tiles. Bits of granite or marble set in mortar, then polished.

Thermocouple. An electric device for measuring temperature.

Thin-set mortar. A setting adhesive for tiles.

Three-four-five method. An easy way to check whether a corner of a large area is square. Measure 3 feet along one side and 4 feet along the other. If the corner is square, the diagonal distance between those two points will equal 5 feet.

Three-way switch. Operates a light from two locations.

Threshold. The plate at the bottom of some—usually exterior—door openings. Sometimes called a saddle.

Tile nippers. A cutting tool for making small notches and curves in tile. It resemble pliers but has carbide-tipped edges.

Timber. A structural or framing member that is 5 inches or larger in the smallest dimension.

Time-delay fuse. A fuse that does not break the circuit during the momentary overload that can happen when an electric motor starts up. If the overload continues, this fuse blows like any other.

Throw mortar. To place mortar using a trowel.

Toe-kick. Indentation at the bottom of a floor-based cabinet. Also known as toe space.

Toenail. To drive a nail at an angle to hold together two pieces of material, usually studs in a wall.

Tongue-and-groove joint. A joint made using boards that have a projecting tongue on the end of one member and a corresponding groove on the other member .

Top plate. The topmost horizontal element of a stud-frame wall.

Trap. The part of a fixture drain that creates a water seal to prevent sewer gases from penetrating a home's interior. Codes require that all fixtures be trapped.

Transformer. A device that reduces or increases voltage. In home wiring, transformers step down current for use with low-voltage equipment such as thermostats and doorbell systems.

Travelers. Two of the three conductors that run between switches in a three-way installation.

Tread. The level part of a staircase.

Trim tile. Tiles that are shaped to turn corners or define the edges of an installation. Includes, cove trim, bullnose, V-cap, quarter round, inside corner, and outside corner.

Trimmers. See Jack studs.

Trowel. Any of several flat and oblong or flat and pointed metal tools used for handling and/or finishing concrete and mortar.

Tuckpointing. Refilling old masonry joints with new mortar.

U

Underlayment. Cement-like product that is used to level floors prior to laying down the surface material. Sometimes used to refer to the subfloor material or material laid on the subfloor. See also Subfloor.

Underwriters knot. A knot used to secure wires in a lamp socket.

Underwriters Laboratories (UL). Ttesting agency that examines electrical components for hazards.

Uniform Plumbing Code (UPC). Nationally recognized guidelines prescribing safe plumbing practices. Local codes take precedence over the UPC when the two differ.

Union. A fitting used with threaded pipe to facilitate disconnecting the line without having to cut it.

Utility knife. A razor-blade knife with a retractable blade.

V

Valley. An intersection of roof slopes.

Vapor barrier. A waterproof membrane in a floor, wall, or ceiling that blocks the transfer of condensation to the inner surface.

Veneer. A thin layer of decorative wood laminated to the surface of a more common wood.

Veneer tape. A ribbon of reinforced wood veneer applied to plywood or other rough wood with glue or heat-sensitive adhesive.

Vent. The vertical or sloping portion of a drain line that permits sewer gases to exit the house. Every plumbing fixture must be vented.

Vent stack. The upper portion of a vertical drain line through which gases pass directly to the outside. The main vent stack is the portion of the main vertical drain line above the highest fixture connected to it.

Vitreous tile. Ceramic tiles with a low porosity, used indoors or outdoors, in wet or dry locations.

Volt (V). A measure of electrical pressure. Volts × amps = watts.

Voltmeter. A device that measures voltage and performs other tests.

W–Z

Wall box. A rectangular enclosure for receptacles and switches. See Junction box.

Wall anchor. A fastener such as the toggle bolt or Molly that is used to secure objects to hollow walls, or a concrete anchor used to secure objects to concrete or masonry walls.

Warp. Any of several lumber defects caused by uneven shrinkage of wood cells.

Water hammer. A loud noise caused by a sudden stop in the flow of water, which causes pipes to repeatedly hit up against a nearby framing member.

Water supply system. The network of pipes and fittings that transports water under pressure to fixtures and other water-using equipment and appliances.

Watt (W). A measure of the power an electrical device consumes. See Amp, Kilowatt, and Volt.

Weep holes. Openings made in mortar joints to facilitate drainage of built-up water.

Wet saw. A power tool for cutting tile. A pump sprays water to cool the blade and remove chips.

Wet wall. A strategically placed cavity (usually a 2×6 wall) in which the main drain/vent stack and a cluster of supply and drain-waste-vent lines are housed.

Whaler. A doubled 2×4 secured to the outside of a concrete form to strengthen it against the pressure of the concrete as it is poured.

Wye. A Y-shaped drainage fitting that serves as the starting point for a branch drain supplying one or more fixtures.

Yard. The unit of volume by which ready-mix concrete is sold; equal to 1 square yard (27 cubic feet).

Zoning. Ordinances regulating the ways in which a property may be used. See also Building codes.

METRIC CONVERSIONS

U.S. UNITS TO METRIC EQUIVALENTS			METRIC UNITS TO U.S. EQUIVALENTS		
To Convert From	Multiply By	To Get	To Convert From	Multiply By	To Get
Inches	25.4	Millimeters	Millimeters	0.0394	Inches
Inches	2.54	Centimeters	Centimeters	0.3937	Inches
Feet	30.48	Centimeters	Centimeters	0.0328	Feet
Feet	0.3048	Meters	Meters	3.2808	Feet
Yards	0.9144	Meters	Meters	1.0936	Yards
Miles	1.6093	Kilometers	Kilometers	0.6214	Miles
Square inches	6.4516	Square centimeters	Square centimeters	0.1550	Square inches
Square feet	0.0929	Square meters	Square meters	10.764	Square feet
Square yards	0.8361	Square meters	Square meters	1.1960	Square yards
Acres	0.4047	Hectares	Hectares	2.4711	Acres
Square miles	2.5899	Square kilometers	Square kilometers	0.3861	Square miles
Cubic inches	16.387	Cubic centimeters	Cubic centimeters	0.0610	Cubic inches
Cubic feet	0.0283	Cubic meters	Cubic meters	35.315	Cubic feet
Cubic feet	28.316	Liters	Liters	0.0353	Cubic feet
Cubic yards	0.7646	Cubic meters	Cubic meters	1.3079	Cubic yards
Cubic yards	764.55	Liters	Liters	0.0013	Cubic yards
Fluid ounces	29.574	Milliliters	Milliliters	0.0338	Fluid ounces
Quarts	0.9464	Liters	Liters	1.0567	Quarts
Gallons	3.7854	Liters	Liters	0.2642	Gallons
Drams	1.7718	Grams	Grams	0.5644	Drams
Ounces	28.350	Grams	Grams	0.0353	Ounces
Pounds	0.4536	Kilograms	Kilograms	2.2046	Pounds

To convert from degrees Fahrenheit (F) to degrees Celsius (C), first subtract 32, then multiply by ⁵⁄₉.

To convert from degrees Celsius to degrees Fahrenheit, multiply by ⁹⁄₅, then add 32.